W9-BKG-377
110°E
120°E
130°E
Lake Baikal
RUSSIA
Amur
Heihe
GREATER KHINGAN RANGE
Hailar
MONGOLIA
MONGOLIAN PLATEAU
Qiqihar
NORTHEAST CHINA PLAIN
Jiamusi
Songhua
Ussuri
La Perouse Strait
Harbin
Lake Khanka
Baicheng
Changchun
Jilin
Xilinhot
Liao
Xar Moron
Tumen
Tsugaru Strait
GOBI DESERT
40°N
Fushun
Shenyang
Benxi
Yalu
Anshan
East Sea (Sea of Japan)
YIN MTS.
Baotou
Datong
Beijing
Tangshan
NORTH KOREA
Korea Bay
ORDOS DESERT
Tianjin
Dalian
Bo Hai
Baoding
Shijiazhuang
LÜLIANG MTS.
Yellow (Huang)
Taiyuan
NORTH CHINA PLAIN
Yellow Sea
SOUTH KOREA
JAPAN
Shandong Peninsula
Jinan
Handan
Qingdao
CHINA
Tsushima (JAPAN)
Korea Strait
Xianyang
Wei
Zhengzhou
Xi'an
Xuzhou
Jeju I. (S. KOREA)
QIN LING
Yancheng
30°N
DABIE MTS.
Nanjing
Wuxi
Shanghai
Suzhou
Three Gorges Dam
Yangzi (Chang)
Hangzhou Bay
East China Sea
Yichang
Wuhan
Hangzhou
Ningbo
Changde
Nanchang
Changsha
WUYI MTS.
Ryukyu Islands (JAPAN)
Fuzhou
Taibei
Tropic of Cancer
Guilin
Shaoguan
Taiwan Strait
Philippine Sea
Zhangzhou
TAIWAN
Hongshui
Guangzhou
Xi
Shantou
Kaohsiung
Nanning
Shenzhen
20°N
Qinzhou
Hong Kong (Xianggang)
Yangjiang
Luzon Strait
Gulf of Tonkin
South China Sea
0 100 200 300 400 500 miles
0 100 200 300 400 500 km
Haikou
Babuyan Islands (PHILIPPINES)
Hainan Island
110°E
120°E
130°E

# *Encyclopedia of Modern China*

# *Encyclopedia of Modern China*

VOLUME 1

**A–E**

*David Pong*

EDITOR IN CHIEF

**CHARLES SCRIBNER'S SONS**

*A part of Gale, Cengage Learning*

Detroit • New York • San Francisco • New Haven, Conn • Waterville, Maine • London

**Encyclopedia of Modern China**

David Pong, Editor in Chief



For product information and technology assistance, contact us at
**Gale Customer Support, 1-800-877-4253.**
For permission to use material from this text or product,
submit all requests online at **www.cengage.com/permissions.**
Further permissions questions can be emailed to
**permissionrequest@cengage.com**



**Library of Congress Cataloging-in-Publication Data**

Encyclopedia of modern China / David Pong, editor in chief.
p. cm. --
Includes bibliographical references and index.
ISBN 978-0-684-31566-9 (set : alk. paper) -- ISBN 978-0-684-31567-6 (v. 1 : alk. paper) -- ISBN 978-0-684-31568-3 (v. 2 : alk. paper) -- ISBN 978-0-684-31569-0 (v. 3 : alk. paper) -- ISBN 978-0-684-31570-6 (v. 4 : alk. paper) -- ISBN 978-0-684-31571-3 (e-book)
1. China--Civilization--1644-1912--Encyclopedias. 2. China--Civilization--1912-1949--Encyclopedias. 3. China--Civilization--1949---Encyclopedias. I. Pong, David, 1939–.

DS755.E63 2009
951.003--dc22 2009003279

*Gale*
27500 Drake Rd.
Farmington Hills, MI 48331-3535

ISBN-13: 978-0-684-31566-9 (set)
ISBN-13: 978-0-684-31567-6 (vol. 1)
ISBN-13: 978-0-684-31568-3 (vol. 2)
ISBN-13: 978-0-684-31569-0 (vol. 3)
ISBN-13: 978-0-684-31570-6 (vol. 4)

ISBN-10: 0-684-31566-1 (set)
ISBN-10: 0-684-31567-X (vol. 1)
ISBN-10: 0-684-31568-8 (vol. 2)
ISBN-10: 0-684-31569-6 (vol. 3)
ISBN-10: 0-684-31570-X (vol. 4)

This title is also available as an e-book.
ISBN-13: 978-0-684-31571-3 ISBN-10: 0-684-31571-8
Contact your Gale sales representative for ordering information.

Printed in the United States of America
1 2 3 4 5 6 7 13 12 11 10 09

# *Dedication*

For my loving wife Barbara

For our children, Amanda, Cynthia, and Myra

And for justice, peace, and security of life everywhere

# *Editorial Board*

# *Editorial and Production Staff*

**PROJECT EDITOR**

Alan Hedblad

**ART EDITOR**

Scot Peacock

**CONTRIBUTING EDITORS**

Douglas Dentino
Jason Everett
Andrew Specht
Jennifer Wisinski

**MANUSCRIPT EDITORS**

Sheryl A. Ciccarelli
Lauren Therese Grace Colton
Judith Culligan
Anne C. Davidson
Jessica Hornik Evans
Alan Thwaits

**EDITORIAL ASSISTANTS**

Caitlin Cowan
Bethany Gibbons
Camille Reynolds
Jaclyn Setili

**PROOFREADERS**

Carol Holmes
Kathleen Wilson
Amy Unterburger

**CAPTIONS**

Sheryl A. Ciccarelli

**CARTOGRAPHY**

Mapping Specialists, Ltd., Madison, Wisconsin

**CUSTOM GRAPHICS**

GGS Creative Resources, a division of PreMedia Global Inc.

**INDEXER**

Laurie Andriot

**EDITORIAL TECHNICAL SUPPORT**

Mike Lesniak
Amanda Sams
Mike Weaver

**PRODUCT DESIGN**

Pamela A. E. Galbreath

**COMPOSITION**

Evi Abou-El-Seoud

**MANUFACTURING**

Wendy Blurton

**DIRECTOR, NEW PRODUCT DEVELOPMENT**

Hélène Potter

**PUBLISHER**

Jay Flynn

# *Contents*

# *List of Maps*

# *Introduction*

China's rise since the 1980s has shown contemporary and modern China in a new light. The reforms implemented after the passing of Mao Zedong have produced dramatic results. It is still too early to fully evaluate the overall impact of these reforms, but an economy with a sustained double-digit growth rate for some two decades cannot be brushed aside as an accident. Nor can China's rise be viewed narrowly as an economic phenomenon, for without the aggregate energy and ingenuity of the people, the leadership of the country, or even the structure of the political system, China would not be where it is today. To be sure, there is much to be desired in China's leadership and political system. Who can say that the nation would not have attained even greater achievements, or that the quality of life for its citizens would not have improved even more, had the mix of ingredients been somehow different? Furthermore, we must also factor in the historical and cultural contexts. There is much to describe, analyze, and understand about modern China. In these volumes, we have brought together nearly five hundred authors to write 936 entries and sidebars about this extraordinary country from 1800 to the present; topics range from the daily life of common folks to the ever-changing structure of the banking system that is part of the engine of China's recent transformation.

Overall assessment of China's modern development has shifted dramatically in the past generation, loosely defined as a thirty-year span. Upon Mao Zedong's death in 1976, the country's future was in a quandary. The Great Helmsman was gone, leaving the nation in the hands of a mediocre successor who, lacking vision or daring, could do no more than promise to carry on whatever Mao had laid down. This was hardly a comforting message, as the legacy of the late Mao was one of political upheaval. Although the country's leadership was soon passed on to abler hands, it was still wary of instability even as late as 1989. During June of that year, the outside world speculated on the breakup of the Communist regime as prodemocracy demonstrators brought matters to a head in Tiananmen Square. Today, China is still a country in search of a solution, one that would bring national dignity and a steady political course, as well as prosperity and security for its citizens. The nation's quest for these objectives in the past century and a half has been nothing short of a prolonged struggle with no end in sight. Deeply sensitive to this quest and to the tensions that inform China's past and shape its present, members of the editorial board set about selecting a rich and balanced collection of topics intended to describe the complexity of the country's history and culture as well as to elucidate its current successes and predicaments.

A little more than a year before Mao died, another Chinese leader across the Taiwan Strait had also passed on. Chiang Kai-shek, who had finally been given the opportunity to guide his regime's development under American protection and the benefits of American aid, had begun to produce a vibrant economy in Taiwan by the mid-1970s. Then, with martial law lifted in 1987, Taiwan emerged as a serious model of development, one of the four Asian Tigers. Coincidental with the opening up of the mainland's economy under Deng Xiaoping's new policies, Taiwan's new wealth found fertile ground for investment on the opposite shore. Yet political tensions between the two parties persist, even as their economic relations hum along. Cross-strait relations will surely continue to capture our attention. The *Encyclopedia of Modern China* explores these issues in a set of well-conceived entries that establish a firm foundation for readers as they continue monitoring future developments.

Still, the world's main focus must be trained on the People's Republic. Since the turn of the present century, the positive effects of the economic reforms have been sufficiently prolonged to generate confidence among the Chinese people and their political leaders. China's rise is not just propaganda hype; it is real. China is now a factor to be reckoned with in practically every aspect of international life. By the time of the April 2009 meeting of the G-20 nations in London, China had risen to star level, even as the world was dazzled by the freshness and the excitement of the new American president, Barack Obama. China's own new generation of leaders and the political and financial institutions that they helped to build are examined in numerous entries.

The "rise of China" perspective demands that we look at the history of the past two centuries in terms of whether China should be considered a "latecomer" or "late bloomer." Past attention has been focused on China's failures—losing its modernization race with Japan, fumbling in its quest for national unity, and taking the wrong turns in its search for political form, a record that makes for a checkered if interesting story. The recent history of China provides a fresh perspective, a new framework with which to view its past as not just a string of failures but also as building blocks or lessons learned on a path to big-power status. Insofar as material or economic transformation is concerned, China's past failures perhaps should no longer be perceived as such, for as long as there was progress, such failures were nonetheless steps, even if baby steps, toward a higher goal. China has been playing catch-up since the middle of the nineteenth century. It is still catching up, but the gap has narrowed and may even close in the foreseeable future. This is a possibility no one dared envision in times past except in ignorance, as a few did in the nineteenth century, or in moments of extreme euphoria, as when in 1958 Mao promised parity with the West in fifteen years. There are entries aplenty in these volumes that will help the reader reconstruct this fresh view of China's modern past.

Historically, the rise of latecomers has been accompanied by ugly episodes in their march toward modernity. The histories of Germany and Japan come readily to mind. These are stories laden with immense human costs inflicted on the peoples of Germany and Japan, but most importantly, on other peoples around them. China's rise is not unencumbered with unpleasant developments. What separates China from the examples just mentioned is that its rise took place initially under prolonged foreign encroachments and aggression, and then, after 1949, under extended periods of relative international isolation. The ugly episodes, other than several border wars and clashes, were ones in which the Chinese turned against themselves. The Great Leap Forward and Famine and the Cultural Revolution, each the subject of study in these volumes by a world-renowned authority, are perhaps the greatest examples. Were these human costs inseparable from China's path toward modernity? Could they have been avoided? From a moral standpoint, one could easily come up with a straightforward answer. But the world has never before witnessed the transformation of a country so extensive, involving a population so huge and a people so steeped in history and culture. China's modern trajectory has been and will be different. It goes without saying, therefore, that simple answers will not help us understand the complexity that is China.

China is expected to soon overtake Japan as the world's second-largest economy, though it still has some way to go before it is anywhere near where the U.S. economy is now. By the end of the first decade of the twenty-first century, China's gross domestic product on a per capita basis, though improving, still ranks low in the world. China can best be characterized as an ongoing project. Its development has been pockmarked with contradictions and paradoxes. Its rise in economic power serves as a constant reminder that it is still in many ways a poor country, where the tallest buildings in the world are constructed by hordes of migrant workers from the countryside. Its capitalist practices serve to highlight its authoritarian rule as the government continues to regulate traffic on the information highway. Its growing military sector, often perceived as a threat to regional stability, seems only to undermine the nation's desire to provide statesmanlike leadership in global politics. And its fear of social turmoil is countered by policies that tend to provoke dissidence, especially in border regions such as Tibet and Xinjiang. Indeed, China has many dimensions. It is a country that begs to be understood, and yet its leaders are not often its best spokespersons. One needs only to read the entries on "Poverty" or "Dissidents" to peer into China's underside.

It is our hope that these volumes will provide reliable and sophisticated renditions of the myriad facets of China. If, for example, China's national-minority problems seem intractable, highlighted even more by the election of the first African-American president in the United States, it may behoove us to look at the nature of China's multiethnic communities. How do China's Muslims or Tibetans, each bound by a deep religious faith and firmly entrenched in a distinct geographical homeland, render China's problems different from those in a multiethnic society like the United States? And if China's ever-widening gap between the rich and the poor is somehow attributable to the nation's huge population, how should one approach the question of birth planning in China? And if its rampant capitalistic practices are to blame instead, how should such a large and populous society have strategized for development? Many of the country's contemporary issues have long historical roots. We invite the reader to not only use this encyclopedia to find intelligent answers to these and other questions, but also to explore the larger issues and to see the bigger picture using the bibliographies, primary sources, and other tools that are provided in these pages.

Modern and contemporary China is not only a rich mosaic in itself, but, like a diamond, it reveals different and ever-changing facets depending on the angle from which it is perceived. Different people see things differently, and people can disagree. As editor in chief for this encyclopedia, I come from the perspective that diversity itself can be a source of strength and excellence. This conviction, translated into a deliberate policy, has resulted in an editorial board of great diversity. To be sure, the associate editors on the board are great scholars in Chinese studies and are widely recognized as authorities in their own fields, but they also represent extremely varied backgrounds and origins. The five of them come from as many countries—Australia, Great Britain, China (Hong Kong), France, and the United States—and hail from four continents. This *Encyclopedia of Modern China* is as much the creation of a group of top scholars as it is the product of an international enterprise.

The importance of the international character of this encyclopedia project cannot be overstressed. Following in broad outline the procedures established with the publisher, the editorial board determined collectively a list of articles, composite entries, and sidebars, drafting scope outlines for each essay and suggesting scholars to write them. As a result of the board's truly diverse background, we managed to draw from a wide pool of talent around the world. We discussed the possibility of commissioning essays written in languages other than English, then translating them. This was the level of our commitment. In the end, only one entry written in French required this service, as other authors who were not fluent in English teamed up with scholars who possessed greater facility in the language.

## PUSHING BOUNDARIES

It is often said that encyclopedias are summations of existing scholarship; they do not produce new knowledge. There is an element of truth in this. Indeed, authors may not necessarily engage in firsthand or archival research in the course of writing an encyclopedia entry. Yet, in the process of putting these volumes together, we became aware that new research was being introduced in the entries. Indeed, when we drafted our lists of entries and pondered what they might include, some editorial board members observed that for many topics on modern China, the research has not yet been done. In part, this is the function of a growing and dynamic field of scholarship, but equally important is the fact that we have included topics in new fields—for example, popular culture, race, ethnicity, identity, and gender, covering of course women but also sexuality and transgender issues. Many authors also infused their entries with various forms of consciousness introduced into the scholarly world by Orientalism, postcolonialism, and diaspora studies. As a result, we are not only providing a good reference but also, in many instances, pushing boundaries. We would like to extend our thanks and gratitude to the many authors who were generous with their unpublished research and were willing to share their insights with our readers.

An encyclopedia is a work presenting various branches of knowledge in discrete treatises; ours is a collection of entries on topics that span the spectrum of China's history, culture, and society from 1800 to the present. Opinion will differ as to how big such an encyclopedia should be. Weighing various considerations—usefulness, readership, accessibility, and cost—we started with a working framework of 1.2 million words in four volumes of approximately five hundred pages each. We also thought that we should have about six hundred entries, but this number soon became irrelevant as the members of the editorial board, each compiling a slate of topics in their respective "domains," produced a list that was twice as long. By eliminating potential duplications and by consolidating related topics, we trimmed the number to just under 870 entries plus nearly 70 sidebars. A more important consideration was the proportion of biographies vis-à-vis the other entries. This was by no means an easy decision. One can imagine a biographical dictionary of modern China with the number of entries running literally into the thousands. However, we came to the conclusion that, given the space, the work would be more useful if it were made up largely of topical and thematic studies, with only the most important individuals given biographical treatment (especially since extensive biographical materials on many major figures from modern China are available from Gale in its Biography Resource Center and other printed and digital publications).

In sum, this *Encyclopedia of Modern China* presents up-to-date scholarship, pushing boundaries as it provides solid reference. It will definitely contribute to a synthesis of the field, and is thus poised to be of great significance in the years to come. The historical reassessment relating to China's role in world affairs and the reappraisal of the dynamics of political power, economic institutions, social and cultural developments, and the trajectory of China's development featured in this encyclopedia will certainly have a lasting impact on Chinese studies. The fact that this set will also be an accessible resource for the general public means that it will help shape new perspectives on China in the public arena.

The *Encyclopedia of Modern China* will enable readers to create their own picture of modern and contemporary China, generating their own interpretation of this or that event by reading one topic in the light of another. The section on primary sources contains a number of rare documents, including one titled "New Population Theory" that, to our knowledge, is the first English translation of the Chinese original. Cross-references and bibliographies, attached to the end of each entry, will help the reader navigate the volumes and locate additional information on the topics covered. We have also designed a "Thematic Outline of Contents" with more than two dozens categories, as well as a chronology, an annotated general bibliography, and a comprehensive glossary of Chinese characters. When combined with the subject index, these features add context for the reader, making the encyclopedia a very user-friendly set.

## ACKNOWLEDGEMENTS

It would not be an exaggeration to say that credit goes first to the five associate editors, whose expertise and dedication are largely responsible for the excellent quality of this reference work. From the development of the table of contents and the writing of scope descriptions, to the careful review of submitted entries, all of the associate editors offered a great deal of their time and energy. Operating from vastly different time zones and academic calendars, not to mention their personal research agendas, they often had to disrupt their work, vacation time, and weekends to keep the project moving forward. I am sure that sacrifices were made in their family and personal lives as well. I would like to introduce the associate editors to our readers:

- Julia F. Andrews is the Bliss M. & Mildred A. Wiant Designated Professor of Chinese Literature and Culture, in the Department of the History of Art, Ohio State University. She is also Associate Director of the East Asian Studies Center at the university, and author of *Painters and Politics in the People's Republic of China, 1949–1979* (University of California Press, 1994), which won the Joseph Levenson Prize. Her research interests are in Chinese painting and modern Chinese art.

- Jean-Philippe Béja is Senior Research Fellow at the Institute of Political Science, Centre d'études et de recherches internationales, Centre national de la recherche scientifique, Centre d'Études Français sur la Chine contemporaine (CNRS/CERI-Sciences-Po, CEFC), Hong Kong. His research topics are state-society relations, especially regarding intellectuals and the Communist Party, and the prodemocracy movement. Among his books is *A la recherche d'une ombre chinoise: Le mouvement pour la démocratie en Chine* (1919–2004), Editions du Seuil, 2004.

- Flemming Christiansen holds the Chair in Chinese Studies at the University of Leeds, United Kingdom, and is Director of the National Institute of Chinese Studies of the White Rose East Asian Centre. Among his authored and co-authored books are *Chinatown, Europe. An Exploration of Overseas Chinese Identity in the 1990s* (RoutledgeCurzon, 2003) and *Village Inc. Chinese Rural Society in the 1990s* (Curzon, 1998). His research interests include urban-rural issues, social and political change, and social stratification in China.

- David Faure, Professor, Department of History, the Chinese University of Hong Kong, focuses his research in Chinese business history, lineages in South China, local history, and the history of Hong Kong. Among his numerous publications are *Emperor and Ancestor: State and Lineage in South China* (Stanford University Press, 2007) and *China and Capitalism: A History of Business Enterprise in Modern China* (Hong Kong University Press, 2006).

- Antonia Finnane, Professor, School of Historical Studies, University of Melbourne, Australia, is the author of *Speaking of Yangzhou: A Chinese City, 1550–1850* (Harvard University Press, 2004), which won the Levenson Prize, and *Changing Clothes in China: Fashion, History, Nation* (Columbia University Press, 2008).

In addition, I would also like to mention the contributions from Professor Marianne Bastid-Bruguière of Centre National de la Recherche Scientifique (Paris) and Professor Xiaobo Lu of Columbia University, New York, who made valuable suggestions in the early planning stages. Delia Davin, Emeritus Professor of Chinese Studies, University of Leeds, is also worthy of special mention. Davin contributed more than twenty entries to this set, and wrote the introductions to each of the primary source documents that appear collectively in volume 4. Special thanks also to Carsten Herrmann-Pillath, Professor at the Frankfurt School of Finance & Management, who contributed nearly thirty articles on important economic concepts. My colleague at the University of Delaware, Associate Professor Jianguo Chen, has provided invaluable advice on matters related to Chinese literature. I would also like to thank Robert Gardella, Professor Emeritus of History at the United States Merchant Marine Academy, for putting together such a useful Chronology for our readers.

No effort has been spared to produce this reference work. Starting with a target of 2,000 pages in 4 volumes, we finished with about 2,500 pages, though still in 4 tomes. Throughout the process, the staff at Gale has worked closely with us. My thanks go first to Ms. Hélène Potter, Director of Publishing, Gale / Charles Scribner's Sons, who developed this project, and has given me free hand in shaping the work. What was envisaged to be a reference with 600 entries became one with 936, including the sidebars. In the section of primary source documents, which, like everything else, turns out to be bigger and richer than originally planned, we have included not only some unusual pieces, but also, for the first time, rendered into English the interesting and important essay "New Population Theory" (*Xin renkoulun*) by the economist and one-time President of Peking University, Ma Yinchu, which is reproduced in its entirety here.

Hélène was certainly generous in her support of such enhancements, but her main contribution was in the overall guidance she provided from beginning to end. To someone unfamiliar with the world of large-scale commercial publishing, Hélène provided indispensable insight and guidance. Her great personal interest in this project and its subject matter was a major reason for the quality of these volumes. From the time she invited me to serve as editor in chief in October 2006, she has never stopped being a cheerleader and an adviser.

Since around July 2007, Alan Hedblad, a senior editor at Gale / Charles Scribner's Sons, has worked with me on a regular basis, exchanging e-mails several times a day, shunting entries back and forth, in an endless quest for perfection. His ability to manage such a large project, organize its materials and resources, is most impressive. And he goes about his job with such equanimity, wisdom, and poise!

In the earlier stages, I had the good fortune to work with Melissa McDade, managing editor. Melissa guided us patiently through the first learning stages, familiarizing the editorial board with databases, scopes, and the like. Her hard work took us through the first eight months or so, until the first draft of the scopes was done. All the while, she had the able assistance of editor Douglas Dentino.

For the style and readability of the work, we must thank primarily copyeditors Judy Culligan and Alan Thwaits. Trained in Chinese studies, Alan Thwaits also compiled and edited the large glossary of Chinese characters.

I would like to acknowledge the wonderful art work, which is under the purview of Scot Peacock, who handled all the images, including the selection of hundreds of photographs, artwork, maps, tables, and graphs. For the research, review and editing of the primary sources, we would like to extend our appreciation to my student-assistant Kevin Impellizeri and to Gale's Andrew Specht, and likewise to Jennifer Wisinski who researched and edited the fact boxes that go with the entries on provinces. Jason Everett helped to finalize the fact boxes and handled all file preparation and coding for typesetting. I am sure that many more at Gale's Farmington Hills offices have had a contributing hand in producing this wonderful project. They are listed on the "Editorial and Production Staff" page.

In closing, I would like to thank my dearest wife, Barbara, without whose encouragement, good cheer, understanding, and support throughout the past two-and-a-half years, I would not have been able to complete this titanic undertaking. Our children, Amanda, Cynthia, and Myra have not only been great cheerleaders, but their own resourcefulness in building their young careers has been nothing short of inspiring. I dedicate these volumes to them.

***David Pong***
Newark, Delaware
Easter Sunday, 12 April 2009

# *List of Articles*

## E



## F

## N



## O



## P

## T



## U



## V



## W

## X



## Y



## Z

# *List of Contributors*

***Amer, Ramses***
Senior Research Fellow, Center of Pacific Asia Studies
Deparment of Oriental Languages, Stockholm University
ASEAN, RELATIONS WITH
SOUTHEAST ASIAN STATES, RELATIONS WITH
VIETNAM, RELATIONS WITH

***Andrews, Julia F.***
Professor, Department of the History of Art
The Ohio State University
ART EXHIBITIONS ABROAD
COMMERCIAL ART: PICTURE BOOKS (*LIANHUANHUA*)
FEDERATION OF LITERARY AND ART CIRCLES
LIN FENGMIAN
LIU HAISU
LUO ZHONGLI'S *FATHER* [SIDEBAR]
ORACLE BONES [SIDEBAR]
RUSTIC REALISM IN ART

***Andrews-Speed, Philip***
Professor of Energy Policy, Centre for Energy, Petroleum and Mineral Law and Policy
University of Dundee
ENERGY: HYDROLOGICAL POWER
ENERGY: OVERVIEW
ENERGY: WIND POWER

***Antony, Robert J.***
Department of History
University of Macau
PIRACY, MARITIME

***Arlt, Wolfgang Georg***
Professor of International Tourism
West Coast University of Applied Sciences, Heide, Germany
TOURISM: TRAVEL ABROAD

***Baark, Erik***
Division of Social Science
Hong Kong University of Science and Technology
SCIENCE AND TECHNOLOGY POLICY

***Bachman, David***
Professor, International Studies
University of Washington
CHEN YUN
PEOPLE'S LIBERATION ARMY: MILITARY DOCTRINE

***Bailey, Paul J.***
Professor of Modern Chinese History
School of History, Classics and Archaeology, University of Edinburgh
EDUCATION: 1800–1949
FILIAL PIETY
SOCIALIZATION AND PEDAGOGY

***Baker, Hugh D. R.***
Emeritus Professor of Chinese, School of Oriental and African Studies
University of London
CANTONESE
FAMILY: OVERVIEW
LINEAGE

***Bakich, Olga***
Research Associate, Center for European, Russian, and Eurasisan Studies
University of Toronto
RUSSIAN ÉMIGRÉS

***Bakken, Børge***
Department of Sociology
University of Hong Kong
EDUCATION: MORAL EDUCATION

***Bartlett, Beatrice S.***
Professor Emeritus, Department of History
Yale University
ARCHIVES, PUBLIC: ARCHIVAL RESOURCES OUTSIDE CHINA
ARCHIVES, PUBLIC: HISTORICAL PRESERVATION AND GOVERNMENT HISTORICAL PUBLICATIONS
GOVERNMENT ADMINISTRATION, 1800–1912

***Bastid-Bruguière, Marianne***
Research Professor Emeritus, Member of the French Institute
The National Center for Scientific Research (CNRS), Paris
GIQUEL, PROSPER
ZHANG ZHIDONG

***Baumler, Alan***
Associate Professor of History
Indiana University of Pennsylvania
OPIUM, 1800–1950

***Bays, Daniel***
History Department
Calvin College
MISSIONARIES
MORRISON, ROBERT

***Becker, Jasper***
Publisher
*Asia Weekly* Magazine
PENG DEHUAI

***Béja, Jean-Philippe***
Senior Research Fellow at CNRS, CERI-Sciences-Po, Paris
CEFC, Hong Kong
DEMOCRACY WALL
DISSIDENTS
LIU BINYAN
LIU XIAOBO
PRODEMOCRACY MOVEMENT (1989)
RIGHTS DEFENSE MOVEMENT

***Bender, Mark***
Department of East Asian Languages and Literatures
Ohio State University
MINORITY NATIONALITIES: ETHNIC MINORITY CULTURAL EXPRESSION

***Benton, Gregor***
Professor of Chinese History
Cardiff University, Wales
CHEN DUXIU
TROTSKYISM

***Berg, Daria D.***
University of Nottingham
PUBLISHING INDUSTRY

***Betta, Chiara***
Department of Historical Studies
University of Bristol
JEWISH COMMUNITIES AND REFUGEES
PARSIS
SASSOON, VICTOR [SIDEBAR]

***Bian, Morris L.***
Associate Professor of History
Auburn University
UNIT (*DANWEI*)

***Bian, Yanjie***
University of Minnesota
NEPOTISM AND GUANXI

***Bo Zhiyue***
Senior Research Fellow
National University of Singapore
ECONOMIC REFORM SINCE 1978: COMMISSION FOR THE REFORM OF THE ECONOMIC SYSTEM
HANGZHOU
HOUSEHOLD RESPONSIBILITY SYSTEM (*BAOGAN DAOHU*)
LIAONING

***Bohr, P. Richard***
Professor of History and Director of Asian Studies
College of Saint Benedict and Saint John's University
NIAN UPRISING
RICHARD, TIMOTHY
WHITE LOTUS

***Bonnin, Michel***
Professor
École des Hautes Études en Sciences Sociales (EHESS), Paris
PRODUCTION AND CONSTRUCTION CORPS [SIDEBAR]
RED GUARDS
SENT-DOWN EDUCATED YOUTH

***Brady, Anne-Marie S.***
Associate Professor, School of Political and Social Sciences
University of Canterbury, Christchurch, New Zealand
PROPAGANDA

***Braester, Yomi***
University of Washington
FENG XIAOGANG
NANJING ROAD [SIDEBAR]
NEW YEAR'S MOVIES
ZHANG YIMOU

***Brandt, Loren***
Department of Economics
University of Toronto
AGRICULTURAL PRODUCTION: OVERVIEW
STANDARD OF LIVING

***Brandtstädter, Susanne***
Associate Professor, Department of Social Anthropology
University of Oslo
SOCIAL RITUALS

***Brautigam, Deborah***
School of International Service
American University
INTERNATIONAL DEVELOPMENT AID

***Bray, David***
Department of Chinese Studies
University of Sydney
HOUSING: OVERVIEW

***Brook, Timothy***
Department of History
University of British Columbia
LOCAL GAZETTEERS
NANJING MASSACRE
WAR CRIMES

***Brown, Kerry***
Royal Institute of International Affairs
London
GANG OF FOUR [SIDEBAR]
UNITED KINGDOM, RELATIONS WITH
XI'AN

***Bruun, Ole***
Associate Professor, Institute for Society and Globalization
Roskilde University, Denmark
MONGOLIA, PEOPLE'S REPUBLIC OF, RELATIONS WITH

***Buck, David D.***
University of Wisconsin–Milwaukee
HEILONGJIANG
JILIN
JINAN
SHANDONG

***Buoye, Thomas***
University of Tulsa
DEATH PENALTY SINCE 1800

***Burke Mathison, Christina Wei-Szu***
Department of History of Art
The Ohio State University
LIN FENGMIAN
LIU GUOSONG (LIU KUO-SUNG)
PANG XUNQIN

***Cabestan, Jean-Pierre***
Professor and Head, Department of Government and International Studies
Hong Kong Baptist University
CENTRAL STATE ORGANS SINCE 1949: CENTRAL MILITARY COMMISSION
CENTRAL STATE ORGANS SINCE 1949: CHINESE PEOPLE'S POLITICAL CONSULTATIVE CONFERENCE
CENTRAL STATE ORGANS SINCE 1949: NATIONAL PEOPLE'S CONGRESS
CENTRAL STATE ORGANS SINCE 1949: OVERVIEW
CENTRAL STATE ORGANS SINCE 1949: PRESIDENT AND VICE PRESIDENT

CENTRAL STATE ORGANS SINCE 1949: STATE COUNCIL, COMMISSIONS, MINISTRIES, AND BUREAUS
CONSTITUTIONS SINCE 1949
FOREIGN POLICY FRAMEWORKS AND THEORIES: ONE-CHINA POLICY AND "ONE COUNTRY, TWO SYSTEMS"
INSPECTION AND AUDIT
POLICE, SECRET
PROVINCIAL AND SUBPROVINCIAL GOVERNMENT STRUCTURE SINCE 1949: COUNTIES
PROVINCIAL AND SUBPROVINCIAL GOVERNMENT STRUCTURE SINCE 1949: MUNICIPALITIES UNDER CENTRAL CONTROL
PROVINCIAL AND SUBPROVINCIAL GOVERNMENT STRUCTURE SINCE 1949: OVERVIEW
PROVINCIAL AND SUBPROVINCIAL GOVERNMENT STRUCTURE SINCE 1949: PROVINCES

***Cai, Yuan Peter***
University of Adelaide, Australia
PAN-ASIANISM

***Cao, Cong***
Neil D. Levin Graduate Institute of International Relations and Commerce
State University of New York
HIGH TECHNOLOGY
RESEARCH IN ENGINEERING
RESEARCH IN THE SCIENCES
RESEARCH ORGANIZATIONS
SCIENTIFIC COMMUNITY
SCIENTIFIC EXCHANGES
SURVEYS OF NATURAL RESOURCES [SIDEBAR]

***Carroll, Peter J.***
Department of History
Northwestern University
SUZHOU

***Chan, Alfred L.***
Professor
Huron University College, University of Western Ontario
WANG DAN [SIDEBAR]

***Chan, Cheris Shun-ching***
Department of Sociology
University of Hong Kong
EMPLOYEES' HEALTH INSURANCE

***Chan, Daniel Kam Yin***
Conjoint Professor, University of New South Wales, School of Public Health & Community Medicine
Bankstown-Lidcombe Hospital
COMMUNITY CARE

***Chan, David K. K.***
Associate Professor and Program Leader of East & Southeast Asian Studies, Department of Asian and International Studies
City University of Hong Kong
HONG KONG: EDUCATION IN HONG KONG SINCE 1842

***Chan, Gerald***
Professor of Political Studies
University of Auckland, New Zealand
INTERNATIONAL RELATIONS: SINCE 1949

***Chan, Kai Yiu***
Department of History
Tunghai University, Taiwan
LIU HONGSHENG

***Chan, Phil C. W.***
Faculty of Law, National University of Singapore
HONG KONG: NATIONALITY ISSUES SINCE 1983
PRIVACY
STRIKES
YOUTH

***Chan, Wellington K. K.***
National Endowment for the Humanities Distinguished Professor of Humanities, and Professor of History
Occidental College
SINCERE DEPARTMENT STORES
WING ON DEPARTMENT STORES

***Chang, Arnold***
Independent Scholar and Artist
CONNOISSEURSHIP
ZHANG DAQIAN (CHANG DAI-CHIEN)

***Chang, Bi-yu***
Centre of Taiwan Studies
School of Oriental and African Studies, University of London
FILM INDUSTRY: TAIWAN

***Chang, Chia-ju***
The City College of New York–Brooklyn College
LEE, ANG

***Chang, Chiung-Fang***
Assistant Professor of Sociology, Department of Sociology, Social Work, and Criminal Justice
Lamar University
MINORITY NATIONALITIES: LARGE NATIONAL MINORITIES

***Chang, Maria Hsia***
Professor Emerita, Department of Political Science
University of Nevada at Reno
BANKING: PEOPLE'S BANK OF CHINA
FASCISM
MONEY AND BANKING, 1800–1949

***Chang, Shih-Ming Li***
Associate Professor, Department of Theatre & Dance
Wittenberg University
DANCE

***Chang Yu-ting***
Texas A&M University
MARRIAGE
SEX RATIO

***Chappell, Hilary***
École des Hautes Études en Sciences Sociales, Paris
HOKKIEN (MIN)

***Chen, Jianyue***
Assistant Professor of History
Northeast Lakeview College
COMFORT WOMEN [SIDEBAR]

***Chen Lei***
Law Faculty
National University of Singapore
COMPANIES: CORPORATE LAW

***Chen, Wenhong***
Department of Sociology
Duke University
FINANCIAL MARKETS

***Cheng, Joseph Yu-shek***
Professor of Political Science
City University of Hong Kong
COMMUNIST PARTY
COMMUNIST PARTY ORGANIZATION AND STRUCTURE [SIDEBAR]
ECONOMIC DEVELOPMENT: GREAT WESTERN DEVELOPMENT SCHEME
FOREIGN POLICY FRAMEWORKS AND THEORIES: OVERVIEW
JIANG ZEMIN
SPECIAL ADMINISTRATIVE REGIONS

*Cheng, Yinghong*
History, Political Science, and Philosophy Department
Delaware State University
INFLUENCES ABROAD: INFLUENCE OF MAOIST PROPAGANDA ON WESTERN AND THIRD-WORLD YOUTH

*Cheung, Sui-wai*
Department of History
The Chinese University of Hong Kong
BAOJIA SYSTEM
IMPERIAL HOUSEHOLD DEPARTMENT
INSTITUTIONAL LEGACIES OF THE TAIPING UPRISINGS [SIDEBAR]

*Chiang, Yung-chen*
DePauw University
HU SHI

*Choi, Eun Kyong*
Assistant Professor
Ajou University, South Korea
TAXATION SINCE 1978

*Chongyi, Feng*
Professor
University of Technology, Sydney
CLASSICAL SCHOLARSHIP AND INTELLECTUAL DEBATES: DEBATES SINCE 1949
HUNDRED FLOWERS CAMPAIGN

*Chou, Bill K. P.*
Assistant Professor, Department of Government and Public Administration
University of Macau
MACAU

*Christiansen, Flemming*
Department of East Asian Studies
University of Leeds
CHINESE OVERSEAS: DIASPORA AND HOMELAND

*Chua, Ying*
Assistant Professor, Art History Department
Ithaca College
ART SCHOOLS AND COLLEGES
CAI GUO-QIANG
OIL PAINTING (*YOUHUA*)
XU BEIHONG
XU BING

*Chung, Jae Ho*
Director of the Institute for China Studies
Seoul National University
CENTRAL-LOCAL RELATIONSHIPS
KOREA, RELATIONS WITH (NORTH AND SOUTH)

*Cini, Francesca*
Freelance Sinologist and Consultant
AFRICAN STATES, RELATIONS WITH
INVESTMENTS IN AFRICA: INFRASTRUCTURE AND NATURAL RESOURCES [SIDEBAR]

*Clausen, Soren*
Institute of History and Area Studies
University of Aarhus
HARBIN

*Claypool, Lisa*
Assistant Professor of Art History and Humanities
Reed College
ART MUSEUMS
REN XIONG

*Cody, Jeffrey W.*
Getty Conservation Institute, Los Angeles, California
ARCHITECTURE, HISTORY OF: WESTERN ARCHITECTS AND BUILDINGS IN CHINA

*Cohen, Paul A.*
Edith Stix Wasserman Professor of History and Asian Studies, Emeritus, Wellesley College
Associate, Fairbank Center for Chinese Studies, Harvard University
BOXER UPRISING

*Comtois, Claude*
Professor of Transport Geography
Université de Montréal
TRANSPORT INFRASTRUCTURE: AIR TRANSPORT
TRANSPORT INFRASTRUCTURE: OVERVIEW
TRANSPORT INFRASTRUCTURE: ROAD NETWORK

*Cong, Xiaoping*
Associate Professor of History
University of Houston
EDUCATION: HIGHER EDUCATION BEFORE 1949
PRIVATE SCHOOLS [SIDEBAR]

*Conn, Peter*
Professor, English
University of Pennsylvania
BUCK, PEARL S.

*Connelly, Marisela*
Professor, Center for Asian and African Studies
El Colegio de México
CHIANG CHING-KUO (JIANG JINGGUO)
DENG XIAOPING
HU YAOBANG

*Conner, Patrick*
Martyn Gregory Gallery
London
INFLUENCES ABROAD: NINETEENTH-CENTURY CHINOISERIE AND CHINESE EXPORT

*Cook, Sarah*
Institute of Development Studies at the University of Sussex
INTERNATIONAL DEVELOPMENT PROGRAMS IN CHINA: OVERVIEW
INTERNATIONAL DEVELOPMENT PROGRAMS IN CHINA: UNITED NATIONS DEVELOPMENT PROGRAMME
INTERNATIONAL DEVELOPMENT PROGRAMS IN CHINA: WORLD BANK

*Crespi, John A.*
Colgate University
BAI HUA

*Croizier, Ralph*
Professor Emeritus of History
University of Victoria
INFLUENCES ABROAD: MAOISM AND ART

*Crossley, Pamela*
Dartmouth College
EMPERORS, 1800–1912

*Culp, Robert*
Associate Professor, History & Asian Studies
Bard College
ZHEJIANG

*Dabringhaus, Sabine*
Institute for History
Albert-Ludwigs University of Freiburg
CIXI, EMPRESS DOWAGER

*Dal Lago, Francesca*
Leiden School for Area Studies
Leiden University
CHANG YU (SANYU)
NEW WAVE MOVEMENT, '85
PAN YULIANG
POLITICAL POP AND CYNICAL REALISM

*Dang, Suzhen*
Institute of Geographic Sciences and Natural Resources Research
The Chinese Academy of Sciences
RIVER SYSTEMS: HUAI RIVER

*Davin, Delia*
Emeritus Professor of Chinese Studies
University of Leeds
ALL-CHINA WOMEN'S FEDERATION
COMMERCIAL ART: PRODUCT DESIGN
COMMUNIST YOUTH LEAGUE
DOMESTIC VIOLENCE
ECONOMIC DEVELOPMENT: UNDP HUMAN DEVELOPMENT REPORT ON CHINA, 2005
EXTRATERRITORIALITY
FOREIGN CONCESSIONS, SETTLEMENTS, AND LEASED TERRITORIES
HIV/AIDS
HUNAN AND HUBEI
LIFE CYCLE: BIRTH
LU ZUOFU
MIGRANT WORKERS
NATIONALISM
POPULATION POLICY: BIRTH-PLANNING POLICY
RURAL DEVELOPMENT SINCE 1978: RURAL INDUSTRIALIZATION
SOCIAL CLASSES SINCE 1978
SONG QINGLING
WANG SHIWEI
WOMEN IN POLITICS
WOMEN, EMPLOYMENT OF
WORKERS, INDUSTRIAL, 1860–1949
XIAFANG
YANG ZHENNING

*Davis, Walter B.*
Assistant Professor
University of Alberta
ART, HISTORY OF: 1911–1949
ART, NATIONAL ESSENCE MOVEMENT IN
CHINESE PAINTING (*GUOHUA*)
WANG ZHEN (WANG YITING)
WU SHUJUAN (WU XINGFEN)

*DeBevoise, Jane*
Chair, Asia Art Archive
GU WENDA

*Deng, Danielle Xiaodan*
Texas A&M University
MARRIAGE
SEX RATIO

*Deng, Kent G.*
London School of Economics
MONEY AND MONETARY POLICY, 1800–1927
TAXATION AND FISCAL POLICIES, 1800–1912
URBAN EMPLOYMENT TO 1949

*Denton, Kirk A.*
Department of East Asian Languages and Literatures
The Ohio State University
HU FENG
LEAGUE OF LEFT-WING WRITERS
LITERATURE SINCE 1800
LU XUN

*Dittmer, Lowell*
Professor of Political Science
University of California at Berkeley
COMMUNIST PARTY HISTORY REVISED (1981)
FOUR BASIC PRINCIPLES [SIDEBAR]
HISTORY: OVERVIEW, SINCE 1949
HOW TO BE A GOOD COMMUNIST [SIDEBAR]
LIU SHAOQI
POLITICAL CULTURE SINCE 1900
POLITICAL SUCCESSION
RESOLUTION ON PARTY HISTORY [SIDEBAR]
ZHOU ENLAI

*Doar, Bruce G.*
The University of Sydney
AVANT-GARDE FICTION
BUDDHISM
FUZHOU
MAO DUN
NEW DEMOCRACY, 1949–1953
NEW LEFT
NINGBO (NINGPO)
PEI, I.M.
PROSTITUTION, HISTORY OF
SOCIALISM
WANG MENG
XIE JIN
YAN FU
YAN'AN FORUM
ZHAO SHULI

*Dong, Madeleine Yue*
Professor, Department of History
University of Washington
BEIJING

*Dray-Novey, Alison J.*
Professor of History
College of Notre Dame of Maryland
POLICE, 1800–1949

*Dubois, Thomas David*
National University of Singapore
Department of History
RELIGIOUS ORGANIZATIONS

*Duckett, Jane*
Professor of Chinese and Comparative Politics
University of Glasgow
MEDICAL CARE SINCE 1949
RURAL COOPERATIVE MEDICAL SYSTEMS

*Edgren, J. S.*
Editorial Director, Chinese Rare Books Project
Princeton University
NIANHUA (NEW YEAR PICTURES) [SIDEBAR]
WOODBLOCK PRINTING (XYLOGRAPHY)

*Edmonds, Richard Louis*
Visiting Professor, Committee on Geographical Studies
University of Chicago
EARTHQUAKES SINCE 1800

*Elleman, Bruce A.*
U.S. Naval War College
NAVAL FACTORS IN THE CHINESE CIVIL WAR [SIDEBAR]
RED ARMY [SIDEBAR]

*Elman, Benjamin A.*
Professor of East Asian Studies and History
Princeton University
CLASSICAL SCHOLARSHIP AND INTELLECTUAL DEBATES: 1800–1864
EXAMINATION SYSTEM, 1800–1905

*Erickson, Andrew S.*
Assistant Professor
U.S. Naval War College
MILITARY REGIONS [SIDEBAR]
PEOPLE'S LIBERATION ARMY: COMMAND STRUCTURE OF THE ARMED SERVICES
PEOPLE'S LIBERATION ARMY: MILITARY ENTERPRISES AND INDUSTRY SINCE 1949
PEOPLE'S LIBERATION ARMY: OVERVIEW

*Evans, Harriet*
Professor, Chinese Cultural Studies, School of Social Sciences, Humanities and Languages
University of Westminster
SEXUALITY

*Eyferth, Jacob*
University of Chicago
HANDICRAFTS
SICHUAN

*Fang, Xiaoping*
Postdoctoral Research Fellow, China Research Centre, Faculty of Arts and Social Sciences
University of Technology Sydney
MEDICINE, WESTERN, SINCE 1949

*Faure, David*
Department of History
The Chinese University of Hong Kong
HAKKA
LIN ZEXU

*Fell, Dafydd*
Lecturer in Taiwan Studies, Department of Political Science and International Studies and Centre for Financial and Management Studies
School of Oriental and African Studies, University of London
CHEN SHUIBIAN
LI DENGHUI (LEE TENG-HUI)
TAIWAN, REPUBLIC OF CHINA: DEMOCRATIC PROGRESSIVE PARTY
TAIWAN, REPUBLIC OF CHINA: POLITICS SINCE 1945

*Field, Stephen L.*
J. K. and Ingrid Lee Professor of Chinese
Trinity University
FENGSHUI

*Finnane, Antonia*
Professor, School of Historical Studies
University of Melbourne
CLOTHING SINCE 1800
DEMOCRATIC PARTIES: CHINA ZHIGONG (PUBLIC INTEREST) PARTY
PEASANTRY SINCE 1900
URBAN CHINA: CITIES AND URBANIZATION, 1800–1949
URBAN CHINA: ORGANIZING PRINCIPLES OF CITIES
YANGZHOU

*Fisher, Nevan Andrew*
Assistant Professor of History
Nazareth College, Rochester, N.Y.
ANHUI

*Flath, James*
Department of History
University of Western Ontario
MONUMENTS
PROPAGANDA ART: NEW NIANHUA

*Fok, Silvia Siu Har*
The University of Hong Kong
STARS (XINGXING) PAINTING GROUP, 1979–1983

*Fonoroff, Paul*
Film Critic and Movie Historian
FILM INDUSTRY: HONG KONG

*Fraser, Sarah E.*
Department of Art History
Northwestern University
ARCHAEOLOGY AND WESTERN EXPLORERS
ARCHAEOLOGY, POLITICS OF

*Frederiksen, Lynn E.*
Freelance Choreographer and Dance Teacher
DANCE

*Fung, Edmund Shiu Kay (Feng Zhaoji)*
Professor of Asian Studies
University of Western Sydney
BEIYANG CLIQUE
CLASSICAL SCHOLARSHIP AND INTELLECTUAL DEBATES: INTELLECTUALS, 1900–1949
DEFENSE, 1800–1912
POLITICAL PARTIES, 1905–1949
REVOLUTION OF 1911
WARS AND THE MILITARY, 1800–1912

*Galikowski, Maria*
Senior Lecturer, Chinese Programme
The University of Waikato
ART, HISTORY OF: SINCE 1949
ART, POLICY ON, SINCE 1949
PROPAGANDA ART: ART PRODUCTS OF THE CULTURAL REVOLUTION
PROPAGANDA ART: OVERVIEW
PROPAGANDA ART: POSTERS
SOCIALIST REALISM IN ART

*Gallagher, Kelly Sims*
Director, Energy Technology Innovation Policy, John F. Kennedy School of Government
Harvard University
ENERGY: ELECTRICITY GENERATION
ENERGY: OIL AND NATURAL GAS

*Gao, Mobo C. F.*
Professor
The University of Adelaide
VILLAGES SINCE 1800

*Gao, Yan*
Ph.D. Student, Department of History
Carnegie Mellon University
NATURAL RESOURCES

*Gao Yunxiang*
Assistant Professor of History
Ryerson University
OLYMPICS, 2008 BEIJING OLYMPIC GAMES
OLYMPICS
SPORTS FIGURES
SPORTS

*Gardella, Robert*
Emeritus Professor
United States Merchant Marine Academy
COMMERCIAL ELITE, 1800–1949
TEA SINCE 1800

*Gerth, Karl*
Faculty of History
Merton College, Oxford University
CONSUMPTION AND CONSUMER CULTURES
NATIONAL PRODUCTS MOVEMENT

*Girardot, Norman*
Religion Studies Department
Lehigh University
LEGGE, JAMES

*Goldblatt, Howard*
Director of the Center for Asian Studies
University of Notre Dame
MO YAN

*Gong, Haomin*
Assistant Professor of Chinese and Asian Studies
St. Mary's College of Maryland
QIAN ZHONGSHU

*Goossaert, Vincent*
Centre National de la Récherche Scientifique & École Pratique des Hautes Études
Paris, France
DAOISM
RELIGIOUS POLICY
RELIGIOUS SPECIALISTS SINCE 1800
STATE CULT

*Gordon, Leonard H. D.*
Professor Emeritus of Chinese History
Purdue University
SUN YAT-SEN (SUN YIXIAN)

*Gottschang, Thomas R.*
Professor of Economics
College of the Holy Cross, Worcester, MA
GEOGRAPHICAL REGIONS, NATURAL AND HUMAN
INTERNAL MIGRATION AND INTERNAL COLONIZATION SINCE 1800

*Green, Colin*
Department of History
Kwantlen University, Vancouver, Canada
MILITARY CULTURE AND TRADITION

*Greene, J. Megan*
Associate Professor of History
University of Kansas
ACADEMIA SINICA (ZHONGYANG YANJIUYUAN)

*Gregory, John S.*
Emeritus Professor
La Trobe University, Melbourne
MORRISON, GEORGE E.

*Grieder, Jerome B.*
Professor Emeritus of History and East Asian Studies
Brown University
CLASSICAL SCHOLARSHIP AND INTELLECTUAL DEBATES: DEBATES, 1900–1949
DEMOCRATIC IDEAS, REFORMS, AND EXPERIMENTS SINCE THE 1880S

*Groot, Gerry*
Senior Lecturer, Centre for Asian Studies
University of Adelaide
DEMOCRATIC PARTIES: ALL-CHINA FEDERATION OF INDUSTRY AND COMMERCE
DEMOCRATIC PARTIES: CHINA ASSOCIATION FOR PROMOTING DEMOCRACY
DEMOCRATIC PARTIES: CHINA DEMOCRATIC NATIONAL CONSTRUCTION ASSOCIATION
DEMOCRATIC PARTIES: CHINESE PEASANTS AND WORKERS DEMOCRATIC PARTY
DEMOCRATIC PARTIES: DEMOCRATIC LEAGUE OF CHINA
DEMOCRATIC PARTIES: JIUSAN (SEPTEMBER THIRD) SOCIETY
DEMOCRATIC PARTIES: OVERVIEW
DEMOCRATIC PARTIES: REVOLUTIONARY COMMITTEE OF THE NATIONALIST PARTY
DEMOCRATIC PARTIES: TAIWAN DEMOCRATIC SELF-GOVERNMENT LEAGUE
UNITED FRONT WORK

*Gu, Yi*
Ph.D. Candidate
Brown University
PHOTOGRAPHY, HISTORY OF: ART PHOTOGRAPHY

*Gunn, Edward Mansfield, Jr.*
Professor of Chinese Literature, Department of Asian Studies
Cornell University
CAO YU
LANGUAGE AND LANGUAGE POLICY
LAO SHE
LEXICOGRAPHY
LIN YUTANG
PLAYS (*HUAJU*)
ZHU ZIQING (ZHU ZIHUA)

*Halperin, Mark*
Department of East Asian Languages and Cultures
University of California, Davis
WALEY, ARTHUR

*Hamilton, Robyn*
University of Auckland
QIU JIN

*Hang, Xing*
Ph.D. Candidate
University of California, Berkeley
AGRICULTURAL PRODUCTION: ANIMAL HUSBANDRY

*Hansson, Anders*
Chinese University of Hong Kong
SERVILE STATUSES

*Harris, Kristine M.*
Department of History and Asian Studies Program
State University of New York at New Paltz
HU DIE
LI XIANGLAN
RUAN LINGYU

*Harwit, Eric*
Professor, Asian Studies
University of Hawaii
AUTOMOBILE INDUSTRY

*Hayford, Charles W.*
Independent Scholar
Northwestern University
CHINA HANDS
CHU ANPING
HOU HSIAO-HSIEN [SIDEBAR]
INTERPRETERS OF THINGS CHINESE TO THE WEST
MAY FOURTH MOVEMENT
STILWELL, JOSEPH
WESTERNIZATION
WONG KAR-WAI [SIDEBAR]

*He, Baogang*
Professor
Deakin University, Australia
PROVINCIAL AND SUBPROVINCIAL GOVERNMENT STRUCTURE SINCE 1949: VILLAGES

*He Jinli*
Visiting Assistant Professor of Chinese
Trinity University
ART SOCIETIES SINCE 1800

*He Lei*
Texas A&M University
MARRIAGE

*He Xi*
History Department
Chinese University of Hong Kong
HAINAN

*Heberer, Thomas*
Professor, Institute of East Asian Studies
University of Duisburg–Essen, Germany
CADRE SYSTEM
CORRUPTION
ENTREPRENEURS SINCE 1949
HARMONIOUS SOCIETY
HENAN
MINORITY NATIONALITIES: CULTURAL IMAGES OF NATIONAL MINORITIES
MINORITY NATIONALITIES: OVERVIEW
PRIVATE ENTERPRISES
PROVINCIAL AND SUBPROVINCIAL GOVERNMENT STRUCTURE SINCE 1949: STREET COMMITTEES, COMMUNITIES
PROVINCIAL AND SUBPROVINCIAL GOVERNMENT STRUCTURE SINCE 1949: TOWNSHIPS
SOCIAL AND COMMUNITY ORGANIZATIONS

*Heep, Sandra*
Research Group on the Political Economy of China
Trier University, Germany
CHINA INVESTMENT CORPORATION [SIDEBAR]

STATE ADMINISTRATION OF FOREIGN EXCHANGE (SAFE) [SIDEBAR]

*Henderson, J. Vernon*
Eastman Professor of Political Economy
Brown University
URBAN CHINA: OVERVIEW
URBAN CHINA: URBANIZATION SINCE 1949

*Heng, Michael Heng Siam (Wang Zhaoxing)*
Senior Research Fellow, East Asian Institute
National University of Singapore
FOUR MODERNIZATIONS

*Henningsen, Lena*
Institute of Chinese Studies
University of Heidelberg
MA, YO-YO

*Herrmann-Pillath, Carsten*
Professor, Frankfurt School of Finance & Management
BRANDS
CENTRAL PLANNING
COMPANIES: COLLECTIVES
COMPANIES: JOINT VENTURES
COMPANIES: OVERVIEW
DOMESTIC TRADE: SINCE 1950
ECONOMIC DEVELOPMENT: ECONOMIC REGIONS
ECONOMIC DEVELOPMENT: OVERVIEW
ECONOMIC REFORM SINCE 1978: DUAL-TRACK PRICING
ECONOMIC REFORM SINCE 1978: OVERVIEW
FIVE-YEAR PLANS
INCOME
INDUSTRIAL DEVELOPMENT SINCE 1949
INDUSTRIAL POLICY SINCE 1949
IRON RICE BOWL [SIDEBAR]
LABOR: MOBILITY
LABOR: UNEMPLOYMENT
MA YINCHU [SIDEBAR]
PRICE SYSTEM
RURAL DEVELOPMENT, 1949–1978: COLLECTIVIZATION
RURAL DEVELOPMENT, 1949–1978: CREDIT COOPERATIVES
RURAL DEVELOPMENT, 1949–1978: LAND REFORM OF 1950
RURAL DEVELOPMENT, 1949–1978: OVERVIEW
RURAL DEVELOPMENT, 1949–1978: PEOPLE'S COMMUNES
SERVICE SECTOR (TERTIARY INDUSTRY)
SOCIAL CLASSES BEFORE 1949
SOCIALIST MARKET ECONOMY
STATE-OWNED ENTERPRISES
WORK POINTS SYSTEM [SIDEBAR]

*Hesketh, Therese*
Senior Lecturer, Center for International Health and Development
University College London
FAMILY: ONE-CHILD POLICY

*Hevia, James*
The New Collegiate Division and the Department of History
University of Chicago
WADE, THOMAS

*Higgins, Roland L.*
Keene State College
LATE IMPERIAL CHINA [SIDEBAR]

*Hill, Emily M.*
Associate Professor, History
Queen's University, Canada
OPIUM WARS
SMUGGLING
TREATY PORTS

*Ho, Eliza*
Ph.D. Candidate
Ohio State University
FAN CHANGJIANG
LINGNAN SCHOOL OF PAINTING
PHOTOGRAPHY, HISTORY OF: DOCUMENTARY PHOTOGRAPHY
PHOTOGRAPHY, HISTORY OF: PROPAGANDA PHOTOGRAPHY
PICTORIAL MAGAZINES SINCE 1880

*Hockx, Michel*
SOAS, University of London
LITERARY SOCIETIES

*Holz, Carsten A.*
Social Science Division
Hong Kong University of Science and Technology
STATISTICS

*Holzman, Marie*
Solidarité Chine, Paris, France
FANG LIZHI
WEI JINGSHENG [SIDEBAR]

*Hong Xiao*
School of Languages, Cultures and Linguistics, University of Canterbury, Christchurch, New Zealand
DIALECT GROUPS

*Hong, Zaixin*
Associate Professor of Art History
University of Puget Sound
ART MARKET, 1800–1949
LITERATI PAINTING (*WENRENHUA*)

*Honig, Emily*
Department of History
University of California at Santa Cruz
GENDER RELATIONS

*Horesh, Niv*
University of New South Wales, Australia
COPPER AND SILVER, 1800–1950
INTERNATIONAL DEVELOPMENT PROGRAMS IN CHINA: INTERNATIONAL MONETARY FUND

*Howell, Jude*
Centre for Civil Society
London School of Economics and Political Science
GOVERNMENT-ORGANIZED NONGOVERNMENTAL ORGANIZATION

*Hsu, Berry F. C.*
Professor, Department of Real Estate and Construction and Deputy Director, Asian Institute of International Financial Law
University of Hong Kong
CHINA SECURITIES REGULATORY COMMISSION [SIDEBAR]
FINANCIAL REGULATION

*Hsueh Yeh (Xue Ye)*
Associate Professor
The University of Memphis
TEACHER EDUCATION

*Huang, Alexander C. Y.*
Assistant Professor of Comparative Literature and Asian Studies
Pennsylvania State University
MODEL OPERAS AND BALLETS
TAIWAN, REPUBLIC OF CHINA: MILITARY FORCES

*Huang, Grace C.*
Assistant Professor, Department of Government
St. Lawrence University
POLITICAL CONTROL SINCE 1949

*Huang Jianli*
Department of History
National University of Singapore
NATIONALIST GOVERNMENT, 1927–1949

*Huang, Nicole*
Associate Professor of Chinese Literature
University of Wisconsin–Madison
CHANG, EILEEN (ZHANG AILING)

*Huang, Sophia Wu*
Agricultural Economist
Economic Research Service, U.S. Department of Agriculture
AGRICULTURAL PRODUCTION: FRUIT AND VEGETABLE FARMING

*Huang, Yanzhong*
Associate Professor, Director of the Center for Global Health Studies
John C. Whitehead School of Diplomacy and International Relations, Seton Hall University
SEVERE ACUTE RESPIRATORY SYNDROME

*Huchet, Jean-François*
Director, French Centre for Research on Contemporary China (CEFC)
Hong Kong (CEFC)
FOREIGN INVESTMENT SINCE 1949

*Huenemann, Ralph W.*
Professor Emeritus
University of Victoria, Canada
BANKING: BIG FOUR
BANKING: OVERVIEW
BUILD-OPERATE-TRANSFER (BOT) CONTRACTS
FOREIGN CURRENCY RESERVES
TRANSPORT INFRASTRUCTURE: RAILWAYS SINCE 1876

*Hussain, Athar*
Professor & Director, Asia Research Centre
London School of Economics
SOCIAL WELFARE: OVERVIEW
SOCIAL WELFARE: PENSIONS
SOCIAL WELFARE: SOCIAL WELFARE SINCE 1978

*Hwang, Dongyoun*
Associate Professor of Asian Studies
Soka University of America
WANG JINGWEI

*Hyer, Eric*
Associate Professor
Brigham Young University
SOUTH CHINA SEA

*Ikels, Charlotte*
Professor of Anthropology
Case Western Reserve University
LIFE CYCLE: OLD AGE

*Ip, Manying*
Associate Professor in Asian Studies
University of Auckland
CHINESE OVERSEAS: CHINATOWNS
CHINESE OVERSEAS: OVERVIEW
CHINESE OVERSEAS: RETURNED OVERSEAS CHINESE

*Ip, Olivia*
Associate Professor, Department of Management
The City University of Hong Kong
LABOR: TRADE UNIONS

*Isett, Christopher M.*
University of Minnesota, Twin Cities
LAND TENURE SINCE 1800

*Jacka, Tamara*
Associate Professor, Research School of Pacific and Asian Studies
Australian National University
WOMEN, STATUS OF

*Janku, Andrea*
SOAS
University of London
GE GONGZHEN
LOCUST PLAGUES SINCE 1800

*Jeans, Roger B.*
Professor of History, Emeritus
Washington and Lee University
FEDERALISM
LIBERALISM
ZHANG JUNMAI (CARSUN CHANG)

*Jeffreys, Elaine*
China Research Centre
University of Technology, Sydney
SELLING AND BUYING SEX IN CONTEMPORARY CHINA [SIDEBAR]

*Jensen, Mads Holst*
Human Rights and Business Department
Danish Institute for Human Rights
LABOR: CHINA AND THE INTERNATIONAL LABOUR ORGANIZATION

*Jiang, Hong*
Assistant Professor of Geography
University of Hawaii at Manoa
DESERTIFICATION

*Jin Qiu*
Associate Professor of History
Old Dominion University
LIN BIAO

*Johnson, Kay Ann*
Professor of Politics and Asian Studies
Hampshire College
ADOPTIONS

*Johnston, Charles S.*
AUT University
HUTONG

*Jones, Andrew F.*
University of California, Berkeley
RADIO

*Judge, Joan*
Associate Professor, Division of Humanities/School of Women's Studies
York University
FOOTBINDING

*Kamata, Mayumi*
Ph.D. Candidate
Ohio State University
ART, JAPANESE INFLUENCE ON
LI HUA

*Kang, Min Jay*
Associate Professor of Architecture
Tanjiang (Tamkang) University
TAIBEI (TAIPEI)

*Katz, Paul R.*
Institute of Modern History
Academia Sinica
POPULAR RELIGION

*Keck, Frédéric*
Centre national de la récherche scientifique, Paris, France
AVIAN INFLUENZA

*Keenan, Barry C.*
Professor of History
Denison University
ACADEMIES (*SHUYUAN*)

*Keister, Lisa A.*
Department of Sociology
Duke University
FINANCIAL MARKETS

*Kelly, David*
Professor of China Studies, China Research Centre
University of Technology Sydney
CHINESE MARXISM: FEUDALISM
INDIVIDUAL AND THE STATE, 1800–1949

*Kent, Ann E.*
Visiting Fellow
ANU College of Law, Australian National University
INTERNATIONAL ORGANIZATIONS, RELATIONS WITH, 1900–1949
INTERNATIONAL ORGANIZATIONS, RELATIONS WITH, SINCE 1949

*Kernen, Antoine*
University of Lausanne, Switzerland
HEAVY INDUSTRY
SHENYANG

*Kerr, David*
Durham University, United Kingdom
EUROPEAN UNION, RELATIONS WITH

*Kinkley, Jeffrey C.*
Professor of History
St. John's University, New York
SHEN CONGWEN
XIAO QIAN (XIAO BINGQIAN)

*Klingberg, Travis*
Ph.D. Candidate, Department of Geography
University of Colorado at Boulder
LEISURE

*Köll, Elisabeth*
Associate Professor
Harvard Business School
RONG ZONGJING
ZHANG JIAN

*Kozyrev, Vitaly*
School of Arts and Sciences
Endicott College
ARMY AND POLITICS
DOMESTIC TRADE: 1900–1949
INTERNATIONAL DEVELOPMENT PROGRAMS IN CHINA: ASIAN DEVELOPMENT BANK
INTERNATIONAL RELATIONS: TREATIES SINCE 1949

*Krebs, Edward S.*
Independent Researcher and Translator
Douglasville, GA
ANARCHISM
SHAANXI

*Krug, Barbara*
Rotterdam School of Management
Erasmus University, Rotterdam
PUBLIC FINANCE SINCE 1900

*Kulacki, Gregory*
Union of Concerned Scientists
ENERGY: NUCLEAR POWER
ENVIRONMENT

*Kuo, Jason C.*
Professor, Department of Art History & Archaeology
University of Maryland, College Park
ART HISTORY AND HISTORIOGRAPHY

*Kuo, Margaret*
California State University, Long Beach
MARRIAGE LAWS

*Kwon Tai-Hwan*
Department of Sociology
Seoul National University
KOREAN COMMUNITY IN CHINA

*Kwong, Julia*
Distinguished Professor Emerita, Department of Sociology
University of Manitoba
EDUCATION THROUGH LABOR, REFORM THROUGH LABOR
EDUCATION: PRIVATE SCHOOLS SINCE 1980S

*Kwong, Luke S. K.*
Professor
Department of History
University of Lethbridge
HUNDRED DAYS' REFORM
KANG YOUWEI
SCRAMBLE FOR CONCESSIONS

*Laamann, Lars Peter*
Lecturer in the History of China, History Department
School of Oriental and African Studies, University of London
DRUGS AND NARCOTICS

*Ladds, Catherine*
Department of History
Colorado State University
CHINESE MARITIME CUSTOMS SERVICE

*LaFleur, Robert André*
Professor of History and Anthropology
Beloit College
CALENDAR
FESTIVALS

*Lai Chi-kong*
Reader in Modern Chinese History
University of Queensland
CHINA MERCHANTS' STEAM NAVIGATION COMPANY
FASHION
HAIRSTYLES
LI HONGZHANG
LU ZUOFU

*Lai, Delin*
Department of Fine Arts
University of Louisville
ARCHITECTURE, HISTORIOGRAPHY OF, SINCE 1800
ARCHITECTURE, HISTORY OF: ARCHITECTURE TO 1949

*Lai, Walton Look*
Department of History
University of the West Indies, Trinidad and Tobago
CHINESE OVERSEAS: COOLIE TRADE

*Lai Yu-chih*
Curator, Painting and Calligraphy Department
National Palace Museum
REN YI (REN BONIAN)

*Laing, Ellen Johnston*
Research Associate, Center for Chinese Studies
University of Michigan
COMMERCIAL ART: CALENDARS

*Lam, Tong*
Assistant Professor, Department of History
University of Toronto
SOCIAL SCIENCES

*Lam, Willy Wo-Lap*
Adjunct Professor of China Studies
Akita International University, Japan & The Chinese University of Hong Kong
HU JINTAO
THREE REPRESENTS [SIDEBAR]
WEN JIABAO
ZHU RONGJI

*Lam, Wing*
Independent Policy Researcher
Hong Kong
INTERNATIONAL DEVELOPMENT PROGRAMS IN CHINA: FOOD AND AGRICULTURE ORGANIZATION
INTERNATIONAL DEVELOPMENT PROGRAMS IN CHINA: OVERVIEW
INTERNATIONAL DEVELOPMENT PROGRAMS IN CHINA: UNITED NATIONS DEVELOPMENT PROGRAMME

INTERNATIONAL DEVELOPMENT PROGRAMS IN CHINA: WORLD BANK

*Landsberger, Stefan R.*
Associate Professor of Contemporary Chinese History, Leiden University
Professor of Contemporary Chinese Culture, University of Amsterdam
DAQING [SIDEBAR]
DAZHAI [SIDEBAR]
PERSONALITY CULTS

*Larus, Elizabeth Freund*
University of Mary Washington
TAIWAN, REPUBLIC OF CHINA: FOREIGN RELATIONS SINCE 1949

*Lary, Diana*
Department of History
University of British Columbia
CIVIL WAR, 1946–1949
GUANGXI
WARLORD ERA (1916–1928)
YUAN SHIKAI

*Laurenceson, James*
Lecturer
University of Queensland
BANKING: NONPERFORMING LOANS

*Lee, Joseph Tse-Hei*
Department of History
Pace University
PATRIOTIC RELIGIOUS ASSOCIATIONS [SIDEBAR]
PROTESTANTISM
THREE-SELF PATRIOTIC MOVEMENT

*Lee, Ngok*
Public Policy Research Institute
Hong Kong Polytechnic University
ARMAMENTS

*Lee, Paul Tae-Woo (Lǐ TàiYǔ)*
Professor, Department of Logistics and Shipping Management;
Director, Shipping, Port and Logistics Research Center
Kainan University, Taiwan
TRANSPORT INFRASTRUCTURE: SHIPPING SINCE 1949

*Lee Pui-tak*
Centre of Asian Studies
University of Hong Kong
FOREIGN INVESTMENT, 1800–1949

*Lee, Tahirih V.*
Associate Professor of Law
Florida State University College of Law
SHANGHAI MIXED COURT

*Leese, Daniel*
Munich University
HEBEI
LITTLE RED BOOK (QUOTATIONS FROM CHAIRMAN MAO) [SIDEBAR]

*Leibold, James*
Asian Studies and Politics Programs
La Trobe University
IDENTIFICATION AND BELONGING

*Leonard, Jane Kate*
Professor Emerita of History
University of Akron
GRAND CANAL
HISTORY: OVERVIEW, 1800–1860
SEA TRANSPORT EXPERIMENT, 1826 [SIDEBAR]
WEI YUAN

*Leung, Edwin Pak-wah (Liang Bohua)*
Professor and Chairman,
Department of Asian Studies
Seton Hall University
LIUQIU ISLANDS

*Leung, Joe Cho Bun*
Professor, Department of Social Work and Social Administration
University of Hong Kong
SOCIAL POLICY PROGRAMS: MINIMUM LIVING STANDARD GUARANTEE SYSTEM
SOCIAL WELFARE: SOCIAL CARE

*Leung, Vincent*
Doctoral Candidate, Department of East Asian Languages and Civilizations
Harvard University
COSMOLOGY

*Lew, Alan A.*
Department of Geography, Planning, and Recreation
Northern Arizona University
TOURISM: DOMESTIC
TOURISM: FOREIGN

*Lewis, Greg*
Professor of History
Weber State University
FILM INDUSTRY: OVERVIEW

*Li, Danke*
Associate Professor, Department of History
Fairfield University
PHYSICAL EDUCATION

*Li, Dian*
Department of East Asian Studies
University of Arizona
XU ZHIMO

*Li, He*
Merrimack College
LATIN AMERICAN STATES, RELATIONS WITH

*Li, Hongshan*
Department of History
Kent State University, Tuscarawas Campus
STUDY ABROAD

*Li, Hui*
Faculty of Education
The University of Hong Kong
EDUCATION: KINDERGARTEN

*Li, Jun*
Assistant Professor, Department of Educational Policy and Administration
Hong Kong Institute of Education
CONFUCIANISM
EDUCATION: POLICY AND ADMINISTRATION SINCE 1976
VOCATIONAL EDUCATION

*Li, Lanying*
School of Economics and Management
Zhejiang Forestry University
AGRICULTURAL PRODUCTION: FORESTRY AND TIMBER TRADE

*Li, Lillian M.*
Department of History
Swarthmore College
FAMINE SINCE 1800
SILK SINCE 1800

*Li, Linda Chelan*
Department of Public and Social Administration
City University of Hong Kong
ECONOMIC REFORM SINCE 1978: FISCAL DECENTRALIZATION

*Li, Lydia W.*
Associate Professor
University of Michigan School of Social Work
FAMILY: ROLES OF THE ELDERLY

*Li, Vivian Y.*
Ph.D. candidate

University of Michigan, Ann Arbor
ART EXHIBITIONS ABROAD
LUO ZHONGLI'S *FATHER* [SIDEBAR]
PROPAGANDA ART: PEASANT PAINTINGS
RUSTIC REALISM IN ART

*Li Xiaobing*
Professor of History
University of Central Oklahoma
KOREAN WAR, 1950–1953

*Liang, Wannian*
Professor, Deputy Director-General, Beijing Health Bureau
Beijing Municipality of Health
COMMUNITY CARE

*Liang Zhiping*
Research Professor
Institute of Chinese Culture, Chinese National Academy of Arts
CUSTOMARY LAW, 1800–1949

*Lifen Pu*
Ph.D. Candidate
University of Hong Kong
CHINA SECURITIES REGULATORY COMMISSION [SIDEBAR]
FINANCIAL REGULATION

*Lijun, Sheng*
Senior Research Fellow, Lee Kuan Yew School of Public Policy
CROSS-STRAIT RELATIONS [SIDEBAR]NATIONAL UNIVERSITY OF SINGAPORE

*Lin, Hsiao-ting*
Research Fellow, Hoover Institution
Stanford University
LHASA [SIDEBAR]
QINGHAI
SONG ZIWEN (T. V. SOONG)
TIBET

*Lin Su-hsing*
Assistant Professor, Department of Visual Communication Design
Shu-Te University, Taiwan
COMMERCIAL ART: ADVERTISING
COMMERCIAL ART: CARTOONS, COMICS, AND MANHUA
COMMERCIAL ART: GRAPHIC DESIGN
COMMERCIAL ART: PICTURE BOOKS (*LIANHUANHUA*)
FENG ZIKAI
LI KERAN

*Lin, Wei*
Art Department
Transylvania University
DUNHUANG [SIDEBAR]

*Little, Daniel*
Chancellor and Professor of Philosophy
University of Michigan–Dearborn
PEASANTRY, 1800–1900
PEASANTS

*Liu, Changming*
Institute of Geographic Sciences and Natural Resources Research, Chinese Academy of Sciences
Division of Geoscience, Resources & Environment, Beijing Normal University
RIVER SYSTEMS: HUAI RIVER
RIVER SYSTEMS: OVERVIEW
RIVER SYSTEMS: PEARL RIVER
RIVER SYSTEMS: RIVER COMMISSIONS
RIVER SYSTEMS: WATER CONTROL
RIVER SYSTEMS: YANGZI RIVER
RIVER SYSTEMS: YELLOW RIVER

*Liu Ji'an*
Ph.D. candidate, Ontario Institute for Studies in Education, University of Toronto
Senior Editor, *China Education Daily*, Beijing
INTERNATIONAL STUDENTS

*Liu, Xiaomang*
Institute of Geographic Sciences and Natural Resources Research
Chinese Academy of Sciences
RIVER SYSTEMS: PEARL RIVER
RIVER SYSTEMS: YANGZI RIVER

*Loo, Becky P. Y.*
The University of Hong Kong
TRANSPORT INFRASTRUCTURE: POSTAL AND TELECOMMUNICATION SERVICES

*Lou, Jingjing*
Assistant Professor, Beloit College
EDUCATION: EDUCATION IN RURAL AREAS

*Louie, Andrea*
Associate Professor
Michigan State University
IDENTITY, CHINESE

*Louie, Kam*
University of Hong Kong
ROOT-SEARCHING LITERATURE
SCAR (WOUND) LITERATURE

*Lu, Hanchao*
School of History, Technology, and Society
Georgia Institute of Technology
BEGGARS
SHANGHAI

*Lu Hu*
Department of Chinese Studies
National University of Singapore
CHINESE OVERSEAS: TAN KAH KEE

*Lu, Tracey L-D*
Associate Professor, Anthropology Department
The Chinese University of Hong Kong
ARCHAEOLOGY, HISTORY OF
MAJOR ARCHAEOLOGICAL DISCOVERIES [SIDEBAR]

*Lu, Yixu*
School of Languages & Cultures
University of Sydney
QINGDAO

*Lufkin, Felicity*
Lecturer, Folklore and Mythology
Harvard University
FOLK ART

*Luk, Michael Yan-lung*
The Centre of Asian Studies
The University of Hong Kong
COMMUNIST THOUGHT IN CHINA, ORIGINS OF

*Luo, Baozhen*
Department of Sociology
Georgia State University
LEISURE AND CULTURE FOR THE ELDERLY
LOVE AND FRIENDSHIP
SOCIAL WELFARE: CARE AND AID FOR THE DISABLED

*Ma, Qiusha*
Associate Professor, Department of East Asian Studies
Oberlin College
MEDICINE, WESTERN, 1800–1949

*Ma Xiaofeng*
Professor
Capital Normal University, Beijing
TEACHER EDUCATION

*Mackerras, Colin*
Department of International Business and Asian Studies, Griffith Business School
Griffith University
GUIZHOU
ISLAM
MEI LANFANG

NINGXIA
PROVINCIAL AND SUBPROVINCIAL GOVERNMENT STRUCTURE SINCE 1949: AUTONOMOUS REGIONS
YUNNAN

***MacKinnon, Stephen R.***
Arizona State University
WARS SINCE 1800

***MacPherson, Kerrie L.***
The Kadoorie Institute, University of Hong Kong
*Author's note: Research supported by the University Grants Council, project HKU747907H*
CITY AND REGIONAL PLANNING
HOUSING: 1800–1949
LAND USE, HISTORY OF
SHOPS

***Madsen, Richard***
Distinguished Professor of Sociology and China Studies
University of California, San Diego
CATHOLICISM
MORALITY

***Maeda, Tamaki***
Department of Art History, Visual Art, and Theory
University of British Columbia
INFLUENCES ABROAD: NINETEENTH- AND TWENTIETH-CENTURY JAPANESE BUNJINGA (LITERATI) PAINTING

***Man Bun, Kwan (Guan Wenbin)***
Associate Professor, Department of History
University of Cincinnati
FOREIGN LOANS, 1800–1949
TIANJIN (TIENTSIN)

***Marmé, Michael***
Department of History
Fordham University
SOCIOECONOMIC INDICATORS

***Mathews, Gordon***
Professor, Department of Anthropology
Chinese University of Hong Kong
DIAOYUTAI, SOVEREIGNTY OVER [SIDEBAR]

***Matsubara, Kentaro***
Faculty of Law
University of Tokyo
CIVIL LAW, 1800–1949 [SIDEBAR]
CODIFIED LAW, 1800–1949

***Mazzone, Marian***
Department of Art History
College of Charleston
ART, SOVIET INFLUENCE ON

***McCord, Edward A.***
Associate Professor of History and International Affairs
George Washington University
MILITIA

***McDonnell, Brett H.***
Professor and Associate Dean for Academic Affairs
University of Minnesota Law School
TOWNSHIP AND VILLAGE ENTERPRISES

***McDougall, Derek***
Associate Professor
University of Melbourne
AUSTRALIA, RELATIONS WITH

***McKeown, Adam***
Associate Professor of History
Columbia University
CHINESE OVERSEAS: EXCLUSION IN RECEIVING COUNTRIES

***McNally, Christopher A.***
Research Fellow, Politics, Governance, and Securities Studies
East-West Center
CHONGQING

***Meisner, Maurice***
Harvey Goldberg Emeritus Professor of History
University of Wisconsin–Madison
CHINESE MARXISM: CLASS, THEORY AND PRACTICE
CHINESE MARXISM: MAO ZEDONG THOUGHT
CHINESE MARXISM: POSTREVOLUTIONARY MARXISM OTHER THAN MAO ZEDONG THOUGHT

***Mengin, Françoise***
Senior Research Fellow, Centre d'Études et de Récherches Internationales
Sciences Po, Paris
FRANCE, RELATIONS WITH

***Meyer, Maisie J.***
London School of Jewish Studies
HARDOON, SILAS AARON [SIDEBAR]

***Miao, Yen-wei***
Assistant Professor
National Chengchi University, Taiwan
LITTLE, ALICIA

***Miles, Steven B.***
Associate Professor
Washington University in St. Louis
RUAN YUAN

***Miller, Joseph T.***
Academic Advisor in Liberal Arts and Sciences and Adjunct Professor in Political Science
University of Illinois at Urbana–Champaign
CHINESE MARXISM: DEMOCRATIC CENTRALISM AND THE MASS LINE
CHINESE MARXISM: OVERVIEW
COMINTERN IN CHINA
UNITED STATES, RELATIONS WITH

***Mitter, Rana***
Professor of the History and Politics of Modern China
Institute for Chinese Studies, University of Oxford
MANCHUKUO (MANZHOUGUO)
MARCO POLO BRIDGE INCIDENT, 1937

***Mittler, Barbara***
Professor, Chair and Director, Institute of Chinese Studies
Heidelberg University
MUSIC, IMPACT IN THE WEST
MUSIC, WESTERN AND RUSSIAN INFLUENCE ON
NEWSPAPERS
TAN DUN

***Mok, Ka-ho***
The University of Hong Kong
EDUCATION: COST OF EDUCATION SINCE 1978

***Moore, Oliver***
Lecturer in Art History and Material Culture of China
University of Leiden
GAMES AND PLAY

***Mortensen, Eric D.***
Assistant Professor of Religious Studies
Guildford College
MINORITY NATIONALITIES: MOSUO AND NAXI NATIONALITIES

***Mühlhahn, Klaus***
Professor of History
Indiana University
GERMANY, RELATIONS WITH

PENAL SYSTEMS SINCE 1949
PENAL SYSTEMS, 1800–1949

***Murdock, Michael G.***
Associate Professor, History Department
Brigham Young University—Hawaii
THREE PRINCIPLES OF THE PEOPLE (*SANMIN ZHUYI*)

***Murowchick, Robert E.***
International Center for East Asian Archaeology and Cultural History, Department of Archaeology
Boston University
HERITAGE PROTECTION

***Murray, Dian H.***
University of Notre Dame
SECRET SOCIETIES

***Muscolino, Micah***
Georgetown University
AGRICULTURAL PRODUCTION: FISHERY AND AQUACULTURE

***Nedostup, Rebecca***
Associate Professor, Department of History
Boston College
NANJING (NANKING)

***Newby, Laura J.***
University of Oxford
GANSU
MUSLIM UPRISINGS
XINJIANG

***Ng, Emil M. L. (Man-Lun)***
Professor and Family Institute Associate Director
University of Hong Kong
HOMOSEXUALITY
LAW ON THE PROTECTION OF WOMEN AND CHILDREN
RAPE
SEX EDUCATION
SEXUAL DYSFUNCTION
TRANSSEXUALITY AND SEX-CHANGE OPERATIONS

***Ng, Peter Tze Ming***
Professor of the Department of Educational Policy and Administration, and Director of the Centre for Religious and Spirituality Education
The Hong Kong Institute of Education
EDUCATION: CHRISTIAN UNIVERSITIES AND COLLEGES

***Ng, Sek Hong***
The University of Hong Kong
LABOR: TRADE UNIONS

***Ng, Wing Chung***
Department of History
University of Texas at San Antonio
CHINESE OVERSEAS: SENDING AREAS

***Ngo, Tak-Wing***
Leiden University and Erasmus University, Rotterdam
HONG KONG: GOVERNMENT AND POLITICS SINCE 1997
HONG KONG: OVERVIEW
HONG KONG: POLITICAL PARTIES AND SOCIOPOLITICAL CONSTITUENCIES
TSANG, DONALD [SIDEBAR]
TUNG CHEE-HWA (DONG JIANHUA) [SIDEBAR]

***Nie, Jing***
Ph.D. Candidate, Comparative Literature
University of California, Davis
FILM INDUSTRY: SIXTH GENERATION FILMMAKERS

***Niquet, Valérie***
Ifri
Institut Frances des Relations Internacionales
SPACE PROGRAM

***Notar, Beth E.***
Associate Professor, Department of Anthropology
Trinity College, Hartford, CT
MINORITY NATIONALITIES: BAI NATIONALITY

***Notar, Isabella***
Assistant Professor, Department of History
Mount Saint Mary's University
CHINA'S AGENDA 21

***Nyíri, Pál***
Professor of Global History from an Anthropological Perspective
Vrije Universiteit, Amsterdam
TOURISM: OVERVIEW

***Ong, Lynette H.***
Assistant Professor of Political Science
The University of Toronto
RURAL DEVELOPMENT SINCE 1978: AGRICULTURAL BANKING
RURAL DEVELOPMENT SINCE 1978: AGRICULTURAL POLICY

***Ownby, David***
Professor, Department of History and Center for East Asian Studies
Université de Montréal
FALUN GONG
QIGONG

***Padovani, Florence M-A***
Shanghai Academy of Social Sciences
PEASANTRY SINCE 1900

***Paine, S. C. M.***
Professor of Strategy & Policy
U.S. Naval War College, Newport, RI
SINO-JAPANESE WAR, 1894–1895

***Parris, Kristen***
Department of Political Science
Western Washington University, Bellingham, WA
WENZHOU

***Peng Liu***
Independent Scholar
RIVER SYSTEMS: OVERVIEW
RIVER SYSTEMS: RIVER COMMISSIONS
RIVER SYSTEMS: YANGZI RIVER

***Perdue, Peter C.***
Department of History
Yale University
IRRIGATION AND MANAGEMENT OF WATER RESOURCES
ZUO ZONGTANG

***Pereira, Alexius A.***
Department of Sociology
National University of Singapore
SPECIAL ECONOMIC ZONES

***Peterson, Glen***
Department of History
University of British Columbia
CHINESE OVERSEAS: REMITTANCES AND INVESTMENT SINCE 1800 [SIDEBAR]
ILLITERACY

***Pong, David***
Professor and Director of the East Asian Studies Program
Department of History, University of Delaware
MARGARY AFFAIR, 1875–1876
QING RESTORATION
REFORM UNDER THE QING DYNASTY, 1800–1912
SELF-STRENGTHENING [SIDEBAR]
SHEN BAOZHEN
ZENG GUOFAN

*Pong, Myra*
Doctoral Candidate, Institute of Development Studies (IDS)
University of Sussex
BANDUNG CONFERENCE, 1955 [SIDEBAR]

*Postiglione, Gerard A.*
Professor and Head, Division of Policy, Administration and Social Science
Faculty of Education, University of Hong Kong
EDUCATION: HIGHER EDUCATION SINCE 1949

*Poston, Jr., Dudley L.*
Texas A&M University
MARRIAGE
SEX RATIO

*Potter, Pitman B.*
Professor of Law
Law Faculty, University of British Columbia
LAW SINCE 1949

*Prazniak, Roxann*
Associate Professor of History
Robert D. Clark Honors College, University of Oregon
QING DYNASTY IN 1800

*Puk, Wing-kin*
Department of History
Chinese University of Hong Kong
SALT, 1800–1949

*Putterman, Louis G.*
Professor of Economics
Brown University
TRANSITION ECONOMY

*Qiu, Jack Linchuan*
School of Journalism and Communication
The Chinese University of Hong Kong
CENSORSHIP

*Quintanilla, Sonya R.*
Curator of Asian Art
San Diego Museum of Art
INFLUENCES ABROAD: INFLUENCE OF CHINESE ART ON INDIA'S NATIONALIST MOVEMENT

*Radchenko, Sergey*
Fellow in International History
London School of Economics
INNER MONGOLIA
RUSSIA, RELATIONS WITH

*Rawnsley, Ming-Yeh T. (Cai Mingyeh)*
Research Fellow, Institute of Communications Studies
University of Leeds
KAOHSIUNG (GAOXIONG)
TAIWAN, REPUBLIC OF CHINA: SOCIAL CHANGE SINCE 1945

*Reed, Christopher A.*
Department of History
The Ohio State University
LITHOGRAPHIC AND MODERN PRINTING

*Rhoads, Edward*
Professor Emeritus of History
University of Texas at Austin
GUANGDONG

*Rioux, Yu Luo*
University of Colorado at Boulder
MUSEUMS

*Riskin, Carl*
Queens College, City University of New York
Weatherhead East Asian Institute; Columbia University
ECONOMIC REFORM SINCE 1978: GRADUALISM
RURAL DEVELOPMENT, 1949–1978: GREAT LEAP FORWARD

*Roberts, Claire*
Senior Curator of Asian Arts and Design, Powerhouse Museum, Sydney
Research Fellow, The Australian National University
HUANG BINHONG
PAN TIANSHOU

*Rohlf, Gregory*
Associate Professor
University of the Pacific, Stockton, California
STATE FARMS [SIDEBAR]

*Rose, Caroline*
University of Leeds
JAPAN, RELATIONS WITH
PEACE SETTLEMENT AFTER WORLD WAR II

*Rosen, Stanley*
Director, East Asian Studies Center and Professor, Department of Political Science
University of Southern California
CULTURAL REVOLUTION, 1966–1969

*Rosenbaum, Arthur L.*
Claremont McKenna College
CHANGSHA
EDUCATION: TEXTBOOKS AND MORAL EDUCATION, 1900–1949

*Ross, Heidi*
Director of the East Asian Studies Center
Indiana University, Bloomington
EDUCATION: EDUCATION IN RURAL AREAS

*Rowe, William T.*
John and Diane Cooke Professor of Chinese History and Chair, Department of History
Johns Hopkins University
DOMESTIC TRADE: 1800–1900

*Saari, Jon L.*
Professor Emeritus
Northern Michigan University
LIFE CYCLE: INFANCY AND CHILDHOOD

*Sabban, Françoise*
Professor, École des Hautes Études en Sciences Sociales (Paris)
Centre d'Études sur la Chine Moderne et Contemporaine
FOOD SINCE 1800

*Salmenkari, Taru*
Researcher, Institute for Asian and African Studies
University of Helsinki
POLITICAL REPRESENTATION

*Sautedé, Eric*
Lecturer and Research Coordinator
Macau Inter-University Institute
INTERNET
TELEVISION

*Schak, David C.*
Department of International Business and Asian Studies
Nathan campus, Griffith University
CIVIL SOCIETY
POVERTY

*Scharping, Thomas*
Modern Chinese Studies
University of Cologne, Germany
POPULATION POLICY: OVERVIEW
POPULATION POLICY: POPULATION CENSUSES

POPULATION POLICY: POPULATION GROWTH PROJECTIONS

***Schucher, Günter***
GIGA Institute of Asian Studies
Hamburg, Germany
LABOR: MARKET
LABOR: OVERVIEW

***Seybolt, Peter J.***
Professor Emeritus of History
University of Vermont
ANTI-JAPANESE WAR, 1937–1945
FLYING TIGERS [SIDEBAR]

***Shao Yiyang***
Associate Professor, Art History and Theory Department
Central Academy of Fine Arts, Beijing, China
ART EXHIBITIONS SINCE 1949

***Shen, Kuiyi***
Professor, Art History
University of California, San Diego
EPIGRAPHIC SCHOOL OF ART
FEDERATION OF LITERARY AND ART CIRCLES
MODERNIST ART OF THE 1920S AND 1930S
NEW PRINT MOVEMENT
WU CHANGSHI (WU JUNQING)

***Shen, Shuchi***
Ph.D. candidate, Department of Art and Archaeology
School of Oriental and African Studies, University of London
ART, HISTORY OF: 1800–1911

***Shi Xiaoling***
Ph.D. candidate
University of Arizona
LI RUI

***Shi, Yaohua***
Department of East Asian Languages and Cultures
Wake Forest University
ARCHITECTURE, HISTORY OF: ARCHITECTURE, 1949–1979
LIANG SICHENG

***Shichor, Yitzhak***
Professor Emeritus
The Hebrew University of Jerusalem
MIDDLE EASTERN STATES, RELATIONS WITH

***Shiroyama, Tomoko***
Graduate School of Economics
Hitotsubashi University
COMPRADOR
FOREIGN TRADE, 1800–1950
GREAT DEPRESSION

***Skar, Lowell***
Assistant Professor of History
University of Michigan–Dearborn
ACUPUNCTURE

***Smith, Richard J.***
Rice University
HART, ROBERT

***So, Billy K. L.***
Professor of History
The Chinese University of Hong Kong
LAW COURTS, 1800–1949

***Song, Lina***
Chair in Economic Sociology and Social Policy
Nottingham University
LABOR: LABOR AND PERSONNEL ADMINISTRATIONS

***Stainton, Michael***
York Centre for Asian Research
Toronto, Canada
NATIONALIST PARTY

***Steinhardt, Nancy***
Department of Asian &Middle Eastern Studies
University of Pennsylvania
IMPERIAL PALACES

***Steuber, Jason***
Cofrin Curator of Asian Art
Samuel P. Harn Museum of Art, University of Florida
COLLECTIONS AND COLLECTING

***Stoecklin, Daniel***
Associate Professor
Institut Universitaire Kurt Bösch
CHILD PROTECTION [SIDEBAR]

***Sturman, Peter C.***
Department of History of Art and Architecture
University of California at Santa Barbara
CALLIGRAPHY

***Sui, Yujie***
Head, Associate Professor
Department of Social Work, Renmin University of China, Beijing, PRC
FAMILY: ROLES OF THE ELDERLY

***Suleski, Ronald***
Director, Rosenberg Institute for East Asian Studies
Suffolk University, Boston
MANCHURIA

***Sun Huei-min***
Assistant Research Fellow, Institute of Modern History
Academia Sinica
LEGAL TRAINING AND THE LEGAL PROFESSION, 1800–1949

***Sung, Yun-Wing***
Department of Economics
The Chinese University of Hong Kong
FOREIGN TRADE SINCE 1950

***Sutton, Donald S.***
Professor of History and Anthropology
Carnegie Mellon University
LIFE CYCLE: DEATH AND FUNERALS
MIAO UPRISINGS
MILITARISM
SUICIDES [SIDEBAR]

***Swanström, Niklas L.P.***
Director
Institute for Security and Development Policy
CENTRAL ASIAN STATES, RELATIONS WITH

***Szonyi, Michael***
Department of East Asian Languages and Civilizations
Harvard University
CHINESE OVERSEAS: HISTORICAL PATTERNS OF GOVERNMENT POLICY AND EMIGRATION
FUJIAN

***Tam, Siumi Maria***
Associate Professor, Department of Anthropology
The Chinese University of Hong Kong
SHENZHEN [SIDEBAR]

***Tan, Qingshan***
Professor, Department of Political Science
Cleveland State University
MOST-FAVORED-NATION TREATMENT

***Taneja, Pradeep***
School of Social and Political Sciences
University of Melbourne
INDIA, RELATIONS WITH

*Tang, Jinhong*
Indexer
CCH Australia
LIBRARIES, ORIGINS AND EARLY DEVELOPMENT OF

*Tang Kwong-Leung*
Director and Professor of Social Work
University of British Columbia
URBAN EMPLOYMENT AND UNEMPLOYMENT SINCE 1949

*Tang, Xiaobing*
University of Michigan
GU HUA
SHAO XUNMEI

*Teiwes, Frederick C.*
Emeritus Professor of Chinese Politics, University of Sydney
*Note: The author wishes to thank the Australian Research Council for its support*
CHINESE MARXISM: MASS MOVEMENTS
HUA GUOFENG
MAO ZEDONG
SINO-SOVIET SCHISM
TIANANMEN INCIDENT (1976)

*Teng, Siow Song*
East Asian Institute
National University of Singapore
TEXTILES

*Thelle, Hatla*
Senior Researcher
Danish Institute for Human Rights, Copenhagen, Denmark
HUMAN RIGHTS SINCE 1949
RURAL DEVELOPMENT, 1949–1978: FIVE GUARANTEES
SOCIAL POLICY PROGRAMS: FOOD-FOR-WORK SCHEME

*Thompson, Roger R.*
Associate Professor of History
Western Washington University
CIVIL SERVICE EXAMINATIONS, 1800–1905 [SIDEBAR]
CONSTITUTIONALISM
CONSTITUTIONS BEFORE 1949
ELECTIONS AND ASSEMBLIES, 1909–1949
FENG GUIFEN
GOVERNMENT ADMINISTRATION, 1912–1949
JIANGSU
JIANGXI
REGIONALISM
SHANXI

*Thomson, Elspeth*
Energy Studies Institute
National University of Singapore
ENERGY: COAL

*Thurman, Robert*
Jey Tsong Khapa Professor of Indo-Tibetan Buddhist Studies
Columbia University
DALAI LAMA

*Todd, Daniel*
Professor of Geography
University of Manitoba
TRANSPORT INFRASTRUCTURE: PORTS

*Tong Chee Kiong*
Special Academic Advisor
Universiti Brunei Darussalam
FAMILY: RITUALS

*Tong, Q. S.*
School of English
University of Hong Kong
CULTURAL POLICY

*Tran, Emilie*
Assistant Professor, Coordinator of Social Sciences, School of Management, Leadership and Government
Macau Inter-University Institute
ELITE GROUPS [SIDEBAR]

*Tran, Lisa*
Assistant Professor, Department of History
California State University, Fullerton
GENTRY [SIDEBAR]
HISTORY: OVERVIEW, 1860–1912
HISTORY: OVERVIEW, 1912–1949
IMPERIALISM

*Tsai, Kellee S.*
Department of Political Science
Johns Hopkins University
MICROFINANCING

*Tsai Weipin*
Royal Holloway, University of London
ZHONGGUO

*Tsu, Jing*
Assistant Professor of Modern Chinese Literature, Department of East Asian Languages and Literatures
Yale University
YU DAFU

*Tu, Chung-min (Zhongmin Du)*
Assistant Professor, Department of Foreign Languages and Literatures
University of Delaware
DING LING

*Tubilewicz, Czeslaw*
School of History and Politics
University of Adelaide
EAST CENTRAL EUROPEAN STATES, RELATIONS WITH

*Tuohy, Sue M. C.*
Department of Folklore and Ethnomusicology
Indiana University
CUI JIAN
MUSIC, POPULAR
MUSIC, PROPAGANDA, AND MASS MOBILIZATION

*Unger, Jonathan*
Professor and Head, Contemporary China Center
The Australian National University
RURAL DEVELOPMENT SINCE 1978: OVERVIEW

*Van Dyke, Paul A.*
Assistant Professor
University of Macau
CANTON SYSTEM [SIDEBAR]
EAST INDIA COMPANY, 1800–1834

*Vassilev, Rossen*
Ohio State University
NORTHERN EXPEDITION
EIGHTH ROUTE ARMY [SIDEBAR]
NEW FOURTH ARMY [SIDEBAR]
SNOW, EDGAR
WHAMPOA MILITARY ACADEMY [SIDEBAR]

*Vertzberger, Yaacov Y. I.*
Professor
The Hebrew University of Jerusalem
PAKISTAN, RELATIONS WITH

*Vickers, Edward*
Senior Lecturer in Comparative Education
Institute of Education, University of London
EDUCATION: EDUCATION SINCE 1949
FORBIDDEN CITY
WORLD HERITAGE SITES [SIDEBAR]

*von Spee, Clarissa*
Curator
British Museum, London
WU HUFAN

*Wachman, Alan M.*
Associate Professor of International Politics
The Fletcher School of Law and Diplomacy, Tufts University
TAIWAN, REPUBLIC OF CHINA: OVERVIEW

*Wagner, Rudolf G.*
Professor of Chinese Studies
University of Heidelberg
ENCYCLOPEDIAS
GORDON, CHARLES
HONG XIUQUAN [SIDEBAR]
JOURNALISM
MAJOR, ERNEST
TAIPING UPRISING

*Walt, Melissa J.*
University of Washington
ARCHITECTURE, HISTORY OF: ARCHITECTURE SINCE 1979
FURNITURE
WOMEN IN THE VISUAL ARTS

*Wang, Ban*
William Haas Professor in Chinese Studies, Department of East Asian Languages and Cultures
Stanford University
LIANG QICHAO

*Wang Danning*
Instructor
Anthropology Department, The Chinese University of Hong Kong
URBAN CHINA: DEVELOPMENT ZONES
URBAN CHINA: REAL ESTATE MANAGEMENT

*Wang Di*
Professor, Department of History
Texas A&M University
CHENGDU

*Wang, Fei-ling*
Professor, Sam Nunn School of International Affairs
Georgia Institute of Technology
HOUSEHOLD REGISTRATION

*Wang Hsien-chun (Wang Xianqun)*
Institute of Modern History
Academia Sinica
SINO-FRENCH WAR, 1884–1885
WEIGHTS AND MEASURES

*Wang, Ke-wen*
Professor of History
Saint Michael's College
CHIANG KAI-SHEK (JIANG JIESHI)

*Wang, Mark Y. L.*
Associate Professor of Geography, Department of Resource Management and Geography
The University of Melbourne
THREE GORGES AND GEZHOUBA DAMS [SIDEBAR]
WUHAN

*Wang, Q. Edward*
Professor of History
Rowan University
CLASSICAL SCHOLARSHIP AND INTELLECTUAL DEBATES: 1864–1900
GONG ZIZHEN
HISTORY: INTERPRETING MODERN AND CONTEMPORARY CHINA
WANG GUOWEI

*Wang, Rujie*
Associate Professor of Chinese
The College of Wooster
BA JIN
GAO XINGJIAN

*Wang, Wensheng*
Assistant Professor of History
University of Hawaii at Manoa
POLITICAL CULTURE 1800–1900

*Wang, Ya Ping*
School of the Built Environment
Heriot-Watt University
HOUSING: HOUSING SINCE 1980

*Wang, Yiman*
Assistant Professor, Department of Film & Digital Media
University of California, Santa Cruz
CHEN KAIGE
SUN DAOLIN
ZHAO DAN
ZHOU XUAN

*Wang, Yiyan*
Department of Chinese Studies
University of Sydney
JIA PINGWA

*Wank, David L.*
Professor of Sociology and Director of the Graduate Program in Global Studies
Sophia University/Tokyo
XIAMEN (AMOY)

*Wasserstrom, Jeffrey*
Department of History
University of California, Irvine
STUDENT ORGANIZATIONS AND ACTIVISM, 1900–1949

*Weng, Qihao*
Professor of Geography
Indiana State University
GUANGZHOU (CANTON)

*Wilson, Michael D.*
School of Education
University of Leeds
EDUCATION: ADULT EDUCATION
TAIWAN, REPUBLIC OF CHINA: EDUCATION

*Wolf, Arthur P.*
Department of Anthropological Sciences
Stanford University
LIFE CYCLE: MARRIAGE

*Wong Chack-kie*
Professor, Social Work Department
The Chinese University of Hong Kong
SOCIAL POLICY PROGRAMS: SMALL WELFARE

*Worthing, Peter*
Associate Professor of History
Texas Christian University/Fort Worth, Texas
MILITARY, 1912–1949

*Wright, Tim*
Professor of Chinese Studies
White Rose East Asia Centre and School of East Asian Studies, University of Sheffield
COAL-MINE ACCIDENTS [SIDEBAR]
INDUSTRIALIZATION, 1860–1949
MINES AND METALLURGY, 1800–1949

*Wu, Fulong*
Cardiff University
GATED COMMUNITIES [SIDEBAR]
URBAN CHINA: SMALL-TOWN CHINA
URBAN CHINA: URBAN HOUSING

*Wu, Guoguang*
Chair in China and Asia-Pacific Relations, Centre for Asia-Pacific Initiatives
University of Victoria
ZHAO ZIYANG

*Wu, Jiaping*
Department of Resource Management and Geography
University of Melbourne, Australia
DALIAN

*Wu Yongping*
Professor and Deputy Dean, School of Public Policy and Management
Tsinghua University, Beijing
TAIWAN, REPUBLIC OF CHINA: ECONOMIC DEVELOPMENT SINCE 1945

*Wue, Roberta*
Assistant Professor, Department of Art History
University of California, Irvine
SHANGHAI SCHOOL OF PAINTING

*Xiang Biao*
Research Council United Kingdom Academic Fellow, Institute of Social and Cultural Anthropology
University of Oxford
CHINESE OVERSEAS: EMIGRATION AND GLOBALIZATION
HUMAN TRAFFICKING [SIDEBAR]
LABOR: OUTMIGRATION

*Xu, Haigen*
Nanjing Institute of Environmental Science, Ministry of Environmental Protection, China
Nanjing, China
ENDANGERED SPECIES, PROTECTION OF

*Xu Jiang*
Assistant Professor
Department of Geography and Resource Management, The Chinese University of Hong Kong
URBAN CHINA: URBAN PLANNING SINCE 1978

*Xu, Xueqing*
Associate Professor
York University
MANDARIN DUCK AND BUTTERFLY LITERATURE

*Yao, Pauline J.*
Independent Scholar and Curator
ART IN NEW MEDIA

*Ye, Yang*
University of California, Riverside
GARDENS AND PARKS

*Yeh, Anthony G. O.*
Chair Professor and Director, Centre of Urban Studies and Urban Planning
The University of Hong Kong, Hong Kong SAR
URBAN CHINA: URBAN PLANNING SINCE 1978

*Yeh, Michelle*
Department of East Asian Languages and Cultures
University of California, Davis
AI QING (AI CH'ING)
GUO MORUO
LIN HUIYIN
LING SHUHUA
LITERATURE OF NATIONAL DEFENSE
POETRY: CLASSICAL POETRY
POETRY: MISTY POETRY
POETRY: MODERN POETRY
YANG MO (YANG CHENGYE)

*Yen, Chuanying*
Senior Research Fellow
Institute of History and Philology, Academia Sinica
ART EXHIBITIONS, 1850–1949

*Yick, Joseph K. S.*
Professor of History and Honorary Professor of International Studies
Texas State University–San Marcos
ZHU DE

*Yin, Runsheng*
Department of Forestry
Michigan State University
AGRICULTURAL PRODUCTION: FORESTRY AND TIMBER TRADE

*Ying, Hu*
Department of East Asian Languages and Literatures
University of California, Irvine
BINGXIN
TRANSLATION OF FOREIGN LITERATURE
WANG SHUO

*Yip, Ka-che*
Professor, Department of History
University of Maryland, Baltimore County
ANTI-CHRISTIAN/ANTI-MISSIONARY MOVEMENTS
EPIDEMICS
HEALTH CARE, 1800–1949

*Yu Maochun*
Naval Academy
YAN'AN

*Yung, Bell*
Professor of Music
University of Pittsburgh
PEKING OPERA AND REGIONAL OPERAS

*Yung Sai-shing*
Department of Chinese Studies
National University of Singapore
GRAMOPHONE AND GRAMOPHONE RECORDS

*Zader, Amy*
University of Colorado, Boulder
AGRICULTURAL PRODUCTION: RICE

*Zamperini, Paola*
Assistant Professor of Chinese Literature
Amherst College
SAI JINHUA

*Zhan, Heying Jenny*
Department of Sociology
Georgia State University
SOCIAL WELFARE: CARE AND AID FOR THE DISABLED
SOCIAL WELFARE: FAMILY-BASED CARE

*Zhang, Enhua*
University of Massachusetts
LONG MARCH

*Zhang, Heather Xiaoquan*
Senior Lecturer, Department of East Asian Studies
University of Leeds
RURAL DEVELOPMENT SINCE 1978: THREE RURAL ISSUES
SOCIAL POLICY PROGRAMS: OVERVIEW

*Zhang, Hong*
Associate Professor of East Asian Studies
Colby College, Maine
FAMILY: INFANTICIDE

*Zhang, Jingyuan*
Georgetown University
CAN XUE
WANG ANYI
YU HUA

*Zhang Rui*
Beijing
ART MARKET SINCE 1949

*Zhang, Yongjin*
Professor of East Asian Studies
University of Bristol
INTERNATIONAL RELATIONS: 1800–1949
INTERNATIONAL RELATIONS: TREATIES, 1800–1949
UNEQUAL TREATIES [SIDEBAR]

*Zhao Yuzhong*
Assistant Professor, Faculty of Arts

Kunming University of Science and Technology
MINORITY NATIONALITIES: BAI NATIONALITY

***Zheng, Yiran***
Ph.D. Candidate, Department of East Asian Studies
University of Arizona
HOUSING: 1949–1980
MEDICINE, TRADITIONAL
NATIONAL FLAGS AND NATIONAL ANTHEMS
ORACLE BONES [SIDEBAR]

***Zheng Zhenzhen***
Professor, Institute of Population and Labor Economics
Chinese Academy of Social Sciences
EDUCATION: WOMEN'S EDUCATION
POPULATION POLICY: DEMOGRAPHIC TRENDS SINCE 1800

***Zhihao, Qin***
Institute of Agro-Resources and Regional Planning
Chinese Academy of Agricultural Sciences, Beijing
CLIMATE

***Zhong, Xueping***
Tufts University
ZHOU YANG

***Zhu, Yanfei***
Department of History of Art
Ohio State University
LIU HAISU
LUO GONGLIU
SCAR (WOUND) ART
SCULPTURE AND PUBLIC ART

***Zhu, Ying***
Associate Professor of Cinema Studies, Department of Media Culture
Co-coordinator of Modern China Program, College of Staten Island, The City University of New York
FILM INDUSTRY: FIFTH GENERATION FILMMAKERS

***Zurndorfer, Harriet T.***
Sinological Institute, Faculty of Humanities
University of Leiden
HUIZHOU
SINOLOGY

# Thematic Outline

*The following classification of articles, arranged thematically, gives an overview of the variety of entries and the breadth of subjects treated in the encyclopedia. Along with the index in volume 4 and the alphabetical arrangement of all entries, the thematic outline should aid in the location of topics. Ideally, this feature will facilitate a kind of browsing that invites the reader to discover additional articles, related perhaps tangentially to those originally sought. Because the rubrics used as section headings are not mutually exclusive, certain entries in the Encyclopedia are listed in more than one section below.*



**1. ARCHAEOLOGY, ARCHITECTURE, HISTORICAL STRUCTURES**

Archaeology and Western Explorers
Archaeology, History of
Archaeology, Politics of
Architecture, Historiography of, since 1800
Architecture, History of: Architecture to 1949
Architecture, History of: Architecture, 1949–1979
Architecture, History of: Architecture since 1979
Architecture, History of: Western Architects and Buildings in China
Beijing
Dunhuang [sidebar to Archaeology, History of]
Forbidden City
Gardens and Parks
Heritage Protection
Huizhou
Hutong
Imperial Palaces
Lin Huiyin
Major Archaeological Discoveries [sidebar to Archaeology, History of]
Monuments
Museums
Oracle Bones [sidebar to Archaeology, History of]
Pei, I. M.
World Heritage Sites [sidebar to Tourism: Overview]

**2. ARTS—LITERATURE**

Ai Qing (Ai Ch'ing)
Avant-garde Fiction
Ba Jin
Bai Hua
Bingxin
Buck, Pearl S.
Can Xue
Cao Yu
Chang, Eileen (Zhang Ailing)
Chen Duxiu
Cultural Policy
Ding Ling
Federation of Literary and Art Circles
Gao Xingjian
Gu Hua
Guo Moruo
Hu Feng
Jia Pingwa
Lao She

League of Left-Wing Writers
Lin Yutang
Ling Shuhua
Literary Societies
Literature of National Defense
Literature since 1800
Lu Xun
Mandarin Duck and Butterfly Literature
Mao Dun
Minority Nationalities: Ethnic Minority Cultural Expression
Mo Yan
Plays (huaju)
Poetry: Classical Poetry
Poetry: Misty Poetry
Poetry: Modern Poetry
Qian Zhongshu
Root-Searching Literature
Scar (Wound) Literature
Shao Xunmei
Shen Congwen
Translation of Foreign Literature
Wang Anyi
Wang Meng
Wang Shiwei
Wang Shuo
Xiao Qian (Xiao Bingqian)
Xu Zhimo
Yan'an Forum
Yang Mo (Yang Chengye)
Yu Dafu
Yu Hua
Zhao Shuli
Zhou Yang
Zhu Ziqing (Zhu Zihua)

**3. ARTS—PERFORMING ARTS**

Bai Hua
Chen Kaige
Cui Jian
Cultural Policy
Dance
Feng Xiaogang
Film Industry: Fifth Generation Filmmakers
Film Industry: Hong Kong
Film Industry: Overview
Film Industry: Sixth Generation Filmmakers
Film Industry: Taiwan
Hou Hsiao-hsien [sidebar to Film Industry: Taiwan]
Hu Die
Lee, Ang
Li Xianglan
Ma, Yo-yo
Mei Lanfang
Minority Nationalities: Ethnic Minority Cultural Expression
Model Operas and Ballets
Music, Impact in the West
Music, Popular
Music, Propaganda, and Mass Mobilization
Music, Western and Russian Influence on
New Year's Movies
Peking Opera and Regional Operas
Ruan Lingyu
Sun Daolin
Tan Dun
Wong Kar-wai [sidebar to Film Industry: Hong Kong]
Xie Jin
Zhang Yimou
Zhao Dan
Zhou Xuan

**4. ARTS—VISUAL**

Ai Qing (Ai Ch'ing)
Art Exhibitions, 1850–1949
Art Exhibitions Abroad
Art Exhibitions since 1949
Art History and Historiography
Art in New Media
Art Market, 1800–1949
Art Market since 1949
Art Museums
Art Schools and Colleges
Art Societies since 1800
Art, History of: 1800–1911
Art, History of: 1911–1949
Art, History of: since 1949
Art, Japanese Influence on
Art, National Essence Movement in
Art, Policy on, since 1949
Art, Soviet Influence on
Cai Guo-Qiang
Calligraphy
Chang Yu (Sanyu)
Chinese Painting (guohua)
Collections and Collecting
Commercial Art: Advertising
Commercial Art: Calendars
Commercial Art: Cartoons, Comics, and Manhua
Commercial Art: Graphic Design
Commercial Art: Picture Books (lianhuanhua)
Commercial Art: Product Design
Connoisseurship
Cultural Policy
Dunhuang [sidebar to Archaeology, History of]
Epigraphic School of Art
Feng Zikai
Folk Art
Furniture
Gu Wenda
Huang Binhong
Influences Abroad: Influence of Chinese Art on India's Nationalist Movement
Influences Abroad: Maoism and Art
Influences Abroad: Nineteenth- and Twentieth-Century Japanese Bunjinga (Literati) Painting
Influences Abroad: Nineteenth-century Chinoiserie and Chinese Export
Li Hua
Li Keran
Lin Fengmian
Ling Shuhua
Lingnan School of Painting
Literati Painting (wenrenhua)
Lithographic and Modern Printing
Liu Guosong (Liu Kuo-sung)
Liu Haisu
Luo Gongliu
Minority Nationalities: Ethnic Minority Cultural Expression
Modernist Art of the 1920s and 1930s
Museums
New Print Movement
New Wave Movement, '85
Nianhua (New Year Pictures) [sidebar to Woodblock Printing (xylography)]
Oil Painting (youhua)
Pan Tianshou
Pang Xunqin
Photography, History of: Art Photography
Photography, History of: Documentary Photography
Photography, History of: Propaganda Photography
Pictorial Magazines since 1880
Political Pop and Cynical Realism
Propaganda Art: Art Products of the Cultural Revolution
Propaganda Art: New Nianhua
Propaganda Art: Overview
Propaganda Art: Peasant Paintings
Propaganda Art: Posters
Ren Xiong
Ren Yi (Ren Bonian)
Rustic Realism in Art
Scar (Wound) Art
Sculpture and Public Art
Shanghai School of Painting
Socialist Realism in Art
Stars (Xingxing) Painting Group, 1979–1983
Wang Zhen (Wang Yiting)
Women in the Visual Arts
Woodblock Printing (xylography)
Wu Changshi (Wu Junqing)
Wu Hufan
Wu Shujuan (Wu Xingfen)
Xu Beihong

Xu Bing
Yan'an Forum
Zhang Daqian (Chang Dai-chien)

**5. CITIES AND URBANIZATION**

Art Museums
Beijing
Changsha
Chengdu
Chongqing
City and Regional Planning
Dalian
Foreign Concessions, Settlements, and Leased Territories
Fuzhou
Gardens and Parks
Gated Communities [sidebar to Urban China: Urban Housing]
Guangzhou (Canton)
Hangzhou
Harbin
Hong Kong: Overview
Housing: 1800–1949
Housing: 1949–1980
Housing: Housing since 1980
Housing: Overview
Huizhou
Hutong
Jinan
Kaohsiung (Gaoxiong)
Lhasa [sidebar to Tibet]
Liang Sicheng
Macau
Nanjing (Nanking)
Nanjing Road [sidebar to Shanghai]
Ningbo (Ningpo)
Qingdao
Shanghai
Shenyang
Shenzhen [sidebar to Special Economic Zones]
Suzhou
Taibei (Taipei)
Tianjin (Tientsin)
Treaty Ports
Urban China: Cities and Urbanization, 1800–1949
Urban China: Development Zones
Urban China: Organizing Principles of Cities
Urban China: Overview
Urban China: Real Estate Management
Urban China: Small-Town China
Urban China: Urban Housing
Urban China: Urban Planning since 1978
Urban China: Urbanization since 1949
Wenzhou
Wuhan
Xi'an
Xiamen (Amoy)
Yangzhou

**6. COMMUNICATIONS AND TRANSPORTATION**

China Securities Regulatory Commission [sidebar to Financial Regulation]
Grand Canal
Harbin
Internet
Radio
Sea Transport Experiment, 1826 [sidebar to Grand Canal]
Television
Transport Infrastructure: Air Transport
Transport Infrastructure: Overview
Transport Infrastructure: Ports
Transport Infrastructure: Postal and Telecommunication Services
Transport Infrastructure: Railways since 1876
Transport Infrastructure: Road Network
Transport Infrastructure: Shipping since 1949

**7. ECONOMICS—BUSINESS, INDUSTRY, ECONOMIC DEVELOPMENT**

Agricultural Production: Animal Husbandry
Agricultural Production: Fishery and Aquaculture
Agricultural Production: Forestry and Timber Trade
Agricultural Production: Fruit and Vegetable Farming
Agricultural Production: Overview
Agricultural Production: Rice
Anhui
Automobile Industry
Banking: Big Four
Banking: Nonperforming Loans
Banking: Overview
Banking: People's Bank of China
Brands
Build-Operate-Transfer (BOT) Contracts
Canton System [sidebar to Foreign Relations before 1949]
Central Planning
Chen Yun
China Investment Corporation [sidebar to Foreign Currency Reserves]
China Merchants' Steam Navigation Company
China's Agenda 21
Chinese Maritime Customs Service
Chinese Overseas: Remittances and Investment since 1800 [sidebar to Chinese Overseas: Overview]
Chinese Overseas: Tan Kah Kee
Chongqing
Coal-Mine Accidents [sidebar to Energy: Coal]
Commercial Elite, 1800–1949
Companies: Collectives
Companies: Corporate Law
Companies: Joint Ventures
Companies: Overview
Comprador
Consumption and Consumer Cultures
Copper and Silver, 1800–1950
Daqing [sidebar to Industrial Policy since 1949]
Dazhai [sidebar to Rural Development, 1949–1978: Overview]
Democratic Parties: All-China Federation of Industry and Commerce
Domestic Trade: 1800–1900
Domestic Trade: 1900–1949
Domestic Trade: Since 1950
East India Company, 1800–1834
Economic Development: Economic Regions
Economic Development: Great Western Development Scheme
Economic Development: Overview
Economic Development: UNDP Human Development Report on China, 2005
Economic Reform since 1978: Commission for the Reform of the Economic System
Economic Reform since 1978: Dual-track Pricing
Economic Reform since 1978: Fiscal Decentralization
Economic Reform since 1978: Gradualism
Economic Reform since 1978: Overview
Energy: Coal
Energy: Electricity Generation
Energy: Hydrological Power
Energy: Nuclear Power
Energy: Oil and Natural Gas
Energy: Overview
Energy: Wind Power
Entrepreneurs since 1949
Environment
Famine since 1800
Feng Guifen
Financial Markets
Financial Regulation
Five-Year Plans
Foreign Currency Reserves
Foreign Investment, 1800–1949
Foreign Investment since 1949

**8. ETHNICITY, NATIONALITY, AND POLITICAL IDENTITY**

Provincial and Subprovincial Government Structure since 1949: Autonomous Regions
Qinghai
Russian Émigrés
Sassoon, Victor [sidebar to Jewish Communities and Refugees]
Tibet

**9. FAMILY—INDIVIDUALS, GENDER, SEXUALITY, SOCIALIZATION**

Adoptions
All-China Women's Federation
Ba Jin
Child Protection [sidebar to Youth]
Comfort Women [sidebar to Anti-Japanese War, 1937–1945]
Ding Ling
Domestic Violence
Education: Kindergarten
Education: Women's Education
Family: Infanticide
Family: One-Child Policy
Family: Overview
Family: Rituals
Family: Roles of the Elderly
Filial Piety
Footbinding
Gender Relations
Homosexuality
Law on the Protection of Women and Children
Leisure and Culture for the Elderly
Life Cycle: Birth
Life Cycle: Death and Funerals
Life Cycle: Infancy and Childhood
Life Cycle: Marriage
Life Cycle: Old Age
Lineage
Little, Alicia
Love and Friendship
Marriage
Marriage Laws
Morality
Population Policy: Birth-Planning Policy
Privacy
Prostitution, History of
Qiu Jin
Rape
Sai Jinhua
Selling and Buying Sex in Contemporary China [sidebar to Prostitution]
Sex Education
Sex Ratio
Sexuality
Social Rituals
Social Welfare: Family-Based Care
Socialization and Pedagogy
Suicides [sidebar to Life Cycle: Death and Funerals]
Transsexuality and Sex-Change Operations
Women, Employment of
Women, Status of
Women in Politics
Women in the Visual Arts
Youth

**10. GEOGRAPHY, REGIONS**

Anhui
City and Regional Planning
Climate
Desertification
Dialect Groups
Diaoyutai, Sovereignty over [sidebar to Japan, Relations with]
Earthquakes since 1800
Economic Development: Economic Regions
Economic Development: Great Western Development Scheme
Education: Education in Rural Areas
Endangered Species, Protection of
Energy: Hydrological Power
Energy: Oil and Natural Gas
Environment
Fujian
Fuzhou
Gansu
Geographical Regions, Natural and Human
Grand Canal
Guangdong
Guangxi
Guizhou
Hainan
Hebei
Heilongjiang
Henan
Huizhou
Hunan and Hubei
Inner Mongolia
Irrigation and Management of Water Resources
Jiangsu
Jiangxi
Jilin
Liaoning
Liuqiu Islands
Local Gazetteers
Macau
Manchuria
Minority Nationalities: Overview
Natural Resources
Ningxia
Production and Construction Corps [sidebar to Rural Development, 1949–1978: Overview]
Provincial and Subprovincial Government Structure since 1949: Autonomous Regions
Provincial and Subprovincial Government Structure since 1949: Provinces
Qinghai
River Systems: Huai River
River Systems: Overview
River Systems: Pearl River
River Systems: River Commissions
River Systems: Water Control
River Systems: Yangzi River
River Systems: Yellow River
Shaanxi
Shandong
Shanxi
South China Sea
Special Administrative Regions
Surveys of Natural Resources [sidebar to Natural Resources]
Taiwan, Republic of China: Overview
Taiwan, Republic of China: Social Change since 1945
Three Gorges and Gezhouba Dams [sidebar to Energy: Hydrological Power]
Tibet
Villages since 1800
Xinjiang
Yunnan
Zhejiang

**11. GOVERNMENT**

Baojia System
Cadre System
Central Planning
Central State Organs since 1949: Central Military Commission
Central State Organs since 1949: Chinese People's Political Consultative Conference
Central State Organs since 1949: National People's Congress
Central State Organs since 1949: Overview
Central State Organs since 1949: President and Vice President
Central State Organs since 1949: State Council, Commissions, Ministries, and Bureaus
Central-Local Relationships
China Investment Corporation [sidebar to Foreign Currency Reserves]
China's Agenda 21
Chinese Maritime Customs Service
Chinese Overseas: Historical Patterns of Government Policy and Emigration

**12. HEALTH AND MEDICINE**



**13. HISTORY AND HISTORIOGRAPHY**

Architecture, History of: Architecture since 1979
Architecture, History of: Western Architects and Buildings in China
Archives, Public: Archival Resources outside China
Archives, Public: Historical Preservation and Government Historical Publications
Art History and Historiography
Art, History of: 1800–1911
Art, History of: 1911–1949
Art, History of: since 1949
Chinese Marxism: Feudalism
Chinese Marxism: Mao Zedong Thought
Civil War, 1946–1949
Communist Party History Revised (1981)
Communist Thought in China, Origins of
Companies: Overview
Constitutions before 1949
Constitutions since 1949
Dance
Defense, 1800–1912
Democratic Ideas, Reforms, and Experiments since the 1880s
Domestic Trade: 1800–1900
Domestic Trade: 1900–1949
Domestic Trade: Since 1950
Earthquakes since 1800
Education: 1800–1949
Education: Christian Universities and Colleges
Education: Education since 1949
Education: Higher Education before 1949
Education: Higher Education since 1949
Education: Kindergarten
Education: Textbooks and Moral Education, 1900–1949
Education: Women's Education
Elections and Assemblies, 1909–1949
Emperors, 1800–1912
Epidemics
Film Industry: Hong Kong
Film Industry: Overview
Film Industry: Taiwan
Food since 1800
Footbinding
Forbidden City
Foreign Concessions, Settlements, and Leased Territories
Foreign Investment, 1800–1949
Foreign Investment since 1949
Foreign Loans, 1800–1949
Government Administration, 1800–1912
Government Administration, 1912–1949
Grand Canal
Heritage Protection
History: Interpreting Modern and Contemporary China
History: Overview, 1800–1860
History: Overview, 1860–1912
History: Overview, 1912–1949
History: Overview, since 1949
Hong Kong: Education in Hong Kong since 1842
Hong Kong: Overview
Identification and Belonging
Industrial Development since 1949
Industrialization, 1860–1949
International Organizations, Relations with, 1900–1949
International Organizations, Relations with, since 1949
International Relations: 1800–1949
International Relations: Since 1949
Late Imperial China [sidebar to History: Overview, 1860–1912]
Law Courts, 1800–1949
Legal Training and the Legal Profession, 1800–1949
Liberalism
Literature since 1800
Local Gazetteers
Opium, 1800–1950
Oracle Bones [sidebar to Archaeology, History of]
Political Culture 1800–1900
Political Culture since 1900
Political Parties, 1905–1949
Public Finance since 1900
Qing Dynasty in 1800
Qing Restoration
Reform under the Qing Dynasty, 1800–1912
Resolution on Party History [sidebar to Communist Party History Revised (1981)]
Revolution of 1911
Salt, 1800–1949
Self-strengthening [sidebar to History: Overview, 1860–1912]
Student Organizations and Activism, 1900–1949
Taiwan, Republic of China: Overview
Tibet
Transport Infrastructure: Railways since 1876
Urban China: Cities and Urbanization, 1800–1949
Warlord Era (1916–1928)
Wars and the Military, 1800–1912
Wars since 1800
Westernization
Workers, Industrial, 1860–1949
Yan'an

**14. IMPERIALISM**

Anti-Christian/Anti-Missionary Movements
Anti-Japanese War, 1937–1945
Archaeology and Western Explorers
Architecture, History of: Western Architects and Buildings in China
Archives, Public: Archival Resources outside China
Bandung Conference, 1955 [sidebar to International Relations: Since 1949]
Boxer Uprising
Catholicism
Chinese Maritime Customs Service
Comfort Women [sidebar to Anti-Japanese War, 1937–1945]
East India Company, 1800–1834
Extraterritoriality
Foreign Concessions, Settlements, and Leased Territories
Foreign Investment, 1800–1949
Foreign Loans, 1800–1949
Handicrafts
Harbin
Hart, Robert
Health Care, 1800–1949
Imperialism
Influences Abroad: Influence of Chinese Art on India's Nationalist Movement
Influences Abroad: Influence of Maoist Propaganda on Western and Third-World Youth
Institutional Legacies of the Taiping Uprisings [sidebar to Taiping Uprising]
Interpreters of Things Chinese to the West
Investments in Africa: Infrastructure and Natural Resources [sidebar to African States, Relations with]
Lin Zexu
Manchukuo (Manzhouguo)
Margary Affair, 1875–1876
Missionaries
Most-Favored-Nation Treatment
Nanjing Massacre
Opium Wars
Pan-Asianism
Scramble for Concessions
Shanghai Mixed Court
Treaty Ports

**15. INTERNATIONAL RELATIONS**

African States, Relations with
Anti-Christian/Anti-Missionary Movements
Anti-Japanese War, 1937–1945
Architecture, History of: Western Architects and Buildings in China

Art Exhibitions Abroad
Art, Japanese Influence on
Art, Soviet Influence on
ASEAN, Relations with
Australia, Relations with
Bandung Conference, 1955 [sidebar to International Relations: Since 1949]
Boxer Uprising
Canton System [sidebar to Foreign Relations before 1949]
Catholicism
Central Asian States, Relations with
Chang, Eileen (Zhang Ailing)
China Hands
China's Agenda 21
Chinese Maritime Customs Service
Chinese Overseas: Emigration and Globalization
Chinese Overseas: Exclusion in Receiving Countries
Chinese Overseas: Historical Patterns of Government Policy and Emigration
Cixi, Empress Dowager
Comintern in China
Companies: Joint Ventures
Dalai Lama
Diaoyutai, Sovereignty over [sidebar to Japan, Relations with]
East Central European States, Relations with
East India Company, 1800–1834
Economic Development: UNDP Human Development Report on China, 2005
European Union, Relations with
Flying Tigers [sidebar to Anti-Japanese War, 1937–1945]
Foreign Concessions, Settlements, and Leased Territories
Foreign Currency Reserves
Foreign Investment, 1800–1949
Foreign Investment since 1949
Foreign Loans, 1800–1949
Foreign Policy Frameworks and Theories: One-China Policy and "One Country, Two Systems"
Foreign Policy Frameworks and Theories: Overview
Foreign Trade, 1800–1950
Foreign Trade since 1950
France, Relations with
Germany, Relations with
Giquel, Prosper
Gordon, Charles
Guangzhou (Canton)
Hardoon, Silas Aaron [sidebar to Jewish Communities and Refugees]
Hart, Robert
Health Care, 1800–1949
Heilongjiang
India, Relations with
Influences Abroad: Influence of Maoist Propaganda on Western and Third-World Youth
International Development Aid
International Development Programs in China: Asian Development Bank
International Development Programs in China: Food and Agriculture Organization
International Development Programs in China: International Monetary Fund
International Development Programs in China: Overview
International Development Programs in China: United Nations Development Programme
International Development Programs in China: World Bank
International Organizations, Relations with, 1900–1949
International Organizations, Relations with, since 1949
International Relations: 1800–1949
International Relations: Since 1949
International Relations: Treaties, 1800–1949
International Relations: Treaties since 1949
International Students
Interpreters of Things Chinese to the West
Investments in Africa: Infrastructure and Natural Resources [sidebar to African States, Relations with]
Japan, Relations with
Korea, Relations with (North and South)
Korean War, 1950–1953
Labor: China and the International Labour Organization
Latin American States, Relations with
Lin Zexu
Margary Affair, 1875–1876
Middle Eastern States, Relations with
Mongolia, People's Republic of, Relations with
Morrison, George E.
Olympics
Olympics, 2008 Beijing Olympic Games
Pakistan, Relations with
Peace Settlement after World War II
Russia, Relations with
Sino-Soviet Schism
Southeast Asian States, Relations with
Taiwan, Republic of China: Foreign Relations since 1949
United Kingdom, Relations with
United States, Relations with
Vietnam, Relations with
Wade, Thomas

**16. LEARNING—EDUCATION, SCHOLARSHIP, RESEARCH**

Academia Sinica (Zhongyang Yanjiuyuan)
Academies (shuyuan)
Art Museums
Art Schools and Colleges
Civil Service Examinations, 1800–1905 [sidebar to Examination System, 1800–1905]
Classical Scholarship and Intellectual Debates: 1800–1864
Classical Scholarship and Intellectual Debates: 1864–1900
Classical Scholarship and Intellectual Debates: Debates, 1900–1949
Classical Scholarship and Intellectual Debates: Debates since 1949
Classical Scholarship and Intellectual Debates: Intellectuals, 1900–1949
Confucianism
Economic Development: UNDP Human Development Report on China, 2005
Education: 1800–1949
Education: Adult Education
Education: Christian Universities and Colleges
Education: Cost of Education since 1978
Education: Education in Rural Areas
Education: Education since 1949
Education: Higher Education before 1949
Education: Higher Education since 1949
Education: Kindergarten
Education: Moral Education
Education: Policy and Administration since 1976
Education: Private Schools since 1980s
Education: Textbooks and Moral Education, 1900–1949
Education: Women's Education
Encyclopedias
Examination System, 1800–1905
Guo Moruo
Hong Kong: Education in Hong Kong since 1842
Hu Shi
Illiteracy
International Students
Interpreters of Things Chinese to the West
Language and Language Policy
Legge, James
Lexicography
Liang Sicheng
Libraries, Origins and Early Development of
Lin Huiyin

Liu Haisu
Luo Gongliu
Morrison, Robert
Physical Education
Private Schools [sidebar to Education: 1800–1949]
Research in Engineering
Research in the Sciences
Research Organizations
Ruan Yuan
Sent-down Educated Youth
Severe Acute Respiratory Syndrome
Sex Education
Sinology
Social Sciences
Study Abroad
Taiwan, Republic of China: Education
Teacher Education
Vocational Education
Waley, Arthur
Wang Guowei
Xiafang
Yan Fu

**17. MILITARY, DEFENSE, AND WARFARE**

Anhui
Anti-Japanese War, 1937–1945
Armaments
Army and Politics
Beiyang Clique
Boxer Uprising
Central State Organs since 1949: Central Military Commission
Chiang Kai-shek (Jiang Jieshi)
Civil War, 1946–1949
Comfort Women [sidebar to Anti-Japanese War, 1937–1945]
Defense, 1800–1912
Eighth Route Army [sidebar to People's Liberation Army: Overview]
Elections and Assemblies, 1909–1949
Flying Tigers [sidebar to Anti-Japanese War, 1937–1945]
Giquel, Prosper
Gordon, Charles
Guangxi
Institutional Legacies of the Taiping Uprisings [sidebar to Taiping Uprising]
Korean War, 1950–1953
Lin Zexu
Long March
Mao Zedong
Marco Polo Bridge Incident, 1937
Militarism
Military Culture and Tradition
Military Regions [sidebar to People's Liberation Army: Overview]
Military, 1912–1949
Militia
Nanjing Massacre
Naval Factors in the Chinese Civil War [sidebar to Civil War, 1946–1949]
New Fourth Army [sidebar to People's Liberation Army]
Northern Expedition
Opium Wars
Peng Dehuai
People's Liberation Army: Command Structure of the Armed Services
People's Liberation Army: Military Doctrine
People's Liberation Army: Military Enterprises and Industry since 1949
People's Liberation Army: Overview
Police, Secret
Production and Construction Corps [sidebar to Rural Development, 1949–1978: Overview]
Red Army [sidebar to People's Liberation Army: Overview]
Sino-French War, 1884–1885
Sino-Japanese War, 1894–1895
Stilwell, Joseph
Taiwan, Republic of China: Military Forces
War Crimes
Wars and the Military, 1800–1912
Wars since 1800
Whampoa Military Academy [sidebar to Military, 1912–1949]
Zhu De

**18. POLITICS—LEADERS, ORGANIZATIONS, EVENTS AND IDEAS**

All-China Women's Federation
Anarchism
Anti-Christian/Anti-Missionary Movements
Archaeology, Politics of
Army and Politics
Art, Policy on, since 1949
Bai Hua
Beiyang Clique
Censorship
Central Planning
Chen Duxiu
Chen Shuibian
Chen Yun
Chiang Ching-kuo (Jiang Jingguo)
Chiang Kai-shek (Jiang Jieshi)
China Hands
Chinese Marxism: Class, Theory and Practice
Chinese Marxism: Democratic Centralism and the Mass Line
Chinese Marxism: Feudalism
Chinese Marxism: Mao Zedong Thought
Chinese Marxism: Mass Movements
Chinese Marxism: Overview
Chinese Marxism: Postrevolutionary Marxism other than Mao Zedong Thought
Chu Anping
Cixi, Empress Dowager
Comintern in China
Communist Party
Communist Party History Revised (1981)
Communist Party Organization and Structure [sidebar to Communist Party]
Communist Thought in China, Origins of
Communist Youth League
Constitutionalism
Constitutions before 1949
Constitutions since 1949
Cross-Strait Relations [sidebar to Taiwan, Republic of China: Foreign Relations since 1949]
Cultural Revolution, 1966–1969
Dalai Lama
Democracy Wall
Democratic Ideas, Reforms, and Experiments since the 1880s
Democratic Parties: All-China Federation of Industry and Commerce
Democratic Parties: China Association for Promoting Democracy
Democratic Parties: China Democratic National Construction Association
Democratic Parties: China Zhigong (Public Interest) Party
Democratic Parties: Chinese Peasants and Workers Democratic Party
Democratic Parties: Democratic League of China
Democratic Parties: Jiusan (September Third) Society
Democratic Parties: Overview
Democratic Parties: Revolutionary Committee of the Nationalist Party
Democratic Parties: Taiwan Democratic Self-Government League
Deng Xiaoping
Dissidents
Fascism
Federalism
Feng Guifen
Four Basic Principles [sidebar to Deng Xiaoping]
Four Modernizations
Gang of Four [sidebar to Cultural Revolution, 1966–1969]
Gong Zizhen
Harmonious Society
Hong Kong: Government and Politics since 1997
Hong Kong: Nationality Issues since 1983

**19. POLITICS—POLITICAL CRITICS, DISSIDENTS**



**20. POPULAR AND MATERIAL CULTURE**



**21. POPULAR AND MASS MOVEMENTS**

**22. POPULATION AND DEMOGRAPHICS**



**23. PRESS, MEDIA, JOURNALISM**



**24. RELIGION AND PHILOSOPHY**



**25. SCIENCE AND TECHNOLOGY**



**26. SOCIAL STRUCTURE**

**27. SPORTS AND RECREATION**



**28. TAIWAN**

# *Major Chronological Periods*

**Qing Dynasty, 1644–1912[1]**

**Shunzhi, 1644–1661**

**Kangxi, 1662–1722**

**Yongzheng, 1723–1735**

**Qianlong, 1736–1796[2]**

**Jiaqing, 1796–1820**

**Daoguang, 1721–1850**

**Xianfeng, 1851–1861**

**Tongzhi, 1862–1874[3]**

**Guangxu, 1875–1908**

**Xuantong, 1909–1912**

**Republic, 1912–1949**

**People's Republic, 1949–**

**Cultural Revolution, 1966–1969[4]**

NOTES

1. The Qing Dynasty, founded by the Manchus, was first proclaimed in 1636 in Shenyang, their capital before the conquest of China. Some historians prefer to think of 1636 as the beginning date of the dynasty. In a reference work about China, we consider it appropriate to consider the Qing a Chinese dynasty, beginning in 1644, the year the Manchus captured Beijing. The ending date of 1912 is based on the abdication of the last emperor on February 12, 1912. The proclamation of the Republic on January 1, 1912 does not automatically make December 31, 1911 the last day of the Qing. It would be an error to think of the Qing having ended in 1911, a matter confused by the frequent reference to "the 1911 Revolution," which brought down the Manchu ruling house, but only in 1912.

2. The usual terminal date given for the Qianlong reign is 1795. Strictly speaking, the Qianlong emperor did not abdicate until February 9, 1796 (Chinese New Year's Day). As it was his wish, for reasons of filial devotion, to not outlast the sixty-one-year rule of his grandfather, the Kangxi emperor, he ended his rule deliberately on the very last day of his sixtieth year. According to the Chinese calendar, then, there is no confusion, but the situation is different when the date is translated into the Gregorian calendar. For the sake of simplicity, the vast majority of historians simply end Qianlong's reign in 1795, making it mathematically correct that he had not exceeded the record his grandfather had set. Such is the dictate of filial piety!

3. A similar situation to the Qianlong-Jiaqing transition developed at the end of the Tongzhi reign. The emperor died on the 5th day of the 12th lunar month of his 13th year on the throne, which fell on January 12, 1875. According to the Gregorian calendar, this would have given him a fourteen-year reign, one year more than it was according to the lunar calendar. The established convention, therefore, is to terminate his reign in 1874, to make it conform to the Chinese lunar calendar. Since the Tongzhi emperor never exercised real power, this manipulation of the reign date is of no great *practical* consequence.

4. The case for terminating the Cultural Revolution in 1969 is based on the declaration of the Ninth Party Congress of the Chinese Communist Party that the Great Proletarian Cultural Revolution was a success. As a mass movement, it had come to an end. As an elite power struggle, it did not end until the death of Mao Zedong and the arrest of the Gang of Four respectively in September and October 1976. Even then the dust had not fully settled. Many who fell victim to the violence and persecution of the time are inclined to regard the Cultural Revolution as the "ten lost years." Many scholars on the subject also take this view.

# *Timeline*

| DATE | EVENT IN CHINESE HISTORY | EVENT IN WORLD HISTORY |
|---|---|---|
| **1800** | Bailianjiao (White Lotus) Rebellion in Sichuan, Hunan, Hubei and Shaanxi, defeated by regular army and local militia (1796–1804); Jiaqing Emperor assumes full control following death of Qianlong Emperor in 1799. | |
| **1802** | Fearing its seizure by France, British occupy Macau. | Britain makes Peace of Amiens with France; temporary peace in Europe. |
| **1803** | | United States under President Jefferson makes Louisiana Purchase from France. |
| **1805** | Russian ships forbidden to trade at Guangzhou (Canton); pirate fleets active along Southeast China coast (1805–1810). | Nelson wins battle of Trafalgar vs. combined Franco-Spanish fleet. |
| **1807** | Robert Morrison, first Protestant missionary, arrives at Guangzhou. | Slave trade abolished throughout British Empire. |
| **1808** | British reoccupy Macau. | |
| **1809** | Qing government issues six regulations on Sino-foreign trade. | |
| **1810** | | Revolts in Mexico, New Granada and Rio de la Plata vs. Spain. |
| **1811** | Uprising of the Tianlijiao (Celestial Order Sect) in Shandong and Hubei (1811–1814). | Luddite riots vs. factory industrialization in Britain. |
| **1812** | | Napoleon's Russian campaign ends in disastrous retreat. |
| **1813** | Eight Trigrams Rebellion—attack on Imperial Court in Beijing fails; East India Company granted control of China trade for twenty additional years. | British Parliament abolishes East India Company's monopoly of trade with India. |
| **1814** | Pope Pius VII authorizes Jesuit missionaries to return to China. | Congress of Vienna determines political order of post-Napoleonic Europe (1814–1815). |
| **1815** | Missionary Robert Morrison begins *China Monthly Magazine* at Malacca. | |

| | | |
|---|---|---|
| **1816** | British East India Company decides upon increasing opium importation into China; Lord Amherst's mission to Beijing fails due to protocol considerations. | |
| **1818** | Missionary William Milne establishes Anglo-Chinese College at Malacca. | |
| **1819** | | Simon Bolivar defeats Spain, becomes president of Gran Columbia; British East India Company establishes settlement at Singapore. |
| **1820** | Opium imports result in China's balance of trade falling into deficit (1820–1825); Jiaqing Emperor dies. | |
| **1821** | Daoguang Emperor's reign begins. | Jose de San Martin and Simon Bolivar liberate Peru from Spanish rule. |
| **1822** | | Brazil declares its independence from Portugal. |
| **1824** | Missionary Robert Morrison helps to translate the Bible into Chinese. | Dutch cede Malacca to British. |
| **1825** | | Decembrist military coup in Russia fails; Nicholas I becomes czar. |
| **1826** | Establishment of Guangdong naval patrols to check opium trade. | |
| **1829** | | Greek independence from Ottoman Empire established; Mexico abolishes slavery. |
| **1830** | | Revolution in France overthrows Charles X and establishes liberal "July Monarchy" under Louis Philippe. |
| **1831** | Protestant missionary Charles Gutzlaff itinerates north along China coast. | |
| **1832** | Prohibition of British ships sailing north along the China coast. | Reform of British Parliament. |
| **1834** | End of East India Company's trade monopoly; Lord Napier's trade mission to Guangzhou fails. | |
| **1835** | Missionary Robert Morrison establishes a Western school at Guangzhou. | Afrikaners (Boers) begin Great Trek to escape British rule in South Africa. |
| **1836** | Emperor orders suppression of the opium trade. | Chartism begins in England. |
| **1838** | Lin Zexu appointed Imperial Commissioner for opium suppression. | |
| **1839** | Opium War (1839–1842) begins; British trade blockaded by China; clash of Chinese and British warships near Guangzhou; Palmerston sends naval squadron to China. | |
| **1840** | Liz Zexu relieved as Imperial Commissioner for opium suppression. | |
| **1841** | Chuenpi Convention rejected by both China and Britain; Sanyuanli incident: 10,000 gentry-led Cantonese attack retreating British. | |
| **1842** | Treaty of Nanjing; Hong Kong ceded to Britain. | British are forced to withdraw from Afghanistan. |
| **1843** | Taiping leader Hong Xiuquan begins preaching Christianity in Guangdong. | |
| **1844** | U.S. and France sign treaties with China; Imperial decree allows Chinese to convert to Catholicism (and in 1845, to Protestantism). | |

| | | |
|---|---|---|
| **1845** | Foreigners refused permission to enter walled city of Guangzhou, initiating protracted conflict. | Potato blight causes widespread famine in Ireland (1845–1846). |
| **1846** | Anti-British disturbances in Guangzhou and Fuzhou. | U.S.-Mexican War, resulting in cession of all territory north of Rio Grande to U.S. (1846–1848). |
| **1847** | Hong Xiuquan and Feng Yunshan establish the Bai Shangdi Hui (God Worshippers' Society) | |
| **1848** | Court takes action to suppress piracy along China's eastern coast. | Revolutions of 1848—urban uprisings throughout much of continental Europe; Marx and Engels issue *Communist Manifesto*; California Gold Rush begins. |
| **1850** | God Worshippers win major military victories in Guangxi; Daoguang Emperor dies. | |
| **1851** | Nian Uprising (1851–1868); Taiping Uprising (1851–1864); Treaty of Ili; Xianfeng Emperor ascends to the throne. | Gold rush in Australia begins. |
| **1852** | Taipings advance into Hunan and Hubei. | British take south Burma. |
| **1853** | Taipings capture Nanjing, making it their capital; Small Sword (Triad) Uprising in Shanghai region (1853–1855). | |
| **1854** | Foreign Inspectorate of Chinese Customs established in Shanghai. | U.S. Naval squadron forces Japan open to limited foreign trade; Crimean War: Russia defeated by Britain, France and Ottoman Empire (1854–1856). |
| **1855** | Panthay Rebellion (1855–1873); defeat of Taiping Northern Expedition; Yellow River floods, changes course (from south to north of Shandong promontory). | |
| **1856** | Arrow War (Second Opium War) (1856–1860). | |
| **1857** | Anglo-French forces capture Guangzhou. | "Sepoy Mutiny" in India vs. British East India Company fails, bringing India under direct control of the British Crown. |
| **1858** | Gold Coin Uprising; Shanghai Tariff Convention; Treaty of Tianjin; Treaty of Aigun. | French forces end the Ngyuen Dynasty in Annam and begin territorial expansion. |
| **1859** | British and French forces defeated in engagement at Dagu forts. | Construction of Suez Canal begins (completed in 1869); John Stuart Mill publishes *On Liberty.* |
| **1860** | Anglo-French forces seize Beijing and burn the Summer Palace; Beijing Convention; Supplementary Treaty of Peking; Xianfeng Emperor flees to Rehe. | Vladivostok founded. |
| **1861** | Self-strengthening Movement (1861–1895); Zongli Yamen established; Xianfeng Emperor dies. | Civil War between Federal and Confederate forces in the U.S., ending in Federal victory (1861–1865); Russian serfs emancipated. |
| **1862** | Northwest Muslim Rebellions (1862–1878); Tongzhi Emperor's reign begins; Tongzhi Restoration era begins (1862–1874); Beijing Tongwenguan (Interpreters College) established. | France occupies parts of Cochin-China. |
| **1863** | International Settlement in Shanghai created by merging British and American concessions. | |
| **1864** | Fall of Nanjing to Qing army, Taiping Rebellion suppressed. | |
| **1865** | Jiangnan Arsenal is established in Shanghai. | |
| **1866** | Shipyard and naval academy established at Mawei near Fuzhou. | Prussia defeats Austria in Seven Weeks' War. |

| | | |
|---|---|---|
| **1867** | | Meiji Restoration in Japan, ending Tokugawa Shogunate (1867–1868). |
| **1868** | Burlingame mission to U.S. and Europe (1868–1870). | |
| **1869** | Alcock Convention. | |
| **1870** | Tianjin Massacre. | Franco-Prussian War, leading to Prussian victory and establishment of united German Empire (1870–1871). |
| **1871** | Yili Crisis (1871–1881). | Paris Commune. |
| **1872** | China Merchants' Steam Navigation Co. founded; thirty Chinese students sent to study in U.S. | |
| **1873** | Foreign envoys received in audience by Tongzhi Emperor for first time without kowtow protocol. | French annex Hanoi and Red River Delta in Vietnam. |
| **1874** | Japan sends military expedition to Taiwan, provoking Sino-Japanese crisis. | |
| **1875** | Margary affair; Tongzhi Emperor dies; Guangxu Emperor succeeds to the throne. | |
| **1876** | Chefoo Convention; famine ravages northern China (1876–1878). | |
| **1877** | First Chinese embassy established in London. | Failure of Satsuma Rebellion vs. modernization in Japan. |
| **1878** | Qing army recaptures Xinjiang, with exception of Yili Valley. | |
| **1879** | Japan annexes the Ryukyu (Liuchiu) Islands. | |
| **1880** | China rejects Treaty of Livadia with Russia over concessions regarding Yili. | |
| **1881** | Treaty of St. Petersburg signed; Russia agrees to return Yili to China. | |
| **1882** | Uprising in Korea, China stations troops there. | Chinese exclusion act prohibits Chinese immigration into U.S. |
| **1883** | Liu Yongfu's Black Flag Army defeats the French near Hanoi. | |
| **1884** | Sino-French War (1884–1885); Xinjiang becomes a province. | International Berlin Conference decides the political future of much of Africa, beginning the imperialist "Scramble for Africa." |
| **1885** | Taiwan established as a province separate from Fujian; Tianjin Military Academy established. | Indian National Congress is founded. |
| **1886** | | Burma comes under the rule of British India. |
| **1887** | Sino-Portuguese Treaty formally cedes Macau to Portugal; Guangxuehui (Society for the Diffusion of Christianity and General Knowledge) established by missionaries and foreigners in Shanghai; Kaiping coal mines established. | French Indochina established. |
| **1889** | Empress Dowager's regency ends, Guangxu Emperor begins to rule in his own right; Beiyang Fleet established. | Meiji Constitution is proclaimed in Japan. |
| **1890** | Hanyang iron and steel works, Daye iron mines, and Pingxiang coal mines inaugurated. | |
| **1891** | Rebellion of the Jindan Jiao (Golden Elixir Sect) is suppressed in North China. | Construction of trans-Siberian railroad begins in Russian Empire; Triple Alliance among Germany, Austria, and Italy. |

| Year | China | World |
|---|---|---|
| **1892** | | Franco-Russian Alliance. |
| **1893** | Zhang Zhidong founds a modern school in Wuhan, stressing mathematics and science, commerce and foreign languages. | Laos incorporated into French Indochina. |
| **1894** | Sino-Japanese War (1894–1895); Sun Yat-sen founds Xingzhonghui (Revive China Society) in Honolulu. | Court martial and false conviction of Col. Alfred Dreyfus in France for treason. |
| **1895** | Treaty of Shimonoseki; Taiwan and the Pescadores ceded to Japan; Triple Intervention. | |
| **1896** | Sino-Russian secret alliance is concluded, sanctioning Russian involvement in Manchuria. | Italian invasion of Ethiopia is routed at Battle of Adowa. |
| **1897** | Scramble for concessions (1897–1899). | |
| **1898** | Hundred Days of Reform; coup against reforms staged by Empress Dowager and Court conservatives; Boxer Uprising (1898–1900). | Victory in Spanish-American War establishes U.S. as a global power, Spain cedes Cuba, Puerto Rico, Guam, and the Philippines to U.S.; Hawaii annexed by the U.S. |
| **1899** | | U.S. proposal of "open door" policy in China; Boer War (1899–1902). |
| **1900** | Eight-Power Allied invasion defeats Boxers and Qing forces. | |
| **1901** | Boxer Protocol (1901–1902); Empress Dowager initiates reforms. | |
| **1902** | Empress Dowager's edict bans footbinding. | Anglo-Japanese Alliance signed; Triple Alliance renewed; U.S. annexes Philippines. |
| **1903** | British troops of Younghusband Mission penetrate into Tibet. | |
| **1904** | Russo-Japanese War (1904–1905) fought on Chinese soil (Manchuria). | Britain and France sign the Entente Cordiale; Russo-Japanese War results in Japanese victory (1904–1905). |
| **1905** | Imperial Civil Service Examination System abolished; Sun Yatsen forms Tongmenghui (China United League) in Tokyo; Anti-American trade boycott protesting racist policies (1905–1906) . | Revolution in Russia leads to granting of a constitution; Anglo-Japanese alliance renewed for 10 years. |
| **1906** | Qing government announces intention of establishing a constitutional monarchy. | All-India Muslim League is founded. |
| **1907** | Qing Court authorizes creation of provincial assemblies. | Anglo-Russian entente defines spheres of influence in Persia, Afghanistan, and Tibet. |
| **1908** | Guangxu Emperor and Empress Dowager Cixi die; outline of Qing Constitution issued. | |
| **1909** | Xuantong Emperor (Puyi) ascends the throne; Provincial assemblies are established. | |
| **1910** | Bubonic plague epidemic breaks out in Manchuria. | Japan annexes Korea, renaming it Chosen. |
| **1911** | Wuchang Uprising; Outer Mongolia secedes from China. | Porfirio Diaz overthrown, Mexican Revolution begins. |
| **1912** | January 1, Sun Yatsen declares the founding of the Republic; Puyi (Xuantong Emperor) abdicates. | |
| **1913** | Song Jiaoren assassinated in Shanghai; Second Revolution. | |
| **1914** | Japanese seize German possessions in Shandong. | World War I begins, involving Central Powers vs. Entente Powers (1914–1918); Panama Canal opens. |

| | | |
|---|---|---|
| **1915** | Twenty-one Demands (of Japan); Yuan Shikai declares himself emperor. | |
| **1916** | Yuan Shikai dies; Warlord era begins. | |
| **1917** | China enters World War I on Allied side; New Culture Movement (1917–1923). | February Revolution forces Czar's abdication; October (Bolshevik) Revolution overthrows successor Kerensky government in Russia. |
| **1918** | Japanese loans to China reach a peak. | Armistice ends World War I in Western Europe. |
| **1919** | May Fourth Movement; Chinese delegation refuses to sign Versailles Treaty; John Dewey lectures in China. | Paris Peace Conference; Treaty of Versailles signed by Germany; British kill hundreds of Indian protesters at Amritsar. |
| **1920** | China joins the League of Nations; Bertrand Russell lectures in China (1920–1921). | League of Nations established. |
| **1921** | Chinese Communist Party (CCP) is formed in Shanghai. | Washington Conference limits Pacific fleets, affirms independence of China. |
| **1922** | China Seaman's Union strike begins in Hong Kong. | Fascist march on Rome; Mussolini forms government in Italy; World Court (Permanent Court of International Justice) established. |
| **1923** | Sun-Joffe Manifesto establishes alliance between Guomindang and Soviet Union; First GMD-CCP United Front established (1922–1927); GMD is reorganized with Soviet assistance (1923–1924). | |
| **1924** | Whampoa Military Academy is founded, Chiang Kai-shek is made its first commandant; Rabindranath Tagore lectures in China. | |
| **1925** | Death of Sun Yatsen; May Thirtieth Incident. | |
| **1926** | Warship Zhongshan incident, Chiang Kai-shek's first break with CCP; Northern Expedition (1926–1928). | General Strike disrupts British industry, is outlawed in 1927; Germany admitted to League of Nations. |
| **1927** | Chiang Kai-shek annihilates Communists in Shanghai, ending the First United Front; Canton Massacre; Nanchang Uprising; National Government under Guomindang established at Nanjing. | Inter-Allied military control of Germany ends. |
| **1928** | Zhang Zuolin assassinated by Japanese army; Japanese send troops to Shandong. | Kellogg-Briand Pact renouncing war as instrument of national policy is signed by 63 nations. |
| **1929** | CCP sanctions Li Lisan line of urban insurrections. | Wall Street Crash of New York Stock Exchange, beginning of global depression. |
| **1930** | Civil war as Yan Xishan, Feng Yuxiang, and Li Zongren oppose GMD government. | Gandhi organizes Salt March in India, is arrested and imprisoned; London Naval Conference results in the Washington Naval Treaty. |
| **1931** | Futian Incident; Manchurian Incident; the Chinese Soviet Republic (Jiangxi Soviet) is established. | |
| **1932** | Japanese army attacks Shanghai; Manzhouguo established by Japanese. | |
| **1933** | Fujian Rebellion (1933–1934); Fifth Encirclement Campaign. | Hitler elected German chancellor; declaration of Third Reich with emergency powers after Reichstag fire; Japan withdraws from League of Nations; U.S. goes off gold standard. |
| **1934** | New Life Movement; Communists driven out of Jiangxi Soviet, Long March (1934–1935) begins. | Hitler purges Nazi Party; declares himself Fuhrer of Germany. |

| | | |
|---|---|---|
| **1935** | Zunyi Conference. | Second London Disarmament Conference. |
| **1936** | Xi'an Incident, kidnapping of Chiang Kai-shek. | Spanish Civil War between Republic and Nationalist rebels, leading to Nationalist victory (1936–1939); Rome-Berlin Axis proclaimed; Japan withdraws from the Second London Naval Disarmament Conference. |
| **1937** | Anti-Japanese War (Second Sino-Japanese War) (1937–1945); Second United Front (1937–1945); Battle of Taiyuan; Rape of Nanjing (Nanjing Massacre). | Italy joins anti-Comintern Pact; leaves League of Nations. |
| **1938** | Battle of Taierzhuang. | Anschluss—Hitler annexes Austria; Munich Conference yields to German demands on Czechoslovakia. |
| **1939** | Flooding in Yellow River basin, famine in Hubei Province kills 200,000. | Nazi-Soviet Pact agrees to partition Poland; World War II begins with German invasion of Poland. |
| **1940** | Hundred Regiments Campaign; Wang Jingwei establishes puppet government in Nanjing. | German victory in western Europe, occupation of Low Countries and fall of France; Japan attacks Burma. |
| **1941** | New Fourth Army Incident marks effective end of Second United Front. | Japan attacks Pearl Harbor, Hong Kong, Singapore, invades Malaysia, south Indochina and Philippines; Germany invades U.S.S.R. |
| **1942** | Yan'an rectification campaign (1942–1944). | |
| **1943** | Cairo Conference: Chiang Kai-shek, Winston Churchill and Franklin D. Roosevelt agree to Japan's unconditional surrender, return of Manchuria and Taiwan to China. | Russian victory—German army at Stalingrad destroyed; Cairo and Teheran Conferences. |
| **1944** | Operation Ichigo. | D-Day: Allied landings in France, opening second front in Europe. |
| **1945** | Marshall Mission begins: unsuccessful U.S. effort to mediate between GMD and CCP. | Yalta Conference; Potsdam conference; Allied victory over Germany; atomic bombs at Hiroshima and Nagasaki, Japan surrenders; U.S. occupation of Japan (1945–1952); United Nations established. |
| **1946** | Chinese civil war (1946–1949). | International Court of Justice begins (established in 1945) |
| **1947** | February 28th Incident (Taiwan); North China land reform and rectification (1947–1948). | New constitution proclaimed in occupied Japan; India and Pakistan become independent. |
| **1948** | Battle of Huai-Hai, decisive PLA victory over Nationalist forces. | Gandhi assassinated. |
| **1949** | CCP Common Program; Mao Zedong proclaims inauguration of PRC. | Soviet Union tests an atomic bomb. |
| **1950** | Marriage Reform Law; Land Reform; Sino-Soviet treaty establishes alliance; China enters Korean War (1950–1953). | North Korea invades South Korea, beginning Korean War (1950–1953); Senator Joseph McCarthy begins his attack on Communist subversion in U.S. (his activities are censured by U.S. Senate in 1954). |
| **1951** | Chinese send troops into Tibet; Three-Anti's and Five-Anti's Campaign (1951–1952). | Japan-U.S. Security Treaty. |
| **1952** | Sino-Japanese Peace Treaty signed in Taibei by GMD government. | |
| **1953** | Official beginning of First Five-year Plan. | |
| **1954** | U.S.-Taiwan Mutual Defense Treaty; Gao Gang and Rao Shushi expelled from CCP leadership; Zhou Enlai represents China at the Geneva Conference. | French defeat in Indochina, Geneva Accords result in divided Vietnam; Southeast Asia Treaty Organization formed. |
| **1955** | Hu Feng Affair marks continued cultural and intellectual purges in PRC; Bandung Conference. | |

| | | |
|---|---|---|
| **1956** | Hundred Flowers Movement (1956–1957). | Egypt nationalizes Suez Canal, prompting invasion and subsequent withdrawal by Anglo-French and Israeli forces; Hungarian Uprising; Polish Uprising. |
| **1957** | Anti-Rightist Campaign; Mao Zedong visits USSR. | EEC (Common Market) established in Europe. |
| **1958** | Beidaihe Resolution; Great Leap Forward (1958–1960); Second Taiwan Straits Crisis. | |
| **1959** | Lushan Plenum (Peng Dehuai dismissed); Tibetan uprising against Chinese Communist occupation; Dalai Lama flees to India. | Cuban revolutionary forces gain power under Fidel Castro. |
| **1960** | Great Leap Forward famine—20–30 million deaths; Sino-Soviet split becomes open. | Treaty of Mutual Cooperation and Security between the United States and Japan. |
| **1961** | Wu Han's article and play openly criticize Mao Zedong. | East Germany (DDR) builds wall isolating western areas of Berlin. |
| **1962** | War between China and India; Socialist Education Movement launched. | Cuban missile crisis, resolved through U.S.-Soviet negotiations; Uganda and Tanganyika become independent. |
| **1963** | | U.S. President John F. Kennedy assassinated in Dallas, Texas; Malaysia formed; Kenya becomes independent. |
| **1964** | PRC explodes an atomic bomb; "Learn from the PLA" movement launched; PLA publishes first edition of Quotations from Chairman Mao (The Little Red Book). | |
| **1965** | China aids Vietnam's struggle vs. the U.S. | U.S. astronauts walk in space. |
| **1966** | Beginning of Cultural Revolution (1966–1969); Mao Zedong's swim in the Yangzi; Mao mobilizes Red Guards; Liu Shaoqi and Deng Xiaoping criticized. | Sukarno falls. |
| **1967** | Revolutionary "seizures of power" erupt; PLA military interventions restore order; China successfully explodes first hydrogen bomb. | Israel defeats Arabs in Six-Day war, capturing Jerusalem, West Bank and Golan Heights. |
| **1968** | May 7th cadre schools established to "reeducate" party officials and intellectuals. | Soviet invasion of Czechoslovakia ousts Dubcek's reformist government; North Vietnam launches TET offensive in South Vietnam; Alliance between India and U.S.S.R; Martin Luther King killed. |
| **1969** | Military clashes occur along Sino-Soviet frontier; CCP's Ninth Party Congress declares the official end of the Cultural Revolution though power struggle and political turmoil continue; Lin Biao is designated Mao's successor. | Strategic Arms Limitation Talks (SALT) begin. |
| **1970** | China successfully launches its first space satellite into orbit. | |
| **1971** | PRC replaces ROC in United Nations; Lin Biao dies in plane crash; "Ping-Pong Diplomacy." | Civil war in Pakistan, establishment of Bangladesh. |
| **1972** | U.S. President Nixon visits Beijing; Shanghai Communique; Japan recognizes PRC. | U.S. returns Okinawa to Japan |
| **1973** | Paris Agreement. | OPEC petroleum crisis following Arab-Israeli War; Watergate investigation; U.S. devalues dollar; Britain, Denmark, Ireland join European Common Market. |
| **1974** | Campaign launched to criticize Lin Biao and Confucius. | Worldwide inflation. |
| **1975** | Chiang Kai-shek (Jiang Jieshi) dies in Taiwan; Zhou Enlai introduces the "Four Modernizations." | End of Vietnam War, Saigon occupied by North Vietnamese forces; Helsinki Accord. |

| | | |
|---|---|---|
| **1976** | Deaths of Zhou Enlai, Zhu De and Mao Zedong; Tangshan earthquake in Hebei kills 240,000; arrest of the "Gang of Four." | ASEAN Treaty of Amity and Cooperation (Southeast Asia). |
| **1977** | Deng Xiaoping returns to power; Hua Guofeng champions the "Four Modernizations." | |
| **1978** | Deng Xiaoping launches free market reforms and open door policy; Jiang Jingguo becomes president in Taiwan. | |
| **1979** | U.S.-China normalization; Deng Xiaoping visits U.S. and Japan; Gaoxiong (Kaohsiung) Incident in Taiwan; Third Indochina War (Sino-Vietnamese War); Democracy Wall Movement; One-child policy is introduced. | Iranian Revolution, overthrow of Shah Reza Pahlevi; Vietnam invades Cambodia. |
| **1980** | Trial of the "Gang of Four" (1980–1981); Special Economic Zones established; PRC admitted to World Bank and International Monetary Fund. | Beginning of Iran-Iraq War (1980–1988). |
| **1981** | CCP denounces the Cultural Revolution and reappraises Mao Zedong. | |
| **1982** | Policy for retirement of government officials is introduced. | U.K. defeats Argentina in war over Falkland (Malvinas) Islands. |
| **1983** | Campaign vs. "spiritual pollution" launched. | |
| **1984** | Sino-British Joint Declaration (Hong Kong to return to PRC on July 1, 1997); fourteen coastal cities open to foreign trade and investment. | |
| **1985** | | Chernobyl nuclear reactor accident in Ukraine, U.S.S.R. |
| **1986** | Deng Xiaoping calls for political reforms. | Ferdinand Marcos falls from power; Corazon Aquino becomes president of the Philippines. |
| **1987** | Sino-Portuguese Joint Declaration (Macau to return to PRC on December 20, 1999); Zhao Ziyang succeeds HuYaobang. | Gorbachev announces policies of glasnost (openness) and perestroika (restructuring) in U.S.S.R. |
| **1988** | Inflation and corruption lead to controversy over price reforms in PRC; Li Denghui (Lee Teng-hui) succeeds Jiang Jingguo in Taiwan. | Mikhail Gorbachev becomes president of U.S.S.R.; Vietnamese troops begin to pull out of Kampuchea |
| **1989** | Tiananmen Square Democracy Movement and suppression; Jiang Zemin ousts Zhao Ziyang as CCP head; normalization of Sino-Soviet relations. | Berlin Wall dismantled; overthrow of Ceausescu in Romania; democratization in Poland and Hungary; Emperor Hirohito dies, Crown Prince Akihito succeeds to the throne. |
| **1990** | Curbs on economic growth, heightened political control in China; promulgation of the Basic Law, post-1997 Hong Kong Constitution. | Reunification of Germany; Iraq invades and annexes Kuwait. |
| **1991** | Normalization of Sino-Vietnamese relations; PRC's first stock exchange opens in Shanghai. | "Desert Storm" operation liberates Kuwait from Iraqi control; breakup of Yugoslavia and beginning of civil war among Serbs, Croats and Muslims; U.S.S.R. collapses. |
| **1992** | Deng Xiaoping "southern tour" promotes faster economic growth; CCP calls for a "socialist market economy." | Canada, Mexico and U.S. form NAFTA. |
| **1993** | Wang-Koo Meeting in Singapore on improving PRC-Taiwan relations. | European Union created. |
| **1994** | Construction of Three Gorges Dam begins. | Nelson Mandela wins South Africa's first multi-racial democratic election. |

| | | |
|---|---|---|
| **1995** | Chinese intellectuals call for political reform. | War in Bosnia among Serbs, Muslims and Croats, ended by Dayton Accord. |
| **1996** | Crisis in Taiwan Straits—PRC holds war games coinciding with Taiwan's presidential elections. | |
| **1997** | Deng Xiaoping dies; Hong Kong restored to PRC rule. | Japanese financial crisis precipitates economic crisis throughout Southeast Asia. |
| **1998** | Asian financial crisis slows growth in PRC, Taiwan and Hong Kong. | |
| **1999** | Resolution on Taiwan's future (DPP); China recovers Macau; crisis in Sino-U.S. relations caused by NATO's accidental bombing of PRC's Belgrade embassy. | Panama regains control of the Panama Canal. |
| **2000** | Chen Shuibian of DPP elected President of Taiwan; PRC intensifies crackdown of Falungong sect. | |
| **2001** | U.S.-China crisis concerning military aircraft collision over South China Sea; Jiang Zemin's "three represents" speech sanctions opening CCP membership to wider social interest groups; China enters WTO. | Terrorist attacks on New York City and Washington, D.C. kill over three thousand. |
| **2002** | Chen Shuibian's speech refers to Taiwan and PRC as "two countries." | |
| **2003** | SARS epidemic in China—government launches emergency public health campaign. | Anglo-U.S. invasion of Iraq overthrows Saddam Hussein's regime. |
| **2004** | Hand-in-Hand rally (Taiwan); campaign against corruption in PRC. | Massive tsunami in eastern Indian Ocean kills over 200,000. |
| **2005** | Death of Zhao Ziyang; widespread anti-Japanese demonstrations in Chinese cities; Donald Tsang (Zeng Yinquan) replaces Tung Chee-hwa (Dong Jianghua) as chief executive of the Hong Kong SAR. | |
| **2006** | Forum on China-Africa Cooperation in Beijing; CCP proclaims goal of a "Socialist Harmonious Society." | |
| **2007** | China launches first lunar probe; widespread Tibetan rioting in Tibet, Gansu, and Sichuan. | Severe cyclone Sidr hits Bangladesh killing up to 10,000 |
| **2008** | Beijing Olympic Games staged; Sichuan earthquake kills over 69,000; milk powder contamination scandal revealed. | Global financial crisis begins, sparked by failures in U.S. banking and credit system; piracy off the Somali coast, begun in the 1990s, reaches new heights; Fidel Castro resigns as president, succeeded by his younger brother, Raúl. |
| **2009** | Global economic downturn brings sharp export declines, rising unemployment; PRC plans massive fiscal stimulus to counter these problems. | Barack Obama takes office as U.S. President; G-20 summit deals with global issues of financial regulation, fiscal stimulus and monetary policy. |

# A

## ACADEMIA SINICA (*ZHONGYANG YANJIUYUAN*)

On the same day in April 1927 that the Guomindang (GMD Nationalist Party;) established its new government, it also decided to construct a new, centralized research academy, Academia Sinica, which was subsequently founded in June 1928. Its creators, the most prominent of whom was Cai Yuanpei (1867–1940), envisioned the new academy as an organization that would oversee and coordinate scientific as well as social scientific and humanistic research conducted in all of the Republic of China's state-sponsored research institutes and universities, in addition to conducting research in its own institutes, to which the best and brightest of China's academicians and independent researchers would be recruited. The intent of the new Nanjing government was to harness China's intellectual power and put it to work whenever possible in the service of the state.

### STRUCTURE AND BUDGET

At the time of Academia Sinica's creation there were already several smaller research institutes scattered across China's urban centers of Beijing, Shanghai, and Nanjing. Academia Sinica incorporated a number of these preexisting institutions into its organization, and rapidly constructed nine institutes: meteorology, astronomy, physics, chemistry, geology, engineering, psychology, history and philology, and sociology, most of which were located in the new capital city of Nanjing. Other institutes, such as agriculture and forestry, botany, zoology, and medicine, were planned for the future. By 1949 the academy had expanded to include thirteen institutes. Academia Sinica was not the only state-funded research institution, however, and the GMD government continued to finance research in the graduate schools of the national universities, as well as in the Beiping Research Academy and other institutes that conducted investigations in geology, agriculture, and industry.

Academia Sinica was a government organ under the direct control of the Executive Yuan. Although its organic charter stipulated that it was politically independent, the government still controlled two of the most critical parts of the institution: The president of the academy was appointed by the GMD government, and the budget was appropriated by the government's Ministry of Finance. Academia Sinica was, however, permitted to appeal to private sources of funding as well. In 1928 the academy was granted a start-up budget of 500,000 yuan by the Nanjing government, and received a matching sum from the China Foundation for the Promotion of Education and Culture. It was also awarded a monthly operating budget of 100,000 yuan, a sum that grew gradually over the next few years before leveling off. At least until the 1970s, however, the academy's budget was always uncertain and often much smaller than necessary.

### RELOCATION TO TAIWAN

When, in 1949, many academicians moved with the GMD to Taiwan, only two of Academia Sinica's institutes, mathematics and history and philology, were able to reestablish themselves in Taiwan more or less as they had been in mainland China. Much of the equipment, resources, and personnel of the other institutes remained in China after 1949, and the process of rebuilding these institutes in

Nangang, a suburb of Taibei (Taipei), lasted into the 1960s. Of the institutes and scholars that remained in China, some, particularly in the sciences, were absorbed into the Chinese Academy of Sciences created by the People's Republic of China in 1950.

In spite of its links to the state, Academia Sinica was (and still is) theoretically autonomous. In practice, it has been compelled to respond to both direct and indirect political pressure. Throughout the 1930s and into the 1940s, for example, the academy participated in the Republic of China's defensive modernization program, and many members willingly contributed their time and energy to war-related research. Even in this atmosphere of cooperation, however, there were tensions between academicians and the state, especially when it came to the selection of leadership for the academy, and in 1940 academicians protested the appointment of Zhu Jiahua (1893–1963) as president of the academy on the grounds that he was too politicized.

Following the move to Taiwan, however, circumstances changed. The academicians who moved with the GMD were, by and large, supporters of the party, and thus less likely to perceive government pressure as problematic. As a result, in the 1950s and 1960s the academy eagerly sought ways to shape itself to suit the needs of the state, and some of the new institutes that it created reflected this phenomenon. In 1955 the academy established a new Institute of Ethnology, in which anthropological research on Taiwan's aborigines could be conducted. This research was deemed by the Institute of History and Philology—which was actively engaged in the GMD state's cultural sinification project in Taiwan—to be outside the scope of its work, even though that work involved the study of archaeological materials. With the creation of the Institute of Ethnology, Taiwan's aborigines were set apart and defined as different, exotic, primitive minorities, as juxtaposed against Han Chinese, whose customs were defined as standard. These two institutes helped with the intellectual reconstruction of Taiwan as China. Further work along these lines was conducted by the Institute of Modern History, also established in 1955, in which modern history was clearly defined as the history of modern China.

Not all of Academia Sinica's new and reconstructed institutes served such explicitly political purposes, but they still served the needs of the state. The Institute of Botany, in which research on rice and sugar cultivation was conducted, was among the earliest institutes to be reconstructed, as were the Institutes of Zoology and Physics. Other new institutes constructed in the 1960s included an Institute of Economics, the Institute of American Culture, and the Institute of Organic Chemistry. By contrast, institutes that the GMD had found threatening on the mainland, such as the left-leaning Institute of Sociology, were not reconstructed in Taiwan.

Whereas in the 1950s and 1960s the academy had eagerly positioned itself to serve the GMD state, by the 1970s academicians were less enthusiastic to compromise the intellectual integrity of the institution, and for some time resisted pressure from the Legislative Yuan to establish an Institute of Three Peoples' Principles. Similarly, in the early 1990s, the academy was resistant to Taiwanese nationalist-inspired political pressure to establish an Institute of Taiwan History, although it did so in 1993, and in so doing became the first state-sponsored research institution in Taiwan to clearly identify Taiwan as something more than a mere subset of China.

At least as important, however, have been the Academia Sinica's contributions to the sciences. From the late 1950s on, the academy has worked with other government institutions and industry to promote industrially relevant scientific education and conduct applied research. Nangang is now home to one of Taiwan's plethora of new science parks, this one devoted to software and biotechnology, and it is expected that the academy will collaborate with the industries that set up in that area.

**BIBLIOGRAPHY**

Chen Shiwei. Legitimizing the State: Politics and the Founding of Academia Sinica in 1927. *Papers on Chinese History* 6 (1997): 23–41.

Wu Dayou. *Zhongyang yanjiuyuan shi chu gao* [A brief history of Academia Sinica]. Taibei: Academia Sinica, 1988.

***J. Megan Greene***

## ACADEMIES (*SHUYUAN*)

As the 1800s opened, a seminal educator founded two academies of lasting influence. Ruan Yuan (1764–1849) founded Gujing Jingshe in Hangzhou (its codirectors were appointed in 1802) and Xuehaitang in Guangzhou (its eight directors were appointed in 1826). The curriculum of both affirmed the reformist agenda of eighteenth-century evidential research (*kaozhengxue*) scholars. But Ruan's more subtle objective was to reinstitute a sophisticated understanding of the scholarly legacy of the Han dynasty commentator Zheng Xuan (127–200) so that attacks by evidential research scholars on the Song-Ming neo-Confucian reading of the classics would remain more balanced.

As the great Xuehaitang scholar Chen Li (1810–1882) put Ruan's case, the error of a lack of balance was committed by ham-handed critics such as Wang Su (195–256) at the end of the Han dynasty, as well as by narrow Qing dynasty critics such as the evidential scholars Wang Niansun (1744–1832) and his son Wang Yinzhi (1766–1834). Finding fault just to improve one's scholarly reputation was learning the wrong lesson from Zheng Xuan. The correct scholarly legacy of Zheng Xuan should be for a scholar to identify a commentarial tradition or lineage that interpreted the meaning of one of the canonical Confucian classics, and then carefully emend that commentary utilizing broader scholarship. Ruan Yuan demanded that critical scholarship not miss the point of focusing on what was correct in the ancient classics.

As other newly founded nineteenth-century academies took inspiration from the two institutions patronized by Ruan Yuan, a syncretic mix of the best of Song–Ming neo-Confucianism with eighteenth-century evidential research scholarship became common in better academies. Officials and scholars following Ruan Yuan's lead, with varying degrees of emphasis on statecraft added, included: Zeng Guofan (1811–1872) in Jiangning, Chen Li in Guangzhou, Zhang Zhidong (1837–1909) in Sichuan, Liu Xizai (1813–1881) in Shanghai, Huang Tifang (1832–1881) in Jiangsu, and Huang Yizhou (1828–1899) in Zhejiang and in Jiangsu. Headmasters at top academies were known for their contributions to scholarship, and many academies were centers of research and publication.

Following the suppression of the Taiping Uprising (1851–1864), an expanding number of academies were founded in several provinces. In provinces that suffered the depredations of Taiping fighting, officials collaborated with local elites to rebuild and expand the number of prewar academies. The result was a tripling of the number of prewar academies in many prefectures. Certain officials who patronized academies were powerful enough to refuse gentry contributions to academy endowments—fearing self-interest; but in many county academies gentry funds were accepted, and those academies were only quasi-official. The large educated elite produced by this expanded number of academies fed into the prerevolutionary mix of reformers before the 1911 revolution.

By the 1880s, Western subjects started to enter the curriculum of many new institutions, and in the 1898 reform movement, reform advocates made the claim that academies should be converted into components of a modern public school system. As the century turned, "New Policies" reforms of the national government converted existing prefectural-level academies into public high schools, and existing provincial-level academies into modern universities.

Two of the first and most prominent university graduate programs in Chinese studies owed clear debts to the traditions of the classical academies. Peking University's Graduate Institute of National Studies (Guoxuemen) was inspired in 1921 by the university president, Cai Yuanpei (1868–1940). He insisted that faculty expertise be grounded in research and that good teaching accompany this research: "An academy headmaster took research as a lifetime calling, and in addition, there was freedom to do research in the *shuyuan* [academies]. That is why research was able to develop freely. Nowadays, there are too many subjects and courses in universities, leaving no room for research." (Ding 1996, p. 229). The Tsinghua University Graduate Institute of Chinese Studies (Qinghua Guoxue Yanjiu Yuan) was crafted by Hu Shi (1891–1962), and its founding regulations read: "The system of this graduate institute is modeled on that of former academies, and on the English university system, emphasizing individual study under the specialized guidance of professors." (Keenan 1994, p. 147). The same debt to academy models seen in those graduate programs was true of the foremost governmental research institute in China, Academia Sinica (Zhongyang Yanjiu Yuan), which formed in 1932. Meanwhile, a classically educated graduate of Southern Quintessence Academy (Nanjing Shuyuan), Tang Wenzhi (1865–1954), had founded and managed for thirty years (1920–1950) the Wuxi National Studies Institute (Wuxi Guoxue Zhuanxiu Guan), which trained classicists and philologists using classical academy pedagogy. In those thirty years, more that 1,700 scholars were trained at the private Wuxi Institute.

The young Mao Zedong established Hunan Self-study University in August of 1921. His teacher, Yang Changji, had noted the similarity of the humanistic education in classical academies to the quality of learning in the modern model of Western liberal arts universities. The organizing regulations of Hunan Self-study University stated: "This university intends to combine the strength of both the ancient *shuyuan* and modern schools; it adopts methods of self-study and develops research in all areas of learning" (Ding 1996, p. 238). While mass education was also added as a populist objective in this predecessor of many revolutionary institutions, the legacy of classical academy traditions was clear.

In the mid-1980s, a flurry of academic discussion over a revival of Confucianism (*ruxue*) occurred in China and overseas. One major participant, a man named Jiang Qing, resigned his post teaching public policy in the People's Republic of China, and enlisted the private support of businessmen to build a classical academy, Yangming Jingshe (Yangming Retreat), in the hinterland province of Guizhou. Jiang Qing wanted to create an environmental context for both the practice and the study of classical Confucian texts. His private *ruxue* academy was functional by 2007, and was organized so students read classical Confucian texts in the morning, then discussed together in the afternoon, and sang in the evening. The underlying intent of the first classical academy to be founded in China since 1901 was to help reestablish *ruxue* as an integral component of China's national identity.

**SEE ALSO** *Education: 1800–1949; Ruan Yuan.*

**BIBLIOGRAPHY**

Abe Hiroshi. Borrowing from Japan: China's First Modern Educational System. In *China's Education and the Industrialized World: Studies in Cultural Transfer*, eds. Ruth Hayhoe and Marianne Bastid, 57–80. Armonk, NY: Sharpe, 1987.

Bell, Daniel A. *China's New Confucianism: Politics and Everyday Life in a Changing Society*. Princeton, NJ: Princeton University Press, 2008.

Ding Gang. The *Shuyuan* and the Development of Chinese Universities in the Early Twentieth Century. In *East-West Dialogue in Knowledge and Higher Education*, eds. Ruth Hayhoe and Julia Pan, 218–244. Armonk, NY: Sharpe, 1996.

Ji Xiaofeng, ed. *Zhongguo shuyuan cidian* [A dictionary of academies in China]. Hangzhou, PRC: Zhejiang Jiaoyu Chubanshe, 1996.

Keenan, Barry C. *Imperial China's Last Classical Academies: Social Change in the Lower Yangzi, 1864–1911*. Berkeley: Institute of East Asian Studies, University of California, 1994.

Makeham, John. *Lost Soul: "Confucianism" in Contemporary Chinese Academic Discourse*. Cambridge, MA: Harvard University Asia Center, 2008.

Miles, Steven B. *The Sea of Learning: Mobility and Identity in Nineteenth-century Guangzhou*. Cambridge, MA: Harvard University Asia Center, 2006.

*Barry C. Keenan*

## ACUPUNCTURE

The term *zhenjiu* (literally "to needle" and "to burn or cauterize") refers to health-inducing therapies for adjusting the flow of the body's vitalities (*qi*) within internal channels, either by inserting fine-gauge needles into specific points on the skin (acupuncture) or by burning cones of ground mugwort (*Artemisia vulgaris*) leaves on or over these points (moxibustion), treatments known in English as *acumoxa*.

Acupuncture and moxibustion derive from a combination of minor surgery and bloodletting with ideas about the body and its place in the cosmos from early imperial China. For most of its 2,000-year history, acupuncture was less popular than moxibustion due to the latter's greater accessibility, lower cost, and less invasive techniques. Popular appeal, elite interest, and state support for acumoxa therapies ensured a significant, but limited, role for them in imperial times. Extant books, charts, figures, case studies, and commentaries came to identify around 360 points systematically arrayed over the skin. These points were linked to twelve to fourteen channels of energy flow that connect to the human body's eleven main organs. Ming (1368–1644) and Qing (1644–1912) dynasty physicians systematized acumoxa therapy, but many treated it skeptically and used it sparingly. Popular literature shows acupuncture, often done by women, as a less prestigious treatment than receiving drugs.

Acumoxa therapies developed after 1800 in relation to biomedicine and state politics. The Qing Imperial Academy banned acupuncture in 1822. Later nineteenth-century threats to the Qing state led some Chinese physicians to stress acupuncture as a distinctive part of their medical learning in new acupuncture associations, books and journals, and correspondence courses that used the language of modern science and technology. The success of Chinese physicians in thwarting a parliamentary motion in 1929 seeking to ban the practice of traditional medicine is often seen as the start of modern traditional Chinese medicine, of which acupuncture was key. Some Republican-era doctors saw China's poverty and lack of public health care as a chance to promote acupuncture as an inexpensive alternative to drug-based medicine. Cheng Dan'an (1899–1957), a physician trained in Western anatomy and physiology, visited Japan in the early 1930s and redefined acupuncture points and meridians in relation to the peripheral nerve distributions of Western medicine. After returning home in 1933, Cheng opened the first modern acupuncture college in Jiangsu, and taught the classical theory he had systematized to suit modern students and readers. His students, writings, and political activities did much to shape the development of acupuncture.

Since the mid-twentieth century, acumoxa therapies have been part of the newly constituted "traditional Chinese medicine" created in the People's Republic of China (PRC), and acupuncture became the hallmark of Chinese medicine around the world. The Chinese Communist Party (CCP) oversaw this maturation of acupuncture within traditional Chinese medicine. Earlier CCP views of Chinese medicine as "feudal superstition" gave way to its promotion in Yan'an, laying the basis for the later combination of the practical value of acumoxa with revolutionary CCP goals. Acumoxa was presented as the embodiment of a "new," "scientific," and "unified" medicine.

Since 1949, the PRC has stressed acumoxa therapies in its health-care system. Mao Zedong's 1950 call to combine Western and traditional medicine was followed in 1951 by the publication of *New Acumoxa Studies* by the Western-trained doctor and Communist Party member Zhu Lian (1909–1978), which describes "new acumoxa" and the political and scientific motivations behind it. Since 1954, the government has promoted Chinese medicine and acupuncture as signal parts of China's cultural heritage. Research organizations for acupuncture have sprung up all over China in special clinics within hospitals. Organizations researching traditional Chinese medicine and pharmacology, many with acumoxa labs, have been established at the provincial, municipal, and autonomous regional levels.

Since the 1960s, acupuncture has become the focus of much scientific research, training, and clinical practice by physicians in and beyond China. Acumoxa therapies are widely used in traditional Chinese medicine, and public support for them in China remains strong. Although most Chinese believe in the superior diagnostic powers of biomedicine, many prefer acumoxa treatment for chronic diseases where the side effects of biomedicine are a concern.

The regular use of acumoxa in clinical settings has not been matched by modern, internationally acceptable, scientific research. Most of the thousands of studies done since 1970—seeking to identify biomedical mechanisms permitting acupuncture anesthesia and surgical analgesia, exploring possible biomedical correlates to the meridians or channels, and determining how acupuncture points relate to needling sensation between acupuncture points and the organs—have included too few subjects, used little or poor patient blinding, had bad or no control groups, and were characterized by multiple sources of bias. Several reviews of this literature have drawn negative conclusions due to these methodological flaws. Some randomized controlled trials have focused on these methodological issues, but no firm conclusions have been reached on how acupuncture works.

Acupuncture has long been practiced in Taiwan, Singapore, Japan, and Korea, and it is becoming part of health-care systems around the world, partly due to PRC efforts to globalize traditional Chinese medicine. In 1971 the *New York Times* reporter James Reston (1909–1995) brought acupuncture to the attention of Americans by describing his acupuncture anesthesia for an emergency appendectomy at a Chinese hospital while part of President Richard Nixon's entourage to China. A 1975 call by the World Health Organization (WHO) for acupuncture courses in Beijing, Shanghai, and Nanjing has provided many American and European practitioners with valuable training and hospital experience unavailable in their own countries. In 1980 WHO promulgated a list of conditions effectively treated with acupuncture, including respiratory, gastrointestinal, gynecological, and nervous disorders, and chronic pain tied to back injuries and arthritis. Acupuncture is also considered helpful in reducing the side effects of chemotherapy and surgery. Acupuncture can be used most effectively in treating chronic problems, but it has limited effectiveness against acute disorders that require surgery or emergency care.

**SEE ALSO** *Medicine, Traditional.*

**BIBLIOGRAPHY**


Academy of Traditional Chinese Medicine. *An Outline of Chinese Acupuncture.* Beijing: Foreign Languages Press, 1975.

Birch, Steven, and Ted Kaptchuk. History, Nature, and Current Practice of Acupuncture: An East Asian Perspective. In *Acupuncture: A Scientific Appraisal,* eds. Edzard Ernst and Adrian White, 11–30. Oxford: Butterworth Heinemann, 1999.

Ernst, Edzard. The Recent History of Acupuncture. *American Journal of Medicine* 121, 12 (2008): 1027–1028.

Lo, Vivienne. Introduction: Survey of Research into the History and Rationale of Acupuncture and Moxa since 1980. In *Celestial Lancets: A History and Rationale of Acupuncture and Moxa,* Lu Gwei-Djen and Joseph Needham, xxv–li. New ed. London: Curzon, 2002.

Scheid, Volker. *Chinese Medicine in Contemporary China: Plurality and Synthesis.* Durham, NC: Duke University Press, 2002.

Sierpina, Victor S., and Moshe A. Frenkel. Acupuncture: A Clinical Review. *Southern Medical Journal* 93, 5 (2005): 330–337.

Sivin, Nathan. *Traditional Medicine in Contemporary China: A Partial Translation of Revised Outline of Chinese Medicine (1972), with an Introductory Study on Change in Present-day and Early Medicine.* Ann Arbor: Center for Chinese Studies, University of Michigan, 1987.

Taylor, Kim. A New, Scientific, and Unified Medicine: Civil War in China and the New Acumoxa, 1945–49. In *Innovation in Chinese Medicine,* ed. Elisabeth Hsu, 343–369. Cambridge, U.K.: Cambridge University Press, 2001.

White, Adrian, and Edzard Ernst. 2004. A Brief History of Acupuncture. *Rheumatology* 43, 5 (2004): 662–663.


***Lowell Skar***

## ADOPTIONS

China is often presumed to lack traditions of adoption because of the influence of Confucianism, with its heavy emphasis on patrilineal biological ties in organizing family and society. Normative texts argued against adoption, and traditional Chinese law prohibited adoption outside patrilineal surname lines. However, in practice, adoption has a long and varied tradition in China and has been documented as quite common for hundreds of years. A number of strains in Confucianism and in popular culture support adoptive ties outside as well as inside bloodlines and encourage the adoption of both boys and girls to build family and kinship.

### EARLY MODERN PRACTICE

James Lee and Wang Feng (1999), providing evidence of relatively high adoption rates in China dating back to the eighteenth century, argue that the traditional Chinese family system was characterized by high levels of adoption compared to Europe's low-adoption kinship practices. China's rate of adoption probably varied from 1 to 10 percent of live births at various times and places.

During late imperial times and earlier, there is much evidence of a variety of adoption practices, varying by region, class, and ethnicity. In legal documented practice, the only legitimate reason for adoption was to obtain a male heir for the patrilineal family. The adoptive heir was supposed to be obtained from close male relatives, ideally if not exclusively from a brother. But in popular practice there were many other purposes for adoption, purposes involving girls as well as boys, and adoption from strangers was probably common. In Southeast China and elsewhere, adoption was often used to obtain a "little daughter-in-law," or future bride, for a son. But girls were also adopted as daughters by childless couples and by unmarried adults. Sometimes girls were adopted under the belief that this would overcome infertility and lead to the birth of a son. Sonless couples might adopt a daughter's husband to provide a male heir. Adoption could thus involve an adult. Adoptions were also prompted to provide homes for orphans and abandoned children. In other words, a variety of formal and informal adoption practices, serving sundry purposes, could be found in China in the past. Although adoption often carried a lesser status and might create weaker bonds than biological ties, when biology failed, bringing unrelated children and sometimes young adults into the family was a common way to build family and kinship.

## THE IMPACT OF THE ONE-CHILD POLICY

In contemporary China, adoption has continued to be practiced, although patterns have altered. The adoption of little daughters-in-law has virtually disappeared, while adopting girls as daughters has become the most common form of adoption, with nonrelative adoption more common than adoption from relatives. Demographic evidence indicates that after an apparent initial drop in the mid-twentieth century to below 1 percent of live births, adoption increased from 1980 through the 1990s with the advent of the one-child policy, reaching 2.1 percent of live births in 1986, or nearly 1 million adoptions, according to a sample survey. Demographers found that the majority of these adoptions were girls and that the number of adoptions, as well as the proportion of girls, were increasing each year, although the vast majority of adoptions were not officially registered. Smaller local studies in the 1990s and 2000s confirmed these patterns and further indicated that half or more of all adoptions were of foundlings.

The increase in adoption and in the availability of girls was a direct result of the high-pressure birth-planning campaigns waged throughout China beginning in the 1980s. The government, under its one-child policy, sought to implement rules restricting couples to one child, later loosened slightly in most of the countryside to two children if the first was a girl. In a largely rural society with waning but still strong preferences for a son, people used adoption as a means to hide a second or third daughter and to be able to try again for a son. At the same time, because the value of daughters was also increasing, people without daughters were often happy to adopt other families' excess daughters. Some "adoptions" were merely a ruse to hide a child temporarily, especially those of relatives and close friends living in other areas. But actual adoptions, involving the permanent transfer of the child into a new family, either through arrangement or outright abandonment, were also suspected by the authorities as a means to hide children.

Consequently, birth-planning officials quickly moved to block this loophole with regulations that forbade adoption except by childless couples over thirty-five. Birth parents who hid a child by adopting it out would be punished and would not be allowed an additional birth if they were caught. Adoptive parents who had another child or who were too young were also subject to birth-planning penalties if caught. In 1991 these birth-planning regulations became part of the nation's first adoption law, one of the most restrictive adoption laws ever enacted.

The combination of strict, often coercive birth-planning campaigns and highly restrictive one-child adoption regulations created waves of female-infant abandonment that surged throughout the country from the late 1980s through the first years of the twenty-first century, particularly in the Yangzi River area and areas extending south and southwest. Although spontaneous adoption of these abandoned female infants continued despite the restrictive one-child adoption law, usually in violation of the law and hence unregistered, increasing numbers of abandoned children reached the orphanages in unprecedented numbers by the early 1990s. Conditions even at the best state orphanages were over crowded and extremely poor, with insufficient funds for medical care and staffing. As a result, mortality rates were very high, and babies languished with little attention.

## INTERNATIONAL ADOPTION

Having severely restricted the pool of legally qualified domestic adopters to bolster population-control policies, the government turned to international adoption, limited entirely to children living in orphanages, to lessen the number of children in state orphanages and, more important, to provide a source of funding for these severely underfunded, highly stressed welfare institutions. As international adoption to the United States, Canada, and Europe gradually increased from a few hundred per year in the early 1990s to a peak of 13,000–14,000 in 2005, more resources were brought into the institutions through adoption fees and charitable international organizations, sometimes funded by adoptive parents. By 2008 over 100,000 Chinese children, mostly girls, had been adopted internationally, over 70,000 to the United States.

While international adoption helped improve conditions in many orphanages and provided a partial solution for the abandonment crisis, it also created further incentives for orphanage directors to favor international adoption over domestic adoption and to rely on a continuing supply of healthy infants for international adoption to finance the care of the disabled, unadoptable population that remained in the orphanages. Thus, even though the government in 2000 slightly eased legal restrictions on domestic adoption from orphanages (but not on the much higher number of adoptions that occur outside orphanages), a financial bias in favor of international adoption became built into the system. This

***An American mother playing with her adopted daughters, Guangzhou, December 8, 2001.*** *Limited by China's One Child Policy, some families choose to abandon female newborns at state-run orphanages, hoping that a future child might be male, a common preference in traditional Chinese culture. Consequently, the abundance of orphaned girls in China has led to a large number of foreign adoptions, with the financial proceeds of these transactions subsidizing the existing overcrowded institutions.* © LYNSEY ADDARIO/CORBIS

was coupled with continued opposition from birth-planning officials to even minor exceptions to the one-child adoption rule. As a result, many domestic adopters continued to have a hard time adopting from orphanages, especially those that did international adoptions, despite eased regulations. While overall domestic adoption from orphanages increased in the 2000s, orphanages that did international adoptions often had long waiting lists of domestic adopters while continuing to process international adoptions in record numbers.

International adoption continued to grow until peaking in 2005. Yet evidence suggests that the numbers of healthy abandoned children began to decline in many orphanages a year or two after the 2000 census. As the supply of healthy children declined while international adoption applications continued to climb to new heights, waiting times for foreigners also lengthened, international adoption requirements stiffened, and a number of scandals involving baby trafficking to orphanages surfaced in Yunnan and later in Hunan. Documented cases of forcible confiscation of overquota birth children and unregistered domestically adopted children by local officials for placement in orphanages for international adoption also surfaced as overcrowding in orphanages turned to a shortage of healthy children. Meanwhile, children with moderate to severe special needs continued to come into orphanages, changing the composition of the child population in state care.

Finally in 2006, international adoptions began to fall, reflecting the new situation in Chinese orphanages. By 2008 the number of international adoptions from China were nearly half the number in 2005; adoptions to the United States fell from a peak of 7,900 in 2005 to 3,900 in 2008. The dearth of healthy babies in most major orphanages is said to be due to decreased abandonment in the context of increasing wealth, lowered fertility, and increased domestic adoption, much of which continues to take place before abandoned children reach the orphanage and remains unregistered. Registered domestic adoption, including adoption from orphanages, went up to a peak of 50,000 in 2000, when legal restrictions were slightly relaxed, then remained around 40,000 thereafter. The trends in unregistered adoption are unknown but probably remain several times higher than registered adoptions. It is possible that unregistered adoptions, which climbed steadily through the 1980s and 1990s and probably reached over 1 million annually, will decline as abandonment declines and as fertility desires in general fall to new lows below the population replacement level. As in the past, this will depend partly on the fate of the one-child policy and the vigor with which it is enforced.

An additional factor affecting trends in domestic and international adoption may be the recent enactment of the Hague Convention governing international adoption, which China has signed. According to the Hague Convention, domestic adoption should always take precedence over international adoption. From the beginning China's international adoption program has violated this principle, being born of coercive government population-control policies that not only stoked abandonment but also intentionally restricted domestic adoption, and thus necessitated the turn to international adoption to fund and ease overcrowding in state orphanages. By 2008, more than fifteen years later, efforts to bring China's adoption program were brought more in line with the norms of the Hague Convention by lessening the policy bias against domestic adoption and allowing international adoption to decline. This may mark the end of international adoption for healthy children and the adopting out only of children with moderate disabilities, which make them difficult to place in China.

**SEE ALSO** *Family: Infanticide; Family: One-Child Policy; Life Cycle: Birth; Population Policy; Women, Status of.*

**BIBLIOGRAPHY**

Greenhalgh, Susan. Planned Births, Unplanned Persons: "Population" in the Making of Chinese Modernity. *American Ethnologist* 30, 2 (May 2003): 1–20.

Johansson, Sten, and Ola Nygren. The Missing Girls of China: A New Demographic Account. *Population and Development Review* 17, 1 (March 1991): 35–51.

Johnson, Kay Ann. *Wanting a Daughter, Needing a Son: Abandonment, Adoption, and Orphanage Care in China.* St. Paul, MN: Yeong and Yeong Book Co., 2004.

Lee, James, and Wang Feng. *One Quarter of Humanity: Malthusian Mythology and Chinese Realities, 1700–2000.* Cambridge, MA: Harvard University Press, 1999.

Stuy, Brian. The Hague Agreement and China's International Adoption Program. Research-China.org, 2006. http://research-china.blogspot.com/2006/06/hague-agreement-and-chinas.html.

Waltner, Ann. *Getting an Heir: Adoption and the Construction of Kinship in Late Imperial China.* Honolulu: University of Hawaii Press, 1990.

Zhang, Weiguo. Child Adoption in Contemporary Rural China. *Journal of Family Issues* 27, 3 (2006): 301–340.

***Kay Ann Johnson***

# ADULT EDUCATION

**SEE** *Education: Adult Education.*

# AFRICAN STATES, RELATIONS WITH

The People's Republic of China's first large-scale approach to African governments took place at the Bandung Conference, held in 1955 in Indonesia. Despite its own poverty, China provided aid and maintained diplomatic ties with

African countries, presenting itself as a poor but principled alternative to the Cold War powers. For half a century, the theory of non interference in other countries' domestic affairs has been a pillar of Chinese politics. Forged to protect Chinese domestic policy from foreign influence, it is now shared by African governments.

During the 1960s and the 1970s, China's support for Africa was mostly directed at revolutionary movements and new governments born from decolonization. China wanted (and still wants) to be the major actor in the developing world. At that time, it needed support to recover its United Nations seat from Taiwan. More recently, China, in its turn, began supporting the African states' pleas for a permanent seat on the UN Security Council.

After Mao Zedong's death, China's foreign policy priorities shifted to developed countries because China needed foreign investments to finance its economic development. The year 1989 was a turning point, both for China generally and for its relations with African countries. Banned and isolated by Western governments after the Tiananmen massacre, China turned again toward its former allies in Africa, building a so-called "win-win" cooperation strategy to recover its position on the international scene.

By 1993, as its economic development accelerated, China started to import oil, and the government realized how badly the country needed not only foreign investments but also natural resources. China first targeted North African countries, which were soon followed by many sub-Saharan countries. Chinese leaders also made official visits to Africa, which led to some thirty oil agreements, with no political strings attached except a pledge to support the one-China principle.

In October 2000, the first Sino-African cooperation summit was held in Beijing with the aim of building a long-term strategy. The summit was followed by an operational forum in 2003 in Addis Ababa, Ethiopia. China promised to help its African partners with investment in infrastructure and public works, including roads and rails to reach extraction sites, as well as government buildings such as parliaments and presidential houses. As was the case with former colonial powers, a dual interest in both Africa's natural resources and its political support in the international arena motivated this approach. But, if those countries could operate for many years without obstacles, China today faces opposition from the international community, which has established international treaties to protect human rights and promote good governance.

Between 2000 and 2006, China ignored this new context, filling all gaps left by former colonial powers such as France and offering better economic deals than the United States. Its support of Sudan, Zimbabwe, Angola, and the Ivory Coast—all banned or sanctioned by the United Nations for violations of human rights or high levels

## INVESTMENTS IN AFRICA: INFRASTRUCTURE AND NATURAL RESOURCES

Reliable statistics concerning China's economic activities in Africa are rare. Only in late 2004 did media and experts begin to focus attention on China's business with Africa, and data began to be published regularly. China's president's travel to France and Africa in January 2004 and China's abstention from voting the UN resolution on Dafur in May could explain this rise of interest. Ideological thinking remains the main driver in the release and interpretation of such data. Western sources tend to give larger estimates of Chinese investments in Africa, while official data from China understate the totals. Estimates are difficult to make in part because the distinction between trade, project financing by China's financial institutions, and direct investment by Chinese enterprises is not often clear.

China's investments in Africa are mostly directed at the search for natural resources in exchange for infrastructure financing. By the end of 2005, China had invested in twenty-seven major oil and natural gas projects in fourteen African countries. In 2006 China Exim Bank, the country's official export-credit agency, acknowledged having approved at least $6.5 billion in loans for Africa, 79 percent of which went for infrastructure investment. The World Bank, however, estimates that all of China Exim Bank's loans to sub-Saharan Africa in the infrastructure sector alone amounted to more than $12.5 billion by mid-2006.

Some Western sources estimate that in 1990 China had $49 million in foreign direct investment in Africa, $600 million in 2003, and $900 million in 2004. Chinese official data (see Table 1) moderate the standard Western view of China as steadily increasing its presence in Africa. The peak of 2000 could be explained with the impulse given to the China Africa relations by the establishment of the China-Africa Cooperation Forum (CACF). However, more recent official data from China has corresponded more closely to Western estimates, and if the trend for the first nine months of 2007 is confirmed, Chinese nonfinancial direct outbound investment in Africa will reach $870 million corresponding to 4.6 percent of the total $18.72 billion of Chinese nonfinancial direct outbound investment for that year.

In this case the Africa share would have more than doubled in three years.

***Francesca Cini***

**Official Chinese investments in Africa**

| Year | US$ | Source |
|---|---|---|
| 1993 | 14 million | CMC quoted by OECD 2006 |
| 1994 | 28 million | CMC quoted by OECD 2006 |
| 1995 | 17 million | CMC quoted by OECD 2006 |
| 1996 | 56 million | CMC quoted by OECD 2006 |
| 1997 | 81 million | CMC quoted by OECD 2006 |
| 1998 | 88 million | CMC quoted by OECD 2006 |
| 1999 | 95 million | CMC quoted by OECD 2006 |
| 2000 | 214 million | CMC quoted by OECD 2006 |
| 2001 | 72 million | CMC quoted by OECD 2006 |
| 2002 | 62 million | CMC quoted by OECD 2006 |
| 2003 | 107 million | CMC quoted by OECD 2006 |
| 2004 | 317 million | China National Statistics Bureau |
| 2005 | 392 million | China National Statistics Bureau |
| 2006 | 370 million | Chinese customs in Agence France Presse, January 30, 2007 |
| 2007 | 650 million (9 months) | *People's Daily*, December 28, 2007 |

Note: CMC is the Chinese Ministry of Commerce; OECD is the Organization for Economic Cooperation and Development.

***Table 1***

of corruption—brought China contracts worth billions of dollars. In 2006 Angola became China's single largest source of oil and in 2007 its first African commercial partner, outrunning South Africa. The PRC also imports 60 percent of Sudan's oil. Zimbabwe sells China uranium and platinum and buys fighter jets from Beijing. By 2008 China had agreed to finance two-thirds of a $402 million information technology park in the Ivory Coast, where it is also building the "biggest Parliament ever."

The PRC's economic involvement in Africa has increased dramatically. According to Chinese official statistics, annual China-Africa trade was $12 million in 1956 when Chinese-Egyptian diplomatic relations were established; the figure had reached $10 billion during the first years of the twenty-first century. The annual bilateral trade value declared in 2007 was $73 billion. Gabon granted China exclusive rights to exploit untapped iron-ore reserves in exchange for the promise to build the necessary infrastructure. China and Niger reached a similar agreement concerning uranium exploitation. In 2006 China obtained 45 percent on the exploitation of a Nigerian oil extraction site. Chinese companies also contributed to the rebuilding of Sierra Leone and the Ivory Coast, both ravaged by war. These are only a few examples. But these relations are not balanced, as South Africa is the only African investor in China as of 2008.

Chinese president Hu Jintao visited Africa three times beginning in 2003, and it has become a rule for the Chinese foreign minister to visit Africa as his first destination every year. The year 2006 was crucial for Sino-African relations. On January 12, China published an official document titled "China's African Policy" in which the one-China principle is designated "the political foundation for the establishment and development of China's relations with African countries." This policy led Liberia, Senegal, Chad, and Malawi to sever diplomatic ties with Taiwan, leaving the island with only four minor allies on the continent. Reaffirming its status as "the largest developing country in the world" sharing with Africa "the historical experience of struggle for national liberation," China has successfully defied Western powers on the continent.

But in the months following the promulgation of the new policy, China's mostly unnoticed "conquest" of Africa encountered its first obstacles. The United States increased its military presence on the continent, while France became concerned about the PRC's growing influence in its former colonies. In addition, the international media began to denounce China's investments in Sudan, Zimbabwe, and Angola. The media declared China responsible for the killing campaign in Darfur through its investments in Sudan, and they accused China of not behaving as the responsible stakeholder it claimed to be. During the summer of 2006, Amnesty International and Human Rights Watch wrote open letters to the Chinese government asking it to pressure Sudan (whose estimated economic growth of 11 percent in 2006 comes mostly from Chinese investments) into accepting UN peacekeeping forces. In addition, such Hollywood stars as Mia Farrow and Steven Spielberg launched a campaign to boycott the 2008 Olympic Games in Beijing.

In this context, the November 2006 Sino-African Forum held in Beijing was both the apotheosis of China's success in Africa and the beginning of a more responsible foreign policy. Meant to be a dress rehearsal for the Olympics, the forum was attended by forty heads of forty-eight African states (out of fifty-three). Posters of Africa were pasted all over Beijing, where the Chinese government tried out the "clear sky" experience promised for 2008. President Hu Jintao declared that the mainland would provide $5 billion in loans and preferential buyer credits to encourage Chinese investment in Africa, cancel the debts of the poorest countries, and double the trade volume to reach $100 billion by 2010.

At the same time, the Chinese leadership has begun putting pressure on the Sudanese government, causing Khartoum to accept the deployment of United Nations–African Union Mission in Darfur (UNAMID) forces in autumn 2007. China also loosened its ties with Zimbabwe. Money and diplomatic efforts have helped calm the situation in Zambia, where anti-Chinese sentiments were voiced by a pro-Taiwan political leader. During his February 2007 trip to Zambia, Hu Jintao cancelled $8 million of Zambia's debt, and announced $800 million in investments in copper mines and the creation of the first free-trade zone in Africa.

***United Nations peacekeepers from China on duty in Darfur, Sudan, January 29, 2008.*** *With Western colonial influence diminishing in Africa during the late twentieth century, China entered this power vacuum, promising infrastructure investment to many politically unstable countries. In exchange, African nations such as Sudan, Angola, and Zimbabwe provided China much needed natural resources to fuel their economic boom at the turn of the century.* AP IMAGES

This new approach has not prevented China from selling arms, fuelling conflicts in countries less-covered by the international media, such as DRC, Mali, Niger, Ethiopia, and Somalia. But the picture would not be fair and complete without mentioning China's burgeoning relations with Africa's more democratic countries, as shown by China's agreement to build a $634-million railroad in Mauritania, as well as aid of $56 million to strengthen the Intranet system of the Senegalese government.

## BIBLIOGRAPHY

L'Afrique du Sud entre le "choix moral" de Taïpeh et le rapprochement avec Pékin [South Africa between the "Moral Choice" of Taipei and the Rapprochement with Beijing]. *Marchè tropicaux* 2652 (September 6, 1996): 1937.

Aicardi de Saint-Paul, Marc. La Chine et l'Afrique entre engagement et intérêt [China and Africa Mingled in Interest and Engagement]. *Géopolitique africaine* 14 (2004): 51–65.

Amnesty International. China: Secretive Arms Exports Stoking Conflict and Repression. Index number: ASA 17/033/2006. June 11, 2006.

Amnesty International. Sudan/China: Appeal by Amnesty International to the Chinese Government on the Occasion of the China-Africa Summit for Development and Cooperation. Index number: AFR 54/072/2006. November 2006.

Amnesty International. Sudan: Arms Continuing to Fuel Serious Human Rights Violations in Darfur. Index number: AFR 54/019/2007. May 8, 2007.

Bezlova, Antoaneta. Politics-China: Sudan—Showcase for New Assertiveness. Inter Press Service (IPS) News Agency. September 21, 2007.

China's Rise in Africa. *China Security* 3, 3 (2007).

Ching, Frank. China Makes Its Own Rules: Foreign Interference Is All Right if It's to Beijing's Advantage. *Far Eastern Economic Review* 159, 38 (1996): 36.

*Financial Times*. Friend or Forager? How China Is Winning the Resources and the Loyalties of Africa. February 2, 2006.

Gaye, Adama. *Chine-Afrique: Le dragon et l'Autruche*. Paris: l'Harmattan, 2006.

Human Rights Watch. China-Africa Summit: Focus on Human Rights, Not Just Trade—Chinese Leadership Should Pressure Sudan, Zimbabwe on Human Rights. November 2, 2006.

Jamestown Foundation. *China Brief* 5, 21 (October 13, 2005).

Lafargue, François. China's Presence in Africa, *China Perspectives* 61, 2 (2005).

Lafargue, François. États-Unis, Inde, Chine: La compétition pour le pétrole africain [United States, India, China: Scramble for Africa's oil]. *Monde Chinois* 6, 19 (2005–2006).

Naidu, Sanusha, guest ed. China in Africa. *Inside AISA* (Africa Institute of South Africa) 3 and 4 (Oct/Dec 2006).

Ndyae, A. K. En avant pour la Chine [Go Ahead for China]. In *Nouvel Horizon*. February 23, 2006.

Niquet, Valérie. La stratégie africaine de la Chine [China's African Strategy]. *Politique étrangère*. February, 2006.

*People's Daily Online*. China's African Policy. January 12, 2006. http://english.people.com.cn.

Tuquoi, Jean-Pierre. La Chine pousse ses pions en Afrique [China Moves Its Pawns in Africa]. *Le Monde*, January 11, 2006.

Wild, Leni, and David Mepham, eds. *The New Sinosphere: China in Africa*. London: IPPR, 2006.

***Francesca Cini***

# AGRICULTURAL PRODUCTION

*This entry contains the following:*



## OVERVIEW

Analysis of Chinese agriculture for much of the period since 1800 is handicapped by severe data limitations relating to acreage and production. These problems are especially serious for the nineteenth century—there was no regular reporting system for agriculture under the Qing (1644–1912)—and are compounded by uncertainty at critical junctures in Chinese history over the size of the Chinese population, a key input into any assessment of Chinese agriculture. It was not until 1953 that China carried out a credible population census, which put China's population at 583 million. Data issues are even more pronounced at a subnational or regional level.

This entry begins by offering a brief sketch of Chinese agriculture circa 1800. To provide a perspective on the dynamics of Chinese agricultural growth over the next two centuries, the discussion draws heavily on Dwight Perkins's (1969) seminal work, which covers the much-longer period between 1368 and 1968. This entry updates Perkins's analysis to include the years under collectivized agriculture up through 1978, and then the important post-1978 reform era. A central issue in the examination of Chinese agriculture over this period is the relationship between agriculture and population growth. The role of institutions is also important.

### CHINESE AGRICULTURE CIRCA 1800

By the beginning of the nineteenth century, China already had a population in the vicinity of 300 million. Estimates of G. William Skinner (1977) for the mid-nineteenth century suggest that more than 90 percent of the population lived in rural areas—the remainder lived in cities and towns—and probably three-quarters or more of the labor force derived their incomes directly from farming. Much of Chinese agriculture was made up of relatively small family farms.

China was self-sufficient in food, but agriculture operated under a relatively severe land constraint. Although China's land mass was roughly comparable to that of the United States today, less than 15 percent of China's land area was arable. In 1800, land per capita was not much more than half an acre, and slightly higher in the north than the south. Expanded opportunity to double-crop in the south, made possible by the region's longer growing season and public and private investments in water control, drainage, and irrigation, helped to support higher population densities. Overall, up to a third of acreage in China was irrigated, and possibly as much as half of all acreage in the south.

Estimates suggest that 80 percent of China's sown area was devoted to grain, primarily rice in the south, and wheat and millet in the north. Smaller amounts of acreage were in miscellaneous grains such as sorghum, barley, and buckwheat. Almost all grain production was consumed directly, with upwards of 80 percent of total calories consumed coming from grain. Exhaustion of land productivity levels and of opportunities to expand cultivated area in more densely populated regions limited the size of the animal-husbandry sector. As a result, the contribution of proteins from animal and dairy products to Chinese diets was very small, as was the role of draft animals in farm production.

Land productivity in China, however, was still among the highest in the world. In 1800, grain (unhusked) output was roughly 1.5 metric tons per hectare, or 600 kilograms per acre. By comparison, grain yields in 1800 were nearer

**Grain production and consumption in China: 1766–2005**

| Year | Cultivated area (million hectares) | Percentage in grain | Cultivated area in grain (million hectares) | Grain output (million metric ton) | Population (million) | Output per capita (metric ton) | Yield (metric ton per hectare) |
|---|---|---|---|---|---|---|---|
| 1766 | 63 | 0.80 | 50 | 77.0 | 270 | 0.285 | 1.53 |
| 1850 | 78 | 0.80 | 62 | 111.2 | 390 | 0.285 | 1.78 |
| 1873 | 81 | 0.80 | 65 | 99.8 | 350 | 0.285 | 1.54 |
| 1933 | 98 | 0.80 | 78 | 142.5 | 500 | 0.285 | 1.82 |
| 1957 | 112 | 0.80 | 90 | 195.1 | 647 | 0.302 | 2.18 |
| 1977 | 135 | 0.81 | 109 | 283.3 | 950 | 0.298 | 2.60 |
| 2005 | 127 | 0.67 | 85 | 484.0 | 1308 | 0.370 | 5.68 |

SOURCE: Perkins, Dwight. *Agricultural Development in China 1368–1968*. Chicago: Aldine Publishing Company, 1969; Zhongguo Tongji Nianjian, miscellaneous years; author's own calculations.

*Table 1*

to a metric ton per hectare in Great Britain, and even less in India. The high yields in China were supported by high levels of labor input, irrigation covering a third or so of cultivated area, extensive application of organic fertilizers, and crop rotations refined over centuries that helped to maintain long-run soil fertility. Multiple-cropping (more than one crop on a piece of land per year) as well as intercropping (planting of more than one crop on a piece of land at the same point in time) also played an important role.

The remaining 20 percent of acreage was used for cash crops that included soybeans, oilseeds such as rape and sesame, cotton, and mulberry trees. The latter were especially important to two of China's most important traditional industries, namely, sericulture and textiles, both of which were tightly integrated with household farming activity at the time. Regionally, cotton cultivation was significant in the Lower and Middle Yangzi and parts of North China. Mulberry cultivation was heavily concentrated in the Lower Yangzi and Pearl River deltas.

At the beginning of the nineteenth century, Chinese agriculture was also relatively commercialized. Wu Chengming (1985) estimates that overall roughly 20 percent of agricultural output was marketed. Much of this was locally sold, but crops such as rice and cotton entered into regional and occasionally national markets, and helped to facilitate specialization in both agriculture and nonagriculture activity. Grain from the surplus Upper and Middle Yangzi provinces, for example, helped to feed the historically grain-deficit areas of the Lower Yangzi, the capital city of Beijing, and southern coastal cities.

Prices that farmers received for their crops were a product of domestic demand and supply, with prices highly integrated in localities linked by low-cost water transport (Chuan Han-sheng and Kraus 1975). The role of international factors in Chinese agriculture was negligible at this time, including the import or export of agricultural commodities.

In most years, Chinese agriculture was able to feed the population easily, but successive years of crop failure could lead to localized and regional famine. Pierre-Étienne Will and R. Bin Wong (1991) argue that throughout the first half of the Qing these problems were often mitigated by an effective public granary system that provided organized relief in affected areas. The same system appears to have been much less effective in the nineteenth century for reasons that remain open to debate.

## GROWTH AFTER 1800

Dwight Perkins (1969) provides a valuable framework for analyzing how Chinese agriculture accommodated an enormous increase in population over a period covering the six hundred years between 1368 and 1968. The two margins on which agricultural production could expand were the *extensive* margin, through an increase in cultivated area, and the *intensive* margin, through increases in yields, or output per unit of cultivated area.

This entry will focus on the period since 1800. If the Chinese population was in the vicinity of 300 million in 1800, by the mid-1950s it had doubled to 600 million, and by 2005 it had doubled again to 1.3 billion. In the wake of the huge devastation and loss of life caused by the Taiping Uprising (1851–1864), China's population at the beginning of the twentieth century was nearer to 400 million, and probably slightly over 500 million by the 1930s. Skinner's careful forensic work on early nineteenth-century Qing population registers suggests a population slightly less than 400 million in 1850.

It is not until the mid-1950s that credible estimates of agricultural output actually exist. Perkins contends however that over much of the six-hundred-year period he analyzes, per capita grain consumption moved within a fairly narrow range of 250 to 300 kilograms of unhusked grain per year. If per capita grain availability had been much higher, the number of draft animals and hogs per capita would have been much larger than other sources suggest, and a lower percentage of calories would have been coming directly from grain. A lower boundary on grain consumption is 200 kilograms per year, which provides the minimum calories required for subsistence.

With the role of grain imports and exports minimal, estimates of China's population enable Perkins to "fix" the size of China's grain production at key points in time. Combined with his estimates of cultivated acreage, and assuming that roughly 80 percent of acreage was in grain, Perkins is able to estimate the contribution of the intensive and extensive margins to growth in output. Table 1 provides estimates of cultivated area, grain output, population, output per capita, and grain yields for key years.

Over the entire six centuries that Perkins examines, the contributions to the growth in output in cultivated area and yields are roughly equal. The same is also true for the century and a half after 1800. Between 1800 and the 1950s, cultivated area expanded by 60 percent, from roughly 70 million hectares to 112 million. This increase is potentially misleading, however. A significant portion of this expansion can be attributed to the opening up of the Northeast to migration beginning in the last half of the nineteenth century. Settlement in Sichuan and the Southwest (Guizhou and Guangxi) played a similar role at the end of the eighteenth and beginning of the nineteenth century. In the more densely settled areas of China, notably the Pearl River Delta and the Lower Yangzi, land under cultivation remained more or less fixed.

Improved seeds (e.g., early ripening varieties of rice from present-day Vietnam), intercropping, new crop rotations, and new crops were the source of much of the yield growth. In the nineteenth and early twentieth century, the introduction and spread of corn and sweet potatoes were especially important among new crops, and often allowed an extension of cultivation to otherwise marginal lands.

Following Ester Boserup (1965), Perkins contends that the increases in yields from these innovations are hard to disentangle from concurrent increases in labor inputs. For example, early-ripening varieties allowed an increase in the degree of double-cropping, but this would not have been possible without an increase in the size of the population and thus the labor force that was needed to alleviate labor bottlenecks during peak periods. An increase in population density was also the primary source of the increase in fertilizer, which continued to be night soil and animal manure. Similarly, capital deepening by allocating more labor to water control was facilitated by the increase in the size of the labor force.

This logic represents an important reversal of the usual Malthusian causality in which agricultural development determines the level of population. More generally, Perkins's analysis suggests that a long, slow growth in population density could occur over an extended period of time without diminishing returns to labor and declining food availability because of a combination of slow improvement in new seeds, intensification of cultivation, and increasing specialization.

One important development for Chinese agriculture at the end of the nineteenth century was its integration into the international economy. As a consequence of falling oceanic transport costs and the introduction of the telegraph, prices of China's traditional exports such as tea and silk, as well as those of such major farm commodities including rice, wheat, and cotton, increasingly came to follow international price trends (Brandt 1989). Previously, these prices were determined within China, and reflected domestic demand and supply considerations. These new ties were especially pronounced in areas of China linked by low-cost water transport, and in the early twentieth century, by rail.

Generally rising terms of trade for agriculture in the international economy between the 1870s and 1920s, combined with an increase in the size of China's nonagricultural population, contributed to a rising commercialization and specialization in China's farm sector that built on earlier patterns. Only a relatively small percentage of the marketed output actually made its way into the international economy, with most of it sold domestically in local, regional, and national markets. By the late 1920s and early 1930s, upwards of 40 percent of farm output was sold. This process helped agricultural output to grow at least as rapidly as the population over the course of much of the late nineteenth and early twentieth century, and possibly faster (Rawski 1989).

The 1930s marked the beginning of a sharp reversal for agriculture. With the onset of the world depression, the terms of trade for agriculture deteriorated significantly. Subsequently, agriculture was disrupted by the Anti-Japanese War (1937–1945) and then the civil war (1946–1949).

## AGRICULTURE UNDER THE PEOPLE'S REPUBLIC

The 1950s witnessed a major reorganization of Chinese agriculture with the establishment of the People's Republic of China (PRC). Following land reform in the early 1950s that redistributed upwards of 40 percent of cultivated area to poorer households, households were soon reorganized into agricultural collectives, and family farming was eliminated. Economic planners hoped that the reorganization would enable them to exploit untapped potential in China's traditional agriculture, and facilitate the mobilization of a grain surplus to feed a rapidly expanding urban population. Domestic autarky in food production was also pushed.

By the mid-1950s however, China had already exhausted most, if not all, of the potential gains from its traditional agricultural technology. Agricultural output and China's ability to feed its population also became very sensitive to shifting institutional winds. The deaths of between twenty-five and thirty million people during the Great Leap famine (1959–1961), generally acknowledged now to have been a product of bad policy as opposed to bad weather, is a poignant reminder (Li Wei and Dennis Tao Yang 2005).

Future increases in farm output would have to come from the development and use of new high-yielding varieties of the kind associated with the green revolution. These new varieties, which needed to be adapted through breeding to suit local growing conditions, also required significant application of chemical fertilizers, pesticides, and controlled water use. Experimental work on these varieties began in China in the early 1930s, and resumed under government auspices after 1949 (Wiens 1982).

This research and development paved the way in the 1960s and 1970s for a rapid expansion in the area under high-yielding varieties in both rice and wheat. This was complemented by significant investment in rural infrastructure for water control and irrigation, as well as investment in chemical fertilizer production. In principle, these investments should have contributed to significant increases in yields and output. In other parts of Asia, high-yielding varieties contributed to as much as a doubling of yields within a span of two decades.

Much of this promise went unfulfilled in China, and the country experienced enormous difficulty in feeding the growth in its population; in all likelihood, per capita food-calorie consumption declined throughout much of the 1960s and 1970s from the levels of the mid-1950s, and in the mid-1970s average consumption may have been lower than the levels in the 1930s. By the late 1970s, upwards of 250 to 300 million individuals living in rural China found themselves below China's own stark poverty line. In the 1970s, China had to frequently resort to emergency food imports to feed its urban population, which in percentage terms had actually declined between the mid-1950s and the mid-1970s.

Nicholas Lardy (1983) argues that these improvements in farm technology were insufficient to offset the huge disincentive effects associated with collectivized agriculture, including a highly egalitarian distribution of income within communes. Cropping intensification in the form of triple-cropping was pushed to uneconomic extremes. Small private plots, an important complement to collective agriculture in the 1950s, were also occasionally prohibited. These weaknesses were compounded by poor terms of trade (price of agricultural goods relative to nonagricultural goods) for agriculture, marketing restrictions, and a policy of local grain self-sufficiency. Indeed, the degree of specialization in agriculture and the size of the interregional trade in grain and other agricultural products were less than they had been in the 1930s. Growth in the production of nongrain crops lagged even more, and overall, productivity in agriculture likely fell significantly over this period.

The difficulty experienced by Chinese agriculture in feeding its population likely contributed to renewed deforestation and environmental degradation. Hillsides were often terraced and other marginal lands converted to grain production by local authorities in the hopes of increasing grain production and procurement. Cultivated area under production, much of it likely marginal in quality, increased over the period. Data for earlier years on forest coverage are problematic, but it appears that only with the reforms of the farm and forestry sectors after 1978 was there a reversal in some of these trends (Zhang Yuxing and Song Conghe 2006).

## POST-1978

China's food problem was at the core of the major overhaul of its agricultural sector beginning in the late 1970s. The hallmark of these reforms was the introduction of the household responsibility system and the reinstitution of family farming after nearly a quarter century of collective agriculture. The precursor to the household responsibility system was similar reforms carried out in the aftermath of the Great Leap famine in order to promote a rapid recovery of output, but these experiments were abandoned for ideological reasons within a few years.

The household responsibility system was complemented by other important reforms relating to pricing, crop choice, marketing, and input market liberalization. Between 1978 and 1984, rates of growth of grain production nearly doubled over those in the 1970s, while cash-crop production, including cotton and oilseeds, increased even faster. Agriculture sidelines such as fishery and livestock also exhibited rapid growth. The rapid growth in cash crops and agriculture sidelines was inextricably tied to China's newfound ability to feed its population, which allowed land and labor to move out of grain production. By 2005, 67 percent of sown area was in grain, down from 81 percent in 1977.

A careful analysis of the sources of growth in the cropping sector by Justin Lin (1991) attributes more than half of the rapid growth between 1978 and 1984 to the incentive effects associated with the broad set of institutional reforms mentioned above. Underlying this was "untapped" potential from technological development and investment in the 1960s and 1970s, which ideology and institutions prevented China from fully exploiting.

Rates of growth in agriculture have slowed appreciably since the mid-1980s, but the gross domestic product in the entire agricultural sector has continued to grow at nearly 4 percent per annum. With China successful in solving its basic food (grain) problems, much of this growth has been in agriculture sidelines, which by 2008 represented nearly half of the value of agricultural output. There has also been increasing specialization in the cropping sector, with China becoming an important exporter of more labor-intensive, higher-valued products such as horticultural and animal goods, including aquatic products, and increasingly, an importer of land-intensive grain and oilseeds. Once again, prices of agricultural commodities in China largely follow behavior in international markets.

Rapid productivity growth and mechanization in agriculture have allowed a significant transfer of labor out of agriculture into the manufacturing and service sector. Official estimates of the share of labor in agriculture are probably too high, but alternative estimates suggest that in 2008 roughly 35 percent of the labor force was engaged in agriculture, down from 70 percent in 1978. Rapid growth in agriculture was also instrumental in the reversal of China's trade balance in food and agricultural products from negative to positive, which in the 1980s helped to ease a macro foreign-exchange constraint.

Central to the sustained growth in yields and productivity has been public and, to a much lesser extent, private investment in agricultural research and plant breeding. The same will be true going forward. Well-defined property rights in agriculture will also likely be important. The household responsibility system allocated use rights to land to households, and over time other important rights with respect to crop choice, land rental, and so forth have also been solidified. Land ownership, however, remains vested in villages, and household land tenure is occasionally subject to the capriciousness of local government officials.

**BIBLIOGRAPHY**

Boserup, Ester. *The Conditions of Agricultural Growth: The Economics of Agrarian Change under Population Pressure.* Chicago: Aldine, 1965.

Brandt, Loren. *Commercialization and Agricultural Development: Central and Eastern China, 1870–1914.* New York: Cambridge University Press, 1989.

Buck, John L. *Land Utilization in China.* Chicago: University of Chicago Press, 1937.

Chuan Han-sheng and Richard Kraus. *Mid-Ch'ing Rice Markets: An Essay in Price History.* Cambridge, MA: Harvard University Press, 1975.

Lardy, Nicholas. *Agriculture in China's Modern Economic Development.* New York: Cambridge University Press, 1983.

Li Wei and Dennis Tao Yang. The Great Leap Forward: Anatomy of a Central Planning Disaster. *Journal of Political Economy* 113, 4 (2005): 840–877.

Lin, Justin. Rural Reforms and Agricultural Growth in China. *American Economic Review* 82 (1991): 34–51.

National Bureau of Statistic (NBS). Zhongguo Tongji Nianjian [Statistical yearbook of China]. Beijing: China Statistics Press, annual.

Perkins, Dwight. *Agricultural Development in China, 1368–1968.* Chicago: Aldine, 1969.

Rawski, Thomas G. *Economic Growth in Prewar China.* Berkeley: University of California Press, 1989.

Skinner, G. William. Regional Urbanization in Nineteenth-century China. In *The City in Late Imperial China*, ed. G. William Skinner, 211–249. Stanford, CA: Stanford University Press, 1977.

Wiens, Thomas. *The Microeconomics of Peasant Economy: China, 1920–1940.* New York: Garland, 1982.

Will, Pierre-Étienne, and R. Bin Wong. *Nourish the People: The State Civilian Granary System in China, 1650–1850.* Ann Arbor: Center for Chinese Studies, University of Michigan, 1991.

Wu Chengming. *Zhongguo zibenzhuyi yu guonei shichang* [Chinese capitalism and domestic markets]. Beijing: China Social Science Publishing, 1985.

Zhang Yuxing and Song Conghe. Impacts of Afforestation, Deforestation, and Reforestation on Forest Cover in China from 1949 to 2003. *Journal of Forestry* 107, 7 (2006): 383–387.

***Loren Brandt***

## FRUIT AND VEGETABLE FARMING

China's small-scale but intensive farm sector is the world's largest producer of vegetables and fruits. About 110 commonly produced vegetable varieties and numerous temperate and tropical fruits are grown in its diverse agroclimatic zones. After the 1949 establishment of the People's Republic, China experimented with collective agriculture and emphasized grain and cotton production. Economic reforms begun in 1978 gave farmers more freedom in planting decisions, allowing them to divert land from grains to more lucrative cash crops like vegetables and fruits. Under a generally free market structure since 1984, vegetables and fruits have become two of the most dynamic segments in China's agriculture.

### INTENSIVE CULTIVATION, WITH POLICY FOCUSED ON SUPPLYING CITY RESIDENTS

China's vegetable production is complex and labor-intensive. For China's numerous self-sufficient small farms, vegetable cultivation is an integral part of a household enterprise that also includes raising pigs, chickens, and other crops. With warm temperatures and abundant rainfall in Central and

South China, farmers can use multiple-cropping and intercropping to produce large quantities of vegetables from small plots of land. Greenhouses and plastic sheeting are used in colder regions of northern China to extend the growing season. China's intensive vegetable farming, however, is susceptible to insect and disease outbreaks, particularly in the warm and humid south. China has a long history of using different disease- and insect-control practices, including traditional rotation of various types of vegetables. In recent years, farmers have increased their use of chemical pesticides.

Under central planning, authorities established networks of specialized vegetable production teams and state-owned marketing companies in areas surrounding cities to supply urban residents' vegetable needs. Since the late 1980s, the government has launched various "vegetable basket" programs to ensure stable supplies of vegetables and other nonstaple foods to urban consumers. Important measures include facilitating the extensive use of low-cost Chinese-style greenhouses, establishing regional "production bases," and building wholesale and retail markets. Production has moved from city suburbs to the rural hinterland as an integrated national market has developed. Supermarkets began to displace small vendors, and private distributors began to displace state-owned companies in the 1990s.

## REFORMS REVOLUTIONIZE VEGETABLE PRODUCTION, CONSUMPTION, AND EXPORT

China's National Bureau of Statistics estimates that vegetable farming area swelled fivefold after 1980, reaching 17.3 million hectares in 2007. The United Nations Food and Agriculture Organization estimates that China accounts for nearly half of the world's vegetable production. Chinese customs statistics show that vegetable export volume rose 150 percent from 2000 to 2007. Exports in 2007 were equivalent to about 1.4 percent of the volume of output (565 million tons). Imports are negligible. Aided by foreign investment in advanced and large-scale operations, China emerged in the 1990s as a fast-growing exporter, particularly of fresh and frozen vegetables, with neighboring Asian countries, especially Japan, the main markets. Most of China's vegetable production, however, is for the domestic fresh-vegetable market; vegetables are an important part of the Chinese daily diet, with cabbages, radishes, cucumbers, onions, eggplants, tomatoes, and peppers the main crops. The composition of vegetable production has diversified since 1980 from traditional cabbage and other low-priced vegetables to a mix that reflects consumers' changing demands. In addition, farmers and regulators are paying more attention to the quality and safety of vegetables as consumers become more discriminating.

## DYNAMIC CHANGES IN FRUIT FARMING

The fruit sector—traditionally a sideline activity in China's agriculture and a minor part of the national diet—has seen similar explosive development. The "Layout Plan for China's Advantageous Agricultural Products," launched in 2003, aimed to consolidate production of apples and citrus in designated regions. Unlike vegetables, fruits are perennial crops that mature and are harvested over a two- to three-month period, and they are easier to store. China's fruit policies focus on encouraging farmers to plant different-maturing varieties to extend the supply season and on improving postharvest treatment and storage facilities, while also improving quality. Assuring the availability of fruit varieties suitable for both the processing and fresh markets is also increasingly important. China's fruit growers use chemical pesticides as well as labor-intensive methods to control disease and insects.

China's orchard area rose nearly sixfold after 1980, to 10.5 million hectares in 2007, when China produced 181.4 million tons of fruit, including apples (43 percent of world production), citrus (17 percent), pears (63 percent), bananas (9 percent), and grapes (9 percent). The high volume of fruits has led to increased exports—apples and mandarins are the dominant fresh exports—largely to its Asian neighbors, as well as Russia. Apple juice and canned mandarins are the leading processed exports, mainly to the United States, Europe, and Japan. The processed fruit industry—a small part of China's fruit sector—is export-oriented because Chinese people traditionally do not consume much processed fruit. Most of China's fruit is for the domestic fresh market. However, imports of tropical fruits, grapes, oranges, and apples have increased to meet the demands of China's increasingly affluent and sophisticated consumers. Fruits are popular as desserts and snacks, and imported fruits are a luxury item often given as gifts.

### BIBLIOGRAPHY

Buck, John Lossing. *Land Utilization in China: A Study of 16,786 Farms in 168 Localities, and 38,256 Farm Families in Twenty-two Provinces in China, 1929–1933*. 1937. New York: Council on Economic and Cultural Affairs, 1956.

China National Bureau of Statistics. *Rural Statistical Yearbook*. Beijing: China Statistics Press, various issues.

Plucknett, Donald L., and Halsey L. Beemer, eds. *Vegetable Farming Systems in China: Report of the Visit of the Vegetable Farming Systems Delegation to China*. Boulder, CO: Westview, 1981.

U.S. Department of Agriculture, Foreign Agricultural Service. Attaché Reports. http://www.fas.usda.gov/scriptsw/AttacheRep/default.asp.

***Sophia Wu Huang***

*This paper does not necessarily reflect the views of the Economic Research Service or the U.S. Department of Agriculture.*

## RICE

Rice has played a significant role in shaping the political and physical landscape of China. As the main grain in southern areas of China, rice is integral to people's diet and the overall economy. Prior to 1911, Chinese grain distribution worked through a grain tribute system. Rice and other grains were the primary form of payment for the local land tax. Grain was shipped to the imperial palace in Beijing and used to pay central government officials. Much of the rice in the nineteenth century was grown using traditional technology and land intensification methods developed before the Ming dynasty (1368–1644).

Rice production is both land- and labor-intensive. As a semiaquatic plant, rice requires a great deal of water. Fields are flooded before transplanting and left wet throughout most of the season. Paddies are typically drained a month before harvesting. Over time, the Chinese have developed intricate systems of irrigating and draining fields with nearby water sources, and have terraced sloped land, especially in the mountainous regions of southwest China, to hold and drain water efficiently. Rice is planted in the spring and harvested in the fall, requiring a great deal of human labor. Growing seasons range from 90 to 200 days, with 120 days as average.

There are two main varieties of rice in China: indica and japonica. Indica rice is long-grain and grown in southern, hot climates. The grains are long and the cooked rice is fluffy. Japonica rice is usually grown in temperate climates where seeds thrive with abundant sunlight and more extreme temperature variation between night and day. The grains are round and short. Today 60 percent of China's rice is indica, 29 percent is japonica, and 11 percent are indigenous varieties such as upland glutinous rice grown in mountainous southwestern China.

Rice production has thrived primarily in the Yangzi River Valley and further south where the climate is moist and warm. Cultivation has expanded as far north as the Yellow River and into the northeast as well as west to areas of Sichuan and Yunnan near the Tibetan Plateau. Northeastern China, which traditionally relies upon wheat, corn, and soybeans as primary crops, has seen the growth of japonica rice as a commodity grain since the 1990s.

Throughout the nineteenth century and into the early twentieth century, rice trading took on new dimensions. Of primary importance was the industrialization of urban areas. Rural households in western regions such as Sichuan and Hunan produced a surplus to sell to urban areas along the industrialized eastern coast. Additionally, the presence of Chinese rice merchants and traders in Southeast Asia ensured that China could import rice to meet its demands.

Manual labor and the use of natural fertilizers allowed for rice production to sustain the intensive practices necessary to keep it growing. Farming households maintained individual plots of land, consumed their own harvests, and sold the surplus at the market. During the planting and harvest seasons families extended labor to other households in exchange for assistance with their own fields. Taxes were paid to local officials and landlords through gains from surplus rice. High taxes, tenant farming, and corrupt landlords enabled the Communists to form a rural base to come to power.

Mao Zedong's radical attempt at collectivized agriculture brought major transformations in the production and distribution of rice. Mao had garnered the support of the peasants with land reform. Beginning in the 1950s, households and villages were encouraged to pool their land, labor, and tools together to begin the process of collectivization. Agricultural output quotas were established. After meeting their quota of grain to give to the state, communes were entitled to their surplus rice and other grains through collective canteens. In urban areas grain was distributed through rations.

After the 1978 reforms Chinese rice production increased dramatically due to technological improvements and political change. The high quantities of rice produced in the 1980s were attributed to high-yielding hybrid rice developed by the Chinese scientist Yuan Longping (b. 1930). Along with the introduction of hybrid rice came the use of synthetic chemical fertilizers and pesticides, which increased production yields. The second factor leading to increased rice production was the introduction of the household responsibility system (*baogan daohu*): Rural reforms dismantled the collective agricultural system and redistributed land from collectives to individual households.

Today, China remains the world's largest producer of rice. According to world rice production statistics, China produced 185,490 of the world's 650,193 metric tons of paddy rice in 2007 (International Rice Research Institute 2008). The Chinese rice industry faces challenges in the areas of food security, the production of high quality rice grain, reliance on synthetic pesticides and fertilizers, increasing grain prices, little market or political incentive for farmers to produce grain, increasing water pollution and/or shortage, and the use of agricultural biotechnologies such as genetic modification.

**SEE ALSO** *Food since 1800.*

**BIBLIOGRAPHY**

Anderson, Eugene N. *The Food of China.* New Haven, CT: Yale University Press, 1988.

Buck, John Lossing, Owen L. Dawson, and Yuan-li Wu. *Food and Agriculture in Communist China.* New York: Praeger Publishers, 1966.

Hinton, Harold. *The Grain Tribute System of Imperial China (1845–1911).* Cambridge, MA: Harvard University Press, 1970.

International Rice Research Institute. 2008. Statistics Portal. http://beta.irri.org/statistics.

Oi, Jean. *State and Peasant in Contemporary China: The Political Economy of Village Government.* Berkeley: University of California Press, 1989.

Perkins, Dwight. *Agricultural Development in China, 1368–1968.* Chicago: Aldine, 1969.

***Amy Zader***

## ANIMAL HUSBANDRY

Due to varied topography and climates over its vast landmass, China boasts a diverse variety of domesticated animals. Traditionally, sheep, cattle, and horses were concentrated in the grazing regions of the northeast, northwest, and southwest, areas with low population density that make up 54 percent of the country's area. In the rest of China, where intensive agriculture predominated, swine and poultry were the animals of choice due to their suitability as sidelines, though horses and water buffalo remained important as draft animals. From the 1950s to 1970s the boundary between pasture and farming regions shifted northward due to the increased cropping of grasslands.

From the nineteenth century to 1978, when economic reforms began, China's total meat production and consumption increased modestly, with fluctuations due to famines and political turmoil. Since then, total production grew at 7.9 percent per annum, from 13.6 million tons in 1978 to 28.5 million in 1990, while per capita consumption increased from 30 pounds to nearly 51 pounds (Miyazaki et al. 1994, pp. 172–173). In general, animal husbandry in China still suffers from low productivity in its breeding and distribution networks. However, with rising incomes, urbanization, and lower agricultural population, farm sizes are expected to increase, and meat production to become more rationalized and mechanized through the introduction and development of new technologies. Animals are becoming specialized to produce meat and milk, rather than as sidelines or for draft purposes.

### SWINE

China's native pig breeds can be broadly categorized into two types: the northern type, which have big frames, low-hanging bellies, and inferior meat quality; and the southern, which have smaller bodies, thinner skin, and a higher fattening rate. The importation of exotic breeds began in 1800, and from the 1950s to 1970s crossbreeds were made with breeds introduced from across Europe and North America. The rapid spread of new technologies such as artificial insemination and embryo transplants have hastened the process, triggering fears among scientists that the hardy native breeds, which are better adapted to the local environment, are in danger of extinction.

Pig farming in China goes back at least 6,000 to 7,000 years. At the beginning of the nineteenth century pigs were raised in the countryside as a part of small-scale, intensive agricultural practices. They lived in crude shelters built near or against residences, and subsisted on a diet high on forage—mostly table scraps and roughage-such as stalks and straws—and low on coarse grains and other concentrates. Besides meat, pigs also provided bristles and cooking oil, and their manure went to fertilize the soil. After 1949 collective pig farms came into operation.

With the onset of economic reforms, many households dropped out of sideline production as the cities offered more job opportunities. Urbanization, in turn, resulted in greater consumption of pork per capita, rising from 24.7 pounds per year in 1979 to 40.8 pounds in 1991 (Miyazaki et al. 1994, pp. 172–173). The proliferation of restaurants in cities and small towns, along with growing consumer expectations and sophistication, increased demand for specialized, higher quality breeds producing leaner meats. In response, private and state-owned operations have expanded in size and scale. In 1990 China boasted 42 percent of the world's swine inventory and was the leading pork producer, with a 35 percent share (Miyazaki et al. 1994, p. 7).

Feeding practices also have changed dramatically, as reliance upon cooked domestic table scraps gave way to processed, fermented feeds high in concentrates. These consist of chopped straw, stalks, and weeds mixed with water and supplemented by carbohydrates, ammonia, edible salt, and other minerals. Since 1971 Chinese scientists have been developing ways of replacing the fermentation process by breaking down coarse fibers into complex carbohydrates with cellulose molds.

### SHEEP AND CATTLE

There are several native breeds of beef-grade, yellow cattle. Of these, the Mongolian is found mainly in the north, and the Kazakh in the northwest. Their production of meat and milk is limited by the poor ecological conditions of the grassland. The Qinchuan, Nanyang, Jinnan, and Luxi are typical breeds found within the agricultural zone that are known for their big draft capacity and greater beef production. Other important draft animals are the water buffalo, used mainly in South China, and the yak, commonly found in Tibet. The major dairy cows, known as the Chinese Black and White, result from a cross with Holstein and Friesian cattle imported from the United States, Japan, and Canada. Others such as the Binzhou, which primarily inhabit northeastern Heilongjiang, have dual-use purposes. Dairy cattle are raised on collective and small private pastures, or by herders for subsistence purposes. Milk is marketed and processed at state-owned processing plants located outside big cities such as Beijing and Shanghai.

China's 113 million sheep (1991) are categorized according to their grade of wool, ranging from fine to

***Kazakh sheep herder, Xinjiang Uygur Autonomous Region, September 18, 2007.*** *In the autonomous region of Xinjiang, nomadic Kazakh sheep herders continue to care for livestock following traditional transhumance methods, driving flocks into the mountains for summer grazing and into the desert plains during the winter months.* **CHINA PHOTOS/GETTY IMAGES**

coarse. The fat-rump, coarse-carpet wool sheep, found primarily in Inner Mongolia and Xinjiang, was traditionally dominant due to its ability to adapt to the harsh climate. Recently, crosses with exotic breeds such as the Merino have led to finer, higher grade wools, though in general their production remains limited. As with pigs, artificial insemination and embryo transplantation are key technologies used to increase cattle and sheep numbers and improve their quality, and provincial governments have invested heavily in them.

Most cattle and sheep are found in the grazing regions of China. For thousands of years, herding practices there ranged from free roaming in areas such as the vast deserts of Xinjiang, to transhumant in Inner Mongolia, where herders moved their animals to areas with more abundant forage during the winter. The typical feed of cattle and sheep consisted of wild grasses, tree leaves, and green manure crops; during the barren winter months they relied upon rice and millet straws provided by local farms. These practices reflected the harsh conditions of the grasslands, with its short growing seasons and adverse climatic fluctuations. Beef and mutton production were traditionally very low nationwide; the animals were consumed primarily for subsistence by minorities in the grazing areas. In the 1950s to the 1970s, misguided policies to transform pastures into farmland contributed to severe overgrazing and desertification. After reforms began increased production to meet growing urban demand placed further pressures on the fragile ecosystem of the grassland. In response, the government enacted regulations to protect grasslands and set up seed testing and replication stations, and it established a shelterbelt some 4,350 miles long known as the "Green Great Wall" (*lüse changcheng*). However, the cattle and sheep industry still suffers from low productivity due to the lack of a developed infrastructure to transport meat to urban markets and limited property rights, which encourages the "tragedy of the commons," when herders maximize the number of livestock grazing on the grasslands in spite of the danger of long-term environmental degradation.

Nevertheless, the future points toward greater rationalization of the production process for livestock. The rise of increasingly sophisticated middle-class consumers benefiting from urbanization and industrialization has led to greater demand for land-intensive meats such as beef and mutton. Although pork still dominates China's total meat production, its proportion fell from 82 percent in 1979 to 80 percent in 1991. Meanwhile, per capita consumption of beef and mutton increased dramatically, from 0.4 pounds to 1.5 pounds per year and from 0.4 pounds to 0.9 pounds per year, respectively, in the same period. Per capita milk consumption also jumped, from 4 pounds to 9.8 pounds per year (Miyazaki et al. 1994, pp. 172–173). The cattle and sheep industry holds the most promise for using mechanization to meet the growing demand. For instance, the electronic detection of mastitis helps to eradicate a disease very common to dairy herds, and implanted identification tags simplify the monitoring of a cow's performance and body temperature. New technologies to be implemented in the future include on-farm extraction of milk, sanitization of meat by means of irradiation, and the use of robots in meat slaughter and milking.

**BIBLIOGRAPHY**

Miyazaki Akira, James R. Simpson, and Xu Cheng. *China's Livestock and Related Agriculture: Projections to 2025.* Wallingford, U.K.: CAB International, 1994.

Wiens, Thomas B. Animal Sciences. In *Science in Contemporary China*, ed. Leo A. Orleans, 345–371. Stanford, CA: Stanford University Press, 1980.

***Xing Hang***

## FORESTRY AND TIMBER TRADE

China had abundant forests in the ancient times, but as its population grew, farmland expansion and fuel gathering, coupled with protracted wars, frequent fires, and excessive royal constructions, resulted in the extensive destruction and degradation of its forests (Fan 2002). By the time of the Opium War (1839–1842), China's forests had dwindled to about 160 million hectares. Thereafter, when the regimes of the Qing dynasty weakened, military and merchant forces from Europe, Russia, and Japan came to occupy its land and exploit its natural resources. This foreign invasion and plundering caused further destruction of China's forests, especially in the northeast. The Guomindang government estimated that in 1934 China had a forest area of 91 million hectares; by 1947 it had dropped to 84 million hectares (Xiong 1989).

Customs records show that China's importation of timber products began in 1868, and the imports peaked in 1907 at an annual gross value of 265 tons of silver (Xiong 1989). China's export of timber products started in 1903, and it reached a value of 756 tons of silver in 1923. Western powers increased exports of wood products to China during the Great Depression to alleviate domestic economic pressures. Following Japan's expansion of its Chinese occupation in 1931, however, the gross value of China's wood products exports decreased to less than 38 tons of silver (Xiong 1989). The primary export products included roundwood, lumber, poles, and other finished products, and the main destinations were Japan and Southeast Asia (Xiong 1989). In 1947 China's imports of wood products surpassed 300,000 cubic meters of roundwood equivalent, including logs, lumber, and railway sleepers from North America and some neighboring countries. At that time, the timber trade was dominated by foreign entities, especially British and U.S. firms; although China's domestic sector of wood products manufacturing and trade was not yet well established, a timber-marketing network came into existence.

### NATIONALIZATION AND COLLECTIVIZATION

After the founding of the People's Republic of China in 1949 the international timber trade came to an abrupt halt due to the political isolation from the West. Under national land reform, timberland owned by landlords, bureaucrats, and merchants was confiscated and allotted to peasants who were landless or lacked sufficient timberland. Self-sustaining peasants were allowed to maintain their own small woodlots. The large natural forests in the northeast, southwest, and some other regions were nationalized, and more than 130 state-run forest enterprises gradually were set up to produce timber—a commodity that was desperately needed for the recovery and growth of the new economy. Later, forest management and wood products manufacturing were incorporated into the mission of these enterprises. Nationalization also was extended to relatively large tracts of forests in the south that either had been confiscated from landlords and others or unclaimed (in certain remote places); state forest farms and logging entities were formed to manage these forests and produce timber (Yin 1998).

Until 1956 trees and forests in rural areas had remained largely privately owned, and most forest management activities were carried out by individual owners. Thereafter, however, a campaign was launched to reorganize the countryside by amalgamating the existing co-ops into People's Communes, purportedly to promote more efficient operation and adequate attention to public work. As a result of collectivization, private ownership of productive means and compensation for them were no longer honored, family forest plots were absorbed into collective timberland, and local timber markets were replaced by government planning control (Qiu 1998). Peasants were left with only a few trees scattered around their houses, cemetery yards, and temples. Tree planting and afforestation was carried out in mass drives, but management of existing forests was largely

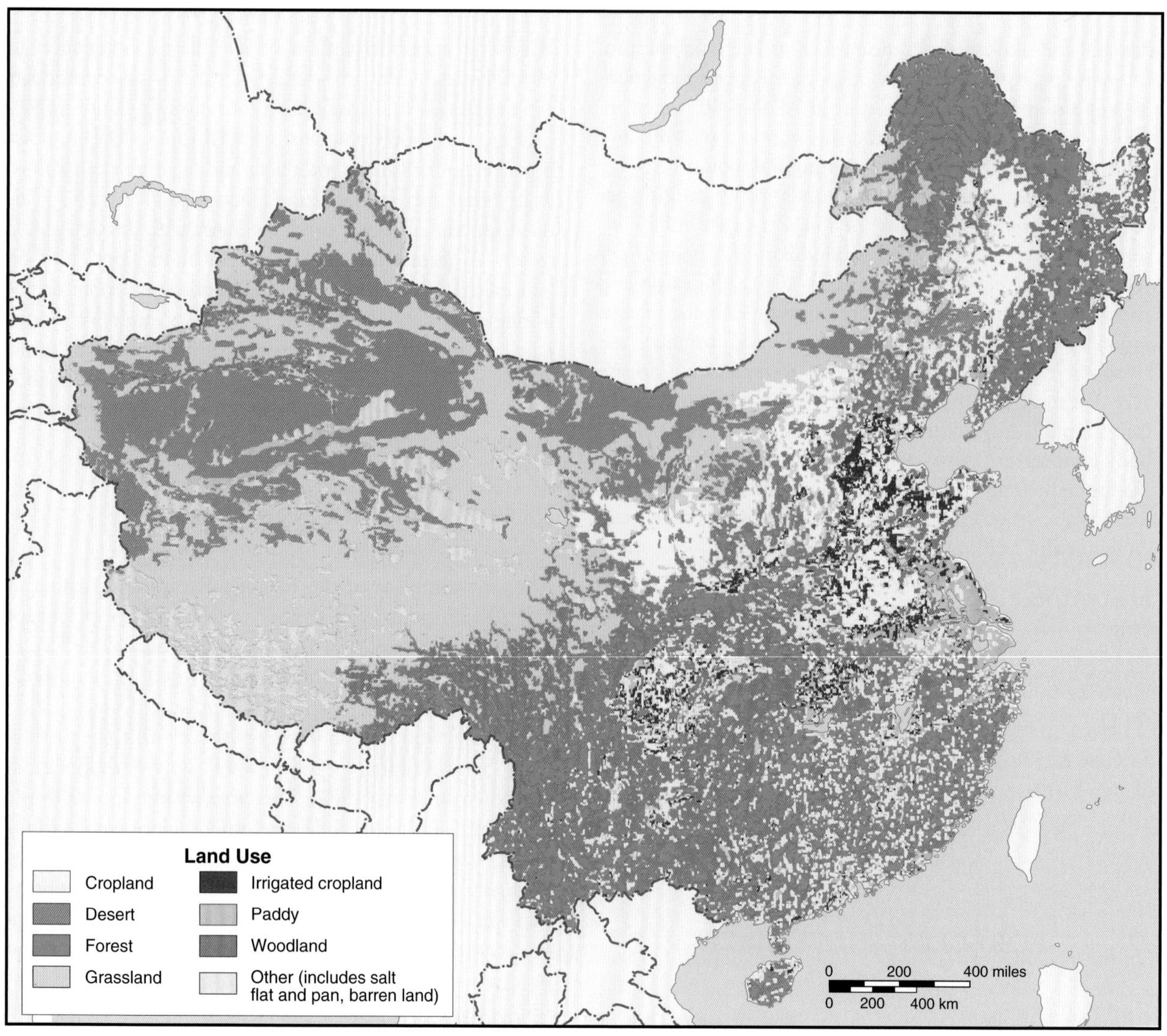


neglected. To meet wood production and distribution quotas set by the government, state-run procurement and shipment stations were instituted in the timber-producing regions. Meanwhile, more state and communal forest farms were born (Yin 1998).

Since the early 1960s, forestry in China has been organized into three regional/operational categories: the Northeast/Southwest National Forest Region, the Southern Collective Forest Region, and the Central/North/Northwest Farm Forest Region (Yin 1998). Natural forests in the northeast and southwest were owned and managed predominantly by the large state enterprises of central and provincial governments, whereas the primary and secondary forests in the south were largely owned and managed by the local collectives. Forestry in other parts of the country was very limited, and its main goals were the establishment and maintenance of agroforest and shelterbelt systems for the provision of locally used fuel, timber, and other products and environmental benefits.

## FORESTRY REFORM AND DEVELOPMENT

After the end of the Cultural Revolution the forest sector gradually was reformed. Some collective forestland was contracted to households, individually or in groups, for management. The government procurement quota was reduced and ultimately abolished, and the purchase price was increased and marketized. In the national forest regions, similar management responsibility and market liberalization measures were implemented. Nonetheless, there have been few systematic and sustained attempts to transform the institutional framework, including not only land-use and property rights but also the pricing mechanism, taxation policy, harvesting regulation, and forest administration. Due to the still unfavorable incentive structure, active and efficient forest investment and management have not been taken up enthusiastically by farmers and enterprises. In recent years, a new round of tenure and institutional reforms has been launched to build a market-based forest economy to improve productivity and sustainability.

Nevertheless, China's afforestation and reforestation accomplishments are remarkable. According to the latest forest inventory, the nation has a forest area of 175 million hectares, of which plantations account for 54 million hectares and the forest stock is 13.6 billion cubic meters; the annual increment is 497 million cubic meters, whereas the annual removals amount to 365 million cubic meters (State Forestry Administration 2005). This is in contrast to 8.6 percent forest coverage, with a stocking volume of 11.6 billion cubic meters in the early 1950s (Chinese Forestry Society 1986). However, the per capita forest area is 0.13 hectares, only 22 percent of the world average. Furthermore, forest productivity remains low. Of all the forestland, 99.4 million hectares is collectively owned and 73.3 million hectares is state owned, but collective forests carry only 45 percent of the stocking volume (State Forestry Administration 2005). The country has adopted a classified management scheme of commercial forests, environmental forests, and multiple-use forests.

China also has developed a vibrant and competitive wood products industry, increasing production and export of furniture, panel, paper, paperboard, and other finished products with expanded use of imported timber and other raw materials. In 2006 the gross production value of the forest sector was 1,065 billion yuan and the total trade value was over $50 billion—$26.3 billion for imports and $24.4 billion for exports. China's timber consumption in 2006 reached 320 billion cubic meters of roundwood equivalent, of which roughly one half came from international sources (State Forestry Administration 2007).

In addition, China has implemented major ecological restoration programs to deal with its increasingly severe environmental problems, including the Sloping Land Conversion Program, the Natural Forest Protection Program, the Desertification Combating Program, the Wildlife Conservation and Nature Reserve Development Program, and the Shelterbelt Expansion Program. It is expected that the state's investment of over $50 billion over ten years will result in further expansion of China's forest area and stock and greatly improved environmental conditions (State Forestry Administration 2007).

**BIBLIOGRAPHY**

Chinese Forestry Society. *Senlin Shihua* [A Brief History of China's Forestry]. Beijing: China Forestry Publishing House, 1986.

Fan, Baommin. *Zhongguo Qingchao yilaide Linzhenshi Yanjiu* [China's History of Forestry Policy since the Qing Dynasty]. Beijing: Beijing Forestry University, 2002.

Qiu, Junqi. *Zhongguo Qingchao yilaide Linzhenshi Yanjiu* [Forest Economics]. Beijing: China Forestry Publishing House, 1998.

State Forestry Administration. *Deliuci Quanguo Senlinziyuan Qingcha Zhuyaojieguo* [The Main Findings of the Sixth Successive National Forest Inventory]. Beijing: China Forestry Publishing House, 2005.

State Forestry Administration. *Zhongguo Linye Nianjian* [China Forestry Yearbook]. Beijing: China Forestry Publishing House, 2007.

Xiong, Datong. *Xiandai Zhongguo Linyeshi* [Modern History of Chinese Forestry]. Beijing: China Forestry Publishing House, 1989.

Yin, Runsheng. Forestry and the Environment in China: The Current Situation and Strategic Choice. *World Development* 26, no. 12 (1998): 2153–2167.

***Lanying Li***
***Runsheng Yin***

## FISHERY AND AQUACULTURE

With China's vast coastline and extensive inland waterways, fishing has long been an important economic activity. In imperial times China's fishing population was quite diverse: some households fished seasonally and farmed the rest of year; others, like the Tanka (*danmin*) of South China, lived on boats as virtual outcaste groups. Over the course of the Qing Dynasty (1644–1912), fishing and aquaculture expanded with commercialization. During the eighteenth and nineteenth centuries, the push of population pressure and the pull of profits led many coastal residents to use the sea as their fields, promoting growth in marine fisheries and cultivation of clams, oysters, and seaweed. Freshwater fisheries also flourished, but by the nineteenth century widespread land reclamation impinged on lakes and rivers, causing declines in some regions. In rural southeast China, aquaculture was connected to commercial silk production. The "mulberry tree and fish pond" (*sangji yutang*) system, which many view as an ecologically integrated agricultural system, used mud from carp ponds to fertilize mulberry trees. Mulberry leaves fed silkworms, while fish fed on organic matter from trees and silkworm droppings.

Marine fisheries continued to expand with China's economy in the Republican period, as market integration tied fishing grounds more closely to consumption centers. However, sail-powered Chinese junks faced fierce competition from imported fish products and Japan's mechanized fishing fleet, which encroached on waters off China's coast in the 1920s and 1930s. Under these pressures, coastal fishing grounds began to show signs of overexploitation. Under the Nationalist regime, foreign-trained Chinese fishery experts tried to counter Japanese competition by using scientific management to modernize China's fishing industry, but the Second Sino-Japanese War (1937–1945) and Chinese civil war stymied their plans and seriously disrupted all types of fishery production from 1937 to 1949.

***Fish leap out of the water as men pull on nets, bank of Qiandao Lake, Zhejiang, June 28, 2007.*** *China's abundance of lakes and rivers has fostered a thriving fishing industry, making the country a leading exporter of fish. However, overaggressive fishing techniques and poor pollution controls in the late twentieth century have resulted in new government controls to preserve the future of the industry.* AP IMAGES

Fishery output quickly recovered after the founding of the People's Republic of China, increasing from around 448,000 tons in 1949 to around 3 million tons in the 1960s. Expansion partly resulted from reforms like centralized marketing facilities for which fishery experts had advocated since the Republican era. In the early 1950s local cadres organized the fishing population into mutual-aid teams and cooperatives that received low-interest loans, making it possible to upgrade to more effective equipment. From 1956 to 1958 fishing cooperatives combined to form production brigades that took over production decisions and ownership of boats and gear. This changed somewhat after the Great Leap Forward, as fishing production teams contracted with brigades for part of production value, giving the incentives to increase yields. Catches consisted mostly of marine fish species like yellow croaker, hairtail, and cuttlefish. In the 1970s these fish stocks declined and previously less-favored species grew in importance. Inland fisheries also suffered after the 1960s as a result of massive dam construction, land reclamation, and industrial pollution.

Fishery production stagnated with the political turmoil of the decade of the Cultural Revolution (1966–1976), but following China's post-1978 economic reforms fisheries experienced rapid growth. Relaxed government controls alongside increased prosperity and demand combined to stimulate fishing efforts. Catches boomed from around 7 million tons in 1985 to 25 million tons in 1995, making China the world's largest fish producer. Continuous increases in fishing efforts led to the collapse of many species, and catches of immature fish and subprime species replaced them. Hoping to protect threatened fish populations, after 1999 the government's goal shifted from the long-standing emphasis on greater production to "zero growth" in marine fisheries. Yet several trends impede conservation efforts and put greater demands on declining marine resources. Attracted by increasing fish prices, many of the migrants who flooded to China's coastal regions from rural areas started to fish with small boats in inshore waters, using particularly damaging types of gear. Furthermore, local officials allow fishers to defy higher-level restrictions on fishing to boost production and bring in badly needed revenue.

As natural resources declined, aquaculture stepped in to meet demand for Chinese fish products on domestic and international markets, growing from 29 percent of China's total fishery production in 1979 to 64 percent in 2003. At the beginning of the twenty-first century China produced about 70 percent of the world's farmed fish, with aquaculture enterprises crowding offshore waters as well as inland rivers, lakes, and reservoirs. Fish farming comprises several organizational forms, with a handful of state-owned farms existing alongside many household enterprises and partnerships. Aquaculture employs over 4.5 million people, including many female workers in small-scale fish farms. However, China's polluted water supply has raised serious concerns about the effect of farmed fish on public health. Intensive fish farming also poses threats China's aquatic ecosystems, because uneaten fish food, fertilizers, veterinary drugs, and fish droppings generate considerable pollution.

**BIBLIOGRAPHY**

Chen, Weizhong. Marine Resources, Their Status of Exploitation and Management in the People's Republic of China. *FAO Fisheries Circular No. 950.* Rome: Food and Agriculture Organization of the United Nations, 1999.

Jia, Jiansan, and Jiaxin Chen. Sea Farming and Sea Ranching in China. *FAO Fisheries Technical Paper No. 418.* Rome: Food and Agriculture Organization of the United Nations, 2001.

Muscolino, Micah. *Fishing Wars and Environmental Change in Late Imperial and Modern China.* Cambridge, MA: Harvard University Asia Center, forthcoming.

Ouyang Zongshu. *Haishang renjia: Haiyang yuye jingji yu yumin shehui* [Sea people: The marine fishery economy and fishing people's society]. Nanchang: Jiangxi gaoxiao chubanshe, 1998.

Wang, Ning. *Making a Market Economy: The Institutional Transformation of a Freshwater Fishery in a Chinese Community.* London: Routledge, 2005.

Yin Lingling. *Ming Qing Changjiang zhong xia you yuye jingji yanjiu* [Research on the fishery economy of the Middle and Lower Yangzi during the Ming and Qing]. Jinan: Jilu shushe, 2004.

Zhong, Gongfu. The Mulberry Dike–Fish Pond Complex: A Chinese Ecosystem of Land-Water Interaction on the Pearl River Delta. *Human Ecology* 10, 2 (1982): 191–202.

***Micah Muscolino***

## AI QING (AI CH'ING)

### *1910–1996*

Ai Qing, the penname of Jiang Haicheng, was born into a wealthy landowner's family in Zhejiang province on March 27, 1910. After graduating from middle school, he was admitted to the National Hangzhou West Lake Art Academy. Encouraged by the principal of the school, the eminent painter Lin Fengmian (1900–1991), he went to France to study painting. While there, he was exposed to modernist poetry and became particularly fond of the Belgian poet Émile Verhaeren (1855–1916) and the Russian poet Vladimir Mayakovsky (1893–1930). It was in 1932 that he wrote his first poem (under the penname E Qie).

Ai Qing returned to China in May 1932. He soon joined the League of Leftist Artists and helped found the Spring Earth Painters Association in Shanghai. For his leftist activities opposing the Nationalist regime, he was imprisoned in July. While incarcerated, he wrote poetry, using the penname Ai Qing for the first time, and translated Verhaeren into Chinese. "Dayanhe" (The Dayan river) pays tribute to the peasant woman whom his family hired to nurse him for five years after his birth. The woman loved him as if he had been her own son, and because of her the poet identifies with the poor and the oppressed rather than with his wealthy family. Ai Qing also wrote poems about Europe: "Ludi" (Reed pipe) quotes the French poet Guillaume Apollinaire (1880–1918) and expresses his conviction as a poet; "Bali" (Paris), on the other hand, critiques the materialism and decadence of urban culture. In 1936 he published his first book of poetry under the title *Dayanhe* in Shanghai.

Ai Qing was released from jail in October 1935. After the War of Resistance against Japan broke out in July 1937 and the North fell, he went to Wuhan. There he wrote "Xue luo zai Zhongguo de tudi shang" (Snow is falling on the land of China), in which he records the horrific suffering of Chinese people and looks to poetry to provide a glimmer of hope in the suffocating darkness. In the next few years he traveled all over China, never ceasing to write poetry and edit journals on the road. During the war he published six books of poems, including two long narratives, as well as a collection of commentaries on poetry, titled *Shi lun* (On poetry). In 1941 he went to Yan'an and attended the historic "Yan'an Forum on Literature and Art" the following year. Ai Qing was arguably the most famous poet during the War of Resistance. His poems express deep love for the land and the people, and memorialize the valor of Chinese soldiers, realistically represented in a simple yet moving language.

After 1949 Ai Qing occupied important positions in the cultural establishment, including chief editor of the leading national journal *Shi kan* (Poetry journal). As a high-ranking official, he also traveled to Europe and South America and wrote poems about the experiences. In 1958, during the Anti-Rightist Campaign, Ai Qing was labeled a rightist and was exiled, first to Heilongjiang province in Manchuria, and then to Xinjiang province in the Northwest. Persecution continued through the Cultural Revolution (1966–1969) and its aftermath. It was not until 1979 that he was "rehabilitated" and allowed to write and publish again. After a hiatus of two decades, a new collection of poems titled *Guilai de ge* (Songs of return) appeared in 1980.

Also in 1980, after almost half a century, Ai Qing revisited France. In 1985 French President François Mitterrand bestowed on him the Commandeur de l'Ordre des arts et des letters. The best-known poet in China, he was involved in the controversy over Menglongshi (Misty poetry) in the early 1980s, in which he sided with the establishment and criticized the new poetry of the younger generation. Ai Qing died in Beijing on October 10, 1996. By then, his poetry had long been canonized in the standard curriculum in China.

**SEE ALSO** *Art Schools and Colleges; League of Left-Wing Writers; Lin Fengmian; Poetry.*

**BIBLIOGRAPHY**

Ai Qing. *Selected Poems of Ai Qing.* Ed. Eugene Chen Eoyang. Trans. Eugene Chen Eoyang, Peng Wenlan, and Marilyn Chin. Beijing: Foreign Languages Press, 1982.

Palandri, Angela Jung. The Poetic Theory and Practice of Ai Qing. In *Perspectives in Contemporary Chinese Literature*, ed. Mason Y. H. Wang, pp. 61–76. Michigan: Green River Press, 1983.

***Michelle Yeh***

## ALL-CHINA WOMEN'S FEDERATION

The All-China Women's Federation (ACWF), also known in English by its abbreviated Chinese title, Fulian, is China's official women's organization. Its declared objectives are to represent and safeguard the interests of women and to promote equality between men and women. Since 1995 it has often been defined as a nongovernmental organization (NGO), a status that allows it to cooperate with foreign NGOs more easily, and to work in partnership with them on aid projects. It enjoys considerable official standing, advises the government on issues relating to women and children, and receives government funding. At the national level, it has six departments dealing with women and development, education and training, law, children, international liaison, and publicity. There are ACWF offices at all provincial and county levels. Local women's federations at the township or neighborhood level and in factories and enterprises are group members of the national federation.

### HISTORY

The ACWF was established in April 1949 under the Chinese Communist Party. Its role was to represent women and promote their interests while organizing them to support and implement the policies of the Communist Party and the new government. The federation brought together women's associations that had existed in Communist-controlled areas before the establishment of the People's Republic and women's organizations based in the big cities, such as the Young Women's Christian Association and the Women's Christian Temperance Union. The ACWF national committee reflected this alliance. It included both well-known Communist women leaders such as Cai Chang (1900–1990), Deng Yingchao (1904–1992; wife of Premier Zhou Enlai), and Kang Keqing (1911–1992; wife of Minister of Defense Zhu De), and prominent nonparty women such as Song Qingling (1893-1981), He Xiangning (1878–1972), and Xu Guangping (1898–1968; widow of Lu Xun).

The ACWF accepted the Communist Party's analysis that only the success of a socialist revolution could bring about the liberation of women. In the 1950s it carried out programs deemed by the Communist Party to be effective for the promotion of women's liberation. These included campaigns to implement the new marriage law, to recruit women into the labor force, to ensure equal treatment for women in land reform and collectivization, to improve health, hygiene, and childcare, and to increase female literacy. The most contentious policy was marriage reform. The new marriage law, based on monogamy and the free choice of partners, prohibited child marriage and liberalized divorce. It met with strong resistance, especially from male peasants, older women, and some rural cadres. Women were persecuted, beaten up, and even murdered for trying to divorce their husbands or marry men they had chosen themselves. Women's Federation cadres played an important role in supporting individual women's struggles to realize their rights under the law and in promoting family change, but the law ultimately met with limited success.

Throughout its existence the ACWF has had to deal with the tensions that arise from its position as a party-led women's organization. Although the party insisted that women's liberation was an integral part of the revolution, it condemned what it called "narrow feminism." In theory, this referred to giving gender concerns priority over class revolution. In practice, it could mean pointing out that sexual equality was still far from being achieved in Chinese society. In the 1950s and early 1960s, the ACWF steered a careful path, supporting the current party line on women while working for women's rights.

The ACWF came under severe criticism early in the Cultural Revolution. It was accused of opposing gender interests to class interests, of making too much of family problems, and of distracting women from politics. Its critics argued that there was no need for a separate women's organization, and it was temporarily closed down in 1968. Leading members such as Cai Chang, Deng Yingchao, and Kang Keqing were forced to make self-criticisms of their "bourgeois attitudes." When the ACWF reopened in 1973, its new leftist leadership campaigned against patriarchy in the family, and, under the Maoist slogan "What men comrades can do, women comrades can do too," demanded the entry of women into areas of work previously closed to them. However, after Mao's death in 1976, when his wife Jiang Qing (1914–1991) and her associates were discredited, these campaigns that had been associated with Jiang Qing's bid for succession were dropped. By the late 1970s, the survivors of the old ACWF leadership had been restored.

## THE ACWF IN THE POST-MAO PERIOD

The early period of the economic reforms brought new difficulties for Chinese women. They were disproportionately affected by widespread layoffs in state industry and by reductions in health and childcare provision. Working conditions for male and female workers in new privately owned industries were often appalling. The one-child family policy, introduced in 1980, revealed how strongly son preference had survived. Desperate to have at least one son, parents concealed first-born daughters. Cases of female infanticide were reported. Later, with the introduction of scanning, widespread sex-selective abortion gave rise to serious distortions in sex ratios.

These developments made it impossible to argue that sex equality had already been achieved, and an invigorated ACWF developed initiatives for the new era. It denounced suggestions that unemployment could be solved by getting married women to give up work. It launched campaigns against domestic violence and female infanticide. It organized rural women to find new forms of income generation and urban women to upgrade qualifications that would enable them to compete successfully in the market.

In the 1990s, the organization underwent further change. International agencies and aid donors working in China introduced ideas about targeting women in development projects. In 1995 the United Nations–sponsored Fourth World Conference on Women held in Beijing allowed the ACWF to assume a high profile. New ideas about gender and gender roles were introduced by Chinese women returning from postgraduate studies in the West,

***Woman exercising at a facility in Chongqing, November 22, 2006.*** *Founded in the late 1940s, the All-China Women's Federation (ACWF) promoted greater rights for women in China, particularly in areas of employment, marriage law, and education. In the twenty-first century, the ACWF continues to provide a voice for millions of women, raising awareness of contemporary issues, such as selective abortions of female fetuses by couples favoring a male child.* CHINA PHOTOS/GETTY IMAGES

by international exchanges and conferences, and by the translation of feminist literature from abroad.

### CURRENT ROLES AND SIGNIFICANCE

The ACWF today is involved in poverty alleviation in the countryside, training women for income generation, and working to eradicate illiteracy. In the cities it offers training programs designed to help unemployed and migrant women. It participates in drafting laws on marriage, adoption, family planning, and protection of women and children. It also helps women migrants, and sponsors women's studies and research into women's history. However, the ACWF remains constrained by its official position. It must carry out government policy toward women and cannot be too critical of the treatment of women. Thus, for example, local Women's Federation cadres are involved in the implementation of population policy, checking that women have not become pregnant without permission and putting pressure on them to abort out-of-plan pregnancies.

Scholars differ in their evaluations of the ACWF. Some see it as hopelessly compromised by its association with the party/state, lacking all possibility of independent thought or action. They argue that its official monopoly on advocacy and action for women hinders the development of independent women's organizations. For them, the official gender policy, at least in the Maoist years, pushed women to conform to male norms rather than exploring what real sexual equality might be. Others believe that the ACWF has been able to keep women's issues on the agenda throughout the history of the People's Republic and to achieve real advances for women just because it has official status. They praise the practical work of the ACWF for ordinary women and argue that it has mitigated the effects of economic liberalization and globalization on Chinese women. For them, the ACWF's adoption of the NGO label is justified. Since the 1990s they say it has become less hierarchical, and open to alliances with other organizations while acting as a women's pressure group on the Chinese state.

**SEE ALSO** *Song Qingling; Women, Status of.*

### BIBLIOGRAPHY

Davin, Delia. *Woman-work: Women and the Party in Revolutionary China.* Oxford: Clarendon Press, 1976.

Hershatter, Gail. *Women in China's Long Twentieth Century.* Berkeley: University of California Press, 2007.

Hsiung Ping-chun, Maria Jaschok, and Cecilia Milwertz, eds. *Chinese Women Organizing: Cadres, Feminists, Muslims, Queers.* Oxford and New York: Berg, 2001.

Judd, Ellen. *The Chinese Women's Movement between State and Market.* Stanford, CA: Stanford University Press, 2002.

Zhang Naihua. The All-China Women's Federation, Chinese Women and the Women's Movement, 1949–1993. Ph.D. diss., Michigan State University, East Lansing, 1996.

*Delia Davin*

## AMOY

**SEE** *Xiamen (Amoy).*

## ANARCHISM

China's defeat in the Sino-Japanese War in 1894–1895 was a crowning blow after repeated humiliations in earlier decades of the nineteenth century. Even more important to many intellectuals were problems of injustice and corruption in China's social and political order. Anarchism offered a systematic analysis of and response to all such problems, and Chinese intellectuals who adopted anarchist principles did so for some combination of this broad range of concerns.

### EARLY ANARCHISM IN CHINA, 1905–1910

Two major forms of anarchism developed in China, both originating in European intellectual life of the previous several decades. The earliest notions about anarchism came by way of Japan and drew on revolutionary activism elsewhere, especially on Russian populism, which emphasized assassination and other forms of "propaganda by the deed." A number of assassination attempts occurred in China during the first decade of the twentieth century.

Early Chinese anarchists in Japan emphasized traditional thought and values. The activist couple Liu Shipei and his wife He Zhen gave shape to the anarchist ideas of the group that formed in Tokyo. Liu posited an anarchist society based on natural communities in the Chinese countryside, while He Zhen became the first to expound anarchist feminism in China. Liu and He presented their views in *Tianyi bao* (Heaven's justice) and *Heng bao* (Natural equality). Personal and political considerations made the anarchist careers of this radical couple brief.

The second model for anarchism emphasized the rationality of science and natural law. This anarchism influenced Chinese who sojourned in Europe, especially in France, in the early 1900s. The Chinese anarchist group that formed in Paris developed an avant-garde, science-oriented form of anarchism. Their greatest inspiration was Peter Kropotkin, the great Russian anarchist leader who had abandoned violence in favor of sophisticated theory and popular organizing. His anarchism rested on observation of history and society, and he emphasized the concept of mutual aid (*huzhu*), which became a watchword for Chinese activists of all viewpoints by the late 1910s.

The Paris group criticized superstition and backward social customs. They urged the application of modern science in every aspect of life, thus launching a major theme among subsequent generations of intellectuals. Three individuals formed the nucleus of the Paris group: Zhang Jingjiang, Li Shizeng, and Wu Zhihui. Zhang managed his family's business importing European goods to China. Li, who studied biology, started an enterprise to prepare bean curd (*doufu*) for sale. These activities launched the group on a practical footing and provided outlets for their evolving anarchist ideas. Wu joined them later and wrote eloquently in their anarchist journal *Xin shiji* (The new century). Begun in 1907, this journal emphasized the scientific basis of anarchism, ridiculed superstition in Chinese life, and challenged the Qing government's authority.

## LIU SHIFU, THE EPITOME OF CHINESE ANARCHISM

Liu Sifu (1884–1915), who adopted the name Shifu in 1912, became China's most consistent anarchist. Liu's evolution as an anarchist reflects all the influences described above. He went to Japan to study in 1906 and joined the Tongmeng Hui (Revolutionary Alliance). Following a failed assassination attempt in May 1907, Liu studied the Paris group's *Xin shiji* and other journals during three years in prison and completed his transition to theoretical anarchism. Essays written then also show Liu's attraction to the Buddhist ideal of the self-sacrificing bodhisattva, which characterized his entire career.

After the Republic was established in early 1912, Shifu used only pacifist means to propagate anarchism. He organized family and friends into an anarchist commune in Guangzhou. The group launched *Min sheng* (Voice of the people), which commented on social movements within China and abroad and published translations of anarchists such as Kropotkin and Emma Goldman. The group taught Esperanto, and in *Min sheng* Shifu publicized the worldwide Esperanto movement, a great idealistic community on the eve of World War I. Yuan Shikai's crackdown in late 1913 abruptly ended Shifu's activities in Guangzhou, and his group relocated in Shanghai, where they continued to publish *Min sheng* regularly despite declining funds. Shifu contracted tuberculosis, but as a strict vegetarian inspired by Leo Tolstoy, he refused to eat meat to gain strength; he died in spring 1915.

Shifu had broken with Sun Yat-sen's concept of a new Chinese state. He castigated Sun as a state socialist like Marx, anticipating the enmity of Chinese anarchists to the Chinese Communists, who organized some years later. Shifu stood as a powerful exemplar of anarchist principles, but his idealism was difficult for less austere individuals. Members of his group continued their anarchist mission as ordinary laborers in Shanghai, organizing labor there and in Guangzhou. Some in the group carried their influence as far as Singapore.

In France, meanwhile, the old Paris group of anarchists continued the practical aspect of their work in a work-and-study program during and after World War I. This assisted many young Chinese with sojourns in Lyons or Paris for study-abroad experiences. Such major figures as Zhou Enlai and Deng Xiaoping participated. Mao Zedong himself was strongly attracted to anarchist ideas during the late 1910s and early 1920s during the formative stage of his development. The ultimate choice of Marxism reflected this generation's acceptance of discipline and authority as essential to making revolution.

## HIGH TIDE AT MAY FOURTH, DECLINE DURING THE 1920s

Anarchists were prominent in the May Fourth incident in 1919, which gave shape to the Communist revolution in China after World War I. Arif Dirlik has shown the high degree of anarchists' involvement in this action, regarded by Chinese Communists as the springboard of their movement. By the early 1920s, however, anarchism weakened in the face of the Nationalist and Communist movements, both emphasizing military means to advance national development. By the late 1920s members of the Paris group of anarchists became senior advisors in Chiang Kai-shek's Guomindang (Nationalist Party), their opposition to Marxism taking precedence over whatever else remained of their anarchist principles.

During this later period some anarchists emphasized free thought and individual expression. A few remained creatively faithful to anarchist principles. Chief among these was the novelist Ba Jin (Li Feigan), who took his pen name from the Chinese form of the names of Mikhail Bakunin and Peter Kropotkin. Ba Jin died in 2004 at the age of 100, a revered symbol of the positive achievements of China's revolutionary twentieth century. His humanism reflected his anarchist principles.

The Communist leadership recognized the anarchist movement as it undertook to evaluate the Cultural Revolution (1966–1969). Seeking sources of the "ultraleftism" deemed responsible for that chaotic decade, they commissioned efforts to collect materials on the earlier anarchist movement. The compendia published as a result of those efforts have proved indispensable for research on Chinese anarchism. But it is not at all clear that anarchism played any role in that tragic decade, the causes of which would seem to lie deep in China's history and in the nation's tortured transition to a workable form of modernity.

### BIBLIOGRAPHY

Dirlik, Arif. *Anarchism in the Chinese Revolution*. Berkeley: University of California Press, 1991.

Krebs, Edward S. *Shifu: Soul of Chinese Anarchism.* Lanham, MD: Rowman and Littlefield, 1998.

Müller, Gotelind. *China, Kropotkin, und der Anarchismus.* Wiesbaden, Germany: Harrassowitz Verlag, 2001.

Scalapino, Robert A., and George T. Yu. *The Chinese Anarchist Movement.* Berkeley: Center for Chinese Studies, Institute of International Studies, University of California, 1961.

Zarrow, Peter. *Anarchism and Chinese Political Culture.* New York: Columbia University Press, 1990.

***Edward S. Krebs***

## ANHUI

Anhui was formed as a distinct province in 1667, split from the larger administrative unit of Jiangnan in the early decades of the Qing dynasty. Although there remains some debate over the creation of the name, it is generally accepted that *Anhui* was derived from a combination of the first characters of the names of two important cities: Anqing and Huizhou. With such a varied geography, however, provincial identity and cohesiveness were difficult to maintain, because the three zones of Anhui often had more in common with subregions of neighboring provinces than with each other. Linguistic and cultural differences among peoples living in these zones further contributed to the social and political disunity that has plagued provincial governance into the present.

Located in central East China, Anhui is an inland province of great geographical and cultural diversity. Landlocked on all sides, Anhui is bordered by six provinces: Shandong to the north, Jiangsu to the northeast, Zhejiang to the southeast, Jiangxi to the south, Hubei to the southwest, and Henan to the northwest. The Huai and Yangzi Rivers divide Anhui into three distinct zones, each with unique cultural and economic bases. The Huai River flows through the northern third of Anhui, and the flat dry plains that extend north of this river define the first zone. Known as Huaibei, this region shares much in common with the North China Plain, and wheat, soybeans, vegetable oilseeds, and cotton are the primary agricultural crops. The middle and lower reaches of the Yangzi River wind through the southern third of the province and help delineate the remaining regions. The area contained between the Yangzi River to the south and the Huai River to the north comprises the second zone. This region is hilly and fertile, especially suitable for rice agriculture, silk cultivation, and fish farming; higher mountains lie in the far west of this region, creating a natural boundary with Hubei and Henan. The third zone is south of the Yangzi River and heavily mountainous. Famous for the granite peaks of the rugged Yellow Mountains (Huangshan), and for its historic Huizhou merchant culture, this area is densely forested with hardwoods and bamboo and is a producer of timber, ink, and world-class teas.

| ANHUI |
|---|
| **Capital city:** Hefei |
| **Largest cities (population):** Anqing, Hefei (4,910,000 [2007]), Huangshan City |
| **Area:** 139,600 sq. km. (53,900 sq. mi.) |
| **Population:** 61,180,000 permanent residents (2007) |
| **Demographics:** Han, 99%; Hui, 0.6% |
| **GDP:** CNY 734.57 billion (2007) |
| **Famous sites:** Mount Huangshan; Xidi and Hongcun villages |

In Huaibei the soil is relatively poor, and during the first decades of the nineteenth century the Huai River and its tributaries flooded frequently and severely, devastating the meager harvests and pushing the population into further misery and indebtedness. The floods, often followed by periods of drought, led to numerous uprisings, revolts, and banditry, and north Anhui experienced constant political and social instability.

### TAIPING AND NIAN REBELLIONS

In February 1853 Anqing (Anking), the provincial capital on the north bank of the Yangzi River, fell to Hong Xiuquan's rebellious Taiping army. The city was laid waste, its vast storehouse of government cash reserves and munitions appropriated by the rebels and used the following month to take Nanjing.

While Taiping forces controlled the Yangzi River Valley, Nian rebels took charge of northern Anhui and further contributed to provincial destabilization and impoverishment. Nian discontent coalesced into outright revolt against authority after repeated flooding of the Yellow River caused it to change course in 1855. The redirection of the river to the north of the Shandong Peninsula drastically reduced the flow of tributary waters into the Huai River Basin, which, in turn, led to severe drought across Huaibei. This effectively destroyed the agricultural productivity of the region for years afterward. By 1861 Qing government forces had rallied. Anqing was recaptured from the Taipings in September of that year, but only after a prolonged siege made conditions so extreme that human flesh was openly sold for human consumption in the city streets (Fisher 2005, p. 129). The leading Confucian statesman and military general Zeng Guofan, together with his protégé Anhui-born Li Hongzhang, were instrumental in the suppression of the

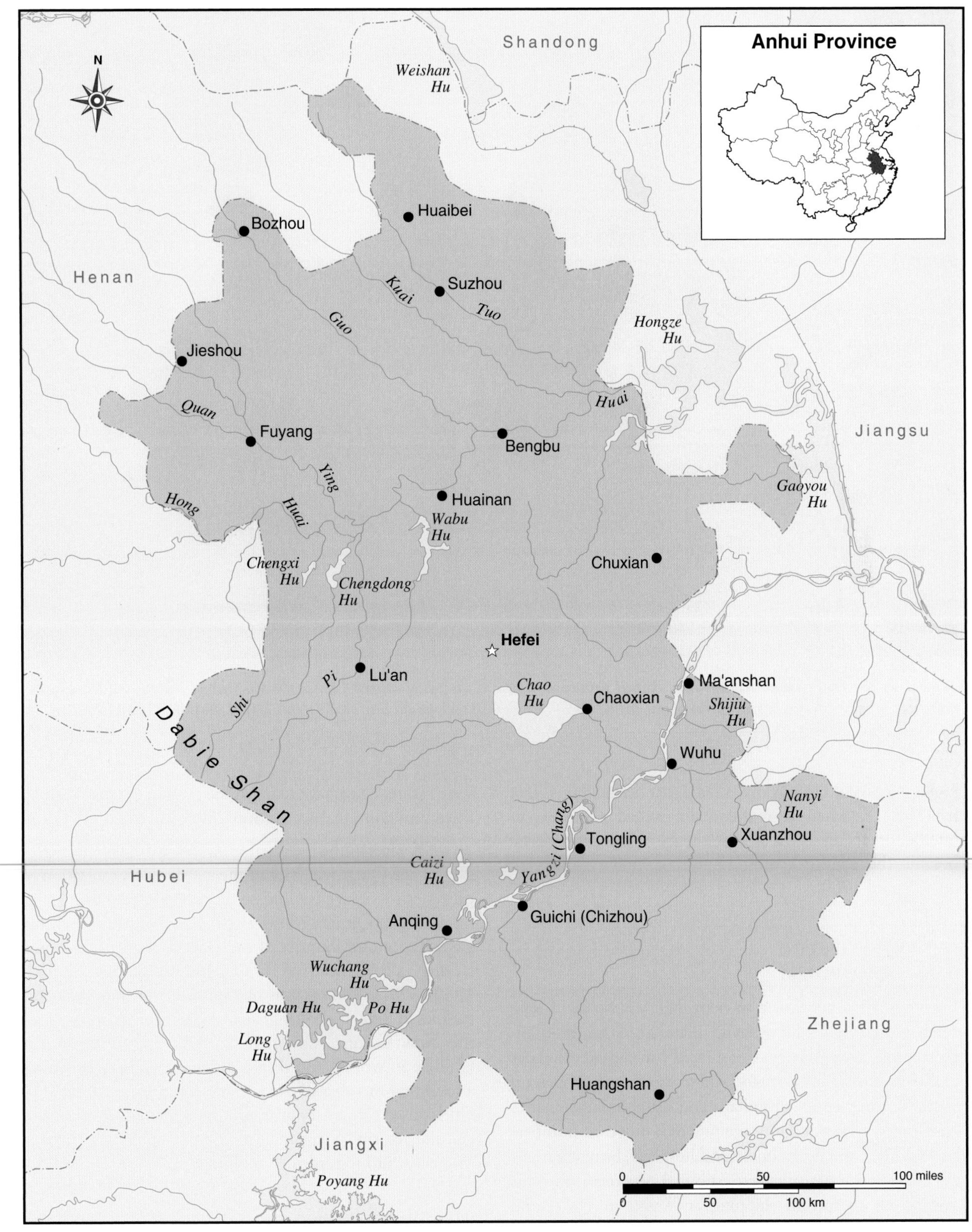


Taipings, and Anhui was considered a crucial linchpin to reasserting national government control. After Anqing's recovery Zeng and Li launched some of their early self-strengthening reforms from the provincial capital, and the city produced China's first steam-powered ship in 1865. Li also began to gather recruits here for his personally loyal and

***Winter in the Huangshan Mountains, Anhui province, 2006.*** *Situated in eastern China, the province of Anhui contains a wide variety of landforms, from agricultural plains in the north to snow-capped mountains in the south.* © FRANK LUKASSECK/CORBIS

highly successful Huai Army, a force that defeated the Nian by 1868. The Huai Army eventually swelled to more than 60,000 forces and served as Li's primary base of power as he became the country's most important military and civil official until 1900.

## DYNASTIC DECLINE AND WARLORDISM

Provincial elites continued to exert their autonomy as long as their patron Li Hongzhang maintained his hold on power, but times were changing rapidly in the later decades of the nineteenth century, and Anhui was forced to open up to the outside world. Protestant and Catholic missionaries from the West poured into the province in record numbers and opened churches, schools, and hospitals, bringing modern education and medicine to Anhui. A new treaty port was opened up to foreign shipping at Wuhu in 1877, and commercial development began to change the economy of the surrounding countryside, slowly eroding Huizhou's commercial importance. Despite slow improvements in infrastructure, it took decades for the population to recover from the devastating effects of rebellion and famine, which were estimated to have reduced the population of Anhui by fifteen million inhabitants (Sun 2002, p. 161).

The start of the twentieth century saw the rapid implosion of the Qing dynasty and the steady decentralization of power as successive warlords took control of Anhui. Anhui native Duan Qirui (1864–1936), the leader of the Beiyang government and founder of the Anhui Clique, dominated Beijing politics from 1916 until his ouster in the mid-1920s. Other leading sons of Anhui left to pursue opportunities in Beijing or Shanghai, becoming key proponents of the New Culture movement and the use of vernacular Chinese in writing and language reform. Chen Duxiu was a founding member of the Chinese Communist Party; Hu Shi focused less on politics and more on intellectual and cultural reform, but gradually his cosmopolitanism slowly propelled him toward the Guomindang.

## WAR AND RESISTANCE

Once the Guomindang consolidated its hold on power after the 1927 Northern Expedition, Anhui's central location once again gave the province strategic importance, yet it was never as solidly under Nationalist control as its immediate neighbors to the east and south. Ruinous taxes, often collected years in advance, continued to meet stiff resistance from the peasantry and local elites, and this sometimes became violent. The chronic poverty of Huaibei and the remoteness of the mountains in the far western and southern reaches of the province made these areas particularly suitable for Communist activity. In 1938, however, invading Japanese forces swept up the Yangzi River Valley, and most of Anhui fell swiftly under Japan's military control. The provincial government relocated outside occupied territories, and as a consequence, Anqing permanently lost its status as capital; eventually it was supplanted by Hefei further to the north and center.

During the early years of the war Anhui became an important base of operations for the New Fourth Army. The mountainous terrain in the south provided the perfect cover for the Communist forces to rally. In early winter 1941 this same region became infamous for the New Fourth Army Incident, a dire blow to the fragile alliance between the Communists and the Guomindang (Sun 2002, p. 158). When the war against Japan ended in 1945, Anhui reverted to Nationalist control, but it remained a hotbed of discontent, with resentment toward gentry landowners reaching critical proportions.

## 1949 TO 1990

Communist victory brought sudden change to the status quo. The new central government in Beijing reorganized the province into two separate prefectures, North and South Anhui, but these administrative divisions were short-lived, and the province was reunited in 1952. The dominion of Anhui's old elite was finally destroyed by extensive land-reform campaigns. Long-standing grievances of peasants who had endured generations of hardship and suffering were unleashed in violent and bloody confrontations against the wealthy landowners. After land reform, the countryside was reorganized by the state and forcibly collectivized. The provincial government was left-leaning and conservative, aligned with Beijing's most extreme elements. Economic policies focused almost exclusively on agricultural initiatives, with little or no attention paid to the development of heavy industry. Anhui remained one of the poorest provinces in China, and fallout from mass campaigns such as the Great Leap Forward and the Cultural Revolution was especially severe.

Deng Xiaoping's rise to power following the death of Mao Zedong marked a sudden transformation in national priorities and approaches, but Anhui was slow to change. Despite the fact that Huaibei peasants were among the first to experiment with the household responsibility system and with a limited free market, the annual growth rate of the provincial economy lagged far behind the national average. Provincial leaders were still known for their conservatism, and the reputation of Anhui as a province that men, women, and children left to become wandering beggars or migrant workers became legendary. This perception remains today.

## 1990 TO THE PRESENT: ECONOMY, CULTURE, AND REGIONALISM

In the early 1990s provincial authorities became more pragmatic and encouraged the growth of primary and secondary industries, ending the province's exclusive reliance on agriculture. The abundant natural resources and mineral wealth of the province were systematically developed, and huge coal reserves and copper and iron ore deposits were mined for energy use and industrial output. Anhui's proximity to Shanghai, and the development of crucial transportation and communications hubs that link the province with all parts of China, have made Anhui particularly suitable for the production of light manufactures. A string of cities located along the central and lower reaches of the Yangzi River fully benefit from new economic policies, and factories, petrochemical operations, iron- and steel-making companies, and automotive plants have proliferated there. Although the agricultural sector continues to employ the majority of Anhui's working population, it no longer dominates the economy as it once did. Apart from agriculture and industry, tourism has emerged as a new growth area for the provincial economy. The mountainous zone south of the Yangzi River attracts domestic and international tourists, and the government has plans to develop tourism in Huangshan and historic Huizhou, a protected zone of the World Heritage Foundation.

In 2007 the provincial capital of Hefei was a bustling city of nearly 5 million, the largest city in a province of more than 61 million people. Apart from its principle role as the seat of government, Hefei has become a leading producer of household electrical appliances. It is also home to the University of Science and Technology (USTC) (Zhongguo Keji Daxue), widely considered one of China's top universities in the fields of applied and theoretical research. In Hefei there is a residual culture of suspicion among government officials, especially toward foreigners. This attitude is eroding quickly as the province seeks to attract foreign investment into the region, but conservatism persists among the general population as social and cultural opportunities remain limited.

**SEE ALSO** *Huizhou.*

## BIBLIOGRAPHY

Anhui Provincial Government. Official Web site. http://www.ah.gov.cn/.

Bianco, Lucien. Peasant Uprisings against Poppy Tax Collection in Su Xian and Lingbi (Anhui) in 1932. *Republican China* 21, 1 (November 1995): 93–128.

Calvert, Philip J. Provincial State-building and Local Elites in Anhui: 1929–1935. Ph.D. diss., University of Washington, 1991.

Fisher, Nevan A. A House Divided: Christmas Church and the Protestant Community of Anqing. Ph.D. diss., University of Virginia, 2005.

Frean, Nicola. Warlordism in Anhui. *Asian Profile* 12, 4 (1984): 307–323.

Perry, Elizabeth J. *Rebels and Revolutionaries in North China, 1845–1945.* Palo Alto, CA: Stanford University Press, 1980.

Spence, Jonathan D. *The Search for Modern China.* 2nd ed. New York and London: W.W. Norton, 1999.

Sun, Wanning. "Discourses of Poverty: Weakness, Potential, and Provincial Identity in Anhui." In *Rethinking China's Provinces,* ed. John Fitzgerald, 153–177. London and New York: Routledge, 2002.

Wo guo di yi tai zhengqiji, di yi sou lunchuan zai Anqing shizhi chenggong shimo [The successful trial launch in Anqing of my country's first steam powered ship]. *Anqing Wenshi Ziliao, Gongshang jingji shiliao, zhuanji di yi* [Anqing research materials, business and economic history edition] pt. 1, 14 (1986): 38.

***Nevan A. Fisher***

# ANTI-CHRISTIAN/ ANTI-MISSIONARY MOVEMENTS

Anti-Christian and anti-missionary movements in nineteenth-century China were, in the main, responses to the activities of Western Christian missionaries on the part of both the Chinese literati and common people. While the former were concerned with the challenge posed by the foreigners to their political, social, moral, and religious authority, the latter found their lives impacted negatively, to a significant extent, by the intrusion of the missionaries and the misconduct of converts. By the early decades of the twentieth century, however, most anti-Christian activities were carried out by modern intellectuals and members of political parties who denounced the missionaries for preaching unscientific and outdated ideas that were deemed to be obstacles to China's efforts to regain national sovereignty and achieve modernization. After 1949, China's government, insisting that all religious practices were a form of superstition, placed religious organizations, Christianity included, under strict control, although it has since the late 1970s adopted a policy of relative toleration.

## THE NINETEENTH CENTURY

Before 1860, the relatively small number of Western missionaries and the restrictions on their movements imposed by the Qing government lessened the potential for conflict between the Chinese population and foreigners. However, the influx of Western missionaries after the 1860 Beijing Convention, which opened China to travel by foreigners and protected missionaries in their proselytizing activities, created conditions for violent confrontations. Many Chinese literati found such Christian doctrines as original sin or the virgin birth of Jesus absurd and fundamentally contrary to Confucian beliefs. In addition, social teachings and educational activities that promoted interaction between the sexes challenged established social and cultural practices.

Abuses of treaty privileges by some missionaries—such as intervention in lawsuits on behalf of converts, or the taking over of Chinese properties on questionable grounds and converting them into edifices for religious or other uses—all deepened the mistrust of Chinese who found themselves powerless vis-à-vis religious establishments backed by the political and military might of the foreign powers. For Chinese literati who claimed sole political, moral, and religious leadership, activities of foreign missionaries directly threatened not only their position and authority but also their fundamental beliefs. The fact that a domestic rebel group, the Taipings (1851–1864), adopted Christian doctrines in their attack on traditional values seemed to validate their fears that Christianity and the missionaries were destroying China's traditional order and way of life. Not surprisingly, some Chinese literati were active in producing anti-Christian literature with sensational charges of sexual misconduct and other crimes allegedly committed by the missionaries and their converts.

On the other hand, responses of the common people in the countryside to the intrusion of missionaries and their often aggressive tactics of conversion tended to take the form of direct action like riots or violent attacks. Many of them interpreted their misfortunes as resulting from a growing foreign threat to their lives and livelihood. Their resentment, often fueled by bitter attacks of the literati, tended to focus on the special privileges enjoyed by the missionaries, the protection of converts, and the disruptive consequences of Christian teachings and practices in the social and religious life of rural communities. The spatial expansion of missionary activities in the second half of the nineteenth century was accompanied by the proliferation of anti-Christian and anti-missionary cases that ranged from attacks on converts, their property, and churches to attacks on the missionaries themselves, often resulting in loss of life. Such activities culminated in the Boxer Uprising in 1898 to 1900, the suppression of which by an international expeditionary force led to another humiliating treaty imposed on China by the foreign powers.

## THE TWENTIETH CENTURY

By the turn of the century, missionary activities were increasingly being criticized for nationalist and anti-imperialist reasons. Many modern intellectuals embraced science, with its potential for technological advances and social betterment, as the key to achieving modernity and national power. Such ideas were promoted by intellectual leaders and student activists during the May Fourth movement in the late

***An armed Roman Catholic priest, center, with two soldiers, preparing for self-defense during the Boxer Uprising, c. 1900.*** *In the latter part of the nineteenth century, Western missionaries arrived in large numbers to convert Chinese citizens. Resentment over the domination of Western countries coupled with the perceived threat to traditional Chinese culture by Christian teachings led to widespread hostility against foreigners, culminating in the failed Boxer Uprising at century's end.* HENRY GUTTMANN/HULTON ARCHIVE/GETTY IMAGES

1910s and early 1920s. To them, Christianity, like all religions, was not only unscientific but also impeded the unfettered development of the individual. At a time of heightened nationalism, missionaries, supported and protected by the foreign political, economic, and military establishment, were viewed as partners in the Western imperialistic encroachment of China.

Beginning in 1922, when anti-Christian organizations opposed the meeting of the World Christian Student Federation in Beijing, Christian missionaries encountered mounting attacks from intellectuals, students, and the Guomindang and the Chinese Communist Party. With their professed aim of building a strong sovereign and independent state capable of national reconstruction and resisting foreign domination, these groups considered mission schools a tool of denationalization and were a serious infringement of the state's authority to determine national educational policy. Moreover, the schools were "poisoning" Chinese minds with unscientific and outdated religious ideas. The restoration of educational rights became one of the objectives of the anti-Christian movements. Widespread anti-Christian and anti-imperialist demonstrations and disturbances broke out after the May Thirtieth Incident of 1925, when Chinese demonstrators against foreign imperialism were fired upon by the police of the International Settlement in Shanghai, and during the Northern Expedition of 1926 to 1927.

Organized anti-Christian and anti-missionary movements gradually subsided after the Nationalist regime was established in 1928. Although the Nationalist party-state was anxious to foster ideological oneness and assert its ideological and moral authority, it was reluctant to challenge mission activities as it sought support from the West in China's domestic reconstruction. At the same time, the Nationalists also tried to curb student activism and mass movements that would pose a threat to their power. Cooperation between the Nationalist government and missionaries proved to be fruitful in such areas as famine relief, medicine, and education before and during the war against Japan. The Communists, on the other hand, continued their anti-religious, including anti-Christian and anti-missionary, activities in areas under their control during the 1930s and 1940s. After they came to power in 1949, they continued to denounce Western Christian bodies as agents of Western imperialism, and Chinese Christian churches had to sever all foreign ties.

The anti-Christian and anti-missionary movements had prompted some missionaries to reevaluate the objectives and methods of their work in China. Some had begun to work toward the eventual devolution of control before the Communist victory. Significantly, nationalist and anti-Christian sentiments in the prewar period hastened the process, led by some Chinese Christian leaders, of the indigenization of the church—both in its theology and forms of worship.

**SEE ALSO** *Boxer Uprising; Catholicism; Missionaries; Protestantism; Three-Self Patriotic Movement.*

**BIBLIOGRAPHY**

Bays, Daniel H., ed. *Christianity in China: From the Eighteenth Century to the Present.* Stanford, CA: Stanford University Press, 1996.

Cohen, Paul A. *China and Christianity: The Missionary Movement and the Growth of Chinese Antiforeignism, 1860–1870.* Cambridge, MA: Harvard University Press, 1963.

Yip, Ka-che (Ye, Jiachi). *Religion, Nationalism, and Chinese Students: The Anti-Christian Movement of 1922–1927.* Bellingham: Western Washington University, 1980.

***Ka-che Yip***

# ANTI-JAPANESE WAR, 1937–1945

The eight-year Sino-Japanese War that began on July 7, 1937, with a skirmish near the Marco Polo Bridge (Lugouqiao) in North China was the culmination of many years of violent incidents that marred the relationship of the two countries. For more than half a century, a resource-poor, rapidly modernizing Japan had challenged the authority of a succession of Chinese governments and steadily acquired territory and privileges at the expense of Chinese national sovereignty. Japanese actions differed little from those of imperialist Western nations in China during the period of dynastic collapse and ensuing political chaos in the late nineteenth and early twentieth centuries except in scope and violence, a difference that eventually resulted in full-scale war.

## EARLY BATTLES

Sustained Chinese military action following the Marco Polo Bridge incident in 1937 surprised the Japanese. For six years after its troops had invaded Manchuria in northeast China in 1931 and created a puppet government there, Japan had been nibbling away at Chinese territory in Inner Mongolia and North China with little resistance. Chiang Kai-shek (Jiang Jieshi), chairman of the national government and generalissimo of the army, had largely acquiesced to Japanese encroachment in pursuit of a policy of "internal pacification before external resistance," his main concern being elimination of Communism. For a growing number of Chinese, even among Chiang's own troops, that policy was anathema in the face of persistent Japanese aggression.

Underestimating Chinese resolve, the Japanese hoped to end the conflict quickly with a few decisive blows. Beiping (Beijing) and Tianjin were taken with little resistance by the end of July. The next target, Shanghai, proved to be a different story. The 300,000 troops, 500 aircraft, and more than 300 tanks the Japanese eventually committed to the battle that began in August 1937 met fierce resistance from a relatively poorly equipped Chinese army of roughly half a million men (only about 20 percent of whom were well trained). For three months the battle raged before outgunned Chinese units were forced to withdraw. Heavy losses were incurred on both sides. Chiang had committed his best troops and would pay a high price politically as well as militarily, having to rely thereafter on less able and reliable troops (60 percent of his elite troops were casualties of the Shanghai battle).

Pursuing a Chinese army in disarray and hundreds of thousands of fleeing civilians, the Japanese army pushed west from Shanghai to the capital city of Nanjing, capturing it in December 1937. The infamous Nanjing massacre (or Rape of Nanjing) that ensued was perhaps the most notorious atrocity in this brutal eight-year war. Casualty estimates range widely from a few thousand to 300,000; the very existence of a massacre is denied by some Japanese even today, but evidence of a slaughter of considerable magnitude is abundant.

In North China, the Japanese also met determined resistance and suffered heavy losses in the Battle of Taiyuan, before taking the city in November 1937 after nearly two months of combat. Thereafter, Japanese troops moved swiftly down the east coast of China using the Chinese rail system. Nationalist general and governor of Shandong Province, Han Fuju (1890–1938), disastrously disobeyed orders and allowed the Japanese to cross the Yellow River and race through Shandong without a fight. Chiang Kai-shek had him executed for insubordination. A major Chinese victory in the Battle of Taierzhuang in Jiangsu Province in April 1938 was a temporary respite from the Japanese onslaught, but soon thereafter the Japanese took Xuzhou, a critical railway junction, and continued to move west and south. By late 1938 Japanese troops had occupied Guangzhou (Canton), bringing almost all of the major cities and rail lines along the east and south coasts of China under their control.

## FLYING TIGERS

Flying Tigers was the popular nickname of the American Volunteer Group (AVG) that operated within the Chinese Air Force in 1941 and 1942. It was primarily the creation of Claire Chennault (1890–1958), a retired U.S. Army Air Corps officer who had become aviation advisor to Chiang Kai-shek (Jiang Jieshi). Most of the pilots were volunteers from the U.S. Army, Navy, and Marine Air Corps who resigned from the U.S. military and went to work for a private contractor when they joined the AVG. Approved by President Franklin D. Roosevelt, this was a necessary ploy to disguise American aid to China because the U.S. was not yet at war with Japan. Chennault oversaw the recruitment and training of the pilots and the purchase of the shark-face P-40 fighter planes they flew. He also designed a combat strategy that proved to be very effective against Japanese planes, many of which were faster and more maneuverable than the P-40s. Chennault's pilots fought in teams; attaining an altitude advantage, they would dive on their prey, firing the P-40's six machine guns, and escape before Japanese escort planes could catch them. Their success was extraordinary. They are credited with destroying at least 115 Japanese planes (one estimate is 297) in the year and a half they were active, suffering combat losses of only fourteen AVG pilots. Chennault also trained a small number of Chinese cadets, some of whom eventually joined the AVG. As the U.S. entered the war, the AVG as subterfuge was no longer necessary. On July 4, 1942, the AVG was disbanded; many of the pilots joined the U.S. Army Air Force's Twenty-third Fighter Group, later absorbed by the Fourteenth Air Force commanded by Chennault in China. The name Flying Tigers continued to be used commonly by the U.S. press and the general public to refer to U.S. Army Air Force units in China throughout the war years.

**BIBLIOGRAPHY**

Ford, Daniel. *Flying Tigers: Claire Chennault and His American Volunteers, 1941–1942.* Rev. ed. Washington, DC: HarperCollins/Smithsonian Books, 2007.

***Peter J. Seybolt***

With the fall of Nanjing, the national government of China moved up the Yangzi River to Wuhan and prepared for a determined stand. From June through October 1938, Japanese troops moved toward the city, fighting numerous battles north and south of the Yangzi River. To slow the Japanese advance from the north, Chiang Kai-shek ordered that the Yellow River dikes near Zhengzhou be breached. The resulting flood destroyed the homes and property of approximately ten million Chinese civilians in four provinces, an estimated million of whom died from drowning, starvation, and disease. The Japanese advance was slowed by only a few weeks. Another self-imposed tragedy occurred when panicky Chinese troops burned the city of Changsha in November 1938, killing an estimated twenty thousand people before the Japanese even arrived. (Ironically, Changsha would later be successfully defended three times before the Japanese finally occupied the city in 1944.)

### STALEMATE AND GUERRILLA WARFARE

Wuhan was finally taken by the Japanese in late October 1938, by which time the national government of China had moved up river, beyond the defensible Yangzi gorges, to Chongqing, where it would remain throughout the war, refusing to capitulate despite continuous heavy bombing by Japanese planes. There followed several years of relative stalemate in which the Japanese sought to consolidate and exploit their gains, and military actions by both the Nationalists and Communists primarily took the form of guerrilla warfare behind enemy lines. Two important exceptions were the eventual success of Chinese Nationalist troops under American generals Joseph Stillwell (1883–1946) and Albert Wedemeyer (1897–1989) in opening the Burma Road between China and India in 1945 after nearly three years of grueling seesaw combat, and the major Japanese offensive in 1944, Operation Ichigō, intended to strengthen control of railroads, link Japanese forces in China and Indochina, and destroy U.S. air bases in southern China. Those goals were achieved, but at great cost for both sides.

### CHINESE COLLABORATORS

The Japanese were not alone in their attempt to seize control in China; they were aided by millions of Chinese collaborators. It had always been Japanese policy to rule China indirectly, through puppet governments manipulated by Japanese "advisors." Such governments had been successfully established before and during the war, in Manchuria, Inner Mongolia, and parts of North and Central China. In 1940 they all were subordinated, at least nominally, to a new "national government" in Nanjing headed by Wang Jingwei. For many years, Wang had been a high-ranking member of the Guomindang and a frequent critic and rival

***Japanese soldiers raising the Japanese flag, Nanjing, China, December, 1937.*** *Internal conflicts between Nationalists and Communists weakened China's military strength in the 1930s, allowing the Japanese quick victories in cities like Nanjing. During "the Rape of Nanjing," Japanese forces ravaged the city, executing an estimated 300,000 civilians.* AP IMAGES

of Chiang Kai-shek. He characterized his formal collaboration with the Japanese as the culmination of a "peace movement" designed to save the nation from the horrors of war and oppression of Japanese rule. Whatever his intentions and expectations, tight Japanese control of his policies and actions made him little more than a puppet. Historians in China have condemned him and his fellow collaborators as unprincipled opportunists and traitors to the Chinese nation.

Estimates of the strength of the collaborationist army range from one million to two million troops in late 1944. They included a significant number of Nationalist troops formerly loyal to Chiang Kai-shek (62% of the total by Chinese Communist Party estimate), many of whom professed a greater fear of Communism than of Japanese imperialism. There was also a motley array of other combatants, including many former bandit gangs and paramilitary units led by secret societies and local elites that had arisen in great profusion, especially during the chaotic early months of Japanese invasion. Many collaborated with the Japanese, but only when convenient to do so. Much of the fighting in local areas during the years of strategic stalemate pitted Chinese of different allegiances against each other, with the Japanese playing a relatively minor role.

## THE FRAGILE COMMUNIST-NATIONALIST UNITED FRONT

Among the Chinese maneuvering for power and influence during the war period, the Nationalist and Communist parties were by far the most powerful. Having fought each other for years, they agreed shortly after the war began to establish a united front against the foreign invader. That uneasy alliance was sustained, officially, throughout the war years, but was severely tested on numerous occasions by armed conflict, including three major military confrontations by mid-1943.

The Communist strategy during the war was to infiltrate rural areas behind enemy lines in North and Central China and create base areas where they could exercise significant political control and harass the Japanese and their collaborators through guerrilla warfare. By mid-1940, their authority extended to an estimated 100 million people, a number that was reduced by half in the next three years as Japanese, puppet, and Nationalist forces all sought to roll back Communist expansion. Continuous Japanese and puppet "mop-up" and rural pacification campaigns took a heavy toll on Communist-led forces and on the rural populace. The Communists fought only one major frontal engagement with Japanese forces during the entire war (the successful Hundred Regiments Campaign, August 20 to December 5, 1940), but their guerilla warfare tactics seriously undermined the intentions and effectiveness of the Japanese and their collaborators.

By the end of the war, the Communists had again greatly expanded their area of influence, creating more than twenty base areas where their reform efforts would win popular support and lay a solid foundation for the Communists' final showdown with the Nationalists after the war with Japan had ended.

## JAPAN'S SURRENDER

The Japanese surrender in August 1945, hastened by the use of nuclear weapons by the United States and invasion of Manchuria by the Soviet Union, was a major victory for the Chinese. For eight years they had engaged more than three million Japanese troops, approximately half a million of whom were killed or died of other war-related causes. The number of war-related deaths among Chinese is staggering. Estimates vary widely, but approximately twenty million is a figure commonly used by both Nationalist and Communist historians in China (some put the figure as high as thirty million), and it is widely accepted elsewhere.

## COMFORT WOMEN

Comfort women were women recruited by the Japanese military before and during World War II to provide sexual service for its troops. During the Russo-Japanese War (1904–1905), unregulated sexual activity led to widespread venereal disease in the Imperial Army and weakened its combat effectiveness. So, during the 1932 Battle of Shanghai, the Japanese military established a system of comfort women, also aimed at reducing incidents of rape and stopping leakage of military secrets. When the Sino-Japanese War (1937–1945) started, the system was renewed. Initially, no Chinese women were used for fear of exacerbating anti-Japanese sentiments. Only after the Battle of Taierzhuang of early 1938 were Chinese women recruited to meet the demands of the increased number of Japanese soldiers.

According to Chinese estimates, the number of comfort women in China ranged between 100,000 and 200,000, with more than 10,000 comfort stations across 20 provinces. The nature of the abuse makes it difficult to verify these figures by independent research. Lack of documentary evidence further adds to the difficulty.

Most comfort women came from poor families. There were cases in which girls were kidnapped or tricked by false promises of legitimate employment. Comfort women received pay and underwent routine medical checks, but often had to tolerate physical abuses. After the war, they remained silent about their traumatic life as comfort women. While Tokyo long denied their existence, Beijing avoided the issue to promote relations with its neighbor. By the late 1980s few Chinese knew the term *comfort women.*

The first government leader to raise the issue of comfort women with Tokyo was South Korean President Roh Tae-woo during an official visit in May 1990. In November 1990, South Korea established the Korean Council for the Women Drafted for Sexual Slavery by Japan to encourage surviving victims to tell the truth. In 1991 the Japanese historian Yoshimi Yoshiaki discovered incriminating documents indicating direct involvement of the Japanese military in recruiting comfort women and managing comfort stations. Yoshimi's discovery, published by *Asahi Shimbun* (Asahi newspaper) on January 11, 1992, forced Tokyo to admit and apologize for the use of comfort women. Soon Taiwan also published similar documents.

Against this backdrop, former comfort women from South Korea and the Philippines filed separate lawsuits in 1993 asking Tokyo for an official apology and compensation. Encouraged by these lawsuits and with reluctant support from their government, some Chinese victims filed similar lawsuits in 1995. So far all have failed, as the Japanese courts rejected them by citing statues of limitations, the immunity of the state at the time of the acts concerned, and the nonsubjectivity of the individual in international law.

The courts' decisions make any future lawsuit an uphill endeavor. Lack of statistics further complicates the issue. Yet the issue of comfort women will continue to affect Sino-Japanese relations. On March 2, 2007, Japanese Prime Minister Abe Shinzō denied that the Japanese military had forced women into sexual slavery during World War II. China responded by establishing a museum of comfort women in Shanghai on July 5, 2007, portraying the system of comfort women not only as sexual slavery, but also as a crime against morality and humanity.

### BIBLIOGRAPHY

Funü Jiuen Jijin Hui [Taiwan Women Rescue Fund], ed. *Taiwan weianfu baogao* [Reports on Taiwan comfort women]. Taibei: Taiwan Shangwuyin Shuguan, 1999.

Hicks, George L. *The Comfort Women: Japan's Brutal Regime of Enforced Prostitution in the Second World War.* New York: W.W. Norton, 1997.

Min, Pyong Gap. Korean "Comfort Women": The Intersection of Colonial Power, Gender, and Class. *Gender and Society* 17, 6 (December 2003): 938–957.

Reilly, James. China's History Activists and the War of Resistance against Japan: History in the Making. *Asian Survey* 44, 2 (March–April 2004): 276–294.

Schellstede, Sangmie Choi, ed. *Comfort Women Speak: Testimony by Sex Slaves of the Japanese Military.* New York: Holmes and Meier, 2000.

Soh, Chunghee Sarah. The Korean "Comfort Women": Movement for Redress. *Asian Survey* 35, 12 (December 1996): 1226–1240.

Su Zhiliang, Rong Weimu, and Chen Lifei, eds. *Taotian zuinie: Erzhan shiqi de Rijun "weianfu" zhidu.* [A monstrous sin: The Japanese military system of "comfort women" during World War II]. Shanghai: Xuelin Chubanshe, 2000.

Taiwan-sheng Wenxian Weiyuanhui [The Taiwan Provincial Documentary Committee]. Tai-Ri guanfang dangan weianfu shiliao huibian [A collection of official Taiwan documents on comfort women during the Japanese occupation]. Nantou, Taiwan: Taiwan-sheng Wenxian Weiyuanhui, 2001.

Tanaka, Yuki. *Japan's Comfort Women: Sexual Slavery and Prostitution during World War II and the US Occupation.* London: Routledge, 2002.

Yoshimi, Yoshiaki. *Comfort Women: Sexual Slavery in the Japanese Military during World War II.* New York: Columbia University Press, 2001.

***Jianyue Chen***

Tragically, foreign war was followed by nearly four years of civil war before peace prevailed. In China today, the eight-year war of resistance is viewed as a period of appalling suffering and sacrifice, but also as one of national triumph, a turning point marking the end of more than a century of foreign imperialism and the beginning of a new era of unity and resurgence.

SEE ALSO *Harbin; Manchukuo (Manzhouguo); Marco Polo Bridge Incident, 1937; Stilwell, Joseph.*

**BIBLIOGRAPHY**

Barrett, David P., and Larry N. Shyu. *Chinese Collaboration with Japan, 1932–1945: The Limits of Accommodation.* Stanford, CA: Stanford University Press, 2001.

Hsu Long-hsuen and Chang Ming-kai. *History of the Sino-Japanese War, 1937–1945.* Trans. Wen Ha-hsiung. Taibei (Taipei): Chung Wu, 1985.

Pong, David, ed. *Resisting Japan: Mobilization for War in Modern China, 1935–1945.* Norwalk, CT: EastBridge, 2008.

Jiang Weiguo (Chiang Wei-guo), ed. *Kangri yuwu* [Resistance against Japanese oppression]. 10 vols. Taibei (Taipei): Liming Cultural Enterprise, 1978.

Zhang Bofeng and Guang Jianping, eds. *Kangri zhanzheng* [Anti-Japanese War]. 7 vols. Beijing: Chinese Social Science Academy, Modern Chinese History Research Institute, 1997.

Zhongguo kangri zhanzhengshi xuehui, zhongguo kangri zhanzheng jinianguan [Chinese Anti-Japanese War History Institute of the Chinese Anti-Japanese War Memorial Office], ed. *Zhongguo kangri zhanzhengshi congshu* [Chinese Anti-Japanese War history series]. 12 vols. Beijing: Beijing Publishing House, 1995.

***Peter J. Seybolt***

# ANTI-RIGHTIST CAMPAIGN

SEE *Hundred Flowers Campaign.*

# ARCHAEOLOGY AND WESTERN EXPLORERS

European explorers mounted scores of important expeditions in western China in the late nineteenth and early twentieth centuries, from about 1860 to about 1920. This period coincides with colonial expansions in China. Whereas colonial inroads on the east coast after the Opium Wars (1839–1842; 1856–1860) resulted in great economic benefit, the impetus for exploration in the western regions was less rooted in monetary concerns and more motivated by political aspirations to control the vast area of Central Asia between the Russian empire and the British-controlled India and China's western regions. Acquisition of geographic and scientific knowledge was central in the explorations in Xinjiang, Tibet, Gansu, Xikang, and Yunnan—indeed, the first explorers were cartographers, geologists, zoologists, and botanists. Beyond reconnaissance and surveying activities, the lure of antiquities and archaeological treasure quickly brought new explorers on the heels of the discovery of the Bower manuscript in Kucha in 1899 (Hopkirk 1980, pp. 43–46; Giès 1996, p. 10). This necromantic and medicinal text written in fifth-century Brahmi Sanskrit sparked broad interest in philology and archaeology that led to major discoveries and questionable collection tactics throughout western China and Inner Asia for the next twenty years. Archaeological discoveries by Western explorers in China were on par with those in Egypt, Greece, and other parts of the Mediterranean; plunder and treasure from monuments and ruins along the Silk Route captured public attention as part of a broad interest in "exotic" colonial locales.

European, Russian, and Japanese explorers concentrated primarily on three areas: Tibet; the northern Silk Road extending from Xinjiang to Persia; and the southern Silk Road, incorporating the area from Dunhuang south around the Taklamakan to Pakistan and India. Sven Hedin (1865–1952), a Swedish cartographer and mountaineer with a doctorate in geography, was among the first foreign explorers. He conducted extensive, multiple expeditions to the Taklamakan and Gobi Deserts, the Pamirs, and Tibet. The first of these, in 1893 to 1897, were to unexplored areas largely unknown to both Chinese and Europeans. Hedin's much admired maps, which constitute part of the prolific publications on the geography and cultures of the region, were the product of targeted, well-orchestrated missions; for example, he located the headwaters of the Brahmaputra River (as well as the Indus and Sutlej) in 1907, correcting long-held notions about the relationship of the Himalayas to the Nile (Hedin [1925] 2003). His explorations in Xinjiang extended into the Republican period, when he directed a collaborative Sino-Swedish venture to explore paleolithic remains in 1927 to 1935. Just a few years earlier another Swede, the geologist Johan Gunnar Andersson (1874–1960), teamed up with the Geological Survey of China and identified the neolithic Yangshao culture in Gansu Province in 1921 (Trigger 2006, pp. 265–266), revealing and thereby changing conceptions of China's earliest history.

Exploration of northwest China and Central Asia was an international affair. In 1908 the Russian colonel Petr Kozlov (1863–1935) identified and excavated Kharakoto, the cultural center of the Tangut or Western Xia empire (1032–1227) in Inner Mongolia; before that he had led a Mongolian-Tibetan expedition in 1898 to 1901. A regular stream of Russian scientists explored Xinjiang and points west across Central Asia between 1876 and 1898. By the turn of the century, many expeditions were mounted in search of treasure. In 1900 to 1901 Sir Aurel Stein (1862–1943) on behalf of the British mounted the first of his four expeditions. The German explorers Albert Grünwedel (1856–1935) of the Ethnological Museum, Berlin, and Albert von le Coq (1860–1930) both removed extensive paintings, sculpture, and murals from the Turfan region on the northern Silk Route in 1902 to 1903 and 1904 to 1905, respectively. Count Otani Kozui (1876–1948) of Japan ventured to Buddhist ruins in 1902 to 1903, and the French archaeologist and philologist Paul Pelliot (1878–1945) began his explorations in 1906 (Giès 1996, p. 11). They dug the forgotten oases and cave shrines of the Silk Route, including Tumshuq, Dunhuang, Khotan, Niya, Toqquz-Saraï, Duldur-Âqur at Ming-oï, Subashi, and Kumtura. The desert climate preserved vast quantities of millennia-old material culture indexing the missing cultural links to trade across Asia and Europe from the first century BCE to the fourteenth century CE.

Indisputably, the most spectacular discoveries came from Dunhuang in present-day Gansu Province, where some 490 Buddhist cave temples decorated with thousands of meters of wall paintings document the development of Buddhist lay and monastic religious practice from the fifth to the thirteenth centuries. In June 1900 Wang Yuanlu (c. 1849–1931), the caves' caretaker, discovered a cache of over 42,000 manuscripts and portable paintings on silk and paper. The secular and religious documents include letters, lecture notes, account books, talismanic texts, ritual diagrams, irrigation and labor contracts, and marriage and divorce papers, as well as thousands of Buddhist sutras written in a range of Silk Road languages including Chinese, Tibetan, Sanskrit, Tocharian, and Khotanese (Whitfield 2004b). In 1906 to 1907 both Stein and Pelliot removed thousands of texts to Europe. Now these materials are reunited with the wall paintings in a digital research environment (Fraser, 2004). Bamboo slips found at the base of nearby desert watchtowers built by the imperial Han court contain inventories of imperial army provisions; these predate the cave texts by six centuries.

**SEE ALSO** *Archaeology, History of; Archaeology, Politics of.*


**BIBLIOGRAPHY**

Almond, Philip C. *The British Discovery of Buddhism.* Cambridge, U.K., and New York: Cambridge University Press, 1988.

Andersson, Johan Gunnar. Researches into the Prehistory of the Chinese. *Bulletin of the Museum of Far Eastern Antiquities* 15 (1943): 7–304.

Fiskesjö, Magnus, and Chen Xingcan. *China Before China: Johan Gunnar Andersson, Ding Wenjiang, and the Discovery of China's Prehistory.* Stockholm: Museum of Far Eastern Antiquities, 2004.

Fraser, Sarah E. An Introduction to the Material Culture of Dunhuang Buddhism: Putting the Object in Its Place. *Asia Major* 17, part 1 (2004): 1–14.

Giès, Jacques. The Pelliot Expedition (1906–1909). In *The Arts of Central Asia: The Pelliot Collection in the Musée Guimet*, trans. Hero Friesen and Roderick Whitfield, 10–16. London: Serindia, 1996.

Hedin, Sven Anders. *My Life as an Explorer.* [1925]. Washington, DC: National Geographic Society, 2003.

Hopkirk, Peter. *Foreign Devils on the Silk Road.* Amherst: University of Massachusetts Press, 1980.

Kolb, Charles C. Review of Meyer, Karl E., and Shareen Blair Brysac, *Tournament of Shadows: The Great Game and the Race for Empire in Central Asia.* H-Russia, H-Net Reviews. April 2000. http://www.h-net.org/reviews/showrev.php?id=4018.

Lopez, Donald S., ed. *Curators of the Buddha: The Study of Buddhism Under Colonialism.* Chicago: University of Chicago Press, 1995.

Trigger, Bruce G. *A History of Archaeological Thought.* 2nd ed. Cambridge, U.K.: Cambridge University Press, 2006.

Weinberg, Roberto, and Owen Green. Central Asiatic (Tibet, Xinjiang, Pamir) Petrological Collections of Sven Hedin (1865–1952)—Swedish Explorer and Adventurer. *Journal of Asian Earth Sciences* 20 (2002): 297–308.

Whitfield, Susan. *Aurel Stein on the Silk Road.* Chicago: Serindia Publications, 2004.

Whitfield, Susan, ed. *The Silk Road: Trade, Travel, War, and Faith.* London: British Library, 2004.


*Sarah E. Fraser*

## ARCHAEOLOGY, HISTORY OF

The study of antiquities by Chinese scholars dates back to at least the seventh century BCE, when prehistoric ceramics and bronze items were discussed and recorded, and a chronology of three ages, characterized by tools made of stone, jade, and bronze, was proposed (Zhang Guangzhi 1986a). Scholars of ancient China meticulously examined ancient texts for authenticity, accuracy, structure, function, meaning, and changes due to transcription. They subjected languages, antiquities, history, and geography to the same scrutiny, reaffirming political authority and the historical record based on as much evidence as they could collect. This inductive methodology is referred to as *kaozhengxue* (literally, the examination of evidence/documents) (Qi Longwei 2003, p. 4).

Antiquarianism (*jinshixue*, literally, the study of metal and lithic items) came of age during the Northern Song dynasty (960–1127 CE), with a focus on the documentation of bronze vessels and stone tablets, and the deciphering of inscriptions on these items. Such endeavors were enthusiastically promoted by Emperor Huizong (1082–1135 CE), who was an incompetent ruler but a talented artist with a keen interest in antiquities. The Chinese term *kaogu*—literally meaning "examining the past"—first appeared as a book title during this period, and was adopted as the Chinese equivalent of *archaeology* in the late nineteenth century (Wei Juxian 1936).

## EIGHTEENTH- AND NINETEENTH-CENTURY DEVELOPMENTS

The study of antiquities diminished after the collapse of the Song dynasty, but was revived and flourished again in the second half of the Qing dynasty (1644–1912). Emperor Qianlong (1711–1799) played an important role in this revitalization by editing a book recording the royal collection of antiquities and promoting the study of antiquities. Before the reign of Qianlong, *jinshixue* focused on inscriptions on stone and bronze items, but during and after the Qianlong period, bronze mirrors, seals, seal clays, and ancient coins also became subjects of *jinshixue*. More than nine hundred *jinshixue* monographs were published in and after the Qianlong period, compared to twenty-two publications during the Song dynasty, apparently the outcome of more scholarly participants and diversified study subjects (Xia Nai et al. 1985).

After the Qianlong reign, the Qing dynasty was greatly weakened by rebellions and foreign aggression. Chinese intellectuals began to question the traditional philosophies, including Confucianism, by which the country had been guided for more than two thousand years. In this context, some scholars set about rediscovering China's past, trying to find solutions to its present crises. Examining artifacts, an additional source of history, was part of this project. Antiquarianism in nineteenth-century and early twentieth-century China was characterized by the meticulous and critical examination of ancient texts, the discovery and deciphering of ancient Chinese characters on oracle bones from Anyang and on documents from the Dunhuang grottoes, and the detailed recording of bronze, stone, and other antiquities in private and public collections.

**Leading Scholars** Many prominent scholars contributed to the strength of antiquarian studies in this period. Among the most influential was the political reformer and historian Liang Qichao (1873–1929). Liang defined *kaozhengxue* as a fundamental approach for historical study and urged historians to collect ethnographic data as references for the study of social evolution in China, which for him was the ultimate goal of history (Xu Guansan 1986).

Historian and epigraphist Sun Yirang (1848–1908) was the first person to decipher inscriptions on oracle bones and to elaborate the significance of these inscriptions. Antiquarian and epigraphist Luo Zhenyu (1866–1940) is well known for collecting and deciphering inscriptions on oracle bones and bronze vessels dated from the sixteenth to eleventh centuries BCE. Between 1910 and 1937, Luo published numerous works on this subject. He also studied bronze mirrors, grave goods, tiles, seals, and documents found in Dunhuang, and many other antiquities (Xia Nai et al. 1985). Luo's protégé, Wang Guowei (1877–1927), a versatile historian and antiquarian, was the first scholar to use artifacts to cross-check the validity of historical documents and to reach an understanding of the history, societies, and geography of China through a combination of textual and archaeological sources (Xia Nai et al. 1985).

Both Luo and Wang had a strong influence on Gu Jiegang (1893–1980), the founder of the Doubting Antiquity school, so-called because this school took a skeptical stance toward historical documents (Gu Jiegang 2002). Gu argued that it was not sufficient just to identify the authenticity of ancient texts and antiquities, because the contents of many authentic Chinese historical documents were accumulations of ancient myths and could not be fully trusted; rather, unearthed artifacts, as well as ethnological and ethnographic data, should be used to study the history of ancient China.

Antiquarianism and *kaozhengxue* undoubtedly had an influence on the development of archeology in China, but they do not explain its origins. Modern archaeology was introduced into China by Western scholars and explorers at the beginning of the twentieth century.

## DEVELOPMENTS FROM 1900 TO 1949

On June 22, 1900, a Daoist Wang Yuanlu (c. 1850–1931) discovered a secret cave containing thousands of ancient scrolls in Dunhuang, Gansu Province. Before and after that time, many Western explorers came to China with varying agendas.

**Western Explorers and Archaeologists in China** The English colonial administrator Douglas Forsyth (1827–1886) arrived in Xinjiang in 1873 and took the liberty of removing a number of artifacts from China. Hungarian explorer Aurel Stein (1862–1943) visited northwest China three times (1900–1901, 1906–1908, and 1913–1916) to collect antiquities for the British Museum. He excavated several archaeological sites in Xinjiang, and also removed artifacts from China. In 1907 he persuaded Wang Yuanlu to sell hundreds of bundles of Dunhuang scrolls and three boxes of Buddhist paintings to him. The American art historian Langdon Warner (1881–1955) traveled to northwest China in 1924 to 1925 to collect antiquities for the Fogg Museum at Harvard University. Warner took a large quantity of ancient manuscripts and artifacts from Xinjiang and Dunhuang back to the United States without permission from the Chinese government. French sinologist Paul Pelliot (1878–1945) visited northwest China in 1906. After digging in Xinjiang, he traveled to Dunhuang, where he selected and removed the most important Buddhist manuscripts and artifacts. Swedish explorer Sven Hedin (1865–1952) carried out numerous expeditions in western China between the 1890s and 1935, discovering many archaeological sites and artifacts (Xia Nai et al. 1985).

Notwithstanding the significance of these explorers and their activities, there is a general consensus that the beginnings

## ORACLE BONES

"Oracle bones" made from turtle shells or animal bones were used by the ruling house of the ancient Shang dynasty (about 1600–1046 BCE) to foretell the future. The inscriptions carved on them, known as oracle bone script (*jiaguwen*), form the first well-developed system of writing Chinese characters. As the earliest surviving documents in the Chinese script, they have fascinated historians, collectors, and calligraphy enthusiasts since their existence became known in the early decades of the twentieth century.

Carefully prepared by cleaning, drying, polishing, and trimming the scapulae of large quadrupeds such as oxen or deer or the plastrons or carapaces of tortoises, the oracle bone was then drilled with regularly placed indentations to prepare it for the augury. During the course of rituals dedicated to spirits of heaven, earth, or the ancestors, a hot point was applied to notches on the bone or shell as a question was asked of the spirit. The process produced cracks that were read as answering the king's question in the negative or affirmative. Questions might concern the proper site for a new capital, a suitable day for a military action, or even the health of a member of the royal family. After the results of the king's divination were interpreted, they were incised, along with the question, and the oracle bone cached with others that preceded it.

The existence of these primary sources for ancient Chinese history were unknown until the very end of the nineteenth century, when some were sold as "dragon bones" by peasants who had found them in the vicinity of the last Shang capital, in Xiaotun village, Anyang. Marketed by Chinese apothecaries in the capital as medicine, they were ground up and consumed. It is said that in 1899 a scholar of ancient scripts, Wang Yirong, noticed by chance that some of the medicinal bones had potentially legible archaic characters incised on their surfaces. This discovery stimulated the work of subsequent epigraphers and collectors, including Liu E, Wang Xiang, Meng Dingsheng, Duan Fang, Hu Shicha, and Luo Zhenyu, and ultimately led to recovery of buried oracle bones in scientifically excavated archaeological sites. Following the early generations of epigraphic scholars, the first official archaeological excavation was performed by the newly founded Academia Sinica (the highest research institution in Republican China) in 1928. The scholars Dong Zuobin and Li Ji successively led the first two excavations. From 1928 to 1937 more than 20,000 oracle bones were unearthed during fifteen excavations. Government-sponsored scientific archaeology resumed after 1950, and the work of deciphering and understanding the contents of the divinations has shed new light on China's early history. Now about 150,000 fragments of oracle bones may be found in museums and collections around the world, with the majority in mainland Chinese collections.

The oracle bones are important in a number of ways. Most significantly, they confirmed the existence of one of China's earliest named kingdoms, the Shang dynasty, which was recorded in early histories but suspected of being only legendary by skeptical nineteenth-century scholars. They thus document the early origins of Chinese civilization, and the Chinese written language. Further research into the oracle bones has determined a chronology of the royal house itself, along with the names of the diviners, and many details about the governance and activities of kings who lived almost 4,000 years ago. Most surviving oracle bones date to the last period of the Shang dynasty. The topics of divination provide rich material for historical studies of Shang religion, institutions, astronomy, geography, medicine, education, agriculture, farming, military, and so on.

At present, between 4,500 and 5,000 Chinese characters have been identified on oracle bones, but more than half remain to be deciphered. The archaic writing style also has served as inspiration for calligraphers and painters in the twentieth century.

### BIBLIOGRAPHY

Keightley, David N. *Sources of Shang History: The Oracle Bone Inscriptions of Bronze Age China*. Berkeley: University of California Press, 1978.

Keightley, David N., ed. *The Origins of Chinese Civilization*. Berkeley: University of California Press, 1983.

Kwang-Chih Chang. *Shang Civilization*. New Haven, CT: Yale University Press, 1980.

Loewe, Michael, and Edward L. Shaughnessy, eds. *The Cambridge History of Ancient China: From the Origins of Civilization to 221 BC*. Cambridge, U.K.: Cambridge University Press, 1999.

***Yiran Zheng***
***Julia F. Andrews***

## DUNHUANG

Dunhuang is an oasis town in the Gobi Desert in northwest China's present-day Gansu Province, near one of the most spectacular surviving monuments of early Chinese painting and sculpture. The name *Dunhuang*, meaning "blazing beacon," first appeared in the second century BCE during the Han dynasty, when the Dunhuang Prefecture was established. Situated at a crucial junction of the northern and southern branches of the ancient Silk Road, the garrison town was the gateway to China and a meeting place of East and West. As a bustling trading and cultural center, this region hosted diverse groups of people and exchanges of ideas, religious beliefs, and customs. Buddhism came to China through Dunhuang, and from the fourth century onward, the area further developed into a vibrant center of religious devotion and pilgrimage. In particular, the renowned Mogao (Peerless) Grottoes, also known as Qianfodong (Thousand Buddha Caves), vividly document China's early art, religion, and culture, of which few traces have survived outside Dunhuang.

Excavation of cave temples into a cliff overlooking the now barren river at the Mogao site was begun by the monk Yuezun in 366 CE during the Sixteen Kingdoms period (366–439), and continued through the fourteenth century, during the Mongol-ruled Yuan dynasty (1279–1368). Subsequently abandoned for many centuries, and virtually buried by shifting desert sands, the cave complex was rediscovered in the early twentieth century. Approximately 492 caves with remains of Buddhist art and other artifacts, some in an excellent state of preservation, have survived. They contain about 54,000 square yards of wall paintings and over 2,400 painted stucco sculptures. Discoveries of a cache of forgotten manuscripts at the Mogao caves yielded a rich harvest of literary texts, silk and paper paintings, woodcuts, and embroideries. Many are now in museum collections in China and abroad. The large treasure of well-preserved art provides remarkably diverse and extensive examples of early Chinese and Central Asian painting and sculpture, and offers an unparalleled visual display of Buddhist art and culture spanning nearly 1,000 years. The murals, painted stucco sculptures, inscriptions, and artifacts, which are some of the earliest to survive in China, provide insights into the region's history of architecture, calligraphy, music, medicine, politics and economics.

After a golden age that lasted from the Northern Wei (386–534) to the Tang dynasty (618–907), the central Chinese government lost control of Dunhuang from the late eighth to the early thirteenth centuries, when it came under the successive rule of Tibetans, the local Zhang and Cao clans, and finally the Tangut Western Xia kingdom (1032–1227). As a result of Dunhuang's strategic position and this complex history, the cave excavations at Mogao enjoyed the sponsorship of a varied mix of patrons, including Chinese, Tibetans, Tanguts, Uygurs, and people from other Central Asian kingdoms. Numerous donors' portraits bear witness to the lives of people from different ethnic groups and social strata. The works at Mogao, therefore, demonstrate a unique combination of styles and themes from China proper, Tibet, and western regions, particularly Central Asia and India, ranging from hybrid Indo-Sinitic styles to those that reflect the metropolitan cultures of the ethnic groups that contributed to formation of the site. They attest to the wealth of cultural and artistic developments at Dunhuang throughout the history of the Silk Road.

Because of its religious, cultural, and artistic significance, the impact of Dunhuang art has been far-reaching. Today, the Mogao Grottoes are lauded as the "Museum in the Desert" and the "Library on the Walls." They attract tourists, pilgrims, artists, and scholars from all over the world, and were recognized by UNESCO as a World Heritage site in 1987. Many of the rare manuscripts now held in museum and library collections may be viewed on the Web site of the International Dunhuang Project.

### BIBLIOGRAPHY

Duan, Wenjie. *Dunhuang Art: Through the Eyes of Duan Wenjie*. Ed. Tan Chung. New Delhi: Abhinav Publications, 1994.

International Dunhuang Project Web site. http://idp.bl.uk/.

Whitfield, Roderick, and Susan Whitfield. *Cave Temples of Mogao: Art and History on the Silk Road*. Los Angeles: Getty Conservation Institute and the J. Paul Getty Museum, 2000.

***Wei Lin***

***Inscribed oracle bone, Shang dynasty, 1300–1200*** **BCE.** *Once sold in the 1800s as dragon bones and ground to a powder for the treatment of malaria and other maladies, oracle bones have been traced back to the Shang dynasty. Diviners heated animal bones and interpreted the cracks, then inscribed their predictions on the resulting fragment, leaving modern archaeologists some of the earliest known Chinese writings.* © **ROYAL ONTARIO MUSEUM/CORBIS**

of archaeology in China should be dated to 1921. In that year, Swedish geologist Johan Gunnar Andersson (1874–1960) conducted the systematic excavation of the site of a Neolithic culture at Yangshao, in the Middle Yellow River Valley. Geology and paleontology were also introduced into China around this time, facilitating the establishment of archaeology (Chen Xingcan 1997).

**National Identity and Ownership** While these important developments were underway, China was in political chaos. The Qing dynasty was overthrown in 1911 and the Republic of China was established in 1912, but the following decades were marked by warlordism and civil conflict, and the influences of the Western imperial powers.

During this period, the conventional account of the origins and development of Chinese civilization was being questioned by both Chinese and Western scholars, with Egypt or the Middle East being proposed as the "homeland" of Chinese civilization (Chen Xingcan 1997). This proposal was viewed by some Chinese intellectuals as having not only

**Western Paradise of the Pure Land, *Dunhuang, c. 618–907.*** *Considered by many scholars one of the greatest repositories of ancient Buddhist art, the caves near Dunhuang feature a variety of paintings and sculptures. From the fourth through the fourteenth centuries, monks carved temples into the sides of sandstone cliffs and decorated their interiors with religious murals, many still preserved in the remaining 492 caves situated along the famous Silk Road.* © PIERRE COLOMBEL/CORBIS

academic but also political and social implications, in that it provided a justification for Western domination of China. These intellectuals vowed to locate a Chinese "homeland" for Chinese civilization so as to strengthen people's confidence in Chinese culture and the nation (Li Ji 1998). They viewed archaeology as the most essential and reliable approach to this objective.

At the beginning of the twentieth century, China had no laws governing the ownership of antiquities, although their purchase and sale were forbidden by the Qing authorities (Liu Shiping and Meng Xianshi 2000). In 1930, mainly in response to the loss of the Dunhuang manuscripts and artifacts, the Nationalist (Guomindang) government passed the first Antiquity Preservation Law, which was to be implemented in 1933 (Wei Juxian 1936). The legislation stated that archaeological remains belong to the nation, that excavations must be conducted by public academic institutes, that the export of antiquities must be controlled, and that a central antiquity-preservation committee should be established to monitor the excavation, preservation, and study of antiquities (Wei Juxian 1936, appendix). This was the first legislation in China to clarify the national ownership of antiquities and set up regulations for archaeological work. However, because of the weak national government at Nanjing and unstable social conditions from the 1930s to 1949 due to the Second World War and the Civil War, the legislation was never effectively implemented.

**Leading Scholars** Johan Gunnar Andersson continued to be recognized as an important scholar. He came to China in 1914 as a mining advisor to the Chinese government, but he was interested in archaeology and conducted archaeological surveys in northwest and north China from the 1920s to the 1930s (Chen Xingcan 1997). Andersson discovered and excavated the first Neolithic remains at Yangshao with Chinese scholars in the 1920s. He and Canadian paleontologist Davidson Black (1884–1934) also discovered the Zhoukoudian site near Beijing in 1927, where fossils of the Beijing (Peking) man (*Homo erectus*) were unearthed over a period of nearly forty years from 1927 to the 1960s

(Xia Nai et al. 1985). Among Andersson's many books was *Children of the Yellow Earth* (1934), the best-known work on the prehistoric archaeology of China at that time. Andersson introduced archaeological fieldwork methods and research approaches into China, laying the foundations for the discipline.

Other geologists, paleontologists, and paleoanthropologists were also active in China during the 1920s and 1930s. Chinese geologist Ding Wenjiang (V. K. Ting, 1887–1936), who was in charge of the Geological Survey Institute in the 1920s, supported and worked with Andersson to discover many prehistoric remains in the Yellow River Valley (Xia Nai et al. 1985). Geologist and archaeologist Pei Wenzhong (W. C. Pei, 1904–1982) led the excavations at Zhoukoudian from 1928 to 1935, and discovered the first skullcap of the Beijing man in 1929. Pei returned to China to continue his work on Paleolithic archaeology after obtaining a Ph.D. in archaeology from the University of Paris in 1937.

The "father of Chinese archaeology," however, is Li Ji (1896–1979), who in 1926 became the first Chinese archaeologist to lead an excavation in China. He held a Ph.D. from Harvard University, where he received training in archaeology and physical anthropology. Li was the first director of the national archaeology team of the Institute of History and Philology, founded in Beijing in 1928. Li became determined to trace the origin of Chinese people and civilization. To reach this goal and to remedy the lack of archaeological data from the Bronze Age, Li and his colleagues selected Anyang, one of the ruined capitals of the Shang dynasty (sixteenth century–1046 BCE), as their fieldwork site, and conducted fifteen excavations between 1928 and 1937 (Li Ji 1998), collecting rich and crucially important data for the study of Chinese civilization. Li continued to conduct research on Chinese archaeology after moving to Taiwan with the Institute of History and Philology in late 1948.

The first archaeological research section in tertiary education in China was established in 1922 at Peking University, with antiquarian Ma Heng (1881–1955) as the first director. Ma taught courses primarily on antiquarianism, but he also led archaeological surveys in the 1930s. He was appointed curator of the Forbidden City Museum in 1933, and retained this post until 1952.

**Devouring the Prince,** ***from the Mogao Caves, Dunhuang, c. 557–581 CE.*** *Established in the Han dynasty to connect the Northern and Southern Silk Roads, Dunhuang thrived as an important bridge between Western and Eastern merchants. Many Buddhist monks entered China through this city, leaving behind religious murals painted in the temple caves of Mogao, located just south of the city.*

**Important Discoveries** The most important archaeological discoveries of the first half of the twentieth century (1912–1949) include the Beijing man at Zhoukoudian, the Yangshao culture and the Longshan culture in the Yellow River Valley, the Bronze Age remains in Anyang, and the manuscripts and artifacts found in Dunhuang (Xia Nai et al. 1985).

The Zhoukoudian site, located approximately 50 kilometers southwest of Beijing, includes a small hill called Longgushan (Dragon Bone Hill). Andersson and Austrian paleontologist Otto Zdansky (1894–1988) discovered fossils at the site in 1921. Excavations continued until 1980, although activities were suspended in the 1930s and 1940s. Hundreds of human remains representing more than forty *Homo erectus* and *Homo sapiens sapiens* individuals, together with more than 100,000 artifacts and animal remains, were discovered in various layers at different locations on Longgushan (Xia Nai et al. 1985). The Zhoukoudian discovery counts among the earliest evidence of the presence of *Homo erectus* in the world, and shows the existence of human beings and cultures in East Asia during the Pleistocene and Holocene eras.

The discoveries of the Yangshao and Longshan artifacts reveal the cultural development of Neolithic China. Characterized by painted pottery and stone tools, the Yangshao culture gives a picture of farming societies in the Middle Yellow River Valley some 7,000 to 5,000 years ago (Xia Nai et al. 1985). The Longshan culture, discovered by archaeologist Liang Siyong (1904–1954) in the Lower Yellow River Valley in 1928, is characterized by delicate black pottery and walled towns dating to approximately 4,800 to 4,000 years ago (Xia Nai et al. 1985). These discoveries established the basis for the Neolithic chronology of human settlement in the Yellow River Valley.

Anyang, the last capital of the Shang dynasty, is located in northern Henan Province. Between 1928 and 1937, Li Ji and his colleagues excavated more than 46,000 square meters at Anyang, discovering the remains of over fifty dwellings, as well as bronze-casting workshops, burial sites, ten royal tombs, more than 24,000 oracle bones, thousands of pits containing sacrificed human remains, thousands of bronze, stone, and pottery items, and numerous other artifacts and archeological remains (Li Ji 1998; Xia Nai et al. 1985). The Anyang archaeological remains are among the most important discoveries of Bronze Age archaeology in China, providing crucial information for the study of the origin and development of Chinese civilization, particularly the chronology of the Shang dynasty (Li Ji 1998).

## ARCHAEOLOGY IN THE PEOPLE'S REPUBLIC

The People's Republic of China was formally proclaimed on October 1, 1949. The excavation at Zhoukoudian had resumed in September 1949, after a twelve-year suspension. The State Administration of Cultural Heritage (SACH), established in November 1949, was responsible for the management of archaeological remains and monuments, as well as for museums and libraries in China (SACH 2002).

In the 1950s, the newly established state had close ties with the former Soviet Union, from which it received economic aid along with political and ideological advice. Not surprisingly, the political and ideological paradigms of archaeology in the Soviet Union were also transmitted to China. In this decade, Chinese archaeology was clearly defined as a subdiscipline of history. This definition was consistent both with Chinese antiquarianism and with Soviet Marxism. Soviet archaeology was viewed as a correct model in China, and Chinese archeologists accordingly adopted Soviet field methods and theoretical interpretation. With the Sino-Soviet split in the early 1960s, China became isolated, and until 1978 Chinese archaeology was largely cut off from international trends.

**Developments from 1949 to 1978** From 1949 to 1978, archaeological work in mainland China was carried out by local scholars belonging to either the civil (government) or academic sections. The former was headed by SACH, and consisted of antiquity-management committees founded in the 1950s and 1960s in provinces, cities, and counties, as well as archaeologists in some public museums. Archaeologists working with these committees and museums were accountable to both SACH and local governments, but they were paid by local governments.

The academic section consisted of research institutes and archaeology programs in universities, the two national organizations being the Institute of Archaeology of the Chinese Academy of Social Sciences (CASS) and the Institute of Vertebrate Paleontology and Paleoanthropology. The former was established in 1950 and was responsible for archaeological studies from the Neolithic to the historical epoch, while the latter was founded in 1957 and focused on Paleolithic archaeology in China (Xia Nai et al. 1985). This division of academic responsibilities remains largely unchanged today.

Although there was no direct link between scholars working in these two institutes and in other organizations, the two national institutes were viewed as leaders of the discipline in the 1949–1978 period. These institutes employed the most experienced and knowledgeable archaeologists, and local archaeologists often sought advice from senior counterparts in the two institutes.

Archaeology was established as an undergraduate major in Peking University in 1952, and subsequently at ten other universities. Most of these programs were affiliated with the history department of the relevant university (Xia Nai et al. 1985). Working with SACH, the archaeology program at Peking University trained more than three hundred personnel

## MAJOR ARCHAEOLOGICAL DISCOVERIES

To date, more than 40,000 archaeological sites dated from the Paleolithic to the historic periods have been located in mainland China, and more than twelve million artifacts have been discovered (ICOMS China 2002). They greatly enrich our understanding of human evolution and cultural development in China.

- Fossils of both *Homo erectus* and *Homo sapiens sapiens* were discovered at Zhoukoudian, near Beijing, in 1921. The former species is dated to approximately 200,000 to 500,000 years ago, and the latter to approximately 13,000 to 30,000 years ago. Although all the fossils were lost during World War II, their discovery provides crucial and rich information for our understanding of human evolution and distribution not only in Asia, but also in the world (Xia 1985).
- The Neolithic Cishan and Peiligang cultures were found in the 1970s in the middle Yellow River Valley. The former is dated to approximately 7,700 to 8,000 years ago and the latter to 7,500 to 8,500 years ago. The Xinglongwa culture, dated to 7,400 to 8,000 years ago, was found in the 1980s in Northeast China. These archaeological cultures evidence the earliest foxtail and broomcorn millet farming in the world (Lu 1999; Zhao 2004).
- The Jiahu archaeological assemblage with rice remains in the Huai River Valley was found in the 1980s. This assemblage belongs to the Peiligang Culture and is dated to between 7,500 and 8,500 years ago. As Jiahu is geographically located between the Yellow and the Yangzi River Valley, the discovery raises questions on the Neolithic cultural dynamics between the two river valleys, as well as on the expansion of rice cultivation in East Asia (Lu 1999).
- The Pengtoushan and Bashidang culture, dated to approximately 7,500 to 8,500 years ago, was found in the middle Yangzi River Valley in the 1990s, manifesting the earliest rice cultivation in East Asia to date (Lu 1999).
- The Hongshan culture in Northeast China was first discovered in 1935; it is dated to about 5,500 years ago. The Longshan culture in the Yellow River Valley, dated to 4,000 to 4,500 years ago, was found in 1928, and the Liangzhu culture in the lower Yangzi Valley, discovered in 1934, is dated to between 4,200 and 5,300 years ago. These archaeological cultures demonstrate complex societies in several regions, and evidence shows that ancient Chinese civilization in the Yellow River Valley was integrated with elements from these cultures (Liu 2004).
- Remains of ancient cities dated to the Bronze Age (2,220–4,100 years ago), namely Erlitou, Yanshi, Zhengzhou, and Anyang, have been discovered since 1928. Erlitou is now considered to have been the probable capital of the Xia dynasty (approximately 3,600-4,100 years ago), once thought to be a legendary kingdom, whereas Yanshi, Zhengzhou, and Anyang were capitals of the Shang dynasty (2,100-3,600 years ago) (Liu 2004). These discoveries help to establish the chronology of Bronze Age China, and provide rich information about the social structure, language, beliefs, customs, and material cultures of Chinese civilization.
- The *bingma yong* (terracotta army) of the First Emperor of the Qin dynasty (221–206 BCE), perhaps China's most spectacular archaeological discovery, was unearthed in 1974 to 1976 just outside Xi'an (Xia 1985); these thousands of life-sized terracotta sculptures of ancient soldiers enrich our understanding of the art, technology and burial customs of the First Empire of ancient China.
- Remains of the capitals of the Han (206 BCE–220 CE) and Tang (618–907CE) dynasties near or at present-day Xi'an city, Shaanxi Province, have been excavated since the 1950s, along with royal and noble burials dated to the same periods (Xia 1985).

All these discoveries help us to understand the material culture, social structures and cognitive aspects of historical China, as well as the cultural exchanges between the East and the West through the Silk Road.

**BIBLIOGRAPHY**

ICOMS China. *China Principles.* Beijing: State Administration of Cultural Heritage, 2002.

Liu, Li. *The Chinese Neolithic.* Cambridge University Press, 2004.

Lu,Tracey L-D. *The Transition from Foraging to Farming and the Origin of Agriculture in China.* Oxford: Bar International Series No. 774, 1999.

Xia, Nai, et al, eds. *Zhongguo kaoguxue da baike* [Encyclopedia of China's archaeology]. Beijing: Chinese Encyclopedia Press, 1985.

Zhao, Zhijun. Study on the origin of dry-land agriculture in North China based on the floatation result from the Xinglonggou site, Inner Mongolia. *Dongya Guwu*, Vol. A (2004): 188–199.

***Tracey L-D Lu (Lu Liedan)***

from different parts of mainland China over four terms from 1952 to 1955. These graduates were then sent back to their hometowns to head archaeological projects.

In the 1950s, while many projects for building infrastructure, factories, and other social and cultural facilities were underway, archaeological work focused on salvage excavations and was controlled by SACH and the Institute of Archaeology CASS—the former issued licenses and provided funding, and the latter gave academic advice. Beginning in the 1950s, the Institute of Archeology CASS also led excavations at Anyang, Yangshao, the Ding Mausoleum of the Ming dynasty (1368–1644 CE), aristocratic and imperial burial sites of the Tang dynasty (618–907 CE) near present-day Xi'an, and many other important archaeological sites in the Yellow River Valley. In the late 1950s, the institute also launched two journals, *Kaogu* (Archaeology) and *Kaogu Xuebao* (Acta archaeologica sinica) (Xia Nai et al. 1985), which remain the most prestigious archaeology journals in China today. In 1965 the institute set up the first radiocarbon laboratory in China.

During the Cultural Revolution, studying antiquities was viewed as politically incorrect, and between 1966 and 1972 archaeological work was largely suspended. However, with the support of Premier Zhou Enlai, some salvage excavations continued, leading to the important discovery of the Mancheng Han Burials in Hebei Province in 1968. This excavation brought to light two burial suits made of gold thread and jade, fabricated for a royal couple more than 2,000 years ago. Excavations and surveys gradually resumed after 1972 (SACH 2002), the year an exceptionally well-preserved body more than 2,000 years old was found in another Han tomb at Mawangdui, Changsha City, Hunan Province. Hundreds of artifacts made of wood, bamboo, lacquer, and bone were found at this site. The well-known terracotta army of Qin Shihuang (259–210 BCE) was discovered in 1974 near Xi'an, and the site has been under continuous excavation since that time. All these discoveries are evidence of the high degree of technology and craftsmanship in ancient China, and they facilitate the understanding of the material culture, social structure, aesthetic sense, arts, customs, and beliefs of the past. These discoveries have also been used by the Chinese government for civil and patriotism education, and to promote nationalism.

Between 1949 and 1978, archaeology in mainland China developed mostly independently of international trends. Although the fieldwork methods and some analytical approaches were similar to those practiced in other areas of the world, Marxism and Maoism dominated the ideological domain, and the only theoretical framework for Chinese archaeology was cultural evolution. Archaeology was expected to reveal the material cultures created by the ancestors of the Chinese people, to promote patriotism, and to preserve national heritage (Xia Nai et al. 2005). Theoretical homogeneity and political influence are notable characteristics of Chinese archaeological work during this period.

**The 1980s and After** The reform and opening policy implemented in mainland China from 1978 caused enormous economic, social, political, and ideological changes, which had an impact on academic developments. In the field of archaeology, the effects were apparent in academic structures, funding models, collaboration, research methods, and theoretical frameworks.

Although all archaeologists in China still belonged to the public sector after 1978, and the basic structure involving civil and academic sections remained unchanged, many provincial and city institutes of archaeology have emerged. These institutes are accountable to the relevant local government and are responsible for local archaeological projects.

Several factors have contributed to the emergence of these smaller institutes. First, many local governments, especially those in the coastal areas, benefited from economic development after 1978, and were able and willing to pay for local archaeology teams that could focus on the origin and development of local cultures. Second, numerous construction projects have been carried out in many parts of China since the 1980s. National legislation on heritage preservation and management was introduced in 1982 and revised in 2002, requiring archaeological survey and salvage excavations before any construction took place. The result was a greater demand for archaeological teams. Finally, since the 1970s, the archaeology programs in eleven Chinese universities have trained many young archaeologists, providing human resources for the new institutes.

Economic development and construction have also led to changes in the funding model for archeological work. In the past, such work was funded solely by the central or local government or SACH. Now, both public and private companies must pay for salvage excavations before carrying out construction projects (Lu Liedan 2002). Thus, the total funding available for archaeological work has increased.

In brief, the academic field of Chinese archaeology has been expanding since the 1980s. SACH still plays a vital role in managing archaeological excavations and research through the licensing system. SACH has the power to refuse new licenses to archaeologists who have not published their data within the stipulated time period. It also monitors excavations, and, most importantly, it coordinates nationwide salvage excavations, including those for the Three Gorges Project in the 1990s and the South-North Water Transfer Project in the early twenty-first century. SACH is also responsible for authorizing international collaboration on archaeological works, the framework for which was set out in the Regulation for Foreign Participation in Archaeological Work in 1991. Before that time, foreign participation was not allowed in mainland China, mainly because of the loss of archaeological remains to Western explorers in the late nineteenth and early twentieth centuries.

***Archaeological site at Yin, in the province of Henan, May 25, 2005.*** *Renowned Chinese archaeologist Li Ji began to excavate Yin, the ancient capital of the Shang dynasty, in 1928, discovering thousands of oracle bones in the process. Work continues on Yin into the twenty-first century, with scholars finding artifacts such as this burial pit containing sacrificial horses and chariots.* © CHINA NEWSPHOTO/REUTERS/CORBIS

On the other hand, local institutes have more financial and human resources and have become more influential in the field, while the two national institutes struggle to cope with the ever-increasing demand for excavations and research (Lu Liedan 2002). Generally speaking, the field of archeology in China today is much less centralized now than it was between 1949 and 1978.

This decentralization has had a significant impact on contemporary developments in Chinese archeology. While increased financial and human resources mean more fieldwork, more equipment for local institutes, more research, and more journals, academic collaboration between the two national institutes and local organizations seems less close than it was before 1978.

Another factor worthy of note is the impact of returned overseas students, who have brought new research methods and theories to the field of archeology in China since the 1980s. Such techniques as flotation, phytolith analysis, use-wear analysis, isotopic analysis, residue analysis, and neutron-activation analysis have been applied to archaeological research in China since the mid-1980s. The application of these methods facilitates data retrieval and has helped archeologists develop a more comprehensive, concrete, and holistic understanding of the societies and peoples of China's past.

Although Marxism and cultural evolution remain important theoretical frameworks, other models, such as the "new archaeology" and cognitive and interpretive archaeology, have been introduced into mainland China since 1978. Academic publications in English and other Western languages have also been translated into Chinese, and some are even used as university textbooks. Overall, academic discussion in mainland China has become more lively and diversified.

In addition, many important discoveries have been made since the 1980s. The discovery of two ritual pits in

***Painted pottery jar, Neolithic Age, c. 2000* BCE.** *As early as 600* BCE, *the Chinese began discovering archaeological artifacts, categorizing objects into different time periods. Although the importance of studying archaeology decreased during the Cultural Revolution in the 1960s and 1970s, local and national governments have increased funding for preservation in the twenty-first century.* © CHRISTIE'S IMAGES/CORBIS

Sanxingdui in 1986 revealed a completely unknown civilization more than 3,000 years old in the Upper Yangzi Valley, raising many questions about Bronze Age archaeology in China. The temples and statues of a goddess, found in Hongshan in northeast China, illustrate local beliefs dating back more than 5,000 years, while the Liangzhu burials discovered in the Lower Yangzi Valley indicate the existence of segmental societies moving toward civilization (Yang Xiaoneng 1999). To date, the consensus is that Chinese civilization developed based on the interaction and integration of cultures spread across a vast area from northeast China to the Yellow and Yangzi river valleys. In other words, peoples living in different regions of ancient China all contributed to the origin and development of Chinese civilization.

**Heritage Conservation** In China, archaeological remains, monuments, and historical buildings are defined as *guwu* (antiquities) or *wenwu* (relics). After 1978 China adopted the concept of conserving its natural and cultural heritage (*yichan*), including archaeological sites and artifacts, as defined by the United Nations Educational, Scientific, and Cultural Organization (UNESCO) in its 1972 World Heritage Convention.

The UNESCO Convention was ratified by the People's Congress of China in 1985 (ICOMOS China 2002), producing significant impacts on both archaeology and archaeologists in China. In 1987 six heritage sites in China were entered on the UNESCO World Heritage list, four of which were archaeological sites. By 2008 twenty-six cultural, seven natural, and four combined cultural and natural heritage sites in China had been put on the list; many were archaeological sites or included significant archaeological elements.

In 1997 SACH decided to draw up technical guidelines for the conservation of China's cultural heritage, including archaeological sites. With the help of Australia ICOMOS (International Council on Monuments and Sites) and the Getty Conservation Institute in Los Angeles, the *China*

*Principles* were promulgated in 2002. The document adopts many ideas of the 1964 Venice Charter, an international charter for the conservation and restoration of monuments and sites, and the 1999 Australia ICOMOS Burra Charter for the conservation of places of cultural significance, but it proposes modified approaches to suit China's context (ICOMOS China 2002). The ratification of the UNESCO World Heritage Convention and the promulgation of the *China Principles* were important steps toward international standards and practices in the management of archaeological remains in China.

Consequently, Chinese archaeologists no longer focus solely on excavations and written reports. Many now work with scholars from other disciplines to design and implement management plans for archaeological sites and artifacts. In 2008 the Institute of Archaeology CASS set up a Conservation and Research Center of Cultural Heritage, dedicated to the conservation and management of archaeological remains (Institute of Archaeology CASS 2008). Archaeology in contemporary China has closely connected to heritage management.

**Leading Scholars** Many archaeologists contributed to the development of archaeology after 1949, among them Liang Siyong (1904–1954), Jia Lanpo (1908–2001), Pei Wenzhong (1904–1982), Su Bingqi (1909–1997), and Xia Nai (1910–1985).

Liang Siyong, the second son of Liang Qichao, obtained a masters degree in archaeology and anthropology from Harvard University, and returned to China to work at the Institute of History and Philology in the 1930s. His excavation at Hougang in the 1930s identified the cultural sequence from Yangshao, to Longshan, to the Shang dynasty (Xia Nai et al. 1985), thus establishing a chronology from the middle and late Neolithic to the Bronze Age in the Yellow River Valley. Liang also edited the first archaeological fieldwork report, *Chengziya*, in 1934. He fell ill with tuberculosis in the 1940s, but was appointed as the first deputy director of the Institute of Archaeology CASS from 1949 to 1954, and contributed to the establishment of the institute (Xia Nai et al. 1985).

The most important figure in the history of the institute is arguably Xia Nai, who was "the architect of Chinese archaeology" (Zhang Guangzhi 1986b, p. 442) from 1949 to 1985. Xia studied for his Ph.D. at University College London from 1935 to 1939. He returned to China in 1941 and worked at the Institute of History and Philology from 1943 to 1949. He was appointed the second deputy director of the Institute of Archaeology CASS in 1950, before becoming director in 1962 (Zhang Guangzhi 1986b). Xia shouldered the main responsibilities for the establishment, planning, and management of the institute for thirty-five years, and he made significant contributions to the study of the cultural dynamics between China and the West in ancient times, as well as to the Neolithic chronology of China.

As noted above, Pei Wenzhong discovered the first skullcap of Beijing man. He also made significant contributions to Paleolithic archaeology in China by studying stone artifacts found in Zhoukoudian and several other Paleolithic sites (Xia Nai et al. 1985).

Jia Lanpo was another leading scholar of Paleolithic archaeology. He was in charge of the excavation at Zhoukoudian from 1935 to the 1950s, discovering many more fossils. From the 1950s to the 1970s, he also conducted numerous excavations in the Yellow River Valley, establishing the Paleolithic chronology of this area (Xia Nai et al. 1985).

Su Bingqi received his tertiary education in mainland China, and taught in the Archaeology Department of Peking University from 1952 to 1982. Apart from training the next generation of archaeologists, his contributions include typological analysis of Bronze Age remains from the Yellow River Valley, and the analysis of eight regional clusters of Neolithic cultures in mainland China as illustrations of cultural diversity (Liu Li and Chen Xingcan 2001).

Other prominent scholars include: Su Bai, a specialist in the archeology of Buddhism who applied typological analysis to establish the chronology of grottoes in China; Yan Wenming, a leading scholar on the origin and development of agriculture and Neolithic cultures in China; and Lu Zun'e, who discovered several important Paleolithic sites and human fossils, including skulls found in Jinniushan and Nanjing. Lu also introduced use-wear analysis into China in the 1980s.

To summarize, before 1949 archaeologists in China mainly focused on Paleolithic, Neolithic, and Bronze Age archaeology, but since then they have expanded their research to include Buddhist archaeology and historic archaeology up to the Qing dynasty. In recent years, archeological specialization has grown to include zooarchaeology, radiocarbon dating, and many cross-disciplinary fields. Archaeology in twenty-first-century China is moving toward becoming a multidisciplinary field with diverse theoretical frameworks.

**SEE ALSO** *Archaeology and Western Explorers; Archaeology, Politics of; Liang Qichao.*

**BIBLIOGRAPHY**

Chen Xingcan. *Zhongguo shiqian kaoguxueshi yanjiu: 1895–1949* [A history of prehistoric archaeology in China from 1895–1949]. Beijing: Sanlian Book Press, 1997.

Gu Jiegang. *Gu shibian* [Analyzing ancient history]. Reprint. Shijiazhuang, PRC: Hebei Education Press, 2002.

ICOMOS China. *Principles for the Conservation of Heritage Sites in China (China Principles)*. Beijing: SACH, 2002. http://www.icomoschina.org.cn/download/ChinaPrinciples08.2004.pdf

Institute of Archaeology CASS. Wenhua Yichan Baohu Zhongxin Juxing le Guapai Yishi [The Establishment of the Cultural Heritage Conservation and Study Center]. 2008. http://www.kaogu.cn/cn/detail.asp?Productid=8603.

Li Ji (Li Chi). *Kaogu suotan* [Issues on archaeology]. Wuhan, PRC: Hubei Education Press, 1998.

Liu Li. *The Chinese Neolithic: Trajectories to Early States*. Cambridge, U.K.: Cambridge University Press, 2004.

Liu Li and Chen Xingcan. Archaeology of China. In *Encyclopedia of Archaeology: History and Discoveries*, ed. Tim Murray, Vol. 1, 315–333. Santa Barbara, CA: ABC-CLIO, 2001.

Liu Qingzhu, ed. *20shiji Zhongguo baixiang kaogu dafaxian* [100 major archaeological discoveries in the twentieth century in China). Beijing: China Social Sciences Press, 2002.

Liu Shiping and Meng Xianshi. *Dunhuang bainian* [One hundred years of Dunhuang]. Guangzhou, PRC: Guangdong Press, 2000.

Lu Liedan (Tracey L-D Lu). *The Transition from Foraging to Farming and the Origin of Agriculture in China*. Oxford: J. and E. Hedges, 1999.

Lu Liedan (Tracey L-D Lu). The Transformation of Academic Culture in Mainland Chinese Archaeology. *Asian Anthropology* 1 (2002): 117–152.

Qi Longwei. *Kaozhengxue jilin* [Collecting essays on *kaogzhengxue*]. Yangzhou, PRC: Guangling Bookshop, 2003.

State Administration of Cultural Heritage (SACH). *Zhonghua Renmin Gongheguo wenwu bowuguan shiye jishi 1949–1999* [Chronology of heritage and museum management in the People's Republic of China from 1949 to 1999]. Beijing: Cultural Relics Publishing House, 2002.

Wei Juxian. *Zhongguo kaoguxue shi* [A history of Chinese archaeology]. Shanghai: Commercial Press, 1936.

Xia Nai et al, eds. *Zhongguo kaoguxue da baike* [Encyclopedia of China's archaeology]. Beijing: Chinese Encyclopedia Press, 1985.

Xu Guansan. *Xinshixue 90 nian* [Ninety years of new historiography]. Hong Kong: Chinese University of Hong Kong Press, 1986.

Yang Xiaoneng, ed. *The Golden Age of Chinese Archaeology: Celebrated Discoveries from the People's Republic of China*. New Haven, CT: Yale University Press, 1999.

Zhang Guangzhi (Kwang-chih Chang). *The Archaeology of Ancient China*. 4th ed. New Haven, CT: Yale University Press, 1986a.

Zhang Guangzhi (Kwang-chih Chang). Xia Nai (1910–1985). *American Anthropologist* 88, 2 (1986b): 442–444.

***Tracey L-D Lu (Lu Liedan)***

## ARCHAEOLOGY, POLITICS OF

Politics and archaeology are inseparable, as the events of the last one hundred years in China confirm. Government-sponsored archaeological projects during the Republican period (1912–1949) were indirectly part of larger Guomingdang (GMD) efforts to control the territories of the former Qing empire and create a unified nation-state. After 1949, when the rapidity of archaeological finds outpaced independent interpretation and the development of critical methodological structures, internal political agendas forcefully shaped the study of material culture (Von Falkenhausen 1993). Scholars cite the close link between modern political agendas and the study of antiquities in the late nineteenth and twentieth centuries (Marchand 1996; Trigger 2006). Global enthusiasm for archaeological wonders paralleled colonial expansion and object acquisition in the Mediterranean, as well as in Africa, Latin America, and Asia during this period. In China, except for a few early excavations sponsored by the Smithsonian Institution (and the digs in Gansu Province by Johan Gunnar Andersson), archaeology was for the most part homegrown at its inception, pursued by Republican intellectuals whose cultural politics emerged out of a growing nationalism in the post–May Fourth (1919) period. Traditional conceptions of history and received wisdom were jettisoned in favor of what were perceived as neutral, Western-style scientific inquiries based on hard data acquired through fieldwork (Gu [1926–1941] 1982; Fu 1928).

The official beginning of large-scale archaeology was in late 1927 and early 1928 when Fu Sinian (1896–1950), the acting head of the newly established Institute of History and Philology, Academia Sinica (*Lishi yuyan yanjiusuo*), appointed Li Ji (1896–1979) head of the institute's archaeology section, and authorized Dong Zuobin (Tung Tso-pin, 1895–1963) to make test digs at Anyang, Henan Province (Fu Archives, December 20, 1928; Brown 2008). Very quickly, this area became the focus of almost all archaeological work in China for the next nine years. Fifteen campaigns unearthed oracle bones that represented some of the earliest written records, as well as ritual bronzes, jade, marble sculpture, and the remains of late Shang (twelfth to eleventh century BCE) palatial structures. In summer 1937 during the Japanese invasion this work came to a halt as abruptly as it had begun. The entire collection of archaeologically excavated materials, along with the contents of the National Museum (*Zhongyang Bowuguan*), historic documents from the dynastic period, and private libraries of archaeologists, were packed and shipped by boat, rail, and road to Guiyang, Changsha, Chengdu, and Chongqing (Fu Archives, August 30, 1938). The ensuing exodus of officials to the interior would occur in reverse almost ten years later in 1946, when the collections were sent back to the coast after the war. Ultimately, many of the objects and much of the data from the early archaeological research were shipped to Taiwan, where they remain today. The survival of these excavated materials and their wartime plight was likened at the time to the very survival and rebirth of Chinese culture.

Although state-sponsored archaeology had a limited run (less than a decade) before the major digs at Anyang were disbanded, the policies developed during these formative years were critical to the pursuit of archaeological activity for the remaining years of the twentieth century. First was the issue of regional versus central control.

***Buried terracotta figures dating to the third century* BCE*, Qin Terracotta Warriors and Horses Museum, Lintong, Shaanxi province.*** *First unearthed in 1974, this pit contains over 8,000 clay soldiers, all buried to protect the final resting place of Chinese emperor Qin Shi Huang. The figures have become known as the Terracotta Army, with each earthen soldier given unique facial features and full battle dress.* CHINA PHOTOS/GETTY IMAGES

Henan provincial officials regularly challenged the Academia Sinica's ownership of excavated objects from 1928 to 1937; at issue was whether a national entity superseded local authority. Even after agreements were signed, bold, extensive looting (sanctioned by local authorities) threatened the integrity of the excavations. Second were the issues of race, ethnicity and Han identity. In his 1923 Harvard University dissertation, Li Ji categorized China's ethnic groups and posited Han-centered origins of Chinese culture; the findings at the Anyang digs were to mirror his early theories (Li 1928). And, later, when Republican scholars of the Institute of History and Philology conducted ethnographic and linguistic surveys of the Southwest—where the Guomingdang government was based during the war—researchers were also concerned with creating a race- or ethnic-based theory of China's origins identifying cultures dependent on and inferior to a Han center in the Yellow River Valley. With an Anyang-centered, Yellow River heartland occupied by Han Chinese, the research agendas of archaeology, anthropology, and ethnography reinforced the age-old narrative of a distinct, superior Han imperial culture that controlled primitive frontier peoples in the Southwest and Northwest. Li's theories about the racial features of Anyang skeletons have since been discredited (Keightley 1978). Third, researchers were keen to locate China as a political entity in the ancient period with distinct cultural origins independent from Europe, Africa, or Mesopotamia. Excavating both Chengziya and Anyang, Liang Siyong (Liang Ssu-yung, 1904–1954) identified contiguous Neolithic and Bronze Age strata, which was used to dispel contemporary diffusionist models that world cultures emanated from one African or Mesopotamian source (Fu, Liang, et al. 1934). These three factors were immensely important to the strong links between Chinese archaeology, politics, and nationalism.

In the post-1949 period, despite the limited resources of the new state, archaeology received strong government support; and its scholars in turn promoted research that supported a unique Chinese cultural identity aimed at the international audience and a Marxist agenda applicable in domestic contexts, which emphasized the contributions of laboring classes in ancient production. Until the anti-rightist campaign in 1957, a handful of professional archaeologists, led in part by the British-trained Egyptologist Xia Nai (1910–1985), who later became the director of the all-powerful Institute of Archaeology (*Kaogu Yanjiusuo*), quickly trained hundreds of new archaeologists to do the cultural and political work of the nation. Materials, labs, and instruments were limited, but it was the weight of strict ideological expectations and restrictions on research questions, culminating in the iconoclasm of the Cultural Revolution period (1966–1976), that crippled archaeological work. No degrees in archaeology were awarded, and from 1966 to 1972 archaeological work was suspended (Von Falkenhausen 2004). Xia Nai's xenophobia deprived scholars of international exchange and the benefits of nonnative interpretive models (Tong 1995); his vehement rejection of foreign data and models was rooted in an essentialized notion of China's cultural purity and its technological independence during the ancient period. Yet, these three decades from 1949 to 1979, while dramatic and tumultuous, were also extremely productive. The spectacular finds of these early years, typified by the discovery of the Mawangdui tombs in 1972 and the Qinshihuang multi-pit tumulus in 1974, remain unmatched. Guo Moruo (1892–1978) promulgated the application of Maoist class struggle to archaeological analysis (Guo [1930] 1989); during this period most research followed a narrow Marxist conception of culture. And in the spirit of using the past to promote the present, Mao embraced comparisons to Qinshihuang and the First Emperor's efforts to unify disparate political entities into a unified state (Brook, Frolic 1997).

Ironically, the paradigm of ancient states leading teleologically to a unified country (as the Qin, est. 221 BCE) not only mirrored the contemporary (post-1949) political sweep toward a centralized socialist government, but also echoed pre-1949 theories about the primacy of the Yellow River Cultures as the locus of Chinese civilization (Tong 1995; Von Falkenhausen 1993). Not until the early 1980s, when a new, multicenter paradigm of interregional Neolithic cultures was advanced by Kwang-chih Chang (1931–2001) in the U.S. and Su Bingqi (1909–1997) in the PRC, did the theory of a sole geographical source of Chinese culture, which held sway for the first six decades of Chinese archaeology, begin to change (Von Falkenhausen 1997; Chang 1986, 2002). And, yet, the older model still continues to have its appeal at the highest levels (Li Xuejin 2002). Deng Xiaoping's relaxation of central control across regional centers in the early 1980s impacted archaeological models and new scholarly networks developed region-based research agendas (Von Falkenhausen 1995; Evasdottir 2004). But the lack of iron-fisted central control in the last two decades meant that looting was once again a serious problem.

**SEE ALSO** *Archaeology and Western Explorers; Archaeology, History of.*

## BIBLIOGRAPHY

Brook, Timothy, and B. M. Frolic. *Civil Society in China.* Armonk, NY: Sharpe, 1997.

Brown, Clayton D. Li Ji: The Father of Chinese Archaeology. *Orientations* 39, 3 (April 2008): 61–66.

Chang, Kwang-chih. *The Archaeology of Ancient China.* 4th ed. New Haven, CT: Yale University Press, 1986.

Chang, Kwang-chih. Reflections on Chinese Archaeology in the Second Half of the Twentieth Century. *Journal of East Asian Archaeology* 3, no. 1–2 (2002): 5–13.

Chen Xingcan. *Zhongguo shiqian kaoguxueshi yanjiu* [Research on the history of Neolithic archaeology]. Beijing: Sanlian, 1997.

Evasdottir, Erika. *Obedient Autonomy: Chinese Intellectuals and the Achievement of Orderly Life.* Vancouver: University of British Columbia Press, 2003.

Fu Sinian (Fu Ssu-nien). [The purpose of (our) work at the Institute of History and Philology]. Planning Meeting for the Institute of History and Philology, Academic Sinica. (Guangzhou, May Minguo 17 [1928]): 1–10.

Fu Sinian (Fu Ssu-nien), Liang Siyong (Liang Ssu-yung), et al. *Zhengziya: Shandong Lichengxian Longshanzhen zhi heiyao wenhua yizhi.* [Chengziya: Ruins of black pottery culture of Licheng County, Longshan Township, Shangdong Province]. Nanjing: Guoli zhongyang yanjiuyuan lishi yuyan yanjiusuo. Minguo 23 (1934).

Fu Ssu-nien Archives. Archives of the Institute of History and Philology. Fu Ssu-nien Library, Academia Sinica, Taibei, Taiwan.

Gu Jiegang. *Gushi bian* [Symposium on ancient history]. [1926–1941]. Beijing: Pushe, 1982.

Guo Moruo. *Zhongguo Gudai Shehui Yanjiu* [Research on ancient Chinese society]. 1930. Shanghai: Shanghai Shudian, 1989.

Keightley, David N. Review of Li Chi, *Anyang. Journal of Asian Studies* 38, no. 1 (November 1978): 171–173.

Ledderose, Lothar. Aesthetic Appropriation of Ancient Calligraphy in Modern China. In *Modern Expressions*, ed. Judith Smith and Maxwell Hearn, 212–245. New York: Metropolitan Museum of Art, 2001.

Li Chi. *Formation of the Chinese People, an Anthropological Inquiry*. Cambridge, MA: Harvard University Press, 1928.

Li Chi. *Anyang*. Seattle: University of Washington Press, 1977.

Li Xueqin. The Xia-Shang-Zhou Chronology Project: Methodology and Results. Trans. Sarah Allan. *Journal of East Asian Archaeology* 4, no. 1–4 (2002): 321–333.

Marchand, Suzanne L. *Down from Olympus: Archaeology and Philhellenism in Germany, 1750–1970*. Princeton, NJ: Princeton University Press, 1996.

Tong, Enzheng. Thirty Years of Chinese Archaeology (1949–1979). In *Nationalism, Politics, and the Practice of Archaeology*, ed. Philip L. Kohl and Clare Fawcett, 177–197. Cambridge, U.K.: Cambridge University Press, 1995.

Trigger, Bruce G. *A History of Archaeological Thought*. 2nd ed. Cambridge, U.K.: Cambridge University Press, 2006.

Von Falkenhausen, Lothar. On the Historiographical Orientation of Chinese Archaeology. *Antiquity* 67 (1993): 839–849.

Von Falkenhausen, Lothar. The Regionalist Paradigm in Chinese Archaeology. In *Nationalism, Politics, and the Practice of Archaeology*, ed. Philip L. Kohl and Clare Fawcett, 198–217. Cambridge, U.K.: Cambridge University Press, 1995.

Von Falkenhausen, Lothar. Obituary, Su Binggqi. *Artibus Asiae* 57, no. 3–4 (1997): 365–366.

Von Falkenhausen, Lothar. Obituary, Yu Weichao. *Artibus Asiae* 64, no. 2 (2004): 295–312.

*Sarah E. Fraser*

# ARCHITECTURE, HISTORIOGRAPHY OF, SINCE 1800

Although China has a long tradition of architecture, until 1929 scholars interested in architectural history focused on the terminology of ancient texts, anecdotes associated with buildings, and the locations of certain places in a city. In 1929 the Zhongguo Yingzao Xueshe (Institute for Research in Chinese Architecture) was established. By 1945, when the society was disbanded, its researchers had investigated 2,783 buildings scattered in more than 190 counties in China and had produced measured drawings for 206 of them. Yet the society's work was not merely positivist records of its investigations but also an effort to legitimate Chinese architecture in the modern global context.

## WESTERN PERSPECTIVES

Chinese architecture entered the purview of the West in the seventeenth century. At one time the Chinese paradigm was admired by Western patrons and architects, as reflected in the chinoiserie designs of the mid-eighteenth century. In most of the following century, however, especially after China was defeated by Britain in the Opium War of 1839–1842, its architecture fell into disrepute in the dominant narratives of architectural history. For instance, in his influential *History of Indian and Eastern Architecture* (1876), James Fergusson described Chinese architecture as an enigma because it lacked the monuments of Western architecture. He commented, "There really are no buildings in the country worthy of the people or their civilization." He praised this architecture for its polychromy, although he commented,

> The Chinese are the only people who now employ polychromy as an essential part of their architecture; so much so, that colour is with them far more essential than form; and certainly the result is so singularly pleasing and satisfactory, that for the lower grades of art it is hardly doubtful that it should always be so. It is almost as certain that, for the higher grades of art, colour, though most valuable as an accessory, is incapable of the same lofty power of expression which form conveys to the human mind. (p. 688)

Banister Fletcher, in the fourth edition of his influential *History of Architecture on the Comparative Method* (1901), positioned Chinese architecture in the category of "non-historical styles," echoing Hegel's term "unhistorical history," which the latter applied to China and India because he saw no development, by which he meant increase in rationality, over time.

## A JAPANESE PERSPECTIVE

In East Asia the Japanese architectural historian Itō Chūta first questioned both Western scholars' Eurocentric views of Chinese architecture. He argued in his book *Shina kenchiku shi* (A history of Chinese architecture, 1925) that Eastern architecture was a system parallel to Western architecture. Within this system, Chinese architecture, the only living tradition so unique that it deserves people's admiration, influenced a broad area inhabited by one-third of the world's population. Itō's work was an effort to justify Chinese architecture in the global context and to legitimate its Japanese derivation.

## THE REVIVAL OF TRADITIONAL CHINESE ARCHITECTURE

Zhu Qiqian (1872–1964), former minister of the interior of the Beiyang government in the early Republic of China, established the Zhongguo Yingzao Xueshe in 1919 after his discovery of *Yingzao fashi* (Building methods, 1103), a Song dynasty treatise on building construction that he reprinted in 1925. This was a time of fundamental change in Chinese social and intellectual history. On the one hand, the devastation of World War I disillusioned Chinese who had taken Western civilization as the model of progress and made them more conscious than ever of Chinese identity in the quest for modernization. On the other hand, the New Culture Movement, which started in 1916, set the task of revaluating Chinese culture in light of science and global culture during China's modernization. Liang Qichao, an advocate of reform, proposed a "cultural history" of China, to include Chinese architectural history, as a means of revolutionizing traditional dynastic histories. Hu Shi, a central figure in the New Culture Movement, advocated ordering the national heritage (*zhengli guogu*), which in literature and history studies meant punctuating, paragraphing, and annotation ancient texts so that they could better serve China's modernization. The work of the Zhongguo Yingzao Xueshe reflected the ideals of both Liang and Hu.

Key scholars of the Zhongguo Yingzao Xueshe were Liang Sicheng (1901–1972), the eldest son of Liang Qichao; Liu Dunzhen (1897–1968); and Liang's wife Lin Huiyin (1904–1955). Liang and Lin graduated from the University of Pennsylvania in 1927; Liu graduated from Tōkyō Kogei Daigaku (Tokyo Polytechnic Institute) in 1921. They combined textual study with modern archaeological methods of carrying out extensive field research on the remains of Chinese architecture from the 1930s to 1940s, even during the Second Sino-Japanese War (1937–1945). Their fieldwork enabled them to interpret the terms and construction methods elaborated in *Yingzao fashi*, as well as in the Qing-dynasty treatise *Gongcheng zuofa zeli* (Construction methods, 1723), and further, to discover the structural and stylistic characteristics of formal Chinese architecture in different dynasties. With the assistance of Lin and other colleagues, Liang published his findings in *Zhongguo jianzhu shi* (A history of Chinese architecture, 1985) and *A Pictorial History of Chinese Architecture* (1984). The complete collection of his academic works, including his annotations of Song and Qing construction manuals, was published in 2001. Liu published extensively in the society's journal, and the complete collection of his academic works was published in 2007.

## DIALOG WITH THE WEST

Because of their American educational background, Liang and Lin were more cognizant of Western scholarship and engaged more in dialog with it. In their writings they argued first that the frame structure was an essential structural characteristic of Chinese architecture, one that it shared with Gothic architecture as well as modern international-style architecture. Second, the bracket-arm set (*dougong*) was a basic module in Chinese architectural design, playing a role similar to that of the order in Greco-Roman architecture. Third, some unique features of Chinese architecture, such as the bracket-arm set and the concave roof, were created for functional purposes. Fourth, as identified with reference to J. J. Winckelmann's description of Greek art, Chinese architecture developed from the vigorous style of the Tang (618–907) and Liao (916–1125) dynasties, to the elegant style of the Song (960–1279) and Yuan (1279–1368) dynasties, to the rigid style of the Ming (1368–1644) and Qing (1644–1911) dynasties. Whether a structure accurately represented a style could be a criterion for dating that structure.

By drawing similarities between Chinese architecture and both Greco-Roman architecture and Gothic architecture, Liang and Lin showed that Chinese architecture was as great a system as its Western counterparts. Emphasizing the structural rationality of Chinese architecture, they disproved Fergusson's notion that polychromy was more essential to it than form, and legitimated the modern revival of Chinese architecture. By delineating a progression parallel to Western classical architecture, they also disproved Fletcher's notion that Chinese architecture is nonhistorical. It is also worth noting that neither Liang, Lin, nor Liu discuss in their writings the significance of geomancy (*fengshui*), which the American architect Henri K. Murphy, known for his "adaptive architecture," regarded as an essential characteristic of Chinese architecture.

From 1929 on, the society was absorbed into the national academic-research system. This is reflected directly in the sources of funding for this organization from two official organizations: the China Foundation for the Promotion of Education and Culture (Zhonghua Jiaoyu Wenhua Jijin) and the Board of Trustees for the Administration of the Indemnity Funds Remitted by the British Government (Zhong-Ying Gengkuan Dongshihui). The new mission of the society included the work of the Central Committee for the Protection of Monuments (Zhongyang Guji Baoguan Weiyuanhui). After 1939 the society was funded directly by the Ministries of Education and of Finance. Its personnel became affiliated with the Institute of History and Philology of Academia Sinica (Zhongyang Yanjiu Yuan) and the Preparatory Office of the National Central Museum (Guoli Zhongyang Bowuyuan). The findings of its expeditions became part of the museum's documentary project on Chinese architecture. Up until 1944 membership in the society included not only people from the finance sector and architects interested in the revival of Chinese architecture, but also officials involved with Chinese cultural affairs. Liang Sicheng was elected as a member of Academic Sinica in 1948; Liu Dunzhen became dean of the Engineering School of National Central University in 1945. Thus by the 1940s research on Chinese architectural history had become an integral part of the official task of cultural reconstruction.

### MARXIST HISTORY OF ARCHITECTURE

After 1949 the study of Chinese architectural history, like other areas of the humanities and social sciences, was put under the guidance of Marxism. In 1959 the Institute of Building Science (Jianzhu Kexue Yanjiuyuan) of the National Construction Committee started writing an official textbook of Chinese architectural history, *Zhongguo gudai jianzhu shi* (A history of traditional Chinese architecture), with Liu Dunzhen, who had distanced himself from Liang Sicheng by criticizing Liang's "idealism" in 1955, as chief editor. Through eight revisions, the book was completed in 1964, but its publication was delayed by the Cultural Revolution and its aftermath until 1980. The narration of the book follows the chronological sequence of Chinese history from the "primitive period" (chapter 1); to the "slave period" (chapter 2), encompassing the Shang dynasty (sixteenth century–1046 BCE) and Zhou (1046–256 BCE) dynasties; to the "feudal period" (chapters 3–7), encompassing the dynasties from the Qin (221–206 BCE) to Qing (1644–1911). Though the core historical data in the book were the result of the Zhongguo Yingzao Xueshe research and the evolution of Chinese architecture is still delineated by styles, the book categorizes structures into such types as cities, palaces, dwellings and gardens, Buddhist temples and pagodas, and mausoleums to highlight the influence of political, social, and cultural changes on architecture. This typological narrative is continued by a considerably expanded five-volume work with the same title, coauthored by Liang and Liu's students Liu Xujie, Fu Xinian, Guo Daiheng, Pan Guxi, and Sun Dazhang, and published from 2001 to 2003.

**SEE ALSO** *Hu Shi; Liang Qichao; Liang Sicheng; Lin Huiyin.*

**BIBLIOGRAPHY**

Fairbank, Wilma. *Liang and Lin: Partners in Exploring China's Architectural Past.* Philadelphia: University of Pennsylvania Press, 1994.

Fu Xinian, Guo Daiheng, Liu Xujie, et al. *Chinese Architecture.* Trans. and ed. Nancy Steinhardt. New Haven, CT: Yale University Press, 2002.

Itō Chūta. *Shina kenchiku shi* [A history of Chinese architecture]. Tokyo: Yūzankaku, 1931.

Lai Delin. Liang Sicheng, Lin Huiyin: Zhongguo jianzhushi xiezuo biaowei [A historiographical study of Liang Sicheng and Lin Huiyin's writings on Chinese architectural history]. *Ershiyi shiji* 64 (April 2001): 90–99.

Li, Shiqiao. Writing a Modern Chinese Architectural History: Liang Sicheng and Liang Qichao. *Journal of Architectural Education* 56 (2002): 35–45.

Liang Sicheng. *Liang Sicheng quanji* [The complete works of Liang Sicheng]. Beijing: Zhongguo Jianzhu Gongye Chubanshe, 2001–2007.

Lin Zhu. *Koukai Lu Ban de damen: Zhongguo Yingzao Xueshe shilüe* [Opening the gate of Lu Ban: A brief history of the Society for Research in Chinese Architecture]. Beijing: Zhongguo Jianzhu Gongye Chubanshe, 1995.

Liu Dunzhen. *Liu Dunzhen quanji* [The complete works of Liu Dunzhen]. Beijing: Zhongguo Jianzhu Gongye Chubanshe, 2007.

Liu Dunzhen, ed. *Zhongguo gudai jianzhu shi* [A history of traditional Chinese architecture]. Beijing: 1980.

Steinhardt, Nancy. China: Designing the Future, Venerating the Past. *Journal of the Society of Architectural Historians* 61, 4 (December 2002): 537–548.

Steinhardt, Nancy. The Tang Architectural Icon and the Politics of Chinese Architectural History. *Art Bulletin* 136, 2 (June 2004): 228–255.

Zhao Chen. "Minzu zhuyi" yu "gudian zhuyi": Liang Sicheng jianzhu lilun tixi de maodunxing yu beijuxing zhi fenxi [Nationalism and classicism: An analysis of the contradiction and tragedy of Liang Sicheng's architectural theory]. In *Zhongguo jindai jianzhu yanjiu yu baohu*, ed. Zhang Fuhe, vol. 2, 77–86. Beijing: Qinghua Daxue Chubanshe, 2001.

**Delin Lai**

# ARCHITECTURE, HISTORY OF

*This entry contains the following:*



## ARCHITECTURE TO 1949

The modern transformation of Chinese architecture initiated from China's communications with the West, first in the sixteenth century when Portuguese merchants and missionaries arrived in Macau, then in the eighteenth century when Italian Jesuits were hired as artists and architects by the Manchu court, and ultimately in the nineteenth century when China was forced to open to the West after the Opium War of 1839–1842. These interactions brought to China new architectural types, styles, and technologies. However, the discipline of architecture did not become a part of the Chinese modern system of knowledge until the early twentieth century. After signing the humiliating Boxer Protocol in 1901, the Qing government launched a series of reforms that included urban renewal campaigns in Beijing and other cities. Construction of Western-style office buildings and privately owned shops were symbols of modernity. Architecture was also listed as a course in Chinese higher-education curriculums issued by the Qing court in 1902, though study required a knowledge of Japanese. The first modern Chinese architectural book, *Jianzhu xinfa* (*New Methods of Architecture,* also known in English as *Building Construction*), was written by Zhang Yingxu, a Japanese-trained mechanical engineer, and published in 1910 (Lai 2007).

The Qing dynasty was overthrown in 1912, but the modernization of Chinese architecture continued. Before the emergence of Chinese architects, however, it was civil engineers who played the role of building designers. The fact that China had no less than four departments of civil engineering in universities by 1911 indicates that building construction as a science had formed in China in the first decade of the twentieth century. In the 1910s, indigenous architects started businesses in such cities as Shanghai, and an increasing number of Western-trained Chinese architects returned home. They introduced to China a new concept of architecture as the combination of science and art. The first department of architecture in Chinese higher education was established in 1923 by two Japanese-trained architects at the Jiangsu Provincial Polytechnic Institute in Suzhou. Before the Second Sino-Japanese War, which started in 1937, China had departments of architecture at the National Central University in Nanjing, the National Northeastern University in Shenyang (discontinued in 1931 when the Japanese army occupied the city), the National Beijing University in Beijing, and the Provincial Xiangqin University in Guangzhou. The Chinese Society of Architects, the core organization of Chinese architects, was established in Shanghai in 1927. It enabled the profession to uphold a consistent standard. By 1940 the society had 41 American-trained architects, including 16 graduated from the University of Pennsylvania, among its 82 members, together with 5 who had returned from France, 4 from Britain, 4 from Germany, 2 from Belgium, 1 from Japan, and 25 trained in China. These numbers demonstrate the strong influence on modern Chinese architecture not only of the United States but also of the École des Beaux Arts in Paris, which was the dominant force in architectural education worldwide when those Chinese were students in college. Architectural journals, such as *Zhongguo Jianzhu* (The Chinese architect) and *Jianzhu Yuekan* (The builder), also emerged and fostered the evolution of professional knowledge (Lai 2007).

The 1920s was also a period of surging nationalism in China. The Nationalist government consciously put architecture on the agenda of modern state-building. During the 1920s and 1930s the central government and local governments organized several large architectural competitions, including those for the Sun Yat-sen Mausoleum in Nanjing (1925–1931, won by Lü Yanzhi), the Sun Yat-sen Memorial Auditorium in Guangzhou (1926–1931, won by Lü Yanzhi), the National Library in Beijing (1926, won by V. Leth-Moller & Co.), the Greater Shanghai Plan (1930–1931, won by Zhao Shen, redesigned by Dong Dayou), the National Central Museum in Nanjing (1935–1948, won by Su, Yang & Lei Architects, revised by Liang Sicheng), and the headquarters of the Guangdong provincial government (1936, won by Robert Fan, not constructed). These competitions were mainly for three categories of projects: commemorative structures, government office buildings, and buildings for public education. Without exception, the judges selected Chinese-style designs, thereby encouraging a classical revival in Chinese architecture.

The design of the Sun Yat-sen Mausoleum, the most important monument in the Republic of China, combined Western technology with the Chinese architectural tradition. It also referred to such Western models as the tomb of Napoleon and the Lincoln Memorial as models. Moreover, its bell-shaped site plan conveyed the symbolism of awakening China. It thus embodies the ideals of the founding father of the Republic of China for a modern nation. (Lai 2005).

Yang Tingbao was an eminent student of Paul Philippe Cret and arguably the most productive Chinese architect of his time. His works are of remarkable stylistic diversity, and they demonstrate a consistent pursuit of proportional excellence in the Beaux-Arts tradition. The Communication Bank of Beijing (1930) and the Central Archives of the KMT (Nanjing, 1934) are his two representative works. They revealed his effort of using the Beaux-Arts principle of proportion to codify the designs of a Chinese style (Lai 2007).

It is also worth noting that this "Chinese revival" was initiated by Western church architects in the late nineteenth century, when Christian churches, facing the anti-foreignism of Chinese society, sought an indigenous approach. Among numerous examples of this style is the St. Joseph Cathedral in Guiyang, which was designed by an unknown architect under the patronage of French Catholics in 1876. Its east façade is in the form of a Chinese commemoration arch, and the bell tower adjacent to its west façade a Buddhist pagoda. This design was thus one of the earliest efforts to create an architecture that would combine Western function with a Chinese style in general, and Christianity with Confucianism and Buddhism in particular.

The American architect Henry K. Murphy was one of the most important architects of the Chinese Revival architecture. His works included Jinling (Ginling) College for Girls in Nanjing (1918–1923) and Yanjing (Yenching) University in Beijing (1919–1926), both run by American missionaries (Cody 2001). Murphy's design showed "frankness of construction" and "lavish use of gorgeous color," two of the main characteristics of Chinese architecture he highlighted. This suggested the influence of Western architectural aesthetics of the nineteenth century, such as structural

**Sun Yat-sen Memorial Hall, Guangzhou, completed in 1931.** *After the fall of the Qing dynasty, China experienced a renewed sense of national pride as citizens sought to modernize the country. Many public building projects completed during this time feature traditional Chinese elements, such as multi-leveled sweeping roofs, as seen in this picture of the Sun Yat-sen Memorial Hall in Guangzhou.* © LIU LIQUN/CORBIS

rationalism and Gottfried Semper's view of polychromy. His application of the Qing dynasty's official style of architecture as the model of the revivalist design also influenced some Chinese architects, including Lü Yanzhi and Dong Dayou, the designer of the governmental headquarters of greater Shanghai, both of whom had worked for him before practicing on their own. Murphy also helped the Nationalist government in planning Guangzhou (1926) and Nanjing (1928).

The search for a Chinese style of modern architecture accompanied the study of Chinese architectural history. The Institute for Research in Chinese Architecture was established in 1929. The key historians included Liang Sicheng, his wife Lin Huiyin, and Liu Dunzhen. By 1945, when the society disbanded, its researchers had investigated 2,783 buildings scattered in more than 190 counties and had produced measured drawings for 206 of them (Lin 1995). In evaluating Chinese architecture, they used the principle of structural rationalism, which had been widely applied in architectural criticism of classical and Gothic architecture since the nineteenth century and was still popular in criticism of the modernist architecture of the 1930s. Their writings on Chinese architecture can thus be seen not only as a record of their investigations but also as an effort to authenticate Chinese architecture in a global and modern context. The National Central Museum in Nanjing, which Liang participated in designing in 1935, reflected Liang's ideal for a renaissance of Chinese architecture. Its language came from the most vigorous period of Chinese culture, which were the Tang, Liao, and Northern Song dynasties, and referenced the aesthetics of Western classical and modernist architecture (Lai 2007).

Besides Chinese revival architecture, popular in buildings of Christian universities and Chinese governmental headquarters, modern architecture (the architectural styles of Art Deco, Art Moderne, and International Style) also became influential after the early 1930s, especially in foreign-controlled cities or settlements, including Hong Kong, Dalian, and Shanghai. These styles have been popular in commercial architecture, specifically in hotels, cinemas, ballrooms, banks, and hospitals. Modernist principles, including those of the International Style, were also introduced to China after 1933. They formed a challenging force against revivalist architecture (Lai 2007). However, the Second Sino-Japanese War (1937–1945) and the civil war (1946–1949) that followed retarded the development of modern Chinese architecture. Only Beiping (Beijing), the wartime capital Chongqing, and the Japanese-occupied territories, such as Taiwan and the cities in the northeastern provinces, received relatively large-scale municipal construction.

**SEE ALSO** *Gardens and Parks; Liang Sicheng; Lin Huiyin.*

**BIBLIOGRAPHY**

Cody, Jeffrey W. *Building in China: Henry K. Murphy's "Adaptive Architecture," 1914–1935*. Hong Kong: Chinese University Press, 2001.

Gong Deshun, Zou Denong, and Dou Yide. *Zhongguo xiandai jianzhu shigang* [An outline of modern Chinese architectural history]. Tianjin: Tianjin Kexue Jishu Chubanshe, 1989.

Lai, Delin. Searching for a Modern Chinese Monument: The Design of the Sun Yat-sen Mausoleum in Nanjing. *Journal of the Society of Architectural Historians* 64, 1 (March 2005): 22–55.

Lai, Delin. *Zhongguo jindai jianzhushi yanjiu* [Studies in the history of modern Chinese architecture]. Beijing: Qinghua Daxue Chubanshe, 2007.

Lin, Zhu. *Koukai Lu Ban de damen—Zhongguo Yingzao Xueshe shilüe* [Opening the gate of Lu Ban: A brief history of the Society for Research in Chinese Architecture]. Beijing: Zhongguo Jianzhu Gongye Chubanshe, 1995.

Rowe, Peter G., and Seng Kuan. *Architectural Encounters with Essence and Form in Modern China*. Cambridge, MA: MIT Press, 2002.

***Delin Lai***

## ARCHITECTURE, 1949–1979

Chinese architecture after 1949 is often divided into the following periods according to the prevailing socioeconomic conditions and political dictates: 1949–1952, modernism with socialist characteristics; 1953–1957, Soviet influence; 1958–1964, the Ten Great Constructions of Beijing; and finally 1965–1979, construction dogmatism during the decade of the Cultural Revolution.

### MODERNISM WITH SOCIALIST CHARACTERISTICS, 1949–1952

During the first years of the People's Republic, private practices continued to operate along with the newly established state design institutes. Architects had a relatively free hand. This was partly because there was as yet no party line on architecture and planning, most cadres being unacquainted with design and construction issues. Boxy modernist structures were common, thus continuing a trend from the 1930s and 1940s. To address the acute housing shortage in cities such as Beijing and Shanghai, slums were cleared and replaced with vast residential estates called "workers' new villages." Phase 1 of Caoyang New Village in Shanghai, for instance, consisted of 4,000 small studio apartments. The two- and three-story buildings were grouped along a creek. The informal, organic plan was influenced by the garden-city model. Although most workers' new villages were designed to minimum standards, public and institutional buildings showed remarkable refinement and ingenuity.

Wuhan Hospital (1952–1955) and Beijing Children's Hospital (1952–1954) were the works of the Austrian-trained Feng Jizhong (b. 1915) and the French-trained Hua Lanhong (b. 1912), respectively. While both architects designed from within to meet the functional needs of the modern hospital, they handled the massing and the details—the fenestration and the chimney and water tower in the case of Hua's children's hospital—with considerable deftness. Other well-known modernist examples from the period include the Bauhaus-influenced Wenyuan Building (1953–1954) on the campus of Tongji University in Shanghai and the ensemble of twelve agricultural-exhibition pavilions (1951) in Guangzhou. The former was designed by the twenty-six-year-old Huang Yulin (1927–1953), whose promising career was cut short by cancer, and Ha Xiongwen (1907–1981), and the latter by about ten architects under the direction of the Guangzhou Municipal Construction and Planning Commission. The most imaginative of the exhibition pavilions were perhaps those devoted to aquatic and forestry products. The aquatic pavilion, the work of Xia Changshi (1903–1996), who had been schooled in Germany, featured a circular inner courtyard around a fountain. Moored to the right of the entrance appeared a playful, boat-shaped, quasi-expressionist structure. In the forestry pavilion, by Tan Tiansong (1901–1971), the recessed central bay was almost entirely glazed. Two slim columns running through the upper part and the marquee lent vertical emphasis to the entrance hall. The two shorter wings consisted of two vertically and horizontally staggered boxes with Γ-shaped ribbon windows. The overall abstract, geometric composition of the facade of this modest building suggested ever so subtly the multi-trunked, luxuriant banyan tree, ubiquitous in subtropical Guangdong.

## SOVIET INFLUENCE AND NATIONAL STYLE, 1953–1957

With the launch of the First Five-Year Plan came Soviet funding, Soviet blueprints, Soviet experts, and Soviet dogmas. Structuralism, formalism, and cosmopolitanism were out; socialist content in national form was in. Modernist experiments thus effectively came to an end, although a few modest structures that combined function and regional character were allowed. Ironically, some of the most iconic classic motifs of the national style (*minzu fengge*) came straight from China's feudal palace architecture. The dominant building type consisted of bombastic and extremely wasteful government buildings. The new socialist architecture in fact differed little from the official architecture of the 1930s and 1940s under the defeated Nationalist government, except in scale. The designs of these typically huge buildings were sometimes modified from preexisting plans to conform to the orthodox national style. The Friendship Hotel in Beijing, for example, recycled the design of the Xinqiao Hotel but added a double-eaved hip and gable roof. The forbidding group of central-ministry buildings, the so-called Four Ministries and State Planning Commission complex, likewise evolved from a simpler design. The architect, Zhang Kaiji (1912–2006), topped the buildings with traditional Chinese-style big roofs at the insistence of the Soviet advisers.

Away from Beijing, a small number of attempts at regionalism stood in marked contrast to the high-profile government buildings in the capital. The Lu Xun Memorial Museum in Shanghai (1956), by the veteran architect Chen Zhi (1902–2002), is an unassuming structure with white-washed walls, black unglazed roof tiles, and "horse-head" gables, all characteristics of the architecture of this celebrated writer's native place. Another modest project, the Faculty and Staff Club at Tongji University, was animated by a flowing spatial disposition that adroitly dealt with a complex building program. Instead of an imposing central facade, the club's informal elevation and plan had the intimate feel of a vernacular house.

## THE TEN GREAT CONSTRUCTIONS AND STRUCTURAL EXPERIMENTS, 1958–1964

The so-called Ten Great Constructions of Beijing were jump-started in 1958 in preparation for the tenth anniversary of the People's Republic of China. The Great Hall of the People, the Museums of Chinese Revolution and Chinese History, the Chinese People's Military Museum, the Beijing Train Station, the Beijing Workers Stadium, the National Agricultural Exhibition Hall, the Diaoyutai State Guest House, the Nationalities Cultural Palace, and the Overseas Chinese Building were completed within a year, reflecting the Great Leap Forward, then in full swing. Thousands of architects in Beijing and from other cities participated. More than four hundred proposals were submitted for the Ten Great Constructions, including a version from Tongji University advocating "transparency" and "democracy," symbolized by glass-curtain walls for the Great Hall of the People. The prominent architectural historian and planner Liang Sicheng (1901–1972) put forward a set of criteria for evaluating the design proposals, with Chinese and modern at the top and Western and archaic at the bottom. In the end, all ten built structures were monumental in scale, with squat horizontal masses projecting power and authority in a blend of Beaux Arts and classical Chinese styles. Liang criticized the design of the Great Hall of the People by Zhang Bo (1911–1999), a former student, as both Western and archaic.

Tiananmen Square also took its present shape during this period. The 1958 planning guidelines for Beijing called for expanding and completing the transformation of the former Imperial-City domain before the Gate of Heavenly Peace into one of the world's largest public squares. In the center a new Monument to the People's Heroes, designed by Liang Sicheng, was prominently aligned along the central axis of old imperial Beijing. Two enormous structures, the Great Hall of the People and the Museums of Chinese Revolution and Chinese History, flank the square on the west and east. The 1,640-foot-wide, 2,822-foot-long, 18.8-square-mile square was not without its critics. Liang himself characterized the proposal as beyond human scale. Six Shanghai-based architects put their names to a joint letter to Premier Zhou Enlai voicing their concern that the square would become a vast desert. These criticisms, however, did not prevent the radical remaking of Tiananmen. The addition of Chairman Mao's Mausoleum in 1977 in the center of the square made it even more politically charged.

The disastrous emphasis on speed and scale during the Great Leap Forward did give rise to a few structurally innovative buildings. For instance, Tongji University's main dining hall (1962), which doubled as an auditorium, was clearly adapted from Pier Luigi Nervi's Palazzetto dello Sport in Rome. Like the Italian architect's famous design for the 1960's Olympic Games, the Tongji dining hall included a continuous ribbon of window under the roof. A 184-foot-long barrel vault of ferroconcrete pans, a technique pioneered by Nervi, replaced his shallow dome at the indoor stadium. The 52,530-square-foot facility at Tongji could accommodate 3,300 people for dining and 5,000 for performances and meetings.

The designs of sports stadiums in Beijing and Zhejiang, a train station in Fuzhou, an airport in Chengdu, and other predominantly utilitarian structures were also driven mainly by function and economy. Fascinating experiments in modernism took place in overseas projects financed by the Chinese government, but they were little known at home.

***Great Hall of the People, Tiananmen Square, Beijing, c. 1990.*** *To celebrate the tenth anniversary of the People's Republic of China, government officials planned the construction of one significant building for each year of the country's existence. The Great Hall of the People, home to National People's Congress, serves not only as a legislative building but also a site for prominent state events, including U.S. President Richard Nixon's 1972 visit to Beijing.* © JOSEPH SOHM/VISIONS OF AMERICA/CORBIS

In Ulaanbaatar, Mongolia, for instance, the hotel, department store, and apartment buildings by Gong Deshun (b. 1923) were all elegant, well-proportioned, boxy modernist structures.

## THE CULTURAL REVOLUTION, CONSTRUCTION DOGMATISM, AND EXPLORATIONS IN REGIONALISM, 1965–1979

In March 1966 the Chinese Society of Architects met in Yan'an. The theme of the conference was how to "foreground politics" and "revolutionize" architecture. The responses were iconographic references to Cultural Revolutionary encomiums about Chairman Mao and the Chinese revolution. Torches and solar representations abounded in new constructions, particularly in ceremonial structures such as the exhibition halls of Mao Zedong Thought. The upper corners of the exhibition hall in Changsha, the capital of Chairman Mao's home province Hunan, were topped by ornaments of torch flames flanking a sculptural program of flapping red flags and a portrait of Chairman Mao against an aureole background (Chairman Mao, the Red Sun). The Guangdong Exhibition Hall next to a revolutionary shrine, the Guangdong Peasants Lecture Hall (Guangdong Nongmin Jiangxi Suo), likewise resorted to a decorative scheme of torches and solar motifs, extending all the way to the lamp posts, the wrought-iron fence, and, most prominently, the facade, which featured a gigantic torch flame atop a huge plinth. The composition thus graphically represented Chairman Mao's saying, "A single spark can start a prairie fire."

Along with politicization was construction dogmatism over a technique called rammed dry earth (*gandalei*), first made popular at the Daqing oilfields. This simple and economical method was used extensively in worker housing. It quickly became politically orthodox nationwide, along with the rest of the Daqing model, regardless of local conditions. Even in industrial construction, rammed dry earth became obligatory.

Compared with declamatory buildings laden with political symbolism, explorations in regionalism were less conspicuous but all the more significant. Particularly remarkable are the Mineral Spring Resort Hotel (1972–1974) and the Children's Palace (Shaonian Gong, 1965) both in Guangzhou. The hotel sensitively reinterpreted traditional Chinese garden architecture using modern materials and construction techniques. The Children's Palace used inexpensive local materials and regional styles in a straightforward modern manner. Other noteworthy examples of regional modernism—the Ethnographic Museum (1978) and the Ministry of Post and Telecommunications' Sanatorium in Guilin—can be found in neighboring Guangxi Province.

With the repudiation of the Cultural Revolution in 1976 and the policy reform and opening up to the outside world adopted at the 1979 Third Plenum of the Tenth Congress of the Chinese Communist Party, Chinese architecture entered a new chapter, influenced by myriad new ideas and trends.

**SEE ALSO** *Architecture, Historiography of, since 1800; Art, History of: since 1949; Liang Sicheng.*

**BIBLIOGRAPHY**

Rowe, Peter, and Seng Kuan. *Architectural Encounters with Essence and Form in Modern China*. Cambridge, MA: MIT Press, 2002.

Shi, Yaohua. Reconstructing Modernism: The Shifting Narratives of Chinese Modernist Architecture. *Modern Chinese Literature and Culture* 18, 1 (Spring 2006): 30–84.

Wu, Hung. *Remaking Beijing: Tiananmen Square and the Creation of a Political Space*. Chicago: University of Chicago Press, 2005.

Zou Denong. *Zhongguo xiandai jianzhu shi* [A history of modern Chinese architecture]. Tianjin: Tianjin Kexue Jishu Chubanshe, 2001.

Zou Denong. *Zhongguo jianzhu shi tushuo, xiandai juan* [An illustrated history of Chinese architecture, modern period]. Beijing: Zhongguo Jianzhu Gongye Chubanshe, 2001.

***Yaohua Shi***

## ARCHITECTURE SINCE 1979

Deng Xiaoping's economic reforms (1979) yielded dramatic results in China's architecture. Economic expansion and the rapid growth of urban populations helped fuel a boom in architecture, as established urban areas made room for residential and commercial construction. In Beijing, entire neighborhoods have been relocated to accommodate the boom, and in Shanghai, plans for World Expo in 2010 take in 1,300 acres of riverfront property, requiring the relocation of 50,000 residents and hundreds of factories.

Beijing and Shanghai have been centers of China's architectural revolution. Beijing, as the nation's administrative capital, boasts buildings with historical associations to both imperial and post-1949 China; Shanghai has long been China's commercial and financial center. The urban landscape of both cities was altered dramatically after 1979, with high-rise buildings transforming the skylines of both cities. Change is not limited to Beijing and Shanghai, however; many of China's large and not-so-large cities, including Guangzhou, Harbin, Kunming, and Ningbo, have undergone similarly impressive makeovers.

In 1982 the construction of the Fragrant Hills Hotel signaled a new era in Chinese architecture. Located near Beijing, this sprawling hotel sparked intense interest among Chinese designers and critics. The hotel was designed by I. M. Pei (b. 1917), a Chinese-born architect trained at the Massachusetts Institute of Technology. Pei's ancestral home is Suzhou's Lion Grove Garden, one of China's most famous traditional gardens, with a history that dates back to the Yuan dynasty (1279–1368). Four decades removed from China, Pei produced a design that recalled the vernacular architecture of his youth in southeast China, combining courtyards, gardens, and traditional details with his hallmark modern architectural style.

As new projects were developed, debates arose over the use of vernacular forms and whether certain styles should be privileged. Some new buildings reflected the idea that traditional Chinese forms should be echoed in China's new buildings. The Beijing Library (1987), for example, included a pitched parapet that recalls traditional architecture and embodies the idea of a national form.

In the 1980s large numbers of Beijing's traditional courtyard homes and *hutongs* (labyrinthine neighborhoods of courtyard houses and alleyways) were demolished. Old neighborhoods, some with buildings dating to the seventeenth century, fell to make room for growth within the city. Courtyards and lanes gave way to glass and steel towers. Residential relocation from the city center to its periphery became a contentious issue. Many long-time *hutong* residents protested that the compensation was inadequate and the social impact traumatic, but population pressures and property developers prevailed. In 2007 Beijing's population neared 17.5 million, a number unsustainable by the low-profile, sprawling layout of traditional Beijing. Historic preservationists rallied to bring attention to the rapidly disappearing vestiges of Beijing's vernacular residential architecture. A few *hutongs* survive, and their maintenance and renovation is part of Beijing's emerging new appearance. Preservation efforts extended to twentieth-century factories as well. In this way, both traditional and Mao-era buildings have been repurposed as new spaces with courtyards and modern amenities, in an effort to acknowledge the old in the face of rapid change.

Shanghai's transformation included the construction of a new district, Pudong, on the eastern side of the Huangpu

***China Central Television headquarters, Beijing, July 17, 2008.*** *Prior to the 2008 Summer Olympics, Chinese officials in the capital city began an ambitious building campaign designed to accommodate the event and also display China's rising economic power to the world. Many of the designs feature modern elements, such as this combination of leaning skyscrapers housing China Central Television's headquarters.* AP IMAGES

River, where growth could be concentrated. Nearly as large as Singapore, Pudong rapidly became a center of high-profile construction projects that altered the skyline of Shanghai and stimulated economic development throughout the region. Pudong's pioneering landmarks include the eighty-eight-story Jin Mao Tower (1999), whose tapering, stepped form derives from the shape of a traditional pagoda. It was designed by the Chicago architectural firm Skidmore, Owings, Merrill, and until 2007 was China's tallest building. At 101 stories, the Shanghai World Financial Center (2008), designed by Kohn Pedersen Fox Associates of New York, features a square base that transitions to a blunt, chisel-like top pierced by a trapezoidal aperture whose purpose is to relieve wind pressure and building stress in typhoon conditions.

In 2001, the 2008 Summer Olympics joined population pressures and economic development as spurs to the construction surge in Beijing. The central axis of Beijing's imperial plan was extended northward so that the Olympic green would conform to the city's ancient symmetrical layout. Deadline-driven changes included infrastructure improvements such as subway and airport upgrades, as well as construction of venues that would be used for the Olympic games. Experimental and controversial buildings credited to international design firms predominated. Foster and Partners designed the city's new monument to air travel, the new international terminal at Beijing's airport (2008). Though its swooping form invokes comparison to a Chinese dragon, Norman Foster's (b. 1935) design inspiration was Berlin's iconic Tempelhof Airport of the 1930s. Paul Andreu's (b. 1938) conception for the National Theater (2005) located three auditoriums beneath an egg-shaped titanium and glass dome set within a reflecting pool. Herzog and de Meuron's National Stadium (2008), the centerpiece of Beijing's Olympic park, is distinguished by the sculptural effects of crisscrossing beams and struts that envelope its massive elliptical form. Nicknamed the "Bird's Nest," the stadium's tangle of steel girders contrasts with the design of the nearby National Aquatics Center. PTW Architects, the building's Australian designers, imagined an innovative form that plays off the stadium. Using technologically advanced engineering and materials, its blue exterior is clad in layers of inflated translucent plastic: The building not only evokes the notion of bubbles, it is itself sheathed in bubbles.

Architecture as landmark has become a familiar phenomenon in early twenty-first-century Beijing. China Central Television (CCTV), the state television authority, chose an innovative design by the Dutch architect Rem Koolhaas (b. 1944) to house its headquarters. Koolhaas's design reinvents the modern skyscraper idiom, rejecting monolith for asymmetry. Only fifty-one stories tall, the building's novel form includes two asymmetrical towers joined by an angled cantilevered connector, features that distinguish the building in terms of both design and structural challenge, and earned it the nickname "Big Shorts."

Beijing's growth has necessitated some of the city's changes, as officials seek ways to accommodate the burgeoning population. The influx of people to the capital includes migrant workers from rural areas, who are a source of labor for the city's construction projects. It is estimated that more than one million unskilled workers have supplied the labor for Beijing's massive urban transformation. They also have made possible many of the innovative designs that characterize much of Beijing's new architecture. Crews work around the clock to meet deadlines, and the source of labor is virtually inexhaustible. Large crews and low wages have allowed architects and engineers to undertake projects whose costs elsewhere would be prohibitive.

In terms of educational and professional qualifications, Chinese architects were no match for the celebrity architects who competed for China's biggest architectural commissions, and most projects before 2008 went to foreign architects. When China's system of higher education was reorganized in 1952, architectural training was concentrated into eight schools, whose graduates supplied the nation's state-run design institutes. After 1978, however, the number of trained architects and architectural students was insufficient to meet demand. By 1986, 46 schools offered programs in architectural studies, and by 2004, that number had reached 120. State-run firms were no longer the only option; private practice became a possibility. The concept of private architectural practice was revived in response to demand and opportunity, beginning with joint ventures in the 1980s. In 1993 Yung Ho Chang (b. 1956) founded China's first private architectural firm, Atelier Feichang Jianzhu, and since then private practice has become common. With the increased profile of architecture, the profession has flourished and Chinese architects have received increased attention both domestically and internationally.

**BIBLIOGRAPHY**

Chan, Bernard. *New Architecture in China.* London: Merrell, 2005.

Dawson, Layla. *China's New Dawn: An Architectural Transformation.* Munich: Prestel Verlag, 2005.

Luna, Ian, and Thomas Tsang, eds. *On the Edge: Ten Architects from China.* New York: Rizzoli, 2006.

Xue, Charlie Q. L. *Building a Revolution: Chinese Architecture since 1980.* Hong Kong: Hong Kong University Press, 2006.

***Melissa J. Walt***

## WESTERN ARCHITECTS AND BUILDINGS IN CHINA

Western architects practicing in China from the early nineteenth to the early twenty-first centuries have exerted significant but highly variable influence upon Chinese builders, designers, and others involved in the field of architecture. That influence can be measured not only by a selection of buildings that have survived the cataclysmic historical changes in China in the past 200 years, but also by documentary evidence that attests to the myriad places and ways in which Western architects interacted with Chinese builders. One of the most important ways was how architecture, as a discipline with an evolving, rigorous set of design methodologies in the West, came to be understood by Chinese, who did not have professional architects as such. Instead, buildings in China were commonly erected by *jiangren* (builders), some of whom worked for the emperor and thus were restricted by imperial construction rules that extended back to the Song dynasty, when the building manual *Yingzao fashi* was published (1103). Builders outside the imperial system commonly used other manuals, such as the *Luban jing* (1453), to erect many magnificent works.

## EARLY WESTERN INFLUENCES

Chinese *jiangren* began to interact more intensively with Western practitioners as early as the eighteenth century. For example, between 1751 and 1783, at the Yuanmingyuan imperial Garden of Perfect Clarity in Beijing, the Italian Jesuit architect Giuseppe Castiglione (1688–1766) erected more than forty Baroque-style pavilions that greatly impressed the Qianlong emperor (r. 1736–1796). In the southern city of Guangzhou, British commercial agents erected thirteen residential/commercial structures known as "factories" (i.e., residences of factors) that reflected the growing Western presence.

It was after the Opium Wars of the mid-nineteenth century that Western architectural influence began to spread more widely throughout China, largely through the treaty port system, which between the 1840s and the 1910s permitted Western commercial agents to operate in an expanding constellation of cities. By the early twentieth century, traders from England, France, Germany, Russia, and Japan had established themselves. They employed Western architects to erect stylistically eclectic structures with many functions, from commerce and residence to entertainment and religion. The construction of churches was particularly troubling to many Chinese, as was evident in both Guangzhou and Beijing when French Catholics erected tall churches in these cities in the late 1860s and early 1870s, respectively. The earliest British architects in China, including Thomas Kingsmill (1837–1910), William Kidner (1841–1900), William Dowdall (1843–1923), and Henry Lester (1840–1926), diversified their practices to include surveying and real estate management. French architects established themselves relatively later than the English; by about 1900 French firms such as Charrey and Conversy, Joseph-Julien Chollot, and the Crédit Foncier d'Extrême-Orient were thriving, particularly in Shanghai and Tianjin. German firms such as Becker and Baedeker, Curt Rothkegel, and Lothar Marcks also benefited from trading and quasi-colonial entrenchments, especially after 1898 when the city of Qingdao became a German treaty port. At approximately the same time, Russian architects in Harbin (Heilongjiang) and Japanese architects in Manchuria began to practice widely.

As internal strife intensified during the late Qing period and many Chinese flocked to cities for security and prosperity, Chinese associations (*huiguan*) also began to promote architectural works, which led to curious encounters between foreign architects and Chinese builders. Furthermore, foreign architects often hired Chinese carpenters, masons, and laborers. Between about 1900 and 1937, when many commercial cities experienced periods of boom and bust, imported technologies such as reinforced concrete, raft foundations, and mechanized cranes, hoists, and mixers facilitated the construction of taller buildings. One of the most notable, the Hong Kong and Shanghai Bank headquarters (1926) on the Shanghai Bund, combined all of these technologies and became an object lesson for how to build up-to-date, foreign structures in a Chinese urban context. Shanghai's Park Hotel, designed by László Hudec (1893–1958), was the tallest building in the world (outside of North America) when it was completed in 1934. Western architects also became involved in erecting new building types for the post-Qing republican state, including university campuses, civic centers, and transportation buildings. One of the best known of these architects was the American Henry K. Murphy (1877–1954), who designed Yenching University in Beijing and Ginling College for Women in Nanjing in an "adaptive" architectural mode by merging Chinese traditional forms with Western construction technologies.

## DEVELOPING A CHINESE ARCHITECTURE

Between 1911 and 1937 approximately fifty Chinese students who aspired to be architects were given scholarships to study at U.S. universities, where they were strongly influenced by French beaux-arts design paradigms that had become well established in the United States. This so-called "first generation" (*di yidai*) of Chinese architects returned to their homeland in the 1920s and began to practice, compete, and establish university programs teaching architectural design. The first Chinese architectural association, *Zhongguo Jianzhushi Xuehui*, was established in Shanghai in 1928. However, after Japan defeated China in Manchuria in 1932 and began full-scale invasion of China in 1937, much building activity ceased until the early 1950s, after the establishment of the People's Republic of China (PRC) in 1949.

Between 1953 and 1960 Soviet influence in Chinese architecture became more significant as academic architectural programs, design institutes, and large-scale Socialist building programs proliferated. In 1959, for the ten-year anniversary of the establishment of the PRC, ten major buildings that exemplified the ideals of the revolution were premiered. They included ministries, museums, and exhibition halls that demonstrated the dominant Soviet influence. Then, as a result of the disastrous Great Leap Forward (1958–1962) and the Great Proletarian Cultural Revolution (1966–1969), building activity again slowed to a crawl. It was not until 1978 that architectural activity began to rebound, concomitant with reforms initiated by Deng Xiaoping.

Since the 1980s, as China has made it easier for Chinese professionals to work with foreign partners, many domains of architectural practice have been transformed. For example, some Chinese architects began to work with foreign designers in joint venture projects. One of the earliest of these was in Shanghai, where the American architect John Portman designed a center initially named after him on Nanjing Road, directly behind the Shanghai Exhibition Center, built with Soviet assistance in 1953. In the 1990s and early 2000s, many other Western architects received Chinese commissions. Some of the most prominent were the Jinmao Tower in Shanghai (Skidmore, Owings, and Merrill), the Beijing National Stadium (known colloquially as the "Bird's Nest"; Herzog and Demeuron), and the National Opera (Paul Andreu) in Beijing.

Powerful design institutes have given way to the proliferation of private architectural firms. University programs, architectural journals, and building sites have shifted toward increasingly globalized influences. As the Chinese economy has expanded rapidly, so too has the extent of hybridizing influences upon Chinese architecture, fueled in part by the work of Western and Japanese architects who have been drawn to China to design and build innovative structures, and also spurred on by Chinese architects, city planners, and other persons of influence who have partnered with foreign colleagues and clients in an attempt to create a distinctively Chinese architecture for the twenty-first century. Preparations for the 2008 Olympics in Beijing and the 2010 World Exposition in Shanghai further encouraged these collaborations.

**SEE ALSO** *Beijing; Gardens and Parks; Shanghai; Tianjin (Tientsin); Wuhan.*

**BIBLIOGRAPHY**

Campanella, Thomas J. *The Concrete Dragon: China's Urban Revolution and What It Means for the World.* New York: Princeton Architectural Press, 2008.

Cody, Jeffrey. The Woman with the Binoculars: British Architects, Chinese Builders, and Shanghai's Skyline, 1900–1937. In *Twentieth-Century Architecture and Its Histories*, ed. Louise Campbell, 251–274. Otley, U.K.: Society of Architectural Historians of Great Britain, 2000.

Cody, Jeffrey. *Building in China: Henry K. Murphy's "Adaptive Architecture," 1914–1935.* Hong Kong and Seattle: Chinese University Press and University of Washington Press, 2001.

Farris, Johnathan. Thirteen Factories of Canton: An Architecture of Sino-Western Collaboration and Confrontation. *Building and Landscapes* 14 (2007): 66–82.

Huebner, Jon W. Architecture and History in Shanghai's Central District. *Journal of Oriental Studies* 26, no. 2 (1988): 209–269.

Rowe, Peter G., and Seng Kuan. *Architectural Encounters with Essence and Form in Modern China.* Cambridge, MA: MIT Press, 2002.

Ruan, Xing. *New China Architecture.* Hong Kong: Periplus, 2006.

Strassberg, Richard. War and Peace: Four Intercultural Landscapes. In *China on Paper: European and Chinese Works from the Late Sixteenth to the Early Nineteenth Century*, ed. Marcia Reed and Paola Dematte, 89–137. Los Angeles: Getty Research Institute, 2007.

Warner, Torsten. *German Architecture in China: Architectural Transfer.* Berlin: Ernst & Sohn, 1994.

Wu, Jiang. *Shanghai bainian jianzhushi* (1840–1949) [One hundred years of Shanghai's architecture (1840–1949)]. Shanghai: Tongji Daxue Chubanshe, 1997.

Zheng, Shilin, ed. *Shanghai jindai jianzhu fengliu* [The evolution of Shanghai architecture in modern times]. Shanghai: Tongji Daxue Chubanshe, 1999.

*Jeffrey W. Cody*

# ARCHIVES, PUBLIC

*This entry contains the following:*

HISTORICAL PRESERVATION AND GOVERNMENT HISTORICAL PUBLICATIONS
*Beatrice S. Bartlett*

ARCHIVAL RESOURCES OUTSIDE CHINA
*Beatrice S. Bartlett*

## HISTORICAL PRESERVATION AND GOVERNMENT HISTORICAL PUBLICATIONS

China's present-day archival enterprise is one of the largest and most active in the world. As of 2005, China had approximately four thousand archival repositories with upwards of thirty thousand full-time employees. The items in the largest and most prevalent type of repository, the Comprehensive Archives (Zonghe Dang'an Guan), numbered close to 200 million, with more than fifty million items processed and open for research and approximately nine million photographs. These accomplishments are supported by high-level government supervision through a State Archives Board (Guojia Dang'an Ju), and a solid program of laws, meetings, publications, a newspaper, and education, as well as annual prizes to encourage excellence in archival work. There is an enormous professional organization (Zhongguo Dang'an Xuehui) with a membership of thousands. Publications include well over one hundred published book titles (some in large multivolume sets) and more than fifty journals on the subject of archival activities, including two national journals; in addition, nearly every one of China proper's eighteen provinces has its own archives journal. Archival education is carried out at several levels of professional training, ranging from an archival college and departments in twenty-six universities, to radio and television extension courses both to train lower-level staff and update those who long ago earned their degrees.

A record of all this activity appears in substantial yearbooks published occasionally since 1989 (the first volume having covered the earliest decades, 1945 to

1988). The government supervises and controls virtually all archives in the country; the few private archives left from earlier times (for example, the business archives in Shanghai) have now been organized as part of this prodigious government drive. Significant numbers of materials also survive in several installations in Taiwan (possibly as much as 10 percent taken from the mainland in 1948 and 1949) and Hong Kong. Although comparisons are difficult, it may well be that China's current archival endeavor is the largest and most active in the world, a situation attributable to the large population and the long-standing archival tradition.

## CHINA'S ARCHIVES FOLLOWING 1949

Immediately on coming to power on October 1, 1949, when Mao Zedong stood in front of the Imperial Palace to announce victory, the government displayed its intense concern for archives by ordering protections for documents of both the former and present governments, as well as Communist Party materials, including the large holdings of the former Republic's Bureau of Documents (Dang'an Guan) and the Archives Section of the Northeastern Library (Dang'an Bu). Other strictures followed with detailed requirements for saving and handing over old documents, preventing archival materials from leaving the country, and setting up new offices to carry out this work. Although we cannot know how thoroughly the new government was able to enforce these regulations, they were widely known and probably deflected many thefts and disappearances of the kind that had bedeviled past archival efforts.

The year 1949 marks the principal chronological division between China's two main groups of archival remains: "historical" and "contemporary." The three officially designated historical types are: Ming-Qing (1368–1644 and 1644–1912); Republic (1912–1949); and History of the [Chinese Communist] Revolution (late Qing to 1949). In addition, scattered historical documents survive from much earlier than the Ming, but sequential runs sufficient for research are available only from the early Qing and are best beginning with the Yongzheng reign (1723–1735). The chief open historical collections are the Ming-Qing materials held in the Number One Archives in Beijing (Zhongguo Diyi Lishi Dang'an Guan) and the Republic's in the Number Two Archives in Nanjing (Zhongguo Di'er Lishi Dang'an Guan). In addition, both these historical topics are well represented in local archives across the country, as well as in several sites on Taiwan. The History-of-the-Revolution materials are housed with post-1949 documents in Beijing's Central Archives (Zhongyang Dang'an Guan), which is generally closed to external researchers. Although China supposedly has a thirty-year rule, which would now open materials through the late 1970s, access to post-1949 holdings is rare but occasionally does take place.

## THE FATE OF CHINA'S EARLY ARCHIVES

Most but not all the earlier dynasties' documents have been lost to fires, insects, floods, and civil wars, but there are significant survivals, some of which were carried off to foreign countries in the late nineteenth and early twentieth centuries. In spite of the loss of a great many, probably the majority, of original pre-Qing documents and copies, we know that Chinese governments have been maintaining archives since at least the Han, and possibly since the time of Confucius (c. 500 BCE). Probably thousands or tens of thousands of documents did once exist; some copies and summaries have survived in the form of quotations and excerpts in historical compendia. Many lost items have ended up overseas, a fact that indubitably led to the government's 1949 prohibitions against export of archival documents. (Treasures such as the large cache of Han dynasty [207 BCE to 220 CE] bamboo slips unearthed in the 1920s at Edsen-gol in northwest China were sent to the LOC during World War II and returned to Academia Sinica outside Taibei in 1965.)

There are now strict prohibitions against removing archival documents or, in some cases, copies of archival materials from the country, and the post office has been known to confiscate archival Xeroxes and handwritten copies entrusted to the mails.

## ARCHIVES THAT ARE CATALOGUED AND OPEN

Aside from some of the local archives, the Ming-Qing and Republic sections of the official historical archives are generally the only holdings catalogued and open to external researchers. These two holdings, plus the History-of-the-Revolution materials, have another distinction: Since 1995, projects to index them electronically have been underway in Beijing's and Nanjing's "Union finding-list centers for historical archival materials" (Quanguo lishi dang'an ziliao mulu zhongxin). Three levels of finding-lists have resulted: fonds or record groups (generally government agencies, *danwei*, known by the Chinese archival term *quanzong*), cases, and documents. One remarkable feature of these finding aids is that the reach of the index is planned to extend to archival units all across the country, whether in major municipalities, provinces, autonomous regions, prefectures, or county seats. The indexes were probably developed first for the government-sponsored project to revise the official Qing history.

## QING MATERIALS

Because the surviving Qing materials are by far the most complete and the most accessible, the following description is largely based on the Beijing, Taibei, and local Qing holdings. Nearly all Qing documents were handwritten—little before the twentieth century was printed: Printing was expensive, copyists' wages were cheap, and copyists enjoyed immense personal satisfaction in executing a line of well-formed characters. As a result, many Qing archival documents are works of beauty, the characters well-shaped and of good size (*kaishu*). This may also have reflected the need to produce readable documents for declining imperial eyesight: We know, for instance, that the Qianlong emperor (r. 1736–1796) could not see well in his eighth decade, and similar declines may have befallen other aging emperors.

Qing documents have survived well because most were written on buff-colored cloth-based paper. Provincial reports were rendered in accordion style and read from right to left, unless there was also a Manchu version, which ran left to right. Archival record books held together with twisted paper thongs have likewise survived well. Some still bear proofreading slips, yet another manifestation of the care attending the production of these materials. On the other hand, some documents were hastily copied for reference files, but these were not submitted for the imperial perusal.

Topics covered in these documents may seem broad, describing a wide range of political and economic activities, but they were limited to government interest. Nonetheless, imperial concerns had a long reach. Although we shall not find drafts or original and corrected eighteenth-century novels or diaries of famed individuals, such as those held in Western rare-book libraries, the Qing archives contain substantial holdings on traditional Chinese opera because that was a favorite imperial entertainment. Imperial curiosity and interests are also reflected here: When a male heir in the fifth generation was born to the Qianlong emperor's line, he ordered provincial reports on all males throughout the empire enjoying similar good fortune. Maps and diagrams abound, some submitted with provincial reports, some prepared at the capital. There are also genealogies of the imperial family, as well as those of certain Manchu banner families. The Number One Archives also possesses some green-headed tallies prepared for imperial audiences, as well as numerous dictionaries necessary to clerical work, particularly for translating between Manchu and Chinese.

## PURPOSES AND USES OF THE QING ARCHIVES

The purpose of such a large Qing archival project was to maintain policy reference files, but it also generated materials for a future official history of the dynasty, a requirement established in the Tang era (618–907), when the government viewed an official history as a means of circulating its narrative of events. Traditional official histories were done in stages, and the following description of the Qing project for preparing the official biographies based on archival research will supply one example of these varied programs. Biographies were important, frequently taking up half a multivolume official history and offering the drama of personal narratives. The first level of work was the Qing's "Long Draft Record" (*Changbian dang*), in which document summaries were particularly referenced for possible future biographies. Once it became necessary to draft a biography, these archival indexes, of which thousands now exist, were then used to locate materials, which could then be copied for a "biographic packet" (*zhuan bao*), to which could be added funeral notices and eulogies. A draft might follow, with corrections and eventual incorporation into the biography section of the "State History" (*Guoshi*), another Tang practice generally followed in subsequent eras. The final incarnation would be placement in the official dynastic history.

The Qing archives were similarly used to prepare other steps on the road to publication. The Qing "Court Diaries" (*Qijuzhu*), of a tradition even more ancient than the Tang, are now held, with some of their drafts, in Qing archives in both Beijing and Taibei. They too played a role in compiling other parts of the dynastic histories. Although most archival materials were kept secret during the dynasty, some were published in court circulars known as the "Peking Gazettes" (*Jingbao*) and others were printed—often in revised form—in accounts of military campaigns or other dynastic achievements (*fanglue*). Today the materials are pored over chiefly by academics, but some, particularly the local holdings, have been used successfully in modern concerns, such as real-estate claims.

## PROTECTION OF ARCHIVAL MATERIALS

China's archives survival was not left to chance: Various protections and defenses have long been in place, although with varying success. Some measures seem exaggerated today: As protection against fire, one Han archive was surrounded with a moat, and the Ming taxation and population registers were housed on islands in a lake, but today no vestige of either survives. A Kangxi (r. 1661–1722) edict required that all palace lamps be kept under guard when used. Qing palace memorial transmission operated with sets of locks and monitored keys. A document logbook summarized and registered all Grand Council documents from the eighteenth century on. During the Ming, and possibly earlier, official copies were required at the time of an individual report's submission. The Qing carried this further, from the mid-eighteenth century creating reference copies for most provincial reports and establishing a regular copying program focused on record books as well. Some of the latter were copied and recopied, happily making it possible today to locate a copy to compensate for a missing or fragmentary remain. The Qing copying program included detailed inventories, which today may be used to reassure us that for mid-Qing and later documents, archival survival is the rule, at least at the central-government level. Not even the Cultural Revolution was allowed to interfere with these valued remains.

Today's archival protections frequently include camphor to prevent insect infestation, spacious temperature- and humidity-controlled vaults, and stiff boxes to keep paper-covered albums from rubbing against each other and causing fraying. To prevent thievery or other depredations, some archives have instituted a variety of measures, including restricting the use of pens, requiring face masks, and monitoring users with hidden cameras.

**BIBLIOGRAPHY**

Bartlett, Beatrice S. The Secret Memorials of the Yung-cheng Period (1723–1735): Archival and Published Versions. *National Palace Museum Bulletin* 9, 4 (1974): 1–12.

Bartlett, Beatrice S. A World-class Archival Achievement: The People's Republic of China Archivists' Success in Opening the Ming-Qing Central-Government Archives, 1949–1998. *Archival Science* 7, 4 (2007): 369–390.

Bartlett, Nancy, and Wang Lan, guest eds. *Janus: Archival Review* 2 (1999). Entire issue on the current archival situation in China.

Cole, James H. Archives. In *Twentieth Century China: An Annotated Bibliography of Reference Works in Chinese, Japanese, and Western Languages*, comp. James H. Cole, 60–81. 2 vols. Armonk, NY: Sharpe, 2004.

Editorial Committee for the *Quanguo Minguo dang'an tonglan*, comp. *Quanguo Minguo dang'an tonglan* [Compendium on the nation's Republic archives], Pt. 1. Beijing: Zhongguo Dang'an Chubanshe, 2005.

Organizing Committee Thirteenth International Congress on Archives, ed. *Zhongguo dang'an shiye* [Archives work in China]. 9 unpaginated fascicles. Beijing: Dang'an Chubanshe, 1995.

Wilkinson, Endymion. *Chinese History: A Manual*. Rev. and enlarged ed. Cambridge, MA: Harvard University Press, 2000. See especially, Archives, 484–488; Private Documents, 493–494; Archives, 717–718; Central Archives, Published Archival Documents, Provincial and County Archives, 903–939; and Taiwan and Manshukoku, 1035–1038.

*Zhongguo dang'an nianjian* [Chinese archives yearbook]. Beijing: Dang'an Chubanshe. Published irregularly since 1989.

***Beatrice S. Bartlett***

## ARCHIVAL RESOURCES OUTSIDE CHINA

Four significant collections of China's historical archives are now held outside of China. These consist of original documents written in the languages of China (chiefly Chinese and Manchu, with some Mongolian and Tibetan) and formerly held in China. The institutions holding three of the collections offer sufficient datable runs of materials to allow researchers to create and document narratives, thereby allowing significant research. Most of these documents were sold to foreign collectors and scholars in the early twentieth century, prompting China's new government to regulate foreign sales and archival security in 1949 and 1950. Since then, high-level officials in the government have been concerned with preserving China's archival wealth; accordingly, the argument that such materials are in danger if left in Chinese hands and are better overseen by foreigners should be abandoned.

Major overseas research holdings include oracle bones, Buddhist and government documents found in Dunhuang and the dry-air regions of the surrounding western desert, and small holdings of Qing documents. In addition, many universities and libraries in Europe and North America have their own small holdings, but these generally lack the continuous runs necessary for sustained research.

Chinese regard the oracle bones (*jiaguwen*, turtle shells and animal bones inscribed with divination questions and, in some cases, the answers) as their earliest historical documents. The oracle bones date from the late Shang, (c. 1200–1046 BCE, and early Zhou, c. 1046–771 BCE). Endymion Wilkinson estimates that, of the total 155,000 published inscriptions, about 26,700 (or 17%) are held outside of China, but it is unclear how much is in the form of drawings, rubbings, and photographs and how much consists of original bones, shells, and fragments. Major holdings are located in Japan, Canada, the United Kingdom, and the United States.

By far the largest and best organized of all foreign Chinese document holdings is the enormous number of mainly Buddhist remains that survive in the Dunhuang area and date from the fourth to the eleventh century. The principal hoard was sequestered in the "Library Cave" (Cave 17) in about 1000 CE and only discovered around the turn of the last century, precipitating foreign scholars and explorers to rush to purchase large quantities of its treasures. Today, the International Dunhuang Project, founded in 1994 at the British Library in London, oversees sixty thousand items located around the world. The National Museum in New Delhi is additionally believed to possess large, but generally less known, holdings. Additional small holdings of Dunhuang materials are located in Paris, St. Petersburg, Berlin, and Beijing. The International Dunhuang Project makes its numerous already-published documents available for research online, but is not able to assist with the use of unpublished materials.

Whereas research on most subjects covered in the Dunhuang materials requires access to the overseas holdings, the two principal groups of Qing archival sources outside of China, those at the Public Record Office in London and the Toyo Bunko (East Asian Library) in Tokyo, cover significant but narrow topics, meaning that most scholarly research using Qing archives can be successfully completed in China. Nonetheless, overseas consultation is essential for many subjects encompassed in the two collections.

The Public Record Office holdings related to China consist mainly of documents collected during the nineteenth century by the British Legation in Beijing, supplemented by some documents seized in the course of the Arrow War (1856–1860). They total approximately twenty thousand items dating from 1793 to 1911. Most consist of diplomatic correspondence and documents concerning the Arrow War, with two thousand documents of the Guangdong provincial government extracted from the Arrow War materials. All series have been generally described, indexed, or at least listed. No series is complete, and all must be supplemented by other sources.

The Tokyo Qing documents in the Toyo Bunko are in Mongolian, Tibetan, Manchu, and Chinese. The most significant group is 2,400 Manchu-language documents of the Beijing Bordered Red Banner office purchased from a Shanghai bookseller in 1936 and covering the two centuries from 1723 to 1922. Although this is not a complete run of materials from this office (more exist in Beijing's Number One Historical Archives), it is a sizeable portion, exhibiting the continued use of Manchu late in the dynasty. Many of these documents have been published in Manchu transcription, and some have also been translated into Japanese.

Although the Russians carried off archives when in Beijing in 1900 and Manchuria after World War II (1937–1945), it is believed that these were returned to China in the 1950s. Dr. Grimsted's 1972 work on the archives of the Soviet Union describes several Chinese and Tibetan holdings, but it is not clear that these are archival holdings taken from China; they may simply represent the Russian side of diplomatic, commercial, or other exchanges.

**BIBLIOGRAPHY**

Cao Jinyan and Shen Jianhua, comps. *Jiaguwen Jiaoshi zongji* [Union reproduction and translation (into modern Chinese) of inscribed oracle bones]. 20 vols. Shanghai: Shanghai Cishu Chubanshe, 2006.

Cole, James H., comp. Archives. In *Twentieth Century China: An Annotated Bibliography of Reference Works in Chinese, Japanese, and Western Languages*, Vol. 1, 60–81. Armonk, NY: Sharpe, 2004.

Grimsted, Patricia Kennedy. *Archives and Manuscript Repositories in the USSR: Moscow and Leningrad.* Princeton, NJ: Princeton University Press, 1972.

Hopkirk, Peter. *Foreign Devils on the Silk Road: The Search for the Lost Cities and Treasures of Chinese Central Asia.* Amherst: University of Massachusetts Press, 1980.

International Dunhuang Project. http://idp.bl.uk/.

Kanda Nobuo, ed. *The Bordered Red Banner Archives in the Toyo Bunko.* Vol. 1: *Introduction and Catalogue.* Tokyo: Toyo Bunko, 2001.

Keightley, David N. *Sources of Shang History: The Oracle-Bone Inscriptions of Bronze Age China.* Berkeley: University of California Press, 1978.

Pong, David. *A Critical Guide to the Kwangtung Provincial Archives Deposited at the Public Record Office of London.* Cambridge, MA: Harvard University East Asian Research Center, 1975.

Rao, Zongyi. Haiwai Jiagu luyi [Record of oracle bones transferred overseas]. *Journal of Oriental Studies* 4, 1–2 (1957–1958): 1–22.

Rong, Xinjiang. The Nature of the Dunhuang Library Cave and the Reasons for Its Sealing. Trans. Valerie Hansen. *Cahiers d'Extreme-Asie* 11 (1999–2000): 247–275.

Toyo Bunko. http://www.toyo-bunko.or.jp/.

Whitfield, Susan, and Frances Wood, eds. *Dunhuang and Turfan: Contents and Conservation of Ancient Documents from Central Asia.* London: British Library, 1996.

Wilkinson, Endymion. Oracle-Bone Inscriptions. In *Chinese History: A Manual*, rev. and enlarged ed., 389–406. Cambridge, MA: Harvard University Press, 2000.

Wilkinson, Endymion. Archives. In *Chinese History: A Manual*, rev. and enlarged ed., 484–488. Cambridge, MA: Harvard University Press, 2000.

Wilkinson, Endymion. Dunhuang and Turpan Documents. In *Chinese History: A Manual*, rev. and enlarged ed., 826–835. Cambridge, MA: Harvard University Press, 2000.

Wilkinson, Endymion. Foreign Archival Sources on China. In *Chinese History: A Manual*, rev. and enlarged ed., 1039–1045. Cambridge, MA: Harvard University Press, 2000.

Xu Wen. Yingguo gonggong dang'an guan suo cang de Zhongwen dang'an [Chinese-language archives in the Public Record Office, England]. *Lishi Dang'an* 1981, 2 (1981): 129–130.

**Beatrice S. Bartlett**

# ARMAMENTS

Since the establishment of the People's Republic of China in 1949, threat perceptions changed and caused Chinese military doctrine and strategy to evolve. The development of Chinese armaments and weapons systems were guided and steered by decision makers who took full account of these evolutionary changes. Thus Mao Zedong's "people's war," which was the prevailing strategy up to 1979, was both pragmatic and well suited to the People's Republic at a time when Chinese armaments fell far behind developments in the West.

Nevertheless, the People's Republic succeeded in detonating its first atomic bomb in October 1964 and in establishing in 1966 the Second Artillery Corps, which was responsible for developing ballistic missiles.

The evolution from people's war to "people's war under modern conditions" up to 1985 witnessed much improvement in weapons systems, as well as the beginnings of a modern military-industrial complex. By the time of the "limited war" strategy up to 1991 and the strategy of "limited war under high technology" from 1991 on, Chinese development of armaments had crossed a few thresholds and had somewhat narrowed the technological gap with the West. Nevertheless, the People's Republic over the decades encountered problems associated with procurement, technology assimilation, reengineering, and retrofitting. The upgrading of avionics for the F8-II fighter and the imposition of embargoes on lethal weapons by the European Union are but two examples of these problems.

## THE DEVELOPMENT OF CHINA'S ARMAMENTS AND WEAPONS SYSTEMS

The development of China's armaments and weapons systems is principally guided and steered by the Central Military Commission's policy with regard to China's threat perceptions and by military doctrine and national strategy in response to these threats. Such development is the main support for China's security policy.

In 2009 China's military doctrine remains that of "active defense," and its war-fighting principles are encapsulated in the latest national strategy of "local wars under conditions of informationization." Projected demands on joint operations and the latest developments in research and development, as well as in command, control, communication, computers, intelligence, surveillance, and reconnaissance ($C^4$ISR), including the need to close the technology gap with the United States, all provide strategic goals for the development of weapons systems. The Commission on Science, Technology, and Industry for National Defense provides the necessary guidance. Thus *China's National Defense in 2006* aims to lay a "solid foundation" for the modernization of its defense forces by 2010, securing "major progress" by 2020, and "winning in informationized wars" by the mid-twenty-first century. Setting these priorities rests with the Central Military Commission and its relevant departments.

According to *China's National Defense in 2006*, China's immediate goal for defense modernization is 2010, and major progress is expected in the decade starting in 2010. Such progress is in turn linked to threat perceptions and strategic security issues. At the top of its list of priorities are developing a truly blue-water navy, developing a missile-defense system in response to the U.S. Theater Missile Defense initiative in the Asia-Pacific, and building weapons systems that can counter continuing U.S. arms sales to Taiwan.

China's need to develop a truly blue-water navy requires building aircraft carriers comparable to the Russian Admiral Kuznetzov (ex-Tibilisi) class and upgrading naval fighters and battle-group capabilities. Features of Kuznetzov-class carriers include a displacement of 459,000 tons and a 14° ski-jump ramp. Air support comprises Su27K/Su33 Flanker D fighters and Su-25 UTG Frogfoot helicopters. It is debatable whether China can achieve this objective by 2020. Preparations for an invasion of Taiwan also require upgrading amphibious-attack capabilities. Beyond these is the objective of winning the informationized war by the 2050s.

In the arms competition over the Taiwan Strait, high on the agenda of the People's Liberation Army is the development of state-of-the-art surface combatants (cruisers, destroyers, frigates, and corvettes), together with their associated missile systems, and fighters capable of taking on Aegis-class destroyers, PAC-3 missile systems, and F-16C/D fighters, which the United States could sell to Taiwan.

## WEAPONS INVENTORY, 2008

In May 2008 China and Russia jointly expressed concern over the U.S. development of a missile shield in the Asia-Pacific. China's response to the U.S. development of the Theater Missile Defense initiative includes upgrading its ballistic-missile technology, as illustrated by its destroying its own satellite with laser technology in January 2007 and by its launching the lunar probe project.

Because China's national military strategy focuses on "local war under conditions of informationalization," its weapons systems require upgrading to the state of the art in relevant areas. In terms of the capabilities of its military-industrial complex, China lags behind leading nations by at least two generations, although in some areas, such as strategic forces, the technological gap is narrower. Table 1 presents an inventory of China's weapons according to *The Military Balance, 2008* (Hackett 2008).

## ARMS IMPORTS

Reliance on arms imports and development of indigenous weapons systems are China's two major sources of sustainable development. The second source is especially important for narrowing the technological gap, but it requires development of a viable military-industrial complex capable of leapfrogging to state-of-the-art technology. Reliance on Russian arms imports—including naval surface combatants, submarines, fighters, and missile systems—will continue. Urgent modernization of the Air Force requires achieving in-flight-refueling capability, acquiring an early warning and control system, and importing Il-76 cargo aircraft from Russia.

A U.S. Department of Defense report estimated in 2006 that Russian arms exports to China constituted 95 percent of China's total arms import, providing state-of-the-art fighting capabilities for China's Navy and Air Force. These sales included Sovremenny-class destroyers armed with SS-N-27B missiles for the Navy, and Su-27 and Su-30 fighters for the Air Force.

## CHINA'S MILITARY-INDUSTRIAL COMPLEX AND TECHNOLOGY BASE

The Commission on Science, Technology, and Industry for National Defense and the Central Military Commission's General Armament Department oversee and coordinate

**Weapons inventory (the military balance, 2008)**

| | |
|---|---|
| | **Strategic missile forces**<br>(Second Artillery Corps: 20 brigades in 6 armies) |
| Inter-continental ballistic missiles (ICBM) | 46 (DF-31; DF-4; DF-5A) |
| Intermediate range ballistic missiles (IRBM) | 35 (DF-21) |
| Short range ballistic missiles (SRBM) | 725 |
| | **Ground forces**<br>(18 groups garrisoning 7 military regions) |
| **Equipment by type** | |
| Main battle tanks | 6,650+<br>Type-59 I/II (5,000+); Type-79 (300); Type-88A/88B (1,000); Type-96 (1,200); Type-98A/99 (160) |
| Armored personnel carriers | 3,500+ |
| Artillery | 17,700+<br>Self-propelled 1,200<br>Multiple rocket launcher 2,400<br>Mortar: Self-propelled 82mm Type-82; towed from 81mm to 160mm |
| Anti-tank missiles | 7,200 |
| Helicopters | Including 7 SA-321 Super Frelon; 31 WZ-9; 8 SA-342 Gazelle; 260 support; Mi-6 Hook; 19 S-70C2 Black Hawk; 61 AS-365 Dauphin 2/Z9 Dauphin 2 |
| Air defense. SAM | 284+ |
| Radar.land | Cheetah; RASIT; Type-378 (vehicle) |
| | **Navy**<br>(3 fleets and aviation divisions) |
| Submarines | 62 |
| Strategic (SSBN) | 3 |
| Xia | 1 (CSS-N-3) SLBM |
| Jin | 2 (CSS-NX-4) SLBM 3rd and 4th being built |
| Tactical | 59 |
| SSN | 6 |
| Han | 4 (Type 091) SSM |
| Shang | 2 (Type 093) 533mm TT 3rd being built |
| SSG | 1 mod. Romeo (SSG) SSM |
| SSK | 51<br>Kilo 12 (SS-N-27) ASCM; 533mm TT; Ming 19 (Type ES5E) 533mm TT; Romeo 8 (Type ES3B) 533mm TT; Song 10 (CSS-N-8) SSM 533mm TT; Yuan 2 533mm TT; |
| SS | 1 Golf (SLBM trials) |
| Principal surface combatants | |
| Destroyers | 29<br>Luyang: 2 YJ-83 SSM; Grizzly SAM; 324mm TT (Ka-28 Helix A ASW)<br>Hangzhou: 4 (RF Soveremenny) (SS-N-22) Sunburn SSM; Grizzly SAM; 533mm ASTT; RBU 1000 Smerch 3; 130mm (Panther ASW/ASUW; Ka-28 Helix ASW)<br>Luyang II: 2 each with 2 quad each with YJ-62 SSM;<br>Luda III: 1 with 2 triple each with HY-2 SSM;<br>Luda Type-051: 11 each with 2 triple 324mm ASTT;<br>Luhai: 1 with 4 quad each with YJ-83 SSM;<br>Luhu: 2 each with 4 quad each with YJ-83 SSM;<br>Luzhou: 2 each with 2 quad YJ-83 SSM;<br>Luda II: 1 with 2 triple 324mm ASTT;<br>Luda mod Type-051DT: 3 each with 2 quad each with YJ-1 SSM |
| Frigates | 46<br>Jiangwei Type I: 11 each with 2 triple each 1 SY-1 SSM;<br>Jianghu Type II: 9 each with 1 triple with SY-1 SSM;<br>Jianghu Type III: 3 each with 8 YJ-1 SSM;<br>Jianghu Type IV: 1 with 1 triple with 1 SY-1 SSM;<br>Jianghu Type V: 6 each with 1 triple with SY-1 SSM;<br>Jiangwei I: 4 each with 2 triple each with 1 YJ-8 SSM;<br>Jiangwei II: 10 each with 2 quad each with YJ-83 SSM;<br>Jiangkai: 2 each with 2 quad each with YJ-83 SSM |

continued

*Table 1A*

the defense industrial sector responsible for the production of major weapons systems. There is no indication of any policy toward privatizing major defense enterprise groups, nor is there any evidence of horizontal sharing of technological information between the civil and defense sectors.

**Weapons inventory (the military balance, 2008)** (CONTINUED)

| | |
|---|---|
| Amphibious | 1 Yudao;<br>1 Yudeng (capacity 6 tanks; 180 troops);<br>13 Yuhai (capacity 2 tanks; 250 troops);<br>22 Yuliang (capacity 5 tanks; 250 troops);<br>10 Yunshi (capacity 6 tanks);<br>7 Yukan (capacity 10 tanks; 200 troops);<br>10 Yuting (capacity 10 tanks; 250 troops; 2 helicopters);<br>10 Yuting II (capacity 4; 10 tanks; 250 troops);<br>10 Yukei (capacity 10 tanks or 150 troops);<br>120 Yunnan;<br>20 Yuchin;<br>Air-cushion vehicles 10 LCAC |
| Naval aviation | Bombers 130: 100 H-5, F-5, F-5B (torpedo-carrying); 30 H-6D;<br>Fighters 346: including 50J-8B; 20J-8D;<br>Fighters (ground attack) 296: including 48 Su-30MK2;<br>Helicopters (anti-submarine): including 252-9C; 10 Ka-28 Helix A |
| Marines | Army 3 divisions; Marine infantry 2 brigades |
| **Air Force**<br>(32 air divisions and commands air operation in each of 7 military regions) | |
| **Aircraft** | |
| Bombers | 82<br>50H-6E/H-6F/H-6H; 20H-6 (Tu-16) Badger |
| Fighters | 1,179<br>400 J-7II/J-7IIA Fishbed; 296 J-7E Fishbed; 24 J-7G Fishbed; Su J-8 Finback; 11 J-8F Finback; 28 J-8IIB Finback; 24 J-8IID Finback; 40 J-8III Finback; 62 J-10; 116 Su-27SK (J-11) Flanker |
| Fighters (ground attack) | 557<br>73 Su-30 MKK Flanker; 70 JH-7/JH-7A; 408 Q-5C Fantan / Q-5D Fantan |
| Air-borne early warning | 4+<br>A-50 Mainstay; 4 Y-8 |
| Tankers | 296<br>15 B-737-200; 5 CL-601 Challenger; 2 11-18 Coot |
| Helicopters | Support 56: 6 AS-332 Super Puma; 50 Mi-8 Hip<br>Utility 24: 20 Z-9 Dauphin 2; 4 Bell 214 |
| Air defense | SAM 1,578+<br>Missiles: Tactical 4,500+ |

SOURCE: Hackett, James, ed. *The Military Balance, 2008*. London: Oxford University Press for the International Institute for Strategic Studies, 2008.

*Table 1B*

China's military-defense industries face organizational problems leading to overproduction and overcapacity, whereas researchers lag far behind state-of-the-art benchmarks. Financial support for research and development in defense industries in the form of investments from the People's Liberation Army has been estimated to be in the range of US$4–5 billion per annum.

Cole and Godwin (1999) evaluate China's production and research-and-development capabilities according to the U.S. Defense Department's Military Critical Technologies List, Part 1: Weapons Systems Technologies, and make the point that China has little or no capacity in all but two categories: nuclear weapons and nuclear-materials processing.

Nevertheless, indigenous developments in conventional and nuclear capabilities indicate attempts to narrow the technological gap through arms acquisitions from Russia and Israel and reverse engineering. According to Shambaugh, Chinese mastery of the following technologies is improving: "fission and fusion; atoms, hydrogen, and other radiation devices; inertial guidance; solid fuel propulsion; advanced warhead design (particularly miniaturization and MIRVing); submarine-launching and various land-base modes; and so on" (p. 243). Chinese ability to produce the fourth-generation J-10 fighter is a distinctive example of attempts to narrow the technological gap.

The civilian sectors that have made contributions to indigenous military development include information technology, missiles, shipbuilding, and civil aviation. In May 2008 the formation of the Commercial Aircraft Corporation of China was announced, signaling China's ambition to be a part of the jumbo-jet market. The goal is to produce a large transport aircraft for military purposes by 2015 and to enter into the civilian market by 2020.

**Estimates of expenditure, 2000–2006**

unit: US$ billion

| | 2000 | 2001 | 2002 | 2003 | 2004 | 2005 | 2006 |
|---|---|---|---|---|---|---|---|
| China official | 15 | 18.4 | 22.6 | 22.6 | 24.4 | 29.8 | 35 |
| U.S. low estimate | 42.2 | 45 | 49.3 | 49.3 | 59.2 | 64.5 | 70 |
| U.S. high estimate | 61.5 | 66.1 | 66.1 | 71.8 | 86 | 93 | 105 |

SOURCE: Cordesman, H., and M. Kleiber. *Chinese Military Modernization: Force Development and Strategic Capabilities.* Washington, DC: CSIS Press, 2007, p.53.

*Table 2*

### ARMS EXPORTS

Chinese arms exports have been on the decline. They peaked in 1988 at US$3.25 billion, while average per annum sales in the 1980s were US$1.5 billion. In 2006 China ranked ninth on the list of leading suppliers, with sales of US$800 million (the United States ranked first, with sales of US$16.9 billion). Its arms sales go mainly to developing nations, especially Pakistan, Bangladesh, Iran, and Myanmar. Typically, it sells small arms, tanks, and fighter aircraft. Revenues from sales do not go directly to the People's Liberation Army, but it benefits indirectly in the form of support for the armed forces and defense establishments.

### DEFENSE BUDGET

Estimates of China's defense budget fall into three categories: (1) Chinese official estimates, (2) U.S. low estimates, and (3) U.S. high estimates. Estimates (2) and (3) include in the calculations all military-related expenditures incurred. Table 2 presents the three types of estimates for 2000 to 2006.

According to *The Military Balance, 2008* (Hackett 2008), the Chinese Eleventh Five-Year Program (2006–2011) makes no reference to defense-related spending, whereas the official defense budget in 2007 shows a major increase of 25 percent when compared with the previous year, reaching US$46.7 billion when converted at market exchange rates. This official budget does not truly reflect overall military spending.

Analysts have identified the following areas where subsidies are forthcoming for expenditures for items not included in the official budget:

- Subsidies for production and research and development from other sources
- Expenses for development of strategic and nuclear weapons by the Second Artillery Corps
- Revenue accrued from arms exports and, more important, expenses for arms imports and procurement
- Expenses for paramilitary forces
- Revenues from commercial and other activities of the People's Liberation Army

It is generally agreed that the official budget is around half of total expenditures for the armed forces, that the Central Military Commission, like other ministries, has been undertaking comprehensive budgeting reforms, and that the general distribution of funds for equipment, human resources, and operations observes a ratio of 1:1:1.

SEE ALSO *People's Liberation Army: Military Doctrine.*

#### BIBLIOGRAPHY

Ball, Desmond. Assessing China's ASAT Program. Australian Special Report 07-14S (June 14, 2007). Nautilus Institute, RMIT University, Melbourne, Australia. http://nautilus.rmit.edu.au/forum-reports/0714s-ball/.

Cole, B., and P. H. B. Godwin. Advanced Military Technology and the PLA: Priorities and Capabilities for the 21st Century. In *The Chinese Armed Forces in the 21st Century*, ed. L. M. Wortzel, 159–216. Carlisle Barracks, PA: U.S. Army, Wan College, Strategic Studies Institute, 1999.

Cordesman, H., and M. Kleiber. *Chinese Military Modernization: Force Development and Strategic Capabilities.* Washington, DC: CSIS Press, 2007.

Hackett, James, ed. *The Military Balance, 2008.* London: Oxford University Press for the International Institute for Strategic Studies, 2008.

Information Office of the State Council of the People's Republic of China. *China's National Defense in 2006.* Beijing: State Council of the People's Republic of China, 2006. http://www.china.org.cn/english/features/book/194421.htm.

Office of the Secretary of Defense. *Annual Report of Congress: Military Power of the People's Republic of China, 2006.* Washington DC: Office of the Secretary of Defense, 2006.

Shambaugh, David. *Modernizing China's Military: Progress, Problems, and Prospects.* Berkeley: University of California Press, 2002.

Watts, A. J. *Jane's Warship: Recognition Guide.* London: Harper Collins Publishers, 2006.

*Ngok Lee*

## ARMY AND POLITICS

In imperial China, the military was used to suppress domestic upheavals and often as a means to effect the transition to a new dynastic cycle. In the mid-nineteenth century, however, the military's foray into political life did little to resolve the crisis of the Manchu Qing dynasty or reinvigorate the traditional mode of political control. On the contrary, the increasingly modernized military became a party to the conflict to determine the nation's political form and set about saving the nation.

Institutionally, the collapse of traditional political organization and intensified state building throughout the late nineteenth and twentieth centuries then led to a greater role for the army in modern China. Over the century-long period of modern nation building, the political role of the army grew along four specific dimensions. First, as state organization weakened in postimperial China, the military repeatedly helped resolve the problem of administrative control and maintenance of order. Second, army organization laid down patterns for generation change in the ruling elite. Third, the army was instrumental in changing complex relationships between the bureaucratic state and semiautonomous local communities, and thus in setting the foundation for new forms of collaboration between the two. Fourth, the military dominated in the political decision-making process at every stage of China's modern transformation.

## THE LATE QING PERIOD

In the 1830s to 1850s, the hierarchic military organization of the Qing, based on the stagnant 220,000-strong hereditary Eight Banners Army, proved to be ineffective in times of social unrest and conflict with the Western powers. Eventually the court had to appeal to the power of semiofficial local militias, organized by provincial commanders into local networks. Philip Kuhn (1980) has characterized such reliance as an unprecedented collaboration between the provincial bureaucracy and traditionally semiautonomous local communities. Despite the existing tradition of mobilizing irregular militias (*tuanlian*) under control of local elite, this remarkably high level of military organization undermined the Qing bureaucracy. As a web of vertically organized militia units, the so-called provincial armies, controlled by a number of prominent officials (such as Zeng Guofan, Li Hongzhang, and Zuo Zongtang), were instrumental to suppressing the Taiping rebels in 1853 to 1861. The Qing court sanctioned the subsequent self-strengthening and further development of local armies over the next three decades, and regional armies (like the Anhui army Li Hongzhang, or the Hunan army of Zeng Guofan) were considered part of the Qing military establishment.

Unlike regional armies, the New Armies, established shortly after China's bitter defeat in the first Sino-Japanese War (1894–1895), were nonpersonal and more professional, and they enjoyed greater political autonomy from Beijing. The New Armies were not merely a new stage of military bureaucratization and professionalization. Under the influence of prominent reformers of the late Qing period, the New Armies embraced the state militarist nationalism prevalent in Europe during the late nineteenth century. During the 1911 Revolution, the army opened the way to politics, and after 1911 the armed forces were applied to any domestic political conflict, whether to protect the constitution or to enforce commanders' personal hegemony.

## THE WARLORD PERIOD

The warlordism of 1912–1928 thus emerged as a political phenomenon. Militarist rulers had a clear political agenda of self-government aimed at restraining centralized bureaucratic control. Edward McCord (1993) sees the New Armies' antimonarchical war in 1915–1916 against Yuan Shikai's imperial ambitions as a turning point in the rise of warlordism. Yuan's incessant efforts to prevent the drift of political power into the hands of local military commanders slowed down but never reversed the process of political disintegration. Following his death provincial commanders were free to use their armed forces to achieve political supremacy. In the 1910s and 1920s, proliferation of military factions resulted in a fourfold rise of number of armed men to over 2 million.

These forces of local militarization aided warlords in recruiting for their armies. Military organization also helped to preserve the role of local elites by means of its engagement with governmental bodies. Warlords nonetheless could not dispense with the services of the local elite in civil administration. Hence, warlordism arose as an alliance of regional military rulers and local village elites under the banner of modernization and national reconstruction. This alliance was cemented by the newly found need to arrange for the collection and distribution of local tax revenues.

## THE EARLY REPUBLICAN PERIOD

In Republican China, the two dominant actors—the Nationalists and the Communists—sought to consolidate military force throughout the country and to form a new political elite by building Bolshevik-style parties and maintaining direct political control over the army. There arose a new party-army alliance rooted in the Whampoa Military Academy (Huangpu Junxiao) near Guangzhou (Canton), established in 1924 with support of Soviet Russia for training Nationalist Party officers. In 1925 two Whampoa-trained regiments formed the first division of the National Revolutionary Army, an effective instrument of war against the warlords and for politically unifying the country. This army's military control of eastern China in 1925–1927 enabled Chiang Kai-shek (Jiang Jieshi), its commander-in-chief, to assume power in the Nationalist government as a key political leader. In Nationalist China (1928–1949), Whampoa graduates held many command positions and by the late 1940s served as top military commanders or heads of governmental bodies at the central and provincial levels. During the Anti-Japanese War (1937–1945), the army was the main source of Nationalist Party members.

## THE COMMUNISTS DURING THE REPUBLICAN PERIOD

The army proved to be a leading force in the Communist Party's long path to power. Its strategy of a "people's war" helped the isolated Communist Party to survive in Northwest China in the late 1930s to early 1940s. This strategy sought to unite peasantry, party, and army under a party-army alliance that helped organize the socioeconomic life of the population. From 1937 to 1945 the Communist Party expanded its zone of control to border districts and liberated areas, where army-protected party cadres effectively restored order and control. One-third of newly established administrative units at the grassroots level were led by army representatives. In 1945 a quarter of the members of the Communist Party's Central Committee were military. The rise of peasant nationalism during the Anti-Japanese War helped the Communists to consolidate mass support and to compete effectively with local elites in control and mobilization. The army provided attractive career opportunities. By the end of war the Communist Army grew from a microscopic unit of about 40,000 soldiers in 1937 to an organized force of 1 million. Military service moved thousands of young peasants to the fore of political life, while the influence of the older gentry elites weakened. By liberation in 1949 the "brotherhood" of the People's Liberation Army underpinned the emerging new political culture of the People's Republic.

## THE MAOIST PERIOD

The Communist Party's rise to power never reduced the political role of the army. Military-Administrative Committees were established as centralized control units in every liberated district, and army commanders held top positions in civil administration. Top military officers were key political figures in Mao's China. For Communist Party leaders, symbiotic relationships with military commanders of the People's Liberation Army served as the foundation of their political power. Mao Zedong frequently appealed to the army in his numerous political campaigns, particularly during the decade of the Cultural Revolution (1966–1976), which started with a heavy blow against the fonts of power in the military and party and ended with the army's support of the anti–Cultural Revolution forces in the Communist Party's leadership.

Prominent military commanders of People's Liberation Army performed a crucial role in elaborating the main strategic decisions in China's domestic and foreign policies. In the late 1960s Mao and his military aids were highly concerned about the external threat, and these laid the foundation for a dramatic shift in Beijing's foreign-policy priorities. Concentration of heavily equipped Soviet troops in the Soviet Far East and in Mongolia (in accordance with the 1967 Soviet-Mongolian mutual defense treaty) and Sino-Soviet border clashes in 1969 inspired Mao's strategic decision to break the deadlock in China's relationship with the United States. These policies resulted in the signing of the historic Shanghai Communiqué in 1972 and the normalization of Sino-U.S. relations seven years later. During the period of Soviet global expansion in the mid-1970s, the army's concerns about China's weaknesses were a driving force behind the Four Modernizations program, as well as China's gradual turn toward its pragmatic, growth-oriented foreign policy.

At the end of the Maoist era, most of the army's top commanders (Ye Jianyin, Xu Xiangqian, Chen Xilian, and Deng Xiaoping) and powerful security forces supported the campaign, initiated by Hua Guofeng, Mao's successor, against the radical advocates of the Cultural Revolution. The army was instrumental in conducting military control at the local level since early 1977, and a thoroughly planned rectification campaign was fortified by intensive mass media pressure, including the military press. In 1977–1978 more than 70 top-ranking army officers were dismissed, and 6 famous army military commanders were rehabilitated. After the eleventh party congress in August 1977, 46.7 percent of the Central Committee's members were from the military. The privileges of army servicemen were secured, and army officers filled many administrative positions in the country. In December 1978 Deng Xiaoping, as the party leader and chairman of the Central Military Commission of the party's Central Committee, announced his strategy of reform.

## THE REFORM PERIOD

In the reform years, the issue of the independent political role of the army has remained topical. Post-Mao political struggle raised the question of party dominance over the military. The success of economic reforms has been beneficial for the military. The army was allowed to be involved in profit-making market-economy operations until the late 1990s. Unprecedented economic growth has enabled the Chinese leadership to improve the army's economic condition, restructure the People's Liberation Army to make it more professional, and modernize the defense industry. The most critical test of the party-army relationship occurred in June 1989 during the prodemocracy movement in Tiananmen Square. The army proved its loyalty to party leaders, and subsequent political developments in the 1990s demonstrated the strength and influence of military factions, led by Army Marshal Yang Shangkun and his supporters.

As China develops its armed forces along new organizational principles and renewed military doctrine, the party's direct-command role over the army tends to decrease. In 1982, parallel to the party's Central Military Commission, an identically named commission responsible to the National People's Congress was established. After the fifteenth party congress, the army was no longer represented in the Politburo of the Communist Party Central Committee. In October 2007 (the seventeenth party congress) the People's Liberation Army lost its seats in the Secretariat of the Communist Party Central Committee. Compared to its standing after the sixteenth party congress, the military's representation in the Central Committee dropped from 22.2 to 21.1 percent. Seeking to create a more professional, less politicized People's Liberation Army, capable of guaranteeing reforms and development and securing national integrity and China's new role in the regional and global arena, Hu Jintao, chairman of the party and the Central Military Commission, seemed likely to put the army under more effective control of the bureaucratic state and participatory political institutions.

**SEE ALSO** *Beiyang Clique; Central State Organs since 1949: Central Military Commission; Chiang Kai-shek (Jiang Jieshi); Deng Xiaoping; Li Hongzhang; Lin Biao; Mao Zedong; Military, 1912-1949; Peng Dehuai; Warlord Era (1916-1928); Wars since 1800; Zeng Guofan; Zhu De; Zuo Zongtang.*

**BIBLIOGRAPHY**

Blasko, Dennis J. *The Chinese Army Today: Tradition and Transformation for the 21st Century.* London: Routledge, 2006.

Dreyer, Edward. *China at War, 1901–1949.* New York: Longman, 1995.

Elliott, Mark C. *The Manchu Way: The Eight Banners and Ethnic Identity in Late Imperial China.* Stanford, CA: Stanford University Press, 2001.

Firbank, John K., and Kwang-Ching Liu, eds. *The Cambridge History of China.* Vol. 11: *Late Ch'ing, 1800–1911, Part 2.* Cambridge, U.K.: Cambridge University Press, 1980.

Finkelstein, David M., and Kristen Gunness, eds. *Civil-Military Relations in Today's China: Swimming in a New Sea.* Armonk, NY: M. E. Sharpe, 2007.

Fung, Edmund S. K. *The Military Dimension of the Chinese Revolution: The New Army and Its Role in the Revolution of 1911.* Vancouver: University of British Columbia Press, 1980.

Graff, David A., and Robin Higham, eds. *A Military History of China.* Boulder, CO: Westview Press, 2002.

Johnson, Chalmers. *Peasant Nationalism and Communist Power: The Emergence of Revolutionary China, 1937–1945.* Stanford, CA: Stanford University Press, 1962.

Kuhn, Philip A. *Rebellion and Its Enemies in Late Imperial China: Militarization and Social Structure, 1796–1864.* Cambridge, MA: Harvard University Press, 1980.

Li, Nan, ed. *Chinese Civil-Military Relations: The Transformation of the People's Liberation Army.* London: Routledge, 2006.

McCord, Edward. *The Power of the Gun: The Emergence of Modern Chinese Warlordism.* Berkeley, CA: University of California Press, 1993.

Swaine, Michael D. *The Role of the Chinese Military in National Security Policymaking.* Santa Monica, CA: Rand, 1996.

Van de Ven, Hans, ed. *Warfare in Chinese History.* Leiden, Netherlands: Brill, 2000.

Wakeman, Frederic, and Richard Louis Edmonds, eds. *Reappraising Republican China.* Oxford: Oxford University Press, 2000.

Whitson, William W., and Chen-hsia Huang. *Chinese High Command: A History of Communist Military Politics, 1927–71.* New York: Praeger, 1973.

Worthing, Peter M. *A Military History of Modern China: From the Manchu Conquest to Tian'anmen Square.* Westport, CT: Praeger Security International, 2007.

***Vitaly Kozyrev***

## ART EXHIBITIONS ABROAD

Before the twentieth century, exhibitions of Chinese art in the West reflected the taste for chinoiserie, focusing mainly on ceramics and decorative arts. Foreign interest in Chinese paintings and other antiquities emerged at the turn of the century following a flurry of archaeological finds, including the discovery of a sealed chamber filled with paintings, sutras, and documents at the Dunhuang Buddhist caves in 1900. Interest in such finds resulted in increasing numbers of exhibitions of early Chinese art, such as shows at the galleries of the Parisian art dealers Madame Langweil and Charles Vignier, the London exhibition of Chinese pottery and porcelain at the Burlington Fine Arts Club in 1910, and various exhibitions in both London and Paris of tomb figures from the Wei period (386–556) to Tang dynasty (618–907).

Following World War I, the pursuit of cultural internationalism among intellectuals yielded another revival of Chinese art in Europe, as seen in exhibitions ranging from antiquities and porcelain to contemporary paintings. One of the earliest exhibitions of contemporary Chinese painting in Europe was held in Prague in 1928 at the Galerie Rudolfinum, organized by Vojtech Chytil, an artist recently returned from ten years in Beijing. This show was followed by no fewer than eight Chinese art exhibitions over the subsequent three-year period, a phenomenon that is believed to have strongly affected Czech modernism.

At the same time, Chinese artists and administrators who had traveled abroad, including the painters Xu Beihong and Liu Haisu, began to see art exhibitions as necessary to cultural education and as a way to publicize the greatness of the Chinese nation. A series of well-received, joint Sino-Japanese painting exhibitions was held between 1921 and 1931, four of them in Japan. By the 1930s Chinese art leaders and government officials began actively organizing and promoting showings of Chinese art in Europe. From 1933 to 1935 alone, there occurred at least seventeen exhibitions of twentieth-century Chinese ink paintings in fourteen European cities in eight countries, such as *Ausstellung Chinesischer Maler der Jetztzeit* (Exhibition of contemporary Chinese painters) at the Frankfurter

Kunstverein in Frankfurt, *Mostra di Pittura Cinese* (Masters of Chinese painting) at the Palazzo Reale in Milan, and *Chinesische Malerei der Gegenwart* (Chinese contemporary art) in Berlin. In some instances, contemporary ink paintings were displayed along with ink paintings from the Song, Ming, and Qing dynasties. As Jo-Anne Birnie Danzker (2005) notes, modern works chosen by Chinese curators for exhibition in Europe tended to be ink paintings rather than oil paintings, as the latter were not well received by European audiences.

The whirlwind of activity centering on Chinese art culminated in the blockbuster *International Exhibition of Chinese Art* held in London from 1935 to 1936, which displayed 750 antiquities, paintings, and other imperial treasures from the Palace Museum collection under the auspices of the Nationalist government. The sheer magnitude of high-quality works that had never before been viewed in the West profoundly influenced the interest and study of Chinese art history. Though largely from the palace collection, the show was supplemented by works on loan from the noted Chinese porcelain collector Sir Percival David (1892–1964) as well as collections worldwide. The outbreak of the war with Japan in 1937 put a damper on exhibitions sent from China to foreign countries, although a number of benefit exhibitions were organized abroad by individuals or small groups of artists to support the war effort.

## THE SECOND HALF OF THE TWENTIETH CENTURY

After the Communist victory in 1949, few exhibitions from China traveled to the West, and most of these were to the Soviet-controlled Eastern bloc countries. For example, in 1955 a Chinese arts and crafts exhibition was held in Prague and a woodcut show in Warsaw, and in 1957 a Chinese ink painting exhibition was displayed in Moscow.

In 1961 *Chinese Art Treasures*, a major exhibition of classical masterpieces from the National Palace Museum in Taiwan, was sent by the exiled government of the Republic of China to Washington, D.C., and other cities. Consisting of 251 works, including 122 paintings, from the former imperial collection, it toured five American cities from 1961 to 1962. Most Americans had never before seen such an array of high-caliber Chinese paintings, especially by early landscape masters such as the eleventh-century artists Guo Xi and Fan Kuan. The related colloquia (1969 in Princeton and 1970 in Taibei) were also critical in stimulating the field of Chinese painting.

Although several American museums, including the Museum of Fine Arts in Boston, the Freer Gallery of Art in Washington, D.C., and the Nelson-Atkins Museum of Art in Kansas City, had assembled fine collections of Chinese painting during the first half of the twentieth century, great economic dislocations in China during the post–World War II period yielded an increased availability of Chinese paintings on the world art market. The modernist aesthetic that prevailed in that period made some American museums and collectors receptive to the formal and conceptual appeal of Chinese landscape painting, and they eagerly acquired examples that appeared on the market. These developments spurred increasingly sophisticated scholarly studies of Chinese painting, much of which was made public in the form of museum exhibitions. The 1954 *Chinese Landscape Painting* show at the Cleveland Museum of Art was an important early example but was followed by a series of more focused scholarly exhibitions. Asia Society and the China Institute in New York served as venues for many of these exhibitions. In 1962, for example, James Cahill, who had helped organize *Chinese Art Treasures*, curated a small exhibition of lyrical Southern Song album leaf paintings for Asia Society. Five years later, for the same host, he curated a remarkable exhibition of seventeenth-century paintings, *Fantastics and Eccentrics in Chinese Art*; in 1971 he produced *The Restless Landscape: Paintings of the Late Ming* and in 1981, *Shadows of Mt. Huang: Chinese Painting and Printing of the Anhui School*, both for the University Art Museum at the University of California, Berkeley. In 1968 the Cleveland Museum presented *Art under the Mongols*, and in 1971, one of the first scholarly exhibitions in the West of Chinese calligraphy opened at the Philadelphia Museum of Art. Richard Edwards at the University of Michigan organized two important monographic exhibitions, one on *Shitao* (Tao-chi) in 1967 and one on Wen Zhengming (Wen Cheng-ming) in 1976. Beginning in 1973, Wen Fong curated numerous exhibitions of paintings from the Metropolitan Museum of Art and Princeton University Art Museum as well as private collections. These exhibitions and the publications associated with them established painting as the focus of Chinese art study and appreciation in the United States, although many European scholars continued to focus on the archaeological, religious, and decorative arts that formed the strength of European collections.

As the decade of the Cultural Revolution (1966–1976) drew to a close, China began a period of foreign diplomatic outreach by means of ping-pong tournaments and art exhibitions. The first shows of archaeological finds from the People's Republic of China (PRC), such as the display of ceramic shards in Tokyo and the 1973 *Genius of China* exhibition in Paris and London of 385 discoveries ranging from the Neolithic (6500–1600 BCE) to the Yuan period (1279–1368), refined the international understanding of early Chinese art. A similar exhibition was held in Toronto, Washington, and Kansas City in 1974 and 1975. These shows were usually centrally planned, with objects requisitioned from local areas for inclusion in the shows sent abroad from Beijing.

Once the United States resumed diplomatic relations with the mainland, American audiences were exposed to a more focused scholarly examination of the PRC's recent archaeological discoveries in the 1980–1981 show *The Great Bronze Age of China*, which included several pre-Han works such as archaic bronzes, early jades, and life-sized terracotta soldiers. A similar exhibition drawing on recent archaeological findings in the mainland, *Kiln Sites of Ancient China: Recent Finds of Pottery and Porcelain*, took place in 1980 in London and Oxford. The focus on paintings continued, as seen in the 1981–1982 show *Ming and Qing Dynasties: Painting from Twelve Chinese Provinces*, which traveled to five Australian cities, and in the 1996–1997 exhibition *Splendor of Imperial China: Treasures from the National Palace Museum, Taipei*, which was organized by the Metropolitan Museum of Art and the National Palace Museum. Although it included ceramics and antiquities, the latter prominently featured calligraphy and paintings from the last millennium of Chinese history.

A distinctive feature of exhibitions abroad in the late twentieth century was an openness to different curatorial models that combined works from China with those held in Western collections. In 1992, for the exhibition *1492: Art in the Age of Exploration*, the Palace Museums of Taiwan and Beijing were permitted for the first time to lend their works to the same exhibition, an unprecedented breakthrough. Chinese museums of the twenty-first century are permitted to manage their own affairs, and have sent numerous exhibitions abroad on various topics in archaeology and painting, as well as lending individual items to large thematic exhibitions. Exhibitions of individual Chinese painters of the past, such as Bada Shanren (1626–1705) and Dong Qichang (1555–1636), continued, while showings of modern masters, including Wu Guanzhong (b. 1919) and Zhang Daqian (1899–1983), accelerated.

Art produced in the modern period began to receive a modest degree of attention in the late 1970s, but it was not until the 1990s that major American museums began to exhibit it once again, with the 1998 show *A Century in Crisis* at the Guggenheim Museum Soho in New York and Guggenheim Museum Bilbao in Spain, which presented not only ink paintings but also oil paintings and woodcuts, and the 2001 ink painting exhibition *Chinese Art: Modern Expressions*, at the Metropolitan Museum of Art.

## CONTEMPORARY CHINESE ART

In the 1990s globalization and its application as a curatorial strategy in the contemporary art world proved advantageous and timely for experimental artists looking for alternate exhibition spaces in conservative post-1989 China. In 1989 a watershed—and controversial—exhibition of Chinese contemporary art, *Magiciens de la Terre* (Magicians of the earth), was shown at the Centre Georges Pompidou and Grande Halle de la Villette in Paris. This exhibition, which featured artists from all over the world but chose Chinese artists who worked in Western or international forms, was groundbreaking in the complicated issues it raised, such as cultural authenticity and colonial and neocolonial influences. In sharp contrast to the situation of the 1930s, the Chinese works that have attracted the greatest share of critical attention in the West since the 1990s have been in Western or new media, such as oil paintings, installations, performance art, photography, and video. In 1990 *Chine Demain pour Hier*, curated by Chinese art critic Fei Dawei and sponsored by the French Ministry of Culture, was billed as the largest exhibition of contemporary Chinese art ever mounted in the West, and displayed works by such rising stars as Cai Guo-Qiang, Gu Wenda, and Huang Yong Ping (b. 1954).

Two large-scale exhibitions focusing solely on Chinese contemporary art opened in 1993: *China Avant-Garde*, organized by the Haus der Kulturen der Welt in Berlin, and *China's New Art, Post-1989*, which opened in Hong Kong and then traveled to Sydney and various North American venues between 1994 and 1997. Tsong-zung Chang and Li Xianting, the curators of *China's New Art*, divided the show's 200 works by 50 artists into themes such as Political Pop, Cynical Realism, and Wounded Romanticism, coining some of the terminology later scholars used to describe Chinese contemporary artworks. Smaller shows in 1993, such as *Fragmented Memory: The Chinese Avant-Garde in Exile* at the Wexner Center in Columbus, Ohio, and *Silent Energy* at the Museum of Modern Art in Oxford, brought increased recognition to contemporary Chinese artists, which led to the invitation of thirteen Chinese artists to participate in the Venice Biennial in 1993 and the São Paulo Biennial in 1994. Later Venice Biennials continued to spotlight Chinese artists, and in 2005 China finally opened an official pavilion with the exhibition *Virgin Garden: Emersion*. The 1998 show *Inside Out: New Chinese Art*, which contained works in various formats, such as oil paintings, photographs, and installations, and also featured art from Taiwan and Hong Kong, traveled extensively in the United States, Australia, Mexico, and Hong Kong. Chinese artists continue to exhibit in international biennials abroad, and in the twenty-first century Chinese museums began to hold their own international biennials, often with foreign curators, in China.

Group survey shows dominated exhibitions of Chinese art in the first decade of the twenty-first century, each trying to chart the rapid changes that China and the Chinese people have undergone in the post-Mao era, such as *Alors, la Chine?* at the Centre Georges Pompidou in 2003 and *Between Past and Future: Contemporary Chinese Photography* in 2004 at the International Center for Photography and

Asia Society in New York. As contemporary Chinese art grew in prominence on the international art scene and matured in the late twentieth and early twenty-first centuries, art institutions began organizing individual shows of the foremost artists. *Word Play: Contemporary Art by Xu Bing* opened at the Arthur M. Sackler Gallery in Washington, D.C., in 2001. Huang Yong Ping's retrospective, *House of Oracles,* opened in 2005 at the Walker Art Center in Minneapolis and toured two other North American venues and Beijing, and the retrospective of Cai Guo-Qiang, *I Want to Believe,* opened at the Guggenheim Museum in New York in 2008.

**SEE ALSO** *Archaeology, Politics of; Cai Guo-Qiang; Chinese Painting (guohua); Folk Art; Gu Wenda; Liu Haisu; Oil Painting (youhua); Xu Beihong; Xu Bing.*

**BIBLIOGRAPHY**


Andrews, Julia F., and Kuiyi Shen, eds. *A Century in Crisis: Modernity and Tradition in the Art of Twentieth-Century China.* New York: Guggenheim Museum, 1998.

Birnie-Danzker, Jo-Anne, Ken Lum, and Zheng Shengtian. *Shanghai Modern, 1919-1945.* Munich: Museum Villa Stuck and Hatje Cantz, 2005.

*The Chinese Exhibition: A Commemorative Catalogue of the International Exhibition of Chinese Art.* London: Faber and Faber, 1936.

Fong, Wen C., and James C. Y. Watt. *Possessing the Past: Treasures from the National Palace Museum, Taipei.* New York: Metropolitan Museum of Art; Taibei: National Palace Museum, 1996.

Gao, Minglu, ed. *Inside/Out: New Chinese Art.* San Francisco: San Francisco Museum of Modern Art; New York: Asia Society Galleries; Berkeley: University of California Press, 1998.

Pejc?ochová, Michaela. *Masters of 20th-Century Chinese Ink Painting from the Collection of the National Gallery in Prague.* Prague: National Gallery in Prague, 2008.

Wong, Aida Yuen. *Parting the Mists: Discovering Japan and the Rise of National-Style Painting in Modern China.* Honolulu: University of Hawaii Press, 2006.


*Vivian Y. Li*
*Julia F. Andrews*

## ART EXHIBITIONS, 1850–1949

Although China has a long history in art, in the past art appreciation was limited to the small circle of the educated elite, including courtiers and the literati. For the educated elite, art activities such as poetry, painting, and calligraphy were part of their own self-cultivation and means of communication between friends of the same social status. By the Ming (1368–1644) and Qing (1644–1912) periods, besides literati painting, exquisite objets d'art were popular among high officials, rich merchants, and landowners, yet art collections were still circulated only among the well-to-do.

In the quest for modernity and national prosperity, the government, early in the twentieth century, strove to promote modern commercial and industrial production and to develop a public education system. For the former, commercial expositions were introduced from Japan and the West in the capitals of major provinces. Included in these early expositions were school children's paintings and handcrafts. Such expositions effectively demonstrated to local authorities how public education could enhance the national capacity to produce modern merchandise. Moreover, officials and parents welcomed children's art work in school exhibitions. The Chinese were invited to take part in the international exhibition of educational products, held by Columbia University in New York in 1912. With this encouragement, the Ministry of Education of the Republic of China organized the National Children's Art Exhibition in Beijing two years later to promote painting and handcrafts in public schools. In general, school children's study of art functioned at three different levels: educational attainment, potential commodities, and art work.

In July 1918 the Shanghai Art School launched its first exhibition, commonly recognized as the first public art exhibition in China. Less than six years earlier, the young Liu Haisu (1896–1994) and his friends established this modest school for technical skills in painting. The exhibition, obviously modeled after those of the public schools, was a milestone. Earlier in Shanghai there had been charity exhibitions of traditional painting and calligraphy, but this was the first exhibition focusing on Western-style painting. Paintings on display were appreciated by the audience as modern art based on academic training. The resulting publicity helped the school to establish its reputation as a pioneer professional school for Western art in China.

The success of this exhibition encouraged Shanghai artists to organize modern-art exhibitions for the general public themselves. The first modern-art exhibition group, Tianma Hui (Pegasus Society), was organized in 1918 around Liu Haisu and Jiang Xin (1894–1939), an artist trained at Tokyo Art School and a teacher at Shanghai Art School.

After 1920 a new generation of painters who returned from study abroad to Shanghai became increasingly visible. In 1922 Liu Haisu first proposed a national art exhibition and was supported by Cai Yuanpei (1868–1940), the minister of education and later president of Academia Sinica. In April 1929 the first National Art Exhibition sponsored by the Ministry of Education was held in Shanghai. It was divided into seven genres: painting and calligraphy, bronze and stone, Western painting, sculpture, architecture, handcrafts, and photographs. Traditional Chinese art, rather than contemporary or Western art, was given pride of place. Growing concern over the loss of national treasure abroad turned the show partly into a showcase for antiquities. Like earlier expositions, the exhibition included shops and restaurants, in addition to performances of traditional opera and girls' gymnastics.

In the 1930s, international exhibitions exposed foreign audiences to Chinese art, old and new. In 1933 an exhibition of modern Chinese art organized by Xu Beihong (1895–1953) opened in Paris, with follow-up exhibitions in Berlin and Frankfurt, Moscow, Brussels, and Milan. In 1935 the International Exhibition of Chinese Art in London opened at the London Royal Academy of Arts. National treasures selected from the former imperial collection, along with archaeological finds from Academia Sinica were exhibited. The preview in Shanghai was received with national pride by enthusiastic viewers. In the subsequent National Art Exhibitions in 1937 and 1943, antiquities, traditional Chinese arts, as well as Western art depicting Chinese subject matters, captured the energy of artists and spectators.

Art exhibition thus gradually developed as a showcase for modernity and a venue for public appreciation of art. Sponsored by the government, major art exhibitions displayed outstanding collections of Chinese antiquities to promote national identity both at home and abroad.

**SEE ALSO** *Art Exhibitions since 1949; Collections and Collecting.*

**BIBLIOGRAPHY**

Tsuruta Takeyoshi. Minkokuki ni okeru zenkoku kibō no bijutsu tenrankai: Kinhyakunenrai Chūgoku kaiga shi kenkyū, 1 [National art exhibitions during the Republican period: A study in the history of Chinese painting over the past one hundred years, part 1]. *Bijutsu kenkyū*, no. 349 (1991): 18–42.

Wu Fangzheng. Zhongguo jindai chuqi de zhanlanhui: Cong chengji zhan dao meishu zhanlanhui [Early modern Chinese exhibitions: From school exhibitions to fine-art exhibitions]. In *Zhongguo shi xin lun: Meishu yu kaogu* [New perspectives on Chinese history: Art and archaeology], ed. Yan Juanying. Taibei: Lianjing Chubanshe, 2008.

Yan Juanying, ed. *Shanghai meishu fengyun, 1872–1949: Shenbao yishu ziliao tiaomu suoyin* [Art in Shanghai, 1872–1949: An index of art materials published in Shenbao newspaper]. Taibei: Institute of History and Philology, Academia Sinica, 2006.

***Chuanying Yen***

## ART EXHIBITIONS SINCE 1949

After 1949, when the People's Republic of China was established, most major art exhibitions in China were organized by the Artists' Association with the Ministry of Culture. The largest, the National Art Exhibition, is a competition for artists and also a national symbol of cultural accomplishment. In a socialist country such as China, investing a large amount of capital and human resources to develop art has clear aims: to publicize socialist ideology, promote socialist morality, maintain national solidarity, and improve art education.

The National Art Exhibition was meant to be held every five years, but it was interrupted by the Cultural Revolution (1966–1969). From 1949 to 2005 ten National Art Exhibitions were held in the National Art Gallery, each drawing thousands of participating artists and stimulating intense competition from local and state winners. For example, the oil painting section of the Seventh National Art Exhibition in 1989 received 587 entries, each of which had already won their local competitions. Only 356 of those works were selected for exhibition, and fifty were awarded prizes (two gold, eleven silver, and thirty-seven bronze awards). Because the number of works selected for competition and awarded prizes in the National Art Exhibition was used as a criterion to judge the provincial government's administrative achievement in culture, the intensity of the competition was very much like an all-nation sports game until mid-1990s.

Socialist realism was the dominant style, but after the Cultural Revolution and especially under the reform and opening-up policy introduced in 1978, Chinese art exhibitions began to change. The Second National Youth Exhibition in December 1980, for example, was notable for its rich variety of styles and subject matter. Luo Zhongli's (b. 1948) monumental work *Father*, in the style of American photo-realism, won the first prize. This poignant portrayal of a poor peasant returns to socialist realism from the perspective of Marxist humanism. In May 1985 the Exhibition of Young Artists of Progressive China took place in Beijing. The most remarkable work in this show was Zhang Qun (b. 1962) and Meng Luding's (b. 1962) surrealistic *Adam and Eve in the New Age*, which depicted the enlightenment of the new age and the awakening of individualism.

The Sixth National Art Exhibition of October 1984 was the largest national art exhibition to celebrate the thirty-fifth anniversary of the founding the People's Republic. More than 3,000 works were exhibited simultaneously in nine cities, including a full range of fifteen categories of art, some in modernist art styles. For a government-supported national exhibition in China, this was a great advance with regard to its artistic standards, but it was conservative in comparison with what was happening at that time internationally in modern art.

In the reform-oriented political atmosphere after 1978, some groups independent from the Artists' Association emerged and began to experiment with modern art.

In 1978, Stars (*Xin xing*) was one of the first groups to privately organize a modern exhibition by themselves, eventually having their work exhibited in the National Art Gallery. On February 5, 1989, China National Art Gallery hosted its first major Chinese modern art exhibition, *Zhongguo xiandai yishuzhan* (Chinese Modern Art Exhibition, or China/Avant-garde). Unexpectedly, the artist Xiao Lu (b. 1962) fired two gunshots at her own installation, causing the early closure of the exhibition.

In a sense, the gunshot during the China/Avant-garde exhibition was an omen for the incident that took place in Tiananmen Square on June 4, 1989. In a tense political atmosphere, the Seventh Art Exhibition of July 1989 was notable for its representation of Chinese academist (*xueyuanpai*) oil painting of the 1980s, which retained the formality of the original genre but moved closer to symbolism and surrealism. Meanwhile, pure abstract painting appeared in the National Art Exhibition for the first time.

The 1990s saw a major shift in Chinese social, political, and cultural life, as well as an economic boom and the transition toward a market system. Younger, independent curators began to play a more important role in the mid-1990s, organizing contemporary exhibitions such as the 1992 Guangzhou Biennale, the 1994 Shanghai Avant-garde Art Documents Exhibition, and *In the Name of Art*, a 1996 Shanghai installation art exhibition that was the first of its kind in China. That same year, Hangzhou had its first video art exhibition. In 1998 Shanghai hosted the first conceptual photography exhibition, *Variations on Video Images*, and in 1999 the first exhibition held in a shopping mall, *Art for Sale*.

The most significant contemporary art exhibition in the new millennium was the Shanghai Museum's *Shanghai Spirit: Shanghai Biennale 2000*, which featured works by both international and domestic contemporary artists. Many people believed such a big exhibition held in a state-run gallery was the first sign of the legalization of international styles of contemporary art in China.

Since 2001 the Ministry of Culture has supported Chinese contemporary art exhibited overseas. The two most prominent examples were the first major contemporary Chinese art exhibition, *Living in This Moment*, in Berlin in 2001, and China's first official participation an international biennale, at the São Paulo Biennale 2002. The first fully official contemporary art exhibition, September 2003's Beijing Biennale, organized by the Artists' Association and Ministry of Culture, demonstrated China's determination to join the international art world. Another indicator was China's first official attendance at the Venice Biennale, in June 2003, and its decision to set up its own permanent national pavilion.

Exhibition practices in China, especially since the 1990s, suggest the development of Chinese visual culture is breaking out of isolation and beginning to celebrate a more open-ended style that re-endows art with new freedom in its connection with the daily life of Chinese contemporary society.

**SEE ALSO** *Art Exhibitions, 1850–1949; Art, History of: since 1949; Art in New Media; Art Market since 1949; Art Museums; Art, Soviet Influence on; Chinese Painting (guohua); Collections and Collecting; New Wave Movement, '85; Oil Painting (youhua); Socialist Realism in Art.*

**BIBLIOGRAPHY**

Liu Xilin, ed. *Zhongguo Meishu Nianjian 1949–1989* [Annual of Chinese art, 1949–1989]. Guilin, China: Guangxi Meishu Chubanshe, 1993.

Shao Dazhen, and Li Song, eds. *20 shiji beijing huihuashi* [Twentieth-century Beijing art history]. Beijing: Renmin Meishu Chubanshe, 2007.

Shao Yiyang. Chinese Modern Art and Academy, 1980–1990. Ph.D. diss., University of Sydney, 2003.

***Shao Yiyang***

## ART HISTORY AND HISTORIOGRAPHY

Although China had a long tradition of writing on the history of calligraphy and painting, art history as a modern discipline did not come into being in China until the beginning of the twentieth century, when Chinese art history began to be examined in a global context. This entry examines the shift from traditional ways of writing about art in Chinese to methods characteristic of modern art history over the course of the period since 1800.

### 1800–1911

Up until the end of the nineteenth century the basic literature of art in China was in the form of compilations such as *Guochao huazheng lu* (Painting Annals of the Present Dynasty, preface dated 1735), a collection of Qing artists' biographies edited by Zhang Geng in the early eighteenth century. The tradition of cataloging private collections continued into the nineteenth and twentieth centuries. One of the most important catalogs was *Xuzhai minghua lu* (Catalog of Famous Painting in the Xuzhai Collection), compiled and published by the Shanghai collector-dealer-businessman Pang Yuanji (1864–1949) in 1909, with a sequel in 1924. Many of Pang's paintings were purchased by foreign collectors such as Charles Lang Freer (1854–1919), and today they are shown at the Freer Gallery of Art in Washington, D.C.

In 1889 Kang Youwei wrote and published *Guang yizhou shuangji* (Expansion of the Pairs of Oars for the

Boat of Arts)—later reissued as *Shujing* (The Mirror of Writing)—undoubtedly one of the most important and influential publications on art and art history in modern China. The treatise was reprinted eighteen times in its first seven years, but was banned by imperial orders after the Hundred Days' Reform. When the Reform failed, six of Kang Youwei's fellow reformers (including his younger brother) were executed, and Kang himself fled China, remaining in exile for sixteen years. After the end of the Qing dynasty (1644–1912) Kang's treatise was reprinted many times in China. It also was translated into Japanese by two distinguished Japanese scholar-calligraphers, Nakamura Fusetsu (1866–1943) and Ido Reizan (1869–1935), and published in 1914. Within one year, the translation had been reprinted three times; by 1927, it was in its eleventh edition. The work is one of the most influential modern classics by a Chinese writer in Japan, and has been instrumental in the shaping of modern Japanese calligraphy.

The late Qing dynasty, from about 1800 to 1912, saw a renaissance in the art of Chinese calligraphy that made a fresh challenge to the sole orthodoxy of the millennium-old *tiexue* (the school based on ancient handwritten calligraphic works); this challenge was posed by the more innovative *beixue* (the school based on ancient monumental inscriptions engraved on stelae). Although clearly indebted to its predecessors such as *Nanbei shupai lun* (Discourse on the Northern and Southern Schools of Calligraphy) by Ruan Yuan (1764–1849) and *Yizhou shuangji* (Paired Oars for the Boat of Art) by Bao Shichen (1775–1855), Kang Youwei's *Shujing* was far more comprehensive and radical and was meant to be both a history of Chinese calligraphy and, more significantly, an argument for the aesthetic superiority of the *beixue* school. Most importantly, although it was written in the Chinese historiographical tradition in which history was conceived as a mirror that reflects the past (as in *Zizhi tongjian* [The Comprehensive Mirror of Good Governance] by the great historian Sima Guang [1019–1086]), Kang Youwei's treatise intended to guide the creation of new art. The significance of *Shujing* lies in the fact that it is both a treatise in aesthetics and art history and, like many of the books discussed below, an embodiment of cultural history in modern China.

Since its publication in 1889 *Shujing* has played a tremendously important role in promoting the *beixue* movement and in stimulating heated discussions about how to deal with the past in creating a viable "modern" style in Chinese calligraphy. Its impact is evident in the many times it has been reprinted and in the caliber of Kang's many followers, such as Xu Beihong (1895–1953) and Liu Haisu (1896–1994), who made important contributions to modern Chinese art history.

### 1911–1949

Beginning in the early twentieth century a great deal of biographical and critical literature written between the Tang and the Qing periods (618–1912) was assembled into compendia such as *Meishu congshu* (A Collectanea of the Fine Arts) compiled by Huang Binhong (1865–1955) and Deng Shi (b. 1877), first published in 1911 with sequels in 1913, 1928, 1936, and 1947. Two other very useful reference works were compiled in the same era: *Shuhua shulu jieti* (Annotated Bibliography of Works on Painting and Calligraphy) by Yu Shaosong (1885–1949) was published in 1932, and *Lidai zhulu huamu* (List of Entries from Painting Catalogs of All Dynasties) by the American John C. Ferguson (1866–1945) under his Chinese name Fu Kaisen in 1934.

As Julia Andrews and Kuiyi Shen have pointed out, these publications were only the raw material from which history might be written—none were synthetic art histories in the modern sense. Art history in the twentieth century was a Western discipline based in European concepts of human evolution and progress, and in its most basic form covered the history of artistic style. In the very last years of the Qing dynasty most Chinese scholars deemed traditional Chinese painting to be in a severe decline, and instead favored Western-style artistic practice, which was, however, viewed ahistorically, simply as a skill. Thus, there would have been little need to understand its history. It was not until Cai Yuanpei (1868–1940) returned from his study in Germany that a higher purpose was publicly identified for art in modern China. In the view of Andrews and Shen, Cai clearly separated the study of art from utilitarianism, and provided a philosophical basis for training young people in the fine arts and art history (2006). By the end of the 1920s he had institutionalized the study of art within the national system of higher education.

It was under such active promotion by Cai and other thoughtful intellectuals that the importance of art was reevaluated within the new social and economic world of early Republican China. Art was no longer regarded merely as a tool, but as a core humanistic activity that had a history. This theoretical stance necessitated the introduction of art history into art schools and colleges. To assist in the art education of students and the public, publications of Chinese art history books in the Western sense began to appear in considerable quantity. Contemporary Japanese scholars offered an excellent model of how to write about Chinese art history. For instance, Ōmura Seigai (1868–1927), a faculty member of the Tokyo School of Fine Arts, published his lecture notes as *Tōyō bijutsu shōshi* (A Concise History of Eastern Art) to provide a general introduction to Asian art history. Later, he published a more specialized textbook, *Shina kaiga shōshi* (A Concise History of Chinese Painting). Nakamura Fusetsu (1868–1943), Ōmura's colleague, coauthored with Oga Seiun *Shina kaigashi* (History of Chinese Painting), which adopted a new and highly systematic approach to Chinese art. It divided Chinese art history into three broad periods: ancient, through the Sui dynasty (end 618 CE); medieval, from Tang through Yuan (end 1368); and early modern, from Ming through Qing (end 1912). This book "introduced to Chinese readers a solution to the problem of how to appreciate China's past art while still condemning its late Qing decline" (Andrews and Shen 2006, pp. 21–22).

When Chinese professors in the new art departments and schools realized that they lacked art history teaching materials, they turned to Japanese models. Chen Shizeng (1876–1923), a Tokyo-trained scholar, was one of the first writers to provide a significant theoretical response to some of the challenges posed by Cai in his "art education" program. Chen's 1921 essay "Wenrenhua zhi jiazhi" (The Value of Literati Painting) was a defense of literati painting in early Republican China, when literati painting, increasingly associated with the "Four Wangs" orthodoxy of the Qing dynasty, was under severe attack by contemporary scholars led by Kang Youwei and Chen Duxiu. Repetitive and unoriginal late Qing literati paintings came to be seen as a visual symbol of the decadence of the Qing regime and the nation's culture in decline. Most critics of the period thought that literati painting should be replaced by painting that was realistic, and Western oil painting was viewed as the solution. Thus, Chen's article "was important as a counterargument to the wholesale Westernization and attack on Chinese tradition that dominated the discourse of the May Fourth period" (Andrews and Shen 2006, p. 11). Chen regarded the value of literati painting as the spirit of Chinese art. He defended traditional Chinese culture from the sudden influx of Western culture, and pointed out a new way for the development of modern Chinese painting. Chen's 1925 *Zhongguo huihua shi* (History of Chinese Painting) followed the text of the Nakamura-Oga book, including its periodization, and even used the same terms to label his historical periods: *ancient*, *medieval*, and *early modern*.

The introduction of Western concepts of historical progression, as mediated through Japan, was of paramount importance to the writing of Chinese art histories of the 1920s. Nonetheless, an alternative scheme of periodization was proposed in the small *Zhongguo meishu xiaoshi* (A Concise History of Chinese Art) written by Teng Gu (1901–1941) in 1925. In the introduction Teng Gu, who was trained at the Tokyo Imperial University, wrote that he was strongly influenced by the theory of evolution as popularized in China by Liang Qichao (1873–1929). His text was divided into four organically progressing periods: birth and development (prehistoric to Han); intercourse (Han, Wei-Jin, Southern, and Northern dynasties); florescence (Tang through Song); and stagnation (Yuan through Qing). Teng Gu studied at Berlin University from 1929 to 1932 and wrote his doctoral dissertation on Tang and Song painting theories. His 1933 *Tang Song huihuashi* (A History of Tang and Song Painting) appropriated the stylistic and formalistic approaches of German-speaking art historians. In the 1930s, as the imperial collection was opened to public view and important private collections were well presented in different exhibitions (including the preview shows for international exhibitions), there was a boom in publication of reproduction albums and pictorial compilations. Painting and calligraphy were the dominant forms of Chinese visual art during that period, and the majority of early art histories were written by painters and devoted to the art they best understood. Teng Gu was one of the few who attempted to bring sculpture, architecture, and other arts into the picture.

Pan Tianshou, an art professor at the new national art college in Hangzhou, in his 1926 *Zhongguo huihua shi* (History of Chinese Painting) also followed the Nakamura-Oga book, including its periodization and the same terms to label his historical periods. Notably, in his article "Yuwai huihua liuru zhongtu kao" (Research on the Introduction of Western Painting in China) appended to the second edition of *Zhongguo huihua shi*, Pan examined three periods of Western-style painting in China and argued that Chinese painting and Western painting should develop separately.

*Zhongguo huaxue quanshi* (Complete History of Chinese Painting), one of the most important Chinese art history books of the 1920s, was published by Zheng Chang (1894–1952) in 1929. Zheng stated in the beginning of the book that "[t]here are two systems of painting in the world: Western painting, born on the Italian peninsula; and Eastern, originating in China, then absorbing West Asian, especially Indian elements, and then spreading to Japan and Korea. Italy is the mother of Occidental painting, and China is the ancestor of Oriental painting. This is the position of our nation's *guohua* in world art history" (Zheng p. 1; quoted in Andrews and Shen 2006, p. 25). He went on to describe his own contribution as an attempt to "collect, synthesize, organize chronologically, and use scientific methods to distinguish the origins of the schools and their relationship between the rise and fall of politics and religion" (quoted in Andrews and Shen 2006, p. 26). Zheng went beyond the oversimplified negation of late Qing literati painting and proposed to place it in a realm of poetry and self-expression, and thus opened the door to its continuing development in the modern world. This effort was widely appreciated at the time, and it was followed in the 1930s by a proliferation of more specialized publications, as well as a series of successful European exhibitions of Chinese art. This kind of art history book, which recognized the greatness of China's pre-Qing past, made possible a sense of cultural pride with which to face the humiliations China had endured over the previous decades. Chinese art history gained some confidence in the future potential of Chinese art.

Other important writers on Chinese art history during this period include Fu Baoshi (1904–1965), who wrote about late Ming artists, and Cen Jiawu (1912–1996), who adopted an anthropological and archaeological approach in his studies on Tang and Song art; both Fu and Cen were trained in Japan.

## 1949 TO THE PRESENT

Since the People's Republic was established in 1949, Chinese art historians have built on the scholarship inherited from Republican China. First of all, scholars combined archaeological discoveries with historical documentation to better serve art historical research; in addition, many important and useful reference works were published, such as Ding Fubao and Zhou Yunqing's *Sibu zonglu yishu bian* (A Reference Book on Art Compiled from the Complete Works of the Four Branches of Learning, 1957). Second, Western (including Marxist) theories and methods were applied to the study of Chinese art. Wang Sun's 1956 *Zhongguo meishushi jiangyi* (Lectures on the History of Chinese Art), based on his lectures at the Central Academy of Fine Arts, is a good example. Third, artworks were examined in their original context, including political, economic, and social conditions. Fourth, art in remote areas gained attention and was studied in the context of cultural communications between Chinese and other cultures; studies of folk art, the art at cave temples, and the art of the Liao (916–1125), Jin (1115–1234), and Western Xia (1032–1227) periods also flourished. Examples include Xie Zhiliu's 1955 *Dunhuang yishu xulu* (An Introduction to the Art at Dunhuang).

During the Cultural Revolution, art history research was severely limited. Since the 1970s and 1980s, however, Chinese scholars and museum curators began to reevaluate earlier conclusions and theories, rewrite histories, and find new methodologies, including interdisciplinary comparisons and technological examinations. They also began to bring together the diverging views of Chinese art history, "Marxist or formalist, that developed in China and the West respectively between 1950 and 1980" (Andrews and Shen 2006, p. 4). The archaeological excavations and subsequent research resulted in a tremendous amount of literature, not only in China but also in Europe and the United States. Historians of Chinese art actively exchange their research results and their views at conferences and symposia both inside and outside China. Recent critical and historical reevaluations of the Mount Huang school of painting, the Orthodox school of painting, the Suzhou school of painting and Dong Qichang, for instance, took place in international symposia and conference proceedings with many contributions from overseas scholars, indicating Chinese art historians' high degree of openness to new approaches.

Of all the works on connoisseurship published in recent years, Xu Bangda's *Gu shuhua jianding gailun* (An Introduction to Connoisseurship in Ancient Painting and Calligraphy, 1981) may be the most systematic treatise (Beijing: Wenwu chubanshe, 1981); it was revised and published in Shanghai by the Shanghai renmin meishu chubanshe in 2000 and revised again and published in Beijing by the Zijincheng chubanshe in 2005. The fact that this book has been published by three different publishers over a period of fourteen years, and that each version contains different illustrations, suggests its usefulness and popularity among students of Chinese calligraphy and painting. Xu Bangda's most monumental work so far, however, must be the four-volume set *Gu shuhua wei e kaobian* (Examination and Identification of the Forging of Ancient Calligraphy and Painting). In a favorable review of the work, Thomas Lawton, the former director of the Freer Gallery of Art and the Arthur M. Sacker Gallery of Art in Washington, D.C., summarizes the importance of this work: "There is no better guide for young scholars who want to learn more about the connoisseurship of Chinese calligraphy and painting than the writings of Xu Bangda. His keen observations make them not only an invaluable reference work, but also extraordinarily instructive. Serious consideration should be given to using *Gu shuhua wei e kaobian*, together with *Gu shuhua jianding gailun*, as textbooks for seminars on Chinese connoisseurship. Older, more opinionated specialists should appreciate the rare opportunity of being able to match wits—and convictions—with one of China's most distinguished specialists" (Lawton 1987, p. 187). It is important to mention the contributions made by other senior Chinese scholars (such as Xie Zhiliu, Qi Gong, Liu Jiu'an, Yang Renkai, and Fu Xinian) who, like Xu Bangda, served on the Committee on the Authentication of Ancient Chinese Calligraphy and Painting (*Zhongguo gudai shuhua jianding zu*) from 1984 to 1992. The committee, also known as the Group for Authentication of Ancient Calligraphy and Painting, has published its work in two major publications: *Zhongguo gudai shuhua mulu* (Catalog of Ancient Chinese Calligraphy and Painting, 1984–1993) and *Zhongguo gudai shuhua tulu* (Illustrated Catalog of Selected Works of Ancient Chinese Calligraphy and Painting, 1986–1995); both were published under the auspices of the Cultural Relics Research Protection Bureau (*Guojia wenwuju*). These publications will certainly enhance the writing of a more comprehensive history of Chinese calligraphy and painting.

In the twenty-first century the appearance of the *Kaifang de yishushi congshu* (Open Art History) series from the major publisher Sanlian Shudian in Beijing indicates the openness of Chinese scholars to a synthesis of traditional Chinese and non-Chinese approaches to art history. In this series, important works by scholars working outside China on Chinese art (such as Lothar Ledderose in Germany,

Craig Clunas in the United Kingdom, and Hung Wu in the United States) are translated into Chinese. Another new trend is the increasing attention paid to modern Chinese art, as seen in *Xiandai Zhongguo shufashi* (A History of Modern Chinese Calligraphy, 1993) by Chen Zhenlian and *Zhongguo xiandai huihuashi* (A History of Modern Chinese Painting, 1997–2003) by Li Zhujin and Wan Qingli. The latter publication also indicates the increasing collaboration among scholars and publishers in China, Hong Kong, Taiwan, and elsewhere.

**SEE ALSO** *Calligraphy; Chinese Painting (guohua); Kang Youwei; Liu Haisu; Pan Tianshou; Xu Beihong.*

**BIBLIOGRAPHY**

Andrews, Julia F., and Kuiyi Shen. The Japanese Impact of the Republican Art World: The Construction of Chinese Art History as a Modern Field. *Twentieth-century China* 32 (November 2006): 4–35.

Burnett, Katharine P. A Study of the Collection of Pang Yuan-chi. M.A. thesis, University of Michigan, Ann Arbor, 1986.

Chen, Shizeng, and Ōmura Seigai, *Zhongguo wenrenhua zhi yanjiu* [The study of literati painting]. Shanghai: Zhonghua Shuju, 1922.

Chen Zhenlian. *Xiandai Zhongguo shufashi* [A history of modern Chinese calligraphy]. Zhengzhou: Henan Meishu Chubanshe, 1993.

Ding Fubao, and Zhou Yunqing, eds. *Si bu zong lu yishu bian* [A reference book on art compiled from the completed works of the four branches of learning]. Shanghai: Shangwu yinshuguan,1957.

Ferguson, John C. *Lidai zhulu huamu* [List of entries from painting catalogs of all dynasties]. Nanjing: Jinling Taxue, 1934.

Hong, Zaixin, ed. *Haiwai zhongguohua yanjiu wenxuan* [Anthology of overseas writing on Chinese painting studies]. Shanghai: Remin Meishu Chubanshe, 1992.

Kang Youwei. *Guang yizhou shuangji* [Expansion of the pairs of oars for the boat of arts]. Beijing: Privately published, 1899.

Kong, Lingwei. Minguo, xinzhongguo meishushi yanjiu shuping [Discussion on art historical research in Republican China and New China]. *Meishu Yanjiu* [Research on fine arts] 4 (2008): 4–12.

Kong Lingwei. "Xinshixue" yu jindai zhongguo meishushi yanjiu de xingqi ["New historical study" and the rise of Chinese art historical research in modern China]. *Xin Meishu* [New fine arts] 4 (2008): 49–59.

Kuo, Jason C. Reflections on Connoisseurship of Chinese Calligraphy and Painting. In *Perspectives on Connoisseurship of Chinese Painting*, 7–32. Washington, DC: New Academia Publishing, 2008.

Lawton, Thomas. Review of *Gu shuhua wei e kaobian* by Xu Bangda. *Ars Orientalis* 17 (1987): 184–187.

Li Zhujin and Wan Qingli. *Zhongguo xiandai huihuashi* [A history of modern Chinese painting]. Taibei: Shitou, 1997–2003.

Pan Tianshou. *Zhongguo huihuashi* [History of Chinese painting]. Shanghai: Shangwu Yinshuguan, 1926.

Teng Gu. *Tang Song huihuashi* [A history of Tang and Song painting]. Shanghai: Shenzhou guoguang she, 1933.

Wang, Huan. Pan Tianshou he *Zhongguo huihuashi* [Pan Tianshou and *History of Chinese Painting]. Wenyi Pinglun* [Studies on literature and arts] 6 (2008): 78–80.

Xu Bangda. *Gu shuhua jianding gailun* [An introduction to connoisseurship in ancient painting and calligraphy]. Beijing: Wenwu Chubanshe, 1981.

Xu Bangda. *Gu shuhua wei e kaobian* [Examination and identification of the forging of ancient calligraphy and painting]. Nanjing: Jiangsu Guji Chubanshe, 1984.

Xue, Yongnian. "Fansi zhongguo meishushi de yanjiu yu xiezuo" [Reflections on the study and writing of Chinese art history]. *Meishu Yanjiu* [Research on fine arts] 2 (2008): 52–56.

Yu Shaosong. *Shu hua shu lu jie ti* [Annotated bibliography of works on painting and calligraphy]. Peking: Beiping Tushuguan, 1932.

Yuan, Tung-li. *The T. L. Yuan Bibliography of Western Writings on Chinese Art and Archaeology.* London: Mansell, 1975.

Zhang Heng. *Zen yang jian ding shu hua* [How to authenticate calligraphy and painting]. Beijing: Wenwu Chubanshe, 1966.

***Jason Kuo***

## ART IN NEW MEDIA

The arrival of art forms that exist outside the conventional genres of painting and sculpture is a relatively contemporary phenomenon in China. Initiated by the cultural shifts of the mid-1980s, interest in art using new media such as installation, video, performance, and other types of mixed media grew out of a core desire to challenge existing value systems and reinvent the language of art in China. During the 1980s artists were surrounded with an influx of new ideas and concepts, largely as a result of increased exposure to Western art, philosophy, and culture. Many began to apply new stylistic approaches to the standard forms of painting and sculpture; others made more radical gestures with experimental and experiential art forms such as installation art, video, and performance. At the outset, some of these experimentations existed outside of the academy and official spheres of art production, and thus were branded in China as "new wave" or, by the late 1980s, as "avant-garde." Western journalists and critics tended to refer to them as "anti-official."

Political and economic shifts in the 1990s brought renewed attention to these "avant-garde" practices, and soon the successes of Chinese artists abroad provoked the attention of the wider international art market. Folded into a broader rubric of "experimental art," art in new media met with a lack of exhibition opportunities and institutional support on the domestic scene, until official recognition finally came with the 2000 Shanghai biennial, the first biennial in China to feature international and Chinese artists side by side in a state-run museum. This landmark show signaled a general acceptance of the art forms of installation, video, and performance, and paved the way for further developments locally and globally.

### THE 1980s

Chinese experimental art grew out of the heady days of the 1980s, against a backdrop of economic reforms, cultural renaissance, and newly opened doors to the West. Art of this

***Chinese artist Gu Dexin's installation of apples in a wire cage, titled* 2006-10-7, *London, England, October 6, 2006.*** *The world of Chinese art enjoyed a flurry of activity beginning in the mid-1980s, after years of tight control by the government. Experiments in new media included video, performance, mixed-media arts, and installation.* © LUKE MACGREGOR/REUTERS/CORBIS

decade can be characterized by a core idealism and collective spirit, which was manifested in the implementation of radical ideas in forms of art previously absent or banned in the People's Republic of China (PRC). This included the formation of collectively-minded art groups such as Xiamen Dada, the Southern Art Salon, the Pond Society, the artistic group New Measurement Group and Tactile Art. Loosely termed the '85 New Wave movement, these activities—consisting of small temporary exhibitions, happenings or events, and publications—grew steadily in momentum and attention, culminating in the milestone *China/Avant-Garde* exhibition at the prestigious National Gallery of Art on February 5, 1989. However brief, the show legitimized an escalating movement and promised to redirect contemporary Chinese art.

## THE 1990s

Following the Tiananmen Square incident and the resulting events in 1989, experimental art shifted gears from deep optimism to cynicism, mockery, and self-exile. Despite political conservatism, the 1990s was a period of extreme growth and internationalization in the Chinese art world, powered in part by the commercial successes of oil painters and sculptors, but significantly also by the emigration of Chinese artists to Europe and the United States. The sensation surrounding these émigrés, whose work often dealt with issues of language, cultural translation, and imperialist critiques, eventually brought attention to those on the mainland who were responding to personal trauma and rampant urbanization. The idealistic intent and collective spirit of the 1980s was largely replaced by a desire for individual commercial success in the 1990s, leading artists to set their sights firmly upon the West for exhibition opportunities, access to collectors, and acclaim on the international stage. The period is marked by the intertwining of dualities: inside and outside, traditional and modern, Chinese and non-Chinese, local and global. Major touring exhibitions that were designed for non-Chinese audiences outside of China, such as *China's New Art: Post-89* and *Inside Out: New Chinese Art* (1998) were important precursors to the landmark *2000 Shanghai Biennale* held at the Shanghai Art Museum.

## INSTALLATION ART

Seeking to break art out of the official constraints and viewing conventions associated with large-scale national exhibitions, Chinese artists looked to installation art as a new way of engaging with viewers on a more direct, physical level. Often described as "theatrical," "experiential," or "immersive," installation art emphasizes how objects are positioned in a space and how our bodies respond. Among the earliest installation works in China was *Today No Water* (1986) by Wu Shanzhuan (b. 1960), in which the walls of a small room are plastered with political slogans and everyday advertising text, all written and installed in a manner resembling the style of Cultural Revolution–era "big character posters." Wu's work thus creates a confined conflation of public space and revolutionary space. Another seminal installation work is Xu Bing's gesture toward counter-monumentality and iconoclasm in *Book from the Sky* (1987–1991), which evokes historical vehicles of writing and authority but simultaneously undermines them through meaninglessness and the refusal of legibility. Artists such as Ai Weiwei (b. 1957) execute large-scale installations that modify, repurpose, or reconceptualize existing traditional Chinese wood crafts and ceramics, whereas others such as Gu Dexin (b. 1962) explore aspects of time and decay through arrangements of organic materials such as meat and fruit. Paris-based Huang Yong Ping (b. 1954) is perhaps the most prolific when it comes to strategies of historical, political, and artistic cultural resistance, and his usage of esoteric materials, combined with an emphasis on nonsubjectivity, chance, spontaneity, nonintentional creative process, and noninterference, transcends logical systems integral to Western modernity and modernism.

## VIDEO ART

The plasticity of video as an art form has allowed for many different levels of experimentation in China, ranging from its use as a new mode of individual expression to an emphasis on its aesthetic qualities. The first exhibition featuring video work by a Chinese artist was Zhang Peili's (b. 1957) *Document on Hygiene No. 3* in 1991. The video shows the artist engaging in an absurd action—repeatedly washing a chicken with soap and water in a basin. Similar works by Zhang such as *Water: Standard Pronunciation, Ci Hai* (1992), and works by Yan Lei (b. 1965) share this spirit of mockery and self-exploration. Other artists turned the lens toward the outside world, as in *Forever* (1994) by Zhu Jia (b. 1963), in which a camera is attached to the moving wheels of tricycle cart, giving audiences a kaleidoscopic view of the streets of Beijing. Following the seminal *Image and Phenomena* exhibition at the Zhejiang Academy in 1996—the first-ever survey of experimental Chinese video art—video art in China gained new ground and international recognition. The growth in attention led Zhang Peili and the curator Wu Meichun (b. 1969) to establish China's first New Media Art Department at the China Academy of Art in Hangzhou in 2000. Recent developments in video art, epitomized by the younger-generation artist Yang Fudong (b. 1971), have leaned toward more cinematic approaches and disjointed narratives that center on the role of the individual in a modern, globalized world.

## PERFORMANCE

On February 5, 1989, the day of the official opening of the *China/Avant-Garde* exhibition at the National Gallery of Art, the artist Xiao Lu (b. 1962) removed a gun from inside her coat and fired two shots into her own installation, *Dialogue*, before being quickly escorted away by security guards. Her actions led to the premature closing of the exhibition and launched an effective (though temporary) ban on official support for performance art in China that lasted through most of the 1990s. In 1994, inspired by his dirty and downtrodden surroundings in Beijing's East Village, Zhang Huan (b. 1965) smeared his naked body with a mixture of fish oil and honey and seated himself in the public toilet for an hour. Entitled *12 Square Meters*, his gesture aimed to express human tenacity and human vulnerability as well as the collective trauma of the individual within a vastly changing, urbanizing society. His work is central to "body art" performance in China, which involves explicit display of the body combined with aspects of gender reversal and self-mutilation. Other artists, especially those in the southern regions, responded to the rampant pace of urbanization in Chinese cities with works such as Chen Shaoxiong's (b. 1962) *Seven Days of Silence* (1991) and *Safely Crossing Linhe Road* (1995), in which the artist Lin Yilin (b. 1964) chose to move a wall of concrete blocks—one by one—from one side of a busy intersection to the other, thereby turning a seemingly simple task into a disruption of normal activities of daily life.

**SEE ALSO** *New Wave Movement, '85; Political Pop and Cynical Realism; Xu Bing.*

### BIBLIOGRAPHY


Berghuis, Thomas. *Performance Art in China.* Hong Kong: Timezone 8, 2007.

Doran, Valerie, and Melanie Pong, eds. *New Art from China, Post–1989.* London: Marlborough Fine Art, 1993.

Gao Minglu, ed. *Inside Out: New Chinese Art.* Berkeley: University of California Press, 1998.

Hou Hanru. *On the Mid-Ground.* Hong Kong: Timezone 8, 2002.

Koppel-Yang, Martina. *Semiotic Warfare: The Chinese Avant-Garde, 1979–1989.* Hong Kong: Timezone 8, 2003.

Wu Hung, ed. *Reinterpretation: A Decade of Experimental Chinese Art (1990–2000).* Guangzhou, China, and Chicago: Guangdong Museum of Art and Art Media Resources, 2002.

***Pauline J. Yao***

## ART MARKET, 1800–1949

The art market expanded both domestically and internationally in modern China. Before the First Opium War (1840–1842), four major types of art trades had been popular. First, contemporary literati and professional artworks were traded in old commercial centers such as Yangzhou. Second, antiques and artworks by deceased artists, which traditionally fell into the category of *gudong* (antiquities) and had a broad range of contents, had important markets in the old capitals of Shenyang and Beijing (where Liu Li Chang was the most famous). Third, folk art such as *muban nianhua* (New Year woodblock prints), originating in traditional centers such as Tianjin Yangliuqing, facilitated yearly festivities. And fourth, overseas China trade art was monopolized by *shi san hang* (the hong merchants) in Guangzhou (Canton).

After 1842, however, all these trades were in one way or another altered by the introduction of various Western art business models. Among all the treaty ports Shanghai was the most cosmopolitan, and it was there that contemporary painters, calligraphers, and seal engravers found safe haven during the Taiping Uprising (1850–1864). There a commercial system developed defining a new interdependent relationship between artists and patrons, and supporting the new painting style of *Haipai* (the Shanghai school). Prior to the mid-nineteenth century most patrons in Yangzhou had been merchants near the bottom of the social stratum. They sought works that appealed to the traditional upper-class taste for literati artists. Artists, also conventionally, followed the tradition of *runli*, charging according to a set price list, an old practice dating back to the seventeenth century or even earlier. In Shanghai, however, townsmen were becoming more sophisticated in their art consumption. There, artists found that they had to negotiate their rights and interests with the market through associations and agencies. Numerous associations of artists helped them in these transactions. Until 1949, fan and stationary shops played a major role in the art business, for painted fans had long been highly desired collectables. Also important was the department store gallery in Shanghai, which distributed Western-style *yuefenpai* (calendar posters), *lian huan hua* (storytelling books), and so on, painted mostly by commercial artists. There was no significant Chinese market in this era for Western art in oils or sculpture, whereas abroad various expositions fostered the interest in contemporary Chinese arts such as ceramics, lacquers, textiles, jade carvings, and snuff bottles.

The two Opium Wars of the 1840s and 1850s effectively ended the overseas China trade art from Canton. Later on, the market for *muban nianhua* declined due to the introduction of modern printing technology. However, the antique art business did not falter. The collecting of ceramics, bronze vessels, sculpture, furniture, and similar items in Shanghai, Tokyo, London, Paris, Berlin, Stockholm, and New York continued. After 1900 an international market for *guhua* (antique Chinese painting) began to take shape as Western collectors and museums became increasingly interested in early representational painting styles. A modern Shanghai antique marketplace was created in 1922 by the guild of the Shanghai antique dealers. As the century progressed, modern business practices—art exhibitions, publications, auctions, advertisements, gallery sales, and packaging strategies—were integrated into a globalized market for Chinese art, setting up new models for the dealers in the rest of the country. But China did not, even at the height of the Shanghai art trade in the Republican era, develop a system comparable to that of Western dealers and galleries, but instead relied on the traditional art societies.

**SEE ALSO** *Art Exhibitions, 1850–1949; Art Exhibitions since 1949; Beijing; Collections and Collecting; Folk Art; Handicrafts; Heritage Protection; Museums; Nanjing (Nanking); Shenyang; Wu Changshi (Wu Junqing); Yangzhou.*

**BIBLIOGRAPHY**

Bahr, Abel William. *Old Chinese Porcelain and Works of Art in China: Being Description and Illustrations of Articles Selected from an Exhibition Held in Shanghai, November, 1908.* London and New York: Cassell, 1911.

Chen Yongyi. *Jindai shuhua shichang yu fengge qianbian: yi Shanghai wei zhongxin (1843–1948)* [Modern calligraphy and painting market and the vicissitude of style: the case of Shanghai]. Beijing: Beijing Guangming Ribao Chubanshe, 2007.

Chen Zhongyuan. *Gu dong shuo qi zhen: liu li chang* [About the mysteries and treasures of antiques in Liu Li Chang]. Beijing: Beijing Chubanshe, 1997.

Crossman, Carl. *The Decorative Arts of the China Trade: Paintings, Furnishings, and Exotic Curiosities.* Woodbridge, U.K.: Antique Collectors' Club, 1991.

Deng Zhicheng. *Gu dong suo ji quan bian* [A complete collection of the miscellaneous accounts on antiques]. Beijing: Beijing Chubanshe, 1996.

Huang Binhong. Hu bin guwan shichang ji [Report on the antique market in Shanghai]. *Yiguan huakan* [Pictorial of art perspective] 2 (1926).

Jayne, Horace H. F. The Current Oriental Art Market. *Parnassus* 1, no. 8 (December 1929): 27–28.

Laing, Ellen. *Selling Happiness: Calendar Posters and Visual Culture in Early Twentieth-century Shanghai.* Honolulu: University of Hawaii Press, 2004.

Liang Jiabin, and Quan Zenghu. *Guangdong shi san hang kao* [The studies of the hong merchants in Guangdong]. Shanghai: Guoli Bianyiguan, 1937.

Wang Zhongxiu, Mao Ziliang, and Chen Hui. *Jinxiandai jinshi shuhuajia runli* [Remuneration rate of modern and contemporary seal-cutters, calligraphers, and painters]. Shanghai: Shanghai Huabao Chubanshe, 2004.

Xu Zhihao. *Zhongguo meishu she tuan manlu* [List of modern Chinese art societies]. Shanghai: Shanghai Shuhua Chubanshe, 1994.

*Zhonghua minghua: Shi Deni cangpin yingben* [Chinese pictorial art: E. A. Strehlneek collection]. Shanghai: Commercial Press, 1914.

***Zaixin Hong***

## ART MARKET SINCE 1949

In the first three decades after the establishment of the People's Republic of China (PRC) in 1949, the Chinese art market was centrally controlled by the government and insignificant to the development of the Chinese art scene. Like the Chinese economy, the art market was heavily influenced by the political atmosphere. During these three decades under a planned economy, all the resources of art markets were controlled and distributed by the state. Most artists lived on government salaries, and their works could be sold only to the government or to state-owned galleries. In about 1957, all previously private galleries and antique shops, such as Rongbaozhai in Beijing and Duoyunxuan in Shanghai, which sold art supplies such as ink, decorated stationary, and Chinese painting paper, as well as Chinese paintings and antiques, were nationalized. Cultural relics shops (*wenwushandian*) were another major venue for selling art work, where most buyers were foreign tourists. In addition to fuelling political and ideological propaganda, art works also were meant to decorate the empty walls of newly completed government buildings or to sell to foreign tourists or to buyers abroad in exchange of foreign currencies. However, this ended in the 1980s when the government initiated economic reforms that challenged the insufficiencies of the planned economy and promoted a "planned market economic system." At that time an art market began to take form in China.

In the market's formative stage, ceramics and Chinese ink paintings were especially popular among domestic collectors, whereas the buyers of Chinese oil paintings were mainly diplomats or foreigners working or living in China. As a result, the business of antique shops such as Rongbaozhai revived, and local secondhand markets such as Beijing's Guanyuan and Panjiayuan also became major nonofficial places to sell art works. Art galleries displaying oil paintings appeared in upscale hotels of Beijing and Shanghai in the early 1990s, selling mostly to international tourists. In 1992 the previously promoted planned market economy was replaced by a "socialist market economy." This strengthening of economic reform was based on party leaders' notions of developing the economy to improve people's living conditions.

A direct result of the new economic reform was the emergence of art auction houses, such as China Guardian (*Jiade*) in Beijing and *Duoyunxuan* in Shanghai. In 1993 and 1994, respectively, Duoyunxuan and Jiade held their first auctions, featuring Chinese ink paintings, oil paintings, and ceramics. Although the revenue from these auctions was low (Duoyunxuan's first auction made 8.29 million HK dollars), these sales signified that China's art market had entered a more mature stage, with both a primary market (galleries and antique shops) and a secondary market (auction houses). In the next decade private art galleries, antique shops, and auction houses gradually became major forces of the Chinese art market.

The boom in Chinese contemporary art at the turn of the twenty-first century was a direct result of the boom in the Chinese economy and the rise of China's international status. The driving force of the transformation of the art market was the auction house. Both Sotheby's and Christie's began to feature contemporary Chinese art at their Hong Kong auctions, attracting attention from international collectors. Within four years, market prices for the works of major Chinese artists such as Zhang Xiaogang (b. 1958), Yue Minjun (b. 1962), and Fang Lijun (b. 1963) jumped from tens of thousands of U.S. dollars to several million, pulling up the overall value of Chinese contemporary art at market. Art districts such as 798 Factory, Moganshan Street, and Dafencun appeared in Beijing, Shanghai, and Shezhen, respectively, encompassing hundreds of local and international galleries, artists' studios, and art bookstores. With the rapid growth of the economy, more and more nouveau riche became collectors: In 2007 Sotheby's and Christie's announced that over 50 percent of their buyers at Hong Kong sales were Asian, a significant jump since the early 2000s. A by-product of the rapid expansion of China's art market is the patriotic deed of buying and returning to China looted Chinese treasures from overseas. In 2007 the Macao casino tycoon Stanley Ho (b.1921) bought a sculpture of a horse head from the plundered Yuanmingyuan palace via a private sale at Sotheby's and donated it to China. The 2000s also saw the emergence of private art museums as domestic and international collectors wanted to exhibit their collections in formal environments; examples are Guan Yi's collection of Chinese avant-garde art works and Ma Weidu's collection of Chinese ceramics and furniture. In November 2007 the Belgian philanthropist Guy Ullens (b. 1936) opened Beijing's Ullens Center for Contemporary Art in 798, featuring contemporary art from his own and others' collections.

In this recent stage of its development, the Chinese art market has flourished in almost every way, from the

***The art installation* Life, *by Yue Minjun, on display for auction in Hong Kong, November 21, 2007.*** *Until the 1980s, artists in China worked for the central government, creating items offered for sale in state-owned galleries. With the opening of the economy at century's end came similar relaxations on the art market, allowing successful artists to command significant sums from international collectors.* © **ALEX HOFFORD/EPA/CORBIS**

increased production of artists to the growing number of galleries, from the skyrocketing revenue of auction houses to the record sale prices at market. Regarding the future of the Chinese art market, there are two opposing viewpoints. Optimists attribute the fast growth of the market to its long stagnation during the first four decades of the PRC, and believe that continued growth is inevitable. Pessimists predict a crash in the art market, because the feverish speed of its growth is evidence of irrationality that needs to be corrected.

SEE ALSO *Art Exhibitions, 1850–1949; Art Exhibitions since 1949; Collections and Collecting; Museums.*

BIBLIOGRAPHY

Andrews, Julia F. *Painters and Politics of the People's Republic of China, 1949–1979.* Berkeley: University of California Press, 1994.

Central Committee of the Chinese Communist Party. Guanyu jingji tizhi gaige de jueding [Decisions on Reform of the Economic System]. October 12, 1984.

Christie's Web site. http://www.christies.com.

Ma Weidu. *Mashuo Taoci* [Mr. Ma on Ceramics]. Beiing: Zhongguo Qingnian Chubanshe, 2002.

Hai Yan. Shinian paimai de shige huati [Ten Topics of Ten Years of Art Auction]. *Yishushichang* [Art Market] 4 (2003): 10–12.

Sotheby's Web site. http://www.sothebys.com.

*Zhang Rui*

## ART MUSEUMS

Just as the term *meishu*, or "fine art," is a neologism of modern China, the *meishuguan* (literally, "hall or gallery of art"), or art museum, is an invention of the twentieth century. *Meishu* was borrowed from the Japanese (*bijutsu*), a term coined in 1872 from an unidentified European language, possibly the French *beaux arts* or the German *kuntsgewerbe*. *Meishu* appears in Chinese art periodicals of the early twentieth century, including the *Guocui xuebao* (National essence journal) and the *Shenzhou guoguangji* (Cathay art book). The periodicals functioned as exhibitions of ancient and contemporary objects and paintings in print, and they defined the patrimony and ideals of the modern nation. They revealed a new desire on the part of elites to reconceptualize what art was and how art publicly related to the state. Collecting art and exhibiting it was deemed to be one means by which political as well as cultural authority could be asserted and national community created. The art museums that supplanted these periodicals thus became a critical space for interaction between state and curators, artists, and museum visitors.

The first museums (*bowuguan*) in China included art in their collections, but were not devoted strictly to visual arts. In 1913, roughly one year after the fall of the Qing dynasty (1644–1912) and the establishment of the Republican government, the writer Lu Xun (1881–1936) suggested that the government build a central art museum (*Zhongyang meishuguan*). The earliest art museum was not to be established until 1930, in Tianjin, but in 1914, art was promoted nationally with the establishment of the Exhibition Hall of Antiquities (Guwu Chenlie Xuo) in the Forbidden City, followed by the founding of the Palace Museum in 1925. Such museum collections, however, were essentially historical and archaeological in scope. The Liaoning Museum and other prefectural museums owned and showed primarily, but not exclusively, premodern art (which includes antiquities, but also categories not considered high art in premodern times, such as ceramics, lacquers, furniture, and so forth). The Shanghai Museum, established in 1937, was one of the first to mount shows of important objects and contemporary paintings belonging to local collectors. Ye Gongchuo (1880–1968), the first curator, was also a member of the Chinese Painting and Calligraphy Society. The outbreak of war with Japan ended whatever might have developed there.

After 1949, as part of the new economic model, museums showed work by living artists (sometimes on a rental basis, as at the Palace Museum). The China Art Gallery (Zhongguo Meishuguan), located in central Beijing, opened its doors in 1962. It and regional art museums of the Maoist era (1949–1976) exhibited socialist realist paintings and

***Tang Contemporary Art Gallery, 798 Art Zone, Beijing, October 26, 2007.*** *Once a light-industrial district, Beijing's 798 Art Zone features an eclectic collection of art galleries housed in the area's former warehouses. The open spaces of the East German-designed buildings provide an unusual backdrop for the works of China's contemporary artists.* © ROBERT WALLIS/CORBIS

folk art as a means of supporting the people's revolution, following Mao Zedong's demands in the famous talks at the Yan'an Conference on Literature and Art in 1942. By producing "correct" paintings depicting the revolution and its heroes, martyrs, and leaders, artists effectively were producing work that could be displayed in state-supported art museums, and that could be consumed by museum visitors as truthful, patriotic representations of everyday life under socialism.

The dynamic between artist, museum visitor, and state, mediated through the art museum, was to change dramatically after Mao's death and the end of the decade of the Cultural Revolution in 1976. As state-approved models of revolutionary art slowly began to be reassessed, or their style put to new purposes, the China Art Gallery became the site for a series of protests about the "drab uniformity of the Cultural Revolution." The Star (Xingxing) artists, denied official exhibition space in the gallery in the fall of 1979, displayed paintings and sculpture on the park railings outside the building. Their show was closed down, then moved, but remained in the public eye; a year later, having registered with the Beijing Artists Association, the Stars exhibited at the China Art Gallery again—this time, inside. An estimated 200,000 visitors attended.

This artist-state confrontation was echoed ten years later, in February 1989, at the China/Avant-Garde exhibition at the China Art Gallery. The grounds in front of the museum were draped in funereal black banners depicting the "No U Turn" traffic sign; there was no turning back. Invited artists participated, and others, uninvited, set up their own installations. Wu Hung notes that "many 'accidents' happened during the exhibition, including a premeditated shooting performance, [which] made a big stir in the capital" (2002, p. 84). The exhibition's controversies and its censorship by the state served as precursors to the terrible events later that spring in Tiananmen Square.

In the 1990s, art museums began to compete with an increasing number of independent art galleries, artist studios, and experimental display forums. Exhibition spaces expanded. At the end of the decade, art museums across China began to participate in international biennial and triennial exhibitions, transforming them once again into socially and culturally relevant institutions, and bringing them into the media spotlight. In order to raise their stature, many prominent *meishuguan* have recently changed their English names from "gallery" to "museum." These include the China Art Gallery, now called the National Art Museum of China (NAMOC), and the Shanghai Art Museum (as opposed to the Shanghai Bowuguan, still called the Shanghai Museum).

Yet this new prominence brought with it a new set of troubling issues; today, China's art museums are plagued by problems of ownership and identity. What counts as official or unofficial art? For whom are the displays curated? How do curators and artists balance the local with the global? Art critic and curator Hou Hanru observed of major biennial and triennial exhibitions in Chinese art museums, there "is a conscious effort by different local art communities to emancipate a space for more freedom of imagination and expression on the global map, and on the other hand, the biennial/triennial embodies a desire by the authorities to promote a coherent identity in an increasingly competitive world of cultural production" (2005, p. 32).

**SEE ALSO** *Art Exhibitions, 1850–1949; Art Exhibitions since 1949; Lu Xun; Museums; Socialist Realism in Art.*

**BIBLIOGRAPHY**

Asian Art Museum, Chong-Moon Lee Center for Asian Art and Culture. *The Elegant Gathering: The Yeh Family Collections.* San Francisco: Author, 2006.

Claypool, Lisa. Zhang Jian and China's First Museum. *Journal of Asian Studies* 64, 3 (2005): 567–604.

Hamlish, Tamara. Preserving the Palace Museum and the Making of Nationalism(s) in Twentieth-century China. *Museum Anthropology* 19, 2 (1995): 20–30.

Hou Hanru, ed. *The Second Guangzhou Triennial, Beyond: An Extraordinary Space of Experimentation for Modernization.* Guangzhou: Lingnan Meishu Chubanshe, 2005.

Ju, Jane C. The Palace Museum as Representation of Culture: Exhibitions and Canons of Chinese Art History. In *When Images Speak: Visual Representation and Cultural Mapping in Modern China,* ed. Huang Kewu, 477–507. Taibei: Zhongyang Yanjiu Yuan, Jindai Shi Yanjiusuo, 2003.

Shaping the Forbidden City as an Art-Historical Museum in the 1950s. *China Heritage Newsletter* 4 (December 2005).

Tseng, Alice Y. *The Imperial Museums of Meiji Japan: Architecture and Art of the Nation.* Seattle: University of Washington Press, 2008.

Wu Hung (Wu Hong). *Remaking Beijing: Tiananmen Square and the Creation of a Political Space.* Chicago: University of Chicago Press, 2005.

Wu Hung (Wu Hong), with Wang Huangsheng and Feng Boyi, eds. *The First Guangzhou Triennial, Reinterpretation: A Decade of Experimental Chinese Art (1990–2000).* Guangzhou: Guangdong Museum of Art, 2002.

***Lisa Claypool***

## ART SCHOOLS AND COLLEGES

In the early years of the twentieth century, China experienced an unprecedented interest in Western art education as artists sought to revitalize a tradition considered long stagnant and conservative, and to create and teach a new art that would be both modern and Chinese. This eagerness to learn from the West was an effect of nineteenth-century incursions of Western military and economic might, combined with widespread domestic disorder. As China experienced traumatic changes in almost all aspects of its traditional existence during this turbulent period, reform of the educational system seemed necessary.

The introduction of Western art into the school curriculum may be traced to the first decade of the 1900s when the Manchu monarchy established, as part of a major effort to modernize China, a comprehensive system of schools modeled on Japanese and Western prototypes. The basic curricula emphasized science and technology, and students were trained to observe reality, and to record it objectively on paper or on canvas. In primary schools, middle schools, university preparatory schools, specialized colleges, and technical institutes, Western art or *tuhua* (literally, "drawing and painting") was incorporated into all levels of the curriculum.

In particular, the Liangjiang Higher Normal School (Liangjiang Shifan Xuetang) in Nanjing, Jiangsu Province, the Beiyang Normal School (Beiyang Shifan Xuetang) in Baoding, Hebei Province, were established in 1906 to train art teachers to meet the increasing demand created by the new educational system. Most early art teachers in China were first hired from Japan and were mainly graduates of the Tokyo School of Art. They taught in major cities throughout the country. By 1912, partly as a result of the unstable political situation, most would return to Japan, and be replaced by recent graduates of the new Chinese normal schools or by Chinese students newly returned from overseas.

With the appointment of Cai Yuanpei (1867–1940) as the first minister of education in 1912, Cai's philosophy of aesthetic education was injected into the previously entirely functional curriculum. The adjusted aims for art courses were now twofold, combining the more scientific early approach with one that was more idealistic: first, developing the ability to freely draw and paint objects to be represented based on thorough observation; and second, developing an artistic conception and cultivating an aesthetic sensitivity. At the university level, subjects such as architecture, art history, and aesthetics were also introduced as elective courses in 1913, thus inaugurating the systematic study of art in China as an academic discipline.

In such major cities as Beijing, Nanjing, Shanghai, and Hangzhou, art schools and departments were established with the assistance of promising young artists responding to Cai's educational reforms. For example, Li Shutong (1880–1942), one of the earliest Tokyo School of Fine Arts graduates from China, began teaching Western art in Hangzhou in 1912 at the Zhejiang First Normal School (Zhejiang Diyi Shifan Xuexiao). And, in 1918, the National Beiping College of Art (Guoli Beiping Meishu Xuexiao), ancestor of Beijing Art Academy and today's Central Academy of Fine Arts, was established as the first national art school, with departments of traditional Chinese painting, design, and Western-style painting and later music and drama. Noted early principals of the academy include Zheng Jin (1883–1953), Lin Fengmian (1900–1991), and Xu Beihong (1895–1953).

With the establishment of the new capital and of National Central University in Nanjing in 1927, Cai Yuanpei, who served briefly as head of the Higher Education Council (Daxueyuan), also created an art department there, headed first by academic realist painter Li Yishi (1886–1942), and later by Xu Beihong, who was a proponent of a similar point of view. Of the three most influential art programs in Republican China, the earliest, the Shanghai Art Academy, founded in 1913, was private, and two, the National Hangzhou Arts Academy, founded in 1928, and the National Central University Art Department, founded in 1927, were public. The most prominent director of the Shanghai Art Academy, Liu Haisu (1896–1994), was strongly influenced by Japanese artists of the 1910s and 1920s and promoted postimpressionist styles. Lin Fengmian, who had studied in France, tried to implement slightly more up-to-date forms of modernism. The three schools thus became centers of different Western styles and created a budding pluralism in the art world of the 1930s. However, this period of experimentation in different Western art styles would end with the outbreak of war with Japan in 1937, which led the public colleges to retreat inland and merge their students and faculty. Throughout the eight-year war and the ensuing civil war, from 1945 to 1949, the artistic and political climate of China pressed artists to turn their attention to survival and war efforts in the face of an increasingly dire national crisis.

After liberation in 1949, the Central Academy of Fine Arts was established in a merging of the National Beiping Art College and the fine arts department of the Huabei University in Beijing. Xu Beihong was appointed principal, and the academy became the model for all art schools across the country. Under the new Communist government, art acquired the function of serving the workers, peasants, and soldiers as outlined in Chairman Mao Zedong's famous 1943 *Yan'an Talks on Literature and Art*. Socialist realism also emerged as the officially sanctioned style, and art production came under the strict control of the government in the following years.

With the success of Deng Xiaoping's open-door policies in the late 1980s, the situation has changed rapidly, with artists now trained for the booming commercial economy. Current stars of the art world include graduates Fang Lijun, Zhang Huan, and Xu Bing from the Central

Academy of Fine Arts; Gu Wenda, Wang Jinsong, and Zhang Peili from the Zhejiang Academy of Fine Arts (also known as China National Academy of Fine Arts); and Zhou Chunya, Zhang Xiaogang, Guo Jin, and Guo Wei from the Sichuan Academy of Fine Arts.

**SEE ALSO** *Chinese Painting (guohua); Lin Fengmian; Liu Haisu; Oil Painting (youhua); Xu Beihong.*

**BIBLIOGRAPHY**

Andrews, Julia F., and Kuiyi Shen. *A Century in Crisis: Modernity and Tradition in the Art of Twentieth-century China.* New York: Guggenheim Museum, 1998.

Kao Meiching (Kao Mayching). The Beginning of the Western-style Painting Movement in Relationship to Reforms in Education in Early Twentieth-century China. *New Asia Academic Bulletin* 4 (1983): 373–400.

Sullivan, Michael. *Art and Artists of Twentieth-century China.* Berkeley: University of California Press, 1996.

Zhu Boxiong and Chen Ruilin, eds. *Zhongguo xihua wushi nian 1898–1949* [Fifty years of Chinese Western painting, 1898–1949]. Beijing: Renmin Meishu Chubanshe, 1989.

*Ying Chua*

# ART SOCIETIES SINCE 1800

In the nineteenth century Chinese art societies evolved from traditional, spontaneous, entertainment-directed literati art groups to organized modern societies with widespread cultural and commercial appeal. Large-scale art exhibitions organized by art societies created popular demand for original works and significantly enlarged the commercial market. Shanghai was the center of art societies and the burgeoning art market. The Xiao Penglai Calligraphy and Painting Society, the first Modern Art Society in China, organized in 1839 by Jiang Baoling (1781–1840), functioned to bring together painters and calligraphers for mutual financial support. The Shanghai Tijinguan Epigraphy, Calligraphy, and Painting Society, established in about the mid-1890s, was a bridge between artists and the art market. Its social impact was enriched by one of the founding members, Wu Changshi (Wu Changshuo) (1844–1927), a renowned painter of birds and flowers.

## PROSPEROUS TIME, 1900–1936

From the beginning of the twentieth century until the May Fourth movement in 1919, nearly thirty art societies came into existence, almost three times the known number in the nineteenth century. Their members assembled to discuss not only art, but also social and political issues. Two types of art societies were formed in this period: those that aimed to carry forward traditional art forms and to preserve cultural relics, and those organized to promote aesthetic education inspired by Western aesthetics and culture. Societies of the first type included the Yuyuan Calligraphy and Painting Charitable Society (1909), the Shanghai Calligraphy and Painting Study Society (1910), the Society for Research in Chinese Painting (1919), the Society for Preserving Ancient Art (1920), and the Chinese Painting Society (1931). Societies of the second type included the Peking University Society for the Study of Painting Methods (1918), established by Cai Yuanpei (1868–1940), the president of Peking University; and Liu Haisu's Jiangsu Provincial Education Committee Fine Art Study Society (1918), whose art exhibitions had a profound social impact. These groups emphasized applying new methods and ideals (e.g., modernism and European aesthetic sensibilities) in educating the new generation.

From 1919 to 1936 several hundred art societies were founded. Whereas the first decades of the new century were dominated by art societies that aimed to preserve China's artistic "national essence," after 1919 more Western-study societies were established. The Storm Society was the most influential one; their debates over modern painting styles attracted widespread attention because they reflected deeper concerns about cultural identity and aesthetic theory.

During the Anti-Japanese War (1937–1945) and the Chinese civil war, the center for art societies transferred from Shanghai, Beijing, and Guangzhou (Canton) to Wuhan, Chongqing, and Yan'an. Many woodcut and cartoon art societies were organized and held exhibitions to mobilize social criticism and military resistance. The National Woodcut Society for Anti-Japanese War was established in Wuhan in 1938.

## AFTER 1949

A rather different type of society was the state-sponsored professional organization, the Chinese Artists Association, a prototype of which was established in 1949 for the purpose of educating artists for service to the state ideology. It dominated artistic production in the early years of the People's Republic of China and in certain subsequent periods. Privately organized societies were banned until after the Cultural Revolution (1966–1969), when a few small groups came together. The best publicized exhibition, that of the Star Group in 1979, promoted a new modernist trend. It was followed by the '85 New Wave movement, comprised of innumerable art societies advocating freedom of artistic expression; they were encouraged in their iconoclasm by liberal party officials. Other casual groupings of artists, such as the Yuanmingyuan Artists' Village, the early studios at 798, the Beijing East Village, and other groups that might resemble societies have caught the attention of the international art market.

## ART SOCIETIES

**YUYAN CALLIGRAPHY AND PAINTING CHARITABLE SOCIETY**

Yuyuan Calligraphy and Painting Charitable Society was established in 1909. Wu Changshi was a founding member. Its goals were to serve artists' economic needs and to aid victims of famines and floods.

**CHINESE PAINTING SOCIETY**

A group of artists in Shanghai, including many disciples and followers of Wu Changshi, established the Chinese Painting Society in 1931 to promote traditional Chinese painting and prevent Western cultural domination. They issued a journal, *Chinese Painting Monthly.*

**WOMEN'S CALLIGRAPHY AND PAINTING SOCIETY**

In 1934 Li Qiujun (1899–1971) and a group of other famous women artists in Shanghai organized the Women's Calligraphy and Painting Society. Different from the art societies that aimed for social revolution or promoted Western art styles, this group focused on Chinese women's self-expression in a time of social cultural transformation. The society held four art exhibitions and four issues of their special journal; it disbanded in 1937 when the Japanese army invaded Shanghai.

**ART SOCIETIES OF THE WOODCUT MOVEMENT**

At the instigation of Lu Xun (1881–1936), many art societies of the woodcut movement adopted the styles of European avant-garde prints to express their awareness and hatred of China's depraved political, social, and diplomatic circumstances in the 1930s and 1940s. The increasingly critical attitude toward the government aided the Communist victory in 1949.

**STORM SOCIETY**

Ni Yide (1901–1970), Pang Xunqin, and other artists trained in Tokyo and Paris formed the Storm Society to "devote our whole lives to the undisguised expression of our fierce emotion." They held annual exhibitions until 1935. The Storm Society played an important role in bringing Western art forms into China in the 1930s.

***He Jinli***

**SEE ALSO** *Art Exhibitions, 1850–1949; Art Exhibitions since 1949; Art Market, 1800–1949; Art Market since 1949; Art, National Essence Movement in; Art Schools and Colleges; Chinese Painting (guohua); Commercial Art: Cartoons, Comics, and Manhua; Epigraphic School of Art; Modernist Art of the 1920s and 1930s; New Print Movement.*

**BIBLIOGRAPHY**

Andrews, Julia F., and Kuiyi Shen, eds. *A Century in Crisis: Modernity and Tradition in the Art of Twentieth-century China.* New York: Guggenheim Museum, 1998.

Li Zhujing (Chu-tsing Li), and Wan Qingli. *Zhongguo Xiandai Huihua Shi* [Chinese Modern Art History: Late Qing and the Republican Period]. Shanghai: Wenhui Chubanshe, 2003.

Xu Zhihao. *Zhongguo Mieshu Shetuan Manlu* [A Record of Chinese Art Societies]. Shanghai: Shanghai Shuhua Chubanshe, 1994.

***He Jinli***

# ART, HISTORY OF

*This entry contains the following:*



## 1800–1911

No period in history has challenged Chinese art as greatly as the early modern period. In the nineteenth century the challenge of modernization under the impact of the West and Japan threatened China's culture and society, its worldview, and its very self-identity. Such social changes were also reflected in the visual culture of nineteenth-century China. Among these reflections, the development of the antiquarian studies (*jinshixue*, also known as the studies of epigraphy) and the Shanghai School of Painting (*Haishang huapai*) were the most representative and significant of the era.

### CALLIGRAPHY

From the eighteenth century on, collecting and studying ancient bronzes, jades, and stone inscriptions on stelae, known as Epigraphic School of Art (*Jinshi xuepai*), was very popular. Evidential research, the pursuit of ancient learning and textual scholarship (*kaozheng* or *kaoju*), sought to recover and verify historical and cultural premises in ancient writings and the classics. Such study of ancient writings and antiques gave rise to studying, as ancillary pursuits, seal carving, epigraphy, and ancient painting.

In the nineteenth century, three important essays—*Nanbei shupai lun* (The Northern and Southern schools of calligraphy) and *Beibei nantie lun* (Northern stelae and Southern copybooks), both by Ruan Yuan (1764–1849), and *Yizhou shuangji* (Two oars of the boat of art) by Bao Shichen (1775–1855)—provided the theoretical basis for epigraphic studies (Fong 2001, pp. 26–27). These works offered grounds for theories of calligraphy; more significantly, they also promoted the stele script (*bei ti*) of the Northern Wei (386–534). Nineteenth-century scholars came to see the stele script as the legitimate successor to Han and Wei calligraphy, and their evaluations of inscribed stelae ended the dominance of the copybook script (*tie xue*) in Chinese art history.

After 1888 Kang Youwei (1858–1927) produced *Guang yizhou shuangji* (Two oars of the boat of art, expanded, 1889). Kang's writing was produced in an atmosphere of nationalism rising in response to Western incursions into China. This book also initiated a preference for virile strength as an aesthetic ideal in calligraphy in a challenge to the well-established aesthetic hegemony of Wang Xizhi (307–360) and his followers. New archaeological findings led to the studies of epigraphy (*jinshixue*) being supplemented by studies of oracle-bone scripts (*jiaguwen*) unearthed in a Shang site in Anyang (Hunan Province) and of the cursive-clerical scripts (*caolishu*) found on clay seals and bamboo slips excavated in Northwest China. Archaeological discoveries further legitimated the development of antiquarian studies and archaic calligraphy practice. Representative calligraphers of the Epigraphic School of Art include Deng Shiru (1743–1805), Zhao Zhiqian (1829–1884), Wu Changshi (1844–1927), and Kang Youwei. Among them, Deng Shiru was the foremost advocate of reviving ancient methods of seal carving and calligraphy. Building on Deng's aesthetic perspective, Zhao Zhiqian employed ancient seal and clerical scripts (*zhuanshu*, *lishu*) in ink paintings and appropriated these archaic scripts to better accommodate his dense diagonal or slanted compositions. By blending traditional methods and modern practice, Zhao and his fellow scholar-artists gave new life to the Epigraphic School of Art.

At the turn of the twentieth century, Wu Changshi raised the Epigraphic School of Art to new heights. For example, he applied the stele script of stone-drum inscriptions into running script (*xingshu*) and cursive script (*caoshu*). Wu's bold and forceful methods created exceptional beauty in an archaic style of writing. His calligraphy in his paintings combined dynamic brushwork and forceful, well-balanced structures in each character.

Echoing Kang Youwei's concern about assimilating the Northern Wei stele script to large running and cursive scripts, these nineteenth-century calligraphers emphasized simplicity and unadorned forms. Late in the Qing period (1644–1912), the ever-increasing experiments in epigraphic style became the mainstream in the field of calligraphy. The art world was encouraged to revive archaic styles and formal simplicity.

## PAINTING

The Shanghai School of Painting (*Haishang huapai*) played a major role in the art of nineteenth-century China. While the Shanghai School was formed mainly by sojourning artists drawn to Shanghai from the mid-nineteenth century to the first few decades of the twentieth century by the lure of trade, the term *Haipai* was originally linked to vulgar commercial art appealing to the consumer culture of metropolitan Shanghai (Yang 2007, pp. 45–46).

Catering to middle-class merchants, these artists depicted plebian subject matters in colorful images, and in doing so they portrayed the newly developed urban culture. Instead of landscape painting, contemporary consumers of art favored a wide range of figure painting, portraits, and auspicious flower-and-bird subjects (pines, peonies, cranes, goldfishes with wisteria), these auspicious subjects signifying longevity, good fortune, or prosperity. In contrast to the concern about reviving antiquity among advocates of the Epigraphic School of Art, the Shanghai School of Painting explored novel visual presentations and assimilated new subjects of daily city life.

Shanghai was declared a treaty port after China was defeated in the First Opium War (1839–1842). This brought the development of finance, industry, and commerce, and increased the expansion of urban material resources and cultural consumption by the urban elite. The commercial environment in Shanghai thus created a demand for art from newly affluent professionals and merchants, both foreign and domestic. As a result, the ever-increasing number of painting societies, art associations, fan shops, and art agents fueled the expanding Shanghai art world and changed the cultural ambience of the city. The Duckweed Blossom Society (Pinghuashe Shuhuahui, 1862) was founded by twenty-four leading artists who shared common interests in cultural activities and antiquity. The Shanghai Tijinguan Epigraphy, Calligraphy, and Painting Society (Haishang Tijiguan Jinshi Shuhua Hui, late nineteenth century to 1926) organized numerous artistic gatherings that enabled the artists to exchange ideas and be introduced to potential patrons. By the end of the Qing dynasty, the Yu Garden Charitable Association of Calligraphy and Paintings (Yuyuan Shuhua Shanhui, 1909) further enhanced the social ties between charitable events and commercial art activities. The founding of art associations thus provided a supportive environment for social networking among sojourning artists, the social elite, and collectors. The activities sponsored by these art societies further stimulated the commercialization of traditional Chinese painting and calligraphy.

Yang Yi's *Haishang molin* (Ink forest of Shanghai, 1988 [1919]) records more than 600 artists active in Shanghai during the Qing period, and intensive art dealing opened a booming market for art in this most diverse urban metropolis. The art historian Shan Guolin (1998, p. 21) has identified three phases of the Shanghai School of Painting:

1. The formative period (1840s–1850s): Representative artists were Zhu Xiong (1801–1864), Zhang Xiong (1803–1886), Ren Xiong (1823–1857), and Wang Li (1813–1879).
2. The mature period (1860–1900): Representative artists were Hu Yuan (1823–1886), Xugu (1823–1896), Zhu Cheng (1826–1900), Zhao Zhiqian, Pu Hua (1832–1911), Qian Huian (1833–1911), Ren Xun (1835–1893), and Ren Yi (also known as Ren Bonian, 1840–1895).
3. The late period (1900–1930): Representative artists were Wu Changshi, Wu Qingyun (d. 1916), Gao Yong (1850–1921), Ni Tian (1855–1919), Ren Yu (1853–1901), and Wang Zhen (1867–1938).

In its formative and mature periods, the Shanghai School of Painting, focusing on Chinese traditional arts, epigraphy, and Western drawing techniques, attained its full development. In the late period, Chinese painting became weaker, pushed out of the mainstream by the importation of modern Western art and its techniques. It nevertheless continued to have admirers and collectors, including many far beyond Shanghai.

The figure paintings of the Shanghai School were much inspired by Chen Hongshou (1598–1652), Gai Qi (1744–1829), Fei Danxu (1801–1850), and the Eight Eccentrics of Yangzhou. Hu Xigui (1839–1883) and Wu Guxiang (1848–1903), in particular, gained public favor by painting the popular genre of female beauties, following in the steps of Gai Qi and Fei Danxu.

Flower-and-bird paintings in Shanghai primarily adhered to the style of the seventeenth-century master Yun Shouping (1633–1690), and the unconventional masters Jin Nong (1687–1763), Hua Yan (1682–1756), and Li Shan (1686–1762) of the Yangzhou School of Painting (*Yangzhou huapai*). The inspiration of Yun Shouping's elegant coloring and delicate touch can be found in the paintings of Wang Li, Zhu Xiong, and Zhang Xiong, while the individual styles of the Yangzhou painters are obvious in the art works of Xugu, Zhu Cheng, and Ren Yi.

The Buddhist monk Xugu earned his living by selling poems and paintings. He was especially gifted in drawing flowers, plants, small animals, fruits and vegetables, landscapes, and auspicious objects. In his style he applied dry, free, linear, and rhythmic brushwork to achieve an abstract flavor, yet his works are nevertheless imbued with the lyricism of traditional Chinese paintings.

Among Shanghai artists of the nineteenth century, the most famous were the Three Xiongs (Zhang Xiong, Zhu Xiong, and Ren Xiong) and the Four Rens (Ren Xiong, Ren Xun, Ren Yi, and Ren Yu), all of whom had a great impact on the development of the Shanghai School of Painting. A talented figure painter, Ren Xiong used angular contours to portray himself as a martial-arts figure in his self-portrait. What he delivered in the painting's inscription was a negotiation of idealism and realism. This image reveals a self-consciousness that extends beyond artistic portrayal to the painter's multiple self-identifications. Perhaps the artist aimed to convey his uncertain loyalty and disappointment in the corrupt Qing government. Ren Xiong also specialized in ancestral-portrait techniques, in which he received training from a local portraitist in Xiaoshan (Zhejiang Province) in his early years. Also influential in Shanghai was a younger brother of Ren Xiong, Ren Xun, who emulated Chen Hongshou's archaic painting style and the nail-head rat-tail brushstroke. His creativity is apparent in the flower-and-bird genre, his work characterized by skillful use of the brush and a varied range of ink tones.

Ren Yi, a follower of Ren Xiong and Ren Xun, vividly depicted popular legendary figures, historical heroes, and beauties. Painting in genres ranging from flowers and birds to everyday subject matter, historical stories, and portraiture, Ren Yi was a multitalented artist who achieved great fame in art circles in his day. The portrait of his friend Gao Yong reflects Ren Yi's keen interest in realistic styles and anatomical effects. In this painting, he vividly presented the skeletal and muscular structure of Gao's face. Having many bright highlights contrasted against shadows, the sitter appears demonstrative and realistic. Combining accurate anatomical observation with Chinese linear drawing techniques and light ink washes, Ren Yi portrayed a three-dimensional subject well. Perhaps it was Western art skills or the newly invented technology of photography available in the international settlements in Shanghai that stimulated and enriched his artistic vocabulary.

Ren Yi was also well regarded for his flower-and-bird painting, in which he emulated the Song dynasty (960–1279) boneless (*mogu*) style. In his later works he developed freer brushwork, sensitive coloring, and a more spontaneous boneless style, and applied it to figure painting to create a watercolor effect. In his novel usage of traditional technique, Ren Yi was also one of the first artists to use the foreign red pigment in traditional ink paintings. The visual immediacy in Ren's experimental work enjoyed tremendous popularity, especially among the Canton and Fujian merchant-compradors of Shanghai. Overall, Ren Yi reunited Chinese and Western art techniques and representations. Such features represent the innovation and modernity of the Shanghai School of Painting during China's transitional period.

During the last two decades of the nineteenth century, the visual culture of China was vibrant and captivating. Wu Jiayou (also known as Wu Youru, d. 1893) adapted painting to the lithographic techniques of the *Dianshizhai huabao* (Dianshi Studio pictorial, 1884–1898). To accommodate the growing demand for commercial art, Shanghai publishing houses adopted lithography, as well as graphic design. The subjects presented in lithographic images ranged from traditional folk stories to daily news, beauty competitions, and exotic foreign objects.

Though artists were exposed to Western techniques and art, the impact of Western art on the Shanghai School of Painting was limited largely to the adoption of foreign pigments and lithography, contrasts of light and dark to strengthen facial interpretations, and pencil sketches to impart a realistic effect to portraiture. There was no thorough Westernization in the Shanghai School of Painting, nor did these painters experiment in oil painting or other Western materials. Though Shanghai was a modern metropolitan city, the Shanghai School of Painting was partially rooted in the tradition of the Epigraphic School of Art, literati painting, and the folk arts, enough so that the artists tried to find a balance between these traditions and the newly imported techniques.

Zhao Zhiqian and Wu Changshi were often regarded as leading painters of the Shanghai School of Painting, and their pursuit of and accomplishments in embodying in a single work the three perfections (*sanjue*; namely, poetry, calligraphy, and painting) profoundly inspired other scholar-painters in the city. In their flower-and-bird paintings, they applied metal-and-stone scripts and seal-carving techniques, calligraphic brushwork, and greater free-hand brushwork (*daxieyi*) to initiate a new trend of boldness. Their exaggerated compositions—with an emphasis on bright color washes, heavy ink tones, and forceful brushstrokes—gave the works of Wu and Zhao a distinctive style and also gave these artists a distinctive status in modern Chinese painting.

Wu was also at the forefront of the Xiling Association of Seal Carvers (Xiling Yinshe), established in Hangzhou (Zhejiang Province) in 1904. It encouraged seal-carving studies (in the epigraphic tradition) by regularly holding private gatherings and cultural activities. As a leading painter, Wu was the most reputable artist to integrate the literati painting tradition with satisfying the demand of domestic and overseas bourgeois patronage at the beginning of the twentieth century. Wu's art also inspired later artists, such as Qi Baishi (1863–1957) and Huang Binhong (1865–1955).

Competing with Shanghai, Guangdong also produced noteworthy artists, such as Ju Chao (1811–1865) and Ju Lian (1828–1904). Following the style of Yun Shouping, Ju Lian excelled in the boneless style and was famous for applying the new painting techniques of splashed water (*zhuang shui*) and sprinkled powder (*zhuang fen*) to flower-and-bird painting. Both artists were precursors of the Lingnan School of Painting (*Lingnan huapai*) during the early twentieth century.

## ASSESSMENT

The Epigraphic School of Art was stimulated by evidential research and archaeological practice, which combined to establish a refreshing new set of aesthetic criteria in calligraphy and painting. From mid-century on, the visual presentations of the Shanghai School of Painting were a hybrid of literati painting, popular culture, and Western technique. Shanghai art also deeply influenced later artists, such as Qi Baishi, Zhang Daqian (1899–1983), Zhu Qizhan (1892–1996), and Pan Tianshou (1897–1971). Such professional and commercial production for a booming bourgeois class in Shanghai opened up an exciting new era of art in China.

**SEE ALSO** *Art Societies since 1800; Calligraphy; Epigraphic School of Art; Lingnan School of Painting; Lithographic and Modern Printing; Pictorial Magazines since 1880; Ren Xiong; Ren Yi (Ren Bonian); Shanghai School of Painting; Wang Zhen (Wang Yiting); Wu Changshi (Wu Junqing); Zhang Daqian (Chang Dai-chien).*

## BIBLIOGRAPHY

Andrews, Julia, and Kuiyi Shen. *A Century in Crisis: Modernity and Tradition in the Art of Twentieth-Century China.* New York: Guggenheim Museum, 1998.

Croizier, Ralph. *Art and Revolution in Modern China: The Lingnan (Cantonese) School of Painting, 1906–1951.* Berkeley: University of California Press, 1988.

Fong, Wen C. *Between Two Cultures: Late-Nineteenth- and Twentieth-Century Chinese Paintings from the Robert H. Ellsworth Collection in the Metropolitan Museum of Art.* New York: Metropolitan Museum of Art, 2001.

Shan, Goulin. Painting of China's New Metropolis: The Shanghai School, 1850–1900. Trans. Julia Andrews and Kuiyi Shen. In *A Century in Crisis: Modernity and Tradition in the Art of Twentieth-Century China*, ed. Julia Andrews and Kuiyi Shen. New York: Guggenheim Museum, 1998.

Shanghai Bowuguan [Shanghai Museum]. *Chinese Paintings from the Shanghai Museum, 1851–1911.* Edinburgh: NMS Publishing, 2000.

Yang, Chia Ling. *New Wine in Old Bottles: Art of Ren Bonian in Nineteenth-Century Shanghai.* London: Saffron, 2007.

Yang, Yi. *Haishang molin* [Ink forest of Shanghai]. Taibei: Wen Shi Zhe Chubanshe, 1988. First edition, 1919.

***Shuchi Shen***

## 1911–1949

In the four decades following the Republican revolution of 1911 and the establishment of the Republic of China (1912–1949), Chinese artists faced daunting aesthetic and practical problems. How ought they to modernize their nation and their art? Should artists maintain or abandon ties to their nation's past? Ought they to embrace the possibilities offered by foreign artistic traditions? How should their art address China's rapidly changing economic, political, and social conditions? In what ways could artists make a living and pursue their aesthetic interests in the midst of extensive warfare and social upheaval? Artists responded to these challenges by reformulating traditional Chinese art, mastering new media and forms of expression from the West, and adapting to shifting conditions of production.

### TRADITIONAL CHINESE PAINTING (*GUOHUA*) AND CALLIGRAPHY

By the end of the Qing dynasty (1644–1912), painters of the Orthodox school, which championed the creative emulation of scholarly painting from the past, had settled into formulaic repetition of a few masters' brushwork, thereby robbing Chinese literati art of much of its vitality. The most innovative of China's professional masters had passed away. Chinese calligraphy written in the classical tradition of Wang Xizhi (307–365) was in decline. However, over the course of the Republican period, as enthusiasts of Western art were mastering new media and forms of expression from abroad, producers of traditional Chinese painting (*guohua*) and calligraphy reversed the waning fortunes of their arts.

During the 1910s and 1920s, traditionalist artists sought inspiration outside the lineages and modes that had dominated art of the nineteenth century. Calligraphers like Wu Changshi (1844–1927) and Kang Youwei (1858–1927) turned away from decorative reiteration of standard script and developed seal-script and archaistic forms of semicursive script, such as *zhangcao*, through study of inscriptions on stone drums and steles of the Eastern Zhou (770–256 BCE) and Northern Wei (386–534) periods. Many *guohua* painters found alternatives to the models and approaches espoused by the Orthodox school. Shanghai's Wu Changshi used his epigraphically informed brushwork to structure renderings of popular subjects like plants and rocks. His approach was highly influential, giving direction to such artists as Wang Zhen (1867–1938), Chen Hengque (1876–1923), Qi Baishi (1864–1957), and Pan Tianshou (1898–1971). Painters like Wu, Wang, and Qi applied popular imagery to literati effect, developing reputations as scholarly painters even as they painted works for sale. This reception highlights the substantial diminution of the expectation, widespread in late imperial China, that literati artists were not to sell their works but to exchange them for such loftier purposes as self-expression and personal friendship. In Beijing, Jin Cheng (1877–1926) and Chen Hengque promoted the emulation of Tang (618–907) and Song (960–1279) masters and the Qing individualists Shitao (1642–1718) and Zhu Da (1626–1705).

In returning to China's past, traditionalist artists aimed to revitalize Chinese pictorial art and calligraphy and thus to enable them to compete with the art of other nations. Many *guohua* painters and calligraphers, concerned that Chinese civilization might perish at the hands of the West, joined the National Essence movement. Forming artistic societies dedicated to preserving traditional Chinese art as an irreplaceable medium of Chinese culture, they published journals and catalogs and mounted exhibitions. Chen Hengque argued that *guohua* could be a modern art as capable of personal expression as was avant-garde painting in the West, and Liu Haisu (1896–1994) made a case for this claim by exhibiting his Chinese ink paintings in Europe. Traditionalists like Wu Changshi, Wang Zhen, Qi Baishi, and Zhang Daqian (1899–1983) cultivated networks of collaborators and patrons abroad, especially in Japan. Joining forces with Japanese Sinophiles and traditionalists, they sought to counter Western art's claim to modernity, forming international artistic groups and mounting a series of joint art exhibitions in China and Japan during the 1920s and early 1930s. When the Ministry of Education mounted its First Chinese National Art Exhibition in 1929, *guohua* painters and calligraphers had succeeded in securing a place for their arts. The market for traditional painting and calligraphy was thriving. In the 1930s and 1940s, artists like Huang Binhong (1865–1955) and Fu Baoshi (1904–1965) had the freedom to develop nuanced explorations of various streams of China's painting tradition.

Not all producers of *guohua* believed that their nation's tradition alone could supply what was needed to revitalize China's native painting. Some opted for a more radical reformulation of *guohua*. Gao Jianfu (1879–1951), Gao Qifeng (1889–1933), and Chen Shuren (1884–1948) of the Lingnan school aimed to create a new, national painting by including in it some of the lyricism, Western-inspired naturalism, and subject matter of Japanese-style painting (*nihonga*), which they had encountered in Japan. The French-trained Xu Beihong (1895–1953), who was an admirer of European academic art, incorporated European line drawing and techniques for rendering light and shade into works that he produced with Chinese materials. Xu's protégé Jiang Zhaohe (1904–1986) also espoused Western naturalism. However, unlike Xu, Jiang made a practice of realistically portraying China's lower classes and documenting their contemporary travails. Lin Fengmian (1900–1991), who had studied in France, fused some of the European avant-garde's interests in lighting, color, and composition with traditional Chinese subjects and materials to produce boldly brushed images characterized by serenity and melancholy.

**Eagle** *by Gao Jianfu, 1929. During the 1910s and 1920s, some artists specializing in traditional Chinese paintings, called* guohua, *called for a complete reinvigoration of the art by incorporating Western and Japanese influences. As part of the Lingnan school, Gao Jianfu advocated these changes, pressing for artists to introduce new subject matter and naturalist techniques in their artwork.* GAO JIANFU/FOTOE

## WESTERN-STYLE DRAWING AND PAINTING

In the final decade of the Qing dynasty, political and educational reformers made Western-style drawing and painting part of the national educational curriculum. Japanese instructors in China and Japan exposed Chinese students to Western materials, techniques, and subject matter. In the 1910s, Li Shutong (1880–1942), who had studied under the European-trained Kuroda Seiki (1866–1924) at the Tokyo School of Fine Arts (Tōkyō Bijutsu Gakkō), returned to China to help pioneer the teaching of Western art, and a group of art enthusiasts, including the teenage Liu Haisu, privately founded what would become one of China's most important art schools, the Shanghai Art Academy (Shanghai Meizhuan). In 1912 China's first minister of education, Cai Yuanpei (1867–1940), began promoting aesthetic education as a means of developing an ethical and cosmopolitan worldview. His views helped inspire the social concern and iconoclasm of the New Culture movement and the May Fourth movement, which called for the transformation of Chinese society through a radical remaking of Chinese literature and art.

Around 1920, a second wave of Chinese students began to return from Japan, where teachers at the Tokyo School of Fine Arts and the Kawabata Academy of Painting (Kawabata Gagakkō) in Tokyo had encouraged them to explore various schools of European modernism. Such oil painters as Chen Baoyi (1893–1945), Guan Liang (1900–1986), Guan Zilan (1903–1986), and Ni Yide (1901–1970) exhibited works in Shanghai that drew heavily upon postimpressionist styles developed in Japan by Yasui Sōtarō (1888–1955) and Umehara Ryūzaburō (1888–1986). Chinese artists of the 1930s, many of whom had studied in Japan and France, turned to such European modes as dadaism, constructivism, and surrealism. Ni Yide, Pang Xunqin (1906–1985), and Qiu Di (1906–1958) attempted to create a Chinese avant-garde in Shanghai by forming the Storm Society (Juelan She).

Art schools in China played an important role in the development of Chinese interest in Western-style drawing and painting. The Shanghai Art Academy, directed for many years by Liu Haisu, taught students to work in the open air and caused a stir with its use of nude models. The National Hangzhou Art College (Guoli Hangzhou Yishu Zhuanke Xuexiao), which Cai Yuanpei and Lin Fengmian founded in 1928, encouraged students of Western-style art to explore European modernist styles, and it published important art journals. The art department of the National Central University (Guoli Zhongyang Daxue) in Nanjing, which from 1928 was headed by Xu Beihong, taught European academic painting.

Following the Japanese invasion of 1937, Western-style painting suffered greatly. Many art academies were forced to move or to close. Social disruptions and shortages of supplies caused fewer artists to paint in oils. Paintings produced in the war years tended to be more somber in subject matter and tone, with many artists creating introspective and meditative works. Others created propaganda images for the purpose of combating Japanese aggression.

## GRAPHIC ARTS

In the 1930s and 1940s, Chinese artists began to exploit the woodblock print for modernist artistic aims and political purposes. In the 1920s, the influential writer Lu Xun (1881–1936), who keenly wished to address China's pressing social and political problems through literary and artistic means, collected, displayed, and published European modernist woodblock prints. Beginning in 1931, he helped art students from several Shanghai art schools study woodblock printing and produce their own creations. Artists with leftist sensibilities began producing woodblock prints that criticized the Nationalist government and Japanese aggression. Eschewing traditional Chinese practice and materials, they carved their own blocks and often printed with European oil-based inks. Their works were stylistically indebted to work of contemporary European woodcut artists and bore little relation to traditional Chinese woodblock prints. Prior to 1937 artists like Chen Tiegeng (1908–1970), Li Hua (1907–1994), and Hu Yichuan (1910–2000) produced works that, although frequently political in nature, experimented widely with European modernist styles. After the Japanese invasion, however, participants in the modern Chinese woodcut movement tended to create works that were more ideological, naturalistic, and immediately legible. Many print artists, long having been harassed by Nationalist authorities, threw their lot in with the Communists. At the Lu Xun Academy (Lu Yi) at Yan'an, Hu Yichuan, Jiang Feng (1910–1982), and others made the woodcut a potent medium of party propaganda by printing works in the manner of brightly colored folk prints. Graduates of the school worked in teams to convey the Communists' intentions to peasants in China's western regions. Jiang Feng, Yan Han (b. 1916), and Shi Lu (1919–1982) thus established their Communist bona fides and positioned themselves for influential careers in the People's Republic of China.

A number of talented graphic artists of the Republican period found employment in a variety of institutions and produced images in multiple media and across numerous genres. Ding Song (1891–1972), who was a faculty member and dean of the Shanghai Art Academy, also worked as an editor at such publications as *Pictorial Shanghai* (*Shanghai huabao*), for which he created satirical political cartoons. Xie Zhiguang (1900–1976), in addition to being an accomplished painter of *guohua*, made a living creating calendar posters and newspaper advertisements. Feng Zikai (1898–1975) was equally adept at *guohua* and book illustration. Zhang Guangyu (1900–1964) designed labels, advertisements, and calendar posters before producing cartoons, or *manhua*, that satirized China's political corruption and disarray. Ding Song's son, Ding Cong (b. 1916), moved fluidly between book illustration, woodcuts, and cartoons, producing numerous pictorial works that commented on contemporary politics and social issues. After Lu Xun and other contributors to the May Fourth movement helped make artistically creative cover designs commonplace, Chen Zhifo (1895–1962), Tao Yuanqing (1893–1929), and Qian Juntao (1906–1998) worked as professional designers, drawing inspiration for their elegant book covers from such eclectic sources as Japanese textiles, Russian constructivism, and ancient Chinese pictorial reliefs.

## SCULPTURE

By the beginning of the twentieth century, China's long tradition of sculptural production was in decline. Buddhist institutions had greatly reduced their commissions, depriving sculptors of a vital form of support, and sculpture continued to bear its premodern stigma of being a craft. Cai Yuanpei, who knew of sculpture's preeminence in the West, sought to make it an important part of Chinese art education, and the May Fourth movement laid stress on public art. Even so, the subject was one of the least popular in China's art academies, and publicly sponsored sculptural projects, such as the Nationalist Party's 1927 commission of large-scale sculptures of Sun Yat-sen, were few in number.

A few art students, such as Li Jinfa (1900–1976), Teng Baiye (1900–1980), and Hua Tianyou (1902–1986), studied sculpture abroad, returning to China to teach the subject in such schools as the Shanghai Art Academy and the National Hangzhou Art College. Jiang Xin (1894–1939), who had graduated in oil painting from the Tokyo School of Fine Arts and studied sculpture in Paris, set a standard for cosmopolitan artistic activity, not only teaching at the Shanghai Art Academy and seeking commissions for his sculpture but also helping found a women's fashion company and becoming a darling of the Shanghai media. Due largely to the demands of patrons, most sculptural works of the 1920s and 1930s were naturalistic in style, with the manner of Auguste Rodin (1840–1917) marking the limit of Western sculptural modernism to which Chinese artists were willing to venture. During the 1930s and 1940s, military conflict with Japan and China's civil war resulted in relatively little sculptural production, and most of the public monuments that were erected were destroyed during the war. However, sculptors of the 1920s and 1930s were important forerunners of later sculpture in the People's Republic.

**SEE ALSO** *Art, Japanese Influence on; Art Schools and Colleges; Art Societies since 1800; Chinese Painting (guohua); Commercial Art; Epigraphic School of Art; Lin Fengmian; Lithographic and Modern Printing; Liu Haisu; Lu Xun; Oil Painting (youhua); Sculpture and Public Art; Woodblock Printing (xylography); Xu Beihong.*

**BIBLIOGRAPHY**

Andrews, Julia F., and Shen Kuiyi. *A Century in Crisis: Modernity and Tradition in the Art of Twentieth-century China.* New York: Guggenheim Museum, 1998.

Danzker, Jo-Anne Birnie, Ken Lum, and Zheng Shengtian, eds. *Shanghai Modern, 1919–1945.* Ostfildern-Ruit, Germany: Hatje Cantz, 2004.

Kao, Mayching, ed. *Twentieth-century Chinese Painting.* New York: Oxford University Press, 1988.

Sullivan, Michael. *Art and Artists of Twentieth-century China.* Berkeley: University of California Press, 1996.

***Walter B. Davis***

## SINCE 1949

The establishment of the Communist regime in mainland China in 1949 represented a momentous watershed for art and artists. The principles followed by the League of Left-wing Artists (Meishujia lianmeng) since the 1930s and formalized in Mao's Yan'an Forum of 1942 were now disseminated among artists via art educational institutions and the newly established and thoroughly politicized Chinese Artists Association (Zhongguo meishujia xiehui).

### ART FOR THE MASSES

Art was enlisted in the service of the Communist Party, and artists were forced to follow the party line or risk official censure or worse. Under the influence of Soviet-inspired socialist realism, art methods and content became highly circumscribed. Art was "to serve the workers, peasants, and soldiers," (*wei gong, nong, bing fuwu*) and its purpose was to reflect the endeavors of "the people" in forging a socialist utopia in alliance with the Chinese Communist Party (CCP). Art was no longer to be an elitist activity, produced solely by and for intellectuals; during extreme political swings to the left, such as during the Great Leap Forward (1958–1960) and the decade of the Cultural Revolution (1966–1976), professional artists were sidelined and "the masses" were encouraged to "take up the brush and paint."

Folk art, such as the ubiquitous New Year Picture (*nianhua*), achieved much greater prominence in official pronouncements, exhibitions, and publications because of its traditional links with the laboring classes, especially the peasants. The authorities remained highly ambivalent, however, about both traditional-style Chinese painting (*guohua*) and Western-style oil painting (*xiyanghua*). Its long and close associations with China's social elite meant that Chinese painting was considered to have only tenuous links with "the masses." In addition, it did not lend itself readily to the depiction of "the white-hot heat of revolution." Landscape and bird-and-flower paintings were particularly disadvantaged in this respect, portraiture less so. Nevertheless, as part of China's rich cultural heritage, Chinese ink painting could not be discarded completely. (Special allowances were even sometimes made for a number of elderly painting masters such as Qi Baishi (1864–1957) and Yu Fei'an (1889–1959), who were permitted to continue working in their own personal styles.) Instead, artists were encouraged to imbue Chinese ink painting with themes depicting the new China, and to utilize techniques commonly associated with academic oil painting, such as modeling and single-point perspective. Results of this policy were, however, seldom successful, as evidenced by the negative reports commonly presented at cultural conferences on the "new-style" Chinese painting.

Chinese ink painters did try various means to subvert political dictates and keep the true spirit of their art form alive, even during the most radical stages of CCP rule. Some continued to paint fairly conventional ink paintings but then gave them revolutionary-sounding titles, or included some nominal political element such as a small, lone figure of Mao in an otherwise typical Chinese landscape. In rare instances, Chinese painting could even be used as a means to implicitly critique Communist Party policies; Huang Yongyu's *The Winking Owl* (*maotouying*, 1973), was famously criticized by Mao's wife, Jiang Qing (1914–1991), for supposedly revealing Huang's hatred of the Cultural Revolution. The image carries connotations of the wise owl (the Chinese intellectual), with its one eye open and the other closed, expressing the Daoist sentiment of pretending in turbulent political times to be ignorant of everything, and yet to be fooled by nothing.

Western-style oil painting (*xiyanghua*), with its roots in the formal realism of the nineteenth-century European academies, lent itself much more readily to the dictates of political exigencies and socialist realism. Realist oil painting could easily accommodate the kinds of themes of which the CCP was so fond—"epic" paintings that glorified party leaders and party history; peasants reaping a bumper harvest; workers avidly reading the works of Mao; soldiers of the People's Liberation Army (PLA) grimly decrying the evils of capitalism and imperialism; and everyone celebrating the successes, at home and internationally, of Communism.

Most modern Western art was criticized as decadent and reactionary, particularly impressionism, because its emphasis on light and color meant that form took precedence over content, which contravened the tenets of socialist realism. Lin Fengmian (1900–1991) and Pang Xunqin (1906–1985), key advocates of the "new style painting" (*xin huapai*) that encouraged the adoption of modern Western art styles, were forced to make self-criticisms. Reproductions of modern Western art were still passed around secretly among artist friends, or between art professor and student, but it wasn't until the end of the

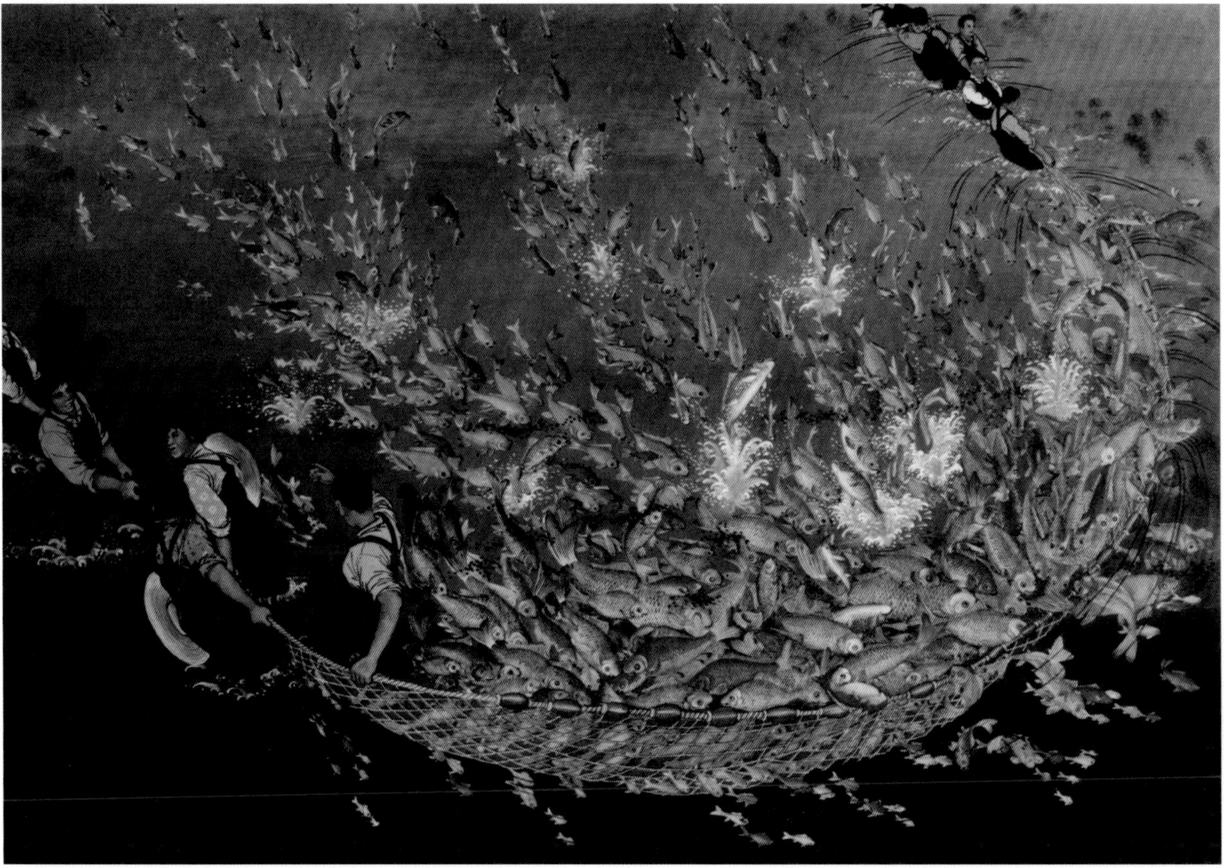

**The Fish Pond of the Commune,** ***by Dong Zhengyi, 1973.*** *After 1949, the Chinese Communist Party commanded great influence over the arts, dictating that all works should promote socialist ideals. Citizens outside the traditional art community were called upon to create artistic works glorifying the efforts of soldiers, workers, and peasants.* SNARK / ART RESOURCE, NY

1970s that individuals could openly espouse an interest in such work. These constraints on subject matter and style meant that, with the exception of the work of certain accomplished artists such as Dong Xiwen (1914–1973), Western-style oil painting tended to become increasingly formulaic and repetitious, especially during the Cultural Revolution years.

## ART IN THE REFORM ERA

The death of Mao Zedong in 1976 and the rise of the more pragmatic Deng Xiaoping saw the gradual opening up of China to the outside world and increasing liberalization in cultural matters. Artists were able to learn for the first time of the modernist developments in art in North America and Europe since the 1950s, and many of them began to incorporate modernist elements in their work. Informal art groups began to flourish, bringing together artists working in similar idioms, or with similar aims. Among these, the Stars (*Xingxing huahui*), mainly young amateurs, were the most prominent. They staged a wildcat, open-air exhibition in 1979, the first of its kind in the People's Republic of China (PRC), displaying both realist and more abstract pieces in media ranging from oils and ink painting to woodcuts and sculptures, much of it clearly political or social critique, often with satirical undertones.

In the wake of the Stars exhibition came a veritable explosion of creative activity over the next decade, encompassing a wide range of styles including abstract expressionism, surrealism, hyperrealism, dada, and pop, as Chinese artists learned of, experimented with, then modified or discarded the various twentieth-century art "isms" imported from North America and Europe.

The 1980s before the Tiananmen Square protests of 1989 is often regarded as an era of "humanism" when artists, encouraged by debates in the political and intellectual arena, sought to bring art back to reality, and back to the realm of the individual, after the collective utopian madness of the Cultural Revolution. Initially, this was framed as rather timid but nevertheless direct interrogations of the validity of aspects of the Cultural Revolution by "scar" (*shanghen*) painters; subsequently, it was manifested as representations of ordinary people, often peasants or minorities, the lowly and the dispossessed, caught in everyday situations and depicted in realist idioms ranging from a Millet-style naturalism to hyperrealism. The '85 New Wave movement in the mid-1980s then further developed this tentative exploration of the human condition in two main directions—rationalist painting (*lixing huihua*) and "current of life," or "élan vital" (*shengming zhiliu*). Rationalist painters such as Wang Guangyi (b. 1956) and Zhang Peili (b. 1941), utilizing a cool palette and elements from symbolism and surrealism, sought to establish a solid, pure, and unadulterated ground of human existence, to engender a sense of the sublime as an antidote to the irrationality of China's recent history and a guard against an uncritical wholesale adoption of Western modernism. The current of life painters—Mao Xuhui (b. 1956), Zhang Xiaogang (b. 1958), and others—following the French philosopher Henri Bergson's precept that life involves the irrational, the violent, and the instinctual, produced highly expressionistic, vivid renditions of the human form to convey a sense of human nature at its most basic, its most raw, and thus in a sense its most authentic.

The late 1980s also saw a renewed interest among some artists in Daoism and Chan, which were viewed as valuable means to negate or deconstruct dominant metanarratives, whether of Chinese tradition or contemporary official discourse. The notable artists Gu Wenda (b. 1955) and Xu Bing (b. 1955) use the motif of Chinese characters, inverting them, placing them on incongruous backgrounds, crossing them out, or combining them with foreign words. Their speciality is incorporating in paintings and mixed media installations invented characters—that is, characters that have no shared cultural meaning. Xu Bing's large installation *A Mirror to Analyze the World* (1989), shown at the controversial *China Avant-Garde* exhibition in Beijing in 1989, for example, consisted of 300 square meters of wide paper strips hung along the walls and ceiling of the gallery and depicting 3,000 invented characters, each of them different, which the artist had painstakingly produced over three years using traditional woodblock printing methods. Such work interrogates the meaningfulness of communication symbols, and questions whether the 3,000-year tradition of reverence for the written character in China (and, by extension, for Chinese high culture as a whole) has led to a spiritual dead end.

The Tiananmen Square massacre in June 1989 and its aftermath caused many artists to reassess their social roles and the purpose of their art. As China entered a new phase of rapid economic growth and commercialization there was a detectable shift among some artists from the more ideal-based approach of the 1980s, where art was perceived as having the power to help shape society and values, to a more mundane view of art as satire, as spectacle, as entertainment, as commodity. Political pop and cynical realism were the two main trends embodying this new view. Political pop (or political parody) is a hybrid of Communist political imagery (Communist Party leaders, PLA soldiers, etc.) and American pop art, occasionally fused with other elements appropriated from, for example, Chinese folk art. Most common were parodies of the Mao cult—a series of the same Mao image, differing only in terms of color and tone, done Andy Warhol–style; or Mao juxtaposed next to a Coca Cola can, the American singer Whitney Houston or other iconic symbols of American pop culture.

Merged to some extent with political pop was cynical realism, pursued by young artists in their twenties and thirties who had largely escaped the political turmoil experienced by older artists, and who no longer took the metanarrative of "saving China" as a serious endeavor. Instead, in an increasingly individualistic and materialistic world, they sought to express the ordinary, the banal, and the absurd in everyday life, usually in a realist idiom with expressionist overtones. Representative artists include Wang Jingsong (b. 1963), whose group portraits present a caricatured and satirical vision of China's new middle class, and Fang Lijun (b. 1963), whose "young bald men" are caught in bored poses or smiling inanely, indifferent and self-mocking, a metaphor for China's youth, who feel powerless against massive political and economic forces over which they have no control, and who live from day to day, pursuing their own simple pleasures.

Chinese artists in the new millennium work with a dazzling array of media, from the traditional tools used for Chinese ink painting to oils, acrylic, and, more recently, photography, video, and other digital media, as well as computer-generated imaging. Styles range from Chinese painting in the traditional idiom to abstract installations and daring performance-art pieces that challenge not only official discourse but also, at times, the moral and aesthetic sensibilities of the viewer. This new level of creative innovation and assuredness has not gone unnoticed outside China's borders, and mainland art is currently highly sought after by the international art market, as evidenced by the presence in Beijing and Shanghai of international auction houses such as Sotheby's and Christie's, and the increasingly high prices that some Chinese artists command at auction. Chinese artists are regularly invited to exhibit overseas, and Chinese art is now an integral part of major events such as the Venice Biennale and ArtBasel. As China's influence in the world continues to rise, and as it

***A depiction of Mao Zedong as a clown by artist Feng Zhangjie, Hong Kong, December 20, 2001.*** *With the establishment of the People's Republic of China, Communist leaders required artists to promote party dogma in their work. However, by the end of the Cultural Revolution, government restrictions loosened, allowing artists to use Western art movements to express other perspectives of China, such as the Pop Art-inspired portrait of Mao Zedong pictured here.* PETER PARKS/AFP/GETTY IMAGES

becomes increasingly integrated with the global system, Chinese art looks set to become a mainstream feature of the international art scene.

## TAIWAN

Although until the late 1980s artists in Taiwan worked, like their mainland counterparts, within an authoritarian political framework, at least culturally the atmosphere was more liberal. Their artistic preoccupation was similar to that of many mainland artists in the 1920s and 1930s—how to reconcile aspects of the Chinese painting tradition with the modernist styles that were emerging in North America and Europe. During the period of Taiwan's occupation by the Japanese (1895–1945), Japan, which had been undergoing a period of comprehensive Westernization since the 1860s, became the major conduit for early twentieth-century European art trends, especially impressionism, expressionism, and fauvism.

The establishment of the Communist regime in 1949 produced an influx of refugee artists from the mainland into Taiwan. These included prominent masters working in the traditional painting idiom such as Pu Xinyu (1896–1963), Zhang Daqian (1899–1983), and Huang Junbi (1899–1991), who added luster and prestige to the local painting scene. Others were drawn to the exciting new art developments taking place in the West, and advocated infusing Chinese ink painting with modernist styles borrowed from the West. Liu Guosong (Liu Kuo-sung), the founding member of the influential Fifth Moon Group (*Wuyue huahui*) and arguably Taiwan's most renowned artist of the 1950s and 1960s until his move to Hong Kong in 1971, was the most prominent advocate of this syncretic approach. Liu continued over the decades to adapt and revitalize his painting techniques, producing startling and impressive takes on the traditional Chinese naturescape by imbuing it with an original, cosmic quality. After the opening up of the mainland in the 1980s Liu's work became hugely popular there, and he continues to inspire innovation in Chinese ink painting.

The last two decades have seen major diversification of the Taiwanese art scene. The lifting of martial law in 1987 and the political liberalization that followed have been accompanied by rapid economic growth, urbanization, and commercialization, all of which provide Taiwan's artists with new creative material that is best expressed through a variety of media, including the latest digital technology. As part of a widespread movement in the 1970s and 1980s to return to Taiwan's "cultural roots," Taiwanese artists began to seek an authentic visual expression of their homeland as people there grappled with a plethora of modernization issues—materialism, the environment, and Taiwan's historical and political identity. Like their mainland and Hong Kong counterparts, Taiwan's artists live and work in a globalized economic and cultural environment that is dominated by commercialism and fierce competition. Opportunities for exhibiting and selling work has increased, due partly to official support in the form of government-sponsored institutions such as the Taipei Fine Arts Museum (*Taibei shili meishuguan*) and MOCA Taipei (*Taibei dangdai yishuguan*), and partly to the privately owned galleries and glossy magazines that have mushroomed in the last twenty years that supply space for showing artwork. But Taiwanese artists are now, more than ever, exposed to and at the mercy of the vagaries of the international art market, and they have to vie for international recognition with mainland artists, who are currently the darlings of the Asian art world.

## HONG KONG

Working within an historical context different from that of artists on the mainland and in Taiwan but still sharing certain cultural ideals and artistic preoccupations with both, Hong Kong artists have striven to forge a unique identity for themselves. This has proved a challenging task. Inhabiting a small island with the reputation of being a "cultural desert" and caught between the two sovereign powers of China and Great Britain, Hong Kong artists until recently have found it difficult to achieve the prominence in international art forums enjoyed by their mainland and Taiwanese counterparts. Historians tend to note only one prominent Hong Kong artist in the early twentieth century—the remarkably versatile and prolific Chen Fushan (Luis Chan, 1905–1995)—though a thriving prewar art scene did exist in Hong Kong, where literati and Lingnan school painting sat side by side with Western-style oil and watercolor painting.

The Communist victory on the mainland brought in its wake an influx into Hong Kong of well-established Chinese ink painters, mainly from South China, such as Yang Shanshen (Yang Shen-sum, 1913–2004) and Ding Yanyong (Ting Yin-yung, (1902–1978). There then emerged a series of art coteries in the 1950s and 1960s with the purpose of exploring possible new directions in art. The leading light in these associations was Lu Shoukun (Lui Shou-kwan, 1919–1975), but he was joined by only slightly lesser luminaries including the painters Jin Jialun (King Chia-lun, b.1936), Irene Chou (b. 1924), and Wucius Wong (b. 1936), and the sculptor Wen Lou (Van Lau, b. 1933), to name a few. Their advocacy of new Chinese ink painting (*xin shuimo*) reveals their concerns with imbuing the traditional-style ink painting system with new techniques or materials in order to render it more "modern." As with the Chinese literati of old, landscapes continued to be a favorite subject, though couched in a distinctly more experimental and expressive idiom. In the main, these painters tended to eschew direct depictions of the Hong Kong landscape, though Lu Shoukun, for example, did produce some recognizable examples of Hong Kong rural areas or fishing villages.

The generation of artists from the 1980s has revealed artistic leanings different from those of its predecessors. Unlike the older group, which had its roots in the mainland or, to a lesser extent, Taiwan, and therefore maintained a strong connection with the Chinese painting tradition, these young artists were born in Hong Kong. Many also gained their formal art training in the West, and so they tend to be drawn to more modern and contemporary Western art styles. A major catalyst for these artists was the approaching handover of Hong Kong to the PRC in 1997, and anxieties about Hong Kong's future, especially in the wake of the 1989 Tiananmen Square massacre. The looming handover, together with an awareness among Hong Kong artists of the international interest in politically critical art on the mainland, gave rise to a plethora of works, ranging from painting to photography and installation, that foregrounded Hong Kong's unease about its future as part of the PRC.

**SEE ALSO** *Art History and Historiography; Art Market since 1949; Chinese Painting (guohua); New Wave Movement, '85; Oil Painting (youhua); Political Pop and Cynical Realism; Scar (Wound) Art; Socialist Realism in Art; Stars (Xingxing) Painting Group, 1979–1983; Yan'an Forum.*

**BIBLIOGRAPHY**

Andrews, Julia F. *Painters and Politics in the People's Republic of China, 1949–1979.* Berkeley: University of California Press, 1994.

Clarke, David. *Hong Kong Art, Culture, and Decolonization.* London: Reaktion Books, 2001.

Cohen, Joan Lebold. *The New Chinese Painting, 1949–1986.* New York: Harry N. Abrams, 1987.

Galikowski, Maria. *Art and Politics in China, 1949–1984.* Hong Kong: Chinese University Press, 1998.

Gao Minglu, ed. *Inside Out: New Chinese Art.* Berkeley: University of California Press, 1998.

Kao, Mayching, ed. *Twentieth-century Chinese Painting.* Oxford, U.K.: Oxford University Press, 1988.

Köppel-Yang, Martina. *Semiotic Warfare, the Chinese Avant-garde, 1979–1989: A Semiotic Analysis.* Hong Kong: Timezone 8 Limited, 2003.

Laing, Ellen Johnston. *The Winking Owl: Art in the People's Republic of China.* Berkeley: University of California Press, 1989.

Lü Peng. *Zhongguo dangdai yishushi* [Nineties art China, 1990–1999]. Changsha, China: Hunan Meishu Chubanshe, 2000.

Lü Peng, and Yi Dan. *Zhongguo xiandai yishushi, 1979–1989* [A history of modern art in China]. Changsha, China: Hunan Meishu Chubanshe, 1992.

Sullival, Michael. *Art and Artists of Twentieth-Century China.* Berkley: University of California Press, 1996.

***Maria Galikowski***

## ART, JAPANESE INFLUENCE ON

After the humiliation of China's defeat in the Opium War (1839–1842) and Japan's successful modernization through the Meiji restoration (1868–1912), Sino-Japanese relations in art underwent a significant change for the first time in the long history of the two nations' cultural interactions. China had been the sophisticated source of artistic inspiration for Japan for centuries. In the modern era, while Japan's admiration for Chinese culture continued, China looked to Japan as a model for modernization. Indeed, China began to view itself through the filter of Japan.

In the early twentieth century Japan was a geographically and linguistically convenient destination for Chinese students to study European artistic forms and practices. One of the first artists to study Western art in Japan was Li Shutong (1880–1942), who in 1905 entered the Tokyo School of Fine Arts, then headed by the French-trained oil painter Kuroda Seiki. Kuroda adopted a systematic pedagogical method for his *yōga* (Western-style painting) students and promoted the early impressionism that he practiced himself. Following the Japanese master, Li Shutong mastered impressionistic techniques infused with academic realism. After Li completed his studies in Japan, he was appointed as an art teacher at Zhejiang First Normal School in Hangzhou in 1912. There, Li introduced the practices he had absorbed in Japan: instead of copying reproductions or sample paintings made by a teacher, he drew from his own observations of plaster casts, still lifes, and nude models.

### IMPORTING NEW STYLES

In the 1920s younger Chinese oil-painting students came back from Japan with newer styles and ideas. Those artists, including Chen Baoyi, Ni Yide, Guan Liang, Zhu Jizhan, Xu Xingzhi, and Guan Zilan, experimented with various modern styles that prevailed in Japan while they were at the Tokyo School of Fine Arts, Kawabata Academy of Painting, and other art schools. Younger Japanese teachers such as Fujishima Takeji, Nakamura Fusetsu, and Yasui Sōtarō attracted Chinese students who were interested in more up-to-date European styles. Fujishima, who studied in Europe two decades after Kuroda, encouraged his students to break away from academic tradition and realistic representation. Under their Japanese teachers, the Chinese students of this period absorbed the styles of postimpressionism and fauvism, utilizing the newer vocabulary of European art.

The third generation of Chinese artists who studied in Japan during the 1930s witnessed the avant-garde trends of dadaism, constructivism, and surrealism. Zhao Shou (1912–2003) was one of the Western-style painting students who exemplified the Japanese experience of this group. Zhao's teacher Satomi Katsuzō was involved in the group of artists called the Independent Art Association (Dokuritsu Bijutsu Kyōkai), which took an approach to art different from the already established Japanese academic art world. Having seen the challenge to the Japanese government–sponsored salon, Zhao Shou and his friends, who were interested in modernist styles, particularly surrealism, formed the Chinese Independent Art Association in Tokyo in 1934. Since the Meiji period (1868–1912) a great number of associations were founded by Japanese artists who shared styles and ideas about art and exhibited their work together. This trend motivated Chinese artists. Kuroda Seiki's White Horse Association (Hakuba-kai) might have inspired the Heavenly Horse Painting Society (Tianma huahui), founded later, in 1919.

As the term *meishu* (fine art) was adopted into the Chinese language from the Japanese word *bijutsu*, *guohua* (national painting), which originated from the Japanese neologism *kokuga*, also came into the vocabulary of Chinese art. In the wake of modernization and Westernization, *guohua* was challenged for its traditional Chinese style and content, which reminded the Chinese of the corrupt old regime of the Qing dynasty. To revitalize art for China, the artists of the Lingnan school from Canton, including Gao Jianfu (1879–1951), his brother Gao Qifeng (1889–1933), and Chen Shuren (1883–1948), looked to Japan for their inspiration to synthesize East and West. The Gao brothers sailed to Japan in the first decade of the 1900s and, seeking to understand how Japanese artists interpreted European artistic concepts, studied various Western styles and techniques such as perspective, chiaroscuro, French academicism, and postimpressionism. However, they were more attracted to the new Japanese-style painting, *nihonga*, a hybrid of Western realism and Japanese subject matter with a touch of Asian lyricism. The influence of *nihonga* painters such as Takeuchi Seihō can be easily traced, especially in Gao Qifeng's animal paintings. The infusion of different styles derived from *nihonga* became the point of departure for the concept of the New National Painting.

## BLENDING OF CULTURES

The first half of the twentieth century saw unprecedented interaction between the Chinese and Japanese art worlds. This was the case not only for oil painters but also for artists working in the traditional medium. Among the ink painters who had strong affiliations with Japan were Wu Changshi, Wang Yiting, Qi Baishi, Feng Zikai, and Jin Cheng, to name a few. While the Lingnan school artists attempted to modernize their painting by integrating Eastern and Western styles to find a new nationalist voice, other *guohua* artists also faced the social change following the fall of the Qing dynasty in 1912 and were challenged by the question about the position of Chinese tradition in the modern era. In the late Qing and the early Republican period, in keeping with the attack on Chinese traditional culture, Chinese literati painting (*wenrenhua*), a highly esteemed painting tradition practiced by educated gentlemen as self-cultivation, was considered inferior to realistic Western-style painting. As a number of paintings attributed to Song (960–1279) and Yuan (1279–1368) literati masters entered Japan during the Taishō period (1912–1926), Japanese scholars such as Naitō Konan and Ōmura Seigai took a new interest in Chinese literati and began to reevaluate their work. This marked a departure from the Edo period (1603–1867), during which *daimyō* (feudal lords) and Buddhist monks had expressed appreciation for the Chinese court style.

In his essay "The Revival of Literati Painting," Ōmura observed that the supremacy of painting lies in its ability to transcend objective representations. This notion encouraged the traditionalist Chen Shizeng (Hengke) in his belief in the merit of literati painting. In 1922 Chen translated and published Ōmura's essay, along with his own "The Value of Literati Painting," as *The Study of Chinese Literati Painting*, in which he argued that literati painting is the equivalent of Western modernist painting because of its subjective and expressive qualities.

Searching for the new idiom of *guohua*, Chinese artists found their own cultural heritage in Japanese art. The ink painters Chen Zhifo (c. 1895–1962) and Fu Baoshi (1904–1965) appropriated the Chineseness preserved in Japanese art, particularly in *nihonga*. In the case of Chen, after he viewed contemporary *nihonga* paintings influenced by court painters of the Southern Song period (1127–1279), he revived Song and Ming dynasty (1368–1644) academic realism in his works. Chinese *guohua* artists conserved the legitimacy of that tradition by using Chinese art history as a base for modernization. Thus Japanese art provided a source of inspiration for Chinese traditionalists but did not require them to compromise their own agenda.

## GRAPHIC DESIGN AND PRINTS

Outside the realm of Western-style and ink paintings, graphic design and modern printmaking in China began to flourish in the first half of the twentieth century. Chinese commercial design in the 1920s and 1930s testified to crucial connections with Japan. As the publishing industry prospered, Chinese professional graphic designers began to develop a modern style of design. The book cover designs by the graphic artist Tao Yuanqing (1893–1929), though he never studied in Japan, exhibited his taste for Japanese art. This stylistic tendency may have been nurtured by his teachers at the Shanghai Art Normal School, Feng Zikai and Chen Baoyi, who had a strong affinity for the Japanese art world. Tao's designs employed simplified forms and asymmetrical composition, qualities often found in Japanese graphic art. Tao's friend Qian Juntao (1906–1998) also followed Japanese pictorial idioms in his designs and, like modernist Japanese graphic artists, experimented with typography as an integral part of composition. Both Tao and Qian were introduced by the printmaker Lu Xun (1881–1936) to the Uchiyama Bookstore, run by Uchiyama Kanzō, in Shanghai, where the young artists likely encountered contemporary Japanese graphic design and may have appropriated the motifs and flavors that appealed to them.

In the modern woodcut movement, Lu Xun played an important role in the establishment of print as a modern medium. He was also a vital figure in bridging Chinese and Japanese printmaking. He collected a great number of foreign art books and prints from Europe and Japan, which he made available for young Chinese students to study. Lu Xun also subscribed to Japanese journals devoted to printmaking such as *Shiro to Kuro* (White and black) and *Hangeijutsu* (Art of printmaking), through which Chinese and Japanese printmakers interacted. With the encouragement of Lu Xun, Li Hua, who was a central figure of the Modern Woodcut Society in Guangzhou, in 1935 sent his coterie journal *Modern Woodcut* to the publishing house of *Shiro to Kuro* and *Hangeijutsu* in hopes that the Chinese and Japanese artists could learn from each other. The Japanese responded positively to the proposal and an exchange of works ensued, some of which were published in journals in China and Japan. In the summer of 1931 Lu Xun gave a lecture at the workshop of woodcut prints in which he introduced prints from various schools, including Japanese *ukiyo-e* and German expressionism. He also invited Uchiyama Kakitsu (brother of Uchiyama Kanzō) from Japan to serve as an instructor of print techniques.

From the end of the 1930s through the late 1970s, the political climate in China, along with the changing relationship between the two countries, diminished the significance of Japanese art in the Chinese art world. After the recantation of the Cultural Revolution (1966–1969) in the late 1970s, it seems that some artists once again incorporated Japanese elements, such as the flat picture plane and decorativeness, in their pictorial vocabulary. The subject of Sino-Japanese relations in art during the final decades of the twentieth century awaits further study.

**SEE ALSO** *Chinese Painting (guohua); Commercial Art: Picture Books (lianhuanhua); Li Hua; Lingnan School of Painting; Literati Painting (wenrenhua); Lu Xun; Modernist Art of the 1920s and 1930s; New Print Movement; Shanghai School of Painting; Wang Zhen (Wang Yiting); Wu Changshi (Wu Junqing).*

**BIBLIOGRAPHY**

Andrews, Julia F., and Kuiyi Shen. *A Century in Crisis: Modernity and Tradition in the Art of Twentieth-Century China.* New York: Guggenheim Museum, 1998.

Andrews, Julia F., and Kuiyi Shen. The Japanese Impact on the Republican Art World: The Construction of Chinese Art History as a Modern Field. *Twentieth-Century China* 32, 1 (2006): 4–35.

Wong, Aida Yuen. *Parting the Mists: Discovering Japan and the Rise of National-style Painting in Modern China.* Honolulu: Association for Asian Studies, University of Hawaii Press, 2006.

***Mayumi Kamata***

# ART, NATIONAL ESSENCE MOVEMENT IN

In the final decades of the Qing dynasty (1644–1912), many Chinese intellectuals were frustrated by failures of the imperial government and worried that avaricious foreign powers might destroy Chinese civilization. A new intelligentsia began to understand Chinese culture as separable from the existing political order and took it upon itself to defend China's cultural identity. Some thinkers looked to Japan, where in the late 1880s and 1890s the Society for Political Education (Seikyōsha) had reacted against widespread Westernization of Japanese society by calling for "preservation of the national essence" (*kokusui hozon*). As early as 1904 some Chinese intellectuals were arguing that China, too, must preserve its national essence (*guocui*). Over the next four decades they worked to maintain the media that they believed transmitted this cultural identity—traditional Chinese scholarship, poetry, and art.

## INSTITUTIONAL AND THEORETICAL CHALLENGES

Between 1902 and 1911 China's new national education system made Western-style drawing and painting a fixture of its curriculum, officially ignoring traditional Chinese painting. Many aspiring artists traveled to Japan and Europe to study Western art. In 1912 the Chinese Republic's minister of education, Cai Yuanpei (1868–1940), who was a keen supporter of Western art, called for reform of the Chinese people's moral sensibility through aesthetic education. This prompted intellectuals of the May Fourth movement, such as Chen Duxiu (1880–1942), to espouse the complete abandonment of traditional Chinese art. By the end of the 1920s, Western art was firmly established in China's educational curricula, and advocates of Western materials, techniques, and pedagogical approaches occupied key administrative positions in all of China's major art academies.

## EARLY ASSOCIATIONS AND ACTIVITIES

Admirers of traditional Chinese culture responded to these challenges by forming associations dedicated to maintaining China's national essence. One of the earliest of these groups, the Society for the Preservation of National Learning (Guoxue baocun hui), was founded in Shanghai in 1905. Although not an artistic association *per se*, the group published essays on the arts and collotype reproductions of traditional Chinese paintings and calligraphy in its *Guocui xuebao* (National Essence Journal). Members of the society also undertook independent publishing projects. Deng Shi (1877–1951), who edited *Guocui xuebao*, founded a press that produced two of the most important Chinese art series of the twentieth century—*Shenzhou guoguang ji* (the Glories of Cathay), which printed reproductions of traditional paintings and calligraphy, and *Meishu congshu* (Collectanea of the Arts), which published seminal premodern texts on the visual arts.

Soon artists took up the charge of protecting China's cultural identity. In 1909 painters and calligraphers in Shanghai, including Gao Yong (1850–1921), Qian Huian (1833–1911), Wu Changshi (1844–1927), and Wang Yiting (1867–1938), joined with several artists who worked in Beijing, notably Jin Cheng (1878–1926) and Cheng Zhang (1869–1938), to found the Yu Garden Calligraphy and Painting Charitable Association (*Yuyuan shuhua shanhui*). Like other artistic associations of the first two decades of the twentieth century, it enabled its members to socialize while helping them to negotiate the novel economic realities of a major artistic center. However, the association also aimed to preserve the national essence and relieve people's suffering by donating half of the proceeds from its members' collaborative works to charity. In 1910 some of the society's artists helped the businessman, revolutionary, and art collector Li Pingshu (1854–1927) form the Shanghai Calligraphy and Painting Research Society (*Shanghai shuhua yanjiuhui*), which aspired to preserve the national essence by strengthening modern artists and collectors' relationships with art of their nation's past.

## TRADITIONALIST ACTIVITIES OF THE 1920s

Although Cai Yuanpei's call for aesthetic education inspired cultural iconoclasm, it also helped reestablish the legitimacy of traditional Chinese art by deeming aesthetic pursuits worthy of study in China's educational institutions. By the end of the 1910s, artists such as Chen Hengque (1876–1923) were teaching Chinese art in public and private schools. Over the course of the 1920s, traditionalists sought to counter the presumption that art had to be Western to be modern, and they responded vigorously to the May Fourth movement. They began to use the terms *Chinese painting* (*zhongguohua*) and *traditional Chinese painting* (*guohua*, literally "national painting") to distinguish works produced with traditional materials and techniques, and they sought to identify and promote this art as an essential component of China's national essence.

Conservatives in Beijing were quick to form national essence artistic associations, founding the Society for the Study of Chinese Painting (*Zhongguo huaxue yanjiuhui*) in 1920. One of the group's leaders, Jin Cheng, lectured on China's ancient art and encouraged students to overcome the moribund orthodoxy of Qing academic painting by emulating works of Tang (618–907) and Song (960–1279) masters. Chen Hengque made a case for traditional painting as a form of modern art. In a 1921 essay titled "The Value of Literati Painting" (*Wenrenhua Zhi Jiazhi*), he argued that literati painting, which expressed the taste of the literati and represented a spiritual component beyond itself, could avoid the failure of literal copying of motifs and brushwork, just as postimpressionism had freed European artists from the strictures of naturalistic representation.

Members of the Society for the Study of Chinese Painting also promoted *guohua* by displaying traditionalist art in large exhibitions. Jin Cheng and his fellows worked closely with Japanese traditionalists, primarily practitioners of Japan's literati painting (*nanga*) and Japanese-style painting (*nihonga*), to organize international exhibitions of contemporary artists' work in cities such as Beijing, Shanghai, Tokyo, and Osaka. When Jin Cheng died in 1926, members of the society honored him by forming a new association called the Lake Society (Hu she). This group published *Hu she yuekan* (Lake Society Monthly), which reproduced works by ancient and contemporary artists and serialized Jin Cheng's lectures. The journal circulated nationally and thus reported on the activities of artists across China.

The movement to preserve China's cultural identity also flourished in Shanghai, where traditionalists formed national essence associations such as the Shanghai Calligraphy and Painting Society (Shanghai shuhuahui, 1922), the Chinese Epigraphy, Calligraphy, and Painting Study Society (Zhongguo jinshi shuhua yiguan xuehui, 1925), the Shanghai Chinese Calligraphy and Painting Preservation Society (Shanghai Zhongguo shuhua baocunhui), and the Bee Painting Society (Mifeng huashe, 1929). These groups supported artists economically by establishing price lists and connecting artists with buyers. Through the efforts of editors such as Huang Binhong (1864–1955) they also produced scholarly journals such as *Yiguan* (Arts Overview) and *Guocui yuekan* (National Essence Monthly), which articulated pointedly nationalistic goals for the practice, study, and collection of traditional painting and calligraphy. Members of these societies contributed their art and organizational expertise to the Sino-Japanese joint exhibitions that took place in the 1920s and early 1930s, helping raise many Chinese artists to national prominence and staking a claim for the continuing vitality of China's traditional art in an international context.

Traditionalists such as Di Baoxian (1872–1941) also exploited the possibilities of Shanghai's modern publishing industry. His Youzheng Book Company reproduced works from his large family collection in the series *Famous Chinese Paintings* (*Zhongguo ming hua*), hoping that by following Japan's example of publishing and protecting its national essence, China might resist foreign powers' plundering of its own cultural inheritance.

## NATIONALIZATION AND DEMISE

By the end of the 1920s, proponents of China's national essence had so revived traditional Chinese painting and calligraphy that these arts featured substantially in the Ministry of Education's First Chinese National Art Exhibition of 1929. By 1930 the Lake Society and the Bee Painting Society had begun to develop national constituencies, and the final issue of the latter group's *Mifeng huaji* (Bee Pictorial) issued a call that "*guohua* artists must unite." In 1931 Huang Binhong, Ye Gongchuo (1881–1965), He Tianjian (1891–1977), Qian Shoutie (1897–1967), Zheng Wuchang (1894–1952), and other Shanghai artists established a new, national group to promote traditional Chinese painting and prevent Chinese art from being eclipsed by Western civilization. The Chinese Painting Society (*Zhongguo huahui*) boasted about 300 members from Beijing to Hong Kong, and it published *Xiandai Zhongguo huaji* (the Modern Chinese Painting Pictorial) and *Guohua yuekan* (Chinese Painting Monthly). The latter was a highly ideological professional journal that sought to popularize ancient and modern masterpieces, and several of its editors, such as He Tianjian and Zheng Wuchang, published prolifically on the theory, practice, and reform of *guohua*. Central members of the Chinese Painting Society also edited other important publications of the day, such as the popular periodical *Meishu shenghuo* (Art and Life), and thus were able to present members' works and exhibitions to a national reading public.

As the presumption of Western art's modernity grew stronger during the 1920s and as Japan steadily eroded China's territorial integrity in the 1930s, calls for preservation of China's national essence grew increasingly shrill. National essence societies and the traditionalists who joined them continued to play prominent roles in the Chinese art world until the establishment of the People's Republic of China in 1949, when elimination of the art market and reform of the educational system demolished institutional support of traditional Chinese art, and Communist ideological orthodoxy tolerated neither private associations nor ostensibly feudal forms of art.

**SEE ALSO** *Art Exhibitions Abroad; Chinese Painting (guohua); Huang Binhong; Wang Zhen (Wang Yiting); Wu Changshi (Wu Junqing).*

**BIBLIOGRAPHY**

Andrews, Julia F., and Kuiyi Shen. *A Century in Crisis: Modernity and Tradition in the Art of Twentieth-century China.* New York: Solomon R. Guggenheim Museum, 1998.

Hengque, Chen. "Wenrenhua Zhi Jiazhi." Reprinted in *Jindai Zhongguo Meishu Lunji,* ed. He Huaishuo, 49–52. Vol. 2. Taipei: Yishujia Chubanshe, 1991.

Kao, Maycning, ed. *Twentieth-century Chinese Painting.* New York: Oxford University Press, 1988.

Schneider, Laurence A. National Essence and the New Intelligentsia. In *The Limits of Change: Essays on Conservative Alternatives in Republican China,* ed. Charlotte Furth, 57–89. Cambridge, MA: Harvard University Press, 1976.

Shen, Kuiyi. A Debate on the Reform of Chinese Painting in Early Republican China. *Tsing Hua Journal of Chinese Studies* 26, no. 4 (December 1996): 447–469.

Sullivan, Michael. *Art and Artists of Twentieth-century China.* Berkeley: University of California Press, 1996.

***Walter B. Davis***

# ART, POLICY ON, SINCE 1949

Communist policies on art evolved gradually following the founding of the Chinese Communist Party (CCP) in 1921. By 1924 a Department of Propaganda was beginning to direct cultural policy in Communist-held areas, and by 1930 the first branch of the League of Left-wing Artists (meishujia lianmeng) was operating in Shanghai, and eventually other urban areas. The purpose of the league was to organize the work of left-leaning artists in support of the Communist cause. The league and other similar leftist groups often provoked the ire of the Nationalist government, which sought to curb their activities by forcibly disbanding associations and jailing members.

During the 1930s prominent figures in the CCP began to formulate ideas on the social function of art in order to bring cultural policy in line with Soviet cultural theorists. These ideas were finally synthesized by Mao Zedong in the famous Yan'an Forum of 1942, which systematically outlined the ideological imperatives for left-wing artists. The Yan'an guidelines, which exhorted artists to reorient their work to meet the needs of the revolution and the broad mass of the people, became the theoretical underpinnings of cultural policy in post-1949 China. To underscore its commitment to the guidelines, the party almost immediately began to carry out small-scale purges against those who expressed heterodox views. Jiang Feng (1910–1982), who later became the key party bureaucrat in charge of art until his downfall in 1958, was severely criticized and kept isolated from his colleagues for many months. Much harsher purges of prominent figures in the art establishment occurred after 1949, particularly during the Great Leap Forward and the decade of the Cultural Revolution (1966–1976).

## OFFICIAL POLICY AFTER 1949

After the establishment of the People's Republic in 1949, the policies outlined at the Yan'an Forum were crystallized at the First and Second All-China National Congresses of Literary and Art Workers (Zhonghua quanguo wenxue yishu gongzuozhe daibiao dahui, 1949 and 1953), and disseminated via the newly formed All-China Federation of Literary and Arts Circles (Zhongguo wenxue yishujie lianhehui). The federation encompassed several national cultural associations that were charged with implementing party policy and overseeing training in the cultural field. In the area of art, this task went to the Chinese Artists Association (Zhongguo meishujia xiehui), which was dominated by the Yan'an veterans and party stalwarts Jiang Feng, Cai Ruohong (b. 1910), and Wang Chaowen (b. 1930).

The purpose of the Chinese Artists Association was stated in its constitution—to actively promote the socialist cause, to follow the party's Marxist-Leninist art policies, and to make socialist realism the guiding theory for art production. In practice, this meant that the association had to organize the participation of artists in mass political movements, and to "guide" artists' creative work to ensure that it aligned with the needs of the party and the broad mass of workers, peasants, and soldiers.

Despite its subordination in terms of policy-making to the Ministry of Culture, which in turn came under the umbrella of the Department of Propaganda, the Artists Association nevertheless wielded a great deal of power, because it had responsibility for arranging art exhibitions and overseeing art publications. It thus controlled artists' access to the public through a laborious process of censorship. Exhibiting work or publishing it in one of the official art periodicals required the permission of the local Artists Association committee. Exhibiting and publishing regularly usually meant one had to be a member of the Artists Association, especially at the national level. The selection process for exhibitions was lengthy and bureaucratic, ensuring that only those works considered ideologically sound would get through the county- and provincial-level selection committees' censorship process, before a final decision was made by a panel of key members of the Artists Association in consultation with others, such as the head of The Central Academy of Fine Art (Zhongyang Meishu Xueyuan) and the head of the People's Fine Art Publishing House (Renmin Meishu Chubanshe).

The state directly controlled the curriculum and teaching methods of art educational establishments. The policies implemented in art colleges to a large extent paralleled those governing the lives of professional artists in general. Emphasis was given to the principle of "observing and learning from real life" (*tiyan shenghuo*)—going into villages and factories to observe the peasants and workers, and then reproducing in painting or sculpture their real-life (i.e., positive) experiences under socialism. Though artists were exhorted to be both "red and expert" (*youhong, youzhuan*), that is, to have a high level of political awareness and to be technically adept, in reality, political considerations generally took precedent over artistic ones. Attention was to be given to more "popular" art forms such as New Year pictures, murals, and propaganda posters. Chinese painting came under severe strain at several junctures, and a number of professors such as Pan Tianshou (1897–1971) found themselves demoted, but there were also periods of relative political liberalization, such as the early 1960s, when Chinese painting was encouraged as a national treasure. Western modernist art trends came in for severe criticism; they were banned from the educational curriculum and from appearing in front of the public in any form.

The extreme period of the Cultural Revolution saw the criticism and purge of all key art establishment figures. Many professional artists were labelled "bourgeois intellectuals" or "feudal remnants." Official arts journals, with the exception of *Zhongguo wenxue* (Chinese Literature), ceased publication in 1966. The Artists Association was suspended and temporarily taken over by one of the many rebel groups that had responded to Mao Zedong's call to seize the organs of power. Finally, in July 1969 most professional artists and art teachers were sent to "May Seventh" cadre schools (*"wuqi" ganxiao*) or military farms to work as laborers. Much of the artwork produced before 1966 was labelled "bourgeois" or "revisionist." Nevertheless, art continued to perform an important ideological function, playing an instrumental role, for example, in the creation of a personality cult around the figure of Chairman Mao.

## DEVELOPMENTS IN THE POST-MAO ERA

Since Deng Xiaoping's political reforms of 1979, liberalization in the social and cultural arenas has gradually unfolded, gaining particular momentum over the course of the 1990s. As opportunities arose for artists to exhibit in spaces other than those sanctioned by officialdom, and to publish their work in new art magazines run by editors who dared to break with the stifling ideological strictures of the past, the Artists Association and its organizational machinery became increasingly irrelevant as a means of mediating art policy and censoring work for public consumption. By the 1990s a semiautonomous system of art discourse and art practice had been firmly established as an effective alternative.

China's current orientation as a modernizing state seeking to become an integral member of the international community has entailed the rethinking of art policy, especially with regard to contemporary or avant-garde art. This fact, coupled with the current international popularity of artwork that a few decades ago would have been considered by the Chinese authorities as political heresy, has resulted in a new strategy of official cooptation of contemporary and "dissident" art and artists, as evidenced by the number of new government-financed modern art museums and galleries, and the official sponsorship of major exhibitions, especially the biennials and triennials that have mushroomed in China's key centers. These new arenas and exhibiting opportunities have drawn into the mainstream artists formerly labelled "dissident," thus rendering them less politically problematic.

Though the authorities are largely tolerant of most contemporary art, anything that is openly critical of China's top leaders or that touches on a particularly sensitive issue can still result in the closing of an exhibition. However, such official action tends to be reserved for images that are considered to be in poor taste, offensive, or in some way a breach of public order, thus bringing China more in line with current international practices.

**SEE ALSO** *Censorship; Federation of Literary and Arts Circles.*

**BIBLIOGRAPHY**

Andrews, Julia F. *Painters and Politics in the People's Republic of China, 1949–1979.* Berkeley: University of California Press, 1994.

Clark, John. Official Reactions to Modern Art since the Beijing Massacre. *Pacific Affairs,* (fall 1992): 334–352.

Galikowski, Maria. *Art and Politics in China, 1949–1984.* Hong Kong: Chinese University Press, 1998.

Holm, David. *Art and Ideology in Communist China.* Alderley, U.K.: Clarendon Press, 1991.

Jiang, Joshua J. H. The Extermination or Prosperity of Chinese Artists—Mass Art in Mid-Twentieth Century China. *Third Text* 18, 2 (March 2004): 169–182.

Laing, Ellen Johnston. *The Winking Owl: Art in the People's Republic of China.* Berkeley: University of California Press, 1989.

*Maria Galikowski*

## ART, SOVIET INFLUENCE ON

Chinese reliance on the Soviet model of socialist art began in the 1920s. Lu Xun, one of twentieth-century China's most important writers, was an early devotee of political art and literature from the new Soviet Union. Drawing on the Soviet model, Chinese socialist realism remained the official state style for almost four decades. The high point of Soviet influence on Chinese art was in the years between the founding of the People's Republic of China in 1949 and the Sino-Soviet split in the early 1960s. Mao Zedong and the party leadership instructed Chinese artists to learn the fundamentals of socialist art from the Soviet example, and the government fostered direct cultural exchanges between the nations to train Chinese artists correctly. The most important exchanges included sending a small number of Chinese artists to study at the Repin Art Academy in Leningrad between 1953 and 1960, holding Soviet art exhibitions in China, bringing the Soviet artist Konstantin Maksimov to teach painting in Beijing in 1955, and installing Soviet-trained Chinese artists, such as Luo Gongliu, as teachers at the Central Academy of Fine Arts (CAFA) to continue the instruction. However, this pattern of exchange did not result in a wholesale grafting of the Soviet style onto Chinese art. The Chinese were also intent on selecting elements from the Soviet model to fit Chinese purposes and adapting the academic realism inherent in the Soviet model to fit the needs of Chinese art.

Lu Xun's interest in Soviet art and literature in the 1920s and 1930s furnished one political precedent for using the Soviets as a model throughout the twentieth century. Lu Xun was captivated by the social reforms that the Russian Revolution promised, especially because the revolution occurred in a nation long beset by autocratic rulers, economic and social injustices, and an immense peasant underclass. The revolutionary spirit of Russian social reformers expressed in literature and art from the late nineteenth century forward served as a dynamic example for Lu Xun's efforts to inspire China to social reform. He translated Russian/Soviet literature into Chinese and exhibited and published Soviet prints for inspiration. The woodcut artists of the 1920s and 1930s, including those at Yan'an, the Communist base, thus had direct access to Soviet works as models for creating graphically powerful prints with a narrative structure to communicate political content. Lu Xun exhibited a number of European printmakers, most notably the German Käthe Kollwitz (1867–1945), who often depicted the sufferings of the poor, to showcase social and political content rendered in an effective style. The art of the Soviet Union, however, would become the preferred source under the Communists.

### OIL PAINTING

Among the intensive cultural and technical exchanges between China and the Soviet Union during the 1950s was the development of oil painting in China, particularly oil paintings that could record the historical events and personages of the new People's Republic. The genre of oil painting was considered the correct format for this purpose, building on the tradition of history painting in the West. Chinese artists were not entirely unfamiliar with Western oil painting. In the early years of the PRC, Western art had been taught in some Chinese schools as a technical and illustrative tool and as a means of naturalistic representation when accuracy was called for. Some Chinese artists had traveled to Japan or Western Europe to learn Western oil painting, both academic and modern in style. Xu Beihong was the most successful of this generation of painters; his style is marked by a preference for the academic and realistic rather than the avant-garde. His prominence made academic art more popular than modern art. Given that the Chinese already had a preference for realism, the clear political content, narrative methods, and conservative style of Soviet art was greatly appealing to the Chinese.

### THE SOVIET INFLUENCE AFTER 1949

The Soviet Union became China's primary ideological and trading partner after 1949. From the Soviets, Chinese artists would learn the basics of socialist content—the standard subjects of workers, peasants, and soldiers, and hagiographic images of party leaders—and, even more important, oil painting techniques. Statements by students of this era, at the Repin Academy and in Maksimov's class, discussed the value of technical instruction in oil painting, and their works reflect a high level of technical skill. Articles on the technical and compositional elements of Soviet painting appeared in the art journal *Meishu* and exported journals such as *China Reconstructs*. Journals also published examples of work of the nineteenth-century Russian realist movement known as Peredvizhniki (the Wanderers), an important precursor of socialist realism. Ilya Repin, for whom the Repin Academy was named, was a primary member of the Wanderers. Young Chinese artists sought to emulate the high degree of academic skill in these paintings. Although for the Soviets the Wanderers were a part of history, for the Chinese their populist subjects and empathy for the people dovetailed with many of the current directives in Mao Zedong's Yan'an Forum on Literature and Art.

From 1956 to 1960, during the period when Nikita Khrushchev rose from Soviet Communist Party leader to premier, the Chinese began to turn away from the Soviet Union. The political separation necessitated a new artistic policy for China. Chinese leaders such as Zhou Yang criticized the excessive realism of the Soviet style and emphasized the inspirational messages that could be expressed through revolutionary romanticism. Artists were urged to look toward Chinese folk art, national forms, and the spirit of the people for guidance. Although Chinese artists continued to rely on the technical foundation of the Soviet academic style, they increasingly turned to Chinese forms and content in the decades that followed.

**SEE ALSO** *Lu Xun; Oil Painting (youhua); Russia, Relations with; Socialist Realism in Art; Woodblock Printing (xylography); Xu Beihong; Yan'an Forum.*

**BIBLIOGRAPHY**

Andrews, Julia F. *Painters and Politics in the People's Republic of China, 1949–1979.* Berkeley: University of California Press, 1994.

Clark, John. Realism in Revolutionary Chinese Painting. *Journal of the Oriental Society of Australia*, 22–23, 1 (1990–1991): 1–30.

Fokkema, D. W. *Literary Doctrine in China and Soviet Influence, 1956–1960.* The Hague: Mouton, 1965.

Golomstok, Igor. *Totalitarian Art in the Soviet Union, the Third Reich, Fascist Italy, and the People's Republic of China.* Trans. Robert Chandler. London: Collins Harvill, and New York: Icon Editions, 1990.

Laing, Ellen Johnston. *The Winking Owl: Art in the People's Republic of China.* Berkeley: University of California Press, 1988.

*Marian Mazzone*

## ASEAN, RELATIONS WITH

The relationship between China and the Association of Southeast Asian Nations (ASEAN) has to a large extent been defined by two factors: first, the impact on Southeast Asia of relations between the major global powers; second, China's relations with ASEAN's largest member-state, Indonesia.

### RELATIONS BETWEEN 1967 AND 1991

ASEAN was established on August 8, 1967, during the Vietnam War (1957–1975) and in a context in which the five founding members—Indonesia, Malaysia, the Philippines, Singapore, and Thailand—were facing internal challenges from communist movements. China's support for these movements made it a threat to the ASEAN states. China's policy toward ethnic Chinese was also a concern, since four of the member-states had large Chinese minority populations, while Singapore had a majority Chinese population.

When ASEAN was established, none of its member-states had diplomatic relations with China. Indonesia had cut off diplomatic relations following a failed coup in 1965. However, China established diplomatic relations with Malaysia on May 31, 1974, the Philippines on June 9, 1975, and Thailand on July 1, 1975.

Although ASEAN did not officially support any actor in the Vietnam War, both Thailand and the Philippines provided military bases to the United States. Furthermore, the perception was that ASEAN had sided with the United States in the conflict, while China supported the opposite side.

Relations between ASEAN and China failed to evolve after the end of the war in Vietnam and Cambodia in 1975, although China's rapprochement with the United States, the emerging conflict between China and Vietnam, and the conflict between Cambodia and Vietnam eventually led to a geostrategic situation in which China and ASEAN pursued similar policies toward the situation in Cambodia—that is, actively opposing the Vietnamese military presence there. In the late 1970s, China also revived and changed its policy toward "overseas Chinese" in light of the initiation of economic reforms in China. China's leaders started to look to the overseas Chinese community for support of China's economic reconstruction.

The convergence of geostrategic interests, along with a gradual shift in China's policy toward ending its support of communist movements in ASEAN countries, led to improved relations with ASEAN in the 1980s. With the end of the Cold War, the reduction of the U.S. military presence in the region, and the normalization of relations between China and Indonesia on August 8, 1990, China's relations with ASEAN expanded. Full diplomatic relations were also established with Singapore on October 3, 1990, and with Brunei Darussalam (a member since 1984) on September 30, 1991. ASEAN's policy shift toward China under the banner of "constructive engagement" also contributed to improved relations.

## RELATIONS SINCE 1991

The ASEAN policy of constructive engagement promoted an expansion in diplomatic interaction and economic relations with China, a country that had earlier been perceived as a threat to the association and its member states. Significant economic growth in several ASEAN countries in the 1990s before the Asian financial crisis, along with China's deepening economic reforms, contributed to increases in both trade relations and investment in China by the ASEAN states. Diplomatically, relations also expanded and deepened. China was invited to attend the ASEAN Ministerial Meeting for the first time in 1991, and China became one of the founding members of the ASEAN Regional Forum in 1994. China became a full ASEAN "dialogue partner" at the association's Twenty-ninth Ministerial Meeting in 1996. China responded to the 1997 Asian financial crisis by not devaluing the yuan, a move that was much appreciated by ASEAN members whose economies were severely hit by the crisis.

Since 2000, ASEAN's relations with China have developed significantly. At the 2001 ASEAN–China Summit, the two sides agreed to focus their cooperation on five priority areas—agriculture, information and communications technology, human resource development, Mekong River Basin development, and two-way investment.

At the 2002 ASEAN–China Summit, the parties agreed on the Joint Declaration of ASEAN and China on Cooperation in the Field of Non-traditional Security Issues and on the Declaration on the Conduct of Parties in the South China Sea. The Declaration of Conduct is of considerable importance, in that China's claims in the South China Sea overlap with claims of several ASEAN states, namely, Brunei Darussalam, Indonesia, Malaysia, the Philippines, and Vietnam.

At the 2003 ASEAN–China Summit, China became the first ASEAN dialogue partner to accede to the Treaty of Amity and Cooperation in Southeast Asia. The Joint Declaration of the Heads of State/Government of the Association of the Southeast Asian Nations and the People's Republic of China on Strategic Partnership for Peace and Prosperity was signed at the same time.

In terms of economic cooperation, the parties, in November 2002, signed the Framework Agreement on Comprehensive Economic Co-operation, which provides for an ASEAN-China Free Trade Area (ACFTA) by the year 2010. ACFTA will initially encompass Brunei Darussalam, China, Indonesia, Malaysia, the Philippines, Singapore, and Thailand; by 2015, the newer ASEAN member countries of Cambodia, Laos, Myanmar, and Vietnam will also be included. In November 2004, ASEAN and China signed an agreement on trade in goods and an agreement on a dispute settlement mechanism of the Framework Agreement on Comprehensive Economic Co-operation.

China's relationship with ASEAN has also been strengthened through the ASEAN+3 process that encompasses China, Japan, and the Republic of Korea. ASEAN +3 cooperation was initiated in December 1997 with the convening of an informal summit; it was institutionalized in 1999 when the countries involved issued a Joint Statement on East Asia Cooperation at the third ASEAN+3 Summit in Manila. Among the documents providing guidelines for ASEAN+3 collaboration are the Report of the East Asia Vision Group of 2001 and the Report of the East Asia Study Group of 2002. The ambition is to promote a multifaceted collaboration between ASEAN and the three countries to the north to complement the partnerships that ASEAN has established with each of them. The areas of collaboration encompass the following: security dialogue and cooperation, transnational crime, trade and investment, the environment, finance and monetary policy, agriculture and forestry policy, tourism, and culture and the arts. Increasing ties are also evident in China's participation in the East Asian Summit, another ASEAN initiative, which held its first meeting in Kuala Lumpur in December 2005.

**SEE ALSO** *Vietnam, Relations with.*

**BIBLIOGRAPHY**

Association of Southeast Asian Nations (ASEAN). http://www.aseansec.org/.

Ba, Alice. China and ASEAN: Renavigating Relations for a 21st-century Asia. *Asian Survey* 43, 4 (2003): 622–647.

Ba, Alice. Who's Socializing Whom? Complex Engagement in Sino-ASEAN Relations. *Pacific Review* 19, 2 (2006): 157–179.

Cheng, Joseph Yu-shek. The ASEAN-China Free Trade Area: Genesis and Implications. *Australian Journal of International Affairs* 58, 2 (2004): 257–277.

Lai Hongyi and Lim Tin Seng, eds. *Harmony and Development: ASEAN-China Relations.* Singapore: World Scientific, 2007.

Saw Swee-Hock, Sheng Lijun, and Chin Kin Wah, eds. *ASEAN-China Relations: Realities and Prospects.* Singapore: Institute of Southeast Asian Studies, 2005.

Suryadinata, Leo. *China and the ASEAN States: The Ethnic Chinese Dimension.* Singapore: Singapore University Press, 1985.

***Ramses Amer***

## AUSTRALIA, RELATIONS WITH

Australia established diplomatic relations with the People's Republic of China (PRC) in January 1973, one of the first acts of the newly elected Labor government led by Prime Minister Gough Whitlam (1972–1975). Although it had been Labor policy to recognize the PRC, the decision was facilitated by the Sino-American rapprochement that had occurred in the previous year. Australia had previously followed the U.S. policy of containing China, but not to the extent of imposing a trade embargo; Australia made significant wheat sales to China during the 1960s.

In recognizing the PRC, the Labor government was motivated not just by the aim of protecting and developing Australia's economic relationship with China, but also by a desire to promote cooperative relations and strategic stability within the Asia-Pacific region. Such a goal was difficult without China's full participation. In relation to the Sino-Soviet conflict, the Labor government sought to follow an evenhanded approach, rather than siding with China.

There was a change of emphasis under the conservative Coalition government that held office from 1975 to 1983. While pre-1972 Coalition governments had been diplomatically hostile to China, Prime Minister Malcolm Fraser (1975–1983) strengthened the relationship. He saw China as a de facto ally in countering a more assertive Soviet Union, and encouraged the United States to adopt a similar approach. Fraser's approach was most obvious at the time of the Third Indochina War (which began in late 1978), with Australia siding with China (as well as the United States and the Association of Southeast Asian Nations [ASEAN]) in opposition to Vietnam's intervention in Cambodia; Vietnam was closely allied to the Soviet Union.

With the election of a Labor government in 1983, there was a return to a more evenhanded policy as far as the Indochina issue was concerned. Nevertheless, Prime Minister Bob Hawke (1983–1991) placed a strong emphasis on the relationship with China as a key element in his government's focus on Australia's role in the Asia-Pacific region. Prime Minister Paul Keating (1991–1996) continued Hawke's approach, while also developing a hedging strategy that involved promoting Australia's relationships with Indonesia and Japan.

The massacre in Tiananmen Square on June 4, 1989, was a major setback for Sino-Australian relations. Hawke had assumed that economic modernization in China would be accompanied by political liberalization. He reacted emotionally to the news of the massacre, with all Chinese in Australia on visitors' visas being allowed to stay for four years and then to become permanent residents (over 27,000 people). In other respects, however, Australia's reaction to Tiananmen Square was cautious, and by January 1990 the ban on Australian ministerial visits to China had been lifted. This was consistent with the Australian approach of not allowing human rights issues to undermine the substantive security and economic interests that underpinned the Australian relationship with China.

During the period of the conservative John Howard government (1996–2007), there was initially some setback in Sino-Australian relations when Australia gave support to the United States in the Taiwan Strait crisis of March 1996. Within a few years, however, the relationship had again become strong, with the Australian economy benefiting substantially from the export of raw materials to China. This economic interest reinforced the Australian perception that the strategic relationship with China should be strengthened. At the same time, the hedging strategy was evident in the development of Australian relations with Japan, India, Indonesia, and other Southeast Asian countries, and most particularly the United States. The Australian ability to balance its relationships with China and the United States was symbolized in the visits by presidents George W. Bush and Hu Jintao to Australia in October 2003, with the two leaders addressing the Australian Parliament on consecutive days. This balanced approach was expected to continue under the Labor government elected in November 2007; Prime Minister Kevin Rudd is a fluent Mandarin speaker.

The Sino-Australian trade relationship steadily developed from the time of normalization. By 2006 to 2007, China was taking 13.6 percent of Australian exports, and providing 15.0 percent of Australian imports. Raw materials exported included iron ore, copper, coal, and wool. Imports were manufactured goods, particularly clothing, computers and telecommunications equipment, and toys. China saw its relationship with Australia providing a means of enhancing its energy security, particularly through the provision of coal and liquefied natural gas; in 2006 there was an agreement allowing the export of Australian uranium to China for peaceful purposes. In May 2005 Australia and China began negotiating a free-trade agreement.

Students from China were an important export earner for Australia. In 2005 there were 81,184 Chinese students in Australia, the single largest group of international students. China also became a major source of immigrants for Australia, with 206,591 people born in China living in Australia according to the 2006 census (about 1 percent of the population).

While Australia ended its diplomatic recognition of the Republic of China in the context of recognizing the PRC, it has maintained an important "unofficial" relationship with Taiwan, focusing particularly on economic aspects. However, China's increasing economic importance has diminished Taiwan's bargaining power in its relationship with Australia. Australia has made clear that it would not automatically support the United States if there were conflict with the PRC over Taiwan.

**SEE ALSO** *International Relations; Vietnam, Relations with.*

**BIBLIOGRAPHY**

Parliament of Australia, Senate Foreign Affairs, Defence and Trade References Committee. *Opportunities and Challenges: Australia's Relationship with China*. Canberra, Australia: Senate Printing Unit, 2005.

Thomas, Nicholas, ed. *Re-orienting Australia-China Relations: 1972 to the Present*. Aldershot, U.K.: Ashgate, 2004.

Zhang, Jian. Australia and China: Towards a Strategic Partnership? In *Trading on Alliance Security: Australia in World Affairs, 2001–2005*, eds. James Cotton and John Ravenhill, 89–111. Melbourne, Australia: Oxford University Press, 2007.

***Derek McDougall***

## AUTOMOBILE INDUSTRY

The first cars in China arrived in 1901 and were used mainly in the developed city of Shanghai. Over the following several decades, nearly all of the vehicles in the country were imported, and many were owned by foreign residents. The nation's low income levels, ready availability of human-powered carriages, and lack of paved roads were major impediments to the expansion of the industry, and little indigenous production appeared until the middle of the twentieth century.

Following World War II (1939–1945) and China's civil war, the new communist government turned its attention in the 1950s to reviving the economy and developing a state-owned heavy industrial sector. Truck production took a leading role, because the vehicles were needed for transportation of rural produce, as well as for military transport. The Chinese looked to their main communist ally, the Soviet Union, for technical advice on launching vehicle manufacturing.

The First Auto Works (FAW) opened in the northeastern city of Changchun in 1956, and began producing Jiefang or "Liberation" model 4-ton trucks, modeled on a similar Soviet vehicle. Soon, other vehicle factories followed in Nanjing, Shanghai, and other cities. National production reached some twenty thousand vehicles in 1960.

Passenger car production began on a small scale in 1958, with manufacture of fewer than one hundred vehicles per year. The main models were FAW's Red Flag limousine and Shanghai's Phoenix passenger car. Many of the vehicles were reserved for the political leadership. China also imported passenger cars from Poland and other parts of Eastern Europe.

Though early vehicle production depended on parts imported from the Soviet Union, worsening relations between the two countries led China to expand its parts production sector. By the mid-1960s, all of the parts for the Liberation truck were made domestically. Manufacture of trucks continued to grow even during the Cultural Revolution (1966–1969), with production in the early 1970s topping 100,000. The new Second Auto Works (SAW) began production in 1970, and by the mid-1970s China had some fifty mainly small-scale vehicle assembly plants scattered around the nation.

Passenger car production lagged, however, as revolutionary policies discouraged official purchases of personal vehicles. Moreover, under the nation's egalitarian policies, private citizens lacked the financial resources to buy a car. Urban residents rode public buses or bicycles for local transport. Following the death of revolutionary leader Mao Zedong in 1976, however, the new reformist government of Deng Xiaoping turned to foreign corporations to quickly develop passenger car production.

### JOINT VENTURES IN THE 1980s AND 1990s

With China's economic and political reforms of the 1980s, demand for passenger cars to serve as taxis for tourists and transport for government officials soared, leading to a surge in imported vehicles. The resultant strain on foreign currency reserves inspired the government to turn to foreign investors for capital and technology to rapidly develop an indigenous production capability.

Among the first foreign auto companies to invest in China were American Motors (later taken over by Chrysler), Volkswagen (VW), and Peugeot. They formed enterprises in

Beijing (Beijing Jeep), Shanghai (Shanghai Volkswagen), and Guangzhou (Guangzhou Peugeot). Of the three, only Volkswagen's venture prospered, as it was able to source good-quality parts in the Shanghai vicinity, and it received substantial support from the local government. Beijing Jeep suffered from the lack of a broad market for its products, and Peugeot's plant was unable to develop parts suppliers in the mainly light-industrial southern part of the nation. By the end of the 1980s, Volkswagen (which subsequently formed another joint venture with FAW) controlled as much as 60 percent of China's passenger car market, and made large profits from its investment. In the mid-1990s, annual passenger car production exceeded 250,000 vehicles.

Volkswagen had achieved much of its success by using variations of its Santana and Jetta model cars. By the mid-1990s, the Chinese government saw the need to bring in more foreign capital and technology to further develop the sector's capacity and product variety. While keeping to earlier constraints on foreign investment, which included a maximum of 50 percent foreign ownership in a joint venture, the Chinese welcomed General Motors (GM), Citroën, Toyota, Honda, Nissan, Ford, Hyundai, and nearly every other major vehicle maker to set up operations in a variety of Chinese cities.

In the first years of the new millennium, as Chinese incomes rose, vehicle prices fell, car loans become more accessible, and the urban and intercity road networks expanded, private purchases of vehicles increased dramatically. Between 2001 and 2007, passenger vehicle production and sales rose nearly eightfold, from 800,000 to more than six million. Production of trucks, buses, and other commercial vehicles, which relied more on domestic technology, stayed relatively constant, rising from 1.7 million to about 2.5 million. China had become the second largest vehicle market in the world, after the United States.

The increase in car production and sales was mainly facilitated by fierce price competition among the many new manufacturing entrants to the field. Prices for cars fell from nearly $38,000 for VW's Santana in 1988, to

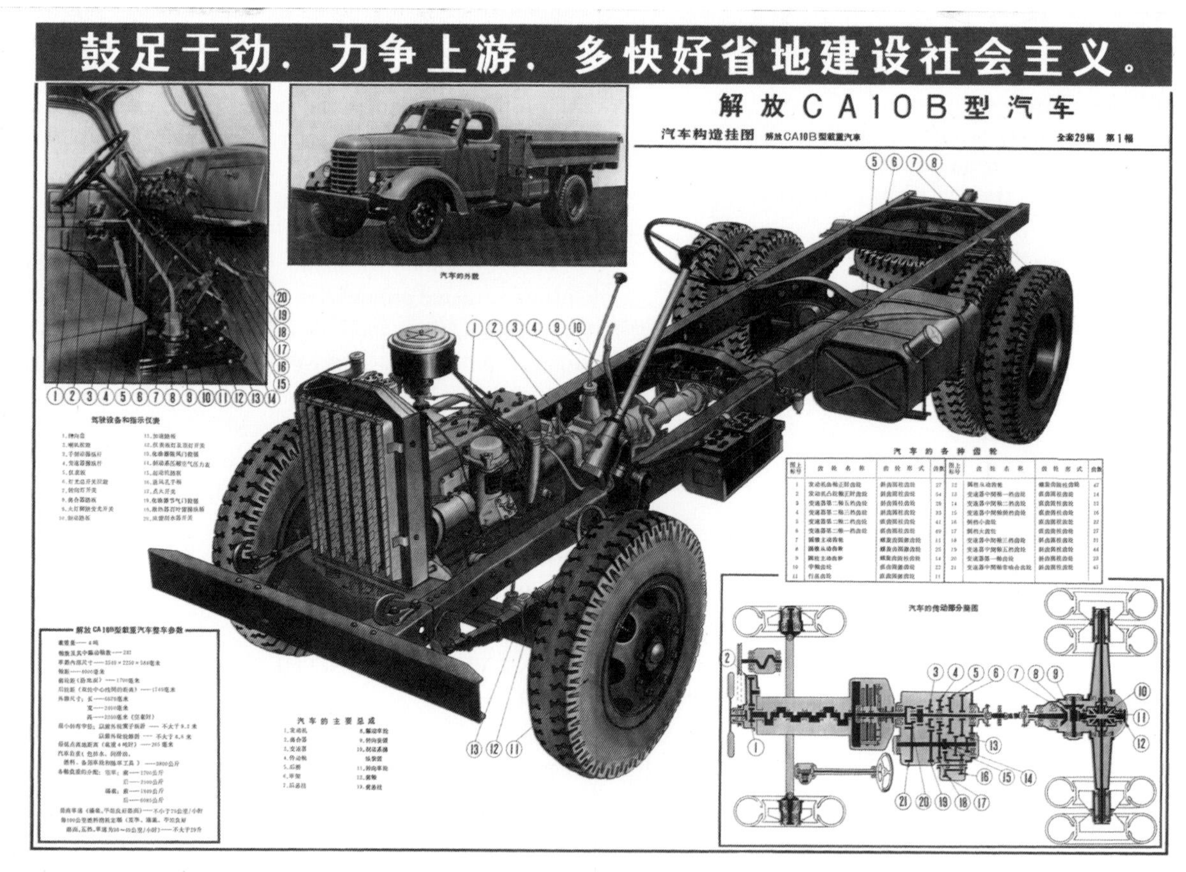


***Poster promoting the Jiefang, an early Chinese-made truck.*** *Based on Soviet designs, the Jiefang was the first heavy-duty truck manufactured in China for both civilian and military use. Meaning "liberation" in English, early Jiefangs were built in the mid-1950s, with later versions used by the Chinese military until the end of the twentieth century.* COURTESY INTERNATIONAL INSTITUTE OF SOCIAL HISTORY

less than $10,000 for a GM Sail in 2003. Suzuki made a small car in China costing less than $5,000. Also at the low end of the automobile market were two emerging Chinese manufacturers, Chery and Geely, companies that did not have investment ties to foreign makers.

In rural areas, so-called "transformed tractors," three- or four-wheeled vehicles that were categorized as farm machinery, appeared as inexpensive transportation tools in the late 1900s and early 2000s. Costing some $2,000 or less, these car- and truck-like vehicles were not officially classified as automobiles, but still played an important transportation role in the vast stretches of China's countryside.

### CHINESE CHALLENGERS AND THE FUTURE OF THE SECTOR

Though the purely Chinese automobile companies had only a small percentage of the vehicle market, they saw steady growth in the early years of the 2000s. By 2007, municipally owned Chery sold nearly 300,000 cars in China, for a 4 percent market share, and the private company Geely had some 3 percent of the market. Both companies were also expanding production overseas in developing nations, and were making inroads in exporting their cars. The Shanghai Automotive Industrial Corporation, which was the joint venture partner of both VW and GM, also set its sights on becoming a major carmaker in its own right.

China's 2001 entry into the World Trade Organization left protection for its vehicle industry, with 25 percent tariffs remaining to shield the market from imported cars. Foreign carmakers also stood to see difficulty in setting up comprehensive distribution networks without the support of a Chinese partner. However, most major foreign producers were already making their cars within the country. China's car import level therefore remained relatively low, in the range of about 2 to 6 percent for most of the decade.

A potential brake on the industry could come with a slowing of China's overall economic growth. More stringent controls on urban vehicle use to combat problems of air pollution and traffic congestion, as well as efforts to improve mass transit systems, could also cut private vehicle sales, as could rising costs of gasoline. However, in the middle of the new decade, China embarked on programs to develop more fuel-efficient cars, and Toyota introduced its hybrid technology at its FAW joint venture site.

Would China become a global automotive exporting power, one to rival the Japanese or South Korean examples? Until at least the mid-2010s, deficiencies in quality and design seemed destined to keep purely Chinese cars out of the most developed nations. Joint venture makers were mainly interested in tapping the Chinese market, rather than cannibalizing their own overseas sales. However, Chinese makers announced that sales in the United States and Europe figured prominently in their long-term goals. With improved quality and continued low prices, Chinese vehicles could, in the long run, follow the examples of South Korea and Japan, and become major competitors for the global automobile market.

**SEE ALSO** *Companies: Joint Ventures; Heavy Industry; Industrial Policy since 1949; Transport Infrastructure: Road Network.*

**BIBLIOGRAPHY**

Harwit, Eric. *China's Automobile Industry: Policies, Problems, and Prospects*. Armonk, NY: M.E. Sharpe, 1995.

Harwit, Eric. The Automobile Industry in China after WTO Entry. *Harvard China Review* 5 (Spring 2004): 107–111.

Harwit, Eric. Chinese Overseas Investment: Cases in the Automobile and Telecommunications Sectors. In Takahashi, Goro, ed., *Kaigai-shinshutsu suru chugoku-keizai* [The overseas advance of the Chinese economy]. Tokyo: Nippon Hyoronsha, 2008, pp. 184-98.

Sperling, Daniel, Zhenhong Lin, and Peter Hamilton. Rural Vehicles in China: Appropriate Policy for Appropriate Technology. *Transport Policy* 12 (2005) 105-119.

*Zhongguo qiche gongye nianjian* [China automotive industry yearbook]. Tianjin: CATARC Press: Annual.

*Eric Harwit*

## AVANT-GARDE FICTION

The emergence in China in the mid-1980s of avant-garde fiction (*xianfeng xiaoshuo*, rarely *qianwei xiaoshuo*), the experimental writing of a small group of young Chinese novelists including Mo Yan, Ma Yuan (b. 1953), and Can Xue, was welcomed by critics as a reclamation of literature from the requirement to present cultural and political comment and as a shift in literary concerns away from society toward the individual and the self. Variously referred to as "pure literature" (*chun wenxue*), "experimental fiction" (*shiyan xiaoshuo*), "meta-narrative" (*yuan xushi*), or "new wave fiction" (*xinchao xiaoshuo*), avant-garde fiction was regarded as postmodernist experimentation within the construction of Chinese literary modernism.

By the 1980s fiction had developed far beyond the confined and often sentimental scar fiction of the immediate post–Gang of Four era. The literary fashions of scar literature (*shanghen wenxue*), misty poetry, absurd drama, reportage fiction (*jishi wenxue*), roots fiction (*xungen wenxue*), and a modernist but realist mainstream generally denoted as "literature of the new age" (*xin shiji wenxue*) had followed each other in rapid succession. Mainstream fiction was beginning to tackle themes that would not have been permissible in the post-1949 period, or even in the May Fourth period and later. These rapid literary changes took place against a backdrop of dramatic socioeconomic and cultural change, and were nurtured by a major translation enterprise through which Chinese readers rapidly become acquainted with developments in world literature and cultural thought.

Avant-garde fiction was the logical outgrowth of these earlier developments, and its appearance signalled the emergence of a generation who had not endured the Cultural Revolution and who had not served time in the countryside as "educated youth." The major innovations of avant-garde fiction were in narrative, and it incorporated some of the sensibilities of the more personal misty poets. Common elements were irony, dislocation, irreverence, discordance, and trauma. Avant-garde works often touched on themes of aberrational behavior from a first-person perspective, recalling the preoccupations of Creation Society writers in the 1930s.

A later group of young writers including Ge Fei, Yu Hua, Su Tong, Sun Ganlu, and Bei Cun, all of whom were born in the 1960s, are sometimes called "post–new wave" (*houxinchao*) or second-generation avant-garde writers. This second group was actively promoted by major southern literary magazines such as *Zhongshan* (Bell mountain) in Nanjing, and *Shouhuo* (Harvest) and *Shanghai Wenyi* (Shanghai literature) in Shanghai. Although the high point of the literary movement was limited to the period 1986 to 1989, the term *avant-garde* was still being applied to the work they were producing in the first half of the 1990s. By the twenty-first century the term had fallen from use, and the avant-garde school had been absorbed into the mainstream of fiction writing. Although works by different avant-garde authors often shared narrative strategies, the term generally was not applied to a form or style of fiction, but only to the work of these particular writers.

Mo Yan (b. 1955), the penname of Guan Moye, is one of the most successful of the avant-garde novelists. Born in Shandong to a poor farming family, Mo Yan joined the army at age twenty and published his first novel, *Chunye yu feifei* (Falling rain on a spring night), in 1981. Three years later he was given a teaching position in the army's Cultural Academy's Department of Literature. In 1985 he came to the attention of critics with the publication of his novella *Touming de hongluobo* (The transparent carrot); a collection of his fiction under the same title appeared in 1986. Around that time he began to be influenced by the Western authors William Faulkner (1897–1962) and Gabriel García Márquez (b. 1927). Mo rose to national and international prominence in 1987 after his 1986 novella *Hong gaoliang* (*Red Sorghum*) was adapted into a successful film by Zhang Yimou. Much of his fiction, including *Red Sorghum*, *Jiu guo* (*The Republic of Wine*, 1992), and *Tiantang suantai zhi ge* (*The Garlic Ballads*, 1995), is set in Gaomi in rural Shandong. His writing has a hallucinatory quality that echoes rural ghost stories and evokes the magical realism that is a hallmark of much of China's avant-garde fiction; at the same time he documents the barbarity of history's violence. Mo has acknowledged that he is also influenced by Japanese literature, and the translations of his work into Japanese are very popular. In 1991 he graduated from the Lu Xun Literature Academy of Beijing Shifan Daxue. In 1997 he was awarded China's most lucrative literary prize, the Dajia Award, for his full-length novel *Fengru feitun* (*Big Breasts and Wide Hips*), for which he also received the Kiriyama Prize in 2005. In 2006 Mo Yan published his first traditional-style Chinese episodic novel (*zhanghui xiaoshuo*), *Shengsi pilao* (*Life and Death Are Wearing Me Out*).

Can Xue (b. 1953), the penname of Deng Xiaohua, is one of the most original of the avant-gardists and the only female writer in the group. Born in Changsha, Hunan, her parents suffered greatly following the anti-rightist movement (1957), and she was raised by her grandmother. Because of the Cultural Revolution, she did not receive a high school education. Her early life is documented in her short memoir *Meili nanfang zhi xiari* (The beautiful summer in the south, 1986). In 1985 she published her first short story, "Wushui shang de feizaopao" (Soap bubbles in the dirty water), and soon came to the attention of scholars in Japan and the United States. In 1988 her short story collection *Huangni jie* (Muddy street) was published in Taiwan; no mainland publisher was willing to publish it. Can Xue has acknowledged the influences of Dante, Kafka, Borges, and Calvino, and in 2008 she was preparing an annotated edition of Dante's *Inferno*. Representative works are *Canglao de fuyun* (Old floating cloud, 1991) and *Shan shang de xiao wu* (The cabin in the mountains, 1985). Like Mo Yan, there is a distinct element of magical realism in Can's work. Her writing explores inner realities and presents nightmarish images of uneasiness and physical discomfort.

Born in Zhejiang Province in 1960, Yu Hua came to critical attention in 1987 with the publication of his first short story "Shiba sui chumen yuanxing" (Leaving home at eighteen). In 1988, with the publication of *Xianshi yizhong* (A kind of reality) and several other works, he was acknowledged as having inherited the mantle of Can Xue, Mo Yan, and Ma Yuan. In 1988 several critics likened him to Lu Xun, his fellow provincial. He is best known for his 1992 novel *Huozhe* (*To Live*), which was made into a film by Zhang Yimou in 1994. Yu Hua has disowned Zhang's cinematic interpretation of his work; nevertheless, it is his most famous novel, along with Xu Sanguan mai xue ji (*Chronicle of a Blood Merchant*, 1995). He produced little work for almost a decade, but in 2005 published a novel, *Xiongdi* (*Brothers*), that was a best-seller in China. In 1998 Yu won the prestigious Premio Grinzane Cavour award for literature. His work has been widely translated into several languages.

Su Tong, the penname of Tong Zhonggui (b. 1963), was born in Suzhou, Jiangsu Province. He is another of the second wave of avant-garde writers. He is best known in the English-speaking world for *Qi-qie chengqun* (*Wives and Concubines*), which was published in 1990 and later adapted as the movie *Hong denglong gaogao gua* (*Raise the Red Lantern*) by Zhang Yimou. In 2007 Su Tong examined the historical mythology surrounding Meng Jiangnü, the grieving widow whose husband was killed during the construction of the Great Wall, in *Bi nu* (Emerald slave).

These four writers exemplify how the appearance of avant-garde fiction marked a turning point away from Chinese traditional values in the literary sphere. Avant-garde was less a movement than a term applied by critics to some writers and not to others, including Zhang Xianliang (b. 1936) and Liu Suola (b. 1955), who have written some works that are equally experimental. In the twenty-first century, most of the writers once designated avant-garde have moved toward more accessible and sometimes picaresque writing while retaining their distinctive styles; a notable exception is Can Xue, who has remained uncompromisingly literary and distinctive.

**SEE ALSO** *Can Xue; Mo Yan; Poetry: Misty Poetry; Scar (Wound) Literature; Yu Hua; Zhang Yimou.*

**BIBLIOGRAPHY**

Jing Wang. *High Culture Fever: Politics, Aesthetics, and Ideology in Deng's China.* Berkeley: University of California Press, 1996.

Jing Wang, ed. *China's Avant-garde Fiction: An Anthology.* Durham, NC: Duke University Press, 1998.

Yang Xiaobin. *The Chinese Postmodern: Trauma and Irony in Chinese Avant-garde Fiction.* Ann Arbor: University of Michigan Press, 2002.

Zhang Xudong. *China's Modernism in the Age of Reforms: Cultural Fever, Avant-garde Fiction, and the New Cinema.* Durham, NC: Duke University Press, 1997.

***Bruce Doar***

## AVIAN INFLUENZA

Avian influenza (AI), popularly known as Bird flu (*qin liu gan*), is an infectious disease transmitted from birds to humans. It is caused by an influenza virus of the type A, composed of hemaglutinin (H) and neuraminidase (N) with multiple strains (H2N2, H3N2, H5N1, H7N7…). It can be either low pathogenic or highly pathogenic, depending on the form of the site of cleavage. Whereas the low pathogenic strain remains in the lungs, the highly pathogenic strain provokes serious damage in the whole body, causing fever, cough, sore throat, muscle aches, and, in severe cases, breathing problems and pneumonia that may be fatal.

At the end of 2008, according to the World Health Organization (WHO), H5N1 had infected 30 persons in China (mostly in Guangzhou and Shanghai), killing 20 (a lethality rate of 67%), and 391 persons in the whole world, killing 247. After the first cases were reported in Hong Kong in 1997 (when a 3-year-old child died in May), the disease was diagnosed in southern China, Vietnam, Cambodia, Thailand, Indonesia (133 cases), Turkey, Egypt, Nigeria, and Pakistan. All of these cases were traced to contacts with infected birds, except for a few cases in Indonesia and Pakistan that were possibly linked to transmission between humans. Comparison with the H1N1 virus that caused the 1918 "Spanish flu" allowed WHO authorities to predict a possible pandemic of sixty million casualties if the virus mutates to an interhuman form. This prediction does not take into account the difference between the situations in 1918 and today in terms of antivirals and immunity.

Most of the influenza viruses of the twentieth century were identified in Hong Kong (H2N2 in 1957, H3N2 in 1968), due to its proximity to South China, where viruses emerge, and to its transparent public health policy and its competitive microbiological research. Hong Kong has been particularly alert to AI after the SARS crisis in 2003, which was first thought to have been caused by H5N1 but later identified as caused by a coronavirus. Public awareness of emerging infectious diseases rose after the Chinese government hid the SARS victims in Guangzhou and Beijing in 2003. Measures of control of the avian population (such as vaccination of poultry, closures of bird parks, and one-day suspensions of the retail markets) and techniques of preparedness (such as drills on the borders between regions, contingency plans in companies, and rooms reserved in hospitals for patients infected with H5N1) have been transferred from Hong Kong to the rest of China.

In Hong Kong, a massive culling of 1.5 million chickens in December 1997 and the closing of poultry farms (from 300 farms in 1997 to 50 in 2007) cleaned the avian population, but the consumption of poultry meat did not diminish, because live poultry is imported from Guangdong and frozen poultry from the United States.

The Qinghai Lake outbreak in May 2005 raised questions about whether the virus spreads more easily via migratory birds or domestic poultry, and, in domestic poultry, through traditional or industrial breeding. On December 9, 2008, a poultry farm in Hong Kong was infected despite strict biosecurity measures, which raised a debate about whether the virus could have mutated, evading the vaccine, or passed through the "one-day chicks" smuggled from Guangdong. The specter of a future pandemic raises burning

***Worker spraying pigeons with disinfectant, Gansu province, November 7, 2005.*** *More commonly known as bird flu, avian influenza remains a concern throughout China, as health researchers fear the virus will gain the ability for human to human transmission. As bird flu outbreaks occur, government authorities take precautions to limit public exposure to birds, including closing live poultry markets, vaccinating birds on poultry farms, and disinfecting bird-infested areas.* AP IMAGES

issues on the current relations between humans and between humans and animals.

SEE ALSO *Epidemics; Rural Cooperative Medical Systems.*

**BIBLIOGRAPHY**

Abraham, Thomas. *Twenty-first Century Plague. The Story of SARS, with a New Preface on Avian Flu.* Hong Kong: Hong Kong University Press, 2007.

Kleinmann, Arthur, et al. Asian Flus in Ethnographic and Political Context: A Biosocial Approach. Spec. issue. *Anthropology & Medicine* 15, 1 (2008).

Peiris, Malik, Menno de Jong, and Yi Guan. Avian Influenza Virus (H5N1): A Threat to Human Health. *Clinical Microbiology Reviews* 20, 2 (2007): 243–267.

Tambyah, Paul, and Ping-Chung Leung, eds. *Bird Flu: A Rising Pandemic in Asia and Beyond.* Singapore: World Scientific, 2006.

World Health Organization. Cumulative Number of Confirmed Human Cases of Avian Influenza A/(H5N1) Reported to WHO: 16 December 2008. http://www.who.int/csr/disease/avian_influenza/country/cases_table_2008_12_16/en/index.html.

***Frédéric Keck***

# B

## BA JIN

### *1904–2005*

Born in 1904 and raised in a landed gentry class in Chengdu, the capital of Sichuan Province, Ba Jin (Li Yaotang) lived to be a centenarian who witnessed nearly all of the great social upheavals in modern Chinese history. His education began in China's interior but brought him to Nanjing, Shanghai, and eventually Europe as he became a translator, publisher, writer, and the chairman of the China Writers' Association. It is no wonder that in several of his fictional works, personal liberation or intellectual enlightenment is signified by a hero or heroine's journey from Sichuan to a metropolis such as Beijing or Shanghai, illustrating Ba's deep contempt for provinciality and cultural conservatism.

To a large extent, Ba Jin's outlook and experience as a writer and thinker are representative of modern Chinese history as understood in terms of intellectual progress. He was seven years old when the Qing government was toppled in the 1911 Republic Revolution. By the time he turned fifteen, students in Beijing had taken to the streets to protest a corrupt government, setting off waves of angry protest that culminated in the May Fourth movement that rejected Chinese cultural traditions as archaic and responsible for keeping China stagnant. At forty-five he witnessed the founding of the People's Republic of China, a new political order and the dictatorship of the proletariat under which he would write for the remainder of his life. To the extent that a writer is also a product of his age, Ba Jin's fiction is shot through with the popular slogans of the Republican revolution, the rhetoric of May Fourth antitraditionalism, the language of the Communist revolution, and, most important of all, the discourse of anarchism.

Ba Jin's literary imagination was informed by his study of anarchism and works of Russian literature. Between 1926 and 1928, during his study abroad in France, he translated into Chinese the Russian anarchist Peter Kropotkin's *The Conquest of Bread* (*Mianbao yu ziyou*) from French and German texts, and his unfinished *Ethics, Origin, and Development* (*Lunlixue de qiyuan he fazhan*). Between 1929 and 1930 he translated Kropotkin's *The Memoirs of a Revolutionist* (*Wode zizhuan*). In his 1939 article "On the History of Russian Social Movements," (Eguo shehui yundong shihua) Ba Jin introduced anarchism not so much as a social program or project but as a personal philosophy that would free the Chinese individual from all familial ties and obligations. In other words, he found anarchism deeply satisfying not because of its actual political goals in changing a society by overthrowing governments, abolishing cultural institutions, or assassinating dictators, but because of its rhetoric of personal liberty and self-autonomy for the individual, a rhetoric that he would soon adopt as the aesthetic for his novels. In the West, the discourse of anarchism developed mainly as a critique of capitalism and industrial civilization in which a government could nationalize natural resources and wealth without the consent of the people. In contrast, in China, the nation was just emerging from its agrarian roots, with little nationalized industry or regimented production from which to free the citizens. Since the beginning of the twentieth century Chinese anarchists had been critical of the feudal family structure, the central location of Confucian culture. In 1907 Han Yi, the pen name of a Chinese anarchist, published his article "On Destruction of the Family" (Hui jia lun), arguing that the traditional family stood in the way of social progress. Another anarchist, Li Shizeng (1881–1973) called for "ancestor revolution," believing that the patrilineal values at the core of Confucian civilization were responsible for China's stagnation.

As a member of an anarchist group, Ba Jin naturally shared this critical view and felt it was necessary to adopt anarchism in China because it was a powerful and much needed ideology with which to replace Confucianism as China's state religion on filial piety and absolute obedience. For Ba Jin, the discourse of anarchism was an intellectual enlightenment that made him more conscious of the human conditions he had a duty to improve if China was to become a modern nation. His pen name, *Ba Jin*, is made up of two of the syllables taken from the names of two anarchists he admired, Mikhail Bakunin (1814–1876) and Peter Kropotkin (1842–1921), with *jin* being the pinyin Romanization of *kin*. As aptly pointed out by the scholar Mau-sang Ng:

> Indeed the writings of Kropotkin were to remain a source of inspiration and comfort to Ba Jin throughout his early period, especially in times of distress. As he wrote in the preface to the translation of Kropotkin's *Ethics*, "At the time when the revolution was crushed in Russia, Kropotkin frantically wrote his *Ethics*, and I was moved by the same spirit when at the time of the great massacre of Chinese people I put all my strength into the translation of this book." (Ng 1988, pp. 186–187)

These literary activities gave Ba Jin insights into and appreciation of Russian literary works, especially works by Ivan Turgenev such as *Fathers and Sons* (1862) and *Virgin Soil* (1877), which he took pains to translate (as *Fu yu zi*, 1943, and *Chunü di*, 1944, respectively). Needless to say, "[it] is clear from the Chinese response to Russian literature that, for the 1920s intellectuals, the Russian hero held up a mirror to themselves" (Ng 1988, p. 213). In 1931 his famous novel *Jia* (*Family*) came forth as testimony to his faith in anarchism.

For anarchists, the traditional family of premodern China was a link in the social hierarchy that a Chinese person experienced most directly and intimately as a form of political oppression that should be abolished to emancipate the individual. Ba Jin's novel *Family* was written within and mediated through this discourse; the story dramatizes the problems of feudal institutions such as footbinding, concubinage, arranged marriage, and ancestor worship. Structurally, this full-length novel about the ups and downs of a family is not very different from many classical Chinese novels such as the eighteenth-century *The Dream of the Red Chamber*, but thematically, it belongs to a completely different intellectual tradition. *Family* signifies, among other things, a tension or antithesis of society and human nature, which perhaps is best articulated by the French philosopher Jean-Jacques Rousseau (1712–1778), who believed that man was good when in the state of nature. Both nihilism (which rejected all existing values) and anarchism (which viewed government and authority as harmful and unnecessary) grew out of this intellectual enlightenment. Thus the central hero of *Family*, Juehui, can be seen as embodying the tendencies of both nihilism and anarchism to interrogate existing values, to question authority, and to accustom people to the romantic idea of man as good in nature. In this sense, one can read *Family* as a variation of Turgenev's *Fathers and Sons*, in which the young nihilist hero Bazarov tells his brother Pavel that he will abandon nihilism when Pavel can show him a single cultural institution in contemporary life that is worth preserving. Such contempt for society is also borne by *Family's* Gao Juehui, who finds social discrimination against the servant class morally incomprehensible. Turgenev's Bazarov, who like Juehui comes from an aristocratic and landholding family, prefigures his Chinese counterpart.

In a sense, *Family* is an intense dialogue between European Enlightenment liberalism and Confucian humanism as seen by intellectuals of the May Fourth generation. Although the story can be read as a clear indictment of the latter by the former, the work is in fact much richer and more nuanced than a presentation of an ideological position. Ba Jin tells a human tale of our ambivalence to change and tradition, with all views represented by a wide range of characters who signify many degrees of attraction to and repulsion by Confucian values. Evil acts are committed hypocritically in the name of filial piety and kindness: indulgence in lust, wanton disregard of another's will, and absurd filial piety when lives are lost as maids are treated as slaves and concubines.

A great master of fiction, Ba Jin was extremely skillful as he choreographed the conflict of human desires to belong and to be free, creating drama out of the complex human existence that offers man no easy solutions. Although oppressive in many ways, the traditional family is nonetheless depicted as the location of meaning, a platform on which all characters perform to achieve their individual identity. On this center stage, Juehui is not a star beyond reproach. His romance with the maid Mingfeng is self-serving in that it gratifies his ego as a savior and redeems his life as a member of the landlord class. Again there are echoes of Turgenev's *Fathers and Sons*, in which the aristocratic nihilist Bazarov falls in love with a young woman of humble origin, Anna Odintsova, as a way to redeem his own meaningless existence, and also Fyodor Dostoyevsky's *Crime and Punishment* (1866), in which the nihilist protagonist Raskolnikov falls in love with the peasant woman Sonia. *Family*, therefore, is not only an indictment of Confucian morality but also a critique of Western anarchism and feminism. Ba Jin makes reference to Henrik Ibsen's *A Doll's House*, a declaration of women's independence in a capitalist society that treats women as playthings, and almost a bible to educated women of the May Fourth generation. The grievances of *Family's* female characters thus amount to a collective accusation of traditional female decorum and chastity, but these characters are also products of a feudal society, and they still dream of being married and becoming housewives as the ultimate form of female self-fulfillment.

It is not without a sense of irony that we come to see Ba Jin's life as a cultural hero who put so much faith in the total emancipation and freedom of the individual from conventional mores and debilitating moral obligations. Despite or because of his status as a celebrity and famous writer, he was persecuted by the Red Guards during the Cultural Revolution (1966–1976), like many other writers and intellectuals, including his wife, Xiao Shan (1921–1972). During his lifetime Ba Jin supported the establishment of a museum of the Cultural Revolution, to serve as a reminder of the dark side of modern Chinese history.

**SEE ALSO** *Literary Societies; May Fourth Movement.*


**BIBLIOGRAPHY**

PRIMARY WORKS

*Jia* [*Family*]. 1931. Garden City, NY: Anchor Books, 1972.

*Di si bing shi* [Ward number four]. 1946. Hangzhou, China: Zhejiang Wenyi Chubanshe, 2003. Translation published as *Ward Four: A Novel of Wartime China*. Trans. Haili Kong, Howard Goldblatt. San Francisco: China Books, 1999.

*Han Ye* [Cold nights]. 1947. Beijing: Renmin Chubanshe, 1986. Translation published as *Cold Nights: a Novel*. Trans. Nathan K. Mao. Hong Kong: Chinese University Press, 1978.

SECONDARY WORKS

Kropotkin, Peter. *Wode zizhuan* [The memoirs of a revolutionist]. Trans. Ba Jin. Beijing: Sanlian Shudian, 1939.

Kropotkin, Peter. *Lunlixue de qiyuan he fazhan* [Ethics, origin, and development]. Trans. Ba Jin. Chongqing: Wenhua Shenghuo Chubanshe, 1941.

Ng, Mau-sang. *The Russian Hero in Modern Chinese Fiction*. Hong Kong and Albany: Chinese University Press and State University of New York Press, 1988.


***Rujie Wang***

## BAI HUA

***1930–***

The Chinese poet, screenwriter, playwright, and fiction writer Bai Hua is known for a versatile and sometimes contentious output as a professional author affiliated with China's literary bureaucracy. Born in Xinyang, Henan Province in 1930, he began his literary career in 1947 doing propaganda work for the People's Liberation Army (PLA). During the early 1950s he was employed as a writer for the Kunming Military District and the PLA's General Political Department. His poetry and short fiction from the 1950s offer romantic depictions of military life and local color in the southwest border regions of China where he was stationed. Like many intellectuals, he fell afoul of the Maoist regime during the anti-rightist campaign in 1957. Banned from writing and stripped of army as well as party membership, he worked in a movie equipment factory until permitted to write for the Shanghai Haiyan Film Studio in 1961. In 1964 he returned to the army as a member of the Wuhan Military District Drama Troupe, until the outbreak of the Cultural Revolution in 1966 again interrupted his creative activity.

Bai Hua re-entered the literary scene in the late 1970s with a succession of poems, novels, and screenplays, many of which responded boldly to the post-Mao cultural and political thaw. He is most widely known for coauthoring the screenplay *Kulian* (Unrequited love, 1979), a work subjected to nationwide criticism in 1981 during the first major cultural-political campaign since the death of Mao Zedong in 1976. Filmed under the title *Taiyang he ren* (Sun and man) but never screened publicly, *Kulian* depicts the suffering of an artist who returns to China from the United States only to find himself attacked and eventually driven to death by radical Maoist elements during the Cultural Revolution. After being singled out by senior PLA staff for dangerous "bourgeois liberal" tendencies, the screenplay was censured on political grounds in a number of high-profile journals and newspapers into the autumn of 1981. Unlike targets of Mao-era campaigns, however, Bai Hua was not imprisoned or otherwise punished for his political malfeasances, but carried on with literary work unscathed after producing a self-criticism. Since 1985 Bai Hua has been a professional author in the China Writers' Association. His career in PRC literary officialdom is that of an outspoken yet fundamentally loyal Chinese establishment writer-intellectual.


**BIBLIOGRAPHY**

Doleželová, Anna. Two Waves of Criticism of the Film Script *Bitter Love* and of the Writer Bai Hua in 1981. *Asian and African Studies* 19 (1983): 27–54.

Kraus, Richard. Bai Hua: The Political Authority of a Writer. In *China's Establishment Intellectuals*, ed. Timothy Cheek and Carol Lee Hamrin, 185–211. Armonk, NY: Sharpe, 1986.


***John A. Crespi***

## BANKING

*This entry contains the following:*



### OVERVIEW

The decades of the 1930s and 1940s witnessed massive military, political, and economic turmoil in China, beginning with warlordism and the Japanese invasion in World War II (1937–1945) and continuing thereafter with the civil war between the Nationalist and Communist forces. To pay for the civil war, the Nationalist government printed more and more money, creating severe hyperinflation (according to the wholesale price index in Shanghai, an item that cost one yuan in September 1945 cost about 105,000,000,000 yuan in May 1949).

## BANKING UNDER CENTRAL PLANNING (1949–1978)

The Communist government moved quickly to stabilize this monetary chaos. A new central bank, the People's Bank of China, was established in 1948 through the amalgamation of several regional banks. Once inflationary expectations had been brought under control through such mechanisms as the indexing of wages, a new currency was issued. (This currency is named the *renminbi* or "people's currency" and is therefore often referred to in English by the abbreviation RMB. However, the RMB's unit of account is the *yuan*, and therefore, under the nomenclature conventions of the international currency markets, another commonly used abbreviation is CNY, for "Chinese yuan.")

In the 1950s, as China moved to copy the Soviet Union's economic system of central planning, the banking system was reshaped accordingly. Nearly all the banks that had survived from an earlier era were incorporated into the People's Bank of China or closed down, and the foreign banks were also closed down or severely limited in their activities. The Bank of China—which was established as the Hu Bu in 1905, became the Da Qing Bank in 1908, and was given its present name in 1912—remained nominally independent but was effectively incorporated into the People's Bank of China as its foreign-exchange trading arm. In a parallel development, the Communications Bank, which had been established in 1907, was incorporated into the Ministry of Finance, where it functioned briefly as the conduit for the government's investment grants to state-owned enterprise (SOEs) but became dormant when it was replaced in 1954 by the newly created China Construction Bank. Virtually all the policy functions of a central bank and the deposit-taking and lending functions of commercial banks came to be concentrated in the People's Bank of China, although this monopoly was supplemented to a modest degree by the deposit-taking functions of small credit cooperatives that operated in rural areas. In 1963, in the wake of three years of deep crisis in agriculture, the Agricultural Bank of China was established to supplement the rural credit cooperatives; like the other banks, the Agricultural Bank was ultimately controlled by the Ministry of Finance and the State Planning Commission.

Paradoxically, as the People's Bank of China gained a near-monopoly in the banking sector, it simultaneously lost much of its economic importance. This paradox has its roots in the inner workings of Soviet-style central planning. Under central planning, all significant industrial and commercial activity becomes governmental activity, carried out by state-owned factories and stores, which make very few independent decisions but rather carry out detailed instructions from a central planning agency (the State Planning Commission in China's case). These instructions are typically embodied in multiyear plans, which China initiated with its First Five-Year Plan (1953–1957). Factories were told how much they would receive in raw materials, how many workers they would employ, and how much final output they must produce. They were also told the prices for all of these transactions. In other words, the State Planning Commission had the power to dictate whether a factory would make money or lose money on its operations. Factories that made money remitted all of their net earnings to the Ministry of Finance, and factories that lost money received offsetting subsidies. So long as the Ministry of Finance received more revenue from the profitable enterprises than it paid out in subsidies to the money losers, this system could be sustained year after year. Thus, there was no expectation that money-losing firms would go out of business or that their workers would lose their jobs (hence the Chinese saying that workers in state-owned enterprises had "iron rice bowls"—that is, secure lifetime employment).

Furthermore, the State Planning Commission decided which enterprises would expand their output in the future and provided (as nonrepayable grants, not loans) the money to pay for an enterprise's new plant and equipment. Thus the classic commercial banking function of financial intermediation (accepting deposits from savers and on-lending these funds to enterprises that plan to expand) became of vestigial importance in the centrally planned economy. The People's Bank of China continued to accept households' savings deposits, but these were quite small, because the State Planning Commission kept urban wages and agricultural procurement prices low. Much larger sums flowed through the banking system as enterprise-to-enterprise payments, but these transactions were dictated entirely by the State Planning Commission, so the People's Bank of China and China Construction Bank were merely the bookkeepers for these accounts. Under this system, a key banking skill (the capacity to assess which potential borrowers should receive loans and which should be refused) withered away from disuse.

## COMMERCIAL BANKING SINCE THE REFORMS—PHASE 1: "REFORM WITHOUT LOSERS" (1978–1991)

China's historic shift from a centrally planned economy toward a market economy can be dated precisely to the Third Plenum of the Eleventh Central Committee of the Party, which was held in December 1978. The first phase of these reforms, which lasted about a decade, has been called the period of "reform without losers" (Lau, Qian, and Roland

2000), because it was a period in which workers in money-losing SOEs were largely shielded from significant job losses.

The banking system has played a major role in, and been deeply affected by, China's economic reforms. The People's Bank of China was formally separated from the Ministry of Finance in 1978, and in turn the Bank of China, China Construction Bank, and the Agricultural Bank of China were all freed from People's Bank of China control in 1979. Equally important, new banks and quasi-banks were permitted to begin operations. One of the first of these, the China International Trust and Investment Corporation, was founded in 1979. Others were soon to follow, such as the China Investment Bank, which was established to manage World Bank loans after the PRC joined the World Bank and the International Monetary Fund in 1980.

A crucial next step in the evolution of the banking reforms occurred in 1984, when the People's Bank of China formally became China's central bank and gave up all of its commercial banking operations, with the Agricultural Bank of China assuming this business in rural areas and the newly created Industrial and Commercial Bank of China assuming the People's Bank of China's retail operations in urban areas. At the moment of its founding, the Industrial and Commercial Bank of China became the largest commercial bank in China and one of the largest in the world—a position it still holds.

During the 1980s, state-owned enterprises were gradually weaned from the old system under which free grants from the state budget covered operating losses and capital expenditures. If this policy had been ruthlessly implemented, it would have forced weak SOEs to close down, thus shattering many rice bowls. However, the government was extremely wary of the social instability that could arise if job losses were widespread. In order to sustain "reform without losers," the government required the nominally independent but still state-owned commercial banks (the "Big Four": China Construction Bank, Agricultural Bank of China, Bank of China, and Industrial and Commercial Bank of China) to provide loans to money-losing factories. Unsurprisingly, these loans were often not repaid, and the banks quickly accumulated a dangerously high proportion of nonperforming loans on their books. This trend was clearly unsustainable, especially in light of the increasing competition that the Big Four faced from the other banks that were being established. (The extent and variety of this emerging competition within the banking sector can be seen in Figure 1.)

***Figure 1***

## COMMERCIAL BANKING SINCE THE REFORMS—PHASE 2: "REFORM WITH LOSERS"

Following the political and economic crisis of 1989, there was considerable uncertainty, both within China and in the outside world, whether China would continue pursuing its reforms. These doubts were not resolved until the summer of 1992, when Deng Xiaoping made his famous southern tour and declared: "Development is the only hard truth. It doesn't matter if policies are labeled socialist or capitalist, so long as they foster development" (Naughton 2007, p. 99). This message was reinforced at the Fourteenth Congress of the Party in October 1992, which endorsed the concept of a "socialist market economy" (a deliberately ambiguous phrase, of course, but one in which the key new word is *market*).

For the banking sector, the shift to "reform with losers" quickly became apparent. In 1994 the government created three new policy banks—the Development Bank of China, the Export-Import Bank of China, and the Agricultural Development Bank of China—with the clear message that in the future, money-losing, politically motivated programs and projects should be financed through these banks, not the commercial banks. This message was reinforced in 1995 when the Commercial Bank Law was promulgated. The new law, especially articles 4, 7, 35, and 41 taken together, stipulates unambiguously that a commercial bank must exercise careful due diligence in examining the creditworthiness of potential borrowers and will bear all of the risk of bad loans. In short, money-losing SOEs could no longer expect to be bailed out by the commercial banks.

### IMPLICATIONS OF WTO ACCESSION

During the discussions that led up to China's accession to the World Trade Organization (WTO) in 2001, some of the most difficult and protracted negotiations concerned the commitments that China would undertake for the liberalization of the banking sector. The final version of the accession document provided for a five-year transition period for financial services, which meant that—at least in principle—after 2006 foreign banks would be permitted to compete on a level playing field with the domestic banks. That is, foreign banks would be free to establish branches in any location (no geographic restrictions), to deal with any and all customers, to do business in local currency, and generally to enjoy "national treatment" (be governed by the same rules that apply to Chinese banks). Of course, establishing a credible brand name and a widespread network of local branches can take many years, but there is no doubt that the WTO liberalization will lead to more intense competition for the Chinese banks, especially in the coastal cities.

SEE ALSO *Financial Regulation; Microfinancing; Money and Banking, 1800-1949; Rural Development since 1978: Agricultural Banking.*

### BIBLIOGRAPHY

China Banking Regulatory Commission. http://www.cbrc.gov.cn.

Lardy, Nicholas R. *China's Unfinished Economic Revolution.* Washington, DC: Brookings Institution Press, 1998.

Lau, Lawrence, Qian Yingyi, and Gérard Roland. Reform without Losers: An Interpretation of China's Dual-Track Approach to Transition. *Journal of Political Economy* 108, 1 (2000): 120–143.

Naughton, Barry. *The Chinese Economy: Transitions and Growth.* Cambridge, MA: MIT Press, 2007. See especially chap. 19: Financial System, 449–484.

People's Bank of China. http://www.pbc.gov.cn.

People's Bank of China. *China Financial Outlook 1994.* Beijing: China Financial Publishing House, 1994.

Wu Jinglian. *Understanding and Interpreting Chinese Economic Reform.* Mason, OH: Thomson South-Western, 2005. See especially chap. 6: Reform of the Banking System and Development of the Securities Market, 217–254.

Xu Xiaoping. *China's Financial System under Transition.* London: Macmillan, 1998.

***Ralph W. Huenemann***

## PEOPLE'S BANK OF CHINA

When the Chinese Communist Party installed the new government of the People's Republic of China, nationalization and consolidation of banks was its highest priority. The process began on December 1, 1948, with the formation of the central bank—the People's Bank of China—from the merger of three regional banks and the confiscated assets of some private banks. Headquartered in Beijing, the People's Bank of China was conceived as the foundation of the banking system, overlapping in function with the Ministry of Finance and performing all the functions of a central reserve bank.

In the early years of the People's Republic, the People's Bank of China put an end to the raging inflation and brought the country's finances under central control by absorbing the remaining semiprivate banks. By the mid-1950s, a Stalinist planned economy was in place. The banking system was centralized under the Ministry of Finance, which exercised firm control over all financial services, credit, and the money supply. Under the ministry's supervision, the People's Bank of China provided and dominated all banking services. Although the People's Bank of China lost many of its responsibilities during the tumultuous decade of the Cultural Revolution (1966–1976), it was restored to its leading position in the late 1970s.

In December 1978 the government began economic reforms that would leave their mark on every sector of society. Reform of the banking and finance sectors was last, because of banks' critical role in the planned economy: that of supplying loans to and maintaining the state-owned enterprises.

In 1983 the People's Bank of China was put in charge of reforming the banking sector. Reform began with decentralization of the banking system and diversification of banking services in the 1980s. In the 1990s banks were liberalized (less specialization and greater competition) and legalized through the institution of rules, regulations, and laws, including the People's Bank of China Law, which went into effect on March 18, 1995. In the 2000s, regulation of the banking system began through the newly created China Banking Regulatory Commission. The most difficult aspect of China's economic and banking reforms is weaning state-owned enterprises of their dependency on bank loans, many of which are nonperforming. At the same time, corruption in the banking sector must also be rectified. Both problems continue to challenge the Chinese authorities.

The People's Bank of China remains China's central bank, with an extensive range of powers and functions, including the following:

- *Policy and rule making.* The bank formulates and implements the government's monetary and interest-rate policies, as well as promulgating ordinances, regulations, and rules concerning financial supervision and control and banking operations.
- *Treasury.* The bank issues currency (the renminbi), controls the money supply, manages the state's foreign exchange and bullion reserves, holds state-owned

enterprises' deposits, and is the lender of last resort to other state-owned banks and financial institutions.

- *Administration.* The bank examines and approves the establishment, merger, and dissolution of financial institutions and insurance companies.
- *Service.* The bank provides services to state-owned specialized banks and financial institutions, including allocating funds, providing information (banking statistics, investigation, analysis, and forecasting), and training personnel.
- *Dispute resolution.* The bank arbitrates disputes between/among other state-owned banking and financial institutions.
- *Supervision.* The bank directs, controls, and supervises the entire banking industry, including other state-owned banks, nonbank financial institutions, and insurance companies.

In organizational structure, the People's Bank of China is headed by a governor, who is assisted by deputy governors. The governor is nominated by the premier of the State Council and confirmed by the legislature, the National People's Congress; the deputy governors are appointed and removed by the premier. As a body at the ministerial level on par with the Ministry of Finance, the People's Bank of China is directly under the control of the State Council. To perform its work, the central bank has branches and subbranches throughout China. At the end of 1992 there were 30 branches at the provincial level, 315 branches in prefectures and cities under provincial governments, and 2,056 subbranches.

### BIBLIOGRAPHY

Ma, Jun. China's Banking Sector: From Administrative Control to a Regulatory Framework. *Journal of Contemporary China* 5, 12 (July 1996): 155–170.

Tokley, I. A., and Tina Ravn. *Banking Law in China.* Hong Kong: Sweet and Maxwell, 1997.

Xie Ping, Financial Services in China. United Nations Conference on Trade and Development, Geneva, 1995. Working paper no. 94.

***Maria Hsia Chang***

## BIG FOUR

Since China's economic reforms, references to the Big Four commercial banks have become commonplace. The four banks in question are the Industrial and Commercial Bank of China, China Construction Bank, Agricultural Bank of China, and Bank of China. These four banks are the largest in China and dominate their sector. They are also large by world standards. Thus, referring to them as the Big Four makes sense. However, a fifth bank, the Bank of Communications, is emerging as a claimant for inclusion in this elite grouping, partly because it is reasonably large in its own right, but more importantly because it has been a leader and catalyst in several important reforms (such as floating shares in Hong Kong and seeking strategic alliances with foreign banks) that were later pursued by the Big Four. One indication of this emerging shift from Big Four to Big Five is that the China Banking Regulatory Commission, in its statistical compilations, now groups the five banks together, referring to them collectively as the state-owned commercial banks. According to the commission, the five controlled 53.2 percent of the total assets of China's banks at year-end 2007.

### HISTORICAL ROOTS

The Big Five have varied historical roots. The Bank of China and the Bank of Communications were both founded in the early years of the twentieth century and were already major banks during the Republican period; China Construction Bank and the Agricultural Bank of China were established as specialized banks during the Maoist era; and the Industrial and Commercial Bank of China was created in 1984 out of the urban retail banking operations that were spun off from the People's Bank of China when it was stripped of its commercial banking activities to become solely the central bank.

When these five banks were established or resurrected as commercial banks in the reform period, they naturally carried with them the specializations of the earlier years: The Bank of China was the acknowledged expert in foreign-exchange dealings; China Construction Bank had special strengths in project evaluation (reinforced when the China Investment Bank was folded into China Construction Bank in 1994); the Agricultural Bank of China focused on retail banking in rural areas, while the Industrial and Commercial Bank of China had a parallel emphasis in urban areas; and the Bank of Communications reestablished its special position as China's first joint-stock bank. However, these distinctions have become increasingly blurred over time, and the five now compete with each other (and with the numerous smaller banks and quasi-banks) for business generally. An example of the effects of this competition can be seen in the realm of foreign-exchange transactions. During the era of central planning, the Bank of China, operating as an arm of the People's Bank of China, handled all of China's foreign-exchange dealings. However, after 1985 the regulatory authorities gradually authorized competing banks to deal in foreign currencies, and by 1996 the Bank of China's share of the market in foreign trade settlement had fallen to about two-fifths (Naughton 2007, p. 65).

### THE REFORM PERIOD

During the period of "reform without losers" (from 1978 into the 1990s), the Big Four banks came under heavy political pressure to support money-losing state-owned enterprises (SOEs) with soft loans that often degenerated into nonperforming loans. By the late 1990s, all four banks were probably insolvent (had liabilities greater than assets). The dangers that lurked in a fragile banking system became especially evident with the Asian financial crisis, which started in Thailand in 1997 and spread quickly to Indonesia, South Korea, Malaysia, and elsewhere in the region. Reform of China's banks could be postponed no longer.

As a first step, in 1998 the Chinese government issued 270 billion yuan worth of special bonds and injected these funds into the banks' balance sheets to raise their capital adequacy ratios (Naughton 2007, p. 462). Then in 1999, the government created four entities called *asset management companies*, one for each of the Big Four: Great Wall Asset Management Company for the Agricultural Bank of China, Orient Asset Management Company for the Bank of China, Huarong Asset Management Company for the Industrial and Commercial Bank of China, and Xinda Asset Management Company for China Construction Bank. The asset management companies took over 1.4 trillion yuan of the banks' nonperforming loans at face value and then sold them into the global capital markets for whatever they would fetch—about 20 percent of face value on average. For the Agricultural Bank of China, which had the weakest loan book of the four banks, Great Wall Asset Management Company recovered only about 10.4 percent of the face value of the nonperforming loans (*People's Daily* 2005). In addition to creating the asset management companies, the central government offered substantial further cash injections to the big banks, but only if they undertook major reforms, including such steps as writing down more of their nonperforming loans against their own profits, laying off redundant staff, closing unprofitable branches, finding foreign banks as strategic partners, and so forth.

As the mechanism for these further cash injections, the government created the Central Huijin Investment Corporation in 2003. In 2004 the reforms carried out by China Construction Bank and the Bank of China were judged adequate to warrant further cash injections. The two banks were restructured as joint-stock banks, and Huijin invested US $45 billion (from China's foreign-exchange reserves) in their new shares, thus effectively taking majority ownership of the banks. Following the precedent of the Bank of Communications, which had floated an initial public offering (IPO) in the Hong Kong stock market in June 2005, China Construction Bank was given permission to float an IPO (sell some of its shares) in Hong Kong in October 2005, with the Bank of China following suit with an IPO in June 2006. Meanwhile, the Industrial and Commercial Bank of China was also pursuing reforms, received a cash injection of US $15 billion in 2005, and in October 2006 was authorized to float an IPO in Hong Kong and Shanghai, which raised the equivalent of US $22.7 billion and was the world's largest IPO to that date. (The Agricultural Bank of China, with its close links to the rural areas, has always been the most troubled of the Big Four, and it remains to be seen whether it will be able to carry out the kinds of reforms instituted by the other three. But, of course, precisely because it is most troubled, it is the one most in need of recapitalization.)

### FOREIGN PARTNERSHIPS

Strategic foreign partnerships have been an important element in recent reforms and have occurred in both directions. Important inbound deals (foreign-bank investment in Chinese banks) have included investments by HSBC Bank in the Bank of Communications (2004), Bank of America in China Construction Bank (2005), Royal Bank of Scotland in the Bank of China (2006), and Goldman Sachs, Allianz AG, and American Express in the Industrial and Commercial Bank of China (2006). Important outbound deals have included the Industrial and Commercial Bank of China's purchases of 20 percent of South Africa's Standard Bank (2007) and 80 percent of Macau's Seng Heng Bank (2008).

### BIBLIOGRAPHY

Agricultural Bank of China. http://www.abchina.com.

Bank of China. http://www.boc.cn.

Bank of Communications. http://www.bankcomm.com.

China Banking Regulatory Commission. http://www.cbrc.gov.cn.

China Construction Bank. http://www.ccb.com.

*People's Daily Online*. China's Asset Management Companies Face Reform Pressure. August 10, 2005. http://english.peopledaily.com.cn/.

Industrial and Commercial Bank of China. http://www.icbc.com.cn.

Naughton, Barry. *The Chinese Economy: Transitions and Growth*. Cambridge, MA: MIT Press, 2007. See especially chap. 19: Financial System, 449–484.

Xu Xiaoping. *China's Financial System under Transition*. London: Macmillan, 1998.

***Ralph W. Huenemann***

## NONPERFORMING LOANS

China's experience with nonperforming loans (NPLs) can be traced back to the early 1980s when the government began turning its reform energies to the inefficient state-owned enterprise (SOE) sector. Prior to this time, SOEs received most of their funding directly from the government budget, and any profits they made were remitted in full. A series of policy initiatives was introduced, modeled around the Contract Responsibility System. The standout feature of this system was that SOEs were permitted to retain a proportion of any profits they earned (Chai 1998). While this did bolster the incentive that SOEs had to be more efficient, it also had the effect of shrinking the government's traditional tax base.

Government revenue as a proportion of gross domestic product (GDP) fell from 28.4 percent in 1979 to a low of 10.7 percent in 1994, even as pressure on the budget to underwrite the infrastructure that was necessary to sustain China's budding economic miracle was growing (McKinnon 1994). Rapidly rising household-sector income also led to a buildup of savings deposits in the banking system. Together, these developments provided the backdrop to a policy shift that sought to replace the reliance of SOEs on budgetary grants with bank loans. The hope was that by making SOEs more dependent upon funds that required repayment, they would become more conscious of the need to be efficient, and at the same time, pressure on the budget might be relieved.

This hope proved largely naive, however, as the reality was that SOEs remained wholly state-owned, as did the banks lending to them. Thus, these loans came to be viewed as being "from the state, to the state," and SOEs felt no great compulsion to make timely repayments. In any case, after years of making loans according to government directives, banks were ill equipped to extend credit based on commercial considerations. The situation was exacerbated by the decentralization in decision-making power away from Beijing that took place in the early 1980s, allowing local bank branches to become, in part, captive to the preferences of local government officials.

All the while, market forces were increasingly determining prices throughout the economy, and SOEs found themselves facing increasing competition from a rapidly developing non-state-enterprise sector. In the absence of reliable official figures, best estimates suggested that the NPL ratio in China's banking system had reached around 25 percent by the mid-1990s and 40 percent by the end of the decade. Nearly all of China's major banks were technically insolvent in the sense that the value of their NPLs was larger than their own capital (Lardy 1998). They were, however, able to remain liquid—making loans and meeting the demand for withdrawals—because households continued their buildup of savings deposits.

Household confidence in the banking sector remained high because the biggest banks were government-backed and the explicit government debt to GDP ratio remained low. Households also had few other investment options—the stock market was still in its infancy, as were real-estate markets, and the capital account remained largely closed. While this meant that the rise in NPLs never resulted in a banking-sector crisis, the need to address the problem nonetheless grew on several fronts. Firstly, the rising stock of NPLs effectively represented an increase in outstanding government debt, and ignoring the problem would only have made it worse. Secondly, over time the household sector was gaining access to an increasing number of investment options, and this raised the possibility of a liquidity crunch if households moved away from savings deposits. Thirdly, in the late 1990s many of China's neighbors experienced an economic crisis hatched in the banking system, despite these countries having a lower NPL ratio than did China, and this raised fears of China's vulnerability. Fourthly, in 2001 China joined the World Trade Organization (WTO) and committed to significant banking-sector liberalization. A massive stockpile of NPLs would have made it impossible for domestic banks to compete with new foreign entrants.

Several measures were introduced to deal with the NPL problem. Firstly, the government created Asset Management Companies that were charged with taking on existing NPLs and seeking their disposal. Secondly, government agencies such as the Ministry of Finance and the People's Bank of China undertook large recapitalization programs, particularly in the biggest banks. Thirdly, the prudential and supervisory structure surrounding banks and their borrowers was overhauled. A Commercial Banking Law was introduced that obligated banks to extend credit based on commercial considerations. Transparency in lending quality was improved through the introduction of an NPL classification system modeled on international standards. A national corporate and personal credit registry was established. The old, provincial-based structure of the People's Bank of China was replaced by a regional structure aimed at minimizing meddling by local officials. Fourthly, ownership reform took place with respect to both SOEs and the banks. While many large SOEs remained majority government-owned and continued to receive support, small and medium-sized ones were sold off or allowed to go bankrupt. Nearly all of China's largest banks now have equity stakes held by nonstate investors, including foreigners.

On the whole, the impact of such measures on the NPL ratio has been impressive. According to the latest official data, which is still contestable but certainly more credible than earlier figures, the NPL ratio in China's banking sector fell to 6.2 percent by the end of the third quarter of 2007. However, it is too early to say that China has put the NPL problem behind it. Firstly, one reason why the NPL ratio has fallen is simply because there has been rapid lending growth. For example, in the first three quarters of 2007, official data shows that the absolute amount of NPLs in China's largest banks actually increased, even as it declined as a proportion of total lending. Secondly, the booming macroeconomy has meant that the quality of lending has yet to be stress tested. Thirdly, Asset Management Companies are likely to develop into considerable financial burdens for the government because they are highly leveraged and their rate of cash recovery has been low. Fourthly, the NPL ratio in most of China's banks still has a way to go. For example, while the NPL ratio for the banking sector as a whole stood at 6.2 percent in 2007, the ratio for foreign banks operating in China stood at just 0.5 percent.

**BIBLIOGRAPHY**

Chai, Joseph C. H. *China: Transition to a Market Economy.* Oxford: Clarendon, 1998.

Lardy, Nicholas. *China's Unfinished Economic Revolution.* Washington, DC: Brookings Institution, 1998.

McKinnon, Ronald. Financial Growth and Macroeconomic Stability in China, 1978–1992: Implications for Russia and Other Transitional Economies. *Journal of Comparative Economics* 18, 3 (1994): 438–469.

***James Laurenceson***

# BAOJIA SYSTEM

The *baojia* system (or community self-defense system) was a neighborhood household registration system in the Qing dynasty (1644–1912) instituted to prevent crime. The Qing government instituted its system in the first year of the dynasty, but the system had origins as far back as Emperor Wen (r. 581–604) of the Sui dynasty. Civilians were registered in *pai* (registration units). Every ten neighboring households constituted a *pai*, headed by a *paitou*; every ten *pai* constituted a *jia* (tithing), headed by a *jiatou*; and every ten *jia* constituted a *bao* (security group), headed by a *baozhang* (Hsiao 1967, p. 43).

By appointing headmen for these groupings, the Qing government sought to grasp settlement and control rural society. The law stipulated that each household be given a door placard affixed with an official seal. The number and names of adult males were recorded on this placard. If any these inhabitants left the household, his destination was recorded; if a new person came into the household, his origin was ascertained and recorded. It was forbidden to take in strangers and suspicious characters unless a thorough questioning of them had been made. The *paitou* was responsible for keeping watch over his *pai*, and he reported to the *jiatou*, who oversaw ten *pai*. At the end of the month, the *baozhang* received reports from the different *jiatou* and gave assurance that all was well in the neighborhoods to the official inspector. Failure to comply was punished. The law also tried to keep track of people not living in villages. It required inns to keep registers of guests. Paper placards were also given to Buddhist temples and Daoist shrines (Hsiao 1967, pp. 44–45).

The *baojia* system had three main features. First, households and inhabitants in neighborhoods and villages were registered. Second, all acts that violated imperial law or disturbed the local order were detected and reported. Third, local inhabitants themselves operated the system, while local officials supervised its operation without taking any direct part in it (Hsiao 1967, p. 45). If the *baojia* system worked as planned, the Qing government could rely on local communities to maintain social order, and there would be no need for the state to expand the bureaucracy.

## DIFFICULTIES

Practice, however, did not correspond exactly to theory. Throughout the entire eighteenth century and first half of the nineteenth, though the central government repeatedly restated the importance of implementing the *baojia* system, the result was far from satisfactory. Qing emperors laid the blame on local officials. As early as 1726 the Yongzheng emperor asserted that there was no better method of bandit suppression than the *baojia* system, and criticized local officials for regarding it as an old formality, finding it troublesome to operate, and not operating it in earnest. Some local officials offered the excuse that it was difficult to arrange the villages into *jia* and *bao*, since the number of households they contained was not always divisible by ten. Others in the frontier provinces gave the pretext that it was inconvenient to apply a system of the interior provinces to a frontier province, since Han Chinese and ethnic minorities intermingled and dwelled together. In 1769 the Qianlong emperor also criticized the attitudes of local officials toward the *baojia* system. He complained that officials saw the *baojia* system as impractical and treated it as a mere formality (Hsiao 1967, pp. 46–47, 73).

It was unfair to lay all the blame for the failure of the *baojia* system on local officials. In 1769 a high Guangdong official reported to the Qianlong emperor that even discovered causes of theft went unreported to the local yamen by *baojia* headmen (Hsiao 1967, p. 73). In other words, local inhabitants cooperated poorly with the local government in implementing the *baojia* system.

Kung-chuan Hsiao argues that illiteracy might have hindered household registration. Under the *baojia* system, each household was required to have a door placard on which the names of its male members were written. The average villager could seldom fulfill this simple requirement. Few door-placard entries were accurate. The compilation of registers from the door placards presented another difficulty. Perhaps the difficulty in registration was writing. Most *baojia* heads were illiterate and could not check entries even with the best of intentions (Hsiao 1967, p. 75). This explanation is problematic, however, even if we accept the view that common villagers were generally illiterate. Chinese villages had a long tradition of using writing in their daily lives. Villagers, literate or not, were somehow able to compile genealogies to trace their origins and to make wooden tablets with names inscribed to represent the souls of their dead ancestors (Faure 2007).

The major difficulty in implementing the *baojia* system was absence of incentive in local communities to cooperate with the state. *Baojia* headmen had no police authority or weapons to arrest suspects or bandits. Their duty was only to watch over neighbors and report crime suspects to local officials. Without police authority, they found no reason to cooperate with the government, and without weapons, they feared revenge from suspects if they reported the latter to local officials. The post of *baojia* headman was onerous, with little prestige and much responsibility (Kuhn 1980, p. 26). The outbreak of the White Lotus Rebellion between 1795 and 1804 demonstrated the failure of the *baojia* system as an instrument of social control. Hsiao, in his work on imperial control in the nineteenth century (1967), concluded that the *baojia* system could operate only in times of peace.

### *BAOJIA* AND MILITIAS

Since the *baojia* system was incapable of dealing with a social crisis, in the mid-nineteenth century, following the outbreak of the Taiping Uprising, the court approved the establishment of local defense militias commonly called *tuanlian* at the time. Unlike *baojia* headmen, militias were armed. With the establishment of militias, many villages became militarized and formed the military confederations that characterized Chinese rural society in the late nineteenth century (Kuhn 1980).

The distinction between *baojia* and *tuanlian* blurred in Republican times (1912–1949). In 1929 the Nationalist government in Nanjing, seeking to crush bandits and Communists in rural areas, encouraged provincial governments to set up *baojia* again. However, the rules for setting up *baojia* included establishing local militia and buying weapons (Wen 1971, pp. 365–430). The *baojia* were transformed into local militia in essence.

### BIBLIOGRAPHY

Faure, David. *Emperor and Ancestor: State and Lineage in South China.* Stanford, CA: Stanford University Press, 2007.

Hsiao, Kung-chuan. *Rural China: Imperial Control in the Nineteenth Century.* Seattle: University of Washington Press, 1967.

Kuhn, Philip A. *Rebellion and Its Enemies in Late Imperial China: Militarization and Social Structure, 1796–1864.* Cambridge, MA: Harvard University Press, 1980.

Wen Juntian. *Zhongguo baojia zhidu* [The Chinese *baojia* system]. Taibei: Taiwan Shangwu Yinshuguan, 1971. First published, 1933.

***Sui-wai Cheung***

## BEGGARS

The Chinese word for *begging* appeared as early as in the oracle bone writing of the eighteenth century BCE and continued to be used in the literature of the Bronze Age. Records describing begging in public appeared in Chinese documents as early as the third century BCE. The modern Chinese word for beggar, *qigai,* first appeared no later than the early years of the Song dynasty (960–1279). By the last imperial dynasty, the Qing (1644–1912), throughout the country mendicancy had long been an established, albeit despised, way of life. The ubiquity of begging continued until the Communists took power in 1949. The Maoist regime effectively reduced mendicancy and to a great extent eliminated it in major cities. But within a few years after the economic reform launched in 1978, beggars were back to the streets again.

### THE MEANING OF "BEGGAR"

In China, as elsewhere in the world, *beggar* in most cases refers to a person who requests something in public in a supplicating manner. However, historically the notion of mendicancy in China has been richly ambiguous and the word *beggar* ingeniously connotative. Thus one can also find references to beggars who worked, performed services, extorted, and coerced, all of which were considered begging techniques. Now and then an authentic beggar was a street entertainer of various sorts: singer, dancer, acrobat, snake-charmer, monkey-trainer, and in festivals, pageant players. More than occasionally he or she could also perform as a porter, errand runner, door guard, fortune-teller, story-teller, prostitute, barber, mourner-for-hire, debt-collector-for-hire, night watchman, or even policeman or picket. Beggars typically were not criminals, but swindlers, thieves, and gangsters were not uncommon among them. Knights-errant and town eccentrics were also found in the ranks of mendicants, and such characters became favorite topics in both popular and literary writings. Paradoxically, the beggars' lives of extreme poverty and misery helped create a rich culture of the underclass.

### BEGGARS AND MAINSTREAM SOCIETY

There were ongoing and often lively interactions between the world of beggars and mainstream society. Major historical characters and cultural icons in China belonged not just to "regular" society but also to the underclass; among them the most famous was Zhu Yuanzhang (1328–1398), a teenage vagrant who rose from a mendicant to be the founding emperor of the Ming dynasty (1368–1644). By capturing mainstream society's imagination, beggars' culture had a profound influence on public opinion regarding poverty, morality, and individuality as well as everyday life issues such as cuisine, clothing, and child rearing. For instance, two popular dishes served in upscale restaurants are called *jiaohuaji* (beggar's chicken) and *Fotiaoqiang* ("Buddha jumps over the wall"—the name suggesting that Buddha himself would escape from the temple to taste this delicacy, which originated from a sort of hobo dish). China has a long tradition of seeing failure as the mother of success and adversity as a way of honing one's ability. Mendicancy is frequently viewed in this way: although beggars may be seen as outcasts

***A farmer from Anhui begs on the streets of Beijing, July 23, 2003.*** *During the tenure of Mao Zedong, police routinely returned rural citizens caught begging in urban areas back to their birthplace. However, at the beginning of the twenty-first century, government policy softened, as citizens caught begging became eligible for social assistance rather than deportation.* © REUTERS/CORBIS

of accepted social organizations, the potential for improvement through adversity ensures them a place in society.

## CHARITIES AND BEGGARS' GUILDS

Government-sponsored charities for beggars were recorded as early as the fifth century, and periodic charities for vagrants provided by religious institutions and local communities were also common and customary. But general mismanagement of philanthropic institutions, along with inadequate budgets, made them ineffective in coping with the persistent and mounting problem of poverty. Impoverished vagrants receiving little or no assistance from the state improvised an extraordinary variety of begging techniques, thus making the whole of society accountable for their misfortune. With little social assistance, beggars organized themselves after a fashion to assure some degree of security and fairness within the group and to increase their chances of survival outside it.

Beggars' guilds—in Chinese often referred to as the derogatory *bang* (gangs)—arose spontaneously but at the same time were semi-officially acknowledged by local authorities. For instance, county governments or chambers of commerce tacitly allowed the head of a beggars' guild to levy a certain fee on local retail stores in exchange for immunity from the daily importuning of beggars. The guild contained the local beggars on its turf, constrained them to follow its rules and customs, and protected their interests with organized acts and collective undertakings to obtain the maximum from the community. Such beggars' guilds were widespread in China prior to the early 1950s and proved to be more successful than any government program in coping with the problem of street people.

## BEGGARS UNDER SOCIALISM

As a result of the sweeping changes brought by the Communist revolution and the reforms after the death of Mao, beggars came to differ in certain ways from their counterparts in old China. In general, the level of poverty in China in the late twentieth and early twenty-first centuries was much less alarming than that in the early twentieth century or in the time of the famine following the Great Leap Forward (1958–1960). Post-Mao reform created a vibrant yet indifferent social environment in which disadvantaged groups, chiefly peasants in less developed areas, were noticeably marginalized and neglected. Beginning in the mid-1980s the most recognizable side effect of reform was the reemergence of a large army of beggars in Chinese cities. No official statistics are available on the number of street beggars in China, but in the first decade of the twenty-first century each of China's major cities was thought to have more than 20,000.

The beggars' world in contemporary China bears some remarkable similarities to that of pre-1949 China. As in the prerevolutionary period, beggars are mostly former farmers, and beggars' social organization repeats old patterns. Virtually all begging methods that were practiced in Qing China and the Republican era (1912–1949) have been resurrected to a certain extent, as have the gangs and the beggar barons. Inside the beggars' world the hallmark of their organizations, often achieved through mafia-type negotiations, is a monopoly over begging turf.

Reforms initiated by Deng Xiaoping in the late 1970s through the late 1990s, along with the Communist Party's call in the 2000s for building a *hexie shehui* (harmonious society), resulted in more humane government policies on the treatment of street people. In June 2003 Premier Wen Jiabao signed into law a set of regulations aiming to transform government detention centers, where beggars were held for labor before being deported to their hometown, into relief centers, where they would be eligible to receive some aid. In other words, the centers would become charity homes of some sort rather than police substations. These policies took a positive step toward protecting basic human rights of street people; but implementation of the rules has varied significantly by locality, and the long-term effects of the policies on beggars remain to be seen.

**SEE ALSO** *Poverty; Social Classes before 1949; Social Classes since 1978; Social Policy Programs.*

**BIBLIOGRAPHY**

Fernandez-Stembridge, Leila, and Richard Madsen. Beggars in the Socialist Market Economy. In *Popular China: Unofficial Culture in a Globalizing Society*, ed. Perry Link, Richard P. Madsen, and Paul G. Pickowicz, 207–230. Lanham, MD: Rowman & Littlefield Publishers, 2002.

Lu, Hanchao. Becoming Urban: Mendicancy and Vagrants in Modern Shanghai. *Journal of Social History* 33, 1 (Autumn 1999): 7–36.

Lu, Hanchao. *Street Criers: A Cultural History of Chinese Beggars.* Stanford, CA: Stanford University Press, 2005.

Schak, David C. *A Chinese Beggars' Den: Poverty and Mobility in an Underclass Community.* Pittsburgh, PA: University of Pittsburgh Press, 1988.

***Hanchao Lu***

# BEIJING

Beijing has been, except for a few brief intervals, the capital city of China since the thirteenth century. It has been a provincial-level municipality administered directly by the central government since the founding of the People's Republic of China (PRC) in 1949. Beijing Municipality borders Hebei Province to the north, west, south, and for a small section to the east. The southeastern part of Beijing borders Tianjin Municipality. Beijing is recognized as the political, educational, and cultural center of the PRC. It is also an important economic center.

## THE CITY'S NAME

From the mid-seventeenth century to 1911, Beijing was the informal name of the capital city of the Qing empire, though it was officially called Jingshi (Our National Capital). After the 1911 revolution that overthrew the Qing, the city was named Beijing (Northern Capital) and served first as the capital city of the newly established Republic of China and later as the seat of an unstable, nominally national government from 1916 to 1928. The city was renamed Beiping (Northern Peace) in June 1928 after the Nationalist Party chose Nanjing (Southern Capital) to be the capital city, and it was marginalized during the Nationalist period (1928–1937). During World War II, the Japanese made it the seat of the puppet Provisional Government of the Republic of China and called it Beijing during their occupation of the city from July 1937. When Japan surrendered on August 15, 1945, the city's name was changed back to Beiping. The Chinese Communist forces negotiated successfully with the occupying Nationalist army and entered the city without a fight in January 1949. At the founding of the PRC on October 1, 1949, the city's name was changed back to Beijing, and it regained its status of the national capital (Naquin 2000).

## POPULATION AND AREA

In 1800 Beijing was the world's largest city, with a population of roughly 1.1 million people segregated by their ethnicities, with the Manchus living in the northern (or Inner) city and the Hans living in the southern (or Outer) city (Han Guanghui 1996). The segregation ended after the fall of the Qing dynasty in 1911. Wars and political changes were the most influential factors in the city's population fluctuation in the nineteenth and the early twentieth centuries. The battles between the Boxers and the Eight Allied Forces in 1900 and the moving of the capital to Nanjing in 1928 resulted in an exodus and decline in the city's population, as did the Japanese occupation from the late 1930s to the mid-1940s. The city's population has increased since 1949, particularly during two periods of high growth. The population of the

municipality grew from 2.03 million in 1949 to 7.92 million at the beginning of the 1970s. This growth included natural growth, in-migration, and increase from the expansion of the municipality. Beijing has seen a second period of major population growth since the 1980s. The city's population during this time has been characterized by a decrease in the natural growth rate but a large increase in in-migration that has led to a dramatic expansion in its total population (Guojia Tongji Ju Zonghe Si 1990). The population of Beijing, defined as the total number of people who reside in the municipality for six months or more per year, was about 15.81 million at the end of 2006. The city's birth rate has been significantly lower than the national average (Renkou Yanjiu Zhongxin 2007). In 2008, Beijing was China's second-largest city in terms of population, after Shanghai. All of China's fifty-six official ethnic groups are present among Beijing's population, but the overwhelming majority of the city's residents are Han.

Both Beijing Municipality as a whole and its urban area have grown significantly since 1949. At the time of the founding of the PRC, Beijing Municipality consisted of its urban area inside what remained of the city walls and gates (and what later became the Second Ring Road) and immediate suburbs. Since the 1950s, several surrounding counties have been incorporated into the municipality. By annexing farmland surrounding the city, Beijing has further expanded its urban area since the late 1980s. In 2009 Beijing Municipality covered an area of about 750 square kilometers and consisted of sixteen districts and two counties.

## URBAN PLANNING AND ARCHITECTURE

Processes of modernization have had a significant impact on Beijing's spatial layout and architectural styles, and the relationship between modernization and preservation has been much debated. Imperial Beijing embodied masterful urban planning, with the Forbidden City located in the center of the city and protected by rings of walls marked by grand gates and watchtowers. The city's most significant structures were arranged carefully along a north-south axis. These included, from north to south, the Bell and Drum Towers, the Scenic Hill, the Forbidden City, the Gate of Heavenly Peace (Tiananmen), the Zhengyang Gate, the Temple of Heaven, and the Temple of Earth.

The city has witnessed several fundamental transformations of its landscape since the late nineteenth century, starting with the burning down of the Yuanmingyuan by the allied forces of Great Britain and France in 1860 during the Second Opium War (1856–1860). The spatial integrity of the city itself was first broken when a section of the city walls was destroyed by the Eight Allied Forces during the suppression of the Boxer Uprising (1900). During the early Republican period, many imperial ceremonial spaces were transformed into museums and public parks. Tiananmen Square first emerged as a public space during this time, and it has witnessed three rebuilds and expansions since 1949 (Wu Hong 2005). New commercial areas that hosted modern-style stores, such as Wangfujing and Xidan, in addition to the old commercial center Qianmen, also developed during the Republican period. Among the most visible changes in the city's landscape was the disappearance of the city walls. Because they were barriers to transportation, especially in the east-west direction, they began to be torn down in the early twentieth century to make way for transportation needs, and had completely disappeared by the late 1960s (Dong 2003).

The first wave of large-scale construction in Beijing in the twentieth century was ten landmark buildings constructed in the late 1950s for the tenth anniversary of the founding of the PRC, including the Great People's Hall, several museums, and state hotels. The post-1978 period saw another wave of construction. This period witnessed the construction of new commercial centers, residential areas, and the ring roads that now define the city's geography, as well as the development of new districts, such as Zhongguancun in the northwestern part of the city, which has become a center of information technology in China.

***Forbidden City (center), Beijing, August 17, 2005.*** *The main capital of China since the thirteenth century and an important center of commerce into the twenty-first, Beijing contains both traditional forms of architecture and modern skyscrapers, as evidenced by the location of the emperor of China's fifteenth-century imperial palace amid a sea of modern structures.* © XIAOYANG LIU/CORBIS

As a result of its complex history, urban Beijing displays an array of architectural styles, blending the old and the new, among which three types predominate. The central part of the city still maintains some traditional architecture from imperial China. This part of the city was first established during the Mongol-led Yuan dynasty (1279–1368) but was primarily constructed during the Ming (1368–1644) and the Qing (1644–1912) dynasties. Many of the imperial structures reflect aesthetic elements of Ming architecture—for example, the Imperial Palace compound and the Temple of Heaven; others, such as the Tibetan Buddhist temple Yonghegong and the imperial resort Yiheyuan, were built during the Qing dynasty. Religious structures, such as the Daoist temple Baiyunguan, also exemplify such traditional architectural style. Some *siheyuan*, a traditional form of vernacular architecture with rooms on four sides making a square housing compound, have survived in central Beijing. Connecting the *siheyuan* are *hutong*, small alleyways that usually run east-west. Most *siheyuan* and *hutong* are now disappearing as they are being leveled to make space for high-rises, but some have been preserved and restored, for example in the Nanchizi area.

Some buildings constructed in the 1950s adopted traditional Chinese architectural elements in their ornamentation; others reflected a socialist cosmopolitanism by adopting Soviet designs—for example, the Soviet Exhibition Hall completed during the First Five-Year Plan (1953–1957) (Duanfang Lu 2007). The following thirty years marked a low tide for construction in Beijing and brought buildings that stressed frugality and were bland in style. Most of these buildings have been dismantled since the 1980s. From the last decade of the twentieth century on, international modern styles began to dominate, due in part to the entering of international architectural and investment firms into the Chinese real-estate market. In preparation for the 2008 Olympic Games (Li, Dray-Novey, and Kong Haili 2008), Beijing added to its landmarks an international airport, a national theater, and a headquarters for the television network CCTV. All three were designed by internationally eminent architects from

Europe and separate themselves from major symbolic structures from earlier periods.

## ECONOMY

Beijing's economy reflects general trends in the country, but as the national political and cultural center, Beijing has been relatively well developed economically throughout history. Beijing was an important center for trade with Mongolia until the end of the nineteenth century. Imperial Beijing's economy focused on supplying and servicing the court, officials, and candidates from the whole country who came to attend the civil service examinations (Belsky 2006). A large amount of grain was shipped from the south, via the Grand Canal from the Ming until the late Qing and then by sea, to satisfy the demands of the capital. Beijing's economy declined during the first half of the twentieth century due to political instability: warlord rule from 1915 to 1928; loss of its status as the capital city to Nanjing in 1928; Japanese occupation from 1937 to 1945; and three years of civil war from 1946 to 1949. Except for some very limited development in coal production, a power plant, some printing factories, and rail transportation, the modern economic sector was almost nonexistent during the Republican period (1912–1949).

After 1949, Beijing developed both light and heavy industries, including automobile and textile production, as well as the Capital Steel Company that was located on the western outskirts of the city in the major industrial area Shijingshan. Since the 1980s, the city has seen significant growth in the sectors of real estate, information technology, financial services, import and export businesses, and automobile production. Beijing is also a major transportation hub, with dozens of railways, roads, and highways connecting the city with the rest of the country. A new airport terminal completed in 2008 makes Beijing the focal point of many international flights to and from China. In order to improve Beijing's air quality, some of the city's industries began to be closed down in the 2000s. Agriculture is carried out outside of Beijing's urban area, primarily to supply the city's needs. Support for the central and municipal administrations, research and educational institutions, news media, and publishing houses continue to be key elements of the city's economy.

## MAJOR HISTORICAL EVENTS AND CULTURAL IDENTITY

Beijing has been the stage for many of the most important historical events in modern China (Strand 1989), including the Boxer Uprising and its suppression in 1900, which resulted in the establishment of the Legation Quarter in the southeast corner of the city, as well as the May Fourth movement in 1919. The Cultural Revolution started in Beijing in 1966, as did the 1989 student movement. Because of its special status as the nation's capital and its significance in the nation's history, Beijing became a focal point of national sentiment and identity during the twentieth century.

Beijing is home to a large number of China's leading universities and research institutes, including the Chinese Academy of Sciences, the Chinese Academy of Social Sciences, People's University of China, and Beijing Normal University. Beijing University (or Peking University, founded in 1898) and Qinghua University (or Tsinghua University, founded in 1911) have long been considered the country's two best universities.

Beijing is a major hub for the entertainment industry and hosts a large number of artists. It is also the center for state-owned mass media, as well as for China's avant-garde art. In the Republican era, Beijing and Shanghai were seen as rivals, especially with reference to literature and the visual arts. This comparison and contrast between the two cities has reemerged in the postsocialist period. Although in the early twenty-first century Beijing's preeminence in the world of arts is unquestioned, this dichotomy remains salient.

When Beijing lost its status as the capital city during the Nationalist period, its past became a central resource for creating the city's identity, and Old Beijing and its way of life were turned into emblems of Chinese tradition. For example, the Beijing Opera (or Peking Opera, *Jingju*), performed through a combination of song and spoken dialogue, was deemed a representative form of traditional Chinese culture, in spite of its relatively recent development in the late nineteenth century and its many modern transformations in the early twentieth century (Goldstein 2007). Since the 1990s, the city has seen a revival of interest in the culture of "Old Beijing," which is reflected in fine arts, films, television programs, design, fashion, food, the large number of books published on life in Old Beijing, and the development of tourist attractions (Dong 2003).

**SEE ALSO** *Gardens and Parks; Hutong; Imperial Palaces; Urban China: Cities and Urbanization, 1800–1949; Urban China: Urbanization since 1949; Urban China: Organizing Principles of Cities.*

### BIBLIOGRAPHY

Belsky, Richard. *Localities at the Center: Native Place, Space, and Power in Late Imperial Beijing.* Cambridge, MA: Harvard University East Asia Center, 2006.

Dong, Madeleine Yue. *Republican Beijing: The City and Its Histories, 1911–1937.* Berkeley: University of California Press, 2003.

Goldstein, Joshua. *Drama Kings: Players and Publics in the Re-creation of Peking Opera, 1870–1937.* Berkeley: University of California Press, 2007.

Guojia Tongji Ju Zonghe Si, ed. *Quanguo ge sheng, zizhiqu, zhixiashi lishi tongji ziliao huibian* (1949–1989) [A collection of historical statistics of the provinces, autonomous regions, and special municipalities]. Beijing: Zhongguo Tongji Chubanshe, 1990.

Han Guanghui. *Beijing lishi renkou dili* [Beijing historical demographic geography]. Beijing: Beijing University Press, 1996.

Li, Lillian M., Alison Dray-Novey, and Kong Haili. *Beijing: From Imperial Capital to Olympic City*. New York: Palgrave Macmillan, 2008.

Lu Duanfang. Architecture and Global Imaginations in China. *Journal of Architecture* 12, 2 (2007): 123–145.

Naquin, Susan. *Peking: Temples and City Life, 1400–1900*. Berkeley: University of California Press, 2000.

Renkou Yanjiu Zhongxin, Zhongguo Shehui Kexue Yuan, ed. *Zhongguo renkou nianjian* [China population yearbook]. Beijing: Zhongguo Shehui Kexue Chubanshe, 2007.

Strand, David. *Rickshaw Beijing: City People and Politics in the 1920s*. Berkeley: University of California Press, 1989.

Wu Hong. *Remaking Beijing: Tiananmen Square and the Creation of a Political Space*. Chicago: University of Chicago Press, 2005.

***Madeleine Yue Dong***

## BEIJING OPERA

**SEE** *Peking Opera and Regional Operas.*

## BEIYANG CLIQUE

The term *Beiyang clique* refers originally to a group of militarists associated with the Beiyang Army created by Li Hongzhang in the 1870s. The Beiyang Army evolved into the modern New Army after Li's death in 1901, when Yuan Shikai succeeded him as viceroy of Zhili, charged with military training at Xiaozhan, near Tianjin. By 1905 six Beiyang divisions of the New Army had been formed. Yuan established the Baoding Military School in 1903, which along with the Tianjin Military Preparatory School, founded in 1885, graduated a generation of officers for the Beiyang divisions. They were the best trained and best equipped of all the New Army units. Many would become leading political figures in the early Republic, most prominently Xu Shichang (1855–1939), Cao Kun (1862–1938), Duan Qirui (1865–1936), Feng Guozhang (1859–1919), and Wu Peifu (1874–1939).

Early in 1909, shortly after the death of the empress dowager Cixi the previous November, Yuan was dismissed by the new regent, Prince Chun (1883–1951), and forced into "retirement" until the outbreak of the 1911 Revolution, when he was recalled. Coming to the dynasty's aid, Yuan was particularly well served by Duan Qirui, who commanded the Second Army Corps in Hubei. As a reward for his loyalty, Duan was named military governor of Hunan and Hubei. Subsequently, Yuan reached a negotiated settlement with the revolutionary army over the abdication of the Manchu emperor and managed to make himself president of the new Republic.

The new Republic was often referred to as the Beiyang government because of the domination of the Beiyang Army. Yuan fought off the revolutionary forces in the so-called Second Revolution of 1913 following the assassination of the Nationalist Party luminary Song Jiaoren (1882–1913). Afterward, he placed four of his loyal lieutenants as military governors in the south: Duan Qirui in Anhui, Feng Guozhang in Jiangsu, Li Chun in Jiangxi, and Tang Xiangming (1885–1975) in Hunan. The Beiyang Army now extended its reach to the Yangzi (Chang) River region, while Yuan consolidated his position in the capital. But Yuan's control of the Beiyang Army was incomplete. When he declared himself emperor in December 1915, he met strong opposition from many of his lieutenants, including Duan and Feng, as well as from the outlying provinces, forcing him to back down a few months later.

Following Yuan's death in June 1916, the Beiyang Army split into cliques: Duan's Anhui clique, Feng's Zhili clique (led by Cao Kun after Feng's death and later taken over by Wu Peifu), and Zhang Zuolin's (1873–1928) Fengtian clique. Interclique hostilities broke out between 1922 and 1924. In Beijing, the domination of the military was unmistakable: Duan served as premier during much of 1916 to 1920, and Feng assumed the presidency of the Republic from 1917 to 1918, followed by Xu Shichang until 1922 and by Cao Kun from 1922 to 1924. The Beiyang clique was factionalized, while other militarists held sway in different parts of the country: Yan Xishan (1883–1960) in Shanxi, Feng Yuxiang (1882–1948) in Shaanxi, Tang Jiyao (1883–1927) in Yunnan, and Lu Rongting (1858–1928) in Guangxi, to mention just a few. Meanwhile, the revolutionary movement led by the Nationalists in the south was gathering momentum. All of this helped to plunge China into political and military fragmentation. The country was not reunified, if nominally, until the rise to power of the Nationalists in 1928. The domination of the Beiyang clique in Chinese politics then came to end, with some of its troops absorbed into the armies of the new government.

The history of the Beiyang clique illustrates the domination of the military in the early Republic and the internecine wars that undermined the principle of civil supremacy, which for centuries had been a feature of Chinese governance. Civil-military relations were never the same again in modern China.

**SEE ALSO** *Army and Politics; Military, 1912-1949; Warlord Era (1916-1928); Yuan Shikai.*

### BIBLIOGRAPHY

Ch'i Hsi-sheng. *Warlord Politics in China, 1916–1928*. Stanford, CA: Stanford University Press, 1976.

Fung, Edmund S. K. (Feng Zhaoji). *The Military Dimension of the Chinese Revolution: The Role of the New Army in the Revolution of 1911*. Vancouver: University of British Columbia Press, 1980.

Gillin, Donald. *Warlord: Yan Hsi-shan in Shansi Province, 1911–1949*. Princeton, NJ: Princeton University Press, 1967.

MacKinnon, Stephen. *Power and Politics in Late Imperial China: Yuan Shi-kai in Beijing and Tianjin, 1901–1908*. Berkeley: University of California Press, 1980.

McCord, Edward A. *The Power of the Gun: The Emergence of Modern Chinese Warlordism*. Berkeley: University of California Press, 1993.

McCormack, Gaven. *Chang Tso-lin in Northeast China, 1911–1928: China, Japan, and the Manchurian Idea*. Stanford, CA: Stanford University Press, 1977.

Sheridan, James. *Chinese Warlord: The Career of Feng Yü-hsiang*. Stanford, CA: Stanford University Press, 1966.

Wou, Odoric. *Militarism in Modern China: The Career of Wu Pei-fu, 1916–1939*. Folkstone, U.K.: Dawson, 1978.

***Edmund S.K. Fung (Feng Zhaoji)***

# BINGXIN

***1900–1999***

An important modern Chinese writer, Bingxin was known for her poetry, short stories, and essays. Her distinctive style made a major contribution to the burgeoning new literature of the early twentieth century.

## LIFE

Bingxin was born as Xie Wanying into an enlightened literary family in Fujian. Her father served as a Qing Imperial Navy officer and later as an officer in the Republican Navy. The ocean, by which she spent much of her childhood, would become a dominant image in her works. She was first taught by her mother and then privately tutored in traditional Chinese literature. When the family moved to Beijing in 1914, Bingxin enrolled in Bridgman Academy for Girls, an American missionary school. Upon graduation, she entered Beijing Union College for Women, also run by American missionary educators and a year later part of Yanjing University.

As a college student, Bingxin participated in the New Culture movement as she worked for the Beijing Nüxuejie Lianhehui (Beijing Federation of Women Students). In August 1919, three months after the May Fourth movement, she sent an essay to the popular *Beijing Chenbao* (Beijing Morning Post), where a cousin of hers worked as an editor. This essay, written in the vernacular, was an eyewitness account of the courtroom proceedings concerning students involved in the aftermath of the movement. After a few more successful essays, she published her first short story, "Liangge jiating" (Two Families), a study in contrast between a chaotic family and an idealized modern family. The story came out under her new pen name Bingxin (Pure in Heart), which the publishers modified to "Ms. Bing Xin," and this is the name under which she would become widely known.

She quickly found herself drawn into the literary world, her essays, fiction, and poetry appearing in print nearly every week over the next few years. Initially majoring in medicine, by her sophomore year she had switched to literature. She became an early member of the literary association founded by Zheng Zhenduo, Shen Yanbin (Mao Dun), Xu Dishan, and others, a major literary society of early-twentieth-century China that favored realistic literature and championed writers' responsibility to society. Although Bingxin's own literary path did not completely coincide with the association's stated goals, she contributed steadily to its chief journal *Xiaoshuo Yuebao* (Fiction Monthly).

After graduating from college, Bingxin received a scholarship to study in the United States. She spent the next three years at Wellesley College and in 1926 obtained her master's degree in English literature, her thesis being "An English Translation and Edition of the Poems of Lady Li I-an (1926)," a distinguished woman poet of the Song dynasty (960–1279).

After returning to China, Bingxin taught at Yanjing University, a position she held until 1936. In 1929 she married the American-trained sociologist Wu Wenzao. While teaching and raising three children, Bingxin continued her literary production, including a translation of *The Prophet* by the Lebanese poet Kahlil Gibran (1883–1931), which came out in 1931. During the Sino-Japanese War of 1937–1945, she and her family moved to Chongqing, where she wrote a series of fourteen short stories about women from the perspective of a male persona simply named "a gentleman."

In Japan during the last years of the civil war of 1946–1949, Bingxin and her family elected to return to China in 1951. She served in prominent cultural committees in the newly founded People's Republic and traveled to many countries in Europe, Asia, and Africa on official delegations. During the decade of the Cultural Revolution (1966–1976) and its aftermath, like most writers of her generation, Bingxin was denounced and stopped writing for more than ten years. In the 1970s she resumed writing and published many memoirs. She died in Beijing in 1999.

## ESSAYS

Bingxin began and ended her long writing career with essays. "Xiao" (Smiles, 1921), one of her earliest and shortest, is representative of her lyrical style and is often anthologized. The essay is about three smiling faces: one a painting of an angel, the other two belonging to a child and an old woman, meeting in the past and now called to mind by the angel. Together the portraits form a succession of snapshots, their clarity and intensity of emotion akin to an Imagist poem.

Her most famous essay series, "Ji xiao duzhe" (Letters to Young Readers), began just before she left for America. During a protracted period of illness, which she spent at the Sharon Sanatorium near Boston, the epistolary essays accumulated and were serialized in *Beijing Chenbao* from 1923 to 1926. Twenty-nine essays were collectively published in 1926 and subsequently were frequently reprinted in textbooks—a fact that established Bingxin's reputation as China's earliest and much beloved children's writer. Neither fairy tale-like nor overtly instructive, her letters were written in an intimate and unreserved style, as if they were conversations between an older sister and her younger siblings. They tell of fond memories of her family and describe her travels around the world. Throughout her career she continued to write such letters and published them as "Zai ji xiao duzhe" (More Letters to Young Readers, 1950s) and "San ji xiao duzhe" (Still More Letters to Young Readers, 1970s).

## POETRY

Bingxin stumbled into modern poetry when in 1921 an editor of *Beijing Chenbao* decided to publish one of her prose submissions in verse format. Her poetry thus at one stroke broke down the barrier between prose and poetry, as well as between departments in the periodical. Over the next few months, more than three hundred of her short poems were serialized in *Beijing Chenbao* and gained her an immediate following among young readers. They were soon republished in two collections: *Fanxing* (Myriad Stars, 1921) and *Chunshui* (Spring Water, 1923). Strongly influenced by the Bengali poet Rabindranath Tagore (1861–1941), her lyrical poems sing of love and nature. Here is one poem in its entirety:

> Creator,
> If in eternal life
> Only one wish is granted,
> I will plead in all sincerity:
> "Let me be in my mother's arms,
> Let Mother be in a small boat,
> Let the small boat be on a moonlit sea."
> (Yeh, p. 22)

Some of her poems appeared in *Xinyue* (Crescent Moon), a periodical founded by the poets Xu Zhimo, Wen Yiduo, and others who were influenced by Tagore and the British Romantic poets. These poets, like Bingxin, sought to create a new type of Chinese poetry that was formally regular and concise. Bingxin later translated Tagore's collected poems *Gitanjali* (Song Offerings) and *The Gardener*, both translations published in 1951.

## SHORT STORIES

Many of Bingxin's short stories dwell on the barriers between human beings. "Chaoren" (Superman), written in 1921, is the most frequently anthologized. It is about a young man influenced by Friedrich Nietzsche and determined to become a superman, in Nietzsche's sense, independent of human emotions and relationships. One day he gave money to a sick boy downstairs so that he would stop his loud groans. The gratitude of the child and his mother broke down the young man's barriers. Remembering his own mother, he accepts the boy's gift of a basket of golden flowers and writes him a letter: "I want to take a silk string, and string the pearls of tears and tie the two ends onto a crescent moon. I want to pick all the stars in the sky and fill the crescent basket. Doesn't it also make a basket of golden flowers? . . . All the sons of the world are good friends, for we are forever connected."

## STYLE

Early in her writing career Bingxin established her style, combining her distinct writer's persona, her pervasive philosophy of love, and her unique lyrical language.

Resonant of her pen name Bingxin (Pure in Heart), which she used consistently throughout her long career, much of her literary output consists of eulogies to unblemished love. When there is pathos in her work, it is caused by the loss of such love. Such love is often evoked in conjunction with the boundless ocean and is ideally realized in motherly love. Bingxin often presented such love in very specific forms, as in memoirs of her own mother; yet she also treated it philosophically as the only true meaning of life, and as such made it mystical and universal, as most prominently seen in her own poetry and her translations of Tagore and Gibran.

Bingxin's focus on love and nature partook of the May Fourth zeitgeist of humanism and romantic pantheism, but also departs significantly from the mainstream. Unique among her generation of writers, Bingxin avoided the young rebel bristling against parental oppression in her works. Also absent is the theme of heterosexual love, a topic that dominated early-twentieth-century Chinese literature. From the 1930s on, despite her continued popularity, Bingxin was often criticized for being narrow in her focus and overly feminine in style.

Yet to describe her style as conventionally feminine is to miss its considerable strength. In contrast to the heavily Europeanized Chinese passing as vernacular at the early stage of the New Culture movement (1915–1925), her language seamlessly absorbs elements of the classical literary language. While her syntax is mostly vernacular, her expression is more concise, her diction more evocative. Because one of her major sources is classical poetry, especially the more descriptive and forthright poetry of the Yuan dynasty (1279–1368), her prose is characterized as much by a gentle flow as by a staccato rhythm, which gives her style its unique supple energy. The effectiveness of this style lies in its successful blend of the vernacular and literary, and constitutes a significant contribution to modern Chinese literature.

**SEE ALSO** *Literary Societies; Women in the Visual Arts; Xu Zhimo.*

**BIBLIOGRAPHY**

WORKS BY BINGXIN

Bing Xin. *Bing Xin quanji* [Collected works of Bing Xin]. Fuzhou: Haixia Wenyi Chubanshe, 1995.

Bing Xin. *The Photograph*. Trans. Jeff Book. Beijing: Chinese Literature Press, 1992. A collection of fourteen essays and short stories.

SECONDARY STUDIES AND ANTHOLOGIES

Bouskova, Marcela. On the Origin of Modern Chinese Prosody: An Analysis of the Prosodic Components in the Works of Ping Hsin. *Archiv Orientalni* 32, 5 (1949): 619–643.

Dooling, Amy D., and Kristina M. Torgeson, eds. *Writing Women in Modern China: An Anthology of Women's Literature from the Early Twentieth Century*. New York: Columbia University Press, 1998.

Meng Yue and Dai Jinhua. *Fuchu lishi dibiao: Xiandai funü wenxue yanjiu* [Emerging from the horizon of history: Studies in modern Chinese women's literature]. Zhengzhou: Henan Renmin Chubanshe, 1989.

Larson, Wendy. Female Subjectivity and Gender Relations: The Early Stories of Lu Yin and Bing Xin. In *Politics, Ideology, and Literary Discourse in Modern China: Theoretical Interventions and Cultural Critique*, ed. Tang Xiaobing and Liu Kang, 278–299. Durham, NC: Duke University Press, 1993.

Yeh, Michelle, ed. and trans. *Anthology of Modern Chinese Poetry*. New Haven, CT: Yale University Press, 1992.

***Hu Ying***

## BOXER UPRISING

The Boxer Uprising of 1900, a violent anti-Christian and antiforeign eruption, constituted an important turning point in the history of the late Qing dynasty (1644–1912). The movement that gave rise to it—its proper name was Yihequan or "Boxers United in Righteousness"—had its inception in northwestern Shandong Province in the last years of the nineteenth century. *Yihe boxing* referred to a particular method (or style or school) of Chinese boxing (a form of martial arts practice, generally very different from what westerners think of as boxing).

The Boxers United in Righteousness (henceforth "Boxers") consisted mostly of poor farmers, seasonal agricultural workers, and unemployed drifters. Their organization was nonhierarchical, centering on boxing grounds in rural areas and altars in cities (often, in both cases, attached to temples). The Boxers represented a composite of two major streams of influence: the notion of invulnerability, derived mainly from the Big Sword Society (Dadaohui), which became active in southwestern Shandong from the mid-1890s, and the mass spirit-possession rituals practiced by groups calling themselves Spirit Boxers (Shenquan), which emerged around the same time in the northwestern part of the province. The Boxers became energized in the winter of 1898 to 1899, mainly as a result of the flooding of the Yellow River, which broke through its dikes in August 1898 and turned much of Shandong's northwest into a disaster zone. Shortly after this, for reasons still not fully understood, the Boxers began to engage in anti-Christian activities and to brandish antiforeign slogans.

### EXPANSION OF THE MOVEMENT

From Shandong, in the winter of 1899 to 1900, the Boxers streamed northward across the Shandong-Zhili border and in the following months spread through much of the North China plain. Several factors fueled this expansion. One was the possession ritual, which was easily mastered and, by putting people at the bottom of the social scale in direct touch with the gods, was enormously empowering. Another was the serious drought that settled over North China after the winter of 1898 to 1899. This created a sizable pool of young males who, idled by the lack of farm work, were bored and had free time on their hands. Also, the longer the drought lasted, the more the population was afflicted by hunger, which made joining the Boxers, who often had ample supplies of grain and food, a way to fill one's belly.

Just as important as actual hunger was hunger anxiety, which became increasingly intense as the drought endured. Widespread anxiety made people more willing to risk their lives in desperate actions. It also made them more susceptible to religious constructions of reality linking the absence of rain to the anger of the gods over the growing inroads of Christianity and other forms of foreign influence. Such constructions were widely disseminated in Boxer notices beginning in the winter of 1899 to 1900, precisely the moment the Boxer movement exploded beyond the confines of its original Shandong home.

In Zhili, in particular, another factor favoring the movement's spread was the weakness of authority in the province, coupled with (and partly resulting from) deep divisions at the Qing court over how to respond to the Boxers. The province was a logical site for an anti-Christian and antiforeign explosion. Its two largest cities, Tianjin and Beijing, both had sizable foreign populations; the recent advent of the railway and telegraph had created visible symbols of foreign penetration, as well as causing job losses in the transport and other sectors; and, not least, Zhili was one of the most heavily missionized provinces in China, with a Christian population of well over 100,000. Not surprisingly, the Boxer War of 1900, which pitted the Chinese

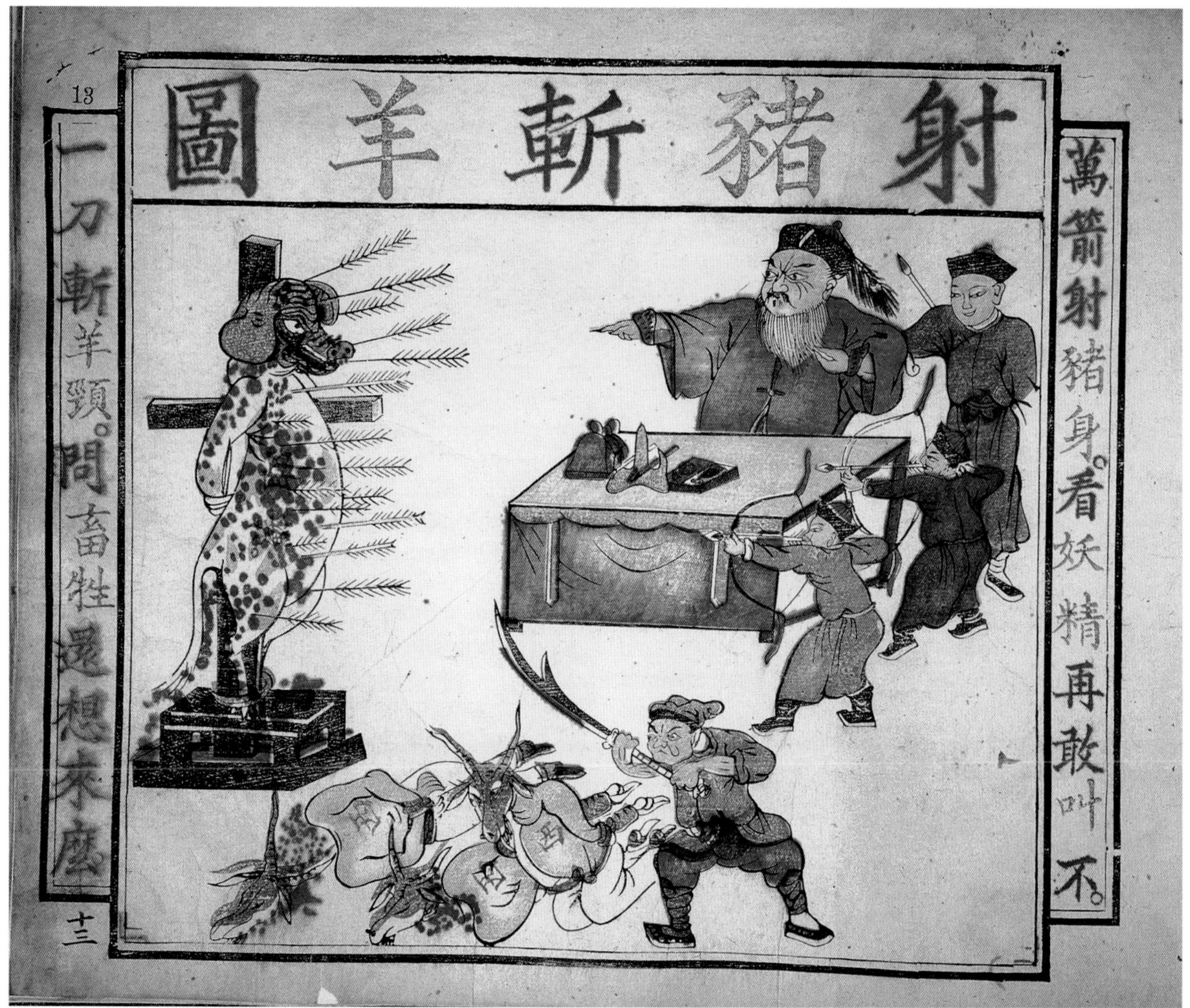


***Chinese woodcut depicting anti-Christian sentiment, c. 1890.*** *In 1900, anti-Western sentiment among the Chinese turned into full-scale hostility against foreigners. Initiated by impoverished citizens from Shandong, the resulting Boxer Uprising looked to purge China of outside influences, particularly those Christian in nature.* THE ART ARCHIVE/CHURCH SOCIETY/THE PICTURE DESK, INC.

army and Boxers (now renamed *yimin* or "righteous people") against the foreign powers, was mainly centered in Zhili.

## WAR AND AFTERMATH

The Boxers' geographical reach widened dramatically after the throne's declaration of war against the powers on June 21, 1900, extending into Shanxi and Henan, and beyond North China into Inner Mongolia and Manchuria. The uprising's character also changed after this date. Prior to the end of May, it had been largely an intramural Chinese affair, only one foreign missionary having been killed (on December 31, 1899). It was not until the summer of 1900, when full-scale warfare broke out and Boxer violence was often abetted by the antiforeign and anti-Christian actions of local officials, that the real bloodbath began, with well over two hundred foreigners (primarily missionaries) being felled, along with untold thousands of Chinese (most of them Christians). The uprising's end came with the arrival in the capital of a joint international force on August 14. The sieges of the legations and Northern Cathedral that had been under way since June were now lifted, the court fled to Xi'an, Beijing was placed under foreign occupation, brutal reprisal raids were carried out against the Chinese population mainly in Zhili, and foreign looting of Chinese national treasures in the capital was rampant.

The signing of the Boxer Protocol on September 7, 1901, imposed on China a stiff diplomatic settlement, the detailed provisions of which were less important than the impact it had on the Chinese government and population.

The huge indemnity (450 million taels or $333 million) intensified the already considerable grip of the powers over China's finances and forced the Qing, in a desperate effort to generate new revenues, to begin laying the foundations for a modern state. The draconian character of the settlement, together with the generally poor showing of the Chinese military in the summer of 1900 and the court's humiliating flight, placed the weakness of the Qing on full view and energized the forces of reform and revolution in Chinese society. The court also, however charily, embarked after 1900 on a program of reform that went far beyond anything previously tried and completely reshaped the environment in which Chinese politics were carried on. This environment proved to be one in which the dynasty itself was unable to survive.

### SYMBOLIC AFTERLIFE

Ever since the Boxer Uprising took place, there has been a powerful tendency in China (not to mention the West) to caricature its participants. The caricaturing has varied among different groups, reflecting different political and intellectual commitments. Thus, Chinese intellectuals, at the time of the New Culture movement in the second decade of the twentieth century, saw the Boxers as symbolizing everything about the old China that they wanted to replace: the xenophobia, the irrationality, the barbarism, the superstition, the backwardness. But Chinese revolutionaries, as a reflection of the growing political radicalism of the 1920s, reworked the Boxers into a more positive set of myths, centering on the qualities of patriotism and anti-imperialism—an affirmative vision that reached a high-water mark during the Cultural Revolution of the 1960s and 1970s. Chinese historians have often found it difficult to move beyond such oversimplified constructions of the Boxer experience, a major reason being that the Boxers (who were at once antiforeign and antimodern) raised, in the most striking way, what has perhaps been the central issue of cultural identity in the last century or so of Chinese history: ambivalence with respect to the West.

**SEE ALSO** *Anti-Christian/Antimissionary Movements; Cixi, Empress Dowager; Imperialism.*

### BIBLIOGRAPHY

Bickers, Robert, and R. G. Tiedemann, eds. *The Boxers, China, and the World.* Lanham: Rowman & Littlefield, 2007.

Buck, David D. *Recent Chinese Studies of the Boxer Movement.* Armonk, NY: Sharpe, 1987.

Cohen, Paul A. *History in Three Keys: The Boxers as Event, Experience, and Myth.* New York: Columbia University Press, 1997.

Esherick, Joseph W. *The Origins of the Boxer Uprising.* Berkeley: University of California Press, 1987.

***Paul A. Cohen***

## BRANDS

With the maturation of the Chinese corporate sector and the increasing globalization of Chinese companies, branding has emerged as a crucial strategic issue. This has been accompanied by the gradual displacement of the Chinese *paizi* (a state-registered trademark) by the more general *pinpai*, which is related to the term *ming pai* (name brand, famous brand) used by official brand recognition agencies. The need to develop genuinely Chinese brands became especially urgent after China's entry into the World Trade Organization, which further opened up the Chinese market for foreign companies, including sectors (especially services) that were previously sheltered. Chinese companies' weakness in branding turned out to be a major competitive disadvantage. Thus brand development and brand promotion have been defined as a task of government, with supervision assigned to the State Administration of Quality Supervision, Inspection, and Quarantine, which set up the National Commission for Brand Promotion in 2002. Building global Chinese brands is a new long march supported by the highest levels of government. The central government and the provincial governments bestow brand awards and prizes, such as the label "Chinese famous brand," (Zhongguo mingpai) on successful companies. These efforts aim at boosting customer confidence at home and abroad by means of piggybacking on the reputation of official bodies.

### HISTORICAL BACKGROUND: BRANDING AND CONSUMERISM BEFORE THE 1950s

In imperial China famous local businesses, such as handicraft shops and restaurants, began to make use of advertising and brands. One of the oldest (and still viable) brands in China is Tongrentang, which was founded in 1669 and received imperial recognition as a purveyor of Chinese medicine to the imperial court in 1723. One of the few traditional brands to survive the anticapitalist policies of the 1950s and 1960s, the Tongrentang family enterprise was transformed into a state-owned company; in the 2000s it was owned by the Beijing city government, with members of the founding Yue family still serving as advisors. Most traditional brands, particularly those for certain foods and drinks, were closely associated with their regions of origin. For example, the famous Maotai, a distilled liquor produced in the town of Maotai and internationally traded under the name Moutai, remains on the list of the twenty strongest Chinese brands. Regions of origin traditionally were important in the tea business, as with the Longjing denomination for green tea grown in an area in Zhejiang province, but were not directly linked with particular companies. Strong traditional brands include local services, such as Quanjude Peking duck restaurant, which was founded in 1864 and received state recognition as a registered trademark in 1999, growing into a national chain of restaurants.

As a result of China's slow emergence as an industrialized country, traditional brands did not feature products of modern industry. The developmental gap between China and the Western industrialized countries, but also Japan, became an issue of national concern in the 1920s, when a movement sought to foster "China-made" products. After the breakdown of the traditional order, Western-style consumption patterns became part and parcel of the attempt to modernize Chinese society. The entire lifestyle of the urban Chinese became a target of nationalist reformers, with efforts at changing the dress code or standards of personal hygiene. As a consequence, foreign products beat out Chinese products even in areas where the latter could have been competitive, as in soap production. Especially in Shanghai, foreign products were present in every sphere of urban life, even the most intimate.

In the early twentieth century, Western and Japanese economic domination in everyday life became the target of national boycott movements, with anti-American boycotts in 1905, anti-Japanese boycotts in 1915, and antiforeign boycotts in the wake of the humiliating events of the 1919 Treaty of Versailles, when the victorious nations (of which China was a member) ceded the rights to Shandong Peninsula to Japan. It became a question of national honor to buy *guo huo* (national products), with national campaigns especially targeting female consumers. After the October 1911 Wuchang Uprising, which led to the collapse of the Qing dynasty, the National Products Preservation Association was established to develop standards to identify genuinely Chinese products, depending on the degree of involvement of foreign capital, technology, and input. Companies that established independent Chinese brands received much public attention and government support, emerging as the group of "national capitalists" that was later identified by the Chinese Communist Party, first as an integral part of the renewed Chinese modernization effort, and later as an object of class suppression. Out of this short period of industrial development, only a few brands, such as Warrior shoes, established in 1935, have survived.

The post-1949 period of radical collectivization and anticapitalist movements failed to suppress the emergence of new brands under Communism. One notable example is the Flying Pigeon bicycle, production of which started in 1950. The company received a state quality award in 1954, after which the brand emerged as one of the most sought-after items for the average Chinese consumer, even during the decade of the Cultural Revolution (1966–1976). With ISO 9001 certification from the International Organization for Standardization, which assures the attainment of international benchmarks of management practices and quality control systems to customers; the brand is present in more than fifty countries today.

In summary, the history of brands in China in the first half of the twentieth century reflects the emergence of consumerism as a part of the national modernization effort in connection with the state-led industrialization drive. Thus brands emerged as a critical element in the interaction between societal change and government economic policies. The anticapitalist movements of the 1950s and 1960s suppressed this interaction, but after the launch of economic reforms in 1978 the conjoined forces of societal change and government policy reemerged with a vengeance. The relationship between the economic policies of the state and consumerism marks a crucial difference between Western and Chinese brand awareness.

## GROWTH AND DIVERSIFICATION OF CHINESE BRANDS AFTER 1978

With the wave of consumerism sweeping across China after 1978, brands once again turned into a central feature of everyday life. At the same time, branding was increasingly seen as a core concern in industrial development strategy. From 1978 to the late 1990s, this concern was seen mainly in the renewed strength of international brands yet again permeating the Chinese market. At the beginning of the new millennium, Chinese companies' drive to "go global" posed a critical challenge, given their almost complete lack of internationally competitive brands. The issue of branding defined a central weakness of the Chinese modernization effort between 1978 and 2008: China had positioned itself as the manufacturer of the world while relying mainly on foreign brands as suppliers and partners for outsourcing. Whereas foreign brands with the "made in China" label hidden inside face no substantial difficulties in penetrating global markets, "made in China" without foreign branding remains a symbol for low-quality, cheap goods. This apparent contradiction has intensified the search for genuinely Chinese brands.

Thus brands returned as a concern for national policy. In particular, many of the newly emerging entrepreneurs in the state and private sectors explicitly pursue corporate branding as a national task to increase China's reputation in the world and to contribute to national competitiveness. For example, the computer manufacturer Lenovo claims to be the vanguard of Chinese goods in global markets, and the tech products company Aigo, a sponsor of Formula 1 car racing that was omnipresent at the 2008 Beijing Olympics, derives its international name from its Chinese name, *aiguozhe*, which means "patriot." For many entrepreneurs, brand nationalism provides additional impetus for success beyond the opportunity to receive government support, still a crucial ingredient of business success in China.

In the twenty-first century, aside from the basic need for branding in corporate competitive strategies there are two main motivations for developing genuinely Chinese brands. The first is to establish brands with roots in Chinese traditional culture, however that may be perceived, thus creating a Chinese-style consumerism. The other is to display Chinese manufacturing prowess and technological expertise, reflecting the success of the state-led modernization program.

The first motivation shows a continuity with views on gender and consumerism from the 1920s. Educated consumers show a very strong awareness of international luxury brands, with Shanghai women viewed as the national avant-garde. Brand consumption is part and parcel of *mianzi xiaofei* (face consumption), that is, a traditional concern for proper outward appearance and status, as well as the culture of gift giving. Thus in the past two decades many brands have emerged that explicitly claim to present a Chinese alternative to Western luxury brands and their implied lifestyles. A foremost example is Yue-Sai cosmetics, a company established by the Chinese-American celebrity Kan Yue-Sai in 1990 and bought by L'Oréal in 2004. Kan Yue-Sai, challenging what she saw as the mismatch between Western aesthetic principles and Chinese ethnic norms of beauty, created cosmetics in a Chinese palette. A similar motivation underlies the creation of Chinese brands in lingerie, such as the Ordifen label, which in 2007 announced the revival of Tang dynasty styles, and in fashion, such as the popular Fish label, which represents a design philosophy rooted in traditional Chinese patterns of colors and shapes, and building on metaphors enshrined in Chinese characters. These movements fit into a general revival of traditional Chinese dress; a particularly salient example is the *qipao*, a dress that after 1949 survived in Hong Kong and Taiwan with a limited group of female users, but that has been revived as a national emblem of feminine beauty. Traditional culture is evoked in many other areas, even by companies with foreign roots, such as the Tsingtao brewery.

Beyond consumerism, Chinese culture plays an important role in branding strategies that emphasize corporate culture, for example, in the context of corporate social responsibility. A notable example is Broad Corporation, which represents an increasing number of companies that adopt an explicitly Chinese corporate culture. Broad, a leading producer of air-conditioning technologies, not only emphasizes the ethical foundations of business, but even built a "Broad Town," which includes a corporate university and recreation facilities for employees. This emphasis on traditional values is merged with a strong branding of innovative capacities. Even globalized companies seek roots in traditional culture. The corporate culture motto of Haier, a major manufacturer of white goods, or home appliances, is *you sheng yu wu*, which is borrowed from the Daodejing and can be rendered only very approximately in English (the official company translation is "being itself is a product of not-being").

Regarding the second motivation to display Chinese prowess and expertise, Chinese companies increasingly strive to switch from being original equipment manufacturer (OEM) suppliers (selling their products for use as components in other companies' branded products) to branded manufacturers. Most companies, however, operate very carefully in these endeavors. One strategy is to buy-in foreign brands and reputation, as in the Lianxiang company's high-profile acquisition of IBM's personal computer branch; in its strategic drive for globalization, the company rebranded itself as Lenovo after discovering that the previous Legend label was already a trademark in many other countries. The IBM brand was to be maintained for five years of transition, while Lenovo took over highly successful brands as the ThinkPad. There are also many examples of failed buy-ins of foreign brands, as in the case of TCL, a global producer of television sets.

Such mergers of Western and Chinese brands often symbolize the transfer of the newest Western technological standards to the Chinese public. The newly created Roewe brand resulted from the buy-in of Rover automotive technology (though not the Rover brand itself, which belongs to Ford Motor Company) by Shanghai Automotive Industry Corporation. At the same time, OEM suppliers have begun to move into independent branding strategies, mostly in the area of telecommunications. The major examples are Huawei and ZTE, which, though still far from being renowned to the global public, are among the technological leaders in their business, using Vodafone mobile phones with ZTE technology inside.

Such cautious strategies are often related to Mao Zedong's strategy to "encircle the cities from the villages." By contrast, other Chinese companies, such as Haier, have pursued an aggressive strategy of independent global branding. The Haier name itself signals a merger of Western and Chinese business, derived from Libuhaier, the Chinese name of the German company Liebherr, from which the first refrigerator technology was transferred. In Haier's corporate cartoon series, *Haier Brothers*, this merger is symbolized by the two heroes, a black-haired, Chinese-looking brother and a fair-haired, German-looking brother. Yet Haier pursues an aggressive strategy to establish itself as a truly global brand, with original design and strong emphasis on research and development. Such independent branding strategies are also pursued by some of the most dynamic upstarts in Chinese industry, such as Chery automobiles, which moved within a decade from alleged copying of Western designs (the notorious QQ3) to original design. The Chinese public admires companies such as Chery as symbols of the Chinese ascendance to a global economic power.

***Television celebrity and cosmetics manufacturer Yue-Sai Kan at home in Shanghai, September 24, 2005.*** *Originally the host of several television programs in China, Yue-Sai Kan used her public image to become a highly successful entrepreneur, developing luxury-style goods with an Asian perspective.* AP/VII/LAUREN GREENFIELD

## THE FUTURE OF BRANDING IN CHINA

A conspicuous feature of branding in China is the fusion of product brands and corporate brands, which is different from the benchmark conceptions of branding, which concentrates on product identities, hence the product brand, and less on the corporate entity owning the brands. As a result, given the sometimes very high degree of diversification of the growing Chinese conglomerates, corporate brands which cover a number of diverse products lose their focus, if the branding strategy does not shift towards product branding. As global mergers and acquisitions play an increasingly important role—once brands have become valuable but seem to be hampered by their involvement in larger corporate structures—this fusion will be dissolved by corporate brand takeovers. Furthermore, professional brand management techniques are increasingly undermining Chinese corporate practice, thus also building the bridge between domestic and global branding. Thus, for example, the fashion company Bosideng explicitly features different brands, including the original Bosideng trademark.

The need to develop brands is also increasingly linked with the urge to strengthen the protection of intellectual property rights in China. Chinese brands, like foreign brands, are endangered by domestic counterfeit products. For example, one of the oldest Chinese brands, Wangmazi scissors, established in 1651, went bankrupt in 2004, after the domestic market was virtually inundated by a flood of fake products. Thus Chinese brand owners are a powerful force demanding better protection of intellectual property rights in China. Technology-based companies are pursuing the development of management techniques in strategic use of patents.

Whether Chinese brands' plans to go global signals a convergence toward a global consumer culture or increased diversification of cultures remains to be seen. In the 2000s global brands underwent a process of localization in China; this followed the increasing turn toward traditional values in Chinese society, for example in personal hygiene products, which successfully turned international product lines into "Chinese brands." Many brands seen as being "Chinese" are designed and promoted by Chinese and foreign joint ventures, such as the food and beverage company Danone-Wahaha JV. Western companies, such as Shanghai Libo Beer, also have become increasingly aware of the regional diversity of China and the potential breeding grounds for local and regional brands. In terms of demographics, changes will come about as a result of a "graying China" coexisting with a highly volatile youth subculture. Finally, after the successful pursuit of a branding strategy for Shanghai, some are calling for a similar drive to establish a brand for China as a whole.

**SEE ALSO** *Companies: Corporate Law; Domestic Trade: 1800–1900; Domestic Trade: 1900–1950; Domestic Trade: Since 1950.*

**BIBLIOGRAPHY**

Gerth, Karl. *China Made: Consumer Culture and the Creation of the Nation.* Cambridge, MA: Harvard University Press, 2003.

Gilmore, Fiona, and Serge Dumont. *Brand Warriors China: Creating Sustainable Brand Capital.* London: Profile Books, 2003.

Wang Jing. *Brand New China: Advertising, Media, and Commercial Culture.* Cambridge, MA: Harvard University Press, 2008.

*Carsten Herrmann-Pillath*

# BUCK, PEARL S.

***1892–1973***

Pearl Comfort Sydenstricker was born in Hillsboro, West Virginia, the daughter of Presbyterian missionaries who had come to the United States from China for a year of home leave. Her parents, Absalom and Carie Stulting Sydenstricker, returned to Zhenjiang when Pearl was five months old. She lived most of the next forty years in China, mainly in a number of cities and towns in the Yangzi (Chang) River valley. Tutored from early childhood in both English and Chinese, she grew up bilingual and, as she liked to say, "culturally bifocal."

Pearl Sydenstricker attended college in the United States, at Randolph-Macon Woman's College in Virginia, graduating in 1914. She had intended to remain in America, but returned to China immediately after graduation to nurse her mother through her final illness. Pearl married her first husband, the agricultural economist J. Lossing Buck, and lived with him for several years in the town of Nan Xuzhou in rural Anhui Province. Her experiences among the impoverished farmers of Anhui provided the materials for many of Buck's novels and stories. In 1920 Buck gave birth to a daughter, Carol. Severely retarded, Carol would spend most of her life in an institution. In the mid-1920s, the Bucks adopted another daughter, Janice.

Buck's first novel, *East Wind, West Wind* (1930), received generally favorable reviews and earned a modest commercial success. Her next book, *The Good Earth* (1931), became an instant best seller. Along with almost uniformly enthusiastic reviews, the novel won the Pulitzer Prize, and, in 1935, the William Dean Howells Medal as the best work of American fiction published in the first half of the 1930s. In 1937 *The Good Earth* was adapted as a movie, produced by Metro-Goldwyn-Mayer. Like the book, the film enjoyed immense commercial and critical success, and was nominated for several Academy Awards.

*The Good Earth* made an unparalleled contribution to American cultural history. In *Scratches on Our Minds* (1958), sociologist Harold Isaacs determined that Buck's novel was the principal source from which Americans had derived whatever images and ideas they had about China. Isaacs concluded, "No single book about China has had a greater impact than … *The Good Earth.* It can almost be said that for a whole generation of Americans [Pearl Buck] 'created' the Chinese, in the same sense that Dickens 'created'... Victorian England."

Faced with the increasing dangers of the Chinese civil war and Japanese aggression, Pearl Buck moved to the United States in 1934. Shortly thereafter, she and Lossing Buck divorced. She then married her publisher, Richard Walsh, with whom she would adopt six more children.

In 1938, several years after returning to the United States, Buck was awarded the Nobel Prize for Literature. She was the third American and the first American woman to win the award. She was also one of the youngest recipients of the prize, and her selection received a decidedly mixed reception among academics and literary critics. She is reported to have said "[Theodore] Dreiser should have won," and Dreiser is reported to have agreed.

For the remaining four decades of her life, Buck continued to write. By the time of her death, she had published over eighty books in a wide assortment of genres. Fifteen of her novels were main selections of the Book-of-the-Month Club and the Literary Guild. *All Men Are Brothers* (1933), her translation of the Ming dynasty novel *Shuihu Zhuan*, was the first English rendering of the complete text of this classic Chinese novel. In 1936 she published separate biographies of both her parents, the titles of which capture her views: Her father's life is called *Fighting Angel*; her mother's *The Exile*. Buck also published two volumes of her own memoirs, poetry, and several children's books, including the prize-winning novel *The Big Wave* (1947), which was named by the Child Study Association as the best book of the year. Buck's novels and nonfiction books were translated into over sixty languages.

Along with her indefatigable publishing, Buck played a leading role in a long list of activist and humanitarian organizations throughout her American years. She and Richard Walsh founded the East and West Association in the early 1940s, part of their effort to promote cultural understanding between the United States and Asia in the midst of wartime anxieties. Buck and Walsh were also instrumental in the campaign that led to the repeal in 1943 of the notorious Chinese Exclusion Act, a discriminatory anti-immigration law first enacted in 1882 and periodically renewed for over sixty consecutive years.

Buck's loyalty to the people of China shaped her attitudes toward both Chiang Kai-shek (Jiang Jieshi) and Mao Zedong. She regarded Chiang as fundamentally corrupt, and she considered Mao a murderous fanatic. For these quite sensible and brave positions, she earned the enmity of the left and right in both China and the United States.

Buck joined the National Association for the Advancement of Colored People in the mid-1930s, eventually becoming a life member. She published articles in support of civil rights in both *Crisis*, the association's magazine, and *Opportunity*, published by the Urban League. During World War II, Buck chaired the Committee against Racial Discrimination, which lobbied unsuccessfully against discrimination in wartime industries. She was a trustee of Howard University for many years. In a Madison Square Garden rally in 1942, Walter White, executive secretary of the National Association for the Advancement of Colored People, told a crowd of 50,000 that only two white Americans understood the experience of black Americans, and both were women: Eleanor Roosevelt and Pearl Buck.

In the 1930s and 1940s Buck also emerged as a leading advocate for women's rights. At a time when opposition included most organized women's groups, she gave speeches around the country in support of the Equal Rights Amendment. In 1942 a collection of her essays on the subject was published as the book *Of Men and Women*, which the *New York Times* likened to the earlier work of Virginia Woolf in importance to the women's movement.

Buck was also vocal and active in support of the rights and welfare of children. In 1949, frustrated by the refusal of U.S. adoption agencies to attempt to find homes for minority and mixed-race children, she founded Welcome House, the first international and interracial adoption agency in the world. In its nearly sixty years of existence, Welcome House has assisted in the adoption of over six thousand children. Some years later Buck established the Pearl S. Buck Foundation, which assists impoverished families in several Asian countries. Buck's book about her daughter, *The Child Who Never Grew* (1950), proved to be a landmark in public discussion of mental illness and retardation.

Throughout the four decades of her American life, Pearl Buck had always hoped to return to China. When Richard Nixon flew to Beijing in 1972, the eighty-year-old Buck secured a journalist's credentials and began making arrangements to join the press plane. Her application for a visa was rejected by the Chinese government, apparently in final retaliation for her long opposition to Mao and the communist regime. She died just a few months later, on March 6, 1973, in Danby, Vermont.

**SEE ALSO** *Mao Zedong.*

**BIBLIOGRAPHY**

Buck, Pearl S. *My Several Worlds: A Personal Record.* New York: John Day Company, 1954.

Conn, Peter. *Pearl S. Buck: A Cultural Biography.* New York: Cambridge University Press, 1996.

Doyle, Paul A. *Pearl S. Buck.* Boston: Twayne Publishers, 1980.

Harris, Theodore F., in consultation with Pearl S. Buck. *Pearl S. Buck: A Biography.* New York: John Day, 1969.

Isaacs, Harold. *Scratches on Our Minds.* New York: John Day, 1958.

Liao, Kang. *Pearl S. Buck: A Cultural Bridge across the Pacific.* Westport, CT: Greenwood Press, 1997.

Stirling, Nora. *Pearl Buck: A Woman in Conflict.* Piscataway, NJ: New Century Publishers, 1983.

**Peter Conn**

# BUDDHISM

Although most historians believe that the heyday of Chinese Buddhism was in the Tang dynasty (618–907) and earlier, and that Buddhism never recovered from the persecution of 845, Buddhism has in fact retained a strong cultural presence in China to the present day. Tibetan Buddhism, in particular, was a major religion ascribed to by many of the Yuan, Ming, and Qing emperors, and it retains a popular resilience in all Tibetan ethnic areas, while belief in Guanyin remains widespread and continues unabated at a popular level. Buddhist beliefs have coexisted with local or folk religions, and Buddhist intellectual concepts pervade traditional Chinese culture, even though organized Buddhism waned in the nineteenth and twentieth centuries.

## LATE-QING EFFORTS TO REVIVE BUDDHISM

Attempts on the part of a minority of Buddhists to adjust to the modern world were first made only toward the end of the Qing dynasty (1644–1912). The layman Yang Wenhui (Renshan, 1837–1911) became interested in Buddhism in the 1860s, and after moving to Nanjing in 1866 he founded the Jinling Sutra Carving Society (Jinling Kejing Chu), setting himself the task of reprinting and distributing Buddhist scriptures. In 1878 he served the Chinese court as a diplomat in London and Paris, and on a subsequent posting in London he became acquainted with Nanjō Bunyū (1849–1927), a Japanese monk studying in London, with whose help he was later able to import more than three hundred sutras from Japan that had been lost in China. He also became acquainted with the work of the German orientalist F. Max Müller (1823–1900), confirming his conclusion that Buddhism was the religion most compatible with modern science.

In contrast with the intellectual lethargy that prevailed in most Chinese monasteries in the nineteenth century, Yang in 1895 established the Zhiheng Monastery at the site of his publishing house and invited the poet-monk Su Manshu (1884–1918) to teach Sanskrit and English. During his lifetime, Yang had a number of prominent students, including the radical philosophers Zhang Taiyan (1869–1936) and Tan Sitong (1865–1898), and the later neo-Buddhist Taixu (1890–1947). In 1910 Yang founded the Buddhist Research Society (Foxue Yanjiu Hui), but he died in the following year.

## NEO-BUDDHISM

Yang Wenhui's most prominent student at the Buddhist Research Society, the layman Ouyang Jian, better known as Ouyang Jingwu (1871–1943), is generally credited with initiating the neo-Buddhist movement in China. Ouyang was at first a disciple of Wang Yangming (1472–1529) and neo-Confucianism, but after having embraced Buddhism, Ouyang reestablished Yang's scriptural publishing house and academy as the Chinese Inner Studies Academy (Zhina Nei Xueyuan) in 1914. Ouyang set out to restore the Faxiang school and reedit the masterpieces of Weishi philosophy, a system of metaphysics imported from India from the pilgrim monk Xuanzang in the seventh century. Weishi philosophy was regarded as the summit of Buddhist rationalism, and its aversion to worship recommended it for consideration as a scientific philosophy.

The destruction of World War I (1914–1918) led many Chinese intellectuals to question Western philosophy, and there was a revived interest in China in "oriental thought" exemplified by the debate on the relative merits of Eastern and Western philosophy that emerged in the post–May Fourth intellectual renaissance. Liang Qichao (1873–1929) played a major part in this debate, and the lectures delivered in China by Rabindranath Tagore (1861–1941) in 1923 also did much to promote the ethical endorsement of oriental philosophy as a peaceful and viable alternative to Western philosophies.

The greatest theoretician of the neo-Buddhist movement initiated by Ouyang Jingwu was the monk Taixu, who was ordained into the Linji school of Chan Buddhism at Xiao Jiuhua Si Temple in Suzhou in 1904. In 1909 Taixu traveled to Nanjing and joined the Jinling Sutra Carving Society, and here he was exposed to the intellectual milieu of Kang Youwei (1858–1927), Liang Qichao, and Zhang Taiyan. Taixu saw his own task as effecting a reform or revolution within Buddhism, and after the 1911 revolution he established the Association for the Advancement of Buddhism (Fojiao Xiejin Hui). He would eventually set up three institutes of Buddhist research: one in Wuchang, which for a long time served as his center and where his lectures were popular; another in Xiamen; and a third in Sichuan near the Tibetan frontier. The latter was established with a view to renovating Tibetan Buddhism. These activities brought Taixu into active contact with young monks and reform-minded lay Buddhists, but aroused lively opposition from conservative monks. The leader of organized opposition to Taixu was Yinguang (1861–1940), the intellectual and spiritual leader of the Pure Land school, the most popular form of Buddhism, which taught salvation through faith in Amitabha and in Guanyin. In some senses, this was a clash between modernizing philosophy and conservative religion.

***A statue of Buddha from the Mogao Caves, Dunhuang, 1998.*** *Scholars believe the teachings of Buddha reached China in the first century* CE. *Followers of Buddha grew in number in subsequent years, blending Buddhist teaching with traditional Chinese beliefs, before declining during a wave of persecution under Emperor Wuzong in the mid-ninth century.* © KAZUYOSHI NOMACHI/CORBIS

Taixu was also very active internationally. He participated in Buddhist congresses in Japan, the Philippines, the Dutch East Indies, and Ceylon (Sri Lanka), and in 1928 he gave a series of lectures in Paris, Frankfurt, Berlin, London, and New York. Taixu planned the creation of a worldwide Institute of Buddhism, with its headquarters in China. Although his lectures were published as tracts, his major work was *Zhen xianshi lun* (The true realism), published in 1940. In this he sought to establish the rational doctrine of his school of "pure ideation" or "consciousness-only" (Weishi) using scientific facts.

These ideas were taken up and amplified in a sophisticated form by the neo-Buddhist syncretist Xiong Shili (1885–1968), who sought to reconcile Buddhism not only with science but with neo-Confucianism. Xiong had studied under Ouyang Jingwu at the Chinese Inner Studies Academy in Nanjing, and later headed the academy, until he was recruited by Cai Yuanpei (1867–1940) to teach at Peking University. Xiong was still teaching at the university when he published his major work, *Xin weishi lun* (A new treatise on consciousness-only), in 1932.

The neo-Buddhist movement succeeded in reestablishing the intellectual reputation of Buddhism, but had little impact on the religion's popular status and fate. Its decline continued through the Japanese invasion, even though the Japanese attempted to use the religion in their cultural efforts in China. The religion was alternately accused of collaboration and patriotism. For example, Master Tanxu (1875–1963), who in the 1930s and 1940s built and operated temples throughout Manchuria and northern China, was accused by the Japanese of leading Chinese resistance, and later by the Chinese Communists of collaborating with the Japanese. Tanxu denied both charges, claiming that his work was strictly religious, but in 1948 he relocated from Qingdao to Hong Kong, where he founded the Huanan Buddhist Seminary.

## CHINESE BUDDHISM AFTER 1949

The victory of the Communists in 1949 saw Buddhism brought within the administrative concern of the government of the People's Republic of China (PRC), which initially adopted united front tactics. In 1953 the government set up the Chinese Buddhist Association (Zhongguo Fojiao Xiehui) to regulate the religion, while at the same time working to overthrow any political or social influence of the religion. Buddhist temples and institutions and members of the clergy were ruthlessly attacked in the Cultural Revolution (1966–1969). With the implementation of the reforms in 1979, orthodox Buddhist religious belief was again tolerated, and many of the temples and other cultural monuments destroyed or damaged in the Cultural Revolution were repaired, while the patriotic activities of the Chinese Buddhist Association were encouraged. The Chinese Buddhist Association is also encouraged to forge links with visiting pilgrims and lay Buddhists, returning in a sense to the united front policies of the early 1950s.

Buddhism has flourished in Taiwan and Hong Kong since 1949. There are more than six hundred temples in the Hong Kong Special Administrative Region, and in 1997 the Hong Kong government designated a public holiday in May or June to mark the Buddha's birthday, which replaced the queen's birthday. In 1949 a number of mainland monks fled to Taiwan with remnants of the Guomindang (GMD), and Buddhists on the island came under the authority of the Chinese Buddhist Association (Zhongguo Fojiao Hui), which had been originally set up by the GMD government in Nanjing in 1947. Dominated by monks from the mainland, it was only in the 1960s that Buddhism began to acquire the full independence and success it enjoys today.

Because Chinese can at one and the same time accept Buddhist beliefs and non-Buddhist beliefs, it is fairly impossible to provide statistics on the number of adherents of the faith in the PRC, Hong Kong, or Taiwan. According to a limited survey of 4,500 people conducted by Huadong Normal University in Shanghai in 2007 and reported widely in the Chinese media, 31.4 percent of people over the age of sixteen considered themselves to be religious, marking a break with earlier attitudes during the Maoist period in the PRC.

**SEE ALSO** *Religious Specialists since 1800.*

**BIBLIOGRAPHY**

Carter, James. A Tale of Two Temples: Nation, Region, and Religious Architecture in Harbin, 1928–1998. In *Place, Space, and Identity: Harbin and Manchuria in the Twentieth Century.* Spec issue. *South Atlantic Quarterly* 99, 1 (2000): 97–115.

Ch'en, Kenneth. *Buddhism in China.* Princeton, NJ: Princeton University Press, 1972.

Jones, Charles Brewer. *Buddhism in Taiwan: Religion and the State, 1660–1990.* Honolulu: University of Hawaii Press, 1999.

Welch, Holmes. *The Practice of Chinese Buddhism, 1900–1950.* Cambridge, MA: Harvard University Press, 1967.

Welch, Holmes. *The Buddhist Revival in China.* Cambridge, MA: Harvard University Press, 1968.

Welch, Holmes. *Buddhism under Mao.* Cambridge, MA: Harvard University Press, 1972.

***Bruce Doar***

# BUILD-OPERATE-TRANSFER (BOT) CONTRACTS

In China and elsewhere, a community's basic infrastructural needs (such as electric power, water treatment, roads and bridges, etc.) have often been provided by government agencies rather than by private companies. Because the benefits of such infrastructure tend to be concentrated in a local area, the government in question is often a local government. These traditional arrangements have three significant potential weaknesses: (1) local governments, especially in poorer regions, may have difficulty financing such projects; (2) local governments may not have the technological sophistication to build and manage such facilities; and (3) government ownership of these public utilities may lead to the cost overruns and poor service that often characterize state-owned enterprises (SOEs) generally.

Around the world, governments grappling with these issues have experimented with a variety of mechanisms (known generically as public-private partnerships) that are intended to combine the advantages of both government and private ownership while avoiding the disadvantages of each. One such mechanism is the build-operate-transfer (BOT) contract, which has the following characteristics: a private company (the concessionaire) and a local government agree that the private company will *build* (at its own expense) a particular facility such as a water-purification plant, will *operate* the facility (and receive its revenues) for a predetermined number of years, and will then *transfer* ownership to the government partner at no cost.

The first successful BOT contract in China, signed in 1985 without competitive bidding, was for the Shajiao B thermal power plant in Guangdong province. The concessionaire was Hopewell Power of Hong Kong. The plant came into full operation in 1988, and ownership was transferred to the Shenzhen government on schedule in 1999. Following this precedent, a few other BOT contracts were signed, including the Guang-Shen-Zhu toll road (1987), the Yan'an tunnels in Shanghai (1993), the Jing-Tong expressway in Beijing (1994), the Zhuhai power plant in Guangdong (1995), and the Dachang water plant in Shanghai (1995).

It was only after this decade of BOT activity that the central government of China took formal steps to regularize the practice. The Provisional Regulations on Foreign Investment Build-Operate-Transfer Projects were issued in draft form by the State Planning Commission in 1996. Although brief, this document does confirm several key principles—most notably, that the foreign concessionaire shall be entirely responsible for all costs and potential losses (the local government partner is explicitly forbidden to provide any guarantee regarding the rate of return on the investment) and that the contract shall be awarded through international competitive bidding.

These provisions have several important adverse implications from a concessionaire's point of view. To begin with, the cost of preparing a bid is substantial, this preparatory investment is lost by all bidders except the winning one, and the winning bidder earns a thin profit margin in a high-risk context. Furthermore, the potential concessionaires are typically engineering and construction firms, which do not themselves have adequate internal capital to finance large projects and must therefore turn to banks for much of the funding. The banks, understandably, are reluctant to lend to risky ventures and therefore pressure the concessionaires to seek government guarantees of various sorts, which is precisely what the Provisional Regulations are trying to prevent, or at least curtail. One way to understand this situation is to say that the foreign banks want the projects to have the characteristics of SOEs (in particular, to have what the Hungarian economist János Kornai has called a "soft budget constraint," which means that if the enterprise gets into financial difficulty, it will be bailed out by the government partner), while the Chinese authorities' goal, through BOT contracts and similar mechanisms, is precisely to create local public utilities that do not have the cost overruns and other failings of SOEs. (It is an interesting aspect of the reforms in China that BOT contracts, like the decollectivization of agriculture and a variety of other reforms, emerged on a local level well before they received official approval from the central government.)

Following the promulgation of the Provisional Regulations, formal BOT contracts were signed for the Laibin B power plant in Guangxi (1996) and the Chengdu No. 6B water treatment plant in Sichuan (1999). These projects are often identified as the first BOT contracts in China's power and water sectors respectively, but it is more correct to say that they were the first BOT contracts in their sectors to be officially approved under the Provisional Regulations. Only a handful of other BOT projects have been approved since 1996, which partly reflects the disruptions caused by the Asian currency crisis of 1997, but also reflects the conflicting goals of foreign bankers and Chinese authorities over who will bear the various risks of infrastructure projects.

**BIBLIOGRAPHY**

Asian Development Bank. *BOT in the Water Supply Sector in the People's Republic of China.* Manila, Philippines: Author, 1996.

Chen Chuan and John I. Messner. An Investigation of Chinese BOT Projects in Water Supply: A Comparative Perspective. *Construction Management and Economics* 23 (2005): 913–925.

State Planning Commission. *Provisional Regulations on Foreign Investment Build-Operate-Transfer Projects.* Beijing: Author, 1996.

***Ralph W. Huenemann***

# C

## CADRE SYSTEM

The term *cadre* (*ganbu*) has two meanings. First, it is used to refer to all Chinese Communist Party officials, as well as civil servants in state offices and institutions, in the army, and in "people's organizations," except ordinary soldiers, "low-grade servants," ordinary workers in state-owned firms, and employees in the state-owned service sector. Second, *cadre* also refers to individuals in leading positions. However, it is necessary to differentiate between party cadres, administration cadres, and military cadres. Since the term includes party leaders and the president and the prime minister of China, as well as such officials as village leaders and police officers, it does not represent a homogeneous category.

The cadre system in existence since the 1950s was restructured in 1993 by the Provisional Regulations for the Public Service to comprise fifteen grades (see Table 1). The grade structure is the same at each level in the party, the people's congresses (parliaments), and the political consultative conferences. This grade system also determines salaries and privileges.

Each cadre grade is treated in a particular manner. Privileges increase according to grade level. High-ranking cadres in grades one through five enjoy the greatest privileges in terms of salaries, labor conditions, housing space and standard, medical treatment, and pensions. High-ranking cadres may also have access to servants paid by the state, an official car and driver, the right to travel first class on trains and planes during official trips, and detailed information on China and on foreign countries. This system is similar to the one in place in China during the time of the emperors, when the civil service was also divided into grades—the so-called *ji*-hierarchy. There were two main categories in this hierarchy: civil and military. Beginning in the Tang dynasty (618–907), each category was divided into nine grades, and each grade was subdivided into two classes, an upper (*shang*) and a lower (*xia*) class. Altogether there were eighteen grades, each characterized by special insignia and salaries.

The higher an official's ranking, the greater the share of privileges and material profits included in the official's compensation. The loss of an official position or exclusion from the cadre system means the removal of numerous privileges and a significant reduction in one's living standard. The potential for ascent in such a system, and the social security it offers, motivates individuals to become members of the party and to join some kind of network that guarantees advancement in the hierarchy. The cadre system also encourages conformist behavior toward network groups and patrons.

Communist Party membership is the starting point for a career, material benefits, and social privileges within the cadre system. However, the political monopoly of the party generates opportunism, careerism, clientelism, and corruption. Concurrently, party members have to adapt to political changes, or they might be demoted or expelled.

Although most officials' salaries are relatively low, their privileges are a major compensation. The estimated cost for an official car, for example, may reach tens of thousands of yuan annually, plus the cost of the salary and benefits of the driver. Thus, the state may spend about 100,000 yuan per year for the car and driver of a single official. According

**Fifteen grades of the cadre system**

| Grade | Positions |
|---|---|
| 1 | Premier of the State Council |
| 2–3 | Vice-premier / State councillors |
| 3–4 | Ministers (*buji*) / provincial governors (*shengji*) |
| 4–5 | Vice-ministers (*fubuji*) / vice-governors (*fushengji*) |
| 5–7 | Heads of departments of ministries (*siji*) / heads of provincial bureaus (*tingji*) |
| 6–8 | Vice-heads of departments of ministries (*fusiji*) / vice-heads of provincial bureaus (*futingji*) |
| 7–10 | Heads of subdepartments of ministries (*chuji*) / governors of counties (*xianji*) |
| 8–11 | Vice-heads of subdepartments of ministries (*fuchuji*) / vice-governors of counties (*fuxianji*) |
| 9–12 | Heads of sections of ministries (*keji*) / directors of towns / townships (*xiangji*) |
| 9–13 | Vice-heads of sections of ministries (*fukeji*) / vice-directors of towns / townships (*fuxiangji*) |
| 9–14 | Employees of sections of ministries (*keyuan*) |
| 10–15 | Office employees (*banshiyuan*) |

SOURCE: *Renmin Ribao*, 19 August 1993.

***Table 1***

to official data, approximately 500,000 high-ranking cadres enjoy such privileges.

To become a civil servant paid by the state—a state cadre or *guojia ganbu*—one has to be added to the official staffing schedule by the responsible personnel offices. Organization departments are responsible for party cadres. State cadres are paid out of the official budgets. Their salaries are part of the regular budget, whereas rural cadres have to be paid from extra-budgetary sources. The *bianzhi* system is used to administer the positions of administrative cadres, including all public servants, and to determine the number of staff in an administrative unit. The *nomenklatura* system applies primarily to the ranking order and the leading cadres of the party. However, because the party and its organizational departments are constantly intervening in the personnel and administrative functioning of state institutions, the parallel existence of the *bianzhi* and *nomenklatura* systems has become an obstacle to fundamental administrative reform in China.

In recent years, the party's Organization Department introduced an evaluation procedure for leading officials (the cadre responsibility system) that aimed to assess regularly the officials' performance and success at implementing policies. However, research conducted by Thomas Heberer in China in 2007 revealed that an effective evaluation procedure is not yet in place. Crucial policy areas, such as environmental issues, are not being evaluated, and evaluation is predominantly based on self-assessment.

The *nomenklatura* system, through which the party identifies officials who fit its policies, is facing grave challenges due to the development of the market economy and private entrepreneurship in China. Chinese citizens can now achieve upward mobility and the acquisition of resources outside the party's control. The Communist Party is no longer the sole stakeholder. This development also entails a challenge to the power monopoly of the party.

Since the 1980s, China's political leadership has striven to restructure the cadre system and to reduce the number of officials. Accordingly, a new incentive system was established to support the implementation of reforms and economic development. The former system of lifelong employment was abolished, a strict retirement system was implemented, and new guidelines stipulating the proper age and educational level of officials were issued. To win the support of the political elite, influential members of the leadership were transferred into advisory boards, thus allowing them to keep their privileges even after retirement. This practice, by which officials keep their full salary and basket of privileges after retirement, is known as *lixiu* (leave office for recuperation). In addition, officials can resign and turn their attention to economic activities or become self-employed, a practice called *xiahai* (to throw oneself into the sea). Moreover, the coupling of economic performance to the income and job prospects of cadres has generated new incentives and facilitated the acceptance of developmental goals at the local level.

Party schools at the township to the central level play an important role in educating cadres. Every five years, higher officials at the level of ministers or provincial governors (*shengbuji*) have to attend three-month courses at the Central Party School in Beijing; bureau leaders at the central and provincial level do so every three years. Prospective ministers or provincial heads must study at the Central Party School for one year before being promoted. Promising county party secretaries are invited to attend training courses for three months. This further education includes courses in ideological issues (Marxism-Leninism, Mao Zedong Thought, Deng Xiaoping theory, Three Represents theory, etc.), as well as courses in modern Western political theory and philosophy, practical issues of the world economy, modern technology, international law and international relations, globalization, and defense and national security. Through such training, top officials obtain an overview of global developments and trends.

Local officials are trained in the lower-level party schools. Such schools offer courses in ideological and organizational knowledge, party guidelines and policies, technical skills, and the market economy. Training in party schools leads to the ideological standardization of cadres. Such schools can also help the party identify talented individuals, and can contribute to network building among higher officials at all levels.

In political decision-making processes, there are four types of groups: (1) the *political leading core*, a small group of decision makers at the top; (2) the *political elite*, the remaining leading officials at the central and provincial level; (3) the *political subelite*, leading distinct subareas; and (4) the *local subelite*.

The members of the political leading core wield the central decision-making power and make decisions on most principle issues. This group includes the members and candidates of the Political Bureau, the top leadership of the State Council and the armed forces, the chairman and vice chairmen of the National People's Congress (NPC) and the Political Consultative Conference (PCC), and the prime minister and his deputies—that is, the level of vice prime minister and above. Frequently, decisions are made through informal channels whereby the leading core may include civil and military leaders at the central and regional level in discussion processes.

The political elite encompasses those officials who can decide or influence subareas of the political system: members of the Central Committee, the Standing Committee of the NPC and PCC, the provincial leadership, military leaders, ministers and vice ministers, the heads of the Supreme People's Court and the Supreme People's Procuratorate, and the heads of mass organizations and the academies of sciences and their deputies—that is, the level of vice minister and above. The political elite is comprised of people who have a clearly higher degree of bureaucratic power in steering processes of significance for the entire society.

The political subelite includes leading officials at the central bureau level, top officials at the provincial level, and division commanders and their deputies. This group acts relatively independently within the authority assigned by the higher echelons. Distinct from the political elite, members of the political subelite make operative political decisions, rather than strategic decisions. They function as a link or liaison between the political elite and those in the lower levels.

The local subelite primarily includes the heads of departments at the central and provincial level, as well as leading officials of prefectures, municipalities, districts, counties, and townships.

In the 1990s, the political leading core consisted of about 300 to 350 persons, the political elite about 3,000, and the subelite about 80,000. The local subelite comprised approximately nine million people. China's entire leadership thus comprised less than 1 percent of the country's population. Andrew Walder counted 900 persons in the central party apparatus in 1998, 2,500 at the level of ministers and provincial governors, 39,000 at the prefecture and bureau level, and 466,000 at the county and subdepartment level; altogether approximately 500,000 people were leading some forty million cadres below the county and subdepartment level. Only one-fourth of Communist Party members are considered cadres.

The lower cadre level has the task of implementing the guidelines and policies of the political elite. Cadres at this level have limited decision-making power, and do not belong to the elite. In 2002 about forty-five million people belonged to this category, which is closer to the common people than to the elite. It is important to distinguish between two basic groups of cadres: the political-power elite, which grants its members decision-making power, privileges, and favors, and, in principle, is not controllable by outsiders, and the remaining cadres with little power and without major privileges.

**SEE ALSO** *Communist Party; Social Classes since 1978.*

**BIBLIOGRAPHY**

Brodsgaard, Kjeld Erik, and Zheng Yongnian, eds. *The Chinese Communist Party in Reform.* London and New York: Routledge, 2006.

Lee Hong Yung. *From Revolutionary Cadres to Party Technocrats in Socialist China.* Berkeley: University of California Press, 1991.

Walder, Andrew G. The Party Elite and China's Trajectory of Change. In *The Chinese Communist Party in Reform,* ed. Kjeld Erik Brodsgaard and Zheng Yongnian, 15–32. London and New York: Routledge, 2006.

Zang Xiaowei. *Elite Dualism and Leadership Selection in China.* London: RoutledgeCurzon, 2004.

***Thomas Heberer***

# CAI GUO-QIANG

***1957–***

Cai Guo-Qiang was born in 1957 in the city of Quanzhou in Fujian Province, China. From 1981 to 1985 he trained in stage design at the Shanghai Xiju Xueyuan (Shanghai Drama Institute) and mastered a variety of traditional mediums, such as painting, drawing, and sculpture. Cai was also an active member of the New Wave movement, one of the first experimental art movements in China during the middle to late 1980s. Fascinated by the medium's unpredictability and potential to extend art beyond its traditional boundaries, he started to experiment with gunpowder. In his "The Brand of The Archean Era" series in 1985 and 1986, Cai experimented with gunpowder in a primitive painting style reminiscent of art from the Shang dynasty (sixteenth century–1046 BCE). He created simplistic sticklike figures by sprinkling gunpowder onto the canvas and lit them to create permanent burnt marks on the canvas that formed powerful and evocative works in a new medium of expression.

Moving to Japan in 1986 allowed Cai greater artistic freedom to work on larger-scale gunpowder installations, mainly ephemeral explosions executed around the world, recorded on video, and exhibited with preparatory drawings using ink and gunpowder. His signature series *Project for Extraterrestrials* (1989–1995) consisted of impressive and sometimes unsuccessful massive outdoor and environmental works, and involved the risks and hazards of working with the material. This series also exemplified the artist's wish, through these explosions, to portray to the universe a different image of humans—one not related to war or killing, and aimed at establishing an exchange between viewers and the larger universe around them.

In 1995 Cai migrated to the United States and began his *Century with Mushroom Clouds* series, wherein the artist addressed themes of culture conflict and war in the nuclear age. In these works Cai situates himself standing, his back toward the viewer, and sets off a mushroom-cloud-shaped explosion, with a major national icon (such as the Statue of Liberty, London's Tower Bridge, or the Eiffel Tower) in the background. Other projects, such as *Cultural Melting Bath: Projects for the Twentieth Century* (1997), also included the artist's experiments with alchemy, an extension of his interest in gunpowder, and addressed cultural and racial issues related to the artist's experience as rooted in his Chinese past and as developed in his new American environment. Works such as his *Cry Dragon/Cry Wolf: The Ark of Genghis Khan* (1996) and *Borrowing Your Enemy's Arrows* (1998) address the rising economic and political power of China within the global context. Other representative works include the following:

- His installations—*Inopportune: Stage One* (2004) and *Rent Collection Courtyard* (Venice version, 1999; New York version, 2008)
- His social projects—*Bringing to Venice What Marco Polo Forgot* (1995) and *DMoCA [Dragon Museum of Contemporary Art]*: *Everything Is Museum No. 1* (2000)
- His many collaborative projects, such as *Wind Shadow* (2006), realized with Yunmen Wu Ji (Cloud Gate Dance Theatre) of Taiwan

Recognized as a major artist worldwide, Cai Guo-Qiang has received a number of prestigious awards, including the Forty-eighth Venice Biennale International Golden Lion Prize (1999) and the CalArts/Alpert Award in the Arts (2001), and the Seventh Hiroshima Art Prize (2008). His 2004 exhibition Cai Guo-Qiang: Inopportune at Mass MoCA (Massachusetts Museum of Contemporary Art, North Adams) also won awards for best exhibition and best installation from the International Curators Association. Cai's works have been exhibited internationally at major biennials and museums, and the artist has also curated the first China Pavilion at the Fifty-first Venice Biennale (2005).

Cai held a mid-career retrospective exhibition, *I Want to Believe,* at the Guggenheim Museum, and he worked with fireworks expert Phil Grucci to provide the pyrotechnic displays of the extravagant opening and closing ceremonies of the Beijing 2008 Olympic Games.

SEE ALSO *Art Exhibitions since 1949; New Wave Movement, 85.*

**BIBLIOGRAPHY**

"Cai Guo-Qiang." http://www.caiguoqiang.com. The artist's website.

Chiu, Melissa. *Breakout: Chinese Art outside China.* Milan: Edizioni Charta, 2006.

Friis-Hansen, Dana, Octavio Zaya, and Serizawa Takashi. *Cai Guo-Qiang.* London: Phaidon Press, 2002.

Krens, Thomas, and Alexandra Munroe. *Cai Guo-Qiang: I Want to Believe.* New York: Guggenheim Museum, 2008.

***Ying Chua***

## CALENDAR

The lunar and solar calendars live side-by-side in contemporary China. The rhythms of the lunar year dominate family life, even as the solar calendar affects much of the public realm. Most Chinese calendars published today follow, in rough fashion, the Hong Kong-style calendar, for which the page is read right to left, and a large column to the far right explains the lunar calendar information for the month as a whole. The organization of the individual columns shows the parallel forces of the lunar and solar calendars in contemporary China.

Of the eight distinct rows of information, the first gives the date according to the solar calendar. The rows that follow, however, reflect a distinctly traditional set of assumptions about society, time, and the universe. The second row presents the names of several auspicious stars, while the third row contains a listing of the hours of the day (in two-hour blocks), followed by one of three variables: lucky, middling, and unlucky. The fourth row, with the character for *avoid* in boldface, contains a list of activities that one should shun. These activities—moving earth, digging wells, paying mourning visits, and making nets, to name just a few—give a feel for a society very different from contemporary Hong Kong, Shanghai, or Beijing. Row six, with the character for *appropriate* in boldface, contains a longer list of activities to be undertaken, including meeting friends, erecting beams, studying, and visiting the doctor. Rows seven and eight are little used, but show astral influences and household activities, respectively.

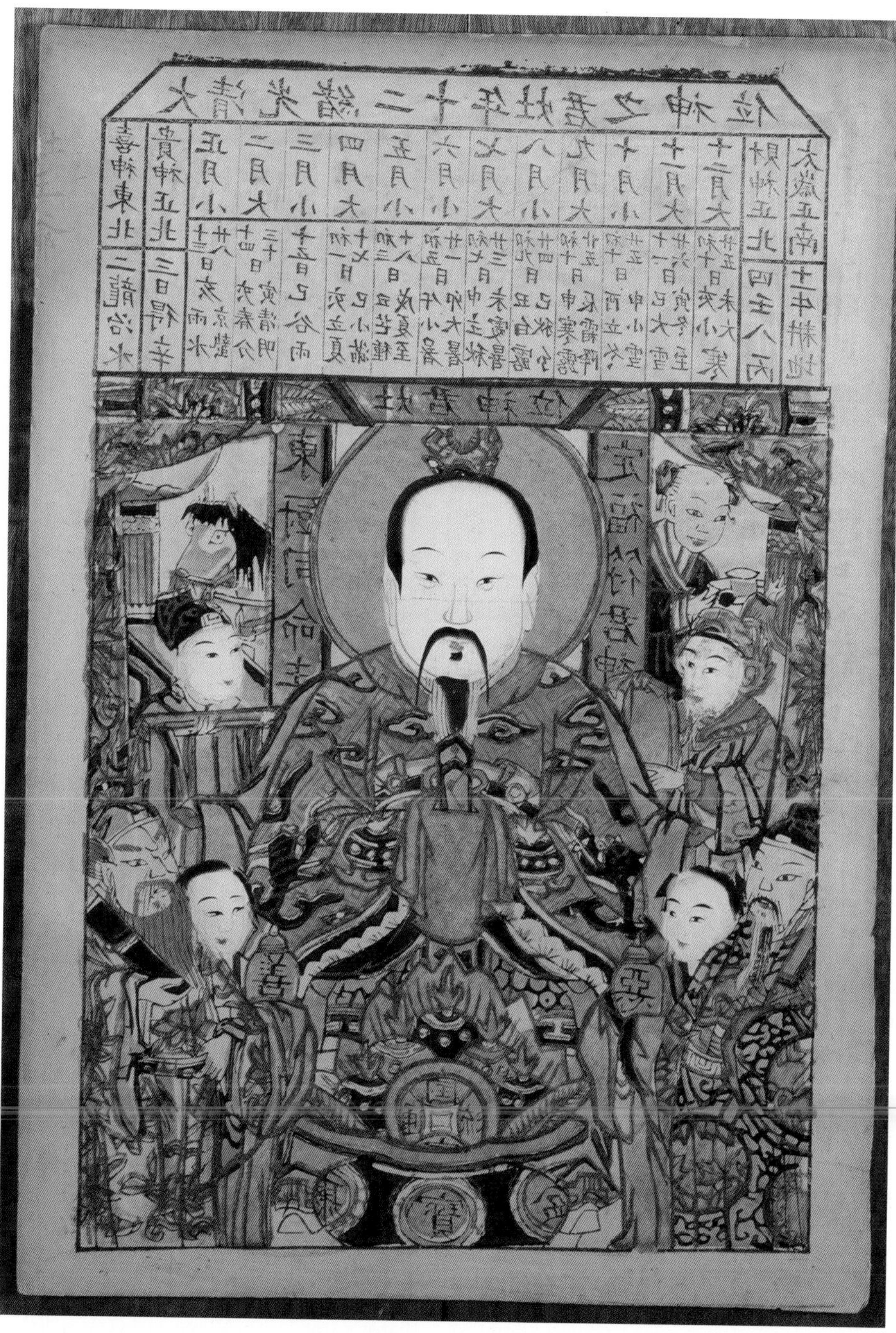

***Woodblock lunar calendar, 1895.*** *This Qing Dynasty lunar calendar shows the year in outline form, organized by months. Full calendars also provide extensive information for each day of the year.* **KITCHEN GOD WITH LUNAR CALENDAR, 1895 (WOODBLOCK ON PAPER), CHINESE SCHOOL, QING DYNASTY (1644-1912)/© ORIENTAL MUSEUM, DURHAM UNIVERSITY, UK/THE BRIDGEMAN ART LIBRARY**

The fifth row—the heart of the calendar—contains the *phase* (metal, fire, water, earth, wood) connected with the day, as well as information about a number of *cycles* that have appeared in calendars in China for centuries. The most significant of these is a character sequence used to count from one to sixty in endless cycles through time. Days, months, and years have been denoted by this system throughout Chinese history, and it remains important in historical studies and even fortune-telling. The last two characters in row five show a duo of *day personalities* related to the twenty-eight *lunar mansions* of the moon's orbit, on the one hand, and a cycle of twelve distinct day-types, on the other, such as *open, closed, danger,* and *smooth.* These day personalities have played a significant role in Chinese traditions, and one can still see hotels and restaurants filled to capacity with weddings on days that meet the right criteria in this section.

The Hong Kong calendar is the closest contemporary reflection of traditional Chinese calendars. Calendars published in Taiwan, Singapore, and the People's Republic of China (PRC) vary in their details, but follow the same guiding calendrical principles—from the numerical and day-personality cycles to the parallel tracking of solar and lunar information. Many calendars in the PRC eschew supposedly "superstitious" information, such as lucky and unlucky stars, hours, activities, and so forth. All calendars observe the lunar-oriented holidays that, to this day, give a sense of rhythm and proportion to life in China.

The greatest political tension in contemporary calendars concerns the reckoning of dates in the PRC and the Republic of China (ROC) on Taiwan. The ROC adopted the Western calendar when it came to power and the republic was proclaimed on January 1, 1912. The ROC recognizes solar-calendar dates for major holidays, such as the Double Ten celebration to commemorate the Wuchang Uprising in 1911 that brought down the Qing government, and reckons the new year from January 1. This system of counting years from the ROC inauguration was in effect until 1949, when the PRC was proclaimed. Republican forces fled to Taiwan, and they continue to use the Republican calendar, making 2009 the year "98" (the ninety-eighth year after the Republic's founding) in almost all government business. In contrast, the PRC uses Western-style dates (e.g., 2009) in most official materials. Just as the Republican and PRC calendars have spent six decades on parallel tracks, so too does every person in China negotiate the parallel forces of the solar and lunar calendars.

**SEE ALSO** *Festivals.*

**BIBLIOGRAPHY**

Aslaksan, Helmer. The Mathematics of the Chinese Calendar. http://www.math.nus.edu.sg/aslaksen/calendar/chinese.shtml.

Dalby, Liza. *East Wind Melts the Ice: A Memoir through the Seasons.* Berkeley: University of California Press, 2007.

Li Shu. *T'ung Shu: The Ancient Chinese Almanac.* Ed. and trans. Martin Palmer. Boston: Shambhala, 1986.

Morgan, Carole. *Le tableau du boeuf du printemps: Étude d'une page de l'almanach chinoise* [The spring cow illustration: A study of a page in the Chinese almanac]. Paris: Collège de France, Institut des hautes études chinoises, 1980.

Smith, Richard. *Fortune-tellers and Philosophers: Divination in Traditional Chinese Society.* Boulder, CO: Westview, 1991.

Smith, Richard. *Chinese Almanacs.* Oxford: Oxford University Press, 1992.

Zhu Wenxin. *Lifa tongzhi* [A comprehensive account of calendrical methods]. Shanghai: Shangwu Yinshuguan, 1934.

*Robert André LaFleur*

# CALLIGRAPHY

From the middle of the Qing dynasty (1644–1912) until well into the twentieth century, Chinese calligraphy as an art form was clearly divided into two distinct approaches to the earlier tradition. The first, labeled the epistle school (*tiexue*), was defined by earlier famous calligraphers' writing (of letters, poetry, and other forms) that was prized, transmitted through collections, and occasionally reproduced in private- and court-sponsored compendia of printed rubbings called *fatie* (model writings). This was the foundation upon which the educated learned to write, and it defined the orthodox classical tradition in calligraphy. The second, known as the stele school (*beixue*), or by the rubric *jinshi* (metal and stone), sought inspiration from largely anonymous inscriptions found on memorial stones (*bei*), ritual bronzes, and other ancient objects. This bifurcated approach to the past took shape as scholarly studies of metal and stone inscriptions grew increasingly popular through the Qing dynasty, peaking in the eighteenth and nineteenth centuries and continuing strongly through the Republican period (1912–1949). There have been significant new developments in the art of writing since, influenced by the sweeping cultural transformations that have taken place in China over the past century, yet the degree to which the mainstream of calligraphy has remained grounded in its own independent tradition, impervious to fundamental change, is remarkable.

## THE EPISTLE TRADITION VERSUS THE METAL-AND-STONE TRADITION

Differences in the epistle and metal-and-stone orientations to calligraphy are manifest in style, aesthetics, and to a certain degree type of script. The model writings known from rubbings, largely circumscribed by a history of canonical masters that stemmed from Wang Xizhi (303–361) and the masters of the Tang dynasty (618–907), were dominated by the three commonly practiced scripts: *kai* (standard), *xing* (semicursive), and *cao* (cursive). In contrast, inscription writing, grounded in archaeological spirit and practice, sought to reexplore the archaic *li* (clerical) script commonly used on stelae of the Han dynasty (206 BCE–220 CE), as well as earlier forms of writing often grouped under the script label *zhuan* (seal). In a well-known essay on calligraphy, the eminent Qing official and historian Ruan Yuan (1764–1849) associated the two approaches to calligraphy with a territorial divide, stelae being associated with the north and epistles with the south. While this geographic split does not bear scrutiny, Ruan's division reflects the fundamental aesthetic difference between the two approaches. Stelae and their calligraphy are rough, powerful, and direct; letters and other occasional writings, especially those associated with Wang Xizhi's influence, were cultivated, graceful, and elegant. Increasingly, as fascination with metal-and-stone inscriptions grew, many perceived the epistle tradition as irrelevant and the models as too far removed from their original sources to be trustworthy. This trend reached a peak in the 1960s, when the respected scholar Guo Moruo (1892–1978) published an article that questioned the validity of Wang Xizhi's famed *Lanting xu* (Orchid Pavilion Preface), the fountainhead of the epistle tradition.

All calligraphers were cognizant of the epistle tradition, and a few of the finest remained wedded to the classical models. Bao Shichen (1775–1855) was not only devoted to the cursive style of Wang Xizhi; he considered himself the great master's "first successor." Such bravado was useful when attempting to measure up against history's best, but it needed to be matched with exceptional skill at handling the brush. Among the few who proved themselves worthy in the modern era are Shen Yinmo (1883–1971) and Wu Yuru (1898–1982).

In contrast, the inscription tradition was fresher and more open to innovation. Initial attention focused largely on a select group of well-known Han stelae written in the clerical script, but increasingly through the latter half of the Qing dynasty, calligraphers adopted new models and experimented freely in an effort to establish personal styles. Two of the more eye-catching styles belong to the monk Dashou (1791–1858), who combined different forms of seal- and clerical-script writing into a monumental mode of writing, and Xu San'geng (1826–1890), who developed a unique style hinting of Sanskrit writing out of an unusual third-century model. Some calligraphers demonstrated singular focus in their exploration of a given style or model, such as the well-known master Wu Changshi (1844–1927), who was particularly enamored with the seal-script writing of the famous Stone Drums (Shigu) of Eastern Zhou (770–256 BCE), but the general trend was an eclectic blending—mixing models and even scripts to create something new. The key ingredient was the ink-and-brush medium, which infused the ancient inscription forms with vitality, added nuance, and gave them an entirely new appearance, especially when written large. Conversely, the distinct set of aesthetic values associated with the ancient metal-and-stone sources—strong, hoary, rough, awkward—was broadly embraced and applied to the handling of the brush, inflecting even the standard, semicursive, and cursive scripts. Among the better-known calligraphers who embodied the inscription spirit and applied it to a range of scripts were Chen Hongshou (1768–1822), He Shaoji (1799–1873), Yang Shoujing (1839–1919), Kang Youwei (1858–1927), Wu Changshi, and Qi Baishi (1863–1957). More recently, the fiercely individualistic artist Shi Lu (1919–1982), who is better known for his paintings, relied on the same inscriptional values in creating distinctive calligraphy with a strong pictorial aspect.

## TWENTIETH-CENTURY DEVELOPMENTS

With its roots deeply embedded in the Chinese literary tradition, calligraphy became a site of contestation amid the widespread efforts to modernize China in the twentieth century. The colloquial-language movement (*baihua yundong*), the development of simplified characters, and the use of pens and pencils all offered serious challenges to the traditional art form. Concurrently, a number of artists interested in modernizing Chinese art experimented with calligraphy, partly encouraged, perhaps, by the attention shown to it by some Western modernist painters. A number of artists active outside of mainland China, including Wang Fangyu (1913–1997; New York) and Yuan Dexing (better known by his penname, Chu Ge [Chu Ko], b. 1931; Taiwan), played with the interaction of semiotic and pictorial elements in characters in their "character paintings" (*shuhua*). A more recent trend in mainland China, exemplified by earlier work of the avant-garde artists Xu Bing (b. 1955) and Gu Wenda (b. 1956), has been to incorporate characters in installation art. In utter contrast to the work of the older generation of modern Chinese artists, some of Xu's most celebrated pieces turn the very notion of comprehension and meaning upside down by employing fabricated, nonsensical characters. However, the application of writing in one's art does not necessarily qualify the art as calligraphy, and much of this recent work should be considered in a different context. As for the more traditional approach, it remains remarkably popular in China today and shows little, if any, sign of decline. Perhaps the best indication of its attraction and resilience is the fact that Mao Zedong, the country's greatest advocate for doing away with the old, was a proud practitioner of epistle-style calligraphy.

**SEE ALSO** *Epigraphic School of Art (jinshi xuepai); Gu Wenda; Xu Bing.*

### BIBLIOGRAPHY

Bai, Qianshen. Chinese Calligraphy in the Mid to Late Qing and Republican Periods (1850–1950). In *New Songs on Ancient Tunes: 19th–20th Century Chinese Paintings and Calligraphy from the Richard Fabian Collection*, ed. Stephen Little, 66–79. Honolulu: Honolulu Academy of Arts, 2007.

Barrass, Gordon. *The Art of Calligraphy in Modern China.* Berkeley: University of California Press, 2002.

Chang, Joseph, Thomas Lawton, and Stephen D. Allee. *Brushing the Past: Later Chinese Calligraphy from the Gift of Robert Hatfield Ellsworth.* Washington, DC: Freer Gallery of Art, Smithsonian Institution, 2000.

Ellsworth, Robert Hatfield. *Later Chinese Painting and Calligraphy.* 3 vols. New York: Random House, 1987.

Krauss, Richard Curt. *Brushes with Power: Modern Politics and the Chinese Art of Calligraphy.* Berkeley: University of California Press, 1991.

Kuo, Jason, and Peter Sturman, eds. *Double Beauty: Qing Dynasty Couplets from the Lechangzai Xuan Collection.* Hong Kong: Xianggang Zhongwen Daxue Wenwu Guan, 2003. English and Chinese. Chinese title given as *Hebi lianzhu: Lechangzai Xuan cang Qingdai yinglian.*

***Peter C. Sturman***

# CAN XUE

## *1953–*

Known by the penname Can Xue ("dirty leftover snow"), Deng Xiaohua was born on May 13, 1953, in Changsha city, Hunan Province. Her father, lead editor at the *Xin Hunan bao* (New Hunan Daily), was condemned as an ultrarightist in 1957, and thereafter the whole family of nine lived in poverty. A few years later, Can Xue's maternal grandmother, whose imaginative mind and rustic rituals the writer later cited as an important influence, died of starvation. Can Xue's education was interrupted in 1966 by the Cultural Revolution, shortly after she finished primary school. She worked as an ironworker and then an assembler in a neighborhood factory for ten years. After the Cultural Revolution, she married a local carpenter in 1978 and gave birth to a son the following year. She and her husband then started a successful tailoring shop. Can Xue began writing fiction seriously in 1983 and published her first story in 1985. Her fame reached its peak in China in the late 1980s.

Can Xue was the only woman among the avant-garde writers of the mid-1980s, and her work then was uniquely innovative. Young writers at that time, fed up with the dominant socialist realist mode of fiction, were experimenting with new ways to express their thoughts through literature. Western modernism served as a catalyst in the new literary trend, and Can Xue has been particularly inspired by Franz Kafka and Jorge Luis Borges. She considers Kafka a "writer of the human soul," and she has been determined to be a Chinese Kafka exploring the unconscious terrain of the human mind.

Can Xue's fiction is a challenge to readers. Though the sentences are not difficult, the narrative is often puzzling and yet strangely fascinating. To enter her fictional world is to experience nightmarish encounters: Everywhere are prying eyes, distrust, nausea, and filth, often in what seems a surreal incoherence. In Can Xue's fiction, things seem to happen randomly, and the narrative itself is often without clear logical connection. Reading her works requires effort, as with many other modernist writings, but the very existence of a voice like hers opened up a refreshing new space for the contemporary Chinese literary scene and became a vital part of the avant-garde moment of the late 1980s.

Although Can Xue insists that her main concern is to portray the unconscious rather than to make any political point, her early works can be seen as allegorical explorations of the police state. For example, the story "Huangni jie" (Yellow Mud Street, 1986) portrays a cancer-prone dysfunctional society whose citizens behave like animals, and of whose lower bodily functions we hear a good deal more than we might like. Arguably, "Yellow Mud Street" is a parable about China, "yellow" referring partly to the imperial color, and "mud" hinting partly at the agricultural tradition. The fictional society is full of suffering, both emotional and physical, and all quests to escape the suffering are futile.

Since 1990, most of the 1980s avant-garde Chinese writers have moved in new literary directions, usually curbing their early flamboyance to attend more realistically to the lives of ordinary people. Can Xue has been highly critical of these changes. In her own writing she has maintained her schizophrenic and paranoiac narrative technique and not significantly changed her themes. This continuity is defensible, as her writings reflect contemporary feelings of insecurity, confusion, disillusionment, and distrust.

The reception of Can Xue's works has been varied. But her historical importance is generally acknowledged, and her works have been translated widely into various languages.

**SEE ALSO** *Avant-garde Fiction.*

**BIBLIOGRAPHY**

Can Xue. *Dialogues in Paradise.* Trans. Ronald R. Janssen and Jian Zhang. Evanston, IL: Northwestern University Press, 1989.

Can Xue. *Old Floating Cloud: Two Novellas.* Trans. Ronald R. Janssen and Jian Zhang. Evanston, IL: Northwestern University Press, 1991.

Can Xue. *The Embroidered Shoes: Stories.* Trans. Ronald R. Janssen and Jian Zhang. New York: Henry Holt, 1997.

Can Xue. *Blue Light in the Sky and Other Stories.* Trans. Karen Gernant and Zeping Chen. New York: New Directions, 2006.

Can Xue. *Five Spice Street.* Trans. Karen Gernant and Zeping Chen. New Haven, CT, and London: Yale University Press, 2009.

***Jingyuan Zhang***

# CANTON

**SEE** *Guangzhou (Canton).*

# CANTONESE

The word *Canton* derives from the name of the province of Guangdong, but it has long been used in English to refer to the province's capital city, Guangzhou. Inconsistently, *Cantonese* is frequently used to describe anyone or anything from the whole province, though there is great diversity of languages, customs, and lifestyles there, and the term is also applied to parts of neighboring Guangxi province where live many people of similar speech and lifestyle.

## THE YUE LANGUAGES

The various Cantonese languages are not all mutually intelligible, but they have enough in common to be classified together as the Yue group, and are spoken by over forty million people in Guangdong and Guangxi. There are also substantial numbers of speakers of Hakka and Min dialects as well as non-Chinese languages in these provinces. Because of the predominance of Guangdong as an emigrant region in the nineteenth and twentieth centuries, one or another form of Cantonese became the lingua franca of many (but not all) overseas Chinese communities. Chinese living in North America, for instance, spoke versions of the Four Counties (*siyi*) variety, while in parts of Malaysia, Fiji, and northern Europe, the language of Guangzhou and the more easterly areas around the Pearl River Delta was used. Recent emigrant waves from Taiwan and mainland China are likely to swamp this pattern with the universalized Mandarin (*putonghua*) language.

## STANDARD CANTONESE

The language of the city of Guangzhou is generally considered to be standard Cantonese. It uses seven tones arranged in three pitches: a high-level and a high-falling tone; a mid-rising and a mid-level tone; and a low-falling, a low-rising, and a low-level tone. All syllables carry more or less equal stress, and even the common function words, such as subordinating and final particles, carry full tone.

The majority of syllables end in vowels, and the only full consonants found in final position are *–n*, *–m* and *–ng*. However, in a survival of the old "entering tone" (*rusheng*), some syllables end with *–p*, *–t*, or *–k*: These endings are stopped (without aspiration or voicing), effectively shortening the length of the syllable rather than having full consonant value.

The grammar of the language is for the most part identical with that of Mandarin, with the principal exceptions that in Cantonese the direct object usually precedes the indirect object; the classifiers (words indicating the type of noun that is to follow a number or a specifying word such as *this* or *each*) may be used both to indicate the possessive and as definite articles in sentence-initial position; and the particle *ma* is not normally used to form questions. There are considerably more classifiers used in Cantonese than in Mandarin, and the number of final particles (one, two, or three syllables long) is also much greater.

In vocabulary, items have been retained that have long passed out of spoken Mandarin. But while retention of ancient vocabulary is a significant feature, it has not prevented Cantonese speakers from devising new terms or from happily accepting words from other languages. The result is an extremely rich blend of registers and a colorful depth of word power and expressiveness.

## HONG KONG CANTONESE

Nowadays, the very similar language of urban Hong Kong offers an alternative standard, largely because of the importance of Hong Kong as a channel for migration and international trade, combined with its success in creating and popularizing a strong cultural image in the realms of film and popular music. Differences from the language of Guangzhou include a far greater borrowing from English, the merging of the high-level and high-falling tones, and a rapid advance of what is known as "lazy mouth" (*lan kou*), the three most noticeable instances of which are the dropping of the initial *ng–* consonant, the replacing of initial *n–* by initial *l–*, and the change from initial *gw–* to initial *g–*.

## WRITTEN CANTONESE

Of the Chinese languages, Cantonese is almost alone in having developed its own set of written characters. These represent vernacular words for which there are no equivalents in standard written Chinese. For instance, the standard negative indicator *bu* 不 is understood in Cantonese and pronounced *bat*, but the most common word for *not* in colloquial speech is pronounced as a vowelless hum (*m*), and the character 唔 is used to represent this. There are several hundred of these special Cantonese characters, some of them not found in standard Chinese, and others borrowed from standard Chinese but used in meanings unknown to it. They have no official standing and are subject to variation at the whim of the writer. Although they have a long history, they have not been held in high regard by the literati, and have been used mainly for representing the colloquial language in novels, cartoon speech bubbles, poetry, and opera scripts, while more esoterically they have been exploited by translators of the Bible and by pornographers. In recent years, in Hong Kong at least, their use has increased in advertisements and tabloid newspapers.

## CANTONESE PEOPLE

The Cantonese are distinguished by their speech, the delicacy of their cuisine, which accentuates the natural flavors of the ingredients, their liveliness and noisy enjoyment of life, their business acumen, and their love of gambling. Their gregariousness appears in their strong sense of family unity, which finds its developed form in huge clan settlements, where hundreds and even tens of thousands of kin of the same surname live together. It shows too in the secret societies of sworn blood brothers that have dominated the criminal world.

Referring to themselves as "men of Tang" (*tang ren*), the Cantonese identify with the glories of the Tang dynasty (618–907). They call their language "the speech of Tang" (*tang hua*), and it is a fact that Tang poetry sounds best when recited in modern Cantonese. The man in the Guangzhou street is proud to be Cantonese, to be different. He is apt to tell you that he is Chinese and speaks Chinese, and that anyone from elsewhere in China is just an "outside-the-province person" (*shengwai ren*) who speaks "Shanghainese" (*shanghai hua*).

**SEE ALSO** *Chinese Overseas.*

**BIBLIOGRAPHY**

Hutton, Christopher, and Kingsley Bolton. *A Dictionary of Cantonese Slang: The Language of Hong Kong Movies, Street Gangs, and City Life*. London: Hurst, 2005.

Matthews, Stephen, and Virginia Yip. *Cantonese: A Comprehensive Grammar*. London and New York: Routledge, 1994.

Snow, Don. *Cantonese as Written Language: The Growth of a Written Chinese Vernacular*. Hong Kong: Hong Kong University Press, 2004.

***Hugh D. R. Baker***

## CAO YU

### *1910–1996*

Cao Yu (Ts'ao Yü), the most celebrated dramatist of the Republican era, was born Wan Jiabao and took the pen name Cao Yu, an anagram of his surname Wan. Since his most famous spoken dramas center on crises within elite families, his early life has attracted attention. He was the son of a failed, reclusive official and a mother who died shortly after giving birth to him. Growing up in Beijing and Tianjin, Cao Yu was taken to Peking Opera and early adaptations of Western theater known as "civilized drama" (*wenming xi*), which made a strong impression on him. Once enrolled in Nankai preparatory school, Cao Yu took an active interest in Western literature and spoken drama, so that even though he entered Nankai University as a student in political science, he soon transferred to Tsinghua (Qinghua) University to study Western languages and literature, where he took courses with Professor Wang Wenxian (James Quincy Wong), who had recently studied with George Pierce Baker at Yale University.

### DEPICTING REPUBLICAN DECAY

By graduation Cao Yu had completed a draft of his first play, *Leiyu* (*Thunderstorm*), published in 1934. Inspired by aspects of the realist plays of Henrick Ibsen and John Galsworthy and the classical tragedy of Jean Racine, *Thunderstorm* presents an elderly North China industrialist whose philandering as a patriarch is meant to suggest the worst of traditional culture and whose attitude toward workers proffers exploitive capitalism. While one son by a former mistress organizes worker strikes, another son by the patriarch's first marriage pursues the mistress's daughter, and he in turn is pursued by the patriarch's young second wife. The play thus suggests that the legacy of the Chinese elite is the collapse of the ideals of morality and filial piety. Amateur performances of *Thunderstorm* in 1934 attracted the attention of the commercial theater company Zhongguo Lüxing Jutuan (China Traveling Dramatic Company), which staged a popular production that brought much public attention to spoken drama and to Cao Yu's work.

Cao Yu continued his explorations of intimate life, foregrounding the decay of the social elite against a backdrop of purposeful struggle of the common people in *Richu* (1936; *Sunrise*) and *Yuanye* (1937; *The Wilderness*). *Sunrise*, which owes a debt to Anton Chekhov's art of indirection in *Three Sisters*, presents a naive young intellectual's futile attempt to rescue a suicidal film actress turned nightclub hostess and a teenage prostitute, all in the shadow of a patron constructing a high-rise building. In *The Wilderness*, which builds on Eugene O'Neill's expressionistic experiment *The Emperor Jones*, a peasant imprisoned on the false charges of a landlord escapes to take revenge on the landlord's family and reclaim his own former bride, only to discover that his individual challenge to his unjust fate is in vain.

Cao Yu's success led in 1936 to an appointment at the newly founded Guoli Xiju Zhuanke Xuexiao (National Academy of Dramatic Arts) in Nanjing, where he married Zheng Xiu, who had studied law at Tsinghua University and was the daughter of a justice of the Supreme Court. After the outbreak of the Anti-Japanese War (1937–1945), the academy was relocated to Jiang'an, a small Sichuan community on the Yangzi River, where Cao Yu continued to write on themes of domestic drama. There he wrote *Beijingren* (1940; *Peking Man*) and an adaptation of Ba Jin's novel *Jia* (*Family,* 1941). *Peking Man*, often regarded as Cao Yu's greatest critical success, blends an expressionistic presentation of the prehistoric hominid Peking Man as a symbol of vitality with a Chekhovian portrait of an extended gentry family sinking into bankruptcy, dominated by an aging patriarch facing death, with younger members struggling between succumbing to a superfluous existence or striking out to find new lives. Also drawn to patriotic propaganda, Cao Yu coauthored *Quanmin zongdongyuan* (Total Mobilization, 1939) with Song Zhidi and turned domestic drama to patriotic dedication in *Tuibian* (Metamorphosis, 1940). The latter portrays a woman physician overcoming mismanagement of a hospital, then faced with returning her wounded son to duty. Cao Yu also took time to adapt the Mexican American Josephina Niggli's *Red Velvet Goat* into the comedy *Zhengzai xiang* (Just Now Thinking, 1940) and to translate *Romeo and Juliet*.

Cao Yu's dissatisfaction with the National Academy of Dramatic Arts and dismay with Nationalist leadership grew during the war. He resigned from the National Academy in 1942 and moved to Chongqing, the interior wartime capital and a center of theatrical production, where a number of his plays were staged. Cao Yu edited the journal *Xiju yuekan* (Drama Monthly) and attempted unsuccessfully to write historical plays. Although Communist critics faulted much of his work, leaders such as Zhou Enlai increasingly recognized his value as an artist and social critic and showed solicitude for his career. After several unproductive years, this induced Cao Yu to turn to a frequent Communist theme of intellectuals frustrated by official corruption, in his play *Qiao* (The Bridge, 1945). This play portrays dedicated civil engineers stymied in their attempts to fulfill needed modernization projects by profiteering financiers and officials. In 1946 Cao Yu accepted a U.S. State Department-sponsored visit to the United States to raise American interest in modern Chinese theater and funds for its development, but he was soured by U.S. policies in China and abandoned his development plan, returning to China to write and direct the film *Yanyang tian* (Sunny Sky, 1947), which pits an idealistic lawyer against a corrupt merchant over the fate of an orphanage.

## TRAVAILS UNDER SOCIALISM

During these years Cao Yu grew estranged from Zheng Xiu, and after the founding of the People's Republic, obtained a divorce in 1950, following which he married his longtime acquaintance Fang Rui (Deng Yisheng), who, he wrote, had inspired the character of the heroine Sufang in *Peking Man*. Accepting criticism of his past failures to adopt Mao Zedong Thought and undertaking self-criticism of the ideological shortcomings of his work, Cao Yu was also appointed to numerous prestigious positions, ranging from vice president of the Zhongyang Xiju Xueyuan (Central Drama Academy, 1949), president of the Beijing Renmin Yishu Juyuan (Beijing People's Art Theater), and chairman of the Zhongguo Xijujia Xiehui (Chinese Dramatists Association, 1952) to member of the National People's Congress (1954–1964). His career as a playwright never fully recovered. Despite joining the Communist Party and receiving an award in 1956 for his play *Minglang de tian* (1954; *Bright Skies*), he had to accept criticisms for its limitations. Written in 1953 in support of resisting the United States and aiding Korea, and in opposition to germ warfare, the play depicts a Chinese scientist's thought reform, which leads him to reject an American agent's plan to enlist him in developing germ warfare.

In 1961 Cao Yu offered his first completed historical play, *Dan jian pian* (Gall and Sword), on the popular tale of the fifth century BCE in which King Goujian of the state of Yue, defeated by his rival King Fucha of Wu, is able to overthrow him after years of submission and patient planning. The focus of the play—the achievements of Goujian's advisors and his debt to their wisdom and dedication—suggested Cao Yu's concern for the role of intellectuals in Mao's unsettled administration. Although important colleagues praised Cao Yu's thoughtful treatment of the story, Maoist critics, such as Yao Wenyuan, found Cao Yu's ideological position wanting. In 1966 Red Guards detained and interrogated Cao Yu, and in 1968 they denounced him as a reactionary writer, arguing that in the play King Goujian's overcoming King Fucha represented Chiang Kai-shek's overcoming Mao Zedong. Cao Yu was assigned to clerical and custodial duties at the dormitories of the Beijing People's Art Theater, where he had been appointed president. In 1974 his second wife, Fang Rui, died of an apparent overdose of sleeping medication. In 1975 Cao Yu was restored to his membership in the National People's Congress and resumed his other appointments. In 1978 he published his final play, another historical drama, *Wang Zhaojun* (*The Consort of Peace*), which the late Premier Zhou Enlai had encouraged him to write. This play recounts the celebrated story of a Han dynasty (206 BCE–220 CE) imperial consort married to a Xiongnu prince. Cao Yu went against convention by depicting her as voluntarily entering into the marriage and thereby providing a historic model of reconciliation and solidarity among the Han ethnicity and ethnic minorities in the People's Republic in the wake of ethnic tensions during the preceding decade. Cao Yu married the former Peking Opera performer Li Yuru in 1979, traveled overseas, and continued to revise earlier editions of his plays for film adaptations and stage revivals.

**SEE ALSO** *Plays (huaju).*

**BIBLIOGRAPHY**

Eberstein, Bernd, ed. *A Selective Guide to Chinese Literature, 1900–1949.* Vol. 4: *The Drama.* Leiden, Netherlands: E. J. Brill, 1990.

Hu, John Y. H. *Ts'ao Yü.* New York: Twayne Publishers, 1972.

Lau, Jospeh S. M. *Ts'ao Yü: The Reluctant Disciple of Chekhov and O'Neill.* Hong Kong: Hong Kong University Press, 1970.

Tian Benxiang. *Cao Yu zhuan* [Biography of Cao Yu]. Beijing: Beijing Shiyue Wenyi Chubanshe, 1988.

***Edward Mansfield Gunn Jr.***

## CARSUN CHANG

SEE *Zhang Junmai (Carsun Chang).*

## CATHOLICISM

Catholics constitute about 1 percent of the Chinese population (roughly about 13 to 14 million people). They are disproportionately rural, although there are sizable Catholic communities in cities such as Shanghai and Beijing. Catholic communities are scattered throughout all of the provinces and autonomous regions of China, including Inner Mongolia and Tibet, and they are found among most of China's ethnic groups.

A typical pattern in rural areas is for entire villages or entire lineages to be Catholic. Under these circumstances, practice of the Catholic faith is intertwined with the whole range of local social, economic, and political life.

### SEVENTEENTH- AND EIGHTEENTH-CENTURY MISSIONARIES

The origins of the present-day Catholic Church in China go back to the work of Western missionaries in the seventeenth century. The leading missionary orders then were the Jesuits, Dominicans, Franciscans, and the Société des Missions Étrangères de Paris. Led by Matteo Ricci (1552–1610), the Jesuits attempted to convert the Chinese cultural and political elites. They dressed like scholar-officials, studied Chinese philosophy and art, and in turn taught their Chinese counterparts about the latest advances in Western science, as well as theology. They also allowed their Chinese converts to practice most of their traditional rituals and to maintain most of their customary way of life. The Jesuits found a receptive audience among late Ming reformist scholars. After the transition to the Qing dynasty, some Jesuits gained access to the imperial court, and one even served as a tutor to the Kangxi Emperor (1654–1722). In 1692 the Kangxi Emperor declared Catholic Christianity an "orthodox teaching," meaning that, along with the mainstream teachings of Confucius, Laozi, and the Buddha, it was to be protected and encouraged by the government.

In contrast, other missionary orders, such as the Dominicans, devoted their efforts to evangelizing at the grass roots, and they typically demanded that Catholic converts give up their traditional rituals and customs. Rivalries between the religious orders in Europe led to the bitter "Rites Controversy," with the Jesuits accused of compromising the Catholic faith by over-accommodating Chinese culture. In the end, the Jesuits lost. In 1704 Pope Clement XI condemned the Jesuit toleration of Chinese rites. In response, the Kangxi Emperor and his successors declared Christianity a "heterodox sect" and proscribed foreign missionary activity.

Although the condemnation of Chinese rites was lifted by Pope Pius XII in 1939, the effects of the Rites Controversy lingered. Denunciation of the Jesuit approach effectively terminated efforts to convert the ruling elite, and subsequent missionary activity focused mostly on peasants, producing the present-day concentration of Catholics in the countryside. Proscription of the Chinese rites led rural Catholics to mark their identity by practicing distinctive funeral rites. This has helped to maintain and reproduce Catholic identity over many generations. Even rural Catholics who are lukewarm in the faith—rarely going to church and failing to abide by Catholic moral teachings—have no choice but to be buried according to Catholic funeral rites if they want to remain connected in death to family and community. Thus a rural Catholic can leave the church only with great difficulty.

### THE NINETEENTH CENTURY

Catholic communities maintained themselves in the eighteenth century, even when they were declared heterodox, suffered some persecution, and were bereft of foreign missionary leaders. When foreign missionaries returned under the protection of Western imperialist powers after the Opium Wars of the nineteenth century, the communities established by the seventeenth century missionaries provided the foundation for new expansion. Conversions were fairly gradual, however. Even in the nineteenth century, much of the expansion of Catholicism can be accounted for by natural population increases rather than by new conversions.

Nineteenth-century missionaries faced obstacles from below as well as above. In the absence of priests, many Catholic communities had been led since the eighteenth century by generations of lay leaders, and sometimes these lay leaders resisted the efforts of newly arrived missionary priests to take charge. Meanwhile, the ruling elites resented the prerogatives of foreign missionaries, who had the military protection of the French government (which often used Chinese attacks against missionaries as an excuse to extend their military power further into Chinese territory) and who enjoyed the benefits of extraterritoriality. Furthermore, the local neighbors of rural Catholics resented the Catholics' refusal to pay for and to participate in traditional rural fairs and community festivals.

Such tensions formed part of the background that led to the antimissionary riots that began in 1860 and reached a peak in the Boxer Uprising of 1899 to 1900, which resulted in violent attacks against Catholic as well as Protestant communities and the murders of hundreds of priests, nuns, and laypeople. The Western powers responded to antiforeign attacks by sending to Beijing an "eight nation army" that suppressed the rebellion and imposed heavy indemnities on the Qing government. This display of power seems to have led to a spurt of new conversions to the Catholic Church.

***A Catholic woman at confession, Taiyuan, Shanxi province, April 7, 2006.*** *Catholic missionaries first arrived in China during the seventeenth century, establishing a Christian presence in rural areas and among the ruling elite. Despite being banned in the eighteenth century, attacked during nationalist rebellions in the late nineteenth century, and persecuted by the Communist government in the twentieth century, the Catholic Church remains a small but enduring presence in China.* © REINHARD KRAUSE/REUTERS/CORBIS

## THE TWENTIETH CENTURY

In the first half of the twentieth century the Catholic Church gradually distanced itself from its imperialist patrons. In the nineteenth century French military protection of the Chinese Catholic Church had been combined with French control over the administration of the Church. The Vatican was eager to break this control, and was able to do so after France had been weakened by World War I. In 1919 Pope Benedict XV warned missionaries against being too tied to the cultures and politics of their home countries, and urged them to learn local languages and cultivate local leaders for the Church. In 1926 Pope Pius XI personally ordained the first group of six Chinese bishops. Until after World War II, however, the Catholic Church in China was still led mostly by foreign missionary bishops under the direct jurisdiction of Propaganda Fidei, the Vatican office for missionary work. Finally in 1946, the Vatican removed the Chinese Catholic Church from the jurisdiction of Propaganda Fidei and gave it the status of a national church, under the formal jurisdiction of a native hierarchy. A majority of its bishops, however, were still foreign. With the Communist victory in 1949, all of the foreign bishops and foreign missionaries were expelled and the leadership of the Catholic Church was completely in Chinese hands.

In the 1950s the Chinese Communist Party steadily worked to bring the Catholic Church under its control. This was in line with the party's efforts to bring all autonomous social organizations under its political control. Despite its relatively small size—about three million adherents in 1949—the Catholic Church was particularly threatening to the party because of its legacies of imperialism and its connections with a foreign power, the Vatican, which was led by a resolutely anti-Communist pope, Pope Pius XII.

The Communist government imprisoned many bishops and priests who dared to oppose it, including the archbishop of Shanghai, Gong Pinmei (1901–2000). In 1957 the government set up the Patriotic Catholic Association to supervise and control the Catholic Church. The Vatican declared that Chinese Catholics should not cooperate with the association. Nonetheless, the Chinese authorities found several bishops who were willing to cooperate, and in defiance of Vatican authority, these bishops consecrated several new bishops. Most ordinary Catholics, however, shunned those bishops who seemed to be collaborators with the Communist-led government. For its part, the government closed most churches and greatly restricted public worship.

During the Cultural Revolution (1966–1969) the persecution of the Catholic Church reached new extremes. All churches were closed, and even Catholic bishops and priests who had joined the Catholic Patriotic Association were denounced and often imprisoned. With the beginning of the Reform Era in 1979, restrictions were gradually loosened. Churches were repaired and reopened and some confiscated property was returned to the Catholic Church. Public church activity, however, still had to be supervised by the Catholic Patriotic Association. In particular, the appointment of new bishops had to be approved by leaders of the association (who were ultimately responsible to the United Front Work Department of the Chinese Communist Party).

Although the government was more flexible in allowing Catholic leaders to decide on their own liturgical and theological matters, many Chinese Catholics still found these arrangements unacceptable. Meanwhile, a parallel leadership structure of the Catholic Church emerged, with the encouragement of the 1978 Vatican directive that gave considerable leeway to "underground" Catholic bishops to train priests and appoint successors without the supervision usually required by the Vatican bureaucracy. Probably about two-thirds of the lay members of the Chinese Catholic Church worship in venues that have not been approved by Chinese government authorities and follow the authority of bishops who are not approved by the Catholic Patriotic Association and government authorities, but claim allegiance to the Vatican. This situation sometimes causes serious divisions within the Chinese Catholic Church, which are exacerbated by the intertwining of the Catholic faith with local rivalries based on lineage and community interests.

The divisions have occurred in a context of ambiguity. Perhaps 90 percent of the bishops officially registered with and approved by Chinese government agencies have also been quietly approved by the Vatican. At the same time, some "underground" bishops are acting independently in ways that the Vatican would not approve.

In 2007 Pope Benedict XVI issued a letter attempting to reconcile divisions within the Catholic Church. He suspended the special faculties given to underground bishops: Now they, too, have to seek direct Vatican approval for their work (although in the absence of any formal relationship between the Vatican and the Chinese government, this approval has to be gained through informal channels). The pope also laid out guidelines for cooperation in worship and pastoral work between officially registered and unregistered Catholic communities. But there is enough ambiguity in the pope's letter and enough historical mistrust and animosity among church factions that some divisions within the Chinese Catholic Church persist.

**SEE ALSO** *Boxer Uprising; Missionaries; Protestantism; Three-Self Patriotic Movement.*

**BIBLIOGRAPHY**

Ladany, Laszlo. *The Catholic Church in China.* New York: Freedom House, 1987.

Madsen, Richard. *China's Catholics: Tragedy and Hope in an Emerging Civil Society.* Berkeley: University of California Press, 1998.

St. Sure, Donald F., and Ray R. Noll. *One Hundred Documents Concerning the Chinese Rites Controversy (1645–1941).* San Francisco: University of San Francisco, Ricci Institute for Chinese-Western Cultural History, 1992.

Tang, Edmond, and Jean-Paul Wiest, eds. *The Catholic Church in Modern China.* Maryknoll, NY: Orbis Books, 1993.

***Richard Madsen***

## CENSORSHIP

Censorship is a constant factor in the development of Chinese media and culture. Before 1949, rulers of the Qing dynasty (1644–1912), as well as warlords and the Guomindang government during the Republican era (1912–1949), all exercised authoritarian control over dissident content in the public domain, from journalism to literary activities to performing arts. The founding of the People's Republic was more than a historical continuation of this trend, as the Communist Party institutionalized its censorship regime on the basis of Leninist principles, which forbade private ownership of press organizations and restricted the role of mass media to being the mouthpiece of the authorities. Owing to rapid media commercialization and the internationalization of the overall cultural market since 1978, the propagandist function of cultural activities has been diluted (Zhao 1998). But this dilution of the propagandist function does not mean a decline of censorship. Whereas in certain areas, such as content production, there are signs of the retreat of censors, in the regulatory, bureaucratic, and technological aspects of censorship, as well as in major censorship cases, evidence is even stronger for the greater scope of censorship, manipulation by more types of censors, and growing sophistication in control efforts (Chan and Qiu 2001).

At the top of the censorship structure is the Communist Party's Central Propaganda Division, which has not only direct power over media and cultural organizations but also indirect control through various government agencies, such as the Ministry of Culture, the State Administration of Radio, Film, and Television, and the General Administration of Press and Publication. Since the late 1980s, the functioning of these state regulatory bodies has been strengthened along increasingly technocratic lines toward the goal of "rule by law." Though this is quite different from a rule of law that would restrict the behaviors of censors, it nevertheless marks a change in the censorship agenda, which used to be dominated solely by ideologues in the Central Propaganda Division (Polumbaum 1994).

The transition from ideological censorship to technocratic censorship finds its best expression through the many government regulations that have appeared since the 1990s. In 1997 the Ministry of Culture issued its Regulatory Measures for Foreign-Related Cultural, Art, and Exhibition Activities (Shewai Wenhua Yishu Biaoyan ji Zhanlan Guanli Guiding), which targeted artistic activities involving foreign partners. In the same year, the State Council passed the Regulatory Measures for Radio and Television (Guangbo Dianshi Guanli Tiaoli), which

***Animated figures of "virtual police officers" from the Beijing Public Security Bureau, August 28, 2007.*** *In 2007, the Beijing Public Security Bureau announced plans to remind Chinese users of the Internet to stay away from material considered objectionable by the Chinese government. Cartoon characters as shown in the photo above will appear on a user's screen with a warning to only view permissible Web sites.* AP IMAGES

prohibits seven types of content, for example, content that jeopardizes national unity. In 2003 the State Administration of Radio, Film, and Television promulgated its Temporary Regulations for Permission of Film Production, Distribution, and Exhibition (Dianying Zhipian, Faxing, Fangying Jingying Zige Zhunru Zanxing Guiding). In 2007 the Central Propaganda Division, the State Administration of Radio, Film, and Television, and the General Administration of Press and Publication jointly issued the Implementation Plan for the Management of Radio and Audiovisual Journalists (Guangbo Yingshi Xinwen Caibian Renyuan Congye Guanli de Shishi Fang'an).

Internet censorship is another rapidly expanding realm of government involvement. In 2000 alone, six regulations were issued to reduce the degree of freedom previously enjoyed by Internet content providers, electronic bulletin-board systems, and chatroom services. This was followed by restrictive measures designed to control bloggers, online gamers, and the transmission of audiovisual materials through Internet channels. Besides devotion of state administrative resources, Internet censorship is unique also in that it has led to the materialization of a considerable technological structure, known as the Great Firewall of China, the largest such effort in the world (Deibert et al. 2008). Private information-technology companies, including Chinese firms and transnational corporations such as Cisco, have actively participated in the construction of the Great Firewall by providing technical and personnel assistance to the censorship regime.

A consequence of this expanding social control is the emergence of major censorship cases that periodically punctuate the contemporary history of media and culture. One such incident, which led to an angry outburst among journalists and intellectuals in April and May of 1989, was the dispute surrounding *Shijie jingji daobao* (World Economic Herald) in Shanghai, in which its editor-in-chief Qin Benli was removed from his job due to his role in the 1989 movement. Another indication of the continued rule of the censors was the suspension of *Bingdian* (Freezing Point), an award-winning weekly publication by *Zhongguo qingnian bao* (China Youth Daily), and the removal of its editor-in-chief Li Datong in 2006 as a penalty for his audacity in discussing controversial topics in the newspaper. Another example can be seen in the banning of *Lingren wangshi* (Past Stories of Peking Opera Stars) and seven other books by Zhang Yihe since 2006 because the author excavated historic relics of the unflattering past of the Communist Party and forcefully criticized the problematic reality of China today.

Although censors have been largely successful in controlling politically incorrect print publications, banned authors and journalists like Li Datong and Zhang Yihe have moved onto the Internet in ways their predecessors like Qin Benli could not have dreamed of. The cat-and-mouse game between censors and dissidents is such a constant dialectic in the history of China's media and political culture that it is defining freedom of expression in China as well.

**SEE ALSO** *Art, Policy on, since 1949.*

**BIBLIOGRAPHY**

Chan, J. M., and J. L. Qiu. Media Liberalization in China. In *Media Reform: Democratizing the Media, Democratizing the State*, ed. Monroe Price, Beata Rozumilowicz, and Stefaan Verhulst, 27–46. London: Routledge, 2001.

Deibert, Ronald, John Palfrey, Rafal Rohozinski, and Jonathan Zittrain, eds. *Access Denied: The Practice and Policy of Global Internet Filtering.* Cambridge, MA: MIT Press, 2008.

Polumbaum, Judy. Striving for Predictability: The Bureaucratization of Media Management in China. In *China's Media, Media's China*, ed. Chin-Chuan Lee, 113–128. Bolder, CO: Westview Press, 1994.

Zhao, Yuezhi. *Media, Market, and Democracy in China: Between the Party Line and the Bottom Line.* Urbana: University of Illinois Press, 1998.

*Jack Linchuan Qiu*

## CENTRAL ASIAN STATES, RELATIONS WITH

China has been increasingly active in Central Asia since the independence of the Central Asian states in 1991. The region is strategically significant to China in many respects, and as such Central Asia occupies an important position in China's foreign policy. China is arguably now the second most important actor in Central Asia after Russia; this represents a notable departure from the situation in 1990, when China had virtually no contact nor trade with the region. Indeed, the success of China's policy toward Central Asia has been considerable and arguably very positive. As a result, there are no open conflicts between China and the Central Asian states, as many of the border conflicts have been resolved, and economic, political, and military cooperation has served to create stronger relations between China and the states of the region. China has also made a move to increase its soft power by promoting the Chinese language and culture, as well as by attracting Central Asian students to China. This has been facilitated by overlapping interests between the Central Asian states and China.

### TRADE AND ENERGY

The Chinese government has been successfully engaged in efforts to increase trade with the Central Asian states. According to data from international financial institutions and the Central Asian republics, the value of trade is lower than Chinese estimates, but it nevertheless represents an

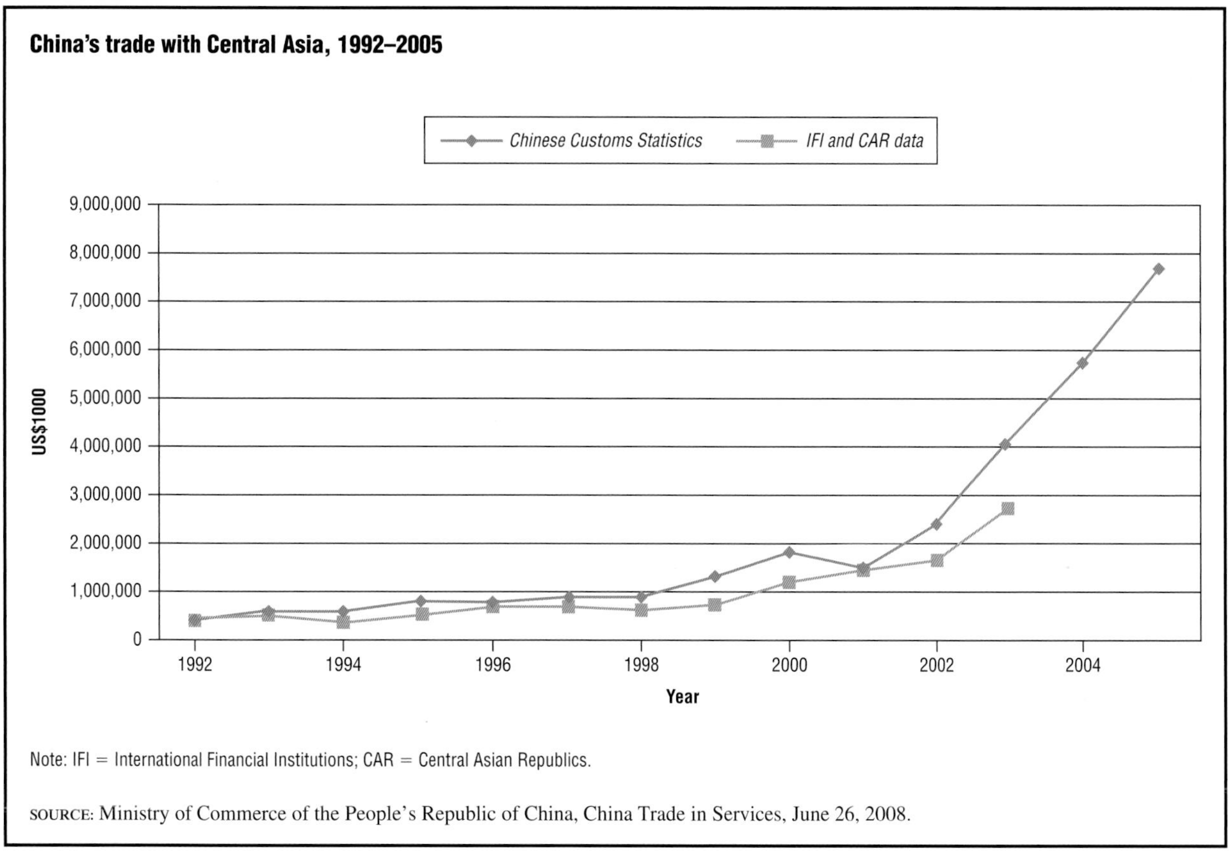


*Figure 1*

impressive increase (see Figure 1). Apart from an increase in overall trade volume, the Chinese government has initiated a strategy to increase trade from the western provinces of China. Xinjiang and China's western provinces account for most of the increase in trade between China and Central Asia, with Xinjiang's trade alone amounting to 80 percent of the total. These estimates do not include the informal economy and illegal trade that are increasing at a much quicker pace than the legal economy.

The relatively underdeveloped state of the Central Asian economies has hampered the further development of trade. Moreover, the lack of infrastructure between China and the Central Asian states has also been a negative factor. To minimize this deficit, China has invested significant resources in not only improving infrastructure, but also to a certain extent in building a stronger economy in Central Asia so as to create a stronger trading partner that can also facilitate its trade with Europe. The construction of a proposed transport corridor through Central Asia to Iran and Europe will enhance the importance of Central Asia, as much of Sino-European trade could be redrawn through Central Asia rather than through the longer and more expensive sea route to great economic benefit—which would also serve to integrate greater Central Asia, Iran, and India. While Central Asia fulfils a function as a trading partner for China, its main potential is found in its transit value for Chinese goods to other markets. Chinese investments in infrastructure will guarantee long-term Chinese influence in the region and increase Central Asian dependency on China.

The energy sector, on the other hand, has developed as the single most important sector, outside of the security sphere. China has increased its demand for external energy resources because its own domestic production is in decline. Central Asia has become an important, albeit still a small, segment of the energy strategy of China. Trade with Central Asia plays a strategically significant role for China's energy strategy in the sense that it will decrease the dependence on sea-lanes, but also reduce the significance of the Middle East for energy imports. Important investments initiated in the late 1990s onward have aimed therefore at creating alternative options; however, the trade with Central Asia remains only a small percentage of China's total energy imports. Notwithstanding this, China has aggressively bought up oil and gas fields in the region, often at a high price, indicating that there is a broader interest behind the acquisitions, namely, economic and political control over resources and development.

## SECURITY

The single most important aspect of China's foreign policy toward Central Asia is its security concerns. This entails internal security and border security, as well as ensuring the stability and security of Central Asia. Many of China's security concerns have centered on the spread of separatism, extremism, and terrorism in Xinjiang. China has taken harsh measures against its minority population in Xinjiang through its strike-hard campaign (*yanda*)—this despite relatively little evidence that Uygur separatism and terrorism are actually so great a problem as has been portrayed. The increased trade with Central Asia aims partly at reducing the social tension that exists in Xinjiang today, but also in Central Asia. China has demanded assistance from the Central Asian states in combating Uygur groups that operate from Central Asia. Cooperation in fighting groups of this kind has been far reaching, and joint training exercises, as well as exchanges of information, have attained a level of significance. Collaboration in this area has proven successful in large part because of the interest from Central Asian states in controlling their own opposition groups.

As a result of China's fear of separatism, border security has been an important factor, especially in the light of the terrorist threat, but increasingly also in the case of organized crime and, in particular, the heroin trade, which originates from Afghanistan and is directed through Central Asia to Xinjiang and China. China has thus realized that its western border is insecure and difficult to monitor, with most narcotics arriving through Central Asia.

Apart from China's own security, the Central Asian states' internal security has emerged as an important factor for China. This is because it is much in the interest of China to stabilize the governments of the region, and to reduce the tension in Central Asia. Policies are designed to reduce conflict along China's own border, but also to keep likeminded governments in power in Central Asia. Despite China's reluctance to engage in other states' internal affairs, it has proven supportive in keeping accordant regimes in power, especially in neighboring states.

China has refrained from making Islam an issue in the bilateral relations, much due to the importance that Central Asia has for China but also because China does not want to alienate itself from the Muslim neighbors and its trading partners in the Muslim world.

## SHANGHAI COOPERATION ORGANIZATION

The Shanghai Cooperation Organization (SCO), established in 2001, has emerged as the primary instrument of China in its multilateral contacts with the Central Asian states. During the early days of the organization, it was the main mechanism through which China handled its border disputes with the Central Asian states and combated the "three evils" (terrorism, extremism, and separatism). The functions of the organization have evolved to include direct military and economic cooperation. The SCO is still weak, however, and is undermined by the weakness of the Central Asian states and the emerging power struggle with Russia. Nevertheless, its importance should not be underestimated.

## COMPETING INTERESTS WITH RUSSIA AND THE UNITED STATES

China's encroachment into Central Asia has not gone unnoticed by the other major powers in the world, especially Russia and the United States. Following the breakup of the Soviet Union, Russia is the actor that has lost most influence in the region, due in large part to its own inability after 1991 to sustain its influence, and also because China's strategy has partially supplanted Russia in the region, which has seen a relative and absolute increase in Chinese influence and trade.

Latent Sino-Russian tensions aside, of note has been America's seemingly waning influence in the region. With the war on terror and the U.S. invasion of Afghanistan, American influence in Central Asia did, for a short while, increase significantly—to the concern of both China and Russia. After U.S. criticism of the Uzbek government's involvement in the Andijon incident in 2005, however, American influence has decreased significantly, due also in part to pressure from Russia and China. This loss of influence has served to consolidate China's growing foothold in the region. Apart from its engagement in the security sector, therefore, there has been little U.S. impact, and the long-term scenario would suggest a power struggle primarily between Chinese and Russian interests. Already China has directly challenged Russian energy interests in Turkmenistan and Kazakhstan.

**SEE ALSO** *Drugs and Narcotics; Islam; Russia, Relations with; Sino-Soviet Schism; United States, Relations with.*

### BIBLIOGRAPHY

Burles, Mark. *Chinese Policy Toward Russia and the Central Asian Republics*. Santa Monica, CA: Rand, 1999.

Huang Jinhao (Huang Chin-Hao). China and the Shanghai Cooperation Organization: Post-Summit Analysis and Implications for the United States. *China and Eurasia Quarterly* 4 (2006): 15–21.

Liao Xuanli. Central Asia and China's Energy Security. *China and Eurasia Quarterly* 4 (2006): 61–70.

Linn, Johannes F. Central Asia: National Interests and Regional Prospects. *China and Eurasia Quarterly* 5 (2007): 5–12.

Swanström, Niklas. China and Central Asia: A New Great Game or Traditional Vassal Relations. *Journal of Contemporary China* 14, 45 (2005): 569–584.

Swanström, Niklas. China's Role in Central Asia: Soft and Hard Power. *Global Dialogue* 9 (2007): 1–2.

***Niklas L. P. Swanström***

# CENTRAL PLANNING

The term *central planning* refers to a system of economic coordination that relies on directed allocation of all goods, resources, capital, and labor using one integrated national plan that balances supply and demand for all items. Typically, as in China, plans are differentiated into annual plans, five-year plans, and long-term plans. A national authority, such as China's State Planning Commission, is responsible for drafting and implementing the plans, which are executed by different sectoral and regional units—that is, the different ministries on the central level, as well as the provinces and local administrations. In China, the dualism of sectoral organization and central coordination was replicated at the different levels of regional administration, with planning commissions at the provincial and lower levels.

Central planning was considered essential for the transition to socialism by Marxist theorists. It was considered more efficient than market systems because the administrative equilibration of supply and demand could prevent economic fluctuations and underutilization of resources, especially unemployment. According to Marxist theory, a precondition for setting up central planning is a high level of industrial development and concentration of market power, because coordination between large-scale organizations could be smoothly implemented once the capitalist class structure was destroyed by socialist revolution and public ownership was installed.

Full-fledged approaches to central planning were mainly pursued in the Soviet Union, some Eastern European countries (notably, the German Democratic Republic), and other Communist countries, such as Cuba. Several countries in Eastern Europe (e.g., Hungary) moved to mixed approaches after the 1960s. These mixed systems served as benchmarks for China's early efforts at central-planning reform in the 1980s. With the breakdown of the Eastern European socialist systems, central planning was quickly abandoned worldwide, so that today only a few cases, such as North Korea, remain as practical examples. In practice, central planning was closely connected to goals of national mobilization, such as the Stalinist war economy (corresponding to the introduction of central planning in Nazi Germany) or economic development via "big push" industrialization, as occurred in India.

## THE CELLULAR COMMAND ECONOMY IN CHINA

After 1949, the preconditions for central planning did not exist in China because the country was moving to a public-ownership regime on a very low level of economic development. This was clearly recognized by the Chinese Communist Party, which therefore opted for a mixed system under the auspices of the "new democracy" in the early years of the People's Republic of China. Under the influence of the Soviet Union, however, there was a rapid move toward advanced central planning in the mid-1950s, mainly as a means to implement a strategy of heavy industrialization with a limited number of core projects.

To understand the Chinese system that subsequently emerged, it is important to distinguish between the centrally planned economy and the command economy. A centrally planned economy encompasses all economic transactions in a country, based on quantitative ("material") plans with a high degree of disaggregation and precision. Financial indicators and money flows are instruments of plan control and accounting, but do not play an active role in the economy. By contrast, the command economy does not necessarily build on comprehensive planning, as long as larger parts of the economy remain self-sufficient and demonetized. This situation, known as a *cellular economy*, characterized the Maoist era. Following the ideal of self-reliance (*zili gengsheng*) pursued in external relations, China imposed a relatively high degree of economic autarchy on lower-level administrative units. This was further enhanced by repressing the use of money to a degree unfamiliar to the Soviet model. In particular, China implemented a system of coupons in the consumption-goods sector, corresponding to the abandonment of monetary incentives in the labor system.

The cellular economy reflected one of the strategic aims of decentralization in Maoist thinking, namely, to safeguard regional and sectoral production systems in the case of a foreign invasion by minimizing economic interdependencies. This strategy also helped to cushion the system against major political disturbances, especially the Cultural Revolution, because spillovers among different production subsystems were minimal. However, cellularization does not necessarily imply weak central control. The foremost example is foreign trade and investment and the foreign-exchange regime. Central planning achieved almost total control of all flows of trade and currencies across the national border. Between 1960 and 1978, this resulted in a decoupling of the Chinese economy from the world economy and crucially supported the autarchic Maoist policy.

Another distinctive feature of the Chinese system in contrast to the Soviet system relates to incentive structures. Central planning always faces the problem that economic agents hide information and minimize effort. Therefore,

**Industrial enterprises under central control, 1953–1983**

| | Centrally controlled industrial enterprises (A) | State-owned industrial enterprises (B) | (A) / (B), % (estimated corresponding output share in brackets) |
|---|---|---|---|
| 1953 | 2,800 | | |
| 1957 | 9,300 | 58,000 | 16,0 (39,7) |
| 1958 | 1,200 | 119,000 | 1,0 (13,8) |
| 1965 | 10,533 | 45,900 | 22,9 (42,2) |
| 1970 | 142 | 57,400 | 0,2 (8,0) |
| 1976 | 1,300 | 78,300 | 1,7 (n.a.) |
| 1983 | 2,500 | 87,100 | 2,8 (30–40) |

SOURCE: Ishihara Kyōichi. *China's Conversion to a Market Economy*. Tokyo: Institute of Developing Economies, 1993.

*Table 1*

planners need to implement elaborate mechanisms of control and incentivization. In the Chinese command economy, however, these mechanisms were mainly substituted by political mobilization and moral commitment. In campaigns such as in the Great Leap Forward, this resulted in a synchronization of investment into backyard furnaces, without any plan coordination. Therefore, upon closer inspection, central planning in China actually manifested two opposing principles, which were related to the two main factions in the political struggle—namely, the leftist Maoist forces and the administrators (mainly represented by Chen Yun), who basically followed the Soviet approach in conceptual if not in political terms. The first principle, which may be dubbed the "command economy by mobilization," is rooted in the Yan'an traditions of the Chinese Communist Party. The second principle is "command economy by bureaucracy."

## ADMINISTRATIVE PRACTICE AND PROCESS

The cellular command economy consists of spatial units that are close to self-sufficient, especially the rural people's communes, and of industrial branches and large-scale state-owned enterprises (SOEs) that are likewise nearly self-sufficient. A typical large Chinese SOE was a huge vertically integrated unit with few upstream or downstream relations to other units. Central planning only encompasses interunit relations, and therefore does not penetrate the entire economy. Economic development in China until the 1990s was characterized by cyclical changes to this system, which oscillated between more-centralized planning processes in times of economic recovery (such as after the Great Leap Forward) and reconstruction and far-reaching decentralization in times of Maoist radicalization (as in the wake of the Cultural Revolution). Decentralization did not imply that market forces were strengthened, but that larger economic units were assigned to lower administrative levels.

Central planning requires a comprehensive national statistical system, which simply did not exist in China until the 1980s. Using insufficient data and information, central-planning authorities concentrated on the most-essential goods and sectors, especially after the national disaster of the post–Great Leap famine, which was also caused by a total failure of statistics. For this purpose, goods and materials were divided into priority classes, with central planning prevailing for materials such as steel and essential consumption goods such as rice.

The Chinese planning system was deeply influenced by the regional system of administration that emerged after the establishment of the central-planning system in the 1950s. In most industries, enterprises on different regional levels coexisted, and were not integrated into one coherent plan. For example, the central plan covered the coal production of the central government and provincial government coal mines, but left local mines under the control of local authorities. Thus, total national coal production was allocated via different disconnected systems, the national and interregional central-planning system, and the local system. This situation was also reflected in the assigning of coal to the "commodity" (*wuzi*) category in the context of national and provincial planning and the "merchandise" (*shangpin*) category in the context of local production for household consumers. In many industries, such a fragmented administrative structure resulted in complicated relations among enterprises and different planning authorities. For example, even within the same city, enterprises with provincial and local affiliation would rarely come into direct contact with each other; when they did, it occurred only with the intermediation of higher-level units. This pattern continued until the early 1990s.

The most important means of integrating the cellular economy was the so-called *tiao-kuai* (lines and blocks) system and the corresponding distinction between directive and professional relations among administrative units. *Blocks* were regional units, such as provinces or cities, and *lines* were hierarchical administrative relations within the same administrative sector, such as banking or personnel. Within blocks, the command mode prevailed in the allocation of resources; between administrative units on different levels of blocks, the regulatory mode was dominant. Thus, a regional planning commission would direct the flows of commodities and goods within its jurisdiction (which overlapped spatially with jurisdictions of higher- and lower-level authorities), but would only receive directives regarding net inflows and outflows from higher levels, thus leaving much scope for the design of internal

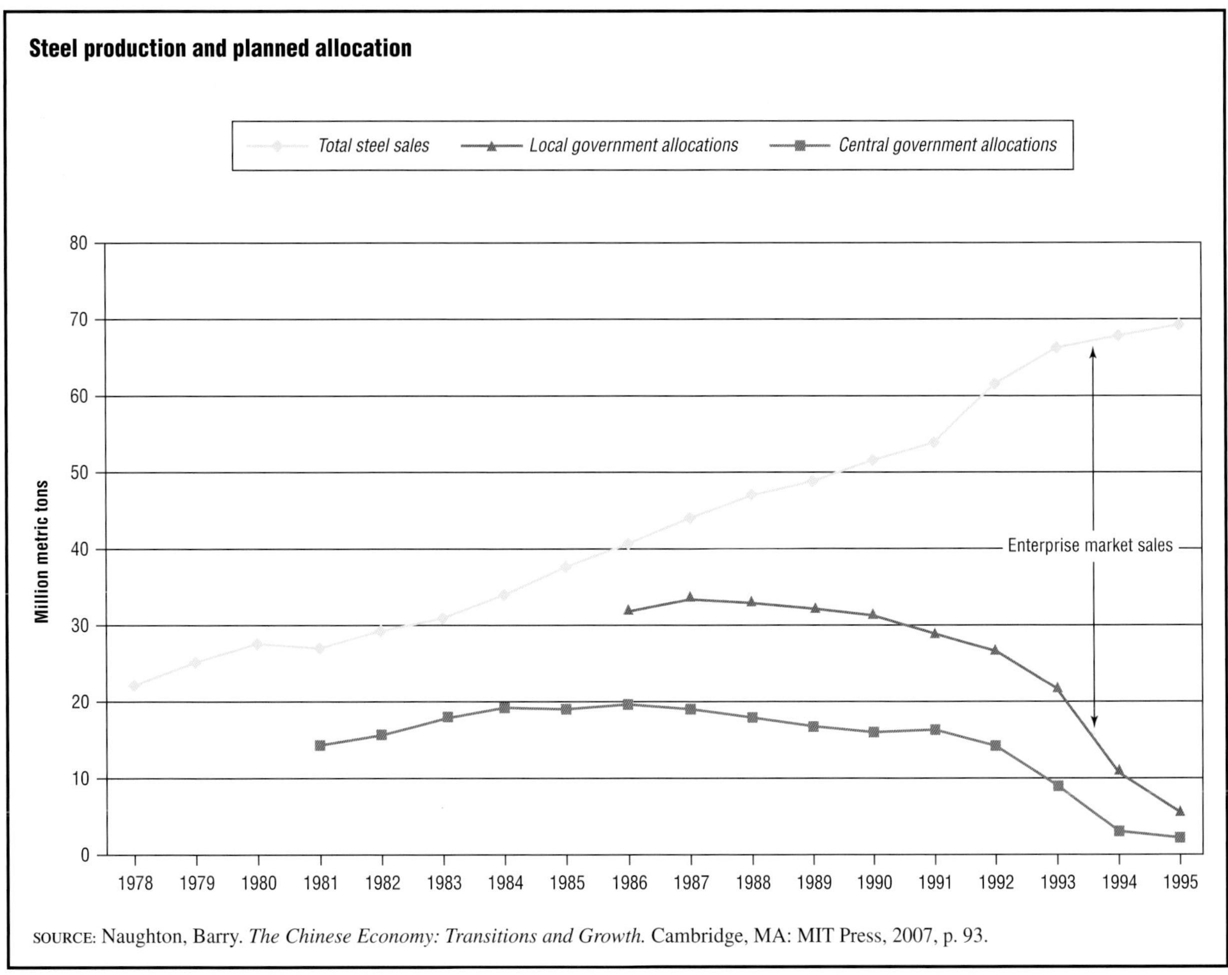


SOURCE: Naughton, Barry. *The Chinese Economy: Transitions and Growth.* Cambridge, MA: MIT Press, 2007, p. 93.

*Figure 1*

processes. At the same time, a regional planning commission would be subordinated to the professional regulations of the higher-level planning commission, regarding, for example, such factors as standards and statistics. The responsibility of higher levels included control of the *nomenklatura,* which also added party control to intergovernmental control.

An important feature of central planning is the use of distorted prices to pursue political aims in the economic system. An example in China is agricultural development and the strategy of forced industrialization. Central planning in agriculture crept into the system despite prevailing ideas in the early 1950s about a mixed-economy approach to maintaining rural markets. However, once depressed prices for rural commodities were imposed to foster industrial development, disincentives emerged for agricultural producers, with the final effect of motivating rural outmigration in the mid-1950s. Thus, establishing the commune system and imposing rigid production quotas were concomitant to adopting price controls as a tool of development policy. The Maoist policy of revolutionizing the countryside matched a rationale in the economic system.

One important implication of this system was the existence of slack in the economy, because the central plan rarely encompassed the entire production capacity. However, economic agents were, at the same time, prohibited from exploiting free capacities because of the suppression of market coordination. The rural communes were a case in point. Via central planning of essential goods such as cotton and rice, production quotas were set up that were obligatory for the regional authorities to fulfill. The suppression of rural markets blocked farmers from using spare working capacity for sideline production beyond self-consumption. In the 1970s, this underemployed labor was activated in the "rural-industrialization" drive, which was itself a reflection of certain dysfunctions of central planning, namely, the undersupply of the rural area with basic commodities (e.g., concrete) and consumption goods (e.g., textiles). This situation was in part responsible for the mobilization of local comparative advantages, which had been materializing in flourishing sideline activities in pre-Communist China, and later proved to be the starting point for the emergence of township and village enterprise (TVEs) in many places.

The oscillations in China's system of central planning were matched by contractions and expansions in subsidiary market sectors in the economy. Interestingly, the expansion of market coordination always accompanied periods of increase in administrative planning, because both were suppressed in Maoist policies. According to the radical leftists, one ideological justification for this was that both systems of coordination rely on financial indicators and money flows, thus presupposing an economically motivated agent. The radical leftists saw the danger of a capitalist resurgence in both the market and administrative central planning, which was a major departure from orthodox Soviet theory.

### TRANSITION FROM CENTRAL PLANNING TO THE MARKET ECONOMY

In the beginning, Chinese economic reforms after 1978 were a step toward both liberalization and centralization. This was possible because of the large scale of underutilized capacities in the economy. The lever that activated this capacity was dual-track pricing. The general strategy of economic reforms was simple: Opening up market relations beyond the scope of the central plan, thus pulling down the walls of the Chinese cellular economy. This was done in the agricultural sector first, and was gradually expanded to other sectors. Thus, even for essential commodities such as steel, the old dual system of central and local allocations was almost entirely substituted by market allocation in the mid-1990s.

Yet, the tools and organizations of central planning maintained an important role in the Chinese economy until the mid-1990s at least. Sometimes central planning was even strengthened, especially in times of economic crisis, such as after 1989. Planning serves a number of different objectives, such as securing the supplies for industrial core sectors and enterprises, maintaining discriminatory prices against market forces, and pushing politically motivated investment projects. One lever is the national credit plan, which, for example, allows for planning in the investment process.

However, with the promulgation of the "socialist market economy" in 1993, the ideal of comprehensive national planning was finally abandoned. This is most obvious from the transformation of one key institution of central planning, the five-year plan. Today, five-year plans are strategic-development plans, highlighting national priorities in investment or scheduling major steps in infrastructure development. These transformations were reflected in major organizational reforms. The State Planning Commission, which was established in 1952, was renamed the State Development Planning Commission in 1998, only to be merged with other high-ranking institutions to result in the National Development and Reform Commission in 2003.

**SEE ALSO** *Heavy Industry; Mao Zedong; Transport Infrastructure: Shipping since 1949.*

**BIBLIOGRAPHY**

Donnithorne, Audrey. *China's Economic System.* New York: Praeger, 1967.

Ishihara Kyōichi. *China's Conversion to a Market Economy.* Tokyo: Institute of Developing Economies, 1993.

Naughton, Barry. *The Chinese Economy: Transitions and Growth,* chaps. 3 and 4. Cambridge, MA: MIT Press, 2007.

***Carsten Herrmann-Pillath***

# CENTRAL STATE ORGANS SINCE 1949

*This entry contains the following:*



## OVERVIEW

Since the enactment of the 1954 constitution, the central state organs of the People's Republic of China have been organized along the Soviet model, with a few subsequent adaptations and a ten-year interruption during the decade of the Cultural Revolution (1966–1976). Like the Supreme Soviet in the now defunct Soviet Union, the National People's Congress (Quanguo Renmin Daibiao Dahui) is the supreme organ of state power. This means that all leading positions are formally elected by the National People's Congress or its Standing Committee: the state president (*guojia zhuxi*), the premier (*zongli*), the ministers (*buzhang*) and commission chairpersons (*weiyuanhui zhuren*) of the State Council (Guowu Yuan), members of the Supreme People's Court (Zuigao Renmin Fayuan), and members of the Supreme People's Procuratorate (Zuigao Renmin Jiancha Yuan). However, candidates to leading positions are all recommended by the Communist Party leadership, which by tradition proposes only one candidate to each position, and party leaders share these positions among themselves.

Between 1949 and 1954, the Chinese People's Political Consultative Conference (Zhongguo Renmin Zhengzhi Xieshang Huiyi) was the de facto parliament of the People's Republic. In 1949 it adopted a Common Program that was used as a constitution until 1954 and elected a two-tier government, the Central People's Government Council (Zhongyang Renmin Zhengfu Weiyuanhui), chaired by Mao Zedong, and the Administrative Affairs Council (Zhengwu Yuan), headed by Premier Zhou Enlai.

After 1954 the Chinese People's Political Consultative Conference was kept as a symbol of the united front between the Communist Party and the other political forces—the eight democratic parties, also represented in the conference—that had accepted to collaborate with and work under the leadership of the Communist Party. Its members (around 2,000 in 2008) are all recommended by the party.

In 1954 Mao Zedong became president of the People's Republic and was succeeded by Liu Shaoqi in this position in 1959. Zhou Enlai was appointed premier of the newly created State Council, and Liu Shaoqi chaired the National People's Congress. However, the Central Military Commission (Zhongyang Junshi Weiyuanhui), chaired by Mao until his death in 1976, remained purely a party institution, although the defense minister always sat in the State Council. The Supreme National Defense Council, which Mao chaired as head of state, was a symbolic advisory body.

The two constitutions promulgated in 1975 and in 1978 did not fundamentally change the organization of 1954. The state presidency was abolished. In 1975 the National People's Congress was clearly operating under the party leadership. And the Chinese People's Political Consultative Conference reappeared as an active body only in 1978.

In 1982 the fourth Constitution not only restored the institutions of the first one, such as the state presidency, but also incorporated what had until then been the party's Central Military Commission. Since March 1983 both commissions have had identical memberships.

The National People's Congress (with around 3,000 delegates) and the Chinese People's Political Consultative Conference meet only once a year, in early March for two weeks. This is called the two-assembly system. Since the early 1980s the Standing Committee of the National People's Congress (174 members since 2008) holds meetings every two months; most laws and appointments are voted on in these sessions. Only constitutional revisions, organic laws, and the most important nominations are approved by the plenary session of the National People's Congress. The top state leaders (president, premier, etc.) are usually elected in the first session of each National People's Congress, which since 1978 has taken place a few months after the latest party congress.

**BIBLIOGRAPHY**

*The Constitution of the People's Republic of China.* Beijing: Foreign Language Press, 1983. Also available at http://english.people.com.cn/constitution/constitution.html.

Saich, Tony. *Governance and Politics in China.* New York: Palgrave, 2001. See chap. 5.

Schurmann, Franz. *Ideology and Organization in Communist China.* Berkeley: University of California Press, 1968.

***Jean-Pierre Cabestan***

## CHINESE PEOPLE'S POLITICAL CONSULTATIVE CONFERENCE

From September 21–30, 1949, the eve of the foundation of the People's Republic of China, the Communist Party leadership decided to convene a Chinese People's Political Consultative Conference (CPPCC, Zhongguo Renmin Zhengzhi Xieshang Huiyi). This political gesture was aimed at demonstrating to Chinese society and the outside world that the Communist Party had succeeded in uniting the nation where the Guomindang (Nationalist Party) had failed. In 1946 the Guomindang had convened a similar conference, at which the Communist Party was represented, but this meeting was unable to mend relations between these two parties and prevent the civil war from resuming.

The CPPCC was thus a symbol of the united front (*tongyi zhanxian*) between the Communist Party and the other political forces opposed to the Guomindang regime. Inspired by both the Anti-Japanese War (1937–1945) and Stalin's establishment of people's democracies in Central and Eastern Europe, this assembly maintained a purported multiparty system. In the CPPCC, Communist Party delegates represented just 30 percent of the 585 delegates and had just 77 alternate members to the plenary session. The other delegates included famous personalities (such as Guo Moruo) and leaders of the eight small democratic parties that had split with the Guomindang (such as the Guomindang Revolutionary Committee, created in 1948) or that tried unsuccessfully before 1949 to constitute a third force between the two major Chinese

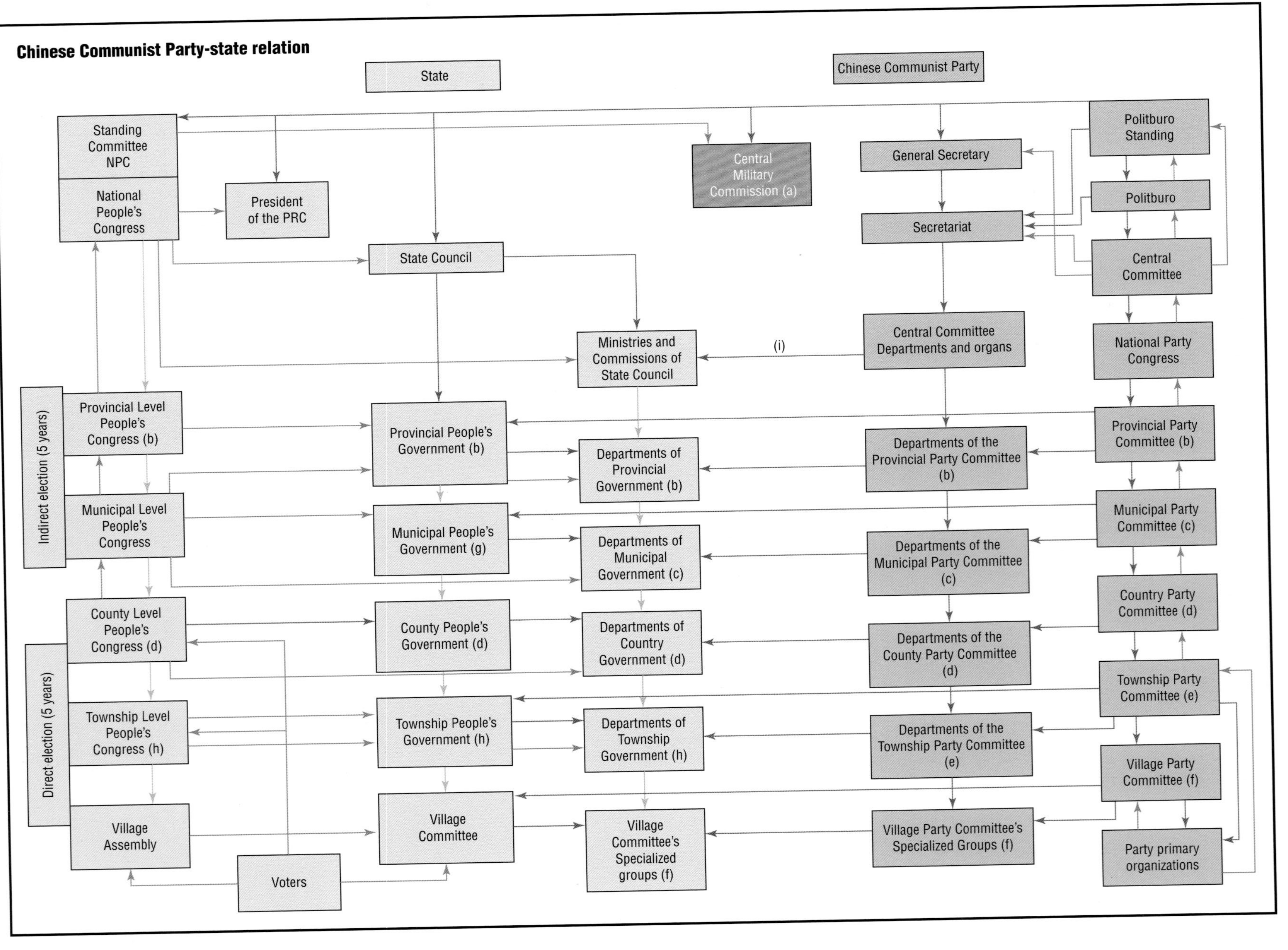
Chinese Communist Party-state relation
State
Chinese Communist Party
Standing Committee NPC
National People's Congress
President of the PRC
State Council
Central Military Commission (a)
General Secretary
Secretariat
Politburo Standing
Politburo
Central Committee
National Party Congress
Central Committee Departments and organs
(i)
Ministries and Commissions of State Council
Indirect election (5 years)
Provincial Level People's Congress (b)
Municipal Level People's Congress
Provincial People's Government (b)
Municipal People's Government (g)
Departments of Provincial Government (b)
Departments of Municipal Government (c)
Departments of the Provincial Party Committee (b)
Departments of the Municipal Party Committee (c)
Provincial Party Committee (b)
Municipal Party Committee (c)
Direct election (5 years)
County Level People's Congress (d)
Township Level People's Congress (h)
Village Assembly
County People's Government (d)
Township People's Government (h)
Village Committee
Departments of Country Government (d)
Departments of Township Government (h)
Village Committee's Specialized groups (f)
Departments of the County Party Committee (d)
Departments of the Township Party Committee (e)
Village Party Committee's Specialized Groups (f)
Country Party Committee (d)
Township Party Committee (e)
Village Party Committee (f)
Party primary organizations
Voters

*Table 1A*

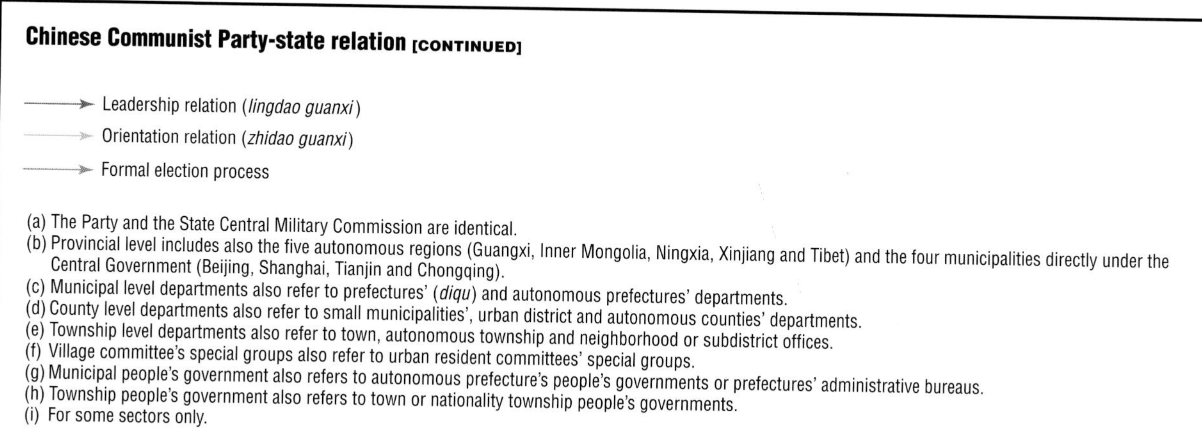


*Table 1B*

political forces (such as the China Democratic League, 1941). The six other democratic parties were the China Democratic National Construction Association (1945), the China Association for Promoting Democracy (1945), the Chinese Peasants and Workers Democratic Party (1930), the Public Interest Party (Zhigong Dang, 1925), the September 3 Society (1944), and the Taiwan Democratic Self-Government League (1947). In 1949 all these parties and famous personalities that had accepted a seat in the CPPCC had accepted Communist Party leadership in politics and over their activities.

In 1949 the first CPPCC, chaired by Mao Zedong, the Communist Party chairman, formally appointed a two-tier government: the Central People's Government Council (Zhongyang Renmin Zhengfu Weiyuanhui), also chaired by Mao Zedong, and the Government Administrative Council (Zhengwu Yuan), headed by Premier Zhou Enlai. It also adopted a Common Program, which served as a de facto constitution until 1954. But the CPPCC's power and responsibilities were highly symbolic and its activities remained tightly controlled by the Communist Party. Provincial and subprovincial CPPCCs were also set up, operating along the same lines.

Acting as a constitutional and national assembly in the first years of the People's Republic, the CPPCC in 1954 was replaced in this role by the newly created National People's Congress, which then adopted the country's first genuine Constitution. Chaired now by Zhou Enlai (who would keep this position until the Cultural Revolution in 1966), the second CPPCC was maintained as a symbol of the united front between the Communist Party and the other political forces.

The CPPCC's activities and raison d'être started to be questioned as early as 1957, during the Hundred Flowers Movement, in which several democratic parties' figures dared to criticize the Communist Party's and Mao's heavy-handedness. In the subsequent anti-rightist movement, some of these leaders (such as Zhang Bojun) were purged, and the democratic parties (which had 100,000 members in 1957, in contrast to 20,000 in 1949) were marginalized. The CPPCC's National Committee (with 1,119 members in 1965) continued to convene every five years, but it was frozen as an institution as soon as the Cultural Revolution (1966–1969) broke out.

The CPPCC was restored and convened its fifth National Committee meeting (with 1,989 members) in March 1978. Chaired by Deng Xiaoping, it contributed to rehabilitating many persecuted intellectuals and political figures, in particular those from the democratic parties, which were also resurrected at the time. And between 1978 and 1982, provincial-, municipal-, and county-level CPPCCs were also gradually restored.

Since then the activities of the CPPCC have stabilized. Elected for five years, as recommended by the Communist Party, and meeting every year in March in Beijing at the same time as the National People's Congress, its National Committee (with 2,237 members at the eleventh conference convened in March 2008) remains a political photograph of China's ethnic, entrepreneurial, scientific, intellectual, and artistic elites. Communist Party members continue to comprise around one-third of its members. Leaders of the eight democratic parties (with around 500,000 members today) sit in larger numbers than before in this assembly.

Since 2002 the CPPCC has been chaired by Jia Qinglin, number four in the Communist Party leadership. The director of the Communist Party United Front Department (Du Qinglin since 2002) partakes ex officio in the CPPCC leadership and conducts its annual sessions and the bimonthly meetings of its Standing Committee (298 members).

The CPPCC actively submits many suggestions and ideas to the government. For instance, between 2003 and 2008 it "handled over 23,000 proposals, compiled over 100 reports on inspection tours, submitted over 270 survey and research reports, organized 4,000 session speeches and provided over 6,600 reports on social conditions and popular sentiment." Nevertheless, the CPPCC has not demonstrated its influence on the Communist Party leadership. Increasingly business-oriented, its members use this assembly as a club to make contacts or enhance their status.

#### BIBLIOGRAPHY

CPPCC Web site. http://www.cppcc.gov.cn/English/news/.

Groot, Gerry. *Managing Transitions: The Chinese Communist Party, United Front Work, Corporatism, and Hegemony.* New York: Taylor and Francis, 2004.

Seymour, James D. *China's Satellite Parties.* Armonk, NY: M. E. Sharpe, 1987.

***Jean-Pierre Cabestan***

## NATIONAL PEOPLE'S CONGRESS

Since the enactment of the first Constitution of the Peoples' Republic of China in 1954, the National People's Congress (NPC, Quanguo Renmin Daibiao Dahui) has officially been the country's supreme organ of state power. However, like the Supreme Soviet in the defunct Soviet Union, the NPC works under the leadership of the Chinese Communist Party. Although its role has expanded, in particular in the legal field, since a new Constitution was promulgated in 1982, it does not enjoy the functions of a real parliament nor does it represent Chinese voters and citizens.

Between 1954 and 1966 the NPC met regularly and endorsed Communist Party decisions and drafts according to constitutional procedures. Chaired by Liu Shaoqi, then number two in the Communist Party, the first NPC was already a very large assembly (1,226 delegates). While the second NPC (1959) kept the same size, the third one (1965) doubled the membership (3,040). The NPC, chaired by Marshal Zhu De after 1959, started to become less active, however, and after the outbreak of the Cultural Revolution (1966–1969), it in fact ceased to operate for nine years (1966–1975).

The radical leaders promoted by Mao Zedong after 1966 drafted a new Constitution, which was promulgated in 1975 by the fourth NPC (2,885 delegates). Clearly stipulating that the NPC worked under Communist Party leadership, this Constitution was replaced three years later by a third Constitution, which somewhat restored the role that the NPC played in the 1950s (the fifth NPC having 3,497 delegates). However, only the 1982 Constitution was bold enough to boost the status of the NPC beyond that in the 1954 model.

### MEMBERSHIP

The NPC (with fewer than 3,000 delegates after 1983) is the summit of a pyramid of people's congresses elected directly by voters at the township and, since 1979, county levels, and indirectly by lower-level people's congresses at the municipal, provincial, and national levels. Since 1979 candidates for the NPC, generally recommended by the Communist Party, must number 33 percent more (20% for indirect elections) than the number of seats available. Although ten citizens can propose an independent candidate, direct elections are tightly managed by the Communist Party. And indirect elections, in particular, of the NPC, do not leave much room for uncertainty. Most NPC deputies are cadres or intellectuals. Workers and farmers comprised less than 20 percent of delegates in 2003. More than two-thirds of delegates are Communist Party members. A few are people involved in the nonpublic economy (133 in 2003, versus 48 in 1998). Though membership composition of the eleventh NPC, convened in March 2008, was not fully published, 360 of the 2,987 delegates came from ethnic minorities, 265 from the military, and 3 were migrant workers.

Elected for five years, the NPC meets every year in March in Beijing for around two weeks. Its Standing Committee (174 members since 2008) meets on a bimonthly basis and can perform most NPC functions. It is the genuine power locus of the NPC.

### FUNCTIONS

Since 1982 the NPC has performed all the functions it had in the 1950s and some new ones: It approves laws, constitutional revisions, the annual state budget, and the activity reports submitted by the State Council, the Supreme People's Court, and the Supreme People's Procuratorate. It also formally elects the state president and vice president, the premier, the chairman of the Central Military Commission, the president of the Supreme People's Court, and the procurator general; and on the recommendations of the four latter leaders respectively, it elects the ministers or commission chairpersons of the State Council and the members of the Central Military Commission, the Supreme People's Court, and the Supreme People's Procuratorate.

Nevertheless, the NPC, being so large, is too unwieldy to exercise much power. For instance, it is not provided with an itemized state budget that it can really scrutinize. It is mainly a forum offered to local officials to make known their problems and grievances.

## POWER

Many of the NPC's functions are performed by its Standing Committee. Only constitutional revisions, organic laws, and the most important nominations must be approved by the NPC plenary session. Of course, the NPC plenary session can express its mood by electing a state leader with relatively low tallies (10%–20% opposition), as was the case with Zeng Qinghong in 2002. It also approved with a mediocre majority some work reports (for instance, that of the Supreme People's Procuratorate in 1998). But it has never opposed a law, a promotion, or a report.

The Standing Committee has demonstrated more autonomy. For instance, in 1986 it opposed the Bankruptcy Law proposed by the reformists, and in 2000 it vetoed the government's Highway Bill, expressing the financial interests of localities opposed to the abolition of the toll system.

Chaired by number two of the Communist Party leadership since 1997 (Wu Bangguo since 2002), the NPC leadership consists of fifteen vice chairmen, including the secretary general. Most of them are former ministers. Members of the Standing Committee considerably overlap (around 70%) the membership of the nine NPC specialized committees: those for ethnic minorities; law; finance and economic affairs; education, science, culture, and health; foreign affairs; overseas Chinese; civil and judicial affairs; environment and resource protection; and agriculture and rural affairs.

More influential is the permanent bureaucracy of the NPC, in particular the Legislative Work Committee (Falü Gongzuo Weiyuanhui) and Budgetary Work Committee (Yusuan Gongzuo Weiyuanhui, created in 1999), both permanent organs of the NPC Standing Committee that take a more active part in drafting or budgetary work. But over 70 percent of all bills remain submitted by the State Council and not by the NPC. And the state budget has never been challenged by the legislature's leadership.

Since the promulgation of the Legislation Law (Lifa Fa) in 2000, the NPC has established burgeoning control of the legality of local regulations. However, it has neither the staff nor, more importantly, the enforcement power to annul illegal local regulations.

### BIBLIOGRAPHY

Cabestan, Jean-Pierre. More Power to the People's Congresses? Parliaments and Parliamentarism in the People's Republic of China. *Asien*, no. 99 (April 2006): 42–69.

Cabestan, Jean-Pierre. The Relationship between the National People's Congress and the State Council in the People's Republic of China: A Few Checks but No Balances. *American Asian Review* 19, 3 (Fall 2001): 35–73.

O'Brien, Kevin. *Reform without Liberalization: China's National People's Congress and the Politics of Institutional Change*. New York: Cambridge University Press, 1990.

Tanner, Murray Scot. *The Politics of Lawmaking in Post-Mao China: Institutions, Processes, and Democratic Prospects*. Oxford: Oxford University Press, 1998.

***Jean-Pierre Cabestan***

# PRESIDENT AND VICE PRESIDENT

The positions of president and vice president were created in 1954 by the first Constitution of the People's Republic of China. These prestigious titles do not convey powers stemming from direct or indirect popular election. Although the president and vice president are formally elected by the National People's Congress, their powers stem from the positions that these officeholders occupy in the Chinese Communist Party.

Interestingly, to differentiate these titles from the ones defined by the 1946 Constitution of the Republic of China, the Chinese terms chosen in 1954 were not *zongtong* and *fuzongtong* (the usual translations of *president* and *vice president*) but *zhuxi* and *fuzhuxi*, which correspond to *chairman* and *vice chairman*. When elected president, Mao Zedong had been chairman of the Communist Party (*dang zhuxi*) since 1945. The president had two particular competences that Mao used occasionally: summoning supreme state conferences and chairing the Supreme National Defense Council. In 1959, tired of the formal obligations attached to this position (such as the accreditation of ambassadors), Mao retired and let Liu Shaoqi succeed him. However, Mao remained Communist Party chairman until his death in 1976. From 1954 to 1959 the vice president was Marshal Zhu De, number four in the Communist Party. From 1959 to 1975 there were two vice presidents: Song Qinglin (Sun Yat-sen's widow) and Dong Biwu.

The fate of Mao's former right hand in the Cultural Revolution—Liu died in jail in 1969—led to the abolition of the state presidency. Mao's one-time designated successor Lin Biao tried in 1970 to restore it, but to no avail. In the 1975 and 1978 Constitutions, there was no president. The obligations of the head of state were then filled by the National People's Congress chairman, Zhu De and, after 1976, Ye Jianying.

The 1982 Constitution restored the positions of president and vice president. Since April 1983 both the president and vice president have been elected by the National People's Congress for five-year terms, renewable only once. Officially, any citizen who is at least forty-five years old and retains his political rights can run for election (Article 79). In reality, only the Communist Party can recommend candidates, and there have always been just one candidate for each position. To date, all presidents and vice presidents have been male.

From 1983 to 1993 the president and vice president were senior, rather conservative but retiring, Communist Party leaders. The first two presidents of the post-Mao era were Li Xiannian (1983–1988) and Yang Shangkun (1988–1993). The first two vice presidents were Liao Chengzhi (because of the sudden death of Ulanhu [Wulanfu]) and General Wang Zhen.

In March 1993, under the new institutional pattern called "three in one" (*san he yi*), Communist Party Secretary General and Central Military Commission Chairman Jiang Zemin was elected president. This arrangement, new to China, was inspired by the Soviet Constitution enacted under Leonid Brezhnev in 1977. Unclear or divided about the vice presidency, the Communist Party leadership then appointed the "red capitalist" Rong Yiren to this position. Later in 1998 Hu Jintao, selected by Deng Xiaoping himself to succeed Jiang and elevated in 1992 to the Communist Party Politburo Standing Committee, was elected vice president. A year later he was appointed vice chairman of the Central Military Commission. He remained in this position for another six years, although he was elected president in March 2003. Since March 2005 the three-in-one pattern has been restored. And in March 2003 Hu had to accept as vice president Zeng Qinghong, number five in the Communist Party leadership and a Jiang protégé. Although Zeng was never promoted to the Central Military Commission, he remained very influential until he retired in October 2007 from the Communist Party leadership and in March 2008 from the state vice presidency.

Since March 2008 the vice president has been Xi Jinping, number six in the party leadership and, for the first time, Hu Jintao's accepted successor, expected to succeed him as president in 2013 when Hu's second term ends.

The state president holds many formal powers: He promulgates laws; appoints the premier and the members of the State Council; declares amnesty, martial law, states of emergency, and mobilization for war; receives ambassadors' letters of accreditation; and ratifies treaties. Unlike their predecessors, Jiang and Hu have been able to utilize these powers to expand their influence. In March 2004 Hu introduced a constitutional amendment aimed at strengthening the state president's role. After the change, Article 81 explicitly stipulated that he "conducts state affairs." Although it might have no implications whatsoever, one can wonder whether Hu Jintao wanted, through this slight alteration, to enhance the prerogatives of the head of state, not only vis-à-vis the chairman of the Central Military Commission, who at the time was still Jiang Zemin, but also vis-à-vis the rest of the party leadership, in particular the Standing Committee of the Politburo, which in principle collectively makes most decisions, and to a lesser extend the premier.

In any case, it remains to be seen whether the state presidency in the future can be disconnected from the control of the Communist Party and, as in the Soviet Union under Mikhail Gorbachev, become a new powerbase.

The vice president does not enjoy any personal powers. He "assists the president in his work" (Article 82). Xi's election has initiated a new pattern, according to which the vice president is presumed to succeed the president. Nevertheless, again, this smooth transfer of power depends on the party, not the state.

**BIBLIOGRAPHY**

*The Constitution of the People's Republic of China*. Beijing: Foreign Language Press, 1983. Also available at http://english.people.com.cn/constitution/constitution.html.

Saich, Tony. *Governance and Politics in China*. New York: Palgrave, 2001. See chap. 5.

Zhu Guobin. *Zhongguo xianfa yu zhengzhi zhidu* [The Chinese constitution and political system]. 2nd ed. Beijing: Falü Chubanshe, 2006.

***Jean-Pierre Cabestan***

## STATE COUNCIL, COMMISSIONS, MINISTRIES, AND BUREAUS

Since 1954, according to the state Constitution, the State Council (Guowu Yuan) has been the "executive body of the highest organ of state power" (Article 85 of the 1982 Constitution), namely, the National People's Congress (Article 57). Though it is "the highest organ of state administration," the State Council directly reports to the Communist Party Politburo Standing Committee, the top leadership group to which the premier has constantly belonged. Between 1954 and 1966, the departments of the Communist Party Central Committee supervised the activities of the State Council in every area. However, since the Cultural Revolution (1966–1969), for domestic political reasons, only matters related to personnel, propaganda, security, and military affairs have remained under the control of Central Committee organs. Hence, in contrast to other Soviet-type regimes, the Chinese central government since the early 1970s has directly managed economic and social affairs, and to do so, it has elevated its numerous commissions, ministries, and bureaus into powerful vertical administrations, organized around major activities, such as agriculture, heavy industries, light industries, water conservancy, railways, etc.

The introduction of major economic reforms after 1978 has gradually but deeply changed the role and organization of the central and local governments, precipitating successive waves of restructuring and streamlining. But the separation of government and enterprises (*zhengqi fenkai*) initiated in 1997 has not totally forced the government out of management. The Communist Party's national development objectives and its desire to keep under its control the industries that it considers of strategic importance have impeded these attempts to simplify. Though smaller, the State Council remains a large and complex bureaucracy.

## EARLY STRUCTURE

Between 1949 and 1954, the People's Republic of China had a two-tier government: the Central People's Government Council (Zhongyang Renmin Zhengfu Weiyuanhui), chaired by Mao Zedong, and the Administrative Affairs Council (Zhengwu Yuan), headed by Premier Zhou Enlai. For instance, the State Planning Commission, established in 1952 and chaired by the powerful Gao Gang (purged in 1954), was directly under the former, while all ministries, including a few technical portfolios headed by non-Communist figures, were attached to the latter.

This complicated structure was replaced in 1954 by the State Council. Headed by Zhou Enlai until his death in 1976, this structure was then weaker than it is today. Formally, it was a large institution, including 10 vice premiers, and 40 ministers and commission chairpersons (in 1965, 16 and 55 respectively). And since most vice premiers were also Politburo members (such as Deng Xiaoping, Chen Yun for the economy, and Lin Biao and Peng Dehuai for the military) or Central Committee department heads (Deng Zihui for agriculture and Li Fuchun for planning), the State Council could also coordinate decisions. Nevertheless, key areas were supervised by Central Committee organs and the Secretariat, then controlled by Liu Shaoqi and Deng Xiaoping, Central Committee secretary general between 1956 and his purge in 1967.

## THE CULTURAL REVOLUTION

The Cultural Revolution led directly to the dismantling of the party apparatus, and in particular the Secretariat and departments of the Central Committee. The State Council survived with Zhou and Li Xiannian, finance minister, but many ministries disappeared, and others were taken over by the military. It was only after 1970 that the structure of the central government was gradually restored. And the first post-1966 State Council was not formally elected by the National People's Congress until 1975. It was a somewhat smaller government, with only 31 ministries and commissions (including two women), but its head was large and divided. There were a total of 12 vice premiers, including Deng Xiaoping and Zhang Chunqiao, one of the radicals promoted by Mao, and for the first time a woman. In January 1976 it was Hua Guofeng, former minister of Public Security, not Deng, who succeeded Zhou as premier.

## RESTRUCTURING

Thereafter the State Council rapidly expanded again as purged officials were rehabilitated. In 1978 it included 13 vice premiers (among them one woman, Chen Muhua) and 46 ministers and commission chairpersons (including another woman). And in 1980, even though Zhao Ziyang replaced Hua as premier and 7 old vice premiers retired (among them Deng Xiaoping and Chen Yun), there were 55 ministerial-level administrations and 51 bureaus. And each ministry included up to a dozen vice ministers.

This bloat convinced Deng to drastically streamline the State Council. In May 1982 the number of vice premiers fell to 2, and the number of ministries and commissions to 41. Only 18 of the 51 bureaus were kept. The number of vice ministers dropped by 82 percent (180 versus 1,000), and the State Council staff was cut by 35 percent (32,000 versus 49,000). However, a new position close to vice premier was then created: state councilor (*guowu weiyuan*), and ten senior officials were promoted to state councilors and continued to coordinate the major sectors of government activity. Moreover, because the State Council had continued to manage most of the economy, except agriculture, and at the same time took on new missions, the number of central ministries increased again. For instance, as early as August 1982, by merging various organizations that reported before to the military, a new commission was created: the Commission of Science, Technology, and Industry for National Defense. A year later, two new administrations were added to the government: the Ministry of State Security and the National Audit Office (*shenjishu*). Then in 1987 a Ministry of Supervision was created. Yet these changes did not increase the portion of women ministers, which stagnated around 3 percent.

Such bloating triggered repeated restructuring and simplification in 1988, 1993, 1997, 2003, and 2008. In 1988, a few months after Li Peng succeeded Zhao Ziyang as premier, State Council personnel was again cut, by 20 percent (from 50,000 to 40,000), and some ministries were successfully turned into national enterprises in the areas of oil, nuclear energy, textiles, and others. But ministries for other sectors, such as the coal industry, resisted change. And some, such as the Ministry of Railways, have avoided restructuring in spite of repeated attempts by Premier Zhu Rongji (in office from 1998 to 2003) and Premier Wen Jiabao (from 2003).

The State Council endorsed by the National People's Congress in March 2008 is on the whole much smaller and better adapted to the central government's new role. It includes only 25 organs (versus 40 in 1993 and 26 in 2003): 21 ministries, 2 commissions (the powerful National Development and Reform Commission and the State Ethnic Affairs Commission), the central bank (the People's Bank of China), and the National Audit Office. Deserving special mention are three new key ministries. The Ministry of Industry and Information has incorporated the project-approval functions of the National Development and Reform Commission and of the Commission of Science, Technology, and Industry for National Defense. The Ministry of Human Resources and Social Security not only manages labor affairs and public servants, but is also in charge of establishing a comprehensive social and health safety net for society. The new Ministry of Environmental Protection underscores the Communist Party's awareness of major air- and water-pollution problems.

### STRUCTURAL RELATIONSHIPS

Chaired by Wen Jiabao and meeting every week, the State Council Standing Committee still includes ten senior officials: four vice premiers (Li Keqiang, in charge of economic restructuring; Hui Liangyu, agriculture; Zhang Deqiang, industry; and Wang Qishan, banking and foreign economic and trade relations) and five state councilors (Liu Yandong, a woman, in charge of education, health, culture, and sports; Mai Kai, concurrently secretary general of the government; Dai Bingguo, foreign affairs; Men Jianzhu, public security and justice; and General Liang Guanglie, also defense minister, the military). In 2008 the Chinese cabinet still includes only three women: Liu Yandong, Justice Minister Wu Aiying, and Minister of Supervision Ma Wen.

The State Council administers economic and social affairs, but the party is also involved, since the party-state divide has little effect. For one, each ministry is controlled by a party group (*dangzu*), generally chaired by a minister. All vice premiers are Politburo members. Important financial and economic matters are coordinated and dealt with by a small group of party leaders (*caijing shiwu lingdao xiaozu*), chaired by the premier. A number of sectors are still supervised by Central Committee organs, including security (the Political and Legal Commission), personnel (the Organization Department), communication, censorship, education, and culture (the Propaganda Department), and the military (the Central Military Commission), or by groups of leaders (foreign policy, Taiwan, Hong Kong, and Macau).

The State Council is the summit of a pyramid, and its structure is duplicated at the four levels of local administration. Coordinate relationships (*kuaikuai*) among local Communist Party committees has always been stronger than the vertical authority (*tiaotiao*) of the government's functional bureaucracies. Hence, China's great devolution of state structure, which sometimes amount to "scattering" (*fensanzhuyi*), may have less effect on diminishing the State Council's power than appears at first glance, particularly in the provinces, which do not financially depend on Beijing.

### BIBLIOGRAPHY

Harding, Harry. *Organizing China: The Problem of Bureaucracy, 1949–1976*. Stanford, CA: Stanford University Press, 1981.

Lieberthal, Kenneth. *Governing China: From Revolution through Reform*. New York: W. W. Norton, 2004.

Saich, Tony. *Governance and Politics in China*. New York: Palgrave, 2001.

***Jean-Pierre Cabestan***

## CENTRAL MILITARY COMMISSION

The Central Military Commission (CMC, Zhongyang Junshi Weiyuanhui) was established as a state organ in March 1983, three months after the promulgation of the December 1982 Constitution. Before this, the CMC was purely a Communist Party organ and was referred to in English as the Military Affairs Commission of the Communist Party's Central Committee. Chaired by Mao Zedong from the Communist Party's Zunyi Conference (1935) to his death in 1976, it later continued to be controlled by the country's de jure or de facto paramount leader: Hua Guofeng from 1976 to 1981, Deng Xiaoping from 1981 to 1989, Jiang Zemin from 1989 to 2004, and Hu Jintao since 2004. Identical since March 1983, the party and state CMCs have remained the top leadership body of the People's Liberation Army.

### FORMALIZATION

What the 1982 Constitution did was to formally include as a central state organ this key and very secretive party organ, whose composition was seldom made public. Nevertheless, the power and the political legitimacy of the state CMC come from the Communist Party. The 1954 Constitution had established a National Defense Council chaired by the state president. But it remained an advisory body, rarely convened, and gradually ceased to function after Liu Shaoqi had replaced Mao Zedong as head of state in 1959.

## CHANGING COMPOSITION

In March 1983 the party CMC, appointed at the twelfth Communist Party Congress (September 1982) and chaired by Deng, was formally elected by the National People's Congress to become the first state CMC. Following the constitutional procedure, the National People's Congress first elected Deng, who then as CMC chairman nominated the CMC vice chairmen and members, who in turn were approved by the National People's Congress. All CMC members are elected for a renewable five-year term. The CMC chairman is responsible to the National People's Congress and its Standing Committee (Article 94 of the Constitution). While Deng was alive, the new system was not stable.

At the thirteenth Communist Party Congress, in November 1987, Deng had Zhao Ziyang, then general secretary of the Communist Party, appointed as the CMC's first vice chairman (*diyi fuzhuxi*), a nomination confirmed by the National People's Congress in March 1988. This position ranked ahead of standing vice chairman (*changwu fuzhuxi*), at the time Yang Shangkun, a clear indication that the paramount official in the Communist Party would eventually become commander in chief of the armed forces. However, the Tiananmen Prodemocracy Movement (June 1989) sealed Zhao's fate and revealed that ultimate political power was still controlled by semiretired Deng and other party elders, who then appointed Jiang Zemin as Zhao's successor. Learning from this difficult experience, Deng decided as early as November 1989 to promote Jiang Zemin to the post of party CMC chairman, and in April 1990 Jiang was formally elected state CMC chairman by the National People's Congress. Of course, at the time, the old military leaders Yang Shangkun (then also state president), Yang Baibing (his half brother), and Liu Huaqing (a navy admiral) still sat on the CMC. However, since 1987 the CMC had gradually become a purely military body, including, ex officio, the chiefs of the main army departments. Its chair was nearly the only civilian (until 1992, the only other civilian was Yang Shangkun, who was more a party leader than an army officer).

Three years later, after having successfully relaunched the economic reforms, Deng, at the fourteenth Party Congress (November 1992), consolidated this evolution—probably his last political initiative. He confirmed Jiang as Communist Party general secretary and CMC chairman, and decided to appoint him state president, creating a new institutional pattern called "three in one" (*san he yi*). These two latter appointments were confirmed by the National People's Congress in March 1993. To make Jiang's job easier, Deng forced the Yang brothers to retire and promoted younger military leaders to the CMC. Apart from Vice Chairmen Liu Huaqing and Zhang Zhen, the other CMC members were Defense Minister Chi Haotian, People's Liberation Army Chief of Staff Zhang Wannian, General Political Department Director Yu Yongbo, and General Logistics Department Director Fu Quanyou.

After Deng's retirement from politics in 1994 and death in 1997, Jiang managed to consolidate his grip on the CMC by promoting a large number of full generals (twenty-seven in 1994–1995) and reshuffling this leadership organ at the fifteenth Party Congress in 1997, when Admiral Liu and General Zhang retired. In 1998 the director of the newly formed General Armament Department, General Cao Gangchuan, joined the CMC—an indication of its professionalization.

State Vice President Hu Jintao's inclusion in the CMC in 1999 was more unexpected. By way of background, Hu was selected by Deng himself to succeed Jiang in 2002 and for this reason was promoted to the Party Politburo Standing Committee in 1992. He was included in the CMC to be familiarized with military affairs. This sequence of events created a new pattern in which China's paramount leader invites his designated or potential successor to sit on the CMC.

Yet his promotion had the effect of delaying Jiang's retirement. Hu succeeded Jiang as Communist Party general secretary in 2002 and as state president in March 2003 (state presidents can serve two five-year terms, but not CMC chairmen). However, Jiang clung to the party CMC chairmanship until September 2004 and to the state CMC chairmanship until March 2005. Ironically, it was the generals that he himself had promoted earlier (Chi Haotian and Zhang Wannian) who convinced Jiang to retire fully in 2004. Having to report to two leaders made the People's Liberation Army uncomfortable, and so could not continue for long.

In September 2004 Hu expanded the CMC from 8 to 11 members to also include commanders of the navy, air force, and second artillery (strategic and tactical nuclear forces), thus deepening the military nature of this body. At the seventeenth Party Congress in October 2007 and the eleventh National People's Congress in March 2008, this new format was confirmed. In 2008 the party and state CMC consist of two vice chairmen, Guo Boxiong and Xu Caihou, as well as the following eight members: Defense Minister Liang Guanglie, People's Liberation Army Chief of Staff Chen Bingde, General Political Department Director Li Ji'nai, General Logistics Department Director Liao Xilong, General Armament Department Director Chang Wanquan, Second Artillery Commander Jing Zhiyuan, Navy Commander Wu Shengli, and Air Force Commander Xu Qiliang. Hu will likely chair the CMC until he retires in

2012–2013. State Vice President Xi Jinping may join the CMC before then.

### INFLUENCE IN THE REFORM ERA

The party and state CMC deals mainly with purely military affairs, its political influence having diminished since the late 1980s. In 1998, for instance, it organized the withdrawal of the People's Liberation Army from business activities, a move ordered by the Communist Party leadership. And after the huge May 12, 2008, earthquake in Sichuan, the CMC played a key role in coordinating relief operations with the State Council. Of course, the CMC debates about and has a say on all foreign-policy and international matters that have a clear security dimension, in particular, border security and disputes, and relationships with Taiwan, the United States, Japan, and Russia. When an international crisis affecting China's security breaks out, CMC leaders or members are invited to join Politburo meetings enlarged by Communist Party leadership to help the top party leadership, and in particular the nine-member Politburo Standing Committee, make decisions—as in the 1995–1996 and 1999 Taiwan Strait crises. In ordinary times, one or two CMC members sit in on groups of Communist Party leaders (*lingdao xiaozu*) dealing with security, foreign policy, or Taiwan affairs. However, this participation remains at the discretion of the party general secretary and armed-forces commander in chief. For over twenty years, the CMC as such is no longer a decision-making locus on these issues.

This does not prevent the CMC from developing its own foreign relations. The CMC Foreign Affairs Bureau coordinates all the international exchanges and cooperation programs (such as port calls and joint exercises) of the People's Liberation Army. All in all, the party and state CMC has remained the top decision-making and coordinating body dealing with military affairs in the People's Republic.

#### BIBLIOGRAPHY

Finkelstein, David M., and Kristen Gunness, eds. *Civil-Military Relations in Today's China: Swimming in a New Sea.* Armonk, NY: M. E. Sharpe, 2006.

Lampton, David M., ed. *The Making of Chinese Foreign and Security Policy in the Era of Reform.* Stanford, CA: Stanford University Press, 2001.

Nelsen, Harvey W. *The Chinese Military System: An Organizational Study of the Chinese People's Liberation Army.* Boulder, CO: Westview Press, 1981.

***Jean-Pierre Cabestan***

## CENTRAL-LOCAL RELATIONSHIPS

The term *central-local relations* refers to the complex interactive relationships between China's central government and its subnational levels of administration. While the definition of *subnational* has varied over the course of Chinese history, the People's Republic has largely adopted a de facto four-tier system linking the provinces, prefecture-level cities, counties, and townships, with some regional and temporal variations. Villages are regarded as grassroots, rather than local, units.

During Mao Zedong's rule (1949–1976), the central government wielded absolute power over the provinces through ideological monitoring, mandatory state planning, budgetary provision, and personnel control. Despite Mao's noble causes, his successive efforts to transform Chinese society ended up as grand failures, suggesting in part that the central government, then without sufficient informational capacity, was only skilled at dictating its own preferences without taking into consideration regional variations and local conditions. In a totalitarian state, local governments had no choice but to carry out whatever order came down from Beijing.

Post-Mao China's transitional reforms have entailed de-ideologization, decentralization, marketization, ownership diversification, liberalization, and internationalization, all of which initially led to the weakening of central power vis-à-vis localities. Among other developments, the dynamics of decentralization—a process of devolving decisional authority from the central government to the provinces and below in an effort to promote local incentives and initiatives—has brought about a wide range of changes to China's central-local relations.

### ECONOMIC DECENTRALIZATION

The impact of decentralization was greatest in various economic arenas. Planning is one area where Beijing's power has been most consciously and consistently weakened over the years. Mandatory targets were cut sharply in the 1980s, and less-binding guidance targets gradually replaced them during the 1990s. With an enhanced level of marketization, the powers of the State Planning Commission, often dubbed the little State Council, were steadily curtailed and eventually restructured in 2003 as the State Development and Reform Commission. Given that the Eleventh Five-Year Plan for 2006 to 2010 was for the first time designated as directional guidelines (*guiha*) as opposed to plans (*jihua*), it can be safely argued that the era of centralized planning is finally over.

Investment is another domain where the impact of decentralization has been highly discernible. Considerable decisional latitude was granted to the provincial and sub-provincial units, as well as to state-endorsed development zones, in authorizing large-scale investment projects without attaining Beijing's prior approval. During the 1990s, many powerful ministries, such as the ministries of machinery, metallurgy, electricity, and electronics, were restructured as lower-level bureaus and no longer allowed to approve investment projects. These bureaus—except for the one in charge of cigarettes—were all abolished in February 2001, leaving the pertinent sectors wide open for market competition with little room for governmental interference.

Beijing's powerful instrument of local control during Mao's rule was budgetary provision. In an effort to promote local discretion and incentives, central-local budgetary relations were drastically transformed in the 1980s. Most of the provinces were permitted to adopt a fiscal contract system with regional variations, which allowed them to retain some revenues of their own, as long as fixed amounts were remitted to Beijing. As the provinces became adept in dyadic bargaining with the center, Beijing's share in total state revenues declined from 57 percent in 1981 to 33 percent in 1993. In order to reassert the center's budgetary control over the provinces, at the Third Plenum of the Fourteenth Central Committee in 1993, Beijing adopted a nationwide tax-assignment reform (*fenshuizhi*) by reversing its earlier pledge that the fiscal contract system would remain until 1995.

By reclassifying tax categories—that is, by dividing the consolidated industrial-commercial tax—Beijing managed to take a big chunk out of the largest tax item, thereby tipping the budgetary balance to its advantage. In January 2002, additional measures were taken to divide enterprise income tax revenues—regardless of their ownership—between the center and the provinces, again favoring the central government. The recentralization of the privilege to offer tax reduction and exemption back to the State Council also strengthened Beijing's efforts to plug a loophole in tax collection. After all these measures were employed, the center's share in budgetary revenue rose sharply, from 33 percent in 1993 to an annual average of 53 percent during the 1994–2006 period.

Another crucial dimension concerns the opening and restructuring of foreign economic relations. By granting various preferential policies and designations to coastal regions with comparative advantages and developmental potentials, Beijing sought to take advantage of selective deregulation. In promoting foreign trade and investment, the central ministries' monopoly on foreign trade was terminated, along with a rapid increase in the number of foreign trade corporations, which totaled more than seven thousand already in 1994. Provinces, cities, and counties were permitted to retain fixed portions of their foreign exchange earnings generated through exports. Provincial and subprovincial authorities, as well as various new designations such as *special economic zones* and *coastal open cities*, were also empowered to authorize large-scale foreign-invested projects worth $30 million in the late 1980s and later $100 million or more. With the launch of the Develop the West and Revive the Northeast schemes in 2000 and 2004, respectively, opening has become a competitive game for all the provinces and localities in China.

## NONECONOMIC DECENTRALIZATION

The extent to which post-Mao decentralization has affected noneconomic domains of central-local relations is more difficult to gauge. As for the cadre-management system, a notable change was introduced in 1983 by which the decisional power of the Central Organization Department (COD) was reduced from "managing two levels" (roughly 13,000 positions) to "managing only one level" (7,000 positions). Despite the change, crucial appointments, such as provincial secretaries, deputy secretaries, governors, and deputy governors, were still made by COD. Since 1990, cadres in key positions at the central economic cities (*jihua danlie shi*) and prefecture-level governments have also been appointed and dismissed by COD. In the reform era, the economic performance of local cadres is considered alongside their ideological compliance as a key criterion for career advancement. Therefore, once Beijing was determined to enlist local support at all costs, provincial leaders, whose fate depends upon COD, were usually left with few options but to comply.

As the number of local units equipped with lawmaking mandates increased during the reform era, grave concerns were voiced about the lack of clear delineation of legislative responsibilities along the administrative hierarchy. A large number of local regulations proved inconsistent with the constitution or national laws. Some provinces and cities even adopted local rules to grant tax reduction and exemption at will, in violation of national laws. While the State Council provided a regulation in 1990, according to which "in such cases [of conflicting laws of different levels of governments], the National People's Congress is to mediate," problems have continued to pile up. While the "Lawmaking Law" (*lifa fa*) was promulgated in March 2000 to better delineate the central-local boundaries of legislative power, there still exists ample room for jurisdictional disputes.

In tandem with the expanded discretion of localities, Beijing has been improving its capacity for administrative monitoring. Since manipulating (inflating or deflating) performance statistics has long been a silent weapon of local officials, the center has sought to strengthen its informational capacity. By 1995 all provincial units had adopted penalties against the violation of the Statistics

Law promulgated in 1983. More importantly, the State Statistical Bureau has sought to arrange its own personnel appointment and budgetary allocation in such a way that interferences from the local administration would be minimized. Furthermore, the information-collecting and auditing capacity of the central government has improved over the years.

## CHALLENGES OF DECENTRALIZATION

One of the most important—yet often neglected—dimensions of post-Mao decentralization concerns the reformist leadership's effort to redress the pernicious effects of using ideological standards in policy implementation by emphasizing the principle of implementing according to local conditions. While its efforts to transform the norms of central-local relations have scored major successes, assuming that the change was bound to have across-the-board effects is a mistake. The effect of decentralization is not indiscriminate among different issue areas, nor is it uniformly manifested in all local units.

The overall impact of post-Mao reforms on central-local relations has not been straightforward. While localities have obtained a significantly expanded scope of discretion, the balance of power between Beijing and the localities has not predominantly tilted toward the latter. Although central-provincial dynamics have at times resembled a zero-sum game, more often than not, Beijing's reduced imposition has not necessarily resulted in a corresponding increase of local discretion. It seems that genuine decentralization may deflect regionalist temptations, thereby paradoxically strengthening the overall control capacity of the center.

In the long run, however, the marginal space—both functional and hierarchical—under Beijing's tight control may decrease in proportion with the overall duration of the decentralization reform. Whereas the reform era has been replete with cycles of decentralization and recentralization, each cycle at its end appears to have generated a set of structures and interests more favorable to local incentives and discretion. More interesting is that the deepening of marketization and ownership diversification may increasingly interact with the decentralization reform in ways that were not foreseen. That is, as the reforms intensify, a wide range of socioeconomic programs—welfare provision, poverty alleviation, interregional equalization, and so on—may become more bottom-heavy in their resource and informational requirements. This unforeseen connection may put central-local dynamics much closer to the crucial concerns of state-society relations in contemporary China within the framework of governance.

Central-local dynamics are also increasingly linked with China's capacity for governance. The turbulent conditions in some minority regions—Xinjiang and Tibet—are haunting Beijing irrespective of whether they pose a grave threat to the regime itself. Furthermore, the numerical and organizational expansion of various local units during the reform era, the growth of invisible economies well beyond state taxation and regulation, the prevalence of cross-border smuggling, drug trafficking, corruption, the breakdown of the *hukou* (household registration) and *danwei* (unit) systems, and widening regional disparities all provide ample room for the entanglement of central-local dynamics with state-society relations.

As long as the central party/government remains the center of power, as is true in many unitary systems, antinomies of decentralization are bound to stay with it. With the considerable strengthening of its capacity for administrative monitoring, Beijing may now find it somewhat easier to enforce its preferences with regard to national priorities, although monitoring still faces problems with nonpriority issues. Given that China has not even opted for a nominal federal structure, as the former Soviet Union had, the issue of centrifugality must be more real to its leaders than would normally be taken for granted. In the long run, therefore, ample possibilities exist that the progress of political reform on the state-society front may eventually spill over to central-local relations in ways that have not been foreseen.

**SEE ALSO** *Archives, Public; Central State Organs since 1949; Provincial and Subprovincial Government Structure since 1949: Overview; Public Finance Since 1900; Urban China: Small-Town China.*

## BIBLIOGRAPHY

Chung Jae Ho. Studies of Central-Provincial Relations in the People's Republic of China: A Mid-Term Appraisal. *China Quarterly* 142 (1995): 487–508.

Chung Jae Ho. Reappraising Central-Local Relations in Deng's China. In *Remaking the Chinese State: Strategies, Society, and Security*, eds. Zhao Jianmin (Chien-min Chao) and Bruce J. Dickson, 46–75. London: Routledge, 2001.

Feng Chongyi and Hans Hendrischke, eds. *The Political Economy of China's Provinces: Comparative and Competitive Advantage.* London: Routledge, 1999.

Fitzgerald, John, ed. *Rethinking China's Provinces.* London: Routledge, 2002.

Goodman, David S. G., ed. *China's Provinces in Reform: Class, Community, and Political Culture.* London: Routledge, 1997.

Huang Yasheng. Central-Local Relations in China during the Reform Era: The Economic and Institutional Dimensions. *World Development* 24, 4 (1996): 655–672.

Yang, Dali L. *Beyond Beijing: Liberalization and the Regions in China.* London: Routledge, 1997.

*Jae Ho Chung*

# CHANG, EILEEN (ZHANG AILING)

***1920–1995***

Few figures of twentieth-century China have attracted as much attention as Eileen Chang (Zhang Ailing). Born with an aristocratic lineage, Chang had a troubled childhood and grew up under the shadow of her parents' broken marriage. Educated bilingually at a missionary school in Shanghai, she displayed her writing talents from an early age. In 1939 she became a first-year student at Hong Kong University, only to see her college education brought to an abrupt end two years later in the bloody Hong Kong Battle, an experience she later captured vividly in the essay "Jinyu lu" (From the Ashes). She bid farewell to the war-torn city of Hong Kong and returned to the equally ravaged metropolis of Shanghai. Becoming a professional writer seemed like a natural choice. What followed was one of the most distinctive literary careers of the twentieth century.

When Eileen Chang first began to write, she wrote in English and for the Nazi-backed English-language journal the *XXth Century*. She wrote film reviews and social commentaries, and soon came to be known as the young Ms. Chang who depicted Chinese life and customs in a witty and accessible prose style for the journal's Western readers. Chang's literary ambitions went beyond Western readership in Shanghai. She soon began to rewrite her English essays into Chinese and published them one after another in popular literary journals of the time. The process was not straightforward translation, but a deliberate act of self-positioning and a rediscovery of a burgeoning middle-class readership in the midst of war and turbulence. For the next year she continued to write steadily, mostly in Chinese, and in spring 1943 Chang published her first short story, "Chenxiang xie: di yi lu xiang" (Aloewood Ashes: The First Incense Burning), in the Mandarin Ducks and Butterflies journal *Ziluolan yuekan* (Violet Monthly). This is regarded as the turning point of her literary career: She became an overnight sensation. The Shanghai readership joyfully embraced this new talent.

Initially, Chang was among the first of a stream of young women authors who were discovered by Zhou Shoujuan (1895–1968), the veteran Butterflies writer and editor-in-chief of the *Violet Monthly*. But unlike other young women authors who continued their writing careers under the umbrella of Butterflies journals, Chang soon went beyond the market of popular fiction and became a principal architect of the cultural life in occupied Shanghai. In a matter of two years she produced the most significant works of her entire writing career, including a collection of short stories, *Chuanqi* (Romances, 1944), and a collection of essays, *Liuyan* (Written on Water, 1945). These two works alone cemented her unique position in the literary history of twentieth-century China. But to Shanghai readers in 1943 to 1945, Chang was more than a successful writer. Her celebrity status in the occupied city was unparalleled.

From the point of view of literary history, Eileen Chang's most important legacy is her construction of an alternative wartime narrative, one that contradicted the grand narratives of national salvation and revolution. In an age of heroes and villains, she highlighted the quotidian, seemingly irrelevant details of daily life, and stories of ordinary men and women caught in wars, revolutions, and drastic social transformations. In both her fiction and essays from the period, her impressionistic view of modern history displays colors, lines, shapes, textures, and moods, which are often crystallized in the drastically changing styles of women's clothes. Chang is at her best when she juxtaposes elements of a historical reality (war, turbulence, blockade, hunger, death, and scarcity) with the domain of domesticity and private life (love, loss, fantasy, emotional yearning, and artistic creativity). What shines through her highly stylized prose is the entanglement of a personalized inward journey and a persistent, although not always explicit, attempt to come to terms with the immediate experience of the war.

In *Qingcheng zhi lian* (Romance from the Ruins), a 1943 novella often considered to be Chang's best work of fiction, the protagonists travel back and forth between Hong Kong and Shanghai around the outbreak of the Pacific War. This is one of Chang's many Hong Kong narratives specifically written for her Shanghai audience. Its title alludes to an ancient Chinese tale in which the beauty of a woman is blamed for the collapse of a kingdom. Chang's modern narrative shares with the ancient legend a sense that war and turbulence are always lurking in the background and will eventually emerge as a substantial force that transforms individuals. As the story unfolds, the young and defiant widow Bai Liusu encounters Fan Liuyuan, a wealthy dandy from an overseas aristocratic family. She decisively leaves the repressive house of her parents and travels to Hong Kong to be with Liuyuan. In Hong Kong, a city depicted as an exotic mirror image of Shanghai, Liusu gradually falls under the spell of Liuyuan's scheme of seduction. She would continue to be Liuyuan's mistress if not for the outbreak of the war, which destroys the city but ironically completes the romance, which ends in happy matrimony.

In another acclaimed story, "Fengsuo" (Blockade), a male office worker meets a woman college teacher on a streetcar during an air raid, when the entire city comes to a standstill. When the blockade ends and the streetcar moves again at the end of the story, their romantic attraction is drawn to an abrupt end, as if nothing had happened. The streetcar caught in the carved-out space of a besieged city is an allegory of life in wartime: As in other works by Chang, there is the omnipresent threat of war—in the air raid and in other manifestations of modern warfare—but life goes on, like the streetcar tracks, pressing forward. Chang's alternative wartime narrative responds to the immediate reality and, more importantly, challenges the way that war, history, and individual lives had been represented in the master narrative of her time.

With the end of the Sino-Japanese War in 1945, Chang was politically weakened because of her brief marriage to Hu Lancheng (1906–1981), a key intellectual player in the Wang Jingwei's collaborationist government, and her professional association with the literary circle surrounding *Zazhi yuekan* (Miscellany Monthly) and several other Japanese-backed literary journals. She continued writing, though sparingly, during the postwar years, often under a pseudonym. Her first novel *Shiba chun* (Eighteen Springs), later reissued as *Bansheng yuan* (Destined for Half a Lifetime), was serialized under the pseudonym Liang Jing in the entertainment newspaper *Yi bao* in 1948. Her situation further deteriorated with the Communist takeover in 1949. In 1952 she left Shanghai for the last time and returned to Hong Kong, where she worked for the next three years at the United States Information Agency (USIA) as a translator. She translated Ernest Hemingway's *Old Man and the Sea* and Ralph Waldo Emerson's essays, among other English-language works, into Chinese. She also translated Chen Jiying's anti-Communist novel *Dicun zhuan* (The Story of Di Village) and other propaganda materials into English for the agency to disseminate in Southeast Asia.

Chang's three years in Hong Kong were productive because she also completed her two major novels, *The Rice-Sprout Song* (1955) and *The Naked Earth* (1956), both of which she wrote first in English and then transcribed into Chinese titled as *Yangge* and *Chidi zhi lian*, respectively. Both books were anti-Communist works commissioned by the USIA and produced at the height of the McCarthy era in the United States. With the completion of these two novels, Chang earned an immigrant visa to come to the United States in 1955. In the next four decades until her death in 1995, Chang severed most of her connections to the outside world and lived as a recluse. Dubbed the "Chinese Greta Garbo," her unsurpassed status as a cultural celebrity in occupied Shanghai, as well as her chosen reclusive life during her four decades in the United States, formed a sharp and puzzling contrast that contributed to her near mythical status.

The reception of Eileen Chang's work is a long and winding narrative of cultural migration. In the first three decades of the People's Republic of China, official literary histories made no mention of Chang and her work; this was due to her association with the collaborationist regime during wartime and the anti-Communist stance of her writing in the early 1950s. But Chang's reception outside of mainland China was a completely different story. In the late 1960s and early 1970s she was rediscovered by a generation of literary historians who were attempting to recanonize literature written in the Chinese language. Scholars such as C. T. Hsia and Shui Jing recognized her significance and assigned her an unparalleled position in literary history. Her works became popular again among readers in Taiwan, Hong Kong, and the Chinese diaspora communities. Her literary legacy had an important impact on a host of writers in Taiwan, where a group of young women authors formed an "Eileen Chang school" in the 1970s.

With a re-examination of literary histories in the post-Mao era, a renewed Eileen Chang "fever" also swept through cities on the mainland. Pirated editions of her early fiction and essays flooded the stalls of street vendors, a phenomenon that went hand in hand with a collective effort to uncover a cultural history of Shanghai from the prerevolutionary era and to redefine the city as a major metropolis on a new global map. As in Taiwan in the 1970s, in mainland China in the 1980s and 1990s a group of young women authors emerged whose writings clearly were inspired by Chang. Many of her stories were adapted into feature films. The name *Eileen Chang* came to stand for the glories of a bygone era. A new wave of frenzied media coverage of this enigmatic figure followed her quiet death in a Los Angeles apartment in summer 1995. Since then, most of her fiction and essays has been translated into English and other languages and widely used in classrooms. Interest in Chang rose again with the release of Ang Lee's 2008 film *Lust Caution*, which was adapted from an obscure story by Chang originally written in Hong Kong in the 1950s.

When Eileen Chang died in 1995, she had lived long enough to witness how the legends surrounding her life had grown in the popular cultures of Taiwan, Hong Kong, mainland China, and other Chinese communities around the world. Although she watched from a safe distance, remaining unaffected most of the time, no cultural history of twentieth-century China would be complete without an account of how the Chang mythology took shape amidst wartime turmoil and subsequently evolved and traveled across national and political boundaries in the following decades. The reception of Eileen Chang's writing is intertwined with war, revolution, migration, and urban transformations.

**BIBLIOGRAPHY**

Chow, Rey. Modernity and Narration—In Feminine Detail. In *Woman and Chinese Modernity: The Politics of Reading between West and East*, 84–120. Minneapolis: University of Minnesota Press, 1991.

Huang, Nicole. Introduction. In *Written on Water*, by Eileen Chang, trans. Andrew F. Jones. New York: Columbia University Press, 2005.

Huang, Nicole. *Women, War, Domesticity: Shanghai Literature and Popular Culture of the 1940s.* Leiden, Netherlands: Brill, 2005.

Lee, Leo Ou-fan. Eileen Chang: Romances in a Fallen City. In *Shanghai Modern: The Flowering of a New Urban Culture in China, 1930–1945*, 267–303. Cambridge, MA: Harvard University Press, 1999.

***Nicole Huang***

# CHANG YU (SANYU)

## *1901–1966*

Chang Yu (which he rendered Sanyu in Paris) was born to a wealthy family in Nanchong, Sichuan Province, on October 14, 1901. He was schooled at home and studied traditional painting with his father and calligraphy with the Sichuan artist Zhao Xi. Between 1918 and 1919 he was in Japan with his brother Chang Bicheng. There he had occasion to exhibit his calligraphic works. He returned to Shanghai in 1920 and in the same year traveled to Paris as part of a work-study program organized by the Chinese Ministry of Culture. His eldest brother Junmin, who owned and managed the successful Dehe Silk Factory in Sichuan, provided financial support. Chang Yu first enrolled at the École Nationale Supérieure des Beaux-Arts, in the atelier of François Flameng, in May 1921. In August of the same year he followed Xu Beihong and his wife Jiang Biwei to Berlin, where living conditions were more affordable than in Paris. He returned to Paris in 1923 and enrolled at the private Académie de la Grande Chaumière, focusing on nude and model drawing.

In 1928 he married fellow student Marcelle Charlotte Guyot de la Hardrouyère, but the couple would divorce a few years later. In 1929 he began a business relationship and friendship with the art collector and dealer Henri-Pierre Roché and began to paint nudes in oil, but in 1932 he tumultuously ended his relationship with Roché. This year marked the beginning of a period of ongoing hardships, heightened by the death of his eldest brother in China.

Through friendship with the Dutch collector and composer Johan Franco, Chang Yu held several exhibitions in Holland in the early 1930s. His financial difficulties made him shift his interests to the idea of developing and marketing a sport of his own invention, ping-tennis, to whose promotion he dedicated much effort, traveling to Berlin in 1936 on the occasion of the Olympics Games. During World War II the artist's financial circumstances worsened to the point that he could not afford even to buy painting materials. In 1948 he traveled to New York to promote ping-tennis, which he believed was his only chance to obtain financial stability. There he met and befriended photographer Robert Frank and lived in his studio for two years. A solo exhibition of Chang Yu's work was organized at the Museum of Modern Art in 1948. He returned to France in 1950. In 1963 he was invited by the minister of education of Taiwan to hold an exhibition in Taibei, but after shipping his paintings he could not implement the plan, nor could he bring his works back. On August 12, 1966, he was found dead of gas poisoning in his studio due to a leak, but speculations had it that he might have wanted to take his own life.

As for artistic style, Chang Yu was fascinated by the practice of drawing since his arrival in Paris. To it, he applied the techniques of Chinese ink painting. This hybrid yet fascinating combination of Western anatomical accuracy and Chinese linear energy would remain one of the distinguishing characteristics of his work, and made him one of the few true modernist painters in the Chinese modern tradition.

**SEE ALSO** *Oil Painting (youhua); Xu Beihong.*

**BIBLIOGRAPHY**

Desroches, Jean-Paul, ed. *Sanyu: L'ecriture du corps* (Sanyu: Language of the Body). Milan: Skira, 2004.

Gao Yuzhen, ed. *In Search of a Homeland: The Art of San Yu.* Taipei: National History Museum, 2001.

Wong, Rita. *Sanyu: Catalogue Raisonné, Oil Paintings.* Seattle: University of Washington Press, 2001. Text in Chinese, French, and English.

***Francesca Dal Lago***

# CHANGSHA

Changsha, the capital of Hunan Province since 1664, is located on the lower reaches of the Xiang River south of the Yangzi River and Lake Dongting. The city is best known for its contributions to modern China's reform and revolutionary movements. Changsha played a central role in the radical reform of 1898 and the 1911 revolution. Its links to Mao Zedong and other leaders of the Communist Party earned the city the sobriquet "cradle of the revolution." Ninety percent of the old city was burned in 1938, so few ancient sites remain. Today Changsha is a modern functional city that serves as the economic, political, and cultural center of Hunan Province, and is classified as one of China's twenty economically advanced cities.

## THE NINETEENTH CENTURY

Changsha began the nineteenth century with a reputation as cultural backwater that produced few scholars or notable officials. More an administrative center than a commercial city, it was overshadowed by Wuhan on the upper Yangzi; closer at hand, Xiangtan controlled trade on the Xiang River. As a consequence of the efforts of scholars at the Chengnan and Yuelu Academies who promoted statecraft and the thought of Wang Fuzhi (1619–1692), Changsha enjoyed a renaissance of scholarly activity just before the Opium War. In autumn 1852 Taiping forces besieged Changsha for four months before finally being driven off. The massive contributions of the Hunanese to the eventual suppression of the Taiping strengthened the power and status of the elite. The most renowned Hunanese gentry who had led the fight against the Taiping left the province to assume high-level positions in the national civil bureaucracy and military. Although the Changsha elite did not produce leaders of comparable prominence on the national stage, those remaining in Changsha nonetheless took special pride in the province's role as a defender of empire and Confucianism. Not surprisingly, Changsha's gentry soon became known for their conservatism. They blocked opening Hunan to foreign residence, ostracized reform-minded gentry such as Guo Songtao (1818–1891), and encouraged the antimissionary riots that rocked the central Yangzi in 1892.

In the years following the Sino-Japanese War (1894–1895), the belief in Hunan's special status stimulated efforts to defend the province through gentry-led reform and modernization. Changsha became a breeding ground for political activism and intellectual discourse. Gentry leaders promoted mines, industries, electric lighting, an arsenal, and telegraphs. Educational reforms started with moderate efforts to include Western subjects and current affairs in the curriculum, but turned more radical. In 1897 Changsha's School of Current Affairs became home to Liang Qichao, Tan Sitong (1865–1898), and other radical thinkers who advocated "people's rights." When the Empress Dowager's coup terminated the Hundred Days' Reform (1898), the reform movement in Changsha came to an abrupt end, but by then the gentry had split into progressive and conservative factions.

## THE TWENTIETH CENTURY

The opening of Changsha as a treaty port in 1904, followed by improved port facilities and a rail connection to Wuhan completed in 1917, transformed Changsha into the primary commercial center and rice market for Hunan. Introduction of a modern school system at the turn of the century consolidated Changsha's reputation as a center of education and culture; it also bred a new generation of reformers and revolutionaries committed to anti-imperialism and opposition to autocratic governance. The most alienated of the students joined revolutionary parties committed to overthrowing the Qing. Following a failed plot in 1904, Huang Xing (1874–1916) and other young revolutionaries from Changsha left for Tokyo, where they joined the Revolutionary Alliance and plotted uprisings in central China in conjunction with the new armies and secret societies. In Changsha the new urban gentry promoted movements for constitutional rule and rights recovery; after 1909 they dominated the newly formed provincial assemblies. The Changsha rice riot of 1910 revealed the existence of large pockets of antiforeignism and popular hostility to the modernizing efforts of the Qing and reformist gentry. In the revolution of 1911, Changsha declared for the revolution on October 22 in a relatively bloodless affair. However, the efforts of the revolutionaries to mobilize secret societies alienated the reformers and constitutionalists. In response, the reformist elite with assistance from the military overthrew the revolutionaries and installed Tan Yankai (1876–1930) in power.

The 1920s and 1930s were a period of moderate growth for the city. The population increased from 271,000 in 1921 to 381,000 in 1931. Imports and exports rose unevenly, modern factories including a cotton mills and engineering works appeared, and modest efforts were made to widen roads. However, progress was slowed by periodic flooding, political disorder, and gross misgovernment under militarists such as Tang Xiangming and Zhang Jingyao, who were nicknamed "Butcher Tang" and "Zhang the Venomous." One contending warlord army after another fought to control this strategically located city. Each change of government brought heavy exactions, violence against the population, and pillage. In July 1930 Changsha was briefly occupied by elements of the Red Army under Peng Dehuai as part of the Li Lisan (1899–1967) line. As was true in the Changsha riots of 1910, handicraft workers attacked foreign-owned properties and modern factories that threatened their livelihoods. Among those killed when Changsha was retaken by the warlords were Mao's wife and sister.

In the popular mind, Changsha is associated with Mao Zedong, who was a student at the Hunan First Normal School from 1913 to 1918. Following his graduation Mao remained in Changsha, where he served as principal of a primary school, edited a radical newspaper (*Xiang River Review* [Xiangjiang Pinglun]), founded a "self-study university," ran a bookstore, organized radical study groups, and formed the Hunan branch of the Communist Party. Other important Communist leaders who lived in Changsha include Liu Shaoqi, Hu Yaobang, and Zhu Rongji.

Changsha was the site of three of China's major victories in the Sino-Japanese War (1937–1945). Chinese forces under General Xue Yue (1896–1998) defeated three Japanese offensives against Changsha in 1939, 1941, and 1942, but the city finally fell in 1944. By then the city was mostly ruined because Nationalist forces had burned the city in 1938 to deny it to the Japanese.

### CONTEMPORARY CHANGSHA

Today Changsha has jurisdiction over more than 4,500 square miles with five districts, three counties, and one city. The current population is slightly over six million, of whom slightly fewer than two million live in the urban district. Changsha is listed as one of China's top twenty "economically advanced" cities, and is the regional hub for economic activity, transportation, distribution, education, and culture. During the 1960s efforts were made to develop heavy industry, especially machine tools and aluminum industry. At the start of the reform era in 1978, Changsha lagged behind the coastal cities, but since the 1990s it has seen rapid growth in both industry and the service sector. In 1992 the government established a national economic and technical development zone. Improved transportation facilities, including a port and airport, have created an "economic circle" with cities one hour away that comprises over 70 percent of Hunan's gross domestic product (GDP). From 2002 to 2006 the circle's GDP grew at an average of 14 percent, compared with the national average of 10 percent. The service sector, which constituted half of Changsha's GDP in 2006, is expected to drive the city's economic development. According to government statistics Changsha has the highest number of students per 10,000 in China and one of the highest literacy rates in China.

Since 1978 the government has begun to restore the city's ancient and recent historical sites. The famous Mawangdui tombs, first excavated in the 1970s, include the 2,000-year-old preserved corpse of Lady Xin Zhui and the earliest versions of the Daodejing. More than 170,000 wood and bamboo slips from the Three Kingdoms period (220–280) were unearthed at Zoumalou. The Yuelu Academy was restored in the 1980s following Song dynasty designs. The Mao Zedong Museum features Mao's living quarters and historical photographs from the 1920s.

**SEE ALSO** *Hunan and Hubei.*

**BIBLIOGRAPHY**

Changshashi tongjiju. *Changsha sishinian* [Forty years of Changsha]. Changsha, China: Huazhong Yinshuachang, 1989.

Clark, Paul. Changsha in the 1930 Red Army Occupation. *Modern China* 7, no. 4 (October 1981): 413–444.

Esherick, Joseph W. *Reform and Revolution in China: The 1911 Revolution in Hunan and Hupei.* Berkeley: University of California Press, 1976.

Guo Wang, Shigai Chen, and Shijing Chen. *Changsha shihua* [Talks on the history of Changsha]. Changsha, China: Hunan Renmin Chubanshe, 1980.

Lewis, Charlton M. *Prologue to the Chinese Revolution: The Transformation of Ideas and Institutions in Hunan Province, 1891–1907.* Cambridge, MA: Harvard University Press, 1976.

Platt, Stephen R. *Provincial Patriots: The Hunanese and Modern China.* Cambridge, MA: Harvard University Press, 2007.

Short, Philip. *Mao: A Life.* New York: Henry Holt, 2000.

***Arthur Lewis Rosenbaum***

## CHEN DUXIU

***1879–1942***

Chen Duxiu was a giant of Chinese thought and politics and a man of great moral passion. Born into a gentry family on October 8, 1879, he was educated in the Confucian classics. However, he turned against tradition and is often described as an iconoclast. In the early 1900s he joined a nationalist organization in Anqing, his native town in Anhui. In 1904 he published *Suhua bao* (Vernacular Magazine), written in vernacular Chinese. In Shanghai he briefly joined an anarchist assassination squad. Through his writings and other activities, he helped prepare the ground for the 1911 Revolution.

Disappointed by the revolution's failure to solve China's crisis, between 1915 and 1919 he led the New Culture Movement, which mobilized students and intellectuals in a campaign to transform Chinese culture. In 1915 he founded the journal *Qingnian* (Youth), later renamed *Xin qingnian* (New Youth), which campaigned against traditional ethics and the use of literary Chinese for written communication. In 1917 he became dean of letters at Beijing National University (Peking University), where he worked with such scholars as Hu Shi, Qian Xuantong, and Zhou Zuoren. As formulated in *Xin qingnian,* their project—part of the New Culture Movement—was to save China by assimilating Western concepts of humanism, democracy, individualism, and the scientific method. An unrelenting critic of Confucian patriarchal thinking, Chen argued that China could never be free as a nation without women's liberation (although he did not always live up to his moral precepts in his own married life and sexual behavior).

On May 4, 1919, a student movement broke out under *Xin qingnian*'s direct influence in protest against the decision of the Paris Peace Conference to transfer German concessions in China to Japan. As its leader and inspirer, Chen was jailed for three months. After his release, he declared himself a Marxist and began to work toward establishing the Chinese Communist Party.

He founded the Communist Party in 1921 and was elected general secretary at its first five congresses. During the Revolution of 1925–1927, the Communist Party, acting on Comintern instructions, joined the Guomindang (Nationalist Party) in a united front. In the spring of 1927, Chiang Kai-shek (Jiang Jieshi) broke with the communists and massacred thousands. Yet the Communist Party's alliance with the Guomindang continued through the latter party's left wing under Wang Jingwei in Wuhan, but in July Wang too turned against the Communists. Chen had earlier advocated that the Communist Party withdraw from the Guomindang, but the Comintern scapegoated him for the defeat.

In August 1927 Chen was dismissed as general secretary. After Chiang's coup in 1927, Stalin refused to concede that the Chinese Revolution had been defeated and called for urban insurrections backed by peasant armies. Chen condemned this policy as "adventurist." In 1929 he read Leon Trotsky's writings and went over to his positions, whereupon he was expelled from the Communist Party. In May 1931 he joined others to form a Chinese section of the Trotskyist International and became its general secretary. He and the Trotskyists tried to rebuild the trade unions and reestablish a presence in the cities. Central to their program was a struggle for a democratic assembly, as advocated at the time by Leon Trotsky. It was chiefly the slogan for democracy that attracted Chen to the opposition. In October 1932 he was arrested on charges of seeking to overthrow the government. He went to jail, where he stayed until the outbreak of the Sino-Japanese War in 1937. In 1938 Communist Party leaders accused him of collaborating with Japan, an echo of Stalin's slander that Trotsky was working for the Nazis. He died on May 27, 1942, in Jiangjin near Chongqing.

## THOUGHT

Chen and the Chinese Trotskyists advocated democracy, unlike the Communist Party leaders after 1927, who accused Chen of "liquidationism" for his democratic policy and denounced the democratic, humanist, and universalist values of the May Fourth Movement as "bourgeois." Having found traditional strategies for change wanting after the degeneration of the 1911 Revolution, Chen fixed on socialism with democracy as the remedy. Although he drew his inspiration from the Bolsheviks, his idea of the Communist Party differed from theirs. He opposed the creation of a strong party chief. Initially he allowed non-Marxists and anarchists to join the party. Even Mao Zedong recognized that under Chen the Communist Party was "rather lively" and free of dogmatism. Although it imported authoritarian habits in the 1920s, only after Chen's dismissal did they become general.

Chen's leftist opposition was born of four different organizations, most of whose members had several years of revolutionary experience. Unlike some of his comrades, Chen was not afraid to challenge policies that bore Trotsky's personal imprimatur. For example, in 1934 he expressed his doubts about Trotsky's belief that the Soviet Union was a workers' state that revolutionaries must defend against bourgeois aggressors. Trotsky admired Chen and remarked that he should learn Chinese so as to be able to read Chen's writings. Chen believed that the essence of great revolutionaries like V. I. Lenin was their refusal to be bound by ready-made Marxist formulas. He was never prepared to accept uncritically the word of foreign communists, especially after Moscow unfairly blamed him for the defeat of 1927.

In the mid to late 1930s, the Moscow show-trials and Stalin's alliance with Hitler caused Chen to rethink his views on democracy. He concluded that Lenin's denial of the value of democracy was responsible in part for Stalinism. To his comrades, it seemed that Chen in his declining years had returned to his original attachment to pure democracy. In those years Chen wrote that democracy is the content and form of human history and must not be equated with the bourgeoisie. He denied the progressive import of proletarian dictatorship and Bolshevism, which he described as Fascism's twin and Stalinism's father. He continued to identify himself as a Marxist, however.

Even after the Japanese invasion in 1937, Chen stuck to his belief that there could be no revolution outside urban culture. While Mao was developing his rural strategy, Chen continued to look toward industrial workers in the belief that peasants cannot make a modern revolution.

## LEGACY

Despite his contribution to politics and letters, after his death Chen's name was blackened for many years by Communist Party leaders because of his conversion to Trotskyism. Not until the 1980s was a more positive evaluation of his merits allowed. The new attitude toward his legacy is epitomized in a comment made by the mainstream historian Tang Baolin: "Chen Duxiu changed often in the course of his life, but he stuck to certain ideas all his life, at least where the five great issues of progress, democracy, science, patriotism, and socialism are concerned. The practice of several decades has proved that the positions he took accord essentially with the truth."

Chen's rehabilitation extended to his bones. His material remains were repatriated to Anqing in Anhui Province for reburial, and his tomb was designated "a major tourist resource and site imbued with human and cultural meaning." In 1989 a group of scholars in Beijing founded the Society for Chen Duxiu Studies. Also in 1989, the students who occupied Tiananmen Square drew direct inspiration from the May Fourth Movement, which Chen led, and copied his slogan calling for science and democracy.

Chen's role has been likened to Lenin's, although he lacked Lenin's gift for theory. Others see him as China's Georgi Plekhanov, since he inspired the rise of communism in his country, or as its Ferdinand Lassalle for his practical bent, his lack of ideology, and his literary merits. His friend Hu Shi called him a lifelong opponent to any authority. His follower Wang Fanxi said that although he was best known as a revolutionary politician, he was also a poet, writer, educator, and linguist. He was, said Wang, China's Vissarion Belinsky, Nikolai Chernyshevsky, Plekhanov, and Lenin rolled into one in that he "traversed the entire gamut of their thinking, from the first awakening of individualism to the struggle for socialist collectivism."

**SEE ALSO** *Chinese Marxism; Communist Party; May Fourth Movement; Trotskyism.*

**BIBLIOGRAPHY**

Benton, Gregor. *China's Urban Revolutionaries: Explorations in the History of Chinese Trotskyism, 1921–1952*. Atlantic Highlands, NJ: Humanities Press, 1996.

Benton, Gregor, ed. and trans. *An Oppositionist for Life: Memoirs of the Chinese Revolutionary Zheng Chaolin*. Atlantic Highlands, NJ: Humanities Press, 1997.

Feigon, Lee. *Chen Duxiu, Founder of the Chinese Communist Party*. Princeton, NJ: Princeton University Press, 1983.

Tang Baolin. *Zhongguo Tuopai shi* [A History of Chinese Trotskyism]. Taibei: Dongda Tushu Gongsi, 1994.

Wang Fan-hsi. *Memoirs of a Chinese Revolutionary*. Trans. Gregor Benton. New York: University of Columbia Press, 1991.

***Gregor Benton***

## CHEN KAIGE

***1952–***

A key figure among China's Fifth-Generation filmmakers, Chen Kaige has had a career that interweaves, parallels, competes, and coextends with the career of fellow director Zhang Yimou.

Chen's filmmaking was shaped by his experiences during the Cultural Revolution (1966–1969), which started when he was enrolled in Beijing's No. 4 High School. His classmates were mostly sons and daughters of high-ranking government officials, making the Cultural Revolution all the more immediate and personal for him. According to Chen's autobiography, *Shaonian Kaige* (The youthful Kaige, 2001), he was pressured as a teenager to denounce his father, also a film director, during the Cultural Revolution—a traumatic moment that he was to explore in many of his films.

Chen's films of the 1980s manifested the ambitious formal and thematic experimentation characteristic of the early films of Fifth-Generation directors. Unlike Zhang Yimou's flamboyant psychosomatic intensity, however, Chen's early aesthetics emphasized meditative quiescence overlying turbulent historical and political undercurrents. Chen's directorial debut, *Yellow Earth* (*Huang tudi,* 1984), shot by Zhang Yimou, garnered major awards in 1985 at the British Film Institute Awards, the Locarno International Film Festival, and the Hawaii International Film Festival, placing the Chen–Zhang duo on the international map of art cinema. Chen's next film, *The Big Parade* (*Da yuebing,* 1986), scored another success, with awards in 1987 at the Montreal World Film Festival and *Torino* International Festival of Young Cinema. Chen's third project, *King of the Children* (*Haizi wang,* 1987), adapted from a novel by Ah Cheng, a writer of "scar literature" (*shanghen wenxue*), was Chen's first cinematic treatment of the Cultural Revolution. It won China's prestigious Golden Rooster Award (Jinji Jiang) for best cinematography and the director's special prize, as well as international awards.

Chen sojourned in the United States between 1987 and 1990. During this period, he had a cameo role in Bernardo Bertolucci's *The Last Emperor* (1987). Upon returning to China, Chen made *Life on a String* (*Bianzou bian chang,* 1991), a tour-de-force treatise on an individual's awakening and iconoclasm against a tradition of deception and dictatorship. A year later, Chen took a commercial turn with *Farewell My Concubine* (*Bawang bie ji,* 1992), so far his best-known film to Western audiences. Adapted from a novel of the same title by Hong Kong writer Lillian Lee (Li Bihua), *Farewell My Concubine* is a China–Hong Kong coproduction starring Leslie Cheung (Zhang Guorong), Gong Li, and Zhang Fengyi. A historical saga covering the most sensational five decades of modern Chinese history, the film centers on a triangular relationship between two male stars of the Peking Opera and a former prostitute who marries one of them. As a spectacular melodrama of modern China, the film garnered a long list of prestigious prizes, including the 1993 Cannes Festival's Palme d'Or, which it shared with Jane Campion's *The Piano. Farewell My Concubine* was also one of the first Chinese films to touch explicitly, albeit subtly, on a taboo issue: homosexuality.

The more commercial style of *Farewell My Concubine* was maintained in Chen's two subsequent films, *Temptress Moon* (*Fengyue,* 1996) and *The Emperor and the Assassin* (*Ci qin,* 1998), both period dramas starring Gong Li. In the new millennium, Chen shifted gears with *Killing Me Softly* (2002), an English-language romance-thriller made with American and British producers. Instead of pursuing a career in Hollywood, however, Chen returned to China and refocused on contemporary Chinese society in *Together* (*He ni zai yiqi,* 2002), a melodrama exploring a father-son rapprochement as a means of working through Chen's own Cultural Revolution trauma.

Chen's next film, *The Promise* (*Wuji,* 2005), a mythic action film following at the heels of Zhang Yimou's box-office hits *Hero* (*Yingxiong,* 2002) and *House of Flying Daggers* (*Shimian maifu,* 2004), was a blockbuster aimed at consolidating and profiting from the East Asian market. Chen and Zhang's new-millennium films signaled the Fifth Generation's negotiation and increasing conformity with the logic of the market, the pressures of global commercialism, and the disintegration of the state-sponsored film industry in post-socialist China. The common strategy is to mobilize big production values, multinational collaboration, computer-generated imagery and digital postproduction, and a transnational star cast (from Hong Kong, Japan,

***Movie still from the film* Farewell My Concubine, *1993. A leading figure among China's Fifth Generation filmmakers, Chen Kaige earned worldwide acclaim with his 1993 work* Farewell My Concubine. *In many of his films, Chen examines the impact of the Cultural Revolution not only on Chinese society at large, but also on personal relationships between family members.* EVERETT COLLECTION**

and Korea, as well as mainland China). This approach has produced mixed results. Depleted of references to history and society, *The Promise* was widely criticized and even parodied for its overreliance on computer graphics, its gratuitous spectacles, and its anemic narrative.

In 2008 Chen returned for inspiration to the early twentieth century theater, and directed *Mei Lanfang*, a biopic of an internationally renowned Peking Opera *dan* (female impersonator). Chen also contributed to the portmanteau films *Ten Minutes Older* (2002) and *To Each His Cinema* (2007), made in collaboration with other internationally acclaimed directors. Chen's further contributions to the profession internationally include service on the juries of the Berlin and Venice international film festivals in 1989 and 1993, respectively.

SEE ALSO *Film Industry: Fifth Generation Filmmakers; Zhang Yimou.*

## BIBLIOGRAPHY

Berry, Chris, and Mary Ann Farquhar. Post-socialist Strategies: An Analysis of *Yellow Earth* and *Black Cannon Incident*. In *Cinematic Landscapes: Observations on the Visual Arts and Cinema of China and Japan*, ed. Linda Erlich and David Desser, 81–116. Austin: University of Texas Press, 1994.

Berry, Michael. Chen Kaige: Historical Revolution and Cinematic Rebellion. Interview in *Speaking in Images: Interviews with Contemporary Chinese Filmmakers*, 82–107. New York: Columbia University Press, 2005.

Chen Kaige. *Shaonian Kaige* [The youthful Kaige]. Beijing: Renmin Wenxue Chubanshe, 2001.

Lau, Jenny Kwok Wah. *Farewell My Concubine*: History, Melodrama, and Ideology in Contemporary Pan-Chinese Cinema. *Film Quarterly* 49, 1 (1995): 16–27.

Yau, Esther. *Yellow Earth*: Western Analysis and a Non-Western Text. *Film Quarterly* 41, 2 (1987–1988): 22–33.

Zhang Xudong. A Critical Account of Chen Kaige's *King of the Children*. In *Chinese Modernism in the Era of Reforms: Cultural Fever, Avant-garde Fiction, and the New Chinese Cinema*, 282–305. Durham, NC: Duke University Press, 1997.

***Yiman Wang***

## CHEN SHUIBIAN
### *1950–*

Chen Shuibian (Chen Shui-bian) was born in Guantian, a small town in Tainan County in Taiwan, in 1950. The son of a tenant farmer, he lived in relative poverty for much of his childhood. Chen proved to be an outstanding student, gaining admittance to the law school of Taiwan's top-ranked National Taiwan University in 1969.

Chen became involved in politics in the aftermath of the Gaoxiong (Kaohsiung) Incident of 1979. Following a pro-human rights demonstration in the southern city of Kaohsiung, the entire leadership of the opposition movement (known as the Dangwai, or outside the party movement) was arrested. Chen served as the defense lawyer for opposition leader Huang Hsin-chieh. Following the trial, Chen participated in the Dangwai movement, winning election to the Taibei City Council in 1981 and serving as publisher for a number of opposition magazines.

He narrowly lost in his bid to win election as Tainan County magistrate in 1985. Three days after the election, his wife, Wu Shu-jen, was hit by a truck and paralyzed from the waist down. Then, in 1986, Chen began an eight-month prison sentence after losing a libel case related to one of his magazines. On release from prison, Chen soon revived his political career, winning election as a legislator in 1989 representing the newly formed Democratic Progressive Party (DPP). Chen's performance in the parliament earned him a reputation as one of the rising stars of the DPP.

In 1994 Chen took advantage of divisions in the Guomindang (Kuomintang; GMD) camp to win the Taibei (Taipei) mayoral election. Instead of focusing on the divisive national-identity issue, Chen appealed to a broader electorate with his emphasis on social issues and the slogan "Happiness, Hope, Chen Shuibian." Chen's new style of political communication owed much to the influence of his team of young advisors led by Luo Wenjia, and contributed to the DPP's increasing appeal to younger voters.

During Chen's four years as Taibei mayor, he proved to be a competent administrator. Key achievements included cracking down on illegal gambling and prostitution, expanding the bus and metro systems, opening new parks, and implementing a new, improved waste-collection system. However, in 1998, despite receiving a larger vote share than in 1994, facing a united GMD, Chen lost his bid for reelection.

Chen subsequently began planning for the 2000 presidential election, aiming to learn from his 1998 defeat and the DPP's disastrous campaign of 1996. First, he attempted to moderate his party's image on the controversial independence issue. In 1999 the party passed the Resolution on Taiwan's Future, which accepted "Republic of China" as Taiwan's national title. Chen's campaign also placed greatest emphasis on political corruption and social welfare, issues that were damaging for the GMD. In addition, Chen's team ran a strong political-communication campaign, which included what are regarded as some of the best political advertisements in Taiwan's history. However, as in 1994, Chen benefited from a GMD split when in addition to the official GMD candidate, Lian Zhan (Lien Chan), former provincial governor Song Chuyu (James Soong) stood as an independent. This allowed Chen to win with only 39 percent of the vote.

During the presidential campaign, both the GMD and the People's Republic of China (PRC) warned that Chen's election could lead to a declaration of independence and war. Chen moved to defuse tensions in his inaugural speech by pledging not to declare independence. In an initial honeymoon period early in his first term, Chen enjoyed public approval rates of 70 percent.

Chen's first term saw some important domestic policy achievements. The most significant reforms included the 2002 Pensions Bill, the 2001 Equal Employment Law, and anticorruption legislation such as the 2004 Political Donations Bill, the 2003 Referendum Bill, and banking reforms. On the economic front, an important consensus was reached at the 2001 Economic Development Conference to lift many of the restrictions on cross-strait trade and investment imposed by former president Li Denghui (Lee Teng-hui).

Nevertheless, by the end of Chen's first term, many were disappointed. Despite a number of conciliatory measures, the PRC refused to resume cross-strait negotiations. Environmentalists were angered when Chen had to reverse his decision over halting construction of the Fourth Nuclear Power Station in 2001. In addition, Chen was criticized for failures in economic management after Taiwan experienced its worst economic recession in living memory, with negative growth in 2002 and record unemployment of almost 5 percent.

Despite these setbacks, Chen was able to win reelection in March 2004. Key factors included a lackluster GMD campaign, the GMD's failure to nominate its most popular politician, Ma Yingjiu (Ma Ying-Jeou), and the DPP's ability to dominate the election agenda. On the eve of the March 2004 election there was an assassination attempt against Chen, in which both he and his vice president, Annette Lu, were slightly wounded. After Chen's narrow victory by less than thirty thousand votes, the GMD challenged the legitimacy of the election, calling for a recount and alleging electoral fraud and that the assassination was staged. Nevertheless, Chen survived both the recount and a GMD lawsuit that called for the election to be nullified.

Chen's second term proved to be even more challenging than his first. His most significant achievement was the passage of constitutional reforms in 2005 that revised the electoral system to a single-member district, two-vote system. But the bitterness created by the controversial presidential election and Chen's failure again to gain a legislative majority in 2004 meant that his second term was dominated by increasingly polarized parties and legislative gridlock. The KMT and its allied parties, known as the Pan-Blue camp, were able to repeatedly block DPP government bills in the legislature. Chen also failed to deliver on his promise for a new Taiwanese constitution.

Chen's government lost its reputation for clean governance after a series of damaging corruption scandals. In 2006 Chen's son-in-law was found guilty of insider trading, and both Chen and his wife were accused of embezzling government funds. This led to large-scale anticorruption demonstrations calling for his resignation, as well as three GMD-initiated recall votes.

In contrast to the relative moderation of Chen's first term, after 2004 Chen appeared more radical. In 2006 he broke one of his inaugural pledges by abolishing the National Unification Guidelines and Council. Moreover, in 2007 he began promoting a referendum on an application to enter the United Nations under the name of Taiwan. Such moves not only kept cross-strait relations tense, but also damaged Taiwan's ties with the United States.

By the end of his second term, Chen's unpopularity contributed to the DPP's disastrous electoral defeats in early 2008. It remains uncertain what Chen's long-term legacy will be. Many of Chen's former supporters have condemned him as he faces prosecution on corruption charges of money laundering. However, Chen, like his predecessor Li Denghui, refuses to fade quietly from the Taiwanese political scene. After leaving office Chen's speeches and court cases still attract front page media attention.

**SEE ALSO** *Li Denghui (Lee Teng-hui); Taiwan, Republic of China: Democratic Progressive Party; Taiwan, Republic of China: Politics since 1945.*

**BIBLIOGRAPHY**

Chen Shuibian. *Son of Taiwan: The Life of Chen Shui-Bian and His Dreams for Taiwan*. Trans. David J. Toman. Taibei and Upland, CA: Taiwan Publishing, 2000.

Fell, Dafydd, Henning Klöter, and Chang Bi-yu, eds. *What Has Changed? Taiwan Before and After the Change in Ruling Parties*. Wiesbaden, Germany: Harrassowitz, 2006.

Kagan, Richard. *Chen Shui-bian: Building a Community and a Nation*. Taibei: Asia-Pacific Academic Exchange Foundation, 2000.

*Dafydd Fell*

# CHEN YUN
***1905–1995***

Chen Yun was a top official in the Chinese Communist Party (CCP) from the early 1930s until the early 1990s. He was the longest-serving member of the Central Committee of the CCP, being a member from 1931 to 1987. Chen played a leading role in Chinese economic policy making in the 1950s and early 1960s, often leading efforts to clean up economic dislocation. He was not active during the Cultural Revolution period (1966–1969), but reemerged after Mao Zedong's death in 1976 and was effectively the second most powerful Chinese leader from 1978 until the early 1990s. In the 1950s and early 1960s, many of his economic ideas could be seen as reformist: He suggested some utility for market allocation and backed a return to individual farming in 1962 (his last major act of policy advocacy during Mao's lifetime). During the 1980s, Chen was certainly more conservative and less experimental than Deng Xiaoping, and Chen is usually portrayed as the "godfather" of the conservative group in the Chinese leadership.

## CHEN AND THE COMMUNIST REVOLUTION

Chen was born in Qingpu County, now part of Shanghai Municipality, in 1905. His parents were poor peasants and died when he was very young. Raised by relatives, he received limited formal education. He was apprenticed to the Commercial Press in Shanghai, where he worked until 1927. He became politically active at the press and joined the Communist Party in 1925. After the worker uprising in 1927 and its subsequent suppression, Chen escaped to Qingpu and became active in the remnant Jiangsu party committee in the late 1920s and early 1930s. Chen's worker background stood him in good stead. In 1931 he became a member of the Central Committee of the party, and he began to work closely with a number of leading party officials, including Zhou Enlai, Kang Sheng, and Wang Ming, in Shanghai. Chen was also a member of the Special Service Committee of the Party Center responsible for security affairs. By late 1932, the CCP was forced to abandon Shanghai, and Chen arrived in the Jiangxi Soviet in early 1933. In Jiangxi, he became a leader in the workers' movement.

In late 1934, the CCP was defeated in Jiangxi and forced to embark on the Long March. At the climactic Zunyi meeting in 1935, Chen supported Mao Zedong as Mao effectively became the top party leader. In turn, Chen was sent to Moscow to brief the Soviet Communist Party about the Long March and Mao's leadership; he remained in Moscow until April 1937. After helping to arrange the repatriation of a column of Long Marchers from Xinjiang, Chen traveled to Yan'an and sided with Mao in a series of political confrontations with Mao's rivals. Chen held top positions in the trade-union movement, and became head of the CCP's organization department during the party rectification campaign of 1942 to 1944, when Mao's leadership was fully consolidated.

By 1945 Chen was among the top ten ranking members of the CCP. With the end of the war with Japan in sight, Chen was dispatched to Manchuria with Lin Biao and other top leaders to establish a CCP presence in the area. Manchuria became a key battlefront during the Chinese civil war, but Chen's role with regard to the military campaigns is obscure. However, he quickly became deeply involved in the economic efforts to support the war effort. In early 1949, Chen traveled to Moscow, and upon his return to China in the summer of 1949, he became the top official in charge of restoring order to the Chinese economy.

## CHEN AND MAO'S CHINA

From 1949 until late 1957, Chen was the top leader directly involved with economic affairs. In the early days of the People's Republic of China, Chen supervised the ending of inflation and the restoration of production and commerce, and in general he managed the rehabilitation of the Chinese economy. He also played important roles in economic planning, particularly after 1953. In 1954 Chen became the first vice premier of China's State Council, and in 1956 his position in the CCP hierarchy was reaffirmed by his membership in the Politburo Standing Committee (a status he had held since at least 1950) and his appointment as vice chairman of the CCP. Chen worked closely with Premier Zhou Enlai, but Zhou's duties were considerably broader than Chen's, and Zhou delegated many economic tasks to Chen.

After the "socialist high tide" of 1955 to 1956, which saw collectivization of the countryside and the effective nationalization of all remaining private industry and commerce, Chen began to articulate a more independent view of China's use of the Soviet model of economic development. Reacting to inflation, economic overextension, lack of incentives, and other ills, Chen proposed a series of measures to promote a more balanced economy (in agriculture, light industry, and heavy industry), a more sustainable rate of development (i.e., a slower rate of growth), the use of the market to supplement the planned economy, and a smaller role for planning in the economy. In the 1950s, Chen's views were characterized as having the government maintain control over large issues, and allowing the market to manage smaller affairs. In the 1980s, these views came to be called the *bird-cage theory.* The market was the bird in the analogy; it should be allowed to fly, but within controlled parameters. If the cage (state economic administration) was too small, the bird would die, and if the bars were too widely separated, the bird would fly away. Mao too would claim he wanted more-balanced growth around this time, but he still wanted a high rate of growth. Others continued to advocate concentration on heavy industry.

In the aftermath of the Hundred Flowers campaign and the subsequent anti-rightist movement, Chen's ideas came under increasing attack by Mao, and by late 1957 to early 1958, Chen's position was significantly weakened. Through the high point of the Great Leap Forward in 1958, Chen played no active role, but when Mao began to allow modest readjustments in 1959, Chen became more active, trying to help modify the great imbalances caused by the impetuosity of 1958. But after the Lushan Plenum of July to August 1959, Chen again disappeared from the scene, as Mao intensified the Great Leap. Only after mid-1960 would Chen reappear, playing a leading role in trying to fix the economy after the full extent of the Great Leap crisis was accepted. Chen continued in these efforts until mid-1962.

Chen was pessimistic about the state of the economy in 1962, and in the summer, he argued to Mao that agriculture should return to household farming. Mao rejected this proposal, and began the process of radicalization that led to the Cultural Revolution. Chen again went into eclipse (CCP histories suggest that he was in persistent ill health). Chen was criticized during the Cultural Revolution, but never formally purged. He was dropped from the Politburo in 1969 and exiled to Jiangxi, but remained in the Central Committee. He returned to Beijing in the early 1970s, but played a minimal role in Chinese politics.

## CHEN AND THE REFORM ERA

With Mao's death in 1976, Chen returned to prominence. In 1978 he was again made a member of the Politburo Standing Committee, and he took charge of yet another round of economic readjustment. In influence, Chen was second only to Deng Xiaoping. Many of Chen's policies of the 1950s and early 1960s were revived, and they contributed to the early economic reform program. But whereas Chen was the leading reformer in China in the 1950s, by the 1980s his views were at the more-conservative end of the political spectrum. At the Party Conference of 1985, for example, Chen was highly critical of excessively high growth rates and the lack of attention being paid to grain production. Deng apparently agreed with Chen, and the growth target for the Seventh Five-Year Plan was lowered to 7 percent per year for the 1986–1990 period. Chen also supported Hu Yaobang's forced resignation as party general secretary. With advancing age and continued poor health, Chen's activities were limited, but he continued to devote his energies to economic affairs, and increasingly, to party discipline and recurring attempts (unsuccessful) to deal with party corruption. Chen adamantly opposed the weakening of party leadership.

Chen sided with the decision to crack down on demonstrators in 1989, and he supported more conservative policies between 1989 and 1992. But Deng Xiaoping's southern tour in 1992 redefined the economic agenda, and in one of his last public articles, Chen admitted that events had passed him by. He died in 1995.

**SEE ALSO** *Communist Party; Deng Xiaoping; Liu Shaoqi; Mao Zedong; Rural Development, 1949–1978: Great Leap Forward.*

**BIBLIOGRAPHY**

Bachman, David. *Chen Yun and the Chinese Political System.* Berkeley: University of California, Center for Chinese Studies, 1985.

Chen Yun. *Chen Yun wenxuan* [Selected works of Chen Yun]. 3 vols. Beijing: Renmin Chubanshe, 1984.

Fewsmith, Joseph. *Dilemmas of Reform in China: Political Conflict and Economic Debate.* Armonk, NY: Sharpe, 1994.

Jin Chongji and Chen Qun, eds. *Chen Yun zhuan* [A biography of Chen Yun]. 2 vols. Beijing: Zhongyang Wenxian Chubanshe, 2005.

Lardy, Nicholas R., and Kenneth Lieberthal, eds. *Chen Yun's Strategy for China's Development: A Non-Maoist Alternative.* Armonk, NY: Sharpe, 1983.

Zhu Jiamu, ed. *Chen Yun nianpu* [A chronology of Chen Yun]. 3 vols. Beijing: Zhongyang Wenxian Chubanshe, 2000.

***David Bachman***

# CHENGDU

Chengdu is the capital of Sichuan Province and one of the major cultural, economic, and political centers in western China. Thanks to its geographically isolated position, it was little affected by the Opium Wars (1839–1842 and 1856–1860), apart from missionary activities, and it also suffered little during the Taiping Uprising (1851–1864). In 1877 Chengdu became the site of the Sichuan Arsenal (Sichuan Jiqi Ju), established as part of the Self-strengthening movement. The arsenal was the first modern factory in Sichuan. After nearby Chongqing was opened as a trade port in 1890, Chengdu became less isolated and began to experience the cultural contact and conflict apparent in cities closer to the coast. In 1895 a large-scale anti-Christian movement broke out in Chengdu, and some churches were burned down. A few years later, a group of local intellectuals participated in the reform movement by organizing the Society of Sichuan Learning (Shuxue Hui) and publishing the *Journal of Sichuan Learning* (*Shuxue bao*). Many new schools were also established at this time.

## LATE-QING AND REPUBLICAN CHENGDU

In the first half of the twentieth century, Chengdu was one of the largest cities in inland China, with a population of around 340,000 at the turn of the century, increasing to around 440,000 by the 1930s. By 1945, due to wartime migration, its population had reached 740,000, falling to 650,000 in 1949. As the capital of Sichuan Province, Chengdu experienced almost all of the political, economic, social, and cultural transformations that occurred from the late-Qing reform period to the Communist victory in 1949.

In the 1900–1910 period, Chengdu, under the influence of the new policies and self-government movement, became a center and model of industrial, commercial, educational, and social reforms in the Upper Yangzi region. Local elites, supported by state power, enthusiastically participated in reforms that built their social reputation and expanded their influence over ordinary people.

The Sichuan Police Force was set up in 1902, symbolizing the establishment of an early form of urban administration. In 1910 the City Council of Chengdu and Huayang (Chenghua Cheng Yishihui) was formed as part of the self-government movement; the council's members were elected. Both the police and the council became the early foundation of the Chengdu municipal government, but the former played a much more important role. In 1911 many residents joined the railroad-protection movement, contributing to the climate of protest that led to the revolution in October of that year. In late November 1911, Sichuan declared independence and organized the Great Han Military Government (*Dahan Sichuan Jun Zhengfu*).

Postrevolution Chengdu suffered from the chaos general to the warlord era. In 1917 two wars erupted in the city—the first between the Yunnan and Sichuan armies in May, and the second between the Guizhou and Sichuan armies in July. Many thousands of people were killed, and thousands of houses were destroyed, leading to a mass of refugees. Despite social disorder, under the influence of Westernization, new publications and new forms of entertainment such as modern drama emerged in Chengdu during the May Fourth and New Culture movements. The city's most famous writer of this period was Ba Jin (1904–2005), whose autobiographical novel *Jia* (Family), written in 1932, deals with intergenerational family conflict and its impact on political and social change during the 1920s.

By 1926, Sichuan's military leaders were able to expel first the Yunnan Army and then the Guizhou Army from the province. After warlord Yang Sen (1884–1977) became governor in 1924, he launched large-scale urban reconstruction in Chengdu by opening new commercial districts and widening the main streets, changing the urban landscape. In 1928 the Chengdu municipal government was established. During this period, the central government barely controlled Chengdu and instead the city was in the hands of five warlords who shared power under the System of Defense Districts (*Fangqu Zhi*). The Nationalist government finally extended its power into Sichuan during 1935 and 1937.

The War of Resistance (1937–1945) brought Sichuan and Chengdu to central stage in national politics. The Nationalist government's move to Chongqing led to the relocation to Chengdu of many offices of the central government, as well as those of other provincial governments. Many social and cultural organizations, schools, and factories from eastern China also arrived in Chengdu. In addition, a huge number of refugees flooded the city, bringing with them many new cultural elements. All this had a profound impact on Chengdu, and changed the relationship between Sichuan and the central government. After the war, Chengdu became a stage of political struggle between the Guomingdang and Communists, mirroring the situation in the country as a whole. Runaway inflation and food shortages led to food riots. On December 27, 1949, nearly three months after the establishment of the People's Republic of China, the People's Liberation Army captured Chengdu.

## SOCIALIST CHENGDU

During the early socialist period, Chengdu gradually developed into an industrial city producing electronics, machinery, metal goods, chemicals, and textiles, among other products. Facilities were also gradually improved, with attention paid to street widening, residential construction, sewerage, and bridges. After 1964, the central government launched the Three Lines of Construction (*Sanxian Jianshe*) defense plan for preparation against future wars, which stimulated a new wave of industrial development in Chengdu. During the Cultural Revolution (1966–1969), the city experienced extreme unrest, even violence. Many factories and schools were shut down, and many young people and government employees were sent to the countryside.

Post-Mao reforms meant rapid development in Chengdu. From 1993 to 1998, the landscape, environment, and living conditions in the city were greatly improved by the dredging of the Funan River, which circles the city, and the construction of parks along its banks. Chengdu also benefited from the central government's ambitious Great Western Development strategy (*Xibu Dakaifa*), launched in 2000 and directed at balancing coastal development by attention to the hinterland.

Today's Chengdu is a large metropolitan area including nine districts, four cities, and six counties, covering more than twelve thousand square kilometers, and holding over eleven million people, of whom nearly five million live in Chengdu city. Chengdu is rivaled by Chongqing, which in 1997 ceased to be part of Sichuan Province when it became a provincial-level municipality. In response to Chongqing's growing economic power, Chengdu has shown its momentum by building up the economy of western Sichuan. With more than three thousand software companies, Chengdu has become one of the ten largest bases for software production in the nation. In 2006 Chengdu's software exports reached $100 million. The manufacture of airplanes, automobiles, steel, electronic products, biomedicine, and machinery has also developed dramatically. In 2006 Chengdu's gross domestic product was $35 billion (U.S. dollars), and the export and import total was $6.95 billion.

Chengdu is an important scientific, educational, and cultural center in western China, hosting many universities and research institutions. Tourism has also become a major economic driving force. In 2006 Chengdu attracted more than forty million visitors. Among its tourist attractions is the Jinsha Museum, the most advanced modern museum in China, which opened in 2007. The museum holds the country's most important archeological discoveries related to the prehistoric civilization of the Upper Yangzi region. Other attractions include the Du Fu Thatched Cottage Park and Wuhou Temple. Chengdu is best known, however, for its leisurely lifestyle, encapsulated in its teahouses and their clients, which do much to sum up the richness of the city's history and culture.

**SEE ALSO** *Ba Jin; Chongqing; Sichuan.*

**BIBLIOGRAPHY**

He Yimin, ed. *Biange yu fazhan: Zhongguo neilu chengshi Chengdu xiandaihua yanjiu* [Reform and development: A study of modernization in interior city Chengdu]. Chengdu, PRC: Sichuan daxue chubanshe, 2002.

Stapleton, Kristin. *Civilizing Chengdu: Chinese Urban Reform, 1875–1937.* Cambridge, MA: Harvard University Asia Center, 2000.

Wang Di. *Kuachu fengbi de shijie: Changjiang shangyou quyu shehui yanjiu, 1644–1911* [Striding out of a closed world: A study of society in the Upper Yangzi region, 1644–1911]. Beijing: Zhonghua shuju, 1993.

Wang Di. *Street Culture in Chengdu: Public Space, Urban Commoners, and Local Politics in Chengdu, 1870–1930.* Stanford, CA: Stanford University Press, 2003.

Wang Di. *The Teahouse: Small Business, Everyday Culture, and Public Politics in Chengdu, 1900–1950.* Stanford, CA: Stanford University Press, 2008.

Zhang Xuejun and Zhang Lihong. *Chengdu chengshi shi* [A general history of Chengdu]. Chengdu, PRC: Chengdu chubanshe, 1993.

*Wang Di*

# CHIANG CHING-KUO (JIANG JINGGUO)

***1910–1988***

The son of nationalist leader Chiang Kai-shek and Mao Fumei, Chiang Ching-kuo (Jiang Jingguo) was born on April 27, 1910, in Fenghua, very close to Ningbo, and died on January 13, 1988. He spent eleven years in the Soviet Union and, after returning to China, lived for several years in the province of Jiangxi, working at the military headquarters in intelligence and in the youth corps, before going to Taiwan. On the island he completed his political career under the shadow of his father, rising to the position of minister of defense and then prime minister, finally succeeding his father as president of the Republic. He contributed to the economic development of Taiwan, supported by a group of technocrats, and began the process of democratization.

## YEARS IN THE SOVIET UNION

Ching-kuo received a traditional education. At the age of fourteen he entered Pudong High School in Shanghai. He began to surround himself with left-wing friends and made the acquaintance of Li Dazhao, founder of the Chinese Communist Party. In 1925 he left with a group of young people to study in the Soviet Union at the Sun Yat-sen University. There he joined the Communist Youth Corps and received classes from the director of the university, Karl Radek. He read Leon Trotsky's writings and was convinced of the correctness of his ideas about the path that the revolution ought to follow. In 1926 Deng Xiaoping also arrived in Moscow and enrolled in the Sun Yat-sen University. Deng and Chiang took part in classes together, but Chiang supported his father's actions in China. He published an article (1926) in the university's Chinese newspaper with the title *Guomin geming he gongchandang* (China's national revolution and the Chinese Communist Party). He criticized the Chinese Communist Party for sowing discord within the Guomindang (Nationalist Party) and accused the Communist Party of seeking to concentrate power in its own hands. He thought that the true strength of the revolution lay with the Guomindang and his father. As a result, his relations with the Communists deteriorated. Nevertheless, when Chiang Kai-shek delivered his coup against the Communists in Shanghai in 1927, Ching-kuo criticized the action severely. In the autumn of 1927 he entered the Central Tolmatchev Military and Political Institute in Leningrad, where he was forced to renounce his Trotskyite ideas. In May 1930 he graduated from this military academy and returned to Moscow to work in the Dynamo Electrical Plant as a machine-tool operator; later on he was sent to a collective farm in Zhukova, near Moscow. In October 1932 he was transferred to the Urals to work in the mines. He fell sick and, after recovering, was sent the Altai region. In 1933 he returned to the Urals to work in an industrial complex. There he met the woman who was to be his wife, Faina Ipatyevna Vakhreva. In 1935 they had a son, Xiaowen, and in 1936 a daughter, Xiaozhang.

## BACK IN CHINA

Chiang Kai-shek's government reestablished relations with Moscow and asked that Ching-kuo be repatriated. In April 1937 he arrived in Shanghai with his family and held conversations with his father in Hangzhou. Ching-kuo became a member of the central committee of the Three Peoples' Principles Youth Corps (*Sanminzhuyi Qingnian Tuan*) and director of its Jiangxi branch. He also served as commissioner and peace preservation commander in the south of Jiangxi. There he put into practice a three-year plan (1940–1943) to improve the living conditions of the population and maintain security. In 1944 Chiang Kai-shek decided to set up a cadet school in Chongqing and appointed Ching-kuo as director. The group of students was rigorously trained and was later to be a source of support for Ching-kuo. During this period he fathered twin sons, Zhang Xiaoci (1942–1996) and Xiaoyan (John Chiang) (b. 1942), by his then-secretary Zhang Yaruo (1913–1942).

Following the defeat of the Japanese in 1945, Ching-kuo took part in the negotiations between the Guomindang and the Soviet Union that resulted in the Sino-Soviet Treaty of Friendship and Alliance. Later, with the conflict between the Guomindang and the Communist Party, Chiang Kai-shek sent his son to Manchuria to supervise the retreat of Soviet troops and prevent the region from being taken over by the Chinese Communists. On failing to achieve this objective, Ching-kuo was criticized and during the following two years kept a low profile. During those years Ching-kuo and Faina had two more sons: Xiaowu and Xiaoyong.

In Shanghai, Ching-kuo helped his father put into practice an economic policy that sought to deal with high inflation but that ended in failure. He also helped his father prepare for the departure to Taiwan in view of the imminent triumph of the Communists. Ching-kuo was appointed president of the Taiwan provincial committee, and he was entrusted with the task of packing artworks, gold, silver, and foreign currency and making the necessary preparations for setting up a nationalist government on the island.

## TAIWAN

Ching-kuo was a key member of the Nationalist secret service in Taiwan. The secret police arrested thousands of

***Chiang Ching-kuo visiting troops on Kinmen Island, February 27, 1975.*** *The eldest son of the Nationalist leader, Chiang Ching-kuo assumed Chiang Kai-shek's position as head of the Kuomintang before serving as president of the Republic of China. During his tenure, Chiang modernized the economy, ended martial law, and pushed for greater inclusion of native Taiwanese in government affairs.* KEYSTONE/GETTY IMAGES

Taiwanese, and the military courts sentenced many to long periods in prison, while hundreds were killed by execution squads. Ching-kuo also established a school for reeducating prisoners known as the New Life Institute (*Xinsheng Zhaodai Suo*) on Green Island (*Lü Dao*). He was the architect of the white terror in Taiwan.

By 1965 Ching-kuo was nominated minister of defense. In fact, Ching-kuo had informal authority over various areas of government, since his seventy-eight-year-old father was no longer able to supervise these matters. He also acted as negotiator with the United States.

Rapprochement between Communist China and the United States in the late 1960s and early 1970s led to a change in strategy in Taiwan. Ching-kuo and the reformers within the Guomindang thought that the international situation and changes within the island called for a gradual and controlled opening up of political participation. The idea was to transform the Guomindang into a popular and democratic political organization, even though this would lead gradually to control of the party by islanders. This entailed co-opting the Taiwanese in the leadership of the Guomindang and at the same time fostering the growth of a moderate opposition.

## THE LEADER

In June 1969 Ching-kuo finally assumed formal leadership of the administration. Chiang Kai-shek nominated him deputy premier. These were difficult times for Taiwan. The United States was beginning to negotiate a rapprochement with China. Ching-kuo traveled to the United States, where he suffered an assassination attempt from which he escaped unhurt. On October 25, 1971, the mainland took over the China seat in the United Nations, and Taiwan was expelled. Little by little, the island lost the diplomatic recognition of a growing number of countries. On May 26, 1972, Ching-kuo became premier. During the 1970s he promoted government spending on infrastructure in a program known as the Ten Major Development Projects: railways, roads, ports, airports, electrification, and capital-intensive industries such as petrochemicals, iron and steel, aluminum, and copper. On April 5, 1975, Chiang Kai-shek died, and Ching-kuo was elected chairman of the Guomindang Central Committee. Ching-kuo surrounded himself with intellectuals, who supported him in implementing his policies. In 1978 he became president of the Republic. He liberalized political life, adopting policies in keeping with U.S. President Jimmy Carter's defense of human rights. The establishment of diplomatic relations between China and the United States in 1979 was a hard blow for Ching-kuo, who followed a double tactic: negotiating with the Carter administration while approaching the U.S. Congress in search of concessions. These efforts resulted in the Taiwan Relations Act, regulating Taiwan-U.S. relations.

Ching-kuo continued to advance political reforms in an attempt to legitimate his government in the international sphere. In 1984 he designated Lee Teng-hui (Li Denghui), a Taiwanese, as vice-president. Within the Guomindang he formed a committee responsible for political reform under three headings: abolishing martial law, giving parliament a greater role in government, and legalizing opposition parties.

In 1986 the Democratic Progressive Party was founded, and though not immediately recognized by the government, it was tolerated. In June 1987 martial law was abolished. By this time Ching-kuo was very ill, and he died in January 1988.

His son John, who in 2005 took his father's surname, Chiang, pursued a political career in Taiwan: foreign minister (1996–1997), secretary general of the Presidential Office (1999–2000), and later a member of the Legislative Yuan.

**SEE ALSO** *Chiang Kai-shek (Jiang Jieshi); Taiwan, Republic of China.*

**BIBLIOGRAPHY**

Chao, Linda, and Ramon H. Myers. *The First Chinese Democracy: Political Life in the Republic of China on Taiwan.* Baltimore, MD: Johns Hopkins University Press, 1998.

Leng, Shao-chuan. *Chiang Ching-kuo's Leadership in the Development of the Republic of China on Taiwan.* Lanham, MD: University of America Press, 1993.

Taylor, Jay. *The Generalissimo's Son: Chiang Ching-kuo and the Revolutions in China and Taiwan.* Cambridge, MA: Harvard University Press, 2000.

*Marisela Connelly*

# CHIANG KAI-SHEK (JIANG JIESHI)

***1887–1975***

A leader of Nationalist China, Chiang Kai-shek (Jiang Jieshi) ruled the Mainland for two decades amid internal upheavals and foreign aggression before spending the last twenty-six years of his life as the head of a government in exile on Taiwan.

## EARLY CAREER AND RISE TO POWER

Chiang, whose courtesy name is Kai-shek in Cantonese, was born in Fenghua County, Zhejiang Province, to a salt-merchant family. The eldest son of his father's third wife, Chiang was close to his mother and bitter about the ill treatment she received from kinsmen after his father died when Chiang was only nine. Early in life Chiang began to show traits that would shape his future: daring, ambitious, irritable, prone to suspicion. At age twenty-one, then a student at the Baoding Military Academy, Chiang was sent to Japan for military studies and training. He graduated in 1910 from the Shinbu Military School (Zhenwu Xuexiao) in Tokyo, an institution established for Chinese students, and received training in the Japanese Army for a year. Like many other Chinese students in Japan at the time, Chiang became attracted to anti-Qing revolutionary ideas. In 1908 he joined the Tongmenghui, the revolutionary organization founded by Sun Yat-sen (Sun Yixian).

When the 1911 Revolution broke out, Chiang returned to China and participated in the uprisings in Shanghai and Hangzhou. In the wake of the overthrow of the Qing dynasty, he followed his faction leader, Chen Qimei, in a power struggle among revolutionaries for the control of the lower Yangzi River valley. In January 1912 Chiang assassinated Chen's rival and had to hide in Japan for months. From 1913 to 1915 he again assisted Chen in the unsuccessful Second Revolution (*Erci Geming*), which Sun Yat-sen organized against the Republic under Yuan Shikai. Both Chiang and Chen joined Sun's Chinese Revolutionary Party (Zhonghua Geming Dang). Chen's death in 1916 at the hands of Yuan's agents deprived Chiang of a mentor and protector. As a result, he spent the next few years without a clear focus in his life or career. He maintained marginal contacts with Sun's revolutionary movement, providing occasional services to Sun's regime in Guangzhou (Canton), and joined business ventures with a few other followers of Sun in Shanghai. It was during this time that Chiang developed ties with the city's powerful underworld, the Green Gang (Qing Bang).

Chiang's political break came in June 1922, when Sun was ousted by his military supporter Chen Jiongming from Guangzhou. A former subordinate and bitter rival of Chen Jiongming, Chiang rushed south and joined Sun on board a gunboat outside of Guangzhou, assisting Sun in his campaign against Chen. The campaign proved futile and they soon retreated to Shanghai, but Chiang's ability and loyalty displayed during those weeks deeply impressed Sun. From then on he became one of Sun's key military advisers and aids. In 1923 Sun recaptured

Guangzhou and appointed Chiang chief of staff of his new southern regime. At the time Sun was accepting advice and assistance from the Comintern and establishing a United Front between his reorganized Guomindang (Nationalist Party) and the newly founded Chinese Communist Party. Later that year he sent Chiang on a three-month study tour in the Soviet Union. Chiang later recalled that he obtained a negative impression of both the country and its designs for China, yet he showed little of that upon returning to Guangzhou. The trip in fact made Chiang the only military figure around Sun who had received Moscow's influence and blessing. He was soon appointed commandant of the new military academy at Huangpu (Whampoa), founded with Soviet support. Although small in size, the Whampoa Military Academy (Huangpu Junxiao) allowed Chiang for the first time to build a power base of his own. Taking the late Qing leaders Zeng Guofan and Hu Linyi as his models, he stressed moral indoctrination and cultivated personal ties with officers and cadets at the academy.

This new power base proved crucial to Chiang's ascent when Sun died in Beijing in March 1925. While at first not a major contender to succeed Sun, Chiang's military strength made him a valuable partner for those who were. As they eliminated each other in the ensuing intraparty struggles, Chiang steadily rose in political importance. By early 1926 he dominated Guangzhou alongside Wang Jingwei, a civilian party leader. Then in March, Chiang ousted Wang in a coup d'état and became the sole leader of the Guomindang regime. His fellow provincials and former business associates in Shanghai now became his major supporters and would remain so for decades to come.

In July 1926, with Soviet and Chinese Communist Party assistance, the young general launched a Northern Expedition against warlords and their government in Beijing in hopes of reunifying China under the Guomindang. With his Huangpu cadets as the core of his troops, Chiang marched the National Revolutionary Army northward from Guangzhou and within months defeated or absorbed dozens of warlords, extending Guomindang control to the Yangzi River valley. As his troops entered his old base in Shanghai in early 1927, Chiang, long dissatisfied with the United Front, decided to purge the Communists from his ranks. In April he broke with the Guomindang center, recently moved from Guangzhou to Wuhan and still supporting the United Front, and slaughtered thousands of Communists, leftists, union workers, and students with the help of the Green Gang. The United Front collapsed and the Wuhan regime, then headed by Wang Jingwei, eventually joined Chiang to form a new Guomindang government in Nanjing. After a brief tactical retirement, Chiang resumed command of the National Revolutionary Army and continued the Northern Expedition until late 1928, by which time all the major warlords accepted the national leadership of the Guomindang.

## THE NANJING DECADE

At age forty-one, Chiang became ruler of a nominally reunified China. With a narrow military background and limited experience in policy making, he was confronted with the task of reconstructing central authority in a poor, weak, and disintegrated country. Chiang had little time for deliberate nation building. The threats he faced were multiple and immediate: The Communist Party, though devastated by the purge, continued its armed revolts in the countryside. The hasty effort to bring the Northern Expedition to a conclusion allowed many regional militarists to maintain their autonomy, and they were ready to challenge the new government whenever opportunity arose. The foreign powers continued to exploit China under the unequal treaties, with Japan the greatest menace among them.

In the following ten years, known as the Nanjing decade, Chiang waged a series of political and military struggles against various alliances between regional militarists and his intraparty rivals, and directed five "bandit-suppression campaigns" to eradicate the Communist Party from its base in Jiangxi. These efforts were largely successful, as his control over the Guomindang and China steadily increased and the Communists were driven to their desperate Long March in 1934. These priorities induced Chiang to avoid confrontations with the Japanese, who occupied Manchuria in 1931 and made inroads into North China and Mongolia in the following years. Describing their strategy as "domestic pacification before external resistance," Chiang and his partners in Nanjing, notably Wang Jingwei, made repeated territorial concessions to Japan in order to concentrate their attention on crushing domestic rivals.

Chiang also tried to reduce the Japanese threat by soliciting Western help. After breaking with Moscow in 1927, Chiang improved relations with the Western powers, especially the United States, which provided several loans to Nanjing in the early 1930s. He partly made up for his lack of foreign-policy experience by marrying Song Meiling (Mayling Soong), who was in effect his fourth wife (before marrying her in 1927, he had to divorce two previous wives and dispose of a concubine). The marriage brought him immense political benefit, as the Song family not only had married another daughter to the late Sun Yat-sen but also was wealthy, influential, and well connected with the West. Educated at Wellesley and fluent in English, Meiling projected a Westernized, pro-Western image for Chiang's regime. Chiang's own conversion to Christianity, a condition for the marriage, further convinced the American public that his "new China" was modern, progressive, and friendly to the United States. Yet Chiang remained eclectic in his adoption of Western models. His Guomindang regime was a Leninist-party dictatorship, a legacy of Russian influence during the United Front, and in the early 1930s he showed interest in Fascism and employed German advisors to strengthen his armed forces.

During the Nanjing decade Chiang's government made moderate progress in improving the infrastructure of the Chinese economy, especially in the coastal cities, where Guomindang control was relatively stable, but it largely ignored the poverty and oppression of rural China. While not necessarily an ally of landlords or capitalists, Chiang's own background and propensity prevented him from initiating radical social and economic reforms. His vision of national reconstruction was exemplified by the New Life movement that he launched in 1934. Mixing elements of Confucianism, Fascism, and YMCA reformism, the movement attempted to restore China's social and moral order by civilizing the daily attitude and behavior of its citizens. It was a dismal failure.

Meanwhile, Chiang's leadership came under increasing popular criticism for its weak-kneed policy toward Japan. In December 1936, while inspecting troops in Xi'an and planning final assaults on Communist Party forces recently relocated just to the north, Chiang was placed under house arrest by his own generals. In captivity he gave in to the generals' demands to stop the anti-Communist campaigns and begin preparations for a war against Japan. When he was dramatically released two weeks later, he was regarded by many as an indispensable leader of the nation.

***Chiang Kai-shek, c. 1948.*** *Leader of the Nationalist forces, Chinese general Chiang Kai-shek rose to power after the fall of the Qing dynasty. At the end of World War II, Chiang led his forces into a losing war with Mao Zedong's Communist Red Army, eventually retreating to Taiwan and governing a U.S.-backed Republic of China on the island.* HULTON ARCHIVE/GETTY IMAGES

## THE WAR AGAINST JAPAN AND CIVIL WAR

War against Japan finally broke out in July 1937 when the Japanese Army started another incident in North China. Hoping to attract Western assistance by demonstrating China's ability and will to resist Japan, Chiang devoted his best troops to the defense of Shanghai in August, which lasted for three months. When that assistance did not arrive, the Chinese forces retreated inland, losing the entire eastern seaboard to the invading Japanese by the end of 1938. Moving his government to Chongqing in the interior, Chiang had to adopt a strategy of trading space for time and waged a war of attrition against the militarily superior Japan. Chiang formed a second United Front with the Communists, in which the Communists agreed to join the war under Guomindang leadership and were allowed to keep their armies. Though from 1938 to 1941 Chiang's government fought a precarious war with scarce resources and little foreign help, his prestige among the Chinese, who saw him as a symbol of national resistance, reached its zenith.

The Japanese attack on Pearl Harbor in December 1941 came as timely relief for Chiang. After the Sino-Japanese conflict became a part of World War II and China an ally of the Western powers, military and financial aid from the United States alleviated Chongqing's war burden and greatly boosted Chinese morale. Unequal treaties with the West were abolished in early 1943. Later that year Chiang attended the Cairo Conference as one of the "Big Four" Allied Powers. Yet the United Front between the Guomindang and the Communist Party was deteriorating. Confident of eventual victory over Japan with American help, Chiang now returned his attention to the Communist threat. He ordered a blockade of the Communist Party base in Yan'an and preserved his best troops and foreign aid for a possible showdown with the Communists in the near future. The United States tried to mediate the conflict, but expected Chiang to be the leader of postwar China and his government a major U.S. ally in postwar East Asia.

Shortly after Japan surrendered in 1945, full-scale civil war erupted between Chiang's Guomindang regime and the Communists. To Chiang's surprise, the long war against Japan had left his party and army demoralized and corrupt, yet had transformed the Communist Party into an experienced and popular force. Rampant inflation and mismanagement of the economy further alienated the urban population from the Guomindang. Chiang's overly ambitious war plans and micromanagement of battles also backfired. The much larger and better-equipped Guomindang forces lost almost every battle in the four-year-long civil war. To rally popular support, Chiang declared the end of Guomindang "tutelage" and convened a National Assembly in 1948, which quickly elected him president, but without Communist Party participation, the new constitutional structure was but a façade. He had to resign from office when the civil war worsened in early 1949. Despite repeated pleas from Chiang and a personal trip by his wife to Washington, D.C., a shocked and disappointed United States gave up on him. By the end of 1949 Chiang and a Guomindang in shambles had been driven out of the mainland by the Communist Party and found refuge on the island of Taiwan.

## ISLAND REFUGE

On the verge of total defeat, Chiang and his followers were saved by the outbreak of the Korean War in June 1950. Fearing expansion of the Communist Bloc, of which the People's Republic had become an important member, the United States decided to provide military and financial aid to Taiwan as part of its global strategy of containment in the emerging Cold War. For the next two and a half decades, American protection and assistance ensured the survival of Chiang and his government in exile on Taiwan.

Chiang ended up ruling Taiwan longer than he governed the mainland. On the island he resumed the presidency of the Republic of China, still recognized by most nations owing to U.S. backing, and was "reelected" four times until his death. While continuing to claim the right to rule over all of China, he controlled the island population (about 15% of which came with him from the mainland) with an iron fist. In the 1950s Chiang's regime, with American support, survived two military confrontations with the People's Republic across the Taiwan Strait, yet in the early 1960s his plan to invade the mainland was also stopped by a less confident United States. The United States maintained military bases on the island, turning it into a critical link in its defenses in the West Pacific. Yet Chiang regarded himself as a nationalist fighting Soviet domination of China and rejected the notion of an independent Taiwan. When Mao Zedong launched the Cultural Revolution in 1966, Chiang initiated a Chinese Cultural Revival movement in Taiwan as an ideological counteroffensive. The movement displayed much of the same concerns and approaches of his New Life movement in the 1930s, but with a new emphasis on the defense of Chinese traditional culture.

Chiang's years in Taiwan were the most secure and comfortable in his life. Only the most loyal had followed him there, and the small island was much easier to govern than the vast mainland. Urged on by the Americans, the Guomindang in the 1950s carried out land reform, which eliminated a potential source of rural unrest. Despite the humiliating loss of the mainland, Chiang was treated as a demigod in China's "last bastion of anti-Communism." Political stability, American aid, solid infrastructure left by the Japanese, and appropriate Guomindang development strategies produced rapid economic growth in Taiwan in the 1960s and 1970s. The U.S. war in Vietnam also benefited Taiwan economically. Yet international support for Chiang's regime gradually declined. As the United States improved relations with the People's Republic in the early 1970s, Taiwan lost control of the China seat in the United Nations as well as diplomatic ties with many countries. Now in his eighties, Chiang's health deteriorated in the face of this diplomatic crisis. Chiang had one son, Jingguo, from his first wife and another adopted from his friend Dai Jitao. By the 1950s it became clear that the Russian-educated Jingguo, who controlled the secret police in Taiwan, would be Chiang's successor. Potential rivals to Jingguo were purged from power one after the other. As Chiang lay ill and senile in the early 1970s, Jingguo ran the island regime as its premier. He took over Chiang's leadership in Taiwan soon after Chiang's death.

Chiang was both a transitional and transformational figure in modern Chinese history. A shrewd player of warlord politics, he was well-equipped to bring the divided country back together by force, bargaining, and political maneuvering. While his background and vision limited his ability as a leader to tackle the complex social, political, and economic problems facing China at the time, his government laid the groundwork for later national integration and reconstruction. Moreover, the long and eventually victorious war that Chiang led against Japan enhanced the Chinese sense of nationhood and elevated China's international status. In Taiwan he survived essentially as an American puppet, his nationalistic rhetoric notwithstanding. He established a de facto dynasty there and enjoyed the aura and authority of an imperial autocrat. Yet Guomindang rule also transformed the former Japanese colony into a modernized, prosperous Chinese society. Chiang's model of "Confucian" authoritarianism and Western-oriented economic development offered a contrast and potential alternative to the turbulent path of Maoism in post-1949 China.

**SEE ALSO** *Nationalist Government, 1927–1949; Taiwan, Republic of China.*

## BIBLIOGRAPHY

PRIMARY SOURCES

Jian Shenghuang, ed. *Jiang Zhongzheng zongtong dang'an: Shilüe gaoben* [The Chiang Kai-shek collections: The chronological events]. Vol. 1–29. Taipei: Academia Historica, 2003–2007.

Mao Sicheng, ed. *Minguo shiwu nian yiqian zhi Jiang Jieshi xiansheng* [Mr. Chiang Kai-shek prior to 1926]. Reprint, Hong Kong: Longmen Bookstore, 1965.

Qin Xiaoyi, ed. *Zongtong Jiang gong dashi changbian chugao* [A preliminary draft of the chronology of President Chiang]. Taipei: The Guomindang Party Archives, 1978.

SECONDARY SOURCES

Cheng, Peter P.C. Taiwan under Chiang Kai-shek's Era, 1945–1976. *Asian Profile* 16, 4 (August 1988): 299–315.

Eastman, Lloyd E. *The Abortive Revolution: China under Nationalist Rule, 1927–1937.* Cambridge, MA: Harvard University Press, 1972.

Eastman, Lloyd E. *Seeds of Destruction: Nationalist China in War and Revolution, 1937–1949.* Stanford, CA: Stanford University Press, 1984.

Fenby, Jonathan, *Chiang Kai-shek: China's Generalissimo and the Nation He Lost.* New York: Da Capo Press, 2004.

Li, Laura Tyson, *Madame Chiang Kai-shek: China's Eternal First Lady.* New York: Atlantic Monthly Press, 2006.

Li Yong and Zhang Zhongtian. *Jiang Jieshi nianpu* [A chronology of Chiang Kai-shek]. Beijing: The Chinese Communist Party History Press, 1995.

Loh, Pichon. *The Early Chiang Kai-shek: A Study of His Personality and Politics, 1887–1924.* New York: Columbia University Press, 1971.

***Ke-wen Wang***

## CHINA HANDS

The term *China Hands* long referred to Westerners respected for their knowledge of, or at least extended presence in, China. The "Old China Hands" of the British Foreign Office made Far East policy in the nineteenth century, but after World War I (1914–1918), Americans gradually challenged the British and saw Old China Hands as representing the colonialist "Shanghai Mind."

But China Hands now most commonly refers to wartime American Foreign Service Officers and military advisers who in the 1950s were blamed for the "loss of China" and in the 1970s were credited with having offered a "lost chance" to maintain relations. After World War I, both the American Department of State and War Department developed China specialists. The Fifteenth Army, known as the "Old China Hands," was stationed in Tianjin, where it was commanded by George Catlett Marshall (1880–1959) in the 1920s. Army officers such as Joseph Stilwell (1883–1946) and David D. Barrett (1892–1977) had language training and were military attaches in the 1930s. Foreign Service Officers John S. Service (1909–1999) and John Paton Davies (1908–1999) were born in China to missionary parents, while John Carter Vincent (1900–1972) and O. Edmund Clubb (1901–1989) became China specialists after joining the foreign service.

After 1941, these China Hands were caught between Allied "Europe first" priorities and Chinese resentment of them. They reported to superiors in Washington whose policies they could not influence to describe situations in China over which they had little control. Their reports contrasted Nationalist war weariness and corruption with the vigor and achievements of the Communists and urged military liaison with Yan'an. Chiang Kai-shek (Jiang Jieshi) resisted until the visit of Vice President Henry Wallace (1888–1965), accompanied by Owen Lattimore (1900–1989), an American raised in China and a scholar of Central Asia. The August 1944 "Dixie Mission" to Yan'an, which included Barrett, Davies, and Service, found Mao Zedong eager to court American recognition and to coordinate militarily. Diplomats and reporters widely foresaw eventual victory for the Communists, though they had differing predictions about the nature of their rule. Patrick Hurley (1883–1963) was appointed U.S. ambassador in late 1944 and flew immediately to Yan'an to promote a coalition government between the Nationalists and Communists. When the project failed, Hurley demanded the removal of Service, Clubb, and Davies, and later alleged that the State Department had sabotaged his efforts.

After 1945, the Cold War changed Russia from U.S. partner to adversary and China from dependent ally into potential victim of Soviet expansionism. General George Marshall, before becoming secretary of state, traveled to China to negotiate a coalition government in which Communists would participate. In Washington, Service was arrested for leaking documents to *Amerasia*, a leftist journal (the case was dropped by the grand jury). Republicans took control of the U.S. Congress in 1946 but lost the 1948 presidential election. One Republican senator charged that the "pro-Communist group in the State Department ... promoted at every opportunity the Communist cause in China." (Kahn 1975, p. 2) The State Department's so-called *China White Paper* (1949) defended support of the Nationalists in a way that infuriated American critics and insulted Chinese Communists as they took power.

Many then asked "who lost China?" They assumed that Mao could not have succeeded without American perfidy. Senator Joseph McCarthy (1908–1957) blamed Marshall for sabotaging Nationalist victory and called Lattimore the "top Soviet agent" in the State Department. Senate and House committees interrogated the China Hands and showed that they had extensive contacts with known Communists. Lattimore was indicted for perjury (the charges were eventually dismissed). Service was accused of presenting Mao as an "agrarian reformer," a phrase Service denied using. Although successive loyalty boards found no specific transgression or even disloyalty, they did allege bad judgment. Service, Clubb, Vincent, and Davies were either forced to resign or were fired. Journalists such as Theodore White (1915–1986) and Edgar Snow (1905–1972) lost their jobs or could no longer write on China. White invented a pocket calendar, then went to report on Germany, while Snow moved to Switzerland. Service designed successful industrial steam traps before being reinstated by the Supreme Court in 1957. When he was not given China responsibilities, he retired to work as a researcher at the Center for Chinese Studies at Berkeley. Davies ran a furniture factory in Peru before being reinstated, while Vincent retired to Cambridge, Massachusetts. Other wartime China Hands fared better, including Everett F. Drumwright (d. 1993) and Edward Rice (1909–2006), who by 1960 were the only Foreign Service Officers with experience in China before 1945.

After Richard Nixon (1913–1994) opened relations with China in 1972, many wondered about a "lost chance" in 1949. Others speculated that the purged China Hands might have kept Vietnam-era policymakers from misreading China's bellicose rhetoric. Skeptics replied that China was committed to the Soviet bloc and better communication would not by itself have transformed relations.

By the end of the twentieth century, China Hand once again meant simply "someone who came to China before I did."

**SEE ALSO** *Civil War, 1946-1949.*

**BIBLIOGRAPHY**

Bickers, Robert. *Britain in China: Community, Culture, and Colonialism, 1900–1949.* Manchester, U.K.: Manchester University Press, 1999.

Evans, M. Stanton. *Blacklisted by History: The Untold Story of Senator Joe McCarthy and His Fight against America's Enemies.* New York: Crown Forum, 2007.

Kahn, E. J., Jr. *The China Hands: America's Foreign Service Officers and What Befell Them.* New York: Viking, 1975.

May, Gary. *China Scapegoat: The Diplomatic Ordeal of John Carter Vincent.* Washington, DC: New Republic, 1979.

Rand, Peter. *China Hands: The Adventures and Ordeals of the American Journalists Who Joined Forces with the Great Chinese Revolution.* New York: Simon & Schuster, 1995.

U.S. Department of State. *The China White Paper, August 1949* (originally issued as *United States Relations with China, with Special Reference to the Period 1944–1949*). 2 vols. Stanford, CA: Stanford University Press, 1967.

***Charles Hayford***

# CHINA MERCHANTS' STEAM NAVIGATION COMPANY

The China Merchants' Steam Navigation Company (Lunchuan Zhaoshangju, or CMSNC) was officially formed on January 14, 1873, to transport the Qing government's tribute rice from the Lower Yangzi to Tianjin and to compete with foreign steamship lines in coastal freight service. The CMSNC was neither a state enterprise nor a family firm; it was, rather, the first indigenous joint-stock company sponsored by the Chinese state. Management was shared between the Qing government and merchants, but much of its capital was raised through shares. Chinese merchants were slow to take up the shares until the joint-stock organization was reorganized under the management of two comprador-merchants, Tang Jingxing (1832–1892) and Xu Run (1838–1911), who became the actual administrators between 1873 and 1885. Tang and Xu were the largest shareholders, under whose leadership the paid-up share capital increased to 476,000 *taels* by the fall of 1874, reaching one million by 1880 and two million by 1882. Even though the company was government sponsored, it was owned and administrated privately by risk-taking shareholders.

## FINANCING AND EXPANSION

Yet the CMSNC had to rely on government loans to supplement merchant capital. Zhili governor-general and commissioner of the northern ports, Li Hongzhang, under whose aegis the CMSNC was formed, accepted the necessity of such loans and regarded them as an important part of his approach to the official-supervision, merchant-management (*guandu shangban*) model exemplified in the CMSNC's operations. Thanks to Li and his influence, loans amounting to 1,903,868 *taels* were made to the company at various points before 1885. With the government loans, the company could repay the short-term high-interest loans made by native banks, and in 1877 the company was able to purchase the Shanghai Steam Navigation Company of the American firm Russell and Company.

In 1876 the CMSNC also began to develop a diversified investment portfolio through the creation of two very profitable insurance subsidiaries and the rapid expansion of its real-estate holdings in the form of wharves, warehouses, and other properties in Shanghai, as well as other ports. After the acquisition of Russell and Company in 1877, the CMSNC owned a fleet of thirty vessels and had the highest tonnage among steamship companies in China. Between 1878 and 1883, the company purchased nine new ships, and extended its operations beyond Chinese waters to the United States, Japan, and Southeast Asia.

The management of the loans exemplifies the Qing government's financial support for the CMSNC. Before 1882, the total of the government loans made to the company was much larger than its total paid-up share capital: The loans represented some 50 to 60 percent of the company's total debts, or 2.2 times more than the maximum paid-up capital between 1876 and 1880. The loans were guaranteed an interest of 7 to 10 percent per annum, a lower rate than the shareholder's annual 10

**Government loans to the China Merchants' Steam Navigation Company, 1872–1883 (in Shanghai taels)**

| Source | Year | Amount of loan | Annual interest rate |
|---|---|---|---|
| Tianjin military funds | 1872 | 120,000 | 7% |
| Wood likin of Nanjing | 1875 | 100,000 | 8% |
| Zhejiang Public funds | 1875 | 100,000 | 8% |
| Coastal defense funds | 1876 | 100,000 | 8% |
| Yangzhou commissary | 1876 | 100,000 | 8% |
| Zhili military funds | 1876 | 50,000 | 10% |
| Baoding military funds | 1876 | 50,000 | 8% |
| Chefoo customs | 1876 | 100,000 | 8% |
| Nanjing provincial treasury | 1877 | 100,000 | 10% |
| Jiangan commissary | 1877 | 200,000 | 10% |
| Shanghai customs | 1877 | 200,000 | 10% |
| Zhejiang silk revenue | 1877 | 200,000 | 10% |
| Jiangxi treasury | 1877 | 200,000 | 10% |
| Hubei treasury | 1877 | 100,000 | 10% |
| Coast-defense funds | 1878 | 150,000 | |
| Coast-defense funds | 1878–81 | 100,000 | |
| Funds for diplomatic missions | 1881 | 80,000 | |
| Tianjin funds for coast-defense | 1883 | 200,000 | |

SOURCE: Lai, Chi-kong. "Lunchuan zhaoshangju guoyou wenti, 1878–1881" (The proposal to nationalize the China Merchants' Steam Navigation Company, 1878–1881). *Bulletin of the Institute of Modern History Academia Sinica* (Taipei), Vol. 17, 1988, p. 21.

*Table 1*

**Tribute grain shipped by the China Merchants' Steam Navigation Company**

| Year | Tribute grain shipped (in Shanghai taels) | Rate of freight (tribute grain shipped × rate of freight) | Total earning |
|---|---|---|---|
| June 1873 | 170,000 | 0.600 | 102,000 |
| 1873–74 | 250,000 | 0.600 | 150,000 |
| 1874–75 | 300,000 | 0.600 | 180,000 |
| 1875–76 | 450,000 | 0.600 | 270,000 |
| 1876–77 | 290,000 | 0.600 | 174,000 |
| 1877–78 | 523,000 | 0.600 | 313,800 |
| 1878–79 | 520,000 | 0.600 | 312,000 |
| 1879–80 | 570,000 | 0.600 | 342,000 |
| 1880–81 | 475,415 | 0.531 | 252,445 |
| 1881–82 | 557,000 | 0.531 | 295,767 |
| 1882–83 | 580,000 | 0.531 | 307,980 |
| 1883–84 | 390,000 | 0.531 | 207,090 |
| 1884–85 | 470,000 | 0.531 | 249,570 |

SOURCE: Lai, Chi-kong. "Lunchuan zhaoshangju guoyou wenti, 1878–1881" (The proposal to nationalize the China Merchants' Steam Navigation Company, 1878–1881). *Bulletin of the Institute of Modern History Academia Sinica* (Taipei), Vol. 17, 1988, p. 20.

*Table 2*

percent guaranteed dividend. Thanks to Li's influence, no interest was paid on the loans between 1877 and 1885. The suspended interest totaled more than 900,000 *taels* over those eight years. This amounted to about half of the paid-up share capital of the company in the 1882–1893 period.

Government connections were also important for preferential shipping arrangements. Part of the CMSNC's success during its first decade of operations resulted from the fact that Li left management to the merchants but used his enormous power to create favorable conditions for company operations. When the company began to make a profit, Li was also instrumental in defending it against the many officials who proposed that the government take over ownership. However, not even Li's influence could shelter the CMSNC from official exactions. From 1883 to 1885, the CMSNC's merchant managers were replaced by officials, and the company's capacity for growth declined.

## DECLINE FOLLOWING THE SINO-FRENCH WAR

The change in policy was occasioned by the Sino-French War (1884–1885) and the resulting financial crisis in Shanghai. With war looming, Li Hongzhang had to divert funds from the CMSNC to the northern fleet. When the merchant directors lost heavily in the financial crisis and were found to be misusing the company's capital for private investments, Li removed them and, in 1885, appointed Sheng Xuanhuai (1844–1916) as CMSNC director-general. Sheng had meanwhile been buying the company's shares, and was the largest shareholder in 1885. During his directorship, between 1885 and 1902, Sheng continued to hold such official posts as customs *daotai* in Chefoo (Yantai) and Tianjin, and he controlled the company's affairs from a distance. He appointed his favorites as top administrators, regardless of their share-holding amounts. Bureaucratic control in the company increased.

Despite the advantages that the CMSNC once enjoyed, profits were not reinvested in technological improvements after the Sino-French War. To be sure, the company was paying off its debts, donating large amounts to the hard-pressed government, and investing in other enterprises in this second period (1885–1902). But capital investment stagnated, and the tonnage of the fleet remained constant. By 1893 the CMSNC had a fleet of only twenty-six ships, while the shipping tonnages of foreign steamship companies in Chinese waters had grown rapidly. In addition, several new shipping companies, including the Nippon Yusen Kaisha (Japan Mail Line, or NYK), shared the growing Chinese shipping market. The loss of mercantile control of the CMSNC led to a more general disenchantment among

Chinese merchants regarding government-sponsored enterprises, and dampened their willingness to invest in other such projects.

When Li Hongzhang died in 1901, the CMSNC was restructured, with CMSNC's shareholders and Sheng Xuanhuai using the board of directors and company law to limit growing bureaucratic control. The new governor-general of Zhili, Yuan Shikai, removed the company's director in an effort to consolidate his own personal control over the CMSNC, but he faced resistance from shareholders. Yuan's control adumbrated important changes in corporate governance, and the government, from 1908, continued to appoint managers under the control of the Ministry of Posts and Communications. While the CMSNC's assets and investments continued to grow after 1902, its market share gradually declined because of strong competition from NYK and other foreign shipping companies operating in Chinese waters. As late as 1903, the CMSNC still retained the largest amount of tonnage on the Yangzi River, although it fell far behind its principal rivals during the Republican period.

### CHANGES AFTER THE 1911 REVOLUTION

In the late 1900s, a newly established board of directors appointed new managers to conduct company affairs, while the government appointed top officers to supervise the company. After the revolution of 1911, the newly established government needed to borrow money from foreign banks and proposed using the company's assets to arrange a loan with the Hong Kong and Shanghai Banking Corporation, provoking strong opposition from CMSNC shareholders. With the privatization of the company in 1912, CMSNC remained under the control of the Ministry of Agriculture, Industry, and Commerce and was required to submit an annual report on its business performance to the government. The company's assets grew from 5.1 million *taels* in 1887 to 15.5 million by 1914.

By the 1920s, CMSNC was headed by descendants of Sheng Xuanhuai and Li Hongzhang, but the company suffered from the military and financial instability of the early Republican period. Warlords used CMSNC steamships to transport soldiers without paying for the service, and the company had serious financial and management problems. In the 1920s, Li's grandson Li Guojie became head of the company, but he was charged with corruption. In 1927 the Nationalist government established a team to investigate the company's management, and in 1932 the government nationalized the company.

**SEE ALSO** *Li Hongzhang; Liu Hongsheng.*

### BIBLIOGRAPHY

Chan, Wellington K. K. *Merchants, Mandarins, and Modern Enterprise in Late Ch'ing China*. Cambridge, MA: Harvard University Press, 1977.

Eastman, Lloyd E. *Throne and Mandarins: China's Search for a Policy during the Sino-French Controversy, 1880–1885*. Cambridge, MA: Harvard University Press, 1967.

Feuerwerker, Albert. *China's Early Industrialization: Sheng Hsuan-huai (1844–1916) and Mandarin Enterprise*. Cambridge, MA: Harvard University Press, 1958.

Hao Yen-p'ing (Hao Yanping). *The Comprador in Nineteenth Century China: Bridge between East and West*. Cambridge, MA: Harvard University Press, 1970.

King, Frank H. H. The Hong Kong Bank in Late Imperial China, 1864–1902. Cambridge, MA: Cambridge University Press, 1987.

Lai Chi-kong. Lunchuan zhaoshangju guoyou wenti, 1878–1881 [The proposal to nationalize the China Merchants' Steam Navigation Company, 1878–1881]. *Bulletin of the Institute of Modern History, Academia Sinica* (Taibei) 17 (1988): 15–40.

Lai Chi-kong. Lunchuan zhaoshangju jingyin guanli wenti, 1872–1901 [Enterprise management of the China Steam Navigation Company, 1872–1901]. *Bulletin of the Institute of Modern History, Academia Sinica* (Taibei) 19 (1990): 67–108.

Lai Chi-kong. Li Hung-chang and Modern Enterprise: The China Merchants' Company, 1872–1885. *Chinese Studies in History* (1991): 19–51.

Liu Kwang-Ching (Liu Guangjing). Steamship Enterprise in Nineteenth-century China. *Journal of Asian Studies* 18, 4 (1959): 435–455.

Liu Kwang-Ching (Liu Guangjing). *Anglo-American Steamship Rivalry in China, 1862–1874*. Cambridge, MA: Harvard University Press, 1962.

Liu Kwang-Ching (Liu Guangjing). British-Chinese Steamship Rivalry in China, 1873–1885. In *Economic Development of China and Japan: Studies in Economic History and Political Economy*, ed. C. D. Cowan, 49–78. London: Allen & Unwin, 1964.

Liu Kwang-Ching (Liu Guangjing). Tong King-sing: Jardine Comprador and China's First Modern Entrepreneur. In *The Thistle and the Jade: A Celebration of 150 Years of Jardine, Matheson & Co.*, ed. Maggie Keswick, 102–127. London: Octopus, 1982.

Liu Kwang-Ching (Liu Guangjing). *Jingshi yu ziqiang* [Statecraft and self- strengthening]. Taibei: Lianjing, 1990.

Pong, David. Keeping the Foochow Navy Yard Afloat: Government Finance and China's Early Modern Defence Industry, 1866–75. *Modern Asian Studies* 21, 1 (1987): 121–152.

Zhang Guohui. *Yangwu yundong yu Zhongguo jindai qiye* [The Westernization movement and modern Chinese enterprise]. Beijing: Zhongguo Shehui Kexue, 1979.

Zhang Houquan, ed. 1988. *Zhaoshangju shi* [A history of the China Merchants' Steam Navigation Company]. Beijing: Renmin Jiaotong, 1988.

***Lai Chi-kong***

## CHINA'S AGENDA 21

The 1992 United Nations Conference on Environment and Development in Rio de Janeiro adopted UN Agenda 21 calling for replacement of the traditional model of "polluting first and treating later" with a new sustainable model promoting economic growth while protecting the environment. The conference called on all nations to create their own Agenda 21 models. The People's Republic of China was one of the first developing countries to respond.

## CHINA'S RESPONSE

At Rio, Premier Li Peng personally committed China to implementation of Agenda 21. The State Council almost immediately assembled a leading group drawn from fifty-two ministries and agencies, and supported by over three hundred international experts, to develop a program for implementation. In March 1994 the State Council approved a program that was carefully reviewed to ensure conformity with international standards for promoting sustainable growth with reduced toxic side effects to water, soil, and air.

In 1996 the Chinese government published *Opinions for Further Implementation of China's Agenda 21*. This document empowered local authorities to: (1) create actions plans that are sensitive to local conditions, (2) implement local pilot projects, (3) guide the construction of experimental communities as models of Agenda 21 development, and (4) instill administrative organs with strong leadership for unified implementation of China's Agenda 21.

By the end of 1996, two-thirds of China's thirty provinces, autonomous regions, and municipalities had organized leading groups and established administrative infrastructure to implement Agenda 21 at local levels. A major focus of Agenda 21 became the Cleaner Production Strategy, as part of China's transition from a planned to a socialist market economy. The State Planning Commission stressed the need for cleaner production as the foundation for China's transition from "extensive" to "intensive" economic growth. The Ninth Five-Year Plan (1996–2000) and long-term targets for 2010 incorporated the Agenda 21 strategy to change China's pollution control from end-of-pipe treatment to preventative technology throughout the manufacturing process.

## RESULTS AND PROBLEMS

In the past, poor institutional and cooperative ties with international organizations hindered China's implementation of sustainable development. But following Agenda 21, bilateral and multilateral agreements with appropriate countries are incorporated into economic planning and administrative practices. The processes promoted by Agenda 21—including the formation and implementation of environmental and social impact assessments—reflect the many issues and practices brought to the forefront to harmonize development with the environment and to predict and limit adverse impacts of large-scale internationally funded projects.

Nonetheless, the main themes of the UN's Agenda 21, including the use of local knowledge in development decisions, were interpreted differently in China or, in some cases, never gained importance in actual government behavior. Local environmental agencies failed to evaluate and audit enterprises, and industries failed to install treatment systems or meet target dates for the elimination of major emission sources. Although environmental and social impact assessments were part of project design, they were often ignored or were given low priority in construction projects. Irrespective of its variable success in guiding local behavior, there *is* a commitment to comply with Agenda 21 in official stated policy.

In the process of formulating and implementing China's Agenda 21, decentralized authority has become more attuned to local problems. The transfer of administrative power to lower tiers of organization, for example, has enabled Shanghai to discourage the sale of low-grade models in the local automobile market, and to limit the number of vehicles permitted to drive on city roads. These local initiatives allowed the city to enforce the principle recognized in Agenda 21 that "whoever causes pollution shall be responsible for its clean-up."

The experience of Shenzhen in mandating yearly emission inspections of vehicles is also representative of the Chinese government's determination to learn from international experience. From 1991 to 1995, five groups were appointed by the Shenzhen city police and transportation departments to perform emission inspections, but the Shenzhen Environmental Protection Bureau was not permitted to participate. When nitrogen-oxide emissions continued to increase, six more groups were authorized in 1997 to perform vehicle inspections. But air quality continued to decline even after additional countermeasures, indicating that poor cooperation between the city's Environmental Protection Bureau and traffic administration was hindering the effectiveness of the inspection program. When Shenzhen allowed Environmental Protection Bureau representatives to supervise inspections according to national regulations, nitrogen-oxide emissions began to drop. Shenzhen's experience shows that exchange and cooperation has a profound influence on vehicle emission-control programs.

One major goal of Agenda 21—the participation of local people in national policymaking—has come up short. Nevertheless, granting local people the power to raise issues has led to effective community activism. In Beijing, for example, plans to build new roads without bike paths were defeated due to public pressure in 2003.

## IMPACT OF GROWTH AND THE 2008 OLYMPIC GAMES

The selection of Beijing to host the 2008 Olympic Games focused international attention on China's Agenda 21.

Could Beijing clean up its air for the games? The empowerment of local authorities across China to set the standards and pace of economic development and environmental protection enabled Beijing's municipal authorities to unleash a construction boom that would test Communist Party strategies to their limits. Meanwhile, thanks to the economic boom on China's east coast, private automobile traffic was adding tailpipe emissions to Beijing's already polluted air. Using flexibility allowed by Agenda 21, Beijing authorities were able to reduce auto emissions beyond central standards.

Mammoth economic growth also focused world attention on China's Agenda 21. By 2007 China surpassed the United States as the leading emitter of carbon-dioxide emissions. Since the economic reforms of 1978, China has raised 400 million people from poverty, but many experts wonder whether the planet can survive a China with per-capita energy use equal to that of the United States.

China's Agenda 21 represents the country's search for a sustainable path between breakneck growth and biodegradation. For long-run solutions to the problems of pollution and poverty, China promotes technical education of the managerial elite—moving away from ideological leaps that wreck the economy and environment—toward pragmatic solutions that promote global partnerships and domestic empowerment, loosening but not dismantling the Maoist structure of self-chosen command.

**BIBLIOGRAPHY**

*China's Agenda 21: White Paper on China's Population, Environment, and Development in the 21st Century.* Adopted at the Executive Meeting of the State Council of the People's Republic of China, March 25, 1994.

Edmonds, Richard Louis. The Environment in the People's Republic of China 50 Years On. *China Quarterly* 159 (1999): 640–649.

Gan Lin. Implementing China's Agenda 21: From National Strategy to Local Action. *Impact Assessment and Project Appraisal* 16, 4 (1998): 277–287.

Kebin He and Chang Cheng. 1999–2000. Present and Future Pollution from Urban Transport in China. *China Environment Series* 3: 38–50.

***Isabella Notar***

# CHINESE MARITIME CUSTOMS SERVICE

The Chinese Maritime Customs Service (the Imperial Maritime Customs Service until 1912) was a foreign-run organization subordinate to the Chinese state and charged with administering duties on foreign trade in China. The extensive range of activities it undertook and the sheer length of its existence render it one of the most distinctive and important institutions of the modern era in China. While its significance is indisputable, the Foreign Inspectorate has been variously regarded as, on the one hand, a modernizing force inaugurating bureaucratic reform and technological innovation in China and, on the other hand, a glaring example of imperialistic oppression in China.

## ORIGINS AND EARLY DEVELOPMENT

As an emergency measure in response to the disruption caused by the Small Swords Uprising in Shanghai in September 1853, a system of consular administration of foreign trade was established by the U.S., British, and French consuls. This system was replaced by a permanent Foreign Inspectorate of Customs on July 12, 1854, briefly headed by Thomas Francis Wade (1818–1895). In May 1855, with the appointment of the first customs inspector general, Horatio Nelson Lay (1832–1898), the system of consular control ended, and the customs administration was brought under the Chinese government's jurisdiction. From this date until 1949 the Maritime Customs Service calculated the duties on foreign trade in the treaty ports, defined as trade conducted in "foreign-type vessels," whether owned by Chinese or foreigners, and trade conducted in Chinese-style vessels chartered by foreigners. The Native Customs establishment continued to supervise the duties levied on domestic trade.

In 1863 Robert Hart (1835–1911) replaced Lay as inspector general. After Hart took the helm, customs began to be fashioned into a powerful and efficient bureaucracy with far-reaching responsibilities. Hart's expansionist impetus was practically granted a free rein by the Zongli Yamen, the Qing department of foreign affairs under whose jurisdiction customs operated after 1861, and later by the Waiwu Bu (Bureau of Foreign Affairs), which replaced the Zongli Yamen in 1901. The Customs Marine Department (permanently established 1881) pioneered lighting of the China coast and was also responsible for mapping and policing China's coast and rivers. In the nineteenth century, customs was closely involved in loan negotiations, currency reform, and financial management. In 1896 China's post office was founded under its auspices.

During the self-strengthening era (c. 1861–1895), customs revenues helped to fund many noteworthy industrial, commercial, military, and educational projects. Customs funds supported the construction of arsenals and shipyards, the acquisition of modern ships and armaments, and the establishment of military academies. Hart was involved in many of these undertakings in an advisory capacity, particularly in the Tongwen Guan (Interpreters' College), a school established in 1862 in Beijing to teach Western languages and learning.

Customs activities also served to promote international understanding of China's trade, politics, and culture. For example, the Statistical Department (created 1873) compiled and published reports on countless China-related topics, ranging from biannual medical reports to Chinese music. Importantly, the customs service compiled and published decennial reports on trade in the treaty ports. These reports, covering the years 1882–1931, were the most reliable source of statistics on China's foreign trade during this period. The customs service arranged exhibits of Chinese arts, industries, and trade at twenty-eight international exhibitions and world's fairs. Furthermore, prominent customs personalities occasionally assumed diplomatic functions, and Hart played a central role in organizing China's first diplomatic delegations to Europe and America.

## STAFF STRUCTURE AND JURISDICTION

The Foreign Inspectorate of Customs operated until the 1940s as a semiautonomous organization directed by the inspector general in Beijing. Although the inspector general was ultimately answerable to the Chinese government, he enjoyed a large degree of financial and political autonomy. Until September 1942, for example, the inspector general was permitted to decide upon the service's annual budget and to appropriate funds directly from customs revenues rather than being allocated a budget by its supervisory board, as was the usual procedure for other government organizations. In the ports a dual system of control existed. The commissioner, invariably a foreign national until the late 1930s, was appointed by the inspector general and was in charge of the administrative side of the work of customs, principally the examination and assessment of cargoes and the calculation of duties. The commissioner was also in charge of the internal administration of customs in his port and managed all employees at the custom house. The Chinese superintendent of customs was appointed directly by the Revenue Board (Shuiwu Ju) and was responsible for the service's political business. Until 1911 the commissioner and his staff did not supervise the actual collection and banking of revenue. Traders paid customs duties directly to authorized, Chinese-owned customs banks selected by the superintendent, which were responsible for the security of the revenue. The superintendent's staff kept a daily record of revenue collections. The superintendent was also in charge of Native Customs establishments in his area of jurisdiction, with the exception of those that came under the control of the Foreign Inspectorate after 1901. In practice, however, the delineation of each party's responsibilities was not so clear-cut, and disputes over the relative authority and jurisdiction of the commissioner and the superintendent arose at regular intervals.

Customs headquarters in Beijing, the Inspectorate General, presided over two main branches: the Revenue Department and the Marine Department. Within the Revenue Department, three different bodies of staff were employed: the executive Indoor Staff, which chiefly performed administrative work and calculated duties; the Outdoor Staff, charged with examining and assessing cargoes and preventative work; and the Coast Staff. The Coast Staff performed much the same work as the Marine Department, whose personnel were variously employed in antismuggling work, maintaining aids to navigation, harbor maintenance, meteorological work, and coastal and riverine surveying.

Over the course of its existence, from 1854 and 1949, customs employed approximately 11,000 Chinese staff and 11,000 foreign staff, with Chinese employees usually restricted to lower-paid and lower-status positions until the late 1920s. Whereas all Chinese employees and most foreign members of the Outdoor Staff and Marine Department were appointed locally in China, the foreign Indoor Staff were recruited in Europe and America, most often through the service's London Office (established in 1874). A Customs College was established in Beijing in 1908 to train Chinese Indoor Staff recruits in customs practice and purpose, but no formal training system existed for the foreign staff. The Inspectorate did, however, cultivate a disinterested commitment to serving customs among its personnel.

## GROWING RESPONSIBILITIES

At the end of the nineteenth century the boundaries of the service's responsibilities were pushed even further forward. Indemnity and loan repayments to foreign governments and institutions had been made from customs funds almost since the service's inception. The Beijing Conventions of 1860, made between China and Britain and France at the conclusion of the Second Opium War, stipulated that indemnity payments of one-fifth of gross Maritime Customs revenue be made in quarterly installments. In the late nineteenth century, as China's foreign debts mounted, customs revenues became increasingly tied up in debt repayment. The Anglo-German loans (1896 and 1898), contracted to help pay the indemnity levied on China by the Treaty of Shimonoseki (1895) at the conclusion to the Sino-Japanese War (1894–1895), were secured against customs revenue. The terms of the 1898 loan also stipulated that revenues from the *lijin* (a tax levied on goods in transit) in four ports and the salt *lijin* in three ports be placed under the control of the inspector general and that fixed quotas be deducted for repayments. Under the terms of the Boxer Protocol of 1901, customs assumed control of the revenues of all Native Customs stations within a 50-*li* (17.9-mile) radius of the treaty ports, a portion of which contributed toward repayment of the Boxer indemnity. In the politically chaotic postrevolutionary period, Hart's successor in 1911, Francis Aglen (1869–1932), even assumed direct control of collection of customs duties for the first time and placed the revenues in foreign banks. Foreign loans and indemnities were henceforth serviced directly from these banks, with the result that the Chinese government effectively lost control over the revenue. Customs also continued to expand territorially in the Republican era; by 1920 there were customs houses in forty-five treaty ports.

Come 1927, the Beijing government of Zhang Zuolin dismissed Aglen for "insubordination" because it disapproved of his conducting negotiations over revenue collection with the southern authorities and Shanghai bankers. The newly established Nationalist government in Nanjing appointed Frederick Maze (1871–1959), Hart's nephew, as his successor. During Maze's time as inspector general (1929–1941), the Foreign Inspectorate, now headquartered in Shanghai, saw a dramatic change in its position in China. The Guomindang's centralized vision of government and anti-imperialist agenda saw the Inspectorate lose a great deal of its autonomy as its activities were drawn closer under the watchful eye of the Customs Administration (Guanwu Shu), the supervisory board established by the Guomindang in Nanjing under which customs operated after 1928 (from 1906 until 1928 customs was answerable to the Revenue Board, controlled by the Beijing government). In 1928–1930 the Nationalist government recovered tariff autonomy from the foreign powers, one effect of which was to make customs the largest single source of government revenues. The government also regained control of the banking of customs duties. In tune with these developments, foreign recruitment was suspended in 1927 and two years later was officially terminated, with the exception of technical experts engaged on a contract basis. Although successive inspectors general had stressed that customs, since its inception, was a *Chinese* institution, and not simply an arm of Western imperialism, it was only in the 1930s that Chinese employees began to rise to the highest positions in significant numbers.

## WARTIME

The tumultuous 1930s and 1940s also brought many challenges and setbacks for the Foreign Inspectorate. In 1932, after the Japanese invasion of Manchuria, customs stations in northern China dropped one by one outside the Inspectorate's sphere of authority, and full-blown conflict with Japan in 1937 led to further losses. Worse came in December 1941, when, with the onset of the Pacific War, Wang Jingwei's collaborationist government took over control of the Inspectorate in Shanghai, a fact that led to the dismissal of all British and American customs employees in occupied China. This coup divided the service into two bureaucracies. While customs in occupied China continued to operate to all intents and purposes as normal under the leadership of Kishimoto Hirokichi—the former customs chief secretary and the first non-British inspector general—the Nationalist government set about creating a rival Inspectorate from scratch in the wartime capital of Chongqing.

In 1943 an American customs commissioner, Lester Knox Little, was drafted as inspector general at Chongqing. The political turmoil of the early 1940s took its toll on customs, however, and by 1945 Little found himself in charge of a depleted customs staff working for a financially drained government. In the wake of the communist victory in 1949 Little moved the Inspectorate to Taiwan, via Shanghai and Guangzhou (Canton). There in June 1950 he resigned as inspector general, the last foreign employee to leave the service.

The People's Republic closed down the Foreign Inspectorate and placed customs under the General Administration of Customs. In the early twenty-first century, customs continues to carry out revenue collection, port management, antismuggling, and statistical work. Since 1949 the customs administration has continued to expand and now employs a staff of 48,000 across 562 customs houses and offices. Post-1949 customs administration owes much to the groundwork laid by the Foreign Inspectorate, particularly in terms of its staff structure, training, and ethos.

**SEE ALSO** *Hart, Robert.*

**BIBLIOGRAPHY**

Brunero, Donna. *Britain's Imperial Cornerstone in China: The Chinese Maritime Customs Service, 1854–1949.* London: Routledge, 2006.

Fairbank, John K. *Trade and Diplomacy on the China Coast: The Opening of the Treaty Ports, 1842–1854.* Cambridge, MA: Harvard University Press, 1964.

Horowitz, Richard S. Politics, Power, and the Chinese Maritime Customs Service: The Qing Restoration and the Ascent of Robert Hart. *Modern Asian Studies* 40, 3 (2006): 549–581.

Wright, Stanley F. *Hart and the Chinese Customs.* Belfast: Mullan, 1950.

***Catherine Ladds***

# CHINESE MARXISM

*This entry contains the following:*

FEUDALISM
*David Kelly*

DEMOCRATIC CENTRALISM AND MASS LINE
*Joseph T. Miller*

MASS MOVEMENTS
*Frederick C. Teiwes*

POSTREVOLUTIONARY MARXISM OTHER THAN MAO ZEDONG THOUGHT
*Maurice Meisner*

## OVERVIEW

Chinese Marxism is not one entity, but rather a changing set of ideas and concepts, always attached to specific conditions and time periods. The development of Marxism in China has been a long and complicated process. Many wonder if anything remains of Marxism in contemporary China.

The earliest Chinese writings on Marxism are found in the works of Zhu Zhixin (1885–1920), a self-described Marxist scholar from well before the revolution of 1911; indeed, there are coincidental parallels between Zhu's work on the possibility and practicality of revolution in China and Leon Trotsky's (1879–1940) writings on "permanent revolution" in Russia at the very same time. According to the contemporary scholar Li Zehou, a central aspect of Marxism that attracted some Chinese intellectuals during the pre-Comintern period was the materialist conception of history, with its dialectical approach to social and economic development. This was, in effect, an understanding of how the seeds of a new social structure might be found in the current social and economic relationships.

With the onset of the Bolshevik Revolution in 1917, Marxism in China moved to a new plateau. Radical intellectuals and revolutionaries began to see Marxism, as further embellished by Lenin's work on imperialism and the Russian experience, as a potentially practical guide to action. Based upon Lenin's theory of semicolonialism and its role in the international struggle, these revolutionaries began to view China as a semifeudal country whose further development was limited by its semicolonial status.

The establishment of the Chinese Communist Party (CCP) under the guidance of representatives from the Communist International (Comintern) in 1921 was a further leap in the development of Marxist thought and practice in China. The CCP was organized as a democratic centralist institution, as required for membership in the Comintern, and this format took Chinese revolutionaries even further into the Marxist-Leninist framework.

Ultimately, however, the conditions on the ground in China in the 1920s and 1930s, particularly the failure of the so-called "Second Chinese Revolution" in 1927, produced splits and differences among Chinese Marxists. Arguments ensued over just how "capitalist" China was. Who would actually lead the Chinese revolution? The industrial working class? The peasantry? The bourgeoisie?

Throughout the 1920s and 1930s, Marxist historians and revolutionary activists both inside and outside the CCP carried on fierce debates over the proper road for the Chinese revolution, including various arguments about the validity of China's semifeudal and semicolonial status. By this time, however, the CCP had almost disappeared from the cities and from the labor movement because of the "White Terror" carried out by Chiang Kai-shek's Nationalist Party (Guomindang).

By 1935, at the end of the Long March, it seemed that the base of the Chinese revolution had been moved clearly to the countryside. Given the formal semifeudal status of China and its semicolonial place in the world, the Chinese peasantry was now to be the primary social force for change in China, led by the CCP under Chairman Mao Zedong. Throughout the 1930s and 1940s, Mao further "Sinified" Marxism to fit the specific conditions that he and the remnants of the CCP were facing. This was the era that produced the notion of the "mass line," whereby the party would learn from the masses, consolidate what it learned, and then bring to the masses policies that fit the conditions. This fit China's needs very well during the Anti-Japanese War and the civil war against the Guomindang that followed.

It was during this period that Mao added the concept of "New Democracy" to the Marxist lexicon of the time. This reflected the reality that there would be no workers' government or proletarian dictatorship in the classical Marxist sense. In China a bloc of four classes—peasants, workers, the petty bourgeoisie (including intellectuals), and the national bourgeoisie—would be the political base of this new society.

Overall, from a classical Marxist perspective, Chinese Marxism, then and now, seems to have redefined or even denied fundamental categories. For example, the concept of "class struggle," clearly tied to the materialist conception of history, seems to have disappeared over the decades in the theoretical and practical aspects of Chinese Marxism. This is probably in reaction to the constant misuse of the term by Mao and his supporters throughout the 1950s and the 1960s. Fears of a repeat of the excesses of the Cultural Revolution (1966–1969) and the social and political instability of that period caused what might be termed an anti-Marxist backlash.

Today, China's leaders claim to be building "socialism with Chinese characteristics," and that their ultimate goal is a "harmonious society," something that seems to echo traditional Confucian concepts rather than those of Karl Marx, or even Mao himself. Or, is this a new term for what used to be called "communism"? Some scholars and commentators point to growing gaps within the fabric of contemporary Chinese society that reflect the greater relevance of classical Marxist categories in this age of neoliberalism and globalization.

**SEE ALSO** *Chinese Marxism: Mao Zedong Thought; Chinese Marxism: Democratic Centralism and Mass Line; Chinese Marxism: Mass Movements; Communist Party.*

**BIBLIOGRAPHY**

Bernal, Martin. *Chinese Socialism to 1907*. Ithaca, NY, and London: Cornell University Press, 1976.

Chan, Adrian. *Chinese Marxism*. London: Continuum, 2003.

Chen Guidi, and Wu Chuntao. *Will the Boat Sink the Water?* New York: Public Affairs, 2007.

Li Zehou. *A Study on Marxism in China*. Hong Kong: Joint Publishing, 1993.

Schram, Stuart. *The Thought of Mao Tse-tung*. Cambridge, U.K.: Cambridge University Press, 1989.

Su Shaozhi, Wu Dakun, Ru Xin, and Cheng Renqian. *Marxism in China*. Nottingham, U.K.: Spokesman, 1983.

***Joseph T. Miller***

## MAO ZEDONG THOUGHT

The "Thought of Mao Zedong" was formally proclaimed to be the guiding ideology of the Chinese Communist Party (CCP) at the party's Seventh Congress held in Yan'an in April 1945, just as the long war of resistance against the Japanese invaders was approaching its triumphant conclusion. During the Anti-Japanese War, the power of the CCP had grown enormously. The eight thousand ragged survivors of the Long March who found sanctuary in northern Shaanxi in the autumn of 1935 had burgeoned a decade later into a powerful Red Army that numbered one million dedicated soldiers. By 1945 the Communists had acquired enormous popular support among the peasantry of North China on the basis of a combination of nationalist and economic appeals, and they governed rural areas with a population of about ninety million. These successes, which proved to be the material foundation for the Communist victory in the massive civil war with the Guomindang that followed, were attributed to the leadership of Mao Zedong and the power of his "Thought." They served to validate the claim of the Seventh Congress, and did so in extravagant fashion, providing new impetus for the flourishing of the Mao cult.

The Chinese Communists did not use the term "Maoism" (*Mao zhuyi*) to describe the contributions of Mao Zedong to the theory and practice of Marxism-Leninism. To do so would have placed Mao on a higher ideological level than Vladimir Ilyich Lenin (1870–1924), and thus explicitly challenged the universal supremacy claimed by Joseph Stalin (1879–1953) as the sole interpreter of Marxist-Leninist orthodoxy in the world Communist movement. Instead, the "Thought of Mao Zedong" was simply presented as the practical application of the "universal truths" of Marxism-Leninism to the specific historical conditions of China.

What then is the content of the "Thought of Mao Zedong," or what outside of China is commonly called "Maoism"? Mao Zedong and his followers consciously saw themselves as the inheritors of the Marxist-Leninist intellectual and political tradition. Indeed, they claimed to have enriched that tradition by applying it to new and unforeseen historical circumstances. Thus, any inquiry into Maoism must begin with an examination of the relationship of the Chinese doctrine to the inherited body of Marxist-Leninist theory.

Mao Zedong's departures from the premises of Marxism were enormous. But those intellectual departures, the basis for the Maoist strategy of revolution, are not necessarily fully apparent in Mao's voluminous writings. Mao, and especially Maoist theoreticians, made great efforts to disguise his heretical departures by encasing them in orthodox Marxist-Leninist formulae and terminology. Thus an understanding of what Maoism is, or what it was during Mao's lifetime, cannot be gained by simply reading the official texts. Rather it is essential to take into account the implications of Maoist practice for Maoist theory. The following discussion will proceed with these considerations in mind.

### PEASANTS

The "Thought of Mao Zedong," first and foremost, appears as a radical (although mostly implicit) rejection of many of the basic premises of the inherited body of Marxist-Leninist theory. Indeed, the departures are so radical that the intellectual links between Karl Marx (1818–1883) and Mao become tenuous.

The first link was shattered when Mao, early in his Communist career, substituted the peasantry for the proletariat as the main revolutionary class. Mao discovered the revolutionary potential of the peasants in 1925 and expressed that belief in its most pristine form in his February 1927 "Report of An Investigation of the Peasant Movement in Hunan." The "Hunan Report" was essentially a celebration of the spontaneous revolutionary energies of the peasantry, "a force so swift and violent that no power, however great, will be able to suppress it." The elemental revolutionary actions of the peasants were not to be subordinated to either the urban working class or to any political party. But Mao soon learned to partly disguise his ideological heresies, insisting that revolutionary peasants were to be guided by "proletarian consciousness." However, "proletarian consciousness" occupies a most ambiguous place in Maoism. It was not an attribute of the actual proletariat, a class that Mao largely ignored after the early 1920s, and especially after the crushing defeat of the urban working-class movement in 1927. Nor did Mao attribute "proletarian consciousness" to the peasantry, however much he praised its spontaneous revolutionary zeal. Rather, "proletarian consciousness" was first attributed to the Communist Party, which had few working-class members after 1927. Eventually, "proletarian consciousness" came to reside in Mao himself and especially his "Thought."

Closely related to the Maoist faith that the peasantry was the truly revolutionary class was a rejection of the Marxist (and Leninist) view of the relationship between town and countryside in the making of modern revolutions. For Marx, from antiquity to modern times, historical progress was centered in the cities, whereas the rural areas were associated with political reaction and periods of historical regression. Mao Zedong inverted the relationship between town and countryside. For Mao, the true sources of revolutionary energies and political purity resided in the rural areas, whereas China's foreign-dominated cities were viewed as alien dens of moral corruption and political reaction. In his February 1927 "Report," Mao measured the relative importance of the cities and the rural areas in the Chinese revolution and came to the extraordinary conclusion that the revolutionary achievements of urban dwellers and the military together merited only three out of ten points, whereas the peasants in the countryside merited the remaining seven. Mao's celebration of the revolutionary potential of the peasantry, reinforced by powerful antiurban biases, was among the intellectual strains that went into the making of a political strategy that sought to mobilize the revolutionary forces of the countryside to "surround and overwhelm" the conservative cities.

## THE ADVANTAGES OF BACKWARDNESS AND CAPITALISM

The Maoist conception of a revolution taking the form of a war of the countryside against the cities was reinforced by a profoundly non-Marxist belief in the "advantages of backwardness." The notion, primarily identified with nineteenth-century Russian populism, suggested that backward countries such as Russia were closer to socialism than the advanced Western countries precisely because of their backwardness, precisely because the moral and social virtues inherent in backwardness had not yet been undermined by modern capitalism. Mao Zedong encountered this populist belief in the anarchist writings he so avidly read around 1918 to 1919. He embraced it, as did many other young intellectuals of his generation. While the young Mao deplored China's backwardness, he saw in that very condition a great reservoir of youthful creativity and revolutionary energy that would soon propel China forward, ahead of all other nations.

Mao Zedong's belief in "the advantages of backwardness" survived his conversion to Marxism in 1920. Whereas Marxism taught that the promise of socialism resided in the activity of the most modern social classes in the most economically advanced capitalist countries, Mao was drawn to the most backward rural areas and to impoverished peasants, who, he believed, were filled with revolutionary activism and an innate desire for socialism. The idea of the advantages of backwardness persisted after the Communist victory of 1949 and found its most extreme expression in the "poor and blank" thesis Mao set forth in 1958, on the eve of the Great Leap Forward campaign. Material poverty and cultural blankness, he proclaimed, were characteristics of the Chinese people, particularly China's peasantry and its youth. But these seemingly negative features held enormous potential for creative revolutionary activity—for, as Mao explained, poor people want change and young people are relatively uncorrupted by the moral evils of the old society. Thus the alleged condition of being "poor and blank" foreshadowed China's imminent leap to a Communist utopia.

Since its Russian populist origins in the mid-nineteenth century, the notion of the "advantages of backwardness" supported a belief that capitalism was not an inevitable stage in historical development, and that modernity and socialism could be achieved without suffering the agonies of a capitalist phase of development. This was a powerful strain in the thought of the modern Chinese intelligentsia since the 1890s. It was a belief that Mao Zedong embraced around 1918 and one that survived his conversion to Marxism. Yet it was not a belief that could be reconciled with the basic premises of Marxist theory. In the Marxian analysis, socialism presupposed capitalism. The modern urban proletariat was the social agent of socialism while large-scale industry was its material basis—and both of course were the unique creations of a capitalist economy.

Yet the Chinese historical situation did not encourage acceptance of the Marxist view of the progressiveness of capitalism. Modern capitalism came to China in the late nineteenth century as part of the massive foreign imperialist impingement, and it developed mainly in the foreign-dominated treaty ports. Thus the general reaction of Chinese intellectuals to this distorted capitalism was to identify capitalism with foreign imperialism, to reject both as alien impingements on the Chinese nation, and to look elsewhere for the sources of China's regeneration. The search for a noncapitalist road of development—and a noncapitalist road to socialism—found its most powerful political expression in Maoism.

There was, however, one notable exception to Mao's hostility to the Marxist view of capitalism. In 1940 he set forth the theory of "New Democracy," which called for an alliance of the four progressive classes in Chinese society (the bourgeoisie, the petty bourgeoisie, the proletariat, and the peasantry) to carry out a "bourgeois-democratic" revolution, which would open the way for the development of capitalism. And Mao seemed to envision a postrevolutionary China that would have a mixed economy, with a flourishing capitalist sector, for the foreseeable future.

Yet the apparent concessions Mao made to Marxist-Leninist orthodoxy were less than they seemed. By setting forth the theory of New Democracy, Mao was partly responding to Moscow's insistence on a "two-stage" revolutionary process, with a bourgeois stage preceding the socialist one, thus giving the appearance of ideological orthodoxy. More importantly, New Democracy responded to the nationalist demand for the Chinese to unite to resist the Japanese invaders. However, with the defeat of Japan in 1945 and the Communist victory in the civil war with the Guomindang in 1949, the theory of New Democracy began to fade in importance—and fading along with it was the appearance of Mao's acceptance of the Marxist view of the progressiveness of capitalism. In 1952 Mao announced the beginning of the "transition to socialism," heralding the end of the capitalist sector of the urban economy. Shortly after there followed the collectivization of agriculture and the abolition of private landownership in the countryside. It is difficult to believe that the theory of New Democracy was more than a tactical move to meet the political needs of the time.

## VOLUNTARISM

Mao Zedong's refusal to accept the Marxist proposition that socialism presupposes capitalism reflected the persistence of his pre-Marxian belief in the decisive importance of ideas and spiritual factors in history. In a land that lacked the Marxian-defined economic and social prerequisites for socialism, a reliance on what Marxist theory defined as the "objective forces of history" relegated the revolutionary to political passivity. But Mao's activistic temperament, and his lack of any real Marxian confidence in objective historical processes, demanded political action in the here and now. Mao thus retained a highly voluntaristic belief that the historical outcome depended on subjective factors—the consciousness, the moral values, and the will of dedicated people. This faith in the supremacy of "men over machines" became a pervasive feature of Mao Zedong Thought and was reinforced by the experience of the revolutionary war, when a relatively small Communist force triumphed over a numerically and technologically superior enemy.

## NATIONALISM

Many of Mao Zedong's departures from Marxist-Leninist orthodoxy had profoundly nationalist implications. His inversion of the Marxist analysis of the relationship between town and countryside was dictated by the fact that China was an overwhelmingly agrarian nation, but certainly reinforced by a perception that China's foreign dominated cities were dens of moral corruption and political reaction. The true sources of China's national regeneration, he believed, resided in the peasants who were bearers of "a fine old culture" not yet corrupted by alien influences. And his belief in "the advantages of backwardness" was largely nationalist compensation for China's impoverishment. It was nourished by a faith that the last shall be first, and the conviction that the energies latent in backwardness would soon propel China to the forefront of nations.

Nationalist sentiments also drew Mao to those aspects of the Chinese tradition that could be selectively incorporated into the theory and practice of Communism. The seemingly innovative military tactics Mao employed in the 1930s and 1940s are striking examples of Mao's use of tradition. The basic principles of Mao's military thought—emphasizing mobility and surprise—were derived from the fifth-century BCE military writer Sun Zi. He also drew from traditional sources, especially Daoism, in his abortive effort to master "dialectical materialism" and his claim to be an innovative Marxist philosopher. Yet the content of Mao's philosophic essays "On Practice" (1937), "On Contradiction" (1937), and "On Dialectical Materialism" (1940) was largely derived from turgid Stalinist treatises, even though they were written in a relatively lively fashion, and filled with allusions to Chinese history and culture.

Nationalist sentiments were also involved in Mao Zedong's call for the "Sinification of Marxism," a slogan first set forth in 1938. The slogan had two meanings, only one of which was fully acknowledged at the outset. On the one hand, "Sinification" meant that Marxism should be presented in a form that would appeal to the Chinese people. As Mao originally put it, Marxism was to be conveyed in "a new and vital Chinese style and manner, pleasing to the eye and ear of the Chinese common people." On the other hand, Sinification also meant the adaptation of Marxism to concrete Chinese historical conditions—and this implied the departures from many of the basic premises of Marxism discussed in the preceding paragraphs.

## THE "THOUGHT OF MAO ZEDONG" AND THE CHINESE REVOLUTION

Maoism, far from being hard-line Marxism, as commonly portrayed, was an ideology that abandoned many of the most fundamental beliefs of Marxism. It was an ideology that rejected the Marxist view that capitalism is a progressive stage in historical development and the necessary precondition for socialism. It was an ideology that turned its back on the urban proletariat, the agent of historical redemption in Marxist theory, in favor of the precapitalist peasantry as the main revolutionary class. It was a doctrine that celebrated the "advantages of backwardness." And Maoism extolled the human will and spirit as the decisive forces in history. At the close of the Mao era, the "Thought of Mao Zedong" had only the most tenuous ties to the Marxist tradition to which Mao laid claim. Yet however far Maoism strayed from the premises of Marxism, it was an ideology that was conducive to carrying out a revolution in a backward and largely agrarian land where a revolution was desperately needed. It is most unlikely that revolutionaries who adhered to orthodox Marxist beliefs could have been successful in the Chinese historical environment.

Yet a Maoist doctrine that had played so vital a role during the revolutionary years became increasingly anachronistic in the postrevolutionary era. And the revival of the more radical features of revolutionary Maoism in the late 1950s, often called "late Maoism," had catastrophic consequences, producing the human and political disasters of the Great Leap Forward and the Cultural Revolution. It was precisely at this time, however, in the 1960s and 1970s, that the worldwide influence of Maoism reached its peak. Maoist ideology, often misinterpreted, had a powerful influence on the widespread student revolts of 1968. Significant Maoist factions split Communist parties in Western Europe and Asia into pro-Chinese and pro-Soviet camps, and Maoism inspired a number of rural-based insurgencies in Latin America, the best known and longest-lived of which was the Shining Path insurrection in Peru. Most of these movements, however, proved transitory, surviving as significant political forces only in the most backward rural areas, most notably in several states in India and in Nepal.

In China itself, the "Thought of Mao Zedong" remains the official ideology of the ruling Communist Party. But Maoist ideology has little to do with the making of socioeconomic policies. Rather, Mao and selected aspects of his "Thought" are merely used as nationalist symbols to legitimize the post-Maoist Communist regime. As Deng Xiaoping said as he embarked on the post-Mao reforms, Mao's portrait still hung in Tiananmen Square because "it is the memory of a man who guided us to victory and built a country." To be sure, the image of Mao and quotations from his "Thought" have sometimes been used in popular protests in the post-Mao era, particularly protests by peasants victimized by corrupt officials. But this, at best, has been a sporadic phenomenon. More commonplace, but perhaps less significant, has been the nostalgic reappearance of Mao and Maoist slogans in popular culture in recent decades—in the names of expensive restaurants, in pop culture portraits, and as lucky charms hanging in taxi cabs. Nothing more surely testifies to the death of the "Thought of Mao Zedong" as a living ideology than the commercialization of the late chairman and his works.

**SEE ALSO** *Chinese Marxism: Overview.*

**BIBLIOGRAPHY**

Chen, Jerome. *Mao and the Chinese Revolution*. New York: Oxford University Press, 1965.

Feigon, Lee. *Mao: A Reinterpretation*. Chicago: Ivan R. Dee, 2002.

Griffith, Samuel B. *Mao Tse-tung on Guerrilla Warfare*. New York: Praeger, 1961.

Meisner, Maurice. *Marxism, Maoism, and Utopianism*. Madison: University of Wisconsin Press, 1982.

Meisner, Maurice. *Mao Zedong: A Political and Intellectual Portrait*. Cambridge, U.K.: Polity Press, 2007.

Schram, Stuart. *Mao Tse-tung*. New York: Simon and Schuster, 1966.

Schram, Stuart, ed. *Mao's Road to Power: Revolutionary Writings, 1912–1949*. 7 vols. Armonk, NY: Sharpe, 1992–.

Schwartz, Benjamin. *Chinese Communism and the Rise of Mao*. Cambridge, MA: Harvard University Press, 1951.

Schwartz, Benjamin. *Communism and China: Ideology in Flux*. Cambridge, MA: Harvard University Press. 1968.

Wakeman, Frederick. *History and Will: Philosophic Perspectives on Mao Tse-tung's Thought*. Berkeley: University of California Press, 1973.

***Maurice Meisner***

## CLASS, THEORY, AND PRACTICE

The division of society into social classes, and the conflict between those classes as the motive force of history, is an essential theme of Marxist theory. It is also the aspect of Marxism that had the greatest impact on the thought of Chinese converts to Communism in 1919 and after. At the same time, it was the part of Marxist theory that the early converts were most reluctant to accept. The reluctance stemmed from the profound nationalist feelings of the early Chinese Communists and their belief that the main enemies were the foreign imperialist powers who had so deeply impinged on China. Nationalism encouraged the belief that the Chinese people were united against the external threat rather than divided into antagonistic social classes.

## MAO ZEDONG AND CLASS ANALYSIS

Still, the severity of exploitation in China, the poverty, and the appalling socioeconomic inequalities could not be ignored, and many Communists soon turned their attention to the internal social class structure of Chinese society as well as to the foreign threat. One of the first to do so was Mao Zedong in his 1926 treatise "An Analysis of the Classes in Chinese Society." Although an elementary work, it broadly anticipated what was to become the Maoist view of China's class divisions and their political implications. With the aim of determining the friends and enemies of revolution, Mao identified six class categories: (1) the landlord and comprador (or urban capitalist) classes, who were wholly dependent on foreign imperialism and thus politically reactionary; (2) the "middle bourgeoisie," urban and rural capitalists who would soon be forced to either join or oppose the revolution; (3) the "petty bourgeoisie," consisting of landowning peasants and lower-level intellectuals, a politically vacillating group whose deteriorating circumstances would probably force them to join the revolution; (4) a massive "semiproletariat" of middle and poor peasants and handicraft workers; (5) the urban proletariat; and (6) a lumpenproletariat made up of peasants who lost their land and were unable to find regular employment. With variations in terminology and emphasis, these were the social groups that Maoist class theory was concerned with until 1949.

It is noteworthy that only the first of the six class categories—the comprador bourgeoisie and the landlords—were definitely enemies of the revolution. The various social groups listed under the next five categories were potential friends of the revolution—and thus amenable to the processes of "ideological remolding" that were to occupy so prominent a place in the Maoist scheme of things. Moreover, while Mao noted that the proletariat numbered only two million in a land of over four hundred million, he nonetheless wrote that the urban industrial proletariat was "the leading force in our revolution." This was clearly a ritualistic bow to the official Marxist-Leninist orthodoxy, for in 1925 Mao had already discovered the revolutionary potential of the peasantry. And in his February 1927 "Hunan Report," he was completely drawn to the spontaneity of peasant revolt, a force he described to be as powerful as "a tornado or tempest." The urban proletariat was barely mentioned in Mao's "Report." Indeed, it was largely dismissed: "if we allow ten points to the accomplishments of the democratic revolution," Mao wrote, "then the achievements of the city dwellers and the military rate only three points, while the remaining seven points should go to the achievements of the peasants in their rural revolution."

From a Marxist-Leninist point of view, this failure to recognize the leading revolutionary role of the urban proletariat was heretical, and it probably would have earned Mao expulsion from the Communist Party had it not been for the counterrevolution of April 1927, when Chiang Kai-shek (Jiang Jieshi) turned his army against his erstwhile Communist allies and nearly destroyed them. The urban revolutionary movement was virtually extinguished, the Communists who survived the counterrevolution fled to the countryside, and the urban proletariat was terrorized into political passivity—and remained so until 1949 when the Red Army, composed almost entirely of peasants, "surrounded and overwhelmed" the Guomindang-ruled cities.

During the Yan'an era (1935–1945), the crucial phase in the development of the Maoist revolution, few members of either the proletariat or the bourgeoisie were to be found on either side in China's civil war. Yet the terms *proletarian* and *bourgeois* appeared ubiquitously in Maoist writings. But they referred not to actual social classes but to the political tendencies attributed to those classes. In the "rectification" campaigns of the early 1940s, which solidified Mao's political and ideological control over the Communist base areas, a good many Communist and other radical intellectuals were punished for harboring "bourgeois" ideas. The "bourgeoisie" and the "proletariat" had become ideological categories that did not necessarily correspond to the actual social classes that bore those names.

## SOCIAL CLASSES AND CLASS ANALYSIS IN THE MAO ERA

The Communist victory of 1949, and the new policies that followed in the early 1950s, radically transformed China's social class structure. Many of the wealthier capitalists fled to Taiwan and elsewhere, and their properties were immediately nationalized by the new Communist state. Those who remained, politically designated "the national bourgeoisie," were usually given low-paying government bonds in return for state ownership of their enterprises. The bourgeoisie lingered on only as a small group of aging pensioners collecting modest dividends on noninheritable state bonds.

The demise of the bourgeoisie as a functioning social class marked the beginning of the end of the period of "new democracy." The theory of "new democracy," set forth by Mao Zedong in 1940, called for a government based on a "bloc of four classes"—an alliance of the proletariat, the peasantry, the national bourgeoisie, and the petty bourgeoisie—to carry out the bourgeois-democratic phase of the revolution. The four small gold stars on the national flag of the People's Republic adopted in 1949 represented the four classes that made up this alliance, surrounding the larger gold star representing the Chinese Communist Party. "New democracy" further envisioned a partly capitalist economy surviving for a lengthy period of time into the postrevolutionary era. But with the proclamation of the "transition to socialism" at the end of 1952, the nationalization of most private enterprises, and the collectivization of agriculture, the idea of "new democracy" faded into irrelevance after the mid-1950s.

In the countryside, the landlord class was more quickly and ruthlessly destroyed during the nationwide land-reform campaign of 1950 to 1952. A good many landlords were killed by angry peasants, but most were simply reduced to the status of ordinary peasant-cultivators, their lands distributed to poor peasants. Thus, by the mid-1950s, both the urban and rural ruling classes of prerevolutionary China, the bourgeoisie and the landlords, had been destroyed. Three main social classes remained (although with significant divisions within them): peasants, urban workers, and intellectuals. Nonetheless, images of the prerevolutionary class structure lived on. During the revolutionary era, an elaborate system was developed for determining and officially recording the class origin of each individual. Those of "low" social origins (poor peasants, workers) were politically and economically favored, while members of the families of former landlords, ex-capitalists, and sometimes intellectuals suffered discrimination.

## THE CULTURAL REVOLUTION

Class labeling was a cruel and pernicious system, and its absurdity was revealed by the Cultural Revolution. Mao Zedong launched the Cultural Revolution with the aim of overthrowing "the bourgeoisie" within the Communist Party, that is to say, party leaders who he believed were pursuing policies that would lead to "the restoration of capitalism." But that was by no means made clear to all who participated in the great upheaval. The "bourgeoisie," many assumed on the basis of the system of class labels, were former capitalists and landlords, and their families and offspring. Thus there was much persecution (by Red Guards and party officials) of citizens not so much on the basis of their class but on their prerevolutionary class origins. Intellectuals in particular were subjected to verbal and physical attacks because they seemed the most "bourgeois" in a society that no longer had a bourgeoisie.

More broadly, zealous Red Guards, lumping together class and political labels, sought out and attacked members of what were variously called the "five black categories" or the "five bad elements," which vaguely included landlords, rich peasants, rightist elements, bad elements, and counterrevolutionaries.

One of the most bizarre "class" phenomena in the Cultural Revolution involved the theory of "natural redness" (or the "bloodline theory"), whereby the sons and daughters of Communist officials (mostly peasants and workers in the old society) claimed special revolutionary credentials by virtue of their birth. The "five red categories" whose children were favored according to this self-serving theory included workers, poor and middle peasants, revolutionary cadres, revolutionary soldiers, and revolutionary martyrs. They generally joined the more conservative Red Guard organizations that defended the existing party apparatus that was under Maoist attack. The more radical Red Guards, more fervently Maoist in attacking the established party apparatus, usually were the children of intellectuals and former bourgeois families. The paradox can be explained by noting that the members of the latter group were discriminated against in the new society because of their prerevolutionary class origins, whereas the former were members of classes who had benefited from the revolution and wished to preserve their relatively privileged status.

## CLASS STRUCTURE IN THE POST-MAO ERA

In the end, despite the fury and destructiveness of the Cultural Revolution, the social structure that emerged was essentially the same as it had been at the beginning of the upheaval. It was not until the massive process of capitalist development that issued from the post-Mao market reforms that the social class structure began to undergo fundamental changes. The most important development has been the emergence of an increasingly wealthy industrial, commercial, and financial bourgeoisie in the great cities. It is a bourgeoisie that remains materially and psychologically tied to the state that nurtured it, but nonetheless operates and profits much like a bourgeoisie in an advanced capitalist country. Officially, they are known as "socialist" or "private" entrepreneurs.

A second new element of the class structure has been the transformation of once-collectivized peasants into de facto owner-cultivators. In addition, the commercialization of the countryside has forced hundreds of millions of peasants off the land to seek work in the cities. Those who have found jobs have become members of the rapidly growing urban proletariat. Others who cannot find regular work have joined the "floating population," some 150,000,000 migrant laborers who seek such temporary work as they find. They are members of a vast reserve army of labor, a group both economically exploited and politically feared in Marxist as well as traditional Chinese terms (*youmin*). It is ironic that as sharp class divisions have emerged, the Communist government no longer speaks of class struggle but rather proclaims China to be a "harmonious society."

### BIBLIOGRAPHY

Hart-Landsberg, Martin, and Paul Burkett. *China and Socialism: Market Reforms and Class Struggle*. New York: Monthly Review Press, 2005.

Kraus, Richard Curt. *Class Conflict in Chinese Socialism*. New York: Columbia University Press, 1981.

Lin Weiran. An Abortive Chinese Enlightenment: The Cultural Revolution and Class Theory. Ph.D. diss., University of Wisconsin-Madison, 1996.

Mao Zedong. Report on the Peasant Movement in Hunan. Vol. 2 of *Mao's Road to Power: Revolutionary Writings, 1912–1949*, ed. Stuart Schram, 433. Armonk, NY: M.E. Sharpe, 1992–.

Nee, Victor, and David Mozingo, eds. *State and Society in Contemporary China*. Ithaca, NY: Cornell University Press, 1983.

Perry, Elizabeth, and Christine Wong, eds. *The Political Economy of Reform in Post-Mao China*. Cambridge, MA: Harvard University Press, 1985.

Selden, Mark. *The Political Economy of Chinese Development*. Armonk, NY: Sharpe, 1993.

Yu Luoke. *Yu Luoke: Yi zuo yu hui yi* [Yu Luoke: Writings and recollections]. Beijing: Zhongkuo wenlian chubanshe, 1999.

***Maurice Meisner***

## FEUDALISM

*Feudalism*, a key term of Western historiography, was translated into Chinese as *fengjian zhuyi*. *Fengjian* may be rendered as "enfeoffment," an act by which a person was awarded land in exchange for a pledge of service. This specific social form is a component of the broader notion of feudalism; the latter often refers to a system of social relations in which inferiors are highly dependent on superiors.

*Fengjian zhuyi* as a rendering of the foreign term has tended to become even more misleading over time: eliding major differences between the Chinese and Western phenomena, it has led to misunderstandings, distortion, and even political persecution. Many scholars advise abandoning using it, although given its wide currency this would be difficult to achieve. One option is, while retaining the term *feudal*, to introduce *fengjian* as a term of specific application to Chinese history.

*Fengjian zhi* (the "enfeoffment system") was a key category of traditional Chinese history. Traditionally regarded as emerging from the slave society of the Xia and Shang states (sixteenth to eleventh centuries BCE), and reaching a peak under the Zhou dynasty (tenth to third centuries BCE), it was assumed to have ended by the Qin (221–206 BCE) and Han dynasties (206 BCE–220 CE), when the power of landed aristocracy was dissolved and the imperial bureaucracy set up in its place. This transition was a fundamental assumption of neo-Confucian formulations of Chinese cultural identity. Under this interpretation (reiterated in 2008 by the intellectual historian Wang Hui), medieval and early modern China was a postfeudal society.

With the formulation of Marxism–Leninism–Mao Zedong Thought as the reigning orthodoxy following the rise of communism in twentieth-century China, this notion was overturned. Modern China (post-1840, that is, after the first Opium War [1839–1842]) was categorized in Marxism–Leninism–Mao Zedong Thought as "semifeudal and semicolonial." The inner core of this usage rested on class analysis: Feudal society was said to be determined by the antagonism between two classes, the landlords and the peasants. Marxism–Leninism–Mao Zedong Thought explained the longevity of feudal society in materialist terms: The peasantry maintained a precapitalist mode of production, producing nearly everything for themselves, in a natural economy rather than for the market. The landlords had little incentive to invest, and change was limited to the rise and fall of various ruling families. After 1840, capitalist elements were introduced under the threat of Western invasion, and the society became "semifeudal and semicolonial." Catastrophic change became the order of the day, dogged however by deep-seated economic and ideological inertia.

Despite certain advantages of this model—simplicity, coherence, and scope—the main force driving its adoption was the anxiety of Marxist theorists to align their thinking with that of the Soviet Union, where the "five-stage theory," as authorized by Soviet leader Joseph Stalin (1879–1953), was the all-powerful orthodoxy. Criticisms, which were beaten down at the time but have emerged with renewed force in recent years, were largely directed at the underlying class theory. Agrarian theorists Liang Shuming (1893–1990) and Fei Xiaotong (1910–2005) argued that landowning tended to be distributed in Chinese society as a function of a given household's status in the patrilineal clan; hence, "class" antagonism between landlord and peasant had to be conceived as intersecting familial ties in ways quite different to what Karl Marx (1818–1883) and others took for granted in the West. Tao Xisheng (1899–1988) and other non-Communist Marxists, drawing on certain ambiguities in the writings of Marx, introduced variant accounts. Zhao Lisheng (1917–2007) and later his student Qin Hui argued that peasant wars, which supposedly arose from land-focused class antagonism, had all along emerged from a deeper structural conflict between officialdom and its subjects—between rulers and ruled.

Sun Yat-sen and his Nationalist (Guomindang) supporters used the charge of "feudalism" to castigate warlords like Chen Jiongming (1878–1933), a champion of electoral democracy and local autonomy. Hence it was the Nationalists who ushered in "party rule" in preference to "self-rule." This underpinned a framework of governance which was preserved down to the present by the Communist Party. The zenith of Maoist influence in the Cultural Revolution was, ironically, to see the Mao himself subject to mocking critique under the code term "feudalism." On his death the Gang of Four Maoist disciples were openly denigrated as feudal fascists.

The cultural ramifications of the feudalism thesis are equally subject to radical revision. Traditional Chinese culture, Confucianism in particular, was criticized as "feudal," and *fengjian*/feudal soon became a general term of abuse for everything from footbinding to arranged marriages and the emergence of warlords. Reaching a fever pitch in the Cultural Revolution (1966–1969), criticism of feudalism inspired by Marxism–Leninism–Mao Zedong Thought has continued in attenuated form to the present: For example, intellectual historians Ren Jiyu and Fang Keli have kept alive the critique of Confucianism (*rujiao*) as a "feudal ideology."

The reform period since 1978 has been marked by renewed vitality of many phenomena once labeled *feudal*, not least being Confucianism itself. Patrilineal clans have reemerged in many regions, making use of the outward forms of modern political and corporate structures. Overuse of the term at the height of the Mao Zedong era has, arguably, resulted in depriving feudalism of its impact as a critical term. Possibly most important has been a return to the traditional perspective noted by Wang Hui, in which China had crucially transcended feudalism at an early stage.

**SEE ALSO** *Chinese Marxism: Mao Zedong Thought; Chinese Marxism: Overview.*

**BIBLIOGRAPHY**

Dirlik, Arif. Feudalism in Chinese History. In *Revolution and History: The Origins of Marxist Historiography in China, 1919–1937*, 95–136. Berkeley: University of California Press, 1978.

Fitzgerald, John. One Nation, One State: Feudalism and Social Revolution. In *Awakening China, Politics Culture and Class in the Nationalist Revolution*, 103–146. Stanford: Stanford University Press, 1996.

Wang Hui. The Liberation of the Object and the Interrogation of Modernity: Rethinking the Rise of Modern Chinese Thought. *Modern China* 34 (2008): 114–140.

***David Kelly***

## DEMOCRATIC CENTRALISM AND MASS LINE

Two of the most significant characteristics of Marxism-Leninism as it developed in China are found in the theory and practice of democratic centralism and the mass line. While these are interconnected under the specific conditions of the Chinese revolution, they have very different origins.

### ORIGINS AND DEVELOPMENT OF DEMOCRATIC CENTRALISM

Since the earliest discussions by Lenin and other Marxists in the period from 1902 up to the onset of the Bolshevik Revolution in 1917, the fundamental concept and practice of democratic centralism—democracy in discussion, unity in action—went through some basic changes. These changes, based on changing conditions within the revolutionary movements and the immediate post-1917 situation in Russia, then had a direct impact on the early conduct of the Chinese revolution under the direction of the Communist International. Further developments in China, especially in the area of the mass line, took place under the leadership of Mao Zedong throughout the 1930s and 1940s.

What had begun as a practical organizational concept for a revolutionary party under the repressive conditions of imperial Russia soon became an organizational concept for the structure and practice of the state in a postrevolutionary society. Pressures of the civil war after the taking of state power in October 1917, along with international isolation and invasion by Western and Japanese troops, eventually led to a decision by the Bolshevik leadership at their Tenth Party Congress in 1921 to institute a temporary ban on factions in the party. Up to that point, the practice of democratic centralism was reflected in lively debates that led to concerted action. But inner-party democracy became constricted, and this constricted form of democratic centralism was soon applied to the organization and practice of the state machinery in the Soviet Union.

### THE INTERNATIONALIZATION OF DEMOCRATIC CENTRALISM

During the Second Comintern Congress in 1920, the Bolshevik leader Leon Trotsky presented "Theses on the Conditions of Admission to the Communist International," the infamous "twenty-one conditions." It is worth quoting point 12 in full:

> The parties belonging to the Communist International must be built on the basis of the principle of *democratic centralism*. In the present epoch of acute civil war the Communist Party will only be able to fulfill its duty if it is organized in as centralist a manner as possible, if iron discipline reigns within it and if the Party centre, sustained by the confidence of the Party membership, is endowed with the fullest rights and authority and the most far-reaching powers. (Adler 1980, p. 95)

In this way, even before the formal ban on factions took place inside the Bolshevik Party, a rather stringent notion of democratic centralism was required of any party or group that wished to join the Comintern. As a result, the parties connected to the Comintern moved toward greater centralism and less inner-party democracy as well.

The Chinese experience certainly reflected this reality, especially after the failure of the so-called Second Chinese Revolution in 1927. Through purges, the leadership of the Chinese Communist Party was changed many times with the support of the pro-Soviet Comintern representatives. The "iron discipline" of the Comintern always set the framework, and the Chinese Communist Party eventually became caught up in the same internal restrictions.

Even after Mao Zedong became the semiofficial leader of the Communist Party at the completion of the Long March in 1935, the period in Yan'an reflected greater and greater centralism with more and more restrictions on inner-party democracy. After all, the Communist Party was the vanguard of the Chinese revolution, and it must be single-minded in its pursuit of victory first over the Japanese imperialists and then over Chiang Kai-shek's Guomindang.

## ORIGINS AND DEVELOPMENT OF THE MASS LINE AND LINKS TO DEMOCRATIC CENTRALISM

It was also during the Yan'an period that Mao began to develop the organizational principle of the mass line. Its clearest statement may be found in his 1943 piece titled "Guanyu lingdao fangfa de ruogan wenti" (Some questions concerning methods of leadership). Here Mao described a process that would bring together the vanguard role of the Communist Party and a high degree of participation by the masses. Party cadres were called upon to personally investigate the conditions of the people and participate in their struggles. They would then bring this knowledge back to the party, whereupon a plan of action could be developed to meet the needs of the people. This was not to be done in a purely empirical fashion, but rather was to be based on the party leadership's understanding and analysis of objective conditions and the end goal of revolutionary success. Party policies would then be brought back to the people and carried out by the cadre concerned.

This was the connection between the mass line and democratic centralism. The Communist Party, being the vanguard, would always make the ultimate policy decisions, but it was hoped that these decisions would be based on clear knowledge of the realities on the ground.

The mass line was carried into the post-1949 era, as was the concept and principle of democratic centralism. Both organizing principles may be seen in the founding documents of the People's Republic of China, as well as in successive constitutions.

Both of these concepts suffered some setbacks to their original meaning and practice from the late 1950s through to the end of the Cultural Revolution and its aftermath (1966–1976). For example, some would argue that the 1958 Great Leap Forward was not an expression of either democratic centralism or the mass line. And since Mao himself attached meaning and substance to the mass-line concept only in connection with the vanguard party, his attacks on the party during the Cultural Revolution would seem to have undermined this principle somewhat.

## DEMOCRATIC CENTRALISM AND THE MASS LINE IN THE POST-MAO ERA

Even though the Communist Party was reconstructed under Deng Xiaoping's leadership as he took China into the massive economic and social reforms of the late 1970s and 1980s, the principles of democratic centralism and the mass line are still held to be fundamental to the day-to-day operation of the People's Republic. In fact, there seems to have been a return to the mid-1950s version of both concepts, with a focus on the notion of the collective leadership of the party, as opposed to that of a strong central leader.

This does not mean that the Communist Party has relinquished its central authority, or that Western-style democracy is on the horizon. Rather, democratic centralism continues to have application in both state policies and the internal workings of the Communist Party. While there are continuing calls for greater inner-party democracy at each successive party congress, it is clear that the upper-level leadership, the Standing Committee of the Politburo, still calls the shots.

As for the mass line, this concept has clearly been eroded over time, even though it gets lip service from the leadership. Party and government officials are still expected to go down to the people to find out what their needs are, but one wonders how effective these investigations are.

There is certainly greater awareness, and official policies do reflect a desire to take care of major problems. But the widespread social protests year after year by those who feel left out of the China "miracle" would seem to raise serious questions about the validity and efficacy of democratic centralism and the mass line as currently practiced in the People's Republic of China.

**SEE ALSO** *Communist Party.*

**BIBLIOGRAPHY**

Adler, Alan, ed. *Theses, Resolutions, and Manifestos of the First Four Congresses of the Third International.* Trans. Alix Holt and Barbara Holland. London: Ink Links, 1980.

Leung, John K., and Michael Y. M. Kau. *The Writings of Mao Zedong: 1949–1976.* Vol. 2: *January 1956–December 1957.* New York: M. E. Sharpe, 1992.

Lieberthal, Kenneth. *Governing China: From Revolution through Reform*. 2nd ed. New York: W. W. Norton, 2004.

Mao Tse-tung. *Selected Works of Mao Tse-tung*. Vols. 2 and 3. Beijing: Foreign Languages Press, 1967.

Saich, Tony. *Governance and Politics of China*. New York: Palgrave, 2001.

Waller, Michael. *Democratic Centralism: An Historical Commentary*. New York: St. Martin's Press, 1981.

***Joseph T. Miller***

## MASS MOVEMENTS

The Chinese Communist Party under the leadership of Mao Zedong was notable for repeated intense mass movements. Table 1 lists the most significant of these movements in the period from the consolidation of Mao's leadership in the 1940s to his death in 1976. While this entire period could be considered one long mobilization, mass campaigns had a rhythm of their own involving preparation, intense attack, and easing off. Moreover, the system as a whole, particularly in the pre–Cultural Revolution period, alternated between mobilization and consolidation phases, the latter reflecting deliberate decisions to repair dislocations caused by campaigns and reduce pressure on the population generally. The final period of Mao's life, the so-called Cultural Revolution decade of 1966 to 1976, marked a distinct change as the party lost control of mobilization. In the post-Mao period, the new leadership sought to break decisively from the disruptions of the Cultural Revolution and earlier campaigns with a (largely honored) promise of no new political movements.

### DISTINCTIVENESS, OBJECTIVES, AND METHODS

While Soviet organizational methods have been copied in China, the Maoist approach is distinctive in important respects. To an unusual extent, Mao sought individual transformation; whereas the Soviet approach can be characterized as making clear what was acceptable and unacceptable, the Chinese method aimed at genuine conversion to socialist values. Moreover, in the pre–Cultural Revolution period, the Chinese were more surgical and less reliant on unpredictable terror than were the Soviets during the Stalinist period, as limits were generally placed on violence and sanctions during movements. Another contrast with Stalinism, where the secret police acted independently of and often against the Communist Party, was the Chinese Communist Party's insistence on control of all mass movements before 1966.

Chinese mass movements have had a range of overlapping objectives as summarized in Table 1. Political objectives were always present, whether that meant indoctrinating cadres in the party line, altering the influence and behavior of different groups in society, correcting deviant tendencies, or restoring regime control. A major objective throughout the 1950s was social transformation as collective socialist structures were imposed on society. Various economic objectives have also been pursued: liberating productive forces (land reform), increasing state control of economic assets (the Three-Anti and Five-Anti Campaigns), improving planning capabilities (agricultural cooperativization and the socialist transformation of industry and commerce), and increasing production (the Great Leap Forward).

**Mass movements under Mao**

| Movement | Objectives | Target groups |
|---|---|---|
| Yan'an rectification (1942–1944) | Political-ideological | Party members |
| North China land reform and rectification (1947–1948) | Political-ideological / economic | Peasants and rural cadres |
| National land reform (1950–1953) | Political-ideological / economic | Peasants |
| Suppression of counter revolutionaries (1951–1953) | Political control | Class enemies |
| Three-anti and five-anti campaign (1951–1952) | Political-ideological / economic | Urban cadres and bourgeoisie |
| Thought reform (1951–1952) | Political-ideological | Intellectuals |
| Agricultural cooperativization (1955–1956) | Social transformation / economic | Peasants |
| Socialist transformation of industry and commerce (1955–1956) | Social transformation / economic | Urban bourgeoisie |
| Hundred Flowers movement (1957) | Political-ideological | Party cadres |
| Anti-rightist campaign (1957) | Political control | Intellectual critics |
| Great Leap Forward (1958–1960) | Social transformation / economic | Whole society |
| Anti-right opportunism (1959–1960) | Political-ideological | Party critics and rural cadres |
| Socialist Education movement (1963–1966) | Political-ideological | Peasants and rural cadres |
| Cultural Revolution (1966–1968) | Political-ideological | Party leaders and whole society |
| Cleansing of class ranks (1968–1969) | Political control | Disruptive elements |
| Criticism of Lin Biao and Confucius (1974) | Political-ideological | Party leaders |
| Criticism of Deng Xiaoping (1976) | Political-ideological | Party leaders |

*Table 1*

While the approach has varied according to movement objectives and the groups targeted, similar methods have been used across campaigns, at least in the pre-1966 period. Organizationally, the Communist Party leadership defined the issues requiring mass mobilization; produced propaganda justifying campaigns and outlining their objectives; set in place a top-down organization, with special offices set up at each administrative level and reaching work units, urban residential street and neighborhood committees, and villages; and made use of work teams sent from higher levels to enforce movement goals. The essence of the organizational approach was to mobilize all resources necessary for success, making campaign goals a priority over normal organizational tasks—often causing major disruptions that had to be rectified in subsequent consolidation phases.

The manipulation of tension to bring pressure on target groups and individuals, and gain support from other elements in society, has been an essential campaign method. This can be seen in rural society, where, from the period of land reform on, class enemies were identified, lower strata of peasants were mobilized against them through orchestrated "speak bitterness" meetings highlighting past exploitation, and the majority were promised concrete economic benefits. Rewards were also used in the cultivation of activists, normally youthful villagers, workers, or employees, who were promoted to official positions as a result of their enthusiastic support of movements.

Small groups built into bureaucratic and productive organizations have played a central role in mass movements in China. Meetings of groups of cadres, workers, and employees, during which directives from above are presented and discussed, are a ubiquitous feature of the system, but such groups are energized during campaigns, meet on a much more frequent basis, and have implemented tension-creating measures. Criticism and self-criticism have characterized these groups; people were required to confront their shortcomings—and those of their colleagues—as defined by the leadership. When the aims of a movement were particularly stringent, these meetings included "struggle sessions" and abject confessions. Additionally, the practice of issuing rough guidelines requiring that a percentage of deviants be uncovered forced arbitrary designation of the innocent. This practice not only led to destructive intra-unit conflict undermining organizational relationships over long periods, it also produced a ritualized process that often resulted in role-playing rather than the true ideological change desired by Mao.

## THE EVOLUTION OF MASS MOVEMENTS SINCE 1949

Mass movements have evolved through a number of periods since 1949, reflecting both objective conditions and leadership preoccupations, particularly those of Mao Zedong. From 1949 to 1956, mobilization focused on the related objectives of national reconstruction, party control, and the establishment of a socialist politico-economic structure on the Soviet model. This focus meant that campaigns addressed concrete problems following a well-developed template, and the results were successful: party control was secured and significant economic growth achieved; key sections of the peasantry and urban population received specific benefits and supported national achievements; and state socialist structures were imposed on society. In the 1956–1957 period, Communist Party leaders declared that socialism had been basically realized, and the large-scale class struggle that had underpinned mass campaigns was largely a thing of the past.

Matters did not turn out as predicted due to a series of misjudgments on Mao's part. From 1957 to 1965, key campaigns created problems that were not inevitable. One of these campaigns, the Hundred Flowers movement, was meant to encourage mild criticism of party cadres by intellectuals and others, but after much hesitancy, an unanticipated torrent of criticism unfolded, leading to the harsh crackdown of the anti-rightist campaign. This campaign not only had a lasting chilling effect within Chinese society, it arguably led Mao to embark on the Great Leap Forward as an alternative project to his failed Hundred Flowers movement. Great Leap excesses resulted in economic depression, massive starvation among peasants, and a demoralized population and cadre corps, as well as significant fissures within the leadership. The need to recover from this situation led to a reduction in major campaigns in the early 1960s, with the rural Socialist Education movement being implemented on a limited geographic basis while undergoing shifting objectives and intensity. Most importantly, the amorphous results of this movement fed into Mao's dissatisfaction with both Chinese society and his leadership colleagues, leading him to launch the Cultural Revolution.

The Cultural Revolution was unique, mixing an effort to revive the revolutionary spirit in society, especially among the youth, with attacks on many of Mao's long-standing loyal colleagues. Most fundamentally, the Cultural Revolution departed from all previous campaign methodology. Rather than the Communist Party guiding the movement through an elaborate structure, it was truly a bottom-up campaign, with young university students playing a dynamic role. Although the themes were set by official propaganda, there was only sporadic organizational guidance, and the previously sacrosanct party committee structure was subject to withering attack and essentially dismantled by 1968. After Mao tired of the political and economic chaos during the summer of 1968, a degree of order was restored, in part using violent methods during the "cleansing of class ranks." But the weakness of the party structure was further evident in the political campaigns criticizing Lin Biao and Deng Xiaoping in 1974 and 1976 respectively, when rebel groups seriously challenged party committees, albeit with much less effect than in the 1967–1968 period.

The post-Mao leadership immediately moved to end this situation, launching a traditional-style campaign to criticize the deposed Gang of Four. More fundamentally, by 1979 the leadership promised no new political campaigns, a promise only briefly reneged in the antispiritual pollution drive of late 1983, the antibourgeois liberalization campaign in 1987, and the post-Tiananmen crisis efforts to restore order in 1989 and 1990. This, however, does not mean that successive post-Mao leaderships no longer rely on mass mobilization. Rather, they use campaigns (although reduced in scope, intensity, and number) to address specific problems. Undoubtedly the most dramatic case was the mobilization of the public to effectively combat the severe acute respiratory syndrome (SARS) epidemic in 2004. Gone are large-scale mass movements meant to reshape the structure of society or carry out Mao's ideological enthusiasms, but the organizational tools to mobilize the population for defined tasks remain.

**SEE ALSO** *Chinese Marxism: Mao Zedong Thought; Communist Party; Cultural Revolution, 1966–1969; Hundred Flowers Campaign; Mao Zedong; Music, Propaganda, and Mass Mobilization; Propaganda; Propaganda Art.*

**BIBLIOGRAPHY**


Bennett, Gordon. *Yundong: Mass Campaigns in Chinese Communist Leadership*. Berkeley: Center for Chinese Studies, University of California, 1976.

Chan, Anita, Richard Madsen, and Jonathan Unger. *Chen Village: The Recent History of a Peasant Community in Mao's China*. Berkeley: University of California Press, 1984.

Lifton, Robert J. *Thought Reform and the Psychology of Totalism: A Study of "Brainwashing" in China*. New York: Norton, 1961.

MacFarquhar, Roderick, ed. *The Hundred Flowers Campaign and the Chinese Intellectuals*. New York: Praeger, 1960.

Perry, Elizabeth J., and Li Xun. *Proletarian Power: Shanghai in the Cultural Revolution*. Boulder, CO: Westview, 1997.

Teiwes, Frederick C. *Politics and Purges in China: Rectification and the Decline of Party Norms, 1950–1965*. 2nd ed. Armonk, NY: Sharpe, 1993.

Whyte, Martin King. *Small Groups and Political Rituals in China*. Berkeley: University of California Press, 1974.


***Frederick C. Teiwes***

## POSTREVOLUTIONARY MARXISM OTHER THAN MAO ZEDONG THOUGHT

After the victory of 1949 and the establishment of the People's Republic of China (PRC), virtually all of the higher leaders of the Chinese Communist Party (CCP) felt the need to establish their credentials as Marxist theoreticians. Unlike the sometimes impressive works of academic Marxists in such scholarly fields as ancient history and archaeology, the Marxist writings of China's postrevolutionary leaders, other than Mao Zedong, are thin in quantity as well as quality. During the Maoist era, for the most part, they simply repeated the official ideological formulations laid down by Mao Zedong. Nonetheless, while the political reports and commentaries of Communist political leaders remained within the confines of "Mao Zedong Thought," differences in emphasis and nuance sometimes reflected significant political and policy differences.

### LIU SHAOQI

Such was the case with Liu Shaoqi, the second highest-ranking leader of the CCP and Mao's heir apparent until his downfall at the outset of the Cultural Revolution in 1966. Liu's writings reveal an emphasis on two main ideological tendencies that eventually deviated from Mao's changing definitions of the meaning of "Mao Zedong Thought." One was Liu's ultraorthodox interpretation of the Leninist scheme of party organization, with the Communist Party's political and ideological infallibility guaranteed by a strict hierarchy of ranks and the unquestioning obedience of lower-ranking members to higher-ranking ones. This view of the absolute primacy of the party was set forth in such works as "How to Be a Good Communist"(1939) and "The Victory of Marxism-Leninism in China" (1949).

Second, Liu was a principal Chinese Communist advocate of the orthodox Marxist (and Stalinist) belief that economic factors were the main historical determinant, ultimately molding politics, society, and ideology. Liu put the latter belief into practice in the early 1960s, when he assumed the leading role in the effort to restore production after the disasters of the Great Leap. For this he was accused of the heresies of "revisionism" and "economism," that is, putting an exaggerated emphasis on the development of productive forces to the neglect of ideological and political correctness.

Moreover, by the early 1960s, Liu's strict Leninist view of the proper functioning of the Communist Party clashed with Mao Zedong's growing distrust of the organization, which, with the outbreak of the Cultural Revolution in 1966, took the extraordinary form of a Maoist assault against the Communist Party and its organizational appendages. Liu Shaoqi was denounced as "the leading person in authority taking the capitalist road," abused, and arrested. He died in prison in 1969.

### ZHOU ENLAI

Zhou Enlai, China's urbane premier and foreign minister during most of the Maoist era, had fully accepted Mao's political and ideological leadership since the Yan'an era while skillfully attempting to moderate the radical excesses of Mao's policies in their execution. Zhou's theoretical writings were very limited, but he did make several notable contributions to the theory and practice of Mao Zedong Thought. At the outset of the Hundred Flowers campaign in 1956, Zhou presented a report titled "On the Question of Intellectuals," at a time when Mao was attempting to win the support of the intelligentsia for China's scientific advancement and economic construction. Addressing the longstanding problem of the social classification of intellectuals, a matter on which Marxist theory was ambiguous, Zhou declared that: "The overwhelming majority of intellectuals have become government workers in the cause of socialism and *are already part of the working class*" (emphasis added). With their class status thus favorably determined, suspicions over the political proclivities of intellectuals in general were removed, at least for a time, and the problem that now presented itself was a scarcity of intellectuals and their expertise. Thus Zhou proposed increases in university enrollments, the recognition of intellectuals as masters of science and technology, that they enjoy a wide realm of professional autonomy, improvements in their working and living conditions, and their recruitment into the party in greater numbers.

In his 1956 report on intellectuals, Zhou Enlai foreshadowed the changes in policy that were to be adopted by the post-Mao regime more than two decades later. He also anticipated the policies that were to proceed under the slogan of "the Four Modernizations," which were to be adopted by Mao's immediate successors. In January 1975, a dying Zhou left his hospital bed to make an impassioned call for the "modernization of agriculture, industry, national defense, [and] science and technology" in order to put China "in the front ranks of the world" by the end of the century.

## LIN BIAO'S PEOPLE'S WAR

While Zhou Enlai emphasized the more pragmatic and rational features of Maoism as a strategy of national economic development, other Communist leaders interpreted Maoism in an extravagant and ultrarevolutionary fashion, increasingly far removed from China's real needs and capabilities. A principal expression of this tendency was Lin Biao's 1965 treatise "Long Live the Victory of People's War." Lin Biao had been the most brilliant of the Red Army's military commanders in the civil war with the Guomindang. In 1959, during the Great Leap, Lin replaced the purged Peng Dehuai as China's minister of defense. From that powerful position, on the eve of the Cultural Revolution, Lin projected the strategy of "people's war" that Mao had pioneered in China into a global revolutionary vision. The "encirclement of the cities from the countryside" was a Maoist strategy that should be emulated by all oppressed nations, Lin declared. Just as the Chinese Communist revolution was won by mobilizing the forces of revolution in the rural areas to "surround and overwhelm" the conservative cities, so the world revolution would take the form of "the countryside" of Asia, Africa, and Latin America encircling "the cities" of North America and Western Europe.

It is unlikely that Mao ever took seriously this messianic world revolutionary vision. Following Lin Biao's demise in 1971, after an ill-fated coup, Mao reemphasized the PRC's customary foreign policy based on the realpolitik pursuit of China's national interest. It was thus that President Richard Nixon (1913–1994) flew to Beijing in 1972 to meet with Mao, preparing the stage for the normalization of relations between the United States and the PRC.

After the death of Mao Zedong in 1976, the Communist leaders who succeeded him still proclaimed their fidelity to Marxism in general and Mao Zedong Thought in particular. But increasingly in the post-Mao years, ideology functioned as a disguise for policies undertaken for reasons other than those that were dictated—or even could be sanctioned—by official doctrine. The general tendency of Marxism in the post-Mao era was toward the disintegration of the doctrine, an acceleration of Mao Zedong's already substantial departures from the premises of Marxist–Leninist theory.

## DENG XIAOPING

Mao Zedong's initial successor, Hua Guofeng (1921–2008), presided over a caretaker regime with a Maoist facade in the transition from the Mao to the post-Mao era. The decisive break with the Maoist version of Marxism came with the accession of Deng Xiaoping as China's "paramount leader" at the end of 1978. Deng Xiaoping had been a Communist since 1924 and a leading member of the Maoist faction of the party during the civil war with the Guomindang and during the early years of the People's Republic. By the end of 1978, Deng had established himself as China's "paramount leader" on a program championing "socialist democracy" and market reforms.

Deng's democratic promises proved transitory but his introduction of market relationships in the countryside and then in the cities earned him the reputation of being a pragmatist who would flexibly employ capitalist means to achieve eventual socialist ends. As Deng put it, it doesn't make any difference whether the cat is black or white, so long as it catches mice it is a good cat. He believed that capitalist methods would speed up the "development of the productive forces" and that, along with a continuing monopoly of political power by the Communist Party, would eventually yield a socialist society. What in fact it has yielded is the world's most massive and rapid process of capitalist development. It is one of the most striking examples in history where the means of economic development overwhelmed the ends that were sought. But if capitalist methods did not yield socialist ends, they did serve China's search for "wealth and power," a nationalist impulse that soon extinguished what remained of the revolution's socialist aspirations.

### JIANG ZEMIN AND HU JINTAO

Nationalism also dominated the ideology and policies of Deng Xiaoping's successors. Jiang Zemin, the leader of the CCP from the mid-1990s to 2002, undertook to incorporate into the Communist political framework the new and expanded social groups that rapid economic development had produced. He thus added to the official canon of Mao Zedong Thought the theory of the "Three Represents." Since the CCP represented China's "advanced productive forces," China's new bourgeoisie (or those officially known as "private entrepreneurs") were to be represented in, and by, the Communist Party. Secondly, since the CCP represented China's "advanced culture," intellectuals were to be recruited into the party in greater numbers. And thirdly, since the CCP "represents the interests of the overwhelming majority of the Chinese people," Jiang claimed, the party need no longer concern itself with class struggle.

It is ironic that this nationalist celebration of an essentially united people "represented" by a single party was proclaimed at a time when income inequalities in China surpassed those of India and the United States. It was left to Hu Jintao, Jiang's successor as head of the CCP, to blur the social results of China's economic advance by adding to Mao Zedong Thought the theory that China had become a "harmonious society."

**SEE ALSO** *Deng Xiaoping; Jiang Zemin; Lin Biao; Liu Shaoqi; Zhou Enlai.*

#### BIBLIOGRAPHY

Brugger, Bill, and David Kelly. *Chinese Marxism in the Post-Mao Era.* Stanford CA: Stanford University Press, 1990.

Dittmer, Lowell. *Liu Shaoqi and the Chinese Cultural Revolution.* Rev. ed. Armonk, NY: Sharpe, 1998.

Kau, Michael Y. M., ed. *The Lin Piao Affair: Power Politics and Military Coup.* White Plains, NY: International Arts and Science Press, 1975.

Liu Shaoqi, *Collected Works of Liu Shao-ch'i.* 3 vols. Hong Kong: Union Research Institute, 1968–69.

Meisner, Maurice. *The Deng Xiaoping Era: An Inquiry into the Fate of Chinese Socialism.* New York: Hill and Wang, 1996.

Su Shaozhi. *Marxism in China.* London: Spokesman, 1983.

Sun Yan. *The Chinese Reassessment of Socialism, 1976–1992.* Princeton, NJ: Princeton University Press, 1995.

Zhou Enlai. On the Question of Intellectuals. *Communist China 1955–59: Policy Documents with Analysis,* eds. Robert R. Bowie and John K. Fairbank, p. 133. Cambridge, MA: Harvard University Press, 1962.

***Maurice Meisner***

# CHINESE OVERSEAS

*This entry contains the following:*



## OVERVIEW

The term *Chinese overseas* broadly denotes all persons of Chinese ancestry residing outside China (mainland China and Taiwan). Scholars use more specific terms to denote different subgroups: *Huaqiao* (Chinese sojourners or Chinese citizens living abroad), *Huaren* (ethnic Chinese with foreign citizenship), and *Huayi* (descendents of Chinese parents). Although these subgroups have different legal or citizenship status in their host countries and in China, they have much in common in terms of their history, their past and present socioeconomic roles, and their geopolitical impacts on their host countries and on China.

The number of Chinese overseas is estimated to be 37 million (Poston, Mao, and Yu 1994) or 35 million (Liu 2006), depending on when they were counted, and they can be found in every continent of the world. They have played significant roles in the socioeconomic developments of their host countries, and have participated in the modern nation-building processes of China and their host countries. Since the 1980s the Chinese overseas have been an important agent of transnational linkages because of the dramatic increase in ethnic Chinese moving out of their original areas of settlement such as Hong Kong and Taiwan, and by the early 1990s, out of mainland China itself.

The Chinese left China in waves of emigration for different reasons. Their pattern of movement is part of the story of globalization, with the "push and pull factors" closely associated with the rise of Western imperialism, economic difficulties, and the political decline of China. Early emigrants, from the seventeenth century onward, were merchants trading beyond China's shores and then settling in various parts of Southeast Asia. Modern Chinese emigration on a massive scale started in the mid-nineteenth century, propelled by "push factors" from within Qing China, when the country suffered Western imperialist invasions such as the Opium Wars (1839–1842 and 1858–1860) and severe economic dislocations that brought about acute internal unrests such as the Taiping Uprising (1850–1864). The breakdown of internal social order coupled with the lack of arable land produced an at-risk population driven to the brink of starvation or vagrancy. Emigration became a strategy for overpopulated villages to ensure survival.

Simultaneously, Western imperial powers were establishing colonies around the world. The shortage of cheap labor for gold and tin mines, coffee, sugar, and rubber plantations, railroad construction, and other enterprises created such a demand for manpower that many Chinese became indentured laborers (coolies), often by force or under false pretenses. Others emigrated as "free migrants." In various Southeast Asian colonies (e.g., Dutch East Indies, British Borneo, British Malaya, French Indochina) the Chinese also were in demand as middlemen and merchants liaising between the Western colonizers and the indigenous people.

From the mid-twentieth century onward, emigration was almost entirely voluntary and prompted by the search for better opportunities. In the 1980s, in contrast with most earlier periods, Chinese migrants often were motivated by a desire to find host countries that enjoyed greater political stability, less competitive education systems, and superior lifestyles. With the growing prosperity of China, however, many migrants keep their options open: Instead of settling down in the host countries, they move frequently between their home and host countries as transnationals.

## IDENTITY

The sense of identity of the Chinese overseas has changed over time. In the early migration periods, most had little intention of staying in their host countries for good. Their ideal was *luoye guigen*—like fallen leaves returning to the ground, most of them thought they would eventually return to China to settle down after a lifetime of hard work. They essentially considered themselves Chinese subjects.

The pull of China was very strong. This feeling was engendered not just by attachment to the motherland, but also by the harsh anti-Chinese laws that various settlement countries had enacted. The new immigrant nations such as the United States, Canada, Australia, and New Zealand, all new frontiers open for settlement, had policies that clearly favored immigrants from Britain and other white European countries. Chinese people were subjected to exorbitant taxes and difficult English-language tests, and they faced a series of discriminatory measures aimed at barring them from entering these countries. Those Chinese who succeeded in entering were barred from citizenship (and therefore had no right to vote) and excluded from much of the welfare of the state. In effect, the anti-Chinese laws of these white settler countries prevented the Chinese from becoming full citizens and kept them segregated and marginalized until the mid-twentieth century, when new laws relaxed the color bar.

In Southeast Asia, where Europeans were setting up colonies but generally had no intentions of settling down themselves (because of the tropical climate, which they disliked), the Chinese were needed as middlemen traders and deliberately allowed into the region in large numbers. Their numbers grew quickly and they settled down in relative prosperity, often becoming the backbone of the economy. Subsequently, when these nations gained their independence after World War II, the Chinese became a target of resentment from the indigenous populations. The new native governments introduced restrictive laws of various degrees of severity (such as forbidding Chinese schools, use of the Chinese language, etc). Turbulent times saw race riots, and the destruction of Chinese property (such as the burning of shops) was commonplace. In Indonesia, for example, race riots with widespread massacres from 1956 to 1966 forced the repatriation of tens of thousands of ethnic Chinese, many of whom had been born in Indonesia and had very little real connection with China.

Until the mid-twentieth century, the Chinese overseas mainly came from three main provinces, all located on the southeast coast where the logistics of emigration was easier. The first was the Fujian Province; most of the Fujianese went to modern-day Philippines, Malaysia, and Indonesia, and some emigrated to Europe, notably France. The second was the Guangdong Province, which sent people to the United States, Australia, and New Zealand. The third region was the Zhejiang (Shanghai dialect group) area, with notable centers in Wonhou, Wencheng, Qintian, and Ningbo. These regions that sent out their able-bodied young men to seek better fortunes overseas thrived on the remittances that the emigrants sent back. Besides supporting their immediate family members, the money went to building village schools and hospitals, as well as private villas constructed for the émigrés' eventual return and retirement. These buildings, with visible European architectural characteristics, became the hallmarks of the *qiaoxiang* (home villages) and are still in evidence today.

The different provincial origins of the Chinese overseas are clearly reflected in the dialects they speak. Whereas many of the Chinese communities in Southeast Asia speak Hokkien (Fujianese dialect), Cantonese remains the lingua franca of the Chinatowns in North America, Europe, and

## REMITTANCES AND INVESTMENT SINCE 1800

China's Qing dynasty (1644–1911) banned emigration and viewed Chinese overseas with hostility and suspicion until the 1870s, when it began to solicit their wealth and skills for China's modernization. The lifting of the emigration ban in 1893 legitimated emigrants' growing ties with China, especially their ancestral homes in South China. Since then every Chinese national government has encouraged family remittances and investment from Chinese overseas. Between 1862 and 1949 Chinese overseas invested a total of US$128 million in China, nearly all of it destined for the two main emigrant provinces of Guangdong and Fujian; 90 percent originated in Southeast Asia, where the majority of Chinese overseas live. Investments in mining, railroads, telephone and telegraph services, electricity companies, trolley and bus companies, maritime shipping, cinemas, and department stores were a major force in the modernization of the emigrant counties and coastal cities of South China. Before 1949 most investments were concentrated in real estate (42%), followed by commercial enterprises (16%) and industry (15%). Chinese overseas also invested heavily in the social welfare of their home counties, sponsoring schools, hospitals, roads, bridges, and other forms of public infrastructure. Remittances also have been important as a means of family support and a major source of foreign exchange for successive Chinese governments. The following list (based of figures from Bolt [2000], Hicks [1993], Li, Lin and Cai [1993], Remer [1933], and Wu [1967]) shows remittance estimates for selected years from the early 1900s to until the Japanese invasion in 1937:

1906: 150 million yuan
1928: 228 million yuan
1933: 306 million yuan
1937: 456 million yuan

Remittances and investments have continued to play an important role in the People's Republic of China. Between 1949 and 1975 family remittances totalled US $4.6 billion. Overseas Chinese investment companies set up in the early 1950s had little success, however, attracting only around US$100 million, and were closed when the Cultural Revolution erupted in 1966. Major changes have occurred since the adoption of the Open Door Policy in 1978. By 1998 to 2000, Chinese overseas (including those in Hong Kong and Taiwan) accounted for 65 percent (more than US $82 billion) of total foreign direct investment. A significant proportion of this investment is linked to the globalization of traditional overseas voluntary associations (such as the Singapore-based International Federation of Fuqing Clans and the Hong Kong-based World Guan Association), which mobilize capital on a global scale for business investments and charitable works in the *qiaoxiang* (emigrant districts). Family remittances to traditional South China *qiaoxiang* have declined in significance as the pre-1949 emigrants and their descendants pass from the scene. However, approximately two million "new migrants" (post-1978 emigrants, often from areas outside the traditional *qiaoxiang*) now remit an estimated US$840 million annually to family members in China.

### BIBLIOGRAPHY

Bolt, Paul J. *China and Southeast Asia's Ethnic Chinese: State and Diaspora in Contemporary Asia.* Westport, CT: Praeger, 2000.

Ch'en, Ta. *Emigrant Communities in South China: A Study of Overseas Migration and Its Influence on Standards of Living and Social Change.* Shanghai: Kelly and Walsh, 1939.

Godley, Michael R. *The Mandarin-Capitalists from Nanyang: Overseas Enterprises in the Modernization of China, 1893–1911.* Cambridge, U.K.: Cambridge University Press, 1981.

Hicks, George L., ed. *Overseas Chinese Remittances from Southeast Asia, 1910–1940.* Singapore: Select Books, 1993.

Li, Guoliang, Lin Jinzhi, and Cai Renlong. *Huaqiao huaren yu Zhongguo geming he jianshe* [Overseas Chinese and ethnic Chinese and China's revolution and construction]. Fuzhou, China: Fujian renmin chubanshe, 1993.

Lin, Jiaqing, et al. *Jindai Guangdong sheng qiaohui yanjiu* [Research on overseas Chinese remittances to Guangdong in modern times]. Guangzhou, China: Zhongshan daxue chubanshe, 1999.

Liu, Hong. Old Linkages, New Networks: The Globalization of Overseas Chinese Voluntary Associations and Its Implications. *China Quarterly* 155 (September 1998): 582–609.

Liu, Hong. New Migrants and the Revival of Overseas Chinese Nationalism. *Journal of Contemporary China* 14, no. 43 (May 2005): 291–316.

Remer, Charles F. *Foreign Investments in China.* New York: Macmillan, 1933.

Wu, Chun-hsi. *Dollars, Dependents, and Dogma: Overseas Chinese Remittances to Communist China.* Stanford, CA: Hoover Institution on War, Revolution, and Peace, 1967.

***Glen Peterson***

Australasia, although Mandarin is increasingly spoken, especially by the younger generation.

## RELATIONS WITH AND ATTITUDES TOWARD CHINA

Qing China (1644–1911) did not encourage migration, and was "neglectful of, and indifferent to" the Chinese overseas (Wang Gungwu 1998, p. 103). Nevertheless, the excessive ill-treatment of Chinese coolies in Cuba and Peru prompted a visit by the Qing commissioner in 1873. That was the first instance of direct Chinese government intervention, albeit rather mild, on behalf of the Chinese overseas. The right of the Chinese to emigrate and to return was established by the government in 1893. By the time the Qing fell in 1911, many consulates had been established around the world, mostly to promote education and the setting up of chambers of commerce. Consular representatives in various overseas cities also protested anti-Chinese activities.

From the mid-nineteenth century until the founding the People's Republic in 1949, the Chinese overseas were loyal to China, but they could feel little pride in their home nation because of the country's frequent political upheavals and helplessness in the face of foreign aggression. Many of them took part enthusiastically in the political movements in China.

During the late Qing period, both reformers under Kang Youwei and Liang Qichao and revolutionaries under Sun Yat-sen appealed to overseas Chinese for financial and moral support. All three leaders personally visited various Chinatowns for fundraising. When the Chinese Republic was founded in 1912, Sun Yat-sen famously honored the overseas Chinese with the slogan *huaqiao wei geming zhi mu* ("the overseas Chinese are the mother of the revolution"). Under Republican China's constitution, overseas Chinese could have six representatives in the national parliament.

After Chiang Kai-shek's success in the Northern Expedition in 1928, the Guomindang (GMD) government established an overseas Chinese affairs bureau. The 1929 Nationality Law—still nominally effective in the Republic of China on Taiwan—established Chinese citizenship for all people of Chinese descent. In 1932 the Overseas Chinese Commission became a ministry with nationwide responsibilities and a detailed agenda of promoting education, investment, and migration. The aim was to enhance links between overseas Chinese links and the GMD government.

When the Communists came to power in 1949 they initially followed in their predecessors' footsteps, but with less enthusiasm. In 1954 Chinese premier Zhou Enlai announced a new policy that encouraged overseas Chinese to opt for local nationality, thereby cutting the legal citizenship link with China. In 1955 the Sino-Indonesian Dual Nationality Treaty was signed, and overseas Chinese were free to choose the nationality they preferred. This essentially remains the policy of the PRC toward the Chinese overseas.

## GENDER IMBALANCE

Like most pioneer communities, the early Chinese overseas communities were mainly male because the purpose of their emigrating was to provide much needed manual labor. The host countries needed Chinese men only as itinerant workers, not settlers. Chinese women seldom migrated (the migration of women to Singapore to work as maids in the early twentieth century was an exception) because the men were expected to return to China at the end of their foreign sojourn. It was common practice for villages to arrange weddings prior to the men's departures so that there was added incentive for them to send regular remittances home. Chinese men might return for home visits once every five or ten years.

Foreign governments also enacted laws that made female immigration difficult, partly to forestall the emergence of a local-born Chinese population. Very often the Chinese overseas lived in ethnic enclaves that had very few Chinese women. Intermarriages with local women occurred when the Chinese men could afford it.

## POLITICAL ACTIVITIES: TONGS, TRIADS, AND ASSOCIATIONS

The earliest overseas Chinese organized mutual aid societies, clan associations, and secret society–style "brotherhoods" (*tongs*) for mutual aid. As visible minorities in foreign lands often facing hostile or indifferent host societies, their banding together was important for the survival of the communities.

These Chinese associations provided newcomers with rudimentary temporary housing, employment advice, emergency medical care, and relief funds. They often were led by local businessmen from their own respective home villages. In time, these societies also handled remittances and made representations to the host governments to uphold the rights and interests of the Chinese community. Two of the best known groups were the Chee Kong Tong (which originated from the late Ming antigovernment Triad brotherhood) and the Guomindang.

During ordinary times the Chinese congregated to share news, chat, eat, gamble, and smoke—generally socializing within their own circle. When news of various political upheavals in China reached the overseas communities, however, many enthusiastically got involved. Political activities of the Chinese overseas communities were China-centered and had little to do with the politics of the host countries. When Japan invaded China, overseas Chinese communities all around the world responded with demonstrations, rallies, and very generous and regular donations to the war of resistance in China. For this reason, when Japan successfully invaded Southeast Asia, the ethnic Chinese were targeted and punished much more harshly than the indigenous peoples, many of whom regarded the Japanese as liberators against their colonial masters. As a result, members of many indigenous Southeast Asian communities became collaborators while the Chinese became anti-Japanese resistance fighters.

### PRESENT-DAY "TRIUMPHAL MODERNS"

In the twenty-first century, China regards the Chinese overseas as potential supporters and allies. Many have shown great patriotism toward Chinese causes, as well as an alertness to opportunities, especially now that China is a new economic powerhouse with sound investment opportunities. Generally, the Chinese overseas have maintained strong trade links with China, and supply much of the foreign investment in China's industries. Some hold the view that the Chinese form a global network of great influence; the diversity of the ethnic Chinese and their conditions and ambiguous belonging suggest otherwise. In some settings, some ethnic Chinese are influential cosmopolitans, but in others they form fragile and marginalized groups in overseas societies.

**SEE ALSO** *Ma, Yo-yo; Pei, I.M.*


**BIBLIOGRAPHY**

Liu, Hong, ed. *The Chinese Overseas*. New York: Routledge, 2006.

Ong, Aiwha, and Don Nonini, eds. *Ungrounded Empires: The Cultural Politics of Modern Chinese Transnationalism.* New York: Routledge, 1997.

Pan, Lynn. *Sons of the Yellow Emperor*. London: Secker and Warburg, 1990.

Poston, Dudley, Michael Mao, and Mei-yu Yu. The Global Distribution of the Overseas Chinese Around 1990. *Population and Development Review* 20, no. 3 (1994): 631–645.

Wang Gungwu. Nationalism Among the Overseas Chinese. In *The Encyclopedia of the Chinese Overseas*, ed. Lyn Pan, 103–105. Singapore: Archipelago Press, 1998.


***Manying Ip***

## HISTORICAL PATTERNS OF GOVERNMENT POLICY AND EMIGRATION

The more than 30 million people of Chinese ancestry who, in the early twenty-first century, reside outside of China are the product of a centuries-long history of emigration. Many of the economic and social factors that have shaped this history, what Philip Kuhn calls the "historical ecology of Chinese emigration," have been largely consistent over time. It is thus other factors, notably government policy, that account for much of the historical and geographic variation in emigration. Two types of government policies are relevant: those of successive Chinese governments toward emigrants and their descendants and those of countries receiving Chinese emigrants. The single most important policy shaping emigration from China to the United States, Canada, Australia, and New Zealand was probably the adoption and eventual repudiation of race-based exclusion by those countries. Only the policies of the Chinese state are treated in this entry. It explores the categories into which migrants were classified for policy purposes, the history of emigration regulatory regimes and other policies related to emigrants and their families, and the intersection of emigrant policies with larger political concerns.

### TERMS AND CONCEPTS

Until the mid-nineteenth century, emigration from China was nominally illegal, so government documents typically describe emigrants as either bandits, fugitives, or temporary sojourners abroad. As the numbers of emigrants grew and the Qing state increasingly recognized the need for a relationship with them, officials sought new terms. By the end of the century, the term *Huaqiao* (Chinese sojourner, often translated as "overseas Chinese") had come into common use. Though the term's etymology implied only temporary absence, in practice it came to encompass permanent migrants and their descendants as well. This led to a problematic relationship with increasingly universalized notions of citizenship, for the term retains a certain ambiguity between Chinese nationals abroad and the larger category of people of Chinese ethnic origin living outside China. Modern scholars generally use the term *overseas Chinese* to describe the former, and *Chinese overseas* to describe the latter. In the twentieth century descendants of emigrants and emigrants who have become naturalized citizens of their adopted countries have frequently been troubled by the ambiguity and have started using such terms as *Huaren* (Chinese people) and *Huayi* (descendants of Chinese). As we shall see below, the government of the People's Republic accepts this basic distinction between Chinese citizens living abroad and persons of Chinese ethnic origin holding foreign citizenship. Following precedents from the Republican period, the People's Republic adopted policies that also identify the categories *guiqiao* (returned overseas Chinese) and *qiaojuan* (overseas-Chinese dependents, that is, emigrants' family members living in China), as relevant categories for policy. The term *qiaowu* (overseas-Chinese affairs) describes the policies formulated to deal with these groups and the institutions charged with implementing them.

## CHRONOLOGY OF REGULATORY POLICIES

Out of concerns that Chinese living abroad might be fugitive loyalists of the preceding Ming dynasty (1368–1644) or potential rebels, the laws of the Qing dynasty (1644–1912) forbade emigration. But by the mid-nineteenth century, ever-growing numbers of emigrants made political recognition of actual large-scale emigration necessary. Businesses known as coolie agencies were active in the export of Chinese labor from South China, sometimes using coercion and deception, to support growing international demand. In 1866 the British, French, and Chinese governments signed a convention to regulate Chinese emigration in the hope controlling such activities. Though the British ultimately rejected its terms, the convention nonetheless became the basis of a Qing policy that reluctantly accepted the reality of emigration. The U.S.–China Burlingame Treaty of 1868 further recognized the principle of freedom of movement between the two countries. The regulation of external migration effectively legalized it, even though formal legalization of emigration did not occur until 1893. An important though unexpected consequence of de facto recognition was to normalize the status of emigrants who returned from abroad. This enabled successful emigrants to play a public role in their home communities and men with overseas connections to take on leadership roles in many parts of South China.

From the 1870s the Qing government adopted a more activist foreign policy that included establishing Chinese consuls charged with protecting the interests of Chinese overseas, as well as dispatching official missions to investigate labor conditions for Chinese in places where there were reports of ill-treatment, such as Cuba and Peru. The Qing state also sought to strike a deal with Chinese overseas, offering them official recognition and support, for example by protecting their rights in China and abroad, in the hope of obtaining their political loyalty, economic investment, and skills. The status of Chinese emigrants was further clarified in the Qing's 1909 Nationality Law. Based on the principle of jus sanguinis (that a child's citizenship is determined by its parents' citizenship), this law made all emigrants from China and their descendants citizens. But Qing efforts to secure the loyalty of Chinese overseas were far from a universal success, as demonstrated by the support many offered to anti-Qing movements. In gratitude for this support Sun Yat-sen (Sun Zhongshan) bestowed on overseas Chinese the epithet "mother of the revolution."

The Nationalist government inherited from the Qing both the principle of jus sanguinis and the view of Chinese overseas as both a responsibility and a potential resource. The status of overseas Chinese as citizens meant that they should be represented in government, so several seats in the National Assembly were assigned to overseas Chinese (a situation that persisted in the Republic of China until the dissolution of the National Assembly in 2005). In the 1920s the Nationalist state also set up a comprehensive administrative structure for formulating and implementing policies on overseas-Chinese affairs (a structure largely carried over into the state structure of the People's Republic). As the threat from Japan increased in the 1930s, the Nationalist government intensified its activities among Chinese overseas in hopes of securing their support for anti-Japanese efforts.

After 1949 overseas Chinese policy became part of the larger international struggle between the Republic of China and the People's Republic, with the two states competing for support from Chinese living abroad. The People's Republic also faced new challenges. The vast majority of Chinese overseas lived in Southeast Asia. As the states of the region became independent, ethnic hostility against Chinese rose. Majority indigenous populations worried that ethnic Chinese in those countries owed their primary loyalties to China, and that state support by the People's Republic for ethnic Chinese was a new form of colonialism. This created difficulties for Chinese overseas, and also in China's foreign relations. Zhou Enlai proposed a solution to the problem at the Afro-Asian Conference of Bandung, Indonesia, in 1955. Zhou declared that persons of Chinese origin must choose whether to remain Chinese citizens or become naturalized citizens of the countries in which they resided, in which case China would renounce all claims on them. Whatever their choice for citizenship, Chinese overseas were urged to integrate fully into the societies in which they lived.

Following Republican precedents, the People's Republic, as an aspect of policy in the early 1950s, guaranteed the rights of relatives in China of Chinese overseas, including the right to receive remittances. But as overall policies became more radicalized in the 1950s, contradictions arose between the transition to socialism and the protected, privileged status of the families of Chinese overseas. By the time of the Cultural Revolution (1966–1969), overseas Chinese descendents lost their privileges and came under political attack, as all foreign connections became suspect. This undermined the position of the People's Republic in the competition with the Republic of China for the support of Chinese overseas. It also meant tight restrictions on any further emigration.

With the repudiation of the Cultural Revolution, the institutions responsible for overseas Chinese affairs were revived, and the political verdicts on Chinese overseas were reversed. They and their families in China were now recognized as a fundamentally patriotic force. New emigration, of students in particular, began to be permitted. To encourage Chinese overseas to contribute to reform, efforts were renewed to deepen their ties to China. But the overall policy of the 1980s had to balance this objective against the larger diplomatic issues inherited from the 1950s. The basic elements of the policy were to encourage Chinese overseas to become naturalized and to integrate into local societies, to protect and even repatriate Chinese nationals as necessary (in practice, the People's Republic was rarely willing to risk its relations with other states by exerting itself against ill treatment of Chinese nationals abroad), and to encourage Chinese overseas' business interests to contribute to Chinese economic growth.

In the post-1978 reform era, China's emigration regime has increasingly converged with international norms, with few formal restrictions on emigration and growing efforts to regulate illegal emigration and human smuggling. With the number of China-born ethnic Chinese in Southeast Asia declining with the passage of time, the long-term strategy for dealing with Chinese overseas has shifted to a more active policy to secure the loyalty of a wider group of persons of Chinese ethnic origin, as well as of the recent waves of new emigrants (*xin yimin*), through liaison work, publicity, and schemes to promote Chinese education abroad.

## PATTERNS AND CYCLES

The history of the relevant terms and the chronology of government policy show that policy on emigration has long been shaped by both domestic and international concerns. Underlying all the policies of successive states have been the dual goals of securing the interests of Chinese citizens abroad while maintaining their ties with China in ways that serve state interests. In the twentieth century these goals have often conflicted with one another. Efforts to foster ties with Chinese overseas aroused suspicion in the countries in which they lived. This suspicion harmed both the Chinese residents of those countries and China's own foreign relations. The fundamental dilemma for the Chinese state was how to limit the relationship with Chinese overseas, so that it did not cause problems for both parties, while simultaneously strengthening the relationship so as to serve state interests, for example by boosting investment in China.

The chronology also illustrates the broad historical pattern of government policies and emigration that Wang Gungwu has labeled the "Chinese overseas cycle." The early to middle nineteenth century saw a shift from formal prohibition to tacit acceptance of emigration. Such acceptance was gradually replaced, reluctantly, by formal acceptance and regulatory intervention. From the end of the century and through the Republican period (1912–1949), there developed a policy of strategic management: regulating emigration and devising policies to secure the loyalty of Chinese overseas to the Chinese state. Early in the People's Republic, the cycle turned back to effective prohibition of emigration, coupled with more restrained efforts to secure the interests and loyalties of Chinese overseas. Since the start of the reform era in the late 1970s, the cycle has turned back to strategic management of emigration, including more liberal policies on emigration and continued efforts to make emigrants and their descendants serve state interests back in China.

A second pattern of variation has to do with the intended scope of government policy. From the earliest policies to those of the early 1950s, the principle of jus sanguinis meant that policies applied to all emigrants and their descendants, that is, to all people of Chinese descent living overseas. The neocolonialist concerns of the 1950s led the government of the People's Republic to narrow its targets of intervention to Chinese citizens abroad only (the Nationalist government on Taiwan retained the original broader conception). Since 1978 the scope of state policy has expanded once again to include new emigrants, as well as ethnic Chinese who have taken foreign citizenship. Like the underlying concerns of policy, the scope of policy has also varied over time to include both domestic and international targets, at various times extending to include families of emigrants who remain in China and Chinese who have returned from abroad.

For more than a century, maintaining and strengthening ties with Chinese emigrants and Chinese communities overseas has been a consistent strategy of successive Chinese states. Changing over time were the purposes for which this strategy was enlisted, the political approaches used in support of the strategy, and the official discourses justifying the strategy, shaped by the changing international and domestic situation in China.

**SEE ALSO** *Chinese Overseas: Exclusion in Receiving Countries.*

### BIBLIOGRAPHY

Fitzgerald, Stephen. *China and the Overseas Chinese: A Study of Peking's Changing Policy 1949–1970*. Cambridge, U.K.: Cambridge University Press, 1972.

Kuhn, Philip. *Chinese among Others: Emigration in Modern Times*. Lanham, MD: Rowman and Littlefield, 2008.

Mette Thunø. Reaching Out and Incorporating Chinese Overseas: The Trans-territorial Scope of the PRC by the End of the 20th Century. *China Quarterly* 168 (2001): 910–929.

Wang Gungwu. Greater China and the Chinese Overseas. *China Quarterly* 136 (1993): 926–948.

Zhuang Guotu. *Zhongguo fengjian zhengfu de huaqiao zhengce*. Xiamen: Xiamen Daxue Chubanshe, 1989.

***Michael Szonyi***

## SENDING AREAS

Since the Song dynasty (960–1279), the provinces of Zhejiang, Fujian, and Guangdong had been involved in maritime trading activities with Japan and different parts of Southeast Asia. Beginning in the late sixteenth century, merchants particularly from the latter two provinces responded to the opportunities presented by indigenous rulers and newly arrived European powers, and established Chinese settlements in various mercantile outposts. After 1800 these earlier streams gave way to an outflow of population from the same coastal region on an unprecedented scale, in part because of the decline of the Qing government and the outbreak of local turmoil and in part because of the growing demand for labor and the prospect of economic gains in Southeast Asia and other parts of the world.

The areas sending Chinese migrants since 1800 can be broken down into smaller, usually spatially concentrated units that corresponded with local dialects. The southern part of Fujian, especially Quanzhou and Zhangzhou, was the home base of the Hokkiens, who left and returned via Xiamen (Amoy). Across the provincial border in eastern Guangdong lay the native region of the Teochews. There, people from Chaozhou and the surrounding districts used Shantou (Swatow) as the domestic anchor for their migration. To the south is the Cantonese area of the Pearl River Delta. Often subdivided into the Four Counties (Szeyap in Cantonese, Siyi in pinyin) of Taishan, Kaiping, Xinhui, and Enping, and the Three Counties (Samyap, Sanyi) of Panyu, Nanhai, and Shunde, these counties and others in the vicinity, such as Zhongshan and Baoan, enjoyed access overseas through Guangzhou, Hong Kong, and, to a lesser extent, Macao. The case of the Hakkas was unique in that they were drawn from scattered locations such as Yongding in southern Fujian, Meixian and Dapu in eastern Guangdong, and Boluo and Huizhou further south. In addition, there were a relatively small number of Hainanese migrants from Hainan Island and of Hokchiu and Hokchia migrants from places around the provincial capital of Fuzhou in northern Fujian.

In Chinese, emigrant districts were called *qiaoxiang* (migrants' native areas). Apart from their coastal location and a common designation, these communities shared other characteristics, including hilly terrains and a scarcity of arable lands, which encouraged emigration. Migration undertaken mainly by adult males over the course of the late nineteenth and early twentieth centuries resulted in demographic imbalances caused by the prolonged absence of men. Economically, since emigrant households were supported by overseas remittances, emigrant communities typically enjoyed a higher level of income and consumption than their neighbors, not to mention the added advantages of an infusion of business activities, investment in local transportation and industries, and contributions to education and charities. The Xinning Railroad, masterminded by the Seattle-based merchant Chen Yixi in his native Taishan, and Xiamen University, founded single-handedly by the Hokkien magnate Tan Kah Kee (Chen Jiageng) are two examples of major projects funded by overseas Chinese. Unfortunately, the resulting economic dependence spelt disaster for the inhabitants of emigrant communities when support was cut off, as happened during the Second Sino-Japanese War (1937–1945). In the early decades of the People's Republic, foreign connections were a political liability and led to state persecution of emigrants' families during times of ideological excesses, particularly the Cultural Revolution (1966–1969).

Since the 1980s, the opening of post-Mao China and the liberalization of immigration policies in many Western countries have ushered in a new era of Chinese international migration. Apart from Guangdong and Fujian, other parts of mainland China have furnished steady flows of prospective migrant workers and traders to locations hitherto unexplored. Whereas migration from Zhejiang before the Pacific War (1937–1945) had led to no more than a sprinkling of Zhejiang natives in France, the Netherlands, and Germany, scholars have documented active migratory circuits in South and Central Europe developed by people from Wenzhou, Wencheng, and Qiantian, all in Zhejiang. Another source of relatively recent migrants, particularly to the United Kingdom in the 1960s and 1970s, is the New Territories of British Hong Kong. June Fourth 1989 (the Tiananmen Square massacre) led to a spike in unintended Chinese migration to a number of Western countries when tens of thousands of overseas students failed to return home. This added many natives of Beijing, Shanghai, Guangzhou, and lesser urban centers to the populations of the United States, Australia, and other immigrant-receiving countries. The last quarter of the twentieth century produced a new generation of migrants from Hong Kong and Taiwan. Generally more affluent and having professional or entrepreneurial backgrounds, this latest group accounts for a significant number of contemporary Chinese migrants in the current age of global dispersion of Chinese.

**SEE ALSO** *Fujian; Guangdong; Zhejiang.*

**BIBLIOGRAPHY**

Chen, Ta. *Emigrant Communities in South China: A Study of Overseas Migration and Its Influence on Standards of Living and Social Change.* New York: Institute of Pacific Relations, 1940.

Lin Jinzhi and Zhuang Weiji. *Jindai Huaqiao touzi guonei qiye shi ziliao xuanji: Fujian* [Selected historical materials on the investments of modern overseas Chinese in Chinese enterprises: Fujian]. Fuzhou: Fujian Renmin Chubanshe, 1985.

***Wing Chung Ng***

## TAN KAH KEE

Chinese people have been migrating abroad since the tenth century, but they began to do so in greater numbers after the Opium War (1839–1842). There were about ten million Chinese living outside of China by 1949, and by 2008 the number had increased to more than thirty million, 80 percent of whom reside in Southeast Asia. Overseas Chinese link their country of residence with China, and their mobility contributes to change in both countries. In China-centric nationalist discourse, however, overseas Chinese (*huaqiao*) are expected to be patriotic toward China even as they reside in other countries, and they are regarded as caring about the motherland and longing to return to their hometowns. Tan Kah Kee (Chen Jiageng) (1874–1961), a China-born businessman living in Southeast Asia, became an iconic representative of this overseas Chinese ideal, and he played an important role in the formation of modern China.

Tan was born on October 21, 1874, in Jimei in Tong'an County, a coastal village adjacent to Xiamen in Fujian Province. After ten years of education in a traditional private school, Tan went to work in 1891 in his father's rice-trading company in Singapore. Later, he started his own business operating pineapple canneries and other ventures. Always ready to enter new industries, Tan was especially successful in running rubber plantations and in manufacturing rubber products. The peak of Tan Kah Kee & Company came in 1924, when the company ran 10,000 acres of rubber plantations with 10,000 employees, and earned eight million dollars annually. As an industrial pioneer, Tan earned the nickname "Henry Ford of Malaya." Due to depressed rubber prices and fierce market competition, however, Tan's business empire declined at the end of the 1920s and was liquidated in 1934, when he was nearly sixty years old.

As a successful businessman, Tan rose steadily to prominence in the Chinese community, and emerged as the leader of Singapore's Fujian community in its fund-raising for the newly founded Republic of China in 1912. In 1928 he launched the Shantung Relief Fund and became the leader of Singapore's entire Chinese community. After the Sino-Japanese War broke out in 1937, Tan became chairman of the Singapore Chinese Relief Fund. In October 1938, after having been elected chairman of South Seas China Relief Fund Union, he established himself as the most prominent leader among Chinese in Southeast Asia. His autography, *Memoirs of Tan Kah Kee* (1946), added color to his reputation. He also headed the Ee Hoe Hean Club for Singaporean millionaires, the Singapore Fujian Association, and the Singapore Chinese Chamber of Commerce.

Tan advocated social reform, tried to modernize Chinese organizations, and funded numerous schools in Singapore. He witnessed the rapid socioeconomic progress achieved by the British administration and Chinese migrants, and was eager to introduce Singapore's modernization experience to China. Tan maintained a cordial working relationship with the British colonial authority, and become a naturalized British subject in 1916. The British regarded Tan as the only person suitable to lead the Chinese community in Singapore, and approved of his role in raising relief funds for China in the 1930s. When the invasion of the Japanese was imminent, the British persuaded Tan to mobilize and lead the Chinese community to defend Singapore. Tan never criticized the British harshly, as he did the Americans after 1946. In 1949 the British authorities began to fear Tan's intimacy with China and his growing influence in Singapore and Malaya, but they did little to impede his efforts.

Tan maintained a strong devotion to Jimei, his hometown in China, and believed that education was the best way to rid the community of poverty and backwardness. In 1904 he established a primary school in Jimei. After 1912, with Tan's help, the school was enlarged to provide education at the preschool, primary, secondary, and pre-university levels. Tan also founded Xiamen University in 1921, and ran it independently for sixteen years. Even when his business came to a close, he did not stop supporting these schools. It is estimated that Tan donated a total of twenty million dollars to education efforts in Jimei and Xiamen. His initiative, selflessness, and persistence won him fame throughout China.

After China lost the Sino-Japanese War (1894–1895), Tan began to participate directly in Chinese politics by joining Sun Yat-sen's (Sun Yixian's) revolutionary organization Tung Meng Hui in 1910. He later became an ardent supporter of the Nationalist government. However, he changed his allegiance after visiting Yan'an and meeting Mao Zedong in 1940. During the civil war from 1946 to 1949, Tan led his overseas Chinese followers in standing firmly by the Chinese Communists, though he continued to proclaim himself nonpartisan. He attended Chinese People's Political Consultative Conference as the chief representative of overseas Chinese in June and September 1949, was elected a commissioner of the people's central government, and was present at the founding ceremony of the People's Republic of China in October. In late October, he accepted the post of commissioner of the Central Overseas Chinese Affairs Commission. He also traveled around China as much as possible, visiting forty cities in fourteen provinces, and publishing his influential travel notes. After traveling back to Singapore for three months, Tan returned to China in May 1950 and stayed there.

Tan was among the few officials who enjoyed some autonomy in the new government. He not only spoke on behalf of overseas Chinese at the national level, but also had a say in the affairs of Fujian Province, the administration of the Jimei schools and Xiamen University, and the construction of Fujian railways and the Xiamen Overseas Chinese Museum. Tan gave devoted support to the new policies of China, though he sometimes criticized bureaucratism. In October 1956, Tan was elected chairman of a new organization called the All-China Federation of Returned Overseas Chinese. He gave up his status as a British subject at the end of 1957. Tan passed away on August 12, 1961, and was laid to rest in a mausoleum he built for himself in Jimei.

**BIBLIOGRAPHY**

Chen Jiageng (Tan Kah Kee). *The Memoirs of Tan Kah Kee*. Eds. and trans. A. H. C. Ward, Raymond W. Chu, and Janet Salaff. Singapore: Singapore University Press, 1994.

Lu Hu. Changing Roles, Continuing Ideas: Tan Kah Kee in 1949 and 1950. *Journal of Chinese Overseas* 5, 1 (2008): pp.1–36.

Yong, C. F. *Tan Kah Kee: The Making of an Overseas Chinese Legend*. Singapore: Oxford University Press, 1987.

***Lu Hu***

## COOLIE TRADE

The term *coolie trade* tends to refer to the Chinese indentured-worker migrations to the plantations of slave and ex-slave America, especially in Cuba and Peru, and also to the smaller flows to the British, French, and Dutch West Indies, in the nineteenth century. Others apply the term *coolie migration* to the entire global movement of Chinese unskilled labor (*huagong*), whether indentured or unindentured, as distinguished from the centuries-old movement of traders (*huashang*), artisans, and skilled workers who migrated mainly to Southeast Asia (Wang 1991, pp. 4–6). While this entry will discuss the trade in its narrow sense, it is worth remembering that the central factors stimulating the growth of all sectors of the Chinese diaspora in the nineteenth century were basically the same: the explosive growth of the global economy (powered by two industrial revolutions, the British and the American) and the consequential widespread demand for labor generated in a variety of labor-scarce local economies all over the globe (most of which became food and raw-material producers for the industrial and industrializing world). Not all the migrations of indentured workers were to countries with a history of slavery—Hawaii, the Malay Peninsula, Transvaal in South Africa (at least officially), and Queensland in Australia being the most obvious examples. More than 7 million of South China's poor sought opportunities overseas in response to a variety of local push factors—among them famine, civil war, and regional ethnic strife—as well as in response to systematic recruiting in the South China region carried on by a multitude of private and government-sponsored agencies, both Chinese and Western. Some country-recruitment practices and some destinations ultimately proved more calamitous than beneficial for those who went there, and this is what eventually distinguished the coolie trade from the coolie migration. The Latin American indentured migrations (Cuba and Peru) were the most calamitous and gave a negative connotation to the term *coolie trade*.

After the First Opium War (1839–1842), Chinese coastal labor became accessible to the Western powers, and by the late 1840s emigration ventures were being organized at Xiamen (Amoy) and off Guangzhou (Canton) by individual shipping firms acting on behalf of various nationalities. Between 1847 and 1852, just under 6,000 migrants were recruited at Xiamen alone for destinations beyond Southeast Asia: Australia, Cuba, Peru, Hawaii, California, French Bourbon (Réunion), British Guiana. The early, mainly British recruiting firms, based onshore and offshore, utilized the services of freelance Chinese recruiters (crimps), whose methods of recruitment ranged from normal persuasion to all forms of deception, intimidation, and force, including kidnapping.

In November 1852 an incensed Xiamen populace rioted against the practices of the British firms and their Chinese recruiters. A confrontation with British soldiers led to several deaths and injuries. After this incident, the importers for Latin America shifted to other ports. By the late 1850s Macau had become the primary base from which most of the Cuba- and Peru-bound Chinese embarked. The British West Indies recruiting efforts, now state-controlled and supervised, were centered in Hong Kong and Guangzhou, with small depots in Xiamen and Shantou (Swatow) in the 1860s.

Between 1847 and 1874, 347 vessels delivered 125,000 Chinese to Cuba, and 276 vessels took about 100,000 to Peru. Between 1853 and 1884, 51 vessels transported about 18,000 Chinese to the British West Indies, mainly to British Guiana (13,539). Suriname (Dutch Guiana) also received about 2,630 Chinese between 1853 and 1874, and 3 vessels delivered 1,000 Chinese to the French West Indies in the 1860s. Smaller numbers went to a variety of other destinations: Brazil, Chile, Panama, and Costa Rica in Latin America, and Trinidad and Jamaica in the British West Indies.

Two things were shared by Chinese immigrants to Latin America and the Caribbean between 1847 and 1874. First, about 96 percent of them came from southern Guangdong province, from the districts surrounding Macau, Guangzhou, and Hong Kong. Only about 4 percent came from northeast Guangdong (via Shantou) or from Fujian (via Xiamen). During this century, most of the Fujianese who emigrated continued to prefer destinations in Southeast Asia. Second, these immigrants came under the indenture or contract system, rather than immigrating as

***Chinese workers panning for gold, California, c. 1855.*** *In the mid-nineteenth century, many impoverished Chinese workers traveled abroad for better economic opportunities. Not all of these migrations proved beneficial for the worker, as in many instances those who became indentured servants received treatment little better than slaves, particularly in Cuba and Peru.* HULTON ARCHIVE/GETTY IMAGES

free migrants under the credit ticket arrangement more common in the United States and Canada. The arrangements for their recruitment, transportation, and distribution in Latin America and the Caribbean were handled by Western, rather than Chinese, intermediaries—a fact that made these migrations substantially different from similar coolie migrations to Southeast Asia and North America. The British system of indenture was handled by state-supervised agencies and vessels, but the Cuba- and Peru-bound shipments were handled by private shippers and planters, many with a history of involvement in the African slave trade.

Because of the deception and coercion surrounding much of the traffic bound for Latin America, there was a high degree of rebelliousness on many vessels. For the 700 voyages to Latin America between 1847 and 1874, at least 68 mutinies were recorded, mostly on ships bound for Cuba and Peru. Many resulted in great loss of life after ships were set on fire or run aground. Catastrophic ship fires following failed mutinies led to loss of all passengers on the *Flora Temple* to Cuba in 1859 (850 lives), the *Napoleon Canevaro* to Peru in 1866 (662), and the *Dolores Ugarte* to Peru in 1871 (600). The average mortality rate on Cuba- and Peru-bound vessels was around 12 percent, at least double that on vessels bound for the British West Indies, which had a 5 to 6 percent mortality rate. In the early 1860s, the Peru-bound mortality rate reached 25 to 35 percent. In response to domestic pressure, the U.S. Congress banned American ships from participating in the coolie trade in 1862.

Under the contract-labor system, Chinese laborers were legally and physically bound to their workplace environment on pain of imprisonment for a specified number of years (five years in British jurisdictions, eight years in Spanish jurisdictions). This differed from the loose debt-bondage arrangement of the credit ticket system, which depended for its enforcement on family, clan, or village connections within the Chinese community itself. Technically, the physical bondage was different from slavery, and laborers' freedoms were safeguarded by law, but often, in places like Cuba and Peru, the discipline and physical treatment were so brutal, and the legal protection so lacking in fact, that it was often difficult to distinguish between indenture and slavery.

## CUBA

In Cuba, the Chinese were employed mainly on the sugar plantations, especially in the province of Matanzas. About 10 percent were employed on tobacco and coffee estates. Cuba, which did not abolish slavery until 1886, used a mixed system of labor, with slaves at one end of the scale, free laborers at the other, and contract or indentured labor in between. Contract labor was the cheapest of the three, paying about 4 or 5 pesos a month, while the wages of free labor might be as high as 10 to 15 pesos. In the field and the factory, the Chinese assisted the slaves. Though officially classified as whites, their labor conditions tended to be identical to those of the black slaves. Some estates had all Asian workers, though most were racially mixed. By the 1870s most plantations had an indentured- and free-labor force of up to 40 percent to supplement their slave-labor force. The Chinese comprised about 2 to 3 percent of the Cuban population.

The legal and physical abuse of the Chinese in Cuba equaled some of the worst features of slavery. The Chinese government, prompted by reports of abuse of Chinese laborers in Cuba, sent an imperial mission to the island in 1873 to investigate the social conditions under which they lived and worked. The resultant Cuba Commission Report was compiled from interviews with more than 1,000 Chinese, as well as from about 85 petitions supported by over 1,600 signatures. The report confirmed the slave-like treatment of the Chinese. The Cuba Commission Report also pointed out that 80 percent of the 68,000 Chinese in Cuba in 1873–1874 had been decoyed or kidnapped from China, and that only about 20 percent of them had received letters of domicile to reside on the island as free men. The mortality rate was around 45 percent over a period of 27 years. Only about 140 ever returned to China, less than 1 percent. Family life was almost nonexistent. The commission found 2 Chinese men married to Chinese women, 2 married to white women, and about 6 married to mulattoes or blacks.

The Macau-based coolie trade was formally banned in 1874, after much pressure from the Chinese, United States, and British governments, and finally from public opinion within Macau itself. By the time Cuba gained its independence from Spain in 1898, the Chinese population (many of whom had fought with the rebels in both Independence Wars) had dwindled to 14,863. A census taken in 1899 enumerated 8,033 day laborers, 2,754 servants, 1,923 merchants, 471 peddlers, 301 used-goods dealers, 287 charcoal vendors, 196 laundrymen, 127 brick masons, 104 carpenters, and 61 barbers, among others.

## PERU

In Peru, the slave trade ended in 1810, and slavery itself in 1854. The silver mines declined after independence in 1824, and in the 1840s and 1850s there emerged new industries based on sugar, guano (seabird excrement used as fertilizer), and later cotton. In 1849 the Peruvian government authorized its planters to import Chinese indentured labor, virtually on the same terms and conditions as those of the traffic to Cuba: eight-year contracts at 4 pesos per month, plus food and clothing; private entrepreneurial control over the recruiting, sale, and distribution of Chinese labor from China to Peru; and private planter jurisdiction over Chinese coolies with little effective state supervision.

Chinese entry into Peru fell into two periods: 1849 to 1856 (when a temporary ban was imposed after revelations of atrocities against the laborers, especially on the offshore guano islands, the Chinchas) and 1861 to 1874 (when the coolie traffic was banned in Macau). About 75 percent of 100,000 Chinese were assigned to the coastal sugar and cotton plantations, and about 12,000 were employed in the guano industry, which was Peru's main export industry in the 1850s and 1860s. Another 10,000 worked on railway construction into the Andes in the 1870s. A large number were also used as domestic servants, cooks, bakers, mill hands, and handymen in commercial establishments.

The horrendous exploitation and high mortality rates in Cuba were duplicated in Peru, especially in the highly profitable guano industry, with its demeaning environment. In the 1840s convict labor, army deserters, and black slaves worked the guano fields. In 1853 the labor force was still mixed: Chinese, black slaves, Peruvians, and Chileans. But Chinese soon became the main element of this labor force, under conditions vividly described by people who protested their exploitation. The average working life of a guano worker was said to be about three years, and suicide was rampant. Although the situation eased somewhat in the late 1860s, the horrors of life on the guano islands were legendary, and remained so up to the decline of the industry in the 1870s.

Until 1854 Peru's coastal-plantation agriculture relied almost entirely on African slave labor. Even more than in Cuba, the Chinese became the dominant labor force on the coastal sugar plantations between the mid-1850s and mid-1870s, and continued to be up to the early 1890s. A shift in the pattern of labor supply and organization began with the end of the coolie trade in 1874, and hastened with the Second War of the Pacific (1879–1883) between Peru and Chile, when many Chinese sided with the Chilean invading army. Peruvian labor from the inland mountainous region was increasingly utilized in the 1880s, and by the 1890s Peruvians had surpassed the Chinese as the dominant group. From 1899 to 1923 about 18,000 Japanese contract workers joined the Peruvian workforce on the sugar plantations.

Even then the Chinese continued to remain in agriculture for most of the 1880s, with the formal indenture system giving way to new forms of labor coercion and recruitment. These included debt bondage, as well as group labor contracts mediated by Chinese labor contractors from the merchant class. As late as 1887, thirteen years after the end of the coolie trade and indenture, an official investigation revealed that most of the 8,503 Chinese in the coastal provinces were still engaged in agriculture.

In the 1870s and 1880s, many Chinese became traders in the region surrounding Lima and other cities. Another 10,000 worked on the construction of railways into the Andes. A few hundred ventured into the Amazon region, where they worked as peddlers, shopkeepers, food growers, and suppliers. They also tapped rubber and panned for gold in the interior and populated most of the small frontier towns.

## BRITISH WEST INDIES

The Chinese in the British West Indies were subject to a distinctively British indenture system. After experiments with a Latin American–type arrangement of private-enterprise recruitment and transportation, mainly in the 1850s, the British in the 1860s opted for a state-controlled system with their own recruiting agencies in Hong Kong and Guangzhou, and smaller temporary locations in Xiamen and Shantou. A paid government emigration agent, acting in collaboration with the Guangdong provincial authorities, oversaw the entire recruitment operation. Attempts were made to avoid recruiting migrants through paid Chinese freelance recruiters or crimps. Greater reliance was placed on individual voluntary appearances at the emigration depots, along with publicity, assistance, and encouragement from European missionaries based in South China. Of the Chinese who went to the British West Indies, about 80 percent (14,120) arrived during the 1859–1866 period.

The Chinese were employed on the sugar plantations along with other immigrants who came in the 1860s: Madeiran Portuguese, Indians, and black immigrants from the smaller West Indian islands and West Africa. Unlike in Cuba and Peru, the Chinese contribution to the revival of the sugar industry was marginal, although they were widely dispersed on 116 out of 153 estates in British Guiana, and 70–76 out of 153–158 estates in Trinidad. Though there were many complaints of injustices at the hands of both planters and officials, especially in British Guiana before a commission of inquiry in 1870–1871, treatment was in general less harsh than it was in the Spanish jurisdictions. The law sanctioned neither the autocratic authority of the plantation owner nor the use of whips and irons, and the court system was allowed to function free from corruption. Moreover, the Immigration Department, through the Protector of Immigrants or Immigration Agent-General, as he was also known, was allowed to play a more interventionist and supervisory role.

By the late 1880s most Chinese, following the termination of their indentures, were off the plantations and had taken up small-scale retail trading activity. Huge numbers left British Guiana for Trinidad, Dutch and French Guiana, and Colón in Panama, where opportunities for self-advancement were greater. A few hundred actually returned to China at their own expense. By the turn of the nineteenth century, the Chinese had become identified as part of a multicultural trading community that included Portuguese, Indians, and many blacks and coloreds.

The indenture system to the British West Indies was officially terminated in 1917, but long before that, between 1866 and 1884, Chinese emigration effectively ended because of diplomatic disagreements on immigration-treaty clauses over the right of return passage and consequent greater costs in comparison with those of Indian immigration. Also, the Dutch experiment in Suriname (Dutch Guiana) ended in the 1870s because of British restrictions on emigration from Hong Kong to non-British destinations. In British Southeast Asia, where free Chinese migrants always outnumbered contract laborers by seven to one, contract indenture ended in the 1910s, but free male immigration was not restricted until 1929 and 1933 (these restrictions did not apply to females or children).

## LEGACY

The turn of the nineteenth century saw an increase in direct Chinese immigration to all the territories to which indentured labor had previously gone, as well as to other parts of Latin America that had never experienced indentured traffic (mainly Mexico). Most of this immigration took place during the exclusion period (1880s–1940s), when Chinese immigration was banned in the United States and Canada, but it has increased with the changes in China's emigration policies since the 1980s.Throughout that long period, they have evolved more normally as ethnic trading minorities in their respective host societies. Even so, they have been the occasional targets of discriminatory laws and host society resentment in some countries, and many have emigrated to North America, where they are a distinct element within the larger Asian-American community.

**SEE ALSO** *Chinese Overseas: Chinatowns; Guangdong; Xiamen (Amoy).*

**BIBLIOGRAPHY**

Campbell, Persia. Chinese Coolie Emigration to Countries within the British Empire. London: P. S. King and Son, 1923.

Chen, Ta. *Chinese Migrations, with Special Reference to Labor Conditions.* Washington, DC: Government Printing Office, 1923.

Helly, Denise. *Idéologie et ethnicité: Les Chinois Macao à Cuba, 1847–1886.* Montreal: Presses de l'Université de Montréal, 1979.

Helly, Denise, ed. *The Cuba Commission Report: A Hidden History of the Chinese in Cuba; the Original English Language Text of 1876.* Baltimore, MD: Johns Hopkins University Press, 1993.

Look Lai, Walton. *Indentured Labor, Caribbean Sugar: Chinese and Indian Migrants to the British West Indies, 1838–1918.* Baltimore, MD: Johns Hopkins University Press, 1993.

Look Lai, Walton. *The Chinese in the West Indies, 1806–1995: A Documentary History.* Kingston, Jamaica: University of the West Indies Press, 1998.

Northrup, David. *Indentured Labor in the Age of Imperialism, 1834–1922.* New York: Cambridge University Press, 1995.

Perez de la Riva, Juan. Aspectos económicos del tráfico de culíes chinos a Cuba, 1853–1874. *Universidad de la Habana* 173 (May–June 1965): 95–115.

Perez de la Riva, Juan. Demografía de los culíes Chinos en Cuba, 1853–1874. *Revista de la Biblioteca Nacional José Martí* 57, 4 (1966): 3–31.

Rodríguez Pastor, Humberto. *Hijos del Celeste Imperio en el Peru? (1850–1900): Migración, agricultura, mentalidad y explotación.* Lima: Instituto de Apoyo Agrario, 1989.

Stewart, Watt. *Chinese Bondage in Peru: A History of the Chinese Coolie in Peru, 1849–1874.* Durham, NC: Duke University Press, 1951.

Wang Gungwu. *China and the Chinese Overseas.* Singapore: Times Academic Press, 1991.

Yen Ching-Hwang. *Coolies and Mandarins: China's Protection of Overseas Chinese during the Late Ch'ing Period (1851–1911).* Singapore: Singapore University Press, 1985.

***Walton Look Lai***

## CHINATOWNS

Chinatowns have been characterized as "towns within cities" (Lai 1973), and they only exist outside of China. They are formed when a sizeable community of overseas Chinese settles down amid a non-Chinese urban environment. Geographically, Chinatowns are often located conveniently close to the inner business districts of the major cities. But the area is usually not up-market, so the buildings are smaller, the roads narrower, and the rents cheaper. Inexpensive land prices and close proximity to the inner city make it possible for small retail and marginal servicing activities to flourish. The Chinese typically engage in labor-intensive, low-capital services like laundry, cooking, fruit shops, and takeouts, catering to the needs of the larger population.

The Chinese call Chinatowns "Tangren jie," literally, Chinese people's street. In the white-immigrant countries of the United States, Canada, Australia, and New Zealand, early Chinatowns were often called "Chinamen's quarters," a derogatory label for the districts or city blocks where Chinese people lived and conducted their social and economic activities. Sometimes Chinatowns are called "huabu," literally, Chinese wharf, because the district was located near the waterfront, as in the case of Limehouse in London.

The clustering of Chinese in Chinatowns was partly voluntary and partly dictated by necessity. When Chinese seeking gold migrated voluntarily to North America in the 1850s, they made San Francisco the largest and oldest Chinatown outside of Asia (Mišc?ević and Kwong 2000). Overt racism and prejudice meant that Chinatowns were safe havens into which Chinese could retreat to a familiar environment and where they could be self-reliant with only minimal contact with the other residents of the city. Early Chinatowns were formed in cities like Manila, Batavia, and Singapore in the mid-nineteenth century, when the segregation of races was considered a useful policy by the respective colonial governments. An ethnic enclave was designated for Chinese people to live in for easier control (Pan 1990). Under Spanish colonial rule, Chinese traders in Manila were confined to the Parian and were not allowed to mix with local Filipinos. The Dutch similarly put the Chinese merchants into ghettos in Batavia, separating them from the native Indonesians.

### EUROPEAN VIEW OF CHINATOWNS

In an anti-Chinese era, Chinatowns were the most visible symbol of the Yellow Peril. Early Chinese settlers were relegated to ghettos, which kept them apart, both socially and spatially, and which accentuated and reinforced their outsider status. "Chinatown, like race, is an idea that belongs to the white European cultural tradition" (Anderson 1987). From the European vantage point, Chinatowns signified all those features that seemed to set the Chinese irrevocably apart: their alien appearance, lack of Christian faith, addictions to opium and gambling, strange eating habits, and odd religious practices. Chinese men wore queues and loose clothing, suggesting a lack of virility and making them the target of white homophobia. In general, the Chinese were accused of keeping themselves apart and resisting assimilation by retreating to the Chinatown ethnic enclave.

Within Chinatowns there are shops, grocery stores, restaurants, and bookshops catering especially to Chinese clients. In older Chinatowns there were gambling houses, opium dens, clan associations, and sometimes triad society headquarters as well as joss (deity) houses. In Western anti-Chinese lore, Chinatowns were vice towns, where decent white people would enter at their own peril. A newspaper headline of the *New Zealand Times* in 1896 is rather typical of the feelings of the time: "Wellington's Chinatown: Plague Spots of Asiatic Vice in Our Midst." Lurid and sensational stories circulated about white slave traders luring young white women into Chinese laundries or fruit shops, plying them with opium, and then forcing them into prostitution. A New Zealand author recalled his boyhood impression of the local Chinatown: "We were told that even if we went near that drab, narrow, little street with its congestion of tumbledown houses, we might be kidnapped, boiled in a copper and made into preserved ginger" (Shum 2003). In the late 1960s, many Chinatowns became depopulated because of social change, and governments took the opportunity to demolish the buildings in the name of desegregation and acculturation.

## FAMILY AND SOCIAL ACTIVITIES WITHIN CHINATOWNS

Though tales of opium dens, gambling houses, and brothels were frequently circulated about Chinatowns, many more mundane everyday activities took place there. Up to the mid-twentieth century, Chinatowns were residential areas as well as centers of business and social activities. Chinatowns were the place where many overseas Chinese families lived and where their children grew up. Often the families lived at the back of shops or upstairs in attics. The practice not only saved on rent, but also enabled all family members to pitch in and to work long hours for the family business. Chinese schools, often run by Chinese churches, taught classes so that children could learn some rudimentary Chinese. Chinese-language newspapers also established themselves within the confines of Chinatowns.

A hallmark of the Chinatown community was the spirit of self-reliance and mutual help. Chinese grocery stores often supplied home-made delicacies like dried vegetables, salted fish, preserved ginger, and steamed buns, besides the imported dried foods and Chinese herbs. Clan associations ran hostels and boarding houses for new arrivals and departing clansmen waiting for boats departing for China. They also maintained accounts to which members of various clan associations contributed for mutual help and charity purposes, such as repatriating elderly men and the bones of deceased Chinese to China.

Chinatown shops were often community centers and also took on advisory roles. Long-established shops, often owned by community leaders, doubled as banks, and offered loans as well as remittance services. They collected mail from China for kinsmen, offered letter-writing services, and loaned out homeland newspapers and magazines. Services like document processing, loans, remittances, and couriers for letters and money were specially appreciated during World War II, when coastal China (where many of the home villages of overseas Chinese were located) was under Japanese occupation or in the shadow of its empire. Transmissions were largely very reliable, often delivered right into the villages, sometimes directly, sometimes via Hong Kong.

## CHINATOWN POLITICAL ACTIVITIES

Chinatowns were also the center of Chinese political activities. Also located in Chinatowns were the headquarters of powerful tongs (secret societies), including the Chee Kong Tong (Zhigong Tang), and of political parties, such as the Guomindang (Nationalist Party). Regional clan associations and secret societies were usually presided over by a national organization, like the Chinese Consolidated Benevolent Association in the United States or the Australian Chinese Association or the New Zealand Chinese Association. Until the 1970s such associations in these new immigrant nations were invariably staunchly pro-Guomindang, with close ties to the ambassadors sent by the Nationalist government in Nanjing and, after 1949, Taibei.

During the Anti-Japanese War (1937–1945), such associations were responsible for highly successful patriotic fund-raising activities that reached well beyond Chinatowns. While political rallies were held in the Chinatowns, dedicated teams of donation collectors were dispatched to smaller and more distant regional centers. Large sums of money were sent to China in aid of the war of resistance or for medical aid.

In Europe, nations differed in their tolerance toward Chinatown political activities. Attitudes were decided by the diplomatic alignment of their national governments with China. For example, Britain did not want their Chinatown activities to be pro-Guomindang, because the government recognized the People's Republic in 1950. France similarly switched recognition to the People's Republic in 1964. In Spain under Francisco Franco, the small Guomindang-oriented community was not allowed to have an organization at all.

## CHINATOWNS REDEVELOPED AND GENTRIFIED

In the early decades of the twentieth century, Chinatowns suffered from bad reputations of dangerous overcrowding and substandard buildings. In the name of maintaining public health and public morality (the buildings were allegedly brothels, gambling houses, and opium dens), Chinatowns were subjected to periodic police raids. From time to time, city councils also intervened to "demolish shanty towns." As the modern metropolis took shape, many old houses in various Chinatowns were pulled down in the interests of slum clearance and traffic management.

Beginning in the 1970s and 1980s, a new class of Chinese middle-class professionals migrated and settled down in suburbs instead of living in Chinatowns. At the same time, illegal migrants continued to move into the cheap housing of old Chinatowns, such as in New York

***Residents of New York City's Chinatown celebrating the Lunar New Year, February 12, 2002.*** *Many urban areas where large numbers of Chinese settled have districts referred to as Chinatowns. While some immigrants, such as those in New York's Chinatown, moved to the area voluntarily, other cities, such as Manila, Jakarta, and Singapore, legally segregated the Chinese into these separate neighborhoods.* SPENCER PLATT/GETTY IMAGES

and Paris, and took up menial work like dishwashing, sewing, cleaning. The commercial sectors of old Chinatowns continued to function as retail centers, but slowly lost their importance as social-exchange and mutual-support centers to the new Chinese community. The shopping areas of such Chinatowns often underwent revitalization and gentrification owing to the rising spending power of their new immigrant clientele.

Since the 1980s, city councils sometimes set up special Chinatown redevelopment committees to cobblestone roads and install new Chinese-style street lights. Often the initiatives were propelled by business opportunities, and sometimes they were seen as friendly gestures toward the Chinese government (Fitzgerald 1996). The Chinese Chamber of Commerce was often involved, and donations were accepted from local businesses.

## NEW CHINATOWN ETHNOBURBS

At the beginning of the twenty-first century, a Chinatown might be a new Chinese-themed shopping mall or an area with stylish Asian supermarkets and expensive seafood restaurants, mixed with clinics offering acupuncture and traditional Chinese medicine. Yet one familiar physical feature is the memorial archway with stone lions guarding the entrance. Within the precinct shops sell Chinese compact discs of "Cantopop" (Cantonese popular music), bilingual almanacs, and phone cards to Asia. More often than not, such Chinatowns also offer chic Japanese sushi bars, Korean noodle houses, and also Thai and Vietnamese restaurants. Here the streetscape is visibly different. Architecture often takes on an oriental flavor, and signs are bilingual. Shops, restaurants, and banks use Chinese on their signboards. Public institutions like post offices, police stations, and street signs are also often bilingual. Such Chinatowns, proud showcases of multiculturalism, can be found in cities like Vancouver, Brisbane, Sydney, and Auckland—the Pacific Rim cities that are the favored destinations of the new Chinese migrants. These Chinatowns are rarely residential areas of the Chinese, but are often more like multiethnic suburbs (ethnoburbs).

The new Chinatowns have been criticized as commercial ventures where "Chineseness" is being marketed to suit foreign tastes. Advocates for the Chinatowns usually argue, however, that they are symbols of the larger community's acknowledgement of the contribution of Chinese pioneers. Many original Chinatowns have been designated as historic places and have attracted the attention of tourist bureaus. Chinatown guided walks are now frequently on offer to visitors in many cities, and placards explaining the history of these old Chinatowns are also common sights. In an acknowledgement of the history and contribution of the overseas Chinese in different urban centers, joint government and community efforts have led to the establishment of Chinatown museums. The rise of new migration trends since the 1980s has definitely revitalized the old Chinatowns.

### IMAGE

Chinatowns have been the background of countless Western movies and novels, offering a backdrop at once mysterious, evocative, and seedy. These Chinese districts have remained an integral part of how non-Chinese think about overseas Chinese. In the early twenty-first century they still serve as nostalgic reminders of a romanticized Orient. Yet when politicians hold rallies or stage walkabouts in Chinatowns to campaign for ethnic-minority votes, they remind everyone of how much Chinatowns have changed through the centuries. In an age of extensive urban redevelopment and planning, Chinatowns have become an integral feature of cities.

#### BIBLIOGRAPHY


Anderson, Kay J. The Idea of Chinatown: The Power of Place and Institutional Practice in the Making of a Racial Category. *Annals of the Association of American Geographers* 77, 4 (1987): 580–598.

Fitzgerald, Shirley. *Red Tape, Gold Scissors: The Story of Sydney's Chinese.* Sydney: State Library of New South Wales Press, 1996.

Lai, David. Socio-economic Structures and the Viability of Chinatown. In *Residential and Neighbourhood Studies in Victoria*, ed. Charles Forward, pp. 101–129. Victoria, Canada: University of Victoria, 1973.

Lai, David. *Chinatowns: Towns within Cities in Canada.* Vancouver: University of British Columbia Press, 1988.

Mišc?ević, Dušanka, and Peter Kwong. *Chinese Americans: The Immigrant Experience.* Southport, CT: Hugh Lauter Levin Associates, 2000.

Pan, Lynn. *Sons of the Yellow Emperor: The Story of the Overseas Chinese.* London: Secker and Warburg, 1990.

Shum, Lynette. Remembering Chinatown: Haining Street of Wellington. In *Unfolding History, Evolving Identity: The Chinese in New Zealand*, ed. Manying Ip, pp. 73–93. Auckland, New Zealand: Auckland University Press, 2003.

Yung, Judy, Gordon H. Chang, and Him Mark Lai. *Chinese American Voices: From the Gold Rush to the Present.* Berkeley: University of California Press, 2006.


***Manying Ip***

## DIASPORA AND HOMELAND

The relationship between the Chinese diaspora and the "homeland," China itself, has changed over time in accordance with the changing nature of state and society in China, and the international economic and political climate. In general, between the nineteenth and twentieth centuries this originally informal, even secretive, relationship, due to the interdict on emigration, began to assume overt political and economic, as well as affective, dimensions.

The diaspora was for the first time politicized in the late Qing, when Liang Qichao and Sun Yat-sen (Sun Zhongshan) began rallying support among ethnic Chinese overseas for their different reform and revolutionary agendas. Sun made use of the British crown colony Hong Kong as a base for his revolutionary attempts in the 1890s and early twentieth century. In these years, Chinese residents of Southeast Asia, Australasia, Japan, and North America were called on by these progressive political leaders to make their voices heard in support of political, economic, and social change in China. Sun was the more influential of the two leaders. While rekindling and using old anti-Qing sentiment still harbored by diasporic Ming loyalists, his main efforts represented political ferment toward modernity, nationhood, and technological progress in the style of Europe and North America, forging a political movement of foreign-trained Chinese, treaty-port opinion makers, and dissidents in China. At the same time, Qing officials sought to promote an imperial version of Chinese nationhood among Chinese overseas, and the 1909 Nationality Law, based on *jus sanguinis,* abandoned the authorities' ban on emigration and declared, for the first time, that ethnic Chinese in exile were part of the Chinese state.

In the face of the various forms of socioeconomic exclusion experienced by ethnic Chinese in colonial and semicolonial settings, nationalist sentiments slowly began to challenge old forms of assimilation and local-place loyalties. The early Republic, founded in 1912, established political representation for overseas Chinese. The Tongmenghui and later the Nationalist Party forged strong and long-lasting bonds of political loyalty with Chinese overseas, tying them closely to the motherland.

In the Southeast Asian diaspora, ethnic Chinese held intermediate positions between European colonial masters and native populations, and were treated differentially in administration, courts of law, and economic policy. Chinese of the same geographical origin often joined together in merchant guilds (*huiguan*) to represent shared interests vis-à-vis colonial authorities, and assumed specific roles in the division of labor (also reflecting colonial preference for divide-and-rule tactics toward the potentially powerful Chinese group), thus typically dividing the diaspora into dialect groups of Cantonese (Siyi, Sanyi/Yuehai) and Teochiu speakers from Guangdong, and Hokkien speakers from Fujian, as well as

***Sandwich board man in New York's Chinatown carries a sign announcing latest war news, December 31, 1938.*** *In many large American urban centers, concentrations of Chinese immigrants preserved their language, heritage, and culture in close-knit neighborhoods, with many earning the generic name of Chinatown.* HULTON ARCHIVE/GETTY IMAGES

Hainanese and Hakka speakers. Chinese nationalism subsumed, rather than replaced, these formations, so that local-place loyalties remained strong.

From the early 1900s onward, successful overseas entrepreneurs and merchants who returned to their local homeland in China were afforded social prestige, and they played an important role in the development of the local society and economy through investments in infrastructure, education, and industry. The nationalist rallying among Chinese globally in the 1930s during the campaign to support China against Japanese aggression provided enormous momentum, and included Nationalists and Communists.

## DIVIDED LOYALTIES

After 1949, the separation between the People's Republic of China (PRC) established in Beijing and the Republic of China (ROC) in Taibei caused a crisis of loyalty among ethnic

Chinese across the world. Political allegiance with the Nationalists prevailed in many Chinese communities, as people held on to their ROC passports. The Cold War, further creating obstacles for contacts with the Chinese mainland, and the resolve of the Nationalist leadership to assert its legitimacy by acting as a custodian of China's cultural tradition against the iconoclasm and censorship of the PRC prolonged the projection of national sentiment onto the Nationalist Party in Taibei. A vigorous overseas Chinese policy also guaranteed continued voting rights for overseas Chinese. The encouragement issued by the PRC at the time of the Bandung Conference in 1955 to overseas Chinese to assume the passport of their state of residence alienated many ethnic Chinese from the mainland. Even so, the PRC involved a number of famous overseas Chinese as specially invited members of the local and national Political Consultative Conferences (*Zhengxie*), and also provided for "returned overseas Chinese" (*guiguo Huaqiao*) fleeing back to China from conflicts elsewhere.

Ethnic Chinese migrants to Europe in the 1960s and 1970s originated mainly in former colonies in Southeast Asia, in Hong Kong, or as refugees from the Cultural Revolution in the mainland. Local-place allegiances became a strong feature of their organization in Europe, as they regrouped. In France, for example, Teochiu, Cantonese, Hokkien, Hakka, and Hainan associations joined together migrants from the various Indo-Chinese Chinatowns, while in Britain, migrants from Hong Kong's New Territories organized themselves according to their origin in dominant lineages and tiny villages. This reflected the lack of a strong *national* focal point in China, and masked Communist and Nationalist political partisanship and activism among ethnic Chinese; as increasing numbers of European states in the 1960s and 1970s established full diplomatic links with the PRC, the overseas Chinese allegiance only reluctantly changed toward the PRC. In some cases, homeland links were maintained through Hong Kong as a proxy for the mainland home, where, for example, Taishan overseas Chinese from the United States would return to find co-native spouses, or where Hakkas maintained close links through the Tsung Tsin Association.

## REBUILDING DIASPORA-HOMELAND LINKS

The resumption in 1977 of the PRC's overseas Chinese work represented a total shift in the attitude to and the mode of dealing with ethnic Chinese. Generally speaking, overseas Chinese property that had been confiscated during political movements was restored, and many "political verdicts" were rescinded. Special travel agencies, hotels, and other services were expanded to facilitate the visit of overseas Chinese to China, and the status and rights of the relatives of overseas Chinese were improved, including, for example, the right to save remittances in foreign currency accounts. Authorities in areas from where many overseas Chinese hailed were able to attract overseas Chinese with reference to lineages and family links. The revival of ancestral temples and rituals of ancestor worship; the resurrection of ancestral graves and old landmarks; invitations to contribute to education, health services, and infrastructure; the establishment of local museums telling the narrative of emigration; and highly efficient official assistance in civil affairs and police matters like marriage, inheritance, passports, household registration, funerals, immigration, and emigration contributed to a rapid development of contacts with overseas Chinese communities.

Hesitance among overseas Chinese, many of whom were still keeping their loyalty to the Nationalists, and in particular to Sun Zhongshan and Chiang Kai-shek (Jiang Jieshi), began to evaporate, as traveling to the mainland ceased to be a statement of politics and became an issue of family reunion and traditional lineage obligation. By thus swaying the core of Chinese migrants from before World War II (1937–1945), at this time in their old age, the overseas Chinese policy of the reform era set in motion a shift of loyalty of great importance for cross-strait relations. Travel, remittances, and donations became important aspects of many places that had experienced emigration in the past, and during the 1980s the overseas Chinese homelands (*qiaoxiang*) began to assert themselves in terms of inward investments and prestige.

The visits by overseas notabilities of local origin, like former governor of Washington state and later U.S. Secretary of Commerce nominee Gary Locke to Taishan, provided positive media exposure. The award of honorary titles and posts to overseas Chinese leaders provided them with social capital. The homeland was often defined opportunistically, as major donations from ethnic Chinese abroad frequently arose from fund-raising activities—the jurisdiction could be a village, a township or town, a county or city, or even a province or the whole nation, depending on whether the overseas Chinese association incorporated members with bonds in a smaller or larger jurisdiction. General Chinese associations would typically donate to national charities like Project Hope whereas regional associations like the Siyi (See Yap), also known as Wuyi (Ng Yap), would typically donate to relevant charitable causes in Jiangmen City in Guangdong. As an overriding principle, though, charitable donations would go to victims of major national disasters (such as floods, blizzards, earthquakes, and so on), symbolically confirming the national spirit of people hailing from particular homelands in China.

There is no doubt that the license given to overseas Chinese homelands in the Chinese mainland to engage in

***Students from the University of Bologna's College of China, Bologna, Italy, November 16, 2005.*** *With the easing of restrictions on international travel during the 1970s, many of China's young students sought educational opportunities abroad, earning undergraduate and graduate degrees at universities in the West.* © SILVIA MORARA/CORBIS

cultural, economic, and political experimentation for the purpose of rallying overseas Chinese support has greatly facilitated the revival of lineage culture, traditional rituals and values, and religious activities, and has also led to rich initiatives in the creation of local cultural institutions otherwise discouraged or suppressed by dominant political ideology. This license has been a major lever for local people to assert more cultural and religious autonomy, at the same time that many often rural and relatively marginal homelands have become part of global networks that provide access and cultural interaction beyond their limiting status in the official hierarchy of jurisdictions in China.

**SEE ALSO** *Sincere Department Stores; Sun Yat-sen (Sun Yixian); Tourism; Wang Jingwei; Wing On Department Stores.*

**BIBLIOGRAPHY**

Douw, Leo, Huang Cen, and Michael R. Godley, eds. *Qiaoxiang Ties: Interdisciplinary Approaches to "Cultural Capitalism" in South China.* London: Kegan Paul International in association with International Institute for Asian Studies, 1999.

Duara, Prasenjit. Nationalists among Transnationals: Overseas Chinese and the Idea of China, 1900–1911. In *Ungrounded Empires: The Cultural Politics of Modern Chinese Transnationalism,* eds. Aihwa Ong and Donald Nonini, 39–60. New York: Routledge, 1997.

***Flemming Christiansen***

## EMIGRATION AND GLOBALIZATION

A total of thirty-five million Chinese traveled abroad for private reasons in 2007, compared to ten million in 2000 (National Bureau of Statistics 2008, p. 2000), up from an average of seven thousand a year between 1949 and 1979 (Ren Yingchao 2001). Long-term emigrants—that is, those who live abroad for more than a year—constitute a minor group (the majority are business visitors and tourists), but their number has increased significantly as well. China has been the top source country of permanent immigrants to Canada since 1998, with thirty thousand to forty thousand arrivals a year (Citizenship and Immigration Canada 2007). More than ten thousand Chinese migrated to Australia permanently from 2005 to 2006 (Australia Department of Immigration and Citizenship 2007). There were 520,000 Chinese (including migrants from Hong Kong and Taiwan) in Japan in 2005 (Statistics Bureau 2008, p. 57) and nearly 500,000 PRC-born permanent residents in the United States in 2006 (Rytina 2008, p. 4). At the same time that emigration from China has considerably liberalized and diversified, the Chinese government has developed new modes of regulation. Emigration represents a case of "Chinese globalization" (Pieke et al. 2004)—global processes that originate in China and remain China-centered but are simultaneously conditioned by various global forces.

## RESUMPTION OF EMIGRATION AND STUDENT MIGRATION

Large-scale, long-distance emigration from China that started in the eighteenth century came to an abrupt halt in the 1950s when the world was divided into nation-states with fixed boundaries and subsequently became engulfed by the Cold War. Migration between China and a number of countries in Asia and Africa and in the Communist bloc did occur, and emigration from South China through family connections resumed in the early 1970s, but the numbers were negligible. Sizable outflows started with student migration after the era of the Cultural Revolution.

As part of the central leadership's Four Modernizations strategy, the Ministry of Education selected three thousand candidates to be sent overseas in 1978; the first fifty arrived in the United States in the same year. In 1981 the government for the first time recognized self-financed overseas study without government sponsorship as a legitimate means of leaving China. By the mid-1990s, China had formed its "twelve-words approach" (support study overseas, encourage returns, guarantee freedom of movement), which signaled that student migration was no longer controlled by the state and had instead became a "societal" phenomenon. From 1978 to 2007, more than 1.2 million students left China, making China the largest source country of international students. More than 90 percent of these students arranged fees themselves. About 900,000 out of the 1.2 million remain overseas and are likely to become long-term settlers (Ministry of Education 2008).

## A NEW EMIGRATION REGIME

In 1986 China introduced identification cards, which enabled citizens to prove their identities independently (without relying on the family's household registration booklet and documents from employers), and thus to produce individualized legal documents as required for international migration. The 1986 Law on the Administration of the Exit and Entry of Citizens grants ordinary citizens private passports, as long as they can provide invitation letters and sponsorships from overseas. From 2001 the Ministry of Public Security dramatically streamlined the application procedure, and by 2005 all urban residents could apply for passports simply by presenting their ID cards and waiting for as little as one working day. The Passport Law effective from January 2007 enshrines citizens' legal entitlement to possess passports. In 2007 Chinese authorities issued 5.5 million passports, excluding diplomatic passports and other types of passes, such as seafarers' papers (Border Exit and Entry Bureau 2008).

Other institutional changes also contributed to the development of the new emigration regime. The reform of the urban housing system, started in 1998, encourages citizens to buy state-owned housing that they were renting. Would-be migrants use the property certificate as security in signing contracts with recruitment agents, taking loans from banks and applying for visas (as required by some embassies). Public notarization offices that were first set up in 1982 have been indispensable in producing legal documents. Foreign embassies in China, and many companies and schools overseas, require documents to be verified by public notarization offices.

Private agents that facilitate emigration for fees constitute an important component of the new regime. First emerging in the late 1980s, they have been licensed and regulated since the end of the 1990s. In the mid-2000s, there were about four hundred education-migration agents (licensed by the Ministry of Education), five hundred that specialize in emigration (e.g., as skilled or investment migrants, licensed by the Ministry of Public Security), and more than two thousand labor-migration agents (licensed by the ministries of labor and of commerce).

The liberalization and commercialization of emigration are accompanied by arguably more systematic government regulation. For example, the old procedure of passport application required "political approvals" from employers and local government officials, a system that put everyone under strict scrutiny but in a decentralized manner. The streamlining centralizes and unifies regulation nationwide. The electronically integrated data system of citizens' criminal records enables swift processing of passport applications. Private agents serve as intermediaries through which the government monitors migration effectively, although this process increases migrants' costs. Various information sources show that illegal emigration is much more contained in the 2000s than it was at the end of the 1980s and early 1990s.

## ECONOMIC RESTRUCTURING AND DIVERSIFICATION IN EMIGRATION

Dynamics in emigration from China are inherently related to economic restructuring at the local, national, and global levels. First, changes in China have created a number of new emigration sites, especially in northeastern China. By the early 2000s, northeasteners made up the largest regional group among Chinese workers in Japan and South Korea. Privatization of state-owned enterprises that started in the early 1990s led to massive labor layoffs and rapid social stratification. The newly rich migrate to seek security, the middle strata migrate for higher wages and business opportunities, and the poor migrate for jobs.

Second, global economic changes provide job opportunities in diverse occupations beyond traditional ethnic enclaves. An increasing number of migrants are highly skilled; among them are Chinese medical doctors, language teachers, and computer engineers. In 2001, 27,330 Chinese were granted H-1B visas for highly skilled professionals migrating to the United States. Sizable numbers of unskilled and semiskilled Chinese migrate to Russia as agricultural workers and to southern Europe and other eastern Asian countries as factory laborers. The "proletarianization" of Chinese emigrants is directly related to the deregulation and informalization of economies in various parts of the world and especially in Japan, South Korea, Italy, and Spain.

Third, changes in world geopolitics opened up new destinations. After the fall of Berlin Wall (1989) and the collapse of the Soviet Union (1991), the Balkans and eastern and central Europe attracted large numbers of Chinese, initially as a route to western Europe but gradually as destinations themselves. Hungary, Romania, and Russia waived visa requirements for Chinese citizens making short visits at the end of the 1980s and the early 1990s (Nyíri 1999). Most of these migrants were traders, petty producers, and service providers. The contribution of Chinese migrants to the creation of an integrated market of daily commodities across Europe and beyond is yet to be properly assessed.

## CHINA-CENTRIC FLOWS AND NETWORKS

The liberalization and diversification of emigration is accompanied by a countertendency toward the flows becoming more China-centered. First, significant new waves of emigration derive from China's economic rise. Chinese traders in Europe, Africa, and Latin America, particularly those from Zhejiang Province, rely on China's position as the world factory for their economic success. China's "stepping out" strategy, which encourages external investment, and Chinese companies' search for energy have induced emigration to Africa, Latin America, and Southeast Asia.

Emigrants' overseas networks have also become increasingly China-centered. New migrants have rejuvenated overseas Chinese nationalism (Liu Hong 2005). Connections with the Chinese government, both national and local, have become an important source of authority and legitimacy for migrant community leaders (see Liu Hong 1998; Pieke et al. 2004; Xiang Biao 2005). Chinese communities in different parts of the world foster ever closer ties with each other, especially through global events such as the World Conference of Chinese Merchants. Although the initiatives often come from overseas, the Chinese state features prominently in the globalization of Chinese networks.

China's central position is paradoxically reinforced by more open and flexible diaspora policies. For example, instead of demanding that former students return to China, the government has advocated a "dumbbell model" since the early 2000s, which means that Chinese who have professional or business affiliations in both China and overseas may move back and forth. This effectively inserts China into market-driven global flows and networks. Indeed, rapid economic growth has attracted 300,000 students back to China between 1978 and 2007.

Another new development is that Chinese emigration has given rise to certain social tensions overseas since the early 2000s. In September 2004, footwear producers in Elche, Spain, burned down warehouses owned by Chinese migrants. Other incidents include a clash with local police in Italy in 2004, regular police raids in Russia since the early 2000s, an anti-Chinese political campaign in Zambia since 2006, and kidnappings and killings in Afghanistan, Ethiopia, Iraq, Nigeria, and Pakistan. The Chinese government established the Interministry Working Meeting on Protecting the Safety of PRC Citizens and Organizations Overseas in 2004, and the Ministry of Foreign Affairs put in place new policy measures in this regard. These developments have attracted widespread attention in China, and the notion of rights protection in an increasingly interconnected world may generate a new type of national consciousness.

**SEE ALSO** *Fujian; Labor: Outmigration; Wenzhou.*

### BIBLIOGRAPHY

Australia Department of Immigration and Citizenship. *Fact Sheet 2: Key Facts in Immigration*. 2007. http://www.immi.gov.au/media/fact-sheets/02key.htm.

Border Exit and Entry Bureau, Ministry of Public Security of the People's Republic of China. *2007 Nian Zhongguo neidi jumin yinsi chuguo zhenjian qingkuang* [Data on processing documents for overseas travels on private purposes by mainland Chinese in 2007]. Beijing: Author, 2008.

Citizenship and Immigration Canada. Canada: Permanent Residents from Asia and Pacific by Top Source Countries. In *Facts and Figures 2006: Immigration Overview*. 2007. http://www.cic.gc.ca/english/resources/statistics/facts2006/permanent/14.asp.

Liu Hong. Old Linkages, New Networks: The Globalization of Overseas Chinese Voluntary Associations and its Implications. *China Quarterly* 155 (1998): 582–609.

Liu Hong. New Migrants and the Revival of Overseas Chinese Nationalism. *Journal of Contemporary China* 14, 43 (2005): 291–316.

Ministry of Education of the People's Republic of China. News release, April 5, 2008. www.moe.edu.cn/edoas/website18/info1207529648459347.htm.

National Bureau of Statistics of the People's Republic of China. Statistical Communiqué of the People's Republic of China on the 1999 National Economic and Social Development. Beijing: Author, 2000.

National Bureau of Statistics of the People's Republic of China. Statistical Communiqué of the People's Republic of China on the 2007 National Economic and Social Development. Beijing: Author, 2008.

Nyíri, Pál. *New Chinese Migrants in Europe: The Case of the Chinese Community in Hungary*. Aldershot, U.K.: Ashgate, 1999.

Pieke, Frank, Pál Nyíri, Mette Thunø, and Antonella Ceccagno. *Transnational Chinese: Fujianese Migrants in Europe*. Stanford, CA: Stanford University Press, 2004.

Ren Yingchao. Yinsi huzhao [Private passport]. Interview with Jin Yan, reporter from *Sanlian shenghuo zhoukan* [Sanlian life weekly]. December 4, 2001.

Rytina, Nancy. *Population Estimates: Estimates of the Legal Permanent Resident Population in 2006*. Washington, DC: Department of Homeland Security, 2008.

Statistics Bureau, Ministry of Internal Affairs and Communication, Japan. Table 2–14: Registered Foreigners by Nationality (1985–2005). In *Japan Statistics Yearbook 2008*, 57. Tokyo: Author, 2008.

Xiang Biao. *Migrant Networks and Knowledge Exchange: How China Researches Out to Its Scientific Diaspora*. Oxford: ESRC Centre on Migration, Policy, and Society, 2005.

***Xiang Biao***

## EXCLUSION IN RECEIVING COUNTRIES

As was the case for migration in most of the world, emigration from southern China increased rapidly after the 1840s. In the 1850s, more than 135,000 Chinese went to the goldfields of California and southeastern Australia, amounting to about a quarter of all Chinese emigration in that decade. European immigrants on these frontiers often responded to the presence of Chinese with mob violence and anti-Chinese legislation, which included discriminatory mining taxes, residential restrictions, heavy immigration taxes, and limitations on the number of Chinese passengers per boat. Many of these laws were overturned in the courts or disallowed by the imperial government in London because they violated domestic rights guarantees and international commitments to free trade and mobility. But the California mining tax of 1852 and several Australian migration and residential restrictions remained on the books until their repeal in the 1860s (see Table 1).

### ANTI-CHINESE RHETORIC AND LEGISLATION

The general framework and vocabulary of anti-Chinese sentiments varied remarkably little around the Pacific region, as activists and legislators watched and learned from each other. Ironically, these sentiments were charged with a spirit of egalitarian self-government and a mistrust of big capital and elite institutions. Two foundations of anti-Chinese rhetoric were a belief in the right of self-governing societies to determine their own membership and a fear that unconstrained capital would degrade the status of the working man. These beliefs were transformed into anti-Chinese convictions through accusations that the Chinese refused to assimilate, were inculcated with a totalitarian culture that was incompatible with free societies, and were willing to work for low wages and send the money home rather than settle and become invested in local working conditions. In short, the Chinese played into the hands of capitalist interests that wanted to dominate and degrade the living standards of laborers rather than build an egalitarian, self-governing community. Depictions of Chinese as dirty, enslaved, heathen, servile, and cunning added an emotional dimension to these accusations. Such depictions culminated in views of Chinese "coolies" as degraded individuals bound to servitude through ignorance and passivity. These views had little basis in fact (less than 4 percent of all Chinese emigrants were ever indentured to Caucasians) but were accepted as truth in countries and colonies around the Pacific by the 1870s.

Anti-Chinese agitation declined in the 1860s, when there was a lull in migration. But a new wave of agitation that rose in the 1870s ultimately led to new anti-Chinese immigration laws being passed in Australia, Canada, Hawaii, and the United States in the 1880s. Unlike earlier laws, these focused more on immigration than on discrimination against resident Chinese and were enacted at a national rather than local level. The Australian colonies agreed to enact coordinated port taxes and passenger-per-boat limits in 1881. The United States prohibited the entry of Chinese laborers in 1882. Hawaii established a quota on Chinese immigrants in 1883. And Canada enacted a fifty-dollar head tax in 1885. Several Latin American countries and Japan also excluded Chinese in the 1890s and early 1900s, despite receiving few or no Chinese immigrants (see Table 1).

All of these laws were plagued with enforcement difficulties. It was far from clear how to effectively patrol enormous borders and coastlines, how to identify and categorize foreign migrants, and how to control the creation of fraudulent documents. Courts often overturned laws and enforcement practices that conflicted with civil rights guarantees. And protests from China and London generated many diplomatic difficulties. In 1897 the South African colony of Natal enacted an immigration act that

**Anti-Chinese immigration laws, 1852–1923**

| Year | Place | Legal Provisions | Fate of Law |
|---|---|---|---|
| 1852 | California | Tax on foreign miners | Voided by Civil Rights Act, 1870 |
| | California | Requirement that shipmasters post $500 bond for landing unnaturalizable passengers | Struck down by California Supreme Court, 1872 |
| 1855 | California | $50 capitation tax | Struck down by California Supreme Court, 1857 |
| | | $450 penalty for landing migrants ineligible for citizenship | |
| | Victoria | Segregated camps | Repealed, 1859 |
| | Victoria | £10 landing fee and limitation of 1 Chinese passenger per 10 tons of ship tonnage. | Repealed, 1865 |
| 1857 | Victoria | Residence tax | Repealed, 1862 |
| | South Australia | £10 and 1 per 10 tons | Repealed, 1861 |
| 1858 | California | Bar to entry of Chinese and Mongolians | Struck down by California Supreme Court, 1862 |
| 1859 | Victoria | £4 overland entry tax | Repealed, 1865 |
| 1861 | New South Wales | £10 and 1 per 10 tons | Repealed, 1867 |
| 1862 | California | Monthly head tax "to discourage the immigration of Chinese" | Struck down by California Supreme Court, 1862 |
| | United States | U.S. citizens banned from participating in the "coolie trade" | |
| 1870 | California | Ban on importation of prostitutes and coolies | Amended, 1874 |
| | United States | Prohibition on eligibility of Asians for naturalization | Repealed, 1943 |
| 1874 | California | Bonds for certain immigrants | Held unconstitutional, 1875 |
| 1875 | British Columbia | Disenfranchisement of Chinese | |
| | United States | Exclusion of felons, prostitutes, and Asian labor under contract | Subsumed under other migration laws |
| 1876 | Queensland | Gold field licensing act | Reserved by governor, 1876 |
| 1877 | Queensland | £10 and 1 per 10 tons | Amended, 1884 |
| 1878 | British Columbia | Quarterly tax | Held unconstitutional, 1878 |
| 1879 | United States | Fifteen Chinese per vessel | Vetoed, 1879 |
| 1881 | New South Wales | £10 and 1 per 100 tons | Amended, 1888 |
| | New Zealand | £10 and 1 per 10 tons | Repealed, 1944 |
| | South Australia | £10 and 1 per 10 tons | Amended, 1888 |
| | Victoria | £10 and 1per 100 tons | Amended, 1888 |
| 1882 | United States | Exclusion of Chinese laborers | Repealed, 1943 |
| 1883 | Hawaii | Quota and passport for returns | Amended, 1887 |
| 1884 | British Columbia | Prohibition on entry of Chinese; registration | Disallowed, 1884 |
| | Queensland | £30 and 1 per 50 tons | Amended, 1890 |
| | United States | Stronger exclusion law | Amended, 1888 |
| 1885 | British Columbia | Prohibition on entry of Chinese | Disallowed, 1885 |
| | Canada | $50 and 1 per 50 tons | Amended, 1901 |
| 1886 | Western Australia | £10 and 1 per 50 tons | Amended, 1888 |
| 1887 | Hawaii | Stricter control of return passports | |
| | Tasmania | £10 and 1 per 100 tons | Amended, 1889 |
| 1888 | Australia | Agreement among colonies to new restriction of 1 per 500 tons | Repealed, 1901–1902 |
| | United States | Scott Act prohibiting return of laborers | Repealed, 1894 |
| 1889 | Ecuador | Exclusion of Chinese | |
| 1890 | Hawaii | New provisions to allow recruitment of limited numbers of laborers | Repealed, 1898 |
| 1892 | United States | Geary Act registering Chinese laborers | Repealed, 1943 |
| 1893 | Hawaii | Admission of merchants, families, teachers and recruited laborers only | Superseded, 1898 |
| 1896 | Guatemala | Exclusion of Chinese | |
| 1897 | Costa Rica | Exclusion of Chinese as "noxious race" | |
| | Natal | Dictation test in European language | Repealed, 1913 |
| | Nicaragua | Exclusion of Chinese | |
| | Western Australia | Dictation test, followed by similar tests in other Australian colonies over the next two years | Repealed, 1901–1902 |
| 1898 | U.S. territories | Extension of U.S. exclusion to new territories of Hawaii, Philippines, Cuba, Puerto Rico | Repealed, 1943 |
| 1899 | Japan | Edict to prohibit laborers without special permission | |
| 1900 | British Columbia | European-language dictation test | Disallowed, 1901 |
| 1901 | Australia | European-language dictation test | Amended, 1905 |
| | Canada | Increase in head tax to $100 | Amended, 1903 |

continued

*Table 1A*

**Anti-Chinese immigration laws, 1852–1923 [CONTINUED]**

| Year | Place | Legal Provisions | Fate of Law |
|---|---|---|---|
| 1902 | Cuba | Exclusion of Chinese | Repeatedly revised through 1959 |
| 1903 | Canada | Increase in head tax to $500 | Repealed, 1923 |
| 1904 | Panama | Prohibition on Chinese, except returning residents and agricultural laborers | Repealed, 1940s |
| | United States | Extension of exclusion to Filipinos | Repealed, 1943 |
| 1905 | Australia | Dictation test in any prescribed language | Relaxed, 1947; repealed, 1973 |
| 1909 | Peru | Prohibition on Chinese without equivalent of £100 | Repealed 1909 |
| 1913 | South Africa | Legislation permitting minister to ban any undesirable immigrants | |
| 1920 | New Zealand | Discretionary immigration permits | Ended, 1987 |
| 1923 | Canada | Exclusion based on U.S. model | Repealed, 1947 |

*Table 1B*

required a fifty-word dictation test in any European language chosen by an immigration official. It was intended for use against Indian immigrants, but London quickly encouraged its use in Australia, New Zealand, and Canada as a way to exclude Asians without resorting to the explicitly discriminatory legislation that had generated severe diplomatic difficulties for the United States. Australia enacted a dictation test in 1901 as one of the first acts accompanying federation. A 1905 amendment changed the test from a "European" language to "any prescribed language," consolidating both the exclusionary and diplomatic effectiveness of the law.

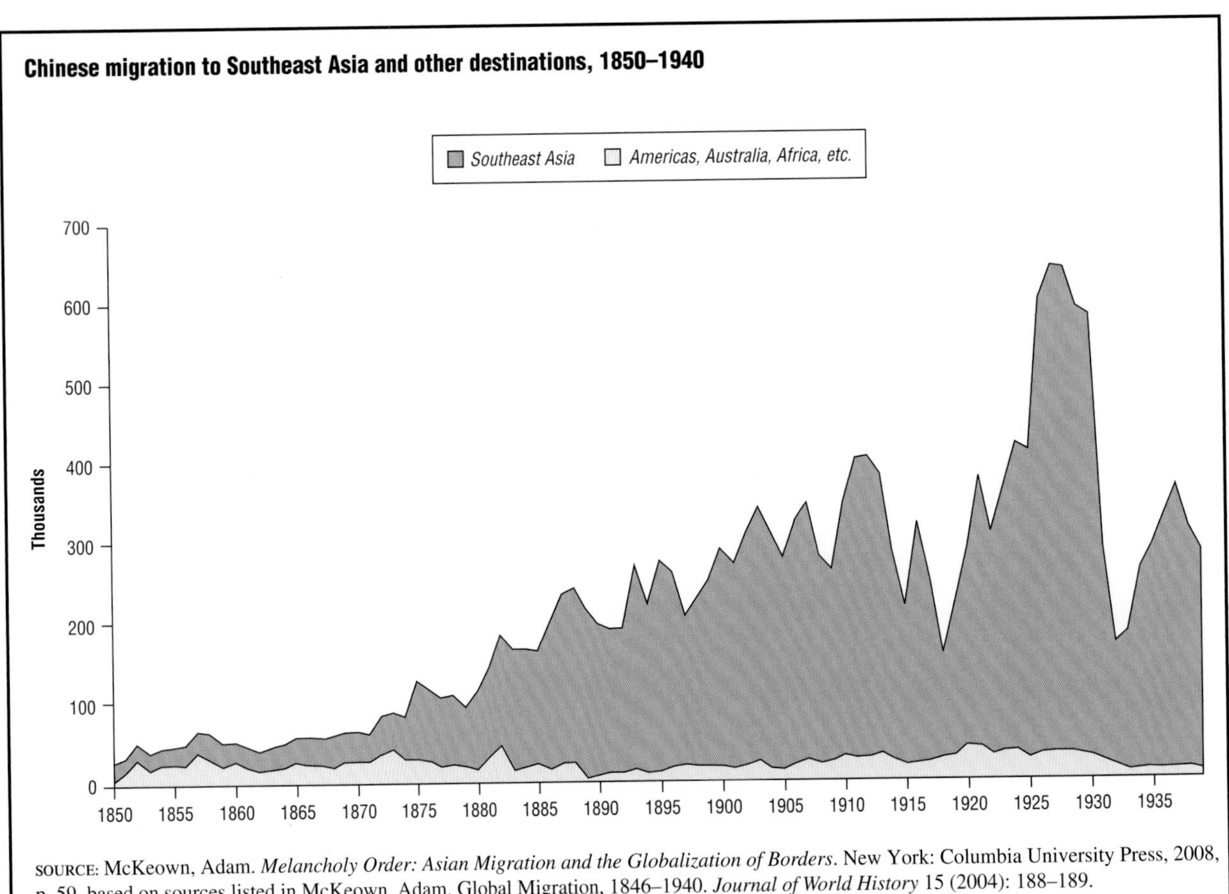


SOURCE: McKeown, Adam. *Melancholy Order: Asian Migration and the Globalization of Borders*. New York: Columbia University Press, 2008, p. 59, based on sources listed in McKeown, Adam. Global Migration, 1846–1940. *Journal of World History* 15 (2004): 188–189.

*Figure 1*

***Insecticide advertisement, Boston, Massachusetts, c. 1880.*** *During the mid-1800s, Chinese immigrants began sailing to California in great numbers, arousing fear in many American citizens. In addition to concerns the unskilled laborers would depress wages for workers already in the United States, many citizens held negative stereotypes about the Chinese immigrants, as reflected in this advertisement for insecticide.* TRANSCENDENTAL GRAPHICS/HULTON ARCHIVE/GETTY IMAGES

Ultimately, the U.S. exclusion laws had the greatest effect, both in the amount of diplomatic tension they generated and because efforts to enforce them shaped many of the techniques and principles of modern migration law around the world. The U.S. exclusion laws prohibited laborers but allowed merchants, teachers, students, family members, U.S. residents, and citizens to enter. The techniques developed to categorize and identify immigrants, and to standardize paperwork related to migration, eventually influenced the standardization of migration laws and international identity documents around the world.

The many diplomatic and legal struggles over exclusion in the 1880s and 1890s also led to the first explicit justifications of migration control in the context of liberal ideals of free mobility. These included many principles of migration control that are now taken for granted: that migration control happens at borders, that migrants have no necessary rights at the borders, and that immigration controls are exclusively the domestic policy of the receiving country.

### THE CHINESE RESPONSE

The Chinese government was deeply humiliated by these laws, by repeated diplomatic failures to mitigate them, and by the widespread perception that China was not able to protect its own people abroad. In the 1880s, many Chinese officials supported plans to self-restrict emigration, arguing that this would preempt the embarrassment of being controlled by a foreign government and show that China was better able to control its own people than foreign governments with leaky borders. The 1905 anti-American boycott organized by merchants in Shanghai and Canton against U.S. exclusion focused especially on the humiliating treatment of merchants and other "exempt" classes by U.S. officials. The boycott failed to compel any change in legislation but it did lead to a mitigation of the harsher enforcement methods. Most significantly, the scale of mass mobilization impressed many observers, and the boycott is often cited as the first concrete manifestation of popular Chinese nationalism.

### LEGACY OF EXCLUSION LAWS

The United States repealed its exclusion laws in 1943 and Canada did so in 1947, both in honor of their wartime alliance with China and as part of the larger global reaction against racism. Migration from China nonetheless remained low after 1949, due to small allotments under immigration quota laws and emigration restrictions from China. The White Australia and White New Zealand policies remained in place until the 1970s and 1980s, respectively, when weakened enforcement and the pressures of multicultural politics led to their final repeal.

Perhaps the most enduring legacy of exclusion is global racial segregation. Before the 1870s, up to 40 percent of Chinese emigrants went to the Americas and Australia. But as Chinese emigration increased twentyfold by the 1920s, migration beyond Southeast Asia remained stagnant, reduced to less than 5 percent of the total (see Figure 1). Had Chinese not been excluded from the Americas and Australia during this period, global migration patterns would have been much more integrated and the contemporary racial distribution of the global population would look much different.


**BIBLIOGRAPHY**

Lee, Erika. *At America's Gates: Chinese Immigration during the Exclusion Era, 1882–1943*. Chapel Hill: University of North Carolina Press, 2003.

Markus, Andrew. *Fear and Hatred: Purifying Australia and California, 1850–1901*. Sydney: Hale & Iremonger, 1974.

McKeown, Adam. *Melancholy Order: Asian Migration and the Globalization of Borders, 1834–1939*. New York: Columbia University Press, 2008.

Price, Charles. *The Great White Walls Are Built: Restrictive Immigration to North America and Australia, 1836–1888*. Canberra, Australia: Australian Institute of International Affairs and Australian National University Press, 1974.

Salyer, Lucy. *Laws Harsh as Tigers: Chinese Immigrants and the Shaping of Modern Immigration Law*. Chapel Hill: University of North Carolina Press, 1995.

Saxton, Alexander. *The Indispensable Enemy: Labor and the Anti-Chinese Movement in California*. Berkeley: University of California Press, 1971.

Ward, W. Peter. *White Canada Forever: Popular Attitudes and Public Policy Toward Orientals in British Columbia*. Montreal: McGill-Queen's University Press, 2002 (1978).

Yarwood, A. T. *Asian Migration to Australia: The Background to Exclusion, 1896–1923*. Melbourne, Australia: Melbourne University Press, 1964.


***Adam McKeown***

## RETURNED OVERSEAS CHINESE

"Returned overseas Chinese" (*guiqiao* or *guiguo huaqiao*) are ethnic Chinese who journeyed to China to settle (intending to stay long term) after a significant period of time spent as residents overseas. These include not only the China-born who emigrated and returned, but also include foreign-born Chinese who migrated to China. The Overseas Chinese Affairs Office of the PRC State Council stipulated this definition in June 1984. Prior to that, the term "returned overseas Chinese" was used to loosely describe anyone who returned, regardless of the length of their intended stay in China. The official classification further subdivides the group into *guiqiao* (returned overseas Chinese) and *qiaojuan* (dependents of overseas Chinese).

Several events can be considered milestones in the evolving relationship between China and Chinese living in other countries. These, in turn, affect the status of the returned overseas Chinese. In 1955 Zhou Enlai relinquished claims to the allegiance of overseas Chinese and encouraged them to take up citizenship in their country of residence. The 1980 Nationality Law abandons *jus sanguinis*, stipulating that Chinese nationals will lose their Chinese citizenship when they opt for a foreign passport. Arguably, the link between China and the overseas Chinese thus became weaker, especially when compared with the policy of the Nationalist government under the Guomindang. However, the People's Republic maintains clear links with overseas Chinese. In 1990 the National People's Congress passed a law "protecting overseas Chinese" and their dependents.

The PRC government has an elaborate policy in place for overseas Chinese, with special administrative institutions spanning both the Communist Party and the State Council. The All-China Returned Overseas Chinese Association was established 1950 as a grassroots organization. High symbolic value and prestige were accorded to returned overseas Chinese, but practical policy never lived up to their august titles (Christiansen 2002, pp. 128–129).

The Chinese returned for many different reasons. Returnees of the 1890s and the early republican era did so to help with the anti-Qing republican revolution inspired by Sun Yat-sen, or to take part in the anti-Yuan Shikai campaigns. After 1949 and in the early 1950s, many scientists and intellectuals returned to answer the patriotic call of serving the new China. In the 1960s and 1970s, Chinese participated in mass evacuations to escape ethnic strife and political persecution in host countries—notable examples include the return of Indonesian Chinese and those from Vietnam and Cambodia (Huang 2005, pp. 26–58).

A broad figure of "over one million returnees by the 1990s" is given by various Chinese sources (see Huang 2005, p. 60). The status accorded the returned Chinese has changed over time. In spite of the initial appeal for their return, they remained outsiders in the communities they entered. Many returned Chinese were resettled in special state farms and factories called *huaqiao nongchang*, and their children were put into reeducation schools (*huaqiao bushi xuexiao*). The conditions of these institutions were far from ideal. The returnees were usually employed at levels far below their skills and professional qualifications. Their children suffered discrimination and were often suspected of being "bourgeois seedlings." During the Cultural Revolution (1966–1969) and its aftermath, returned Chinese became easy targets of many of the worst excesses.

Since the 1980s, the Chinese government has worked to right past wrongs by rescinding unjust verdicts and restoring confiscated property to returned overseas Chinese landowners (Christiansen 2003, pp. 130–131). Renewed efforts have been made to regain their loyalty and goodwill. Many who wish to leave China are allowed to emigrate, and official patronage is once again bestowed on returned overseas Chinese associations. Returned overseas Chinese are looked upon as vanguards of the united front (Zhuang 2001, pp. 285–295), and they are entrusted with general duties of propagating positive images of China in foreign countries, including promoting trade links, attracting foreign investments, and upholding the cause of "one China."

**BIBLIOGRAPHY**

Christiansen, Flemming. *Chinatown, Europe: An Exploration of Overseas Chinese Identity in the 1990s*. London and New York: RoutledgeCurzon, 2003.

Huang Xiaojian. *Guiguo huaqiao de lishi yu xianzhuang* [The history and current developments of the returned overseas Chinese]. Hong Kong: Hong Kong Social Sciences Publishing, 2005.

Zhuang Guotu. *Huaqiao huaren yu Zhongguo de guanxi* [The relationship between China and the overseas Chinese]. Guangzhou: Guangdong jiaoyu chubanshe, 2001.

***Manying Ip***

# CHINESE PAINTING (*GUOHUA*)

The term *guohua*, literally "national painting" but frequently translated as "Chinese painting," usually denotes pictorial works executed predominantly with Chinese ink and pigments on Chinese paper or silk. Over the course of the nineteenth and twentieth centuries, China's political, economic, and social upheavals and its exposure to foreign artistic traditions dramatically transformed the execution and visual form of *guohua*. Traditional Chinese painting, which drew its techniques and subject matter from Chinese painting of the past, gave way to *guohua* that were radically dissimilar in appearance, were produced under novel social conditions, and served different ends.

## THE LATE QING (1800–1912)

Although political reforms of the early nineteenth century greatly reduced imperial expenditures on the arts, professional painters continued to work at the court in Beijing, producing decorative, documentary, and celebratory works. They painted primarily in the manner of the Jesuit missionary Giuseppe Castiglione (1688–1768), combining Chinese materials, compositions, and motifs with Western techniques for rendering perspective and volume. Some members of the royal family painted for the sake of literary and artistic self-cultivation. Artists of the Orthodox school—scholar-amateurs who embraced the aesthetic program of Dong Qichang (1555–1636) and his early-Qing followers—expressed themselves by reinterpreting the compositions, typological forms, and brushwork of select masters from the past, especially southern landscapists of the tenth and eleventh centuries and literati painters of the Yuan Dynasty (1279–1368).

Regional artistic approaches flourished in the Jiangnan area until the Taiping Uprising (1851–1864) ravaged the lower Yangzi River valley. Zhang Yin (1761–1829) and Gu Heqing (1766–after 1830) depicted local topography. Figure painters flourished, and although they were generally not highly esteemed, a few developed

***Landscape by Chen Hengque, 1915.*** CHEN HENGQUE/FOTOE

considerable reputations. Gai Qi (1773–1828) and Fei Danxu (1802–1850) earned renown for their paintings of beautiful women, whom they depicted with large, oval heads and wispy bodies.

After the Treaty of Nanjing (1842) opened five of China's coastal cities to foreign settlement and trade, Shanghai became China's most important economic center. Artists flocked to the city, and fan and stationery shops presented their work to the public. Artistic societies enabled established painters to help younger and newly arrived colleagues negotiate Shanghai's diverse art market. Dominating the market was a newly affluent middle class, with its preference for brightly colored, visually immediate pictures, especially ones in the bird-and-flower and figure genres. Such works frequently portrayed auspicious symbols and characters from popular lore. Critics in the rival artistic center of Beijing scorned this art as belonging to the "Shanghai school" (*haipai*). Today the term has lost its negative connotations and broadly refers to painters who worked in Shanghai or sold their art on its market.

Many Shanghai artists created works that held popular appeal. Zhang Xiong (1803–1886), Zhu Xiong (1801–1864), Zhu Cheng (1826–1900), and Wang Li (1813–1879) styled their bird-and-flower painting after sixteenth-century Suzhou painting and that of Yun Shouping (1633–1690), though they made less use of poetic subtlety and employed brighter palettes and bolder brushwork. Ren Xiong (1823–1857)—whose sources of inspiration included Chen Hongshou (1598–1652), paintings of the Tang (618–907) and Song (960–1279) dynasties, and folk prints—produced figural, floral, and landscape works with lucid compositions, forceful lineament, brilliant color, and sumptuous detail. Ren Xun (1835–1893) and Ren Yi (1840–1895) combined expressionistic (*xieyi*) brushwork with finely detailed (*gongbi*) painting. Other Shanghai school painters infused popular painting with literati tastes. Xugu (1823–1896) affected scholarly reserve through pale colors, dry trembling brushwork, and experiments in rhythm and geometric abstraction. Zhao Zhiqian (1829–1884) and Wu Changshi (1844–1927) created an epigraphic mode in which they structured colorful and expressionistic paintings of flowers and rocks with strokes of ink and color applied in the manner of the seal, clerical, and stone drum scripts of ancient steles.

Artists in Guangdong produced works unique to their region, depicting local subjects such as the kapok plant and inscribing works in vernacular Cantonese. Ju Chao (c. 1824–1889) and Ju Lian (1828–1904) earned fame as bird-and-flower painters, combining "boneless" washes (ones not circumscribed by outlines) with puddling effects created by dropping clear water or powdered mineral pigments onto wet areas of the picture surface.

## REPUBLICAN PERIOD (1912–1949)

By the beginning of the twentieth century, the orthodox school of the Four Wangs (*Si Wang hua pai*) had sapped painting in Beijing of its vitality, and only a few masters in Shanghai continued to innovate. Western drawing and painting were soon vying for practitioners and prestige in China's art academies. By the 1910s some critics were arguing that the subject matter and naturalism of Western painting better suited modern Chinese life than the themes and conventionalized brushwork of traditional painting. Iconoclasts of the May Fourth movement even advocated that *guohua* be totally abandoned.

Some artists sought to revive Chinese painting by infusing it with desirable traits of foreign art. The founders of the Lingnan school—Gao Jianfu (1879–1951), Gao Qifeng (1889–1933), and Chen Shuren (1884–1948)—studied European and Japanese art in Tokyo and attempted to fashion a new national painting that incorporated Western naturalism and the misty romanticism of Japanese-style painting (*nihonga*). Xu Beihong (1895–1953), who studied in Paris and became an influential arts administrator, promoted European academic painting, but he also incorporated Western drawing into his works in Chinese materials.

Many Chinese artists believed that the best way to adapt traditional Chinese painting to modern life was to draw from the past. In Beijing the legal scholar Jin Cheng (1878–1926) broke with Qing orthodoxy by advocating the study of Tang and Song styles. Chen Hengke (1876–1923) found liberation in the early Qing individualists Shitao (1642–1707) and Zhu Da (1626–1705), whose work he encountered while studying in Japan and from whom he drew some of his own bright colors, strong brushwork, and refreshing naïveté. Chen also took advice on painting, calligraphy, and seal carving from Wu Changshi. In 1921 Chen published "Wenrenhua zhi jiazhi" (The value of literati painting), an essay in which he argued that literati painting, like Postimpressionist painting in Europe, was a modern art whose freedom from naturalistic concerns enabled it to express the subjective intentions of the artist. Qi Baishi (1864–1957), who was born poor in Hunan Province and initially worked as a carpenter, developed a painting style grounded in the art of Zhu Da, Shitao, and Wu Changshi. Qi's paintings of fish, shrimp, crabs, frogs, insects, and flowers combined expressive and finely detailed brushwork and were tremendously popular.

Traditionalists in the South also sought to revive and continue *guohua*. Lu Hui (1851–1920) and Gu Linshi (1865–1930) effected a minor revival of literati painting in Suzhou in the 1910s. Wu Changshi led the Shanghai art world during the 1910s and 1920s. His numerous students included the businessman Wang Yiting (1867–1938), who successfully fused Wu's calligraphic style with Ren Yi's subjects and compositions. He Tianjian (1891–1977) and Huang Binhong (1865–1955) were forceful advocates of the art of the past and, through their study of Tang and Song painting, developed innovative landscape compositions and brushwork. Wu Hufan (1894–1968), a collector and connoisseur who embraced the Suzhou literati tradition, earned acclaim for his exquisite interpretations of the antique blue-and-green style.

Traditionalists also promoted *guohua* through organizational and educational efforts. They formed artistic societies dedicated to continuing traditional Chinese painting, which they believed conveyed China's national essence. Members of such groups as the Zhongguo Huaxue Yanjiuhui (Chinese Painting Research Society) and the Zhongguo Hua Hui (Chinese Painting Society) gave public lectures, published journals and histories of Chinese art, and mounted exhibitions. They also allied themselves with traditionalists in Japan, with whom they organized a series of joint exhibitions in the 1920s and early 1930s. The supporters of *guohua* were so successful that traditional painting featured prominently in the Ministry of Education's first national art exhibition in 1929, and the market for it flourished until the establishment of the People's Republic of China.

## THE PEOPLE'S REPUBLIC OF CHINA (1949–PRESENT)

Soon after the Communists founded the People's Republic, they took control of the art world. The commercial market for *guohua* collapsed, and many painters lost their livelihoods. Art authorities dictated that art serve the people and deemed oil painting, Chinese New Year pictures (*nianhua*), and serial illustrations (*lianhuanhua*) suitable for the new Chinese society, not *guohua*. They closed private art schools, and they reorganized public art academies, eliminating departments of *guohua*, dropping traditional landscape and bird-and-flower painting from curricula, and discontinuing the study of old masters' techniques. The only traditional approach that students continued to learn was painting figures in outline and colored washes. When administrators reinstated *guohua* in the mid-1950s, a new generation of artists with little training in traditional techniques propelled the art in new directions. Some called this new art *caimohua*, or "color-and-ink painting," to distinguish it from traditional Chinese painting. Although a few traditional artists—such as Qi Baishi, Wu Hufan, and He Tianjian—were assigned to research institutes and allowed to continue painting roughly in their old styles, mainstream *guohua* preserved little of the subject matter and technique of preliberation painting.

Between 1953 and 1957, arts administrators sought to implement Mao Zedong' s cultural theories, requiring art to convey revolutionary ideals. Soviet socialist realism became the official style of the academies. Different approaches to

**Buddha's Manifestation of Benevolence** ***by Zhang Daqian, 1946.*** *While receiving early training in traditional Chinese painting, Zhang Daqian later expanded upon this knowledge by studying other types of art, including the murals in the Mogao caves near Dunhuang. In the 1940s, Zhang spent several years making paintings of the Buddhist images in the sandstone grottoes, an experience which would influence his subsequent works.* THE METROPOLITAN MUSUEM OF ART, GIFT OF ROBERT HATFIELD ELLSWORTH, 1986. (1986.267.361) IMAGE © THE METROPOLITAN MUSEUM OF ART / ART RESOURCE, NY

socialist-realist figure painting emerged at various art academies. Jiang Zhaohe (1904–1986), a protégé of Xu Beihong and a professor at the Central Academy of Fine Arts (Zhongyang Meishu Xueyuan) in Beijing, used dark ink to model three-dimensional surfaces, and he generated perspective by dramatically foreshortening his figures. During the 1930s and 1940s he had sensitively depicted the suffering of ordinary people, but after 1949 he rendered cheerier subjects that embodied the ideals of the new society. Another approach rose to prominence at the East China branch of the Central Academy of Fine Arts in Hangzhou. Fang Zengxian (b. 1931) and Zhou Changgu (b. 1929), who graduated from the school and then became instructors there, dispensed with heavy shading and modeling, creating a style that shared with other socialist-realist figure painting a concern for anatomical accuracy and Western perspective but favored simpler compositions and more expressively brushed outlines.

*Guohua* painters at other academies also developed novel approaches that gathered local followings. In Nanjing, Fu Baoshi (1904–1965) painted figures from Chinese history in landscape settings. Having studied in Tokyo in the 1930s, Fu taught at the National Central University and Nanjing Normal University. From the 1940s he developed an influential, scribbly painting style that drew heavily from the work of such Japanese painters as Takeuchi Seihō, Yokoyama Taikan, and Kosugi Hōan. In Xi'an, Shi Lu (1919–1982) produced images closely associated with the Northwest. Shi had worked on Communist propaganda in the liberated zones during the civil-war years and joined the party in 1946. After 1949 he worked as a regional arts administrator, and he painted the scenery of the Northwest with a palette of reds and browns. His work was widely acclaimed as conveying the true appearance of China. In Beijing, Li Keran (1907–1989) also drew praise and emulators. While teaching at the Central Academy of Fine Arts, he studied with Huang Binhong and Qi Baishi, and in the 1950s he traveled around China and sketched. His painting displays a focused interest in strong tonal contrasts, and in several compositions he explored the effects of light.

The Cultural Revolution (1966–1969) restricted painters largely to heroic images of Mao Zedong and certain idealized figure types. Artists like Lin Yong (b. 1942) adapted socialist-realist figure painting to the task, adding bolder colors and stirring gestures. From 1971 until Jiang Qing (1914–1992) lost control of the art world in 1976, figural works displayed a predominantly red palette. Crimson hues pervaded other genres well, as traditionalists like Qian Songyan (1899–1985) attempted to integrate socialist iconography into landscapes. Many painters suffered terribly during the Cultural Revolution. Shi Lu and Li Keran were criticized, and Lin Fengmian (1900–1991) destroyed all of his works to avoid humiliation.

Mao's death in 1976 brought an end to the excesses of the Cultural Revolution and prompted painters to envision new iconography and approaches. Tremendous variety has characterized *guohua* of the past thirty years, as artists have sought to come to terms with recent history and to reconcile national identity with participation in the global art world. Neotraditionalists like Xiao Haichun (b. 1944) have produced monumental reinterpretations of traditional Chinese painting. Others, like Wang Jiqian (C. C. Wang, 1907–2003) and Zhang Daqian (Chang Dai-chien, 1899–1983), who were traditionally trained in China but lived their last decades in the United States or Taiwan, have experimented with combinations of traditional and nontraditional materials, formats, and approaches. Still others, like Chen Ping (b. 1960) and Xu Lei (b. 1956), have sought to transform the aesthetics of *guohua* and to articulate through it divergences between the China of today and that of the past.

**SEE ALSO** *Lingnan School of Painting; Shanghai School of Painting; Wu Hufan.*

**BIBLIOGRAPHY**

Andrews, Julia F. *Painters and Politics in the People's Republic of China, 1949–1979.* Berkeley: University of California Press, 1994.

Andrews, Julia F., and Kuiyi Shen. *A Century in Crisis: Modernity and Tradition in the Art of Twentieth-Century China.* New York: Solomon R. Guggenheim Museum, 1998.

Brown, Claudia, and Ju-hsi Chou. *Transcending Turmoil: Painting at the Close of China's Empire, 1796–1911.* Phoenix, AZ: Phoenix Art Museum, 1992.

Kao, Mayching, ed. *Twentieth-Century Chinese Painting.* New York: Oxford University Press, 1988.

Sullivan, Michael. *Art and Artists of Twentieth-Century China.* Berkeley: University of California Press, 1996.

***Walter B. Davis***

## CHINESE SOVEREIGN WEALTH FUNDS

**SEE** *Foreign Currency Reserves.*

## CHONGQING

The city of Chongqing is located at the confluence of the Jialing and Yangzi (Chang) rivers in the southeastern part of the Sichuan basin. Mountainous and hilly in topography, Chongqing became the capital of the Ba kingdom in the eleventh century BCE. After the Qin state conquered the Ba in 316 BCE, Chongqing continued to function as the political center of the region under various dynasties.

Fertile ground, plentiful water resources, and waves of Han migration have made the Sichuan basin one of China's most productive agricultural regions. Due to its strategic location along the upper reaches of the Yangzi, Chongqing also excelled in commerce and developed as a major river port. In 1891 the city became the first inland port in western China to open to foreign commerce. In the 1920s Chongqing evidenced considerable social experimentation and indigenous industrialization, including the reforms guided by Lu Zuofu. His Minsheng Shipping Company, which adopted elements of Taylorism, was China's largest domestically owned private transportation company before 1937.

After the outbreak of the Sino-Japanese War in 1937, Chiang Kai-shek (Jiang Jieshi) made Chongqing China's provisional capital, a status it retained until the end of the war in 1945. Although heavily bombed in Japanese air raids, Chongqing was afforded a degree of protection by its western location, surrounding mountains, and perennial fog. Its role as wartime capital also triggered Chongqing's transformation from an inland port into a heavy industrial city. After the outbreak of the war, many factories and universities located in China's east were moved full-scale to western China, and Chongqing became a center for the steel, machinery, and armament industries.

Following the founding of the People's Republic of China in 1949, Chongqing remained directly under the central government in Beijing, but in 1954 its status was reduced to a city within Sichuan Province. This created conflicts and rivalry between Chongqing and Chengdu, Sichuan's provincial capital. Indeed, Chengdu leveraged its political status to gain in industrial strength, leading many in Chongqing to feel that the city's economy was a victim of internal exploitation by Sichuan's political center. Nonetheless, Chongqing saw further development of its heavy industry under state ownership and planning between 1954 and 1979.

In 1983 Chongqing was granted provincial status in economic affairs, but uneasy political relations between Chengdu and Chongqing continued. Chongqing leaders thus supported moves to separate the city from Sichuan Province. More pressing reasons, though, lay elsewhere.

The Three Gorges Dam project, which began construction in 1994, created enormous challenges, most of all the relocation of over one million people from the reservoir area, and the rebuilding of two cities and numerous county seats and townships. Another salient reason for Chongqing's separation from Sichuan was the city's troubled state-owned industry. Besides Shenyang, Chongqing in the mid-1990s had the heaviest burden of obsolete and money-losing state firms, many in the defense industry. Worker unrest was common, and reform of the state sector was complicated by administrative overlap and confusion.

These factors justified the establishment of Chongqing as a provincial-level municipality directly under the central government on March 14, 1997. Chongqing's split from Sichuan gave it better access to central policy and financial resources. However, the Chongqing municipality also faced considerable burdens, as it emerged in the form of a small province incorporating some of Sichuan's poorest rural counties along the Three Gorges Reservoir. Of Chongqing's thirty-one million inhabitants, barely one-third are urban residents.

The Chongqing municipality's early years were marred by infighting within its leadership and poor economic performance. Chongqing's economy, though, took off after the launching of the Great Western Development Scheme in 2000 and China's economic acceleration after 2002. Greater central investment aided the construction of massive public works, and, as with other cities in China, Chongqing experienced a real-estate boom. Some of Chongqing's old industrial base was also reinvigorated, and the city emerged as China's major exporter of motorcycles. Put together, these features generated some of the best economic performances Chongqing had ever recorded.

Despite economic improvements, Chongqing continues to face challenges in industrial restructuring, poverty alleviation, rapid urbanization, and air and water pollution. Perhaps most important is the ecological management of the area around the Three Gorges Reservoir. In late 2007, Chongqing announced the relocation of four million rural residents, many located near the reservoir, to within one hour's driving distance from the city center by the year 2020. With this undertaking, Chongqing became the site of one of China's most ambitious urbanization programs.

**SEE ALSO** *Chengdu; Lu Zuofu; Sichuan.*

**BIBLIOGRAPHY**

Donovan, G. A. Chongqing vs. Chengdu—Great Expectations. *China Economic Quarterly* Q2 (2006): 46–52.

Hong Lijian. Chongqing: Opportunities and Risks. *China Quarterly* 178 (2004): 448–466.

McNally, Christopher A. Sichuan: Driving Capitalist Development Westward. *China Quarterly* 178 (2004): 426–447.

***Christopher A. McNally***

## CHU ANPING

### *1909–1966*

Chu Anping was born in Yixing, Jiangsu. While still an undergraduate at Guanghua University in Shanghai, he published patriotic and literary essays in leading national journals, which helped to pay his way. After graduation in 1934, he was hired as an editor by Nanjing's *Zhongyang ribao* (Central Daily News), the organ of the Guomindang (Nationalist Party), but he soon left to undertake graduate study in literature at Yenching University in Beijing.

In Beijing he fell under the influence of Hu Shi, Luo Longji, and Xu Zhimo, all independent liberal figures. In 1935 he earned a scholarship to study at the London School of Economics, a sojourn which confirmed his belief in British civic society, especially the emphasis on freedom of speech and organized opposition. When he returned to China, he refused to follow the party line, much less join the Guomindang, a stand that cost him his job at *Zhongyang ribao*. He spent most of the war teaching at Lantian Teacher's College in Hunan and writing a book on British liberal culture.

After the war he returned to Chongqing and founded *Guancha* (The Observer), published from 1946 to 1948 and reaching a peak circulation of some 60,000 copies. The journal was the outlet for a group of third-force intellectuals, many of whom were members of the China Democratic League (Zhongguo Minzhu Tongmeng), though Chu himself did not join. Chu proclaimed that the magazine stood for the classic liberal values of "democracy, freedom, progress, and rationality."

The journal criticized both the Nationalist government and the opposition Communist Party. Chu wrote in 1947 that the question for the Nationalists was how much freedom, but for the Communists the question was whether there would be any freedom at all. He added that the basic spirit of the Communists is "antidemocratic," and that there is "no difference between them and the fascists" in their aim to control people's thinking. The Communist Party goal is "political monopoly, not democracy." In 1957 these words would be used against him.

In the atmosphere of unity and relative relaxation of the Hundred Flowers campaign in 1956, the government established the *Guangming ribao* (Guangming Daily) as a forum for intellectuals and made Chu chief editor. Chu took advantage of the seeming openness to solicit criticism and publish frank reports on the West and essays from members of the Democratic League. Chu's speech to fellow independent figures, titled "Dang Tianxia" (translated either as "The party empire" or "All under the party") attacked one-party rule. He agreed that the party needed to be strong to meet the needs of the people, but asserted that "a party leading the nation is not the same as a party owning the nation." He objected to putting a "party boss into every unit and organization . . . and making everything, no matter how large or small, depend on the reaction of this apparatchik" (Dai 1989).

The speech was published in the official *Renmin ribao* (People's Daily), but in the following anti-rightist campaign, Chu was pilloried. He then abjectly apologized for his words of 1947 and 1957 and for assisting other liberals in their "conspiracy for power," but Mao himself labeled Chu a "cardinal rightist." For many years the circumstances of his death in 1966 were not clear, but it is now accepted that he killed himself because of political harassment.

Even after Mao's death in 1976, Chu was one of five major Beijing intellectuals not to be rehabilitated. The democracy activist Dai Qing published a series of Chu's essays in Hong Kong magazines and in 1989 collected them into a book. In the early twenty-first century Chu's name is frequently invoked in discussions of democracy and liberalism.

**SEE ALSO** *Hundred Flowers Campaign; Newspapers.*

**BIBLIOGRAPHY**

Dai, Qing. The Case of Chu Anping. In *New Ghosts, Old Dreams: Chinese Rebel Voices*, ed. Geremie Barmé and Linda Jaivin, 359–362. New York: Times Books, 1992.

Excerpts from *Chu Anping yu "Dang Tianxia,"* compiled by Qing Dai. Beijing: Zhongguo Huachiao Chubanshe, 1989.

MacFarquhar, Roderick. *The Hundred Flowers Campaign and the Chinese Intellectuals*. New York: Praeger, 1960.

Wong, Young-tsu. The Fate of Liberalism in Revolutionary China: Chu Anping and His Circle, 1946–1950. *Modern China* 19, 4 (October 1993): 457–490.

***Charles Hayford***

# CITY AND REGIONAL PLANNING

City and regional planning from 1949 was predicated on national socialist and collectivist goals and the drive for economic viability and industrial competence. The strategic development of cities and regions therefore was subordinate to the needs of industrial expansion, was centrally planned, and was implemented by state agencies and their local counterparts. This was facilitated by the nationalization of private property and business enterprises and by restrictions on population mobility through work-unit (*danwei*) and household (*hukou*) registration systems. Although master planning (such as in Shanghai and Guangzhou) and city-based regional planning were well established in China's major cities during the Republican period, planning was basically conceived as a municipal responsibility tailored to local requirements, responsive to public and private interests and to foreign and Sino-foreign investment, and financed by local taxes or by transfer of payments or loans from the provinces and the national government. With the establishment of the People's Republic of China (PRC), "consumer" or "parasitic" cities that had developed under capitalism (and imperialism) needed to be transformed into "socialist" and "productive" cities, and were planned accordingly. City and regional planning therefore was subsumed under national economic and social objectives.

## INDUSTRIAL PLANNING IN THE 1950s

There was an initial period of reconstruction to basic urban infrastructure after the war, but faced with a hostile international environment exacerbated by the Korean conflict, the new regime welcomed technical advice and financial assistance from the Soviet Union. Soviet-style large-scale industrial and capital-intensive construction projects meant that urban services, regarded as "unproductive" investments, were a lesser priority. In 1952 the Ministry of Construction Engineering with a National City Planning Bureau was established to coordinate comprehensive development plans mandated through the Provisional Law Regulating the City Planning Process. The First Five-Year Plan (FFYP, 1953–1957) initiated 156 key-point projects, over one-third of which were built in the northeast provinces of Liaoning, Jilin, and Heilongjiang to capitalize on their prior industrial capacity and access to natural resources, as well as their proximity to the Soviet Union. Anshan, for example, received 52 percent of the total national investment in steel. Because industry was state-owned and collectivized, housing, schools, clinics, and recreational facilities were provided and subsidized by the state-owned enterprises (SOEs) and directly affected local urban development.

However, no large construction projects were earmarked for the historically advantaged coastal cities (most of them former treaty ports), despite their concentrations of population, industry, and manufacturing that might have allowed for economies of scale. Policies were aimed at restricting the size of great cities, though large cities such as Shanghai were regionalized by annexation of surrounding counties so that excess population could be dispersed to satellite towns. The number of new cities increased, and land-use and infrastructure plans and planning institutions were established in all cities by the end of 1957. That year also marked the advent of the anti-rightist campaign to root out counter-revolutionaries in the party. It was a reaction to the flood of criticism and general dissatisfaction with living conditions that had blossomed during the government-sponsored Hundred Flowers campaign to encourage cadres and intellectuals to express their opinions. In the following year the government announced the Great Leap Forward, a mandated program of industrialization to surpass the West by spatial "evenization" that would eliminate the distinctions between countryside and city and industry and agriculture by means of collectivization. These radical policies led to one of the largest recorded famines in history, resulting in more than thirty million deaths and a massive influx of twenty million rural residents to cities ill-equipped to handle them.

## DEFENSE PLANNING, 1960–1976

After the Sino-Soviet split in 1960, because of the escalation of tensions due to the Cold War and perceived threats to China's security from regional and international actors, China inaugurated a policy of self-reliance. Planning (which was blamed for the failures of the Great Leap Forward) practically ceased from 1960 to 1962, and planners, viewed as technocrats, were "sent down" (*xiafang*) to factories or rural communes to be reeducated through labor to the proper socialist goals of society. Nevertheless, in 1961 to 1964 the government quietly began preparing the "third front" (*sanxian*), a regional policy of relocating and building strategic industrial complexes away from the coastal cities (the "first front"), which were perceived to be under military threat, to the under-urbanized western areas (the "interior" of the FFYP west of the Beijing-Guangzhou railroad). This was reflected in the revised Third Five-Year Plan (1965–1970) and continued until 1976, with almost half of the national capital and national industrial investments made in third-front regions. Stressing economic "self-reliance" in the face of possible war, the central government devolved control to provincial levels of government (or their municipal counterparts) so as to establish relatively independent industrial systems. Although to some extent these shifts did help to eradicate differences between regions and between the countryside and the city, the launching of the ideologically oriented Cultural Revolution (1966–1976) created social and economic havoc. City and regional planning (and the training of planning professionals) ceased, and urban services deteriorated, constituting the "ten lost years."

## THE REFORM PERIOD: 1980s AND BEYOND

The fall of the Gang of Four and Mao Zedong's death brought to a close the radical economic and social policies of the Cultural Revolution. The dramatic shift in national economic policies in December 1978 at the meeting of the Eleventh Central Committee of the Communist Party set in motion key policy changes redefining the role of cities as generators of development (a return to the key-point city concept), creating special economic zones (SEZs), open coastal cities, and three large triangular coastal development zones for experimentation in market economies. These changes were a recognition that foreign trade and investment were powerful development tools.

The official urban policy announced in 1979 was to pursue a spatially balanced development program of controlling the size of large cities and actively promoting the growth of medium and small cities, which was mapped out at the National Conference on City Development in 1980. Two fundamental changes that shaped city and regional planning were the 1988 Constitution, which enshrined various types of ownership, particularly the separation of property ownership from land-use rights, allowing for the privatization of housing and a land market; and the promulgation of the City Planning Act (1990), a statutory framework to guide master planning that permitted cities, as opposed to the central government, to take the lead in regional development. An apt example (and evidence of a shift in the 1979 policy for balanced urban development) was the sanctioning in 1990 of Shanghai's 135-square-mile Pudong New Area project as the linchpin in revitalizing Shanghai proper and anchoring the future development of the entire Yangzi River region. In 2000 the construction of the Yangshan deep-water port (requiring an investment of US$12 billion over twenty years) was sanctioned to enhance the "outward-oriented" economic policies and to ensure Shanghai's regional and national primacy in the face of intercity and interregional economic competition.

## REGIONAL PLANNING FOR THE TWENTY-FIRST CENTURY

By the turn of the twenty-first century, regional economic coordination was being stressed because of the rapid integration of major cities such as Shanghai and Guangzhou with their development zones, and economic restructuring was initiated to overcome the disparity between the rich developed metropolitan core areas and the underdeveloped peripheries. The keys to coordinated regional development included clearly defined roles for different cities in a region based on their competitive advantages, the elimination of redundant major construction projects, integrated transportation links (both domestic and international), cross-border environmental monitoring, and resource and energy sharing. Predicated on interprovincial cooperative agreements, new regional development alliances were struck. Some were deltaic, such as the Yangzi River Delta (YRD) Metropolitan Region (comprised of Shanghai, southern Jiangsu, and eastern and northern Zhejiang Provinces) and the Pearl River Delta Development Zone, which originally was composed of nine municipalities in Guangdong plus Hong Kong and Macau but later expanded to include cooperative agreements with nine provinces—Guangdong, Guangxi, Jiangxi, Guizhou, Sichuan, Yunnan, Fujian, Hainan, and Hunan—and Hong Kong and Macau, and in 2003 was renamed the Pan-Pearl River Delta (PPRD) Regional Cooperation Project. Other regions followed suit. Commencing in 1999, the Beijing–Tianjin–Hebei Area Development Plan (the "Jing-Jin-Ji" megalopolis) addressed the area's lack of economic competiveness (compared to the YRD and PPRD), uneven resource allocation, and poor environmental management due to a lack of coordinated planning in the "capital area." In 2005 the mayors of Shenyang and six cities in Liaoning Province signed an agreement to promote integration, cooperation, and revitalization (that is, the continued reform of state-owned enterprises) in this industrialized region.

Not surprisingly, with the rapid growth and liberalization of the economy, and the magnetism exerted by better living conditions and employment opportunities in the cities, China's urban population increased from 17.9 percent of the total population in 1978 to 43.9 percent in 2004 (China State Statistical Bureau, 2007); it is predicted to rise to 70 percent of the total population in 2050 (Embassy of the People's Republic of China in the United States of America, 2002). Planning a sustainable urban future, and navigating a plethora of local, regional, urban, rural, and public and private interests and aspirations, despite regional alliances and the drive for regional integration, will continue to challenge the state in the era of globalization.

**BIBLIOGRAPHY**

China State Statistical Bureau, *China Urban Statistical Yearbook 2006*. Beijing: Beijing Statistical Press, 2007.

Embassy of the People's Republic of China in the United States of America. Experts: China's Urbanization Rate Tipped to Rise. Ministry of Foreign Affairs of the People's Republic of China. http://www.china-embassy.org/eng/zt/wto/t36952.htm.

Friedmann, John. *China's Urban Transition*. Minneapolis: University of Minnesota Press, 2005.

Kirkby, Richard J. R. *Urbanisation in China: Town and Country in a Developing Economy, 1949–2000 AD*. London and Sydney: Croom Helm, 1985.

Lin, George C. S. *Red Capitalism in South China: Growth and Development of the Pearl River Delta*. Vancouver: University of British Columbia Press, 1997.

MacPherson, Kerrie L. The Head of the Dragon: The Pudong New Area and Shanghai's Urban Development. *Planning Perspectives* 9 (1994): 61–85.

McGee, Terry, George C. S. Lin, Mark Y. L. Wang, et al. *China's Urban Space: Development under Market Socialism*. London: Routledge, 2007.

Naughton, Barry. The Third Front: Defence Industrialization in the Chinese Interior. *China Quarterly* 115 (1988): 351–386.

Naughton, Barry. *Growing Out of the Plan: Chinese Economic Reform, 1978–1993*. Cambridge, U.K.: Cambridge University Press, 1995.

Yeung, Yue-man. *Developing China's West: A Critical Path to Balanced National Development*. Hong Kong: Chinese University Press, 2004.

***Kerrie L. MacPherson***

# CIVIL SOCIETY

Since Thomas Hobbes (1588–1679) introduced the idea of civil society, it has taken on a variety of meanings. In the early twenty-first century, scholars regard it as an ideal type to which no society completely conforms. Thomas Gold defines it as a "realm between society and the state, where associations of autonomous individuals, participating voluntarily, enjoy autonomy to establish themselves, determine their boundaries and membership, administer their own affairs, and engage in relationships with other associations" (1998, p. 164). For Jürgen Habermas, whose work sparked the recent debate on civil society in China, this realm is a "public sphere" in which there is rational public debate on, inter alia, issues of governance. Civil society is often closely associated with democracy, which, by investing sovereignty in society rather than a regime, makes public-sphere organizations autonomous and allows them to criticize and even challenge the state. By these criteria, has China ever had a civil society?

## CIVIL SOCIETY IN PREMODERN CHINA

Some scholars find evidence of a civil society and public sphere since the Ming dynasty (1368–1644) in such social groups as guilds, literary societies, and charity halls (*shantang*), which had wide scopes of operation and elite participation for philanthropy and the construction and maintenance of local infrastructure. However, the autonomy that such groups enjoyed was by default rather than by right, as is demonstrated by their increasingly common occurrence in the post-Taiping period (1850–1864), when the central government was weak. Under dynastic rule, there was no formal separation of state and society, no social contract through which the state governed at the pleasure of the governed, no proprietorship over one's own person or property, and no individual rights (Rowe 1993). Prior to 1902, only officials were permitted to be concerned with national policy. The meanings of *gong* (public) were not consistent with the notion of a public sphere, and although there were strong moral ideas about public life, there were no clear distinctions as to what or whom the public or private included (Chen 2005). Certainly there were public spirit and civic-mindedness in imperial China, but groups engaged in them lacked the necessary permanence or ubiquity to constitute a civil society. Claims that there was a public sphere or a nascent civil society are sustainable only by defining them to fit one's evidence.

## CIVIL SOCIETY IN THE REPUBLICAN PERIOD

Early in Republican China, Western notions of democracy and modernism were introduced, and especially prior to the Anti-Japanese War (1937–1945), the era was marked by social criticism and political protest. Social groups such as local associations; labor unions; chambers of commerce; academies; religious, benevolent, social, artistic, and intellectual associations; and even political movements proliferated. Although people had considerable de facto autonomy, government suppression of critical groups and individuals was also common (Strand 1989). The Nationalist ideology was classic fascism, featuring a strong state and a disciplined population and leaving little if any room for civil society.

## CIVIL SOCIETY IN THE PEOPLE'S REPUBLIC

The history of the People's Republic divides into two periods: from 1949 to 1978 and from 1978 on, the period of reform and opening up. After assuming control of the government, the Leninist party-state quickly set about replacing previously existing voluntary organizations with state corporatist organizations under party tutelage and collectivizing the rural population, in part to weaken kinship-based collectivities. It also established functional groups in which membership was mandated and the entire population enrolled. During the Cultural Revolution (1966–1969) and its aftermath, distinctions between state and society ceased to exist.

The reform period has been characterized by moves toward a market economy, with more private enterprises and a lessening of totalitarian control over the population. Party and government began to be distinguished, and since 1987 mass organizations have been under legal, rather than party, control. Party soft-liners began to extend legal rights and guarantees to individuals and to devolve economic authority, and social organizations sprang up at the grassroots level. The old political models were criticized, local government was strengthened, and law and legal institutions were developed (He 1997). Social groups (*shehui tuanti*) were allowed to organize, but needed sponsorship by an official body to register.

The transformation to a market economy gave social groups a measure of autonomy. The state recognized that an economy increasingly linked to participation in civic life needed a mediating structure able to generate the horizontal bonds necessary for economic efficiency (Brook 1997). As the state gradually weaned many existing social groups from financial support, they had to support themselves through membership fees and so had to provide services valued by members. Moreover, no longer economically dependent on the state, groups felt less obligated simply to do the state's bidding. Finally, the state lacked sufficient police power to control all groups and intervened only when they challenged the state or system.

With relaxation of control of the population, scholars became aware of discussions of civil society elsewhere in the world and began to examine what it was and whether, how, and in what form it might be useful to China. Since Western social sciences had been labeled pseudosciences during the Maoist period, their initial source of information was Karl Marx, so many regarded civil society as standing in opposition to the state—a position later reinforced by events in eastern Europe. Gradually, they discovered other interpretations, creating a variety of views and even several translations of the term (*gongmin shehui*, *shimin shehui*). Some felt that a strong state was needed to steer China through the necessary reforms, so civil society, since it inherently creates conflict, was undesirable. Others had difficulties reconciling the Western model of civil society and a public sphere with China's long history and tradition in which change had never come from an autonomous society confronting the state. A third view was that civil society in the form of secret societies had run rampant over the past two centuries owing to the weakness of the state, and this fact rendered it unable to foster a normal civil society. These views reflected the long and widely held fear of social disorder (*luan*) that disunity could invite.

Yet some scholars held more favorable views of civil society. One model advocates an approach in which the state is subordinate to society, the people are citizens (not "the masses") and are sovereign, and the economy is market-driven. A neoauthoritarian approach calls for a middle-class society, with the people enjoying property rights and economic freedoms but limited political liberties, and with democracy initially limited to the elites until the state feels that it can be extended. A prominent advocate of this approach recommends that China become a "professional society," in which people are rewarded on the basis of merit and contribution (He 1997, pp. 39–41).

Social groups have grown rapidly since the reforms. There was a slowdown in the period between the Tiananmen Square protests of 1989 and Deng Xiaoping's Southern Tour (1992), during which registration requirements were tightened, but this affected mainly social and intellectual groups rather than economic groups.

A frequently debated question on civil society in China is the level of autonomy of groups in the public sphere. Ma (2006) examined autonomy in four economic associations originally organized by the state and compared them with the Wenzhou trade associations, which sprang from grassroots action. The former have some freedom of action but are all regulated to varying degrees. The Geti Laodongzhe Xiehui (Self-Employed Laborers Association) is controlled most tightly and the Wenzhou associations operate more freely, though do nothing to threaten the state. In fact, they value the state because it keeps order in society and the economy, which is good for business. Because the state needs voluntary associations in the economic realm, it is willing to give them a higher level of autonomy than it affords groups that might be critical of state policy or are otherwise seen as potentially disruptive (Zhang 2004).

No reputable scholar claims that China has a full-blown civil society. Frolic argues that China has a "state-led civil society," made up of social organizations that exist between state organs and enterprises to help the state govern. They "co-opt and socialize potentially politically active elements in the population," coordinate and focus activities, especially in the economic arena, and create links between state enterprises and the private sector and between collective and private interests. Furthermore, they "function as surrogates for a state that is devolving control, rather than serving as centers of citizen resistance to a repressive state" (Frolic 1997, pp. 56–57).

He Baogang regards China, which he labels "a semi-civil society," as a work in progress. Constituent associations are often voluntary, but have links to the state through sponsorship, with state personnel serving as patrons or honorary directors. Having officials as prominent members gives the state some control over association activities, but it also gives organizations a direct line of communication into state deliberations, greatly helping them achieve their goals. Because it is nearly impossible for social groups to have legally guaranteed and enforced autonomy under the present regime, this setup is a win-win situation: While it gives the government some control, it also helps the groups survive and develop and creates the possibility to change the state from within (He 1997).

The Internet is an emerging sphere with potential in civil society. For example, it played a positive role in shaping the public debate over the 2003 outbreak of SARS (severe acute respiratory syndrome). However, while the government has promoted the Internet, it also censors it, permitting communication it approves of and shutting down what it does not (Tai 2006).

From a path-dependency perspective (a view which maintains that choices made in the past guide or restrict choices that can be made in the future), given the totalitarian tendencies of the CCP it is unlikely that a full-blown civil society will emerge in China. However, as demonstrated by the thriving democracy and civil society in Taiwan and the strong democracy movement in Hong Kong, culture is malleable and change is possible.

**BIBLIOGRAPHY**

Brook, Timothy. Auto-organization in Chinese Society. In *Civil Society in China*, ed. Timothy Brook and B. Michael Frolic, pp. 19–45. Armonk, NY: M. E. Sharpe, 1997.

Chen Ruoshui. Gongde guannian de chubu tantao: Lishi yuanliu yu lilun jian'gou [A preliminary exploration into the notion of public morality: Historical origins and theoretical construction]. In *Gonggong yishi yu Zhongguo wenhua*, ed. Chen Ruoshui, pp. 3–41. Taibei: Lianjing Chuban Gongsi, 2005.

Frolic, B. Michael. State-Led Civil Society. In *Civil Society in China*, ed. Timothy Brook and B. Michael Frolic, pp. 46–67. Armonk, NY: M. E. Sharpe, 1997.

Gold, Thomas. Bases for Civil Society in Reform China. In *Reconstructing Twentieth-Century China: State Control, Civil Society, and National Identity*, ed. Kjeld Erik Brødsgaard and David Strand, pp. 161–188. Oxford: Clarendon Press, 1998.

He, Baogang. *The Democratic Implications of Civil Society in China*. Hampshire, U.K.: Palgrave Macmillan, 1997.

Ma, Qiusha. *Non-governmental Organizations in Contemporary China: Paving the Way to Civil Society?* London: Routledge, 2006.

Rowe, William T. The Problem of "Civil Society" in Late Imperial China. *Modern China* 19, 2 (1993): 139–157.

Strand, David. *Rickshaw Beijing: City, People, and Politics in the 1920s*. Berkeley: University of California Press, 1989.

Tai, Zixue. *The Internet in China: Cyberspace and Civil Society*. New York: Routledge. 2006.

Zhang Jing. Neighborhood-Level Governance: The Growing Social Foundation of a Public Sphere. In *Governance in China*, ed. Jude Howell, pp. 121–142. Lanham, MD: Rowman and Littlefield, 2004.

***David C. Schak***

# CIVIL WAR, 1946–1949

The end of the eight-year Resistance War in 1945 did not bring to China the longed-for end to warfare. Instead, within the year, China was at war again. This time the country was embroiled in a vicious civil war between the armies of the national government under the Guomindang (GMD) and of the Communist Party (CCP). The bitter animosity between the two went back to at least 1927, when the GMD almost destroyed the CCP. In 1937 the two parties came together in the Second United Front to resist the Japanese invasion, but the alliance soon broke down and the animosity revived.

The civil war was a titanic struggle between massive armed forces, between major leaders (Chiang Kai-shek and Mao Zedong), between ideologies (Sun Yat-sen's Three Principles of the People and Marxism-Leninism), and between classes (the prosperous versus the poor). The stakes could not have been higher. The ferocious fighting ended in 1949 with the victory of the CCP and the flight of the GMD to Taiwan, a victory that shook not only China but the whole of Asia and the world.

In 1945, despite the victory over Japan, morale among the GMD troops and the GMD's civilian supporters was low. Inflation had undermined the GMD's economic position. The GMD's forces were still much larger than the CCP's, at a ratio of about four to one, but the bulk of them were in the south and west, remote from the great cities of the east, Shanghai, Beijing, and Tianjin. The CCP forces were in the north and northwest, closer to the areas previously occupied by the Japanese. The CCP was a far more significant force than anyone could have imagined eight years before. During the war, some of the CCP's guerrilla forces had evolved into regular armies. The CCP controlled great swathes of land in the rural areas of North China. The party had also instilled a tough discipline in its supporters, and the authority of the leader, Mao Zedong, was unquestioned.

Even before the Resistance War (1937–1945) ended, both the GMD and the CCP were girding themselves for war. Each had a foreign ally. The United States supported the GMD, though with some qualms about Chiang Kai-shek's leadership as a result of the Marshall mission (1945–1946), a failed attempt to stave off the conflict. The CCP had limited support from the Soviet Union, whose forces had entered

## NAVAL FACTORS IN THE CHINESE CIVIL WAR

During the Chinese Civil War (1946–1949), Soviet intervention helped the Communists. In particular, the Soviet Union's decision to deny the Nationalist Navy access by sea limited Chiang Kai-shek's forces to a single railway line, making it easier for the Communists to surround and defeat them.

Following the Soviet Union's entry into the war in early August 1945, Soviet ships helped move the Communists to Manchuria by sea, and gave them arms from Japanese stockpiles. Once in Manchuria, the People's Liberation Army (PLA) used the Soviet-controlled railways to move quickly into the metropolitan centers of Shenyang, Changchun, and Harbin.

Soviet control over the Manchurian ports of Lüshun (formerly Port Arthur) and Dalian (formerly Dairen) further denied access to the Nationalist Navy, which had more than eight hundred vessels and forty thousand men by October 1948. According to *The China White Paper*, the Nationalists complained bitterly in November 1948 that the "most fundamental factor in the general deterioration of the military situation was the nonobservance by the Soviet Union of the [August 1945] Sino-Soviet Treaty of Friendship and Alliance" (U.S. Department of State [1949] 1967, p. 287), which had guaranteed them sea access.

PRC authors understate Soviet assistance because it conflicts with Mao's claim that the Chinese Communist Party (CCP) won the civil war unaided. However, archival documents reveal otherwise. In 1958 Nikita Khrushchev reminded Mao: "On the issue of Port Arthur . . . it was advantageous for you that the Soviet Army was in Port Arthur and Manchuria" (CWIHP 2001, pp. 254–255). Without assistance from the Soviet Union, the CCP might have faced a combined land-sea attack from the Nationalist Army and Navy. With Nationalist access to Manchuria virtually cut off by Soviet forces, the PLA could shift to conventional warfare.

### BIBLIOGRAPHY

Cold War International History Project (CWIHP). New Evidence on the Cold War in Asia. *Cold War International History Project Bulletin* 12, 13 (2001): 243–288.

U.S. Department of State. *The China White Paper, August 1949* (originally issued as *United States Relations with China, with Special Reference to the Period 1944–1949*), Vol. 1. Stanford, CA: Stanford University Press, 1967.

***Bruce Elleman***

Manchuria in the last week of the war on the Allied side and had taken the Japanese surrender there.

### THE COURSE OF THE CIVIL WAR

The civil war broke out as General George C. Marshall (1880–1959) left China. The GMD under Chiang Kai-shek decided to fight the first stages of the war in Manchuria, a decision that turned out to be mistaken. Its armies were initially successful in 1946 and 1947, but by the end of 1947 the tide was turning against them. The CCP went on the offensive. The PLA (Peoples' Liberation Army) had units capable of fighting positional warfare, and several brilliant field commanders, notably Lin Biao. In Manchuria, the PLA acquired weapons and trucks left behind by the Japanese (probably with the help of the Soviet armies), which allowed the PLA to operate more rapidly and effectively than before. At the same time, the morale of the soldiers of the GMD armies was draining away. They were mainly southerners, who found the bitter winter in Manchuria overwhelming. The topography of the region—widely separated cities connected by ribbons of railway—made the GMD forces vulnerable to being cut off; all the PLA had to do was blow up railway tracks.

By early 1948, the CCP was in control of Manchuria, and moving strongly into North China, south of the Great Wall, linking up with guerrilla forces that already controlled parts of the rural north. There were major defections of military units from the GMD to the CCP.

In the civilian arena, the GMD was also losing ground. China's bourgeoisie was suffering from the continuing inflation, which even draconian financial measures could not stop. The measures against "collaborators" that accompanied the government return to cities that had been under Japanese occupation were widely seen as carpetbagging by the victims. The alienation of the bourgeoisie was a disaster for the GMD, since this was its natural constituency. It inspired the formation of a new political party, the Democratic Socialist Party founded by Carsun Chang (Zhang Junmai), but the party had little hope in the polarized world of the civil war. Intellectuals had also, by this stage, turned solidly against the GMD, and many were leaning toward the CCP, which was already waging a highly successful campaign to win their support and the support of the bourgeoisie.

The HuaiHai campaign in late 1948 was fought in the critical zone between the Yellow River and the Yangzi River, where civil wars had often been fought in the past. The campaign was a series of huge battles, in which the GMD armies were decisively defeated. This defeat led to the forced resignation of Chiang Kai-shek as president, in early 1949; he was held responsible for the mistaken strategies of the war to date. His departure came too late. The damage of the mistaken strategies early in the civil war was already done, the GMD armies were critically weakened, the GMD leaders had fallen out amongst themselves, and the GMD's civilian support was draining away. By now it was clear that the CCP would win the war.

The CCP's forces rolled south, crossing the Yangzi River in a triumphal show of force in the spring of 1949. The capital city Nanjing fell at the end of April, less than four years after it had been liberated from the Japanese. The second half of 1949 saw a miserable string of defeats for the GMD forces, which soon turned into a rout as GMD forces fled south in disarray. The rout ended with a brief, hopeless stand on the island of Hainan. In the last months of the year, hundreds of thousands of GMD troops were evacuated to Taiwan.

In early 1949 a great exodus from the mainland started. Several million people, supporters of the GMD and others who feared Communism, fled from China, to Taiwan, Hong Kong, and North America. Most Chinese, however, threw in their lot with the CCP, either because they believed in the socialist solution to China's ills, or because they had no choice but to stay.

On October 1, 1949, before the actual fighting had stopped, Mao Zedong announced the foundation of the People's Republic of China.

### THE OUTCOME OF THE CIVIL WAR

The Communist victory changed the face of China and of the world. It thrilled many people in China, who believed that the country had finally "stood up" (i.e., recovered from decades of humiliation). But it horrified others who believed that the "red menace" had spread to one of the largest countries in the world. Everyone else—the majority—was simply confused and uncertain about what the future held.

**SEE ALSO** *Chiang Kai-shek (Jiang Jieshi); China Hands; Communist Party; Mao Zedong.*

### BIBLIOGRAPHY

Chassin, Lionel. *The Communist Conquest of China: History of the Civil War, 1945–1949.* Trans. Timothy Osato and Louis Gelas. Cambridge, MA: Harvard University Press, 1965.

Pepper, Suzanne. *Civil War in China: The Political Struggle, 1945–1949.* 2nd ed. Lanham, MD: Rowman and Littlefield, 1999.

Westad, Odd Arne. *Decisive Encounters: The Chinese Civil War, 1946–1950.* Stanford, CA: Stanford University Press, 2003.

*Diana Lary*

## CIXI, EMPRESS DOWAGER
### *1835–1908*

Cixi, popularly called the empress dowager (her court title), decisively influenced the last half century of Qing rule. Though she lacked the formal legitimacy of an emperor, she ruled indirectly through a network of family relations, court cliques, and loyal officials. Yet her power at court was unstable and often threatened by internal counterforces and foreign interventions. Both great military events of her reign, the Sino-Japanese War of 1894–1895 and the Boxer Uprising of 1900, prove that the empress dowager was not the omnipotent despot frequently described in Chinese and Western literature.

Cixi was born on November 29, 1835, in the Yehenara clan. Her father was a Manchu clerk belonging to the Bordered Blue Banner. Until 1851, when she entered the palace of the newly enthroned Xianfeng emperor (r. 1851–1861) as a low-ranking concubine, her home environment was that of a middle-ranking Qing official. For a Manchu woman in her position, imperial concubinage was a rare opportunity for social and political ascendance. Her rise at court began in 1853, when the emperor promoted her to worthy lady (*guiren*). This meant that she was allowed to enter the inner realm of the palace. Her status was raised to concubine (*bin*) in 1855. After she gave birth to the later Tongzhi emperor (r. 1861–1875) in 1856, she was promoted to honored consort (*guifei*).

### THE EMPRESS DOWAGER

In 1860, at the end of the Second Opium War, British and French allied forces advanced on Beijing. The emperor fled with his imperial family to the Qing summer residence at Chengde, leaving his half brother Yixin (1833–1898), better known as Prince Gong, to negotiate the peace conditions with the foreign powers. Xianfeng died in August 1861. According to his will, the affairs of state were entrusted to a regency of eight leading court dignitaries, either imperial princes, generals, or state councilors. The child emperor's mother, now called Cixi, was confirmed as empress dowager, together with empress Xiaozhen (1837–1881), the senior consort, now named Ci'an. This event launched Cixi on her political career, as the council of regents could not issue imperial commands without her consent. The Xianfeng emperor before his death is said to have entrusted to Xiaozhen a seal that had to be impressed at the beginning of each edict, and to the boy future emperor, still under his mother's control, a seal that had to appear at the end. When the coregents resisted the growing female influence on the throne, the two empresses dowager allied with Prince Gong, who was also in conflict with members of the regency because of his new style of foreign policy. In a coup d'état, the three abolished the coregents. The government now consisted of Prince Gong, bearing the title of prince counselor (*yizheng wang*), and the two empresses dowager, who were described as "listening from behind screens to reports on governmental affairs" (*chuilian tingzheng*).

With the help of trusted provincial officials like Zeng Guofan, Li Hongzhang, and Zuo Zongtang, the three regents defeated the widespread rebellions of the period (the Taiping, Nian, Muslim uprisings). The management of foreign affairs remained in the hands of Prince Gong as head of the Foreign Office (Zongli Yamen; in full, Zongli Geguo Shiwu Yamen),

***Cixi, Empress Dowager with two maids of honor and guard.*** *Mother of the only surviving son born to the Xianfeng Emperor, Cixi, Empress Dowager, positioned herself to assume de facto control of China upon the emperor's death in 1861. Through manipulation of the imperial court via her son and later her nephew, Cixi ruled China for over forty-five years during the last days of the Qing dynasty.* ARCHIVES LAROUSSE, PARIS, FRANCE / THE BRIDGEMAN ART LIBRARY INTERNATIONAL

founded in 1861. He became Cixi's most important adviser and introduced her to state affairs. In 1875, however, the prince distanced himself from her after she violated the dynastic law of succession by placing her nephew, the Guangxu emperor (r. 1875–1908), on the throne, despite his belonging to the same generation as her late son. Cixi continued to dominate Qing politics indirectly from behind the screens. As a woman, she could not ascend the imperial throne and could not achieve such autocratic powers as possessed by the Qing monarchs of the eighteenth century. Her continuous influence in imperial governance was based on skillful maneuvering between the competing factions at court.

## POWER BASE DURING THE GUANGXU REIGN

Cixi's closest confidants included members of the Council of State (Junji Chu), who formed the "faction of the empress dowager" (*houdang*), in opposition to the "faction of the emperor" (*didang*). The Council of State was an advisory institution that was established at the beginning of the eighteenth century and assumed the routine duties of government. This highly confidential group met in a small building between the inner and outer parts of the palace. Like other inner-court agencies, it was exempted from censorate control.

Another important ally was Li Hongzhang, one of the most important representatives of the self-strengthening movement (Ziqiang Yundong). Cixi was fearful of Han Chinese attempts to overthrow the Manchu dynasty and tried to play off leading reform officials, such as Li Hongzhang, against each other instead of concentrating provincial initiatives into a uniform national strategy of modernization.

Even at court, the empress dowager's authority was never beyond challenge. Though eunuchs failed to gain much power under the Qing dynasty, Cixi relied on them to spy on officials and to assist her in maintaining order at court. In 1869, however, she could not prevent the execution of her favorite eunuch An Dehai, a setback to her authority.

After the death of Ci'an in 1881, Cixi became the sole regent of the dynasty. Now she acted simultaneously as the head of the imperial clan and of the Qing state. When Guangxu reached his full legal age in 1887, Cixi continued to "assist" him for two more years. Residing in the new summer palace Yiheyuan, which she had constructed after the Anglo-French forces destroyed the Yuanmingyuan in 1860, Cixi kept control over the Qing government partly through skillful marriage policy, with Guangxu marrying one of her nieces. This enabled her to retire officially in 1889 without losing her influence at court. Every day she was informed about current correspondence. Replacements at the Council of State occurred only with her consent.

## FROM THE FIRST SINO-JAPANESE WAR TO THE BOXER UPRISING

The period from 1894 to 1900 was dominated by the First Sino-Japanese War and the Boxer Uprising. In 1894 the First Sino-Japanese War erupted in consequence of a struggle over Korea, a long time tributary country of the Chinese empire. The Qing army suffered a devastating defeat against the modern Japanese forces. Li Hongzhang's navy was totally destroyed. Japanese troops even advanced into southern Manchuria. The humiliating outcome of this war was that the Qing empire lost its role as a military power in East Asia. When Li Hongzhang was sent to Japan for peace negotiations, Cixi left the official statements to Guangxu to weaken his personal reputation. The defeat reinforced disunity and conflict at the top of the Qing system. The opponents of reform and self-strengthening used the weakened position of Li Hongzhang and other advocates of modernizing to enforce a more conservative line.

The tension between Cixi and Guangxu increased and escalated into an open struggle over reform policy in 1898. The empress dowager demonstrated her undiminished authority in September of that year by suppressing a reform initiative of Kang Youwei and other young officials who had gained the support of Guangxu. Her third coup d'état ended Guangxu's attempts to resist his aunt's interference in government. He was put under house arrest, and the leading reformers of the Hundred Days' Reform were killed or forced to exile. This coup d'état marked the beginning of the third and final period of Cixi's rule.

In the antiforeign Boxer (Yihetuan) movement of 1900, Cixi and her conservative supporters at court found ideal allies, because the Boxers resisted changes in traditional society. Cixi decided to support the Boxers in their fight against increasing foreign penetration. The traditional peasant uprising escalated into an international confrontation. Foreign diplomats in Beijing blamed the empress dowager for the expansion of the Boxers movement over most of northern China. At the same time, they doubted her legitimacy and accepted only Guangxu as head of the Qing government. One of the first global media events, the Boxer Uprising contributed to the negative image of the empress dowager in the West. When the allied forces entered Beijing on August 14, Cixi fled with the emperor from the capital to Xi'an, leaving Li Hongzhang in charge of the peace negotiations with the foreign powers.

## THE LATE QING REFORMS

Only after the conclusion of the Boxer Protocol in September 1901 did the empress dowager decide to return to Beijing. She arrived there in January 1902. During the following years she launched an extensive reform program, known as the "new policy" (*xinzheng*), falling back on the reform proposals of 1898. The Foreign Office was transformed into a modern Foreign Ministry (Waiwu Bu). It and eleven other ministries represented a new central-government apparatus. Cixi dispatched two reform commissions to Japan, Europe, and North America to study foreign political institutions. Though she sought to change autocratic rule into a constitutional state structure, the cabinet of 1906 was still dominated by the Manchu elite, and Cixi in fact never abandoned her old instrument of rule, the Manchu nobility.

To counter growing anti-Manchuism, the traditional prohibition of marriages between Manchu and Han Chinese was lifted. Yet Cixi's most dramatic reform initiative was the abolition of the traditional examination system in 1905, which for centuries tied study of the Confucian classics to a bureaucratic career. All over the empire, modern schools were established in competition with the existing missionary and private schools. For the first time, study abroad was supported by the state. In 1906 over 12,000 Chinese students lived in Japan.

The creation of chambers of commerce encouraged economic cooperation with foreign countries. To modernize the army, military academies and a military training system were established. Cixi's important contribution to developing China into a modern state during the last years of her life remained unrecognized for decades. Her continuing influence at court until her death is demonstrated by her personally naming the next emperor when Guangxu died on November 8, 1908, one day before her own death.

### RETROSPECT

Throughout her life at court, Cixi secured her preponderant influence in Qing governance with the help of allies from three different power bases. First, she relied on members of the imperial clan, like Prince Gong, who mediated between the empress dowager and the Han Chinese official elite. After his dismissal in 1884, Cixi divided his tasks among three other princes: Prince Chun, the father of the Guangxu emperor, who rose to the position of consultant on national affairs; Prince Qing, who was appointed head of the Foreign Office; and Prince Li, who was entrusted with the Council of State. Second, Cixi's actions were backed by military power. Ronglu, who had grown up with her, commanded the banner troops in the capital and assisted Cixi whenever she needed the authority of the gun. Third, the empress dowager could also count on high Han Chinese officials like Li Hongzhang, who served her on the international stage and repeatedly stood the test in critical missions. After military defeats, Li negotiated the peace settlements with France (1884), Japan (1895), and the Eight Power Alliance in the aftermath of the Boxer War (1901). In 1896 Cixi sent him on a journey around the world to meet monarchs and statesmen and to gain an international reputation for Qing China. In her last years she increasingly turned to Zhang Zhidong and Yuan Shikai.

Cixi was respectfully called Old Buddha (Lao Foye) at court. This name aptly characterized her position. Though the empress dowager emitted authority, she was not formally legitimized to rule the empire. For decades she directed decisions at court through a network of her confidants. In 1910 the journalist J. O. P. Bland and the scholar Edmund Backhouse, in their book *China under the Empress Dowager*, created the myth of Cixi as an irresponsible despot. Though it was later revealed that some of their source material was spurious, their portrait decisively shaped the Western image of Cixi for a long time. In the negative judgment of Chinese authors, still prevalent today, Cixi is even blamed for the decline of the Qing state in general. In the search for reasons explaining China's failure to develop into a constitutional monarchy and to come to terms with the West, Cixi, with her formally dubious status at court, is an ideal scapegoat. A balanced biography remains to be written.

**SEE ALSO** *Boxer Uprising; Emperors, 1800–1912; Hundred Days' Reform; Li Hongzhang; Qing Restoration.*

**BIBLIOGRAPHY**

Ding Richu. Dowager Empress Cixi and Toshimichi: A Comparative Study of Modernization in China and Japan. In *China's Quest for Modernization: A Historical Perspective*, ed. Frederic Wakeman Jr. and Wang Xi, 175–190. Berkeley, CA: Institute of East Asian Studies, University of California, 1997.

Liu Qi, ed. *Cixi shengping* [The life of Cixi]. Beijing: Zhongguo Shehui Chubanshe, 2005.

Zuo Buqing, ed. *Qingdai huangdi zhuanlüe* [Short biographies of the Qing emperors]. Beijing: Zijincheng Chubanshe, 1991.

Zuo Shu'e. *Cixi taihou* [Empress Dowager Cixi]. Changchun, China: Jilin Wenshu Chubanshe, 1993.

***Sabine Dabringhaus***

# CLASSICAL SCHOLARSHIP AND INTELLECTUAL DEBATES

*This entry contains the following:*



## 1800–1864

Those who have evaluated Chinese intellectual history have commonly blamed Confucian scholars of the Qing dynasty (1644–1912) for creating a climate of effete textual criticism. Such accounts, for the most part, deny that Qing Confucians were concerned with larger social and political issues and overlook the significance of their discoveries. The general view is that Confucianism since the Song dynasty (960–1279), that is, Neo-Confucianism, was a synchronic set of classical concepts tied to Song interpretations. Although it showed signs of change (or "unfolding" as the conventional wisdom has it), the Confucian orthodoxy during the Qing period, according to this view, was essentially a reworking of themes and concepts set in place originally by Zhu Xi (1130–1200) and Wang Yangming (1472–1529).

Yet in the early nineteenth century, Fang Dongshu (1772–1851), an advocate of the Cheng Yi (1033–1107) and Zhu Xi orthodoxy known as Song Learning, condemned in ringing fashion the antiquarian currents of the Qianlong (1736–1796) and Jiaqing (1796–1820) reign periods known as Han Learning:

> The Han Learning scholars all have evidence to back up every statement and research to support every word. However, they are only debating on paper with the ancients over glosses, phonetic elements [in Chinese characters], scholia, and textual corruptions. They adduce from various books ancillary evidence by the hundreds and thousands of items. Yet, if they were to apply to themselves their attitudes and activities, or extend them to the people and the country, it would be of no benefit whatsoever.

From the point of view of the twentieth-century Neo-Confucian revival, the Qing dynasty evidential-research movement (*kaozheng xue*) represented a break with the ethical values and humanistic ideals of imperial orthodoxy. From another perspective, however, this seeming betrayal of the Confucian philosophical tradition by Qing philologists can be turned inside out. Imperial orthodoxy, by the late Ming dynasty, had degenerated into a debilitating formalism dedicated to enhance the prestige and power of autocratic rulers, as first described by Huang Zongxi (1610–1695):

> In antiquity, the people of the realm loved and supported their ruler. They compared him to their father. They emulated him as they do heaven and could not go far enough to demonstrate their sincerity. Today, the people of the realm harbor nothing but hatred for their ruler. They view him as an enemy.... Can it be that the greatness of the realm, with all its millions of people and myriads of lineages, is to be enjoyed privately by one man, by one lineage?

Dai Zhen (1724–1777), polymath and philosopher, continued, from a historical perspective, Huang's exposé. Using the text of *Mencius* as a foil to criticize the creeping autocracy since Song times, Dai contended that in the final analysis the fundamental problem lay with the ideological nature of Neo-Confucian orthodoxy and its support for an autocratic state that dominated Chinese political culture:

> The high and mighty use *li* [moral principles] to blame the lowly. The old use *li* to blame the young. The exalted use such principles to blame the downtrodden. Even if they are mistaken, [the ruling groups] call [what they have done] proper. If the lowly, the young, and the downtrodden rely on principles to struggle, even if they are right they are labeled rebellious.... Those on top use principles to blame them for their lowly position. For these uncountable throngs of people, their only crime is their lowly position. When a person dies under the law, there are those who pity him. Who pities those who die under [the aegis] of principle?

Later, Fang Dongshu, outraged by Dai's audacious remarks, retorted,

> [To say] that the principles of heaven are not dependable and that one should rely on the emotions and desires of the people, that they should have an outlet and be allowed to follow their desires, implies that *li* [moral ideals] are attained at the expense of *qi* [human desires] and brings disorder to the Way. However, [Dai Zhen] is merely trying to make it difficult for the Cheng-Zhu [school] without realizing that his is the way of great disorder.

In the twentieth century, the impact of Dai Zhen's political critique was acknowledged by radicals such as Zhang Binglin (1868–1936) and Liu Shipei (1884–1919). Before his turn to anarchism in 1907, Liu Shipei admired Dai's criticism of the oppressive aspects of Confucian orthodoxy. Liu agreed with Dai's account of the autocratic aspects of the Cheng-Zhu imperial ideology. Were Qing evidential-research scholars sterile philologists? Did they commit the crime of overturning Confucian ethical values, leaving a moral vacuum in their wake? Or did they challenge an ideology that, since the Song dynasty, provided theoretical support for the increasingly autocratic Confucian imperium?

## STATECRAFT AND NEW TEXT STUDIES

Many scholars circa 1800 felt that the Han Learning attack on Song Learning ignored the theoretical import of the great principles (*dayi*) contained in the classics. The goal of these scholars remained the mastery and execution of concrete studies (*shixue*). In the Yangzi delta entrepôt of Changzhou, scholars called for more comprehensive literati thought, thought that would go beyond the limited textual studies in typical evidential scholarship by stressing the moral principles contained in Confucius's *Spring and Autumn Annals*, one of the Five Classics. In their hands, evidential research was informed by theoretical and ethical issues associated with Han dynasty (206 BCE–220 CE) New Text studies of the classical canon and was not an end in itself. In the Han dynasty, scholars had to reconstruct the books burned by the First Emperor, and they did this by recovering the clerical script (*jinwen*). Hence, studying the new texts was called *jinwen jingxue*, i.e., "New Text Classical studies." New Text Classical studies of the Qing dynasty drew on these origins in order to revive "Han learning."

The Yangzhou scholar-official Ruan Yuan (1764–1849) is a good example of those influenced by these currents of thought. Although his reputation was made in Han Learning, he was influenced by several New Text scholars who were more concerned with moral philosophy, including Liu Fenglu (1776–1829) and Kong Guangsen (1752–1786). Gong Zizhen (1792–1841), a follower of the Changzhou New Text tradition, praised Ruan's talents in the textual fields associated with evidential scholarship, but he also pointed out Ruan's considerable contributions to philosophy and literature. Ruan contended that Qing scholars did heed questions of human nature and the Way emphasized in Song Learning, and did use the principles of Han Learning to apply these questions to practical use. Yet Ruan went on to write:

> To sum up, the Way of the sages is like the house of a teacher. The [study of] primary and derived characters and their glosses is the entrance. If one misses the path, all steps lead away from it. How can one reach the hall and enter the studio? If a student seeks the Way too high and regards with scorn the art of punctuating a text, it is just as if he were a bird soaring into the heavens from the roof of his teacher's magnificent studio. He gets high all right, but then he doesn't get to see what lies between the door and the inner recesses of the room.

Population pressures, accompanied by increases in competition for land, education, and official status, had a debilitating effect on all levels of Chinese society. Changes in the character of the elite and the increasing competition for access of the educated to power and livelihood produced serious social problems. An atmosphere of corruption pervaded the bureaucracy and the countryside. These were also the years when internal rebellions, especially the Jinchuan (1770–76), Wang Lun (1774), White Lotus (1796–1805), and Eight Trigrams (1813) uprisings, put an end to the long period of relative peace since the late seventeenth century. Foreign trade exacerbated these internal dislocations. The deflationary effects of a silver drain brought on by the British opium trade began to force the Qing state into serious economic depression.

The rise of New Text studies and Song Learning was paralleled and in part provoked by an intense moral concern for the state of the dynasty and involvement with its administrative problems in the late eighteenth and early nineteenth centuries. These concerns made themselves felt in an overt attack on the apolitical stance of evidential-research scholars. In response to external and internal problems, scholar-officials such as He Changling (1785–1848) from Hunan began in the early years of the nineteenth century to emphasize proposals for statecraft (*jingshi*) in their attempts to shore up the sagging imperial bureaucracy. In 1821 He began to compile the *Huangchao jingshi wenbian* (Collected writings on statecraft during the Qing dynasty) as an expression of revived interest in practical administration. Such pragmatically oriented scholar-officials believed that they were avoiding both the scholastic philology associated with Han Learning and the empty speculation of Song to Ming orthodoxy. They took as their inspiration early Qing scholars, such as Gu Yanwu (1613–1682) and Huang Zongxi, who, they argued, had not succumbed to the bookish orientation that plagued eighteenth-century scholarship.

Wei Yuan's (1794–1856) and Gong Zizhen's commitment to New Text classicism grew out of their interest in statecraft proposals. Jiangsu statecraft scholars in the early nineteenth century were not members of a scholarly movement but men who, according to James Polachek, "operated mainly within a framework of bureaucratic and political relationships—relationships, that is, which were structured through hierarchical ties contracted in office, and which functioned, at least in part, to promote the personal and career interests of these literati as a discrete group."

New Text classicism was also the outgrowth of two centuries of philological evidence that had been accumulating through painstaking research by Qing evidential-research scholars. The debate between New Text and Old Text learning was reconstructed by relying on philological and historical research. New Text scholarship during the Qing dynasty tried to revive the political activism of the Western Han dynasty (206 BCE–8 CE). The debates between the various schools of evidential research reveal the more reformist intent among the Changzhou New Text scholars. Moreover, New Text philology abetted the reaction against what were considered sterile textual studies and helped to revive an orientation toward statecraft.

Wei Yuan also was dissatisfied with what he considered petty philology. Wei served at one time or another on the administrative staffs of several important provincial officials interested in statecraft. He was thus able to use these influential positions to blend his earlier concerns about statecraft with his later New Text notions of institutional reform. In 1825 He Changling, then financial commissioner of Jiangsu, invited Wei Yuan to become editor of the *Huangchao jingshi wenbian* collection, which became regarded by nineteenth-century scholars as a valuable source for Qing administrative history and an important starting point for the study of efforts to handle the dual problems of domestic unrest and foreign incursion.

Wei Yuan attempted to reverse what he considered the fascination with textual minutiae in evidential research. The ill-conceived debate over Han Learning versus Song Learning, he thought, was no longer relevant to the challenges that faced the Qing state. Writing in 1841, some time after studying with Liu Fenglu, Wei Yuan noted his misgivings about the status of China's elite class: "Since the middle of the Qianlong Emperor's reign, all literati in the empire have promoted Han Learning. This movement is especially popular north and south of the Yangzi River [that is, Jiangnan].... Such a state of affairs has confined the bright and talented of the realm and tempted them onto a useless path." His intent was to initiate bureaucratic and moral reforms within the framework of the existing political structure.

## THE ATTACK ON HAN LEARNING

Nascent statecraft groups emerged in the early nineteenth century in academies in Changsha and Guangzhou, where the administrative problems facing the empire were more evident. The statecraft movement was initially led by literati whose native origins were outside the Yangzi River delta. In the mid-nineteenth century, the Hunan scholar-official Zeng Guofan (1811–1872), a major exponent of "self-strengthening" in the wake of the intrusion of Western military power in East Asia, patronized Song Learning in local and national academics. Guangdong also emerged as a center for statecraft studies.

As the foreign threat in Guangzhou mounted in intensity during the 1820s, the attention of Ruan Yuan (then governor-general) and faculty members of the Xuehai Tang (Sea of Learning Academy) was drawn to foreign affairs and opium trafficking in Southeast China. In 1821 Ruan adopted what seemed at the time a strict policy toward opium, arresting sixteen opium dealers in Macau and temporarily forcing the opium trade out of the Pearl River. Although Ruan's policy marked the end of the first phase of the trade, in reality opium trading continued uninterrupted, and in fact increased at Neilingding (Lintin) Island. The crackdown was a face-saving device for Ruan Yuan, after attention had been directed to the opium problem by the Daoguang emperor (r. 1821–1850). The latter had just ascended the throne in a reformist frame of mind, and the opium problem was one of his chief concerns.

In an 1824 letter to Ruan Yuan, Fang Dongshu made it clear that he blamed the chaotic situation in Guangzhou vis-à-vis foreigners, on the moral passivity and useless erudition that the Han Learning movement had fostered throughout China. Having personally perceived the effects of opium policies in the 1820s, Fang Dongshu recommended in the 1830s that Ruan's failed policies be rescinded. Han Learning had shown itself to be morally bankrupt, according to Fang. He became associated in the 1830s with calls for the complete eradication of the opium evil. In Guangzhou, the teachers and students at the Yuehua Academy were the leaders of the anti-opium movement.

In a famous memorial of 1836, Xu Naiji (1777–1839) recommended legalizing opium for all except civil servants, scholars, and soldiers, and this was connected with the proposal by a number of directors at the Xuehai Tang that opium restrictions be relaxed. Ruan Yuan himself leaned toward legalizing the trade. These apparent capitulations angered Fang and others in Guangzhou who took a hard line on the opium question. It was no accident that when Lin Zexu (1785–1850), charged by the emperor with the task of eradicating the opium evil, took office in Guangzhou, he established his headquarters at the Yuehua Academy, where hardliners were in the majority.

The Legalizers versus the Moralists in the Guangzhou opium debate reflected in many ways the widening rift between Han Learning and Song Learning. Looking back on the Opium War, Fang wrote in the summer of 1842:

> In my considered opinion on the basis of close observation, the disaster at the hands of the English foreigners was not the result of the recent policy of total prohibition and confiscation of opium. In fact, [the disaster] resulted because of the rapacious and corrupt behavior of the foolish foreign merchants, the vacillating policies of earlier governors-general [that is, Ruan Yuan] who have cultivated a festering sore, and the greed of Chinese traitors who sold out their country.

## HAN AND SONG LEARNING SYNCRETISM

Advocates of Song Learning were not purists, however. Their methods of reasoning and manner of exposition had been heavily influenced by evidential research. Attempts to reassert the Cheng-Zhu orthodoxy did not entail wholesale rejection of evidential-research scholarship. One important outgrowth of this challenge was the attempt to reconcile Han and Song Learning. Evidential research remained popular, but it was becoming difficult to justify in its own terms. Ruan Yuan's increasing emphasis on philosophical themes in the last decades of his life was indicative of the tension within classical discourse in the nineteenth century.

Guangzhou also became a center for the movement to synthesize Han Learning methods with Song Learning political and moral concerns. In a work titled *Hanru tongyi* (Comprehensive meanings of Han scholars) printed in 1858, Chen Li, who by then was one of the most widely respected literati in Guangzhou, contended that the attack on Han Learning for its lack of theoretical significance was unfair. He outlined the philosophical issues that Han dynasty scholars had discussed. Chen also took the other side of the argument in his collected notebooks, published late in his life. He pointed out that those who criticized Zhu Xi for not emphasizing ancient glosses and etymologies in Han commentaries were equally mistaken. According to Chen, Zhu Xi was as concerned with philology as with philosophy, a line of thought later taken up by the modern scholar Qian Mu in his twentieth century study of Zhu Xi's scholarly contributions.

Zeng Guofan, for example, adopted a conservative position in favor of Zhi Xi Learning in scholarship. Conservative scholarship was now tied to reformist politics. Despite growing dissatisfaction, particularly among Hunan and Guangdong scholars, evidential research was still defended by southern literati until the Taiping Uprising (1851–1864). In the nineteenth century, the defense of evidential research by political reformers such as Zhang Zhidong (1837–1909) and others was argued less and less in terms of the utility of an apolitical discourse in the "search for the truth in actual facts" and more in terms of statecraft goals and concerns.

Late Qing intellectual history was severely affected by the conflict between the Taiping and imperial forces. The lower Yangzi's leading cities such as Nanjing, Suzhou, Changzhou, and Yangzhou were devastated. Their libraries and institutions of learning were destroyed. After the rebellion was suppressed, the evidential-research academic community of the Yangzi River delta largely perished, and this cleared the way for the emergence of Hunan and Guangdong gentry as the leading spokesmen for literati interests. The rise to power of such Hunan men as Zeng Guofan, Zuo Zongtang (1812–1885), and Hu Linyi (1812–1861) was thus made possible by the Taiping Uprising.

**SEE ALSO** *Taiping Uprising; Wei Yuan.*

**BIBLIOGRAPHY**


Bastid, Marianne. *Educational Reform in Early Twentieth-Century China.* Trans. Paul J. Bailey. Ann Arbor: Center for Chinese Studies, University of Michigan, 1988.

Borthwick, Sally. *Education and Social Change in China: The Beginnings of the Modern Era.* Stanford, CA: Hoover Institution Press, 1983.

Elman, Benjamin. *Classicism, Politics, and Kinship: The Ch'ang-chou School of New Text Confucianism in Late Imperial China.* Berkeley: University of California Press, 1990.

Elman, Benjamin. *From Philosophy to Philology: Social and Intellectual Aspects of Change in Late Imperial China.* 2nd, rev. ed. UCLA Asian Pacific Monograph Series. Los Angeles: University of California at Los Angeles, 2001.

Elman, Benjamin, and Alexander Woodside, eds. *Education and Society in Late Imperial China, 1600–1900.* Berkeley: University of California Press, 1994.

Keenan, Barry. *Imperial China's Last Classical Academies: Social Change in the Lower Yangzi, 1864–1911.* Berkeley: Institute of East Asian Studies, University of California at Berkeley, 1994.

Polachek, James. *The Inner Opium War.* Cambridge, MA: Council on East Asian Studies, Harvard University, 1992.

Rawski, Evelyn. *Education and Popular Literacy in Qing China.* Ann Arbor: Center for Chinese Studies, University of Michigan, 1979.

Rowe, William. *Saving the World: Chen Hongmou and Elite Consciousness in Eighteenth-Century China.* Stanford, CA: Stanford University Press, 2001.


***Benjamin A. Elman***

## 1864–1900

From the 1860s to the early twentieth century, there were several remarkable changes in classical scholarship in Qing China. Arguably, these changes irrevocably reoriented the Chinese attitude toward the time-honored Confucian tradition, and their cultural heritage in general vis-à-vis modern Western learning. The causes of the changes were both external and internal. Although the Qing, aided by the militia forces organized by local Chinese gentry from southern provinces, defeated the Taiping rebels, its rulers could not restore the traditional political order without reckoning the military and cultural infiltration from the West. As the regime looked for new ways to work with the Western powers diplomatically, the Chinese literati also sought ways by which they could accommodate Western influence rather than reject it outright. This gave rise to several new trends in classical scholarship. One developed new theories for reinterpreting the Confucian tradition in order to better address the problems facing China at the time. The revival of the New Text school (*Jinwen jingxue*) in Confucian learning from the Later Han period (25–220) was a notable example. Another trend expanded the scope of study by looking for useful intellectual resources in the Hundred schools (*zhuzi*), schools of thought that flourished in the age of Confucius but did not fall within the bounds of Confucianism. Neither interest was entirely new but built on or modified previous scholarly traditions. With respect to the study of the Hundred schools, in the eighteenth century some evidential scholars had already examined, out of their philological interest in textual criticism, several works by Confucius' contemporaries for verifying and validating the Confucian classics. In the nineteenth century excellent philological studies of ancient texts, including those of the Hundred schools, continued to be produced by eminent evidential scholars such as Yu Yue (1821–1907) and Sun Yirang (1848–1908).

### THE NEW AND OLD TEXT SCHOOLS

Nevertheless, as an intellectual trend, evidential learning unequivocally declined from the 1820s, owing largely to the changing cultural milieu that encouraged a new outlook on the Confucian tradition as a useful resource for solving the pressing issues associated with the Western intrusion. This new outlook was best embodied by the New Text school, which held that if *Chunqiu* (*Spring and Autumn Annals*) was the key to fathoming the Confucian teaching of the classics, then the *Gongyang zhuan* (*Gongyang Commentary*)—instead of the *Zuo Zhuan* (*Zuo Commentary*) favored by the Old Text school (Guwen jingxue) as well as by most evidential scholars—offered the best tool to unpack the enigmatic message Confucius supposedly embedded in editing the *Chunqiu*. In addition, the New Text Confucians challenged the authenticity of some Confucian texts, particularly certain chapters of the *Shangshu* (*Classic of History*) written in a pre-Han script that allegedly were found in Confucius' residence during the Later Han.

What differentiated the New and Old Text schools most was their interpretations of Confucius' role in ancient China. Whereas the Old Text school viewed Confucius as a transmitter of the cultural heritage before him, the New Text school considered him more a creator who injected new ideas into the inherited traditions. Like the study of the Hundred schools, the reemergence of the New Text school, which had been dormant after the Han's fall, occurred before the mid-nineteenth century, thanks to the scholars of the Changzhou school such as Zhuang Cunyu (1719–1789) and Liu Fenglu (1776–1829). But it flourished in the later part of the century, as shown in the influential and at times controversial works of Pi Xirui (1850–1908), Liao Ping (1852–1932), and Kang Youwei (1858–1927).

The increase in interest in the Hundred schools and the resurgence of the New Text school both gained currency because of the augmented Western presence in China in the period. Many studies of the Hundred schools that appeared in the time, for example, argued that modern Western learning actually originated in ancient China, in the schools of thought that rivaled Confucian teaching, such as Moism and Daoism. This observation, though obviously false, provided a new and different motivation for the scholars to analyze carefully the content and relevance of the Hundred schools, and in their own right. This approach departed from the evidential tradition that had more or less treated their study as only supplementary to that of the Confucian classics.

## NEO-CONFUCIANISM AND THE TI-YONG DICHOTOMY

The rivalry between the New and Old Text schools extended, to some degree, the debate between neo-Confucianism and evidential learning, or between the so-called Song Learning (*Songxue*) and Han Learning (*Hanxue*), from the previous century. Yet in the face of cultural incursions from the West, there were also efforts to mediate the two in order to shore up the Confucian tradition as a whole. The 1851 outbreak of the Taiping Uprising, which had served as a strong reminder of increasing Western influence, provided an important incentive for neo-Confucians such as Zeng Guofan (1811–1872) to seek a way of transcending the divide. Although he was a neo-Confucian, Zeng maintained that the research conducted by Qing evidential scholars on the rituals of ancient China was quite useful and relevant to help restore the Confucian sociopolitical order undermined by the Taiping rebels as well as by the Western invasion. Yet, the best cure for political corruption in government and moral decline in society, he contended, came from the teaching of neo-Confucianism. Zeng thus reiterated the need of mind-tempering, character building, and moral cultivation through quiet-sitting and meditation in order to strengthen and solidify the "substance/foundation" (*ti*) so that "practical knowledge" (*yong*), which included advanced military weaponry and techniques from the West, could be better absorbed and applied.

This idea of the *ti-yong* relationship became prevalent in the "Foreign Matters movement" (*Yangwu Yundong*) during the era of Self-strengthening (1861–1895), or the Qing restoration, which was characterized by the attempt to obtain more knowledge about the West and import more modern technology and industry into the country. The *ti-yong* idea also found its best expression in the writings of Zhang Zhidong (1837–1909), who, though much younger than Zeng, became one of the four most prominent officials along with Zeng in the late Qing. The other two were Li Hongzhang (1823–1901) and Zuo Zongtang (1812–1885), who, like Zeng, established their early careers by suppressing the Taiping rebels and later played equally important roles in the Self-strengthening movement.

## KANG YOUWEI AND CONFUCIUS AS REFORMER

After the Foreign Matters movement came to an abrupt end during the Sino-Japanese War of 1894 to 1895, a sense of national crisis permeated the entire country but was felt most acutely by the members of the literati. The crisis generated more interest in pursuing the radical reforms already called for by Kang Youwei and his disciples such as Liang Qichao (1873–1929) and his followers such as Tan Sitong (1865–1898). Having traveled in 1879 to Hong Kong and in 1882 to Shanghai, where he witnessed first-hand the impact of Western civilization and purchased books translated by the Jiangnan Arsenal and the missionary press, Kang Youwei had developed a critical attitude toward the neo-Confucian practice advocated by Zeng Guofan and his associates. Kang believed that though moral cultivation and character building were important, their significance paled in comparison with developing new ideas in "statecraft learning" (*jingshi zhixue*), which were urgently needed for launching political and institutional reform and coping with the modern woes haunting China at the time.

From 1891 to 1898 Kang preached his ideas by admitting students into the Wanmu Caotang (literally, "thatched hall by ten thousand trees"), a school he founded in Guangzhou. During the same period, inspired by the work of Liao Ping, he published two controversial works: *Xinxue weijing kao* (Liu Xin's falsification of classics) and *Kongzi gaizhi kao* (Confucius as reformer). Drawing on the tradition of New Text Confucianism, Kang challenged the validity of the Confucian texts used by the Old Text school. More importantly, he refuted the conservative image of Confucius portrayed by the Old Text school and accepted by many scholars in the past, and recast Confucius as a creative and committed reformer who advocated constant adjustment to the change of time, an idea Kang himself championed at the time.

In light of the Qing's shattering defeat by Japan in the war, Kang Youwei's reform idea quickly gained sway among certain elements at Qing court and in intellectual circles. To bolster his argument, Kang produced pamphlets that sketched the reform experiences in Japan and elsewhere, urging the Qing to follow suit. These writings, together with the translations of Western social writings by Yan Fu (1854–1921), a student returned from England and an exponent of social Darwinism, played a crucial role in changing the Chinese worldview. Intellectuals came to realize China's weakened position and backward status in the world in comparison with the rising West and newly modernized Japan. Around the same time, Kang also produced a seminal text—*Datongshu* (On grand unity)—which depicts, among other things, an upcoming utopia in the world, following the evolutionary scheme of historical movement Confucius supposedly had anticipated some two millennia earlier. The work perhaps was intended to point to the bright future Kang envisioned if the country accepted his reform. However, this remained quite illusory at the time because the reform, though embraced by Emperor Guangxu (r. 1875–1908), lasted only 103 days in 1898. It was put down by the conservative faction at court; the same faction later was also blamed for the dynasty's shameful defeat at the hands of Western powers in the wake of the Boxer Uprising of 1900.

**SEE ALSO** *Classical Scholarship and Intellectual Debates: 1800–1864; Kang Youwei; Liang Qichao; Qing Restoration; Yan Fu; Zeng Guofan; Zhang Zhidong.*

**BIBLIOGRAPHY**

PRIMARY WORKS

Kang Youwei. *Kang Youwei quanji* [Complete works of Kang Youwei]. Beijing: Zhongguo renmin daxue chubanshe, 2007.

Liang Qichao (Ch'i-ch'ao). *Intellectual Trends in the Ch'ing Period.* Trans. Immanuel C. Y. Hsu. Cambridge, MA: Harvard University Press, 1959.

Liao Ping. *Jinguxue kao* [A study of New and Old Text learning]. Shanghai: Shanghai guji chubanshe, 1999.

Pi Xirui. *Jingxue lishi* [A history of classical study]. Shanghai: Shanghai shudian, 1996.

Zeng Guofan. *Zeng Guofan wenji* [Zeng Guofan's essays]. Beijing: Jiuzhou tushu chuban gongsi, 1997.

SECONDARY WORKS

Chang, Hao. *Chinese Intellectuals in Crisis: Search for Order and Meaning, 1890–1911.* Berkeley: University of California Press, 1987.

Elman, Benjamin A. *Classicism, Politics, and Kinship: The Ch'ang-chou School of New Text Confucianism in Late Imperial China.* Berkeley: University of California Press, 1990.

Liang Qichao. *Zhongguo jin sanbainian xueshushi* [A Chinese intellectual history of the past three centuries]. Beijing: Zhongguo shudian, 1985.

Luo Jianqiu. *Jindai zhuzixue yu wenhua sichao* [The study of the hundred schools and the modern intellectual trends]. Beijing: Zhongguo shehui kexue chubanshe, 1998.

Qian Mu. *Zhongguo jin sanbainian xueshushi* [A Chinese intellectual history of the past three centuries]. 2 vols. Beijing: Zhonghua shuju, 1986.

Tang Zhijun. *Jindai jingxue yu zhengzhi* [Modern classical studies and politics]. Beijing: Zhonghua shuju, 2000.

*Q. Edward Wang*

## INTELLECTUALS, 1900–1949

The Chinese term *zhishi fenzi* (knowledgeable elements) was first used in the 1920s to distinguish intellectuals from the traditional literati (*shi*, or scholar-officials) of imperial times. *Zhishi fenzi* referred to those who had received a certain level of education and who had a profession and a certain amount of cultural and scientific knowledge combined with an interest in arts and literature. The category of intellectuals included persons of letters, as well as engineers, doctors, editors, journalists, administrators, and the like. A narrower definition viewed intellectuals as elites who were not only well-educated but reflective and who devoted a significant portion of their energies to analyzing the problems of China and to finding solutions. What's more, intellectuals inquired about the human condition beyond themselves and the immediate situation of everyday life, and they expressed their ideas through words and writings, communicating and engaging with fellow intellectuals.

In a more specific sense, Chinese intellectuals saw themselves as the conscience of society, with a sense of social responsibility. They were cultural creators, critical thinkers, opinion leaders, moral renovators, and political actors who saw social problems as moral issues and who provided role models for ordinary people. As China entered the twentieth century, intellectuals embarked on a historic mission to save the nation from external invasion and internal decay, convinced that they were destined to play the leadership role in their country's modern transformation.

### EDUCATIONAL ORIGINS

A significant number of modern intellectuals had an educational grounding in classical learning. Their transition from literati to modern intellectuals began in the late nineteenth century, when some scholar-officials questioned the basic premises of Confucianism and its concepts of social order. The transition gathered pace following the abolition in 1905 of the civil service exams, which removed much of the premium on classical studies. In the following years, a new education system was instituted, which adopted curriculums combining modern languages, science, and history with the study of Chinese classics. Modern schools and academies were established in many parts of the country, producing a new generation of educated Chinese with a progressive outlook.

A parallel trend emerged in the treaty ports, also in the last decades of the nineteenth century, involving initially a much smaller number of individuals who had undergone a nontraditional educational experience. Some attended missionary schools. Others enrolled in government academies associated with arsenals and naval dockyards. Still others acquired new knowledge and a modern outlook through exposure to a modern treaty-port environment, especially Shanghai, with its business enterprises, study societies, newspapers, journals, and magazines, as well as church-supported and secular reading rooms.

Women, too, had the opportunity to receive a modern education, first in missionary schools in the late nineteenth century, then increasingly in indigenous schools from the early twentieth century onward. Finding themselves in a new environment, they sought gender equality and women's rights, especially during and in the wake of the May Fourth movement. The famous writer of this period, Ding Ling (1904–1986), subverted male-centered desires by boldly writing about female sexuality and about the torment of liberated Chinese women who struggled against the contradictory claims of political rights and modern theories that made women less than men by nature. Her novel *Miss Sophie's Diary* (1928) is a powerful feminist critique of male ideology. Other writers, such as Bai Wei (1894–1987), Xie Bingying (1906–2000), Shi Pingmei (1902–1928), and Xiao Hong (1911–1942), also contributed to the feminist movement by focusing on things that they desired as women rather than as fellow travelers of revolutionaries.

Increasing numbers of Chinese were educated overseas, some on scholarships and some self-funded, with many topping their early traditional education with a modern one received in Japan, Europe, or the United States. This continued a trend begun in the last quarter of the nineteenth century with government-sponsored and other study-abroad programs. Prominent among those who went abroad was Yan Fu (1854–1921), who attended the Royal Naval College in Greenwich, England, from 1877 to 1879, after studying in the Fuzhou Arsenal Academy. Yan was well-known for introducing Western liberal thought into China through his translations of a number of important British political and sociological works. Back home, returned students played significant cultural, intellectual, and political roles in a changing society. Many leaders of the 1911 revolution and later of the Chinese Communist movement were returned students. The products of a new age, the new intellectuals were exposed to a range of foreign ideas from liberalism to democracy to capitalism to social Darwinism to Marxism, all of which they learned and compressed within a short period of time. The result was intellectual diversity and experimentation amid political uncertainties.

## INTELLECTUAL ORIENTATIONS

As China was transformed from empire to nation-state, educated elites faced an identity crisis that was at once political, cultural, intellectual, philosophical, religious, and psychological. Not only was it necessary to forge a new citizenship, as the reformer Liang Qichao (1873–1929) maintained, but the cultural relations of East and West had to be reappraised. Chinese culture was in need of renewal and creative transformation so that it could meet the challenges of the twentieth century and make a contribution to world civilization. Those who had no faith in Chinese culture being capable of self-renewal became cultural radicals advocating total Westernization. Yet, paradoxically, many were steeped in the tradition that they assaulted. Cultural conservatives, on the other hand, came to its defense with a mindset that was more future-oriented than inward-looking, for many of them, too, had received a modern education, such as the Harvard-trained Critical Review Group (Xuehengpai).

The intellectual community was made up of diverse elements: zealous Westernizers, cultural conservatives, New Confucians, liberals, democrats, anarchists, Marxists, and socialists. Many held liberal, conservative, and socialist ideas simultaneously or at different times; nationalistic, they were concerned about China's myriad problems and articulated rival ideas of saving the nation (*jiuguo*). Some promoted cultural, intellectual change prior to political reform; others sought both simultaneously; still others viewed political change as a higher priority.

Politically, after 1920 the intelligentsia split into reformers and revolutionaries, with the former favoring gradual, piecemeal change and the latter committed to social revolution. Revolutionary intellectuals gravitated to the Chinese Communist Party, whose leaders themselves were intellectuals, while those of a liberal persuasion opposed class struggle, proletarian dictatorship, political tutelage, and one-party rule. They sought democratic change, constitutional government, human rights, and rule of law. Economically, the dominant view was that, as China was underdeveloped and extremely poor, capitalist forms of production must be adopted to create wealth and thereby to lift the population out of poverty. At the same time, there was anxiety to prevent the social and economic equalities that capitalism would bring in its wake. Many saw socialism as the ultimate goal that was compatible with the ancient Chinese ideal of *datong* (the great commonwealth and universal harmony).

## INTELLECTUALS AND THE STATE

Modern intellectuals were no longer linked to state power in the way that the literati had been. As their social and political roles expanded, not all of them sought positions in officialdom; actually, many developed careers outside the establishment, earning their livings as university professors, college teachers, newspaper and journal editors, writers, publishers, artists, and professionals. Many were historians, philosophers, political scientists, and literary critics. Prominent among those in the early decades of the Republican period were Hu Shi (1891–1962), Chen Duxiu (1879–1942), Li Dazhao (1888–1927), and Lu Xun (Zhou Shuren, 1881–1936), to mention just a few, who were on the faculty of Beijing University and whose influence was felt in a variety of ways. New opportunities for extrabureaucratic employment in a variety of fields served to weaken the traditional link between scholarship and officialdom.

Nonetheless, there was no lack of educated elites recruited into the government of the day, including regional military regimes. The first cabinet of the Republic was composed of some of the country's best talents, notably Premier Tang Shaoyi (1860–1938), Foreign Minister Lu Zhengxiang (1871–1949), Minister of Communications Shi Zhaoji (1877–1958), Minister of Education Cai Yuanpei (1867–1940), Minister of Justice Wang Chonghui (1881–1958), Minister of Agriculture and Forestry Song Jiaoren (1882–1913), and Minister of Finance Xiong Xiling (1870–1937). Others also served successive military-dominated governments in various capacities. Hu Shi, though never wanting to be a member of government, maintained ties with some ministers and bureaucrats in order to influence government policy from the outside. He also hoped to work with the progressive, reformist warlord Wu Peifu (1874–1939). Similarly, the Nationalist government in the Nanjing decade (1928–1937) boasted of a large proportion of its members being highly educated, many with Western degrees, such as the diplomatic historian Jiang Tingfu (1895–1965), the educationalist Jiang Menglin (1886–1964), the historian Fu Sinian (1896–1950), the geologist Weng Wenhao (1889–1971), and the banker and financier Song Ziwen (T. V. Soong, 1894–1971). Hu Shi chose to remain a government critic, but in 1938, driven by patriotism, he accepted Chiang Kai-shek's (Jiang Jieshi's) appointment as Chinese ambassador to the United States in an effort to win American support for the war against Japan.

There were many activist intellectuals who sought to change the prevailing sociopolitical order, who were critical of both the Communists and the Nationalist party-state, and who engaged in organized activities, forming minor political parties and groups that were outlawed until 1936. Some had no qualms about joining recalcitrant warlords in opposing the dictatorship of Chiang Kai-shek. The state socialist leader Zhang Junmai (Carsun Chang, 1887–1969), for example, attempted to ally with the Shanxi warlord Yan Xishan (1883–1960) and the Guangxi strongman Li Zongren (1890–1969) in order to help develop these provinces, while supporting the government's anti-Japanese war efforts. Others chose not to be politically involved. The distinguished historian Chen Yinke (1890–1969), for instance, was happy to engage in scholarly pursuits as long as academic freedom and freedoms of thought and expression were allowed. Still others were politically engaged but later withdrew to academe, such as the vocational-education leader Huang Yanpei (1878–1965).

The renewal of civil war after 1945 further split the intellectuals into pro- and anti-Communists. Disaffected by the corrupt, repressive Nationalist government, many in the liberal camp sympathized with the Communist movement. Although they were under no illusion that political life under Communist rule would be more comfortable, they were hoping that the new regime would be better able to solve China's problems. Others had no faith in the Communists, fleeing the mainland in 1949 to seek asylum in Taiwan, Hong Kong, and the West.

**SEE ALSO** *Chen Duxiu.*

**BIBLIOGRAPHY**

Feng Zhaoji (Edmund S. K. Fung). *In Search of Chinese Democracy: Civil Opposition in Nationalist China, 1929–1949.* New York: Cambridge University Press, 2000.

Goldman, Merle, and Li Oufan (Leo Ou-fan Lee), eds. *An Intellectual History of Modern China.* Cambridge, U.K.: Cambridge University Press, 2000.

Grieder, Jerome. *Hu Shih and the Chinese Renaissance: Liberalism in the Chinese Revolution, 1917–1937.* Cambridge, MA: Harvard University Press, 1970.

Grieder, Jerome. *Intellectuals and the State in Modern China: A Narrative History.* New York: Free Press, 1981.

Hao Zhidong. *Intellectuals at a Crossroads: The Changing Politics of China's Knowledge Workers.* Albany: State University of New York Press, 2003.

Ip Hung-yok. *Intellectuals in Revolutionary China, 1921–1949: Leaders, Heroes, and Sophisticates.* London: RoutledgeCurzon, 2005.

Schwartz, Benjamin. *In Search of Wealth and Power: Yen Fu and the West.* Cambridge, MA: Harvard University Press, 1964.

Ye Wenxin (Yeh Wen-hsin). *The Alienated Academy: Culture and Politics in Republican China, 1919–1937.* Cambridge, MA: Council on East Asian Studies, Harvard University, 1990.

Zhang Hao (Chang Hao). *Chinese Intellectuals in Crisis: Search for Order and Meaning (1890–1911).* Berkeley: University of California Press, 1987.

***Edmund S. K. Fung (Feng Zhaoji)***

## DEBATES, 1900–1949

The first half of the twentieth century was a time of intellectual turbulence to match the political uncertainties of the period. It was also a time of intellectual experimentation, largely free of the burden of governing dogma. By the 1900s, in the aftermath of the Boxer Uprising, the institutions and philosophy of imperial Confucianism had been thoroughly discredited. Thereafter the search for new sources of authority, both political and intellectual, went forward in an environment of social crisis and of unprecedented freedom from ideological conformity, until the imposition of Marxist–Leninist–Maoist orthodoxy at mid-century.

In 1905 the Confucian examination system was abolished. That system had been based on a mastery of classical texts and literary styles that for centuries had served to recruit literate talent into the civil bureaucracy, and also had protected the elite status of the gentry class. This act simultaneously destroyed the imperial institution's principal constituency, and rendered superfluous the intellectual class that traditionally had been vocationally committed to public service. For the next several decades an underlying theme of intellectual life would be the effort to endow the intellectuals' role with public significance.

## ANTITRADITIONALISTS AND NATIONALISM

The greatest innovation of the decade preceding the 1911 revolution was a change in the concept of the source of sovereign authority. Liang Qichao, a protégé of Kang Youwei and veteran of the Hundred Days' Reforms of 1898, remained the foremost proponent of a radically modernized constitutional monarchy. But the conspicuous failure of the traditional institutions meant that now for the first time the idea of republicanism attracted a rapidly growing following. How this was to be reflected in institutional ways, however, remained a matter of dispute. Republican forces included both vaguely progressive, Western-oriented spokesmen such as Sun Yat-sen (Sun Yixian) and virulently anti-Manchu, culturally conservative thinkers such as Zhang Binglin (1868–1936). Generally speaking, throughout this period, and indeed beyond mid-century, there was little enthusiasm for the implementation of democratic governing institutions, except as a remote eventual destination. A strong element of elitism dominated political and intellectual discourse, expressed as advocacy of enlightened despotism, or of party dictatorship, or of the guiding role of a "modern" intellectual and bureaucratic elite.

From the turn of the century onward, this combined with an enthusiasm for Darwinism, spurred by Yan Fu's seminal translations of English thinkers such as Thomas Henry Huxley (1825–1895), Herbert Spencer (1820–1903), and J. S. Mill (1806–1873). In the popular mind this idea came down to a simplified belief that the world order is dominated by a struggle that justifies the survival of the fittest. Such an interpretation of China's weakness and vulnerability on the international scene, together with resentment of the recent history of Western imperialist encroachment, created the ardent nationalism that was a major driving force of Chinese politics throughout the twentieth century.

Nationalism of a kind inspired some thinkers who were by temperament and conviction culturally, or even politically, conservative. Zhang Binglin espoused violently anti-Manchu opinions that led him into an uneasy collaboration with republican and radical circles revolving around Sun Yat-sen and Liang Qichao in Tokyo before 1911; he remained, however, adamantly traditionalist in matters of language and culture. Wang Guowei (1877–1927), profoundly influenced by both classical Chinese scholarship and by Arthur Schopenhauer (1788–1860) and the German idealists, became a celebrated philologist and historian of Chinese literature; he never abandoned the Manchu cause, and committed suicide in despair as revolutionary forces approached Beijing in 1927.

The mood of intellectual protest in the 1910s and 1920s, however, was generally antitraditional, often radically iconoclastic. "Down with Confucius & Sons!" was a popular slogan, the assumption being that Confucianism was inseparable from the repudiated institutions of dynastic imperialism. The New Culture movement arose in the 1910s as a reaction against the failure of the political revolution of 1911 to replace the imperial government with substantial republican institutions. Such ideas were encouraged by, and in turn encouraged, the emergence of a modern, popular press as the vehicle of culturally iconoclastic and, increasingly as time went on, politically radical opinion. The most famous and influential new journal was *Xin qingnian* (*The New Youth*, originally subtitled *La Jeunesse*, 1915), edited by Chen Duxiu and sponsored by a group of Beijing intellectuals, many on the faculty of Peking University. It emerged as the epicenter of radical opinion in the late 1910s.

Chen Duxiu apotheosized the spirit of the times as *saiensu xiansheng yu demokelaxi xiansheng* (Mr. Science and Mr. Democracy). These terms left much room for individual interpretation, but generally they were consistent with the antitraditionalist stance epitomized by Hu Shi's call for the adoption of a pragmatically "critical attitude" in weighing any proposal for present action, and in assessing the burden of the past in all its social and cultural manifestations.

Illustrative of the call for emancipation from the shackles of tradition was the vernacular literature (*baihua*) movement (1917), promoted by Hu Shi and other intellectual modernizers, that sought to overthrow the elitist monopoly of literacy by the introduction of a written language based on the spoken, and hence accessible to the many. As this suggests, advocates of the New Culture argued that sweeping cultural and social transformation must precede effective and enduring political change, though they differed as to whether this should be accomplished by gradualist and evolutionary or by violent revolutionary means. This disagreement colored intellectual and political discourse throughout the following decades, as the warlordism of the 1910s and 1920s gave way to the dictatorship of the Nationalist Party.

In the 1920s a modified traditionalism began to find expression, first in a widespread debate over science and the philosophy of life. Critics of "science," which they viewed as a sobriquet for Westernization in general, argued that the underlying spiritualistic humanism of traditional Confucian ethics could be divorced from the distortions of dynastic imperialism, and must not be sacrificed in the pursuit of legalistic and materialistic "modern" goals. This view, promoted by thinkers such as Zhang Junmai, Liang Shuming (1893–1988), and the aging Liang Qichao, reflected a disenchantment with the Western, or specifically European, model in the aftermath of World War I and the Treaty of Versailles. It received its most conservative (or reactionary) expression in the New Life movement inaugurated by Chiang Kai-shek (Jiang Jieshi) in 1934, a nationalistic pastiche of refurbished Confucian moral nostrums and tips on personal hygiene intended to counter the growing influence of Marxism-Leninism.

### RISE OF MARXISM IN CHINA

Marxism had begun to attract attention only in the late 1910s, in the wake of the Bolshevik Revolution in Russia. Its first prominent converts, Chen Duxiu and Li Dazhao (1888–1927), were both members of the Peking University faculty and of the coterie of progressive intellectuals behind *The New Youth*. The issues that came to divide this group—and eventually China's political and intellectual world in general—into liberal and radical factions were first articulated in the early 1920s in a debate on problems and "isms"; that is, the question of whether change should be sought by slow, incremental and nonviolent evolutionary means, as Hu Shi maintained, or by means of sweeping, root-and-branch, and perhaps violent revolution, as Li Dazhao argued. The exigencies of politics, however, soon rendered such strategic disagreements irrelevant to the course of events. The narrowly militaristic and socially conservative policies of the Guomindang's Nanjing decade (1927–1937) and the increasingly ominous threat of Japanese expansion into North China created an environment of crisis that the government sought to contain by resorting to increasingly stopgap and repressive measures that exacerbated the conditions underlying the Communist challenge to GMD authority in the 1930s.

By the time that China confronted the tragedy of full-scale war against Japan in 1937, the cosmopolitanism and skepticism that had characterized the high tide of the New Culture were dead, overwhelmed by the need to respond to this threat to national survival, and by the competing ideologies of Right and Left that sought to address the deepening social and political crisis. The conservative reactionary nationalism espoused by the Guomindang and the evolving ideology of Sinified Marxism shared in common only a strident anti-imperialism and an insistence on party dictatorship; on social and cultural issues they were profoundly opposed. The Guomindang's "New Life" proved intellectually and socially insufficient to contend against the revolutionary enthusiasm of Maoist Marxism in the civil war of the 1930s and 1940s. In 1941 to 1942, in a series of talks on literature and art delivered in the remote Communist capital of Yan'an, Mao Zedong proclaimed the subservience of intellectual inquiry to the claims of ideology, and of intellectuals to the masses. By the late 1940s, as the Communists fought their way from the wilderness to national power, and in the decades that followed the establishment of their authority, Maoist Marxism became China's new orthodoxy.

**SEE ALSO** *Chen Duxiu; Kang Youwei; Liang Qichao; Zhang Junmai (Carsun Chang).*

**BIBLIOGRAPHY**

Chow Tse-tsung. *The May Fourth Movement: Intellectual Revolution in Modern China.* Cambridge, MA: Harvard University Press, 1960.

Goldman, Merle, and Leo Ou-fan Lee. *An Intellectual History of Modern China.* New York: Cambridge University Press, 2002.

Grieder, Jerome B. *Hu Shih and the Chinese Renaissance: Liberalism in the Chinese Revolution, 1917–1937.* Cambridge, MA: Harvard University Press, 1971.

Grieder, Jerome B. *Intellectuals and the State in Modern China: A Narrative History.* New York: Free Press, 1981.

Schwarcz, Vera. *The Chinese Enlightenment: Intellectuals and the Legacy of the May Fourth Movement of 1919.* Berkeley: University of California Press, 1986.

Spence, Jonathan. *The Search for Modern China.* New York: Norton, 1990.

***Jerome B. Grieder***

## DEBATES SINCE 1949

Intellectual debates in China between 1949 and 1978 were manipulated and controlled by the totalitarian party-state. During the reform era after 1978, the party-state evolved into a post-totalitarian regime with diminishing power to impose ideological and intellectual uniformity. This entry describes several intellectual debates that have had a major impact on intellectual life in the People's Republic of China (PRC) since 1949.

### *THE STORY OF WU XUN*

The attack on the film *The Story of Wu Xun* marked the first major instance in the PRC in which the Communist Party intervened in an academic or cultural discussion and turned it into a political denunciation (*da pipan*). The film, written and directed by Sun Yu (1900–1990) and first screened by Kunlun Film Company in 1950, told the story of Wu Xun (1838–1896), a late-Qing educator who endured extraordinary hardship and humiliation as a beggar for the purpose of funding free schools. The film was widely hailed for presenting a hero who made personal sacrifices for the public good and contributed to the development of education, a topic of great interest in China in the early 1950s.

Critics, however, argued that Wu Xun lacked revolutionary spirit. On May 20, 1951, the *People's Daily* published an editorial by Mao Zedong accusing those who made and praised the film as advancing reactionary propaganda to smear the people and the revolution. A nationwide campaign was launched to denounce the film and those associated with it, adding fuel to the ongoing thought-reform campaign to remold the thinking of intellectuals.

### *THE DREAM OF THE RED CHAMBER* AND THE DENUNCIATION OF HU SHI

Yu Pingbo (1900–1990), a Western-educated scholar and an authority in the study of the eighteenth-century novel *The Dream of the Red Chamber,* published an article in the journal *New Construction* in March 1954 to expound his long-held view that the novel was an autobiographical work of its author, Cao Xueqin (1715–1763), who followed principles of Buddhism in his writing. While many established scholars shared Yu's view, two young students, Li Xifan and Lan Ling, published articles in September and October 1954 asserting that Yu denied the significance of the novel as a great realistic work of antifeudalism (*fan fengjian*).

At Mao's direction, meetings were organized and numerous articles were published to criticize Yu's "wrong view of bourgeois idealism" (*zichanjieji weixinzhuyi*). Then Mao and the central leadership of the party shifted to an attack on Hu Shi (1891–1962), Yu's mentor in the 1920s. By March 1955, hundreds of articles had been published in newspapers and journals to denounce Hu's "reactionary thought" in all fields of humanities and social sciences. Articles by high-profile authors were published in the eight-volume *Collection of Essays Criticizing the Thought of Hu Shi* in 1955. The attacks on Hu and Yu amounted to a major campaign by which the party imposed its political view of scholarship on Chinese intellectuals.

### *THE DISMISSAL OF HAI RUI*

In response to Mao's call in 1959, Wu Han (1909–1969), an expert on the history of the Ming dynasty (1368–1644) and a non-Communist deputy mayor of Beijing with close ties to party leaders, published several plays and essays on Hai Rui (1514–1587), a well-known Ming official. Wu's play *The Dismissal of Hai Rui* was first staged in Beijing in early 1961. The plot concerned Hai Rui as he took risks to investigate and punish corrupt officials who bullied peasants. According to the play, the emperor fell prey to the slander of corrupt officials and dismissed Hai Rui.

Wu's play was widely praised by both historians and literary critics, but it also provoked debate on such issues as the difference between "authenticity" in history and "authenticity" in a play about history, the nature of the "concession policy," and the relationship between upright officials and peasants in ancient China. Yao Wenyuan (1931–2005), an editor for the *Liberation Daily* in Shanghai, published an article titled "On the Rewritten History Play *The Dismissal of Hai Rui*" in the November 10, 1965, issue of the *Wenhui Daily*. The article, which was actually commissioned by Mao's wife, Jiang Qing (1914–1991), and revised by Mao himself, charged that Wu Han not only distorted the historical record, but also took the wrong side in the class struggle in offering ideological support for those who wanted to demolish the people's commune and restore the rule of landlords and rich peasants. Most scholars, cultural officials in particular, did not agree with the charge.

On December 21, 1965, Mao told his trusted followers that "the dismissal was the crux of the play," alleging that Wu Han used the play as a historical allegory to implicate Mao for his arbitrary dismissal of Peng Dehuai. Based on this assumption, Mao made arrangements for a full-scale attack on Wu Han and his backers, including Peng Zhen (1902–1997), the party boss of Beijing, and Liu Shaoqi, the president of the PRC. The debate eventually escalated into a major political battle, and touched off the Cultural Revolution.

### THE DEBATE ON THE CRITERIA FOR ESTABLISHING "TRUTH"

The debate to establish criteria for "truth" was a typical case of a political struggle clothed in a philosophical controversy. Hu Fuming, a lecturer in philosophy at Nanjing University, submitted an article on the issue of truth (*zhenli*) to the *Guangming Daily* in October 1977. Hu Yaobang, director of the Propaganda Department of the CCP Central Committee and president of the Central Party School, found the article highly relevant to the fight against the "whateverist group" (*fanshi pai*) led by Hua Guofeng (1921–2008), the all-powerful chairman of the CCP and PLA, and premier of the State Council.

Hu appointed Wu Jiang and Sun Changjiang, two of his aids at the Central Party School, to organize a group of scholars to revise the article for publication in May 1978 in the journal *Trends in Theoretical Fields* and the *Guangming Daily* with the title "Practice Is the Sole Criterion of the Truth." The article directly challenged the dominant party line of "two whatevers" (*liangge fanshi*), as summarized in the statement "We will resolutely uphold whatever policy decisions Chairman Mao made, and unswervingly follow whatever instructions Chairman Mao gave." After half a year of heated debate, the "faction of practice" (*shijian pai*) prevailed over the "faction of whatever," resulting in the "emancipation of thought" from Maoist fundamentalism, the full rehabilitation of Deng Xiaoping, and the change of the party line to embrace a fundamental reform at the Third Plenum of the Eleventh National Congress of the CCP in December 1978.

## THE DEBATE ON HUMANISM AND ALIENATION

The debate on humanism and alienation took place during the early 1980s, with a focus on whether humanism (*rendao zhuyi*) was the central theme of Marxism, whether there was a universal human nature, and whether alienation (*yihua*) could develop under the conditions of socialism. The surge in interest in humanism could be partly attributed to the influence of similar debates in Eastern Europe, but it was primarily a direct consequence of the human suffering that occurred in China during the Cultural Revolution.

Reflection on the Cultural Revolution led to a powerful trend among Chinese intellectuals to rediscover and reinterpret Marxism as a social theory about the alienation and liberation of human beings. This trend culminated in early 1983 with the publication in the *Wenhui Daily* of "A Defense of Humanism" by Wang Ruoshui (1926–2002), a well-known philosopher and deputy editor in chief of the *People's Daily*. A second article, "An Inquiry into Some Theoretical Issues of Marxism" by Zhou Yang, former deputy director of the Department of Propaganda of the CCP Central Committee, appeared in the *People's Daily*. According to these authors, abandoning Marxist humanism had led to a sort of alienation in which the "people's dictatorship" was turned into "dictatorship toward the people," in which "servants of the people" became "masters of the people," and the people became slaves of blind loyalty under the personality cult of Mao.

This argument met with strong criticism from orthodox Marxists and party loyalists, who maintained that there was no abstract human nature beyond class relations; that even if humanism were taken as an "ethical principle," it was wrong to consider humanism as a "concept of history" (*lishi guan*) and a framework for class analysis; and that the Marxist theory of alienation referred exclusively to the special phenomenon under capitalism where wage labor became an alienating force to dominate workers. The orthodox view was summarized by Hu Qiaomu (1912–1992), a member of the Politburo and the Secretariat of the CCP Central Committee, in his article "On Problems Concerning Humanism and Alienation," published in January 1984. Fearing that this trend in humanism might challenge party rule, the leadership launched a campaign to eliminate "spiritual pollution" (*jingshen wuran*), and those who promoted "Marxist humanism" were purged for the crime of advocating "bourgeois liberalism" (*zichanjieji ziyouhua*).

## THE DEBATE BETWEEN LIBERALS AND THE NEW LEFT

The ongoing debate between liberals and the new left began in the late 1990s. Liberals (*ziyoupai*) are scholars and retired officials who have established their belief in liberal democracy; this group includes Li Shenzhi (1923–2003), Qin Hui, Xu Youyu, Zhu Xueqin, Liu Junning, Wu Guoguang, He Weifang, Feng Chongyi, Zhang Boshu, Fan Yafeng, and Wang Yi. The new left (*xin zuopai*) encompasses three overlapping groups: nationalists, populists, and neo-Marxists, including Gan Yang, Wang Hui, Cui Zhiyuan, Wang Shaoguang, Han Deqiang, and Han Yuhai.

Both sides are critical of the reality of "social polarization" (*liangji fenhua*) and "inequalities" (*shehui bujun*), but they differ sharply in identifying the causes and remedies for these social ills. Borrowing neo-Marxism, postmodernism, and postcolonial critique from the West, and reflecting the growing nationalism in China, the new left blames neoliberalism, market-oriented reforms, and the hegemony of global (Western) capital for social injustice and other evils in China. They also warn that globalization is undermining Chinese sovereignty. As a remedy, they propose "institutional renovation" with elements of Maoism.

Chinese liberals, on the other hand, insist that the authoritarian political system of the party-state and inadequate development of the market economy are the main sources of social inequality and other social evils in contemporary China. They argue as well that the future of China lies in the genuine market economy and liberal democracy embodied by the West, and that the current trend of globalization offers the best opportunity for China to achieve its long-overdue goal of modernization.

Liberals have come under attack from a group of neo-Confucians, such as Kang Xiaoguang and Jiang Qing, who see Western hegemony as China's number-one enemy and who advocate Confucian benevolent government (*ren zheng*) as an alternative to liberal democracy. The party-state has not directly participated in this debate, although it continues to harshly suppress liberal intellectuals.

**SEE ALSO** *Cultural Revolution, 1966–1969; Hu Feng; Hu Shi; Hundred Flowers Campaign; Prodemocracy Movement (1989).*

## BIBLIOGRAPHY

Goldman, Merle, and Li Oufan (Leo Ou-Fan Lee), eds. *An Intellectual History of Modern China*. Cambridge, U.K.: Cambridge University Press, 2002.

Liu Yong and Gao Huamin, eds. *Da lunzheng: Jianguo yilai zhongyao lunzheng shilu* [Great controversies: Records of major debates since the establishment of the PRC]. Vols. 1–3. Zhuhai: Zhuhai Press, 2001.

***Feng Chongyi***

# CLIMATE

The climate of China is complex, diverse, and unique, with a monsoon-controlled pattern showing clear latitudinal and longitudinal differentiation. The annual rotation of four seasons (spring, summer, autumn, and winter) with coincident heat and rainfall is a well-known feature of the Chinese climate. Figure 1 shows the monsoon-controlled climatic regimes in China. Formation of the Chinese climate is subject to the interaction of four main regimes that govern climatic dynamics in China: subtropical monsoon, tropical monsoon, plateau monsoon, and west-wind circulation.

## CLIMATIC REGIMES AND REGIONAL VARIATION

Many factors play critical roles in the activities of these regimes. Among them, geographical location, terrain, and territory are especially important. Geographically, China is on the western coast of the Pacific Ocean and in the eastern part of the Eurasian continent, with the Mongolian Plateau in its north, Central Asia in its west, and the Indian Ocean to its southwest. The terrain of China is mainly composed of a three-step ladder: the eastern coastal region with a low altitude, the northwestern region in the middle, and the Tibetan Plateau as the world's highest terrain. China is a vast country, with territory extending 5,200 kilometers from west to east and 5,500 kilometers from south to north.

These unique features determine the atmospheric forces driving seasonal and spatial climate changes in China. Three meteorological forces are especially important in the formulation of China's climate: the Pacific Ocean air mass, the Arctic air mass, and the Indian Ocean monsoon. Under this global context, China's climate is shaped by the Tibetan Plateau and the northwestern desert into a typical monsoon pattern with clear seasonal changes. As a monsoon climate, the summer is subject to atmospheric control from the Pacific Ocean with significant effects from the Indian Ocean. China's winter is mainly subject to the action of Arctic cold air invading through the Mongolian Plateau in northwestern China. The mutual interaction of these two atmospheric forces results in an annual rotation of four seasons in most parts of China. For example, in central China, spring generally runs from February to April, summer from May to July, autumn from August to October, and winter from November to January.

The climate of eastern China gradually changes from a hot and humid tropical atmosphere in the south, to a warm subtropical climate in the middle, to a moderate temperate climate in the north. Distance from the Pacific Ocean generally controls the spatial distribution of precipitation in China. The coastal region has heavy rainfall, while the northwest sees little rainfall and hence is mostly arid and semiarid. The rise of the Tibetan Plateau plays a critical role in altering air and moisture transmission from the Pacific Ocean, Indian Ocean, and Arctic region. Climatic change in China is thus characterized by longitudinal differentiation, with a humid climate in the southeastern coastal region, a semihumid and semiarid climate in the middle, and an arid desert climate in the northwest. There are also many mountains, basins, and plains distributed throughout China. These local topographical bodies, with their different sizes and shapes, render the climate in different parts of China more complex and diverse.

China (including the South China Sea region) can be comprehensively divided into ten climatic zones (Figure 1), with consideration of latitudinal and longitudinal differentiations and local topographical alternations. As seen in Figure 2, there are six climate zones that are very important: the southern, the middle, and the northern subtropical zones; the warm and moderate temperate zones; and the Tibetan Plateau. These six zones occupy more than 90 percent of China's total territory. Economically, the three subtropical zones and the warm temperate zone make up the core of China because three-quarters of the population and its economic activities are concentrated in these zones. The soil fertility and excellent natural conditions for agriculture in these four zones are important reasons why Chinese civilization first expanded and consolidated there.

## TEMPERATURE AND PRECIPITATION

Climate can be analyzed using a number of variables, including temperature and precipitation in China between 1950 and 1980. Precipitation variation in China follows a pattern of decreasing from the southeastern coastal region to the inland northwest. The highest annual precipitation can be observed in eastern Taiwan, southern Tibet, southern Hainan, and southern Guangdong, with more than 2,000 millimeters. The lowest annual precipitation, below 25 millimeters, is found in the center of Taklamakan Desert in southern Xinjiang. Regional differences in annual precipitation are very evident in China. The northeast generally has annual precipitation of 400 to 800 millimeters. The precipitation in the North China Plain is also within 400 to 800 millimeters. Precipitation is above 1,500 millimeters in southern China, and 1,000 to 1,500 millimeters in southwestern China.

As shown in Figure 3, two precipitation isolines are especially important for identifying climatic patterns in China. It is generally agreed that the annual precipitation isoline of 800 millimeters divides eastern China into humid and semihumid regions, while the isoline of 400 millimeters separates the semihumid from the semiarid region. The arid region and desert can be divided using the annual precipitation isolines of 200 millimeters and 100 millimeters.

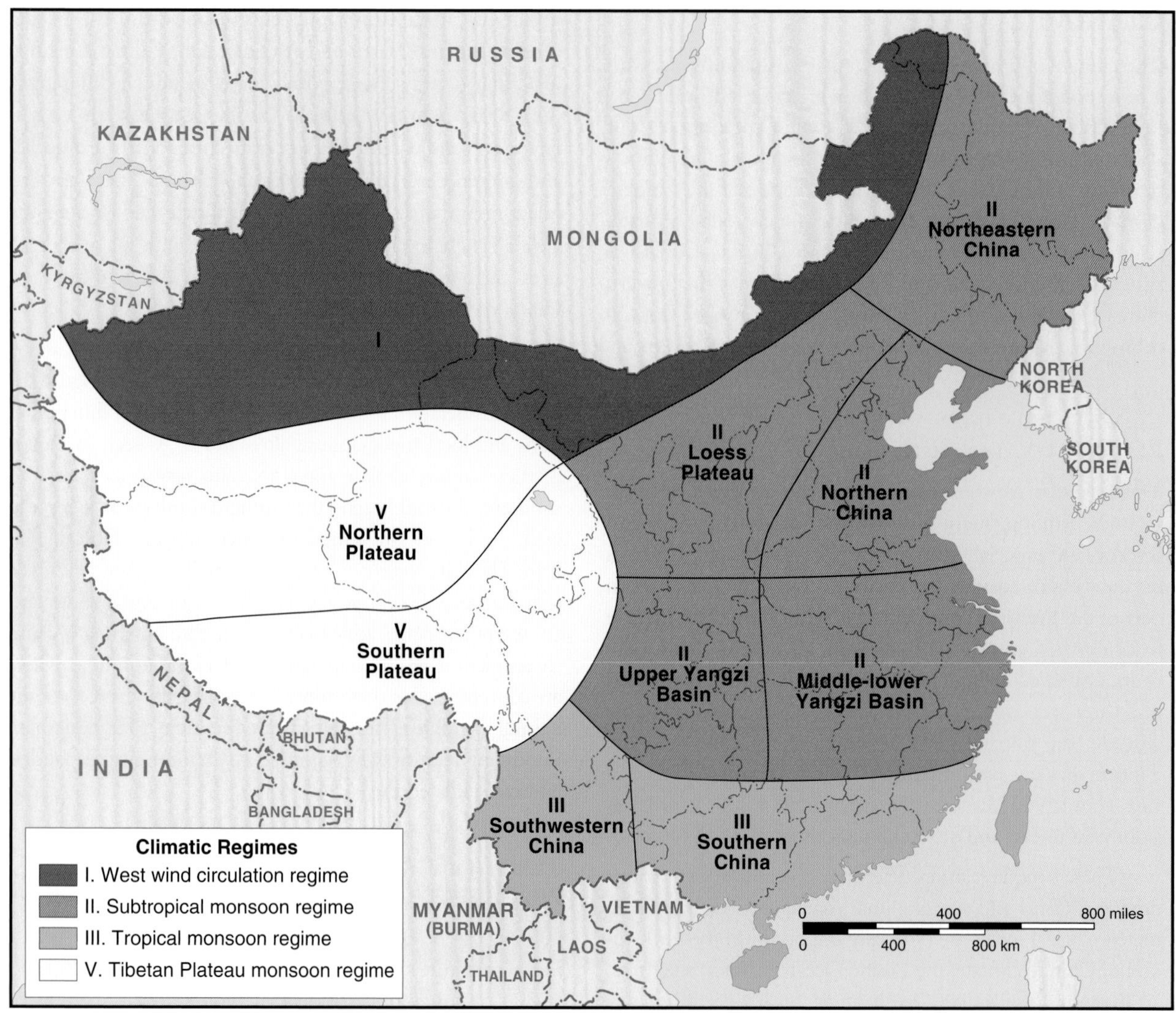


*Figure 1*

Figure 4 compares the annual change in average precipitation between 1970 and 2005 in five typical Chinese cities: Harbin in northeastern China, Ürümqi in northwestern China, Lhasa in Tibet, Wuhan in central China, and Heyuan in southern China. Since China's climate follows a monsoon-dominated pattern, rainfalls in China generally concentrate in the summer, leading to the coincidence of heat and water favorable for ecosystems and agriculture. In winter, the landscape is dry with little rain. The dry season usually runs from autumn to early spring. Spring drought is a serious climatic problem for Chinese agriculture.

Spatial variation of Chinese annual average air temperature is shown in Figure 6. Temperature variation is subject to climatic zones. The regions with the highest annual temperature distribution are in southern China, where subtropical and tropical climates dominate. In particular, southern Guangxi, southern Guangdong, Hainan, and Taiwan have an annual average air temperature of above 24°C. The Tibetan Plateau and northern Heilongjiang Province have the lowest annual average air temperature. The low air temperature in the Tibetan Plateau region is mainly attributable to altitude, while the low temperature of Heilongjiang is mainly due to the province's high latitude.

Though the air temperature is moderate in northwestern China, where a desert climate dominates and there is very little precipitation, the clear difference between summer and winter is unique in the world. As shown in Figure 7a, low air temperature dominates most parts of northern China as a result of cold air from the Arctic north. One important feature highlighted in Figure 7a is a geographical line linking Qinling Mountain with Huai River. The regions north of

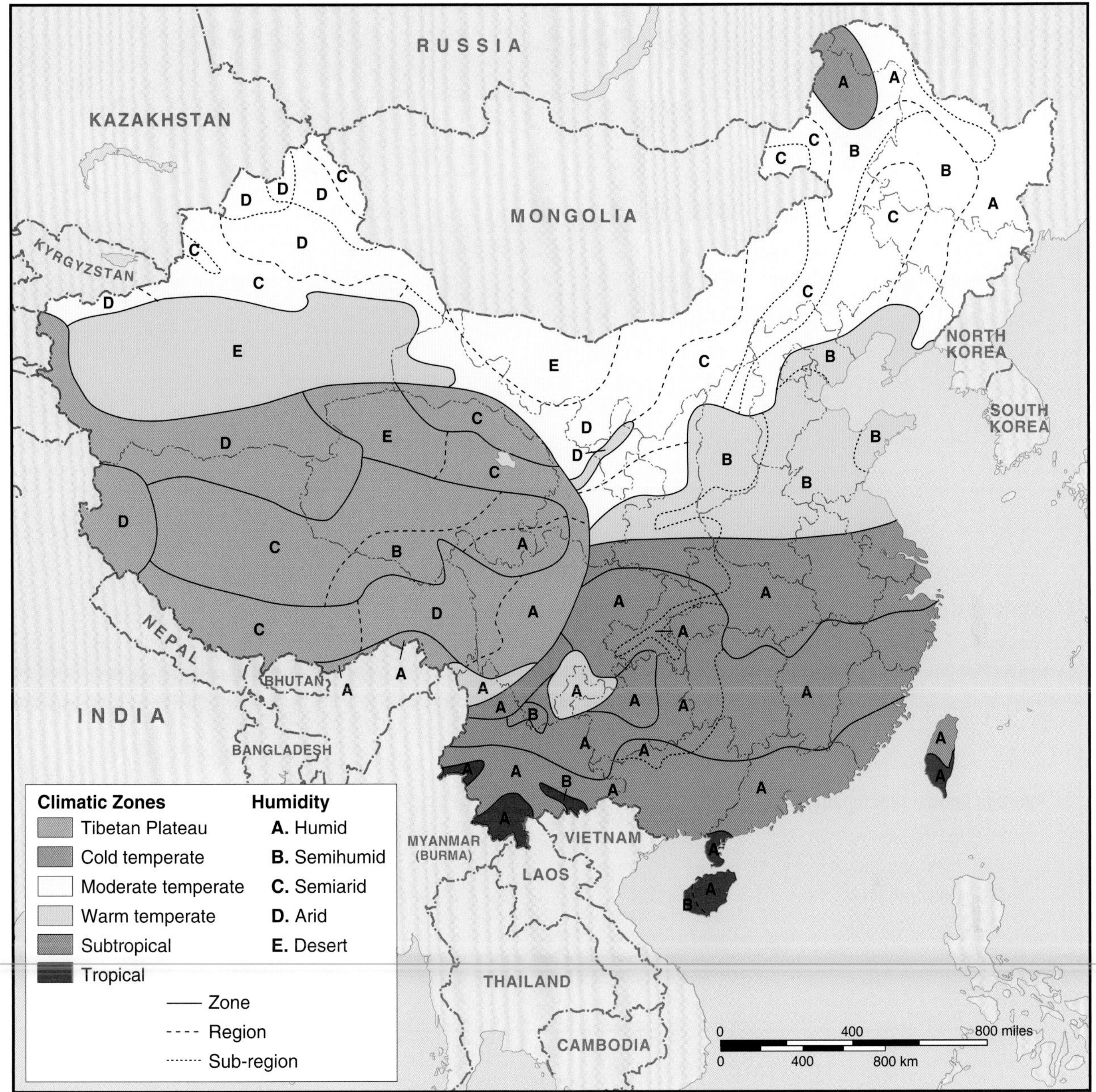


*Figure 2*

this line generally have cold winter air temperatures of below 0°C, while the temperature is above 0°C in regions south of this line. Thus, geographically as well as climatically, this line is called the south-north separation line. This definition is different from the traditional separation of North China from South China by the Yangzi, which runs south of Huai River.

In contrast to the spatial variation of winter air temperature, Figure 7b shows that summer air temperature tends to be similar in most parts of China except the Tibetan Plateau. Whether in the northwestern inland desert, the southern subtropical region, or the northeastern moderate temperate region, high air temperature dominates. In summer, the air temperature during the day is usually above 30°C in China.

In spite of this uniformity in temperature, heat patterns differ in various parts of China. Generally, the northwestern inland region experiences dry heat, while regions south of the Yangzi River experience wet or humid heat patterns. The cities of Nanjing, Chongqing, Wuhan, and Nanchang along the Yangzi River have been nicknamed the "four furnaces under heaven" due to their hot, humid summers. On average, these four cities have 19.3 days per year with a daytime air temperature of above 35°C and 13.2 days per

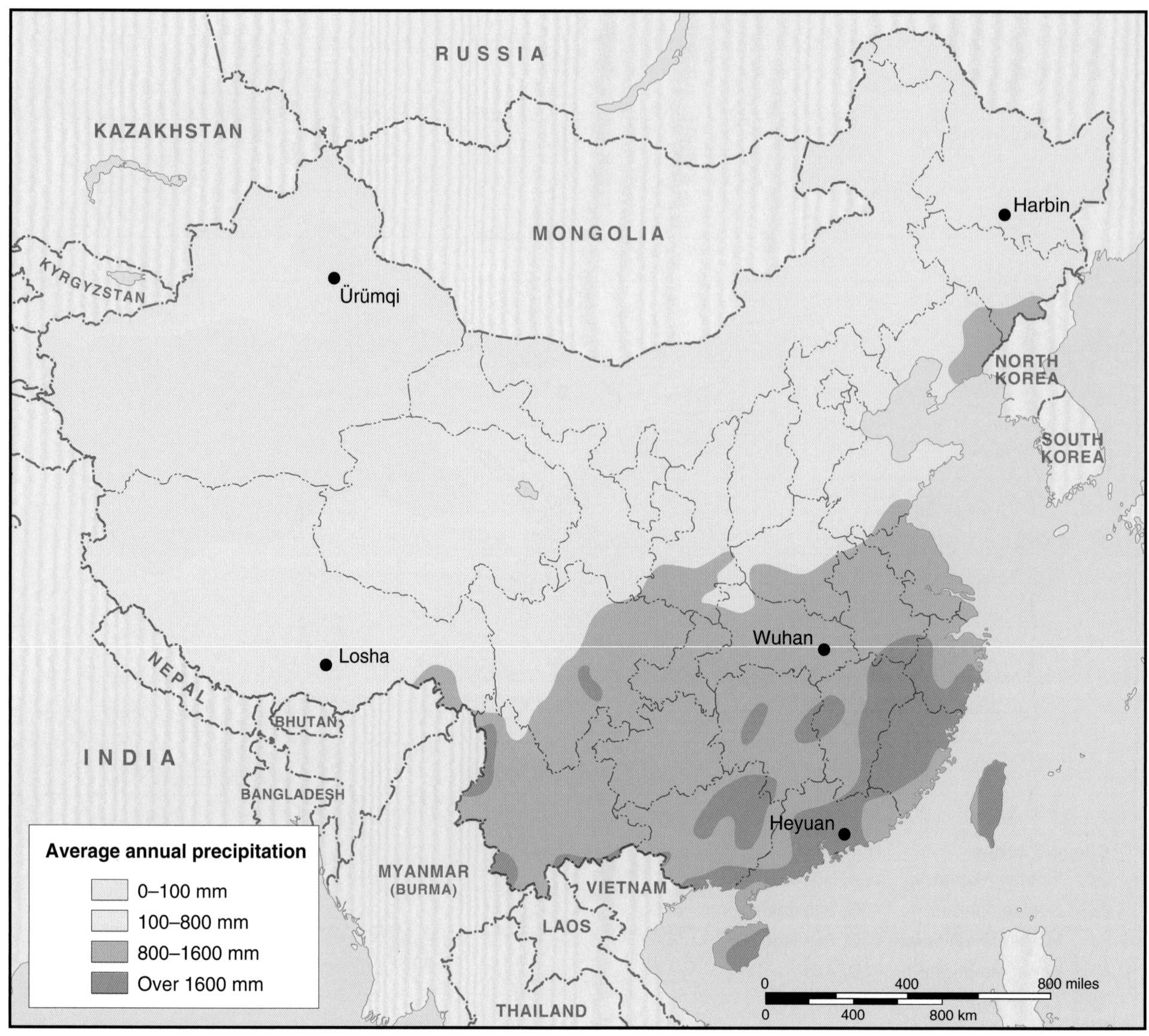


*Figure 3*

year with nighttime air temperature of above 28°C. During these hot days, the humidity in the cities is usually above 90 percent, and there is almost no wind. The "furnace" phenomenon in these cities has intensified in recent decades because of urban expansion. Figure 8 shows the change of annual average air temperature for selected meteorological observation stations in China between 1970 and 2005 at meteorological observation stations in Harbin in northeastern China, Ürümqi in northwestern China, Lhasa in Tibet, Wuhan in central China, and Heyuan in southern China.

## CLIMATE CHANGE

Annual air average temperature for the entire country increased only 0.5 to 0.8°C during the last century, but it is higher than the global average. Nationally, since 1986, China's winters have been warm. Annual average air temperature also shows gradual increases during 1970–2005 period, with the temperature in Wuhan increasing from 15.9°C in 1970 to 18.2°C in 2005, at a yearly pace of 7.1 percent. Similar increases are also seen in Harbin, Lhasa, and Ürümqi (Figure 8).

In the mid-twentieth century, North China had a humid and cool climate, very suitable for agriculture. More recently, scientists have found that the region is undergoing a drying process (An et al. 2004; Huang et al. 2003; Ma and Ren 2007). Thick winter snow was common before the 1950s in North China. Now snow is rarely seen in winter. Water shortages are also severe in North China, which is home to several large cities, including Beijing, Tianjin,

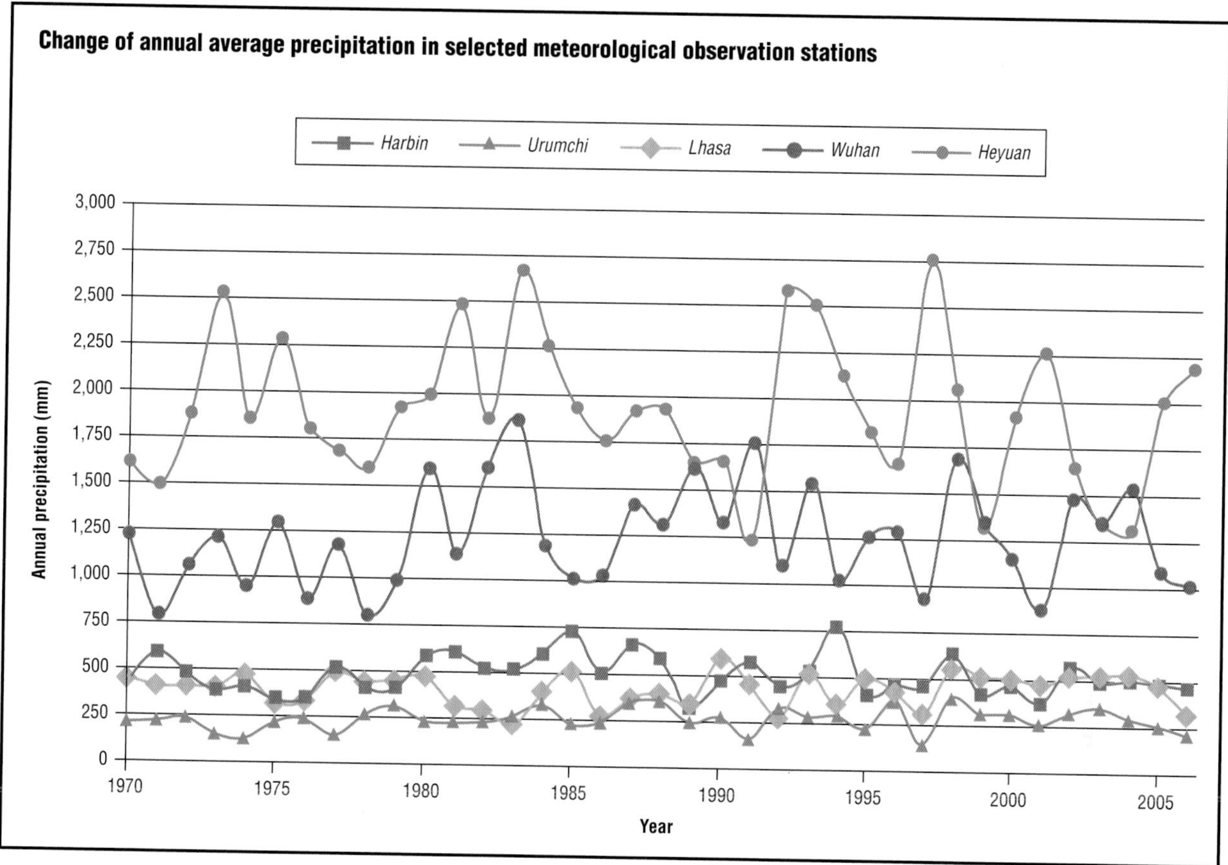


*Figure 4*

Shijiazhuang, Zhengzhou, and Jinan. Overpumping of groundwater for both agriculture and urban uses has led to a drop in the groundwater level, as well as surface subsidence. Several large-scale surface dents have been observed in the western part of the North China Plain. Many small rivers have dried out, and larger rivers, such as the Yongding and Yellow, show a clear decrease in flowing water. Using data from 336 observation stations, Huang Ronghui and colleagues (2003) revealed that summertime precipitation in North China significantly decreased from 1951 to 1994, showing a clear drying trend.

The regional variation of the Chinese climate during the 1980s was found to be sharply different from that in the 1970s. A comparison between the 1980s and the 1970s reveals a remarkable precipitation increase in the Yangzi and Huai river basins, leading to a high risk of flooding in these areas, while a decrease was seen in South China and North China (Zhou et al. 2004). This change could be attributable to El Niño activities in the tropical Pacific Ocean (Huang and Wu 1989; Yan et al. 2001; Huang et al. 2003; Fu et al. 2005).

Extreme meteorological events and climate-related natural disasters are considered by many experts to result from climate change. In recent years, such events have been both intensive and extensive in China (Li et al. 1997; Ye and Huang 1996). The middle and lower reaches of the Yangzi River basin have warm winters. However, an abnormal weather event featuring snow and icy rain hit this region in January 2008, an event not observed in meteorological records dating back to the mid-twentieth century. The abnormal weather brought chaos to highway traffic and disrupted power supplies and communications in central and southern China. For more than ten days, Chenzhou in Hunan Province was isolated without regular power or water. Economic losses in the seven provinces affected by the unusual weather were estimated to be above 33 billion renminbi yuan. Figure 9 shows a mobile signal tower and a communication cable in north Guangxi covered with thick ice due to the high-moisture air with low temperatures during the icy rain period.

Before the disaster struck, the region had suffered from a severe drought for several months, causing the water level of the Yangzi, Dongding Lake, and Boyang Lake to drop to the lowest level on record. Spatial distribution of disastrous weather events shows a drought increase in North and northwest China. The Huai River basin, the coastal region,

**Comparison of average monthly precipitation and air temperature between 1970 and 2005 in Harbin in northeastern China (a), Lanzhou in northwestern China (b), Wuhan in central China (c), and Guangzhou in southern China (d)**

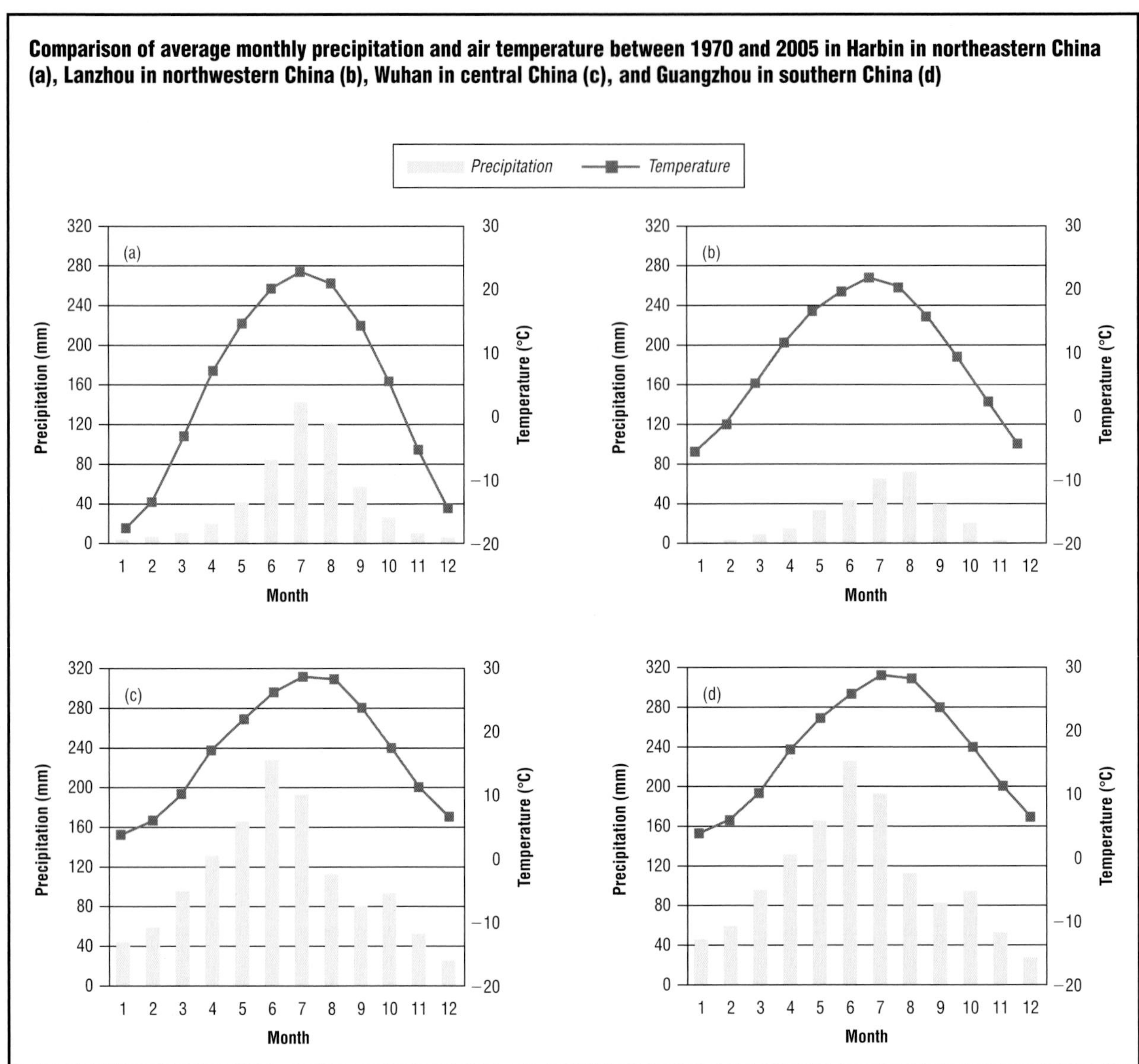


*Figure 5*

and South China face a higher flood risk due to typhoons and tropical cyclones.

Scientists continue to debate whether the climate is changing or exhibiting a normal oscillation, although the majority of scientists in China agree that climate change is occurring. In addition to such global events as El Niño, climate change has been interpreted from various perspectives. The increasingly high pressure of China's large population, with more than 1.3 billion people and limited natural resources, is interpreted as it relates to climate change. Population density in the eastern part of China is high, with as many as 300 to 500 persons per square kilometer. Pressure for food and a better life has led to overuse of the region's limited natural resources, including its farmland, grassland, water, and minerals. Intensive use of land for agriculture has greatly changed the land cover, which results in a change to heat flux and moisture content, the two forces that drive the movement of the earth's climate (Liu and Lin 2007; Xiong et al. 2005; Cai 2001).

On average, 15 percent of China's entire territory is under cultivation. In Shandong and Henan provinces, the amount of land under cultivation in 2005 was 49 percent and 48 percent, respectively. Grassland degradation and desertification have become more and more serious in recent decades as a result of overgrazing and overcultivating. Each year, the

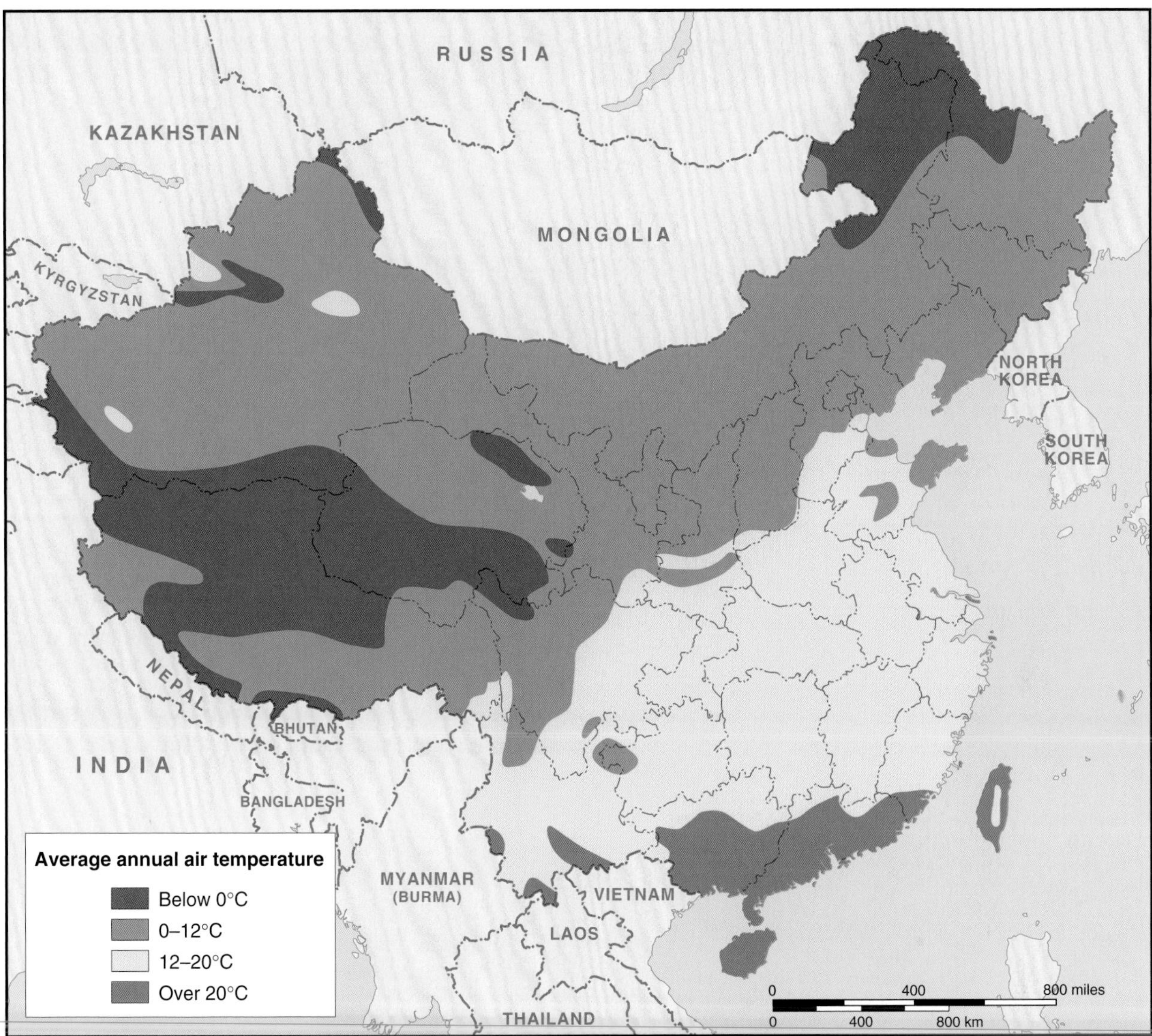


*Figure 6*

acreage of desertification in China increases by some 3,460 square kilometers, leading to an annual economic loss of 54 billion renminbi yuan.

Along with agriculture and pasture activities, urban expansion and industrial development are closely related to climate change in China. Since the late twentieth century, the built areas of cities in China have rapidly expanded. In place of the farmland observed in suburban areas in the mid-1990s, most of China's metropolitan areas are now made up of forests of tall buildings used for housing and commerce.

China's GDP (gross domestic product) doubled between 1995 and 2005, leading to a rapid increase in energy consumption in the form of coal, electricity, and oil, which consequently leads to large $CO_2$ emissions into the atmosphere. China's $CO_2$ emission rate is second only to that of the United States.

Climate change is a complex phenomenon with multiple driving forces. All the factors discussed above, especially land-cover and land-use change, agriculture, grassland degradation and desertification, urban expansion, and economic development, contribute to climate change regionally and globally. Since social and economic development requires the use of energy and land for food, materials, and shelter to satisfy human demand, emission growth and land-cover change is unavoidable, which implies that climate change is an irreversible process. The strategy of humankind in the face of this challenge is to minimize greenhouse emissions, optimize the utilization of natural resources, and adapt to the change.

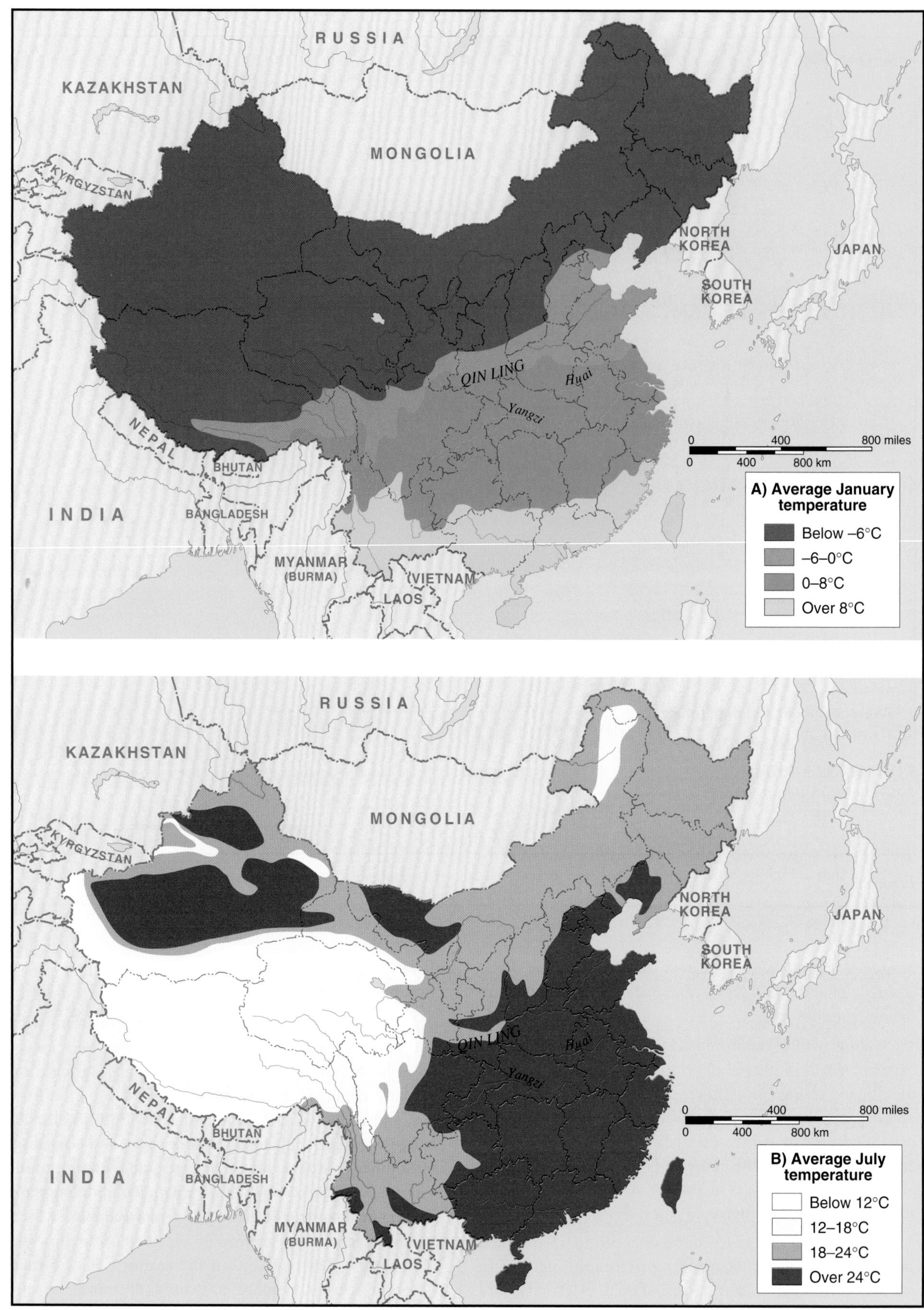
RUSSIA
KAZAKHSTAN
MONGOLIA
KYRGYZSTAN
NORTH KOREA
SOUTH KOREA
JAPAN
QIN LING
Huai
Yangzi
NEPAL
BHUTAN
INDIA
BANGLADESH
MYANMAR (BURMA)
VIETNAM
LAOS
0 400 800 miles
0 400 800 km
A) Average January temperature
Below –6°C
–6–0°C
0–8°C
Over 8°C
RUSSIA
KAZAKHSTAN
MONGOLIA
KYRGYZSTAN
NORTH KOREA
SOUTH KOREA
JAPAN
QIN LING
Huai
Yangzi
NEPAL
BHUTAN
INDIA
BANGLADESH
MYANMAR (BURMA)
VIETNAM
LAOS
0 400 800 miles
0 400 800 km
B) Average July temperature
Below 12°C
12–18°C
18–24°C
Over 24°C

*Figure 7*

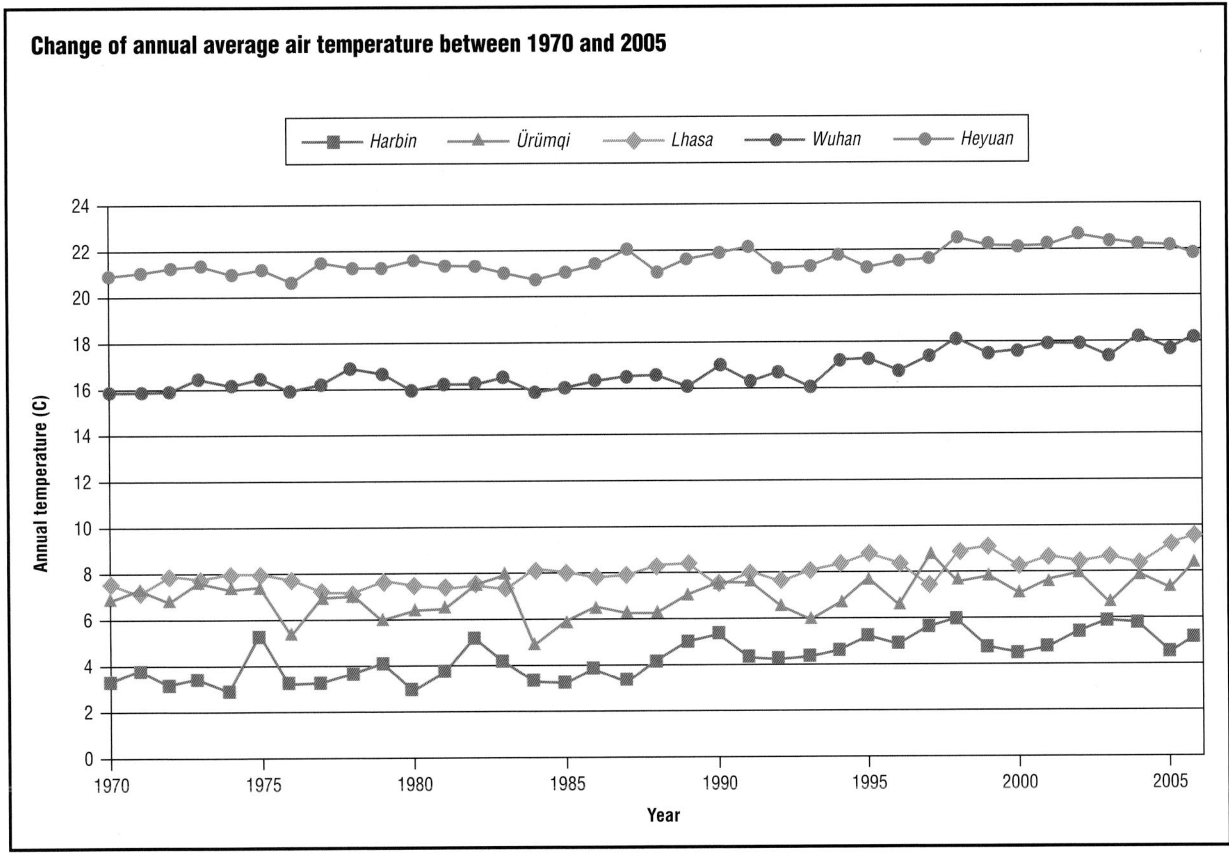


*Figure 8*


**BIBLIOGRAPHY**

An Zhishen, Ding Zhongli, Zhou Weijian, Zhou Jie. Historical Studies of Drying Climates in North China. Beijing: Meteorology Press, 2004. [安芷生, 丁仲礼, 周卫健, 周杰. 中国北方干旱化的历史证据和成因研究。 北京: 气象出版社, 2004, 298页.]

Cai Y. S. Agricultural Adaptation to Climate Change in China. *Journal of Environmental Sciences* 13, 2 (2001): 192–197.

China Statistics Bureau (CSB). *China Statistics Yearbook 2006.* Beijing: China Statistics Publication House, 2006.

Fu Congbin, An Zhisheng, and Guo Weidong. Evolution of Life-supporting Environment in Our Nation and the Predictive Study of Aridification in Northern China: I. Main Scientific Issues and Achievements. *Advance in Earth Sciences* 20, 11 (2005): 1157–1167. [符淙斌; 安芷生; 郭维栋. 我国生存环境演变和北方干旱化趋势预测研究 (I): 主要研究成果. 地球科学进展20, 11 (2005): 1157–1167.]

Huang Ronghui, Li Chongyin., and Wang Shaowu. Mechanism of Drought and Food Climates in China. Beijing: Meteorology Press, 2003. [黄荣辉, 李崇银, 王绍武. 我国旱涝重大气候灾害及其形成机理研究。 北京: 气象出版社, 2003, 483页.]

Huang Ronghui and Wu Yifang. The influence of ENSO on the Summer Climate Change in China and Its Mechanisms. *Advances in Atmospheric Sciences* 6 (1989): 21–32.

Institute of Geography, Chinese Academy of Science (IGCAS). The National Physical Atlas of China. Beijing: China Cartographic Publishing House, 1999.

Li Kerang, Guo Qiwen, and Zhang Jiacheng. Drought Disasters and Anti-Drought Strategies in China. Zhengzhou: Henan Scien-Tech Press, 1997. [李克让, 郭其蕴, 张家城. 中国干旱灾害研究及减灾对策。 郑州:河南科学技术出版社, 1997, 397页.]

Liu Yingjie and Lin Erda. Effects of Climate Change on Agriculture in Different Regions of China. *Advances in Climate Change* 3, 4 (2007): 229–233. [刘颖杰, 林而达. 气候变暖对中国不同地区农业的影响. 气候变化研究进展3, 4 (2007): 229–233.]

Ma Zhuguo and Ren Xiaobo. Drying Trend over China from 1951 to 2006. *Advances in Climate Change* 3, 4 (2007): 195–201. [马柱国, 任小波. 1951–2006 年中国区域干旱化特征, 气候变化研究进展, 3, 4 (2007): 195–201.]

Wu Guoxiong, Sun Sufen, and Chen Wen. Roles of Tibetan Plateau and Northwest Arid Region in Formation of Disaster Climates in China. Beijing: Meteorology Press, 2003. [吴国雄, 孙菽芬, 陈文. 青藏高原与西北干旱区对气候灾害的影响。 北京: 气象出版社, 2003, 337页.]

Wei Jie, Zhang Qingyun, and Tao Shiyan. Formation of Severe Drought Events during the 1999 and 2000 Summers in China. *Journal of Atmospheric Sciences* 28, 1 (2004): 125–137.

[卫捷 张庆云 陶诗言. 1999及2000年夏季华北严重干旱的物理成因分析, 大气科学, 28, 1 (2004): 125–137.]

Xiong Wei, Lin Erda, Ju Hui, and Xu Qinlong. A Study of the Threshold of Climate Change Impact on Food Production in China. *Advances in Climate Change* 1, 2 (2005): 84–87. [熊伟; 林而达; 居辉; 许吟隆. 气候变化的影响阈值与中国的粮食安全. 气候变化研究进展 1, 2 (2005): 84–87.]

Yang Bangliang, Huang Ronghui, and Zhang Renhe. Dynamical Role of Zonal Wind Stresses over the Tropical Pacific in the Occurring and Vanishing of El Niño Part II: Analyses of Modeling Results. *Chinese Journal of Atmospheric Sciences* 25, 2 (2001): 160–172. [严邦良, 黄荣辉, 张人禾. El Niño事件发生和消亡中热带太平洋纬向风应力的动力作用 II. 模式结果分析. 大气科学 25, 2 (2001): 160–172.]

Ye Duzheng and Huang Ronghui. Formation of Drought and Flood Climates in Yangzi and Yellow River Basins. Jinan: Shangdong Scien-Tech Press, 1996. [叶笃正, 黄荣辉. 长江黄河流域旱涝规律和成因研究,济南:山东科技出版社, 1996, 387页.]

***Qin Zhihao***

# CLOTHING SINCE 1800

What people wore in China during the Manchu Qing dynasty (1644–1912) was different from the clothing of earlier times. Nonetheless, it is not generally described in terms of fashion. In her well-known essay "A Chronicle of Changing Clothes," Eileen Chang (Zhang Ailing) wrote, "We cannot really imagine the world of the past—so dilatory, so quiet, and so orderly that over the course of three hundred years of Manchu rule, women lacked anything that might be referred to as fashion" (2003, p. 429). Much the same opinion was expressed by French historian Fernand Braudel in his pioneering discussion of fashion in history *Capitalism and Material Life* (1967). By fashion, these commentators meant observable changes in clothing styles over relatively short spans of time.

This view of clothing in late imperial China fits in with a long-held view of Chinese society itself as changeless over many centuries. It has been modified by research on urban life in pre-1900 China that shows there were short-term changes in the popularity of fabrics, hats, hairstyles, cuts of garments, and colors of cloth worn by the residents of prosperous cities such as Nanjing, Suzhou, and Yangzhou. Such changes in taste were even more obvious in the early twentieth century, when capitalism and industrialization accelerated the popularization of new trends in clothing.

In the late twentieth century, when China was making its way into the world market after nearly three decades of relative isolation and sluggish growth, this earlier history of fashion was rediscovered. Retro elements in contemporary fashion reflect attention to fabric, ornament, trim, and cut in older clothing regimes. China's reengagement with the world exposed it fully to international fashion trends, but this was not a totally new phenomenon. To a surprising degree, Chinese clothing in earlier times shows the effects of cultural interaction between Han and non-Han peoples.

***Chinese woman in traditional dress, c. 1900.*** *During the late Qing dynasty, clothing styles for women included long jackets layered over a skirt. Many pieces of clothing featured detailed embroidery, with embellished shoes for bound feet a treasured part of many women's wardrobe.* 

## LATE QING FASHIONS

The clothes worn by Chinese people at the beginning of the nineteenth century marked them as subjects of the Manchu Qing dynasty (1644–1912). The educated man wore a long gown (*changpao*) with a vest (*majia*) and/or riding jacket (*magua*), cloth shoes or black cloth boots, and a little round melon-skin cap (*guapimao*), or a hat appropriate to his official rank if he had one. An official's formal wardrobe included a surcoat adorned front and back with a large square plaque (*fangbu*) embroidered with the figure of a particular animal (for a military official) or bird (for a civil official). His hair was styled in the Manchu way: shaved at the front, and braided at the back to form a long queue that was sometimes further lengthened with artificial hair or

***Chinese man in traditional dress, c. 1890.*** *In the late nineteenth century, many Chinese continued to wear traditional forms of dress, such as long gowns with jackets for men and flowing jackets with pants or skirt for women. However, the beginning of a new century also brought changes in fashion, with many citizens opting for more streamlined styles, including tighter-fitting suits with stand-up collars for men and one-piece slender dresses for women.* © ALINARI ARCHIVES/THE IMAGE WORKS

black silk. The well-born Han Chinese woman wore a long jacket (*ao*) with loose trousers (*ku*), and a pleated skirt (*qun*) if she was in company. The wife or daughter of an official would wear on her formal jacket a rank badge appropriate to his official rank. Footbinding was widely practiced, and small embroidered shoes were among the most valued items in a woman's wardrobe. Girls put their hair up at puberty and wore it in an often elaborate coiffure. Hairstyles varied regionally and over time. The "suzhou do" (*suzhoujue*) was popular in the late nineteenth century.

Manchu and Han men dressed alike, but Manchu women were readily distinguished from Han women by their distinctive hairstyles, large unbound feet, and long robes. In the nineteenth century, Manchu dress was increasingly influenced by Chinese styles. Platform-soled shoes were worn to give the appearance of small feet beneath the hem of one's robe, and sleeves were cut ever wider, following Han fashion. Han women did not wear Manchu clothing and resisted early attempts to prohibit footbinding, but by the nineteenth century Han women's dress no longer looked like late Ming dress. The long jacket may show the long-term influence of the Manchu robe.

In the early years of the twentieth century, such clothes began to change quite rapidly. The jacket and trousers, central items in the Chinese wardrobe, changed from loose, wrapper-style garments to close-cut, fitted ones. The plain round neckline gave way to a stand-up collar, the so-called mandarin collar that became a signature feature of Chinese dress. Footbinding began to decline among elite families as girls were sent to school in increasing numbers. Leather shoes became popular among both men and women. Felt caps, hombergs, and boaters replaced the old-style melon-skin hats, and controversies erupted among schoolboys over cutting off queues. By the time the dynasty fell in 1912, fashionably dressed women were beginning to venture out of doors, creating fashion scenes evident first in Shanghai and then gradually in other treaty-port cities.

## REPUBLICAN STYLES

During the Republican era (1912–1949), fashions were highly sensitive to politics. In 1912, under the new administration, suits were approved as standard formal wear for men, and queues and footbinding were both banned, though not with immediate effect. Western clothes were very popular among the well-to-do for a year or two, but Chinese styles regained ascendancy, perhaps as a direct response to the failure of the first Republican government, led by Yuan Shikai, to satisfy Republican aspirations or even to provide strong, stable government.

Yet there was no reversion to late-Qing styles. Hems went up, and trousers gave way to stockings, which were worn with the dark skirt and jacket-blouse of the May Fourth era (*duan'ao*). With its bell-shaped sleeves and high collar, the jacket-blouse was a recognizably Chinese style. So too, obviously, was the long gown and jacket (*changpao magua*) worn by men, although both of these garments were now closer fitting than they had been in the nineteenth century. Suits were worn by some progressive young men in the 1920s, but lost popularity in the 1930s. During the Nanjing decade (1928–1937), nationalism informed clothing choices. The Sun Yat-sen suit (*Zhongshan zhuang*), based on Japanese military uniform and designed by the Republican leader Sun Yat-sen, became standard wear for officials in the ruling Nationalist Party, and also for schoolboys. This decade was also the heyday of the Mandarin gown (*qipao*), which displaced the skirt and jacket-blouse to become the definitive Chinese dress of modern times. A one-piece garment that developed in the 1920s from a mixture of styles including the long vest (*chang majia*), and the man's long robe, the Mandarin gown became famous in its most fashionable form, cut close to the figure with long, leg-revealing side-slits.

In the meantime, a recognizable fashion industry had emerged in Shanghai. Mechanized spinning, weaving, and knitting were by now major industries. Around 1924 the popular press began running seasonal fashion features. Soon after, fashion shows made an appearance. The first was organized by graphic artist Ye Qianyu (1907–1996) for the British department store Whitelaw's. In the late 1920s and 1930s pictorial magazines carried photographs of fashionably dressed women and of new fashion designs by artists such as Ye Qianyu and his circle. From Shanghai, new styles spread to other parts of China via advertising posters and the popular press, and increasingly by movies.

During the Nanjing decade attempts were made by the central and some provincial governments to control fashion by regulating the length of sleeves, the height of hems, hairstyles, and even footwear. These regulations were issued in the name of defending Chinese culture and accorded with widespread efforts to revive Confucianism as the moral framework for Chinese society. The Anti-Japanese War created other priorities. After the Japanese invasion in 1937, the supply of cloth became an issue, and as in Europe in the same period, women's fashions during the war were dictated by the need to conserve cloth. The long Mandarin gown of the mid-1930s gave way to a short one late in the same decade.

## SOCIALISM AND FASHION

Needless to say, clothes worn in 1930s Yan'an, the Communist-base area, looked rather different from those worn by high society in Shanghai and Nanjing. The one point of similarity was the Sun Yat-sen suit, which was worn by Nationalist and Communist bureaucrats and political leaders. Other styles available in Yan'an were the army uniform and the country-style homespun jacket and trousers. These had a profound influence on fashions after 1949, when patriotic young men and women, inspired by romantic tales of the Yan'an period, liked to wear the Yan'an-style cadre suit (*ganbu zhifu*)—essentially the Sun Yat-sen suit or a modest variation thereof. Foreigners dubbed this the Mao suit.

Russia was the other source of inspiration for 1950s styles in China. Among women, the Lenin suit (a jacket with a turned down collar and two rows of buttons) and the *bulaji* (the Russian *platye*, a simple frock often made of figured rather than plain cloth) attest to Russian influence. In 1955–1956, the *bulaji* was much publicized during a short-lived campaign directed by Yu Feng (1916–2007) to encourage greater diversity in fashions and especially to get more women to wear skirts. A modified form of the Mandarin gown was also designed for this campaign, but the era of the Mandarin gown proved to be over. While it was still worn behind closed doors until the beginning of the Cultural Revolution in 1966, and very occasionally for performances, it had become a niche garment.

Although China exported cotton during the Mao years, cloth was in short supply at home. This shortage buttressed the antifashion ethos up to the late 1970s restricting the variety of clothes worn. It even affected choice within the antifashion regime, since it could be very expensive or absolutely impossible to buy the cloth to make the antifashion garments in vogue. During the Cultural Revolution, an army uniform was the fashion of the day for young people, but the real thing could be obtained only through connections. To judge from memoirs and anecdotes of the time, mothers around the country were at their wits' end as to how to get cloth to make uniforms for their revolutionary offspring. This fashion received a curious twist in the late 1970s, when the height of winter fashion among the young was a fleecy hat with earflaps, worn with an army coat and a mouth mask tucked into a button hole with its strings trailing down untidily, giving the wearer an air of insouciance suitable to the post-Mao era.

## THE REFORM ERA AND BEYOND

One of the first signs of change in post-Mao China was a relaxation of vigilance about how to dress. Women began to perm their hair and wear makeup. Bell-bottom trousers came into vogue and were a bone of contention between parents and teenagers. Japanese television, films, and imports, including sewing machines, dramatically enlarged fashion possibilities. In this commodity-short society, anything with a foreign label became a desirable accessory. The most famous example was sunglasses, which were worn with the designer label still affixed to the lens.

China's half-open door in the 1980s allowed foreign skills, goods, and money into the country, which in turn facilitated an outflow of Chinese-made goods, particularly textiles and garments. In 1970 China accounted for less than 5 percent of clothing exports from developing economies. By 1980, in the wake of the policy shift toward reform and opening up in 1978, this share had more than doubled. By 2000, on the eve of China's entry into the World Trade Organization, it had been the leading exporter of textiles and garments for five years running.

The importance of the textile and garment industry was reflected in the education system. Early reform-era designers were mostly graduates in fine arts, but fashion-design departments soon emerged in technical and art schools. The need for textbooks stimulated research on costume and textile history. By the mid-1980s, Chinese designers were traveling to Japan to study under the recognized masters of couture. National and international competitions gave Chinese designers exposure and experience. A local fashion industry was reborn.

The rapid growth of the textile and clothing industry in China is viewed with mixed feelings by leading participants in the fashion revolution, who early looked to Japan's success in haute couture as the likely model for China. But instead of becoming a byword for design innovation, China is on the way to being the home of fast fashion, a genre defined by imitation and disposability. The names of top designers such as Zhang Zhaoda (Mark Cheung) and Ma Ke (Coco Ma) are barely known abroad, and even in China are less recognizable than a name like Issey Miyake. Chinese models too find it hard to make a name on the world stage, while Chinese fashion magazines, after a promising beginning in the 1980s, now struggle to compete against foreign titles such as *Elle* and *Vogue*. Thirty years after the beginning of the reform era, China has a thriving fashion industry, but it is one that has yet to make its mark in the world.

**SEE ALSO** *Fashion; Hairstyles.*

**BIBLIOGRAPHY**


Braudel, Fernand. *Capitalism and Material Life, 1400–1800.* Trans. Miriam Kochan. New York: Harper Colophon Books, 1967.

Chang, Eileen [Zhang Ailing]. A Chronicle of Changing Clothes. Trans. Andrew F. Jones. *Positions: East Asia Cultures Critique* 11, 2 (Fall 2003): 427–441.

Chen, Tina Mai. Proletarian White and Working Bodies in Mao's China. *Positions: East Asia Cultures Critique* 11, 2 (Fall 2003): 361–393.

Finnane, Antonia. *Changing Clothes in China: Fashion, History, Nation.* New York: Columbia University Press, 2007.

Garrett, Valery. *Chinese Dress from the Qing Dynasty to the Present.* Tokyo: Tuttle, 2007.

Harrist, Robert E., Jr. Clothes Make the Man: Dress, Modernity, and Masculinity in China, ca. 1912–1937. In *Body and Face in Chinese Visual Culture*, ed. Wu Hung and Katherine R. Tsiang, 171–196. Cambridge, MA: Harvard University Asia Center, 2005.

Hua Mei. *Zhongguo fuzhuang shi* [History of Chinese dress]. Tianjin: Renmin Meishu Chubanshe, 1989.

Ko, Dorothy. *Every Step a Lotus: Shoes for Bound Feet.* Berkeley: University of California Press, 2001.

Roberts, Claire, ed. *Evolution and Revolution: Chinese Dress, 1700s–1900s.* Sydney: Powerhouse Museum, 1997.

Segre Reinach, Simona. China and Italy: Fast Fashion versus *Prêt a Porter*, towards a New Culture of Fashion. *Fashion Theory: The Journal of Dress, Body, and Culture* 9, 1 (March 1, 2005): 55.

Steele, Valerie, and John Major. *China Chic: East Meets West.* New Haven, CT: Yale University Press, 1999.

Zamperini, Paola. On Their Dress They Wore a Body: Fashion and Identity in Late Qing Shanghai. *Positions: East Asia Cultures Critique* 11, 2 (2003): 301–330.

***Antonia Finnane***

# CODIFIED LAW, 1800–1949

A distinction between "principal" and "secondary" legal codes can be observed throughout the imperial period. In most dynasties, the principal code bore the title of *lü* and consisted primarily of penal regulations. The secondary codes, formed through the accumulation of administrative practice, codified various forms of imperial commands that could either supplement or override provisions in the principal legal code. The Da Qing Lüli (Great Qing Code; hereafter referred to as the Qing Code), the principal legal code of the Qing, was distinct in incorporating a specific type of secondary code, the *li*, which supplemented each article of the corpus of primary provisions, the *lü*.

## THE DA QING LÜLI

In the Qing Code, the *lü* regulations, of which there were 436 in total, were inherited directly from the Ming Code (Minglü) with but minor amendments in 1646 and 1725. The structure of the Qing Code was provided by the administrative organization of the state. Thus the Qing Code consisted of seven sections (*pian*), beginning with the names of the punishments and general rules (*mingli*), followed by six sections corresponding to the six ministries of administration. Offenses were thus categorized according to the administrative context in which they might arise, rather than following a judicial framework independent of the executive. To the extent that the analogy of Western criminal law could be applied, most offenses that would come under the category of *malum in se* (inherently wrong criminal conduct) were provided for in the *xinglü* (laws relating to the Ministry of Justice [Xing Bu]), while the other sections dealt mainly with *malum prohibitium* offenses, that is, conduct deemed criminal by virtue of the specific administrative circumstances.

While the *lü* was a legal form dating back at least to the Jiuzhang Lü (Statutes in Nine Sections) of the early Han (206 BCE–220 CE), the *li* had origins in the Wenxing Tiaoli, a secondary code of the Ming. The Wenxing Tiaoli was formulated at the end of the fifteenth century through a process of collecting administrative decisions that might be adhered to as precedence, and restating them as more abstract regulations. The code became the primary vehicle for legal change and refinement throughout the Ming. In 1585 the Wenxing Tiaoli was incorporated into one volume with the Minglü, and in this form it was inherited by the Qing and consolidated as the Da Qing Lüli. After this consolidation, *li* regulations were amended and added to regularly, while the *lü* articles stayed fixed. With the final amendment of 1870, the Da Qing Lüli included approximately 1900 *li* regulations.

## THE ADMINISTRATIVE CODES OF THE QING

While the Qing sustained the tradition of the *lü* penal regulations in the Da Qing Lüli, there was also a separate tradition of codified law in imperial China: nonpenal administrative laws that regulated the institutions and practices of government. These laws under some dynasties took the form of another principal code, the *ling*. These administrative laws were not based on different principles from the penal *lü* regulations, but rather the two forms of law explicitly complemented each other, with the penal code, the *lü*, providing the specific punishment for the breach of a particular administrative regulation. This tradition of the *ling* was not continued into the Qing, and such administrative regulations separate from the *lü* were not given the form of a legal code. However, these regulations were entered into volumes called *huidian* (collected statutes). What distinguished the *huidian* from legal codes such as the *ling* is the fact that the compilation process of the *huidian* did not involve legislative change, but rather was a reflection of the need to provide an updated manual of preexisting laws and institutions. The *huidian* was compiled five times during the Qing, in 1690, 1732, 1764, 1812, and 1899.

The administrative regulations found in the *huidian* were supplemented by the official documentation of cases significant as administrative precedents. These cases, and the rules emerging from them, came to be compiled as separate volumes after the *huidian* of 1764. These volumes were named the *huidian zeli* (collected statutes with model cases, to accompany the *huidian* of 1764) and *huidian shili* (collected statutes with precedent cases, for the *huidian* of 1812 and 1899).

In addition to the *huidian* and *huidian shili*, which concerned themselves with all branches of the central government, official documentation on cases providing administrative precedents was accumulated at different levels, and official compilations were made at these different levels, assembling such cases and the regulations that could be extracted from these cases. At the level of central government ministries, there were the *zeli*, collections of edicts and regulations extracted from precedent cases. The *zeli*, like the *huidian*, was without legislative value, but summarized the norms and practices to be adhered to in the process of administration. Five of the six central government ministries produced such collections, the exception being the Ministry of Justice, for which the aforementioned *tiaoli* in the Da Qing Lüli provided the regulations arising from administrative practice. Next, at the provincial level, there was collection of selected imperial edicts and notices from central government ministries directed at the governor or governor general. These collections, somewhat confusingly, were also called collections of *tiaoli*—although the meaning of the term is different from the supplementary clauses of the Da Qing Lüli mentioned above—and appear to have been compiled for every province, examples being the *Siji tiaoli* of Guangdong and the *Shangyu tiaoli* of Zhili. These collections marked out edicts deemed important at the provincial level, but again their compilation was not an act of legislation. Finally, some provinces compiled collections of commands and directives issued by the governor or governor general, to be followed by officials within the provinces. These were known as *shengli*, among the best known being the *Xijiang zhengyao* (Essentials of Jiangxi government) and the *Hunan shengli cheng'an* (Directives of the governor and precedents of Hunan).

## PRECEDENT

In judging a case and meting out punishment, the Qing official was constrained by the *lü* to cite specifically from the *lüli*, and failure to do so resulted in his own punishment. This provision in the *lü* takes care to point out that an earlier judgment (including any imperial decree) that was not promulgated as law could not be cited as a basis for judgment. Promulgation as law involved incorporating the judgment into the *lüli*; any precedent case or imperial decree, such as those collected in the above-mentioned *huidian* or the *shengli*, did not have the same legal significance. Hence, the compilation of the *lüli* had a legal significance that the compilation of administrative codes did not, in that it provided laws that could be cited in judgments involving punishment.

While the place of precedent cases in the legal process was thus strictly limited, the very process of applying specific provisions of the *lüli* to concrete cases was often problematic, in that many of the provisions arose from concrete cases and were thus in the first instance directed toward an extremely narrow range of occurrences. This necessitated the development of the procedure of application by analogy (*bifu*), and officials came to be required to have a certain knowledge of precedent, especially in how exactly analogies were to be made, linking certain clauses (and not others) to certain cases. Consequently, while the Qing government did not compile an official collection of precedent cases, there was a proliferation of private compilations, such as the *Xing'an huilan* (Conspectus of criminal cases), the *Li'an quanshu* (Compendium of precedent cases), and the *Boan xinbian* (New collection of reversed cases). The demand for such collections arose primarily at the level of local and provincial officials and their advisors, whose judgments were scrutinized by the Ministry of Justice. Consistency of judgments was considered a prerequisite, and the official constantly faced the risk of having a judgment rejected on the grounds that its application of the law was not in line with practice established through precedent.

## LATE QING LEGAL REFORMS

The nineteenth-century crises, centering on the Taiping Uprising and defeat in the Opium Wars, gave rise to the Foreign Affairs movement (*yangwu yundong*), bringing in Western technology, in both industry and social institutions, and promoting the use of such technology in accord with China's cultural heritage. In the context of this movement, in 1864 the missionary W. A. P. Martin translated and published *Wanguo gongfa*, a Chinese translation of Henry Wheaton's *Elements of International Law* that is often credited with the introduction of Western legal concepts in China. As the crises deepened with defeat in the Sino-Japanese War (1894–1895), political failure of the 1898 reform movement, and the Boxer Uprising, Western legal concepts came to be seen as a necessary basis on which a modern state might be built, rather than as a set of technological devices that might be manipulated in accordance with traditional Chinese values and incorporated into the existing legal system. Hence in an important move in 1901, the emperor endorsed a memorial from Zhang Zhidong and Liu Kunyi that recommended a procedure for receiving Western laws closely modeled on the Japanese system. Features of the recommended system included inviting foreign legal experts to China for codification, establishing educational institutions for legal studies while sending students abroad, and using Japanese translations of Western legal terms (rather than original translations) to save time.

In the context of codified law, immediate needs were deemed to be laws on mining, railways, and commerce. Indeed, a commercial code, Da Qing Shanglü, was completed in 1904. For overarching needs, an institution dedicated to systematic revision of the law, the Bureau for the Revision of Laws (Xiuding Falü Guan), was established in 1904, with Shen Jiaben and Wu Tingfang appointed as its ministers. Under their direction, codification took place mainly in two contexts. First, the Da

Qing Lüli was reorganized to take the form of a modern criminal code. One aspect of this change was the modernization of punishments, especially the introduction of a unified form of penal servitude (in place of the various forms of banishment found in the Da Qing Lüli) and the abolition of certain "cruel" punishments (death by slicing [*lingchi*], display of the decapitated head [*xiaoshou*], desecration of the corpse [*lushi*], collective responsibility [*yuanzuo*], and tattooing [*cizi*]). Moreover, judicial torture and flogging as punishment were prohibited. A major impetus in this process was the need to create a legal system sufficiently "modern" for foreign powers to relinquish the extraterritorial privileges that had been granted. These changes—with mixed success in actual implementation—were brought about through the endorsement of a series of memorials in 1905 without forming a new criminal code. All the while, the compilation of such a code was taking place, and this process resulted in the Da Qing Xianxing Xinglü (Qing current criminal code), which took effect in 1910. As with the Da Qing Lüli, this code included certain provisions that in a Western system would be understood as belonging to the sphere of civil law. These provisions would remain in effect into the Republic while it worked on codifying its own civil law.

The second approach taken by the Bureau for the Revision of Laws entailed a much more radical departure from the Da Qing Lüli, with a fundamental reworking of the punishments and a stress on such "modern" notions as equality before the law. A draft of the criminal code, the *xinglü caoan*, was completed under Shen Jiaben's direction at the end of 1907. This process was aided by the invited Japanese scholar Okada Asatarō, and the draft shows strong influences of the Japanese criminal code of the time. Yet the draft was subjected to severe criticisms from such conservative scholar-officials as Zhang Zhidong, who held that ritual propriety and ethical teachings (*lijiao*), unique to the Chinese, could not be maintained under the draft criminal code. As a result of the ensuing debate, the conservative critics succeeded in adding a schedule to the draft that effectively negated Shen Jiaben's program for a "modern" criminal code, this draft endorsed as the *xiuzheng xinglü caoan.* This led to Shen Jiaben's resignation from the post of minister of the Bureau for the Revision of Laws in 1911, months before the Republican revolution.

This approach to compiling a new code that fit into a Western-style legal system, relying on the aid of a foreign legal expert, was not limited to the criminal code. Just as Okada was invited to help compile the criminal code, experts on civil law, commercial law, and criminology were invited to assist in the compilation of Western-style legal codes, and with their assistance, drafts were produced between 1910 and 1911 for a commercial code, a civil code, a criminal-procedure code, and a civil-procedure code. Yet before these drafts could evolve any further, the 1911 revolution broke out, putting an end to the Qing dynasty.

## CODIFICATION UNDER THE REPUBLICAN REGIME

In March 1912, just over two months after the Republic was established, a new draft of the provisional constitution was promulgated, and a bicameral parliament was to be established and to field its first election at the end of the year. In the same month of March, President Yuan Shikai decreed that the above-mentioned draft criminal code of 1911, the *xiuzheng xinglü caoan,* would take effect as the Republic's provisional criminal code, the Zhonghua Minguo Zanxing Xin Xinglü, subject to the omission of certain provisions that were incompatible with the Republican regime. This code remained in force until the Republican Criminal Code (Zhonghua Minguo Xingfa) took effect in 1928.

In the period up to 1928, and especially after 1917, when Sun Yat-sen established a new government in Guangzhou upon the dissolution of the parliament in Beijing, codes were produced by both northern and southern governments. This was motivated in part by the need to support their respective claims to legitimacy. This link between legitimacy and the compilation of modern legal codes was reinforced by the Republic's continued struggle against extraterritoriality, due, at any rate superficially, to the lack of such codes. The codes produced during this period included two competing civil-procedure codes both produced in 1921, the Republican constitution of the Beijing government (Zhonghua Minguo Xianfa, 1925), and the National Government Organization Law (Guomin Zhengfu Zuzhi Fa, 1925) of the Guangdong government.

With the completion of the Northern expedition in 1928, the Republic, now with its capital in Nanjing, was thought to have ended its period of military government (*junzheng*) and entered the phase of political tutelage (*xunzheng*), which in turn would lead eventually to constitutional government (*xianzheng*), according to Sun Yat-sen's theory of revolution. In this context, the enactment of the basic codes followed almost immediately, with the Charter of Political Tutelage (Xunzheng Gangling) stipulated in 1928, the criminal code and the criminal-procedure code enacted in the same year, a company law enacted in 1929, the civil code taking effect in its entirety in 1930, and the civil-procedure code taking effect in 1931.

Thereafter the Republican government continued to renew legal codes throughout the years leading to 1949. New versions of the criminal code, the criminal-procedure code, and civil-procedure code were enacted in 1935. While no major new code was produced during the war years, wartime politics led to extraterritorial privileges finally being relinquished in 1943. In 1946 a new company law was enacted, and in 1947 a new constitution was promulgated.

## CIVIL LAW, 1800–1949

While there is some dispute as to whether China during the Qing dynasty (1644–1912) had "civil law" or not, it is clear that the society operated on a sophisticated system of rights and norms regarding such matters as property, obligations, and family. Moreover, these rights and norms were regularly contested and ruled upon in the magistrate's court.

Procedurally, the distinction between civil and criminal cases was relative. All cases were to be brought before the magistrate, and while crimes of a grave nature (*zhongqing*) automatically went through multiple layers of justice (cases involving the death penalty automatically went as far up as the emperor), trivial cases (*xishi*) could be decided at a lower level. Cases where the punishment was lighter than penal servitude (*tu*), could be decided at the level of the county or subprefectural magistrate. These included most cases of household, marriage, land, and monetary obligations (*huhun tiantu qianzhai*).

The magistrate's decision in such cases could involve both punishment according to the code and a ruling on the original dispute. This latter ruling did not have to cite a specific provision from the code, as decisions on punishments were required to, and hence it was not explicitly legal in the same sense as a penal judgment. Moreover, the execution of these decisions relied heavily on assent and cooperation by the parties, and dissatisfied parties could repeatedly bring the same case to be retried. These aspects of civil justice at the magistrate level, along with the absence of an independent civil code spelling out legal rights and duties in a nonpenal context, have led some scholars to hesitate to mechanically apply the Western notion of civil law to the Qing system.

When the Western distinction between civil and criminal laws came to be recognized in the process of legal reform, the Bureau for the Revision of Laws (Xiuding Falü Guan) was required to newly compile civil and commercial codes. Through the invitation of Japanese scholars (most notably Shida Kōtarō and Matsuoka Yoshimasa), expertise on foreign civil and commercial laws was actively introduced. Moreover, because the authorities recognized that many of the traditional rights and norms that would translate into civil and commercial laws existed in the realm of custom, they initiated a survey of customs. At the same time, the risk of the destruction of traditional values—ritual propriety and ethical teachings—became a hotly contested issue, and such considerations led to the Bureau of Rites (Lixue Guan) compiling laws relating to family and inheritance.

These aspects of civil law could be seen also in the Republic (1912–1949). While the notion of civil law (*minfa*) was understood differently according to the writer and the context, a general consensus appears to have existed as to the scope of such legislation, as well as on the idea that it involved laws governing the relationships between citizens rather than those requiring direct government involvement. Republican codes continued to show strong Japanese influences, particularly in their terminology and structures. Full-scale surveys of customs were carried out, producing such important works as the *Minshangshi xiguan diaocha baogaolu* (Report on a survey of civil and commercial customs). Customary land rights, such as those obtained by conditional sales (*dian*), remained a part of civil law. Thus, traditional practices related to contracts were also preserved. Consideration of such ritual institutions as ancestral property could also be seen in the process of accommodating a civil code to Chinese society.

**BIBLIOGRAPHY**


Bernhardt, Kathryn, and Philip C. C. Huang, eds. *Civil Law in Qing and Republican China*. Stanford, CA: Stanford University Press, 1994.

Faure, David. *China and Capitalism: A History of Business Enterprise in Modern China*. Hong Kong: University of Hong Kong Press, 2006.

Huang, Philip C. C. *Civil Justice in China: Representation and Practice in the Qing*. Stanford, CA: Stanford University Press, 1996.

Huang, Philip C. C. *Code, Custom, and Legal Practice in China: The Qing and the Republic Compared*. Stanford, CA: Stanford University Press, 2001.

Kirby, William C. China Unincorporated: Company Law and Business Enterprise in Twentieth-Century China. *Journal of Asian Studies* 54, 1 (1995): 43–63.

Shiga Shūzō. *Shindai Chūgoku no hō to saiban* [The law and the courts during the Qing dynasty]. Tokyo: Sōbunsha, 1984.

Shiga Shūzō. Shindai shūken gamon ni okeru soshō o meguru jakkan no shoken: Tan-Shin Tōan o shiryō to shite [Some findings on litigation before prefect and county magistrates during the Qing dynasty: The Dan-Xin Archives as a historical source]. *Hōseishi kenkyū* 37 (1987): 37–61.

Shiga Shūzō. Shindai no minji saiban ni tsuite [Civil cases during the Qing dynasty]. *Chūgoku: Shakai to bunka* 13 (1998): 226–252.


*Kentaro Matsubara*

**SEE ALSO** *Customary Law, 1800–1949; Law Courts, 1800–1949.*

**BIBLIOGRAPHY**

Bourgon, Jerome. Abolishing "Cruel Punishments": A Reappraisal of the Chinese Roots and Long-Term Efficiency of the Xinzheng Legal Reforms. *Modern Asian Studies* 37, 4 (2003): 851–862.

Huang, Philip. *Code, Custom and Legal Practice in China: The Qing and the Republic Compared.* Stanford University Press, 2001.

Jones, William C. "Studying the Ch'ing Code: the Ta Ch'ing Lü Li" *The American Journal of Comparative Law* 22 (1974): 330–364

Kirby, William. "China Unicorporated: Company Law and Business Enterprise in Twentieth-Century China" *Journal of Asian Studies* 54, 1 (1995): 43–63

Shiga Shūzō. *Chūgoku hōseishi ronshū: Hōten to keibatsu* [Essays on the history of China's legal system: Law and punishment]. Tokyo: Sōbunsha, 2003.

Shiga Shūzō, Konoma Masamichi, Takamizawa Osamu, et al. *Gendai chūgoku hō nyūmon* [An introduction to contemporary Chinese law]. 4th ed. Tokyo: Yūhikaku, 2006.

Shimada Masao. Shinmatsu ni okeru kindaiteki hōten no hensan [The editing of modern legal codes at the end of the Qing dynasty]. Tokyo: Sōbunsha, 1980.

Tanii Yōko. Kobu to Kobu sokurei [The Ministry of Revenue and its itemized rules]. *Shirin* 73, 6 (1990) 44–80.

Tanii Yōko. Shindai sokurei shōrei kō [Administrative regulations of the Qing dynasty]. *Tōhō gakuhō* 67 (1995): 137–239.

Terada Hiroaki. Shindai no shōrei [Administrative regulations of the Qing dynasty]. In *Chūgoku hōseishi: Kihon shiryō no kenkyū* [Chinese legal history: Research on basic source materials], ed. Shiga Shūzō, pp. 657–714. Tokyo: Tōkyō Daigaku Shuppankai, 1993.

Yamane Yukio. Min, Shin no kaiten [Collected statutes of the Ming and Qing dynasties]. In *Chūgoku hōseishi: Kihon shiryō no kenkyū* [Chinese legal history: Research on basic source materials], ed. Shiga Shūzō, pp. 473–507. Tokyo: Tōkyō Daigaku Shuppankai, 1993.

***Kentaro Matsubara***

## COLLECTIONS AND COLLECTING

Throughout China's history, art collecting has involved gathering, housing, recording, and using materials that address specific aesthetic, cultural, economic, or even political agendas. Agendas may reflect the tastes of individual collectors or of the collector's group. Regarding collectors' tastes, there are a myriad of governing attitudes and definitions. Collecting may be based upon aesthetic principles set by the collector or demarcated by utilitarian purposes behind collecting, such as securing economic, personal, political, academic, religious, scientific, or social objectives. Individual collectors may keep collected items to themselves, and groups sometimes allow access only to members. When collections are shared, however, by access either direct or indirect (i.e., posthumously, by archaeological excavation or collection dispersal, for example) or by exhibition, reproduction, or publication, agendas and tastes become topics for investigating the roles and functionalities of collecting.

Archaeological evidence suggests that collecting in China began thousands of years ago. During the 2005 and 2006 excavation seasons, Shaanxi archaeologists demonstrated that the occupant of a tomb that dates to the Spring and Autumn period (722–481 BCE) collected jades from the Neolithic, Shang dynasty (sixteenth century–1046 BCE) and Western Zhou (c. 1046–771 BCE) periods. The jades were from distant regions: The Neolithic probably came from the Hongshan culture (4700–2920 BCE) in Liaoning, and the Shang and Western Zhou jades match finds from Henan Province's Fu Hao tomb at Anyang and the Guo State at Sanmenxia, respectively. In another example of collecting in ancient China, *Shiji* (records of the historian) and archaeological findings suggest that the Qin dynasty (221–206 BCE) mausoleum of the First Emperor (Qin Shi Huangdi, r. 246–210 BCE) in Shaanxi Province—the site of the terracotta army—was looted and razed in 206 BCE.

In the common era, traditional histories dating to the Han (206 BCE–220 CE) to Tang dynasties (618–907) note that early collectors acquired ink rubbings on paper of bronzes and stone stele. *Jinshi xue* (study of bronzes and stone stele) activities are mentioned as early as the Han; rubbings were commonplace by the sixth century of the Southern and Northern dynasties (386–589). By the Song dynasty (960–1279) the emergence of noted collectors is well documented in historical records and extant materials such as the *Kaogu tu* (1092) and *Bogu tulu* (c. 1125), woodblock printed volumes that illustrated and explicated rubbings that were taken from stone stele, bronzes and jades. Song collectors systematically collected rubbings and developed specific terminology to advance the study of bronzes, ceramics, paintings, and sculptures, and they meticulously cataloged their works in woodblock-printed volumes.

In addition to these early collectors' histories, the imperial collections and members of the literati such as the Ming dynasty artist Dong Qichang (1555–1636) inspired and shaped nineteenth-century notions about how collections could and should be built. Dong and other influential artists produced essays, histories, and standards that circulated among collectors. Under patronage of the Ming and Qing courts, artists and studios were commissioned to create paintings, sculptures, ceramics, bronzes, and other works. The Qing collection under Emperor Qianlong (r. 1736–1796; 1711–1799) embraced traditional Chinese collecting as well as foreign exchanges, particularly with Europeans and Jesuits. Qianlong not only acquired materials for display, such as clocks and astronomical instruments, but also used new materials and processes (e.g., copper-plate printing and new methods of architecture) in commissioned projects such as Yuanming yuan (Garden of Perfect Brightness). During the latter half of Qing dynasty the combination of traditional collecting and global demands to export materials from China produced a distinct hybrid collector.

The Qing official Duan Fang (1861–1911) epitomized the traditional yet international collector. As a traditional collector he published volumes on his painting, bronze, and jade collections. In his official capacity he led an imperial mission to governments in North America and Europe (1905–1906), and while in the United States he stopped in Chicago to visit the Field Museum construction site. Upon his return to China he inscribed (in Chinese and English) and donated to the Field Museum a Daoist stele. He also visited Cairo, where he acquired ancient artifacts (sarcophagi and stone monuments) and commissioned rubbings. Back in China, he welcomed to his residences in Hunan and Jiangsu Provinces foreign visitors including the missionary and art collector John Ferguson (1866–1945). Through Ferguson, works once owned by Duan Fang were published in western journals and books and then later sold by Ferguson to private and institutional collectors from the West such as Charles Lang Freer (1854–1919) and the Metropolitan Museum of Art in New York. Duan Fang also led the 1910 international exposition in Nanjing, which promoted not only Western commercial ties but also arts from China. In addition, he engaged photographers to promote his collections via Chinese and international publications. The use of photography continued with scholarly collectors such as Wu Hufan (1894–1968), who used images of works not only to emphasize his scholarship and collections, but also to advance traditional views on collecting.

Traditional collecting in China suffered after the 1912 overthrow of the Qing dynasty by Republican forces and the civil war between the Nationalists and Communists. International events such as the two wars with Japan (1894–1895; 1937–1945) and the two World Wars affected collecting too. Due to the collapse of the banking systems and societal norms, such as everyday governmental institutions, collectors were forced to liquidate their collections for cash to deal with inflation and emergencies, such as the need to flee a region under disruption from the effects of war. Noted intellectuals such as Wu Dacheng (1835–1902), Luo Zhenyu (1866–1940), and Wang Guowei (1877–1927) also challenged the role and functionality of traditional collecting. For example, Luo and Wang travelled to Japan to emphasize the internationalization of the study and collecting of the arts of China. Rather than solely the expertise of a traditional Chinese scholar, collecting and studying the arts of China was a global endeavor beyond China's borders and traditions.

The internationalization of economies, social sciences, military tactics, and political policies forced changes upon collectors and collecting, since Chinese works were collected beyond China's border en masse. Collecting re-emerged as a mechanism to reform domestic and foreign political agendas, and ideological differences on the roles of collecting meant that collecting was increasingly directed by governmental policies. China's leaders embraced new concepts, such as a national museum collection and a national scientific body, to reinforce and solidify their international reputation. One example of this was the opening of the Qing imperial collection to the public in 1914 and the eventual establishment of the Palace Museum (Gugong Bowuyuan) to house it in 1925. A second example was the establishment in 1928 of the Academia Sinica, the Nationalist government–sponsored research institute that originally comprised several branches, including the National Research Institute of History (Zhongyang Yanjiuyuan) and Philology and its Institute of Archaeology (Lishi Yuyan Yanjiusuo), which influenced how collecting was pursued, studied, shared and published. Although their research incorporated traditional collecting paradigms, collecting functioned as a science rather than an antiquated custom. Along similar conceptual lines, during speeches at the Yan'an Forum on Literature and Art (1942), Mao Zedong outlined how collected works of the past should be combined with Communist Party revolutionary arts to transform China. Establishing an interpretation of the evolution of Chinese history according to a Marxist paradigm, he connected his revolutionary push via the contemporary arts to the trajectory of Chinese societal and governmental evolution to a communist state. With both the Nationalists and Communists interested in the arts, the Palace Museum collections were identified by the Executive Yuan as national treasures and therefore politically important and had to be kept from enemy hands at all cost, especially Mao's. Its collections were packed and moved between cities throughout China and eventually to Taiwan following the Second Sino-Japanese War and the civil war.

For Asian collectors, Japan's interventions within China's borders in the first half of the twentieth century sanctioned archaeological and collecting endeavors. By the Treaty of Versailles (1919), Japan was granted control over former German territories in Shandong Province; a decade later Manchukuo was established in northeast China, and Japan occupied and completely controlled this area from 1932 through 1945. The Japanese government established colonial rule, and Japanese scientists systematically conducted archaeological excavations and removed works to collecting institutions in Japan.

Western collectors such as Aurel Stein (1862–1943), Paul Pelliot (1878–1945), and Langdon Warner (1881–1955) led archaeological expeditions to China for their respective collecting institutions—the British Museum, Musée

Guimet, and Harvard University. After 1911, the circumstances mentioned above allowed foreign collectors opportunities to export materials from China with only occasional resistance due to domestic turmoils resulting from regime change and foreign occupation forces. The removal of sculpture, architectural work, tomb treasure, and other art work was rampant because lack of governmental control, while economic uncertainty made collecting lucrative. In an attempt to curtail the export of China's cultural heritage, the National Commission for the Preservation of Antiquities was established by the Executive Yuan in 1928, and the Law on the Preservation of Ancient Objects (1930) and Detailed Rules for the Implementation of the Law on the Preservation of Ancient Objects (1931) were passed. Nevertheless, with national crises diverting the government's attention from enforcing preservation legislation, works exited China en masse, supplying collectors and exhibitions abroad via international dealers such as Paris-based C. T. (Ching Tsai) Loo (1880–1957) and London-based Sadajirō Yamanaka (1865–1936). Many of the treasures sold by Loo and Yamanaka were donated eventually to national museums. For example, George Eumorfopoulos (1863–1939) collected thousands of objects that are now housed at the British Museum and the Victoria and Albert Museum in London; Charles Lang Freer and Arthur M. Sackler (1913–1987) donated their massive collections to the Smithsonian Institution in 1923 and 1987, respectively.

In 1925 an international loan exhibition of 212 works from European collections of Chinese art was held in Amsterdam by the Vereniging van Vrienden der Aziatische Kunst (Society of Friends of Asiatic Art) at the Stedelijk Museum. Organizers secured loans from foreign museums such as the Musée Cernuschi and Musée d'Extrême-Orient (Palais du Louvre) in Paris and the Ostasiatische Kunstsammlung in Berlin. Acclaimed private collectors such as George Eumorfopoulos in London and Adolphe Stoclet (1871–1949) in Brussels also loaned works. One year later, in Cologne, an Asian art exhibition of 600 works was held by the Freunde Ostasiatischer Kunst (Friends of East Asian Art) with loans from European museums and private collectors. In 1929 Berlin hosted an exhibition by the Gesellschaft für Ostasiatische Kunst and the Preussischen Akademie der Künste. The exhibition showcased 1,272 works loaned from 171 private, institutional, and art-dealer collections in thirteen countries. Between 1935 and 1936 the largest exhibition of art from China ever mounted was shown at London's Burlington House of the Royal Academy of Arts. The International Exhibition of Chinese Art contained 3,080 works from more than 240 international lenders, including Laurence Binyon (1869–1943), Sir Percival David (1892–1964), Eumorfopoulos, and others. Of note were the 984 objects loaned by the Executive Yuan's Chinese Organizing Committee from China's Palace Museum, the National Museum, Academia Sinica, the Beiping Library, the Henan Museum, and the Anhui Provincial Library; these works had been displayed previously in Shanghai in spring 1935. This massive, two-continent exhibition occurred with the Japanese government as an active participant, just before Japan's full-scale attack on China in 1937.

World War II began shortly after the exhibition, and it was not until after 1949 that major exhibitions of the art of China resumed. The works that left China between 1911 and 1949 are still being exchanged and sold today, and collectors in China have been the primary buyers since 2000. International cultural heritage guidelines protecting archaeological and ancient art established by the 1970 UNESCO Convention (1970) and the Association of Art Museums Directors (2008) have affected the collecting of Chinese artifacts. Since foreign governments have increased scrutiny on auction sales and repatriated several works fresh to the market to China, the importance of provenance has now affected the market, with those of pre-1970 histories demanding increasingly higher prices.

**SEE ALSO** *Art Exhibitions, 1850–1949; Art Exhibitions Abroad; Art Exhibitions since 1949; Art History and Historiography; Connoisseurship.*

**BIBLIOGRAPHY**

Chang, Kwang-chih. *The Archaeology of Ancient China.* New Haven, CT: Yale University Press, 1986.

Chen Xingcan. *Zhongguo shiqian kaoguxue shi yanjiu 1895–1949* [Study on history of prehistoric archaeology in China (1895–1949)] Beijing: Shenghuo, Dushu, Xinzhi Sanlian Shudian, 1997.

Chinese Organizing Committee. *Illustrated Catalogue of Chinese Government Exhibits for the International Exhibition of Chinese Art in London.* 4 vols. Shanghai: Shangwu Yinshuguan, 1936.

Cohen, Warren. *East Asian Art and American Culture.* New York: Columbia University Press, 1992.

Elliot, Jeannette Shambaugh, with David Shambaugh. *The Odyssey of China's Imperial Art Treasures.* Seattle and London: University of Washington Press, 2005.

*The International Exhibition of Chinese Art.* London: Royal Academy of Arts, 1935–1936.

Lawton, Thomas. *A Time of Transition: Two Collectors of Chinese Art.* Lawrence: Spencer Museum of Art, University of Kansas, 1991.

Li, Chu-tsing, and James C.Y. Watt, eds. *The Chinese Scholar's Studio: Artistic Life in the Late Ming Period.* New York: Thames and Hudson and Asia Society Galleries, 1987.

Murphy, J. David. *Plunder and Preservation: Cultural Property Law and Practice in the People's Republic of China.* Oxford, U.K.: Oxford University Press, 1995.

Rudoph, Richard C. Preliminary Notes on Sung Archaeology. *Journal of Asian Studies* 22, no. 2 (February 1963): 169–177.

Shaanxi Sheng kaogu yanjiusuo, et al. Shaanxi Hancheng Liangdai cun yizhi M26 fajue jianbao [A brief excavation report on Tomb 26 at Liangdi Village, Hancheng, Shaanxi]. *Wenwu* 1 (2008): 4–21.

Starr, Kenneth. *Black Tigers: A Grammar of Chinese Rubbings.* Seattle and London: University of Washington Press, 2008.

Steuber, Jason. The Exhibition of Chinese Art at Burlington House, London, 1935–36. *Burlington Magazine* (August 2006): 528–536.

Tu Cheng-sheng, Chu Hung-lam, and Chang Hsiu-fen, eds. *Tradition and Innovation: A Guide to the Institute of History and Philology, Academia Sinica.* Trans. Chu Hung-lam. Tabei: Institute of History and Philology, Academia Sinica, 1998.

Von Spee, Clarissa. Wu Hufan: *A Twentieth-century Art Connoisseur in Shanghai.* Berlin: Dietrich Reimer Verlag, 2008.

Wilkinson, Endymion. *Chinese History: A Manual.* Cambridge, MA: Harvard University Asia Center, 2000.

Xiaoneng Yang, ed. *The Golden Age of Chinese Archaeology: Celebrated Discoveries from the People's Republic of China.* Washington, DC: National Gallery of Art and Nelson-Atkins Museum of Art, 1999.

***Jason Steuber***

# COMINTERN IN CHINA

The Communist International (Comintern, also known as the Third International) opened its founding congress on March 2, 1919. Representatives from China attended as observers, since Soviet leaders saw the need for a friendly China on its border. This opening congress was concerned not with colonial emancipation, however, but rather with the promotion of revolution in the West.

With the onset of the May Fourth Movement, Soviet and Comintern leaders took note of a new mass movement in China. It involved many strata within Chinese society and was directed at the forces of imperialism as well as at those aspects of Chinese culture and politics seen as obstacles to modernization. Some in the Comintern saw this as an opening for a Bolshevik movement in China. At the end of 1919, however, Lenin argued that any activities in the Asian region must still be based on "bourgeois nationalism" and aimed at a democratic revolution, on account of the relative "backwardness" there. Differences within the Comintern over this question came to a head at its Second Congress in July 1920.

Two issues decided by this Congress were especially relevant to China. One concerned the requirements for full membership, formally titled "Theses on Conditions for Admission to the Communist International," presented to the Congress on July 20, 1920, by Leon Trotsky. Reacting to the experience of the undisciplined Second (or Socialist) International, Comintern leaders felt that a highly centralized, worldwide organization was necessary to carry out effective action. Formal admission requirements were seen as one way to keep undesirable parties and groups from joining.

The other, connected issue concerned the appropriate attitude and policy toward national and colonial questions. The heated debate and the theses that resulted contained some apparent contradictions with the twenty-one conditions for membership. This became the source for much of the confusion within young communist parties in the colonial and semicolonial world, including China.

## EARLY COMINTERN ACTIVITIES

The earliest Comintern representatives, Grigori Voitinski and his interpreter Yang Mingzhai, were sent to Beijing in 1920. There they first met with Li Dazhao. They then went to Shanghai, where they met with Chen Duxiu. These meetings with two of the founders of Chinese communism resulted in the establishment of the first communist group (not yet a party) in Shanghai in the summer of 1920. More groups quickly followed in Wuhan, Changsha, Guangzhou, and Jinan.

These small groups (*xiao zu*) published movement periodicals, such as *Xin qingnian* (New Youth), which had by this time become the Shanghai group's official organ, and *Gongchanzhuyizhe* (The Communist). They also set up a Socialist Youth Corps, bringing in new activists like Peng Zhuzhi and Liu Shaoqi. A Russian language school was set up in Shanghai, and by the spring of 1921, some of its students were sent to Moscow to study at the Communist University of the Toilers of the East.

Ultimately, the founding congress of the Chinese Communist Party took place in Shanghai in July 1921. The party had only fifty or so members across China at this time. Maring (Hendricus Sneevliet), the first official representative to China of the Executive Committee of the Communist International, attended this congress.

The Chinese Communist Party's first program reflected none of the possible contradictions in Comintern policy in the semicolonial world. It was a straightforward pro-working-class and anti-bourgeoisie platform. By the Second Party Congress in July 1922, however, there was grudging recognition of the possible role that Sun Yat-sen's Guomindang (or Nationalist Party) might play in the democratic revolution. The Communist Party saw no need to ally with Sun at that time, however. Under pressure from the Comintern, this would change.

## PRESSURE TOWARD ALIGNMENT WITH THE GUOMINDANG

In Maring's report to the Executive Committee of the Communist International in July 1922, he reflected a favorable attitude toward the Guomindang as a revolutionary party. In April he proposed to the Chinese Communist Party that all party and Socialist Youth Corps members should join the Guomindang. Chen Duxiu, then General Secretary of the Communist Party opposed this and wrote an appeal to Voitinski to act as mediator with the Comintern on the party's behalf. By April, Stalin had been elevated to the post of General Secretary of the Communist Party of the Soviet Union, a position that expanded his power base. This fact played an important role in the future actions of the Comintern in China.

In the end, the Executive Committee of the Communist International sent instructions for Maring in

August 1922. These instructions made it clear that the Comintern viewed the Guomindang as a revolutionary organization that must be actively supported by the Chinese Communist Party. In fact, the Communist Party was required to help build the Guomindang and wait for the day when the split between its bourgeois and proletarian elements would take place. For now, the main work of the Communist Party lay in organizing the working class into trade unions. Under threat of Comintern discipline, Chen and the Communist Party leadership finally acquiesced, and some Communist Party members actually joined the Guomindang.

On January 12, 1923, the Executive Committee of the Communist International passed a resolution concerning the need for greater collaboration between the Communist Party and the Guomindang. The Guomindang under Sun Yat-sen was considered the only "serious national revolutionary group" in China. For this reason, and because the labor movement in China was still weak, it was necessary for members of the Communist Party to remain in the Guomindang. At the same time, however, the Communist Party was expected to maintain an independent organization without engaging in any conflict with the Guomindang. Contradictions in the compromise policy from the Second Comintern Congress in 1920 were showing through.

On January 26, 1923, Sun Yat-sen and Soviet representative Adolf Joffe signed a joint resolution that declared China to be unripe for communism or the Soviet system. The Soviet Union wanted a friendly and stable China on its doorstep, not a revolutionary and chaotic China. The stage was now set for the First United Front.

In fact, by the time of the Communist Party's Third Congress in June 1923, the "bloc within" strategy held sway. Communist Party members such as Li Dazhao, Chen Duxiu, and Mao Zedong had joined the Guomindang and were helping to establish new Guomindang branches throughout China. Views dissenting with this policy were silenced by continued threats of Comintern discipline. When the Fifth Congress of the Comintern took place in 1924, there were no questions raised about the validity of its China policy.

## DISSENT AND BREAK WITH THE GUOMINDANG, 1924–1927

Some dissent began to appear in Communist Party publications toward the end of 1924. Both *Xiangdao zhoubao* (Guide Weekly) and *Xin qingnian* published articles that seemingly challenged the policy of collaboration between the Communist Party and the Guomindang. Even Chen Duxiu shifted his position somewhat and wrote that the real leadership of any revolution in China must be found in the working class. This careful dissent continued at the Fourth Congress of the Communist Party in January 1925, where a "Resolution on the National Revolutionary Movement" expressed criticism of the Comintern's policy of forced collaboration. The resolution called upon party members not to be naive about the Guomindang and its ultimate goals. The resolution recognized a seeming split between left and right in the Guomindang, but it was careful in its analysis of the way forward.

The May Thirtieth movement of 1925 created pressure for working-class organization and a break with the Guomindang. By then the Communist Party attained a membership of 10,000, and the Socialist Youth Corps had 9,000 members. The Comintern was pleased with these developments and recognized that a working-class movement had become a major force in China. The Executive Committee of the Communist International still opposed a break between the Communist Party and the Guomindang. In fact, the hope was that the Communist Party could now push the Guomindang into the hands of the left wing.

The dominant wing of the Guomindang had other plans, however. Now that Sun Yat-sen had passed away, forces inside the party saw rising militancy among the working class as a threat to important constituencies. There were moves to push Communist Party members out of the Guomindang. A coup carried out by Chiang Kai-shek in March 1926 further exposed this effort. In May 1926 the party passed a resolution to exclude Communist Party members from any positions of authority and to require a full listing of any Communist Party members inside the Guomindang.

Between April and July 1926, Communist Party leaders held a series of meetings, including a plenum of the Central Committee, to try to work out a final proposal for dissolving the collaboration between the Communist Party and the Guomindang. At each point the Comintern representative, now Michael Borodin, opposed any change. In fact, by late 1926 the Guomindang was admitted to membership in the Comintern as a "sympathizing party," and support for the collaboration from the Executive Committee of the Communist International became more insistent.

Every effort by the Communist Party leadership to warn the Comintern about the true nature of the Guomindang was ignored. On April 12, 1927, Chiang Kai-shek entered Shanghai with the Northern Expeditionary Forces and, with some assistance from underworld figures and merchants, proceeded to wipe out the workers and Communist Party members who had held the city for nearly four weeks. The Comintern argued that this betrayal only reinforced the need for the Communist Party to continue to work with the left wing of the Guomindang. Three months later the Guomindang left wing, under the leadership of Wang Jingwei, carried out its own coup against the Communist Party.

All blame was placed on Chen Duxiu, rather than any mistaken policy of the Comintern. Central Committee member Qu Qiubai called an emergency conference for August 7, 1927. Only a few Central Committee members attended as the conference removed Chen as general secretary and blamed his "opportunism" for the failure of the revolution. Qu was then placed in the leadership position, with the support of the Comintern. As a direct result of Comintern policies and the "white terror" of the Guomindang, Communist Party membership fell from around 50,000 to merely 10,000.

### THE END OF THE COMINTERN IN CHINA, 1927–1943

Over the next fifteen years it became increasingly difficult for the Comintern to consistently control the Communist Party and the greater communist movement in China. Mao Zedong and his followers had gone to the countryside to organize a peasant army. Urban efforts by Communist Party members left behind were fitful at best, especially after Japanese moves to occupy greater territory in China from 1931 onward.

Though the Comintern sanctioned a series of new leaders for the Communist Party, from Qu Qiubai to Li Lisan to Wang Ming, it finally had to recognize the rise of Mao Zedong to Communist Party (and movement) leadership in the mid-1930s. The Comintern ultimately agreed to give individual communist parties greater freedom, and by 1943 there was no reason to maintain the fiction of a Communist International in China.

**SEE ALSO** *Russia, Relations with.*

**BIBLIOGRAPHY**

Adler, Alan. *Theses, Resolutions, and Manifestos of the First Four Congresses of the Third International.* Trans. Alix Holt and Barbara Holland. London: Ink Links, 1980.

Degras, Jane, ed. *The Communist International, 1919–1943.* 3 vols. London: Oxford University Press, 1960–1965.

Pantsov, Alexander. *The Bolsheviks and the Chinese Revolution, 1919–1927.* Honolulu: University of Hawaii Press, 2000.

Peng Shu-tse. Introduction. In *Leon Trotsky on China*, ed. Les Evans and Russell Block. New York: Monad Press, 1976.

Saich, Tony. *The Rise to Power of the Chinese Communist Party.* Armonk, NY: M. E. Sharpe, 1996.

Van De Ven, Hans J. *From Friend to Comrade: The Founding of the Chinese Communist Party, 1920–1927.* Berkeley: University of California Press, 1991.

***Joseph T. Miller***

# COMMERCIAL ART

*This entry contains the following:*



## ADVERTISING

The earliest existing evidence for commercial advertisements in China may be traced back to the Song dynasty (907–1279) and includes shop billboards depicted in the handscroll painting *Along the River during the Qingming Festival*, by court painter Zhang Zeduan (1085–1145), and a wrapper from the Liu Needle Shop of Jinan, Shandong Province (Figure 1), which possesses both a commercial logo (a rabbit) and advertising texts.

Between 1760 and 1840, advertising in newspapers was one method among many more important ones, including posters, broadsheets, and tradesmen's cards. Advertising in newspapers and magazines eventually assumed the dominant role among all other media. In terms of share of total advertising expenditures, it retained prominence as late as the 1980s, in spite of the growth of cinema, radio, and television.

Early advertising in newspapers, such as *Shenbao* and *Shibao*, were text-only, and these advertisements often appeared vertically on the side of the page. The first newspaper advertisement to include a picture, in today's terms a display advertisement (*tuwen guanggao*), appeared in the eleventh month, fourteenth day of Emperor Muzong's reign. It was an advertisement for a sewing machine, and it appeared in the same paper in the same place for three months to attract readers' attention. Thereafter, many display advertisements appeared in other Chinese publications, such as *Shenbao* and the magazine *Dianshizhai huabao*, as well as journals, such as *Eastern Miscellany* (*Dongfang zazhi*).

In 1906 the term *guanggao* (advertising) was officially adopted in the Qing government's Regulations for Official Political Newspapers (Zhengzhi Guanbao Zhangcheng). With the founding of the Republic of China in 1912, more types of advertising media joined the ranks, including cinema, signboards, sandwich men who carried boards in front of and behind them on which advertisements could be placed, and so forth. American motion-picture posters and cigarette and medicine advertisements were everywhere on the Shanghai streets and presses in the 1920s and 1930s.

The pioneering graphic artist Li Shutong (1880–1942) articulated the importance of advertising and commercial art in China. Li, who received a good classical education as a child, entered the Western art department at the Tokyo School of Fine Arts (Tokyo Bijutsu Gakko) in 1906, and graduated in

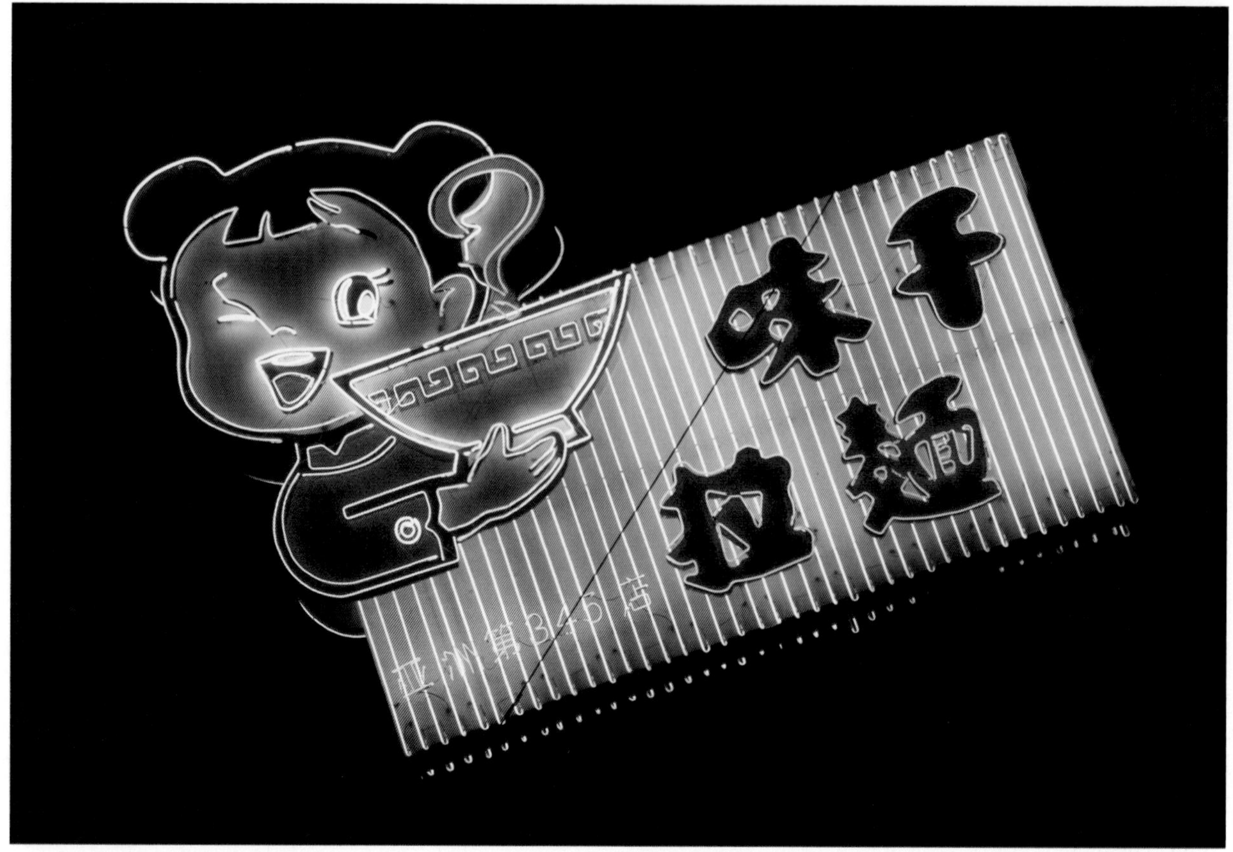


***Neon sign advertising a noodle restaurant, Shanghai, June 19, 2005.*** *After 1949, most forms of advertising came from Communist government propaganda, as competition between companies ceased. Since the adoption of market-based reforms in the 1970s, however, an advertising industry has reemerged, incorporating Western strategies in response to a growing Chinese economy increasingly driven by consumer demand.* © PAUL SOUDERS/CORBIS

1911. In 1912 he returned to Shanghai to teach art and music, and was invited to be the editor of the *Pacific Times* (*Taipingyangbao*). Not only did he draw graphic advertisements for the press, he also introduced advertising theories on its pages. Despite Li's brief involvement in the business world, which he abandoned to become a Buddhist monk, he played a significant role in the development of modern Chinese advertising and commercial art.

Besides the display advertisements found in newspapers, a new kind of advertisement, the cigarette card (*xiangyan paizi*) and calendar poster (*yuefenpai hua*), began to appear in the mid-1850s. By the beginning of the twentieth century, with the explosion of international trade centered in Shanghai, firms such as British American Tobacco transformed the traditional Shanghai calendar with products from their in-house advertising studios. Most of these advertisement calendars and posters depicted beautiful women rendered in close approximation to Western realistic representational style. They retained great popularity among the populace until 1949.

Commercial advertising in China from 1949 to 1978 was very limited. The new Communist government transformed the world of commercial advertising into one that instead produced propaganda, often employing the same artists. With the abolition of private enterprise under the early People's Republic, commercial advertising became unnecessary, and indeed was seen as a vestige of the corrupt capitalist past. Under the policies of economic reform after 1979, business competition resumed and became steadily more intense in China. Advertising as a means of market promotion once again was considered a key competitive element. The demand for advertising services is therefore increasing, and thousands of agencies, both domestic and foreign, have mushroomed almost everywhere in China.

**SEE ALSO** *Fashion; Pictorial Magazines since 1880.*

**BIBLIOGRAPHY**

Berkman, Harold W., and Christopher Gilson. *Advertising Concepts and Strategies*. 2nd ed. New York: Random House, 1987.

Doordan, Dennis P., ed. *Design History: An Anthology*. Cambridge, MA: MIT Press, 1995.

Fan Zhiyu (Fan Chih-yu). *Zhongwai guanggao shi* [Advertising history Chinese and foreign]. Taibei: Sanmin, 1989.

Laing, Ellen Johnston. *Selling Happiness: Calendar Posters and Visual Culture in Early-Twentieth-Century Shanghai.* Honolulu: University of Hawai'i Press, 2004.

Lin Su-hsing. Li Shutong and the Evolution of Graphic Arts in China. *East Asia Journal: Studies in Material Culture* 2, 1 (2007): 86–103.

Wang Shucun. Ji hu jing kai cai tu zhong xi yuefen pai [A note for the Chinese western calendar poster for the lottery, with the scenery of Shanghai]. *Meishu yanjiu* 2 (1959): 57.

Wilmshurst, John, and Adrian Mackay. *The Fundamentals of Advertising.* 2nd ed. Boston: Butterworth-Heinemann, 1999.

*Yinshua zhi guang: Guangming lai zhi dongfang* [Light of printing: Brightness comes from the Orient]. Hangzhou, PRC: Zhejiang Renmin Meishu Chubanshe, 2000.

Zhao Chen. *Zhongguo jindai guanggao wenhua* [China modern advertising culture]. Changchun, PRC: Jilin Kexue Jishu Chubanshe, 2001.

***Lin Su-hsing***

## CALENDARS

Calendar posters (*yuefenpai*) advertising goods and services offered by Western and Chinese firms first appeared in China in the nineteenth century. Combining attractive pictures and useful calendars, and usually distributed free to customers at the New Year, these posters were immensely popular throughout China until the late 1930s. It is estimated that fifty-six commercial artists designed 700,000 posters over the first three decades of the twentieth century.

### PICTORIAL THEMES

During the 1920s and 1930s, three subjects dominated the *yuefenpai* repertoire: pretty women, landscapes, and scenes from legends, novels, or operas. The potential of *yuefenpai* to convey political messages through political motifs was also recognized. Typically, a large picture occupied the center of the vertical format; the calendar was placed at the margins or below the main image. The company name was at the top of the poster, and pictures of the product package or of the advertised product itself were included in the design. Borders of decorative patterns and motifs surrounded the main image.

A survey of posters depicting women reveals new attitudes toward women and their roles in society. In a 1914 poster by Zhou Muqiao (1868–1923), a stern-faced matron stands in a formal, decorous pose. In the late 1920s and 1930s, in examples by Hu Boxiang (1896–1989) and others, women entertainers, fashion models, and sports enthusiasts appear on the posters. Images of sexually appealing smiling women are frequent, sometimes enhanced with mildly erotic overtones.

### POSTER ARTISTS AND WESTERN INFLUENCES

Poster designers worked independently, were employed as staff artists by large corporations such as the British-American Tobacco Company, or worked at commercial art studios. Poster artists were self taught, or learned Western art techniques at the Shanghai Art Academy or in the art department school of the Commercial Press. Several artists were also proficient in traditional Chinese painting.

Zheng Mantuo (1888–1961) used the "rub-and-paint" method, first rubbing a thin layer of carbon for shaded areas and then applying color. Exceptionally vibrant hues characterize the works by Liang Dingming (1898–1959), suggesting Western oil painting. Xu Yongqing (1880–1953) blended Western watercolor and oil painting techniques in his posters depicting famous places in China. Xie Zhiguang (1900–1976) provided representations of beautiful women for calendar posters and also drew black-and-white newspaper advertisements. Hu Boxiang promoted art photography in China, and the special effects of photography are echoed in many of his landscape posters.

In addition to their own ingenuity, artists availed themselves of a variety of visual models. They could copy photographs of lovely celebrities published in pictorials, or borrow renditions of modern Western domestic interiors found in Western magazines for their background settings. The impact of art deco, the prevailing popular artistic style in the West during the 1920s and 1930s, is evident in advertisement posters in the use of color schemes such as blue and yellow, in a distinctly angular form of calligraphy, and in intricate, abstract designs surrounding the central image.

**BIBLIOGRAPHY**

Krasno, Rena, and Yeng-Fong Chiang. *Cloud Weavers: Ancient Chinese Legends.* Berkeley, CA: Pacific View Press, 2003.

Laing, Ellen Johnston. *Selling Happiness: Calendar Posters and Visual Culture in Early Twentieth Century Shanghai.* Honolulu: University of Hawai'i Press, 2004.

Ng Chun Bong, Cheuk Pak Tong, Wong Ying, and Yvonne Lo, comps. *Chinese Women and Modernity: Calendar Posters of the 1910s–1930s.* Hong Kong: Joint Publishers, 1996.

***Ellen Johnston Laing***

## CARTOONS, COMICS, AND *MANHUA*

The Chinese term *manhua*, or sketched drawings, was not common in China until 1925, a period when the mass-media art form known as *manga* also became common in Japan. According to one of its foremost practitioners, Feng Zikai (1898–1975), *manhua* is "a synthetic art, combining painting and texts," and is also "a synthetic art combining intellectual art and graphic art" (Feng, p. 196–199). The birth of *manhua* is usually credited to Feng Zikai; however, the appearance of the term *manhua*, as a noun and an artistic term in China, can be traced back at least to March of 1904, when a column titled *Shishi manhua*, which used *manhua* to depict current affairs, began to appear in the Shanghai-based *Warning of Russian Issues*, which was launched by Cai Yuanpei (1868–1940) and Liu Shipei (1884–1919) on December 25, 1903, and renamed *Warning Bell Daily* on April 25, 1904.

Even before the term *manhua* became widespread in China, a group of commercial artists associated with the new print media contributed comic strips to magazines and newspapers that catered to the interests of a quickly rising middle-class of consumers in Shanghai. One of the earliest and most significant artists was Qian Binghe (1879–1944), author of a famous comic strip titled *The Numerous Guises of the Gibbons* (*Laoyuan baitai*), a cartoon series satirizing the guises that Yuan Shikai (the title is a play on the word *yuan*, or gibbon) assumed in his tireless quest to restore the monarchy, with himself as emperor, during the years of the fledgling Republic (1912–1916).

Along with satirical works, a number of political drawings appeared in the Chinese press. Shen Bochen (1889–1920) was the founder and editor of *Shanghai Punch* (*Shanghai poke*), a bilingual comic monthly based on *Tokyo Punch*, which in turn was derived from the British *Punch*, a weekly magazine of humor and satire. Shen was one of the most influential cartoonists of his generation. *Shanghai Punch*, first published in 1918, may be the earliest cartoon magazine in China.

Trained in both traditional *guohua* techniques as well as the basics of Western painting, the artist-cartoonist Zhang Yuguang (1885–1968) became well-known for using satirical drawings to denounce the territorial seizures of foreign imperialists and to rail against such societal evils as opium or gambling. These cartoons were more often drawn as single-image frames than as comic strips.

## FENG ZIKAI AND HIS CONTEMPORARIES

Numerous works shed a humorous light on everyday life in China. The artists who developed this genre were better educated than earlier cartoonists, and some had received training abroad. The styles of their works were more varied and more closely emulated Western comics. Examples include Feng Zikai, Ye Qianyu (1907–1995), Zhang Guangyu (1900–1964), and Zhang Leping (1910–1992).

Feng Zikai is best known for his lyrical drawings. In 1925, Feng's works became very popular when Zheng Zhenduo (1898–1958), a prominent figure in the Shanghai literary scene, gave him a column, *Zikai manhua*, in his *Literature Weekly* (1921–1929). Throughout his career, Feng's art and writings revealed a strong Japanese influence. Although Feng's poetic and lyrical drawings reveal the unmistakable aesthetic and psychological imprint of the work of Takehisa Yumeji (1884–1934), the style and approach that he developed were all his own, combining traditional Chinese brushstrokes with contemporary social settings, and often lacing them with humor and religious purport.

Ye Qianyu started to draw comics in 1926. His best-known comic strip, *Mr. Wang*, was published in the journal *Shanghai Sketch*, launched in April 1928. Ye's character Mr. Wang cynically symbolized Shanghai life, with his materialism and conformism, his hunger for social success, and his lack of education and culture.

*Shanghai Sketch* was one of more than seventy modern magazines published in Shanghai between 1928 and 1936, a number indicative of the fierce competition to attract consumers from the expanding pool of middle-class and even lower-class readers. This combination of avid demand and support from publishers yielded a peak in the development of the cartoon in China in the years before World War II (1937–1945). Other outstanding cartoonists, such as Lu Shaofei (1903–1995) and Liao Bingxiong (1915–2006), contributed comics to periodicals such as *Shanghai Sketch*, *Modern Sketch*, and *Qingming* (literally, "spring").

## CARTOONS DURING AND AFTER THE WAR

When Shanghai was taken over by the Japanese, many Chinese artists, including Ye Qianyu and Zhang Guangyu, took refuge in Hong Kong. In 1939, they organized a "Modern Chinese Comics Exhibition," which was the first comics exhibition in Hong Kong and had a far-reaching influence on the development of comics on the island.

The war provided its own stimulus to this burgeoning art form. Born in Guangzhou, Liao Bingxiong studied in Shanghai and was known as a satirical writer and member of the Shanghai cartoonists' circle. He joined Guo Moruo's (1892–1978) cartoon propaganda team on the outbreak of war. His best-known works include *Flower Street* (c. 1944), a sardonic evocation of nightlife in the red-light district, and *Gambling with Human Beings* (c. 1945), a savage cartoon showing mahjong gamblers staking not cash but the bound and naked bodies of men and women.

Zhang Guangyu's best-known work was the serial *Journey to the West* (1945), a parodic reprisal of the classical novel of the same name. The journey in this case culminates in Europe, where the travelers find fascism, in the form of Adolf Hitler (1889–1945) and Benito Mussolini (1883–1945), instead of democracy. A sumptuous work, *Journey to the West* includes sixty images, and is highly decorative and rich in comic invention. Not only was the drawing style derived from that of early Chinese art, it also synthesized aspects of the art of Mexico and ancient Egypt that were fashionable in the day.

Ding Cong (b. 1916), the son of designer and cartoonist Ding Song (1891–1972), also stretched the meaning of the word *cartoon* to include ambitious satirical paintings that can be regarded as works of art in their own right. In 1944, Ding Cong painted his best-known work, the satirical handscroll *Xianxiang tu* (literally, "looking at images"). This scroll attacks no individuals in particular, but the picture presented of life under Chiang Kai-shek (Jiang Jieshi) is devastating. Ding Cong's fine drawings of Luoluo tribes people and Zhang Leping's *Refugees* were among the many illustrations that gave Shanghai readers a flavor of the far western regions. Ding Cong also served as art director for the post-war magazine *Qingming*, which caught the mood of thinking men and women as the clouds began to gather after the war. Four issues appeared in 1946 before the magazine was banned in October that year, although it was by no means a Communist organ.

One of the twentieth century's best-known cartoon characters appeared in Zhang Leping's comic strip, *Three Hairs* (*Sanmao*), first published in 1935 in Shanghai. The tragic story of the poor but lovable *Sanmao* immediately became a favorite of both children and adults in Shanghai. After 1949, *Sanmao* continued to appear in publications of the People's Republic of China; however, he was transformed into a happy child, diligent student, and young pioneer by the moral propagandists of the Mao Zedong era. Despite limitations on the permissible targets of satire, and the termination of the commercial role of art under socialism, cartoons and comics remained popular, even during the Maoist years.

**SEE ALSO** *Fashion; Feng Zikai; Pictorial Magazines since 1880.*

**BIBLIOGRAPHY**

Barmé, Geremie. "An Artist and His Epithet: Notes on Feng Zikai and the Manhua." *Papers on Far Eastern History* 39 (1989): 17–43.

Bi, Keguan. "Jindai meishu xianqu Li Shutong [The pioneer of fine arts in modern China–Li Shutong]." *Meishu yanjiu* [Studies of Fine Arts] 4 (1984): 68–73.

Bi, Keguan and Huang Yuanlin. *Zhongguo manhua shi.* [History of Chinese comics]. Beijing: Wenhua Yishu Chubanshe, 1986.

Feng Zikai. *Xiandai Meishu jia hualun Zuopin Shengping: Feng Zikai.* Shanghai-Xuelin Chubanshe, 1996.

Gan, Xianfeng. *Zhongguo manhua shi* [History of Chinese comics]. Jinan, PRC: Shandong Huabao Chubanshe, 2008.

Huang, Dade. "Zhongguo manhua mingcheng yuanqi kao [The origin of the Chinese term—*Manhua*]." *Meishu guancha* [Observations of Fine Arts] 4 (1999): 60–2.

Huang, Dade. "Shijutu kao [Study of the map for current political situations]." *Lao manhua* [Old Comics] 5: 16–22. Jinan, PRC: Shandong Huabao Chubanshe, 1998.

*Lao manhua* [Old Comics] Vol. 1. Shenyang, PRC: Liaoning Huabao Chubanshe, 1998.

*Lao manhua* [Old Comics] Vol. 2-5. Jinan, PRC: Shandong Huabao Chubanshe, 1998.

*Shanghai manhua* [Shanghai sketch]. Reprint. Shanghai: Shanghai Shudian Chubanshe, 1996.

Shen, Kuiyi. "Comics, Picture Books, and Cartoonists in Republican China." *Inks: Cartoon and Comic Art Studies* 4, 3 (1997): 2–16.

Shen, Kuiyi. "*Lianhuanhua* and *Manhua*: Picture Books and Comics in Old Shanghai." In *Illustrating Asia: Comics, Humor Magazines, and Picture Books*, ed. John Lent, 100-120. Honolulu: University of Hawai'i Press, 2001.

Sullivan, Michael. *Art and Artists of Twentieth-century China.* Berkeley: University of California Press, 1996.

***Lin Su-hsing***

## GRAPHIC DESIGN

Graphic design is a term for the modern activity of combining lettering, illustration, photography, cartoons, printing, and other visual elements for purposes of information, instruction, or persuasion. Graphic design yields products such as posters, books, flyers, symbols, brands, packaging, and other elements of contemporary visual culture. As a method of communication, the basic functions of graphic design exist wherever there is civilization, and it is an essential part of the culture and economy of industrialized countries.

### THE INTRODUCTION OF MODERN DESIGN TO CHINA

China was forced militarily to open its doors to the rest of the world after the Opium Wars of the mid-nineteenth century. To China's rich premodern heritage of illustrated books and handicrafts were now added new publications initiated by Western businesspeople. Magazines such as *Dianshizhai huabao* pioneered a hybrid Chinese–British design aesthetic and were produced using photolithography and modern printing presses. After 1895, the Treaty of Shimonoseki gave the Japanese and all foreigners the right to establish manufacturing industries in China. Shanghai experienced two distinct economic boom periods at the turn of the twentieth century. First, there was the expansion that occurred after the Treaty of Shimonoseki (1895), which gave Japan and the foreign powers the privilege to establish manufacturing industries in China, and second, when the Western powers were preoccupied by World War I (1914–1918), which precluded their exports from coming to China, giving native Chinese industries a chance to develop. In this early stage of development in the first two decades of the twentieth century, however, design was still a very limited activity. Most graphic design in China followed European or American models, although contact with Japan spurred the development of Asian innovations.

## PIONEERING COMMERCIAL ARTISTS

Among the pioneers of modern graphic design in China were Li Shutong (1880–1942) and Lu Xun (1881–1936). By 1912 Li had already introduced numerous graphics, which he drew himself, to the pages of the *Pacific Times.* Besides graphic design, Li was also active in promoting advertising art through his published articles and graphics.

Lu Xun, in his work as an editor and promoter of modern literature and philosophy, also became a pioneering patron and sometime practitioner of the art of book-cover design. Although known as a cultural radical, many of his works transformed motifs from past art or archaeology for modern purposes, thus charting a moderate future course for Chinese art and culture. During a time of great upheaval, when young Chinese intellectuals launched fierce attacks on traditional ethics, values, and culture, Lu Xun appreciated the new, but still recognized the importance of selected aspects of China's artistic heritage. Some of his own cover designs reveal his interest in antique motifs, such as *Peach-Colored Cloud* (1923), based on rubbings of archaeological reliefs. He came to recognize the beauty of China's own premodern forms of design, collecting decorated stationary and republishing the collection as a book, *Beiping Decorated Writing Papers* (1934). These various motifs preserved from ancient Chinese art were modified at the hands of Lu Xun and his followers into a new look.

The painter Tao Yuanqing (1893–1929), despite his brief career as a graphic designer, was without doubt one of the most significant book-cover designers of the twentieth century. His talent as a designer was discovered by fellow Zhejiang native Lu Xun, whom he met in Beijing, and he produced covers for many of the most important works of new literature in the late 1920s. The younger designers who followed him praised his unique sensibility and achievement in design. Tao Yuanqing's strong interest in Japanese design informed many of his graphic works, but native Chinese and Western elements were also synthesized into his personal style.

During the late 1920s and 1930s Lu Xun took as one of his missions the promotion of certain kinds of European art. He particularly appreciated the linear qualities of Western graphics, as well as the modern creative process that involved the individual graphic artist both designing and carving his or her own print. His ardent promotion of the woodblock print thus had some impact on Chinese graphic design.

By the middle of the 1930s, several artists who had worked with Lu Xun, including Chen Zhifo (1896–1962), Feng Zikai (1898–1975), and Qian Juntao (1906–1998), also embarked on careers as professional graphic designers and even opened their own design offices in Shanghai.

Chen Zhifo studied graphic design in Japan. In 1919 Chen entered the Tokyo School of Fine Art, where he studied applied art until 1923 and absorbed numerous artistic trends. After he returned to China, Chen set up Shangmei Design Studio, becoming the first professional designer in China, and he trained many young designers. Chen's designs for textiles and book covers show significant influence from Japan and the West.

Feng Zikai, a disciple of Li Shutong, was another prominent graphic designer of this generation, although he was perhaps better known for his cartoons from the mid-1920s. Along with the growth of visual communication in popular literature, Feng became an important designer for book covers and illustrations in the 1930s, designing covers for Kaiming Book Company, the textbook and literature publisher for whom he worked for many years.

Influenced by Lu Xun, Feng Zikai, and Tao Yuanqing, as well as contemporary Euro-American and Japanese design, Qian Juntao's works had a tremendous range, from those with a sweet Japanese flavor to those that reflect an interest in up-to-date European constructivism. Like most Shanghai intellectuals of his day, his work sometimes expressed nationalistic sentiments. To Qian, nationalism and the characteristics of modernity were equally important in his graphic design. In the 1930s and 1940s, Qian's numerous works revealed his own artistic originality and won him a high reputation in the Shanghai art scene. Although modernist painting and literature were not favored by the Communist cultural establishment after 1949, design was less ideologically charged, and Qian Juntao continued to win commissions for his simple, effective magazine and book-cover designs until the end of his long life.

Beyond the relatively highbrow design of the book-cover artists, China's new pictorial newspapers and magazines employed many commercial artists who simultaneously designed mastheads, drew cartoons and ornamental headers, shot photographs, wrote articles, and pasted-up layout for pictorials such as *Shanghai huabao* and *Liangyou.* Among the generation of talented but now virtually anonymous art editors and designers who worked simultaneously for a variety of Shanghai magazines in the 1920s should be counted Ding Song (1891–1972) and Zhang Guangyu (1900–1964). The design projects developed during this period also included advertising billboards, commercial posters, and packaging for all kinds of Chinese commodities. Commercial artists, such as Zheng Mantuo (1888–1961) and Hang Zhiying (1901–1947), were among the most important designers.

## GRAPHIC DESIGN IN THE PEOPLE'S REPUBLIC OF CHINA

After New China was established in 1949, commercial graphics that aimed at selling products were considered symbols of the "Western bourgeois lifestyle" and became almost defunct throughout the first three decades of the

People's Republic. The situation did not change until the Chinese market opened in 1979, when the Chinese government introduced its plan of economic reform and its "open policy" in foreign affairs.

Publication design is another story. After early development in the 1930s, the term *zhuang huang* continued to mean decoration or graphic, but a specialized sector came to be recognized as *shu ji zhuan huang*, or publication design. Book and magazine design was given high priority in China after 1949 because publications were considered to be important means of propaganda. The important book designers after 1949 include Cao Xinzhi (1917–1996), Qiu Ling (1922–), Yu Bingnan (1933–), and Lu Jingren (1947–). Thus, some of the most important developments in early twentieth-century graphic design were developed and refined, and Chinese designers made significant achievements, in the second half of twentieth century.

**SEE ALSO** *Pictorial Magazines since 1880.*

**BIBLIOGRAPHY**

Gao Feng. *Zhongguo sheji shi* [The design history of China]. Taibei: Jimu Wenhua Publishing, 2006.

Hollis, Richard. *Graphic Design: A Concise History*. Rev. ed. London: Thames and Hudson, 2002.

Laing, Ellen Johnston. *Selling Happiness: Calendar Posters and Visual Culture in Early-Twentieth-Century Shanghai.* Honolulu: University of Hawai'i Press, 2004.

Lin Su-hsing. Li Shutong and the Evolution of Graphic Arts in China. *East Asia Journal: Studies in Material Culture* 2, 1 (2007): 86–103.

Livingston, Alan, and Isabella Livingston. *The Thames & Hudson Dictionary of Graphic Design and Designers*. Rev. ed. London: Thames & Hudson, 2003.

Qiu Ling and Zhang Shouyi, eds. *Zhongguo xiandai meishu quan ji: Shuji zhuang zheng* [Comprehensive collections of modern Chinese arts: book cover design]. Beijing: Renmin Meishu Chubanshe, 1998.

Wang Shou Zhi. Chinese Modern Design: A Retrospective. In *Design History: An Anthology*, ed. Dennis P. Doordan, 213–241. Cambridge, MA: MIT Press, 1995.

Zhao Chen. *Zhongguo jindai guanggao wenhua* [China modern advertising culture]. Changchun, PRC: Jilin Kexue Jishu Chubanshe, 2001.

***Lin Su-hsing***

## PICTURE BOOKS (*LIANHUANHUA*)

The immensely popular form of publication referred to as *lianhuanhua* (Chinese picture books) was a low-brow form of entertainment literature enjoyed in urban cities during the Republican period (1912–1949) by readers of limited literacy and economic means. Under the People's Republic (after 1949), the format was adapted as an appealing way to disseminate educational and political concepts to the Chinese masses. With strong support from the party establishment for the training and travel of artists, the often rather coarse and sloppy popular publication was transformed into an art form of great technical skill and imagination.

### REPUBLICAN-ERA PICTURE BOOKS

The sequential use of images to tell a story is an old one in China, be the images religious or secular paintings on walls or scrolls, or xylographically printed images in books. Before the term *lianhuan tuhua* began to appear in 1925, picture books were called by many different names, such as *gongzaishu* or *xiaorenshu* (both terms meaning children's book). The term *lianhuanhua* or *lianhuan tuhua*, which literally means "serial illustrations" or "linked pictures," is believed to have its origins in Shanghai in the mid-1920s. In 1925 the World Book Company (Shijie Shuju) published *Sanguo zhi* (History of the Three Kingdoms), painted by Chen Danxu and issued under the title *Lianhuan tuhua Sanguo zhi* (The picture-book history of the Three Kingdoms). This was the first time the word *lianhuan tuhua* was applied to an illustrated story book. Chinese picture books of the Republican era were often pocket-sized, about three by five inches, with one picture to a page. Inexpensively printed using photolithography, they served a market similar to that for comic books in the West, although in the early days their subject matter was often rooted in Chinese popular culture.

Many picture books took their contents from popular opera stories, such as *Xue Rengui dongzheng* (Xue Rengui goes on an eastern expedition), painted by Liu Boliang in 1920. Besides Liu Boliang, Zhu Runzai (1890–1936) was an important and popular picture-book artist during this period. The themes of Zhu's drawings were adopted mostly from favorite novels and historical romances, including *Sanguo yanyi* (*Romance of the Three Kingdoms*). Other well-known picture-books artists of the 1930s were Zhou Yunfang, Shen Manyun, and Zhao Hongben.

During the 1930s, entertainment culture also inspired picture books. Movies, such as *Genü Hongmudan* (*Singer Red Peony*) and *Huo shao Hongliansi* (*Red Lotus Temple on Fire*), were adapted to the picture-book format. For those who could not afford movie tickets, the cheap picture books, which could be rented from street peddlers, as well as purchased, served as a source of the most up-to-date popular stories.

Most small publishers tried to coordinate their publications with the schedules of performances; the speed of production was thus a major concern for them. Painters were asked to produce such high volume that a great many of these little picture books were drawn quite roughly. Each artist would be in charge of different details, such as architecture, animals, or even the patterns and motifs of clothes.

## PICTURE BOOKS IN THE PEOPLE'S REPUBLIC

As early as the 1930s, leftist intellectuals recognized the didactic potential of this popular form of entertainment. During the Anti-Japanese War, the works of Zhao Shuli were among the earliest to be serialized in picture books sponsored by the Communist Party. Luo Gongliu's charming *Li Youcai ban hua* (The rhymes of Li Youcai) is based on Zhao Shuli's 1943 novel of the same title. An early example of explicitly didactic "revolutionary" picture books was *Xiaoerhei jiehun* (Xiao-erhei gets married), adapted from Zhao Shuli's story and illustrated by Mi Gu in 1950.

After the founding of the People's Republic in 1949, the government began applying the cultural dictates that Mao Zedong had developed in wartime Yan'an to the Shanghai commercial publishing world. While illustrations of traditional fiction deemed to have a modern moral continued to be produced, many picture books were stories of revolutionary heroism, illustrations of new-style plays and movies, biographies of praiseworthy individuals, or adaptations based on contemporary stories.

The Shanghai Cultural Bureau sponsored special classes for artists in 1951 and 1952 to retrain them to produce new, high-quality picture books. The fruits of this and other government support for artists began to appear in the mid-1950s, with development of a fine outline style that combined the best qualities of seventeenth-century woodblock illustration, much admired by Shanghai picture-book artists, with the bold compositions of socialist realism. Among the best examples from the period before the Cultural Revolution (1966–1969) are Zhao Hongben and Qian Xiaodai's *Sun Wukong san da Baigujing* (Monkey beats the white-boned demon, 1961), based on the Ming novel *Xi you ji* (*Journey to the West*), and He Youzhi's *Shanxiang jubian* (Great change in the mountain village, 1962), based on Zhou Libo's contemporary novel of the same title about rural collectivization. The psychological insights the artist He Youzhi has conveyed in his drawings imbue the characters in the otherwise didactic text with liveliness and plausibility, serving perhaps less to praise party policy than to describe the successful struggles the fictional characters underwent as they were required to suddenly change their entire way of life. While picture books were produced in other cities, Shanghai's new picture books enjoyed a heyday during the decade between 1956 and 1966, and the elegant linear style of picture books developed there became standard for the period.

The production of picture books, along with all publications, was radically reduced during the Cultural Revolution (1966–1969). In the 1970s, however, workshops to train young artists were opened. Following the death of Mao Zedong in 1976, the production of picture books boomed, as publishers produced high-quality works to meet pent-up consumer demand. The period between 1978 and 1984 thus marked a second qualitative high point in picture books in the People's Republic, and a new generation of artists emerged to satisfy a seemingly insatiable popular appetite for the little books. The format was so popular during this period that publishers commissioned picture books from many figurative artists who were otherwise known for their work in fine-art formats such as ink painting or oil painting. The resulting picture books spanned a remarkably wide range of graphic styles and pictorial narratives. The Sixth National Art Exhibition of 1984 presented awards to a great variety of works of the previous decade.

If the cultural and economic liberalization of the late 1970s and early 1980s made possible the picture-book boom of the period, the later expansion of television ownership, introduction of computer games, and translation of foreign comics that resulted from the new economic policies sounded the death knell of this art form. The market for picture books collapsed in the late 1980s, and picture books were completely supplanted by these other forms of popular entertainment beginning in the 1990s. The most beautiful picture books of the 1950s and 1960s have been reissued on high quality paper in expensive nostalgia editions. The picture-book classics are now collectors items rather than the cheap, popular entertainment they once were.

**SEE ALSO** *Fashion; Pictorial Magazines since 1880.*

### BIBLIOGRAPHY

Andrews, Julia F. *Painters and Politics in the People's Republic of China, 1949–1979.* Berkeley: University of California Press, 1994. See pp. 246–251.

Andrews, Julia F. Literature in Line: Picture Stories in the People's Republic of China. *Inks: Cartoon and Comic Art Studies* 4, 3 (November 1997): 17–32.

Aying. *Zhongguo lianhuan tuhua shi* [A history of Chinese comic strips]. Beijing: Renmin Meishu Chubanshe, 1984.

Chesneaux, Jean, ed. *The People's Comic Book: Red Women's Detachment, Hot on the Trail, and Other Chinese Comics.* Garden City, NY: Anchor Press, 1973.

Jie Ziping. *Tunse de jiyi: Lianhuanhua.* Taiyuan, China: Shanxi Guji Chubanshe, 2004.

Shen, Kuiyi. Comics, Picture Books, and Cartoonists in Republican China. *Inks: Cartoon and Comic Art Studies* 4, 3 (November 1997): 2–16.

Shen, Kuiyi, and Julia F. Andrews, curators. Literature in Line: Lianhuanhua Picture Stories from China. An online exhibition of original drawings lent by Shanghai People's Art Press, 1997. http://kaladarshan.arts.ohio-state.edu/Exhibitions/Lit_in_line/comhp.html.

Zhu Runzhai. *Zhu Runzhao lianhuanhua xuan: "Sanguo yanyi" baitu* [A selection of comic strips by Zhu Runzhao: 100 illustrations of *The Romance of the Three Kingdoms*]. Beijing: Renmin Meishu Chubanshe, 1984.

***Lin Su-hsing***
***Julia F. Andrews***

## PRODUCT DESIGN

China has a rich tradition of handicraft production. Traditional design reflected a preoccupation with both aesthetic and utilitarian considerations, but the local availability and cost of materials were also important. In elite homes, design and craftsmanship of the highest order were manifest in beautiful traditional furniture made from expensive woods, silk brocade clothes and bedding, embroideries, sandalwood fans, ivory chopsticks, porcelain, lacquerware, and paintings. The design of everyday objects found in the houses of both rich and poor also reflected convenience, cost, and appearance. Even the cheapest baskets, straw mats, bowls, storage pots, and wooden or bamboo chopsticks usually were decorated in some way. Whereas elite culture tended to employ muted or subtly rich colors, popular taste favored the brilliant colors found in folk art, paper cuts, children's clothing, and toys. The traditional design of agricultural tools was affected by the high cost of metal. Plows, scythes, and hoes were made of wood with only small metal cutting parts. Wherever possible, carpenters used wood or bamboo dowels in place of nails. Labor, in contrast, was cheap, and Chinese handicraft industries were often highly labor intensive.

### EARLY MANUFACTURED PRODUCTS

The opening of China to foreign trade in the nineteenth century resulted in an influx of foreign manufactured goods. Chinese consumers, especially those in the rapidly growing coastal towns, embraced modernity and consumer goods enthusiastically. Chinese entrepreneurs were quick to copy imported products or to design cheap substitutes suitable for the Chinese market. They showed great ingenuity in adopting modern materials or manufacturing methods to produce substitutes for traditional handicraft products or goods that suited Chinese demand. By the 1920s and 1930s, goods manufactured in China in both foreign and Chinese-owned factories included products now considered iconic Chinese designs. Huge thermos flasks decorated with brightly colored flowers and birds allowed householders to have constant access to hot water while economizing on the use of fuel. Gaudily painted enamel mugs and washbasins were cheaper, lighter, and more durable than the earthenware utensils they replaced. The rickshaw, a ubiquitous part of Chinese urban life in the first half of the twentieth century, was invented by an American missionary in Tokyo in 1868. It was soon being manufactured in China, where design modifications such as rubber tires, bells, and even glass lanterns were introduced. Only the elite could afford Western-style leather shoes, but traditional cloth shoes were better waterproofed with rubber or composite soles.

Nationalism assisted infant Chinese industry and design. The appeal of imports, often considered to be better designed and of higher quality, was partly outweighed by the movement to show patriotism by choosing "national goods." The Nanyang Industrial Exposition held in Nanjing in 1910 was an attempt to promote industry and design culture in China, emulating the French Industrial Expositions that had begun in 1844 and London's Great Exhibition of 1851. Later exhibitions in Republican China offered awards for good design and quality. However war and poverty limited the development of Chinese design in the first half of the twentieth century.

### DESIGN IN THE PEOPLE'S REPUBLIC

Product design was not a priority in Maoist China. Incomes were low, consumerism was discouraged, and investment was concentrated in heavy industry. China was largely cut off from external design influence, except that of the Soviet bloc. State-owned industry and the shortage of consumer goods meant that producers did not have to compete with each other. Design was the province of engineers. Durability, low cost, and utility were the priorities.

Despite the ethos of thrift, consumers still enjoyed shopping, choosing with careful attention to appearance and quality when they bought the modest items that made up their material culture, such as alarm clocks, thermoses, flashlights, handkerchiefs, towels, pencils, pens, erasers, notebooks, penknives, and soapboxes. Decorative motifs were politicized during the Cultural Revolution (1966–1969), as birds and flowers gave way to revolutionary slogans or the smiling faces of workers and peasants. Yet the basic design of domestic objects changed little in decades. The consumer appetite for novelty found occasional expression: When ballpoint pens in bamboo casing and notebooks with brightly colored plastic covers (made in the factories that also produced Mao's *Little Red Book*) appeared on the market, they were an immediate success.

The culture of design in China has been transformed since the economic reforms. As China attracted vast quantities of foreign investment and was integrated into a globalized system of design, production, and consumption, most domestic manufactures—whether of cars, electronic and electrical goods, or clothes—were at first low-cost copies of goods originally made elsewhere. Designers often were restricted to making cosmetic or cost-effective tweaks to existing designs to adapt them to Chinese needs, rather than developing products from the drawing board based on investigation of user needs and tastes.

Nevertheless, design education developed rapidly. In 2007, the 400 institutions offering courses in industrial design were producing over 10,000 graduates annually. Multinationals and Chinese manufacturers understand that well-adapted design will give them a competitive edge. Consumers are being made more design-conscious by a great range of magazines on design, lifestyle, and fashion.

China's prosperous middle class, though still small as a proportion of the population, is large enough to provide a market of millions interested in acquiring modern homes and the white goods, equipment, and furniture that go with them. Fashion design is another rapidly growing area, boosted by a young urban population that is increasingly interested in appearance. The high degree of computer literacy among urban young people contributes to the rapid spread of new ideas among both designers and consumers.

The innovative design ideas of some leading Chinese companies have won them market share at home and abroad. When the white goods company Haier found that rural consumers in southwest China were blocking their pipes by using domestic washing machines to wash yams, they designed a new machine with bigger pipes suitable for dual washing functions, and the new product became a best-seller in rural China. When their market research revealed that large-capacity machines were needed to wash bulky traditional robes in Saudi Arabia, Haier designed an export model that would take 12-kilo washes—50 percent more than normal capacity. It has enjoyed great success in Saudi Arabia.

Minority areas of design are developing, such as design for sustainable living, avant-garde or art design (often produced by art school graduates), and "nostalgia" design that draws inspiration from traditional Chinese culture. Some quirky designs combine East and West in ways calculated to amuse, such as the Nike shoe with an upper that displays the meridian points of the foot in see-through plastic. Revolutionary retro looks back to (sometimes satirizing) the revolutionary imagery of Maoist China. In the commercial mainstream, by contrast, the homogenizing influence of globalization is undeniable. It is possible to visit a Chinese shopping mall and observe little that is distinctively Chinese in design. Packaging and labelling, however, remain consistently distinguished by the fine graphics that retain a preeminent place in Chinese design.

**SEE ALSO** *Fashion.*

**BIBLIOGRAPHY**

Darmon, Reed. *Made in China*. San Francisco: Chronicle Books, 2004.

Dikötter, Frank. *Things Modern: Material Culture and Everyday Life in China*. London: Hurst and Company, 2007.

Finnane, Antonia. *Changing Clothes in China: Fashion, History, Nation*. Sydney: University of New South Wales Press, 2007.

Hommel, Rudolf P., *China at Work*. [1937]. Cambridge: Massachusetts Institute of Technology Press, 1969.

Wang, Jing. *Brand New China: Advertising, Media, and Commercial Culture*. Cambridge, MA: Harvard University Press, 2008.

Zhang Hongxing, and Lauren Parker, eds. *China Design Now*. London: V&A Publishing, Victoria and Albert Museum, 2008.

*Delia Davin*

# COMMERCIAL ELITE, 1800–1949

The all-encompassing, opaque designation of "merchants" (*shang*) disguised the complex layering of commercial activities in late imperial China, ranging from petty itinerant traders frequenting periodic rural markets, to the canny brokers and middlemen of China's numerous urban centers, to wealthy financial elites involved in facilitating long-distance domestic and foreign trade. Among the last named were the famed salt-monopoly merchants of Yangzhou, the native bankers and remittance agents of Shanxi, the traders and pawnshop owners of Huizhou in Anhui, and the cohong (*gonghang*), incorporating an ensemble of the major authorized foreign trading firms in Guangzhou (Canton). The elite among the merchants never constituted an officially sanctioned political estate in the manner of the anciens régimes of continental Europe, but neither did they suffer the hereditary restraints on upward social mobility so common among their bourgeois counterparts in the premodern West.

## SOCIAL STATUS AND POLITICAL STANDING

Moral and ideological disparagements of trade and its practitioners can be traced back to well before the earliest foundations of the Chinese empire. By the mid-Qing era these tendentious judgments ill accorded with China's burgeoning domestic and foreign commerce. While maintaining a traditional physiocratic predilection that favored agriculture as the foundation of the economy, Qing officials were pragmatic enough to view commerce as a necessity. Since commerce contributed to popular prosperity and the continued welfare of the empire itself, the mid-Qing state largely allowed it to proceed without excessive administrative regulation of markets and onerous levels of taxation.

Even though social preeminence was conventionally accorded to the country's literati, whose political and cultural hegemony appeared unassailable, successful merchants undeniably occupied prestigious positions in Chinese society. This was particularly evident at the local community level, where merchants and scholar-gentry adopted comparable lifestyles and patronage roles displaying their affluence and prominence. In fact, the supposedly hard and fast distinction between the scholar-gentry and the merchant class was becoming increasingly blurred, as indicated by the frequent references to *shenshang* (gentry and merchants) found in mid- to late-Qing documents.

## MERCHANT GUILDS AND THE TRADE TAX

Merchant communities were regionally fragmented in late imperial China, yet far-flung networks of these regional associations loosely bound the entire economy together. Merchant associations took several forms, the most common being regional guilds (*huiguan*), with membership established by place of origin; professional guilds (*gongsuo*), representing a certain line of business or commerce; and trade coalitions or cliques (*bang*), providing assistance for commercial sojourners. Regardless of their designation, these corporate, self-governing bodies served to promote mutual security and mutual welfare among their membership. More significantly, merchant associations were vested by the Qing state with a broad array of discretionary powers that it declined to award to other social constituencies, including the scholar-gentry elite. Merchant associations exercised the authority to adjudicate commercial disputes, stabilize prices for goods and services, establish trade standards and conventions, and limit the free play of competition in the marketplace.

Among their most important functions in the final decades of the Qing era was the power of merchants to determine and remit commercial taxes due to the state. This came about when the Taiping Uprising (1851–1864) devastated large areas of southern and central China, and the embattled Qing state experienced a serious and enduring fiscal crisis that was alleviated by a new form of domestic trade impost, the trade (*lijin*) tax. Introduced in 1853 as a wartime emergency measure, merchants' commercialized tax farming of tax revenues became an essential buttress of fiscal solvency for successive Chinese governments until the 1930s. The trade tax thus presented a paradox: While it opportunely enhanced merchants' political leverage with officials, it was regularly denounced for imposing an unprecedented burden on China's internal commerce.

## LATE QING REFORMS

Also in the decades after the Taiping Uprising, large-scale commercial and industrial enterprises were frequently organized in the latter half of the nineteenth century by variations of a system commonly designated as "government supervision and merchant management" (*guandu shangban*). It had a limited, mixed record in promoting key industrial development projects. At this time, foreign firms trading in the treaty ports came under the protection of Western law. A sector of the Chinese commercial elite in Shanghai and elsewhere, such as compradors (*maiban*) in the employ of foreign firms, became shareholders and even directors of foreign joint-stock companies, setting a precedent for a significant if belated innovation in state policy.

Recognizing the critical need to mobilize indigenous capital for industrial development, in 1904 the Qing government enacted a Company Law (Gongsi Fa). This measure established a modern legalized basis for private commerce and investment, validating the enhanced social and political status of China's commercial elite. An equity capital market and provisions for the legal resolution of commercial wrangles were now available to formally incorporated companies. The first national registration of Chinese companies took place, but the surge in joint-stock registrations was tempered by the fact that the far more numerous single-owner and partnership businesses avoided the entire process.

## CHAMBERS OF COMMERCE

Another aspect of the rising status of merchants in the final decade of the Qing dynasty, after the 1904 reforms in particular, was the official recognition and general encouragement of chambers of commerce (*shanghui*). These organizations had already begun appearing in Chinese cities, most notably in Shanghai, and as many as 794 chambers of commerce were founded throughout the country by the end of the dynasty in 1912. They initially demonstrated their broad political influence by vigorously supporting the anti-American commercial boycott of 1905–1906. In 1907 the chambers moved to form a national federation. The Qing state narrowly envisaged the chambers as a means to link merchants to imperial policies and strengthen official control of a rising sector of society, but its growing political weakness would dictate otherwise.

In the early twentieth century China's chambers of commerce quickly became new flexible instruments for local and even national expression of the interests and power of the commercial elite. Owing to the prolonged debility of centralized state power, the chambers became increasingly autonomous and broadly influential. In the absence of an effective national government, they delivered significant social services in urban localities throughout China, assuming such tasks as road building, establishing local police forces, and providing legal services. They also adopted politically progressive stances, including support for the 1911 Revolution and the May Fourth Movement in 1919. In some major cities, such as Shanghai, the influence of old-style guilds and merchant groups began to yield to that of new-style entrepreneurs and industrialists organized in chambers of commerce.

## THE GOLDEN AGE OF THE 1920s AND THE GUOMINDANG'S RISE TO POWER

The period from 1915 to 1927 has been termed the golden age of China's business elite, a brief era of diminished state power in which they assumed a central role in national development as proponents of economic modernization. Not all scholars, however, see China's bourgeoisie as a relatively independent, politically coherent social force playing a dominant role. The 1920s marked the beginning of what Wen-hsin Yeh terms a "quest for legitimacy and respectability" among Shanghai's as yet insecure bourgeoisie (2007, p. 2). Over the next two decades the city's business elite strove to identify their private pursuit of wealth with national prosperity and celebrated capitalist enterprise as scientific, patriotic, and democratic. China's continual political crises in the 1930s and 1940s would severely test these propositions.

In orthodox Marxist historiography, Chiang Kai-shek's turn against the left in 1927 marks a bourgeois counterrevolution that transformed the Guomindang into the party of Shanghai's capitalists. This view has not been sustained by analyses of Chiang's behavior in the middle to late 1920s and of the Guomindang during the Nanjing-government era (1927–1937). During and after the Northern Expedition (1926–1928), Chiang required extensive funding to pay his troops and buy the loyalty of others, and he extorted the necessary resources from the business and financial elites of Shanghai and the Lower Yangzi region. While these elites thereby purchased a measure of social stability to sustain their economic activities, the Guomindang gained considerable control over the banking and business sectors of the economy and vigorously curtailed the autonomy of the commercial elite and their organizations, such as the chambers of commerce. The Nationalist party-state strengthened itself in urban China at the expense of the elite. The Nanjing decade thus witnessed more coercion and less cooperation between business and government.

### THE IMPACT OF THE ANTI-JAPANESE WAR

China's business elite was mainly preoccupied with survival amid the great turmoil and uncertainty brought on by the Anti-Japanese War (1937–1945). Most business leaders did not relocate their factories and firms from occupied to unoccupied areas of China, thereby failing to conform to the heroic stereotype of wartime national resistance. Nor did the majority of them spend the eight years of warfare collaborating with the Japanese invaders. Navigating precariously between the two extremes of resistance and collaboration, the business elite frequently tended to hedge their bets, as the case of the Shanghai industrialist Liu Hongsheng illustrates. On the one hand, Liu did relocate numerous plants westward to unoccupied Nationalist China, but on the other, he employed family members to continue to manage other businesses under Japanese occupation.

Both during and after the war, Guomindang policy sought to create a militarily secure state, emphasizing state ownership and operation of many essential sectors of the wartime economy. The massive confiscation and nationalization of industries located in the former occupied areas after 1945 served notice that the trend toward a command economy would continue unabated in the postwar era. China's business elite and technocrats were to be coopted to achieve this objective under the dominance of the Nationalist party-state.

### CHANGING POPULAR IMAGES OF THE COMMERCIAL ELITE

During much of the Qing period, official attitudes reflected an ambiguity toward merchants. Official rhetoric often denounced them as "treacherous merchants" (*jianshang*) who habitually put personal profits above public welfare, yet it also frequently proclaimed the need to support merchant transactions and viable market trade. The attitude adopted usually depended upon whether the immediate interests of the state in social order and harmony coincided with the private pursuit of economic gain. A similar ambiguity was still prevalent in late-Qing popular culture. Nonetheless, from the late nineteenth century to the early twentieth, the commercial elite gradually attained a commonly acknowledged measure of legitimacy and social prestige. Negative attitudes toward free markets, private business enterprise, and merchants remained pervasive in Republican China. Nationalist, as well as Marxist, rhetoric greatly contributed to this trend at a time when national crises in the 1930s and 1940s increasingly brought foreign invasion, colonial oppression, and widened class conflict to the forefront of popular consciousness.

**SEE ALSO** *Comprador; Huizhou.*

#### BIBLIOGRAPHY

Bergere, Marie-Claire. *The Golden Age of the Chinese Bourgeoisie, 1911–1937.* Trans. Janet Lloyd. Cambridge, United Kingdom: Cambridge University Press, 1989.

Chan, Wellington K. K. *Merchants, Mandarins, and Modern Enterprise in Late Ch'ing China.* Cambridge, MA: East Asian Research Center, Harvard University, 1977.

Coble, Parks. *The Shanghai Capitalists and the Nationalist Government, 1927–1937.* 2nd ed. Cambridge, MA: Harvard University Press, 1980.

Coble, Parks. *Chinese Capitalists in Japan's New Order:* The *Occupied Lower Yangzi, 1937–1945.* Berkeley: University of California Press, 2003.

Faure, David. *China and Capitalism: A History of Business Enterprise in Modern China.* Hong Kong: Hong Kong University Press, 2006.

Kwan, Man Bun. *The Salt Merchants of Tianjin: State Making and Civil Society in Late Imperial China.* Honolulu: University of Hawai'i Press, 2001.

Mann, Susan. *Local Merchants and the Chinese Bureaucracy, 1750–1950.* Stanford, CA: Stanford University Press, 1987.

Yeh, Wen-hsin. *Shanghai Splendor: Economic Sentiments and the Making of Modern China, 1843–1949.* Berkeley: University of California Press, 2007.

*Robert Gardella*

## COMMUNIST PARTY

Amid the intellectual stirrings of the May Fourth movement, China's educated young men and women began to seriously study socialist and Marxist ideas. The success of the 1917 October Revolution in Russia, soon followed by the renunciation of the unequal treaties, juxtaposed with the carnage of World War I (1914–1918) among the world's leading capitalist nations, doubled the appeal of Marxism in China.

In August 1920, China's first Communist group was set up in Shanghai. From the autumn of 1920 to the first half of 1921, Communist groups were established one after the other in Beijing, Wuhan, Changsha, Jinan, Guangzhou, and other cities, and similar groups were also organized among the Chinese students and residents in Japan and France.

The Communist group in Shanghai drafted the *Manifesto of the Communist Party of China*, which articulated the aspirations of the Communists to create a new communist society that would abolish private ownership, practice public ownership of the means of production, destroy the old state apparatus, and eliminate classes. The manifesto indicated that the Chinese proletariat must wage class struggle to destroy the capitalist system by force; hence, it must "organize a revolutionary political party of the proletariat—the Communist Party" to lead it in the seizure of political power and in the establishment of the dictatorship of the proletariat.

## THE FOUNDING OF THE CCP AND ITS EARLY DEVELOPMENT

On July 23, 1921, the First National Congress of the Chinese Communist Party (CCP) was convened in the French Concession in Shanghai. Attending the congress were twelve delegates representing fifty-three party members in seven localities; Mao Zedong (1893–1976) and Dong Biwu (1886–1975) were among the twelve delegates. The party's cofounders, Chen Duxiu (1879–1942) and Li Dazhao (1888–1927), were unable to attend. The new CCP had set socialism and communism as its goal and was firmly determined to make a revolution. The congress decided that the basic task of the party at this stage would be to establish trade unions of industrial workers and to "imbue the trade unions with the spirit of class struggle." The congress elected Chen Duxiu general secretary; Chen, together with Li Da (1890–1966) and Zhang Guotao (1897–1979), were to form the Central Bureau, the party's leading organ. The CCP believed that earlier revolutionaries had not mobilized the people on a broad scale and, in particular, had neglected workers and peasants.

Two representatives of the Communist International (Comintern), G. Maring (pseudonym of Hendricus Sneevliet, 1883–1942) and Nicolsky, attended the congress as observers. The October Revolution in Russia won the admiration of the CCP, which also rejected the social-democratic line of thinking espoused by the Second International. From the outset, the CCP was a Marxist-Leninist party, a revolutionary party of the working class. Earlier in 1920, the Socialist Youth League had already begun to send students to Sun Yat-sen University in Moscow for political education.

The CCP held its Second National Congress in Shanghai in July 1922, with twelve delegates representing 195 party members. It formulated the program for an anti-imperialist and antifeudal democratic revolution in China, and decided to form a democratic united front. The CCP leadership agreed that the party's most important task should be to overthrow the warlords, to combat oppression by world imperialism, and to unify the country as a genuine democratic republic. On this basis, Maring proposed that members of the CCP and the Youth League should join the Guomindang (GMD), turning it into an alliance of the revolutionary classes, known in history as the first United Front. Meanwhile, Comintern advisors also provided guidance for the GMD, helping it establish the Whampoa Military Academy in 1924 to train an army loyal to the party. The CCP leadership also observed that the Chinese peasants, with their revolutionary enthusiasm, were "the greatest essential factor in the revolutionary movement"; it considered that a large segment of the petty bourgeoisie would also join the revolution because they were living in immense misery.

The CCP held its Third National Congress in Guangzhou in June 1923, and its Fourth National Congress in Shanghai in January 1925. The latter congress resolved that women's liberation was a part of the class struggle. By then, party membership had grown to 994.

The CCP suffered a series of serious setbacks in 1927, beginning with Chiang Kai-shek's (Jiang Jieshi's) betrayal of the United Front in April. After the victory of the Northern Expeditionary Army led by Chiang Kai-shek (1887–1975) over the warlords, the Western powers and Japan intended to cultivate Chiang as the main force to prevent the CCP from controlling southern china. In response, Chiang adopted an increasingly anti-Communist stand, leading to the breakup of the first United Front, as he turned his guns on the Communists and labor activists in Shanghai in April. The left wing of the GMD, led by Wang Jingwei (1883–1944), wanted to maintain an alliance with the CCP to balance against Chiang. At the same time, Soviet leader Joseph Stalin (1879–1953) also desired that the CCP continue to operate within the alliance. Both efforts failed.

## FACTIONALISM AND LINE STRUGGLES

The Fifth National Congress of the CCP was held in Wuhan (Hankou) in April to May 1927, immediately after the debacle in Shanghai. The congress reaffirmed the United Front with the GMD, reflecting Stalin's view, and reelected Chen Duxiu as general secretary. The congress also discussed the agrarian question, because the Comintern had earlier indicated the need to seize real

## COMMUNIST PARTY ORGANIZATION AND STRUCTURE

The Chinese Communist Party is a traditional Leninist party in which power is highly concentrated in the central leadership. Every five years, the party holds a national congress with more than two thousand delegates attending from all provincial units and the People's Liberation Army. Before the national congress, congresses are held at lower levels of the party organization, from village party branches to town/township, county, prefecture, and provincial committees, to elect delegates to participate in the high-level party congresses.

The national congress, the highest organ of power, will elect a Central Committee with over two hundred members and more than one hundred alternate members (without voting power). The Central Committee normally holds a plenary session annually in autumn, and the documents released are the most authoritative. The Central Committee's work is executed by a central secretariat with a Propaganda Department, Organization Department, International Liaison Department, and so forth. The Central Committee in turn elects a Political Bureau with more than twenty members and a Standing Committee of the Political Bureau, usually with seven to nine members.

Party committees not only exist at every level of the government structure, they are also part of practically every organization in China. The party secretary is the real leader in all cases. Where there are fewer than one hundred party members, a party general branch is organized; a party branch will be organized in every unit with more than three members. Through this organizational network, the party exercises leadership as it controls all personnel appointments. The party also leads through its policy programs and the example of its members.

The party exercises leadership over mass organizations like trade unions, women's federations, and youth federations. Party members are the elite, because they are seen as the pioneers of the proletariat, and one has to work hard to qualify for party membership. However, almost everyone in China belongs to a mass organization, and hence the party can reach practically the entire population.

The Communist Party controls the military through its Central Military Commission, party committees in all units, and the political commissar system. The party so far rejects any suggestion of turning the military over to state control.

While party members claim to be the pioneers of the proletariat, Jiang Zemin's "Three Represents" theory reflects the fact that party recruitment since the 1980s tends to emphasize well-educated professionals, administrators, and business executives.

***Joseph Y. S. Cheng (Zheng Yushuo)***

power in the countryside through peasant associations. The position largely supported Mao's report on his investigation in Hunan in January to February 1927.

The Comintern's guidance and Chen Duxiu were later blamed for the "Right capitulationist errors" (surrendering to the imperialist and reactionary forces without insisting on struggling for the revolutionary cause) of the CCP leadership, which included vacillations on certain key questions, blind trust in the GMD and subsequent betrayal by it, and failure to recognize the importance of controlling the armed forces. Though the Nanchang military uprising on August 1, 1927, was another defeat for the Communists, the date has ever since been commemorated as the birthday of the Chinese Red Army. It also marked the beginning of the first civil war between the CCP and the GMD, which ended with the Xi'an incident in December 1936 when the two sides reached an agreement to unite to fight Japan. From the CCP's point of view, this was the agrarian revolutionary war.

Despite its setbacks, the CCP succeeded in establishing itself as a mass party in 1925 to 1927. Mao began to demonstrate his talents in molding his followers into a disciplined force with political and military training during the Autumn Harvest Uprising in Hunan in August 1927. In 1928 Mao articulated in Jinggangshan what would become the famous Three Rules of Discipline and Eight Points of Attention. He also addressed such errors as weak leadership and command, poor discipline, faulty judgment, insubordination and bandit-like behavior, and risky military campaigns, the latter being labeled as "Left" mistakes. Mao emphasized the military's subordination to the party, and, together with Zhu De (1886–1976), worked hard to strengthen the revolutionary base area between Hunan and Jiangxi.

Mao's efforts were disrupted by continuing differences with the central party leadership, then dominated by Li Lisan (1899–1967) after his return from the Sixth National Congress of the CCP held in Moscow in June and July

1928. The venue of the congress demonstrated the significant influence of Stalin, despite his earlier mistakes in guiding the CCP. The congress elected Xiang Zhongfa (1880–1931), a worker, as general secretary to replace Qu Qiubai (1899–1935), who had taken over from Chen Duxiu in August 1927. But it was Li Lisan who headed the new political bureau and enjoyed real power. Significantly, no one from the rural bases attended the congress. In late 1928, Mao and Zhu De, pressed by Chiang Kai-shek's army, had to relocate to the regions between southern Jiangxi and Fujian, where they established the Jiangxi Soviet.

The CCP's military campaign for the summer of 1930 was a failure. With the exception of the soviet bases, the rural population was quite unprepared to follow any revolutionary movement. It was a typical example of the party's tendency to undertake risky and adventurous military campaigns without a sound strategic overview. Meanwhile, the military and rural bases in Central China offered continuing proof of the vitality of the CCP and its revolution, and the Communist military and agrarian experiments demonstrated significant practical value. Mao and Zhu De also established their leadership credentials. In November 1931, Mao was elected president of the Military Committee.

From October 1930 to October 1934, the GMD government mounted five military campaigns to attack the Communist bases. Serious disagreements emerged in the party leadership concerning the conduct of military operations. Finally, the Red Army had to leave the soviet bases and begin its Long March.

**Party membership, 1921–2007**

| Congress | Year | Number of members |
|---|---|---|
| First Party Congress | 1921 | over 50 |
| Second Party Congress | 1922 | 195 |
| Third Party Congress | 1923 | 420 |
| Fourth Party Congress | 1925 | 994 |
| Fifth Party Congress | 1927 | 57,967 |
| Sixth Party Congress | 1928 | over 40,000 |
| Seventh Party Congress | 1945 | 1,210,000 |
| Eighth Party Congress | 1956 | 10,730,000 |
| Ninth Party Congress | 1969 | 22,000,000 |
| Tenth Party Congress | 1973 | 28,000,000 |
| Eleventh Party Congress | 1977 | 35,000,000 |
| Twelfth Party Congress | 1982 | 39,650,000 |
| Thirteenth Party Congress | 1987 | 46,000,000 |
| Fourteenth Party Congress | 1992 | 51,000,000 |
| Fifteenth Party Congress | 1997 | 58,000,000 |
| Sixteenth Party Congress | 2002 | 66,000,000 |
| Seventeenth Party Congress | 2007 | 73,360,000 |

SOURCE: News of the Communist Party of China.

*Table 1*

## THE LONG MARCH, MAO'S ASSUMPTION OF LEADERSHIP, AND THE YAN'AN ERA

During the Long March, the Communists covered 12,500 kilometers in about one year. When the Red Army captured Zunyi in northern Guizhou in January 1935, an enlarged meeting of the Political Bureau was held in which Mao assumed leadership. In early November 1935, the Red Army reached the Shaanxi-Gansu Soviet area; the headquarters of the Central Committee was then set up in Northwest China, marking the beginning of the Yan'an era.

For the Chinese Communist movement, the Long March was an achievement and a political success. The party spread propaganda directly among a population that had been largely ignorant of its objectives. The Long March helped the CCP to achieve a greater independence from Moscow, and the party came to appreciate the principle of self-reliance. Still, more than 100,000 lives were lost during the march.

In anticipation of the war against Japan and to strengthen its appeal to nationalism, the CCP in the next several years downplayed its Marxist ideology. In fact, after the Xi'an incident, the CCP gave up armed insurrection, turned the Soviet Republic into a special region of the Republic of China, and designated the Red Army as a unit of the National Army to bring about the second United Front. Chiang Kai-shek agreed to end the civil war under the pressure of domestic public opinion. The Sino-Japanese War (1937–1945) enabled the CCP to achieve a political and military resurrection. Party membership expanded through the addition of young patriots, who were trained to become loyal cadres. The party also vastly increased its regular and auxiliary armed forces, and considerably expanded the territories under its control as "anti-Japanese guerrilla zones" were formed and then turned into "liberated areas."

From early 1942 to 1944, Mao launched a "rectification campaign" within the party, which served as a model for many future campaigns. Mao removed his principal political opponents, Wang Ming (1904–1974) and the remainder of the "Twenty-eight Bolsheviks." There was an urgent need to ensure the commitment and indoctrination of a party membership that was rapidly increasing, from 40,000 in 1937 to 800,000 in 1940. Mao focused on the evils of ideological differences, refusal to follow the party line closely, and factionalism. The campaign was also the most important exercise of the Maoist sinicization of Marxism-Leninism.

## VICTORY OVER JAPAN AND THE GMD

As the war against Japan turned in favor of China, the CCP became increasingly optimistic about its prospects. Its Seventh National Congress was held in Yan'an from April to June 1945, and it was labeled one of "solidarity and victory." By then, Mao's leadership had been firmly established. Just before the congress, Mao was openly praised for his integration of the "universal truth of Marxism-Leninism with the actual practice of the Chinese Revolution." In the congress, Mao proposed a "democratic coalition government" with the GMD; he indicated that the CCP would long adhere to its New Democracy program in the present protracted stage of the two-stage evolution to socialism. But the CCP would lead the coalition.

The Third Revolutionary Civil War began in the summer of 1946. The CCP had succeeded in buying time to regroup and expand, and in making it appear that the GMD was primarily responsible for the resort to a military solution. Mao proved that he was a great strategist in exploiting negotiations with the enemies.

The Communist's success did not depend entirely on the military achievements of the People's Liberation Army (PLA), the new name of the Red Army. The GMD government was corrupt and repressive, and gradually lost the confidence of the population. In addition, a ruinous inflationary spiral resulted in extreme economic instability, leading to a total collapse of political and social morals. In contrast, the Communists offered effective programs, in particular land reform.

## THE PRC: FROM NEW DEMOCRACY TO SOCIALISM

In "On the People's Democratic Dictatorship," released in June 1949, Mao identified the three main weapons used to defeat the enemy: a well-disciplined party armed with the theory of Marxism-Leninism, an army under the leadership of the party, and a united front led by the party. Mao promised to enforce the people's democratic dictatorship; the "people" comprised the working class, the peasantry, the urban petty bourgeoisie, and the national bourgeoisie.

The first Chinese People's Political Consultative Conference (CPPCC) was held in Beijing in 1949. It served as the national legislature until 1954. The CCP did not seek majority representation for it in the CPPCC; this was not necessary since it controlled all the instruments of power already. But the gesture did support the pretense of a coalition government and democracy. Basically, the party center remained the most important organ of power, and through the party groups in all state institutions, it ensured implementation of the party line.

Through the residents committees in the urban areas and the peasants associations in the countryside, everyone was involved and could be mobilized. The landlord class and its monopoly of power were broken in the land reform. In the urban areas, the Three-Antis campaign and the Five-Antis campaign took place in 1951 and 1952. The former was aimed at the cadres and government employees to combat corruption, waste, and bureaucratism. The latter was directed against bribes, fraud, tax evasion, theft of state property, and leakage of state economic interests in the business community. Regarding intellectuals, the Thought-reform campaign was aimed at the remolding of education and intellectual discourse along acceptable Marxist-Leninist lines. Mao's discussions of the "ten great relationships" in 1956 revealed the Chinese leadership's dissatisfaction with blindly following the Soviet model.

## MAOIST RADICALISM

The Eighth National Congress of the CCP was held in Beijing in September 1956. At home, China claimed to have completed its socialist transformation; internationally, differences with the Soviet Union began to emerge. The party intended to adjust some aspects of China's economic development strategy, as well as make preparations for the rectification of work style throughout the party and correctly handle various kinds of contradictions among the people that were becoming increasingly obvious.

In April 1957, the party formally launched a rectification campaign against bureaucratism, factionalism, and subjectivism—the Hundred Flowers campaign, in which intellectuals were invited to criticize the party. Chinese leaders were probably shocked by the subsequent criticisms against the party and the newborn socialist system, which they interpreted as challenges to the leadership of the party. Mao responded with a nationwide anti-rightist movement, which silenced the intelligentsia until the era of economic reforms.

The people's communes, the final stage of agrarian collectivization, emerged surprisingly in the summer of 1958. The communes and the steel-production targets of the Great Leap Forward stood in obvious contradiction to rational economic thinking. They reflected Mao's power and influence, the erosion of intraparty democracy, and the neglect of scientific input in the decision-making process. Mao was challenged by Peng Dehuai (1898–1974) and was eventually forced to retreat to the second line, while Peng paid for his candor with his career. A collective leadership under Liu Shaoqi (1898–1969) and Deng Xiaoping (1904–1997) asserted itself.

In January 1961, the party leadership put forward the slogan, "readjusting, consolidating, filling out, and raising standards." The economic retreat from radicalism was accompanied by a modified Hundred Flowers campaign in 1961 to 1962. Mao was unhappy with the revisionist tendencies among cadres and peasants. In early 1965, he made it clear that there were people in positions of authority who were taking the capitalist road. Meanwhile, the PLA came to have greater influence on the party and state bureaucracies.

Mao's initial call for a cultural revolution in early 1965 and then an ideological study campaign were ignored. In the summer of 1966, he was able to triumph over Liu Shaoqi. In August, the Eleventh Central Committee Plenum issued the Sixteen Articles, providing the first guidelines for the Great Proletarian Cultural Revolution. The Red Guard movement was organized for the mobilization of the youth to assault the Four Olds, that is, old ideas, culture, customs, and habits.

The party center controlled by Mao then advocated the formation of revolutionary committees at every level of administration throughout the country. The PLA, meanwhile, became more and more involved in the governance because of the chaos. The Ninth National Congress of the CCP, a congress of "unity and of victory," met secretly in Beijing in April 1969. About 45 percent of the new Central Committee members were from the PLA.

After nearly three years of unrest, party rebuilding began at the grassroots level with a campaign of "struggle-criticism-transformation." In addition, the state bureaucracy was slowly revived under Zhou Enlai. In foreign policy, Mao and Zhou decided to approach the United States to deter the Soviet threat. A breakthrough was achieved in July 1971 when the U.S. diplomat Henry Kissinger secretly visited Beijing. The visit led to China's joining the United Nations later in the year and securing permanent membership on the UN Security Council, as well as the rapprochement with the United States symbolized by the Shanghai Communiqué in February 1972, bringing to a climax U.S. president Richard Nixon's (1913–1994) visit to China.

Mao's differences with his designated successor, Lin Biao (1907–1971), gradually sharpened. Lin, after his supporters allegedly plotted to assassinate Mao in September 1971, fled the country with his family, but his plane crashed over Mongolia with no survivors.

The purge of Lin Biao's followers facilitated the reconstruction of the state administration and the reinstitutionalization of the party. Between the fall of Lin Biao and the autumn of 1973, an effort emerged to promote policies similar to those of the post–Great Leap Forward readjustment, which was contrary to Mao's development policies. By mid-1973, the radical leftists led by Jiang Qing (1914–1991) began a counterattack against such moderate policies, which were sponsored by Zhou Enlai and the veteran cadres. It was in this context that the CCP's Tenth National Congress was held, in secrecy, in August 1973. The congress was intended to settle matters following the Lin Biao purge and was not expected to undertake new initiatives.

A campaign to criticize Lin Biao began with the Tenth National Congress; this was soon followed by another campaign to "criticize Confucius," an indirect attack on Zhou Enlai. As these campaigns developed, a revised interpretation of China's first emperor, Qin Shihuang (259–210 BCE), was debated, which apparently was a defense of the revolutionary reforms introduced in the Cultural Revolution era. Deng Xiaoping's appointment as first vice premier and chief of staff of the PLA in early 1975 meant that the radical leftists did not have it all their way and indeed might have lost the full support of Mao. In February 1975, they launched a new campaign to study the theory of the dictatorship of the proletariat and to criticize and restrict "bourgeois rights," that is, capitalist practices that continued to exist under the socialist system in China and were seen as seeds of a capitalist revival, which Deng Xiaoping was allegedly favoring.

In the midst of these intense ideological and power struggles, Zhou Enlai passed away in January 1976. A massive riot erupted in Tiananmen Square on April 5 in his memory. The incident was interpreted by the radicals now in control as a "counterrevolutionary movement," and the blame was fixed on Deng Xiaoping, who was then purged. Earlier, Hua Guofeng (1921–2008), a favorite of Mao, had been appointed acting premier.

When Mao died in September 1976, Hua Guofeng was, for the time being, in the most advantageous position to assume leadership. The radical leftists made a bid for power and exploited their possession of Mao's will, which anointed Jiang Qing as his successor. But Hua, supported by Ye Jianying (1897–1986) and Mao's bodyguard, Wang Dongxing, moved first and arrested the Gang of Four—Jiang Qing, Zhang Chunqiao (1917–2005), Wang Hongwen (1936–1992), and Yao Wenyuan (1931–2005). A campaign vilifying the Gang of Four was initiated.

## ECONOMIC REFORMS AND OPENING TO THE EXTERNAL WORLD

The condemnation of the Gang of Four aroused support for the veteran cadres represented by Deng Xiaoping. In March 1977, a central work conference endorsed the return of Deng to leadership positions. The Eleventh National Congress was then held in August 1977; by then, the party claimed to have a membership of more than thirty-five million. Hua was elected party chairman, and Deng as one of the four vice chairmen.

Deng's influence rapidly expanded at the expense of Hua. At the Third Plenum of the Eleventh Central Committee in December 1978, Deng's political victory was complete. The plenum was hailed officially as "a crucial turning point of far-reaching significance in the history of our party." It rejected the principle of "taking class struggle as the key link," and "made the strategic decision to shift the focus of work to socialist modernization." In sum, the legitimacy of the Chinese Communist regime would depend on its ability to improve the people's living standards.

The Third Plenum made significant economic policy decisions, and gradually led to the breaking up of the communes. Work began on the enactment of a law code, reestablishing China's judicial system and facilitating economic relations with the outside world. An attempt was also made to have a "preliminary basic assessment" of the history of the last thirty years, and to preserve stability inside the party as well as outside it. The thought of Mao Zedong was defined as the "crystallization of the collective wisdom of the CCP." The political rehabilitation of Peng Dehuai in 1978 and Liu Shaoqi in 1980 implicitly corrected some of the major political decisions made in the Cultural Revolution and indicated that Mao had made mistakes.

In August 1980, Deng raised the issue of the reform of the party and state leadership systems. He highlighted the need to prevent overcentralization of power, and spoke against bureaucratism, paternalism, the lifelong tenure system for leading cadres, and "privileges of every description." The Twelfth National Congress of the CCP was then held in September 1982. Hu Yaobang (1915–1989), as party chairman, introduced the concept of a "socialist spiritual civilization," which was a response to the perceived ideological vacuum. In July 1983, the *Selected Works of Deng Xiaoping* was published, partly as study material for a rectification campaign aimed at party consolidation. A secondary campaign against "spiritual pollution," however, also emerged. It clearly reflected a leftist trend and was manipulated to slow Deng Xiaoping's reform programs. This resistance paled at the end of 1984. The Seventh Five-Year Plan (1986–1990) pledged to lay the foundation for the establishment of a socialist economic structure with Chinese characteristics. There was much discussion on political structural reform, that is, decentralization of power and redefinition of the functions of the party.

## THE TIANANMEN SQUARE INCIDENT AND ITS AFTERMATH

Reforms brought high inflation, and the bankruptcy of enterprises was shown to be possible. Large-scale student demonstrations occurred in December 1986, which, instead of offering support for political reforms, brought the downfall of Hu Yaobang. Zhao Ziyang (1919–2005) was named acting general secretary of the party, and a new campaign was organized to combat "bourgeois liberalization," though the reformers were able to limit the scope of the campaign so as not to affect economic reforms.

In the Thirteenth National Congress held in October 1987, Zhao Ziyang announced that the party's central task was to accelerate and deepen China's reforms. Zhao expounded on the important ideological position that China was "in the primary stage of socialism," and that China's socialist economy was a "planned commodity economy based on public ownership."

Serious inflation from 1987 to 1989 severely challenged the legitimacy of the CCP and its reform program. The disparities between the vibrant private economy and the depressed state-owned enterprises gave rise to rampant rent-seeking behavior and corruption among cadres. Corruption was perceived to extend all the way to the top political leadership. Under such circumstances, Hu Yaobang's death on April 15, 1989, triggered large-scale political demonstrations. The demonstrators demanded a reassessment of Hu and the rehabilitation of those sanctioned in the campaign against "bourgeois liberalization." Zhao Ziyang was sympathetic to the demonstrators, but the party elders led by Deng Xiaoping decided that the demonstrations were a political upheaval against the party and socialism. The PLA subsequently carried out a brutal crackdown on the demonstrators on June 4 at Tiananmen Square.

Zhao Ziyang was purged for contributing to the unrest by making divisions in the leadership publicly known. In his place, Jiang Zemin, secretary of the Shanghai party committee, was elected general secretary of the Central Committee. In the wake of the Tiananmen Square incident, dissidents who had fled to the West predicted the downfall of the Chinese Communist regime in a matter of months. They were proven wrong.

In early 1992, Deng Xiaoping's tour of southern China signaled that the economic reforms would not only continue to progress, but would do so at an accelerated pace. The CCP's Fourteenth National Congress, held in October 1992, was significant for the scant attention it drew, because people were too busy improving their own livelihoods. Reformers in China at this stage believed that liberalization and reliance on market forces would solve the country's economic problems, and the congress finally endorsed the concept of a "socialist market economy." *River Elegy*, a documentary film televised in 1988, highlighted the fundamental weakness of the Chinese civilization in achieving modernization, which led to widespread popular historical pessimism among Chinese intellectuals. In response, the CCP launched a "patriotic education" campaign to exploit nationalism and patriotism to fill the ideological vacuum.

## STRENGTHENING THE PARTY IN A MARKET ECONOMY

The introduction of the "household responsibility system" and the abandonment of the people's communes greatly weakened the party organization in rural areas. The *People's Daily* admitted on November 18, 1994, that tyrants were building up mafia-like power bases in the countryside by joining forces with corrupt officials to usurp the power of the party. Chinese leaders realized that dissatisfaction in the countryside had become the most threatening challenge.

In this context, the Fourth Plenum of the Fourteenth Central Committee in September 1994 focused on the theme of party construction. Its communiqué acknowledged that

***Opening of the 16th National Congress of the Communist Party, Beijing, November 1, 2002.*** *Every five years, China's top level Communist Party members meet in a national congress. Held in Beijing's Great Hall of the People, the gathering promotes party members for new leadership positions, appoints individuals to serve on the Central Committee, and makes amendments to China's constitution as needed.* © FRITZ HOFFMANN/CORBIS

"the party was not in control of the party," as well as obvious problems of lax discipline, weak organization, various phenomena of corruption, and so forth. Chinese leaders considered that the party had to be strengthened. There was a reluctance on the part of the intelligentsia to join the CCP immediately after the Tiananmen Incident, and the party had lost its ideological appeal.

Deng Xiaoping's death on February 19, 1997, symbolized the transformation of the regime from a totalitarian to an authoritarian one; it also demonstrated the depoliticization of Chinese society. Chinese people had experienced a significant improvement in living standards since 1978; they therefore feared major changes and chaos.

The Fifteenth National Congress was held in this context in September 1997. The demand for stability meant that Jiang Zemin and other third-generation leaders had gained time and had an opportunity to consolidate power. The important interest groups had to be fully consulted, and their representatives were appointed to leadership positions. Grassroots democracy has been implemented through the holding of democratic elections and the creation of representative assemblies in villages, as well as the holding of direct elections for members of the local people's congresses at the county level (or the district level in urban areas) and below.

## THE CHALLENGES OF GLOBALIZATION

At the World Trade Organization (WTO) meeting in Doha, Qatar, in November 2001, China was admitted into the organization. The party leadership maintains the same approach to the challenges posed by globalization as to those posed by economic reforms: Liberalization that promotes economic growth is acceptable, but it will not be tolerated when it is perceived to be a threat to the party's monopoly on political power.

Economic growth and the development of a market economy have exacerbated contradictions in Chinese society. Together with rampant corruption and the abuse of power by cadres, the disparities have generated considerable dissatisfaction, and they represent the most serious causes for social instability. The party leaders under Jiang Zemin were acutely aware of the potential danger, but they largely failed to initiate the reforms necessary to minimize its risk, despite Jiang's efforts to promote "rule of law" and "rule by virtue." Jiang also offered his "Three Represents" theory, which suggested broadening the base of the party's support to involve the new social strata of executives and professionals and emphasizing the importance of improving economic productivity. The theory was not perceived as a significant ideological innovation, but the approach was generally accepted as an appropriate response of the party to the changing times.

The Sixteenth National Congress of the CCP was held in November 2002. It was a congress of leadership succession and personnel arrangement, not a congress of policy changes and theoretical innovation. There was still very little institutionalization, even when power was supposed to be handed over to the fourth-generation leaders. The Political Bureau and the Political Bureau Standing Committee were dominated by Jiang Zemin's protégés.

Since then, China's official think tanks have been concerned with the country's entry into a complicated and challenging stage of development. They have shown an awareness of the historical experiences of many other countries that, after reaching a gross domestic product (GDP) level of $1,000 per capita, faced political turmoil, the sharpening of social contradictions, rising tensions among ethnic groups, and other social problems. The lessons drawn prompted China's leaders to promote the building of a harmonious society.

The government of Hu Jintao and Wen Jiabao has been acutely aware of the impact on social stability of the widening gap between the rich and poor. The leadership has been working hard to provide a basic social-security net to those who have not been able to enjoy the fruits of economic development, and has been especially responsive to the plight of China's underprivileged groups. Though these efforts entail a significant financial burden for the central government, it has been able to improve social services based on increasing fiscal revenues. The leadership still believes in the strengthening of ideological work to consolidate the legitimacy of the CCP regime.

In the absence of major political reforms, some administrative innovations were introduced. In the Sixteenth National Congress in 2002, the leadership proposed a system of fixed terms, resignation, and responsibility for leading cadres in the party and government.

The Seventeenth National Congress was held in October 2007. At the congress, the leadership claimed that the coming five years would be the pivotal period in the building of a moderately prosperous society; it aimed at planning a peaceful transition in the coming ten to fifteen years. The legitimacy of the Communist regime is now based on its economic achievement: an average annual growth rate of 9.7 percent in the twenty-nine years since the launch of economic reforms. However, Hu Jintao's "scientific outlook on development" places more emphasis on sustainability.

At the end of the Cold War, American political scientist Francis Fukuyama concluded that the evolution of human societies through different forms of government had culminated in modern liberal democracy. The CCP has tried to convince the world that China will be an exception, at least in the foreseeable future. Hu Jintao and other Chinese leaders are well aware of the sharpening social contradictions, and are trying to build a "harmonious society" as a response. It is commonly recognized that their policies are oriented in the right direction. The question is how successful they will be in maintaining political stability in the absence of truly democratic reforms.

The Chinese leadership continues to ignore requests for a reversal of the official verdict on the 1989 Tiananmen Incident. Similarly, it suppressed discussion on the Cultural Revolution during the 2006 fortieth anniversary of its launch and imposed many restrictions on the funeral of Zhao Ziyang in January 2005. This pattern of behavior reveals the party's strong sense of insecurity. Many observers believe that the CCP has become very concerned with the "color revolutions" that emerged in the post-Soviet states, namely, in Georgia in 2003, Ukraine in 2004, and Kyrgyzstan in 2005. In the early years of the twenty-first century, Chinese leaders still follow Deng Xiaoping's advice and continue to avoid open ideological debates. They have tried to generate resources to implement policies that bring relief to the poor. This task has been made easier by the country's rapid economic growth, but real pressure will come when the economy slows down.

**SEE ALSO** *Central State Organs since 1949: Central Military Commission.*

**BIBLIOGRAPHY**

Guillermaz, Jacques. *A History of the Chinese Communist Party, 1921–1949.* Trans. Anne Destenay. New York: Random House, 1972.

News of the Communist Party of China. Party Congresses. http://english.cpc.people.com.cn/66101/index.html.

Party History Research Centre of the Central Committee of the Chinese Communist Party, comp. *History of the Chinese Communist Party: A Chronology of Events, 1919–1990.* Beijing: Foreign Languages Press, 1991.

Perrolle, Pierre M., ed. *Fundamentals of the Chinese Communist Party.* White Plains, NY: International Arts and Sciences Press, 1976.

Sheng Hu and Party History Research Center of the CPC Central Committee, eds. *A Concise History of the Communist Party of China: Seventy Years of the CPC.* Trans. Central Translation Bureau. Beijing: Foreign Languages Press, 1994.

Uhalley, Stephen, Jr. *A History of the Chinese Communist Party.* Stanford, CA: Hoover Institution Press, 1988.

van de Ven, Hans J. *From Friend to Comrade: The Founding of the Chinese Communist Party, 1920–1927.* Berkeley: University of California Press, 1991.

Zhai Wenbo (Winberg Chai). *The Search for a New China: A Capsule History, Ideology, and Leadership of the Chinese Communist Party, 1921–1974, with Selected Documents.* New York: Capricorn, 1975.

***Joseph Y. S. Cheng (Zheng Yushuo)***

## COMMUNIST PARTY HISTORY REVISED (1981)

The leadership of the Chinese Communist Party engaged in a major revision of the party's history in 1980 and 1981. The result was the Resolution on Certain Questions in the History of Our Party since the Founding of the People's Republic of China, which was adopted by the Sixth Plenum of the Eleventh Central Committee on June 27, 1981. It is only the second such document to be adopted in the history of the Communist Party. Though unanimously approved, it was a controversial document, taking over a year to write and going through numerous drafts before formal adoption (in October 1980, for example, it was discussed and critiqued by 4,000 party members). The call of the Third Plenum of the Eleventh Party Congress in December 1978 to "emancipate the mind" had unleashed a relatively open-minded critical review of recent Communist Party history to make way for the revision, but was now becoming dangerously iconoclastic in the view of the leadership. It conceived of this inquiry and resolution as a way of setting forth once and for all the official verdict on what had transpired since Liberation (1949) and thus of drawing the curtain on further critiques, particularly of the role of Mao Zedong, whose iconic status was still deemed essential to the legitimacy of the Communist Party regime. Just as the previous, identically named document (adopted by the enlarged Seventh Plenum of the Sixth Central Committee in 1945, and immediately preceding the convention of the Seventh Chinese Communist Party Congress), provided an authoritative summary of the party's successes and failures and the lessons it had drawn from them and thereby "unified the thinking of the whole Party, consolidated its unity, promoted the rapid advance of the people's revolutionary cause and accelerated its eventual triumph," the present resolution, it was hopefully predicted, "will play a similar historical role." Both resolutions saw themselves as situated at historical turning points in Communist Party history, the first marking the end of the party's experience as an outlaw revolutionary band and the beginning of its role as the ruling party in an era of "new democracy," and the second marking the end of the era of "continuing the revolution under the dictatorship of the proletariat" and the launching of a new program of "reform and opening to the outside world." And as fundamental documents, neither hesitates to challenge and repudiate previously accepted norms and decisions as historical errors and to boldly proclaim new and different rules of the game for the future.

### HISTORICAL REVIEW

The present resolution begins by dividing Communist Party history into two basic periods: the twenty-eight years before the founding of the People's Republic and the thirty-two years since Liberation. Although the resolution focuses on the latter, the former is briefly reviewed in four phases of widely varying lengths: the period of the Northern Expedition (1924–1927), the Agrarian Revolutionary War (1927–1937), the War of Resistance against Japan (1937–1945), and the nationwide War of Liberation (1946-1949). (The sole achievement mentioned for the War of Resistance against Japan was the 1942–1944 party Rectification Movement [Zhengfeng Yundong]. Though hardly a major contribution to the war against Japan, this movement unified the whole party behind the "correct" revolutionary leadership of Mao Zedong.) The characterization and appraisal of this first period closely follows those of the first resolution in affirming that the rise of Mao to a central-leadership position was the "most prominent" reason for the Communist Party's survival and ultimate triumph amid multiple difficulties. The only major innovation of the latter resolution is that Mao Zedong Thought was now collectivized—it came into being through the collective struggle of the Party and the people. Though thus largely unoriginal, Chen Yun reportedly suggested (and Deng Xiaoping gratefully accepted) inclusion of this historical review to demonstrate to critics the substantial historical achievements of Mao and the Communist Party.

After a brief appraisal of the post-Liberation era, focusing on statistical indices of economic development, the post-Liberation era is divided into four periods for closer scrutiny: the seven-year period of the socialist transformation (or socialization of the means of production) (1949–1956), the years of "building socialism in all spheres" (1956–1966), the Cultural Revolution and its aftermath (1966–1976), and the five-year period since the arrest of the Gang of Four (1976–1981). While the pre-Liberation era is defined in terms of the principal contradiction of each period, the post-Liberation era is defined by the tasks to be achieved; only the final period is conceived of in terms of a contradiction. This periodization is followed by an extended theoretical discussion of two key topics: the role of Mao's theoretical contributions and leadership, and the correct prognosis of the forthcoming period of reform and opening to the outside world.

## APPRAISAL OF MAO ZEDONG

Whereas the overall evaluation of Mao's contribution to the period before the founding of the People's Republic is overwhelmingly positive, the evaluation of his contribution to the post-Liberation period is positive in general but predominantly critical in its specifics, with negative verdicts steadily gaining weight and prominence from the socialist transformation, the first period. In the first two periods (1949–1966), Mao both led and acted as an implicit foil to the historically correct line. Disagreeing with the rest of the leadership over the pace and scope of the socialist transformation, he was "impatient for quick results," given to "rash advance," and "overestimated subjective will," and inclined toward "excessive targets," "boastfulness," and "stirring up of a communist wind." Yet these were only differences in degree rather than divergences from the party line, as the leadership had reached consensuses over the decisions to socialize the means of production, implement and then quickly suppress the liberalization of the Hundred Flowers campaign, and launch the Great Leap Forward. During the decade of the Cultural Revolution, Mao's thinking diverged from that of his colleagues in more theoretically systematic ways. Mao advocated continuing the revolution under the dictatorship of the proletariat. Under the premise that class struggle continued to exist during socialism and that class enemies had surreptitiously "sneaked into" the highest ranks of the party leadership, he decreed that politics should take command of economics, culture, and society. This meant that at this historical turning point the relations of production were more important than the forces of production, and that the ideological superstructure took precedence over the economic base—a position that had the effect of elevating his own will over all other considerations. Mao's rising prestige and subjective arrogance led to a feudal overconcentration of power inconsistent with the norms of inner-party democracy, permitted his personal leadership (characterized by leftist errors) to take the place of the collective leadership of the party, and led him to commit "error[s] comprehensive in magnitude and duration." Such errors were not characterized as an error of party line, owing largely to the intervention of Deng Xiaoping (1984), who toned down the criticism and ensured that Mao's leadership was deemed essentially correct. One of the interesting theoretical innovations permitting this seeming discrepancy was that Mao Zedong Thought (or more formally, Marxism-Leninism-Mao Zedong Thought), which was invariably correct, was detached from Mao's leadership, which was not (Mao could and sometimes did violate his own Thought). So conceived, Mao Zedong Thought, which reached maturity during the 1930s and 1940s, was a "crystallization of the collective wisdom of the Chinese Communist Party," including the contributions of many outstanding Communist Party leaders with whom Mao sometimes disagreed. Mao Zedong Thought was thus reformulated to emphasize those points deemed essential by his successors, the most fundamental of which were "to seek truth from facts, the mass line, and independence." The first of these departed from the Cultural Revolution's focus on ideology and politics in favor of the pragmatic application of principle, the second reemphasized an element of informal democracy in policy implementation, while the third, focusing on foreign policy, emphasized self-reliance and pursuit of the national interest.

## NORMS FOR THE FUTURE

The final section of the resolution, "Unite and Strive to Build a Powerful, Modern Socialist China," sets forth the basic norms of the forthcoming era of reform and opening to the outside world. Fundamental here are the Four Basic Principles: upholding socialism, the people's democratic dictatorship, the leadership of the Communist Party, and Marxism-Leninism-Mao Zedong Thought. Here it is emphasized that "socialism and socialism alone can save China," and that "without the Communist Party, there would be no New China." But, according to the resolution, the "socialist transformation was fundamentally completed," and the "principal contradiction our country has to resolve is between the growing material and cultural needs of the people and the backwardness of social production." Thus the fundamental error of the Cultural Revolution was its critique of "productive-forces theory," and the basic task of the party and nation moving forward is that "all our Party work must be subordinated to and serve this central task—economic construction."

## THE NEW SOCIALISM

Despite many changes in the particular features and goals of the subsequent reform and opening period, the basic features of the resolution have since been adhered to with great consistency—owing in part to its ideologically authoritative status, which brooks no legitimate opposition. Thus it has effectively restricted (as it was intended to do) serious critical research by Chinese scholars into recent Communist Party history. To be sure, the resolution has more successfully defined the past than the future, where it has since been superseded by, for example, reports to successive party congresses.

The latter represent periodic ideological adaptations to continuously emerging strains between the principles of "socialism" (study of the precise content of which has been greatly deemphasized) and the sociopolitical implications of the pragmatic expedients eclectically adopted in the course of modernization. Indeed, these reports often beg the questions, what is socialism? and what is left of it? In its construal of socialism in the first two decades since Liberation, the Communist Party focused on two criteria: replacing the chaos of the capitalist market with socialist planning and replacing private property with collective ownership of the means of production. After the discovery in the early 1980s

## RESOLUTION ON PARTY HISTORY

"Comrade Mao Zedong's prestige reached a peak and he began to get arrogant at the very time when the Party was confronted with the new task of shifting the focus of its work to socialist construction. . . .He gradually divorced himself from practice and from the masses, acting more and more arbitrarily and subjectively, and increasingly put himself above the Central Committee of the Party. . . .This meant that conditions were present for the over-concentration of Party power in individuals and for the development of arbitrary individual rule and the personality cult in the Party." (*Resolution*, pp. 46–47)

"The 'cultural revolution,' which lasted from May 1966 to October 1976, was responsible for the most severe setback and the heaviest losses suffered by the Party, the state and the people since the founding of the People's Republic. It was initiated and led by Comrade Mao Zedong. His principal theses were that many representatives of the bourgeoisie and counterrevolutionary revisionists had sneaked into the Party, the government, the army and cultural circles, and leadership in a fairly large majority of organizations and departments was no longer in the hands of Marxists and the people. . . . These erroneous 'Left' theses. . .were obviously inconsistent with Mao Zedong Thought, which is the integration of the universal principles of Marxism-Leninism with the concrete practices of the Chinese revolution." (*Resolution*, pp. 32–33)

"Mao Zedong Thought is Marxism-Leninism applied and developed in China; it constitutes a correct theory, a body of correct principles and a summary of the experiences that have been confirmed in the practice of the Chinese revolution, a crystallization of the collective wisdom of the Chinese Communist Party. Many outstanding leaders of our Party made important contributions to the formation and development of Mao Zedong Thought, and they are systematized in the scientific works of Comrade Mao Zedong." (*Resolution*, p. 57)

**BIBLIOGRAPHY**

*Resolution on Certain Questions in the History of Our Party since the Founding of the People's Republic of China.* Beijing: Foreign Languages Press, 1981.

***Lowell Dittmer***

that the market was still a legitimate part of the economy, at least in the early stages of socialism (where China would remain for a considerable length of time), the market has largely displaced central planning. This leaves collective ownership as the sole criterion of socialism. While this criterion has been honored in the form of the large state-owned enterprises that continue to occupy the commanding heights of the Chinese economy (albeit in diminishing number), private property (including foreign-owned property) has been constitutionally sanctioned and has steadily expanded its role in a now mixed economy. Though this state of affairs has raised occasional theoretical controversy, it will likely not result in any fundamental change in the relations of production until the practical economic success of the "new socialism" becomes more vulnerable to challenge.

**SEE ALSO** *Chinese Marxism: Mao Zedong Thought; Chinese Marxism: Overview; Chinese Marxism: Postrevolutionary Marxism other than Mao Zedong Thought; Communist Party; Cultural Revolution, 1966-1969; Deng Xiaoping; Economic Reform since 1978; Hu Yaobang; Mao Zedong.*

**BIBLIOGRAPHY**

Deng Liqun. *Shi-er chunqiu, 1975-1987: Deng Liqun zi shu* [Twelve years, 1975–1987: Written by Deng Liqun himself]. Hong Kong: Bozhi Chubanshe, 2006. See pp. 159–172.

Deng Xiaoping. Remarks on Successive Drafts of the "Resolution on Certain Questions in the History of Our Party since the Founding of the People's Republic of China" (March 1980–June 1981). In his *Selected Works of Deng Xiaoping (1975–1982)*, vol. 3, pp. 276–297. Beijing: Foreign Languages Press, 1984.

He Fang. *Dang shi biji: Cong Zunyi huiyi dao Yan'an zhengfeng* [Notes on Party history: From the Zunyi meeting to the rectification of Yan'an], vol. 2, pp. 633–706. Hong Kong: Liwen Chubanshe, 2005.

Resolution on Certain Questions in the History of Our Party since the Founding of the People's Republic of China. Beijing: Foreign Languages press, 1981.

Zhonggong Zhongyang Wenxian Yanjiushi (Central Literature Research Office of the Chinese Communist Party). *Guanyu jianguo yi lai dang de ruogan lishi wenti de jueyi zhushi ben* [Notes on the resolution of several historical issues concerning the Party since the founding of the country]. Rev. ed. Beijing: Renmin Chubanshe, 1985.

***Lowell Dittmer***

# COMMUNIST THOUGHT IN CHINA, ORIGINS OF

Marxism was introduced into China in the early twentieth century, when there was a strong interest among intellectuals searching for ways of national survival and regeneration among Western ideas of democracy, nationalism, science, industrialism, and socialism. While the focus of attention, both immediately before and after the 1911 Revolution, was on political action dedicated to establishing a constitutional monarchy or republican democracy, socialism was well recognized as a rising force in the inevitable course of world evolution, and its perceived values of social justice and harmony were much welcomed as good for society and morally right. Most advocates of socialism, including intellectual mentors like Sun Yat-sen and Liang Qichao, tended to take an eclectic approach without committing themselves to one school of thought, except that there were a few distinctive anarchist groups from 1907. Marx was generally praised for his critique of capitalism and "scientific" contribution to social analysis, but his theories of historical materialism and proletarian revolution were only superficially mentioned, rather than understood, while his proposed policies in the *Communist Manifesto* were dismissed by the anarchists as insufficient and less than a genuine form of socialism. In this first wave of socialist ideas, a noteworthy view common to all was that China, in modernizing its economy, should avoid the social inequalities and conflicts experienced by the West. Among socialists, anarchists such as Li Shizeng and Liu Shifu played an important role in popularizing the ideals, values, and terminology of socialism, thereby helping to prepare the intellectual community for the new tide of the 1917 October Revolution in Russia. This tide of revolution cut into the momentous May Fourth and New Culture movements at a critical time, when clamors for Western democracy (*minzhu*) and science (*kexue*) became fused with the mid-1919 patriotic protests against the imperialistic oppressions of the West and Japan. As in other places, it was the October Revolution that gave birth to Communism in China, but the China story was unique in its particulars.

## FIRST REACTIONS TO THE OCTOBER REVOLUTION

Chinese intellectuals in their first reactions to the October Revolution in fact did not see the influence of Marxism or Bolshevism. The revolution was vaguely understood to be a social revolution representing the interests of workers. Some intellectuals with anarchist and socialist leanings, Li Dazhao included, welcomed it as a new historical tide of epochal and messianic significance. He and others who wrote favorably of the revolution tended to merge its socialist spirit rather loosely with the May Fourth ideal of democracy and the new yearnings for international fraternity in reaction to the destructive nationalistic rivalries that brought about World War I. These first reactions thus reflected these people's particular perspective on the changing world and their ideological dispositions, rather than any direct influence of Marxism or Bolshevism, but they set the stage for Marxism and socialism to make a strong impact on the broader circles of May Fourth intellectuals in 1919, when it was finally recognized that Marxism had been the doctrinal frame of reference for the October Revolution.

## THE IMPACT OF MARXISM

Over the next few years Marxism and then Bolshevism exerted their influences in the special circumstances of China under the banner of the May Fourth movement. A short yet distinct first phase saw a dramatic spur of interest in Marxist and similar theories of historical materialism, capitalism, class struggle, and imperialism, which provided Chinese with new vistas and methods of socioeconomic and political analyses, and significantly modified their views on the illnesses of China and the world. Rather than being a future issue for nonindustrialized China, socialism became an immediate concern and was regarded as crucial to the success of all reform programs and actions. Yet at this stage all proponents of Marxism or socialism invariably still shunned a Russian type of revolution as they, like the older generation of socialist thinkers, continued to look for a nonviolent path toward socialism. In this period, Marxism was understood mainly in its pre-Leninist forms; Lenin's ideas were hardly available or recognized at the time.

## GOING THE "RUSSIAN WAY"

A second phase quickly set in as the mood for revolutionary and political action began gathering strength during the nation's patriotic outbursts against the imperialists, as well as the treacherous and authoritarian warlord governments. From around mid-1920s, some of the politicized and more radical-minded intellectuals and students began to look to the "Russian Way" as a possible and even desirable model of national salvation. In the eyes of these people, the Bolsheviks in the Soviet Union had succeeded in emerging triumphant from the chaos of the revolution and commenced an effective program of socialist reconstruction; they had also warded off the challenge of foreign intervention. These successes not only stood in strong contrast to the repeated failures of China in its efforts at national regeneration, but also brought the Soviet Union to the forefront of world civilization, replacing the degenerate capitalist and imperialistic West as the model for China to follow. Established scholars such as Chen Duxiu, Li Dazhao, and Li Da, and young students such as Mao Zedong, Cai Heshen (who converted to communism in France), and Qu Qiubai (who went to Russia as a pilgrim), were typical examples of this new direction of thought, which finally brought them into the fold of Bolshevik Communism. Meanwhile, the Soviet Union's proclaimed abandonment of its imperialist privileges in China (the Karakhan declarations) also helped create a favorable pro–Soviet Union atmosphere. Small Communist groups were formed and, under the guidance of advisors from Moscow, such as Grigori Voitinsky, soon developed into a Chinese Communist Party, founded in July 1921. The party's founders formally adopted Marxism as

***Man viewing portraits of Mao Zedong (left), Vladimir Lenin (bottom center), Josef Stalin (top right), and Karl Marx (top center), at a market in Beijing, October 26, 2002.*** *The 1917 October Revolution in Russia served as inspiration to Chinese intellectuals looking to transform the country into a Marxist society. Consequently, Soviet Communist leaders such as Vladimir Lenin and Josef Stalin and German socialist Karl Marx receive acknowledgment alongside the first leader of the People's Republic of China, Mao Zedong.* AP IMAGES

their espoused doctrine. A wide range of Lenin's revolutionary theories and methods—mainly on the proletarian state and violent revolution, the vanguard party and party organization, and imperialism and world revolution—were introduced and venerated as the source of revolutionary wisdom. Lenin's concept of the vanguard party in particular matched well with the revolutionary activism of the young party and with Chinese traditional notions of elite authoritarianism. An ideological framework was thus formed for the comprehensive development of the party's thought system and revolutionary practice. The Chinese Communist Party became a member of the new Communist International (Comintern), which mentored the Chinese Communist movement until World War II.

## DEFINING THE NATURE OF THE CHINESE REVOLUTION

From 1922 the Communist Party was further equipped with Lenin's concept of the national and colonial question, which identified nationalist movements in colonial and semicolonial countries as an indispensable ally of the proletariat in the world revolution against capitalism. China was thus characterized as a semifeudal and semicolonial nation that had to go through two stages of revolution, in which the bourgeois-democratic revolution must come before the proletarian-socialist revolution. To engineer a national revolution in China, Moscow took strong initiatives from 1922 to support Sun Yat-sen's revolutionary movement and, through the Dutch Comintern delegate Maring (Hendricus Sneevliet), to persuade the Communist Party to collaborate with Sun's Guomindang (Nationalist Party) by joining it as a "bloc within," on the grounds that the Guomindang was a multiclass party with sufficient strengths to carry out the mission of the bourgeois-democratic revolution in China. Though the Communists harbored many political misgivings and disadvantages, this strategy satisfied their nationalistic, voluntarist, and populist instincts, and allowed these instincts to have free rein in the national revolution, which focused on the two tasks of anti-imperialism and antiwarlordism.

### IN SEARCH OF A REVOLUTIONARY MODEL

As the Communist Party's revolutionary movement gained momentum through the Guomindang alliance (called the First United Front), inherent contradictions of its multiparty and multiclass strategies inevitably became a source of continuous ideological polemics and power struggles. In general, controversies over the revolutionary program revolved around such issues as how to deal with the Guomindang and its many factions, what strategies should be adopted in the mass movements and the Guomindang's military Northern Expedition (launched in June 1926), and how to advance the party's interest for the next phase of the revolution. In its class strategy, the Communist Party as a proletarian party naturally placed high hopes in the dynamics of the labor movement, especially during its high tides in 1922–1923 and 1925–1927. Inheriting Lenin's concept of a worker-peasant alliance, the party, from 1923, regarded the peasantry as an auxiliary revolutionary force and quickly discovered its strong revolutionary potentials. Accepting the two-stage theory of revolution and the bloc-within alliance, the party nevertheless also accepted Guomindang leadership and cultivated for the time being the uneasy claim that the bourgeoisie had a significant role to play in the national revolution.

Following Sun Yat-sen's death in March 1925, tensions with the Guomindang gradually multiplied while the national revolution—enjoying massive Soviet aid, vibrant labor and peasant movements, and military successes—dramatically gathered strength. Controversies over revolutionary strategies within the party intensified, and different opinions gradually crystallized into opposing lines. Mikhail Borodin, the powerful Soviet advisor, played a pivotal role in the party's pursuing Stalin's bifurcated policy of simultaneously supporting the Guomindang leadership and advancing the party's aggressive class activities. Party leaders such as Chen Duxiu, Qu Qiubai, Cai Heshen, and Zhang Guotao fell victim to the same influence and vacillated between different positions at different times. When the alliance with the Guomindang finally ruptured in mid-1927, the Communist Party turned toward an even more aggressive model of a Soviet revolution of workers and peasants under Stalin's projection of a "revolutionary high tide," while suffering further setbacks as it was expelled from the cities by the Guomindang's superior armies. Each leadership was in turn discredited: Chen Duxiu, Qu Qiubai, and Li Lisan. In the 1930s Wang Ming, as a representative of the Moscow line, came into new conflict with native leaders such as Mao Zedong, who had now developed their own thoughts on how to conduct the revolution in China. This new round of struggle was to end in the triumph of the native approach, evident first at the Zunyi Conference of 1935 during the Long March and consolidated in 1938 after the outbreak of the Anti-Japanese War of Resistance in July 1937. The left-oriented Soviet revolution was abandoned, as was the right-oriented pro-Guomindang policy that Wang had pursued under Stalin's instructions during the Anti-Japanese War. The framework of the two revolutions was to remain, but its contents became a Sinified version of the revolutionary model known as Mao Zedong's new democracy, which worked toward a broad party-led united front while strengthening the party's autonomy and military position in the countryside for future struggles with the Guomindang.

**BIBLIOGRAPHY**

Bernal, Martin. *Chinese Socialism to 1907*. Ithaca, NY: Cornell University Press, 1976.

Dirlik, Arif. *The Origins of Chinese Communism*. Cambridge, U.K.: Oxford University Press, 1989.

Luk, Michael Y. L. *The Origins of Chinese Bolshevism: An Ideology in the Making*. Cambridge, U.K.: Oxford University Press, 1990.

Meisner, Maurice. *Li Ta-chao and the Origins of Chinese Marxism*. Cambridge, MA: Harvard University Press, 1967.

Schwartz, Benjamin I. *Chinese Communism and the Rise of Mao*. Cambridge, MA: Harvard University Press, 1951.

***Michael Y. L. Luk***

## COMMUNIST YOUTH LEAGUE

The Chinese Communist Youth League (CYL or CCYL, Zhongguo Gongchanzhuyi Qingniantuan) is the youth wing of the Communist Party of China. Its functions are to promote party policy among young people and to train future party members. Membership is open to young people between the ages of fourteen and twenty-eight. The CYL guides the All-China Youth Federation (a mass organization for young people), the All-China Students' Federation, and the children's organization, the Young Pioneers.

### HISTORY

The CYL traces its origins to the Chinese Socialist Youth League, founded in Guangzhou in 1922. It became the New Democratic Youth League in 1949, before adopting its present name in 1957. In the Maoist era, membership was considered an honor, and some young people applied many times before they were accepted or gave up. Criteria were strict; applicants could be excluded on grounds of a "bad class background" or a "low political level," for being insufficiently serious, hardworking, or revolutionary, or for not knowing enough about Marxism-Leninism.

During the Cultural Revolution, the CYL leadership came under attack. It had opposed the distribution of the first Cultural Revolution literature in 1966, and CYL members, many of whom were the children of Communist cadres, were accused of regarding themselves as a hereditary elite. The CYL became less attractive to young people than the Red Guards and was formally disbanded in summer 1966. It was not revived until the 1970s. In the reform era, the CYL has promoted party policy with a special emphasis on the role of young people in modernization.

### IMPACT AND IMPORTANCE

The Communist Party has shown a consistent interest in ideological education for young people. In a 1957 address, Mao Zedong said, "You young people, full of vigor and vitality are in the bloom of life. . . . China's future belongs to you." The Red Guards of the 1960s were encouraged to think of themselves as the "successors to the revolution." Now it is said that the success of the modernization drive depends on China's youth. The CYL is considered a bulwark against autonomous youth activism. However, its task of imposing orthodoxy inculcating socialist values is increasingly difficult in contemporary China's materialist society.

In terms of membership, the CYL is very successful. At the end of 2007, it had 75,439,000 members, just less than 25 percent of the relevant age group. Students accounted for about half its membership, and workers in the agricultural, industrial, and service sectors for 26.9 percent, 7.3 percent, and 14.4 percent respectively. There are branches in public and private workplaces, including one with sixteen members in the Shenyang Wal-Mart store. Despite widespread political cynicism, membership in the CYL is attractive to young people who want to make a career within the state or party bureaucracy. Many former CYL leaders hold party and state offices at the highest level (see list below). At a less elevated level, membership of the Youth League is recognized as a stepping stone for any young person who wants an official career first to obtain a post and subsequently to be considered for promotion. Many CYL members probably also join neither for idealistic nor for careerist motives, but simply because the organization offers a variety of activities and outings.

Chronological list of CYL first secretaries with subsequent career highlights:

- Hu Yaobang (1957–1978): Distinguished career culminating in appointment as general secretary to the party (1981–1987).
- Han Ying (1978–1982): Central Committee member (1973–1982).
- Wang Zhaoguo (1982–1984): Central Committee member and holder of a variety of party posts.
- Hu Jintao (1984–1985): From 1985, Party Committee secretary, first in Guizhou Province, then in the Tibet Autonomous Region; president of China from 2003.
- Song Defu (1985–1993): Central Committee member and party secretary in Fujian Province (2002–2004).
- Li Keqiang (1993–1998): As of 2008, the executive vice premier of China and the seventh-ranked member of the Politburo Standing Committee.
- Zhou Qiang (1998–2006): Central Committee member and from 2008 governor of Hunan Province.
- Hu Chunhua (2006–2008): Central Committee member and from 2008 vice governor Hebei Province.
- Lu Hao (2008–): Central Committee member and governor of Gansu Province.

#### BIBLIOGRAPHY

Chinese Communist Youth League (CYL). http://www.cycnet.com/chinayouth/.

Hooper, Beverley. *Youth in China.* New York: Penguin, 1985.

Li Cheng. *China's Leaders: The New Generation.* Lanham, MD: Rowman and Littlefield, 2001.

*Zhongguo qingnian bao* [China youth daily]. The official CYL newspaper. http://www.cyol.net.

***Delia Davin***

## COMMUNITY CARE

Major changes have occurred in the community health-services system in China since the decision was made by the Chinese government to reform its health system in 1997. The aim of the reform was to introduce an affordable, community-based, health-care system with general practice as the driving force to complement the existing hospital-based system. As of 2008, China had approximately 1.3 billion people and 63,000 medical treatment institutions with three billion attendances per annum. There have been complaints about the cost and the ease of access to health care, especially in the hospital system. As China has embraced a market economy, there has also been a gradual decline in the renowned universal health-care system upon which many workers and farmers relied. The population of China is also aging, adding to the financial burden on health care. In 2005 about 8 percent of China's population was aged sixty-five years and over. This demographic change, along with smaller families, means less family support for older people. It is against this background that China has undertaken reform to develop community health services and train general practitioners (GPs).

### COMMUNITY HEALTH-SERVICES ORGANIZATIONS AND PROBLEMS ENCOUNTERED

Between the founding of the People's Republic of China in 1949 and 1997 reform, the health-care system in China consisted of a three-tiered, vertically organized network of mostly secondary and tertiary hospitals in the urban area and primary hospitals in the rural areas. In other words, the health-care system in the city was entirely hospital-based, without community health services or general practice. To provide the latter service, a number of secondary hospitals were converted into community health services centers, and some of the specialists who used to work in these hospitals retrained as general practitioners (GPs). By the end of 2007, community health services had been established in all thirty-one provinces and autonomous regions in China, with a total of 6,340 community health-services centers and 20,132 affiliated stations (Ministry of Health 2007).

Ideally, a community health-services team would consist of GPs, multiskilled nurses, and public health personnel. Some GPs would be employed by local governments. Apart from providing medical treatment, the team would also be involved in a range of activities, including prevention of disease, rehabilitation, health promotion, medical education, and family planning. Medical treatment would be focused on diseases that can be handled in general practice. People with major illnesses would be referred to tertiary hospitals. The role of the community health team as defined by the central government would be to provide affordable and efficient health care to the masses, and at the same time prevent the spread of communicable diseases, as well as reducing the burden of the pharmaceutical costs on individuals and households (Ministry of Health 1999).

Despite these ideals, the implementation of community health services has faced a number of challenges. The first major obstacle is that the community has not embraced general practice readily. People are not accustomed to community health services, and those with minor illnesses still prefer to be seen by doctors in tertiary hospitals, even though it is more expensive. A visit to a doctor in the outpatient department of a tertiary hospital usually costs three times that of a consultation by a GP in the community health-services center. Despite the difference, patients tend to bypass GPs and go straight to the outpatient departments of big hospitals. GPs have thus failed to establish themselves as gatekeepers for hospitals. According to Ministry of Health statistics, in 2002 there were 1.2 billion consultations in hospital outpatient departments compared to 36 million consultations in community health centers nationwide (Ministry of Health 2003). Moreover, bureaucrats of local governments do not comprehend the importance of the reform, while staff in the district hospitals are reluctant to change their mode of service delivery and do not appreciate the long-term benefits that the reform will bring. Lack of a fair remuneration system is another issue. For instance, some important services, such as public health education and disease prevention as provided by community health-services organizations, have not received appropriate remuneration from the government. In addition, financial resources to support multidisciplinary health-care teams, including allied health services, have not been established.

## A NATIONAL TRAINING PROGRAM FOR GPs AND PROBLEMS ENCOUNTERED

Apart from retraining hospital-based doctors to become GPs, many medical students have been trained specifically to become GPs under a new medical curriculum for GP training developed by the Ministry of Health. In 2000 the National Training Center for General Practitioners was established at the Capital Medical University in Beijing. At the provincial level, the heath bureaucrats in the provinces or cities have included GP medical education in their portfolios and have commenced its implementation. By the end of 2001, sixteen provinces or cities had already established provincial GP training centers. Fifty-eight clinical centers and fifty-six community health-services centers nationwide had been accredited for training (Ministry of Health 2002). A network of GP training centers was progressively being formed. As a result of these efforts, GP training programs have started in seventeen provinces or cities for those who are already working in community health centers. Ten provinces have arranged bedside clinical teaching based in such centers. By 2001, 13,523 GPs had graduated with clinical bedside training (Ministry of Health 2007).

Nationwide, progress has also been made in undergraduate and postgraduate teaching of general practice. Twelve provinces or cities have listed general practice as part of their core (or elective) undergraduate teaching activities in the medical curriculum, and medical students at sixteen institutions study general practice as part of their curriculum. Six provinces or cities (Beijing, Shanghai, Zhejiang, Heilongjiang, Guizhou, and Fujian) have commenced programs in general-practice postgraduate training. By 2002, 639 district hospital doctors had been retrained as GPs (Ministry of Health 2002). The funding for retraining comes mainly from income generated by health-care services, and resources from units and individual workers. Fourteen provinces have begun training GP trainers. By 2007, 1,359 people had been trained as GP trainers in provinces, in addition to the 600 already trained by the Ministry of Health (Ministry of Health 2007).

Despite this progress poorer regional areas still lag behind large cities in the quality and uptake of GP training. The issuing of national licensing and registration examinations for GPs has not been synchronized with GP training, leading to uneven standards of GP practice. Staff morale among GPs is poor due to the lack of opportunities for promotion and professional development.

### PRIORITIZATION OF COMMUNITY HEALTH-SERVICES REFORM BY THE CHINESE GOVERNMENT

The prioritization of community health services by the central government in 2006 is seen as a major step in tackling the underutilization of community health services. The government has met its commitment with generous funding of billions of dollars to improve community health services and the training of GPs. This is welcome news for staff and patients, and it promises a brighter future in the development of a more efficient and more affordable health-care system in China.

**SEE ALSO** *Health Care, 1800-1949; Medical Care since 1949.*

### BIBLIOGRAPHY

Ministry of Health of the People's Republic of China, Division of Primary and Women's Health. *Opinions about Development of Community Health Services in the Cities*. Document no. 326. 1999. 中华人民共和国国务院 (zhong hua ren min gong he guo guo wu yuan); 关于发展城市社区卫生服务的意见 (guan yu fa zhan cheng shi she qu wei sheng fu wu de yi jian).

Ministry of Health of the People's Republic of China, Division of Medical Education. *Survey of Community Health Services and General Practice Training*. 2002. 中华人民共和国卫生部科技教育司 (zhong hua ren min gong he guo wei sheng bu ke ji jiao yu si). 社区卫生服务和全科医学培训现状调查 (she qu wei sheng fu wu he quan ke yi xue pei xun xian zhuang diao cha).

Ministry of Health of the People's Republic of China. *Statistics of Various Health Services Utilization in 2002*. 2003. 中华人民共和国卫生部 (zhong hua ren min gong he guo wei sheng bu)卫生服务利用统计 (wei sheng fu wu li yong tong ji), 2002, 2003.

Ministry of Health of the People's Republic of China. *General Survey of Community Health Services*. 2007. 中华人民共和国卫生部妇幼与社区卫生司 (zhong hua ren min gong he guo wei sheng bu fu you yu she qu wei sheng si), 社区卫生服务调查 (she qu wei sheng fu wu diao cha).

***Liang Wannian*** 梁万年
***Daniel Kam Yin Chan***

# COMPANIES

*This entry contains the following:*



## OVERVIEW

After China launched its modernization drive in the second half of the nineteenth century, the creation of a framework for modern companies was seen as a central task for the nation. Traditionally, the main form of Chinese company was the family enterprise, which has remained true of Chinese business outside mainland China, with such businesses conforming to the legal strictures of the country of residence. In the late Qing dynasty (1644–1912), Chinese family businesses had already developed complex arrangements, in particular exploiting the possibilities of lineage organization. But such businesses had run up against limits in finance and scope.

The establishment of modern companies was thus mainly seen as a task for government. The emergence before 1912 of government-owned and hybrid corporate entities defined another leitmotif of Chinese corporate history that has persisted into the twenty-first century. The results were mixed at best, so that in 1904 the first systematic attempt to create a legal framework for the modern company took the form of the Company Law, followed by new regulations and laws in 1914 and 1929. In principle, these laws allowed for the establishment of public companies and limited liability companies with prescribed governance structures, but their potential was never fully realized because of the lack of corresponding structures in the capital market, regulatory bodies, accounting, and corporate disclosure. After 1929 the Nationalist government reinforced restrictive measures against private business and pushed for nationalization. Thus the major company forms in the Chinese Republic remained the family company and the government-owned company, with the significance of the latter growing in the 1940s as a result of ongoing nationalization.

### THE EVOLUTION OF COMPANY FORMS, 1949–1994

After 1949 the diversity of company forms was rigorously compressed as a result of the introduction of state planning in the economy. Until the launch of the reform policies, the dominant company form had been the state-owned enterprise (SOE). The only significant other form, the urban collective, converged with the SOE after the Great Leap Forward (1958–1960). Behind this uniformity, however, a peculiar governance mechanism emerged from the waves of centralization and decentralization that recurred until the turn of the millennium: the regional property rights system. In this system, companies of different sizes and different strategic significance were assigned to different levels of government (local, provincial and central); the government bodies then assumed the roles of investors, exerting control over retained profits. SOEs also faced different other functional bodies, which might assign particular tasks and responsibilities to the enterprise. Thus the governance structure of the standard SOE featured "too many mothers-in-law," as it was said, whose diverging aims and requirements had to be balanced by interorganizational negotiations.

The main legacy of this system for the reform era was a homogenous industrial structure across regions, as there were strong incentives to build autonomous regional industrial systems to minimize external conflicts and interference. When urban industrial reforms were implemented in 1984, they generated two important trends for the evolution of company forms: First, the low degree of industrial concentration rapidly increased the intensity of competition, such that a downward pressure on SOE profitability occurred, especially on the local level. Second, industrial restructuring mainly took the shape of organizational restructuring, given the reluctance to allow for bankruptcy. These two trends were related, because the profit squeeze contributed to the rise of regional protectionism, that is, local governments as "quasi-owners" interfered with the emerging market process in order protect their fiscal sources and local employment. Thus a major problem was how to overcome the tension between the governance structure implied by the regional property rights system and the policy to increase enterprise autonomy.

One solution was the creation of *qiye jituan* (enterprise groups), which became a ubiquitous SOE company form in the 1990s. The development of the enterprise groups was a major impetus for developing the shareholding system, as restructuring required the settling of balances among different government entities, who might transfer control rights to a group controlled by another entity. Another motivation for the formation of groups was the need to spin off many units of SOEs that did not belong to their core business. The shareholding system allowed for the integration of hybrid ownership forms, such as collectives as part of a group.

The pressure to restructure was heightened by the market entry of two new forms of companies. In the 1980s township and village enterprises (TVEs) grew out of the small-scale industry of the commune, with a highly diversified ownership structure, and operated in a much less regulated market environment, particularly in regard to labor. In the 1990s foreign-invested enterprises (FIEs) expanded considerably. Both developments reflected substantial weaknesses on the part of SOEs and contributed to their rapid decline in the share of industrial production. In both areas a trend toward the dominance of privately owned companies emerged. In the case of TVEs, many collectives were dismantled after the mid-1990s, often via management buyouts. In the FIE sector, the relative significance of the joint venture (which is, in fact, an ownership hybrid, as most Chinese partners of foreign partners were SOEs) declined in favor of the wholly foreign-owned enterprise (WFOE).

## THE COMPANY LAW AND CORPORATE GOVERNANCE SINCE 1994

Facing the difficulties of reinvigorating the SOE sector via restructuring, in 1993 the government promulgated the new Company Law. A unified legal framework for all sorts of companies, the Company Law was in fact directed mainly at the SOEs; after the mid-1990s it was followed by a rigorous policy to establish a modern enterprise system according to the slogan "grasping the large, letting the small ones go." The law was revised in 1999 and 2005, with the clear intention to improve *gongsi zhili* (corporate governance).

The company law distinguishes between the publicly listed company and the limited liability company (LLC). Reflecting the history of industrial restructuring, in fact the categories of a public company and an SOE overlap to a significant degree (in 2008 more than 50% of shares were held by the government). The Company Law mainly paved the way for a formalization of intergovernmental ownership relations in terms of shareholdings, such that the majority of Chinese shares are still not traded on the stock exchange. Further, the law allows the entry of other shareholders via listings at foreign stock exchanges. But it does not change the fundamental nature of the SOE, beyond the still fragile protection of minority shareholders. This structure is reflected in the fact that shareholdings in Chinese-listed companies are highly concentrated, with government units dominating, and that the actual exercise of shareholders' rights in general meetings is limited. The corporatization of SOEs was accompanied by the formalization and organizational separation of the state ownership role in the shape of the State Asset Supervision and Administration Commissions at different levels of government, in direct continuity with the past regional property rights system.

By comparison, the LLC reflects a larger diversity of factual ownership structures and allows for a substantial role of private investors, for example, in the context of sellouts of small-scale SOEs. However, the full impact of the LCC on the evolution of company forms cannot be determined by examining official statistics. The industrial census of 2005 reflects the complex coexistence of old and new company forms, maintaining the categories of "state-owned" and "collectives" and adding "other limited liability companies" and "joint stock limited liability companies," in addition to "private companies," "foreign-invested companies," and a number of miscellaneous categories. In 2007, 22 percent of gross output of Chinese industry was produced by LLC with different underlying ownership arrangements, 10 percent by shareholding corporations limited. Purely privately owned LLC had a share of 17 percent, private shareholding corporations just surpassing one percent. The traditional forms of the SOE and the collective enterprise amounted to 11 percent. These categories are mutually exclusive; at the same time the categories of the Company Law implicitly include state-owned companies. Thus the historical pattern of the first Company Law seems to persist in contemporary China: the dualism between the government-owned or -sponsored company and the privately held business enterprise, with both government and private business exploiting and manipulating legal forms in its own interest.

**BIBLIOGRAPHY**


Keister, Lisa A. *Chinese Business Groups: The Structure and Impact of Interfirm Relations during Economic Development.* Oxford and New York: Oxford University Press, 2000.

Kirby, William C. China Unincorporated: Company Law and Business Enterprise in Twentieth-Century China. *Journal of Asian Studies* 54, 1 (1995): 43–63.

Naughton, Barry. Industry: Ownership and Governance. In *The Chinese Economy: Transitions and Growth*, 297–310. Cambridge, MA: MIT Press, 2007.

Tenev, Stoyan, Zhang Chunlin, and Loup Brefort. *Corporate Governance and Enterprise Reform in China: Building the Institutions of Modern Markets.* Washington, DC: World Bank and International Finance Corporation, 2002.


***Carsten Herrmann-Pillath***

## COLLECTIVES

The Chinese system of classification of enterprises has always been especially fuzzy in the categories of *jiti qiye* (collectives) and *hezuo qiye* (cooperatives). The standard statistical system still differentiates between forms of ownership, as ownership is seen as a fundamental criterion to distinguish socialism from capitalism. But this criterion overlaps with the criteria of size—with the category *zhongxiao qiye* (small- and medium-scale enterprise, or SME) being the latest addition to Chinese regulatory practice—and location (rural versus urban). As China undergoes a rapid urbanization process, serious issues arise in separating the categories of township and village enterprises (*xiangzhen qiye*) in urbanizing rural areas from enterprises with urban registration, while at the same time the former category does include different forms of ownership. Yet the authoritative National Economic Census of 2005 distinguishes only state-owned (28,000 units), collectively owned (152,000), and private enterprises (947,000), as well as an intermediate form of cooperative shareholding companies (52,000), employing 92 million, 72 million, 337 million, and 21 million people, respectively. Most recent data point toward a dwindling significance of these categories, at least in formal terms: In 2007, in gross output of Chinese industry, only 2 percent and less than 1 percent of enterprises were still classified as collectives or cooperatives, respectively; in domestic retail trade, of 26,028 units only 2,180 were registered as collectives and 531 as cooperatives.

Another ambiguity arises from the new legal categories of the Company Law, with the main statistical categories being limited liability company (LLC), 10,500 units of which employ 135 million people, and state-owned enterprise (SOE), a mere 2,000 units of which employ 37 million people, according to the census. However, as the shareholding structure of these units can differ widely, LLCs can include all forms of ownership in the traditional sense. A collective that re-registers as a company according to the Company Law will simply move across categories, without necessarily changing its economic nature.

Finally, beyond the statistics the category of collectives is diffuse in terms of factual ownership and operational modes. Especially in the 1990s, many collectives were in fact privatized while maintaining the designation of a collective ("wearing a red hat"), because this implied certain regulatory advantages and also better access to political resources. Even newly established private firms might choose the umbrella of a collective for their operations. The boundary with the cooperative shareholding companies is also fluid, as many transitional forms of management and employee buyouts exist, with a vast regional diversity. These ambiguities also apply on the other side of the spectrum; that is, for the boundary between collectives and SOEs. As a general rule, the larger a collective enterprise, the closer it is to a de facto SOE, at least until the mid-1990s, when the general policy of privatizing smaller-scale SOEs was adopted.

### COLLECTIVES UNDER MAO

In the late 1940s the Chinese manufacturing sector was still dominated by handicrafts. In Chinese Communist Party–controlled areas, producers' cooperatives had already been established. This process accelerated in the course of the collectivization movement, culminating in an episode of attempts at setting up urban communes during the Great Leap Forward. Although brief, this episode resulted in the almost complete transformation of the urban economy into a tripartite system of state-owned, collective, and individual enterprises. In the last category, designated the *getihu* after the launch of the reforms, were small handicraft and service shops, which enjoyed a certain revival between the Great Leap and the Cultural Revolution (1966–1969), but were suppressed again in the heyday of leftist radicalism. The fluid status of cooperatives also resulted from their fusion with the urban administration system, in which small-scale manufacturing was finally undertaken by the *jumin weiyuanhui* (neighborhood committees), which offered employment opportunities to women.

Collectives in the narrow sense were mainly larger-scale manufacturing enterprises that were not included in the system of state planning, though they were tightly integrated into the state-controlled distribution system. In theory, a collective would be a worker-managed firm, as ownership lies with all employees. In practice, the collectives were subordinate to the subprovincial administration, such that the larger enterprises did not differ in essence from SOEs administered on that level. However, there were some substantial differences between the two ownership types, which contributed to the sharp segmentation of urban society and the labor system into a privileged class of SOE workers and workers in the collectives. Collectives never offered a comparable level of social services and social security; their wage system operated outside the standards set for the SOE, and they could rely only rarely on outside financial support. Until 1978 workers in collectives shared only the privilege of the job guarantee with SOE workers. This different regulatory framework was an incentive for SOEs to cut costs by setting up supplier relations with collectives even in Maoist times, so that many collectives were intimately connected with SOEs when the reforms were launched in 1978.

## THE ROLE OF COLLECTIVES IN THE CONTEMPORARY CHINESE ECONOMY

Collectives played an important role in providing basic consumption goods to the urban population until 1978. With the launch of the reforms, given their loose regulatory environment collectives could exploit the opportunities of the rapid liberalization of light industries and of the consumption goods sector. However, their lack of access to outside capital and knowledge, as well as the diffuse governance structure, threatened their survival. At the same time, however, SOE restructuring was a major reason for their resilience, because many SOEs spun off organizational units in the shape of collectives, thus saving labor costs and even actually shedding superfluous labor.

The role of collectives in safeguarding urban employment was also the driving force in increasing worker participation in collectives, at least in terms of investment. During the 1990s this took the shape of the cooperative shareholding company, which is a mix of different types of ownership relations. Frequently, workers were asked to invest in a company to secure the right to the workplace without obtaining substantial decision rights. That investment might be accompanied by an actual management buyout, hence de facto privatization. On the other hand, shares held by the company might maintain the autonomy of the collective unit, thus in fact preserving the influence of the local administration. However, one aim of the ongoing reforms of the urban administration system is to reduce the direct involvement of city governments in business activities. This is particularly difficult in regions with high unemployment.

Once the enforcement of the Company Law finally unifies the legal forms of companies in China, the role of collectives will wither away. Beneath the surface, however, complex ownership structures will continue to survive, with a wide spectrum of shareholding arrangements that will also include truly collective forms, such as worker participation in company management. Yet the destiny of the majority of collectives is full-scale privatization.

**BIBLIOGRAPHY**

Donnithorne, Audrey. Handicrafts, Small-Scale Industries and Urban Communes. In *China's Economic System*, 219–236. London: Hurst, 1981.

***Carsten Herrmann-Pillath***

# CORPORATE LAW

The corporation as a legal entity was not alien to China's treaty ports prior to the enactment of the first company law in 1904. Before then, business corporations had existed under various "official-supervision-and-merchant-management" (*guandu shangban*) formats. However, the first company law (*gongsilü*) was introduced on January 21, 1904, as part of the Qing government's "new policies" (*xinzheng*). It was patterned on Japanese and English company law and was made up of eleven sections that dealt with the types of company and incorporation, company shares, shareholder's rights, boards of directors, auditors, directors' meetings, general meetings of shareholders, accounts, alteration of articles of association, winding-up, and penalties. Under the new law companies were allowed to register as partnerships with unlimited or limited liability, joint-stock companies with unlimited or limited liability, and sole proprietorships with unlimited liability. The law required an annual company financial report, but provided no uniform system for company accounting. Nor did it require that auditors be independent, except that company directors could not simultaneously be auditors of their own companies. Nevertheless, the 1904 Company Law was groundbreaking because it introduced to early twentieth-century China the concepts of limited liability, publicizing annual company reports, and actually observing the accounting regulations that were in force. Perhaps most significant was the institutionalization of annual shareholder meetings.

In the aftermath of the Qing dynasty's collapse, the 1904 Company Law was superseded by the Republican government's 1914 Company Regulation (*gongsi tiaoli*), which was more detailed and modeled on German commercial law (Bryan 1925, pp. 64–65; Bünger 1933, p. 288). It streamlined the registration process, recognizing four types of companies: unlimited companies (*wuxian gongsi*); limited and unlimited joint companies (*lianghe gongsi*); joint-share companies that had a partnership of both limited- and unlimited-liability shareholders (*gufen lianghe gongsi*); and limited-liability companies by shares (*gufen youxian gongsi*). In practice, the dominant corporate form between 1914 and 1929 was the partnership, a traditional Chinese corporate form imbedded in the Chinese kinship society that included limited partnerships (*gufen hehuo*) and dormant partnerships (*niming hehuo*) (Li 2005, p. 236).

In 1929 the third corporation statute was promulgated under the Nationalist government and came into force on July 1, 1931. The 1929 Company Law (*gongsi fa*) was instrumental in helping the government control domestic and foreign private enterprises. Ultimately, the Nationalist government, driven by the state's ideology, Three Principles of the People (*sanmin zhuyi*), exerted strong control over all aspects of social and economic life, including restricting private capital. A telling example is that the 1929 law capped the voting power of any individual shareholder to 20 percent of the total votes, regardless of the person's share value (Article 129). It also provided for the nationalization of corporations.

In 1946 the Company Law of 1929 was replaced by the New Company Law (*xin gongsi fa*). This law demonstrated the Nationalist government's enthusiasm for developing state capitalism. Additionally, the total abolition in 1943 of the extraterritoriality rights enjoyed by foreign enterprises prompted the call for an up-to-date and less restrictive company law. Consequently, for the first time ever, a section on foreign corporations was introduced in the 1946 law. Thereafter, foreign firms were treated as Chinese companies subject to permission (*renxu*) from the Chinese government (Article 7). Unlike the 1929 law, this new legislation governed state enterprises. The law is still applicable in Taiwan, but it was substantially revised in 1966.

After the People's Republic of China (PRC) was founded in 1949, the 1946 Company Law was repealed without being replaced. Almost all companies were nationalized in one form or another. There were no modern companies in existence in China during the first three decades of the PRC's planned economy. It was not until 1979 that a Sino-foreign joint-venture law was enacted to allow for the establishment of foreign limited-liability companies. In 1986 the General Principle of Civil Law was enacted, laying out the conditions for establishing enterprises with legal personality. But the most significant milestone in China's corporate legislative history was the enactment of the 1993 Company Law (amended in 1999 and 2004) that came into effect on July 1, 1994. This legislation was essential to facilitate state-owned enterprise reform and to establish China's modern corporate system and securities market (Wang and Huang 2006). However, as the country's economic reform proceeded, serious deficiencies in the 1993 law emerged, for instance, the 1993 Company Law was too simplistic and outdated in dealing with the corporate governance issue in newly restructured state-owned enterprises. On October 27, 2005, a revised company law was passed to further extensive market reform and economic development. Specifically, out of the 229 provisions of the old company law, 46 provisions were deleted, 137 were amended, and 41 new provisions were added. Major reforms included significantly reducing the capital requirements for incorporation (Articles 26 and 81); permitting a wider range of noncash capital contributions, provided they can be assessed in dollars and are legally transferable (Article 27); and approving one-member companies (Article 58). The new law also reinforced the directors' duty significantly with the introduction of a new chapter on the qualifications and duties of directors (chapter 6), and made provisions to protect the interests of minority shareholders (Articles 20 and 106).

**BIBLIOGRAPHY**

Bryan, Robert. *An Outline of Chinese Civil Law*. Shanghai: Commercial Press, 1925.

Bünger, Karl. Das Recht der Handelsgesellschaften in China [The right of trading in China]. *Zeitschrift für das gesame Handelsrecht und Konkursrecht* [Journal of Commercial Law and bankruptcy law] 88, 4 (1933): 285–297.

Feuerweker, Albert. *China's Early Industrialization*. Cambridge, MA: Harvard University Press, 1958.

Kirby, William. China, Unincorporated: Company Law and Business Enterprise in Twentieth-century China. *Journal of Asian Studies* 54, 1 (February 1995): 43–63.

Lai Chi-kong. The Qing State and Merchant Enterprise: The China Merchants' Company, 1872–1902. In *To Achieve Security and Wealth: The Qing Imperial State and the Economy, 1644–1911*, ed. Jane Kate Leonard and John Watt, 151–152. Ithaca, NY: Cornell University East Asia Program, 1992.

Li Yu. Beiyang zhengfu shiqi qiyezhidu jianshe zonglun [On the development of corporate system in early republican government]. *Jiangsu Shehui Kexue* [Jiangsu social sciences] 5 (2005): 231–236

Ruskola, Teemu. Conceptualizing Corporations and Kinship: Comparative Law and Development Theory in a Chinese Perspective. *Stanford Law Review* 52, 6 (2000): 1599–1729.

Wang Baoshu, and Huang Hui. China's New Company Law and Securities Law: An Overview and Assessment. *Australian Journal of Corporate Law* 19, 2 (2006): 229–242.

***Chen Lei***

## JOINT VENTURES

The Sino-foreign joint venture (*zhong wai hezi qiye*) was the dominant form of market entry for international companies in China between 1978 and the mid-1990s, after which the wholly foreign-owned enterprise (WFOE) (*waizi qiye*) became more important. Subsequent to China's entry into the World Trade Organization (WTO) in 2001, the joint venture's significance declined further. In 2007 about 20 percent of foreign direct investment (FDI) took the legal form of the joint venture, with the remaining share mainly adopting the form of the WFOE, with the same relation also applying roughly for the volume of FDI. In Chinese industry, 20 percent of gross output are by foreign-funded enterprises (excluding Hong Kong and Taiwan funded ones), with slightly less than 10 percent joint ventures. Beyond the legal forms, mergers and acquisitions as well as minority shareholdings also increased in relative significance in the 2000s as a consequence of the corporatization of a growing number of large state-owned companies in China. At the end of the first decade of the new millennium, however, the joint venture's strategic role was reemerging.

The heyday of the joint venture was between 1992 and 1996, with a peak of more than 50,000 registered projects recorded in 1993. This activity followed Deng Xiaoping's 1992 southern tour, which spurred the rapid revitalization of the Chinese economy after the recession that followed the Tiananmen Square protests of 1989. At this time China's number of state-owned companies was declining as rapidly as it had expanded, and the share of collectives and private enterprises, especially in the southern coastal provinces, was increasing. Between 1997 and 2007 the number of newly registered projects lingered around 10,000 per annum, with the total volume of FDI in the shape of the joint venture declining, in terms of U.S. dollars, from about $25 billion to about $15 billion per year, indicating a trend toward smaller projects. These data refer to the equity joint venture, through which a foreign and a Chinese enterprise form a joint unit with independent accounting and registration as a company according to the Company Law, that is, a limited liability company or a public company. The other legal form of the joint venture, the contractual joint venture, never attained a comparable prominence in Sino-foreign economic relations.

## EVOLUTION OF THE LEGAL FRAMEWORK

The Joint Venture Law of 1979 created the legal framework for this type of venture. Further regulations and amendments followed during the 1980s. In 1993 the establishment of the Company Law set the stage for the convergence of the legal framework among foreign-invested and Chinese companies, a trend that was further strengthened by WTO entry and that reached an end with the amendment of the Company Law in 2005. Through this amendment the Company Law attained full validity for all forms of foreign-invested enterprise unless specific legal provisions for foreign economic relations apply. For example, the special provision of the joint venture law determines that the sharing of profits according to the shareholding ratio is mandatory in equity joint ventures.

The joint venture policy had ramifications for legal developments in other areas. In particular it affected the devolution of responsibilities in the approval process to local authorities as well as the expansion of regional preferences in foreign economic relations, which started with the creation of the first special economic zones in 1980 and quickly included a growing number of open cities in the 1980s and new forms of industrial and technology parks in the 1990s. The main lever of control by the central government remained the allocation of approval rights in terms of size of projects, and in particular the definition and limitation of sectoral restrictions on FDI. These restrictions are at the core of the provisions for China's WTO entry, which limit the role of WFOE in sectors, such as banking or transport, considered to be of national significance; the joint venture thus remains the default strategy. During the first two decades of the reforms, another important legal constraint on joint venture activities was the requirement to meet foreign exchange restrictions, which forced joint ventures to export so as to generate the foreign exchange needed for importing necessary inputs.

## MOTIVATION AND PERFORMANCE

Since its inauguration China's joint venture strategy has concentrated on one dominant goal: the transfer of foreign technological and management knowledge to China—for example, by encouraging foreign companies to contribute patents as investment. Therefore the development of joint ventures has also been strongly influenced by the general technology and industry policy of the Chinese government, which has recurrently defined strategic sectors in which foreign direct investment was especially welcomed and those in which it was discouraged. Roughly speaking, technology transfer was the predominant goal in the first decade, with the subsidiary goal of export promotion increasingly important. The main difference in these goals lies in the exploitation of China's comparative advantage, that is, cheap labor, which would not motivate the transfer of the newest technology. This resulted into a tension between the two policy goals, because export promotion would be based on China's comparative advantage, cheap labor. Technological upgrading would be capital-intensive and labor-saving, and would thus be avoided by investors. However, the goal of technology transfer resurfaced during the 1990s and regained its dominance in the new millennium. As for the foreign partners, from the early days onward their main motivation was market access, with the second motivation being the exploitation of cost advantages. Both motivations were fusing with the growing significance of China as an integral part of global supply chains as the world economy underwent structural changes in the 1990s.

The crucial difference between the joint venture and the WFOE lies in the governance structure. The Joint Venture Law of 1979 cemented the Chinese side's clear formal dominance in the joint venture, authorizing the Chinese side to nominate a chairman. However, specific contractual provisions of a joint venture could relax this formal dominance. The interests of foreign investors who wished to avoid the direct participation of the Chinese side in the management of the project led to the ascendance of the WFOE. However, several factors contributed to the attractiveness and strategic reemergence of the joint venture. In the 1980s, beyond legal restrictions, the joint venture secured access to stakeholders in the government, who were essential in many areas of foreign-invested operations. This function of the joint venture retreated into the background with the increasing intensity of interregional competition in China. For example, in the lower Yangzi River Delta foreign investors would screen many alternatives in the various special zones of Shanghai or the dynamic cities of southern Jiangsu province, which enabled them to cut through red tape and secure advantageous conditions for their investment.

As in the past, a major motivation for concluding a joint venture is the difficulty in overcoming distributional and logistical obstacles to market access. For example, in many services foreign providers would need to make substantial investments to build up a presence across the country, whereas a Chinese partner can offer an existing distribution network. For the Chinese side, access to modern technology remains an important driver of joint venture agreements; however, with the continuous upgrading of indigenous technological capabilities this need for access is diminishing. Since the late 1970s technology transfer has been a contentious issue among foreign investors and their Chinese partners. Investors from different countries have adopted different strategies; Japanese companies, for example, have mostly imposed tight constraints on access to technology, whereas German companies have adopted a much more open attitude. In a number of cases the Chinese joint venture partner extracted technological knowledge from the joint venture and set up a competing business elsewhere.

From the perspective of economic development, joint ventures clearly have played a significant role in enhancing China's technological capacity. They have generated significant spillovers beyond the immediate effects on the foreign partner. Because of the rapid diffusion of modern technology and management practices, joint ventures did not crowd out domestic enterprises but rather played an important role as benchmarks for local competitors. By the end of the 2000s, joint ventures were no longer the avant-garde of globalization in China and faced formidable competition from Chinese companies that had started to invest abroad by themselves.

**BIBLIOGRAPHY**

Tian, Xiaowen. *Managing International Business in China.* Cambridge, U.K., and New York: Cambridge University Press, 2007.

Yan, Yanni. *International Joint Ventures in China: Ownership, Control, and Performance.* New York: St. Martin's Press, 1999.

***Carsten Herrmann-Pillath***

## COMPRADOR

The comprador (*maiban*) was the Chinese manager of a foreign firm in China, serving as middleman in the company's dealings with the Chinese. Widely used in the nineteenth century, the comprador system had declined in efficacy by the early twentieth century. It was replaced in many cases by joint-venture partnerships, which had a similar function within a different company structure.

### RATIONALE FOR THE COMPRADOR SYSTEM

From the late seventeenth century, foreign merchants were allowed to trade with China at Guangzhou under a system known as *hushi*. Under the *hushi* system, foreign merchants were required to funnel all transactions through licensed merchants (*cohong*), who were obliged to pay trade taxes to the Qing government. In the late eighteenth to the early nineteenth century, foreign merchants turned against the *hushi* system because they found the method of estimating the tax amount unclear, but they did not have any way to directly negotiate with the Qing government. Because the merchants' discontent was one of the underlying reasons for the Sino-British Opium War (1839–1842), their obligation to conduct business through licensed merchants was eliminated with the Treaty of Nanjing in 1842.

However, once the licensed merchants were discarded, foreign merchants found themselves lacking the necessary information and skills to trade with inland China outside of the treaty ports. Language was one of the problems that impeded their economic activity in China. Another factor was the complexity of the currency system. The Chinese currency of the early nineteenth century consisted of both coins and *tael* (*sycee*). The variety of silver coins seemed infinite, since coinage differed widely from province to province and even within the same province, and Spanish, Mexican, American, and other foreign coins, as well as coins minted in China, circulated in the country. The Chinese currency system was further complicated by its monetary unit, the *tael*. Historically, the *tael* was a unit of weight, *liang*. The exact weight of a particular *tael* was difficult to determine, because it was not defined by law but fixed by custom. Each monetary *tael* had its own particular gauge, and local custom required that it weigh only slightly more or less than the other *taels*. As an accounting unit, the *tael* was used to varying degrees in almost all of China. Without local knowledge of the monetary system, it was impossible to do business with the Chinese.

Besides the currency system, foreign merchants lacked information about key issues related to their trade, such as the financial status of native banks and leading Chinese merchants, the guild leadership, and so on. Foreign merchants thus had to hire native employees who could cope with indigenous economic and social conditions. Compradors played a number of roles, which changed along with the business methods and other practices of their foreign employers. Immediately after the opening of ports in 1842, compradors mainly served as house stewards, supervising other Chinese servants. As foreign businesses developed after 1860, compradors acted as business managers, taking care of accounting and transactions of bills and drafts. At the same time, some compradors went outside of the treaty ports to purchase tea and silk as so-called upcountry purchasers. It was arguably crucial for any foreign firm operating in China to employ trustworthy and efficient compradors. The Cantonese were the first group to meet the need for compradors, due to their early experience of trading with foreign merchants at Guangzhou. The system of guarantees led to the continued employment of Cantonese as compradors, because they naturally guaranteed their fellow townsmen as their successors.

## COMPRADORS AS INVESTORS IN MODERN INDUSTRIES

Compradors not only received salaries and commissions from foreign merchant houses; they also engaged in trades with their own funds, although their foreign employers tried to prohibit such activities. As Sino-foreign trade expanded from the mid-nineteenth century, some of them accumulated great wealth. Significantly, most compradors invested their money in modern industries. Since they were involved in foreign trade, they first invested in foreign and Chinese steamship companies, such as Shanghai Steam Navigation Company (American), Union Steam and Navigation Company (British), and China Merchants' Steam Navigation Company (Chinese). In fact, compradors sometimes helped foreign firms financially when they were short of money.

Besides steamship navigation, compradors invested in other kinds of modern enterprise. For example, the promoter and investor of Kaiping Mines, China's first large-scale modern coal-mining enterprise, established in 1878, was Tang Jingxing (Tong King-sing, 1832–1892), one of the most famous compradors. Tang was not exceptional in terms of his investment strategy; from 1863 to 1886, compradors invested more than two million dollars in coal mining, which amounted to 62.7 percent of the total capital amount. Other modern enterprises that drew the interest of compradors included textiles, railroads, and insurance. Given that it was very difficult to find investors for new industrial and service enterprises in nineteenth-century China, the compradors' contribution to modern economic development cannot be underestimated.

## THE DECLINE OF THE COMPRADOR SYSTEM

Although compradors played a key role in the expansion of foreign trade, foreign firms gradually found it unwise to depend so heavily on their Chinese employees. The issue of asymmetric information and systems of monitoring shaped the relationship between foreign firms and compradors. Some compradors were suspected of taking extra fees for the transactions they handled for foreign firms. Others, such as compradors working for foreign banks who served as intermediaries for loans to native banks, became involved in risky business ventures under the name of their employer. Once a comprador's venture got into trouble, it could be difficult to decide whom to hold legally responsible. Although foreign firms tried to monitor compradors through contractual provisions or commission-based reward systems, compradors held a structural advantage in the face of management's efforts to control them.

By the turn of the twentieth century, many foreign firms encouraged their clerks to learn Chinese so that they could do business with domestic merchants directly. Japanese firms, such as Mitsui and Yokohama Specie Bank, were the first foreign firms in China to dispense with compradors, followed by Western firms such as Standard Oil Company. Taking another approach, the British-American Tobacco Company and Kailan Mining Administration set up joint ventures with Chinese businessmen to achieve access to mass markets without losing the intermediation services provided by local Chinese.

When China's imports as well as foreign investment in China fell during World War I (1914–1918), the role of compradors declined further. Finally, as the old treaty-port system ended in 1943 with China's new equal treaties, the comprador system disappeared in China.

**SEE ALSO** *Commercial Elite, 1800–1949.*

**BIBLIOGRAPHY**

Cox, Howard, and Chan Kai Yiu. The Changing Nature of Sino-Foreign Business Relationships, 1842–1941. *Asia Pacific Business Review* 7, 2 (2000): 93–110.

Hao Yanping (Hao Yen-P'ing). *The Comprador in Nineteenth Century China: Bridge between East and West.* Cambridge, MA: Harvard University Press, 1970.

Nishimura Shizuya. The Foreign and Native Banks in China: Chop Loans in Shanghai and Hankow before 1914. *Modern Asian Studies* 39, 1 (2005): 109–132.

*Tomoko Shiroyama*

# CONFUCIANISM

Confucianism (*ruxue* or *rujiao*) is a complex and multifaceted philosophy that foregrounds the moral relationships of individuals or groups in a societal context, regulated by propriety (*li*). It has had a profound influence on Chinese sociopolitical systems, worldviews, ethics, education, religions, conventions, individual and community life, and scholarly traditions since around the sixth or fifth century BCE. Based on the teachings of Confucius (Kong Qiu, 551–479 BCE) and his disciples, as recorded in the *Analects* (*Lunyu*), Confucianism was established as the state orthodoxy during the Han dynasty (206 BCE–220 CE) and has dominated the development of Chinese civilization, shaping the political and personal lives of Chinese people. It has also had a tremendous impact in other parts of East Asia, including Japan, Korea, and Vietnam.

In recent decades, Confucianism has enjoyed a resurgence domestically and globally. In the context of rapid economic growth and social change in China, its central tenets—summed up in the five principles of benevolence, righteousness, propriety, wisdom, and trust (*ren*, *yi*, *li*, *zhi*, and *xin*)—have been reasserted and reinterpreted to serve modern life.

## CONFUCIANISM IN THE NINETEENTH CENTURY

At the turn of the nineteenth century, the reigning orthodoxy in China was neo-Confucianism (Lixue), also known as Cheng-Zhu Confucianism after its major exponents, the Song dynasty thinkers Cheng Hao (1032–1085), Cheng Yi (1033–1107), and Zhu Xi (1130–1200), who creatively adopted elements of Buddhism to renovate classical Confucianism. Neo-Confucianism coexisted with another important strand of Confucian scholarship, Han Learning (Hanxue), which was developed in reaction to it. Han Learning, a defining feature of intellectual life in the Qing dynasty (1644–1912), underpinned evidential scholarship, or classical textual study (*kaojuxue*), and played a key role in providing annotations for *Siku quanshu* (*The Four Treasuries*), a major bibliographic compilation of the late eighteenth century. During the Qing dynasty, Confucianism found expression in classical textual study, literary works (*cizhang*), and neo-Confucian ethics and metaphysics (*yili*). In the late eighteenth and early nineteenth centuries, intensive training in writing formal eight-part essays (*baguwen*) in schools preparing one for the Imperial Civi Service Examinations served further to emphasize neo-Confucianism as state orthodoxy.

In the course of the nineteenth century, Confucianism was seriously threatened by challenges from the Western powers engaged in various forms of imperialism to radically expand capitalism, and also from internal political corruption and popular rebellions. From the early nineteenth century, the Qing government suffered from the exploitation of these Western powers. In particular, losing the First and Second Opium Wars (1839–1842 and 1856–1860) forced Chinese politicians and intellectuals to reflect on the tradition of Confucianism and to develop self-strengthening strategies to save the Qing Empire. The internal threats came primarily from political corruption and from the Taiping Uprising (1851–1864) and the Nian Uprising (1851–1868). The Taiping Uprising rejected Confucianism and adapted a form of Christianity as its political ideology.

These threats rocked the political system of the late Qing dynasty, which counted on Confucianism as the sole official orthodoxy. It also challenged the orthodoxy of Confucianism, a philosophy that the Chinese people, from the literati to the masses, had firmly believed in up to then. During this period, many intellectuals and politicians reflected critically on Confucianism and explored new ways to confront these political challenges. Among them were Lin Zexu (1785–1850), Wei Yuan (1794–1856), Zeng Guofan (1811–1872), and Zhang Zhidong (1837–1909), who adopted various approaches to change in the late Qing Self-strengthening movement (Yangwu yundong, 1861–1894).

Lin Zexu was respected mostly for his heroic destruction of banned opium in 1839, but he was also a pioneer who opened Chinese eyes to the outside world, particularly the Western industrialized countries. Rejecting the tendency to ethnocentrism in Chinese culture, he paid serious attention to Western civilization, particularly its technological innovations, and warned that China must strengthen itself by learning from its Western rivals. Lin is viewed as a pioneer of the self-strengtheners and was probably the first Westernizer in China. Deeply influenced by Lin, Wei Yuan became another great Confucian thinker rising to the Western challenge. He spent a few years editing *Haiguo tuzhi* (An illustrated treatise on the maritime kingdoms), which used Lin's collections of world history and geography as a major source. In this work he systematically introduced the latest knowledge about Western history, geography, and technologies, hoping that it would enable China to survive. He showed increasing concern about the Western threat and the need for maritime defense, and he proposed the strategy of controlling the Western powers by mastering their advanced technologies. Lin and Wei stimulated a reexamination of neo-Confucianism in the mid-nineteenth century.

Zeng Guofan, a devout Confucian scholar and army general, crushed the Taiping Uprising and brought about a revival of Neo-Confucianism. He endorsed many ideas from Lin Zexu and Wei Yuan in their reexamination of neo-Confucianism and was fully aware of the threats from the Western powers and the Taiping Uprising. He admired the practical technologies of the West and urged the Chinese to learn from them, although he remained certain of the universality of Confucian values. Unlike Lin Zexu, Zeng faced the urgency of internal rebellions and invasion by external powers at the same time. He focused on practical technologies that could serve both political and defensive purposes. With his efforts and leadership, some modern factories were established for military hardware and transportation, the first steamship was built, the first arms school was opened, and the first students were sent to study in the United States. But he was a strict Confucian believer and practitioner, daily reflecting on his practice of Confucian principles. In addition, he paid much attention to family education with Confucian values.

While Lin Zexu, Wei Yuan, and Zeng Guofan all tried to resist the Western powers by persisting in Confucianism, Zhang Zhidong made the first explicit philosophical commitment to balancing Western learning and Confucianism. His famous formula "Chinese learning as essence, and Western learning for its practical utility" (*Zhongxue wei ti, Xixue wei yong*) made use of concepts drawn from Zhu Xi. Zhang was basically an incremental reformer, but his *Quanxue pian* (Exhortation to study), published in 1898, is widely viewed as the most aggressive declaration of the new eclectic Confucianism before the Hundred Days' Reform (Bairi Weixin) of 1898. In this work he insisted on the continuity of Confucianism as the unshakable orthodox ideology, but opened the door to adopting advanced Western technologies, which he hoped would save the deteriorating Qing dynasty. Zhang's formula of essence and practical utility adapted Lin and Wei's dictum of learning from the West to defeat it, and proposed a combination of Confucianism with Western learning, particularly advanced technologies. Pursuing a philosophy of incremental eclecticism, Zhang took the leadership in the Self-strengthening movement, reformed the old school system and established many new types of schools and colleges, opened modern factories and businesses, and sent many students to Japan and the United States to learn modern technologies from the West. Despite having a profound impact on Chinese society, Zhang's formula of essence and practical utility failed to renew Confucianism in ways that could assure the survival of the Qing dynasty.

## THE SURVIVAL OF CONFUCIANISM

Losing the First Sino-Japanese War of 1894–1895 crushed the dream of the Self-strengthening movement in the late nineteenth century and forced Chinese politicians and intellectuals to consider Zhang's eclectic approach to Confucianism. Though fundamental reform of political and social systems was clearly needed to secure China's future, Confucianism was in no position to provide an ideological foundation for such reform, as it was facing its most serious crisis since Buddhism was introduced into China in the second century.

Unlike the Confucian eclectics, Kang Youwei preferred to view Confucius as a reformer. He warmly embraced Western political systems, together with their advanced technologies, while still revering Confucianism. In his *Datong shu* (Book of great unity), Kang fiercely criticized the old political system, the impractical Civil Service Examinations, and the traditional educational system. At the same time, he urged fundamental and revolutionary reforms in both political and educational systems, including the adoption of a constitutional monarchy, the abolition of the outdated Civil Service Examination System, the establishment of a modern school system, and the equalization of educational opportunity, particularly for women. Notable in his book was Kang's enthusiasm for change and his belief in the possibility of bettering China through Western political systems, as well as technologies. Along with his disciple Liang Qichao (1873–1929), Kang was one of the key leaders of the Hundred Days' Reform (1898), which introduced radical political change to China. However, Kang Youwei's embrace of Western political systems and technologies failed to obtain support from traditional Confucians, including elite politicians and ordinary people, and Confucianism still survived as the dominant ideology, even after the collapse of the Qing dynasty in 1911 and up to the May Fourth movement in 1919.

During the New Culture movement, especially the May Fourth movement of 1919, which was ignited by the Treaty of Versailles, Confucianism was subjected to a serious reevaluation of its role in the development of Chinese civilization and naturally became the target of criticism. The nationwide student movement of the May Fourth era was decidedly anti-Confucian. Many Chinese intellectuals, such as Chen Duxiu (1879–1942) and Lu Xun (1881–1936), saw Confucianism as an obstacle to China's healthy development.

Liang Shuming (1893–1988), the so-called last Confucian, took a different approach. He was originally enthusiastic over Buddhism and Western culture, but by his late twenties Liang turned to focusing on the reconstruction of Confucianism. In his early work *Dongxi wenhua ji qi zhexue* (Eastern and Western cultures and their philosophies), published in 1921, Liang reflected that Confucianism would never catch up with Western culture owing to what he saw as three dimensions of materialism (which China lacked): Conquering the environment and nature, scientific methodology in scholarship, and democracy in social life. He argued that though Confucianism had democratic roots, it needed to be further developed and integrated with Western concepts of democracy and technology. He was optimistic that Confucian ethics, a substitute for religion, could be used as the foundation of sociopolitical life. Liang's efforts toward reinvigorating Confucianism helped Chiang Kai-shek (Jiang Jieshi, 1887–1975) to launch the New Life movement (Xin Shenghuo yundong) in the mid-1930s and also stimulated the Chinese Cultural Renaissance movement (Zhonghua Wenhua Fuxing yundong) of the mid-1960s in Taiwan

***Children dressed in traditional clothing to honor the birthday of Confucius, Changchun, Jilin province, September 28, 2006.*** *The teachings of Confucius continue to influence China into the twenty-first century. While suppressed during the Cultural Revolution, Confucianism has enjoyed a resurgence in popularity among the Chinese, many of whom wish to reclaim traditional values in a changing society.* CHINA PHOTOS/GETTY IMAGES

and Hong Kong. Both of these movements aimed to counter Communist ideology and to promote Confucian values.

Since the 1950s, Confucianism in mainland China suffered a steady decline as the new regime explicitly sought to replace it with the new state orthodoxy of Communism. It was frontally attacked during the 1960s and 1970s, when the Cultural Revolution (1966–1969) brought about nationwide social, political, and economic chaos. Political-ideological movements and struggles trampled on traditional culture in any form, including Confucianism. As a corollary, Liang Shuming, Xiong Shili (1885–1968), Feng Youlan (1895–1990), and He Lin (1902–1992) were all subjected to inhumane treatment, and several of them were finally forced to become Maoists. Meanwhile, many Confucian conventions, historical sites, and artifacts were renounced or destroyed during this period. Only after the turmoil brought about by the Cultural Revolution ended in the late 1970s with Deng Xiaoping's rise to power did Confucianism begin to recover gradually from this nightmare.

By contrast, in Taiwan, Hong Kong, and other overseas Chinese communities, Confucianism remained vital as new Confucianism (*xin Ruxue*). A number of Chinese cultural scholars and philosophers—Zhang Junli (1887–1968), Qian Mu (1895–1990), Fang Dongmei (1899–1977), Xu Fuguan (1903–1982), Tang Junyi (1909–1978), and Mou Zongsan (1909–1995)—devoted themselves to reviving Confucianism or adapting Western or Indian philosophies, including Buddhism, to Confucianism. In 1958 Zhang, Xu, Tang, and Mou jointly published *Wei Zhongguo wenhua jinggao shijie renshi xuanyan* (The Chinese culture manifesto), which appealed for a combination of Western science, technology, and democracy with the Confucian tradition. In addition, Confucianism has also continued as a legacy overseas, in such Confucian societies as Japan, Korea, Singapore, and Vietnam.

## A NEW REVIVAL IN CHINA?

Since the 1980s Confucianism has gradually regained standing in mainland China, both in scholarship and as a system of political thought. Confucius is again hailed as a sage thinker, the paragon of teachers, and the symbol of Chinese culture. In recent years, a wave of enthusiasm for Chinese studies (*guoxue re*) has overflowed in classroom learning, academic research, domestic and international conferences, publications, Internet Web sites, and the mass media, and Confucianism is always at the core of such Chinese studies. Research centers on Chinese culture or Confucianism have been set up under various names in universities, and some prestigious universities have even established graduate schools of Chinese studies. Meanwhile, some advocates of Confucianism have become popular stars in television shows or popular writers for best-selling books about Confucianism. Confucianism, it seems, has been revived, at least on the surface, but whether or not this revival is substantive remains to be seen.

The revival of Confucianism has been stimulated by multiple impetuses. In mainland China, as the state ideology of Marxism–Leninism–Mao Zedong Thought has tended to decline, many Chinese people, including politicians and intellectuals, are seeking alternative ideological resources to overcome the spiritual, ethical, and moral crises encountered in building up a harmonious society, and Confucianism serves as the most appropriate resource for them. Another impetus is China's gradual reemergence as one of the world's superpowers. In this situation Confucianism has returned to respectability as a source of confidence for the Chinese people, after two hundred years of humiliation at the hands of the Western powers. The third impetus is the link between the economic growth of the Asia–Pacific region since the 1980s and the core Confucian value placed on human relationships in the business and industrial world—a link seen as responsible for the economic miracle in this region. Confucianism appeals to politicians, businesspersons, and all those who seek cultural resources that may serve as a practical shortcut for modernization, economic growth, or even simply personal prosperity. Last, it is obvious, at least to Chinese socialist leaders, that Confucianism can be used to combat the corrupting potential of capitalism in an era of intensified globalization, and that the hierarchical social order in human relationships that it fosters can be useful for maintaining political control.

Unlike classical Confucianism, new Confucianism has to be open to the outside world and to enable Chinese thinkers to explore alternative ways to meet the new demands of humanity. Since the shrinking globe has brought greater interrelatedness, interdependence, and interaction among peoples and cultures than ever before, the present revitalization of Confucianism depends largely on how well the Confucian idea of humaneness can communicate Confucianism's unique approach to civil society, and on how well these indigenous Chinese values can contribute to a global ethic and foster a mutually enriching dialogue among civilizations.

**SEE ALSO** *Classical Scholarship and Intellectual Debates; Education: Moral Education; Filial Piety; Kang Youwei; May Fourth Movement; Morality; Qing Restoration; Zeng Guofan; Zhang Zhidong.*

### BIBLIOGRAPHY

Alitto, Guy. *The Last Confucian: Liang Shu-ming and the Chinese Dilemma of Modernity*. Berkeley: University of California Press, 1979.

Chen, Jingpan. *Confucius as a Teacher: Philosophy of Confucius with Special Reference to Its Educational Implications*. Beijing: Foreign Languages Press, 1990.

De Bary, William Theodore. *East Asian Civilizations: A Dialogue in Five Stages*. Cambridge, MA: Harvard University Press, 1988.

Fairbank, John King, and *Merle Goldman. China: A New History.* 2nd enlarged ed. Cambridge, MA: Harvard University Press, 2006.

Feng Youlan. *Zhongguo zhexue shi xinbian* [A new history of Chinese philosophy]. 6 vols. Beijing: Renmin Chubanshe, 1982–1989.

Lee, Thomas H. C. *Education in Traditional China: A History.* Leiden, Netherlands: Brill, 2000.

Levenson, Joseph Richmond. *Confucian China and Its Modern Fate: A Trilogy.* Berkeley: University of California Press, 1968.

Liang Shuming. *Dong xi wenhua ji qi zhexue* [Eastern and Western cultures and their philosophies]. 4th ed. Beijing: Shangwuyin Shuguan, 1923.

Sun Peiqing and Li Guojun, eds. *Zhongguo jiaoyu sixiang shi* [A history of China's educational thought]. 3 vols. Shanghai: Huadong Shifan Daxue Chubanshe, 1995.

Tu, Weiming. *Way, Learning, and Politics: Essays on the Confucian Intellectual.* Albany: State University of New York Press, 1993.

Yu Yingshi. *Xiandai Ruxue de huigu yu zhanwang* [Retrospect and prospect of contemporary Confucianism]. Beijing: Shenghuo, Dushu, Xinzhi San Lian Shudian, 2004.

***Jun Li***

## CONNOISSEURSHIP

The term *connoisseurship* used in its broadest sense refers to expert judgment concerning matters of taste, such as music and art. Connoisseurship of the visual arts, including drawing and painting, involves assessments about authenticity (when, where, and by whom was the object made?) which, in theory, should be objective judgments, as well as about relative quality (is it a fine, mediocre, or poor example of the artist's oeuvre?), and these are subjective judgments. Yet connoisseurship also requires expertise—specific knowledge about a given field of art.

The art critic Holland Cotter has addressed the issue of connoisseurship as it applies specifically to Chinese painting as follows:

> What is connoisseurship? Basically, the assessment of the identity and relative value of a work of art through analysis of external evidence: in the case of Chinese painting, physical materials (ink, paint, silk or paper), style (composition and brushwork), documents (seals, inscriptions, records), and comparable or related works. Who are the connoisseurs of Chinese art? In the West, they are usually art historians, dealers or collectors. In China, traditionally they have been artists. Through a lifelong practice of painting, the theory goes, they develop an intimate second-nature knowledge of the subtleties of style and a nose for discerning the authentic from the bogus that historical knowledge alone cannot match. (Cotter 1999)

In traditional China a painter learned the art of painting just as a calligrapher learned the art of writing: through disciplined copying of selected works from past masters. Through copying, the student learns to recreate the master's technique but also to capture the spirit of the original. Only after mastering the techniques of a variety of models is an artist ready to develop his own personal style by integrating these various stylistic influences. Connoisseurship is learned through firsthand practice of painting and calligraphy. Because the traditional medium of ink brushed on an absorbent ground (usually paper or silk) is extremely sensitive, the slightest variance in pressure or in consistency of ink will yield different results, observable in the finished work. As the student learns to control the brush, his ability to discern subtle differences of ink tonality and line quality will naturally improve. He trains his eyes as he trains his hand. This is why historically many of the best connoisseurs were themselves skilled painters and calligraphers. Traditional Chinese connoisseurship focuses on brushwork and is based on the assumption that every artist develops habitual wrist and arm movements manifested in his brushwork. Every stroke reveals something of the artist's distinctive technique, temperament, and personality. It is up to the connoisseur to become so thoroughly familiar with the brushwork habits of the masters that he can distinguish their authentic works at a glance. Connoisseurs must study as many original works as possible to understand each artist's oeuvre.

In addition to judging the quality of the brushwork, Chinese connoisseurs also trace the work's provenance by reading collectors' seals and inscriptions written on the work, and by comparing the works to those recorded in one or more of the annotated catalogues that Chinese collectors have produced over the centuries. Some of the most highly respected traditional Chinese connoisseurs of the twentieth century were Zhang Heng (1915–1963), Wu Hufan (1894–1968), Xie Zhiliu (1910–1997), Zhang Daqian (1899–1983), and Wang Jiqian (1907–2003). In recent years, as more Chinese connoisseurs have received additional training in universities and museums in the West, they have increasingly learned to combine traditional Chinese techniques of connoisseurship with Western art-historical methodology.

**SEE ALSO** *Collections and Collecting; Wu Hufan; Zhang Daqian (Chang Dai-chien).*

**BIBLIOGRAPHY**

Chang, Arnold. The Small Manifested in the Large, The Large Manifested in the Small: The Connoisseurship of Chinese Painting. *Kaikodo Journal* 12 (Autumn 1999): 43–54.

Cotter, Holland. On Trial at the Met: The Art of the Connoisseur. *New York Times*, December 5, 1999.

Fu, Marilyn, and Shen Fu. *Studies in Connoisseurship: Chinese Paintings from the Arthur M. Sackler Collection in New York and Princeton*. Princeton, NJ: Art Museum, Princeton University, 1973.

Smith, Judith G., and Wen C. Fong, eds. *Issues of Authenticity in Chinese Painting*. New York: Metropolitan Museum of Art, 1999.

Van Gulick, R. H. *Chinese Pictorial Art as Viewed by the Connoisseur*. Rome: Istituto italiano per il Medio ed Estremo Oriente, 1958.

***Arnold Chang***

# CONSTITUTIONALISM

While modern Western constitutionalism is often characterized by its emphasis on an individual's rights, constitutionalism has been practiced since well before the modern era and its concerns for human rights. It is both the practice of politics and the theory of that practice that is at the center of constitutionalism. Seen in this light, China's political elite was grappling with constitutional questions well before the late-Qing reform era. Among the questions discussed in nineteenth-century reformist thought were three of particular importance: How does the individual speak truth to power? How can the political energies of educated men outside government be used for the common good? And how can a country with an enormous population, a complex economy, and pressing social concerns be administered effectively by a relatively small group of provincial and local officials? Such questions were raised by nineteenth-century statecraft scholars such as Wei Yuan and Feng Guifen. Feng Guifen's radical proposals, based in part on his understanding of the West, were discussed by high government officials in the 1890s and anticipated the constitutional reforms promulgated by the Qing government in the post-Boxer era.

When assessing Chinese constitutionalism in the modern era, then, it is important to remember that many of the questions and answers associated with imported ideas were not necessarily new to China's political elite. While a Western-influenced concern about the individual and rights would become an element of modern Chinese constitutionalism, fundamental constitutional concerns about how public and political life should be ordered had been present in China long before the impact of the West.

## CONSTITUTIONALISM IN THE LATE QING

Modern constitutionalism in China is often associated with the late-Qing reform era, beginning in 1895 with Kang Youwei's "ten-thousand-word" petition that called for elected representatives to serve in Beijing where they would critique imperial actions and speak for the people. Kang's 1895 plea echoed the first article of Japan's 1868 Charter Oath, a hallmark of the Meiji era (1868–1912), which reads: "An assembly widely convoked shall be established and all matters of state shall be decided by public discussion." China followed this progressive Western-influenced Japanese constitutional model in the crisis atmosphere of the post-Boxer era.

In 1905 Qing government officials viewed from the sidelines the spectacle of Japan and Russia, which had occupied parts of Manchuria during the Boxer Uprising, fighting one another in this strategic area in China's northeast. Taking a cue from the weakening of autocratic resolve in Russia after its 1905 revolution, and impressed by Japan's prowess, the Qing government announced its intention to begin preparing for an era of constitutional government by dispatching five high-level government ministers and their entourages on a worldwide tour to meet and study foreign governments. High-level officials and the court discussed their reports in the summer of 1906, and on September 1 an imperial edict announced that "while the throne remains the hub of the power, the manifold affairs of the state will be open to public discussion." Local elites celebrated the news in cities like Beijing, Tianjin, Shanghai, Guangzhou, and Shantou.

## "THE PRINCIPLES OF THE CONSTITUTION" (1908)

Many people inside and outside government contributed to the remarkably open debate that ensued about the future direction of China's political reforms. Like Western and Japanese constitutionalism, Chinese constitutionalism in those years addressed fundamental questions, such as how to rationalize the division of political power both functionally and spatially. The other central concern of nineteenth-century constitutionalism—the protection of the rights of the individual—was also under discussion.

Chinese students who had been studying in Japan, some of whom were allies of Kang Youwei and his protégé Liang Qichao, and some who had been leaning toward the revolutionary program of Sun Yat-sen (Sun Yixian or Sun Zhongshan), came home to play important policy-making roles in the government, especially in the ad-hoc bodies responsible for defining a new constitutional order. For example, returned students dominated the proceedings of the government task force drafting electoral regulations for provincial assemblies. These assemblies, as well as local and national assemblies, were outlined in the "Nine-Year Program of Constitutional Preparation" that was announced, along with "The Principles of the Constitution," in August 1908. Some of these principles would inform the many outlines, drafts, and constitutions issued by subsequent regimes in China to the present day, even though constitutionalism in the postimperial era vested sovereignty in the people, a people whose representatives would write the constitution. This goal, however, would require viable constitutional mechanisms by which to assess the will of the people and to protect the rights of individuals—freedoms of speech, press, and assembly—adumbrated in "The Principles of the Constitution."

## CONSTITUTIONALISM IN REPUBLICAN CHINA

The search for these mechanisms in the Republican period was marked by a plethora of constitutions and ongoing constitution-writing. Unfortunately, for the student of Chinese constitutionalism, these discussions often masked a deeply political struggle for power. Sun Yat-sen's Five-Power theory, which attempted to combine Western-style separation of power (executive, legislative, judicial) with traditional central government responsibilities for supervising officials (censorate) and identifying and selecting those officials (examination), would come to dominate the political landscape as his successor, Chiang Kai-shek (Jiang Jieshi), began to consolidate his power in 1927. Like Sun, Chiang was convinced that a strong state was antecedent to a constitution; Sun's three-stage theory of constitutional development required first a military dictatorship and then a period of political tutelage.

This was an anathema to leading intellectuals like Hu Shi and Luo Longji. Both men, whose writings appeared in journals like *Crescent Moon* (*Xinyue*) in the late 1920s and early 1930s, argued that constitutionalism could only be achieved to the degree that China's citizens had their human rights, including freedom of speech, protected by a state free from the domination of any particular political party. Their focus on the individual and on evolutionary development was at odds with both Nationalist and Communist approaches to these fundamental questions. Luo, whose 1928 Columbia University Ph.D. thesis, "Parliamentary Elections in England," informed his thought and actions, worked with both Nationalist and, after 1949, Communist authorities, to realize his vision.

## CONSTITUTIONAL DEVELOPMENTS IN THE PEOPLE'S REPUBLIC OF CHINA

Like the ferment of the late-Qing period, there has been a vigorous debate in recent decades in the People's Republic of China about political reforms, including the issue of a franchise with real power behind it at all levels of society. Yan Jiaqi, for example, argued as an insider in the Chinese Communist Party in the 1980s for a new democratic politics that would be typified by the separation of party and government, freedom of speech, and the creation of procedures whereby leaders would be made accountable to the people. Implicit in Yan's argument was the recognition that the rights guaranteed by China's constitution were not, in fact, guaranteed in practice. Serious reservations remain about how to achieve these goals.

Yan's gradualist, insider position contrasts with the more well-known outsider's call for democracy in "The Fifth Modernization." In 1978 Wei Jingsheng, a former Red Guard and army veteran, had written an essay that was a hallmark of the Democracy Wall movement. Wei's second manifesto, "Human Rights, Equality, and Democracy," echoed topics of moment to Hu Shi and Luo Longji. Wei, like Luo, would be imprisoned for his views. Hu Shi's 1929 essay "What Path Shall We Take," however, emphasized points that many of Wei's opponents could still agree with, including Hu's call for study and specific attention to five evils—poverty, disease, ignorance, corruption, and internal disturbances—that had to be addressed before any fundamental constitutional reform could finally be achieved.

There remain concerns, which date to the late Qing and could be heard in the Republican period as well, about the quality and perspectives of the prospective leaders to be empowered by the ballot; there are many who are uncomfortable with the idea of "people power" unvetted by state authority. This can be explained in part by a fear of elite factionalism, whether local, provincial, or national, that recurs in the history of Chinese political theory and practice. Although the vision of late-Qing thinkers of a constitutional form of government that includes local, provincial, and national assemblies is still discussed, the specter of the 1989 Tiananmen Incident shadows discussions about the fundamental rights of individuals. The modern constitutionalism of the late-Qing period, influenced by Japan, the West, and China's imperial past, marked a new direction for a dialogue between the government and the people of China that continues into the twenty-first century.

**SEE ALSO** *Constitutions before 1949; Constitutions since 1949; Elections and Assemblies, 1909–1949; Hu Shi; Kang Youwei; Liang Qichao.*

## BIBLIOGRAPHY

Beasley, W. G. Meiji Political Institutions. In *The Cambridge History of Japan,* Vol. 5: *The Nineteenth Century,* ed. Marius B. Jansen, 618–673. Cambridge, U.K.: Cambridge University Press, 1989.

Friedrich, Carl J. Constitutions and Constitutionalism. In *International Encyclopedia of the Social Sciences,* ed. David L. Sills, Vol. 3, 318–326. New York: Macmillan, 1968.

Ichiko Chuzo. Political and Institutional Reform, 1901–11. In *The Cambridge History of China,* Vol. 11: *Late Ch'ing, 1800–1911,* eds. John K. Fairbank and Liu Guangjing (Kwang-ching Liu), 375–415. Cambridge, U.K.: Cambridge University Press, 1980.

Kuhn, Philip A. *Origins of the Modern Chinese State.* Stanford, CA: Stanford University Press, 2002.

Meienberger, Norbert. *The Emergence of Constitutional Government in China (1905–1908): The Concept Sanctioned by the Empress Dowager Tz'u-hsi.* Bern, Switzerland: Peter Lang, 1980.

Nathan, Andrew J. *Chinese Democracy.* New York: Knopf, 1985.

Nathan, Andrew J. Political Rights in Chinese Constitutions. In *Human Rights in Contemporary China,* eds. R. Randle Edwards, Louis Henkin, and Andrew J. Nathan, 77–124. New York: Columbia University Press, 1986.

Tan, Chester C. *Chinese Political Thought in the Twentieth Century.* Garden City, NY: Doubleday, 1971.

Thompson, Roger R. *China's Local Councils in the Age of Constitutional Reform, 1898–1911.* Cambridge, MA: Council on East Asian Studies, Harvard University, 1995.

Yan Jiaqi. *Yan Jiaqi and China's Struggle for Democracy.* Trans. and eds. David Bachman and Yang Dali (Dali L. Yang). Armonk, NY: Sharpe, 1991.

***Roger R. Thompson***

# CONSTITUTIONS BEFORE 1949

In 1908 the Qing government promulgated the "Principles of the Constitution," a document that was echoed in the series of constitutional documents issued in the early years of the Republic of China, in the era of Nationalist rule, and in the prototypes used by various Communist regional governments prior to the establishment of the People's Republic of China in 1949. Each set of documents had differences based on conceptions of citizenship, the proper role and function of the ruling political party, the structure and relations within the central government as well as its relationship with regional governments, and the underlying ideologies. However, there were significant similarities and continuities among constitutions associated with late-imperial, republican, and Communist regimes. These similarities over a period of almost four decades suggest that Chinese cultural and social factors influenced the drafters of these documents as significantly as foreign models did.

Among these continuities and similarities are the ways in which the proper relationship between state and individual person is described. Whereas Western models stressed the natural, organic, or prior origin of an individual's rights, whether political, social, or civil, all of China's pre-1949 constitutions stressed that rights were derived from the state. It was taken as a given that there was a harmony of interests between the state and the individual, and should this be violated, it was assumed that the individual, not the state, was probably at fault. Because rights were not deemed to be natural, it followed that successive constitutional documents characterized these rights differently and, in some cases, mentioned them only as a proposition, that is, that some rights could be realized only when China's social and economic development advanced sufficiently to allow the state to grant these rights to individuals. Not only could the state limit rights, it also was empowered to interpret the laws. Whether sovereign power was vested in the emperor, the parliament, the party (Nationalist or Communist), or a people's congress, these bodies could legislate without fear that their decisions could be challenged by another branch of government. As Andrew J. Nathan, a leading scholar of China's constitutions, wrote: "The chief goals of all the constitutions were to strengthen the state and promote collective welfare, rather than to protest individual interests against excessive state power" (Nathan 1986, p. 122). In addition, although every pre-1949 constitution but the first called for popular sovereignty, the structural barriers between the expressed will of the people and state policy were so high that in reality, China's citizens had very little power and influence.

## EARLY CONSTITUTIONS AND DRAFTS, 1908–1931

Five constitutions and two drafts in the pre-1949 period have been identified as especially important. The first, the "Principles of the Constitution" (1908), was promulgated by the Qing government in August 1908. This draft constitution was intended to guide China toward the goal of a complete and definitive constitution. Inspired by the apparent success of Japan in establishing a constitutional government, symbolized by the Meiji emperor's granting of a constitution to the Japanese people in 1889, the Qing "Principles" emphasized that sovereignty was vested in the emperor. The twenty-three articles included fourteen that described the powers of the emperor and nine that outlined the rights and duties of his subjects. The emperor would preside over his subjects, recognizing that they had rights that were codified in laws for the first time in Chinese history. These rights included freedoms of speech, writing, publication, assembly, and association, the right to serve in government or be elected to assemblies, and the right to submit petitions to government. As expansive as this list sounds, because these rights were the gifts from the emperor and could be interpreted only by government officials, the state-centered emphasis—premised on the belief that it was describing a compact between the state and the people characterized by cooperation—could not be missed.

The Provisional Constitution (1912), the Temple-of-Heaven Draft (1913), and the 1923 Constitution, all constitutional documents of the early Republican period, moved Chinese constitutionalism forward in three important areas: All citizens were defined as equal before the law, sovereignty was vested in the people (*renmin* in 1912; *guomin* in 1913) and exercised through a parliament, and a citizen's right to secrecy of correspondence was recognized. Voting rights, which had been left implicit in 1908, were made explicit in each of these documents.

The Nationalist Party, which established its control over much of China during a two-year period from 1927 to 1928, turned some of its attention to writing a constitution in the first years of its national rule, especially after regional rivals Yan Xishan and Wang Jingwei promulgated their own draft provisional constitution, the so-called

"Taiyuan Draft" in October 1930. Influenced by founding father Sun Yat-sen (Sun Yixian), who had become convinced that China would not be ready for democracy until there were sufficient advances in economic development and education, the Provisional Constitution for the Tutelage Period, or the Tutelage Constitution (1931), was designed for this interim period of preparation for full-scale constitutional government. There was an important innovation in this document: Gender was added to race, religion, and class as a basis that could not be used to discriminate against citizens. The Tutelage Constitution called for a permanent constitution to be written by the people through a national assembly whose members would be directly elected. These party-dominated elections were held in 1936, a year before the start of the second Sino-Japanese War; the first assembly could not be held until the war had ended. When the assembly finally convened in 1946 its membership also included Nationalist government and minority appointees.

### 1946 CONSTITUTION AND THE JIANGXI PROGRAM

The end of the "period of tutelage" was heralded on December 25, 1946 with the adoption of a permanent constitution that became effective one week later, on January 1, 1947. No longer was the Nationalist Party privileged in the constitution, and rights and freedoms were expanded further, especially in areas such as academic freedom; citizen compensation for misdeeds of government; rights of election, recall, initiative, and referendum; and the idea of residual rights. These rights, first introduced in the 1923 constitution but absent from the 1931 constitution, were informed by the idea that rights did not need to be specified in order to receive constitutional protection as long as social order and the public interest were not compromised. Similar in spirit was the provision to drop the qualifying phrase "according to law" that had appeared in earlier enumerations of a citizen's rights. The 1946 Constitution also is noteworthy for its expansion of popular sovereignty. Direct elections for the National Assembly were held in 1947 and for the Legislative Yuan in 1948. Indirect elections for the Control Yuan (a supervisory body) were held in 1948. The 1946 constitution also institutionalized the principle of independent judicial review.

Modeled after the Soviet Union's 1924 constitution, the Chinese Soviet Republic (Jiangxi) Constitutional Program (1931; revised 1934) was a Marxist-Leninist-inspired outline for a constitution that contained seventeen articles. Given its ideological origins, the Jiangxi Program differed significantly from earlier Chinese constitutional documents. For example, the Communists limited rights to citizens with the correct working-class background. Neither the "people" nor "citizens" had political rights; these were reserved for "workers" or the "laboring masses." In addition to enumerating the standard freedoms of speech, publication, assembly, and association, the Jiangxi Program echoed earlier constitutional documents in its assertion that some rights were goals for the future. Indeed, for the first time, this understanding was made explicit: Rights were, in a sense, benefits that the government hoped to deliver when adequate economic, social, and political conditions existed.

Constitutions merit attention even if, as often was the case in China, reality did not match the idealistic goals on paper. Dominant political elites and parties impressed these documents with their ideas and goals, and in their pages we can discern power struggles and historic transformations in China's political culture. The constitutional history from 1908 to 1949 provides evidence of the degree to which core Chinese values, especially those that idealized a harmonious relationship between the state and the individual, crossed ideological and political boundaries in a dynamic and fluid environment in which constitution drafters also were responding to influences from Japan, the United States, Europe, and the Soviet Union.

**SEE ALSO** *Constitutionalism; Elections and Assemblies, 1909–1949; Individual and the State, 1800–1949; Liang Qichao; Taiwan, Republic of China: Politics since 1945.*

**BIBLIOGRAPHY**

Ch'ien, Tuan-sheng. *The Government and Politics of China.* Cambridge, MA: Harvard University Press, 1950.

Meienberger, Norbert. *The Emergence of Constitutional Government in China (1905–1908): The Concept Sanctioned by the Empress Dowager Tz'u-hsi.* Bern, Switzerland: Peter Lang, 1980.

Nathan, Andrew J. A Constitutional Republic: The Peking Government, 1916–28. In *The Cambridge History of China,* vol. 12, ed. John K. Fairbank, 256–283. Cambridge, U.K.: Cambridge University Press, 1983.

Nathan, Andrew J. Political Rights in Chinese Constitutions. In *Human Rights in Contemporary China,* ed. R. Randle Edwards, Louis Henkin, and Andrew J. Nathan, 77–124. New York: Columbia University Press, 1986.

Zhao, Suisheng. *Power by Design: Constitution-Making in Nationalist China.* Honolulu: University of Hawai'i Press, 1996.

***Roger R. Thompson***

## CONSTITUTIONS SINCE 1949

In the People's Republic of China (PRC), constitutions are fundamental, if not sacred, political documents describing the state institutions. China's constitutions, however, do not reflect the reality of the country's power structures and are subject to amendment according to the political circumstances and priorities of the Chinese Communist Party (CCP).

In 1949, when the PRC was founded, the CCP convened a Chinese Consultative People's Political Conference (CCPPC) that represented the united front between the party and the other political forces opposed to the Guomindang (GMD) regime. Acting as a national assembly, the CCPPC formally appointed the central government and adopted a Common Program that served as a de facto constitution until 1954. But because the government was headed by Mao Zedong, the CCP chairman, its power and responsibilities were highly symbolic and its activities remained tightly controlled by the CCP.

## THE 1954 CONSTITUTION

In 1954 the PRC promulgated its first full constitution (106 articles), drafted on lines very similar to the constitution of the Soviet Union enacted by Joseph Stalin (1879–1953) in 1936. The new Chinese constitution looked democratic: All state institutions consisted of officials elected, directly or indirectly, by the voters, meaning all citizens that enjoyed political rights. State institutions were organized into three branches: the National People's Congress (then 1,226 delegates) embodied the legislative power; the State Council held the executive power; and the Supreme People's Court and the Supreme People's Procuratorate embodied the judicial power. In addition, all the basic liberties granted in democracies were enshrined in the 1954 constitution; the leading role of the CCP was simply alluded to in its preamble. Two differences with the Soviet constitution should be underlined: The PRC was a unitary and not a federal state, and the constitution instituted a state presidency, specially designed for Mao, who was also CCP chairman.

## THE 1975 CONSTITUTION

The 1954 constitution remained in place until 1975. However, as early as 1959, Mao became increasingly unhappy with the legal formalism it imposed. He thus mainly operated through the CCP that he continued to chair and ceded the state presidency to Liu Shaoqi, then his official successor. In 1966 Mao launched the Cultural Revolution, which froze the implementation of the constitution: The National People's Congress and the local people's congresses stopped convening, and the local governmental councils were replaced by revolutionary committees.

In 1970 Lin Biao, Mao's new designated successor, proposed to draft a new constitution and restore, for himself, the position of PRC president. But Mao opposed this move, and waited for another four years after Lin's fall in 1971 to promulgate a new constitution. This constitution, inspired by the spirit of the Cultural Revolution, was drafted by Zhang Chunqiao (1917–2005), a radical leader and a future member of the famous "gang of four."

The 1975 constitution was short (thirty articles), symbolizing the gradual degeneration of the law under socialism, and it made no secret of the leading role of the CCP. For instance, the National People's Congress was placed officially under the leadership of the Communist Party. But, at the same time, this constitution enshrined the "four great freedoms"—the right to make *dazibao,* or big character posters, being the most famous—supposedly granted by Mao at the beginning of the Cultural Revolution, as well as the right to go on strike, although these rights remained in reality largely suppressed.

## THE 1978 CONSTITUTION

After Mao's death in 1976, Hua Guofeng's appointment as his successor and Deng Xiaoping's gradual rehabilitation led to the drafting of a third—and short-lived—constitution. This third constitution fell half way, in both its spirit and its content, between the first two constitutions. Enacted in March 1978, the new constitution (sixty articles) continued to insist on the CCP's leading role. While people's procuratorates were restored, the revolutionary committees were retained, as were the "four great freedoms" and the right to go on strike.

The famous third plenum of the CCP Central Committee in December 1978 heralded a complete change of orientation, which triggered amendments to the 1978 constitution in 1980. The people's governments were restored, and the "four great freedoms," the last explicit reference to the Cultural Revolution, abolished. But the need to draft a completely new constitution soon emerged.

## THE 1982 CONSTITUTION

On December 4, 1982, the PRC's fourth constitution was promulgated. This new text (138 articles) is in many respects similar to the 1954 constitution. However, it reflects the lessons learned by the CCP leadership during the Cultural Revolution, as well as its new willingness to restore and promote "socialist legality." The CCP is required to operate within the framework of the constitution and the laws. The concept of dictatorship of the proletariat is abandoned and replaced by a more ambiguous notion: the people's democratic dictatorship. The "fundamental rights and duties of citizens" are upgraded and presented in chapter 2, immediately after the general principles (in earlier constitutions, they had appeared at the end of the document). The competences of all state institutions—the State Council or central government, the local people's governments, the national and local people's congresses, the organs of self-government of national autonomous areas, and the judicial organs—are more precisely defined and represent the bulk of the constitution (chapter 3). In addition, the PRC presidency is restored. For the first time since 1949, the constitution implements a state central military commission. Several key state positions (the PRC president and vice president, the chairperson and vice chairpersons of the National People's Congress, the president of the Supreme Court, and the procurator general) are limited to two consecutive terms of five years. Finally, the national flag, the national anthem, and the capital are given constitutional status (chapter 4).

Despite these changes, progress remains limited and superficial. The four basic principles enshrined in the preamble—the leading role of the CCP, Marxism-Leninism and Mao Zedong Thought, the people's democratic dictatorship, and the socialist road—make irrelevant many of the constitutional dispositions. State leaders are formally elected by the people's congresses of the same level, but the party recommends all candidates, and monopolizes all key positions, according to the *nomenklatura* system. For instance, the new central military commission is identical to the party central military commission appointed by the CCP Central Committee. Although elected directly by the voters at the township and the county levels, the people's congresses are still dominated by CCP officials. For these reasons, the constitution does not include any article designed to solve disputes among the various branches of government, as if approval were taken for granted.

Constitutional amendments were introduced in 1988, 1993, 1999, and 2004. Most of these amendments are related to principles or policies introduced by the Communist Party after 1982. For example, since 1988, the state has protected private property, a type of property that became "inviolable" in 2004 (articles 11 and 13). In 1993 the household-based "rural contracted responsibility system" was incorporated into the constitution (article 8), and the phrase "socialist market economy" replaced "economic planning" (article 15). In 1999 the statement that "the People's Republic of China practices ruling the country by law" (*yi fa zhi guo*) and "builds a socialist rule of law" was added to article 5 of the constitution. In 2004, for the first time in the history of the PRC, the state committed itself to "respect and protect human rights" (article 33, paragraph 3). Although these revisions did not expand the role of the constitution, since the early 2000s, they have stimulated among jurists and legal activists a "constitutionalist movement" that is demanding greater respect for the constitution. This movement has now caused some courts to occasionally invoke constitutional disposition to support their judgments. It has also taken the shape of a "rights protection movement" (*weiquan yundong*) that is trying to utilize the constitution as leverage both to enhance the rule of law, and in particular the right of defense, as well as to push for a gradual democratization of the political system. However, the CCP is well aware of these activists' intentions and prevents them from going too far and from threatening the party's power.

**SEE ALSO** *Central State Organs since 1949: National People's Congress; Central State Organs since 1949: President and Vice President; Constitutionalism; Constitutions before 1949.*

**BIBLIOGRAPHY**

Chen Jianfu. The Revision of the Constitution in the PRC: Conceptual Evolution of "Socialism with Chinese Characteristics." *China Perspectives* 24 (1999): 66–79.

Chen Jianfu. The Revision of the Constitution in the PRC: A Great Leap Forward or a Symbolic Gesture? *China Perspectives* 53 (2004): 15–32.

Constitution of the People's Republic of China. Adopted on December 4, 1982. http://english.people.com.cn/constitution/constitution.html.

Li Buyun. *Xianfa yu Zhongguo* [Constitutionalism and China]. Beijing: Falü Chubanshe, 2006.

Zhu Guobin. *Zhongguo xianfa yu zhengzhi zhidu* [The Chinese constitution and the political system]. 2nd ed. Beijing: Falü Chubanshe, 2006.

*Jean-Pierre Cabestan*

## CONSUMPTION AND CONSUMER CULTURES

The subjects of consumption and consumer culture in China are arguably the most important facing the world. It is easy to see why. Underway in urban China is a radical transformation that began with the rise of Deng Xiaoping and the introduction of market reforms at the end of the 1970s. Over the next couple of decades China emerged as the world's factory, churning out the affordable consumer goods essential to contemporary lifestyles abroad. But now China itself is becoming a leading consumer of nearly everything. The ever escalating statistics are stunning. China is already the world's largest consumer of beer, meat, grain, and mobile phones—to select a few random items from a growing list of consumer goods. It also has adopted consumer lifestyles, building new super-sized malls twice as big as the Mall of America and the Mall of Canada. In 2001 Chinese bought only 1 percent of the world's luxury handbags, shoes, and perfume. By 2007 the country had become the third largest consumer of luxury brands, and it may surpass the United States and Japan by 2015.

How will China's consumers shape the lives of its 1.4 billion inhabitants? Will China continue to emulate American forms of consumption through personal automobiles, computers, and large private homes? Political policies, cultural practices, and history will shape consumerism in China. Take Beijing's decision to promote private automobiles and a culture of expressways, drive-in dining, and sprawling suburban and exurban developments. Tax policies and infrastructure investment could easily have led to very different outcomes. Indeed, this particular policy decision may determine not only how Chinese commuters spend their time (on bicycles or public transportation versus in private cars in massive traffic jams). Chinese consumerism may also determine the health of the planet—smog does not need an exit visa.

## TERMINOLOGY

The terms *consumption*, *consumer culture*, and *consumerism* are problematic, especially when applied to China, which has wide regional variation and growing levels of inequality. *Consumption* refers to the selection and use of goods and services and the individual and social consequences. Because all people in all places consume, scholars prefer more focused terms, such as *consumer culture*, which refers to the consumption of branded, mass-produced commodities and the orientation of social life and discourse around such commodities. Here the term *consumerism* is used synonymously with *consumer culture*. Making matters still more complicated, the term *consumer society* suggests the spread of lifestyles and politics centered on consumption to the majority of the population, not merely pockets of consumerism or a consumer culture thriving in an otherwise largely agricultural or proto-industrial country. Thus the more restrictive term *consumer society* applies only to levels of consumerism seen in Western Europe and America in the decades after World War II, in Japan in the 1960s, and in Korea, Taiwan, and Hong Kong in the 1970s and 1980s. In East Asia, however, scholars see broad consumer cultures appearing in major cities such as Seoul, Tokyo, Osaka, Shanghai, and Tianjin by the late nineteenth and early twentieth centuries. By some measures, in the twenty-first century, *regions* such as the Beijing-Tianjin corridor, the Yangzi River Delta area surrounding Shanghai, and the Pearl River Delta area (including Hong Kong, Shenzhen, and Guangzhou) already approach the levels of per capita disposable income, knowledge of mass consumer goods, and availability of mass media required for consumer society.

## CONSUMERISM TO 1949

The grim material conditions during World War II, the civil war (1945–1949), and the Maoist era (1949–1976) misleadingly suggest that Chinese consumerism is strictly a post-Mao phenomenon. But China had elements of consumer culture in imperial and elite circles for centuries. In the wealthiest regions, such as that of the Lower Yangzi Delta, local elites created social capital by exchanging rare gifts and assembling expensive dowries, and they conspicuously consumed by collecting art objects and hosting lavish weddings and funerals. Textiles, liquors, teas, opium, books, and other commodities were consumed well beyond the regions where they were produced. As in Europe, in early modern China consumption habits gradually spread down the social hierarchy for former luxuries such as sugar and tea. Moreover, recent scholarship on the nineteenth century and the Republican era (1912–1949) and a booming domestic nostalgia industry that has reprinted countless photographs from the decades preceding the 1949 Communist victory in China have uncovered more widespread consumer cultures.

It is easy to find evidence in the pre-Communist era of virtually everything imaginable in the material culture of a modern society. Urban China, particularly the treaty ports such as Shanghai and Tianjin, had everything from modern retailing, exhibition halls, and advertising; to modes of transportation establishing more integrated markets such as rickshaws, automobiles, bicycles, and airplanes; to new public environments created within modern schools and workplaces to see and learn of new products; to the energy sources supplying the electricity required by new consumer products and lifestyles. Chinese people, particularly but not exclusively urban elites, used the new objects in their homes, in their leisure activities, and on their persons. A growing number of Chinese altered their appearance from head (hats) to toe (shoes and socks).

It is difficult for historians to reconstruct the exact impact of these commodities and to explain how people used and thought about all the products and services they consumed. Unlike America and Western Europe, China does not have a tradition of detailed probate records revealing exactly what households owned. Contemporary records and the memoirs of foreign travelers readily show that Chinese adopted imports for local, specific, and even individual purposes. For instance, fashionable urban women in the early twentieth-century confidently mixed and matched traditional and imported clothing articles to create their own original styles. This adaptation was predictably common for those least likely to have access to information about or contact with foreigners and how they used their material artifacts. Urban slum dwellers, for instance, built shacks out of discarded iron Standard Oil cans.

Chinese consumers were not always free to purchase whatever they could afford or determine the social significance of the items they bought. In China, modern consumption and consumerism has always been connected with imperialism. During the nineteenth century, Europeans and Americans demanded access to China to sell the fruits of the Industrial Revolution. Through the Opium War (1839–1842), they achieved access through force at a time when the relative superiority of Chinese material culture had declined markedly. Chinese learned to desire imports. In the nineteenth century, the most prominent of these were opium and Western military hardware. But by the end of the century, desire for imports extended to a vast array of consumer goods, all the way to the symbolic heart of China—silk. Japanese silk displaced Chinese silk in foreign markets and increasingly penetrated the domestic market. The sale of imports also benefited from the association of

***Young customer exiting a members-only warehouse store, Beijing, June, 2001.*** *While China established itself as a leading exporter of consumer goods in the 1970s, internal markets for these same goods grew rapidly during the early twenty-first century as the incomes of urban residents increased sufficiently to create a new consumer culture in China.* © BOB SACHA/CORBIS

"foreign" with "better" seemingly everywhere from concepts of male and female beauty, to forms of sport and entertainment, to styles of architecture and personal appearance.

During the first half of the twentieth century, the influx of imports and the desires they stimulated threatened powerful interests. Politicians worried about trade deficits and the new consumer lifestyles exemplified by opium dens. Educated elites, who had begun to read works on Western political economy, feared the loss of sovereignty implicit in the growing foreign dominance of the economy. And manufacturers, faced with inexpensive and superior imports, tried desperately to produce products to compete against new imports. Their concerns took the shape of a National Products movement, which was a multifaceted "Buy Chinese" campaign conducted in cities across the country. Advocates developed countless ways, including skillfully co-opting foreign commodity spectacles like product exhibitions, to exhort, browbeat, and ultimately force fellow Chinese to consume China-made goods. Naturally, most Chinese, particularly those outside of major treaty ports, either were ignorant of such efforts to define consumption along nationalistic lines or ignored them. They were understandably unwilling to adhere to nationalistic admonitions and pay more for poorly made Chinese copies.

## CONSUMERISM UNDER MAO

After it was powerfully reconstituted in 1949, the Chinese state counteracted the ease with which consumers adopted, adapted, and enjoyed imports. The People's Republic threatened to destroy China's nascent consumer culture for four reasons: Mao Zedong's well-known anti-urban biases, the initial decision to follow the Soviet economic model with its emphasis on state-owned heavy industry and neglect of consumer goods, the elimination of private enterprise, and the appeal of autarkic economic growth after a century of imperialism. The Communists gradually forced foreign multinationals out of China and eliminated most foreign brands by imposing higher tariffs and outright bans. After some initial hesitation, which allowed consumer lifestyles to persist into the mid-1950s, the state appropriated all private enterprises, eliminating the trendsetting consumer class of urban capitalists. During the Mao years, the People's Republic radically reshaped consumerism, but never eliminated it from Chinese life. China continued to mass-produce branded goods (albeit new domestic ones), and commodities remained objects of everyday discussion and markers of personal and collective identity. The Communists worked feverishly to eliminate all traces of consumerism, particularly after the shift to ideological over material incentives during the Great Leap Forward (1958–1960) and the decade that opened with the Cultural Revolution (1966–1969). But even the most extreme attempts to eliminate consumerism may have had unintended consequence of heightening commodity consciousness.

Meanwhile, in the 1950s and 1960s, Japan's gross national product grew at an average of 10 percent a year, and the nation became a heavily studied model of high-speed economic growth in the region. This model featured heavy state involvement in economic planning, environmental degradation, and, above all, an emphasis on production and export-led growth at the expense of domestic consumption. Mass consumerism and the formation of a new urban middle class followed. Subsequent decades witnessed similar phenomenon in Korea and the three other Asian tigers (Taiwan, Hong Kong, and Singapore). The spread of consumerism in East Asia culminated in China. In 1978 Deng Xiaoping began depoliticizing daily life and initiated economic reforms that led to growth rates on par with Japan's earlier record levels. The Chinese state staked its legitimacy on economic growth and encouraged citizens to consume—a shift in attitudes and policies toward consumerism embodied in the inapt yet popular 1980s Communist Party slogan "To get rich is glorious!"

## CONSUMERISM AFTER MAO

The market reforms of the late 1970s and 1980s introduced tremendous uncertainty for consumers. Fixed prices shifted toward market prices. This environment created new consumer issues, including resentment and fear of unfair pricing, the sale of imitations through deceptive packaging, food adulteration, false advertising claims, product liability, and warranty issues. The reemergence of markets became sources of media scandals and popular panics and rumors. For instance, in the summer of 1985 a scandal erupted over the sale of supposedly dirty imported used clothing that was sold as new. An investigation by a Beijing textile and clothing association concluded that the clothing was not only dirty but also came from sick people. That winter twenty cities and counties participated in the effort to find and destroy the offending clothing.

This unstable environment gave rise to a consumer movement with academic, bureaucratic, and social dimensions. In 1983 China's most important consumer association, the Chinese Consumers' Association, was established as a state-sponsored consumer-protection organization. By 2001 its 3,000-plus local branches across China had accepted over 6 million consumer complaints. Local efforts also began in this decade. In 1987 the Northeast city of Shenyang passed the first local consumer-protection laws and dozens of provinces and cities quickly followed. The 1980s also saw the beginning of the academic study of consumerism and the publication of consumer magazines and newspapers to protect "consumer rights," as they became known. Finally, in this decade the Chinese Communist Party recast itself as a protector of consumers. The party-state established regulatory agencies such as the National Administration of Industry and Commerce, which regulates trademarks and ads, and the Commodity Inspection Bureau, which requires companies to add product warnings.

From the late 1990s the Japanese model has become a cautionary tale. High savings rates involved suppressing consumption and limiting imports through tariff and nontariffs barriers. These same high saving rates, previously credited for Japan's economic growth, were now blamed for its economic stagnation. Chinese officials feared following the same path, especially since Chinese households saved up to 40 percent of income. Even after China's ascension in 2001 to the World Trade Organization, which reduced tariffs and trade barriers, saving rates remained high. In 1998 Chinese officials began to recognize the importance of stimulating domestic demand and started to shift the economy from a Japanese-style reliance on exports toward domestic consumption-led growth. Policies designed to boost consumption included trying to address the anxieties behind high savings (escalating medical, education, and retirement costs); permitting the establishment of private lending companies; accelerating urbanization; instituting extended holidays around the lunar New Year, May Day, and National Day (October 1); and deregulating the financial sector to facilitate consumer borrowing through mortgages, credit cards, and car loans. By 2008 real estate speculation and the high volume of travel overwhelming the transportation system forced Beijing to reconsider some of these policies.

The growing international environmental crisis and extreme pollution in China—which has sixteen of the world's twenty most polluted cities—raise important questions about the sustainability of modern consumerism. What if, as expected and indeed now *planned* by Chinese bureaucrats, consumerism spreads from the estimated 100 million middle-class consumers in major Chinese cities to secondary and tertiary cities, as well as to towns and villages across the countryside? What will happen as Chinese consumers catch up with the West in per capita consumption of energy and other commodities? New strains on world resources and ecological catastrophes may challenge accepted notions of consumerism based on an individual, acquisitive rationality and, indeed, may test the economic and political organization of the world.

**SEE ALSO** *National Products Movement; Socialist Market Economy; Transition Economy.*

**BIBLIOGRAPHY**

Cochran, Sherman. *Big Business in China: Sino-Foreign Rivalry in the Cigarette Industry, 1890–1930.* Cambridge, MA: Harvard University Press, 1980.

Croll, Elisabeth. *China's New Consumers: Social Development and Domestic Demand.* New York: Routledge, 2006.

Davis, Deborah, ed. *The Consumer Revolution in Urban China.* Berkeley: University of California Press, 2000.

Gamble, Jos. *Shanghai in Transition: Changing Perspectives and Social Contours of a Chinese Metropolis.* London: RoutledgeCurzon, 2003.

Gerth, Karl. *China Made: Consumer Culture and the Creation of the Nation.* Cambridge, MA: Harvard University Press, 2003.

Yan Yunxiang. The Politics of Consumerism in Chinese Society. In *China Briefing, 2000: The Continuing Transformation*, ed. Tyrene White, pp. 159–193. Armonk, NY: M. E. Sharpe, 2000.

***Karl Gerth***

# COPPER AND SILVER, 1800–1950

China's monetary system at the dawn of the nineteenth century was bimetallic—it was based on copper and silver. Chinese currencies were different from those prevalent in the West, where gold, paper, and government regulation had by then begun to play a significant monetary role.

## DENOMINATIONS AND VALUE

The bulk of China's late-imperial monetary system was made up of low-denomination copper-cast coins (*tongqian*), which circulated widely in the rural hinterland of the country, as well as in the more commercialized eastern seaboard. Higher-denomination money was mostly in the form of silver ingots—known to Westerners as *sycee*—or foreign-minted silver dollar coins. The imperial court regulated neither form of silver money until the early twentieth century.

Traditionally, a string (*diao*) of one thousand copper coins was supposed to be on par with one tael or *liang* of silver (approximately 37.5 grams). In practice, however, the copper-silver exchange rate fluctuated according to the availability of either metal at any point in time. Sycee weighed about 50 tael, but there could be considerable variations of ingot weight and fineness even within the same province. The word *sycee* was an English derivative of the Cantonese pronunciation for "pure silk," the equivalent in Mandarin being *dingzi* or *yuanbao*. In South China, a good-quality silver ingot was thought to possess a shiny veneer reminiscent of silk.

The other form of high-denomination money was silver coins imported from Spanish America (*yinyuan*). Such coins were particularly common in coastal cities where merchants exchanged them in return for time-honored Chinese exports like tea and silk. New World bullion was carried onboard Spanish galleons, and trickled into China via Acapulco and Manila. It is estimated that around 400 million Spanish American silver dollar coins (about 280 million silver taels) had been transported across the Pacific by 1821, offsetting a secular decline in mining ventures for monetary purposes in China itself.

## CONTROL OF SILVER

In 1821 Mexico formally gained its independence from Spain, and its symbol of sovereignty—the snake-devouring eagle—replaced Spain's Pillars of Hercules on all coins exported via Acapulco. The net inflow of Mexican-minted silver coins (*yingyang*) into China continued, albeit unevenly, until the breakdown of the Canton (Guangzhou) foreign trade system in the 1830s, and the subsequent Opium Wars (1839–1842, 1856–1860). In the 1850s, imports of Bengali opium finally succeeded in eroding China's longstanding trade surplus with the West. In order to purchase opium from British and other Western trading houses, Chinese merchants had to pay with silver currency. This resulted in a net outflow of the metal, and disruption to the silver-copper exchange rate.

British trading houses had faced enormous difficulty in selling manufactured goods in China: opium and silver coins had been coveted more than anything else that the British could offer in return for tea and silk. Consequently, opium became the great equalizer of trade between British India and China. As a result of the outflow of silver from China overseas, it became dearer domestically, and the traditional 1:1,000 parity with copper was quickly eroded. Yet, in other parts of the world, silver was becoming relatively cheaper during the latter half of the nineteenth century due to a spate of prospecting discoveries and improvements to mining technology.

The late-Qing imperial court (1895–1911) and successive early-Republican governments (1912–1927) saw China disintegrating into warring satrapies, with warlords divvying up the country's dwindling fiscal revenue, expropriating private silver stocks, imposing arbitrary taxes, debasing copper coinage, and issuing unbacked paper currency. Some satrapies went as far as purchasing modern minting machinery to debase their coinage. Thus, copper and traditional casting techniques gradually gave way to alloyed subsidiary coinage.

The breakdown of central authority also precipitated a flight of silver capital from the war-torn hinterland to foreign-controlled and relatively secure Shanghai. There, this capital underpinned the growth of China's embryonic modern industry and financial institutions. When World War I broke out in 1914, Chinese industrialists in Shanghai were well placed to produce substitutes for increasingly expensive Western consumer goods and shipping machinery. At the same time, the surge of Chinese nationalism helped galvanize Chinese banks to support domestic industry and set up clearing mechanisms collaboratively.

In the early 1920s, locally minted Republican silver dollars, subsidiary alloy coins, and privately issued Chinese banknotes superseded China's traditional bimetallic standard in a helter-skelter fashion. It was not until the Guomindang (GMD) had swept to power in 1927 that monetary unification started to be enforced on breakaway provinces as part and parcel of a nation-building agenda.

## REFORM

GMD resolve to bring Chinese currency in line with the West manifested itself in a succession of bold reforms: the enforcement of banknote silver-reserve policy and establishment of an embryonic central bank (1928); the introduction of a gold-pegged Customs Units to offset China's deteriorating terms of trade (1930); the phasing out of cast-copper coins, ingots, and regional tael variations in favor of uniform dollar coinage (1933); and the proclamation of the *fabi* as sole legal tender (1935). *Fabi*, or legal notes, were designed to supplant all currencies commonly used in China that the GMD central government had no control over—be they issued by foreign banks or by wayward provincial governments. A GMD edict required that all other forms of money—particularly silver bullion—be nationalized; they were to be either disposed of or handed over to central-government backed banks in return for *fabi*.

The *fabi* reform effectively severed the centuries-old link between silver and Chinese currency. It came on the heels of what most economic historians see as severe domestic as well as global crises. Pressured by regional mining interests in the U.S. Congress, the Franklin Roosevelt (1882–1945) administration embarked in 1934 on its Silver Purchase Policy, which was designed to lift the United States out of recession. One of the immediate side effects of this policy was that China—now the only country in the world to cling to the silver standard—saw rapid erosion in its terms of trade. This erosion, in turn, slashed exports and crippled the industrial base of China's urban economy.

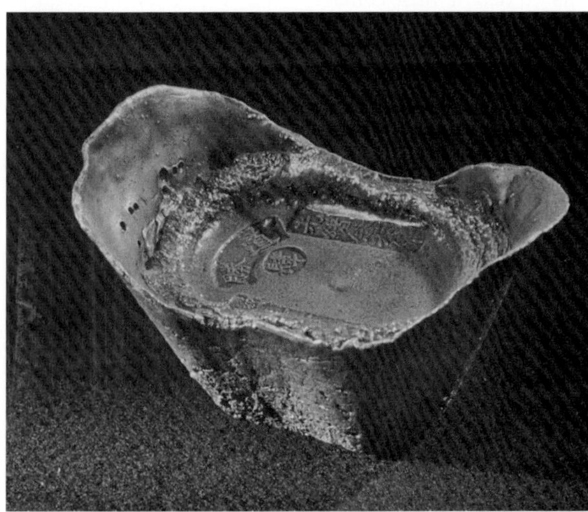

***Silver ingot, 1943.*** *At the beginning of the 1800s, China's monetary system relied primarily on two metals, silver and copper. Much of China's trade with the West involved the exchange of tea and silk for silver coins, a practice that continued until the British discovered an equally lucrative commodity desired by the Chinese, opium.* FRITZ GORO/TIME LIFE PICTURES/GETTY IMAGES

Worse still, China's money supply was being depleted because the U.S. price of silver edged above the official exchange value of the Chinese silver dollar, resulting in incessant waves of sycee exports from Shanghai to America either directly or via London. The implication for China's economy was double-pronged. First, after years of inflation and debasement, China's metallic currency was appreciating artificially on the cross-rates. It made imports cheaper, thus dampening the relative price of agricultural produce and hitting living standards in the rural hinterland. But, much more importantly, it made simple business sense to buy silver dollars in Shanghai with foreign currency and melt them into silver.

After repeated Chinese representations to the Roosevelt administration to change course had failed through late 1934 and early 1935, a daring initiative took shape in discussions between Kong Xiangxi (H. H. Kung), Song Ziwen (T. V. Soong), and Chiang Kai-shek (Jiang Jieshi). Though they were driven by different personal agendas, the three concurred that China should ride on the momentum afforded by U.S. policy to divorce Chinese currency of silver. This move, they hoped, would help the GMD government claw back greater latitude in the monetary realm, and reap a windfall from the sell off of the silver stock while world prices for the metal were at their highest for decades.

At the end of 1935, a year of tense anticipation, a deus ex machina for China's monetary crisis loomed large. The proclamation of the much-awaited *fabi* reform in November saw the Chinese government offering its nationalized silver stock for sale in the United States—including silver that was yet to be advanced by expatriate financial institutions—in return for U.S. dollars.

The *fabi* reform was endorsed by the British government, which sought a rapprochement with a once hostile GMD. The British ambassador to China, Sir Alexander Cadogan (1884–1968), issued a special regulation under the China Order-in-Council 1925, which prohibited payments in silver on Chinese soil by British individuals or institutions, and set out penalties for offenders. Concomitantly, the British made arrangements for a swift transition from silver-based currency to a managed one in the crown colony of Hong Kong.

Short-lived as it may have been, the success of the *fabi* reform had become almost synonymous in much of the pertinent literature in the West with the Leith-Ross mission to China, conducted between September 21, 1935, and June 23, 1936. Recent studies have shown that Sir Frederick Leith-Ross (1887–1968) was instrumental in pulling the British government, diplomatic corps, and business lobby behind the reform. However, these studies also argue that it was the GMD government, not Leith-Ross, who devised the particulars of the reform, and determined its timing without material assistance from the British government and in the face of dogged opposition from British expatriate bankers.

Arguably, the hyperinflation that gripped China from 1937 to 1949 was inevitable in view of the onset of the Sino-Japanese War (1937–1945) and the unbridled military expenditure on both sides. The ultimate collapse of the *fabi* fiat currency and its replacement with a short-lived, nominally gold-pegged paper currency (*jinyuan quan*) in 1948 damaged the GMD's reputation as an economic and monetary reformer.

After 1936, the United States became increasingly involved alongside Britain in attempts to prop up the GMD currency through stabilization boards and wartime credits. The failure of Anglo-American efforts to stem runaway inflation lent credibility to Chinese Communist Party propaganda, and may have played a significant role in its rise to power. It was not until the establishment of a command economy on the mainland in the mid-1950s that inflation finally tapered off.

**SEE ALSO** *Mines and Metallurgy, 1800–1949; Money and Monetary Policy, 1800–1927.*

**BIBLIOGRAPHY**


Brandt, Loren, and Thomas J. Sargent. Interpreting New Evidence about China and U.S. Silver Purchases. *Journal of Monetary Economics* 23 (1989): 31–51.

Burdekin, Richard C. K., and Fang Wang. A Novel End to the Big Inflation in China in 1950. *Economics of Planning* 32, 3 (1999): 211–229.

Friedman, Milton. Franklin D. Roosevelt, Silver, and China. *Journal of Political Economy* 100, 1 (1992): 62–83.

Horesh, Niv. *The Bund and Beyond: British Banks, Banknote Issuance, and Monetary Policy in China, 1842–1937.* New Haven, CT: Yale University Press, 2009.

Kann, Eduard. *The Currencies of China.* Shanghai: Kelly & Walsh, 1927.

Lai Cheng-Chung and Joshua Jr-Shiang Gau. The Chinese Silver Standard Economy and the 1929 Great Depression. *Australian Economic History Review* 43, 2 (2003): 155–168.

Lin Manhong (Man-houng Lin). *China Upside Down: Currency, Society, and Ideologies, 1808–1856.* Cambridge, MA: Harvard University Press, 2006.

Lin Weiying (W.Y. Lin). *The New Monetary System of China: A Personal Interpretation.* Shanghai: Kelly & Walsh, 1936.

Peng Xinwei. *Zhongguo huobi shi* [The history of Chinese currency]. Shanghai: Shanghai Renmin Chubanshe, 1958.

People's Bank of China, comp. *Zhonghua minguo huobishi ziliao* [Materials on the monetary history of Republican China]. 2 vols. Shanghai: Shanghai Renmin Chubanshe, 1989.

Rawski, Thomas G. Milton Friedman, Silver, and China. *Journal of Political Economy* 101, 4 (1993): 755–758.

Salter, Arthur. *China and Silver.* New York: Economic Forum, 1934.

Wei Jianyou. *Zhongguo jindai huobi shi* [The history of currency in modern China]. Shanghai: Qunlian Chubanshe, 1955.

Young, Arthur N. *China's Nation-Building Effort, 1927–1937: The Financial and Economic Record.* Stanford, CA: Hoover Institution Press, 1971.

Zhang Jia'ao (Chang Kia-ngau). *The Inflationary Spiral: The Experience in China, 1939–1950.* Cambridge, MA: MIT Press, 1958.

Zheng Junli, dir. *Wu ya yu ma que* [Crows and sparrows]. Shanghai: Kunlun Studios, 1949. CCP propaganda film.

Zhou Shunxin (Chou Shun-hsin). *The Chinese Inflation, 1937–1949.* New York: Columbia University Press, 1963.


***Niv Horesh***

## CORRUPTION

The Chinese term for corruption, *fubai*, refers in the first instance to the negative side of a system, an organization, structures, or measures. When used to refer to people or a government, *fubai* means moral and ethical degeneration. The word is used mainly for moral matters and stands for everything that does not conform to the ruling moral climate. This can range from crimes committed by party officials to political and ideological misdemeanors violating party norms or the current party line. The word *tanwu*, meaning the abuse of a public position to line one's own pockets, is more similar to the English term *corruption*.

Corruption in the Chinese system has a long history. An emperor who was corrupt had betrayed his heavenly mandate. Excessive public corruption was often the cause of rebellions and uprisings. Corruption hence became associated with phases in the political cycle in which the checks and balances on abuse of power were weakened or nonexistent and the central power had lost its ability to protect society.

In the People's Republic as well, corruption has been an ever present phenomenon, although it was defined differently in different periods according to political aims. In politically radical times, ideological deviation, allegedly anti-socialist or bureaucratic behavior, was identified as corruption. Right after the founding of the People's Republic, the party made considerable efforts to combat corruption, albeit with shifting contents and varying goals. In the 1950s fighting corruption was focused toward capitalists and bureaucrats; during the Cultural Revolution, toward bourgeois or reactionary thought. Thus, the leadership used the reproach of corruption for various political ends. Since the late 1950s the party-state attempted to fight corruption by means of political movements. The movement concept was grounded in the conviction that corrupt behavior was due to individual misbehavior, a flaw of character or awareness. By means of ideological education and reeducation, with the aid of manual labor, officials' corrupt behavior could be thwarted. As this concept was not successful, discipline-control commissions were reestablished in 1978. Since then the party-state has attempted to curb corruption through inner-party cleansings, anticorruption movements, a multitude of laws, and the establishment of surveillance bodies.

In public, however, the topic was mainly taboo. Only at the end of the 1970s, as reform policies began to emerge, were the media permitted to report on cases of corruption. To begin with, the Gang of Four were held responsible for all corruption, but the dramatic increase in corruption in the 1980s made new explanations necessary. The party leadership spoke of "unhealthy tendencies" (*bujiankan de qingxiang*) before reintroducing the term *fubai* (corruption) in the mid-1980s.

Undoubtedly, the reforms after 1978 have favored the increase of corruption. Reasons for the increase are enhanced market and economic liberalization on the one side and the party's continued monopoly on political power on the other. Such liberalization gave rise to a change of values and a new value system competing with or contradicting the old system. Slogans like "Letting some people get rich first" and "It doesn't matter if the cat is black or white, as long as it catches mice" spawned uncertainty in values and rights in society. Discrimination against new ascendant classes (private entrepreneurs, the middle class) and traditional social groups (peasants) also promoted corruption.

In addition, there are factors inherent in the system, such as the overcentralization of the economy, the party's monopoly position, the lack of a clear division between public and private spheres, a lack of transparency, and a lack of checks and balances. There are economic factors (bureaucratic planning, state control of resources), cognitive factors (the failure of the revolutionary model, changes in values), and development deficiencies (shortages of goods and resources, the urban-rural divide). The introduction of reforms has led to an increase in corruption (e.g., through decentralization, opening to the outside world, the extension of market mechanisms, migration, and the diversification of property structures). Since the party's monopoly on power has not been affected, and since no instruments to control cadres have been introduced, officials can freely line their own pockets by using the party monopoly on power to distribute goods and resources. Through decentralization, the local echelons of the bureaucracy have garnered greater decision-making power and hence more opportunities for corrupt behavior. Illegal transfers of arable land, for instance, was favored by the weakening of the surveillance of higher echelons. This happened despite the fact that local leaders are not only agents of the central leadership but also advocates of local interests.

Among the most significant delicts of corruption are illegal transfers of public property into private property, the embezzlement of public funds, and the purchase and selling of public offices or votes. To transfer public property into private property, a manager of a state-owned enterprise may purchase state assets at far below their value, or an official may illegally acquire land, paying only a small or no compensation, or an official may illegally sell land, lining the profits into his own pockets. In many cases, local officials, development companies, and banks are collaborating. Since the turn of the twenty-first century, globalized forms of corruption have emerged: Bribes are paid not in China but abroad (in form of bank accounts, real estate, or expensive voyages) or not until the person bribed has retired. The latter practice diminishes the risk of being detected. It also indicates a high level of trust among the persons involved.

Here, too, China's loss of its guiding ideology plays a crucial role. Party members are no longer goal-oriented toward political objectives but opportunity-oriented toward possibilities for gaining individual advantages, advancing a career, or exploiting power for money. This change in the party's function reinforces corrupt behavior among members of the party.

The costs of corruption for the legitimacy of the political system are high: general distrust toward (particularly local) officials and hence toward the party-state; squandered public resources; political instability; evasion of central policies; and attenuation of innovations, investment, and enterprises' initiatives. Corruption abets growing income disparities and has unintended distribution effects. Consequently, the party's claim to power becomes fragile.

Corruption should be construed to comprise not only criminal acts (such as bribery and embezzlement), but also traditional forms of favoritism-seeking behavior—such as using social connections to officials (*guanxi*), relying on patronage, networks and engaging in nepotism—through which individuals try to gain influence, power, or advantages. Since informal groups and networks of connections ignore state, ethical, moral, social, and political norms to gain power or advantages for those involved, this behavior has to be regarded as part and parcel of corruption.

According to the theory of new institutionalism, *guanxi* networks compete with the legal system in providing a system for accomplishing various tasks. Contracts are bypassed by means of *guanxi*, and this undermines the legal system. As social actors have previously invested heavily into *guanxi*, they are strongly motivated to reap benefits from these investments rather than turning to legal procedures. This, in turn, hinders the development of legality. Owing to their illegal character, corrupt practices cannot be implemented under the formal legal system. *Guanxi* networks provide the infrastructure for corruption, and thus reduce the necessary transaction costs. Even if *guanxi* networks and corruption are not identical, such networks form an alternative system into which corrupt practices might be embedded.

Interestingly, comparative research on corruption has revealed that in countries like China, corruption is not a major constraint to foreign investments. In China, according

***Hand-decorated notice board, Beijing, February 5, 2008.*** *As illustrated in this cartoon drawing on a Communist Party building, government officials actively campaign against corruption and bribery, imploring citizens not to offer excessive gifts to teachers and doctors.* © ADRIAN BRADSHAW/EPA/CORBIS

to a report by the World Bank, corruption is counted as a fixed cost and, moreover, is calculable. Through bribery, personal connections are developed, trust is created, and norms of mutual commitment emerge. China's institutions and bureaucracy are relatively stable, and problems are solved by informal means. Trust between strangers is crucial. In societies with high levels of public trust (trust within society and among members of society) like China, corruption fosters efficiency and is therefore less detrimental to economic development.

As the population is massively discontent with corruption, and because the party leadership has realized that corruption threatens the party's credibility and legitimacy, it continuously carries out anticorruption campaigns. Yet the people are skeptical of the success of such campaigns. The more so as they have not prevented further increases in corruption. Without the approval of higher echelons within the party, criminal prosecution of corrupt officials is not permitted. As party patrons frequently protect culprits, legal bodies are unable to take legal action. This set of circumstances impedes the fight against corruption.

The party leadership attempts to legitimize itself by claiming to be the main force in fighting corruption. But in fact it fights corruption primarily at the lower and middle levels. Owing to its power and multistrand privileges, the political elite is not directly involved in corrupt acts. Hence, the criminal prosecution of corruption is an issue that does not affect the elite, albeit time and again spectacular cases of corruption have been exposed. In a sense, corruption is functional, in that it establishes the legitimacy of the political system. However, corruption can also be detrimental to legitimacy when high-level officials are involved—if such cases become widely known among the people, the party state reacts. Fighting corruption at lower levels distracts attention from corruption at higher levels, and it demonstrates that the party leadership is resolutely opposed to corruption. Yet if the party leadership decisively fought against corruption at the lower levels, it would have to take on most local cadres and hence would be fighting against itself. Thus, fighting corruption also spawns tensions between the center on the one side and the provincial and local levels on the other side. Instead, the central leadership utilizes fighting corruption as a strategy to enforce political directives and goals or in the interest of economic, social, and political stability. Officials counteracting the directives of the center are removed as "corrupt."

Certainly, the number of laws and regulations against market corruption has exploded in recent years. Yet only in single cases are the people concerned severely punished. The risk to corrupt officials lies less in legal persecution than in political condemnation by way of expulsion from the party or disciplinary sanctions that might bring a political career, and the selling of power, to an end. As officials conceive of the party foremost as a career ladder, but one without major income incentives (as salaries of officials are not high), the individual risk is apprehended as rather small. The more so as an expulsion from the party might be compensated by more profitable private economic activities sponsored by companies seeking to lobby the government. Moreover, the expectation of high profits by means of corruption by far outweighs the risk of being detected and facing criminal prosecution. Public prosecution is unlikely as long as corrupt activities do not touch upon sensitive domains, do not affect the general policies of the center or the interests of rival networks, and particularly if one is protected by a patron.

The continuous enacting of new legal regulations and laws that in detail seek to curb or prevent corruption will not solve the problems. It is the political and social system (including traditional patterns of behavior) that favors corruption, not a deficiency of legal regulations. Efficiently combating corruption would require social transparency, public and social monitoring of officials (including freedom of the press), and an independent judiciary. Required is a basket of essential changes, as, for instance, the emerging of public control and checks and balances stemming from nongovernmental organizations, an independent legal system, and new structures of awareness in society.

The establishment of the National Bureau for Corruption Prevention in 2007 signifies a shift in focus from penalization toward prevention. In the future, income, assets, bank accounts, and journeys abroad of local official will be made public. But right after the establishing of this bureau, it was already noted that those goals are not easily realized, as resistance among local officials will be tremendous. It is therefore doubtful that the National Bureau for Corruption Prevention can solve the problem.

**SEE ALSO** *Communist Party; Education: Moral Education; Inspection and Audit; Nepotism and Guanxi; People's Liberation Army.*

**BIBLIOGRAPHY**

Kinkley, Jeffrey C. *Corruption and Realism in Late Socialist China.* Stanford, CA: Stanford University Press, 2007.

Lü, Xiaobo. *Cadres and Corruption: The Organizational Involution of the Chinese Communist Party.* Stanford, CA: Stanford University Press, 2000.

Manion, Melanie. *Corruption by Design: Building Clean Government in Mainland China and Hong Kong.* Cambridge, MA: Harvard University Press, 2004.

Sun, Yan. *Corruption and Market in Contemporary China.* Ithaca, NY: Cornell University Press, 2004.

***Thomas Heberer***

# COSMOLOGY

Cosmology, as a description of the nature and structure of the cosmos, has had a long and complex history in China. The first systematic cosmological statements date back to as early as the fourth and third century BCE, and under the first bureaucratic imperial regimes in China, namely the Qin (221–206 BCE) and Han (206 BCE–220 CE) empires, a *correlative cosmology* emerged as the dominant framework for understanding the universe. Politically, it became a standard language for legitimizing and criticizing the imperial state, and culturally, it served as the conceptual basis for such diverse fields of practice as literature, arts, and religion. It was also the founding paradigm for the indigenous scientific tradition in China, in fields such as alchemy, astronomy, and medicine. Its preeminent status in both the political and cultural spheres persisted until the end of the nineteenth century. Only with the end of the imperial era in the early twentieth century was it at last displaced with the growing predominance of Western science and technology in East Asia. Nevertheless, its displacement was not total, for it continues to persist in particular cultural fields, such as popular religion and traditional medicine, and as such it still figures prominently as a popular worldview in modern China.

## CORRELATIVE COSMOLOGY: BASIC TERMS AND CONCEPTS

To understand how correlative cosmology has figured in modern China, an understanding of its basic terms and concepts is essential. The fundamental premise of this cosmology is that the entire world and all things within it are constituted by a single substance, simply put, that the cosmos is monistic. This basic constituent is called *qi*, sometimes translated as "vital force." While all things are constituted by it, they are distinct from one another because the *qi* of each pertains to a different level of refinement. Generally, the *qi* that makes up an inanimate object is less refined than that of an animate being, and rarefied entities such as the human mind are made up of even more refined *qi*. This all-pervading *qi* is not simply a static mass, however, but is in constant movement throughout the universe, ceaselessly changing and interacting with itself in sundry guises according to a complex set of internal mechanisms and dynamics.

Various rubrics were devised to describe these movements of *qi*. Arguably, the most well-known is *yin-yang* dualism, which classifies all *qi* as being in either a latent (*yin*) or active (*yang*) state, and ascribes all movements and changes within the cosmos to an interplay between these two complementary and mutually implicated qualities. Another important rubric is the five phases (*wuxing*). This denotes the productive and destructive relations between the following five materials: wood, fire, earth, metal, and water. The productive sequence (i.e., wood produces fire, fire produces earth, etc.) and destructive sequence (i.e., fire conquers metal, metal destroys wood, etc.) refer to the different processes of change in the cosmos. In addition, the theory also held that movements in the universe are caused by cosmic resonance (*ganying*) between entities of similar nature (i.e., with the same *qi* composition). Like responds to like, just as plucking a string will cause another string tuned to the same note to resonate and vibrate spontaneously. The all-pervading *qi* in the cosmos is constantly driven by these different dynamic forces, and their spontaneously generated movements are the endless changes that happen to and in all things in the universe. Nothing falls outside this cosmological system—everything is constituted by *qi*, naturally resonates with each other, and is subject to the same spontaneous processes of change.

## COSMOLOGY IN THE LATE QING AND MODERN PERIOD

In early modern China, through to the end of the nineteenth century at least, this correlative cosmology continued to be a predominant worldview. Politically, it was the basis of the state cult. According to the theory of cosmic resonance, improper actions by the state were thought to produce repercussions in the natural world, and natural disasters were seen as signs of improper state actions. Accordingly, the Qing court administered an elaborate program of ritual meant to generate harmonious effects in the cosmos. The grand state rituals were performed in the capital by the emperor himself, and the rest of the ritual program extended all the way down to the county level. Moreover, special rites were carried out to redress supposed disturbances in the cosmos. For instance, the late-Qing court often performed rainmaking rites for the periodic drought in the North China plain, and failure to bring rain reflected on the supposed relative lack of virtue in the emperor and the imperial court at large.

Outside of the political world, correlative cosmology also informed a wide range of cultural practices in late-Qing China. Perhaps most significant, it persisted as the basis for the indigenous scientific tradition, although Western science, with its own distinct cosmology, had been introduced in China since the seventeenth century. Early-modern Western cosmology, as embodied in Newtonian physics, is radically different. For instance, Western cosmology does not recognize any monistic substance like *qi*, but subscribes to an atomistic worldview in which the cosmos consists simply of physical matter made up of indivisible building blocks. In this Newtonian universe, movements are the result not of spontaneous resonance between bits of matter of similar composition but of one entity acting upon another in accordance with natural mechanical law. In the late Qing, though this Western cosmology was basically familiar to the political and cultural elite, it nevertheless did not seriously challenge the dominant correlative cosmology in the study of the natural world and development of medicine. Throughout the early modern period, until the end of the nineteenth century, correlative cosmology remained the fundamental framework for understanding the nature and structure of the universe.

In the first decades of the twentieth century, however, correlative cosmology was significantly displaced from its long-standing preeminent position. The fall of the Qing dynasty in 1912 brought the imperial state cult to an end, and the succeeding modern regimes, namely the Republican government and the People's Republic of China, completely disavowed its validity. Moreover, the impressive power of Western military might, as demonstrated in the series of wars waged against China by the Western powers and Japan at the turn of the twentieth century, also led to a widespread acceptance of the superiority of Western technology and, by extension, its scientific tradition. Hence, both politically and culturally the status of correlative cosmology sharply declined in the modern period. Its devaluation was by no means absolute, however. While it may not be espoused by the state or the elite intellectual community anymore, to the present day it continues to serve as the foundation for a whole host of popular cultural practices, such as traditional medicine and popular religions. All in all, despite its displacement from the official and elite sphere in the past century, correlative cosmology continues to figure prominently in modern China as a popular worldview for understanding the cosmos and the place of human beings within it.

**SEE ALSO** *State Cult.*

### BIBLIOGRAPHY

Bodde, Derk. *Chinese Thought, Society, and Science: The Intellectual and Social Background of Science and Technology in Pre-modern China.* Honolulu: University of Hawaii Press, 1991.

Elman, Benjamin A. *On Their Own Terms: Science in China, 1550–1900.* Cambridge, MA: Harvard University Press, 2005.

Graham, A. C. *Yin-Yang and the Nature of Correlative Thinking.* Singapore: Institute of East Asian Philosophies, National University of Singapore, 1986.

Granet, Marcel. *La pensée chinoise.* Paris: Éditions Albin Michel, 1950.

Henderson, John. *The Development and Decline of Chinese Cosmology.* New York: Columbia University Press, 1984.

Needham, Joseph. *Science and Civilisation in China.* Vol. 2, *History of Scientific Thought.* Cambridge, U.K.: Cambridge University Press, 1991.

Puett, Michael J. *To Become a God: Cosmology, Sacrifice, and Self-Divinization in Early China.* Cambridge, MA: Harvard University Asia Center, 2004.

Wang, Aihe. *Cosmology and Political Culture in Early China.* New York: Cambridge University Press, 2000.

Zito, Angela. Re-presenting Sacrifice: Cosmology and the Editing of Texts. *Qing shi wenti* 5, 2 (December 1984): 47–78.

***Vincent Leung***

# CUI JIAN

## *1961–*

Called the father and godfather of Chinese rock and China's Bob Dylan, Cui Jian is an influential figure in popular music. He is best known for his contributions to Chinese rock music (*Zhongguo yaogun yinyue*) and as a symbol of rebellion and alienation from mainstream society and government, but Cui's output spans from classical and pop music to punk, hip-hop, and jazz. His lyrics allude to problems in the Communist Party, traditional and urban society, and commercialization and obsessions with wealth in post-1980s China. He has been a musical activist for various causes.

Growing up in Beijing in an ethnic Korean family, Cui learned trumpet from his father. He performed with the Beijing Philharmonic Orchestra from 1981 to 1986 and with popular bands. His 1985 performance of "Have Nothing" ("Yiwu suoyou") at a Beijing talent contest and his central position in early underground rock contributed to his reputation as the "father of Chinese rock." His hybrid music combines Chinese traditional and Western popular musical instruments, influences from groups such as the Talking Heads and Rolling Stones, and Northwest Wind (*Xibeifeng*), a style loosely based on folk music from northwest China. His 1987 album *Rock and Roll on the New Long March* (*Xin changzheng lushang de yaogun*) with the band ADO became a rallying point for the countercultural youth scene. In 1989 he performed "Opportunists" ("Touji fenzi") in Tiananmen Square, and "Have Nothing" served as one of the protestors' anthems. His 1991 album *Solution* (*Jiejue*) included "A Piece of Red Cloth" ("Yi kuai hongbu"), which Cui often performed while wearing a red blindfold, and a rock version of the Communist classic "Nanniwan." His performances of these songs were interpreted by some as anti-Communist Party, and the government periodically banned his shows in large-scale venues. Yet Cui continued to perform in China in other venues and overseas, as well as in large-scale venues when the bans were relaxed.

Albums such as the 1998 *Power of the Powerless* (*Wuneng de liliang*) were released through state-run companies, and Cui sang at high-profile events such as the 1988 Seoul Olympics (when he performed "Have Nothing" for a television audience). He launched a 1990 concert tour to support the Eleventh Asian Games, but the Chinese government cancelled the tour after Cui performed "Eggs Under the Red Flag" ("Hongqi xia de dan") while wearing a red blindfold. The government's fluctuating censorship of Cui Jian stemmed from a range of factors, including variations within the party and administrative units in the government as well as the uneven distribution of changing ideologies. At times, particular units within the government made use of Cui Jian and his popularity for their own purposes, such as to generate support and funding for the Olympics. Stricter bans seem to have been precipitated by powerful, older CCP leaders who objected to lyrics and images that negatively reflected on Party history and its cherished images. Such bans, in turn, were loosened in relation to periods of greater opening and relaxation of control over the arts.

Cui also has participated in national and artistic movements, including antipiracy and antilipsyncing movements in 2000 to 2002. He was an organizer for the 2002 Yunnan Snow Mountain Music Festival and the 2005 Gengentala Grassland Festival. He performed in concerts in support of the Beijing Olympics in 2007 to 2008 and in benefits for earthquake victims in 2008. He collaborated with artists in other media and acted in or wrote music for feature films such as Zhang Yuan's *Beijing Bastards* (*Beijing zazhong*, 1989), Jiang Wen's *Devils at the Doorstep* (*Guizi laile*, 2000), and Yu Zhong's *Roots and Branches* (*Wode xiongdi jiemei*, 2001). Cui's 2005 album *Show Your Colors* (*Gei ni yidian yanse*) was based on music composed for the Hong Kong Modern Dance Company.

**SEE ALSO** *Film Industry: Sixth Generation Filmmakers; Music, Popular.*

### BIBLIOGRAPHY

Baranovitch, Nimrod. *China's New Voices: Popular Music, Ethnicity, Gender, and Politics, 1978–1997.* Berkeley: University of California Press, 2003.

Brace, Tim, and Paul Friedlander. Rock and Roll on the New Long March: Popular Music, Cultural Identity, and Political Opposition in the People's Republic of China. In *Rockin' the Boat: Mass Music and Mass Movements,* ed. Reebee Garofalo, 115–127. Boston: South End Press, 1992.

Cui Jian's Official Web site. http://www.cuijian.com.

Jones, Andrew F. *Like a Knife: Ideology and Genre in Contemporary Chinese Popular Music.* Ithaca, NY: East Asia Program, Cornell University, 1992.

Zhao, Jianwei. *Cui Jian zai Yiwu suoyou zhong nahan: Zhongguo yaogun beiwanglu* [Cui Jian laments in "Having Nothing": A record on Chinese rock]. Beijing: Beijing Shifan Daxue Chubanshe (Beijing Normal University Press), 1992.

***Sue Tuohy***

# CULTURAL POLICY

The Chinese Communist Party's cultural policy is an integral part of an overall policy to achieve its political objectives under specific social conditions. Mao's first systematic attempt to define culture and cultural policy appears in his 1940 essay "On New Democracy" (1965a). In an analysis of what he called the "new democratic culture" as historically related to the May Fourth cultural movement, Mao argued for cultural practice supporting the Chinese revolution and his vision of the Communist Party in China's political life. "Any given culture (as an ideological form)," wrote Mao, "is a reflection of the politics and economics of a given society.…The form of culture is first determined by the political and economic form, and only then does it operate on and influence the given political and economic form" (1965a, p. 342). Following a typical analytical exposition of China's "historical characteristics," Mao proposed dismantling the existing order and constructing a "new-democratic culture" to revitalize China. This culture would be "the proletarian-led, anti-imperialist and anti-feudal culture of the broad masses" (Mao 1965a, pp. 372–373).

Mao's "Talks at the Yan'an Forum on Literature and Art" (1965b), not necessarily a policy document when he delivered these speeches (1942), is now generally accepted as the most systematic articulation of Mao's, and hence the Communist Party's, position on literature and art. Its publication marked the emergence of a more coherent policy understanding of cultural practice among the Communist Party's leadership. Central to Mao's analysis of the value of revolutionary art and literature is a political instrumentalism defined by the Marxist revolutionary ideology. Mao argued that art and literature as a specific form of social consciousness were inseparable from social reality, the most salient feature of which was the configuration of the social classes. Forms of cultural practice must respond to the demands of such social reality. "Works of literature and art, as ideological forms," stated Mao, "are products of the reflection in the human brain of the life of a given society. Revolutionary literature and art are the products of the reflection of the life of the people in the brains of revolutionary writers and artists" (1965b, p. 81). The policy implications of his attempt to define art and literature as a mirror of social reality are fully brought out in the dictum that revolutionary literature and art should "follow the correct path of development and provide better help to other revolutionary work in facilitating the overthrow of our national enemy and the accomplishment of the task of national liberation" (Mao 1965b, p. 69).

The immediate revolutionary task at the time Mao delivered these speeches was to resist and eventually defeat the Japanese imperialists. Although politically significant, the talks were not meant to be a sophisticated theoretical exposition of literature or art. Rather, they were almost entirely shaped by a political pragmatism that unapologetically advocated literature and art as part of the Communist Party's revolutionary cause. Subsequently revised and refined (McDougall 1980), they provided an ideological foundation and framework for the cultural policy that would be practiced in the years to come. In fact, shortly after the publication of these talks, the Communist Party's Propaganda Department issued, in November 1943, a directive that presented these talks as the Communist Party's "basic policy" and called on all Communist Party cultural practitioners to study Mao's "Talks on Literature and Art" and to act in accordance with the principles articulated therein (Hu Huilin 2006, p. 200).

## INSTRUMENTS OF CULTURAL POLICY

The Central Propaganda Department (Zhonggong Zhongyang Xuanchuan Bu), the Communist Party's ideological think tank established in 1924, has long been a key department in the organizational structure of the Communist Party, though, like many other party and government departments, it was suspended during the Cultural Revolution (1966–1969) and the years immediately following that period. Within the political and social organization of China, one of the main tasks of the Central Propaganda Department is to establish and consolidate ideological uniformity and homogeneity, as required by the very structure of the Chinese state. The Propaganda Department has thus been a key executive unit in disseminating, promoting, and implementing the Communist Party's policies in the domain of cultural practice. Responsible for supervising ideological work and shaping public opinion throughout the country, it is endowed with the necessary political and administrative authority to coordinate the work of such key departments and organizations as the State Press and Publication Administration (Xinwen Chubanshu), the Chinese Academy of Social Sciences (Zhongguo Shehuikexue Yuan), the *People's Daily* (*Renmin Ribao*), the State Administration of Radio, Film, and Television (Guangbo Dianying Dianshi Zhongju), and the New China News Agency (Xinhua She) (see the Web site of the Central Propaganda Department [Zhonggong Zhongyang Xuanchuan Bu]).

The Ministry of Culture (Wenhua Bu) under the State Council may be considered the civil counterpart of the Propaganda Department. The scope of its responsibilities include proposing specific policies, regulations, and rules governing literary and artistic production; considering and proposing strategies for the development of cultural business in China; promoting experimental art work; coordinating the organization of major national cultural events; formulating policies governing the operation of cultural enterprises; monitoring cultural markets; and so on. Less ideological and more administrative in its given responsibilities, the Ministry of Culture is the highest managerial body concerned with the day-to-day running of practical cultural affairs and cultural establishments. Both the Propaganda Department and the Ministry of Culture have regional and local offices throughout China.

## CULTURAL POLICY DURING THE MAO YEARS

The Communist Party's cultural policy required structural uniformity in the social organization of cultural labor. The founding of the People's Republic in 1949 led to a nationwide deprivatization of cultural entities and establishments. Private performing companies, film studios, museums, cinemas, live theaters, and other establishments were converted to state-owned enterprises. Artists, writers, actors, and actresses had to be on the state payroll to continue their professional careers. State funds were budgeted and allocated for all operational purposes in the broad area of cultural production. The single funding source was determined by the sociopolitical structure of China: Socialism by definition does not permit private ownership of property. Yet such a mode of funding for cultural production in China has had unprecedented benefits for nonmarketable cultural enterprises and practices, especially for the arts and literature in regions inhabited by ethnic minorities.

Before the Communist Party controlled the government, cultural practice in these minority communities had received little attention from central governments. Indigenous forms of cultural production among ethnic minorities arguably survive best without interference from the state. But under the specific conditions of modern China, major ethnic communities had long been faced with the challenges to preserve their traditions: their languages, local forms of cultural production, and customary ways of life. Centralized management of cultural affairs ensured support for marginal forms of cultural production, especially those of ethnic minority groups. Shortly after the founding of the People's Republic, various task forces and steering committees were established at different levels to oversee the collecting, editing, publishing, and translating of some of the most accomplished works of art and literature from the ethnic minorities. Research institutes were set up for these large-scale cultural projects, which would not have been possible without financial support from the state. Local cultural institutions were established to renew and propagate indigenous forms of cultural practice at the grassroots level. But more significant for the preservation of ethnic cultural traditions was the establishment of educational institutions designed to promote studies of these ethnic minorities, especially of their languages. Since the early 1950s the central government, as well as municipal governments, have organized projects ranging from the publication of collections of poetry, mythologies, and local histories to the funding of local museums and the renovation of symbolic architectural structures of ethnic religious traditions, such as the Potala Palace of Lama Buddhism, in Lhasa, the capital city of Tibet. According to a State Council white paper on Chinese policies on ethnic minorities (Guowu Yuan 2007), by 1999 government funds had enabled the establishment of 534 performing companies, 194 theaters, 661 libraries, 82 galleries, 155 museums, and 679 cultural centers in the major regions inhabited by ethnic minorities.

Such state-organized and state-sponsored support of indigenous forms of art and literature is entirely consistent with the Communist Party's basic ideology, especially its utopian belief in the possibilities of universal equality. But such structural centralization necessarily imposed severe constraints on cultural creativity. Creativity in the domain of art is predicated upon its autonomy and freedom from control and regulation, and might be best achieved in a state where artists and writers find themselves moved and directed only by their creative impulses. Hence, in one sense, the practice of cultural policy works against the creative energy of culture. Well before the Communist Party assumed state power, it experienced within its own ideological structure a number of conflicts and political persecutions that were, in the final analysis, attributable to the innate tension between the need for control and the desire for freedom. After the founding of the People's Republic and with the establishment and consolidation of the Communist Party's authority, turmoil in Chinese political and social life continued to manifest this tension until the late 1970s, when China embarked on economic reforms. The first prominent example was Hu Feng. In 1955 Hu Feng, a left-wing literary critic, was arrested and imprisoned for views on literature and art that differed from Mao's in his "Yan'an Talks on Literature and Art" and for his resistance to the possibility of reconciliation with the Communist Party's cultural leaders. This was the first major example of political persecution in the cultural domain. Such persecutions multiplied during the Cultural Revolution (1966–1969), creating so much disruption that pressure started to build from within the system itself for change and reform.

## CULTURAL POLICY IN THE REFORM ERA AND BEYOND

The death of Mao and the fall of the Gang of Four marked the end of an era as well as the end, in practice, of the

Communist Party's monopoly on ideology. In proposing a structural marketization of China's systems of labor, including intellectual and cultural labor, Deng Xiaoping's reform program created genuine opportunities of liberalization in thinking about the state's regulatory role in cultural production. Marketization not only requires that state enterprises, including cultural ones, operate in accordance with the laws of the market, but also presents a challenge to the centralized sociopolitical system. As long as the political system remains intact, however, China's cultural policy must enable cultural production that accords with the state ideology.

In 1985, the Ministry of Culture issued a policy document titled "Some Suggestions for Reforming Repertoire Companies." The outcome was a reform of human resources involving reductions of staff in bloated cultural establishments such as performing companies and cuts in subsidies to these establishments. In 1980, at the beginning of the reform period, there were 3,523 theater and repertoire companies nationwide employing a total of 245,659 professional actors, actresses, and other personnel. Ten years later these two figures had been reduced to 2,787 and 170,000, respectively. The less marketable forms of cultural production were particularly vulnerable when exposed to the market. Without state subsidies, theater companies specializing in local opera, for example, were financially unsustainable, and many were forced to close down (Kang Shizhao 1992). Like all state enterprises, cultural enterprises across the board have been forced to enter the system of market competition, whose modus operandi is very different from that of the centrally planned state.

The market-oriented cultural policy adopted in the reform era, though continuing to acknowledge the need for art and literature to serve the Communist Party's political objectives, aims to reorganize cultural and intellectual labor in accordance with the normative forces of the market. Among the consequences are the disintegration of a sense of accepted standards of cultural and intellectual production and the decline of the social prestige that artists and writers used to enjoy in Chinese society. Admittedly, relaxation of ideological control creates more space for creativity in art and literature, but marketization of cultural labor leads to a new regime of control: the hegemony of the market. The force of the market has left no corner of Chinese society untouched. Repertoire companies send their artists to entertain customers in the cafés of five-star hotels; schools turn their classrooms into hotel rooms during the summer vacation. Serious work in art and literature has increasingly become the business of an elite minority. Pop culture and subpop culture, which pervade China's cultural scene, provide an alternative space for cultural productivity, but at the same time pose a challenge to the once widely accepted understanding that the role of culture is "to learn and propagate the best that is known and thought in the world" (Arnold 1910, p. 37).

In this new era of market reform and economic growth, China's cultural policy is faced with two structural problems. One is the difficulty of reconciling a centralized social structure with marketized diversity of cultural labor. The other is how to regulate China's cultural market in the context of globalization.

**SEE ALSO** *Art, Policy on, since 1949; Censorship; Minority Nationalities: Cultural Images of National Minorities.*

**BIBLIOGRAPHY**

Arnold, Matthew. The Function of Criticism at the Present Time. In his *Essays in Criticism*, first series. London: Macmillan, 1910.

Guowu Yuan [State Council]. *Zhongguo de shaoshu minzhu zhengce ji qi shixian* [China's policies on the ethnic minorities]. 2007. http://cn.chinagate.com.cn/whitepapers/2007-02/13/content_2367033.htm.

Hu Huilin. *Wenhua zhengce xue* [Studies in cultural policy]. Taiyuan: Shuhai Chubanshe, 2006.

Mao Zedong. On New Democracy. In *Selected Works of Mao Tse-Tung*, vol. 2, 339–384. Beijing: Foreign Languages Press, 1965a.

Mao Zedong. Talks at the Yenan Forum on Literature and Art. In *Selected Works of Mao Tse-Tung*, vol. 3, 69–98. Beijing: Foreign Languages Press, 1965b.

McDougall, Bonnie S. *Mao Zedong's "Talks at the Yan'an Conference on Literature and Art": A Translation of the 1943 Text with Commentary.* Ann Arbor: Center for Chinese Studies, University of Michigan, 1980.

Ministry of Culture. 关于艺术表演团体的改革意见 [Some suggestions for reforming repertoire companies]. In Kang Shizhao, ed. Wenhua tizhi gaige [Reforming the cultural system], 187–196. *Zhongguo gaige quanshu* [Compendium on China's reforms], ed. Ma Hong. Dalian: Dalian Chubanshe, 1992.

Wei Tianxiang. *Wenyi zhengce lungang* [Cultural policy issues]. Beijing: Zhonggong Zhongyang Dang Xiao Chubanshe, 1993.

Zhonggong Zhongyang Xuanchuan Bu [Central Propaganda Department]. Zhuyao zhineng [Principal functions]. http://cpc.people.com.cn/GB/64114/75332/5230610.html.

*Q. S. Tong*

## CULTURAL REVOLUTION, 1966–1969

It would be difficult to overstate the importance of the Cultural Revolution for an understanding of the post-1949 history of the People's Republic of China (PRC). In a political system marked by periodic campaigns to accomplish regime goals, it was the first and only campaign in which the masses were not just mobilized by Chinese Communist Party (CCP) officials, but had a major role to play beyond party manipulation, often determining which individuals to attack. Indeed, the CCP itself, which had run all

***Man with dunce cap led through the streets of Beijing, January 25, 1967.*** *In order to promote his Cultural Revolution, Mao Zedong used radical student groups, such as the Red Guard, to impress Chinese Communist Party ideals on citizens. Anyone opposing these ideas often found themselves at the mercy of the Red Guard, including this government official forced to walk through Beijing wearing a hat advertising his offenses.* AP IMAGES

previous campaigns, became a major target. For both outside observers and members of Chinese society, the revelations that appeared in the Red Guard newspapers and other unofficial sources demonstrated for the first time that an ostensibly unified China, seemingly marked by elite cohesion and a common vision, was actually riven by ideological contention and personal animus.

By the time the revived CCP, five years after the death of Mao in 1976 and the arrest of his radical supporters labeled as the Gang of Four, offered its authoritative assessment in 1981, no one, not even Mao, had escaped completely unscathed. In addition to providing detailed information on the hidden history of post-1949 Chinese politics, the turmoil unleashed during the Cultural Revolution played a crucial role in creating the conditions that led directly to the economic reforms that began in December 1978 under Deng Xiaoping, himself an early victim of that movement.

By most independent accounts, the value of agricultural and industrial production had declined significantly in 1967 and 1968. In a similar manner, education was severely affected during these years, particularly at the university level. With virtually all schools closed for four to five years, and then highly politicized in terms of recruitment and curriculum when they began to reopen in the early 1970s, standards dropped precipitously. However, as with post–Cultural Revolution economic reform, the restoration of merit-based unified university entrance examinations, the revival of the "key" school system at all levels, and the urgent upgrading of science and technology, all undertaken between December 1977 and March 1978, signaled the leadership's strong commitment to academic quality and the desire to overcome the losses associated with Cultural Revolution policies.

## THE DEBATE OVER CHRONOLOGY

The scholarly literature has been dominated by two basic approaches to the Cultural Revolution. One approach is to emphasize the elite power struggle, with the Cultural Revolution seen as Mao's final attempt to refashion Chinese politics, society, and culture in a direction that approximated his vision of socialism within a continuing revolution, with the chairman consumed by the fear that China would follow in the footsteps of what he perceived as Soviet "revisionism." At the same time, Mao's ideological concerns

## GANG OF FOUR

The Gang of Four is the name applied to the group of radical leaders that arose during the Cultural Revolution. They were closely associated with Mao Zedong, and almost certainly came into existence through his support. The most prominent of them, Jiang Qing (1914–1991), had been Mao's wife since moving to Yan'an from Shanghai, where she had been an actress, in the late 1930s. A decision by the Central Committee obliged her to keep a low profile during the early years of the People's Republic, but she became increasingly involved in cultural issues from 1961 onward. She was instrumental in encouraging the Shanghai-based writer, Yao Wenyuan (1931–2005), to issue an attack on Beijing vice mayor Wu Han's play, *Hai Rui Dismissed from Office*, in 1965. Yao interpreted the play as an indirect attack on Mao's removal of Minister of Defense Peng Dehuai from office in 1959. Jiang and Yao set up a writing group in Shanghai just before the launch of the Cultural Revolution in 1966, where they were joined by the journalist Zhang Chunqiao (1917–2005). The final member of the group, Wang Hongwen (1936–1992), was the youngest and the only one from a genuinely proletarian background.

Jiang served as the group's chief demagogue, and was active through the earliest, most violent period of the Cultural Revolution, denouncing disgraced leaders, such as President Liu Shaoqi, and acting as an ally to Lin Biao before his own fall from grace. Yao was the chief ideologue, producing articles that gained the approval of Mao and were widely disseminated. Zhang Chunqiao was the political activist, setting up the short-lived Shanghai Commune in 1967 before becoming mayor of Shanghai, a position he held until 1976. Wang Hongwen, a member of a prominent Red Guard group whose daring activities attracted the attention of the other three, was elected into the Central Committee during the notorious Ninth Party Congress in 1969 and became number three in the Party hierarchy during the Tenth Congress in 1973. All four were to become members of the ruling Politburo. If they had a political program, it was embodied in Zhang's "On Exercising All-Round Dictatorship over the Bourgeoisie," a 1975 article that bitterly criticized bourgeois restorationism and stands as the definitive text of extreme leftism in China. Indicative of their reliance on Mao for power, within one month of his death in September 1976 they were arrested, although they were not tried till 1980, during what was widely seen as a show trial under the new leadership of one of their main political opponents, Deng Xiaoping. Their sentences varied from twenty years to death, commuted to life imprisonment. But Jiang Qing's declaration that she was "Mao's dog, and when he said bite, I bit," had particular resonance in China, showing that the Gang of Four had, in fact, been a gang of five. In contemporary China, their notorious reputation only indicates how far the values and ideals they embodied have been abandoned.

***Kerry Brown***

cannot be separated from personal power considerations. The chairman, bitter at being reduced to a mere symbolic figure representing the past glories of the Chinese revolution, sought to regain his decision-making power—which had been greatly truncated within party and government affairs—within the propaganda apparatus and in key sectors of the economy and society in the aftermath of the disastrous results of the Great Leap Forward (1958–1960).

In contrast to the focus on Mao-centered politics from above, a second approach has viewed the Cultural Revolution primarily as a mass movement from below. Regardless of Mao's own motivations for destroying so much of the fabric of the country he had labored so assiduously to create—the key puzzle addressed by scholars of elite politics—and despite his clear initiation of the movement and the attempted manipulation from above, the launching of the Cultural Revolution in 1966 brought to the surface the largely latent tensions and conflicting interests of a wide variety of groups and individuals in Chinese society. This included students and workers—all of whom used the banner Mao had raised to pursue their own aims—forming opposing mass factions and producing a chaotic situation marked by factional struggles, engulfing both the elite and mass levels.

The difference in these two approaches is closely related to the continuing debate over the chronology or periodization for the movement. Officially, the Cultural Revolution lasted ten years and can be divided into three stages, with the first stage beginning in May 1966 and ending with the Ninth Party Congress of April 1969. The second stage concluded with the Tenth Party Congress of August 1973. The third stage ended with the death of Mao in September and the arrest of the Gang of Four in October 1976.

This periodization fits well for those who focus on an elite politics approach to the movement, since the second

***Cartoon depicting the Gang of Four, November, 1976.*** *Jiang Qing, Mao Zedong's last wife, took advantage of her position to create a group of four Communist Party members who actively orchestrated the social and political purges of the Cultural Revolution. Upon Mao's death in 1976, the balance of power in the party shifted to favor Deng Xiaoping, leading to the arrest and imprisonment of all four for their brutality during Mao's reign.* SNARK / ART RESOURCE, NY

and third stages were dominated by the politics of Mao's court and suppression by military or local officials of the mass organizations that had risen during stage one, as the state struggled to regain control over society. Indeed, the Cultural Revolution had initially been declared a success at the Ninth Party Congress, and Lin Biao had been designated Mao's anointed successor. For those who focus on the Cultural Revolution as a mass movement from below, in which Mao was able to use the "cult of personality" astutely to tap into Chinese political culture and harness the anger among ordinary citizens for his own purposes, the Cultural Revolution effectively ended in 1968, with the demobilization of the Red Guard and rebel factions. The intervening years, during which many of the casualties occurred in the name of restoring order, were marked by the enforcement of a rigid conformity from the top down.

## THE COURSE OF THE MOVEMENT

The mobilization of the masses can be said to begin with Mao Zedong, Lin Biao, and Zhou Enlai presiding over the first of eight mass rallies of the newly formed Red Guards—the vanguard of the Cultural Revolution—in August 1966, although by June 1966 all the schools in Beijing had already suspended classes, freeing up the students for their "revolutionary" activities. The seeds for future factional struggles could already be found in the first official document on the Cultural Revolution, the Party Central Committee's Sixteen-point Decision of August 1966, which had Mao's strong endorsement. By pointing the spearhead of attack at the familiar targets of previous movements, namely the representatives of the exploiting classes, the bourgeois academic authorities, and all those preventing the realization of socialism in China, while at the same time suggesting that "the main target of the present movement is those within the party who are in authority and are taking the capitalist road," and also noting that the masses must liberate themselves and "not be afraid of disturbances," there was sufficient confusion with regard to the primary purpose and the objects of the movement to ensure that the mobilized masses, albeit with the "guidance" of supporters at higher levels, could pick and choose among a wide variety of bad people, both inside and outside the party, a situation that would continue for the next two years.

The one institution Mao sought to keep intact was the People's Liberation Army (PLA), but by January 1967 he was compelled to call upon the army to intervene on

## "LITTLE RED BOOK" (*QUOTATIONS FROM CHAIRMAN MAO*)

The international success of the *Quotations from Chairman Mao Tse-tung*, also known as the "Precious Red Book" (Hong Baoshu) in China or "Mao Bible" in the West, is an astounding publishing event. Approximately one billion copies of the *Quotations* were printed during the decade of the Cultural Revolution (1966–1976), and this book ranks second only to the Bible in terms of copies in print.

The compilation of the *Quotations* was inspired, but not directed, by Minister of Defense Lin Biao, who was known for reciting the words of Mao Zedong as part of the increasingly elaborate leader cult. The first edition of the *Quotations* was compiled in December 1963 by the editors of the *Liberation Army Daily*. This project relied heavily on a collection of Mao's quotations thematically arranged in card boxes to ease the daily publication of suitable citations. First published in May 1964 for the internal use of the army, the *Quotations* were meant to strengthen the political reliability of the soldiers and to provide authoritative answers within a climate increasingly characterized by militant rhetoric and instability. The entries accordingly focused on questions of work style, heroism, and the leadership of the Chinese Communist Party (CCP). Despite the book's numerous shortcomings, it included a preface from Lin Biao, and Lin's high prestige as Mao's "closest comrade-in-arms" secured its success and effectively ended all rival efforts to publish more comprehensive collections of quotations from Mao.

The political importance of the *Quotations* reached its apex during the Cultural Revolution (1966–1969). Red Guards and other participants championed the volume as the primary symbol of the Mao cult and their rebellion against so-called capitalist roaders within the CCP. But they soon employed this "magic weapon" to discredit competing factions as well. As the situation in China deteriorated, the *Quotations* became an important symbol of the international student movement in 1968 and contributed to a highly romanticized image of Mao Zedong and the Cultural Revolution, inspiring the emergence of Maoist study groups in the West. With the reestablishment of political order after the CCP's Ninth Party Congress in April 1969, the print numbers of the *Quotations* decreased markedly.

In 1979 the CCP Propaganda Department declared the *Quotations* a "distortion of Mao Zedong Thought by the Lin Biao clique to amass political capital," and copies were withdrawn from circulation. Only in the 1990s, in the wake of the pop-art revival of Cultural Revolution items and aesthetics did illegal reprints of the *Quotations* appear again to be sold as souvenirs to Western tourists. The historical significance of the *Quotations* does not rest with its content but with the specific circumstances that shaped its form, use, and resonance with both domestic and international audiences.

**BIBLIOGRAPHY**

Leese, Daniel. Performative Politics and Petrified Image: The Mao Cult during China's Cultural Revolution. Ph.D. diss., International University Bremen, Germany. 2006. See especially chapter 5. http://www.jacobs-university.de/phd/files/1187983533.pdf.

Mao Zedong. *Quotations from Chairman Mao Tse-tung*. Ed. Stuart Schram. New York: Praeger, 1967.

***Daniel Leese***

the side of the "broad left-wing masses." As the PLA increased its authority and control over the newly formed revolutionary committees set up to restore order in the provinces and cities in 1967, it was inevitable that the army would come into conflict with those mass organizations that it did not favor, leading to armed clashes not just between the military and radical elements among the masses, but also factional struggle within the military in many parts of the country by the summer of 1967. The result, by July 28, 1968, was a meeting between Mao and Red Guard leaders in Beijing at which the chairman, in criticizing the resort to armed struggle, effectively ended the mass-mobilization, radical phase of the Cultural Revolution. By September 7, 1968, revolutionary committees dominated by the military had been set up in all provinces, municipalities, and autonomous regions.

## THE CULTURAL REVOLUTION TODAY

Within China, the official assessment in the 1981 *Resolution on CPC History* was intended to close off any open discussion on the Cultural Revolution, and only a few scholars since then have dared to conduct research on the subject. Chinese youth of the twenty-first century know very little about these events, with their primary source of information coming from their parents and relatives who lived through the movement. At the same time, the current emphasis on making China rich and powerful has fueled a growing materialism and patriotism among youth, so there appears to be relatively little interest in studying the past, particularly such a painful period for many families. Outside China as well, the Cultural Revolution—at one time a beacon to radicals in Europe and the United States who had become disenchanted with the "imperialism" associated with American intervention in Vietnam and the "revisionism" or even "social fascism" associated with the Brezhnev Doctrine used to justify the Soviet invasion of Czechoslovakia in 1968—has largely been forgotten as a "rising"; economically strong China offers very different rewards to those for whom it has become a new beacon.

**SEE ALSO** *Communist Party; Lin Biao; Liu Shaoqi; Mao Zedong; People's Liberation Army; Red Guards.*


**BIBLIOGRAPHY**

Chan, Anita, Stanley Rosen, and Jonathan Unger. Students and Class Warfare: The Social Roots of the Red Guard Conflict in Guangzhou (Canton). *China Quarterly* 83 (1980): 397–446.

Esherick, Joseph W., Paul G. Pickowicz, and Andrew G. Walder, eds. *The Chinese Cultural Revolution as History*. Stanford, CA: Stanford University Press, 2006.

Lee Hong Yung. *The Politics of the Chinese Cultural Revolution: A Case Study*. Berkeley: University of California Press, 1978.

MacFarquhar, Roderick, and Michael Schoenhals. *Mao's Last Revolution*. Cambridge, MA: Belknap Press, 2006.

*Resolution on CPC History (1949–81)*. Beijing: Foreign Languages Press, 1981.

Unger, Jonathan. The Cultural Revolution at the Grass Roots. *China Journal* 57 (2007): 109–137.


***Stanley Rosen***

# CUSTOMARY LAW, 1800–1949

Until the last years of the Qing dynasty, state law focused on matters such as the collection of taxes, public order, and resolution of disputes, while customary law regulated most of the affairs concerning people's daily lives, such as conveyance of land, sale of goods, distribution of family property, tenancy, mortgage, debt, and marriage.

Some aspects of customary law, such as the forms and elements of contracts, can be traced back to the Tang dynasty (618–907) and even to the Han dynasty (202 BCE–220 CE). Over the centuries, some elements of customary law were incorporated into state law. Thus, the Qing Penal Code (Da Qing Lüli) includes references to *dian*, a transfer of possession of immovable property with the option of either redemption or sale at an adjusted price in the future. Likewise, provisions regarding local norms were also incorporated into official provincial pronouncements (*shengli*). Such provincial pronouncements, as compilations of official documents dealing with local governance and the economy within a province, reflected regional differences and local customs. Nevertheless, customary law in China was different from its counterpart in premodern Europe in that such law in China was never comprehensively collected and systematically compiled by any official authority; nor was it cited, relied on, or applied as binding legal norms in any of the imperial courts. In the eyes of officials, the matters that customary law dealt with—household matters, marriage, land, and debt—were only trifles, and customary law itself was no more than folk usage (*xiangsu* or *xianggui*) or local practice (*tuli*), without the status of state law. Even though in practice the courts might resolve a dispute based on local custom, they did not intend to apply it as law, nor could they turn it into law.

## INVESTIGATION AND COLLECTION OF CUSTOMARY LAW IN THE LATE QING AND EARLY REPUBLIC

A major change took place in the status of customary law and its relationship to state law during the late Qing reforms of the early 1900s, when the government decided to adapt Western legal institutions to China. It launched a nationwide investigation, which included investigation of civil and commercial customs, to incorporate best existing practices into the new law and to ensure that legal reforms would fit the conditions of Chinese society. Specific organs for such investigation were established at the central and provincial levels, and a unified methodology and uniform criteria for investigation were produced for this purpose. The project was initiated in 1907, but was terminated four years later because of the dissolution of Qing dynasty and its imperial regime. Before comprehensive formal laws were enacted, the Republican government, in 1918, restarted the nationwide investigation of civil and commercial customs to prepare for the compilation of a civil code and to provide guidelines for civil justice. These investigations produced two compilations of customs, among others: *Zhongguo minshi xiguan daquan* (Corpus of civil customs of China; 1924) and the *Minshangshi xiguan diaocha baogaolu* (Report on investigations of civil and commercial customs; 1930). The compilers classified the customs collected throughout the country in accordance with modern legal categories and arranged them generally according to the framework of the German Civil Code of 1900. However, these and other official compilations were used just as reference works and did not have the force of law.

### CUSTOMARY LAW IN CIVIL ADJUDICATION AND CODIFICATION IN THE REPUBLIC

During the Republic, customs and practices were taken seriously in civil adjudication at different levels. In this regard, the efforts of the Supreme Court (Dali Yuan) from 1912 to 1928 in Beijing were most important and praiseworthy. The court in a series of cases established a set of criteria to identify and recognize a custom as law:

- The people concerned must strongly hold that the custom has the force of law.
- The behaviors claimed must repeatedly occur for a certain period.
- There must be a lack of statutes that can be applied in the case.
- There must be no departure from public order.

Subsequently, in the Civil Code of the Republic (Zhonghua Minguo Minfa), formulated and promulgated from 1929 to 1931, custom was recognized as one of the sources of law, and the status of such customary law was inferior only to that of statute law. In this basic and codified law, such customary practices among people as *dian* and *yitian liangzhu* (dual land ownership) were redefined and changed into a special real right and emphyteusis, respectively. Thus, indigenous Chinese customs were brought into a modernized Western-style legal system. Notwithstanding this effort to integrate the traditional and the modern through law, even at the end of the 1940s, customs and law continued to coexist and even at times to conflict.

**SEE ALSO** *Codified Law, 1800-1949; Law Courts, 1800-1949.*

**BIBLIOGRAPHY**

Huang Yuansheng. *Minchu falü bianqian yu caipan (1912–1928)* [Legal changes and adjudication in the early Republic, 1912–1928]. Taibei: Guoli Zhengzhi Daxue, 2000.

Liang Zhiping. *Qingdai xiguangfa: Shehui yu guojia* [Customary law in the Qing Dynasty: Society and the state]. Beijing: Zhongguo Zhengfa Daxue Chubanshe, 1999.

Sifa Xingzheng Bu (Ministry of Justice and Administration), eds. *Minshangshi xiguan diaocha baogaolu* [Report on investigations of civil and commercial customs]. 3 vols. Taibei: Jinxue Shuju, 1969. First published, 1930.

Tian Tao, Song Gewen (Hugh T. Scogin), and Zheng Qin, eds. *Tiancang qiyue wenshu cuibian* [Contracts and related documents from the Tian Collection]. 3 vols. Beijing: Zhonghua Shuju, 2001.

Zihe Xiusan (Shiga Shūzō). Qingdai susong zhidu zhi minshi fayuan de gaikuoxing kaocha: Qing, li, fa [A general review of litigation in civil courts during the Qing period: Compassion, reason, and law]. In *Ming-Qing shiqi de minshi shenpan yu minjian qiyue* [Civil justice and private contracts in the Ming and Qing Periods], ed. Wang Yaxin and Liang Zhiping. Beijing: Falü Chubanshe, 1998.

*Liang Zhiping*

# D

## DALAI LAMA

The Buddhist monk Tenzin Gyatso (b. 1935) was recognized at the age of three as the Fourteenth Dalai Lama of Tibet, the reincarnation of a long line of Tulkus (buddha-emanations, in Tibetan belief). Enthroned in 1940, he spent the next ten years in intensive Buddhist studies. In 1950, in response to the invasion of eastern Tibet by the Chinese People's Liberation Army (PLA), he was formally installed as head of the government of Tibet, begun in 1642 by the Fifth Dalai Lama.

### CHINESE OCCUPATION FROM 1951

The PLA quickly destroyed the rag-tag Tibetan army and in 1951 imposed a treaty known as the Seventeen Point Agreement for the Peaceful Liberation of Tibet. The Dalai Lama decided to stay in Tibet and work with the Communists, on their promise not to interfere with the culture or governance of Central Tibet, corresponding to the Tibetan provinces of Ü, Tsang, and Ngari, excluding the Tibetan provinces of Amdo and Kham, which were administratively absorbed into four Chinese provinces. In 1954 the Dalai Lama and the Panchen Lama (1938–1989), the second highest ranking lama, who had grown up mainly in China under the Nationalists, went to Beijing, where they met frequently with PRC officials including Mao Zedong, Zhou Enlai, and Deng Xiaoping. The youthful Dalai Lama admired Mao, took interest in the ideals of Communism and saw the benefits of industrial modernization, but was taken aback by Mao's contempt for religion. The two lamas became friends during this visit. The young Dalai Lama was advised by his chamberlain, his tutors, the ex-minister Ngapo, who had gone over to the Chinese during the battle of Chamdo, and the first Tibetan communist, Phuntsok Wangyal, who also served as interpreter; none of these persons had much experience in world affairs or diplomacy.

The Seventeen Point Agreement covered only Central or "Outer" Tibet, so defined by the British since 1913, and did not cover Amdo and Kham to the east, two thirds of the plateau and home to two-thirds of the Tibetan people. This meant that their pledge not to interfere with Tibetan religion and society did not apply to the east, and there the Communist cadres and the military immediately initiated thought-reform, class struggle, suppression of Buddhism, land appropriation and communalization by the state, and destruction of monasteries. Armed resistance by the Khams and Amdo Tibetans was fierce, but eventually ended in their slaughter. The Dalai Lama's telegraphed pleas to Mao went unanswered. In 1956, when he and the Panchen Lama visited India to celebrate the 2,500th anniversary of the Buddha, they both asked Jawaharlal Nehru (1889–1964) if they could stay as refugees; Nehru refused in order to maintain good relations with Mao.

Back in Tibet, the violence in eastern Tibet increased. Once militarily entrenched in Central Tibet, the Chinese ignored the Seventeen Point Agreement and pushed "the revolution" there as well. On March 10, 1959, when the Chinese tried to capture the Dalai Lama, the Lhasa Tibetans rose up against them and were massacred; the official death toll stood at 87,000 Tibetans. However, the Dalai Lama was able to escape to safety in India thanks to the eastern Tibetan fighters, by now somewhat trained and partially equipped by the U.S. Central Intelligence Agency. His last act in Tibet as head of government was to repudiate the

Seventeen Point Agreement, because it had been imposed under duress and was not being honored by the Chinese.

## THE EXILED DALAI LAMA

The Dalai Lama was greeted by Nehru and the international press. India also accepted tens of thousands of refugees who followed him. The Tibetan Government in Exile (TGIE) was established in Dharamsala, and motions on Tibet's behalf were put forward in the United Nations (UN). UN representatives of the Nationalist government in Taiwan, claiming that Tibet was China's "internal affair," prevented diplomatic support from the already ambivalent India, Great Britain, and the United States.

For the next twenty years in exile, the Dalai Lama continued his Buddhist studies and practice, and, with the support of India, led his refugee community of 130,000 worldwide in setting up a constitutional democracy (with an executive cabinet, legislature, and judiciary), a school system, traditional industries such as carpet weaving and artistic production, large monasteries and nunneries, a traditional Buddhist medical institute and clinics, large settlements all over Nepal and India, and even allowing a high-altitude

***Dalai Lama (right) seated with a Hindu priest, Calcutta, India, November 24, 2003.*** *The spiritual leader of Tibet, the 14th Dalai Lama fled his homeland after China crushed an independence movement in the mountainous country. Serving also as head of state from the Indian city of Dharamsala, the Dalai Lama leads a government in exile from that city, while garnering support from the international community for a free Tibet.* © JAYANTA SHAW/REUTERS/CORBIS

Tibetan battalion of the Indian army. Tibet itself was shut off from the outside world; inside, more than one million Tibetans were killed, 6,000 monasteries were destroyed, and the pristine wildlife, forests, and mineral resources of the vast high plateau were devastated.

When Deng Xiaoping took power in China in 1979 he quickly invited the Tibetans to open negotiations on the future of Tibet. Fact-finding delegations of the TGIE were allowed to travel into the country. The Panchen Lama, who had been jailed since 1966, was released in 1978, and during the 1980s he began to restore some of the shattered Buddhist institutions. The fact-finding missions disturbed the exiles, as they came to know directly the horrendous sufferings of their people under occupation. The Dalai Lama expanded his travels abroad, teaching Buddhism to the growing number of Tibetan Buddhists around the world, meeting world religious leaders, and building Western support for Tibetan self-determination.

In 1987, absent meaningful negotiations with Deng, the Dalai Lama sought the help of world leaders. He made his Five Point Peace Plan public in the U.S. Congress, calling on the Chinese to:

1. make Tibet into a "zone of nonviolence" (*ahimsa*);
2. stop transferring Chinese settlers into Tibet;
3. respect human rights and allow democratic freedoms in Tibet;
4. restore the environment; and
5. enter into sincere negotiations about the future.

In 1988 at the European Parliament he qualified his plan by explicitly stating that he was not seeking independence for Tibet, but rather a genuinely autonomous special status within union with China, calling this his "middle way approach." This approach was controversial from the beginning. Many Tibetans felt it compromised their historic independence from all previous Chinese dynasties and the post-1911 Nationalist government, and the Chinese leadership considered it a disguised claim of independence, since they were committed to the claim of primordial ownership of Tibet, maintaining that the Tibetans are only a "minority nationality" of Chinese. However, the Dalai Lama's policy is still accepted by 99 percent of the Tibetans, since a genuine autonomy within the Chinese union is the maximum that a nonviolent liberation campaign can possibly hope for. The Chinese response to the Dalai Lama's internationalization of his people's struggle was to initiate a severe crackdown in Tibet, declaring martial law in 1989, a few months before the Tiananmen Square disturbances. Later that year, the Panchen Lama died of a heart attack. On December 10, 1989, the Dalai Lama was awarded the Nobel Prize for Peace.

Since then, the Dalai Lama has become more well known around the world, along with the true story of Tibet. Numerous world leaders have urged the Chinese leaders to talk to him seriously. The Chinese have become increasingly hardline, forcing Tibetans to denounce the Dalai Lama, pushing nomads and farmers off their lands, moving more Chinese settlers into Tibet, and intensifying resource extraction programs, while presenting all of this as help for Tibet. In 2002 a series of six meetings was begun between the TGIE and the PRC, though the Chinese maintained they were merely discussing the future of the Dalai Lama, so no progress was made toward satisfying the grievances of the Tibetan people. In 2008 some younger exiles mounted an international campaign to highlight China's mistreatment of Tibet in the run-up to the Beijing Olympic Games; inside Tibet, there were more than 200 protest demonstrations, mostly nonviolent. In response, more than 100,000 additional troops were moved into Tibet. In March 2008 the Dalai Lama announced that he was removing himself and future incarnations from any political role, but said that if the Tibetans still need him, he will reincarnate within the exile community, beyond the reach of the Chinese.

In 1959, when Mao was informed that the Tibetan uprising had been quelled but the Dalai Lama had escaped, he is reported to have said, "Ah! We have won the battle but lost the war!" In hindsight, it seems that he could see the extraordinary potential of this figure to represent the cause of Tibet to the world.

**SEE ALSO** *Buddhism; Cultural Revolution, 1966–1969; Mao Zedong; Rural Development, 1949–1978: Great Leap Forward; Tibet.*

**BIBLIOGRAPHY**

Avedon, John. *In Exile from the Land of Snows*. New York: Knopf, 1984.

Goldstein, Melvyn. *The Snow Lion and the Dragon: China, Tibet, and the Dalai Lama*. Berkeley: University of California Press, 1997.

H. H. The Dalai Lama. *Freedom in Exile: The Autobiography of the Dalai Lama*. New York: HarperCollins, 1990.

Shakya, Tsering. *The Dragon in the Land of Snows: A History of Modern Tibet since 1947*. London: Pimlico, 1947

Thurman, Robert. *Why the Dalai Lama Matters: His Act of Truth as the Solution for China, Tibet, and the World*. New York: Atria Books; Hillsboro, OR: Beyond Words, 2008.

***Robert Thurman***

## DALIAN

Dalian is a port city in Liaoning Province covering an area of about 7,750 square miles (12,500 square kilometers). It had a population of 6.1 million in 2007. It is the most important gateway to northeast China, situated on the southernmost Liaodong Peninsula with the Yellow Sea to the east, Bohai Sea to the west, and Shandong Peninsula to the south across the sea. This strategic location, along with its proximity to Japan, Korea, and Russia, placed the area at the center of foreign powers interests. The development of Dalian reflected those strong foreign influences.

In the area of Dalian there was a small fishing village known as Qing Niwakou during Qing dynasty (1644–1912). The region first came to international attention when Japan occupied the Liaodong Peninsula after the Sino-Japanese War in 1895. Soon after, however, Russia, supported by France and Germany, forced the Japanese to relinquish possession of the peninsula, and modern development of the area began when it was leased to Russia in 1898. Under Russian control, Qing Niwakou was renamed Dalny, and a modern port city was planned for extending the Trans-Siberian Railway from Harbin—the South Manchurian Railway—and developing the bounty of resources there. Shipping, smelting, brewing, and timber industries were rapidly developed. Competition for control over northeast China led to the Russo-Japanese War in 1904 to 1905. Following the Russians' defeat, control of the Liaodong Peninsula was transferred to Japan, and Dalny was renamed Dairen. From 1905 to 1945 the Japanese continued to plum the area's great potential; Dairen emerged as the most important industrial base and trade port for exploiting resources in northeast China. After Japan's defeat in World War II, under the terms of the Yalta Agreement Dairen came under the joint control of Russia and China. In 1950 the name of the city changed again, to Lüda, and it merged with its neighboring port to the southwest, Lüshun. China has had sole control over the city since 1955, when Russian forces retreated.

The name *Dalian* was restored with a spatial expansion of the city in 1981. The area of the former Dairen city became Zhongshan District. Today, under the city's jurisdiction there are five more urban districts (Lüshun, Jinzhou, Xigang, Shahekou, and Ganjingzi), three cities (Wafangdian, Pulandian, and Zhuanghe), and one suburban rural county (Changhai).

In 1984 Dalian was selected as one of fourteen coastal cities to be opened to foreign investors. In 1985 the central government designated it a separate economic plan city enjoying provincial-level decision-making. Four state-level development zones were successively installed for attracting foreign investment, including China's first economic and technological development zone, Hi-tech Industrial Park and National Holiday Resort, as well as the only free trade zone and export processing zone in northeast China. Dalian has become the favorite area for foreign investment in northeast China, and it enjoys a high rate of economic growth and has undergone tremendous social and economic transformations. Unlike the development of other coastal open cities in south China that rushed to be a part of the global manufacturing workshop, the development of Dalian exemplifies an alternative model of China's economic miracle under its open-door policy of the last three decades. The focus of the city's development has been to improve its environment and develop environmentally friendly industries. Particularly under the leadership of Bo Xilai, Dalian's mayor from 1992 to 2000, attention was given to urban beautification, razing old buildings, relocating manufacturing to suburban areas, repaving roads, developing urban gardens, and promoting the area's beach resorts.

Dalian is renowned for its green environment and promoted as a model city, and it has received several environmental protection awards from the central government as well as from the United Nations (Wang 2007). Dalian is important to the government's efforts to revitalize northeast China, which has declined since the 1990s. In addition to serving as a transportation hub, the city is an emerging knowledge center in northeast China and eastern Asia, hosting international festivals and exhibitions, and attracting trade, tourism, and software outsourcing businesses. The successful transformation of Dalian serves as a model for the future urban development of northeast China.

**SEE ALSO** *Imperialism; Manchuria; Tourism; Urban China: Cities and Urbanization, 1800–1949; Urban China: Organizing Principles of Cities; Urban China: Urban Planning since 1978.*

**BIBLIOGRAPHY**

Wang Yi. Dalian: The Shining Pearl of the North. *China Daily*, September 6, 2007.

***Jiaping Wu***

# DANCE

Chinese historical dance forms include dances associated with the court, ritual dances, festival dances, theatrical (opera) dance, and folk dance. In the nineteenth century, most of these dances were performed by men, because footbinding among Han Chinese precluded dancing for a majority of women. Court dance was subsumed by opera dance during the Song dynasty (960–1279) and was no longer a separate genre. Folk dance, however, continued as it had from ages past.

Historically, dance helped to define and reinforce social and political structures in China. From the mid-nineteenth century, however, and more particularly from the early twentieth century, the role of dance in China was gradually reshaped by cultural and political forces associated with

China's changing place in the wider world. In the late twentieth century, cultural interchange between China, Taiwan, and Hong Kong, along with the opening of China to the West, created an environment where contemporary dance forms and those from world pop culture and ancient China could mingle in new expressions of dance. The styles of dance performed in China today range from ancient to contemporary, indigenous to imported, through folk dances, court dances, religious ceremonies, social dances, and staged performances.

## SETTING THE STAGE: THE LATE QING DYNASTY TO THE TWENTY-FIRST CENTURY

The Opium Wars (1839–1842 and 1856–1860) required the Qing dynasty (1644–1912) to open up to the Western world, a key event in the emergence of modern China. Concurrently, the California gold rush sparked Chinese emigration to the United States, adding to the complexities of cultural exchange. As Chinese culture became more visible in the West, elements of Western cultures—including new dance forms—were introduced into China. Yu Rongling (1882–1973), a diplomat's daughter, studied dance in both Japan and France, and became a member of Isadora Duncan's (1877–1927) company. After Yu's return to China in 1903, her performances gained the favor of Empress Dowager Cixi and prominence as the first person to bring Western dance to China. At the same time, the influence of Western dance was extended to the education system when a 1907 Chinese translation of a foreign book on dance games (*Wudao youxi*) was introduced into physical-education programs nationwide. Dance as physical education continued to grow from this point onward, and helped provide a receptive context for dance more generally in China.

Early twentieth-century imports included staged performances of modern dance and ballet from Europe, Japan, and the United States, burlesque dances such as the cancan, and ballroom dancing—a form that remains popular to the present day. The advent of Hollywood movies in the 1920s did much to establish the popularity of ballroom dancing, which was to be found in major cities from around 1926. Despite some negative views of Western dance, and particularly of burlesque dancing, most dance forms in China were sustained through the twentieth century, surviving even the turbulent third quarter, when political upheavals altered the cultural landscape of China and the shape of international relations around the globe.

After Mao Zedong and the Communist Party rose to power and Chiang Kai-shek (Jiang Jieshi) and the Guomindang government relocated to Taiwan in 1949, dance followed different trajectories on the two sides of the Taiwan Strait. In the late twentieth century and early twenty-first century, changes in the political climate and the intensity of cultural contact led to a convergence of developments in dance in the two places. The many dance forms evident in the contemporary People's Republic of China (PRC) and Taiwan have passed through a complex history to reach their present stage.

## CLASSICAL DANCE FORMS: CHINESE OPERA DANCE

Established during the Song dynasty, Chinese opera was the most prominent performing art in the late Qing dynasty, and has long been seen as representative of Chinese culture. The highly stylized blend of music, classical court dance, martial arts, acrobatics, poetry, storytelling and drama had been cultivated through centuries of performance, investing traditional characters and stories with a precise technical heritage. Chinese classical dance was preserved within Chinese opera: The ribbon dance (*caichou wu*), sword dance (*jian wu*), water-sleeve dance (*shuixiu wu*), and spear dance (*changqiang wu*) are typical dances in opera, used to fulfill the characterization and plot demands of traditional stories.

In the first half of the twentieth century, two Chinese opera artists made incomparable contributions to Chinese dance. Mei Lanfang (1894–1961) was recognized as the greatest modern Chinese actor of female roles for his virtuosity in the ribbon dance and water-sleeve dance, among others. His solo performances in Europe and the United States brought Chinese opera to the attention and acclaim of Western audiences, and crystallized the image of opera dance as Chinese dance. Denishawn, the modern dance company founded by Ruth St. Denis (1879–1968) and Ted Shawn (1891–1972) in the United States, was inspired by Mei's signature performance, *Farewell My Concubine* (*Bawangbieji*). The company performed their version of this dance during their 1925 tour of China, where audiences were intrigued to see Chinese themes restaged by Western dancers. Denishawn also sponsored Mei in his highly acclaimed 1930 tour of the United States.

Mei Lanfang performed Peking Opera, which had begun in 1790 and was the most prominent of the many Chinese opera forms. Dance is integral to all of these forms, but in *Kunqu*—the oldest extant form of Chinese opera—the dance claims center stage. Ouyang Yuqiang (1889–1962) was a prominent *Kunqu* performer of his day, his renown such that the phrase "Mei in the North, Ou in the South" (Pan Xiafeng 1992) was a common accolade. While historians focus on Ouyang's notoriety in theater, ultimately his influence was most strongly felt in dance. He gave critical guidance to Madame Dai Ailian (1916–2006) from her earliest days in China. Dai was born in Trinidad and studied ballet in London, where she was living in 1937 at the time of the Japanese invasion of China. She helped raise funds for the Hong Kong–based China Defense League, headed by Song Qingling, wife of Sun Yat-sen (Sun Yixian). The league sponsored Madame Dai's trip to Hong Kong in 1940, and she later arrived in Guilin, where Ouyang had founded the Guangxi Provincial Arts Center. With Ouyang's guidance and encouragement, Dai studied classical and folk forms with local artists. Out of these encounters she created several new works, including the highly popular *A Mute Carrying a Mad Woman* (*Yazibeifeng*). Thereafter she traveled throughout China learning and staging minority folk dances, bringing them to broader recognition and acclaim throughout the nation.

Ouyang's support gave Dai the impetus she needed to pursue her goal of developing a national dance, and his assistance to other key figures was no less significant. Wu Xiaobang (1906–1995) and Choi Shunghui (1911–1967) were also beneficiaries of Ouyang's support, serving as artists and leaders at the Central Academy of Dramatic Arts where Ouyang was the president. The workshops that Ouyang developed—the Training Workshop for Dance Movement Cadres headed by Wu and the Dance Research Workshop led by Choi—spurred the growth of dance companies throughout China. Ouyang's influence continued also in the realm of performance, and in 1950 he produced the first full-length Chinese ballet, *Doves of Peace* (*Hepingge*). Furthermore, he trained the first generation of dance historians, including Wang Kefen (b. 1927), elevating the status of dance research in China. Wang's scholarship and exacting research made her the premier authority on dance history in China. Through Ouyang, therefore, the ancient tradition of Chinese opera paved the way for further developments in Chinese dance, and continued to exert an influence as the twentieth century unfolded.

## DANCE SCHOOLS

Opera dance—including acrobatic training—formed a core curriculum for the many dance schools that opened through the mid-twentieth century in China, Taiwan, and Hong Kong, and it continues as core curriculum today. This concentration on opera dance is present even at schools whose primary focus is modern dance. At the same time, the history of cultural exchange in the early twentieth century amplified the focus on Chinese opera. Political camaraderie with Russia meant that the Russian ballet and the theatricality of the Ballets Russes under Sergei Diaghilev (1872–1929) were particularly influential—a connection that remained active through the 1950s and 1960s. The influence flowed both ways, as exemplified by the 1927 Bolshoi production of *The Red Poppy,* a ballet with communist themes set in 1920s China. Furthermore, the backgrounds of dance pioneers such as Madame Dai, Wu Xiaobang, Choi Shunghui, Ye Ning (b. 1913), and Jia Zuoguang (b. 1923) ensured that Western dance concepts and techniques filtered into the development of Chinese dance throughout the twentieth century. Thus different schools developed different ways for utilizing the range of movement vocabularies available to them.

In Taiwan, at schools such as the Chinese Culture University, the classical court dance is derived from opera and practiced as an independent form, albeit one aimed at maintaining the original qualities preserved through the opera. At the Beijing Dance Academy, the opera dance vocabulary is explored through Western ballet and modern dance training techniques to develop a style known as Chinese classical dance. Ballet technique is also employed in the Chinese national dance drama (*wuju*), though the themes and music are purely Chinese. By contrast, Beijing Dance Academy's newest division, the Han-Tang Classical Dance Program (founded by Sun Ying, b. 1929), and Taiwan's Neo-Classic Dance Company (founded by Liu Fengshueh, b. 1925) both minimize the Western dance influence and work toward a more authentic reformation of classical court dance vocabulary.

## FOLK DANCE

Folk dances form the second major area of study in Chinese dance schools. Following Madame Dai's success at bringing minority folk dances to national prominence in the 1940s, and the mandates of the Yan'an Forum of 1942, folk dances throughout China were fostered as integral parts of cultural identity and daily life. In twenty-first-century China, many people can be seen dancing *yangge* (a popular Han folk entertainment) for exercise in the mornings; festivals of dragon and lion dance abound; and schools incorporate folk dances in their offerings. For example, Beijing Dance Academy's folk-dance division specializes in Han folk dance as well as several different minority dances (e.g., Tibetan, Uygur, Korean, Mongolian, Dai, Miao, and Yi). China's most prominent choreographer, Zhang Jigang (b. 1958), a graduate of Beijing Dance Academy and director of the China Song and Dance Ensemble of the People's Liberation Army, is known for his use of authentic folk movement in his contemporary choreography. Zhang was chosen to choreograph the opening ceremony of the 2008 Beijing Olympics—a testament to the place that folk dance holds in modern China.

## CULTURAL REVOLUTION AND BEYOND

Despite the vibrancy of traditional dances, staged performances fell under severe limits during the decade of the Cultural Revolution (1966–1976), even as the importance of dance for promoting and reinforcing the government agenda reached new heights. A small number of performances, known as *The 8 Model Works* or *Yangbanxi*, were created to model the kind of thinking and behavior that the Communist government espoused. Two of these works—*The Red Detachment of Women* (*Hongseniangzijun*)

***Dancers from the National Chinese Opera and Dance Drama Company performing the ballet* The Red Detachment of Women, *Nanning, Guangxi province, November 9, 2006.*** *Using the example of the former Soviet Union, People's Republic of China leaders promote pro-Communist themes through the arts. Propaganda took many mediums in China, including this ballet about a peasant girl's ascension in the Communist Party, performed for U.S. President Richard Nixon during his 1972 visit.* AP IMAGES

and *The White-haired Girl* (*Baimaonü*)—were dances that used the highly popular *wuju* format, with Western ballet technique and structure, as an effective propaganda tool.

Development of dance in China resumed its earlier direction after 1976. Although staged dance forms other than ballet had languished and technical training was severely compromised during the decade of artistic repression, a wide variety of dance was soon flourishing again. Ballroom dance returned full force, even becoming part of traditional morning exercises in parks along with *yangge*, martial arts, singing, and Chinese opera. Readily available teaching materials and, in some provinces, government-sponsored workshops helped to build the ranks of dance leaders in the parks. Meanwhile, young people across the country soon were fully enmeshed in the pop culture dances that arrived with Western music—jazz, tap, hip-hop, and more.

**Popular Culture** The dance scene in large mainland cities quickly came to resemble that of Hong Kong and Taiwan, where the influx of Western culture and the growth of popular dance forms had never abated. As staged forms, jazz and tap are taught through physical-education departments in schools on Taiwan and, along with ballroom dance, are included in the curriculum at Beijing Dance Academy. In China, Taiwan, and Hong Kong, private studios provide the bulk of instruction in popular dance forms, along with a plethora of instructional videos and CDs.

While the popular dance culture was growing, both in social settings and on stage, other concert dance forms also enjoyed a rebirth. Many new works of *wuju* were created, reviving the popularity that the form had attained in the 1950s with such classics as *Precious Lotus Lantern* (*Baoliandeng*), and bringing *wuju* to a second peak of acclaim in 1979 with the seminal work *The Silk Road Flower and Rain* (*Siluhuayu*).

This new *wuju* was inspired by the Dunhuang caves, a national treasure of religious frescoes and sculptures from the fourth through the fourteenth centuries. Dunhuang dance as a distinct, classical form emerged later in the

1980s, with its movement vocabulary and costuming inspired by the images and themes depicted in the Buddhist artworks. Since its inception, Dunhuang dance has become another highly popular dance form in China, Hong Kong, and Taiwan.

**Ceremonial and Religious Dances** Ceremonial and religious dances continue to be a part of Chinese life, as they have been throughout history. For example, *bayiwu*, a dance honoring the great philosopher Confucius, is performed throughout China and Taiwan in formal ceremonies at shrines and at national events. Ritual and religious dances of minority and Han peoples are also performed regularly. Contemporary choreographers have always been inspired by these rituals and, especially in recent years, have created many compelling works exploring identity, spirituality, and history. For example, Buddhist imagery forms the basis for Zhang Jigang's famous *Thousand-Hand Guanyin* (*Qianshou Guanyin*).

**Modern Dance** Chinese modern dance choreographers, springing from this base in the cultural heritage, have been inspired by sources ranging from calligraphy to philosophy and the broad expanse of the human condition. Choreographers draw on a uniquely Chinese experience to explore contemporary themes and bring them to audiences worldwide—an effort aided by the growth of video technology and Internet access. Prominent contemporary choreographers, such as Zhang Jigang in China, Lin Hwaimin (b. 1947) of Cloud Gate Dance Theater in Taiwan, and Willy Tsao (b. 1959) of City Contemporary Dance Company in Hong Kong, are held in high regard as cultural ambassadors. Furthermore, Chinese dance continues to grow through artists living abroad. In the United States alone, a small sampling of the many influential Chinese artists includes Yin Mei (b. 1959), Yunyu Wang (b. 1952), Lan-Lan Wang (b. 1951), Yu Wei (b. 1959), H. T. Chen (b. 1947), and Nai-Ni Chen (b. 1959). Thus in China and throughout the world, these artists and companies of dancers form the dynamic embodiment of modern Chinese identity.

**SEE ALSO** *Mei Lanfang; Model Operas and Ballets; Peking Opera and Regional Operas; Yan'an Forum.*

**BIBLIOGRAPHY**

Chinese Dancer's Association, ed. *Dangdai Zhonghua wutan mingjia chuanlve* [Brief biographies of the contemporary Chinese dance celebrities]. Beijing: China Photography Press, 1995.

Dai Ailian, as told to Luo Bin and Wu Jingshu. *Dai Ailian: Wode yishu yu rensheng* [Dai Ailian: My art and life]. Beijing: People's Music Publishing, 2003.

Dong Xijiu and Liu Junxiang. *Zhongguo wudao yishushi tujian* [A pictorial history of Chinese dance]. Hunan: Hunan Jiaoyu Chubanshe [Hunan Educational Publishing], 1997.

Li Tianmin and Yu Quofang. *Zhongguo wudaoshi* [Chinese dance history]. Taibei: Dajuan Wenhua Youxiangongsi [Dajuan Cultural Co., Ltd], 1998.

Long Yinpei, Xu Erchong, and Ou Jiangping. *Wudao zhishi shouce* [A dance compendium]. Shanghai: Shanghai Yinyue Chubanshe [Shanghai Music Publishing], 1999.

Pan Xiafeng. *Jingju yishu wenda* [An inquiry into the art of Peking Opera]. Taibei: Shangding Wenhua Chubanshe [Shanding Cultural Publishing], 1992.

Wang Kefen. *Dunhuang wudao huajuan* [Dunhuang dance in illustration]. Hong Kong: The Commercial Press, Ltd., 2001.

Wang Kefen. *Zhonghua wudao tushi* [Chinese dance: An illustrated history]. Taibei: Wenjin Chubanshe [Wenjin Publishing], 2002.

Wang Kefen and Long Yinpei. *Zhongguo jinxiandai dangdai wudao fazhanshi* [Recent developments in Chinese dance]. Beijing: People's Music Publishing, 1999.

Wang Kefen, Liu Enbo, and Xu Erchong. *Zhongguo wudao cidian* [Chinese dance dictionary]. Beijing: Wenhuayishu Chubanshe [Cultural Arts Publishing], 1994.

***Shih-Ming Li Chang***
***Lynn E. Frederiksen***

# DAOISM

Daoism during the nineteenth century was a prestigious tradition, without a centralized authority, so that a large array of institutions, persons, and practices were claimed as Daoist without necessarily having much or any relationship to each other. This situation has continued into the contemporary period, in spite of the tremendous changes brought about by twentieth-century political upheavals and attempts by various regimes to redefine and control Daoism. Scholars should be wary of espousing one of the past or present official definitions of Daoism (always restrictive), and recognize the variety of people and groups who can be called Daoist inasmuch as they worship the Pure Deities of Former Heaven (i.e., emanations of the Dao that were never incarnated in human form) as the top of their pantheon, conduct rituals along Daoist paradigms of an ordained priest (*daoshi*) communicating through writing in classical form (petitions in bureaucratic styles, as well as talismans and summonses to lower gods) with those deities, and know (if not necessarily assiduously practice) the self-cultivation tradition and the spiritual and doctrinal heritage found in the Daoist Canon (*Daozang*, 1445 and 1607) and later collections.

A good starting point for the understanding of Daoism in late imperial times is the Daoist clergy. This clergy is usually described, by both scholars and contemporary Daoists, as being constituted of two orders: the older Zhengyi clergy, direct inheritor of the Church of the Heavenly Master (founded in the second century CE), and the Quanzhen order created in the late twelfth century. Besides these two orders that each have a shared coherent scriptural and liturgical foundation, other Daoists, whom scholars now call *vernacular priests* (probably in the majority, although no regime, imperial or modern, has ever been able to track and count them), belong to distinct local ritual traditions, with a role complementary to those of the more elite Quanzhen or Zhengyi.

## ELITE DAOISTS: THE HEAVENLY MASTERS AND THEIR NETWORK

The late imperial Zhengyi order had only one central training and ordination institution: the Zhang Heavenly Master patriarchy. The aristocratic and very well-connected Zhang family has been active and sponsored by the state since at least the eighth century, and was until 1911 invested with the role of overseers of Daoism and protectors of its orthodoxy. It held court on Longhu Mountain (eastern Jiangxi Province), supported by a large retinue of elite Daoist priests, *faguan*, serving as the Heavenly Master's officials.

During the nineteenth century, the Heavenly Masters were most often banned from traveling to the imperial court for audiences, but they still sent some of their *faguan* to serve as court clerics. They enjoyed huge prestige and were invited in all major central China cities to perform rituals, hold ordinations, and select new *faguan*. On Longhu Mountain, they presided over a bureaucratic system of ordination of Daoist clerics and canonization of local saints and gods. The destruction waged by the Taipings and, more importantly, the end of the imperial regime ushered in a decline of the Heavenly Master institution, which moved to Shanghai and then Taiwan, where it now tries to survive.

Most Zhengyi clerics were married and lived at home. The elite (belonging to the Qingwei Lingbao lineages that also produced the *faguan*) managed large urban temples in connection with state cults and merchant guilds. Many maintained relationships with certain temples where they officiated regularly, but they did not live in or manage them. Others concentrated on offering services to families and had little involvement with temples. All of them had a family altar, *tan*, organized around a head priest and acolytes, the latter being family members or disciples. From there they provided ritual services to families and to local communities, notably the large-scale *jiao* communal offerings that were at the core of the religious organization of local society. While such rituals are still crucial in most of Taiwan and in some rural parts of southeast China, where their reappearance after the Cultural Revolution (1966–1969) has been hailed as a Daoist revival, their significance has declined as a whole in twentieth-century Chinese society for both political and sociological reasons (the loosening of traditional territorial communities that organized them).

## THE QUANZHEN CLERGY

Quanzhen Daoists were much less numerous (maybe in the range of 20,000 by the late nineteenth century) than Zhengyi clerics, and were well entrenched only in about half the Qing territory. However, the prestige of their monastic tradition gave them a larger influence and role in transmitting Daoism as a whole than their actual numbers would suggest. Most Quanzhen clerics lived in small temples, just training one or two disciples, but they could undergo advanced training and consecration in one of the twenty-plus large Quanzhen monasteries active during the nineteenth century, most of which are now active again.

Consecrated Quanzhen Daoists take vows of celibacy and vegetarianism, hence the public perception of greater purity associated with Quanzhen Daoism. However, there also were local traditions of clerics initiated within Quanzhen and working as priests to local communities, but married and not consecrated. All of them provide ritual services very similar to that of their Zhengyi co-religionists.

The nineteenth century also witnessed the appearance and development of lay Quanzhen groups, organized around the spirit-writing cult of Lü Dongbin (probably the most important Daoist cult in modern China), whose adherents were initiated as members of a Quanzhen lineage, and taught both Quanzhen liturgy and self-cultivation, while keeping their lay life. These groups are now thriving, notably in Hong Kong, where they have become the mainstream form of Daoism; they represent a typical modern, individualistic, middle-class religiosity.

Besides distinctions based on order and lineage, it is equally relevant to describe Daoists as placed on a hierarchical ladder, with: (1) on top, elite Daoists registered with the imperial state, managing central temples that served both as ritual service centers for the state and for guilds, and as training centers for local clerics; (2) ordinary local temple managers and at-home (*huoju*) Daoists, ministering to the common folk, without large resources but with established hereditary rights (over temples or territorial parishes); and (3) in a marginal situation, mendicant wandering clerics. This basic description shows that Daoism defies any overall definition in terms of elite/popular.

## TWENTIETH-CENTURY ANTI-DAOISM

The late imperial state (both at central and local levels) ignored or occasionally repressed popular aspects of Daoism but cooperated with elite Daoists. This cooperation came to a brutal end in 1912, when the abolition of state cults severed the link between elite Daoists and the state, and a large number of temples used for the state cults and managed by Daoists (such as city god temples, *chenghuang miao*) were destroyed and their clerics expelled. The Republican and later the People's Republic of China (PRC) regimes eventually recognized Daoism as one of the official religions, but the process of recognition was uneasy, with a number of intellectuals and politicians arguing that Daoism was actually not a religion but mere superstition. Daoism had fewer friends in high office than the Buddhists (not to mention Christians and Muslims), and Daoists found it more difficult to resist appropriation of their temples or to secure their restoration. The ruin of the local religious organizations that supported them (village temples, guilds) also dealt Daoists a severe blow.

In this difficult context, Daoists tried to organize and reinvent themselves as a religion in the modern, Western-influenced sense. As early as 1912, tensions arose between the Quanzhen and Zhengyi, whose leaders set up competing national associations claiming to represent the whole of Daoism. Eventually, by the 1930s, newer associations at the local or regional levels managed to overcome such divisions, but they still attempted to register and control non-elite, non-temple-based clerics who resisted such efforts as well as they could. This problem remains a major issue for the Chinese Daoist Association at the beginning of the twenty-first century.

### DAOIST REINVENTIONS

In spite of the difficulties experienced throughout the twentieth century by Daoist clerics as temples were ruined or came under close state control and their rights to perform rituals were curtailed, Daoist individual self-cultivation flourished as never before during the Republican period and again since the 1980s. It had long been the case that Daoist self-cultivation texts and techniques were in large part transmitted to and by nonclerics, in a vast array of contexts ranging from amateur literati practicing for self-healing and attracted by the intellectual sophistication of Daoist "inner alchemy," to cultivational and devotional groups (sometimes called sectarian) and spirit-writing societies—not to mention popular media (ballads, novels, movies). But, during the Republican period, this movement of extraclerical transmission and practice of Daoist self-cultivation became a mass phenomenon, with new religious groups having memberships running in the millions (such as Tongshan she, Zaili jiao, Daoyuan, etc.) and publishing and teaching Daoist scriptures according to a systematic program.

While the above societies moved to Taiwan and continue to thrive and spawn new groups there, they were ruthlessly repressed in the PRC. For that reason, clerics there became again the major representatives and public voices of Daoism, but in a highly constrained situation. The Chinese Daoist Association was set up in 1957, several years later than most other associations for the five officially recognized religions, proof that Daoism, unlike Christianity, Buddhism, or Islam, was not a foreign policy asset and was given lower attention by the regime. The association was run by both Quanzhen clerics and lay reformers, notably Chen Yingning (1880–1969), who was trying to formulate a scientific, unsuperstitious form of Daoism while most clerics were secularized. The association was disbanded during the Cultural Revolution and revived in 1980, and has since then gradually regained control over monasteries and temples over the country, and set up modern training programs, with financial support from Daoists in Hong Kong and elsewhere, and in close cooperation with scholars of Daoism. This scholarship appeared late, during the 1930s, but with the modern reprint of the Daoist Canon (first in a limited edition in 1926 and in more widely distributed reprints since 1977), it has grown fast to become a major force in the modern reinventions of Daoism.

**SEE ALSO** *Popular Religion; Religious Organizations; Religious Specialists since 1800.*

### BIBLIOGRAPHY

Dean, Kenneth. *Taoist Ritual and Popular Cults of Southeast China.* Princeton, NJ: Princeton University Press, 1993.

Goossaert, Vincent. *The Taoists of Peking, 1800–1949: A Social History of Urban Clerics.* Cambridge: MA: Harvard University Asia Center, 2007.

Kohn, Livia, ed. *Daoism Handbook.* Leiden, Netherlands: Brill, 2000.

Lai Chi-tim. Daoism in China Today. In *Religion in China Today,* ed. Daniel L. Overmyer. Spec. issue: *China Quarterly* 174 (2003): 413–427.

Liu Xun. *In Search of Immortality: Daoist Inner Alchemy in Early Twentieth-century China.* Cambridge, MA: Harvard University Asia Center, 2009.

*Vincent Goossaert*

## DEATH PENALTY SINCE 1800

Although often mitigated in practice, offenses from treason to manslaughter merited capital punishment under Chinese law in the Qing dynasty (1644–1912). Executions were public affairs, and the two most common methods were strangulation and decapitation. Strangulation, in which the convict was garroted, was considered the lesser punishment because the body was left intact. Decapitation was deemed harsher because the separation of the head from the torso was thought to deprive the victim's spirit of a refuge in the afterlife. A third form of capital punishment, death by slicing, was reserved for the most serious of crimes, such as rebellion or parricide. The method was not specified by law but usually entailed severing the limbs before slitting the throat. Aside from the pain, the extreme disfigurement supposedly left the corpse unrecognizable to the spirit of the deceased. Despite the deep impression that this form of execution had on the Western psyche, death by slicing was a horrific but rarely used punishment.

Legal, moral, and political considerations combined to make capital punishment an abiding interest of Chinese emperors. Compassionate judicial administration was indicative of the deep regard for human life that was manifested in the special procedures for handling death-penalty cases in Qing law. Capital cases originated at the county (*xian*) level and underwent automatic retrial and review at the prefectural, provincial, and central government levels, culminating in the emperor's final verdict. The judicial review established culpability, cited applicable statutes, and assigned punishments in strict adherence to the code. In the overwhelming majority of capital cases, perhaps as many as 90 percent, the sentences were provisional, pending final approval at the autumn assizes (*qiushen*). As the voluminous extant Qing records indicate, extensive review of capital crimes attested to the concern for the proper adjudication and sentencing of capital crimes.

During the Republican period (1912–1949), China was plagued by civil war and foreign occupation; judicial administration was fragmented at best. The first president of the republic, Yuan Shikai, died in office in 1916 shortly after declaring a new dynasty. From 1916 to 1927 the central government existed in name only and warlords administered territories under their control as they saw fit. In 1927 the Guomindang established a national government in Nanjing but many areas remained beyond the direct control of the new government. Some warlords nominally pledged allegiance to the national government but operated independently. The Communist Party also retained control of rural base areas. Violence was endemic during these decades and the Guomindang, warlords, and Communists used capital punishment against criminals as well as political enemies.

With the establishment of the People's Republic of China (PRC) in 1949, centralized control over criminal justice was gradually restored. The early years of the PRC were marked by political turmoil, and executions for "counterrevolutionary crimes" were not uncommon. During the Mao Zedong years (1949–1976), the judiciary was highly politicized and, although capital punishment

***Chinese citizens allegedly being prepared for execution, Fujian province, 1992 (from a videotape supplied by human rights activist Harry Wu).*** *After the death of Mao Zedong, Chinese government officials have engaged in periodic crime sweeps, known as "strike hard" campaigns, to curtail illegal activity. Human rights activists warn, however, that many of the suspects are executed without a fair trial by a law enforcement organization that harvests the prisoner's organs after death.* AP IMAGES

was used for certain crimes and extrajudicial violence was common during political movements, "reeducation through labor" was the signature judicial punishment.

In the post-Mao era, Deng Xiaoping endorsed highly publicized campaign-style policing, known as "strike-hard" campaigns, which targeted serious crimes with severe punishments, including death. Since 1983 the Chinese government has launched several strike-hard campaigns that have included sentencing rallies culminating in summary executions in sports arenas. Critics have argued that the pressure of campaign-style policing and the deputation of final sentencing in violent crimes to provincial level courts have increased capital punishment. The spectacle of strike-hard campaigns, the brisk implementation of executions, the decentralization of sentencing as well as widely publicized cases of misfeasance, the use of torture to obtain confessions, and the harvesting of transplant organs from executed criminals all have led to domestic and international calls for abolition or reform of capital punishment.

Given the number of capital crimes and the policy of strike-hard campaigns, it is not surprising that China has led the world consistently in use of the death penalty. International and domestic criticisms have contributed, however, to recent changes in capital punishment policy and practice. Lethal injection has gradually replaced the single bullet to the back of the head, and the reported number of executions declined from 1,010 in 2006 to 470 in 2007. Procedural reforms have facilitated legal representation. Most importantly, beginning January 1, 2007, the Supreme People's Court resumed the review of all death sentences. Legal reform notwithstanding, sixty-eight death-penalty crimes, ranging from violent crime to economic offenses and corruption, remain in the criminal code of 1997. Capital punishment remains a controversial human rights issue. Foreign press reports and Amnesty International have alleged a much higher number of executions than those publicly reported, and international organizations have consistently criticized the Chinese judiciary over capital punishment. The decline in reported executions notwithstanding, statements by high judicial officials indicate that the death penalty will not be abolished any time soon.

**SEE ALSO** *Codified Law, 1800–1949; Customary Law, 1800–1949; Penal Systems, 1800–1949.*

**BIBLIOGRAPHY**

Bakken, Børge. *Crime, Punishment, and Policing in China.* Lanham, MD: Rowman & Littlefield, 2005.

Buoye, Thomas. "Suddenly Murderous Intent Arose: Bureaucratization and Benevolence in Eighteenth-Century Qing Homicide Reports." *Late Imperial China* 16, 2 (1995): 62–95.

Lu Hong and Terance D. Miethe. *China's Death Penalty: History, Law, and Contemporary Practices.* New York: Routledge, 2007.

MacCormack, Geoffrey. *The Spirit of Traditional Chinese Law.* Athens: University of Georgia Press, 1996.

Meijer, Marinus J. The Autumn Assizes in Ch'ing Law. *Toung Pao* 70 (1984): 1–17.

***Thomas Buoye***

# DEFENSE, 1800–1912

Defense of the Qing Empire initially fell on the shoulders of the Eight Banners (*baqi*) and the Green Standard Army (*lüying*). By 1800, both had long ceased to be effective as the country was subjected to Western intrusion and increasing social upheavals.

## THE EIGHT BANNERS

Created by the founders of the Qing dynasty (1644–1912) prior to the invasion of the Ming dynasty (1368–1644), the Eight Banners was a military force composed of Manchus, Mongols who had submitted to the Manchu, and the Han of southern Manchuria and some other areas. Of the three ethnic components, the Manchu was by far the largest, estimated at 60 percent of the entire force in the late Qing. The Metropolitan Banners were regular units located in and around Beijing, as well as in Zhili and Fengtian. Some of the "bondservants" (Chinese captured when the Han settlements on the plains of southern Manchuria were overrun by the Qing founders) were organized into separate banner companies. Provincial garrisons were widely distributed among four geographical regions: the capital region, the northeast, the northwest, and the rest of China proper. In addition to these, there were banner units consisting of various frontier peoples who were not formally counted among the provincial garrisons. By the late eighteenth century, the Eight Banners, at one time a first-rate fighting force, had been debilitated by long periods of peace, prosperity, and corruption.

## GREEN STANDARD ARMY

The Han Chinese Green Standard Army was a larger military force, widely dispersed in small garrisons throughout the provinces. Originally the soldiers of commanders of the Ming dynasty (1368–1644) who surrendered to the Qing in 1644 and after, these garrisons were stationed mostly in district or prefectural cities as a constabulary force to maintain local order, and their power could not penetrate the village substructure, where rebellions often arose and flourished. The Green Standard Army was inadequate in times of major social upheaval. Moreover, these troops could be brought together in large bodies only under high commanders specially deputed from the capital during emergencies. The chief officers of each garrison were rotated so that none could establish personal loyalties among his subordinates. As with the Eight Banners, these troops had declined in military power by the late eighteenth century.

### *TUANLIAN*

During the Taiping and other rebellions, the Qing dynasty had to depend on the *tuanlian* (militia units, grouped and drilled locally) or the *yongying* (mercenary armies) for its survival. The *tuanlian* system emerged in the mid-1850s out of the tradition of border-area officials who sought to tighten bureaucratic control over rural society. Such units were later augmented by the militarization of local gentry elite who sought to protect their communities and property from marauding groups of jobless and desperate people, as well as their Confucian way of life from Muslim and pseudo-Christian rebels. Two important examples of militia are the Hunan Army (Xiangjun) formed by Zeng Guofan and the Anhui Army (Huaijun) raised by Li Hongzhang, both of which were trained in traditional fashion, despite the use of some Western arms. Both were loyal to the Qing state, and, as such, local militarization was compatible with the requirements of the imperial state.

Through their loyalty to the throne, and the award of official ranks and titles in return, local elites were drawn into the Qing system and bureaucracy. On the other hand, the *tuanlian* system contributed to the growth of regional power and posed acute problems for the imperial state, even though central power was not seriously undermined. Once the Taipings were suppressed in the mid-1860s, both the Hunan Army and the Anhui Army were ordered by the Qing court to disband. However, while large numbers of troops were demobilized, many were also kept at imperial command to quell other rebellions and to defend China against the West and Japan.

Reform of the armed forces began at this time, culminating with the establishment of the New Army in the first decade of the twentieth century, after the Boxer Uprising.

### NAVAL DEVELOPMENTS

For most of the latter half of the nineteenth century, the navy began to occupy the attention of Qing officials as well. This focus on naval development represented a major change in Chinese military and strategic thinking. Traditionally, China's invaders had mainly come overland from Inner Asia and the far north; they were nomadic or seminomadic horse-riding "barbarians." This threat, linked as it was to the Great Wall and to the army, dominated traditional Chinese military thinking.

Until the second half of the nineteenth century, China had no naval tradition. The only time previously that China had a fleet was in the early fifteenth century, during the reign of the third Ming emperor, Yongle (r. 1402–1424), when Admiral Zheng He (1371–c. 1433) made seven voyages to Southeast Asia and beyond, with at least four of them reaching the Red Sea ports of West Asia and the shores of East Africa. These voyages, however, did not lead to Chinese maritime expansion and ended in 1433. It took another four and a half centuries for the rulers of the Middle Kingdom to realize that a modern navy was a vital means of defense and a chief index of great-power status. In the mid-nineteenth century, the British taught Qing military strategists that the greatest external threat to the Middle Kingdom came from the sea and from the south and east, and that a different military strategy was required for coastal defense. Even so, there was a twenty-year hiatus between the Opium War (1839–1842) and the start of naval development in China in the 1860s.

The establishment in 1866 of the Fuzhou Navy Yard by Governor-General Zuo Zongtang of Fujian and Zhejiang, with Shen Baozhen as superintendent, was a modest start toward building a naval force. With foreign help, especially from the French, fifteen ships had been built by 1874 and a training program was in full operation. Nevertheless, although new ships were purchased from abroad or were built at Fuzhou and Shanghai, these were not organized into a single national fleet. There were conflicts between those who favored ambitious ship-buying programs and those who wanted to build ships in China. Li Hongzhang, the northern commissioner of trade and the governor-general of Zhili from 1870 to 1895, sought to establish a single national naval command, and he preferred to buy the ships. The result of the conflict was a lack of standardization in China's fleet.

On the eve of the Sino-French War (1884–1885), China had over fifty modern ships, more than half of them homebuilt. Of the rest, thirteen were British Armstrong gunboats, two were Armstrong cruisers, and two were German ships. There was still no single national fleet and no unified command. The Fuzhou squadron was wiped out in the war with the French. The loss to France was due not so much to French naval superiority as to the structure of the Chinese leadership and the political organization of the imperial state. The insufficiently trained Chinese naval personnel had no grasp of a naval strategy appropriate to China's new ships.

### THE FLEETS, COASTAL DEFENSE, AND NAVAL TRAINING, 1885–1895

In 1885 the Navy Board was created. The following years, especially between 1888 and 1894, saw the emergence of the Beiyang fleet. Headed by Prince Chun (1883–1951), the Navy Board proved to be ineffectual in its efforts to centralize naval affairs. Li Hongzhang, for all his national ambitions, was still operating in regional fashion. He reorganized his Beiyang flotilla into a fleet of twenty-five ships, acknowledging British and German precedents in staff organization. Commanded by Admiral Ding Ruchang (1836–1895), the Beiyang fleet was divided into seven functional squadrons. It was the largest of China's four fleets, the others being the Nanyang squadron along the coast south of Shandong and two squadrons in Fujian and Guangdong. Coastal defense preparations included shore fortifications at Port Arthur (Luxun), Dalianwan, and Weihaiwei, and numerous forts along the southern coast and the Yangzi.

Elsewhere, coastal defense was still carried out the old way, and the water forces on the Yangzi River remained traditional. The Shanghai defenses used mines that were often poorly mapped, and the Ningbo defenses used torpedoes. In the south, Governor-General Zhang Zhidong built forts but, as late as 1886, still resorted to harbor blocking by dumping stones in the river in the face of a threat from foreign ships.

The naval academies at Fuzhou, Guangzhou, Nanjing, Tianjin, and Weihaiwei were in full operation during the 1885–1894 decade. In Fuzhou, there were two naval schools: a French-language construction school and an English-language naval academy for officers in deck and engine divisions. British officers from the Royal Naval College at Greenwich were engaged to help train early groups of students. Later, bright students were sent to England and Germany for advanced training. In 1888, when Li Hongzhang established the Beiyang fleet, he was well served by the Fuzhou-trained men. The faculty of the academy in Tianjin included William M. Lang of the British Royal Navy, who was given an imperial commission and the title of admiral to run the training program in British fashion and to take charge of the Beiyang fleet's organization and naval yards. He resigned his commission in 1890, after which training at Tianjin went into decline.

## PROBLEMS IN NAVAL DEVELOPMENT

Over the years, China's naval development was hampered by institutional problems and financial difficulties (aggravated by the Qing court's reluctance to change its system of public financing). Many funds meant for the navy were diverted in 1888 and after into building, or refurbishing, the Summer Palace in Beijing. Naval reforms were undertaken with insufficient coordination among officials, each of whom had his own priorities and preoccupations. There was also a lack of leadership from the center. Few high officials in Beijing took a real interest in the navy. And no one, not even Li Hongzhang, could make the naval service into a respected profession or career in China.

## DISASTER IN THE SINO-JAPANESE WAR

The weakness of the Chinese navy was fully demonstrated in the war with Japan (1894–1895). On the eve of the war, the navy had sixty-six large ships, with over 430 torpedo boats. The Beiyang fleet was the strongest; alone it equaled that of Japan in numbers. Li Hongzhang thus was deeply involved in the war, with the Navy Board playing only a subordinate role while the other squadrons looked on. What little help Li received from the southern fleets was given reluctantly. As a result, the Beiyang fleet was wiped out in the 1894 Battle of the Yalu, which demonstrated how disunited China was and how backward it remained in modern warfare.

After the war, the British continued to assist the Qing dynasty with naval reorganization. But the Beiyang fleet never recovered from the Japanese defeat. This led to a reversion of Chinese military and strategic thinking in the post-Boxer decade to the tradition of land defense, when great store was set on the New Army (*xinjun*).

## THE DEMISE OF THE IMPERIAL STATE

After the demise of the imperial state in 1912, the militarization of Chinese society did not cease; it only took a different form. Local elites collaborated with the military regimes at provincial and regional levels to protect themselves and to seek a share of political power in the unstable new order. The New Army in south, west, and central China was largely disorganized, as the revolutionary forces altered the existing military organizations to suit their purposes. New formations of all sorts sprang into existence, with many of the new recruits being unruly elements. In the north, however, the framework of the original New Army organization remained intact, though many divisions had been greatly reduced by war losses and subsequent desertions. Overall, there were too many men under arms. The ascendancy of the military after the 1911 Revolution and the events that unfolded paved the way for a long period of warlord rule in the Republican period.

**SEE ALSO** *Army and Politics; Military Culture and Tradition; Militia; Wars and the Military, 1800–1912; Wars since 1800.*

**BIBLIOGRAPHY**

Fung, Edmund S. K. (Feng Zhaoji) *The Military Dimension of the Chinese Revolution: The New Army and Its Role in the Revolution of 1911*. Vancouver: University of British Columbia Press, 1980.

Kuhn, Philip A. *Rebellion and Its Enemies in Late Imperial China: Militarization and Social Structure, 1796–1864*. Cambridge, MA: Harvard University Press, 1970.

Pong, David. *Shen Pao-chen and China's Modernization in the Nineteenth Century*. Cambridge, U.K.: Cambridge University Press, 1994.

Rawlinson, John L. *China's Struggle for Naval Development, 1839–1985*. Cambridge, MA: Harvard University Press, 1967.

Rhoads, Edward J. *Manchus & Han: Ethnic Relations and Political Power in Late and Early Republican China, 1861–1928.* Seattle: University of Washington Press, 2000.

Spector, Stanley. *Li Hung-chang and the Huai Army: A Study in Nineteenth-Century Chinese Regionalism.* Seattle: University of Washington Press, 1964.

Wang Gungwu. *Anglo-Chinese Encounters since 1800: War, Trade, Science, and Governance.* Cambridge, U.K.: Cambridge University Press, 2003.

***Edmund S. K. Fung (Feng Zhaoji)***

## DEMOCRACY WALL

A brick wall 200 meters long and covered with wooden planks at the angle of the Avenue of Eternal Peace (Chang'an Jie) and Xidan Road became a landmark in the history of the prodemocracy movement in 1978. At this site, discontented citizens of the People's Republic of China (PRC) began posting *dazibaos* (large-character posters) expressing their views on the political movements that had shaken the nation since the Communist Party seized power in 1949.

On December 15, 1978, the April Fifth 1976 movement which commemorated Zhou Enlai's death, was declared a "totally revolutionary" episode by the party. Many discontented citizens understood this decision as a legitimization of a spontaneous expression of political sentiments by ordinary people.

At the time, a group of pragmatists around party vice chairman Deng Xiaoping were engaged in a struggle against the neo-Maoists gathered behind Hua Guofeng and Wang Dongxing. Deng Xiaoping needed all the support possible to impose his pragmatic policies on a leadership still dominated by the neo-Maoists. This might be one of the reasons why he openly supported the posting of *dazibaos* on what was to become the Democracy Wall in a way reminiscent of Mao Zedong's behavior during the Hundred Flowers movement. The Third Plenum of the Eleventh Central Committee, considered to have launched the reform and which signaled the defeat of Hua Guofeng and the neo-Maoists, met in December 1978 in the Great Hall of the People while *dazibaos* were being affixed to the Democracy Wall. The Theoretical Conference, the role of which was to revamp the ideology, met from January to March 1979. The debates in the Great Hall of the People often reflected the discussions on the Xidan wall. This episode of the prodemocracy movement was actually made possible by the struggle at the top, and its end was a result of Deng's victory.

From November 22, 1978, to April 5, 1979, the movement went through its first and most active phase. After a period of repression that followed China's February 1979 war with Vietnam, the movement entered a phase of somnolence. Then, at the end of July, sit-ins, petitions, and a new wave of *dazibaos* appeared at Xidan as a renewed campaign of criticism of Maoist policies was launched following the session of the National People's Congress. At the end of 1979, these activities were suppressed. From the end of 1978 till the end of 1979, democracy walls appeared in many provincial cities, including Shanghai, Guangzhou, Qingdao, and Guiyang. Across the country, *dazibaos* expressed an uncensored discourse by ordinary citizens. One can isolate three categories of content.

### CONTENT OF THE *DAZIBAOS*

At the beginning, the *dazibaos* described the sufferings inflicted on ordinary citizens, peasants of bad class origin, intellectuals sent down to the countryside, and "revisionist cadres" accused by the leadership during the various Maoist campaigns since 1957 and asking for their rehabilitation. The *dazibaos* give a vivid and uncensored image of the sufferings endured by the Chinese people during the last two decades of Mao's rule. These *dazibaos* were in tune with the official line that criticized "leftist excesses," but their uncensored tone made them much more convincing than the official press. These *dazibaos*, and the protests that often took the form of sit-ins by petitioners (*shangfangzhe*), lasted for the duration of the Democracy Wall, and sometimes resulted in rehabilitations, but not always. One of the most famous petitioners, Fu Yuehua, a young woman who denounced a cadre who had raped her, was tried and sentenced to two years in jail in 1979 for disturbing public order.

The second type of *dazibao* that appeared on the wall included the works of writers and artists who did not follow the canons of revolutionary romanticism and socialist realism imposed by Mao since 1949. The poets mimeographed their poems and presented them in journals, the most famous of which, *Jintian* (Today), appeared on the Democracy Wall in December 1978. These writers belonged to the "lost generation": After having been Red Guards, some had been sent to the countryside, others to factories. In their works, poems, and short stories, they wrote about love, about their sufferings in the countryside, about the bitterness of life. The most famous of these works was Bei Dao's poem "Reply," which symbolized the loss of faith of a whole generation: "I don't believe . . . that the sky is blue." Other unorthodox and underground literary journals appeared in the provinces, such as *Hai langhua* (The foam of waves) in Qingdao, Shandong.

The *Jintian* poets were linked to a group of artists who explored new styles of painting and sculpture and refused socialist realism. They resorted to abstract painting or traditional Chinese painting. The most famous were the sculptor Wang Keping and the painters Ma Desheng, Li Shuang,

## WEI JINGSHENG

Born in Beijing on May 20, 1950, Wei Jingsheng is one of the most famous Chinese dissidents. Once nicknamed "the father of Chinese democracy," he was nominated several times for the Nobel Peace Prize, and was awarded the Sakharov Prize for Freedom of Thought in 1996.

Wei Jingsheng grew up within the Chinese Communist system. His parents were high cadres of the regime and taught him the virtues of being "at the service of the people." Having joined the Red Guard in 1966, he had to go into hiding for a year in his father's native province, Anhui, in 1968. He discovered then the huge gap between revolutionary propaganda and real life in the poor countryside, especially during the famine that began during the Great Leap Forward (1958–1960) and lasted until 1962. That turned him into a fierce fighter against dictatorship.

After spending three years in the army, Wei managed to go back to Beijing, where he found a job as an electrician in the Beijing zoo. Taking advantage of the slightly relaxed atmosphere following the death of Chairman Mao Zedong, Wei Jingsheng joined the first democratic movement in Beijing, which developed around the Xidan "Democracy Wall" in winter 1978 to 1979. He became world famous for writing a manifesto, "Di Wuge Xiandaihua: Minzhu" ("The Fifth Modernization, Democracy"), explaining why Deng Xiaoping's program of four modernizations (agriculture, industry, science and technology, and national defense) could never succeed without a true political reform of the system: "We want to be the masters of our own destiny.... Freedom and happiness are our sole objectives in accomplishing modernization. Without this modernization, all the others are merely another new promise" (1995, p. 193). He openly asked for the end of the Communist Party dictatorship.

Having attracted the attention of numerous readers, in December 1978 Wei and a few friends began to publish an underground magazine, *Tansuo* (Exploration). It became the most radical of all the leading publications, with insightful articles on the subject of democracy, shocking exposés of political prisons, and investigative reporting. Clearly disillusioned with Deng Xiaoping's promises to the nation, in the last issue of his short-lived publication Wei wrote that Deng Xiaoping was about to become the next dictator of China. When Deng Xiaoping decided to crack down on critics, Wei Jingsheng was the first to be arrested, on March 29. Six months later he was sentenced to fifteen years in jail. He chose to defend himself, and the text of his eloquent speech, "The Trial of Wei Jingsheng," was smuggled out of Beijing and published in several languages (1995, pp. 200–239).

During the fourteen and a half years Wei spent in jail, he managed to write a few dozen letters to Chinese leaders and to take them with him when he was released from jail in September 1993. These letters, published in New York in book form as *The Courage to Stand Alone* (1996), show a man unbroken by the hardships endured in three different provinces—Beijing, Qinghai, and Hebei—and in three different kinds of prisons. Wei never wavered in his convictions, and immediately took up the fight for democracy as soon as he came out of jail. After only six months of freedom he was arrested again, on April 1, 1994, and after a very quick trial was sentenced on December 13, 1995, to fourteen years in jail. A few days later, Wei was back in the Tangshan jail in Hebei Province.

Thanks to the pressure from human rights organizations and the insistence of U.S. president Bill Clinton, Wei Jingsheng was released in November 1997, only to be expelled from China. As of 2008 he had not been allowed back to his country; he lives in Washington, D.C., where he acts as a lobbyist for China's democracy movement. He also travels frequently to give speeches and interviews on all five continents, and tries to put pressure on Chinese leaders whenever they travel abroad.

Wei has received awards from governments and institutions all over the world, including the Pacific-Asian Human Rights Foundation, which gave him the Human Rights Leader award in July 2008.

### BIBLIOGRAPHY

Holzman, Marie, and Bernard Debord. *Wei Jingsheng, un Chinois inflexible* [Wei Jingsheng, an inflexible Chinese]. Paris: Bleu de Chine, 2005.

Wei Jingsheng. "The Fifth Modernization, Democracy" and "The Trial of Wei Jingsheng." In *Wei Jingsheng: The Man and His Ideas*, ed. Yang Jianli, 189–195; 200–239. Brookline, MA: China in the Twenty-first Century Foundation, 1995.

Wei Jingsheng. *The Courage to Stand Alone*. New York: Random House, 1996.

Wei Jingsheng. *Shifang yilai yanlunji* (Since regaining freedom: Collected works). Hong Kong: Minzhu Daxue, 1997.

***Marie Holzman***

and Ai Weiwei, among others. In January 1979, they organized an exhibition of their group's work called *Xingxing*, the Stars, at the Democracy Wall.

Finally, some *dazibaos* were made by political groups. Besides the *dazibaos* written by the victims of Maoist campaigns, many members of the lost generation affixed posters that contained the results of their reflection on the system. Refusing the official explanations of the causes of the Cultural Revolution, they explained that the Gang of Four would never have existed without Mao. Furthermore, they reflected over the nature of the system. Many reached the conclusion that the tragedy would not have been possible had there been independent organizations to monitor the party. Their *dazibaos* attracted spectators and gave rise to unofficial journals that represented a wide spectrum of political opinions.

**The Radicals** Many people were struck by the maturity of a *dazibao* by Wei Jingsheng titled "The Fifth Democratization: Democracy," in which the author stated that China must get rid of Marxism–Leninism, which he called a "quack doctor's medicine." Wei appealed for an end to the dictatorship of the Communist Party. At the end of December, his *dazibao* was printed in an unofficial journal, *Tansuo* (Exploration). In March 1979, in an article entitled "Democracy or New Despotism?" Wei wrote that because Deng had not opted to transform the system, he might become a new tyrant. Wei was arrested on March 29, 1979, and received a fifteen-year jail sentence.

Another radical group was the Alliance for Human Rights, created by Ren Wanding, a thirty-eight-year-old engineer who posted a *dazibao* asking U.S. president Jimmy Carter to intervene with Chinese leaders to make them respect human rights. The group deemed it necessary to change the system so as to avoid a repetition of the Cultural Revolution. Furthermore, they demanded self-determination for national minorities, a very daring proposal. Ren was arrested on April 4, 1979, and was sentenced to reeducation through labor for two years.

**The Moderates** *Siwu luntan* (April Fifth Forum) was founded by critical Marxists who denounced the dogmatism of Mao. Although ideologically close to the party reformers, they insisted that freedom of association and expression must be respected, so that party leaders would not become despots. Despite their divergences with the radicals, the moderates defended their right to exist. The most moderate group was Beijing Zhi Chun (Beijing Spring), founded by members of the Central Committee of the Communist Youth League. They asked for an acceleration of reforms, but did not question the leadership of the Communist Party. They also demanded respect for freedom of association.

Other groups appeared in the provinces—in Guangzhou, Wuhan, Shanghai, and Guiyang—but they were in general more moderate. He Xin and Wang Xizhe's Renmin Zhisheng (Voice of the People) in Guangzhou was one of the most famous.

### THE END OF THE MOVEMENT

At the end of October 1979, following the sentencing of Wei Jingsheng on October 16, the movement died down, and the authorities prohibited the posting of *dazibaos* on the wall. After having achieved victory over the neo-Maoists, Deng Xiaoping put an end to the movement and reasserted the dictatorship of the party, confirming the prevalence of the Four Basic Principles (socialism, Marxism–Leninism and Mao Zedong Thought, People's democratic dictatorship, and leadership of the party) that he had enunciated in his March 30th speech.

**SEE ALSO** *Classical Scholarship and Intellectual Debates: Debates since 1949; Cultural Revolution, 1966–1969; Deng Xiaoping; Hua Guofeng; Hundred Flowers Campaign; Prodemocracy Movement (1989).*

**BIBLIOGRAPHY**


Goldman, Merle. Hu Yaobang's Intellectual Network and the Theory Conference of 1979. *China Quarterly* 126 (1991): 219–242.

Goodman, David S. G. *Beijing Street Voices: The Poetry and Politics of China's Democracy Movement*. London: Marion Boyars, 1981.

Huang San, Lionel Epstein, and Angel Pino. *Un Bol de Nids d'Hirondelles ne fait pas le Printemps de Pékin*. Paris: Christian Bourgois, Bibliothèque Asiatique, 1980.

Seymour, James D., ed. *The Fifth Modernization: China's Human Rights Movement, 1978–1979*. New York: Coleman, 1980.

Sidane, Victor. *Le Printemps de Pékin: Oppositions démocratiques en Chine, novembre 1978–mars 1980*. Paris: Gallimard/Julliard, Collection Archives, 1980.

Widor, Claude. *Documents on the Chinese Democracy Movement, 1978–1980*. 2 vols. Paris: Éd. de l'École des Hautes Études en Sciences Sociales, 1981.

Widor, Claude, ed. *The Samizdat Press in China's Provinces, 1979–1981: An Annotated Guide*. Stanford, CA: Hoover Institution Press, 1987.


***Jean-Philippe Béja***

## DEMOCRATIC IDEAS, REFORMS, AND EXPERIMENTS SINCE THE 1880s

Embedded in Confucian political thinking from its very beginning is the belief that attention to the physical and moral welfare of the people is the first responsibility of government, and that ultimately it is the people who will judge whether this responsibility has been faithfully discharged; for "Heaven sees as the people see, Heaven hears as the people hear" (*Mencius,* 5A.5). Quite absent from traditional Chinese political theory and practice, however, is any notion that this judgment should be expressed in a way that might involve the direct participation of the populace in their own governance. The tension between what might be called "republican" instincts on the one hand and a steady antipathy to "democratic" processes on the other has marked the Chinese understanding of the concept of democracy since its introduction into political discourse in the later decades of the nineteenth century. Reformers who lived in the treaty ports at that time, such as the journalist Wang Tao (1828–1897) and the physician Ho Kai (1859–1914), were the first to link the solution of China's problems to the liberalization of politics and the introduction of parliamentary forms, though their views of who should be brought into the political process remained highly elitist.

Not until the end of the century, in the explosion of radical publication and propagandizing that followed the debacle of the Hundred Days' Reform in 1898, did democracy become familiar to Chinese readers as one possible alternative to imperial or Manchu autocratic rule. From exile, chiefly in Japan, constitutional monarchists such as Liang Qichao and republican radicals who gravitated toward the evolving revolutionary party of Sun Yat-sen (Sun Yixian) debated the virtues of democracy and its applicability to Chinese realities. Liang's *Xinmin congbao* (New people's miscellany), published in Tokyo, was for several years passionate in its advocacy of democratic ideas as an antidote to the despotic dynastic imperialism that had enslaved the Chinese people and stunted their natural political development. In the end, however, after a 1903–1904 trip to Chinese communities in North America, Liang's allegiance to democracy was overwhelmed by his conviction that the inbred civic backwardness of the Chinese people rendered them incompetent to bear the responsibilities of self-government, and that only enlightened autocratic rule could be relied on to cure China's ills.

The revolutionaries, for their part, made democracy a central pillar of their program, enshrined as one of the Three Principles of the People (*san min zhuyi*) when these were first enunciated by Sun Yat-sen in 1905. The idea of "the power of the people" (*min quan*) remained a slogan of the revolutionary party that Sun founded in that year throughout the following decades of political successes and frustrations; but as with so much of Sun's legacy, what the term might signify in institutional terms remained unclear. With the collapse of the Qing (Manchu) dynasty in 1911–1912 a major revolutionary objective was accomplished, but there was no generally accepted understanding of what should take its place. In 1912 and 1913 nationwide elections were held to create the first provincial and national assemblies—China's first and arguably only free and fair elections, but participated in by only a minuscule electorate, circumscribed by educational and property qualifications to comprise essentially the old gentry elite. In any case the rapid militarization of politics and the ensuing decade and a half of warlord factionalism rendered any consideration of popularly sanctioned government no more than a theoretical enterprise, as evidenced in the several aborted constitutional efforts of those years.

## THE GUOMINDANG GOVERNMENT

In the aftermath of the Northern Expedition (1926–1928), the triumph of Sun Yat-sen's revolutionary party (remodeled along Leninist lines with the aid of Soviet advisers) made the Three Principles of the People central to the ideology of the newly established Guomindang government. The first principle, nationalism (*minzu zhuyi*), was clearly the driving force of the revolutionary regime; socialism (or popular welfare, *minsheng zhuyi*) and democracy (*minquan zhuyi*) were far more problematic commitments. Sun's ideas about democracy had become more guarded over the years of political frustration before his death in 1925; his ultimate successor as party leader, Chiang Kai-shek (Jiang Jieshi), was a far less cosmopolitan and more traditional thinker. These factors, together with the exigencies of nationalist politics and a burgeoning civil war, caused further modifications in the way in which the idea of "people power" would be understood and implemented.

Sun had divided his prospective revolution into three stages: the seizure of power and reunification; the education of the people to assume their newly achieved responsibilities, which would be the task of the revolutionary party; and, eventually, the establishment of a constitutionally founded, participatory political order. In early formulations the crucially important transitional period of "political tutelage" had been limited, first to three, then to six years. By the time the revolution came to power in the 1920s all such restrictions had been dropped. The new Guomindang government accepted Sun's three-stage scheme and declared the first revolutionary stage accomplished. What followed was an extended "period of political tutelage," under the aegis of the party, which quickly degenerated into a period of political indoctrination and one-party dictatorship, with the final constitutional stage indefinitely postponed.

Such an outcome was justified by the familiar argument that the Chinese masses were too inexperienced and immature to assume the burdens of self-government without the guiding hand of politically conscious cadres and technically educated experts. In the 1930s, as China's

***Men reading broadsheets posted on "Democracy Wall," Beijing, December 5, 1978.*** *After the death of Mao Zedong, some protestors took advantage of his absence to begin demanding the prosecution of citizens involved in the excesses of the Cultural Revolution. In Beijing, citizens posted their grievances on what became known as "Democracy Wall," a temporary form of dissent quickly ended by Deng Xiaoping.* DSK/AFP/GETTY IMAGES

political crisis deepened both domestically and internationally, even many intellectuals who had earlier identified themselves with the "liberal" politics of the May Fourth, or New Culture, movement (1915–1925) subscribed to the view that only an enlightened autocracy could meet the need of the moment for technically modern and capable administration. This view did not necessarily equate with support of the Guomindang government, but it represented, in Chinese terms, a repudiation of liberal democratic ideals comparable to events happening at the same time in Italy and Germany. Against this view only a few voices were raised, arguing, like Hu Shi, that political judgment relies not on esoteric knowledge but on the application of everyday common sense to everyday issues; that civic "education" is an autocratic dodge; and that, as Hu put it, "the only way to have democracy is to have democracy."

## EARLY COMMUNIST ERA

A similar insight might seem to guide early Communist attempts to reorganize village social and political life in the "liberated" areas of North China in the 1940s. Following the Maoist doctrine of the Mass Line—denoting a dynamic process of deriving knowledge *from* the masses and on this basis dictating policy *to* the masses—party cadres solicited, and relied on, peasant opinion in shaping the party's response to local conditions over the course of the land reform movements across North China. Often party cadres made it appear that the politicization of village life was a spontaneous process, a result of the release of long suppressed political aptitudes and instincts. In fact, Mao's almost mystical belief in the wisdom of the masses did not translate into confidence in popular self-government. The land revolution mobilized peasant energies to transform the countryside according to a strategy that was participatory only in a manipulative and sometimes coercive sense, in pursuit of the clearly articulated Maoist vision of China's class struggle.

Mao Zedong's celebrated essay "On the New Democracy" (1940), which foreshadowed the political forms imposed in 1949 when the People's Republic of China was established, had nothing to do with the creation of representative democratic institutions of government. It was rather a bold attempt to fit the Chinese Communist movement, with its negligible urban working class element and its great reliance on the peasant masses, into the framework of Marxist-Leninist proletarian-led revolutionary theory. Mao posited a revolutionary alliance of peasants, nationalistic petty bourgeoisie, and workers, peculiar to China, and it was in the name of this coalition that the Communist Party justified its dictatorship after 1949.

## DURING AND AFTER THE MAOIST YEARS

Over the course of the Maoist years (1949–1976), popular participation in politics took the form of government-inspired mass mobilization campaigns, most spectacularly the Great Leap Forward (1958–1960) and the decade of the Great Proletarian Cultural Revolution (1966–1976). In the latter instance what began as a carefully orchestrated intra-party purge spun quickly out of control, and incidents of spontaneous political organization and intense factional infighting proliferated at all levels of the movement, requiring finally the intervention of the People's Liberation Army to restore social discipline. But this was anarchy, not democracy, in action.

In the turbulence of the years after Mao and the Cultural Revolution, "democracy" became a popular catchword in the emerging agenda of political criticism. Maoist ideological dogmatism gave way to a degree of pragmatism in the shaping of economic and social policy, accompanied by some liberalization of Maoist constraints on intellectual and cultural life. The first evidence of this came in 1978–1979, when, briefly, the new regime dominated by Deng Xiaoping allowed the fairly free publication of an outpouring of politically dissident opinion in the form of broadsheets posted on what became known as Democracy Wall in downtown Beijing. In this context, the demands for greater "democracy" meant, essentially, a plea for redressing the wrongs of the Cultural Revolution,

***Demonstrator in Tiananmen Square in front of the "Goddess of Democracy" statue, Beijing, 1989.*** *In the late 1980s, student-led protests against the Communist government became increasingly vocal, spreading throughout China in the spring of 1989. While demonstrations in most cities ended without violence, troops from the People's Liberation Army used deadly force against citizens in Beijing's Tiananmen Square before imprisoning hundreds of protestors.* © DAVID TURNLEY/CORBIS

bringing many perpetrators still in office to justice, a more responsive and transparent style of government, and a greater tolerance of free speech and civil rights generally. The Democracy Wall movement was soon suppressed, but such concerns remained central to the student protests that surfaced again in a minor way in 1986–1987 and exploded in Tiananmen Square from April to June of 1989.

An enduring symbol of the 1989 protests was the "Goddess of Democracy" statue erected in the Square, confronting the portrait of Chairman Mao. The student organizations that formed the nucleus of the movement were loosely democratic in structure, but their demands did not go beyond an elaboration of previously stated reformist aims: open and transparent government, broader tolerance of criticism, freedom of speech, and of assembly and the press. Initially, at least, the protesters did not question the legitimacy of the government, or demand an end to the party's monopoly on decision-making authority, or seek the political empowerment of the masses, urban or rural. Nevertheless, as the movement continued other constituencies became involved, including elements of the bureaucracy, members of the nascent professional elite, and—most ominously from the government's point of view—representatives of the urban working class.

The bloody suppression of the movement on June 4, 1989, made clear the government's hostility to political pluralism and refusal to tolerate any real or potential challenge to its continued insistence on the necessity of one-party rule. At the same time it pressed ahead with economic reforms designed, among other things, to blunt the edge of social and political discontents by satisfying the consumer demands of the urban middle class, which, by the 1990s, was emerging as a significant constituency.

It remains to be seen whether such socioeconomic developments will over time generate demands for political liberalization, as some suggest must be the case. Such was indeed what happened in the Republic of China on Taiwan in the 1980s and 1990s, when economic prosperity created an environment of rising political expectations in which the dictatorial regime imposed on the island by Chiang Kai-shek's Nationalists in 1949 gradually gave way to an active, sometimes boisterous, democratic political system. Is democracy, as the dissident Wei Jingsheng argued on Democracy Wall in 1979, the necessary corollary to economic modernization?

China, however, is larger than the Republic of China, demographically more diverse, and geographically and economically more polarized. In the late twentieth and early twenty-first centuries the coastal provinces and their urban populations benefited from the remarkable generation of wealth far more than have the hinterland provinces and the great majority of the people. Such inequalities might constitute grave impediments in the way of democratization. Moreover, if the Chinese political system were to evolve in time into a genuinely participatory and democratic government it would have to face an issue that no government that came to power in the twentieth century—or at any time in China's long history—had the will to confront: the problem of how to open the political process to the still politically untutored masses of China and empower the people to set the terms of the political settlement under which they would live.

**SEE ALSO** *Constitutionalism; Constitutions before 1949; Constitutions since 1949; Democracy Wall; Dissidents; Elections and Assemblies, 1909–1949; Hu Shi; Human Rights since 1949; Hundred Days' Reform; Hundred Flowers Campaign; Individual and the State, 1800–1949; Kang Youwei; Liang Qichao; Liberalism; Liu Binyan; May Fourth Movement; Nationalist Government, 1927–1949; Political Representation; Political Parties, 1905–1949; Prodemocracy Movement (1989); Student Organizations and Activism, 1900–1949; Sun Yat-sen (Sun Yixian); Three Principles of the People (Sanmin zhuyi); Tiananmen Incident (1976); Treaty Ports; Wang Jingwei; Wang Shiwei; Yan Fu.*

**BIBLIOGRAPHY**

Grieder, Jerome B. *Hu Shih and the Chinese Renaissance: Liberalism in the Chinese Revolution, 1917–1937.* Cambridge, MA: Harvard University Press, 1970.

Grieder, Jerome B. *Intellectuals and the State in Modern China: A Narrative History.* New York: Free Press, 1981.

Meisner, Maurice. *Mao's China and After: A History of the People's Republic.* 3rd ed. New York: Free Press, 1999.

Nathan, Andrew J. *Chinese Democracy.* Berkeley: University of California Press, 1986.

Shi Tianjian. *Political Participation in Beijing.* Cambridge, MA: Harvard University Press, 1997.

Spence, Jonathan. *The Search for Modern China.* 2nd ed. New York: Norton, 1999.

Wei Jingsheng. The Fifth Modernization: Democracy. In *The Fifth Modernization: China's Human Rights Movement, 1978–1979,* ed. James D. Seymour. Stanfordville, NY: Human Rights Publishing Group, 1980.

***Jerome B. Grieder***

# DEMOCRATIC PARTIES

*This entry contains the following:*

## OVERVIEW

In addition to the Chinese Communist Party (CCP), China's political system is notable for the official status of eight so-called democratic parties (*minzhu dangpai*, usually referred to as satellite parties or minor parties and groups outside China). Together with the All-China Federation of Industry and Commerce (Zhonghua Quanguo Gongshangye Lianhe Hui), these minor parties form a key aspect of CCP United Front work, reflecting corporatist principles of both representing and giving access to important interest groups. The eight parties are:

- China Democratic National Construction Association
- China Association for Promoting Democracy
- China Democratic League
- Chinese Peasants and Workers Democratic Party
- Jiusan (September Third) Society
- Revolutionary Committee of the Nationalist Party (Guomindang)
- Taiwan Democratic Self-Government League
- Zhigong (or Public Interest) Party

With the exception of the China Democratic League, most were formed in the 1945–1946 period with the direct support and encouragement of the CCP as part of its anti-Guomindang (GMD) United Front work. The Taiwan Democratic Self-Government League was officially launched in November 1947, and was soon followed by the Reformed Revolutionary Committee of the Nationalist Party.

### POST–WORLD WAR II FORMATION OF THE "SECOND FRONT"

With Japan defeated, the Nationalists were pressured by the United States to reach a settlement with the CCP and build a "strong united and democratic China." The resulting increased political freedom allowed CCP activists to organize a "second front" of anti-GMD political action in urban areas. If the GMD had allowed elections, the minor parties would have acted as CCP proxies and supported CCP positions.

Underground Communist organizers built ostensibly independent political organizations around key personalities and groups, and organized anti-GMD and anti-American protests. When Nationalists attacked these events and then suppressed the parties, they undermined GMD claims to be furthering democracy. At the same time, CCP-backed groups also attacked Democratic League elements, and others attempting to create a "Third Force" between the CCP and GMD. The subsequent open support of the CCP's May 1, 1948, "call for allies" by the minor parties symbolized both the GMD's loss of urban and intellectual support, and the United Front's success in seeking to persuade urban elites that their choices were to support the CCP or the GMD or become passive, but that no alternative third way was viable. This declaration marked the official integration of the minor parties into the CCP's People's Democratic United Front for the New Democratic Era (*Xinminzhu zhuyi Shiqi de renmin minzhu tongyizhanxian*). This integration symbolized the CCP's representation of, and pledge to cooperate with, many classes and forms of ownership for a long time as the CCP prepared the basis for the economic and social transformation to socialism.

### REORGANIZATION AND SUPPRESSION OF MINOR PARTIES AND GROUPS AFTER 1949

After the CCP victory in 1949, all non-CCP-supported minor parties were suppressed, but a new Peoples Democratic United Front was launched to help manage China's transition to socialism. The minor parties and the Democratic League were reorganized and purged to give the CCP's United Front Department (UFD) full control, and their memberships were thereafter generally restricted to particular interest groups. Although some of the leaders and members of these groups were given prominent leadership positions alongside Communists and some non-party personages, their role was largely symbolic. At the same time, leaders and members of minor parties were presented as a model of the transformation of society's politics and thinking to conform with the new demands of socialism. Thought-reform methods such as criticism and self-criticism to eliminate bourgeois thinking became proof of transformation.

For many members of minor parties, this avenue allowed subsequent membership in the CCP. Yet by early

1957, Mao Zedong, worried about problems in the CCP and keen to reinvigorate urban, especially intellectual, support for the party, launched the Hundred Flowers campaign, soliciting criticism of CCP failings from members of minor parties and group. Yet only after considerable encouragement from UFD cadres and especially its head, Li Weihan (1896–1984), did members of these groups respond, with increasingly frank critiques. By June, Mao began denouncing critics as rightists and appointed Deng Xiaoping to launch the anti-rightist campaign, with leaders of the minor parties, such as the Democratic League's Zhang Bojun (1895–1969) and Luo Longji (1898–1965), as major targets. Thought reform and criticism of members of these groups culminated with the Giving of Hearts (*jiao xin*) to the CCP campaign in 1959. Despite their total capitulation, minor party members and leaders were repeatedly targeted in numerous political campaigns.

Only after the failure of Mao's subsequent Great Leap Forward were the minor parties partially rehabilitated to assist with economic reconstruction and morale building among intellectuals as part of a second Hundred Flowers campaign (1960–1964). However, in 1966, as part of the Great Proletarian Cultural Revolution (1966–1969) and calls by Red Guards for dissolution, China's minor parties were effectively disbanded, although Mao insisted that they be maintained in a nominal form. By this stage, the leaders of these groups were almost all ultra-leftists and were usually dual members of both their group and the CCP. Other leaders and members were repeatedly harassed, and many died, were injured, or committed suicide.

### POST-MAO REHABILITATION

After Mao's death in 1976, United Front work in the form of a Patriotic United Front again became important. By 1978 almost all alleged "rightists" were rehabilitated in order to assist China's Four Modernizations by utilizing their still-rare expertise, setting up schools, and providing technical advice. In the mid- to late-1980s, the minor parties were notable for being sources of legitimate expertise-based dissent against some key government projects, especially the Three Gorges Dam. In 1989 many minor parties and their leaders were also publically supportive of the student demonstrations in Tiananmen Square. After 1989 though, these groups lost support among members because the CCP used their names in support of the suppression of the student movement. Initial promises in the early 1990s to give minor parties and groups and nonparty personages more influence in government and allow them to expand to better represent China's rapidly changing social structure soon gave way to more intense control, with emphasis on political education in the Institutes of Socialism run by the UFD.

In 2007 China's minor parties and groups had some 700,000 members. They take part in political activities, particularly through the main United Front body, the Chinese People's Political Consultative Conference. Although a significant part of the conference, minor parties are not allowed to organize within it as party blocs, and it is difficult to convince ordinary Chinese that they are anything but "flower vases" (*huaping*). Nevertheless, they and the Chinese People's Political Consultative Conference can, when requested, provide advice and suggestions and undertake specialist investigations on behalf of the National People's Congress and the government.

The current leaders of these groups do not have significant political or social influence, even within their areas of expertise, and none are major national figures, as their predecessors were. Membership and leadership roles are all tightly controlled through the UFD, and ordinary members have no say in appointments. Outsiders are often appointed at the expense of longtime aspirants. Once accepted, members must attend political training at group-run forums and the UFD's Institutes of Socialism. However, now that CCP membership is readily available to intellectuals and even capitalists, membership in a minor party lacks clear benefits while having costs. Only in response to crises does the CCP allow such groups more extensive responsibilities and take greater heed of their opinions.

### BIBLIOGRAPHY

Groot, Gerry. *Managing Transitions: The Chinese Communist Party, United Front Work, Corporatism, and Hegemony*. New York: Taylor & Francis, 2004.

Jeans, Roger B., ed. *Roads Not Taken: The Struggle of Opposition Parties in Twentieth-Century China*. Boulder, CO: Westview Press, 1992.

Seymour, James D. *China's Satellite Parties*. Armonk, NY: Sharpe, 1987.

Van Slyke, Lyman P. *Enemies and Friends: The United Front in Chinese Communist History*. Stanford, CA: Stanford University Press, 1967.

***Gerry Groot***

## ALL-CHINA FEDERATION OF INDUSTRY AND COMMERCE

Although often mentioned alongside the China Democratic National Construction Association (CDNCA) and long having mutual links and leadership crossover, the All-China Federation of Industry and Commerce (Zhonghua quanguo gongshangye lianhehui, ACFIC) is now China's most important United Front group. It eclipses all the minor parties and groups in both membership and economic and political importance.

Officially launched in 1953 to simultaneously develop, organize, control, restrict, and then socialize China's private business, the federation built on wartime efforts to liaise with business and obtain material support. Although overlapping with the CDNCA, the federation recruited mainly small entrepreneurs and artisans as opposed to the major private businesses and national capitalists represented by the CDNCA.

Through the 1950s, the federation was the key means through which the Chinese Communist Party (CCP) realized United Front work goals of forcing business people to undertake thought reform and acquiesce to the loss of their businesses. The ACFIC and the CDNCA were central to CCP campaigns like the Three-Anti (*sanfan*) and Five-Anti (*wufan*) campaigns of 1950 to 1951 aimed at discrediting private business and forcing its socialization. The federation became largely irrelevant after Mao Zedong's 1956 declaration that the basic transition to socialism had been completed.

In the late 1970s, Deng Xiaoping, seeking to promote China's economic modernizations, sought the help of federation and CDNCA members, encouraging them to use their links in foreign countries to seek investment in China, which had been regarded with suspicion during the Cultural Revolution. The CCP then paid outstanding interest monies to some of the surviving former capitalists owed for the nationalization of their enterprises payments in the 1950s on the condition these funds be invested in new businesses. Since the takeoff of economic reform, the federation has been given the key role of ensuring that business has a voice and representation, in the United Front in particular.

The federation and the CDNCA now have a great deal of influence based on the economic power of their members. The federation, unlike the CDNCA and the minor parties and groups, is not selective in its membership and as a result is much larger than all the minor parties and groups combined. As such, the federation is the most truly corporatist of all the minor parties and groups. Another of its unique features is its ability to fund itself through its own enterprises.

In the early 1990s, aware of the potential of federation members' complaints about state failings to become rallying points for political opposition as highlighted in Western political theory on democratization and in the wake of the student protests of 1989, the United Front Work Department created a new mirror set of chambers of commerce to separate nominally more political issues from day-to-day business problems. However, this attempt failed to have any impact, and the two different names soon came to mark a merely theoretical difference. Today, the use of terms like *chamber of commerce* seems directed at foreigners likely to be confused with any mention of a United Front, although there is growing evidence of industry-specific associations being formed with far greater autonomy than allowed hitherto.

Like the minor parties and groups, the federation is most obviously active in the Chinese People's Political Consultative Conference at all levels, and its opinions and help in solving economic problems make it the most important of the minor parties and groups with which it shares equal political status. One indication of the federation's import is its success in prompting initiatives such as Minsheng Bank, billed as China's first "private" bank, in late 1996. The federation also seems to have been heavily involved in the creation of the first and subsequent investment trusts such as CITIC, the China International Trust and Investment Corporation. Its most famous leader was the so-called red capitalist, Rong Yiren (1916–2005), who was appointed a Chinese deputy president in 1993 and promoted as a non-Communist appointment to government despite having secretly joined the CCP in 1956. In 2007 the federation reportedly had more than two million members across 3,119 branches.

**BIBLIOGRAPHY**

Groot, Gerry. *Managing Transitions: The Chinese Communist Party, United Front Work, Corporatism, and Hegemony.* New York: Taylor and Francis, 2004.

Pu Wenchang, ed. *Jianshe Minjian Shanghui* [Building a non-government chamber of commerce]. Xi'an: Xibei Daxue Chubanshe, 2006.

***Gerry Groot***

## CHINA DEMOCRATIC NATIONAL CONSTRUCTION ASSOCIATION

The China Democratic National Construction Association (Zhongguo Minzhu Jianguo Hui, or CDNCA) is one of seven United Front Department–initiated parties created at the end of World War II (1937–1945) aimed at undermining the Guomindang (GMD) and promoting Chinese Communist Party (CCP) aims among China's educated urban classes.

The CDNCA grew out of the CCP's longstanding United Front work with China's business classes. Communist cadres worked closely with the well-connected Huang Yanpei (1878–1965) and others in the Vocational Educational Society to create the new association in December 1945. The CDNCA then became an active part of the anti-GMD/anti-American "second front" activities in GMD-held cities.

After the CCP's victory in 1949, the CDNCA played an import role in reassuring businesspeople, especially those classified as "national bourgeoisie," that Mao's New Democracy also included them and dissuading them from fleeing abroad. The example of "red capitalist" members of the CDNCA denouncing old ways and committing to socialism was a powerful inducement for others to do likewise. The CDNCA provided a crucial means by which the CCP sought to simultaneously encourage, control, and then transform China's private businesses into socialist ones.

In 1979 Deng Xiaoping lauded CDNCA leaders for promoting the use of foreign capital and talent and encouraging Chinese living in other countries to invest in China. CDNCA associates and members of the All-China Federation of Industry and Commerce were paid monies owing from the nationalization of their assets in the 1950s on the condition the funds were invested in new businesses. Initiatives included the creation of the Chinese International Trust and Investment Company (CITIC) and the revival of China's stock markets. The establishment of special economic zones was another major initiative emanating, at least in name, from these connections and was first proposed in the Guangdong CPPCC (Chinese People's Political Consultative Conference).

In 2007 the CDNCA had a reported 109,000 members. Because CDNCA members are often successful businesspeople, the association represents a group with considerable economic influence.

*Gerry Groot*

## CHINA ASSOCIATION FOR PROMOTING DEMOCRACY

The China Association for Promoting Democracy (Zhongguo Minzhu Cujin Hui, or CAPD) was one of the seven United Front Department–initiated parties created by the Chinese Communist Party (CCP) at the end of World War II (1937–1945) to undermine the Guomindang (GMD) and promote CCP aims among China's educated urban classes.

The CAPD was formed around the longtime leftist radical and National Anti-Japanese Salvation Association leader Ma Xulun (1884–1970) and the underground Communist organizer and labor activist Wang Shao'ao (1888–1970). It was influential in literary, publishing, and academic circles. Since 1978 the CAPD has been generally aimed at schoolteachers; attempts to include radio and television personalities were blocked after 1989.

The CAPD was particularly important as part of the CCP's "second front" in GMD-held urban areas in 1946 and 1947. In conjunction with other United Front–inspired groups, the CAPD organized demonstrations and protests against the GMD and the United States. Public attacks on CAPD leaders by GMD thugs also helped undermine GMD legitimacy and increase support for CCP goals such as a coalition government and opposition to GMD proposals for a national assembly.

In 2007 the CAPD was reported as having 103,000 members.

*Gerry Groot*

## DEMOCRATIC LEAGUE OF CHINA

Unlike the seven other minor parties and groups in the Chinese Communist Party's (CCP) United Front Work, the Democratic League (Zhongguo Minzhu Tongmeng) was not formed as a creature of the CCP, even if it was subsequently captured by it. The League developed from the regular dissolving and reconstituting of political groups in the 1930s. When the League was proclaimed on October 10, 1941, its membership consisted of the remnants of Liang Shuming's (1893–1988) Rural Reconstructionists, Huang Yanpei's (1878–1965) Vocational Education Society, Zhang Junmai's (Carsun Chang's, 1887–1969) National Socialists, elements of the strongly left-wing All-China National Salvation Association, and Deng Yanda's (1895–1931) Third Party, along with a number of other, much smaller groups. The lack of agreement on policies other than resistance to Japan and greater representation in government of intellectuals and experts such as themselves meant that the League lacked clear ideological orientation, coherence, and structure. It was heavily dependent on the influence and reputation of its leaders to attract attention and support. The disparateness of its membership and organization also allowed opportunities for Communists and radicals like Shen Junru (1875–1963) and Zou Taofen (1895–1944) to take shelter in it.

One of the most important political groups in China between 1941 and 1948, the Democratic League was a major target of CCP United Front Work. Initially, this was in order to use the League to help pressure the Guomindang (GMD) to promote increased political freedoms to allow the CCP more freedom of action and to support and protect the CCP from GMD military action. After 1945, preventing the League from not only becoming an independent "third force" between it and the GMD, but also winning its full support and hence symbolizing that progress, peace, and a democratic future lay with the CCP, were crucial to the CCP's efforts to win broad-based support in urban areas for its New Democratic Program.

Thus, when the GMD banned the Democratic League in October 1947, the CCP won a major symbolic victory. The League cemented this victory on May 1, 1948, when radical pro-communist League leaders in exile in Hong Kong responded in the League's name to the CCP's call for allies, and joined the CCP Political Constitution Conference to create a coalition government.

During China's transition to socialism—the new democratic period of 1949 to 1956—the Democratic League played a major role of symbolizing cross-class support and especially support from intellectuals for CCP rule, particularly through the participation of some of its leaders in government. The League also became an important means for organizing the thought reform of China's intellectuals, to transform their allegedly bourgeois and idealistic thinking to the proletarian thinking needed to build a socialist state.

The Democratic League also played a key role in criticizing the CCP in the Hundred Flowers movement of 1956. Likewise, when Mao Zedong then condemned such critics of the CCP and himself as rightists, it was principally League leaders who were held responsible, particularly Luo Longji (1898–1965) and Zhang Bojun (1895–1969). The League struggled on at least in name until the onset of the Cultural Revolution when it was all but dissolved. During the Cultural Revolution many League members and leaders came in for repeated bouts of criticism and even torture with a number committing suicide or dying as a result.

After it was revived in the late 1970s, the League struggled for relevance. The League's journal, *Qunyan* (Tribune), however, became an important outlet for criticism of some CCP policies, such as those concerning the Three Gorges Dam, and in 1988 a League report on Polish minor parties under communist rule advocated greater autonomy for minor parties in China. The most famous League leader after 1978 was the internationally renowned sociologist Fei Xiaotong (1910–2005).

In 2007 Democratic League membership totaled a mere 181,000, a reflection of the relative decline of intellectuals in China since the rise of mass education and the ability of intellectuals to now readily join the CCP.

**BIBLIOGRAPHY**

Groot, Gerry. *Managing Transitions: The Chinese Communist Party, United Front Work, Corporatism, and Hegemony*. New York: Taylor and Francis, 2004.

Zhongghuo Minzhu Tongmeng Zhongyang Wenshi Weiyuanhui [The Central Committee of the Democratic League of Chinese Culture and History Committee], eds. *Zhongguo minzhu tongmeng lishe wenzhai 1949-1988* [A compendium history of the Democratic League of China]. Beijing: Wenwu Chubanshe, 1991.

***Gerry Groot***

## CHINESE PEASANTS AND WORKERS DEMOCRATIC PARTY

The Chinese Peasants and Workers Democratic Party (Zhongguo Minzhu Nong Gong Dang) is nominally one of the seven Chinese Communist Party (CCP)–initiated or supported parties created at the end of World War II (1937–1945) aimed at undermining the Guomindang (GMD) and supporting CCP aims. The Peasants and Workers Democratic Party brought together survivors of Deng Yanda's (1895–1931) radical Third Party of the 1930s in the CCP, GMD, and Democratic League. Party leader Peng Zemin (1877–1956) had extensive CCP connections, and when he and Zhang Bojun (1895–1969) launched the party in 1947, their declaration lauded Mao Zedong's "On New Democracy" and held closely to CCP positions. Using its Third Party links, the Peasants and Workers Democratic Party even raised a small guerrilla force to fight the GMD.

After 1949, the Chinese Peasants and Workers Democratic Party was recognized and stripped of its military connections to become a group representing public officials, teachers, technicians, and doctors. After a demarcation dispute with the Jiusan Society, the Peasants and Workers Democratic Party came to represent doctors trained in Chinese medicine. Today, it has health-care workers as a key constituency, after efforts in the 1990s to expand into new areas were blocked by the United Front Department.

In 2007 the China Democratic League had over 80,000 members.

**SEE ALSO** *Peasantry, 1800–1900; Social Classes before 1949; United Front Work.*

***Gerry Groot***

## JIUSAN (SEPTEMBER THIRD) SOCIETY

The Jiusan or September Third Study Society (Jiusan Xueshe) was one of seven United Front Department–initiated parties created after World War II (1937–1945) to undermine the Guomindang (GMD) and support Chinese Communist Party (CCP) aims. Jiusan grew out of CCP-sponsored "democratic science conferences" held in GMD-controlled Chongqing in 1944. The launch of the society on September 3, 1945, came from a suggestion by Mao Zedong. Its key initial leaders were Xu Deheng (1890–1990) and Da Yijin (b. 1909).

As part of the United Front Department's "second front," Jiusan participated in and helped organize anti-

GMD protests and demonstrations. A notable aspect of Jiusan's work was its attacks on attempts by the Democratic League and others to forge a "middle road" or "third force" between the CCP and GMD.

Reorganized by the United Front Department after 1949, Jiusan came to represent high-level academics, scientists, and lawyers. After a dispute with the Chinese Peasants and Workers Democratic Party, Jiusan also claimed doctors who were trained along Western lines.

In the early 1980s, Jiusan, because of its base among scientists, became an important source of objection to construction of the Three Gorges Dam. Its reports on the project were widely distributed in government circles and were crucial in the central government holding up funding for the dam between 1983 and 1987.

In 2007 the Jiusan Society had 105,000 members.

**SEE ALSO** *Land Use, History of; Land Tenure since 1800; Rural Development since 1978.*

***Gerry Groot***

## REVOLUTIONARY COMMITTEE OF THE NATIONALIST PARTY

Although it was in one sense one of the seven parties created by the Chinese Communist Party (CCP) at the end of World War II (1937–1945) to undermine the Nationalist Party (Guomindang, or GMD) and promote CCP aims, the Revolutionary Committee of the GMD (Guomindang Geming Weiyuanhui) has complex antecedents. When the committee was launched in January 1948, it brought together survivors of Deng Yanda's (1895–1931) Third Party of the 1930s, CCP United Front groups aimed at the GMD, and disaffected GMD members. The committee served as a vehicle for sheltering and attracting GMD defectors, especially its alienated left wing. As a consequence of its target group, the committee's most significant period occurred during the CCP–GMD civil war, when it was used to reach former Nationalists left in the mainland, and its members' personal relations were used to appeal to former comrades in Taiwan.

In the 1990s, the committee suffered from the aging of its membership and difficulty in recruiting new members with any GMD–Taiwan connections. In addition, ignorance of its role and confusion with the GMD proper meant few found membership desirable.

One notable feature of the committee's history was its open support for the 1989 student movement. The party newspaper, *Tuanjie bao* (Unity), and key party leaders openly sided with the student demonstrators, the latter even visiting hospitalized hunger strikers.

In 2007 the committee was reported as having 81,000 members.

***Gerry Groot***

## TAIWAN DEMOCRATIC SELF-GOVERNMENT LEAGUE

The Taiwan Democratic Self-Government League (Taiwan Minzhu Zizhi Tongmeng) is one of seven United Front Department–initiated parties created in the aftermath of World War II (1937–1945) to undermine the Guomindang (GMD) and support Chinese Communist Party (CCP) aims.

Unlike its fellow minor parties, the formation of the league in November 1947 did not occur around a number of prominent figures organized by underground Communists. Rather, the league was fashioned as a new political group for Taiwanese Communists forced to flee Taiwan after the failure of their February 27, 1947, uprising to overthrow the GMD.

The Taiwanese had been members of the Japanese Communist Party, not the CCP, and the league integrated these fellow Communists. In notionally advocating self-government for Taiwan, the league went some way toward recognizing the strong appeal of autonomy to many Taiwanese. The group was notable for its leader, Xie Xuehong (1901–1970), being a woman.

Given the peculiar nature of its origins, the Taiwan Democratic Self-Government League has always been small, and extending membership to mainland Chinese created major dilemmas for the group. After being dissolved in 1966, the league was revived by Zhou Enlai in 1973 specifically to collect information on Taiwan. It remains a part of United Front work directed at bringing Taiwan back under direct mainland sovereignty.

In 2007 the league had approximately 2,100 members.

***Gerry Groot***

## CHINA ZHIGONG (PUBLIC INTEREST) PARTY

The China Zhigong Dang (ZGD), or Public Interest Party, is one of seven parties created or reconstituted after World War II by the United Front Department. Its origins lie in the overseas network of *Hongmen* (secret society) lodges established by Chinese emigrants in the nineteenth century. The term *Zhigong* is derived from the phrase *zhi li wei gong* (exert strength in the public interest), which was initially associated with two Hongmen lodges in North America (one in Victoria, Canada, and the other in San Francisco). More broadly, the adoption of the name marked the reconstitution of the Hongmen into the Zhigong Lodge (-tang), or the Chinese Freemasons Society, which in turn became the basis for the Zhigong Party (-dang). The party in its earlier incarnation was founded at an international meeting of Zhigong affiliates in San Francisco in October 1925. Its first president and vice-president respectively were former Canton governor Chen Jiongming (1878–1933), and former general Tang Jiyao (1883-1927), both of whom had fallen out with the GMD. The party's aims were to protect and promote the interests of Chinese overseas.

In 1931 the party's headquarters were shifted to Hong Kong, where in the postwar period a major party reorganization was initiated by Chen Qiyou (1892–1970), among others. The restructuring was aimed at aligning the party with the Chinese Communist Party (CCP), as clearly stated at its third international convention in 1947. A party member since 1931, Chen Qiyou was the chief ZGD deputy at the first plenary session of the National Committee of the Chinese People's Political Consultative Conference (CPPCC), convened in Beijing on September 21, 1949. He was elected chairman of the ZGD Central Committee in 1952. During the 1950s the minor parties operated under increasingly severe constraints. In 1957 Chen wrote the essay "Great Changes over Ten Years," commemorating the ten years since the party's reform, but the emphasis was more on the CCP than on the ZGD. In that year the anti-rightist campaign was launched, and the ZGD itself was rent by factional struggles as members turned on each other.

The resuscitation of the CPPCC after the Cultural Revolution (1966–1969) allowed the ZGD, too, a new lease of life. In 1997 the ZGD had 540 representatives in local and national People's Congresses. In 2001 it had 18,000 members, and in 2007, 28,000. The year 2007 was also important for the group because one of its leaders, Wan Gang (b. 1952), was appointed a minister of science and technology. Yet the significance of membership of this party remains unclear while the party's interests are so plainly identified with those of the CCP. The current chairman of the party's Central Committee, Luo Haocai (b. 1934), is a Communist Party member who joined the ZGD only in 1992.

Little is understood of the precise nature of the party's links with Chinese overseas, including with the Hongmen, either historically or at present. During the Cold War, ZGD branches among Chinese overseas essentially represented mainland, CCP positions, in opposition to the Guomindang. The CPPCC official Web site describes the ZGD as "a political party based on high and intermediate level personages from among returned overseas and their family dependents, featuring political alliance and dedicated to building socialism with Chinese characteristics." The party's work seems to complement other work aimed at enlisting sympathies and material support from Chinese overseas. The full scope of its activities, like its history, awaits research.

**SEE ALSO** *Secret Societies.*

**BIBLIOGRAPHY**

Fitzgerald, John. *Big White Lie: Chinese Australians in White Australia*. Sydney: University of New South Wales Press, 2007.

Fu Jian Zhi Gong Web site. http://www.fjzg.org.

Lu Meiyuan, and Quan Haosheng, eds. *Guiqiao qiajuan gaishu* [Review of returned overseas Chinese and overseas Chinese relatives]. Beijing: China's Overseas Chinese Publishing House, 2001.

Ma, L. Eve Armentrout. *Revolutionaries, Monarchists, and Chinatowns: Chinese Politics in the Americas and the 1911 Revolution*. Honolulu: University of Hawaii Press, 1990.

National Committee of the Chinese People's Political Consultative Conference Web site. http://www.cppcc.gov.cn.

Wang Peizhi. *Chen Qiyou yu Zhongguo Zhigongdang* [Chen Qiyou and the China Public Benefit Party]. Guangzhou, China: Guangdong Renmin Chubanshe, 2004.

***Antonia Finnane***

## DENG XIAOPING

***1904–1997***

A leader of the Chinese revolution, a Communist committed to the economic advance of his country, and Mao Zedong's successor as paramount leader in the People's Republic of China, Deng Xiaoping played important roles on the national and world stage for a period of nearly half a century before his death in 1997. In the Mao years, he suffered purges several times for challenging ideological orthodoxy. In the late 1970s, he set in motion a program of economic reforms aimed at raising the living standards of the population. In the 1980s, he negotiated with Great Britain for the return of Hong Kong to China. One major blemish on Deng's career was his repression of the prodemocracy movement in 1989. Nonetheless, throughout most of the 1990s, he remained firm in his struggle to speed up economic reforms and ensure a problem-free transition after his period of leadership.

## CHILDHOOD AND YOUTH

Deng Xiaoping was born on August 22, 1904, in the village of Paifang, Guang'an County, in the province of Sichuan, to a family of landlords. He began his education under a private tutor, and at the age of seven he entered a modern primary school, going on to secondary education in Guang'an and to senior high school in Chongqing. In Chongqing, Deng joined the Movement for Diligent Work and Frugal Study (Qingong Jianxuesheng Tuan), directed by Li Yuying (1882–1973), who had been working for years to establish links between China and France.

In early 1920, Deng boarded a ship that carried him and other students to Marseilles, whence they traveled on to Paris. There he went to work in factories that paid little in return for long hours. In 1922 he became a member of the Chinese Communist Youth League in Europe, and came under the strong influence of Zhou Enlai (1898–1976) and Zhao Shiyan (1900–1927). In June 1923, Deng was elected to the executive committee of that organization, which changed its name to the European Branch of the Chinese Socialist Youth League. He assumed responsibility for the league's newspaper, *Red Light*, earning the nickname "Doctor of Duplication."

In the second half of 1924, Deng joined the European Branch of the Chinese Communist Party. Early in 1925, he went to Lyon to engage in political propaganda activities, returning to Paris in July. The French police had him under observation, but Deng eluded them by leaving for the Soviet Union. He spent eleven months in Moscow studying at the Communist University for the Toilers of the East and later at what was to become Sun Yat-sen University.

## RETURN TO CHINA

In 1926 the warlord Feng Yuxiang (1882–1948), who had joined forces with the Nationalists, traveled to Moscow; on his return to China, he brought with him several Chinese Communists, among them Deng Xiaoping, to serve in his army. They arrived in Xi'an in February 1927, and Deng held various posts there: He was director of the political section in the Sun Yat-sen Military and Political Academy, political instructor, and secretary of the underground organization of the Communist Party. Deng was obliged to escape to Hankou, in Hubei Province, in June 1927 due to Feng's threatened onslaught against the Communists following the rupture between the Guomindang (GMD) and the Communist Party. In Hankou, Deng began working in the general party headquarters. When party general secretary Qu Qiubai (1899–1935) moved the headquarters to Shanghai, Deng went with him.

## THE REVOLUTION

In mid-1929, *Deng* was sent to Guangxi and, together with Zhang Yunyi, he organized an uprising in Bose (Poseh); they succeeded in establishing bases in this area and in Pingma. In early 1930, another base was created in Longzhou, with the Eighth Red Army. Deng then returned to Shanghai, where he was appointed political commissar of the new base. On his return to Guangxi, he discovered that the local warlords Li Zongren (1890–1969) and Bai Chongxi (1893–1966) had returned and defeated the Eighth Red Army. The Red Army withdrew to the mountains. Deng spent the spring and autumn working in an agrarian reform program. By June 1930, the Communists had managed to reestablish their base area around Bose.

Following the strategy of party general secretary Li Lisan (1899–1967), which aimed at taking power in urban centers in one or more provinces, Deng and the Communists in Guangxi tried to take cities. Their efforts ended in failure, and the army was decimated. They were obliged to retreat to Jiangxi, not far from Mao's base in Jingganshan. Deng then became secretary of the party committee in Ruijin County, before extending his work to another three counties. In 1932 he was appointed director of propaganda of the party provincial committee in Jiangxi.

In 1933 party leaders Bo Gu (1907–1946) and Luo Fu (1898–1976) migrated to Jiangxi, where they began to criticize the policies implemented by the local leaders. Deng came under attack, accused of ignoring the guidelines set out by party leadership and the Comintern or Third International. Deng was forced to write a self-criticism and was stripped of his responsibilities. Shortly afterward, however, he was rehabilitated and assigned to the Department of Propaganda, becoming also editor in chief of *Red Star*.

Deng took part in the Long March, which began in 1934 as a response to the overwhelming attack of Chiang Kai-shek's (Jiang Jieshi's) forces against the Chinese Communists in Jiangxi. Deng was present at the 1935 Zunyi Conference, where Mao consolidated his leadership. Deng contracted typhoid after the Long March and, on recovering, was made chief of the Propaganda Division of the First Army Group's Political Department. He participated in the Red Army's Expedition to the East in 1936, from Shaanxi to Shanxi.

## WAR AGAINST JAPAN

With the outbreak of the Sino-Japanese War in 1937, the Communist Party joined forces with the GMD in the Second United Front. Deng became deputy director of the political department of the Eighth Route Army. By 1938 he had become political commissar of the 129th

Division commanded by Liu Bocheng (1892–1986), stationed in the Taihang Mountains in southeastern Shanxi. The 129th Division set up a base and created others in the central mountains of Shanxi, from which they fought against both Nationalists and the Japanese.

In August 1940, Liu and Deng participated in the Hundred Regiments campaign. In the second half of 1943, Peng Dehuai (1898–1974), Liu Bocheng, and Nie Rongzhen (1899–1992), the three commanders of the Northern Base Area, were summoned to Yan'an. Deng replaced Peng as the acting secretary of the party's northern bureau.

In the spring of 1944, the Japanese launched the Ichi-Go offensive, while the Communists concentrated on consolidating their positions in the north and east. Deng's main task was to repel the Japanese attacks on the bases in the north and to maintain order by way of social and economic policies. In June 1945, he went to Yan'an to take part in the First Plenary Session of the Seventh Central Committee. For the first time, Deng became a member of the Central Committee.

### THE SECOND CIVIL WAR

When the war with Japan came to an end, the Communists faced civil war with the Nationalists. In 1945 Liu Bocheng and Deng Xiaoping defeated the forces of Yan Xishan (1883–1960) in the Battle of Shangdang in Shanxi. Two years later, they fought the Nationalists in Shandong.

The outcome of the war was decided in three campaigns between September 1948 and January 1949. Deng's military career reached its climax in the 1948 Huai Hai campaign in Central China, which culminated in the taking of Nanjing and led to the collapse of the Nationalist government.

After the establishment of the People's Republic of China in 1949, the national territory was divided into six regions. In the southwest, Deng Xiaoping became vice chairman of the regional committee under the presidency of Liu Bocheng. He also became political commissar of the military command and first secretary of the regional party bureau. The region comprised four provinces: Sichuan, Guizhou, Yunnan, and Xikang. The new leaders succeeded in combating bandits, restructuring the economy, and carrying out agrarian reform. In July 1952, Deng was transferred to Beijing.

### RISE WITHIN THE PARTY

In Beijing, Deng worked on the preparation of a new constitution for the Chinese state, which was promulgated in 1954. But the problems generated in the leadership by the plot of Gao Gang (1902–1955) and Rao Shushi (1903–1975) against Liu Shaoqi (1898–1969) and Zhou Enlai brought about the resignation of Bo Yibo (1908–2007) as finance minister, a post that was then occupied by Deng for a year. When the plot was discovered, Deng himself informed Mao of it. The two conspirators were purged after their case was discussed in party meetings in which Deng had a central role. In June 1954, Deng was appointed general secretary of the Party Central Committee. By April 1955, he had been elected to membership in the Politburo.

At the Eighth Congress of the Chinese Communist Party, held in September 1956, Deng was elected general secretary. In the Politburo, he ascended to the rank of sixth in command, being a member of the Standing Committee. In his speech to the congress, Deng emphasized the need to strengthen collective leadership and democratic centralism within the party.

In 1957, during the Hundred Flowers campaign, Chinese intellectuals criticized, at the urging of Mao, what they considered to be errors committed by party leaders. When their criticism extended to the acts of the party itself, the anti-rightist campaign, in which Deng took an active part, was unleashed.

### THE GREAT LEAP FORWARD AND THE ECONOMIC POLICY OF THE 1960s

The Great Leap Forward, which Mao set in motion in 1958, entailed serious consequences for the country's economy, prompting Zhou Enlai and Chen Yun (1905–1995) to oppose the initiative at the Nanning Conference in January 1958. In late 1958 and early 1959, several party leaders carried out tours of inspection in different provinces to observe the results of the Great Leap. Deng visited Guizhou, where he saw poverty and food shortages. Although he had not opposed the Great Leap Forward, Deng expressed concern for its negative consequences.

Between 1961 and 1965, Deng helped implement the nation's economic policy. He responded to the problems generated by the Great Leap by arguing that production was a priority for economic recovery, no matter what methods were used to increase it. Deng believed that the government should take the country's real circumstances into consideration when designing economic policy, an idea he expressed in a speech to the Communist Youth League on July 7, 1962: "It does not matter if the cat is white or black, as long as it catches mice."

### CAPITALIST ROADER

During the decade of the Cultural Revolution (1966–1976), Deng and Liu Shaoqi were criticized for their working style and their "revisionist" thinking. Mao complained that Deng had pushed him aside after the Great Leap

***Chinese Communist Party Chairman Deng Xiaoping, 1976.*** *Pushed twice to outsider status in the Communist Party, Deng Xiaoping persevered, rising to prominence after the death of Mao Zedong. Scholars credit Deng with energizing China's economy through market-based reforms, admitting publicly the failures of the Cultural Revolution, and securing the return of the British colony of Hong Kong.* © BETTMANN/CORBIS

Forward, and in 1968 Deng was eliminated from his party and government posts, retaining only his party membership. The next year, he was sent to work in Jiangxi. In 1972 Deng wrote to Mao asking permission to return to Beijing. In 1973 he was finally allowed to do so. Deng immediately began working with Zhou Enlai. He served as vice premier, taking charge of the day-to-day affairs of government.

Radicals headed by Jiang Qing (1914–1991) launched attacks on Zhou and Deng. Deng nevertheless recovered his posts on the Politburo and the Military Affairs Commission. In 1974 he delivered a speech on Mao's theory of the Three Worlds to the United Nations General Assembly in New York. A year later, Deng was appointed vice chairman of the Central Committee, first vice premier, and chief of staff of the People's Liberation Army. His priority was economic development and modernization. However, Mao did not approve of Deng's emphasis on stability, unity, and economic development as "key links." For Mao, the "key link" was still the class struggle.

Zhou Enlai died in January 1976, and Hua Guofeng was appointed acting premier. A large demonstration took place on Tiananmen Square the following April 5 under the pretext of rendering homage to Zhou, but the demonstration was also meant as a repudiation of the radicals, who were subsequently suppressed. Hua remained premier and vice chairman of the Central Committee. Deng was accused of being the instigator behind the demonstration, and he was purged again and sent to Guangzhou. When Mao Zedong died on September 8, 1976, marshals Ye Jianying (1897–1986) and Li Xiannian (1909–1992) promised to support Hua if he neutralized the radicals. On October 6, Jiang Qing and her followers were arrested.

## REFORMER

Hua found support in the formula: "Whatever policy originated from Chairman Mao, we must resolutely defend; whatever directions were given us by Chairman Mao, we must steadfastly obey." In 1977 Deng was rehabilitated, recovering his posts in the party, government, and army. Deng thereafter extended his influence in the fields of education, science and technology, military affairs, and foreign relations. In education, he called for excellence in schools. In the army, he fought for the "four modernizations" and professionalism. In foreign relations, he promoted dialogue with the United States, with whom he normalized relations in January 1979.

In order to make his own position prevail and to place his followers in key positions while discrediting Hua, Deng made use of the argument that an essential characteristic of Mao was "to seek truth through the facts." At the Third Plenum of the Communist Party's Eleventh Congress in

## FOUR BASIC PRINCIPLES

The Four Basic Principles (*sixiang jiben yuanze*) were enunciated by Deng Xiaoping in March 1979 at a forum on the principles for the Chinese Communist Party's theoretical work, calling on all Chinese people to "uphold the socialist road, uphold the dictatorship of the proletariat, uphold the leadership of the CCP, and uphold Marxism-Leninism-Mao Zedong Thought." The context was to justify the crackdown on the Democracy Wall movement that had endorsed Deng's return to power but also sought reforms going considerably beyond that, while violating procedural discipline. According to Deng, "certain bad elements have raised sundry demands that cannot be met at present or are altogether unreasonable. They have provoked or tricked some of the masses into raiding party and government organizations, occupying offices, holding sit-down and hunger strikes and obstructing traffic, thereby seriously disrupting production, other work and public order" (Deng 1984, p. 181). Three days later, the Beijing authorities issued regulations to curtail the democracy movement, many of whose leaders were promptly arrested and given lengthy jail terms.

Though often criticized by reformers for vagueness, the Four Basic Principles were welcomed by conservatives as a pretext to suppress controversy or dissent. And the Principles have since been consistently emphasized during periods of retreat from political reform, such as the 1983 "anti–spiritual pollution campaign," the 1987 movement to criticize "bourgeois liberalization," or the post-Tiananmen campaign against "peaceful evolution." Although this has been denied by reformers (for example, Xue Muqiao [1904–2005] saw no contradiction between the Principles and the Hundred Flowers), there is at least an implicit tension between the Principles and many of the reforms; thus, "upholding Marxism-Leninism" has been interpreted as inconsistent with marketization and privatization, and "upholding the socialist road" and "the dictatorship of the proletariat" has been used to suppress "bourgeois liberalization," potentially including some economic innovations. Because of this tension, the focus has consistently been on the third of the Four Basic Principles ("uphold the leadership of the CCP"), reserving to the party leadership the right to evaluate the substantive content of the other three. Although constrictive, the Principles may be said to mark a step toward greater liberalization in that they shift from prescribing what must be done to limiting what must not be done.

### BIBLIOGRAPHY

Deng Xiaoping. *Selected Works of Deng Xiaoping, 1975–1982.* Beijing: Foreign Languages Press, 1984.

***Lowell Dittmer***

December 1978, Deng spoke of the need to leave aside dogmas, to promote debate within the party on the basis of democracy, and to arrive at a balanced judgment of the Cultural Revolution and the role of Mao.

Deng also emphasized the need to "let some people get rich first," and accordingly redefined the notion of equity. He described the superiority of socialism in terms of avoiding polarization, attaining prosperity for all, and eliminating poverty. Equity, according to Deng, must be subordinated to economic construction. Within this climate of greater openness, activities arose that culminated in the placing of large-character posters (*dazibao*) on the Xidan, or "democracy" wall, in Beijing. These criticized the actions taken to suppress the 1976 demonstrations and, in general, commented on political matters. At first, Deng supported the *dazibao* displays, but when criticisms became more acute and the movement spread, he took a hard line, putting a stop to the poster movement and imprisoning its most important exponent, Wei Jingsheng.

At the beginning of the 1980s, Deng eased Hua Guofeng out of the premiership, as well as his party posts, installing Hu Yaobang (1915–1989) as party chairman (and in 1982 as party general secretary) and Zhao Ziyang (1919–2005) as prime minister. The disastrous nature of the Cultural Revolution became undeniable when the trial of the radicals took place between November 1980 and January 1981.

The evaluation of Mao's performance as leader took place the same year, reflecting to a large degree the esteem and respect that Deng felt for Mao. The relation between the two leaders was based on mutual and genuine loyalty; this had been reflected in the protection against physical abuse that Mao granted Deng during the Cultural Revolution, as well as Mao's agreeing to Deng's rehabilitation on several occasions. For Deng, Mao remained a key leader of China.

For his own part, Deng rose to the national leadership not by virtue of rank but through authority based on his experiences and reputation and his vast network inside the party leadership. Deng did not foster a personality cult.

As a national leader, Deng's priority was economic development, and to this end he introduced the concept of "socialism with Chinese characteristics" in 1982. Deng's economic reform involved establishing a system of family responsibility in the countryside (*baochan daohu*); developing rural industry; facilitating rapid growth in the urban economy; restructuring and administration by professionals in industrial concerns; and an open-door policy toward economic relations with the rest of the world, paving the way for foreign investment and stimulating the growth of foreign trade. On the other hand, Deng opposed so-called bourgeois liberalization, and, especially after 1986, he abandoned political reforms emphasizing the separation of state and party functions and the gradual participation of citizens in political affairs.

In international relations, Deng designed an independent foreign policy that, over the years, led to China's assuming an important role on the international stage. Deng's efforts also helped mend relations with the Soviet Union and ensured good relations with other countries, above all those of Southeast Asia. In 1984 he managed, after arduous negotiations with Great Britain, to sign the agreement leading to the return of Hong Kong to Chinese sovereignty in 1997.

## TOWARD TIANANMEN (1989)

Deng had differences with Chen Yun and Peng Zhen (1902–1997) regarding the direction of economic reforms. Chen Yun thought that economic planning should be taken into consideration before market forces. The reforms, which were experimental and implemented in a gradual manner, brought problems concerning inflation, corruption, and inequality, among other things.

In 1986 university students began organizing campus demonstrations to protest corruption and other problems that affected them directly. The astrophysicist Fang Lizhi spoke to the students in Hefei, in Anhui Province, about human and political rights. Deng was categorical in his response to such activities, prohibiting what he saw as bourgeois liberalism and alien ideas that could upset political stability and unity. The effect of the demonstrations was the fall of Hu Yaobang in January 1987, leading to Zhao Ziyang's appointment as general secretary of the party.

The Communist Party's Thirteenth Congress took place in October 1987, after which Deng relinquished his posts on the Central Committee and in the Politburo, although he continued as chairman of the Military Central Committee. His status as the moral leader of both party and state remained intact. The foreign media began referring to him as China's "paramount leader," although the Chinese did not use this term.

Economic and social problems accumulated in 1988, and, following the death of Hu Yaobang in April 1989, students and intellectuals gathered once again in Tiananmen Square in greater numbers than on previous occasions. The international press gave the event wide coverage. On May 20, martial law was declared, and on June 3 to 4, People's Liberation Army soldiers crushed the student-led protest. On June 9, Deng appeared on television to thank the army for their action. Deng and the remaining party leaders had responded with force when they saw the power of the party under threat. Zhao Ziyang was deposed after expressing disagreement with the repression. When the Communist regimes of Eastern Europe fell in 1989, followed in 1991 by the Soviet Union, the Chinese leadership began to fear the same fate if it did not keep the country under control.

## SMOOTH TRANSITION

Conservative economic policies reemerged after the fall of Zhao. Once again, the role of the market and economic planning, the opening to the exterior, and the next steps to be taken in the ongoing economic reform were discussed. The elderly Deng Xiaoping decided to take action to ensure that his efforts to achieve the economic advance of China would not remain inconclusive. In 1992 he undertook a journey to the south, where the economic reform had begun, in an attempt to reactivate the process and give it renewed vigor. He achieved his aim when at the party's Fourteenth Congress in October 1992 his ideas on economic reform and opening to the outside world were given definitive form in congress documents. The final report declared that the characteristics of the new historical period were to be reform and opening to the exterior, efforts that aimed at changing the country's economic structure instead of simply patching it up. The result was to be a system based on a "socialist market economy." It was a triumph for Deng.

Deng handed over power—without the disruptions that had characterized the Maoist era—to Jiang Zemin and the third generation of party leaders, who continued the process of economic reform. Deng's wish to be present at the change of sovereignty of Hong Kong remained unfulfilled, however, when he died in February 1997, four months before the date fixed for the handover.

**SEE ALSO** *Communist Party; Industrial Policy since 1949; Taiwan, Republic of China: Politics since 1945.*

## BIBLIOGRAPHY

Baum, Richard. *Burying Mao: Chinese Politics in the Age of Deng Xiaoping.* Princeton, NJ: Princeton University Press, 1994.

Deng Jixin (Teng Chi-hsin). *Teng Hsiao-p'ing: A Political Biography*. Hong Kong: Cosmos, 1978.
Deng Maomao. *Deng Xiaoping: My Father*. New York: Basic Books, 1995.
Deng Xiaoping. *Fundamental Issues in Present Day China*. Beijing: Foreign Language Press, 1987.
Evans, Richard. *Deng Xiaoping and the Making of Modern China*. Rev. ed. New York: Penguin, 1997.
Gao Yingmao (Michael Ying-mao Kau) and Susan H. Marsh, eds. *China in the Era of Deng Xiaoping: A Decade of Reform*. Armonk, NY: Sharpe, 1993.
Goodman, David. *Deng Xiaoping and the Chinese Revolution: A Political Biography*. New York: Routledge, 1994.
Marti, Michael E. *China and the Legacy of Deng Xiaoping: From Communist Revolution to Capitalist Evolution*. Washington, DC: Brassey's, 2002.
Shambaugh, David, ed. *Deng Xiaoping: Portrait of a Chinese Statesman*. Oxford: Clarendon Press, 1995.
Teiwes, Frederick. Mao and His Lieutenants. *Australian Journal of Chinese Affairs* 19/20 (1988): 1–80.
Teiwes, Frederick. Politics at the "Core": The Political Circumstances of Mao Zedong, Deng Xiaoping, and Jiang Zemin. Contemporary China Centre, Research School of Pacific and Asian Studies, Australian National University. George Ernest Morrison Lecture in Ethnology. 2000. http://rspas.anu.edu.au/ccc/morrison00.pdf.
Yang Bingzhang (Benjamin Yang). *Deng: A Political Biography*. Armonk, NY: Sharpe, 1997.
Yu Guangyuan. *Deng Xiaoping Shakes the World: An Eyewitness Account of China's Party Work Conference and the Third Plenum (November–December 1978)*. Eds. Ezra F. Vogel and Steven I. Levine. Norwalk, CT: EastBridge, 2004.

***Marisela Connelly***

## DEPARTMENT STORES

SEE *Shops*.

## DESERTIFICATION

Dryland environmental degradation, known as *desertification*, is widespread in China, a country faced with serious environmental problems. About one-third of China's land area is considered dryland (arid, semiarid, and dry subhumid), located mostly in northern China. Of this, 2.62 million square kilometers, or 79 percent, is affected by desertification.

Desertification, the decline of vegetation cover and productivity on dryland, manifests in several forms in China. In dry subhumid and semiarid areas, both the grassland cover and the quality of soil have declined, and the land's reduced bioproductivity cannot recover in the short run or without significant human intervention. On arid land, in addition to vegetation decline, salt may build up on areas where irrigation is mismanaged, leading to salinization and alkalization. Where the surface material is sandy, either on sandy land or desert, the decline of vegetation may be followed by the activation of moving sand, a process called *sandification*. On high land on the edge of the Qinghai-Tibetan Plateau, the freezing and melting process may also be accelerated by human activity, leading to vegetation decline (Yang et al. 2005).

Environmental degradation has accelerated since the Communist Party took control of China in 1949. The average annual rate of desertification was 1,560 square kilometers from the 1950s to the 1970s; 2,100 square kilometers in the 1980s; and 2,460 square kilometers in the 1990s. At the turn of the twenty-first century, the annual desertification rate reached 3,436 square kilometers (Meng, Wen, and Ma 2005). While some scholars trace the degradation to historical times, especially the late Qing and the Guomindang periods, it is commonly held that the rate of environmental degradation during the socialist period since 1949 has been markedly higher than during any previous period in Chinese history.

### HUMAN AND ECONOMIC CONSEQUENCES

The human and economic consequences of such severe degradation have been alarming. Desertification has deprived people (many belonging to minority groups) living on marginal lands of their means of livelihood, forcing some to relocate to other areas. The in situ degradation also affects distant regions, as particles from exposed soil are carried by the wind and foul the air in eastern China, East Asia, and even North America.

Studies using 1999 data show that the direct economic cost of desertification accrues to 128 billion yuan (US $16 billion) annually, 1.14 percent of China's annual gross domestic product (GDP). For seriously desertified regions (Inner Mongolia, Gansu, Xinjiang, Qinghai, Ningxia, and Shaanxi), the cost accounts for as much as 23.16 percent of the region's annual GDP (Liu 2006).

### THE ROLE OF HUMAN ACTIVITY IN DESERTIFICATION

Scholars studying China's environment have long recognized the predominant role of human activities in the desertification process. Zhu Zhenda, a leading scholar in the study of China's dryland, points to excessive economic activity among humans as the main factor triggering the process of dryland degradation, with natural factors acting as "background" or "potential" factors (Ding, Bao, and Ma 1998). This understanding of the predominant human role is consistent with studies of desertification elsewhere.

In the 1980s, Zhu further classified desertified land according to primary human activities as follows: 25.4

percent of desertification is led by cultivation on unsuitable land; 28.3 percent occurs because of overgrazing; 31.8 percent is due to excessive fuelwood collection; and 9 percent is due to water misuse and surface industry. Only 5.5 percent of desertification is led by wind erosion of dune sands (Zhu and Liu 1989; see also Wang 2007). Although this assessment was made in the 1980s, overgrazing and cultivation on marginal land remain the main drivers of desertification in China.

Overgrazing has become a serious problem in most pastoral areas in China. According to a 2003 analysis by Lester Brown, from 1950 to 2002, as grassland quality decreased, China's cattle, sheep, and goat population tripled. As of 2002, China had 106 million cattle and 298 million sheep and goats; in comparison, the United States, a country with comparable grazing capacity, had 97 million cattle and 8 million sheep and goats. Brown's analysis referred to a 2001 U.S. embassy report titled "Grapes of Wrath in Inner Mongolia," which noted that the Chinese have "no California to escape to." The reference to the American dust bowl of the 1930s speaks to the serious condition of China's dryland environment.

To better understand human causes of desertification, experts must look beyond direct human activities, whereby the local people, the very victims of desertification, are often blamed. Instead, they have to address underlying human causes, especially those resulting from government policies and the relationship of humans with the environment. These factors are also among the root causes of overexploitation of the environment.

Government policies account for major changes in land-use patterns and environmental consequences. In Inner Mongolia, for example, four waves of disastrous grassland opening have occurred since 1949, each led by government policy change, or forced directly by policies. The first wave of opening occurred in 1956 and 1957, preceding the Great Leap Forward, in China's rush to develop the "socialist economy." The second wave in 1960 and 1961 followed the great famine, produced by astounding policy errors. The more detrimental third wave came during the Cultural Revolution (1966–1669), when the Mongols were persecuted and their pastoral economy was suppressed. During this period, one million hectares of grassland were converted into cropland, leading to lasting devastation of the environment. The fourth wave of grassland opening took place during the post-Mao era. Driven by policies encouraging unchecked economic growth, another one million hectares of grassland were converted into farmland, matching the area of conversion during the Cultural Revolution (Jiang 2005).

This example represents a consistent pattern of environmental degradation during China's socialist period. During both the Mao and post-Mao eras, China's traditional respect for the environment was replaced with human domination. During the Mao era, such domination was expressed in brute political forces of suppression, as is apparent in the era's warlike slogans, such as "fight with heaven and battle with earth" and "conquer the desert." In the post-Mao era, while the direct application of political commands on the environment ceased, such policies have been replaced with single-minded development goals that disregard ecological limits and environmental consequences.

Worth mentioning is the role of population growth and economic development, secondary drivers that are often blamed as the primary source of desertification. While population growth rate was high in northern China's desertification-prone area (more than doubled since 1949), and China's drive for economic development also intensified pressures on the environment, both factors have largely manifested under state policies, serving ancillary roles in inducing desertification while making desertification problems more intractable (see Jiang 1999). Elsewhere in the world, population pressure is rarely an underlying driver of desertification but serves only to exacerbate the complicated process of dryland environmental degradation (see Reynolds and Stafford Smith 2002).

## FAILURE OF GOVERNMENT INITIATIVES

The Chinese government has taken measures to deal with dryland environmental degradation. One of the most notable environmental initiatives is the North China Shelterbelt program *(sanbei fanghulin gongcheng)*, also referred to as the Great Green Wall program. The program started in 1978 and is scheduled to run until 2050; its goal is to establish 35.6 million hectares of forest. By the end of the first stage in 2000, the agency in charge of the program, the State Forestry Administration, claimed to have established twenty-two million hectares of forest, raising forest cover from 5.05 percent to over 9 percent in northern China's project area and bringing desertification under control. Since 1999, another major environmental program, "grain for green" (grain used as subsidies for tree planting), has augmented the afforestation efforts in northern China.

In the meantime, however, desertification has continued to advance over vast areas of northern China, undermining the positive results of the afforestation programs claimed by the Chinese government. While the number of trees planted has certainly increased, environmental improvement has only occurred in limited locales in the background of rapid wholesale degradation.

Several factors help explain the failure of these government programs to check desertification. First, while the programs were enacted to establish forests, they are not aimed at large-scale ecological recovery. Regions outside the programs' coverage area are governed by the rationale

***Workers laying hay to prevent the encroachment of the Maowusu Desert, Baijitan, Ningxia Hui Autonomous Region, August 23, 2006.*** *During the Communist era, damage to China's environment increased, including widespread desertification near existing dry lands. Critics contend livestock overgrazing, agricultural use of substandard land, and population increases all contribute to the desertification process, overwhelming government efforts to reverse the damage.* © MICHAEL REYNOLDS/EPA/CORBIS

that equates development with a narrow notion of economic growth. This lack of integration with the local environment is exacerbated by the State Forestry Administration's overemphasis on establishing forests that never existed on the native landscape of many dryland areas. Planted trees, which are often not well incorporated into the local economy, also contribute to the overdrawing of groundwater and indirectly exacerbate the desiccation of the dryland ecosystem (see Jiang 2005, Cao 2008). Clearly, tree planting is not a panacea for environmental rehabilitation.

Another reason for the failure of China's environmental programs is their narrow ecological discourse. Equating ecology with planting more trees (plus the shrubs and grass that were later added), China's official ecological discourse disregards connectivity and limits of the ecosystem, fails to consider the natural fluctuation of the dryland environment, and negates traditional values and practices (e.g., nomadism) that are better suited for the dryland environment. At the same time, limited space afforded in China for alternative discourses serves to perpetuate environmental overuse.

China's environmental crisis is, at its core, a crisis of policies and consciousness. Unless the Chinese government and society change fundamentally their way of dealing with the dryland environment and begin to respect its limits, desertification cannot be checked and reversed.

**BIBLIOGRAPHY**

Brown, Lester R. China Losing War with Advancing Deserts. Earth Policy Institute Eco-Economy Update. August 5, 2003. http://www.earth-policy.org/.

Cao, Shixiong. Why Large-Scale Afforestation Efforts in China Have Failed to Solve the Desertification Problem. *Environmental Science and Technology* March 15, 2008: 1826–1831.

Ding Dengshan, Bao Haosheng, and Ma Yongli. Progress in the Study of Desertification in China. *Progress in Physical Geography* 22, 4 (1998): 551–557.

Grapes of Wrath in Inner Mongolia: A May 2001 Report from U.S. Embassy Beijing. http://www.usembassy-china.org.cn/.

Jiang Hong. Grassland Management and Views of Nature in China Since 1949: Regional Policies and Local Changes in Uxin Ju, Inner Mongolia. *Geoforum* 36 (2005): 641–653.

Jiang, Hong. *The Ordos Plateau of China: An Endangered Environment.* Tokyo: United Nations University Press, 1999.

Liu Tou. Zhongguo tudi shamohua jingji sunshi pinggu [Assessment of the economic loss of China's desertification]. *Zhongguo shamo* [Journal of desert research] 26, 1 (2006): 40–46.

Meng Shubiao, Wen Suqing, and Ma Dongxue. Woguo fangzhi tudi shamohua de faluu sikao [Consideration of law in China's desertification]. *Hebei faxue* [Hebei law science] 23, 10 (2005): 154–157.

Reynolds, J. F., and D. M. Stafford Smith, eds. *Do Humans Cause Deserts*? Berlin: Dahlem University Pressk, 2002.

Wang Tao. Zhu Zhenda xiansheng dui zhongguo shamo yu shamohua kexue de gongxian [Zhu Zhenda's contribution to China's desert and desertification science]. *Zhongguo shamo* [Journal of desert research] 27, 1 (2007): 2–5.

Yang X., Zhang K., Jia B., and Cai L. Desertification Assessment in China: An Overview. *Journal of Arid Environments* 63 (2005): 517–531.

Zhu, Zhenda and Liu Shu. *Zhongguo de shamohua jiqi zhili* [Desertification in China and its control]. Beijing: Kexue Chubanshe [Science press], 1989.

***Hong Jiang***

# DIALECT GROUPS

What is collectively known as the Chinese language consists of a number of genetically related but mutually unintelligible dialect groups. Dialect classifications have varied, but the one now widely accepted divides Chinese into seven regional groups: Northern Chinese (Mandarin), Wu, Gan, Xiang, Yue (Cantonese), Hakka, and Min. Three more dialect groups have been proposed recently, namely Jin, Hui, and Pinghua, but their statuses are still being debated.

## DIALECTAL VARIATIONS

The regional varieties are dialect *groups* because there are subgroups, dialects, and subdialects within all of them. Northern Chinese is by far the largest dialect group and the one in direct contact with minority languages along the border regions. The other groups are concentrated in the southeast provinces. Linguistic diversity is greater in the southern dialect groups than in Northern Chinese, and the diversity in some Min and Wu dialects is large enough to cause communication difficulties even between neighboring towns. In general, linguistic differences between the groups are greater than those within.

The most important differences separating the dialects are pronunciation and tone, but there are also significant lexical and grammatical differences. The dialects share much of the common lexicon, but pronunciation of the lexical items varies. For example, the word for tea 茶 is pronounced *cha* in Beijing Mandarin, *zo* in Shanghai Wu, and *tsa* in Cantonese. However, to say "drink tea," the three dialects prefer three different verbs: 喝茶 *he cha* in Beijing Mandarin, 吃茶 *chiq zo* in Shanghai Wu, and 饮茶 *iam tsa* in Cantonese. Most Northern Chinese dialects have four tones, but eight or nine tones are common in Yue dialects. A general tendency is that the further south a dialect, the more tones are likely. Tonal variations can occur even among closely related dialects that share pronunciation and tonal categories. For example, the pitch values of the four tones in Beijing are 55, 35, 214, and 51, but in Jinan, also a Northern dialect, the corresponding tones are 213, 42, 55, and 21, making the dialect distinctively different from that of Beijing. In grammar, for example, a direct object follows an indirect object in Northern Chinese, but in many southern dialects they are inverted.

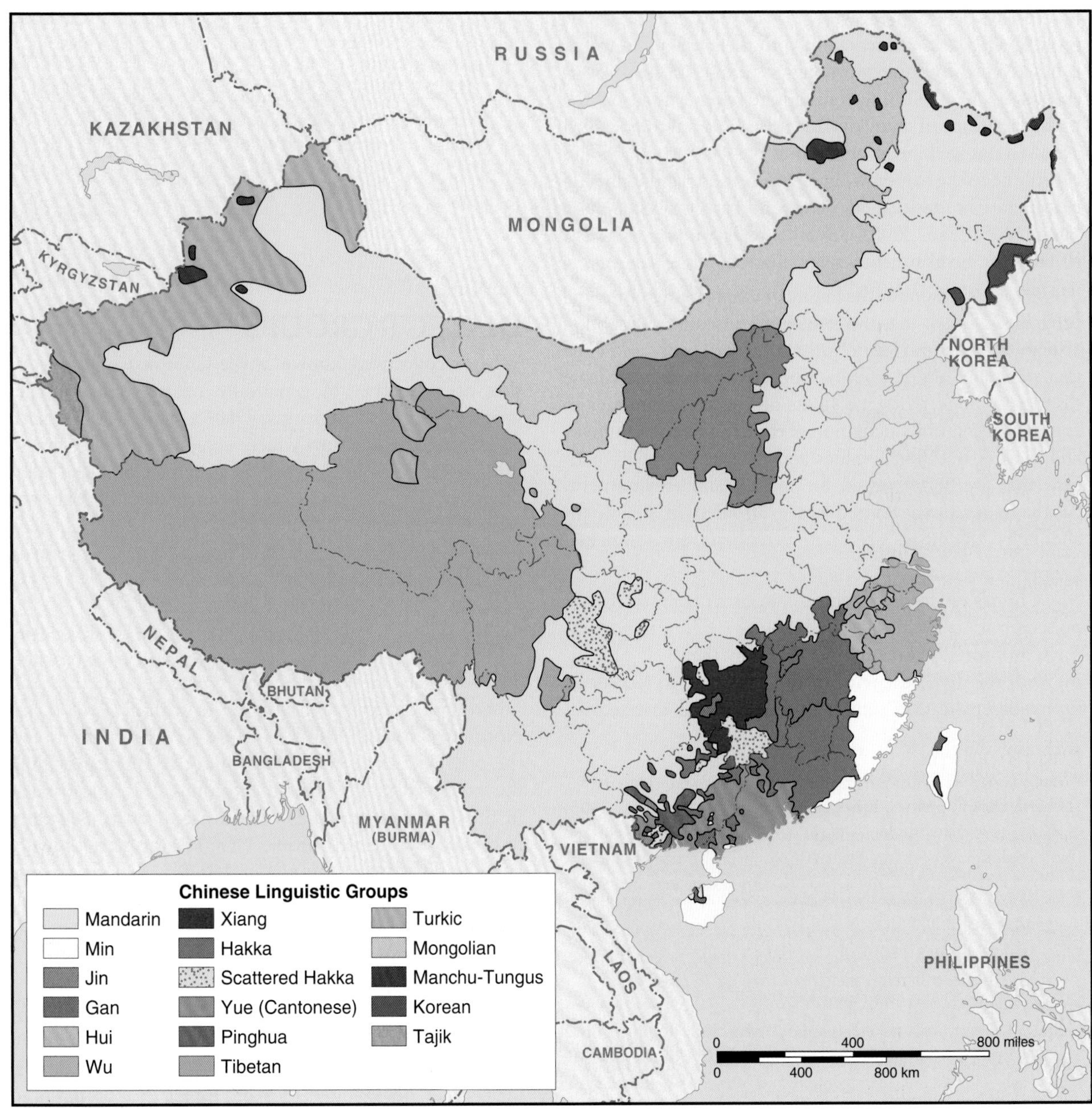


## RELATIONSHIP BETWEEN MODERN STANDARD CHINESE AND DIALECTS

Modern Standard Chinese—that is, Putonghua (common language)—is based on the Northern dialect of Beijing. China's language policy is to promote Putonghua as the common language for the entire country. Putonghua is, by law, the language of government administration and the primary language of education and the mass media. Its use in the service industry is encouraged. However, exceptions are made for local dialects to be used in specified public domains when necessary, which include public-service communications, performing arts, teaching, research, and, with government approval, radio and television broadcasting. Bilingualism in Putonghua and local dialects is widespread. Some degree of Putonghua proficiency is now universal among middle-aged and younger Han Chinese, and the use of Putonghua is increasing among ethnic minorities. For the vast majority of dialect speakers, local dialects remain the languages of the home and other informal communications in local regions.

Intimate contact between Putonghua and local dialects has led to one influencing the other. On the one hand, convergence of dialectal features toward the standard has occurred. On the other hand, expressions once limited to local dialects have entered Putonghua and then been adopted by other dialects. The social and geographic mobility created by the recent economic development has assisted in the further popularization of Putonghua. At the same time, the prosperities of local economies have lent prestige to local dialects. Cantonese and Shanghai Wu have become more popular because of their booming regional economies. Increased contact with Hong Kong and Taiwan in recent decades has also introduced competing linguistic norms from these regions—for example, the use of traditional characters and linguistic features in Taiwan Mandarin and Hong Kong Cantonese—adding further challenges to language standardization, especially where the language contact is intense.

## DIALECTS AND SUBETHNIC IDENTITIES

The current dialectal variations in Chinese owe much to the historical migrations of the Chinese people. As the language spread, it acquired features of the languages it came into contact with, many of which it eventually superseded. The resulting dialects are symbols of regional identities, as children born in the local regions learn and speak local dialects as their first languages. A frequently employed categorization among Han Chinese is local affiliations—for example, *Hunan ren* (people from Hunan) and *Dongbei ren* (people from the northeast)—which are typically identified with local dialects, such as *Hunan hua* (Xiang dialects) and *Dongbei hua* (Northeast Mandarin). An important reason the dialects have persisted is speaker solidarity. With family members and locals where one grew up, dialects are often the only appropriate linguistic varieties to use.

Dialects and accents are important clues in search of *tongxiang* (literally: same country town) for allies and friendship in multicultural situations. The term refers to people from the same town or province and expresses a special relationship between people bound together by regional origins. To be a *tongxiang* is to identify with those who share the same regional origin and the associated cultural understanding and dialect. An organized form of regional identities is *tongxiang hui* (same country town or natives associations). Historically associated with *shangbang* (merchant groups), *tongxiang hui* were once obsolete when China implemented socialist reform and a planned economy in the mid-twentieth century, but they have reappeared with the emergence of a market economy in recent decades. The presence of *tongxiang hui* in many Chinese cities today has contributed to the multilingualism in these cities; the languages used most often among *tongxiang* are their local dialects.

## DIALECTS AND OVERSEAS CHINESE

Prior to the 1980s, the dialects spoken in the overseas Chinese communities were those of the southern groups, in particular Min, Yue, and Hakka, because the coastal provinces of Fujian and Guangdong where the dialects are spoken were the traditional emigration regions. Cantonese was the most prominent Chinese dialect in Western countries where overseas Chinese settled, because the early Chinese in these countries were from the province of Guangdong, where Cantonese was the dominant dialect and lingua franca. In Southeast Asia, where Chinese migrations have a long history, there are many communities of speakers of Min, Yue, and Hakka dialects. The presence of Mandarin as a community dialect of overseas Chinese occurred only recently, as a result of overseas migrations of both Mandarin speakers from Taiwan in the later part of the last century and more importantly, large numbers of mainland Chinese following China's open-door policy of the late 1970s. Many mainland migrants speak a local dialect as their first language but are highly competent in Putonghua.

Owing to different migration histories, cultural and political experiences, and dialects, the overseas Chinese comprise many communities. Their dialects are important defining characteristics of their communities. For example, long-standing Chinese communities in Western countries are Cantonese speaking, while new migrants speak Mandarin. The Chinese in Southeast Asia identify with their own dialects, such as Hokkien (a Southern Min dialect) and Teochiu (Chaozhou, also a Southern Min dialect), and often settle in communities using their dialects.

### BIBLIOGRAPHY

Chen Ping. *Modern Chinese: History and Sociolinguistics.* Cambridge, U.K.: Cambridge University Press, 1999.

Kane, Daniel. *The Chinese Language: Its History and Current Usage.* North Clarendon, VT: Tuttle, 2006.

Li Rulong. *Hanyu Fangyanxue* [Chinese dialectology]. Beijing: Higher Education Press, 2001.

Norman, Jerry. *Chinese.* Cambridge, U.K.: Cambridge University Press, 1988.

Ramsey, S. Robert. *The Languages of China.* Princeton, NJ: Princeton University Press, 1987.

Wang, William S-Y., ed. *Languages and Dialects of China.* Berkeley, CA: Project on Linguistic Analysis, 1991.

Wurm, Stephen A., et al. *Language Atlas of China.* Hong Kong: Longman, 1988.

Yan, Margaret Mian. *Introduction to Chinese Dialectology.* München, Germany: LINCOM Europa, 2006.

Yuan Jiahua. *Hanyu Fangyan Gaiyao* [Essentials of Chinese dialects]. 2nd ed. Beijing: Language Press, 2001.

*Zhonghua Renmin Gongheguo Guojia Yuyan Wenzi Fa* [Law of the People's Republic of China on the standard spoken and written Chinese language]. Beijing: Chinese Democratic Legal Affairs Press, 2000.

Zhou Minglang and Sun Hongkai, eds. *Language Policy in the People's Republic of China: Theory and Practice since 1949.* Norwell, MA: Kluwer Academic, 2004.

**Hong Xiao**

## DIAOYUTAI, SOVEREIGNTY OVER

SEE *Japan, Relations with.*

## DING LING

### *1904–1986*

Ding Ling (Jiang Bingzhi) was a pioneering woman writer in Chinese literary history. Her works express women's problems both on psychological and sociopolitical levels. Ding Ling's life and career reflect the tension between the women's movement and Communist ideology in pre- and postrevolutionary China. A sensitive literary mind, Ding Ling struggled between distinguishing herself as a woman and immersing herself in the revolutionary waves that were attempting to construct a great China. In her writings, she succeeded in reconciling both urges, but in real life, her desire to be a woman with authentic feminine and sexual drives ran counter to her wish to be a loyal Communist in the eyes of the state.

#### THE MAY FOURTH MOVEMENT

Ding Ling was among the most renowned modern Chinese woman writers and the first one who, with full patriotic sentiments, attempted to redeem her country through literature. As one of the few female participants of the May Fourth movement, Ding Ling shared with her male comrades a profound urge to reform Chinese culture in order to strengthen the national defenses against imperialist forces from the West. She was also the first woman writer to openly explore the psychological conflicts in women and to denounce the gender boundaries set by a patriarchal society. The intention to release women from the shackles of traditional Chinese and Confucian values was an intrinsic part of the spirit of the May Fourth movement, which was not in itself a feminist movement. But since women composed half of the Chinese population, the male thinkers of the May Fourth movement regarded the improvement of women's lives to be part of the foundation for improving the whole nation. Thus, the movement's sociocultural reforms included changing certain practices relating to marriage and the traditional family: Concubinage; bound feet; arranged marriages; the equating of woman's illiteracy with virtue; submission of women to fathers, husbands, and sons, and so forth. Ding Ling went even further in exploring openly in one of her first short stories, "Miss Sophie's Diary" (1928), the condition of female sexuality and psychological confusion, as well as her determination to eradicate patriarchal oppression imposed upon women in various institutional forms.

#### EARLY LIFE

Born on September 4, 1904, to a wealthy gentry family, Ding Ling, whose real name was Jiang Bingzhi, was fortunate to be the daughter of an intellectually oriented mother whose vision far exceeded that of other women bound by patriarchal ideology. Even at the death of her dissolute husband and with a three-year-old daughter and an infant son, Ding Ling's mother, in her open defiance against societal pressure to become a reclusive widow, enrolled in a school for women to continue her education. This kind of fortitude and advanced feminist vision greatly shaped Ding Ling's character and self-expectations as a modern Chinese woman. Switching from one school to another in order to fulfill her revolutionary goals, Ding Ling started with her mother's endorsement as an independent young woman as early as her fifteenth year. During her school years, she expressed her feminist views by cutting her hair short and participating in student street demonstrations. At the same time, like any male May Fourth participant, she absorbed numerous translated novels, poems, and dramas imported from the West.

#### GROUNDBREAKING THEMES OF DING LING'S SHORT STORIES

Ding Ling's short stories from the 1920s and 1930s are marked by the fundamental theme of defining female subjectivity through women's internal turmoil, of which "Miss Sophie's Diary" is the representative work. Though exemplifying the boldness and self-doubt of a young, liberated, modern woman in 1920s China, "Miss Sophie's Diary" has had a cross-cultural and cross-temporal appeal for readers from their first encounter with the protagonist. Through its confessional mode and its spiteful narrator, the story is reminiscent of Fyodor Dostoyevsky's *Notes from the Underground* (1864). Every strand of the narrator-protagonist's internal contradictions finds its apex in her ultimate conflict in love. She truly despises the man with whom she frantically falls in love. She is, therefore, imprisoned within her own self-love and self-hatred. Miss Sophie's predicament testifies to her intense desire to understand herself as a woman. It is self-probing and self-exploration that intrigue Miss Sophie.

Despite her concerns with female subjectivity, Ding Ling stood apart from other romantic writers of her time, both male and female. Although she was emotional and effusive in expressing her female characters' inner feelings, Ding Ling's short stories aimed at analyzing the internal psychological interplay of the human mind, rather than the search for ideal romantic love. Being a lover of Western literature, Ding Ling employed her knowledge of Western realism in almost all her stories. In her twenties, she read Gustave Flaubert's *Madame Bovary* (1856) ten times in translation. Like Flaubert's works, almost all

Ding Ling's stories found their source in the author's actual life experiences. For example, her debut work, "Mengke" (1927), was based on her attempt to become an actress in Shanghai. But like Flaubert, she used the raw materials of her own life only as a starting point. She was extremely skillful in transforming her experiences into art. The excellence of this kind of psychological realism lies in the reader being permitted to follow every twist and turn of the protagonist's mental activity, a process normally hidden from others.

Despite their realism, Ding Ling's early works shared one theme with the writings of the romantic tradition: the search for self-identity. This thematic orientation was by no means far from the common interest of all writers and thinkers of the May Fourth generation, who were searching for both self-identity and the identity of the nation. It was a quest pertaining to youth and symbolically referred to the entire country, which was seen in the early twentieth century as being reborn into youth. The period of the so-called Chinese renaissance, in its full revolutionary spirit, ran to the 1970s and the end of the Cultural Revolution. Ding Ling stood, symbolically, as the torchbearer from the beginning to the end of this period. Besides her unique position as a woman writer of the May Fourth generation, another significant trait of her work was her unprecedented representation of the condensed image of both youth and woman in Chinese literary history. Women have been represented in Chinese literature since antiquity, but they were often depicted as the object of male desire, rather than as a subject of interest in their own right. Ding Ling's stories foregrounded young women's psychological conflicts and their subjective desire for self-identity, especially when encountering love.

Ding Ling denied that she ever pursued feminist issues or expressed feminist views in her stories. But from a reader's perspective, Ding Ling's views on women indeed corresponded to liberal feminism and cultural feminism in the Western sense. The difference between Ding Ling and her Western counterparts was that Ding Ling, while critiquing social injustice against women, also called attention to the inner weaknesses of women themselves. Her focus, however, was not placed on the social battle against institutionalized forms of cultural and political discrimination against women, but on how women were able to conquer their own weaknesses and inner disturbances after they were liberated from institutional confinement. Her concern for female and human psychological and spiritual freedom, rather than social freedom, gave an important philosophical dimension and universal significance to Ding Ling's works.

## POLITICAL CAREER AFTER 1931

After 1931, Ding Ling's life took a drastic turn, largely due to the execution of her lover, Hu Yepin, by the Nationalist Party. She became more aggressive and progressive in her march toward Communism. After the 1930s, the thematic orientation of Ding Ling's writings switched from the self-expression of young women to the patriotic and political concerns of the Communist Party. Suddenly, she submerged her urge for self-exploration beneath her passions for a political career. She jumped to prominence in politics and began writing stories for the party apparatus as ideological propaganda. *The Sun Shines over the Sanggan River* (1948) is representative of her work during this time, as are short stories such as "When I Was in Xia Village" (1940) and "Mother" (1932). In these stories, female characters are tougher and are driven toward the so-called Great Self or the party. In "Mother," interpersonal human conflict is transformed into a sisterhood for the sake of the state and party. In "When I Was in Xia Village," a girl named Zhen Zhen succeeds in shedding her self-pity and the villagers' contempt for her after she is raped by Japanese soldiers, and she sets off confidently to find self-fulfillment in service to the nation. These are all patriotic stories exhibiting little artistic craftsmanship. They no longer explore women's internal self, as Ding Ling's earlier works did.

Ding Ling's patriotic literary expressions did not pay off. After the 1940s, she faced the criticism of the party for her "willful" exercise of the pen as a liberal-minded writer. In 1942 her essay "Thoughts on March Eighth" placed her in the center of political turmoil in the Yan'an rectification movement. In the essay, Ding Ling not only discussed the predicament of women in Yan'an, the so-called liberated area, but also uncovered the "dark side" of the Communist Party based on personal politics. The so-called liberated women in Yan'an still encountered social pressure grounded in deep gender discrimination. Stuck in the tension between playing the role of a mother at the cost of career advancement and focusing on self-development and possibly compromising the well-being of their children, the women of Yan'an experienced the brunt of social criticism. Ding Ling insinuated that literary writers, who have special access to the truths of everyday experience, are responsible for articulating the reality of social and political injustice and calling for political reform. Ding Ling's criticism of the Communist Party brought forth a series of debates in the party. Unfortunately, however, all the criticism was silenced by Mao Zedong in his historic "Talks at the Yan'an Forum on Literature and Art," which prescribed the role of art and literature as that of tools for the party. As a punishment, Ding Ling was removed from her position as the editor of *Jiefang ribao* (Liberation Daily).

The criticism intensified after 1958 and culminated in her being deprived of both her prominent position in the party and her personal freedom until 1978. For almost two decades, she disappeared from public view and her very existence was in question to Chinese readers. During this time, she was sent, in political exile, to work in a labor camp in Heilonjiang province, widely known as "northern wilderness." It was not until 1978 that people began to learn that she was still alive. Ding Ling's literary and political reputation was restored in 1978, two years after the end of Cultural Revolution decade. By then she was already seventy-four years old and weakened due to the twenty years of political torments. But unlike other literary figures of the time, she not only survived the Cultural Revolution, but her creative power as a writer did not diminish. "Du Wanxiang" (1979), her last work, is a self-justification in which she identifies herself with the history of the Chinese Communist Party.

Ding Ling died in 1986 at the age of eighty-two. Through "Du Wanxiang" Ding Ling finally triumphed at the end of her life over the psychological confusion that plagued her youth. She came to realize that individual desire for fulfillment leads nowhere without self-transcendence and that one's life becomes meaningful only through serving the needs of other people.

**SEE ALSO** *May Fourth Movement; Women, Status of.*

**BIBLIOGRAPHY**

Barlow, Tani E., and Gary J. Bjorge, eds. *I Myself Am a Woman: Selected Writings of Ding Ling.* Boston: Beacon Press, 1989.

Ding Ling. *Miss Sophie's Diary and Other Stories.* Trans. W. J. F. Jenner. Beijing: Panda Books, 1985.

Feuerwerker, Yi-tsi Mei. *Ding Ling's Fiction: Ideology and Narrative in Modern Chinese Literature.* Cambridge, MA: Harvard University Press, 1982.

***Chung-min Maria Tu (Zhongmin Du)***

## DISABILITY

**SEE** *Social Welfare.*

## DISSIDENTS

In Communist Party–ruled regimes, there is no institutionalized space for the expression of dissent because the party is supposed to represent the interests of the whole people. Expressions of disagreement with the official line are often regarded as a manifestation of hostility toward the people. However, be it in the former Soviet Union or the People's Republic of China (PRC), some citizens have relentlessly criticized the party, and in most cases, paid a heavy price for doing so. Not all opponents to the party are dissidents. For example, in the early years after the establishment of the PRC, some groups—national minorities, bandits, secret societies—put up armed resistance against the Communists. In 1975 groups of Hui in Yunnan put up armed resistance against cadres who wanted to force them to breed pigs, enforcing the official policy of "putting pigs at the center" (*yizhu weizhu*). These episodes of resistance do not belong to the category of dissent.

By *dissident*, we mean a person who uses legal means, mostly writings or peaceful demonstrations, to express disagreement with the Communist Party leadership or to challenge official ideology. The term *dissident* itself appeared in the USSR in the 1960s, and had no equivalent in Chinese for a long time. After 1989, most specialists and actors agreed on the term *chi butong zhengjianzhe* (meaning, those who hold different political views).

Since the founding of the PRC in 1949, various groups of citizens have expressed their disagreement with the official line. Some were party members, others belonged to the so-called democratic parties, and some did not belong to any political organizations. Their political positions varied, some claiming that the leaders had betrayed Marxism–Leninism, while others were opposed to the official ideology. The former were not necessarily treated more leniently than the latter. But the response they met from the party has varied according to the period.

Given the nature of the regime and its pervasive control on information, it is very difficult to establish a precise image of dissent in the PRC. As long as the archives of the bureaus of Public Security and State Security remain closed to historians, researchers will have to count on the memoirs of the dissidents themselves, and on documents released by the party leadership when one faction has been toppled by another, resulting in the rehabilitation of the critics of the previous leadership. The late 1970s, which witnessed the rehabilitation of most of the victims of the Maoist political movements, provided historians with valuable sources on dissent.

Paradoxically, at least until the early 1980s, a large proportion of dissidents belonged to the Communist Party. Intellectuals were predominant, and, although these dissident intellectuals often pretended to be speaking "for the ordinary people," they were never very successful in recruiting the support of workers and peasants. Their supporters were usually students and petty intellectuals such as primary school teachers or, sometimes, petty bureaucrats.

### APPEALING TO MAO TO DENOUNCE THE BUREAUCRACY

The first case of open dissent after the founding of the PRC was that of Hu Feng. Hu had been a famous progressive literary critic since the 1930s. When the Communist Party took over power, he wrote laudatory articles. However, as the new regime consolidated its grip on power, it imposed a strict censorship on literature and art, stifling creativity. Hu Feng, who was convinced that this narrowness of views was due to the sectarianism of the cultural bureaucrats, wrote an open letter to Mao Zedong in which he explained that now that power was in the hands of the proletariat, the party should trust artists and writers and not impose a rigid orthodoxy upon them. Hu denounced the interference of the cultural bureaucrats in creative work.

Directly addressing the chairman to denounce abuses by the bureaucracy was a typical feature of dissent during Mao's reign. When considered in the twenty-first century, this attitude can seem naive, but at the time, the fact that Mao often lashed out at the bureaucracy helped build his reputation as an open-minded leader.

But, as many after Hu Feng were to find out, Mao was not ready to grant intellectuals, whom he considered bourgeois, any freedom of expression. Mao had Hu's letter widely circulated among cadres and intellectuals, and then denounced it as a counterrevolutionary document. And because Hu had consulted with colleagues and disciples who shared his ideas before sending his letter, he was accused of organizing a counterrevolutionary clique and was sentenced to a long jail term. He was to be rehabilitated only in 1980, and the sufferings he had endured deeply affected his mental health. In 1955 the movement to eliminate counterrevolutionaries (*sufan*) that struck the intellectuals who had been on good terms with Hu Feng or supported his ideas resulted in the arrests of thousands of progressive youth who had been active in Guomindang-ruled cities (the famous "white zones") during the civil war. These well-bred Marxists were not ready to submit unconditionally to Maoist orthodoxy, and tried to defend their vision of the socialist revolution, especially the necessity to guarantee freedom of expression to the various forces that supported the regime. Mao showed that he was not ready to accept discussion with them.

More would-be dissidents were to experience the same deception just a year later. This time, it was the turn of the rallied elements of the progressive bourgeoisie and of some of the most valuable members of the elites educated by the regime to express their dissent. It took Mao Zedong a lot of "ideological work" to convince these people to vent their criticism of the regime, because the *sufan* had left deep wounds on the intelligentsia. However, when the Great Leader launched his slogan "Let a hundred flowers bloom, let a hundred Schools contend," many discontented citizens expressed their criticism of the regime. One group was composed of the former leaders of the "Third Force," who had refused to choose between the Guomindang and the Communist Party during the civil war but had finally chosen to cooperate with the latter. Raised on the Western ideals of democracy and freedom, they denounced the omnipotence of the party secretary and, in general, the restriction of basic freedoms. The other group of dissidents was made up of young students who had been admitted to universities after 1949. They too were enraged by the stifling presence of bureaucrats who enforced rigid control over their lives. Some, like Lin Xiling or Tan Tianrong, demanded equality before the law, denounced the excesses of the Land reform, spoke in favor of Hu Feng, and asked for a revision of the verdicts handed over during the *sufan* movement to eliminate counterrevolutionaries. These students expressed their ideas on posters affixed on university walls and in unofficial journals such as *Guangchang* (The square).

The third group of dissidents comprised young writers educated by the party, such as Liu Binyan and Wang Meng, enthusiastic supporters of the new regime who denounced the abuses of cadres in order to help the party correct them. One feature of this generation of dissidents (and in this they are similar to their counterparts in the USSR and Eastern Europe) is that they did not question the legitimacy of the socialist regime, and they believed that Mao was different from Joseph Stalin in that he himself asked the masses to vent their criticisms.

Another feature was that these dissidents did not join the workers and peasants in their criticism of the regime, despite the fact that they pretended to speak for society and that some journalists who were to be labeled rightists did cover workers' strikes or write about peasants who refused to join the cooperatives. They were convinced that rural collectivization and the nationalization of industries were necessary to make China a strong socialist country. But their support for the fundamental tenets of socialism did not save them from the wrath of the party, which launched the anti-rightist movement to get rid of them. Finally, despite (or because of) the Cold War, their struggle never had any resonance in the West.

## HOMEGROWN DISSIDENTS

It took the Cultural Revolution (1966–1969) to see a new generation of dissidents appear on the stage. The fanaticism of the Red Guards was not favorable to the expression of dissent. However, during their stay in the countryside following the disbanding of the Red Guard groups, many youths—the sent-down educated youths—started to reflect over the nature of the regime. They founded informal reading groups, and circulated poems and short stories describing their state of mind and the repression that struck them, inventing the *samizdat* more or less at the same time as their Soviet counterparts. They seized opportunities created by the struggle at the top of the party to express their ideas. In 1974 a *dazibao* (big-character poster) titled *About Legality and Democracy under Socialism* was posted in Guangzhou, demanding an end to the "social fascist Lin Biao system." This new generation of dissidents had been raised under the new regime, and had not been exposed to Western liberal ideas. Their dissent was homegrown. Most of them were not party members, and they had spent part of their youth among peasants. They had a good knowledge of Chinese society.

After Mao's death in 1976, Deng Xiaoping's struggle against neo-Maoists gave them an opportunity to make their writings known to the public by posting them on the democracy walls that appeared in cities at the end of 1978. They distributed mimeographed unofficial journals in which they expressed their criticism of the regime, demanding, as did their 1957 predecessors, the respect of the basic freedoms of association, publication, expression, and demonstration. But, in contrast to their predecessors, most of them had not had the opportunity to get a formal education, and they were closer to the ordinary people. Their *dazibaos* attracted great numbers of readers, but after a few months, they were suppressed by the party. In 1979 and 1981, the most militant activists of the democracy wall movement—Wei Jingsheng, Wang Xizhe, and Xu Wenli—were arrested and sentenced to long jail terms. However, these arrests did not result in a new anti-rightist campaign. Many participants in the movement disappeared into society, interrupting their overt dissident activities. But some of them continued to make their ideas known through various literary publications or in the universities when they had a chance to become professors. They were not open dissidents, but in conferences and in classes, they spread their ideas on democracy and freedom. They thereby played an active role in the intellectual preparation of the 1989 prodemocracy movement, and some of them participated in the events, including former democracy-wall activists Wang Juntao and Chen Ziming. In May 1989 they organized "Conference of all the Cicles of Society" to help rally ordinary citizens around the student movement.

The latest generation of dissidents is composed of the students who led the 1989 protests and continued the fight

***Chinese dissident Wang Dan at a press conference, New York City, June 1, 1999.*** *Chinese authorities arrested and imprisoned Beijing University student Wang Dan for his participation in the 1989 Tiananmen Square protest against the government. While serving a second prison term for anti-government activity, Wang earned a pardon to receive medical treatment in the United States, where he continued his opposition to the Communist leadership.* STAN HONDA/AFP/GETTY IMAGES

for democracy after the June 4 massacre. Some tried to pursue their cause in exile by creating opposition organizations overseas, while others stayed in China and continued the struggle after their prison sentences ended. In contrast to their predecessors, and perhaps due to the presence of exiles overseas, they enjoyed some support in the West, and pressure was put on the Chinese government to exercise restraint in repression. In the 1990s, the party, behaving like its Soviet counterpart in the Leonid Brezhnev years, sent a number of prominent dissidents, such as Wang Juntao, student leader Wang Dan, and 1979 activists Wang Xizhe, Wei Jingsheng, and Xu Wenli, to the West.

Aside from keeping pressure on Western governments to "remember Tiananmen," the exile organizations did not play an important role in China. Those who remained had to continue the struggle under difficult circumstances as the state reinforced its control on the political field. However, times had changed since Mao's reign. Most of the intellectuals and student leaders who had played an important role in the 1989 events were freed and, as they were not given jobs in state institutions, they published their works in Hong Kong first, and then on the Internet. They were a small minority, but they kept meeting and could establish broad informal networks. Since the 1990s, they have kept writing open letters to China's leaders to protest injustice and to denounce arbitrary arrests and discrimination against migrant workers. Of course, their letters are not published in the official press; they appear in the foreign media and the Hong Kong press, and the opposition in exile also gives them a loud echo. Most of these dissidents refuse to compromise with the authorities, and have decided that to "live in truth" (to use Václav Havel's expression) is necessary to avoid being corrupted by the system. The best example of these dissidents is Liu Xiaobo, who prefers not to be published in the PRC rather than to use pseudonyms to achieve that goal. These dissidents have been joined by such individuals as the essay writer Yu Jie and the Internet writer Liu Di, who were too young to participate in the 1989 movement but who have been inspired by its ideals.

Since the development of the Internet, Chinese dissidents have used this media extensively to circulate their ideas. This had led some of them, such as Shi Tao, to be sentenced to heavy jail terms. All of them support the Tiananmen Mothers, a grassroots organization that demands that the government acknowledge its responsibility in the June 4 massacre and give compensation to the victims' families. These dissident activities culminated in Charter 08, the title of which is directly inspired by its Czechoslovak counterpart (Charter 77). This text demands the transformation of the regime into a constitutional democracy, by suppressing the special position of the Communist Party, installing separation of powers, and granting autonomy to national minorities by establishing a federation. The charter resolutely positions itself within the law. It was launched by 303 persons who represent the spectrum of dissidence in China, and has been signed by thousands of ordinary citizens, many of whom are party members or hold positions in the system. Charter 08 marks the first time since 1989 that an open letter has encountered such a response in the population. This does not mean that dissidence has finally been able to mobilize China's various social sectors, but it shows that neither the repression nor the depoliticization provoked by the country's race to riches have succeeded in eliminating dissidents from the political landscape.

**SEE ALSO** *Democracy Wall; Education through Labor, Reform through Labor; Fang Lizhi; Hu Feng; Hundred Flowers Campaign; Internet; Liu Binyan; Liu Xiaobo; Prodemocracy Movement (1989).*

**BIBLIOGRAPHY**

Béja, Jean-Philippe. *A la recherche d'une ombre chinoise: Le mouvement pour la démocratie en Chine1919-2004* [In search of a Chinese shadow: the prodemocracy movement in China 1919-2004]. Paris: Seuil, 2004.

Chan, Anita, Rosen Stanley, and Unger, Jonathan eds. *On Socialist Democracy and the Chinese Legal System: The Li Yizhe Debates.* Armonk, NY: Sharpe, 1985.

China's Charter 08. *New York Review of Books*, January 15, 2009. http://www.nybooks.com/articles/22210.

Goldman, Merle. *Literary Dissent in Communist China.* Cambridge, MA: Harvard University Press, 1967.

Goldman, Merle. *Sowing the Seeds of Democracy in China: Political Reform in the Deng Xiaoping Era.* Cambridge, MA: Harvard University Press, 1994.

Hu Feng. *Hu Feng xuanji* [Selected works of Hu Feng]. Chengdu, PRC: Sichuan Wenxue Chubanshe, 1996.

Widor, Claude. *Documents on the Democratic Movement.* 2 vols. Paris: Editions de l'École des hautes études en sciences sociales; Hong Kong: Observer Publisher, 1981 and 1985.

Zhang Xingying. *Chu Anping wenji* [Chu Anping's collected articles]. 2 vols. Shanghai: Dongfang Chuban Zhongxin, Ershi Shiji Wenxue Beiwanglu Zongshu, 1998.

***Jean-Philippe Béja***

# DOMESTIC TRADE

*This entry contains the following:*



## 1800–1900

China in the nineteenth century was an agrarian society, but it was one of the most commercialized agrarian societies in the world. Most farm families relied on the market to sell at least a portion of their crop and to buy daily necessities, commodities often moved thousands of miles between producer and consumer, and regions of the empire had come to specialize in production of particular goods for interregional shipment. Through entrepôt cities such as Hankou, located at the confluence of the Yangzi and Han Rivers, rice and tea from the Middle Yangzi; cotton, salt, and manufactures from the Lower Yangzi; rice, salt, and medicinal herbs from Sichuan; hides, beans, tobacco, and alcohol from the northwest; millet, beans, coal, and hemp products from North China; timber and lacquer from the southwest; and sugar, fruits, marine products, ironware, and an increasing array of foreign goods from the southeast coast, were exchanged and transshipped (Rowe 1984).

This domestic trade was huge—in the nineteenth century dwarfing the Qing's international trade—but its volume can only be guessed at. One estimate puts the annual rice trade down the Yangzi to Jiangnan at between 1 and 1.5 billion pounds in the 1730s (Ch'uan Han-seng and Kraus 1975, p. 77). As of 1800, probably more than a tenth of the empire's total grain production was sent to market, as was over a quarter of its raw cotton output, over half of its cotton cloth (more than three million bolts per year), over 90 percent of its raw silk, and nearly all of its tea and salt (Wu Chengming 1983, p. 99).

The anthropologist G. William Skinner (1925–2008) divided China into nine "macroregions," based on the flow of goods, persons, and information. Within these macroregions, goods moved up or down discrete regional marketing hierarchies, capped in each case by a "regional metropolis" (Nanjing, Guangzhou, Hankou, Xi'an, etc.). Great as the *inter*regional trade was by the nineteenth century, the *intra*regional trade, circulating within the separate regional marketing hierarchies, was even greater. Trade between regions tended to move only between regional metropolises, which extracted goods from their hinterlands for export and distributed goods imported from other regions. Skinner argues that the discreteness of these regional marketing hierarchies was so great that a "national market" (with prices of commodities moving in tandem across regions) did not exist prior to the increased use of steam-powered transport in the twentieth century, but his argument probably applies better to some commodities than others, such as rice, in which there was considerable interregional arbitrage.

Trade also moved along the coast. After the Kangxi emperor (r. 1661–1722) lifted the maritime ban in 1684—having suppressed the last traces of resistance on Taiwan—the coastal junk trade grew rapidly, especially between Manchuria and the Lower Yangzi. The chief cargo was soybean cake from the north, used as fertilizer in the exhaustively farmed paddy lands of the delta region. By the early nineteenth century, more than ten million catties of wheat and soybeans moved south annually, carried by some 3,500 junks, each capable of bearing 1,500 to 3,000 catties, and making three or four trips per year (Huang 1990, p. 89).

Qing domestic trade was highly diffuse, with many layers of professional peddlers, merchants, and dealers handling the shipment of goods from producers to consumers, typically moving job lots between single stages of the extraction and distribution hierarchy. They sometimes served merely as commission agents, but more often bought and sold for their own accounts. At the apex of the trade were the large interregional shippers who moved goods between one regional metropolis and another. Such men routinely extended credit through a system of prepurchase (*yumai*) to their suppliers, who in turn extended credit to their own suppliers, and on downward to the producer households. In major entrepôts, government-licensed brokers (*yahang*) mediated between shippers, warehoused their goods, made the local market in a commodity, established terms of trade, and standardized weights and measures.

The trade was developed and managed by numerous overlapping diasporas of merchants of common local origin. For instance, the export of Hunan rice downriver to Jiangnan was conducted by merchants from Jiangxi, whereas the extraction of timber from Yunnan was dominated by merchants from Hunan itself. Major commercial cities hosted large numbers of local-origin or common-trade merchant guilds. In the early nineteenth century, the most powerful diasporas were those of Shanxi natives, who dominated remittance banking, and of Huizhou (Anhui) merchants, specializing in the salt, grain, and tea trades. After the midcentury rebellions, these groups receded in favor of merchants from Guangzhou and Ningbo, who enjoyed privileged ties to the overseas trade.

Apart from the many thousands of merchants engaged in the domestic trade, there were an untold number of transport workers: sailors, carters, animal drivers, and many varieties of porters. An even larger number worked in processing of commercial goods (textiles, tea, etc.), usually as sideline employment by agrarian households. A growing share of this processing, however, was accomplished in handicraft workshops owned and managed by a single entrepreneur, in what Marxist historians have described as the "sprouts" of an indigenous Chinese capitalism (*zibenzhuyi mengya*).

Although the domestic trade was not entirely free of government control (the salt trade, for example, was a declared government monopoly), the Qing administration was in general quite solicitous of domestic commerce, and worked actively to encourage maximum circulation (*liutong*) of commercial goods. Price setting and embargoes on regional grain exports were occasionally imposed in times of extreme dearth, but such commandist interventions in the marketplace were unusual and not broadly favored by officials (Rowe 1993). Most domestic trade was only lightly and indirectly taxed, chiefly through the fees paid by brokers for their licenses and recouped through commissions on the transactions they brokered. Beginning in the Taiping era, a commercial transit tax, *lijin,* known to foreigners as "likin" was imposed by provincial administrators to underwrite their antirebel militia and regional armies; after the rebellions' suppression these taxes remained, only somewhat controlled by central imperial authorities.

Transport technologies changed over the course of the latter half of the century, but only slightly. Western steamships made incursions as carriers in the Lower Yangzi trade in the 1860s, because they could run the Taiping blockades better than wind-powered vessels (Liu Kwang-Ching 1962, p. 13–14). But the railroad, which would rapidly transform the shape of long-distance commerce and become an incendiary political issue after 1900, had very modest impact before then because of Chinese concerns for sovereignty and control, despite the strenuous appeals of Westerners. The first rail line in the empire, a short spur near Shanghai built by British interests in 1874, provoked riots and was quickly torn up by provincial authorities. A six-mile rail line was laid in 1880 to connect the Kaiping coal mines near Tangshan to a nearby canal, and extended eight years later to Tianjin. Several other lines were negotiated with foreign powers during the "scramble for concessions" following the Sino-Japanese War (1894–1895), but none of these were completed by century's end (Huenemann 1984).

**SEE ALSO** *China Merchants' Steam Navigation Company.*

**BIBLIOGRAPHY**

Ch'uan Han-seng and Richard Kraus. *Mid-Ch'ing Rice Markets and Trade: An Essay in Price History.* Cambridge, MA: Harvard University Council on East Asian Studies, 1975.

Huang, Philip C. C. (Huang Zongzhi). *The Peasant Family and Rural Development in the Yangzi Delta, 1350–1988.* Stanford, CA: Stanford University Press, 1990.

Huenemann, Ralph William. *The Dragon and the Iron Horse: The Economics of Railroads in China, 1876–1937.* Cambridge, MA: Harvard University Council on East Asian Studies, 1984.

Liu Kwang-Ching (Liu Guangjing). *Anglo-American Steamship Rivalry in China, 1862–1874.* Cambridge, MA: Harvard University Press, 1962.

Rowe, William T. *Hankow: Commerce and Society in a Chinese City, 1795–1889.* Stanford, CA: Stanford University Press, 1984.

Rowe, William T. State and Market in Mid-Qing Economic Thought. *Études chinoises* 12, 1 (1993): 7–39.

Skinner, G. William. Presidential Address: The Structure of Chinese History. *Journal of Asian Studies* 44, 2 (1985): 271–292.

Wu Chengming. Lun Qingdai qianqi woguo guonei shichang [The domestic market in the early Qing]. *Lishi yanjiu* 1 (1983): 96–106.

*William Rowe*

## 1900–1949

Despite the positive trends in population growth and economic development, as indicated by the approximate 5.5 percent growth rate in the industrial sector and 1 to 2 percent in agriculture, China's domestic trade between 1900 and 1949 demonstrated its immunity to structural change and the durability of the traditional market organization. Key determinants of economic development in the first half of the twentieth century—foreign entrepreneurial activity and economic internationalization, the commercialization of the traditional agrarian sector, modernization efforts and state-building experiments of the republican regimes—were not sufficient to revamp the existing market system. As noted by William G. Skinner (1964, 1965), generally the market system was based on more than 60,000 discreet rural basic market areas connected at the "intermediate" and "central" levels by a complex system of trade agencies regulated by merchant guilds and often controlled by local bureaucracies or military commanders. The market organization primarily served the needs of self-sufficient rural communities, but it was also regarded as a lucrative source of revenues of administrative bodies. For most of the period, it remained crippled by a variety of internal levies, the divergent regional currency and measure systems, and the poorly developed transportation system.

By the end of the Qing dynasty (1644–1912), there were several factors that generated strong impulses toward commercialization: the abolition in 1901 of centralized grain supply along Grand Canal, the need to cover immense Boxer indemnity payments partially by increasing exports, and the existence of low customs duties set by the "unequal treaties" that opened the door for increased imports. In the early twentieth century the expansion of the treaty port areas and the increase in state-regulated foreign trade stimulated numerous small handicraft workshops in urban centers to engage in some export-oriented activity, as well as broadening the market for imported products, mainly cotton yarn and cloth. Cotton accounted for one-third of China's imports by value and surpassed opium as the most important single Chinese import. During the Republican era, the growing urban population (5–6 percent of a total population of 500 million in 1938) of northeastern China (Manchuria), the lower Yangzi provinces, and China's eastern and southeastern coastal regions became increasingly involved in commercialized urban markets and export-import activity.

Nonetheless, these processes did not result in a qualitative change of the domestic trade system. Most of the interior provinces remained less dependent on market fluctuations and change in demand in the urbanized areas. Internal transit levies until the mid-1930s helped local governments to cover huge budget deficits. In 1912 more than 10,000 outposts collected 26 million *taels* (a *tael*, or *liang*, was worth about 37.5 grams of silver) of transit fees (*lijin*) throughout the country by levying fifteen categories of goods, including salt, tea, alcohol, opium, tobacco, sugar, silk, and livestock. Albert Feuerwerker (1995) argues that these official extractions were not very burdensome: He estimates transit fees as averaged at 2 percent at each tax station (5–10 percent in the Chinese literature), thus having a smaller effect on the amount of domestic trade than did freight and handling markups of 15 to 100 percent. Thus the main constraint to the marketing structure and size of China's domestic commerce was imposed by the limitations of premodern transportation and communications.

## COMMUNICATIONS AND REGIONAL DIFFERENCES

The geography of China's transportation lines was determined specifically by the development of what John Chang's 1967 article terms the "enclave-export type" of primary production activities. Railway construction was unsystematic and limited to certain areas. According to Feuerwerker, of the railways built in the first half of the century, approximately 50 percent of the total track was located in Manchuria, 32 percent in the rest of China north of the Yangzi River, 22 percent in South China, and 4 percent in Japanese-occupied Taiwan. In the building of a total of 24,845 kilometers of main and branch railway lines by 1945, 9,253 kilometers of line were completed by 1911, and 7,896 kilometers were completed during the Nanjing decade (1927–1937). Of the freight goods in 1932 delivered by railways, the products of mines accounted for about 40 percent, products of agriculture and manufactured products approximately 54 percent, animal products about 4 percent, and timber about 2 percent (*Chinese Yearbook, 1935–36*).

The development of inland navigation played an important role in transportation, but it did not broaden the scope of the carriage of imports far beyond the boundaries of the seacoasts and river shores. In the early 1930s, besides foreign steamship services, there were more than eighty Chinese steamship companies operating in the Chinese market. The military needs and centralization efforts of the Nationalist government in the 1930s resulted in rapid road construction: By 1937 about 116,000 kilometers of roads in Central China were completed, and this helped organize commercial activity in the territories controlled by the Guomindang until their retreat to Southwest Chinese in 1938.

The uneven development of transportation and communication lines and the enclave character of foreign trade dynamics hardly affected domestic commerce because most of the exported output were not retained for domestic processing and fabrication. In the "commercialized" areas, large specialized market centers were formed by the 1920 and 1930s. Grain market centers in Anhui, Jiangsu, Jiangxi, and Hunan were established to satisfy growing demands in food supply in Jiangsu, Zhejiang, Fujian, and Guangdong provinces. Growing urban markets stimulated the commercial activities of local farmers, and in these areas commercialization of farmers' households was the highest in the country: From 1921 to 1925 in seven provinces of East China, the share of marketed rice exceeded 38 percent of total output, whereas in the suburbs of Anhui it reached 56 percent. By the late 1920s the role of imported grains in these coastal market areas grew dramatically: In the Guangdong grain market, the wholesale supply of rice was up to 68.1 percent, secured by imports in 1923, and in Fujian the share of imported rice in the market balance reached 93.2 percent by 1933 (Xu 1997).

The degree of commercialization was high in Manchuria and cotton-producing areas in North China, but overall domestic trade growth in value was performed predominantly in the traditional market system, where approximately 30 percent of total grain output was involved in commercial operations. Thus the rising annual grain output from 120 million tons in 1887, to 169 million tons in the years 1914–1919, to 191 million tons in the years 1931–1937 resulted in the subsequent growth in internal market turnover. Perkins and Feuerwerker estimated that by the mid-1930s the share of farm output shipped to urban areas grew merely from 5 to 10 percent, and exports of agricultural products increased only from 1 to 3 percent (Perkins, 1975, pp. 122–123).

Industrial development in China had some impact, albeit limited, on the development of domestic commerce, especially in the 1920s and 1930s, when production of consumer goods in the industrial sector reached a peak of 45 percent of total output. In the Nanjing period, manufactured goods occupied the most important position in domestic trade, particularly cotton yarn, cotton products, and cigarettes. The share of cotton products manufactured in the Japanese cotton mills reached 40 percent by 1935, and a British factory manufactured more than 50 percent of the cigarettes. But, as Chang points out, industrial production, with its aggregate weight amounting to about 3.4 percent of the net domestic product in 1933, could not change the marketing structure. The Great Depression of the early 1930s had a limited influence on domestic trade in China, mainly because only a small part of the peasantry was involved with markets, and only marginally at that; moreover, as a result of worsening terms of trade and silver outflow from China from 1931 to 1935, the producers returned to the cultivation of traditional grain crops rather than cash crops.

From 1928 to 1937 the Guomindang's economic policy set some grounds for the establishment of the nationwide domestic trade market, although the outbreak of war with Japan terminated these efforts. The restoration of China's tariff autonomy from 1930 to 1933, accompanied by the effect of the worldwide depression, reduced imports, and by the mid-1930s the role of cash crops had decreased. The abolition of transit fees, the local budget reforms between 1931 and 1936, the close of the opium stock exchange in Wuhan in 1936, and the broadening practice of excise collection reduced the dependency of local authorities on transit levies and petty taxes, thus partially eliminating barriers to commercial activity. Nanjing's currency and budget reforms in 1935, as well as the government's attempts to secure measure and weight unification throughout the country, were favorable for commerce interactions.

## THE IMPACT OF THE JAPANESE OCCUPATION

The Japanese occupation of North and East China from 1937 to 1938, and the subsequent political disintegration, dramatically affected the development of the Chinese domestic market. To offer just one example, China's total railway cargo turnover in 1944 dropped to 8.3 metric tons per kilometer from 234.5 metric tons per kilometer in 1936 (Yan 1955). The influx of more than two million people to Sichuan province, the entrepreneurial activity of several hundred small and medium enterprises evacuated from the coastal areas, the growth of state-controlled financial and credit markets, and the development of cooperative production in wartime China had a stimulating effect on trade in the Guomindang-controlled territories. However, galloping inflation and government economic policy resulted in "traditionalization" of market activity by 1943–1944.

From the outbreak of war with Japan in 1937, the Nationalist government considered domestic trade primarily as one of the key sources of budget revenues. As the state strengthened control over forty-six wartime "strategic" commodities, its anti-inflationary policy and the attempts to curb the black markets resulted in the rise of the state as a key operator in domestic commerce. The Chongqing government restored the salt monopoly in the early 1940s, rejecting the prewar policy of liberalization of the salt trade. The government tried to impose a "partnership" with merchants' guilds, while also competing with multiple brokerage agencies by creating a new system of governmental wholesale stores between 1940 and 1942. In 1940 the government's attempts to regulate prices and control key market areas provoked hoarding, inflation, and merchants' speculative activities. In 1941 land tax-in-kind collection and compulsory grain purchases and "rice loans" narrowed the market—not dramatically, however, as the Chongqing government between 1941 and 1945 managed to control only about 8.7 percent of farmers' output in the unoccupied territories. An aggressive policy of governmental control of urban markets caused a depression in industrial production in 1942–1943 because of the state's inability to control the black market of raw materials (the collapse of the Shanxi cotton industry is an illustrative example). The Guomindang failed to control the smuggling of imported goods from Japanese-controlled territories, although the role of imports decreased in the 1940s. In the postwar period the Nationalists continued the policy of market regulation but eventually failed to control inflation and return to the prewar program of a balanced state-merchant partnership policy aimed at the establishment of a unitary market space at the national level.

**SEE ALSO** *Boxer Uprising; China Merchants' Steam Navigation Company.*

**BIBLIOGRAPHY**

Chan, F. Gilbert, ed. *China at the Crossroads: Nationalists and Communists, 1929–1949.* Boulder, CO: Westview Press, 1980.

Chang, John K. Industrial Development of Mainland China 1912–1949. *Journal of Economic History* 27, 1 (March 1967): 56–81.

*China Handbook, 1937–1943.* Chinese Ministry of Information. New York: Macmillan, 1943.

*The Chinese Yearbook, 1935–36.* Shanghai: Commercial Press, 1935.

*The Chinese Yearbook, 1936–37.* Shanghai: Commercial Press, 1936.

Feuerwerker, Albert. *The Chinese Economy, 1870–1949.* Ann Arbor: Center for Chinese Studies, University of Michigan, 1995.

Liu, Ta-Chung, and Kung-Chia Yeh. *The Economy of the Chinese Mainland: National Income and Economic Development, 1933–1959.* Princeton, NJ: Princeton University Press, 1965.

Perkins, Dwight H. *Agricultural Development in China, 1368–1968.* Chicago: Aldine, 1969.

Perkins, Dwight H., ed. *China's Modern Economy in Historical Perspective.* Stanford, CA: Stanford University Press, 1975.

Skinner, William G. Marketing and Social Structure in Rural China. Part 1: *Journal of Asian Studies* 24, 1 (November 1964): 3–44. Part 2: *Journal of Asian Studies* 24, 2 (February 1965): 195–228.

Wu, Zhaoshen. *Zhongguo shuizhishi* [History of the fiscal system in China]. Vol 2. Shanghai, 1937.

Xu, Zhengyuan. Zhongguo jindainongchan shangpinhuade fazhan yu mishi de xingcheng [The development of commercialized rural production and the rice markets in modern China]. *Anhui shixue* [History studies in Anhui province] 1 (1997): 92–94.

Yan, Zhongping. *Zhongguo jindai jingji shitongji ziliao xuanji* [Selected statistical materials on the modern economic history of China]. Beijing: Kexue chubanshi, 1955.

Young, Arthur N. *China's Wartime Finance and Inflation, 1937–1945*. Cambridge, MA: Harvard University Press, 1965.

Young, Arthur N. *China's Nation-Building Effort, 1927–1937: The Financial and Economic Record.* Stanford, CA: Hoover Institution Press, 1971.

***Vitaly Kozyrev***

## SINCE 1950

When the Chinese Communist Party established a planned economy after 1949, taking control of domestic trade was a major step preceding collectivization. The process began with price controls to curtail inflation, and progressed stepwise with increasing restrictions on rural marketing and the gradual transformation of urban traders into cooperatives.

A crucial measure was the establishment in 1953 of the centrally planned grain and oil purchasing system, which was soon extended to other essential rural inputs, in particular cotton. Mandatory purchasing quotas and price controls created serious disincentives for farmers, so the extension of the planning system to include production was a necessary consequence, culminating in the establishment of the people's communes, which also marked the end of unrestricted trading activities. In industry, the buildup of the state-owned sector went hand in hand with the establishment of a unified mandatory distribution system (*tonggou tongxiao*).

Under the centrally planned economy that reigned until 1978, trade was almost entirely controlled by the government. However, there were cycles of retrenchment and expansion of market segments in the rural areas, which reflected the varying intensity of political agitation against rural sideline production. Thus, the traditional system of rural markets (*nongcun jishi*) was never eliminated completely over all of China, but it operated under tight government supervision. In urban areas, there was almost no space for market activities, because the stringent system of household registration was complemented by a system of distribution with coupons, which were inaccessible without registration. Free rural-urban movement of people was blocked.

However, the system did not require all trade to be administered by central-planning authorities. There was a categorization of goods into three classes that correspond to different degrees of national importance. Commodities such as cotton and steel were completely included in the central plan, whereas minor consumption goods were allocated on the local level. The trading system was thus never fully integrated, with government trading organizations on different levels of the administrative hierarchy, and loosely interconnected local, regional, and national flows of goods. Another important distinction was between "commodities" (*wuzi*) and "merchandise" (*shangpin*), which was essentially a distinction between inputs and primary goods on the one hand, and finished goods, mostly consumer goods, on the other hand. For these two groups, there were different distribution systems, which were also strictly vertically organized. As a result, the system caused many inefficiencies due to the blockade of horizontal trading relationships, even within cities.

### LIBERALIZATION AND DEREGULATION OF DOMESTIC TRADE, 1978–1993

After 1978, the mandatory distribution system was gradually dismantled. One of the first steps taken was the liberalization of rural markets and rural sideline production and the opening up of rural-urban trade activities. Simultaneously, the scope of the mandatory state-procurement system was reduced from 135 items to only twenty-six in 1984. Already before industrial reforms began in 1984, an important measure was to liberalize trade of beyond-quota production, even in essential commodities. The main lever was to distinguish between different purchasing modes beyond the mandatory mode. Finally, in the consumption-goods sector, organizational reforms were started with the introduction of urban trading centers in an attempt to overcome the organizational barriers in the old system.

A major effect of these policies, which were extended throughout the 1980s, was the emergence of parallel trading systems—for example, in coal distribution, where local mines accessed markets, while central allocation of coal from large state-owned mines was maintained. Already in the mid-1980s, only 60 percent of steel production was centrally allocated. This process of devolution was speeded up by the crowding out of the state-allocation system by markets via the dual-track price system. The centrally planned trading system also served the purpose of subsidization and taxation by means of mandated, and often distorted, pricing schedules. A case in point was the grain-trading system, which during the 1980s had to offer higher purchase prices to the farmers while maintaining low sales prices for the urban population. This created strong incentives to abolish planned allocation for government agencies that had to fund price gaps. In the mid-1990s, the vast majority of goods and commodities were already being traded with free-market prices, including even sensitive goods such as grain, with regional variations such as the reform spearhead Chongqing. However, the old levers of administrative control remained in place, and were revived for brief periods in times of increasing inflationary pressure, even in the 1990s.

The coexistence of different allocation systems and pricing schemes triggered a peculiar phenomenon: "trade wars" among local governments, leading to rampant local protectionism equipped with all the tools known from international trade, including safety inspections, restraints on licensing, and so forth. These resulted from two determinants. First, as long as administered prices for certain inputs (e.g., cotton and wool) remained below market prices, a massive discrimination against their producers resulted, which created incentives to interfere with trade in these commodities and to build up downstream industries by themselves. Second, many small and medium-sized state-owned enterprises (SOEs) came under strong competitive pressure, thus endangering both the fiscal base of local governments and local employment. This phenomenon in Chinese domestic trade continues to plague foreign investors and poses difficult questions for the implementation of World Trade Organization (WTO) rules in, for example, the retail sector.

By the early 1990s, the organizational structure of domestic trade had been entirely overhauled. During the 1980s, many forms of increased autonomy for state-owned trading enterprises were tested, including profit-retention schemes. But in the end, the complete privatization of small trading units and the gradual transformation of larger ones—for example, via management and employee buyouts—proved to be the most effective solution. Nevertheless, by 1992 only 4.7 percent of SOEs continued to control 40.2 percent of national retail volume.

### MODERNIZATION OF DOMESTIC TRADE

After the announcement of the "socialist market economy" in 1994 and following China's WTO entry in 2001, domestic trade underwent a massive transformation, which was mainly driven by the creation of entirely new business models and the import from advanced industrial economies of such organizational templates as food retailing via chain stores. Initially, this was driven by the restructuring of the state-owned trading system on different levels, mainly by breaking down the barriers between wholesale and retail units—for example, by creating comprehensive trading centers and by allowing for deeper specialization along industries. In the 1990s, national wholesale markets for particular product groups (*chuanye pifa shichang*) emerged, which triggered the development of advanced trading mechanisms, such as futures trade in commodities. This development was supplemented by a fully fledged privatization of the retail sector, which was permeated by a sequence of new business models, such as the spread of supermarkets (*chao shi*), convenience stores (*bianli dian*), and chain stores (*liansuo dian*) in Chinese cities. The country also saw the emergence of modern logistics, which supported the outsourcing of trading functions from large companies. The foundation for the latter process had been prepared by the restructuring of industrial SOEs, which had originally been functionally complete units. Spin-offs of transport units and related trading functions led to a functional separation of logistics. On the other hand, there are new trends toward an increasing organizational integration, especially in the agribusiness sector, where food-processing companies are supplanting wholesale market relations with supplier networks.

WTO entry also opened up domestic trade to foreign-invested companies, which had, in the 1990s, already established a presence via joint ventures, especially in the hypermarket segment. Access to domestic trade is strongly influenced by corresponding access to other services, especially logistics, in order to be able to implement most advanced business models, resulting into many frictions because of institutional diversity across regions. Therefore, an important aspect of the modernization of domestic trade has been the promulgation of numerous trade-related laws and regulations, such as laws on advertisements and product quality, or regulations on wholesale markets, which are intended to regularize the national market. During the 1990s, many government organizations were abolished and merged with different branches of the traditional system, culminating in 2003 in the creation of the Ministry of Commerce, which merged the former Ministry of Foreign Trade and Economic Cooperation, the State Economic and Trade Commission, and the State Development Planning Commission. The Ministry of Commerce works for the further modernization of trade—for example, in e-commerce.

**BIBLIOGRAPHY**

Findlay, Christopher, and Andrew Watson. *Food Security and Economic Reform: The Challenges Facing China's Grain Marketing System*. London: Macmillan, 1999.

Luk, Sherriff T. K., Yin Zhou Xu, and Wan Chun Ye. Distribution: The Chinese Puzzle. *Long Range Planning* 31, 2 (1998): 295–307.

***Carsten Herrmann-Pillath***

## DOMESTIC VIOLENCE

Domestic violence is a modern term used for physical or sexual violence within the household. The comprehensive condemnation of domestic violence is a comparatively new phenomenon. Historically, most human societies have regarded some forms of violence in family relations as permissible and others as deviant. The Confucian emphasis on harmony and a moral order based on a proper respect for a social and family hierarchy gave rise to a tradition in which violence was seen as undesirable. Yet domestic violence could be condoned if used by a family member in authority to enforce the moral order. Within limits, parents could chastise their children, husbands their wives, and older brothers their younger siblings. However, junior family members could never be justified in striking senior ones.

In twentieth-century China, critiques of authoritarian patriarchy and its abuses led to legal prohibitions of the ill treatment of family members. The Communist Party, in particular, opposed wife beating and tended to discourage the corporal punishment of children. However, public opinion has not always kept pace with the law; surveys show that many Chinese still believe that it is natural for a man to beat his wife, that a child who is not hit will be spoilt, and that the state should not interfere in family disputes.

Domestic violence is notoriously difficult to quantify. Where it is regarded as normal, it may not be remarked at all. In other cases, it may be regarded as a shameful secret. This entry is mainly concerned with attitudes toward domestic violence in modern China. Estimates of the prevalence of various forms of domestic violence should be treated as highly tentative.

## FAMILY VIOLENCE IN IMPERIAL AND REPUBLICAN CHINA: LAW AND PRACTICE

The authoritarian Confucian family constituted a hierarchy based on age and gender within which wives, concubines, children, and servants were subject to the authority of adult men, and the younger generation was subject to the older one. Under the doctrine of filial piety, children owed obedience and reverence to their parents, and wives to their husbands. The head of the family was responsible for the behavior of its members and was expected to punish their transgressions.

The Qing Code imposed limits on the degree of violence that a parent or husband could use. The penalties imposed for family violence depended on the status of the perpetrator (Bodde and Morris 1967, pp. 35–38). Thus, whereas a son who struck his father could be decapitated, a parent would be punished for beating a son only if the beating resulted in death. A wife who struck her husband received one hundred blows with heavy bamboo. A husband would be punished for beating his wife only if a tooth or a bone were broken and she personally lodged a complaint. Similarly, between brothers or cousins, the elder could strike the younger with impunity but the younger could be punished for striking the elder. Parents did not have the right of life or death over their children. Infanticide, practiced by poor families or those who did not want to bring up daughters, was prohibited.

New measures in the Civil Code of the Republic (1930) reflected growing opposition to domestic violence (van der Valk 1939, pp. 115–116, p. 137). The ill-treatment of a wife by her husband became grounds for divorce. However, case law indicates that beating was accepted as grounds for divorce only if the beating resulted in injury or was habitual. Slight wounds or occasional beatings were not held to constitute ill-treatment. The code also allowed parents the right to inflict punishment on their children but not in such a way as to endanger the person of the child. An adopted child who suffered gross ill-treatment could terminate the adoptive relationship.

Chinese fiction often negated the ideal of the harmonious family and reflected violence and abuse. For example, the plot of the eighteenth-century novel *Dream of the Red Chamber* turns on the jealousies and cruelty in elite family life, while Ba Jin's novel *The Family* offered an exposé of abusive patriarchy in the early twentieth century. Twentieth-century ethnographic studies recorded violent behavior in more ordinary settings. Angry, jealous, or frustrated men beat their wives, children, concubines, and servants. Mothers-in-law who disliked their daughters-in-law ill-treated them or urged their sons to do so. Sexual jealousy between wives, maids, and concubines, or poverty and the struggle to control household resources, triggered violence. The anthropologist Lin Yaohua recorded an incident in the 1930s in which a little girl died after a beating (Lin 1948, p. 17). Her grandmother had beaten her and her mother and her aunt for spending household money on candy. Many studies of pre-1949 China document violence against children, especially child daughters-in-law, and against concubines and bonded maidservants. In joint households, violence between brothers or between sisters-in-law could arise from disputes over resources or favoritism toward children.

Corporal punishment was widely accepted. Olga Lang's work in the 1930s indicated that in both late Qing and Republican China, most parents beat their children (Lang 1946, pp. 239–243). However, in almost a third of her surveyed families, children were never beaten and beating appeared to be on the decline. Beatings began at age five or six and were abandoned in worker and peasant families at age ten or twelve, when boys began work. Beatings went on for three or four years longer in middle-class families. Boys were beaten more often than girls in urban families, whereas rural families treated boys with more leniency than girls. Children whose fathers had a college education and children whose mothers were factory workers were significantly less likely to be beaten than others. In general, Lang's findings associated

***Punishment of a man convicted of spousal abuse, Beijing, 1901.*** *Traditional Chinese family hierarchy placed men at the head of the household, a power that sometimes led to violence against other family members. Since the Communist reform era, however, the government has become more outspoken against domestic violence and begun providing more resources for abused women.*


urbanization, education, and improved maternal status with a decreased tendency to employ corporal punishment.

## THE PEOPLE'S REPUBLIC

Before 1949, and in the early years of the People's Republic, the Women's Federation campaigned against wife beating as part of a more general attempt to enforce a new marriage law based on the equality of the sexes. Some accounts described young village activists administering beatings to husbands and their mothers who had been cruel to young wives in the family.

Despite these campaigns, violence against young women may actually have increased in the early 1950s. According to official Communist documents, tens of thousands of rural women were beaten or even murdered or driven to suicide in disputes over divorce. An unhappy woman who sued for divorce represented a serious threat to her in-laws. They stood to lose the significant sum they had spent on her bride-price. Moreover, after land reform, women's entitlement to land allowed a divorcing woman to take part of the plot farmed by the family. If the husband or the mother-in-law tried to beat a woman into submission, village cadres were unlikely to intervene in her favor. After all, she was an incomer and her in-laws were fellow villagers. Widows who tried to assert rights to property or to decide over remarriage were also subject to physical abuse.

Although domestic violence no doubt continued in China, after the early 1950s, it received little attention until the 1980s. Various factors then combined to bring violence against women back into prominence. Educated

***A Chinese teenager undergoes physical therapy in preparation for an artificial limb to replace the arm amputated by her stepmother (herself a victim of domestic violence at the hands of her husband), Beijing, September 4, 2005.*** *Pre-Communist Chinese society followed a patriarchal structure, with women often allowed little protection from abusive husbands. With the founding of the People's Republic of China, however, came a greater recognition of equality between the sexes, stronger disapproval of domestic violence, and an increased number of organizations to help battered women and children.* CHINA PHOTOS/GETTY IMAGES

young women produced memoirs of their years in the countryside during the Cultural Revolution, such as Yu Luojin's *A Chinese Winter's Tale*, in which they recalled their horror at the prevalence of wife beating in peasant families. (Their shocked surprise seems to confirm that domestic violence had become comparatively unusual in educated urban families.) Secondly, after the introduction of the one-child family policy, the birth of a daughter meant that the family could never have a son. This sometimes triggered the ill-treatment of mothers who gave birth to girls or even of the baby girls themselves. The influence of Western feminism with its high consciousness of violence against women also reached China in this period. Chinese students returning from abroad, the work of the agencies of the United Nations, and the UN conference for women held in Beijing in 1995 all contributed to a new focus on the status of women.

From the 1980s, the Women's Federation involved itself in advocacy for legislation on women's rights. The 1992 Law on the Rights and Interests of Women asserted that women's freedom of the person was inviolable. It prohibited female infanticide; the cruel treatment, unlawful detention, abduction, or trafficking of women; the maltreatment of women who gave birth to female babies; and the maltreatment or abandonment of aged women. In 2001 a new draft of the marriage law used the imported term "domestic violence" (*jiating baoli*) in forbidding what earlier documents had called the ill-treatment of family members. The security agencies were given the responsibility of combating domestic violence. The Women's Federation and various women's nongovernmental organizations continue to campaign against domestic violence and have set up help lines and refuges for victims

A survey (Parish et al. 2004) of the prevalence of "intimate partner violence" in China indicated that spousal violence is a widespread problem in China, as it is elsewhere. It found that in a sample of just under four thousand men and women aged twenty to sixty-four, 19 percent of respondents reported male-on-female violence within their relationship, 3 percent reported female-on-male violence, and 15 percent reported mutual hitting. Thus 34 percent of women and 18 percent of men had ever been hit during their current relationship. The prevalence of severe pain or injuries resulting from hitting was 12 percent for women and 5 percent for men. Significant risk factors for partner violence were sexual jealousy, patriarchal beliefs, low female contribution to household income, low male socioeconomic status, and alcohol consumption. Partner violence was markedly less common in the developed south and southeast of China than in northern or interior provinces.

By comparison with violence against women, other forms of domestic violence have received comparatively little attention in the People's Republic. The law is ambivalent on the physical punishment of children. The 1992 Law on the Protection of Minors explicitly prohibited corporal punishment in schools and kindergartens. However, the same law, while forbidding the abuse of children in the family, imposed on parents the obligation of education and discipline in relation to their children. In a society where the physical punishment of children is still widely regarded as necessary, this can easily be understood as authorizing it. A questionnaire survey in 1998 of 493 Chinese schoolchildren on their school and home experience found that 51.1 percent had experienced corporal punishment at school, and 70.6 percent had experienced violence at home (Global Initiative 2009).

Elder abuse has been identified as a growing problem in contemporary China. Greatly extended life expectancy has produced an increase in the numbers of frail old people for whom children have a traditional and legal obligation to care. Yan Yunxiang's ethnographic study (2003) of changes in rural family life indicates that in the reform era a greater focus on the intimacy of the couple bond, on the nuclear family, and on consumer goods may be leading some of the younger generation to neglect elderly parents.

**SEE ALSO** *Filial Piety; Gender Relations; Law on the Protection of Women and Children; Marriage Laws; Rape; Women, Status of.*


**BIBLIOGRAPHY**

Ba Jin (Pa Jin). *The Family*. Trans. Sidney Shapiro. Beijing: Foreign Languages Press, 1958.

Bodde, Derk, and Clarence Morris. *Law in Imperial China: Exemplified by 190 Ch'ing Dynasty Cases*. Cambridge, MA: Harvard University Press, 1967.

Cao Xueqin. *A Dream of Red Mansions*. Trans. Gladys Yang and Yang Xianyi. Beijing: Foreign Languages Press, 1978.

Gilmartin, Christina K. Violence against Women in Contemporary China. In *Violence in China: Essays in Culture and Counterculture*, eds. Jonathan N. Lipman and Stevan Harrell, 203–226. Albany: State University of New York Press, 1990.

Global Initiative to End All Corporal Punishment of Children. Country report on China. February 2009 update. http://www.endcorporalpunishment.org.

Honig, Emily, and Gail M. Hershatter in *Personal Voices: Chinese Women in the 1980s*. Stanford, CA: Stanford University Press, 1988.

Jaschok, Maria. *Concubines and Bondservants: A Social History*. London: Zed, 1988.

Lang, Olga. *Chinese Family and Society*. New Haven, CT: Yale University Press, 1946.

Lin Yaohua (Lin Yueh-hwa). *The Golden Wing: A Sociological Study of Chinese Familism*. London: Kegan Paul, 1948.

Parish, William L., Wang Tianfu, Edward O. Laumann, et al. Intimate Partner Violence in China: National Prevalence, Risk Factors, and Associated Health Problems. *International Family Planning Perspectives* 30, 4 (2004): 174–181.

van der Valk, Mark. *An Outline of Modern Chinese Family Law*. Beijing: Henri Vetch, 1939.

Wang Xingjuan. Domestic Violence in China. In *Holding up Half the Sky: Chinese Women Past, Present, and Future*, eds. Tao Jie, Zheng Bijun, and Shirley L. Mow; trans. Amy Russell, 179–192. New York: Feminist Press at the City University of New York, 2004.

Yan Yunxiang. *Private Life under Socialism: Love Intimacy and Family in a Chinese Village, 1949–1999*. Stanford, CA: Stanford University Press, 2003.

Yu Luojin. *A Chinese Winter's Tale: An Autobiographical Fragment*. Trans. Rachel May and Zhu Zhiyu. Hong Kong: Renditions Research Centre for Translation, Chinese University of Hong Kong, 1986.


***Delia Davin***

# DRUGS AND NARCOTICS

From the time of its creation in 1921, the Chinese Communist Party (CCP) shared with the Nationalists the aim of opium eradication. This policy was first put into practice during the First United Front (1923–1927) in Guangzhou (Canton), when idealistic republicans with socialist or communist leanings experimented with radical land reform. During the era of the Jiangxi Soviet (1931–1934), anti-drugs policies were enacted with zeal, becoming a hallmark of Communist rural reform. In line with the moderate New Democracy policies of the later Yan'an years (1936–1945), opium eradication was retained as a theoretical goal. In actual practice, though, narcotic consumption was largely tolerated, and opium poppy cultivation was promoted in order to raise vital revenue for Mao Zedong's resistance against Nationalist and pro-Japanese forces.

## EARLY PRC YEARS

Following the establishment of the People's Republic of China (PRC) in 1949, the CCP embarked on land reforms in the 1950s that created an unprecedented opportunity for change. The Three-Anti's and Five-Anti's Campaigns of the 1950s, which targeted corrupt and criminal elements, facilitated narcotics suppression. Apart from its in-principle position on production of opium crops, the CCP could not afford to be seen as impotent in the fight against this social vice. Yet, in the face of the Korean War and sustained threats from the defeated Nationalists in Taiwan, the PRC leadership initially opted to pursue its antinarcotic policies quietly. The first mass campaign against opiates petered out after intense pressure from forces profiting from its illegal trade. In certain districts opium poppy was grown with official approval throughout the 1950s, partly in order to satisfy the need from China's fledgling pharmaceutical industry, partly because cadres viewed a gradual weaning-off process as the most desirable option.

Nationalist propaganda from Taibei and Washington seized on the mere existence of state-run opium farms as clear evidence that Beijing was drugging China and swamping the Western world with cheap narcotics. Indeed, international surveillance operations during the early 1950s had revealed that narcotics were being smuggled from Chinese ports (especially Tianjin). In truth, drug squads did quickly thwart most illegal activities, and with relative ease. The Five-Anti's movement greatly reduced the ability of the drug underworld to produce and distribute narcotic substances, and social engineering and unparalleled penetration of the state into local society during the Great Leap Forward (1958–1960), the Cultural Revolution (1966–1969), and the last years of the Mao era ensured that even minor attempts at breaking the antinarcotic legislation of the PRC became all but impossible. With the notable exception of the early 1960s, the central government rarely felt the need to intervene, and then merely by means of legal decrees.

## LATER DEVELOPMENTS

In marked contrast to the early campaigns, the antidrug campaigns since the 1980s have been unabashed saber rattling. In a world increasingly reliant on the involvement of China in commerce and diplomacy, the government needs to demonstrate that Beijing is serious in its attempts to drain the international market in illegal drugs.

The reasons are compelling. By the late 1950s the so-called Golden Triangle between China, Burma, and Thailand had emerged as the origin of some 50 percent of the global trade in illegal opiates, especially heroin. With Yunnan Province lying just next door to Burma and Thailand, any opening along the borders was bound to have an effect on China's internal situation. Cross-border smuggling and, importantly, the first confirmed cases of HIV/AIDS in travelers (in particular foreign travelers) caused the central authorities to clamp down on the production and consumption of opiates, first and foremost in this province. Cities such as Baoshan gained such renown in its public fight against narcotics that the confidence of investors in the drug trade began to suffer.

The suppression of the 1989 Tiananmen movement lent a particular rhetorical tone to the narcotics suppression campaign, which by then extended from the former opium-producing province of Yunnan into every corner of China. The attempted eradication of opium in the 1840s by the "patriotic" official Lin Zexu was hailed as part and parcel of a movement to wipe out all elements of "bourgeois liberalism." What precisely made (domestically produced) methamphetamine ("ice," derived from ephedrine), cocaine, and amphetamines "bourgeois" or even "imperialist" was not discussed in the state media, but the effect was to associate the Tiananmen demonstrations with the consumption of drugs.

A later interpretation was that narcotics were being channelled into China from Xinjiang, China's Wild West, by Muslim extremists intent on ruining the PRC. This belief was compounded by separatist attacks against state targets in metropolitan China, notably Beijing and Shanghai.

## DRUG USE IN CONTEMPORARY CHINA

In today's mega-cities a vibrant entertainment sphere for the young has opened up. Many youngsters encounter their first narcotic experience in a nightclub or in the company of friends, often in parks. The predominance of amphetamines seems to indicate that China's dependence on inhaled sedative opiates is well and truly over, and that Shanghai today has more in common with contemporary New York City than with the Shanghai of the 1930s. China's narcotic culture is thus in a process of globalization, in tune with its economic integration into the wider world.

The link between injected drugs and HIV/AIDS is frequently made. According to figures compiled in 1999, more than 70 percent of the infected population are intravenous drug users. The extent of the problem becomes palpable when 2003 estimates by the National Narcotics Control Commission (*guojia jindu weiyuanhui*, NNCC) are taken into account. Out of a total of nearly 3,000 counties and cities in China, 2,200 have been classified as suffering from endemic drug abuse, and there are some 1.05 million recreational users. Female addiction appears to be substantial: Although less than 17 percent of the total number recorded at that time were women, in certain areas female drug abusers accounts for more than one-third of all cases.

There are regional differences in narcotics consumption within China. Sichuan, Guangxi, and Yunnan Provinces, all within relatively easy travel distance from Laos and Burma, have experienced a boom in illegal drugs. Although the smugglers are usually locals, a larger criminal network stretching throughout China to Hong Kong and

***A police officer holds an opium plant while teaching students about the drug and its effects, Nanjing, May 18, 2005.*** *While initially appreciated for its medicinal properties, opium became a troubling import to China during the 1800s, as large segments of the population developed addictions to the drug. After 1949, Communist leaders took a firm anti-drug stance, a commitment the government continues despite a liberalization of other parts of Chinese society.* © CHINA NEWSPHOTO/REUTERS/CORBIS

Taiwan has developed. In addition to "traditional" criminal activities such as prostitution, people smuggling, and drug trafficking, these crime networks (triads) concentrate on international money laundering and Internet fraud. As opposed to the Mafia and to comparable criminal organizations in Russia and the United States, China's gangs usually work discretely and in quasi-legal activities (e.g., local transport, street markets, bars, and public entertainment). In Europe and in the Americas, their commercial activities in Chinatowns are often fully legal (e.g., restaurants, shops).

Traditional triads have successfully infiltrated local government structures, resulting in extra-legal (*weifa*) activities that are not, strictly speaking, against the law. This legal twilight zone clearly has benefited the distribution of illegal drugs since the death of Deng Xiaoping. Another important factor has been the increased capability of producing synthetic drugs within the PRC. Whereas amphetamines were the drug of choice of young clubbers during the 1990s, there has been a trend in the 2000s toward ketamine, particularly in the southern provinces. China thus is evolving from importer to drug-producing country. According to intelligence from the United Nations Office on Drugs and Crime (UNODC), easy access to chemical substances and to laboratories greatly facilitates the production of opiates and methamphetamine.

## ANTI-DRUG CAMPAIGNS

Official education campaigns have tended to focus more on related issues, such as illegal trade, than on drug prevention per se. However, recently there has been a clear change in the level of official recognition accorded to China's drug addiction problem. In 1990 the NNCC was formed from existing drug-suppression agencies belonging to government ministries, the police, and China's customs services. In 1998 the Ministry for Public Security established a dedicated drug-suppression agency (*jinduju*) with branch agencies at provincial, district, and local levels. A majority of these subagencies operate in conjunction with newly created police drug squads. In the same year, China's parliament approved the creation of a national narcotics control foundation (*Zhongguo dupin jijinhui*) to provide financial and educational support. Simultaneous changes in China's legal system produced a gradual shift from a penalizing to a preventative approach. In 2000, China's approximately 1,000 drug rehabilitation centers provided help for 224,000 out-patient habitual drug users, as well as for 120,000 in-patient users. The philosophy guiding the centers can be summarized as "education, moral improvement, recuperation" (*jiaoyu, ganhua, wanjiu*). In a landmark event in October 2005, the UNODC was granted permission to set up a permanent office in Beijing.

**SEE ALSO** *HIV/AIDS; Lin Zexu; Opium, 1800–1950.*

**BIBLIOGRAPHY**

Baumler, Alan. *The Chinese and Opium under the Republic: Worse than Floods and Wild Beasts.* Albany: State University of New York Press, 2007.

Chen Yin. *Baise youling: Zhongguo dupin neimu* [The white spectre: Behind the scenes of China's drug scene]. Beijing: Guangming Ribao Chubanshe, 1993.

Ch'en Yung-fa. The Blooming Poppy under the Red Sun: The Yan'an Way and the Opium Trade. In *New Perspectives on the Chinese Communist Revolution*, ed. Tony Saich and Hans van de Ven, 263–298. New York: Sharpe, 1995.

Choi, Susanne Y. P., Yuet Wah Cheung, and Kanglin Chen. Gender and HIV Risk Behaviour among Intravenous Drug Users in Sichuan, China. *Social Science and Medicine* 62, 7 (April 2006): 1672–1684.

Deng, Rui, Jianghong Li, Luechai Sringernyuang, and Kaining Zhang. Drug Abuse, HIV/AIDS, and Stigmatisation in a Dai Community in Yunnan, China. *Social Science and Medicine* 64, 8 (April 2007): 1560–1571.

Dikötter, Frank, Lars P. Laamann, and Zhou Xun. *Narcotic Culture: A History of Drugs in Modern China.* Chicago: University of Chicago Press, 2004.

Gao, Huan. Female Drug Abuse in China: An Analysis of Its Attributes, Patterns, and Consequences. Paper presented at the annual meeting of the American Society of Criminology, Royal York, Toronto, September 10, 2008. http://www.allacademic.com/meta/p26192_index.html.

Hong Lu. Legal Responses to Trafficking in Narcotics and Other Narcotic Offences in China. *International Criminal Justice Review* 18, 2 (2008): 212–228.

Ma Mozhen, ed. *Zhongguo jindu shi ziliao* [Archival materials on the history of drug prohibition in China]. Tianjin, China: Tianjin Renmin Chubanshe, 1998.

Mili, Hayder. Xinjiang: An Emerging Narco-Islamist Corridor? *Terrorism Monitor* 3, 8 (May 5, 2005).

Ouyang Tao, and Chen Zexian, eds. *Dupin fanzui ji duice* [Drug crime and countermeasures]. Beijing: Qunzhong Chubanshe, 1992.

Polachek, James M. *The Inner Opium War.* Cambridge, MA: Harvard University, Council on East Asian Studies, 1992.

Scott, James Maurice. *The White Poppy: A History of Opium.* London: Heinemann, 1969.

Slack, Edward. *Opium, State, and Society.* Honolulu: University of Hawaii Press, 2000.

Trocki, Carl A. *Opium, Empire, and the Global Political Economy: A Study of the Asian Opium Trade, 1750–1950.* London: Routledge, 1999.

Wang Gungwu. The Nanhai Trade: A Study of the Early History of Chinese Trade in the South China Sea. *Journal of the Malayan Branch of the Royal Asiatic Society* 31, 2 (June 1958): 74–112.

Wang Yongcheng, and First Penal Division of the Supreme People's Court, eds. *Daji dupin fanzui shiyong* [Combating narcotic crime in practice]. Beijing: Renmin Fayuan Chubanshe, 1992.

World Anti-Communist League (China Chapter). *The Chinese Communist Plot to Drug the World.* Taibei: Asian Peoples' Anti-Communist League, 1972.

Yan Xiao, Sybille Kristensen, Jiangping Sun, et al. Expansion of HIV/AIDS in China: Lessons from Yunnan Province. *Social Science and Medicine* 64, 3 (February 2007): 665–675.

Yang Fengrui, ed. *Jin du 2003: Zhongguo jindu baogao* [Annual report on drug control in China, 2003]. Beijing: Shehui Kexue Wenxian Chubanshe, 2004.

Zheng Yangwen. *The Social Life of Opium in China.* Cambridge, U.K.: Cambridge University Press, 2005.

Zhou Yongming. *Anti-drug Crusades in Twentieth-century China.* Lanham, MD: Rowman and Littlefield, 1999.

Zhu Yu, ed. *Gechu duli—gongheguo shouci jindu jinchang shushi* [Cutting out the malignant tumour: true account of the People's Republic's first attempt at prohibiting drugs and prostitution]. Beijing: Zhongyang Wenxian Chubanshe, 1999.

Zou Tao, and Shao Zhenxiang, eds. *"Guanyu jindu de jueding," "Guanyu chengzhi zousi zhizuo fanmai chuanbo yinhui wupin de fanzui fenzi de jueding" shiyi* [Explanatory documents concerning "decisions pursuant to narcotics" and "decisions pursuant to the punishment of persons illegally involved in the contraband, production, peddling, and distribution of obscene items"]. Beijing: Qunzhong Chubanshe, 1991.

*Lars Laamann*

# E

## EARTHQUAKES SINCE 1800

Both the degree of earthquake severity and the land mass affected is greater in China than in any other country. On January 23, 1556, China's Shaanxi Province experienced what is thought to have been the world's most deadly earthquake, killing an estimated 830,000 people. Fortunately, most earthquakes in China are localized and generally do not cause such massive damage. Still, three-quarters of China's cities are located in earthquake belts, and nearly 370,000 people were killed and another one million injured or disabled in earthquakes between 1949 and 2008.

Because the Circum-Pacific seismic belt intersects the Himalaya-Mediterranean seismic belt in China, the country has a high number of earthquakes caused by changes in the earth's structure. It also has earthquakes induced by reservoir impounding and mining. Approximately one-third of China's territory has potential for earthquakes stronger than 7 on the Richter scale. The greatest numbers of quakes occur in the southwest, the northwest, and in Taiwan.

### MAJOR EARTHQUAKES

After a period of relative quiet beginning around 1730, China entered a period of greater earthquake activity after 1880. Since 1897 there have been seven earthquakes rated greater than grade 8 on the Richter scale.

The December 16, 1920, Haiyuan earthquake in Ningxia (then part of Gansu Province and hence often called the Gansu earthquake) measured between 7.8 and 8.5 and killed an estimated 200,000 to 240,000 people, many of whom were buried alive in their cave homes in this loess area. The Haiyuan quake ranks in the top ten deadliest earthquakes in history. Rivers were blocked and a large number of ground cracks and landslides appeared throughout the epicenter area.

The Chayu earthquake of August 15, 1950, in Tibet measured 8.5 in intensity. Although it was an extremely strong earthquake, the population in the area was low, and fewer than 4,000 people died. Collapsing mountains severed the Yarlung Zangbo River in four places, but overall the impact on humans was less than in many weaker quakes.

On July 28, 1976, the Tangshan earthquake, which measured 7.8 on the Richter scale, probably was the deadliest earthquake anywhere in four centuries, resulting in over 240,000 deaths and 400,000 injuries. The quake caused damage over a 115,000-square-mile (300,000-sq-km) area, including the collapse of 5.3 million homes. The location of the epicenter near the surface insured the thorough destruction of Tangshan's water supply, electricity supply, transport, and medical facilities. Reservoirs and dams in the area also were destroyed. The transport networks between Tangshan and Beijing and Tangshan and Tianjin were severely disrupted.

On May 12, 2008, the Wenchuan earthquake in Sichuan Province was more devastating than the Tangshan quake in terms of damage, area affected, and relief effort required. The epicenter was in Wenchuan County, Ngawa Tibetan Autonomous Prefecture, 56 miles (90 km) northwest of Chengdu. Wenchuan had a magnitude of 7.8 to 8 according to different sources, whereas nearby Beichuan and Qingchuan supposedly had readings of 11 or 12. Of the 30,000 aftershocks, over 280 reached 4 on the Richter scale. The event left five million people without homes, killed 69,170 people, injured 368,545, and caused landslides, mudflows, and blockages of rivers on a scale rarely seen. Losses were estimated at 845,100 million yuan.

The Wenchuan earthquake occurred as the result of tectonic stresses caused by the convergence of crustal material slowly moving from the high Tibetan Plateau, to the west, against the strong crust underlying the Sichuan Basin and southeastern China. The area had suffered previous quakes, the most notable being one on August 25, 1933, that killed more than 9,000. With the exceptions of Xinjiang in the northwest, and Jilin and Heilongjiang in the northeast, all regions of China were affected by the quake, and the tremors were felt in Bangladesh, India, Japan, Nepal, Pakistan, Russia, Taiwan, Thailand, and Vietnam. Although the Chinese organized more than 4,000 national earthquake relief workers, and large numbers of soldiers and foreign specialists came to help with relief, the Wenchuan quake was extraordinary as the first in China in which large numbers of private citizens traveled great distances to the area and used their own funds to help with disaster relief.

## WARNING SYSTEMS

China has had primitive warning systems for earthquakes since ancient times. Peasants have claimed that earthquakes can be predicted by unusual phenomena such as changes in groundwater levels, drought, and mass migration of animals. Such phenomena were mentioned in connection with the 2008 Wenchuan earthquake, and Chinese scientists continue to discuss the possibility that animals can feel sonic waves that humans do not detect. They suggest there is reason to continue to research animal behavior in connection with earthquake prediction. In 2006 the scientist Geng Qingguo predicted a possible 7-plus earthquake in the Ngawa Tibetan Autonomous Prefecture where Wenchuan is located based on an analysis of drought; mainstream scientists ignored him. Geng and other experts also predicted the 1976 Tangshan quake, but likewise were ignored.

China has been eager to develop high-tech predictive monitoring systems. That said, the government was not able to predict either the 1976 Tangshan quake or the 2008 Wenchuan quake. The country has had space satellite observation technology in place beginning in the mid-1970s with significant quality improvements in launches since the 1990s. In recent years, China has produced digital maps at 1:50,000, 1:250,000 and 1:1,000,000 scales for the entire country, mapping the geological structure and historic earthquake locations along with the distribution of population and buildings.

A ground earthquake-monitoring network also exists consisting of professional-level monitoring stations, and regional and local stations. At the start of each year, experts hold a seminar to analyze the earthquake activities for that year. A National Earthquake Administration created in 1971 and renamed the China Earthquake Administration in 1998 is directly under the administration of the State Council as mandated by the Law of the People's Republic of China on Protecting Against and Mitigating Earthquake Disasters. The China Earthquake Administration's objectives include selecting which areas require close monitoring, reporting earthquake prone areas to the government, making plans for disasters in such areas, monitoring earthquake damage, educating and coordinating provincial-level earthquake monitoring and disaster mitigation units, organizing research, and liaising with foreign relief organizations.

## SOCIAL IMPACTS OF EARTHQUAKES

Although China is taking measures to deal with earthquakes, sensitive projects such as the Sanxia (Three Gorges) Dam and the Daya Bay nuclear power plant are in earthquake-prone areas. In August 1996 about sixty researchers and experts with the State Commission on Science and Technology drafted a report admitting that the Sanxia Dam may induce moderate earthquakes. Although this study alleviated public concern that the reservoir's huge water storage capacity may induce *major* earthquakes, it demonstrated the increasing potential for earthquakes to be used as a reason to stop unpopular projects.

Some people in China have viewed earthquakes as omens that suggest bad governance or a bad future. The Tangshan earthquake was interpreted as a sign of the fall of the Gang of Four from political power in 1976. In a similar fashion, peasants predicted the 2008 Beijing Olympics were doomed because of the Wenchuan earthquake, though this did not come to pass.

The 7.3 Jiji (Chi-chi) or "921 earthquake" in Taiwan on September 21, 1999, which killed more than 2,400, helped to bring about the downfall of the Guomindang (Kuomintang, Nationalist Party) in the 2000 presidential election. That government was seen as incompetent in managing the disaster relief. Because this was the first democratic change of power on the island, the earthquake had significance beyond the damage and suffering it caused.

### BIBLIOGRAPHY

Edmonds, Richard. Aspects of the Taiwanese Landscape in the Twentieth Century. In *Taiwan in the Twentieth Century: A Retrospective View*, ed. Richard Louis Edmonds and Steven M. Goldstein, 1–18. Cambridge, U.K.: Cambridge University Press, 2001.

Guo Huadong, ed. *Atlas of Remote Sensing for Wenchuan Earthquake Disaster*. Beijing: Chinese Academy of Sciences, 2008.

Li Shanyou, Zhang Mingyu. et al., eds. General Introduction of Engineering Damage of Wenchuan Ms 8.0 Earthquake. *Journal of Earthquake Engineering and Engineering Vibration* 28 Supp. (October 2008): 1–114.

Parsons, Tom, Chen Ji, and Eric Kirby. Stress Changes from the 2008 Wenchuan Earthquake and Increased Hazard in the Sichuan Basin. *Nature* 454 (July 24, 2008): 509–510.

People's Insurance Company of China and Beijing Normal University. *Atlas of Natural Disasters in China*. Beijing: Science Press, 1992.

Zhang, Y. X., H. M. Wang, M. M. Lu, et al. Earthquake Prediction Practice in China's Metropolitan Area around Beijing. *Nature* 454 (July 24, 2008): 451–462.

***Richard Louis Edmonds***

# EAST CENTRAL EUROPEAN STATES, RELATIONS WITH

The communist states of East Central Europe (Albania, Bulgaria, Czechoslovakia, East Germany, Hungary, Poland, Romania, and Yugoslavia) followed the Soviet Union and recognized the People's Republic of China shortly after its establishment in October 1949. In the 1950s they forged close political partnerships with China and offered Beijing economic aid and international support. Not until the Polish and Hungarian incidents in 1956, however, did China develop a distinct foreign policy toward East Central Europe by challenging Soviet leadership in the region.

## UNITY AND DIVERSITY

In the mid-1950s, questioning the applicability of the Soviet model to China's socioeconomic conditions and convinced that the united communist movement guaranteed its security and territorial integrity, Beijing favored East Central Europe's having wide autonomy in its domestic affairs, but opposed any action that would endanger the unity of the international communist movement. Thus Beijing supported Polish demands for freedom in socialist construction and opposed the Soviet military intervention in Poland in mid and late 1956. However, when the Hungarian leadership abolished the one-party system and withdrew from the Warsaw Pact in late 1956, Beijing pressed Moscow to take all necessary measures to smash the "counterrevolutionary rebellion" in Hungary (Zagoria 1966, pp. 55–65).

Having enhanced its prestige and strengthened its position vis-à-vis the Soviet Union in Moscow's own backyard, Beijing embarked on the mission of unifying the Soviet bloc, shattered by the 1956 events. It no longer emphasized diversity of different roads to socialism and equality among socialist states (Brzezinski 1967, p. 281). Fearing potentially contagious revisionism, Beijing cut relations with Yugoslavia in 1958 and forced the Soviets and their allies to follow suit (Byrnes 1962). Its victory, however, was short-lived. Its opposition to peaceful coexistence with the West, its attempts to strengthen the Soviet leadership of the international Communist movement, and its criticisms of economic and political restructuring in East Central Europe alienated the reformist regimes in East Central Europe and made it easier for the Soviets to enlist their support against China when the Sino-Soviet conflict erupted in 1960.

## THE IMPACT OF THE SINO-SOVIET SPLIT

Only the Albanians, viewing improving Soviet-Yugoslav relations as a threat to their national security, begged to differ. In 1960–1961, the Albanian communists sided with Beijing in the Sino-Soviet conflict (Tretiak 1962). When Moscow cut off relations with Albania in 1961, Beijing became Tirana's strategic ally and a chief source of economic assistance, thus positioning itself as an alternative leader of the European communist movement.

Albania demonstrated that the rupture in Sino-Soviet relations provided Soviet allies with an opportunity to challenge Moscow. Romania became the second in East Central Europe to play the China card in order to strengthen its sovereignty. By declaring neutrality in the Sino-Soviet conflict and exchanging high-profile visits with Beijing at crucial junctures in its troubled relationship with the Soviet Union in the 1960s, Bucharest wrought from the Soviets greater autonomy in its domestic and foreign policies (Madsen 1982, pp. 283–288). For Beijing, Romanian pro-China diplomacy demonstrated the effectiveness of its challenge to the Soviet leadership in East Central Europe.

The Cultural Revolution (1966–1969) marked the nadir in China's relations with most East Central European states. Beijing recalled all of its ambassadors, the Red Guards harassed East Central European diplomats and besieged their embassies, and the Chinese reclassified East Central European communist parties (except the Albanian Labor Party) as revisionist. However, the Soviet-led invasion of Czechoslovakia in August 1968 and Moscow's announcement of the Brezhnev Doctrine (justifying Soviet interference in Soviet satellite countries) fundamentally affected China's foreign policy toward East Central Europe. Beijing abandoned its self-imposed diplomatic isolation, upgraded the Soviet Union to the rank of China's principal enemies, and turned anti-Sovietism into the guiding principle of its foreign policy. In East Central Europe, Beijing sought to destabilize the Soviet backyard.

In the late 1960s and early 1970s, China engineered rapprochement with Yugoslavia (which opposed the Soviet invasion of Czechoslovakia) (Johnson 1974, p. 203), strengthened its camaraderie with Albania and Romania, and pursued selective normalization with the remaining states in East Central Europe, hoping to enlist their support for its united front against Soviet "social-imperialism." Chinese efforts to turn Czechoslovakia, Bulgaria, East Germany, Hungary, and Poland against the Soviet Union proved ineffective, however. Horrified by the excesses of the Cultural Revolution and critical of Mao's Three Worlds theory, which highlighted the Soviet exploitation of their economies but left them unclassified (only in 1977 were they explicitly included in the Second World) (Yee 1983, pp. 239–240, n. 2), they all backed Moscow on every issue in Soviet relations with China. Beijing also failed to maintain its partnership with Albania. Tirana was critical of Beijing's reconciliation with Yugoslavia and the West, and criticized the Three Worlds theory as non-Marxist. Following Mao's death, it also censured the purge of the Gang of Four. Facing irreconcilable differences, China, on the eve of Deng Xiaoping's economic reforms, suspended its economic assistance to Albania, thus terminating its militant alliance with Tirana (Biberaj 1986).

## RAPPROCHEMENT

By the early 1980s, in the context of its new policy of maintaining equal distance from both superpowers, China no longer viewed anti-Sovietism as a prerequisite of friendly relations with other states. Increasingly aware of the similarity of views on such issues as economic reforms and peaceful coexistence, Beijing admitted the socialist nature of the East Central European political regimes in early 1983 and gradually restored economic, scientific, and cultural cooperation with all East Central European states. Normalization of political dialogue, however, had to wait until the mid-1980s, when the new Soviet leader Mikhail Gorbachev's policy of rapprochement with China allowed Soviet allies to pursue political relations with Beijing. Having exchanged high-level party and state visits in 1986–1987, China and East Central Europe restored party-to-party dialogue. In the context of this rekindled friendship, Beijing intensified economic cooperation with East Central Europe and extensively studied Hungarian, Polish, and Yugoslav reforms as a source of inspiration and, more often, for legitimization of its own reform measures (Kapur 1990, pp. 164–170). The Chinese reformers appeared particularly interested in the Hungarian model, which combined a planned economy with free-market mechanisms. The 1984 urban reforms in China, for example, were strongly influenced by the Hungarian experience, and the introduction of a two-tier banking system was directly borrowed from the Hungarian economic structure (Talas 1991, pp. 144–152).

The collapse of East Central European communism in 1989, which coincided with the suppression of the student movement in China, not only provided Chinese antireformers with arguments against further economic or political liberalization, but also reduced international support for the Tiananmen massacre. Chinese efforts to forge an ideological coalition with the antireformist regimes in Bulgaria, Czechoslovakia, East Germany, and Romania, all of which supported the Tiananmen solution, failed when those regimes crumbled, leaving China with no ideological allies in East Central Europe.

## THE TAIWAN CHALLENGE IN CENTRAL EUROPE

The 1989 systemic changes in East Central Europe freed the Sino–East Central European partnership from the constraints imposed by the Soviet Union and ended their party-to-party fraternity. Because Beijing perceived East Central European foreign policies as subordinate to those pursued by the West, and since East Central Europe was insignificant for Chinese economic development, Beijing deemphasized relations with the newly democratized states. Yet it could not afford to ignore them, as some of them became vocal critics of China's human-rights record and toyed with the idea of establishing official relations with Taiwan (Tubilewicz 1999, pp. 4–6). While the human rights issue proved to be merely an irritant in bilateral relations, the Taiwan challenge alerted Beijing to the possibility of losing diplomatic ground in postcommunist Europe.

After 1989, Czechoslovakia/the Czech Republic, Hungary, and Poland became the first to welcome Taiwan's pledges of substantial economic assistance and investments. To meet Taiwanese expectations, these countries exchanged representative offices and parliamentarian delegations with Taiwan, engaged in economic and cultural cooperation, and on rare occasions invited Taiwanese dignitaries. In 1991, in response to Taiwan's economic diplomacy, Beijing restored diplomatic dialogue with Central Europe (suspended after 1989), after forcing the new democracies to restate their one-China policies. It also closely monitored their communications with Taibei and did not hesitate to impose political sanctions if vigilance failed. Ultimately, the Central Europeans' dream of conquering the Chinese market, their awareness of Beijing's rising geopolitical clout, and Taibei's reluctance to offer promised aid or investments convinced them of the benefits of sticking to the one-China policy.

## CHINA'S BALKAN FORTRESS

Concerned that the disintegration of Yugoslavia would set a precedent for China's separatist movements in its border regions, Beijing did not support the breakup of Yugoslavia. However, once Belgrade itself acknowledged the inevitable in 1992, Beijing promptly recognized the newly proclaimed Federal Republic of Yugoslavia, as well as Slovenia and Croatia (Tubilewicz 1997). Subsequently, it also recognized Macedonia (1993), Bosnia (1995), and Montenegro (2003).

Its relationship with the post-Yugoslav and other Balkan states (Bulgaria and Romania) was exemplary. In exchange for their adherence to the one-China policy and silence on China's domestic issues, they gained Chinese support in international forums, Chinese foreign aid, and privileged access to the Chinese market. Chinese support in international forums was particularly important to Yugoslavia/Serbia, as Beijing supported the Slobodan Milošević regime and opposed the U.S.-led NATO intervention in Kosovo in early 1999.

Because the Balkan countries avoided direct contacts with Taiwan, Taibei confined its activities in the region to occasional trade visits and contacts with opposition parties. This low-profile approach succeeded in Macedonia, where newly elected democrats recognized Taiwan in January 1999 in exchange for a promise of US$1 billion in aid and investments. In response, Beijing cut off diplomatic ties and vetoed extending the mandate of the United Nations Preventive Deployment Force in Macedonia. The 2001 Macedonian civil war, which broke out partly because the United Nations peacekeeping forces were absent, brought to power former communists who were hostile to Taiwan and created a situation where China's involvement in the resolution of the Macedonian crisis seemed necessary. This and Taibei's reluctance to provide the large amount of economic aid that Skopje expected resulted in Macedonia's restoration of diplomatic relations with China in June 2001 (Tubilewicz 2007, pp. 134–155).

Beijing's diplomatic success in Macedonia displayed its geopolitical influence in the Balkans and its capacity to maintain fraternal relations with major Balkan political forces. In line with its principled opposition to secessionism (and out of loyalty to Serbia), China did not support Kosovo's independence, declared in February 2008. Its recognition of Kosovo's sovereignty depends on Belgrade's policies toward the breakaway republic.

## THE NATO AND EU FACTORS

When the issue of NATO'S eastward enlargement surfaced in the early 1990s, Beijing at first voiced its understanding of Central Europe's security concerns. Soon after, however, in the context of the emerging strategic partnership with Russia, Chinese leadership questioned the rationale for NATO enlargement and implicitly supported Russia's opposition to include its former allies in the NATO structures. Yet, when faced with the dilemma to either explicitly side with Russia on the NATO issue, antagonize the United States and alienate those East Central European countries eager to enter NATO, or take a neutral position by neither voicing opposition nor support, Beijing chose the latter. Its reluctance to side with Russia during two waves of NATO expansion (1999 and 2004) demonstrated the limits of China's support for Russia's diplomacy in Europe, and (more importantly) manifested China's readiness to forgo its tacit sympathies in order to maintain friendly relations with East Central Europe (and the Baltic states in the early 2000s) and the United States (Tubilewicz 1997, pp. 9-10).

After acceding to the European Union in 2004 and 2007, several East Central European states gained in importance in Chinese foreign policy, as they could shape the European Union's common foreign policy on diplomatic and economic issues that Beijing considers significant. Their "traditional friendship" with China notwithstanding, the European Union's new member states (particularly the Central European ones) are dissatisfied with rising trade deficits, critical of China's human rights record, and suspicious of its wider foreign-policy objectives. As such, they are unlikely to form a pro-China voting bloc within the European Union.

**SEE ALSO** *European Union, Relations with; Foreign Trade since 1950; International Relations; Russia, Relations with.*

**BIBLIOGRAPHY**

Biberaj, Elez. *Albania and China 1962–1978: A Case Study of a Bilateral Unequal Alliance.* Ann Arbor, MI: University Microfilms International, 1986.

Brzezinski, Zbigniew. *The Soviet Bloc: Unity and Conflict.* Cambridge: Harvard University Press, 1967.

Byrnes, Robert F. Soviet and Chinese Communist Relations with Yugoslavia. In *Unity and Contradiction: Major Aspects of Sino-Soviet Relations*, ed. Kurt London, pp. 168–180. New York: Frederick A. Praeger, 1962.

Johnson, A. Ross. Yugoslavia and the Sino-Soviet Conflict: The Shifting Triangle, 1948–1974. *Studies in Comparative Communism* 7, 1/2 (Spring/Summer 1974): 184–203.

Kapur, Harish. *Distant Neighbours: China and Europe.* London: Pinter Publishers, 1990.

Madsen, M. Hunter. The Uses of Beijingpolitik: China in Romanian Foreign Policy since 1953. *East European Quarterly* 16, 3 (September 1982): 277–309.

Talas, Barna. *Economic Reforms and Political Reform Attempts in China 1979–1989.* Berlin: Springer-Verlag, 1991.

Tretiak, Daniel. The Founding of the Sino-Albanian Entente. *China Quarterly*, no. 10 (April–June 1962): 123–143.

Tubilewicz, Czeslaw. China and the Yugoslav Crisis, 1990–1994: Beijing's Exercise in Dialectics. *Issues and Studies* 33, 4 (April 1997): 94–112.

Tubilewicz, Czeslaw. Comrades No More: Sino-Central European Relations after the Cold War. *Problems of Post-Communism* 46, 2 (March–April 1999): 3–14.

Tubilewicz, Czeslaw. *Taiwan and Post-Communist Europe: Shopping for Allies.* London: Routledge, 2007.

Yee, Herbert S. The Three World Theory and Post-Mao China's Global Strategy. *International Affairs* 59, 2 (Spring 1983): 239–249.

Zagoria, Donald S. *The Sino-Soviet Conflict, 1956–1961.* New York: Atheneum, 1966.

*Czeslaw Tubilewicz*

## EAST INDIA COMPANY, 1800–1834

In 1699 the British East India Company (EIC) began a direct and regular trade with China, via Guangzhou (Canton), which lasted until 1834. Other East India companies traded with China as well, such as the French, Ostend, Dutch, Danish, Swedish, Prussian, and Trieste. Some of them sent ships to China twice as large as those of the EIC (which in the mid to late eighteenth century ranged from about 500 to 1,000 tons). But overall, the EIC dominated commerce in the port, with other companies handling small volumes in comparison. By 1807 all companies except the EIC had ceased operations in China, partially owing to the Napoleonic Wars, and then the only foreign competitors were private traders. These entrepreneurs consisted primarily of Europeans based in India, indigenous Indian merchants, and Americans, and the majority of them operated small vessels (100 to 500 tons). The Danish Asiatic Company returned to the China trade from 1820 to 1833, but only commissioned five voyages. In 1834 all large monopolistic companies, including the EIC, ceased operations in China, and from this year forward, private traders ruled the commerce.

During its years of operation, the EIC was the most influential company in China. Guangzhou officials depended heavily on large companies, especially the British, to maintain order within the foreign community and to encourage growth. Large vessels received preferential fees and treatment under the Canton system, to the prejudice of small private ships. In return, Qing officials expected EIC officers to help keep private traders in line, even though most of them were not under their jurisdiction. This was a natural response, considering that the Qing government used a similar administrative structure to control Chinese involved in trade, by placing all of them under the supervision of the *cohong* (the small group of Chinese merchants licensed to trade with foreigners). For its part, the company benefited from private traders by encouraging them to purchase EIC opium (and other goods) in India, ship it to China (illegally), and then deposit opium revenues (in silver coin) into the company treasury in Guangzhou. Even though company ships were forbidden from carrying opium to China, the EIC depended heavily on silver from private opium sales to purchase tea and other legitimate goods. It was not difficult to smuggle opium into China and it was a way to avoid the high port fees charged to small ships, so an increasing number of private traders became involved in this lucrative commerce.

Over time, private ships became more efficient (in both licit and illicit trade), with better man-per-ton ratios, quicker turnarounds, less-expensive means of insuring and financing voyages, and the ability to procure exports without having to pay the high fees in Guangzhou (by smuggling or entering the port as a "rice ship"). These improvements in efficiency meant lower operating costs, more voyages per year, and a more competitive trade in both imports and exports. In addition, private traders did not keep expensive retinues in China to manage trade, as the EIC did, but depended on individual agents (called "commission merchants") to place orders and coordinate shipments. By the early nineteenth century, the EIC found it increasingly difficult to compete with small private traders in Asia, which led to its India monopoly being abolished in 1813 and Parliament terminating the company's China monopoly in 1833. Multiple factors influenced this change in policy in Britain such as industrialization and free-trade movements and political reshuffling within the House of Commons. But at the heart of the discussion was the simple fact that large monopolies could no longer compete with the better efficiencies of private traders.

**SEE ALSO** *Commercial Elite, 1800-1949; Foreign Trade, 1800-1950; Opium, 1800-1950; Silk since 1800.*

### BIBLIOGRAPHY

Bowen, H. V. *The Business of Empire: The East India Company and Imperial Britain, 1756–1833.* Cambridge, U.K.: Cambridge University Press, 2006.

Morse, Hosea Ballou. *The Chronicles of the East India Company Trading to China, 1635–1834.* 5 vols. Cambridge, MA: Harvard University Press, 1926–1929.

Van Dyke, Paul A. *The Canton Trade: Life and Enterprise on the China Coast, 1700–1845.* Hong Kong: Hong Kong University Press, 2005.

***Paul A. Van Dyke***

## ECONOMIC DEVELOPMENT

*This entry contains the following:*



### OVERVIEW

The economic development of China after 1978 is historically unique in terms of both speed of growth and extent of structural changes.

In hindsight, the reform policies launched in 1978 represented a radical break between two patterns of growth.

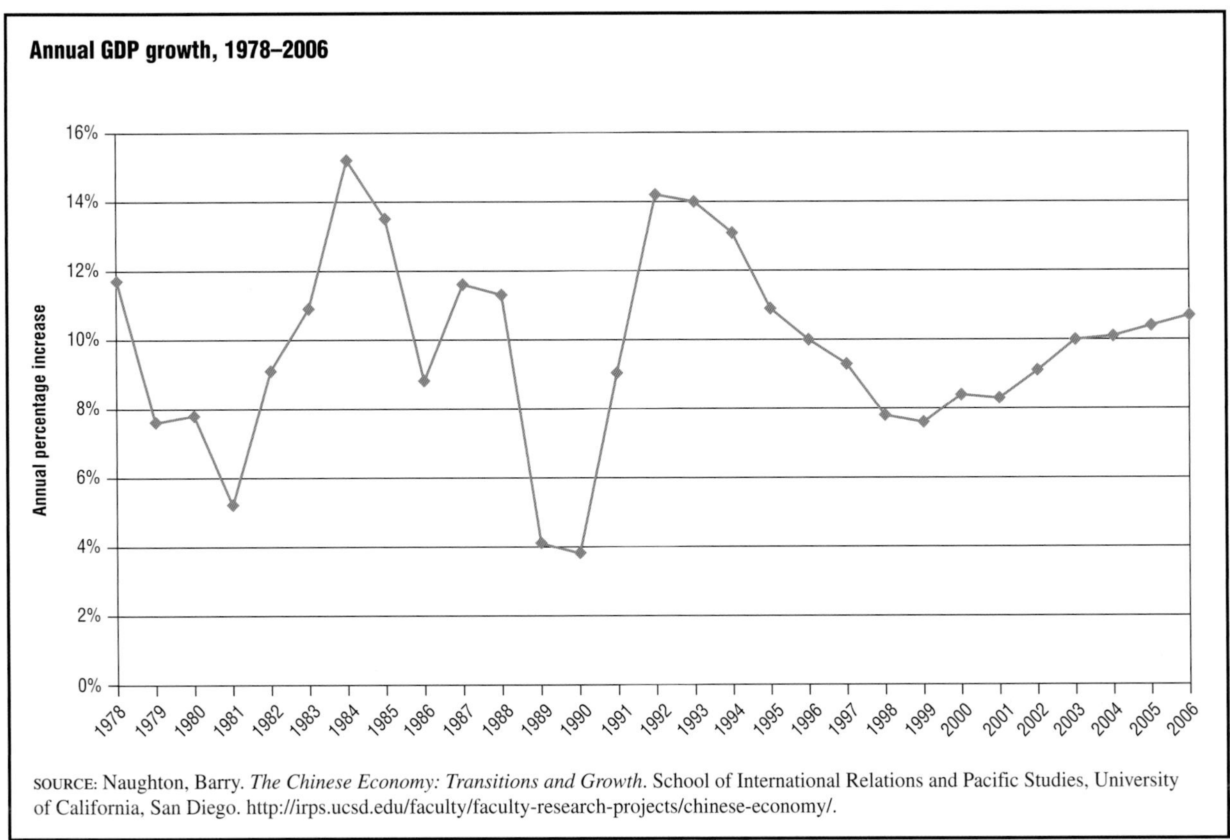


SOURCE: Naughton, Barry. *The Chinese Economy: Transitions and Growth.* School of International Relations and Pacific Studies, University of California, San Diego. http://irps.ucsd.edu/faculty/faculty-research-projects/chinese-economy/.

*Figure 1*

Between 1949 and 1978 China pursued a state-led, big-push industrialization strategy that exploited agricultural surplus to foster heavy industry. Consumer welfare was sacrificed for industrial development. At the same time China secured a relatively egalitarian distribution of income, especially after the shock of the Great Leap Forward.

This planned industrialization caused a convergence of development across regions, because the command economy did not allow for exploitation of regional comparative advantage and state-led investment aimed at relocating industry in the interior provinces. A further distinctive feature of the old system was the almost complete suppression of rural-urban migration after the Great Leap Forward, with even forced urban-rural migration during the Cultural Revolution.

The command economy left a unique legacy for further development after 1978. Sectoral employment shares reflected the low level of income in China in that agriculture accounted for over two-thirds of all employment. Yet in terms of the share of industry in the gross domestic product, China appeared to be overindustrialized. Moreover, compared to the Soviet model, industry was much more regionally dispersed. Both features offered unique potential for growth and caused strongly path-dependent economic development after 1978.

After 1978, although the apparatus of the command economy was dismantled only gradually, the opening of market entry, especially in the countryside, triggered a highly dynamic growth process, with strong effects on both the level and distribution of income. Because industry was regionally dispersed and could rely on production capacities not utilized within the plan, market competition increased its scope to include state-owned industry. Four main periods of economic development can be distinguished:

*1978–1989.* The first decade was characterized mainly by rural reforms, which allowed rural production to diversify again. This diversity induced tremendous gains from trade through specialization and opened the way for the emergence of township and village enterprises. Such enterprises exerted increasing competitive pressure on state-owned industry, which was liberalized only slowly.

*1989–1992.* Following the Tiananmen Incident and the austerity policies initiated in reaction to the

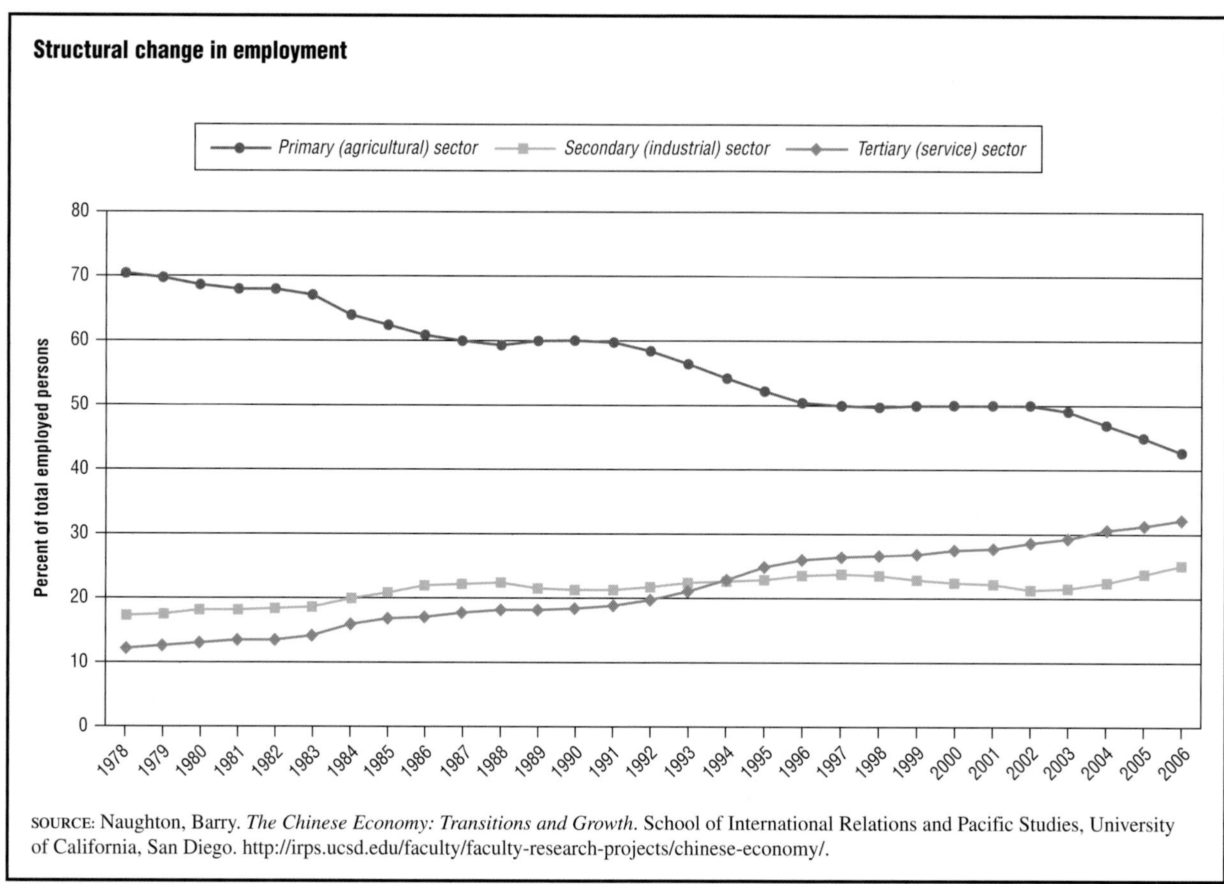


*Figure 2*

outburst of inflation in 1988, growth was suppressed, especially in the rural industrial sector.

*1992–2001.* After Deng Xiaoping's southern tour, the speed of reforms accelerated again, with a rapid further opening-up that led to large influxes of foreign direct investment, especially into the coastal regions. Reforms of state-owned industries intensified.

*2001–present.* Following China's entry into the World Trade Organization, reforms condensed into normalized institutional patterns, featuring mainly a large sector of small- and medium-sized firms and a state-controlled corporate sector. In some regions of China, agriculture emerged as an export sector. The financial sector underwent a slow transformation to a market-oriented banking system.

Against this historical background, economic development underwent structural changes that are recognizable in the growth, and the sectoral and spatial distribution, of income. There are some difficulties in assessing these changes, because measures of income depend on the institutional framework that governs the composition of private and public goods available to the populace. For most of the time, urbanites enjoyed many forms of privileged access to public goods, such as cheap housing, free medical care, and, in the first years, subsidized consumption in individual and collective forms. In contrast, the rural population suffered a breakdown of collective public services since the 1990s, especially in health care.

Generally speaking, the relative income position of the rural population improved in the 1980s and declined continuously after 1992, both in terms of relative monetary income and access to public goods.

The dismantling of urban privileges did not balance these changes, because the urban population could improve its monetary income flows continuously. The main institutional feature explaining this lopsided pattern of development was the system of household registration inherited from Maoist times. This system created barriers for rural residents to move into the cities and hence to enter into the formal urban labor market. It thus acted to protect the income position of urbanites. At the same time, however, economic development led to a significant decline of rural poverty.

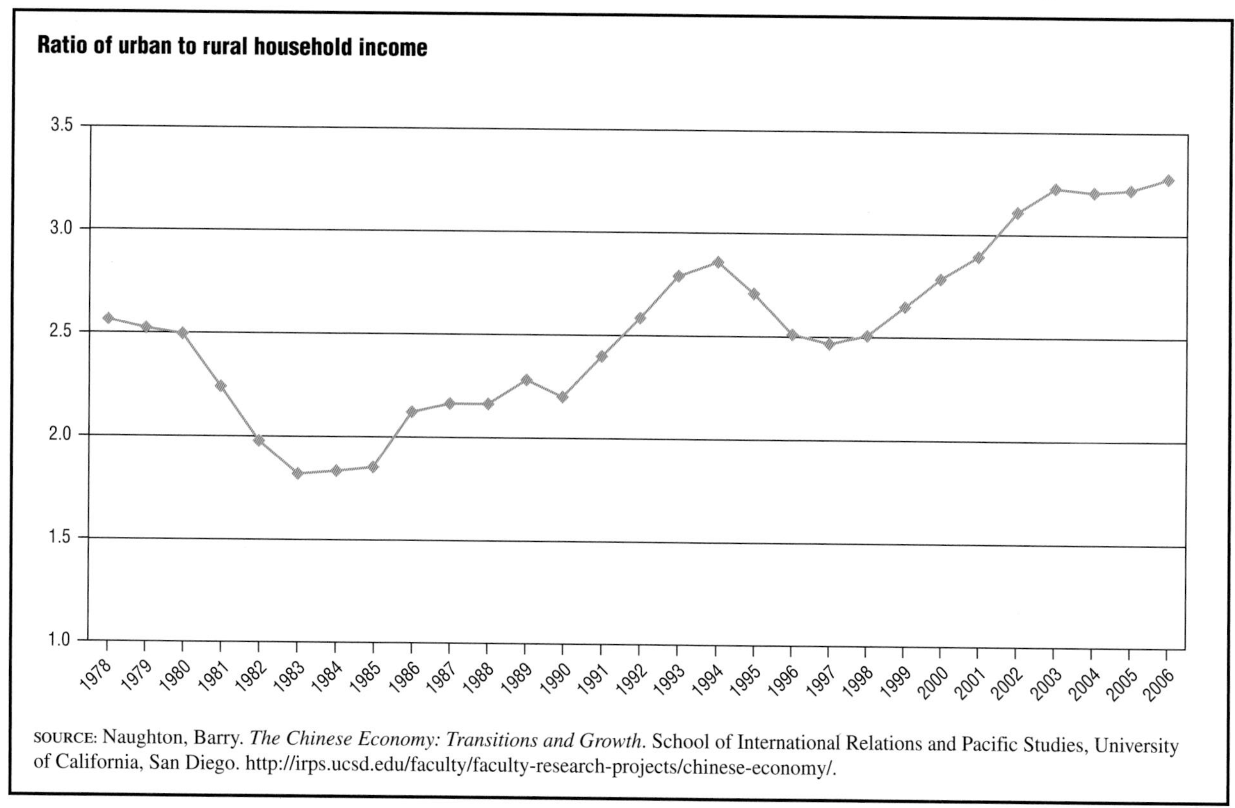

**Ratio of urban to rural household income**

3.5
3.0
2.5
2.0
1.5
1.0
1978
1979
1980
1981
1982
1983
1984
1985
1986
1987
1988
1989
1990
1991
1992
1993
1994
1995
1996
1997
1998
1999
2000
2001
2002
2003
2004
2005
2006

SOURCE: Naughton, Barry. *The Chinese Economy: Transitions and Growth.* School of International Relations and Pacific Studies, University of California, San Diego. http://irps.ucsd.edu/faculty/faculty-research-projects/chinese-economy/.

**Incidence of rural poverty in China**

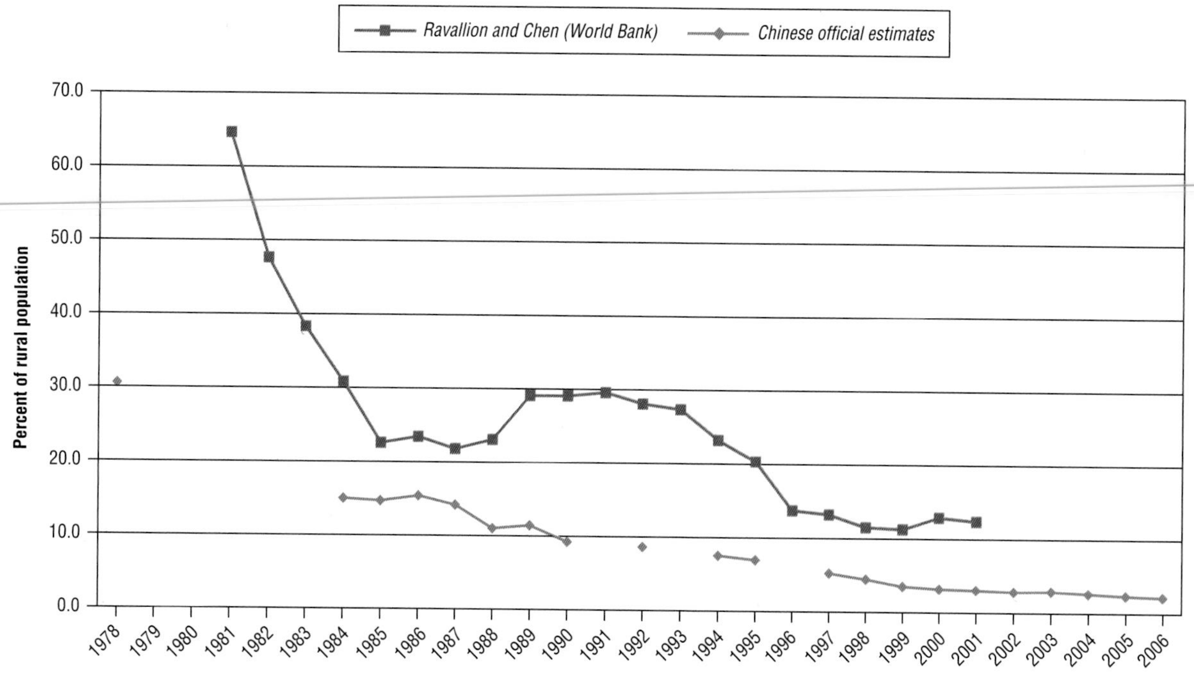

Ravallion and Chen (World Bank)
Chinese official estimates
Percent of rural population
70.0
60.0
50.0
40.0
30.0
20.0
10.0
0.0
1978
1979
1980
1981
1982
1983
1984
1985
1986
1987
1988
1989
1990
1991
1992
1993
1994
1995
1996
1997
1998
1999
2000
2001
2002
2003
2004
2005
2006

SOURCE: Naughton, Barry. *The Chinese Economy: Transitions and Growth.* School of International Relations and Pacific Studies, University of California, San Diego. http://irps.ucsd.edu/faculty/faculty-research-projects/chinese-economy/.

*Figures 3 and 4*

This general picture needs qualification with regard to regional differences. The avant-garde of the early socialist industrialization, the Northeast, suffered increasing disadvantages from its legacy of heavy industry. These disadvantages led to rapidly increasing unemployment, which hampered urban income growth. In the coastal growth cores of the lower Yangzi River valley and the Pearl River delta, rural and urban incomes were boosted by integration with the world economy, and the countryside underwent a rapid process of urbanization. In contrast, the inner southwestern provinces suffered from stalled rural income growth, while the privileged position of its urban areas was maintained.

The rural/urban divide also has a strong impact on the overall measure of development, because it affects the conversion of the gross domestic product into measures of purchasing-power parity. The latter typically results in values that are three to four times higher. This is because the availability of a huge pool of cheap labor acts especially to lower the relative prices of nontradables, such as services and rents. As a result, the purchasing power of the renminbi is much higher than its value calculated by the market exchange rate, and this results in two vastly different assessments of China's relative position in the world economy.

Forecasts of economic development in the decade beginning in 2010 expect a high but slowly declining growth rate, because of the effects of diminishing returns. The growth potential of further structural change of the rural sector remains large, however, especially with regard to employment. China is also on track for increasing productivity gains resulting from technological change. In the longer run, the demographic effects of a rapidly aging population and of an increasing dependency rate will probably dampen economic growth.

**BIBLIOGRAPHY**

Khan, Azizur Rahman, and Carl Riskin. China's Household Income and Its Distribution. *China Quarterly* 182 (2005): 356–384.

Lu, Max, and Enru Wang. Forging Ahead and Falling Behind: Changing Regional Inequalities in Post-reform China. *Growth and Change* 33, 1 (2002): 42–71.

Maddison, Angus. *Chinese Economic Performance in the Long Run.* Paris: Brookings, 2008.

Naughton, Barry. *The Chinese Economy: Transitions and Growth.* Cambridge MA: MIT Press, 2007. See especially chapters 4 and 6.

Organisation for Economic Co-operation and Development. *OECD Economic Surveys: China.* Vol. 2005/13. Paris: OECD Publishing.

***Carsten Herrmann-Pillath***

## ECONOMIC REGIONS

As a geographical notion, *region* refers to a particular area in which a multitude of natural, political, and cultural factors determine patterns of economic specialization and differential concentration of economic activities. In Chinese studies the region plays a central role in understanding the dynamics of economic and social change in the interaction between central political institutions and the large diversity of local conditions. Historical studies of China identify three early economic regions as the infrastructural substrate of Chinese civilization: the large spatial patterns of the Yellow (Huang) River loess (unstratified loamy deposits) region, the fertile areas of the lower Yangzi (Chang) River delta, and the continental border regions. The concept attained paradigmatic status in the notion of the *macroregion*, which was introduced and elaborated analytically by the scholar of China G. W. Skinner. A macroregion is a hierarchically clustered area of economic activity (such as the Jiangnan region) that builds on the system of grassroots marketing areas, and which was interlinked with other regions via long-distance trade mainly managed in the regional centers. China's cultural diversity has important implications for macroregions, with many long-term effects on economic development. An important case in point is the linguistically diverse Southeast Coast, from which the majority of worldwide Chinese migrant populations originated. Global networks of overseas Chinese have been a driving force of foreign direct investment into those areas.

### ALTERNATIVE CONCEPTIONS OF REGIONS

In contemporary China the notion of economic regions is mainly associated with the observation of increasing disparities of economic development, and with the emergence of spatially diverse developmental models resulting from peculiar historical and economic conditions. A natural starting point for identifying economic regions is the agricultural basis, which interacts with the peculiar institutional features of the dualist Chinese development model, clearly separating rural and urban areas in terms of government activity and economic regulation. This dualism leverages the effects of the rural economy on the overall regional disparity across Chinese provinces. Arranging China in agricultural regions, however, results in regions that sometimes cluster provinces of widely varying economic performance (e.g., region IV):

Region I: Middle and lower Yellow River (Beijing, Hebei, Henan, Shandong, Shanxi, Tianjin)

Region II: Northeast (Heilongjiang, Jilin, Liaoning)

Region III: Arid northwest (Gansu, Neimenggu, Ningxia, Xinjiang)

Region IV: Lower and Middle Yangzi River (Anhui, Hubei, Hunan, Jiangsu, Jiangxi, Shanghai, Zhejiang)

Region V: Subtropical-tropical South (Fujian, Guangdong, Guangxi, Hainan)

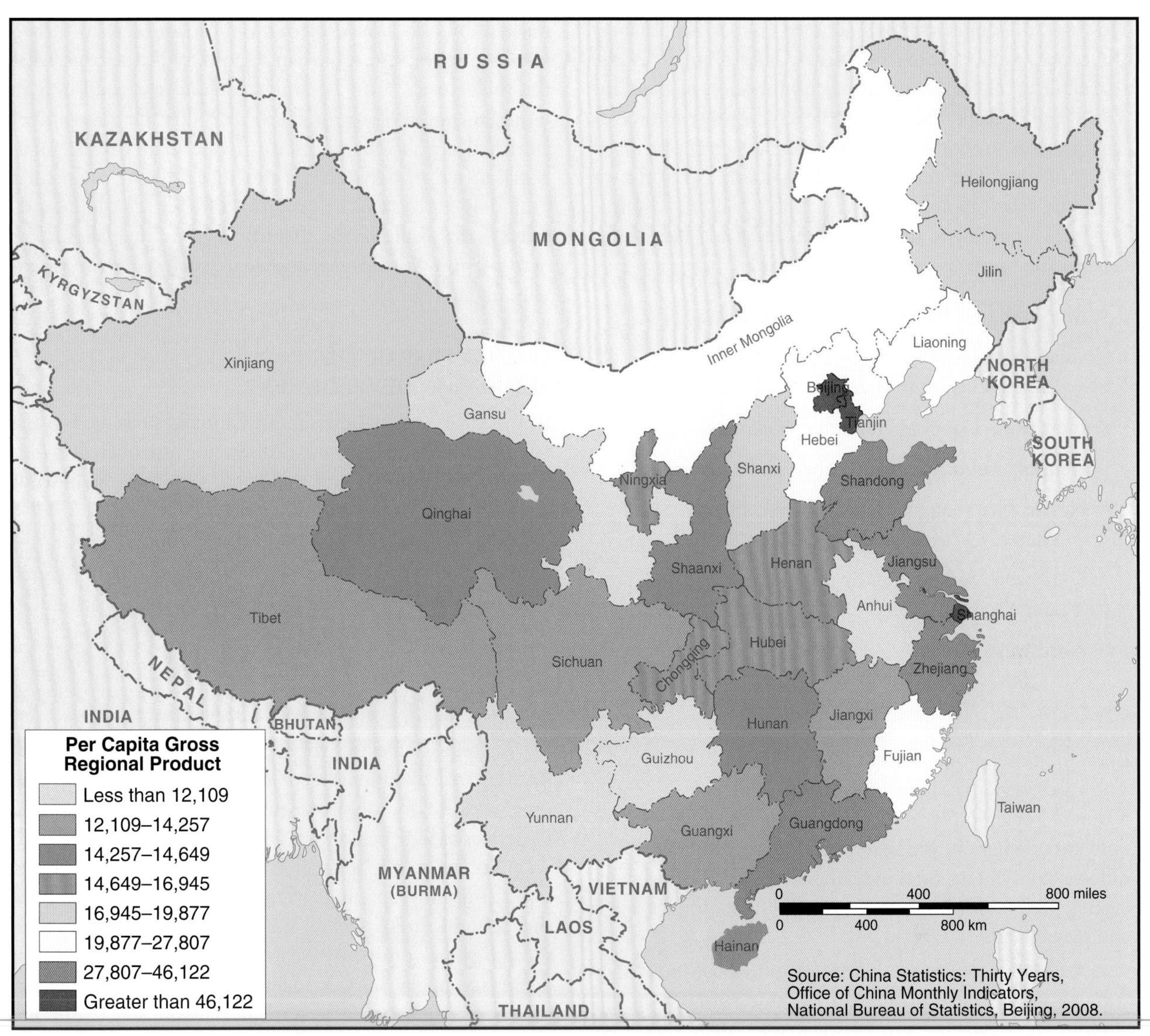


Region VI: Subtropical-tropical Southwest (Guizhou, Sichuan, Yunnan)

Region VII: Mountain plateaus of Qinghai and Tibet

The most common alternative regional division of China is that of the three belts:

Coast: Beijing, Tianjin, Liaoning, Hebei, Shanghai, Jiangsu, Zhejiang, Fujian, Shandong, Liaoning, Guangdong, Hainan, and Guangxi

Center: Neimenggu, Shanxi, Jilin, Heilongjiang, Anhui, Jiangxi, Henan, Hubei, and Hunan

West: Sichuan (Chongqing, since 1997), Guizhou, Yunnan, Tibet, Shaanxi, Gansu, Qinghai, Ningxia, and Xinjiang

Historically, the three belts distinction relates to the "third front" concept of the 1960s, when it was mainly connected with strategic and military thinking that identified the border regions of China as especially vulnerable in a two-front confrontation with the United States and the Soviet Union. As a result, a massive redirection of investment took place, creating centers of heavy industry in the central belt and sometimes even in remote locations, which were lacking competitiveness in the era of market liberalization. However, those regional groupings have always been adapted to the special policy context. Following up the "Western development strategy," the Eleventh Five-Year Plan introduced a new classification in 2006 that separated a northeastern region including Liaoning, Jilin, and Heilongjiang, thus recognizing their common fate as the core region of Chinese heavy industrialization.

In the 1950s some in China developed a more sophisticated concept of regionalization that was closer to macroregions, with the goal of streamlining the planning process along the lines of convergent economic and natural features.

However, this approach never attained political dominance. (In contemporary China one remarkable example is the restructuring of the second-tier administration of the Chinese People's Bank, the Central Bank, according to macroregions, so as to contain the political influence of provincial governments.) The macroregional approach has come to seem the most appropriate given that it clusters Chinese provinces according to their structural and institutional similarities. One such division is the following:

Metropolitan: Beijing, Tianjin, and Shanghai

Coastal: Shandong, Jiangsu, Zhejiang, Fujian, Guangdong, and Hainan

Northeast: Liaoning, Jilin, and Heilongjiang

Central: Anhui, Jiangxi, Hubei, and Hunan

North: Neimenggu, Hebei, Shanxi, Henan, Shaanxi, Gansu, Qinghai, and Ningxia

Southwest: Sichuan, Chongqing, Guizhou, Guangxi, and Yunnan

Northwest: Xinjiang and Tibet

Here, for example, the metropolitan macroregion is based on the similar administrative and structural characteristics of those provinces, without geographic contiguity. The macroregions as listed have significant distinguishing features: For example, the coastal provinces are linked by outward orientation, strong foreign direct investment (FDI) inflows, and vibrant rural industries, and the Southwest by lagging rural industries and low accessibility for foreign trade and investment.

Aspects of economic administration have exerted a stronger impact on subregional divisions, especially in the attempt to bridge the gap between the urban and rural systems. This is done mainly by assigning a stronger coordinating role of urban centers for the surrounding counties. These administrative changes have been particularly pushed by the fast urbanization processes that turned many counties into suburban regions, with the result that the prefecture almost became the basic structural unit in terms of economic regions. In the 2000s the government launched a political process to divide China into "functional areas" in between the province and the prefecture. Functional areas will be assigned different developmental status—for example, to identify regions that should be exempt from further development (such as environmentally fragile regions).

**Regional shares of national totals, 2007 (by percent)**

| | Coastal | Central | Western | Northeastern |
|---|---|---|---|---|
| Area | 9.5 | 10.7 | 71.5 | 8.2 |
| Population | 36.5 | 27.2 | 27.9 | 8.4 |
| GDP | 55.3 | 18.9 | 17.4 | 8.5 |
| Foreign trade | 89.0 | 3.4 | 3.6 | 4.0 |
| Government revenue | 59.6 | 15.2 | 17.3 | 7.8 |
| Graduates from institutions of higher education | 40.4 | 28.7 | 21.3 | 9.5 |
| Hospital beds | 38.1 | 24.6 | 26.1 | 11.2 |

SOURCE: China Statistical Yearbook 2008, pp. 18–21.

*Table 1*

## SPATIAL DISPARITIES IN ECONOMIC DEVELOPMENT

In the 2007 regional division of China as presented in the *China Statistical Yearbook* (2008), the unequal distribution of economic activity stands out, as do the significant differences in levels of economic development.

The question of the appropriate regional division of China is of central importance for assessing the degree and the direction of change of interregional disparities. In the simplest terms, the higher the level of aggregation, the larger the possible estimation errors that result from the hiding of intraregional disparities in the regional averages, which are then used for interregional comparisons. According to some studies on regional disparities in China, total interregional disparity, based on the prefecture as the base unit, account for only one-third as a result of aggregate disparities among belts. Even within-province inequality still accounts for almost one-half of total inequality of GDP per capita, but only one-third of total income per capita. Thus the economic strength of regions converges more closely than the individual prosperity of regions. Further, the regional disparities might in fact mainly reflect disparities within sectors, such as between rural and urban spheres of the economy, which is crucial for drawing the right policy conclusions. There are also difficult measurement issues, such as the divergent price levels across the provinces, the inclusion of which strongly reduces interregional inequality.

Beyond the issue of disparities, the regionalization of China has been affected by the diversity of transition paths after 1978. For example, whereas the Northeast macroregion seems to manifest convergent features resulting from the common heritage of early industrialization (as in Manchukuo, the Japanese puppet state in Manchuria from 1931 to 1945, and the Soviet impact in the 1950s), the southern areas could jump-start economic growth by opening up to the world economy, with the paradigmatic case of Guangdong. Some provinces identify as "models" of transition, such as in the former Jiangnan region, Zhejiang as the model of a private-enterprise economy, and Southern Jiangsu as the model of collective township and village enterprises in the 1990s.

In the past, the differences between the economic regions translated into a lack of integration of the internal market, even including rampant local protectionism. Further development in the future and integration into the global economy will lead toward an integrated national economy. However, this will imply even stronger economic diversification, as the example of other large-scale economies, especially that of the United States, shows. Interregional migration into the most productive regions may help produce a convergence of incomes.

**SEE ALSO** *Economic Reform since 1978; Poverty; Rural Development since 1978; Urban China.*

**BIBLIOGRAPHY**

Cartier, Carolyn. Origins and Evolution of a Geographic Idea: The Macroregion in China. *Modern China* 28, 1 (2002): 79–142.

Tregear, T. R. *A Geography of China*. New York: Aldine Transaction, 2008.

Wan, Guanghua, ed. *Inequality and Growth in Modern China*. Oxford and New York: Oxford University Press, 2008.

***Carsten Herrmann-Pillath***

## GREAT WESTERN DEVELOPMENT SCHEME

In discussions on the development strategy for western China, the Chinese leadership, as well as provincial leaders, often refer to Deng Xiaoping's 1988 statement on the "two macro-situations." Deng predicted that the coastal region's accelerated opening to the outside world would lead to economic growth that, in turn, would facilitate the development of the interior. He asked the interior provinces to support this "macro-situation." He promised that after a period of time the central government would ask the coastal region to support the development of the interior, the so-called second "macro-situation."

The division of China into eastern, central, and western regions was defined at the fourth plenary session of the Sixth National People's Congress in April 1986 when it approved the Seventh Five-Year Plan. Western China includes the provinces of Shaanxi, Gansu, Qinghai, Sichuan, Guizhou, and Yunnan, and the autonomous regions of Tibet, Ningxia, and Xinjiang. The Chongqing municipality, established in 1997, also falls within western China.

### INITIATIVES FROM JIANG ZEMIN AND ZHU RONGJI

Beginning in 1999, President Jiang Zemin and other Chinese leaders clearly made the development of the western region a priority. In June 1999, Jiang Zemin spoke at a forum on the reform of state-owned enterprises (SOEs) and the development of the five northwestern provinces. Jiang stressed that improving the economic conditions in western China was a development strategy related to both the macro-situation and the maintenance of the long-term stability and good governance of the Communist Party and the nation. This development not only had important economic implications, but significant political and social implications as well. In terms of support from the central government, Jiang pledged: (1) priority to infrastructural development projects in the west; (2) support for technological innovations and adjustments in product structure; (3) stronger assistance in increasing capital inputs and reducing debts for the region's SOEs (as part of the arrangements both for the unemployed and in the establishment of a social security system); and (4) enhancement in fiscal transfer payments for the central and western regions.

Premier Zhu Rongji was heavily involved in the planning of the development of the west. Zhu spelled out his priorities as follows: (1) acceleration of infrastructural development, especially projects related to transport links with the coastal areas and the development of water resources; (2) the strengthening of environmental protection; (3) adjustments in the industrial structure; (4) promotion of education, as well as science and technology; and (5) the stepping up of the process of reform and opening up to the outside world, as well as the incorporation of new laws and regulations related to China's entry into the World Trade Organization. Regarding adjustments in the industrial structure, Zhu encouraged industries with comparative advantages and economic activities reflecting regional characteristics. In agriculture, emphasis was placed on products with regional characteristics, water-saving agriculture, and ecological agriculture. In terms of industries, priority was given to the rational exploitation of mineral resources and the development of high-tech and innovative industries. Zhu also highlighted tourism as a growth point in service industries.

Zhu Rongji's priorities and instructions gradually evolved into a grand development strategy for western China. An Office for the Development of the West was established in 2000 within the State Council to oversee the various development programs. The office is thought to have considerable influence over resource allocation through its assessments of development projects sent to the State Council by the western provincial units. The provincial units secure financial support from the central government mainly through appropriations for projects, including infrastructural projects and those for poverty alleviation. The Office for the Development of the West is also responsible for coordination among various central ministries involved in development issues, including the National Development and Reform Commission and the ministries of construction, railways, communications, agriculture, water resources, and so forth.

### POLICIES OF HU JINTAO AND WEN JIABAO

Hu Jintao and Wen Jiabao, who succeeded Jiang and Zhu, respectively, in the early 2000s, continued to support the development of western China. The new leaders were in a better position to do so because the central government had more resources at its disposal by that time, due to China's impressive economic growth. They were also much more concerned about the widening development gap between the coastal and interior provinces; their approach to the development of western China was thus more related to poverty alleviation and the reduction of the sharpening social contradictions. For example, limited funding from the central government (thirty yuan per head in 2006) helped establish a rural cooperative medical insurance system in the west.

Concerning employment, slightly less than half of the labor force is engaged in primary industries. Obviously there is room for manufacturing and construction industries to absorb more surplus labor from the rural and pastoral areas. Heavy industries have been developing considerably faster than light industries. Since economic development and industrial expansion in western China have been heavily dependent on project funding from the central government, heavy industries have been given priority. In terms of the generation of employment opportunities, however, the contribution by heavy industries has been more limited. The slow growth of light industries reflects a general lack of entrepreneurship, and a shortage of employment opportunities in urban areas has reduced the attraction of education as a channel of upward social mobility.

### ENTREPRENEURSHIP, INFRASTRUCTURE, AND INVESTMENT

The predominance of the state sector and the heavy emphasis on infrastructural projects partly explains the lack of entrepreneurship. It is significant that many provincial authorities in western China encourage township and village enterprises (TVEs) to raise rural incomes, yet have no major plans to promote the private sector, which is usually considered to have the greatest potential for economic growth at this stage. TVEs lack funding for development, and the banking system has been slow in responding to their needs. In fact, there is an acute shortage of banking expertise, grassroots cadres, and technicians to support the development of small and medium-sized private enterprises. In contrast to the coastal provinces, western China's rural incomes remain low, and capital accumulation at the family level is insignificant. Those with initiative tend to move to the coastal region in search of opportunities.

More encouraging has been the development of the road and railway networks. Such improvements facilitate the flow of goods and services between the urban centers and rural communities, which in turn will encourage the development of commerce and service industries.

Provincial authorities in western China understand that they must make great efforts to attract investment from the coastal provinces. The inflow of investment will help to retain talented individuals, increase urban employment, and make individual investment in education more attractive. Another important area of development is the establishment of cooperative relationships with leading universities and research institutes in China, enlisting their services both to improve the technological level of enterprises and to develop new products. As in many cases in China, local leadership has a substantial impact on economic development.

According to Chinese official standards, the poverty rate in western China in the 2004–2005 period was 9 percent in rural areas and 13.5 percent in urban areas. Using the international standard of one U.S. dollar per day, the respective poverty rates would be 16.3 percent and 4.1 percent. Obviously, much has yet to be done. The Chinese leadership acknowledges that in the near future the gap between the coastal and interior provinces will continue to widen; the central government can only aim to reduce the rate of widening.

**SEE ALSO** *Minority Nationalities: Overview.*

**BIBLIOGRAPHY**

Gao Zhaoping, Liu Zhong, and Chen Xiaoxue, eds. *Zhongguo xibu dakaifa zhanlue yanjiu* [Study of the grand development strategy of western China]. Xining: Qinghai Renmin Chubanshe, 2000.

Nianjian (*Zhongguo Xibu Ge Sheng*) [Yearbook (various western provinces in China)]. Beijing: Fangzhi Chubanshe and other publishers, various years.

Tongji Nianjian (*Zhongguo Xibu Ge Sheng*) [Statistical yearbook (various western provinces in China)]. Beijing: China Statistical Press, various years.

Yeung Yueman (Y. M. Yeung), and Shen Jianfa, eds. *Developing China's West: A Critical Path to Balanced National Development.* Hong Kong: Chinese University Press, 2004.

Zheng Yushuo (Joseph Y. S. Cheng), "Qinghai's Economic Development Strategy." *Issues and Studies* 39, 2 (2003): 189–218.

*Joseph Y. S. Cheng (Zheng Yushuo)*

## UNDP HUMAN DEVELOPMENT REPORT ON CHINA, 2005

Human Development Reports published by the United Nations Development Programme (UNDP) use the human development index, a weighted index of three measures—life expectancy, educational levels, and per capita gross domestic product—to evaluate human development in different countries. Reports on China written by foreign experts appeared in 1997, 1999, and 2002. The report of 2005 was compiled by a team of Chinese experts, a fact that reflects China's increasing openness to the outside world and willingness to participate in international discussion of problems of economic and human development.

The report acknowledges China's remarkable economic and social achievements since it began economic reforms in the late 1970s. In the 26 years to 2005, gross domestic product grew by an average of 9.4 percent per annum, and the number of people in absolute poverty in the rural areas dropped from 250 million to 26.1 million. China's international ranking on the human development index climbed from 101st in 1991 to 85th in 2003. China now resembles a medium-income country rather than a developing county in terms of life expectancy, primary-school enrollment, and adult literacy.

Although the lives of almost all Chinese have greatly improved over the past thirty years, the report shows that the benefits have been unevenly distributed. There are serious, even worsening, gaps between urban and rural areas, across regions, between the sexes, and among different population groups in terms of income, wealth, education, and health. China now ranks 90th among 131 countries in terms of income equality, the average income of the highest earning decile group being 11 times that of the lowest income decile group. Nationally, life expectancy is 71.4 years, varying from 79.05 in Shanghai to 66.37 in Yunnan province. Urban life expectancy is 75.21; in the rural areas it is 69.55. Urban infant mortality is 14 per thousand, compared with 34 per thousand in the rural areas. Illiteracy is more than 3 times higher in the rural areas than in the urban areas. Illiterate and semiliterate women outnumber men by 2.6 to 1.

The historical, cultural, and geographical roots of these inequities are traced in the report to restrictions on labor mobility; the long-established privileged entitlements of urban residents in health, education, and social security; government spending patterns favoring the cities; and the rapid development of the coastal provinces since the 1980s.

The Chinese government is committed to achieving greater equity through development by building a society of common modest prosperity (*xiaokang shehui*). *Xiaokang* policies have included poverty reduction, special developmental aid for the western regions, reduction of the agricultural tax burden, and a guarantee of minimum social security for the urban poor. However, the report's authors show that much remains to be done. They identify the weak redistributive role of taxation in China as a special problem. The report's ten recommendations for further action include reform of the fiscal system to achieve equitable distribution; unification of the labor market (i.e. removal of restrictions on labor mobility); improvements to public education, healthcare and social security; and greater rule of law and transparency.

The report provides an excellent overview of China's impressive economic progress and its growing economic and social inequalities. It details the Chinese government's effort to address these inequalities, but says nothing directly on the prospect for success. The recommendations with which the report concludes perhaps indicate a belief that government policy could go further. These recommendations focus on inequality across regions and between the rural and urban areas. Oddly, they are silent on gender inequality in education, income, and opportunity even though such inequality is comprehensively described in the report. Also somewhat neglected are weaknesses in governance and administration, in particular, the problem of corruption, although the concern with the rule of law and transparency can be taken as an oblique reference to these problems.

**BIBLIOGRAPHY**

Chan, Chak Kwan, King Lun Ngok, and David Phillips. *Social Policy in China: Development and Well-being.* Bristol, U.K.: Polity Press, 2008.

United Nations Development Programme and the China Development Research Foundation. *China Human Development Report, 2005: Development with Equity.* Beijing: China Translation and Publishing, 2005. http://www.undp.org.cn/downloads/nhdr2005/NHDR2005_complete.pdf (Rates for infant mortality in this report are mistakenly given as percentages; it is clear that the figures given are in fact mortality rates per thousand.)

***Delia Davin***

# ECONOMIC REFORM SINCE 1978

*This entry contains the following:*

## OVERVIEW

Reforms (*tizhi gaige*) have become a permanent feature of Chinese economic policies, with the thirtieth anniversary of their 1978 launch celebrated in 2008. In the first stages, *reform* referred to institutional and organizational changes to the extant Maoist command economy. By 2008 reforms were taking place mainly under the auspices of the World Trade Organization (WTO) and as part of the global integration of the Chinese economy. Yet, a fundamental issue remains whether China is converging on a global institutional benchmark, or to what extent it will maintain unique institutional features over a longer period.

Chinese economic reforms represent a major example of a gradualist transition to a market economy, in contrast to the so-called shock therapy of the postsocialist economies. Upon closer examination, however, China also presents examples of sectoral shock treatments, such as the fiscal centralization measures adopted in 1994. Thus, China's reforms are a complex phenomenon, which can be dissected into sectoral and regional subprocesses with different speeds and scope. There was also no integrated master plan, especially in the first decade. In the 1990s, the conception of a socialist market economy obtained the status of a guidepost, confirming the fundamental fact of a transition from a planned economy to a market economy. China's entry into the WTO in 2001 completed this transition, though also in a gradual fashion because of the transitional periods. Thus, reforms are no longer systemic, but sectoral and regional.

### REFORMS AND STATE CAPACITY

A fundamental characteristic of Chinese economic reforms as compared to other countries is the fact that China's reforms have been closely enmeshed with processes of state building and the formation of workable institutions of government after the Maoist era. For example, the aforementioned fiscal centralization of 1994 took place against the background of a serious weakening of central government control of resource flows in the economy, even triggering widespread fears of a potential unravelling of national unity (see Figure 1). The fragmented nature of economic reforms is also a reflection of far-reaching changes in the role and structure of local governments. Further, the regional diversity of economic conditions and levels of development in China contributed to a corresponding diversity of regional and even local reform strategies. This, in turn, reinforces the lack of systemic unity in the national system. As a result, there is tension between the national legal framework and actual societal practice, which causes recurring international

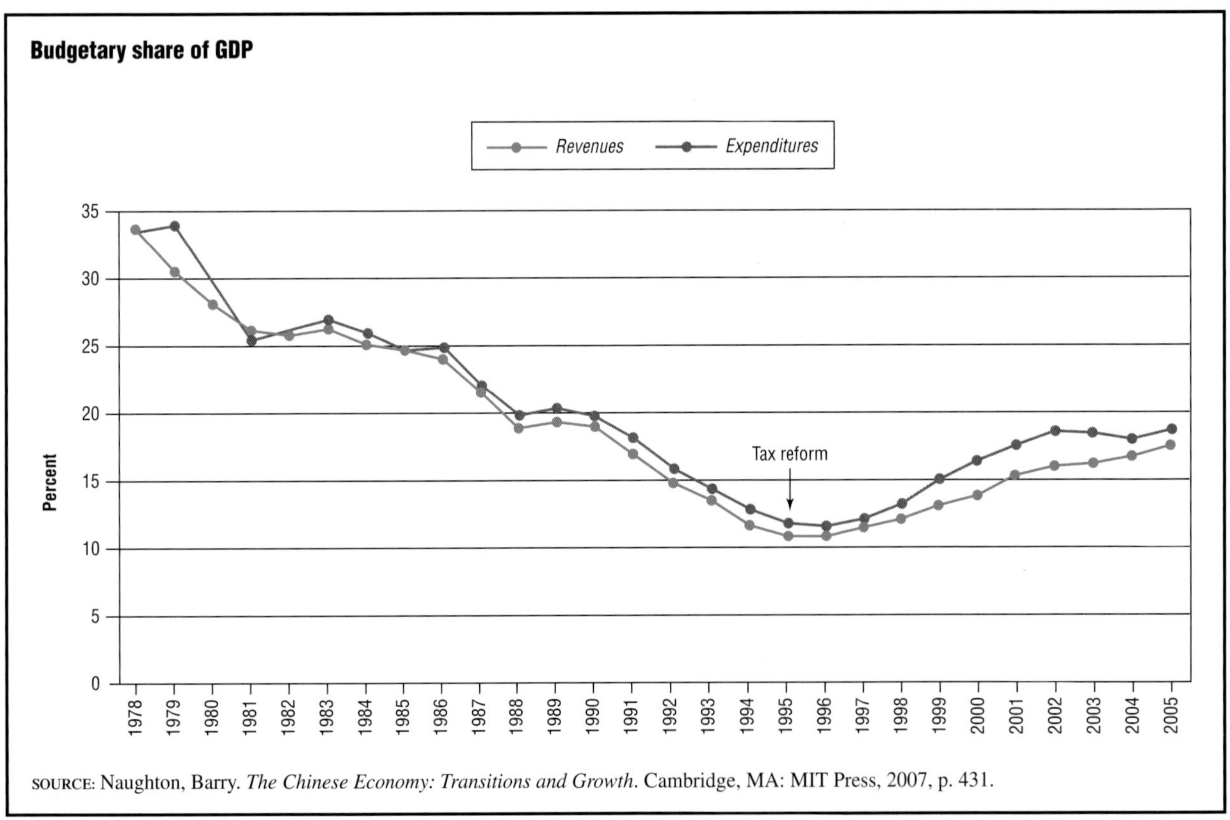


SOURCE: Naughton, Barry. *The Chinese Economy: Transitions and Growth.* Cambridge, MA: MIT Press, 2007, p. 431.

*Figure 1*

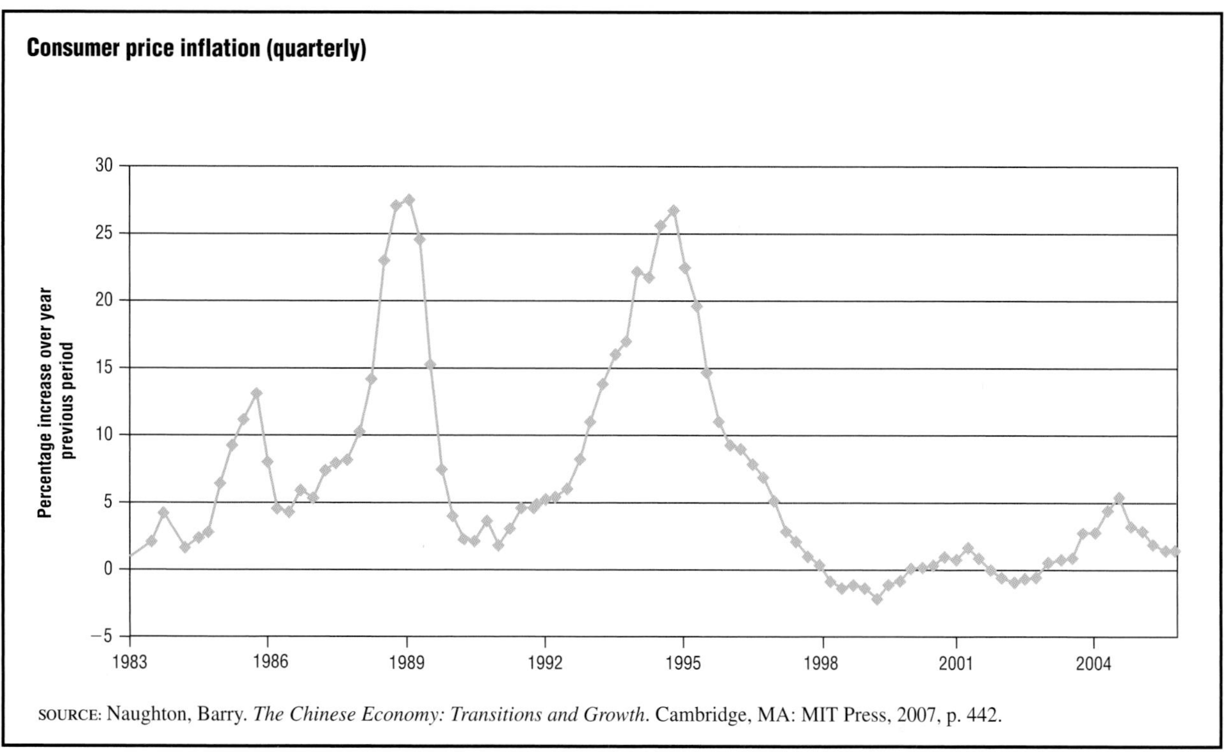


*Figure 2*

conflicts—for example, over the issue of intellectual property rights violations.

In terms of major stages of reform, there was a close correlation with macroeconomic cycles and events (Figure 2). Reforms were launched in agriculture with the transition to the responsibility system, which maintained the socialist ownership structure while expanding the autonomy of farmers. At the same time, however, an early attempt at external opening led to a loss of macroeconomic balance, which was restored by recentralization measures. As a consequence, reforms in urban industry only started in 1984, leading to a divergence of transitional paths in the rural and urban sectors, epitomized in the explosive growth of township and village enterprises (TVEs). Again, a lack of coordination with reforms in the monetary sector entailed a serious loss of macroeconomic control, triggering the inflationary crisis of 1988 and the Tiananmen incident in 1989. The resulting phase of recentralization mainly affected the rural economy, suppressing further growth in the TVE sector.

After 1992, Deng Xiaoping's "southern tour" triggered a resurgence in reform and opening-up, again contributing to an overheating of the economy, with an inflationary peak in 1995. The slowdown was mainly orchestrated via mandatory credit plans. At the same time, however, the gradual institution building enabled policymakers to increasingly rely on more sophisticated measures to steer the transition. After the mid-1990s, major steps were taken toward privatization of the collective sector and small state-owned enterprises (SOEs) while supporting the modernization of the entire SOE sector by gradually developing capital markets and modern systems of corporate governance. Basically, however, the reforms did not challenge one fundamental feature of the socialist system: the dominant role of state ownership, in particular of land, of essential resources, and in key sectors and enterprises. This fact is one of the main reasons why the status of China as a market economy is under dispute in international economic diplomacy.

## POLITICAL ECONOMY OF REFORMS

Given the fragmented nature of the Chinese political system, the forces driving reform relate to complex patterns of interest, in particular those of the central and local political elites. To a large extent, reforms can be also interpreted as a strengthening of central power against lower-level governments, thus eliminating intermediate levels of power in society. Early rural reforms were a prime example of this, breaking up the increasing closure of rural communities under Maoism. Precisely because of the gradual nature of the reforms, over longer periods strong incentives emerged for party and government cadres to take entrepreneurial action on the markets, as in the case of the double-track

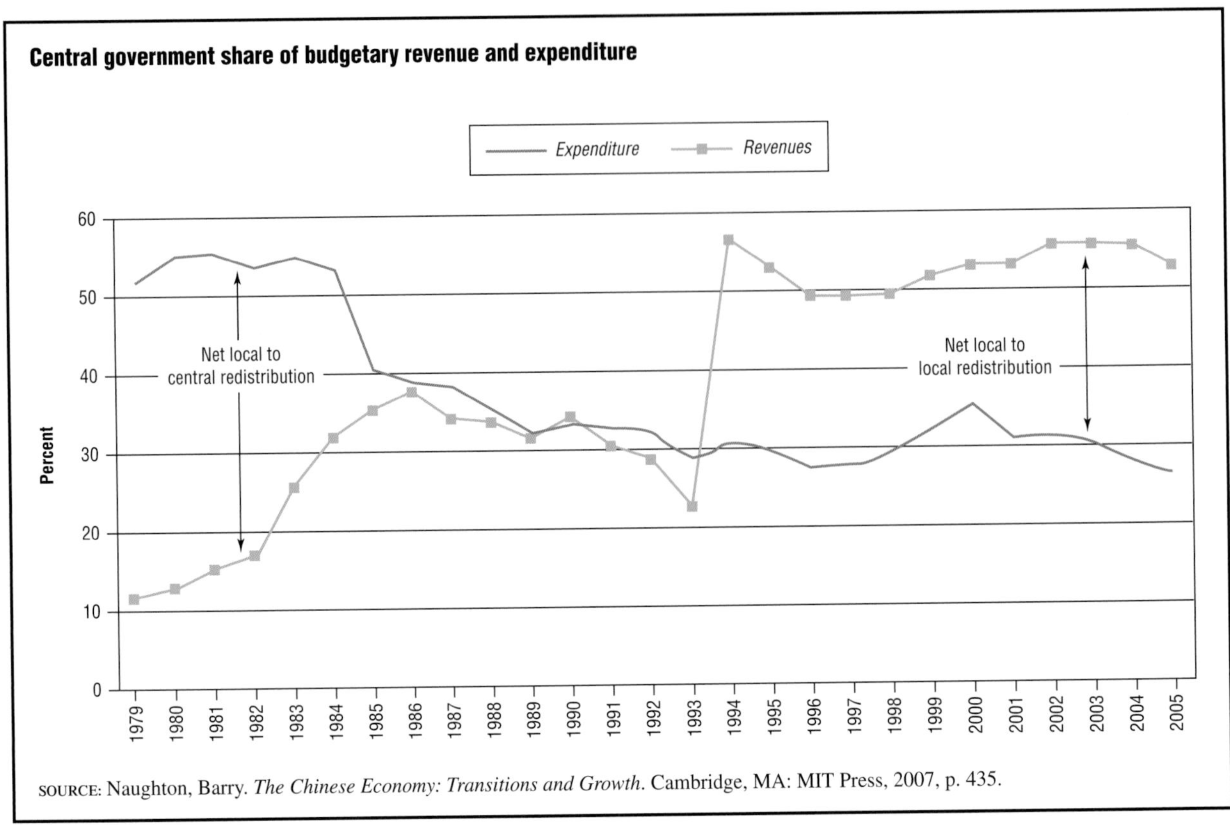


SOURCE: Naughton, Barry. *The Chinese Economy: Transitions and Growth*. Cambridge, MA: MIT Press, 2007, p. 435.

*Figure 3*

pricing system. The fiscal recentralization of 1994 resulted in a lopsided distribution of revenue control and expenditure responsibilities, tightening the budgetary constraints for local governments, which still bear a large share of expenditures (see Figure 3). As a result, strong incentives emerged to privatize loss-making collectives and small SOEs. Thus, understanding economic reforms presupposes an analysis of strategic issues of intrabureaucratic conflict.

This perspective can be broadened to include the larger society. Farmers certainly adopted an active role in the rapid spread of the responsibility system after 1978. At the same time, they expressed preferences to maintain the collective land ownership in the 1990s, while facing a cold expropriation of collective rights through transfers of land use into industrial and service sectors, especially in suburban rural settings. The slow speed of SOE reforms also reflects the interests of the urban workers and pensioners as stakeholders in the related job security and social safety net. Thus, in spite of being elite-driven, to a certain extent interest groups in society also had an impact on the course of reforms. In some areas, the government actively exploited such interests, as in the reforms of the public housing system in the late 1990s, when the SOE sector was largely relieved of the burden of maintaining public housing through a massive sellout to the urban population.

Therefore, economic reforms also contributed to social change in China, which can in turn contribute to political change in the long run. The main driver is the rise of an entrepreneurial class, including both private entrepreneurs and professional managers. The Communist Party actively follows up those social changes by co-opting the new elites into its power structure. This happens at all levels of government, with the local level being the most dynamic. As a result, China today may be described as a fragmented state corporatist system. This politico-economic structure is a major impediment to the emergence of a clear separation between the regulatory state and the market system.

**BIBLIOGRAPHY**

Chai, Joseph C. H., ed. *The Economic Development of Modern China*. Vol. 3: *Reforms and Opening Up since 1979*. Northampton, MA: Elgar, 2000.

Naughton, Barry. *The Chinese Economy: Transitions and Growth*. Cambridge, MA: MIT Press, 2007.

Wu Jinglian. *Understanding and Interpreting Chinese Economic Reform*. Singapore: Thomson.

***Carsten Herrmann-Pillath***

# FISCAL DECENTRALIZATION

Fiscal decentralization has been described, in both the Chinese official accounts and much of the Western-based literature, as the critical institutional reform that set the scene for the Chinese economic reform. The landmark development was the 1980 fiscal reform that allowed provincial governments a "residual claim" to the bulk of newly generated local revenues, and which the central government started with the aim of "tightening up, not letting go (revenues)" (Shirk 1993, p. 164). Fiscal revenues had become so dispersed in the aftermath of the Cultural Revolution (1966–1969) that by the late 1970s the central government had a hard time maintaining fiscal revenue at current levels. The idea of a multiyear fiscal contract thus appealed to the Ministry of Finance for the protection it rendered to central coffers. Local governments played an important part too, as several provinces experimented with new fiscal-sharing schemes during 1976 and 1977 in order to retain more local revenue. The 1980 fiscal reform was thus the product of the interaction of central and provincial considerations in a non-zero-sum game (Li 1998, p. 34).

## EXTENT: HOW DECENTRALIZED WAS THE CHINESE FISCAL SYSTEM AFTER 1980?

The post-1980 fiscal system was generally described as highly decentralized largely due to its diversified nature. Whilst there were a number of general features and patterns across provinces, how revenues and expenditures were shared between each province and the central government, and how much was allotted to each side, were decided in confidential "bilateral" bargaining and "fiscal contracts" concluded between the central government and each and every province individually. Whilst tax laws prescribed a variety of taxes, these central-provincial negotiations included an estimation of total fiscal revenue and expenditure in the province, and, in case of a surplus, designation of a ratio of distribution of the surplus between central and provincial coffers. Alternatively, if a deficit was envisaged, negotiation would focus on the amount of central subsidy to finance the deficit (Wong et al. 1995, chap. 3).

The exact degree of decentralization is, however, difficult to ascertain given the complexity of fiscal flows across government levels and the lack of transparency as to how spending decisions are made. A customary method to define fiscal decentralization is through some measurement of the share of local revenue and/or expenditures. However, the actual central-local distribution of revenues is often unavailable, and revenue figures mostly employed in the economics literature refer largely to revenues collected by central or local governments (see Wong et al. 1995, pp. 92–93, for contracted and earmarked transfers, by province, 1985–1990). Because local governments were charged with the job of revenue collection for the central government until 1994 (when a separate national tax administration bureaucracy was for the first time established to collect central taxes), revenues (collected revenue) had always been, by definition, highly decentralized. Indeed, from this perspective revenues became less decentralized after the 1980 reform: subnational revenue share was 83 percent in 1979 and 60 percent in 1992 (for consistency, all revenue and expenditure figures in the entry are drawn from Chinese official sources). This conclusion is, however, misleading, because local revenue so defined also includes upward remittances to the central government.

Local expenditure statistics include spending financed by locally retained revenue (locally collected revenue minus remittances to the central government) and incoming central transfers; these are thus arguably a better indicator of the resources at local disposal, and of fiscal decentralization, than local revenue (collected) figures. Between 1979 and 1992, the share of local expenditure rose to 59 percent from 49 percent, suggesting increased dispersal of fiscal resources after the 1980 fiscal reform.

In 1994 the fiscal system had further major surgery. Province-specific contracts were scrapped and a rule-based tax-assignment system uniform to all provinces was put in place, with a new national tax administration to collect central revenue. Instead of sharing total revenue, the new system designated each tax category to either the central or provincial coffers, or to both, with each sharing a preset percentage of the tax, uniform across all provinces. For instance, tax/revenue items designated exclusively to central coffers include customs duties, value-added taxes on imports, excise tax, consumption tax, enterprise income tax, and profit remittances of central enterprises and banks; local revenue items include business tax, stamp tax, real-estate taxes, vehicle-utilization taxes, inheritance and gift taxes, agricultural and animal-husbandry tax, slaughter tax, personal income tax, enterprise income tax and profit remittances of local enterprises, state land-sales revenues, capital-gains tax on land, contract tax, and so forth. Value-added tax and securities-trading tax are shared taxes, with the central government getting 75 percent of value-added tax revenues and 50 percent of the securities-trading tax. Personal income tax and enterprise income tax also became shared taxes from 2002 according to a transitional arrangement.

More revenue was consequently centralized: The share of central revenue surged to 55 percent in 1994 from 33 percent a year earlier. In the meantime, the decentralization of expenditure continued. By 2007, subnational spending accounted for three-quarters of total government expenditure. The widening gap between local revenue and spending is filled by central transfer payments, which in 2007 financed nearly half of local spending. A question thus arises: To what extent do the transfers enhance central influence over local spending decisions? More research on the transfers system, central-local negotiations, and decision making on local expenditures is needed.

### SIGNIFICANCE: WAS FISCAL DECENTRALIZATION CONDUCIVE TO ECONOMIC GROWTH?

The literature gives a mixed answer by focusing on different aspects of the question. The "fiscal federalism" literature argues that fiscal decentralization contributed to economic growth through territorial competition. Local officials were motivated to develop the local tax base since they were allowed a residual claim to the collected revenues. Akin to the property rights arguments, the fiscal federalism discourse asserts that subnational governments had operated with hardened budget constraints after the 1980 fiscal reform, and as a result became self-made business entrepreneurs and market reformers (Jin Hehui et al. 2005).

Others disagreed, stressing the lack of evidence of "hardened budgets" (e.g., the proliferation of soft bank loans), the rent-seeking and predatory behavior of many local governments, and continuous economic growth after the recentralizing tax-assignment reform in 1994. In other words, the fiscal federalism arguments cannot stand because their grounds are empirically invalid, incomplete, and irrelevant. More diverse explanations—for instance, the competition between central factions and the central-local linkage mechanisms synchronizing central and local incentives—are more plausible (Sinha 2005; Cai and Treisman 2006).

These two positions are *not* mutually exclusive on closer examination, however. The argument for the motivational effects of the post-1980 fiscal reforms does not preclude predatory government behaviors under some circumstances. Economic growth as an end result is contingent upon a wide range of factors, of which the behavior of local governments is only one. But where local governments are largely predatory, the local economy seldom prospers. The role of fiscal decentralization, and local government actions, in local and national economic development is a complex one. Problems in understanding arise when nuances are dismissed in the interest of a simplified picture. A credible short answer to the question posed above is: yes, but local governments do not act alone, and "conducive to" should not be conflated with "cause."

#### BIBLIOGRAPHY

Cai Hongbin and Daniel Treisman. Did Government Decentralization Cause China's Economic Miracle? *World Politics* 58 (2006): 505–535.

Jin Hehui, Qian Yingyi, and Barry R. Weingast. Regional Decentralization and Fiscal Incentives: Federalism, Chinese Style. *Journal of Public Economics* 89 (2005): 1719–1742.

Li, Linda Chelan. *Centre and Provinces: China, 1978–1993: Power as Non-Zero-Sum*. Oxford: Clarendon, 1998.

Shirk, Susan L. *The Political Logic of Economic Reform in China*. Berkeley: University of California Press, 1993.

Sinha, Aseema. Political Foundations of Market-Enhancing Federalism: Theoretical Lessons from India and China. *Comparative Politics* 37, 3 (2005): 337–356.

Wong, Christine P. W., Christopher Heady, and Wing T. Woo. *Fiscal Management and Economic Reform in the People's Republic of China*. Hong Kong: Oxford University Press, 1995.

***Linda Chelan (Li Zhilan) Li***

## COMMISSION FOR THE REFORM OF THE ECONOMIC SYSTEM

The Commission for the Reform of the Economic System was set up in May 1982 after the Standing Committee of the Fifth National People's Congress approved a State Council proposal on administrative restructuring at its twenty-third meeting on May 4, 1982. The Commission's main tasks were to design the overall plan for reforming China's economic system and to research, prepare for, and provide guidance on the reform efforts.

Premier Zhao Ziyang was the founding chairman of the commission, and his successors include Li Tieying (Politburo member from 1987 to 2002 and state councilor from 1988 to 1998), Li Peng (State Council premier from 1987 to 1998), and Chen Jinhua (chairman of the State Planning Commission from 1993 to 1998). The commission was dissolved in March 1998 after the Ninth National People's Congress approved a State Council proposal on administrative restructuring at its first session. In its place, the State Council Office for the Reform of the Economic System was set up to provide top leadership with relevant research and policy recommendations on reform and opening up.

### ROLE IN ECONOMIC REFORMS

During its sixteen years of existence, the commission played a pivotal role in promoting economic reforms in China. First, under the leadership of Zhao Ziyang, the commission prepared documents for the Twelfth National Congress of the Chinese Communist Party (held in September 1982), which officially ushered in the era of systematic reforms of the economic system in China. Second, the commission assisted in China's transition from agricultural reform to urban reform in 1984 and provided documents for the Third Plenum of the Twelfth Central

Committee (held in October 1984), which adopted a resolution on reforming China's economic system. Third, under the leadership of Li Peng, the commission focused on enterprise reforms in the late 1980s. Finally, in the aftermath of Deng Xiaoping's southern tour of early 1992 and the Fourteenth National Congress of the Communist Party (held in October 1992), the commission was retained in the State Council reshuffle of March 1993 to facilitate the establishment of a market-oriented economy in China. Before 1993 the commission focused on policy recommendations. After 1993 the commission proposed economic legislation.

### WORK STYLE

The commission's work style was typical of the Communist Party's decision-making process, in which local experiments precede national implementations. For comprehensive urban reforms, in February 1983 the commission selected Chongqing as the first experimental site. Chongqing had its own economic planning at the provincial level separate from its parent province, Sichuan Province. The experiment was later extended to Wuhan (capital of Hubei Province), Shenyang (capital of Liaoning Province), Dalian (a coastal city in Liaoning Province), Harbin (capital of Heilongjiang Province), Xi'an (capital of Shaanxi Province), and Guangzhou (formerly known as Canton, capital of Guangdong Province). In April 1984 the commission held a meeting on urban reforms in Changzhou, Jiangsu Province, synthesizing the experiences of these experiments. Subsequently, the commission expanded the experiment to other cities in China.

The commission simultaneously promoted a new administrative system in which municipalities assume leadership roles over counties. From March 1983 this new system was experimentally introduced in some regions. By the end of 1984, 87 percent of all provinces (and provincial-level municipalities) had implemented this system, with the result that 129 municipalities began supervising 571 counties.

To open up to the outside world, the Chinese leadership decided in the late 1970s to set up four special economic zones (Shenzhen, Zhuhai, and Shantou in Guangdong Province; and Xiamen [Amoy] in Fujian Province). Here the commission did not play any role, but in 1984 it was instrumental in opening up Hainan Island and fourteen coastal cities (Dalian, Qinhuangdao, Tianjin, Yantai, Qingdao, Lianyungang, Nantong, Shanghai, Ningbo, Wenzhou, Fuzhou, Guangzhou, Zhanjiang, and Beihai) to foreign investment.

### DECLINING INFLUENCE

The commission played an important role in the reform process, especially in its early period from 1982 to 1987, when Zhao Ziyang was its chairman. Top leaders such as Deng Xiaoping and Zhao Ziyang provided general ideas and directions, and the commission conducted research, came up with specific plans, selected experimental sites, and then made recommendations based on these experiments for national reform policies and legislation.

The commission's importance declined somewhat in later years. While he was chairman of the commission, Zhao Ziyang was State Council premier and a standing member of the Politburo. Li Tieying was only a member of the Politburo during his tenure (from April 1987 to April 1988 and from March 1993 to March 1998). Li Peng too was premier and a standing member of the Politburo, but his tenure as chairman of the commission was brief, from April 1988 to August 1990. Chen Jinhua became a member of the Communist Party's central committee only five months before he stepped down as the commission's chairman in March 1993.

### DISSOLUTION

The commission was dissolved in March 1998 for two reasons. Politically, with Deng Xiaoping's passing in February 1997, China moved into the Jiang Zemin era. The new leadership was not keen on retaining an institution established by Deng Xiaoping and Zhao Ziyang. Administratively, China's reforms became much more complicated. It was no longer feasible to use a single institution to manage the entire reform process.

#### BIBLIOGRAPHY

*Zhongguo Gongchandang zuzhishi ziliao* [Materials on the organizational history of the Chinese Communist Party]. 2 vols. Beijing: Zhonggong Dangshi Chubanshe, 2000. See especially the appendix, October 1949 to September 1997.

***Zhiyue Bo***

## DUAL-TRACK PRICING

Dual-track pricing was a central institutional form of economic reform in China between 1978 and 1993, after which the scope of directive allocation of commodities and goods declined precipitously. This process has been dubbed "growing out of the plan." The system works in a straightforward fashion: Production units operating under material allocation plans were allowed to sell production beyond the assigned quota freely on the market, possibly under an additional regime of price controls that was relaxed simultaneously.

In principle, this system had already been applied as part of the early agricultural reforms, when farmers were allowed to enter into new production activities and free-market relations provided that the still-existing communes fulfilled production quotas for the main commodities, such as grain and cotton. The same principle was later extended to almost all other branches of industry, leading to an organizational dualism in the economy that even affected internal enterprise organization during the transition: A state-owned enterprise (SOE) would have departments that dealt with plan assignments and administrative relations, and at the same time would start to build departments such as marketing and procurement.

The crucial condition for making dual-track pricing workable was the existence of slack in the Chinese economy; that is, the opportunity to put hidden and suppressed production capacity into use rapidly. Further, the emerging markets should not manifest monopolistic structures. Both would have been the result if dual-track pricing had been introduced into a Soviet-style economic system, which operated with high stress on capacity utilization and a tightly concentrated industrial structure. In China, the fragmented and dispersed industrial system and the existence of idle capacities allowed for a rapid expansion of market production with a strong trend toward declining prices, given the increasing intensity of competition and the build-up of additional capacities lured into the market by an initially larger gap between market prices and planned prices. The typical transitional pattern was therefore the opening up of a positive gap between market prices and planned prices in the first stage, triggering rapid market entry by additional, mostly idle, capacities, thus leading to a fall in market prices due to a rapid growth of supply. In the end, the initial gap might even turn negative, giving strong incentives to the incumbents of the planned system to abolish the system altogether, because of the increasing fiscal burden once planned production started to require subsidies in order to survive under market conditions.

Another aspect of this ideal-typical pattern, however, was the rapid growth of corruption and serious misdirection of entrepreneurial activities. As long as a positive gap between market and planned prices existed, huge profits could be reaped by diverting planned allocations into the market. Once market prices became operative, allocating the lower-priced planned allocations was tantamount to the creation of huge rents for those claiming rights to the allocations. This effect also exerted a tremendous influence on interregional and intersectoral relations. Typically, the scope of planning was only slowly decreasing for some core commodities, such as cotton. If the scope of the market increased more rapidly in the downstream industries, value added was redistributed to their benefit. Since commodity production was also concentrated in particular regions, the dual-track system contributed to the sharpening of regional imbalances. The result was several infamous "wool wars," "silk wars," and so forth, where regional authorities tried to establish control over rents by setting up regional downstream industries and even blocking interregional trade. At the same time in these cases, the channelling of scarce commodities into the market was a highly profitable activity.

In sum, dual-track pricing can be seen as a positive contribution to the Chinese transition. Even though the massively dysfunctional phenomena related to rent creation and extraction can be seen as a negative outcome, from the viewpoint of political economy the result was that many incumbents of the old system perceived incentives to put markets into action. Another important positive contribution was the rapid increase in the efficiency of allocation. This occurred because, given the slack in the economy, market prices started to guide production decisions at the margin, which means that statically, efficient allocations would result. Planned prices only affect inframarginal decisions, leading to the distribution of rents. Dynamically, there are negative effects on investment decisions aimed at capturing rents, but positive ones in triggering additional market entries. Thus, given that the system was phased out after a little more than a decade, a positive assessment prevails at the end of the day.

**BIBLIOGRAPHY**

Byrd, William. *The Market Mechanism and Economic Reforms in China.* Armonk, NY: Sharpe, 1991.

Naughton, Barry. *Growing Out of the Plan: Chinese Economic Reform, 1978–1993.* New York: Cambridge University Press, 1955.

Naughton, Barry. Market Transition: Strategy and Process, and Growth and Structural Change. In *The Chinese Economy: Transitions and Growth*, 85–112, 139–160. Cambridge, MA: MIT Press, 2007.

***Carsten Herrmann-Pillath***

## GRADUALISM

The extraordinary changes in China's economic structures, institutions, and policies since 1980 have occurred with startling rapidity by historical standards. Yet compared with the "big bang" approach to economic transition adopted in many European former communist countries, China's reforms have been gradual. The existing institutional organization of the economy was left in place and only gradually amended by replacing old institutions or mutating their functions. Prices were only gradually liberalized, and privatization was delayed, to be implemented only later by degrees. Financial liberalization was held back, then carried out slowly, and indeed is far from complete as of 2008. The political leaders in the early stages of reform—especially Premier and (from 1987 to 1989) Party Secretary Zhao Ziyang and, behind him, Deng Xiaoping—succeeded in moving economic activity out of the sphere of central planning and into the sphere of the market step by step. Throughout this process, employment was maintained, incomes raised, growth encouraged, and macroeconomic stability largely achieved. In stark contrast to the economic implosions that occurred in the former Soviet Union and much of Eastern Europe, economic and human development advanced markedly, which provided an enabling environment for continuing reform.

Barry Naughton (1995) captured China's approach by calling it "growing out of the plan." In essence, the approach was that the state continued to administer a planned economy slackly, while permitting a market economy to expand side by side with it and eventually to eclipse it. The state sharply reduced its investment rate, shifted attention from heavy industry to consumer goods and trade and services. It also began a massive program of urban-housing construction to ameliorate the cramped, degraded housing conditions left by decades of neglect. The result was a better-balanced economy, rapid improvements in living standards, and reduced pressure on the energy sector.

## AGRICULTURAL REFORM

A key element in the success of this approach was that the initial reform occurred in agriculture. Collective farms were almost entirely dismantled between 1979 and 1983, the land parceled out to individual families to work on a leasehold basis, and farm prices were substantially raised. Decollectivization changed the incentive structure in agriculture by making the household the residual claimant on income after tax payments and contracted sales at fixed prices to the collective. The improvement in incentives, along with large increases in fertilizer production, resulted in a remarkably sharp increase in the output of most major crops between 1979 and 1984. In addition, farmers poured resources into profitable nonstaple goods (such as poultry, fruits, and vegetables) and into rural industries. Township and village enterprises began to grow rapidly in employment and production. Up to this point, market liberalization had been minimal. Price changes in the planned economy were administered, not driven by market forces. Although a market, with flexible prices, was taking shape, it was only after 1985 that market liberalization was pursued in earnest.

## INDUSTRIAL REFORM

In industry, reform followed a dual-track approach. State-owned enterprises, after selling planned output to the state at low fixed prices, were allowed to sell above-plan output freely at market-determined prices. The state could thus realize high-priority objectives while providing incentives, at the margin, for market-oriented production. The dual-track system was inherently inefficient and predictably prone to corruption. Nonetheless, it promoted an entrepreneurial, market-oriented outlook on the part of enterprise managements and work forces, and improved resource efficiency at the margin. This system also ensured that a growing fraction of total output would be sold at flexible prices. From 1985, even producer-goods output above planned targets could be legally sold at market prices.

The growth of township and village enterprises and of output from foreign-invested firms and even private enterprises quickly eroded the monopoly of the state in the industrial sphere and subjected state enterprises to increasing competition. State-owned enterprises responded by forming links with nonstate enterprises to supply parts and materials and do subcontracting work, activity that further strengthened the market economy. State-enterprise management was also reformed in various ways, including shifting control from political cadres to economic managers, raising educational standards for management positions, and improving supervision controls. But privatization on any large scale was postponed.

## FOREIGN TRADE & INVESTMENT, FISCAL REFORM, CORPORATE GOVERNANCE, SOCIAL WELFARE

The gradualism of China's transition included its approach to foreign direct investment. Such investment was limited at first to a small number of special economic zones established in 1979 along the coast of South China. These special economic zones were supplemented by others over time, especially in 1984, when fourteen cities in eastern China, including Shanghai, were designated "open cities," with many of the privileges for attracting foreign direct investment in the special economic zones. Confining foreign direct investment initially to enclaves enabled China to gain experience with it and learn to manage it. The foreign investment flowing into these centers and the ancillary economic activity around it occurred largely outside the state plan and were important contributors to the erosion of the planned economy and the growth of the market economy.

China's reform took on new life after 1992, when Deng Xiaoping went to Shenzhen and expressed strong support for continued economic reform and experimentation. Under the vigorous leadership of Zhu Rongji, who played an important role even before becoming premier in 1998 (he retired in 2003), the dual-track system gave way to a unified market, the state sector was reduced in size, township and village enterprises and many small and medium state enterprises were privatized, and China moved more forcefully into the global economy by joining the World Trade Organization in 2001. The central government succeeded in recentralizing fiscal resources to some degree and, in response to burgeoning unemployment occasioned by reform of the state-owned enterprises, began constructing a safety net for the urban population, including

***An American fast food restaurant in downtown Beijing, March 14, 1999.*** *In the late 1970s, China began a slow process of transforming its centrally-planned economy to a market-based one. As China prospered in the 1990s, many Western corporations opened retail outlets in urban areas, capitalizing on an increasing number of citizens with growing incomes.* GOH CHAI HIN/AFP/GETTY IMAGES

unemployment insurance and antipoverty programs guaranteeing minimum livelihood and a restructured pension system. The attention of reformers turned also to establishing effective corporate governance for the newly reformed state enterprises and the newly privatized ones, reforming and vitalizing the banking and financial system, and establishing a suitable regulatory environment for a market economy.

## CONCLUSION: TRANSITION AS A LEARNING PROCESS; PROBLEMS OF GRADUALISM

Chinese leaders characterized their approach to transition as "crossing the river by groping for stones." This captures the sense of trial and error and learning by doing that marked China's reform. There are no reliable blueprints for transforming a planned economy into a mixed capitalist one, and the proliferation of different kinds of capitalism around the globe suggests that each country must find a particular mix of market and control/regulatory institutions suitable to its history and culture. Also, there is a strong link between the political and economic systems. The Communist Party maintaining political power was a crucial ingredient in the gradualist enterprise; a political revolution would have produced a very different economic transition.

While China has maintained strong growth and rising living standards throughout its transition, the period has also seen a proliferation of economic and social problems, including rising income inequality, a weak financial system, and environmental devastation on a large scale. Faced with these and other problems, the leadership has often chosen to maintain stability by promoting rapid growth rather than by addressing the problems themselves, until, that is, they become too large to ignore. The weak fiscal position of the central government relative to the provinces has also discouraged strong redistributive or other non-growth-oriented initiatives from the center (Wong 2008). It is unclear, however, whether gradualism per se is responsible for such problems.

**BIBLIOGRAPHY**

Hope, Nicholas C., Dennis Tao Yang, and Mu Yang Li. *How Far Across the River.* Stanford, CA: Stanford University Press, 2003.

McMillan, John. Avoid Hubris, and Other Lessons for Reformers. *Finance and Development*, September 2004: 34–37.

McMillan, John, and Barry Naughton. How to Reform a Planned Economy: Lessons from China. *Oxford Review of Economic Policy* 8, 1 (1992): 130–143.

Naughton, Barry. *Growing Out of the Plan: Chinese Economic Reform, 1978–1993.* New York: Cambridge University Press, 1995.

Naughton, Barry. *The Chinese Economy: Transitions and Growth.* Cambridge, MA: MIT Press, 2007.

Qian, Yingyi. How Reform Worked in China. In *In Search of Prosperity: Analytic Narratives on Economic Growth*, ed. Dani Rodrik, pp. 297–333. Princeton, NJ: Princeton University Press, 2003.

Sachs, Jeffrey, and Wing Thye Woo. Structural Factors in the Economic Reforms of China, Eastern Europe, and the Former Soviet Union. *Economic Policy* 9, 18 (1994): 101–145.

Wong, Christine. Can the Retreat from Equality Be Reversed? Assessing Fiscal Policies toward Redistribution from Deng Xiaoping to Wen Jiabao. In *Paying for Progress: Public Finance, Human Welfare, and Inequality in China*, ed. Vivienne Shue and Christine Wong. Oxford: Oxford University Press, 2008.

***Carl Riskin***

# EDUCATION, VOCATIONAL

**SEE** *Vocational Education.*

# EDUCATION

*This entry contains the following:*



## 1800–1949

Education played a crucially important role in China's political and cultural life from at least the Tang (618–907) and Song (960–1279) dynasties. During this time printing was developed, facilitating a growth in literacy, and a civil-service examination system that recruited candidates for the bureaucracy based on their knowledge of the Confucian classics was perfected. From this time on, there was a widespread consensus that Confucian moral education was essential to both public order and civilized life (Elman and Woodside 1994, p. 1).

## ELITE AND POPULAR EDUCATION IN THE NINETEENTH CENTURY

By the nineteenth century, however, education in China proceeded along two different paths, which generally did not intersect. Formal education was closely associated with preparation for the civil-service examinations, the curriculum for which progressively narrowed until in the nineteenth century it comprised memorizing designated classical texts by rote and writing formulaic essays (in contrast, early in the Ming dynasty [1368–1644], for example, the examinations tested prowess in calligraphy, mathematics, and penal law, as well as in the Confucian classics). Thus official schools (*guanxue*) at the prefectural and district levels were mainly places where examination candidates on government stipends registered.

Confucian academies (*shuyuan*), first founded during the Song dynasty and funded by officials and local wealthy patrons, had by the nineteenth century become semiofficial institutions promoting the state orthodoxy. In these academies, scholars practiced examination techniques, although some academies continued to provide a wider curriculum, thus continuing the legacy of earlier times, when they were more innovative. For example, the Gujing Qingshe Academy in Hangzhou (established in 1801) examined students in astronomy, mathematics, and geography, while the Gezhi Shixue Academy in Shaanxi Province (established in 1896) taught science, English, and mathematics. By the end of the nineteenth century, there were approximately 4,000 academies in an informal hierarchy that ranged from those located in county seats at the lower end to those established in the provincial capitals at the apex. The most famous tended to be those situated in cities and specialized in preparing students for the provincial and metropolitan civil-service examinations (Pepper 1996, p. 51).

At a more popular level, the traditional Chinese central government—despite occasional interest in promoting a wider network of schools at local levels to inculcate Confucian morality among the populace—more often than not left formal elementary education to local communities, clans, and families to manage. Community schools (*shexue*), for example, date from the fourteenth century and were originally designed to uphold orthodox Confucian values after a century of foreign rule (the Mongol Yuan dynasty [1279–1368]). Imperial edicts were issued at various times in the fifteenth and sixteenth centuries urging local communities to set up such schools. Many of them financially relied on local official support, and hence they were always vulnerable in the wake of personnel or budget changes.

A more genuine community school was the charity school (*yixue*), dating from the early eighteenth century and established specifically for children of the poor to receive instruction in basic literacy. Charity schools were also established in regions inhabited by non-Han Chinese peoples as part of the state's Confucian civilizing mission, a process referred to as *jiaohua* (cultural transformation). One of the most active provincial officials engaged in this activity was Chen Hongmou (1696–1771), the provincial treasurer of the southwestern province of Yunnan, who founded or revitalized nearly 700 charity schools during the 1730s, mainly in rural areas inhabited by the Miao people.

Traditional private elementary schools (*sishu*) might also be established by villages and individual families, and many of these schools (especially in remote rural regions) remained in operation right up until 1949. They were often set up in private homes or temple buildings, and a teacher would be paid (in kind or cash) to take on 5 to 20 pupils—all to be taught together irrespective of age. The buildings and premises of such traditional schools and academies constituted a useful foundation for future educational reform, since many were converted into modern schools from the turn of the twentieth century.

## EDUCATION FOR GIRLS

While most schools generally catered to boys (the civil-service examinations themselves were open only to males), this did not mean that girls (at least those from elite families) were not educated in traditional China, or that female education was considered superfluous. It was not uncommon for the daughters of elite or well-to-do families to be educated at home from the age of four or five and to receive instruction in the same Confucian texts as those of their brothers. At the age of ten their paths diverged, when girls were taught household skills (needlework, weaving), while boys received training in essay competition in preparation for the civil-service examinations (Hsiung 2005, pp. 186–193, 205–217). Sometimes special tutors (who might be male or female) were hired to teach girls in a separate family school. Educated (i.e., morally cultivated) daughters were seen as crucial for family harmony and order (which in turn guaranteed order in the wider public sphere), as well as for the correct future upbringing of children (especially sons).

Growing literacy among women during the eighteenth and nineteenth centuries is confirmed by the increasing number of didactic handbooks specially for girls and young women during the Qing dynasty (1644–1912), a tradition that dates back to as early as the second century CE. Further evidence from the middle and late nineteenth century indicates that there was a basic literacy rate (an ability to read several hundred characters) of 30 to 45 percent among men and 2 to 10 percent among women (Rawski 1979, p. 140).

## PRIVATE SCHOOLS

The term *private school*, in discussions of twentieth-century China, normally refers to schools called *sishu* (*si*, lit. "private"; *shu*, lit. "traditional style schools") that flourished during the first half of the twentieth century but were not included in China's modern school system (that is, a public school system constructed in 1904 by the Qing government on the basis of learning from that of the West and Japan). *Sishu* schools, mostly operated by single teachers in rural areas, provided instruction in basic literacy using traditional curricula and pedagogy. With the development of a public education system in the 1950s, this type of school disappeared.

The roots of *sishu* schools can be traced back to earlier centuries, well before the establishment of China's public education system in the early twentieth century. Imperial China had a widespread school system that included various types of private or collective community schools, such as clan schools (*zuxue*), family schools (*jiashu*), village schools (*cunshu*), charitable schools (*yishu*), and community schools (*shexue*). By 1904, when the first modern education system was established, all types of private and community schools were grouped into one category, *sishu*, in contrast to the numerous state-sponsored "public" schools modeled after the Western style.

Most *sishu* were located in rural areas, but a small number were urban. This type of school often took the form of a one-teacher classroom, in which the teacher gathered a varying number of students from the neighborhood, whose ages may have ranged from around five to teens. Unlike modern schools, which follow rigid schedules, instructional activities in *sishu* were conducted at convenient times for both teachers and students. Most *sishu* teachers were older literati who may have spent a lifetime studying or teaching Confucian classics. Until the schools vanished in the 1950s, their main function was to offer instruction in basic reading and writing skills. The primary schooling phase could sometimes last for ten years, during which time students memorized a set curriculum of Confucian texts, the meaning of which was explained by the teacher only when memorization was complete.

Beginning in the 1920s, the Nationalist government constantly launched a series of programs to reform *sishu* schools in order to "modernize" primary education. Initiatives included sending younger teachers who graduated from modern schools to *sishu*; rectifying old *sishu* teachers; adding special courses, such as civics education, drawing, and physical education, into *sishu* curricula; and replacing Confucian texts with government-issued textbooks. The government also tried to close some *sishu* that were seen as competing with the new modern elementary schools. Some *sishu* were also converted into modern schools. Based on a survey conducted in 1935 by the Ministry of Education, there were 85,291 *sishu* schools with 1,542,961 students in nineteen of twenty-four provinces and five special cities (which were directly subordinated to the central government, rather than the provincial government). About one-third of elementary schools nationwide were *sishu* schools, and one-eighth of all elementary students attended these schools.

*Sishu* schools were seen by some as a remnant of an outdated traditional system that would eventually become extinct. But more and more scholars believe that for the half century of their existence, *sishu* schools reflected the needs of the local society for education in the basic skills of literacy and knowledge of local life. This form of school also helped some young people receive early education and move on to the next stage of education in modern schools.

### BIBLIOGRAPHY

Borthwick, Sally. *Education and Social Change in China: The Beginnings of the Modern Era*. Stanford, CA: Hoover Institution Press, 1983.

Cong, Xiaoping. *Teachers' Schools and the Making of the Modern Chinese Nation-State, 1897–1937*. Vancouver: University of British Columbia Press, 2007.

Deng, Peng. *Private Education in Modern China*. Westport, CT: Praeger, 1997.

Jiaoyu Bu [Ministry of Education]. *Er shi si niandu quanguo sishu tongji* [National statistics on *sishu*-style schools]. Nanjing: Jiaoyu Bu print, 1935.

Liao, T'ai-chu'u. Rural Education in Transition: A Study of the Old-fashioned Chinese Schools [Szu Shu] in Shantung and Szechuan. *Yanjing Journal of Social Studies* 4, 2 (1949): 19–67.

Orb, Richard. Chili Academies and Other Schools in the Late Ch'ing: An Institutional Survey. In *Reform in Nineteenth-Century China,* eds. Paul A. Cohen and John E. Schrecker, 231–240. Cambridge, MA: East Asian Research Center, Harvard University, 1976.

Rawski, Evelyn Sakakida. *Education and Popular Literacy in Ch'ing China*. Ann Arbor: University of Michigan Press, 1979.

Thøgersen, Stig. *A County of Culture: Twentieth-century China Seen from the Village Schools of Zouping, Shandong*. Ann Arbor: University of Michigan Press, 2002.

Wu Ni and Hu Yan. *Zhongguo gudai sixue yu jindai sili xuexiao yanjiu* [A study of private schools in ancient and modern China]. Ji'nan, PRC: Shandong jiaoyu chubanshe, 1997.

**Xiaoping Cong**

## SELF-STRENGTHENING AND EDUCATIONAL CHANGE

Educational reform began in the wake of an increasing external threat from Western and Japanese imperialism from the 1840s on, and from growing internal unrest manifested in large-scale peasant rebellions among both the Han Chinese and ethnic minority peoples during the mid-nineteenth century. As part of the Self-strengthening movement both to reinforce the Confucian political order and equip the country with the means to ward off foreign threats during the second half of the nineteenth century, Qing government officials sanctioned the creation of a number of specialist training schools designed to train experts for government service (army and navy officers, engineers, translators, and interpreters). New schools that provided more of a liberal-arts education (such as St. John's College in Shanghai and Canton Christian College in Guangzhou, which opened in the 1880s) tended to be run by Western Protestant missionaries, who had begun opening schools (including those for girls) in the treaty ports after the Opium War of 1839–1842. These first modern official schools initially had little prestige or status, as the sons of the elite continued to focus their ambitions on the Confucian-based civil-service examinations.

As the threat of Western and Japanese imperialism grew during the 1890s and Chinese commentators began fearing by the late 1890s that the country faced imminent partition, Chinese provincial officials such as Sheng Xuanhuai (1844–1916) and Zhang Zhidong (1837–1909) began establishing official schools with a broader curriculum. The self-strengthening school that Zhang opened in the provincial capital of Hubei in 1893, for example, comprised four departments: Western languages, natural sciences, mathematics, and commercial affairs. Other Chinese officials and reformers—such as Li Duanfen in 1896, Kang Youwei in 1898, and Zhang Zhidong also in 1898—proposed creating a nationwide three-tiered system of modern schools (primary, middle, and higher) incorporating Western subjects in the curriculum. And they suggested that these schools be housed in appropriated traditional schools, Confucian academies, and Buddhist temples.

Proposals such as these to establish a wider network of official schools were not unprecedented. In the eleventh century, for example, the renowned scholar-official Fan Zhongyan (989–1052) had proposed the widespread establishment of government schools at the local level (with the specific aim of preparing examination candidates). And in the seventeenth century the outspoken critic of monarchical absolutism Huang Zongxi (1610–1695) suggested that temples be appropriated to house official schools (with the aim of training candidates for bureaucratic service).

***Students studying at Nanjing University, early 1900s.*** *Much of the higher education in China during the nineteenth century centered around passing civil service exams, tests based on a student's knowledge of Confucian teachings. However, pressured by the rising power of Japan and Western countries, Chinese school leaders began to reform the educational system, offering students more tangible fields of study, such as engineering and military leadership.* © CORBIS

What made the proposals of the 1890s different was the novel emphasis on the importance of educating the people as a whole at a time of perceived national crisis. It is no coincidence that during this period the first Chinese public school for girls was opened in 1898 by reformers and officials: the Chinese Girls' School in Shanghai. (Earlier, Western missionaries had begun to open a small number of schools for girls in the treaty ports from the mid-1840s on with the principal aim of training girls to serve as the future wives of Chinese pastors or as Bible women.) Also in 1898, the Imperial University of Beijing, China's first modern-style institution of higher education, formally opened—later, after the inauguration of the Chinese Republic in 1912, to become Peking University, the country's most prestigious institution of higher learning.

## NEW SCHOOL SYSTEMS IN THE EARLY TWENTIETH CENTURY

Proposals for educational change (including the abolition of the civil-service examinations, increasingly perceived as ill-suited for China's current needs) became more insistent after 1900, when the antiforeign Boxers' siege of foreign legations in Beijing prompted foreign intervention and occupation of the capital. The Qing court—humiliated by the sanctions (including payment of a huge indemnity) imposed by the foreign powers as punishment for its support of the Boxers and shocked by growing internal threats to its rule—sanctioned a program of reform after 1901. Reiterating suggestions first made in the 1890s and pointing to the examples of Western countries and Japan, officials and scholars increasingly linked the attainment of national unity, strength, and prosperity with the creation of a national school system producing a disciplined and hardworking populace. The Qing court also hoped that a school system would inculcate greater loyalty among its subjects. Scholar-gentry reformers preferred to highlight the contributions such a system would make in fostering a more general patriotism and divesting ordinary folk of their backward customs and superstitions, so graphically illustrated (in their view) by the beliefs and activities of the Boxers. In 1905 the government abolished the centuries-old civil-service examination system and created a new government institution—the Board of Education (after 1912, the Ministry of Education)—to oversee a modern system of primary, secondary, and higher schools incorporating a more diverse curriculum of Chinese and Western learning. In the words of one historian (Elman and Woodside 1994, p. 486), the process had begun to establish a vertically integrated system of education controlled at the center and designed for state building—a system that had been lacking in the past. Initially Qing officials were reluctant to permit public education for girls, but two years later in 1907 the government sanctioned the creation of primary and normal schools for girls.

With the formal establishment of a republic in 1912 following the overthrow of the Qing monarchy in the 1911 revolution, a new school system was inaugurated that was to remain in force until 1922. In place of the educational aims promulgated by the Qing government in 1905 (which included inculcation of unquestioning loyalty to the dynasty, reverence for Confucian orthodoxy, and respect for the military), the new system stressed the importance of training modern citizens to fulfill their duties to the nation while also fully enjoying their rights in society (Culp 2007, p. 1). It also prescribed four years of compulsory education (between the ages of 6 and 10), allowed coeducation for the first time (at the lower primary level), and formally sanctioned secondary education for girls. Furthermore, the Confucian classics were totally eliminated from the curriculum (time devoted to their study in the Qing school system had already been gradually reduced between 1904 and 1910). Another significant educational development during the early Republic was the dramatic transformation of Peking University from a corrupt bureaucratic institution catering to the scions of the ruling elite to an intellectual powerhouse and site of vibrant student activism.

## OVERSEAS STUDY

During the early years of the twentieth century, overseas study, especially in Japan, was officially encouraged. Although a number of initiatives had been implemented during the latter half of the nineteenth century to send a small number of Chinese students to the United States and Europe, the scale of overseas study expanded considerably after 1900, when Japan became the principal destination. As an Asian country that had seemingly imbibed the secrets of Western wealth and strength while retaining its own identity, Japan was seen by both the government and elites in China as the ideal place to study. By 1906 there were nearly 9,000 Chinese students in Japan (of whom about 100 were women, another dramatic example of Chinese women's growing public visibility at this time), in what was the largest migration of students abroad anywhere in the world (Harrell 1992, p. 2). Many of them became politicized during their sojourn and, rather than returning to work on behalf of the Qing government, joined antidynastic organizations promoting republican revolution.

## THE 1922 SCHOOL SYSTEM AND THE MOVE TOWARD MASS EDUCATION

During the May Fourth era (1915–1925), a growing class of professional educators lobbied for a new school system, which was inaugurated in 1922. (Some of these educators had studied in the United States and had been influenced by the educational thought of John Dewey, who was invited to China in 1919 to 1921 to give a series of lectures on China's campuses.) This new system emphasized the development of the individual, more autonomy vis-à-vis the state, and greater respect for vocational instruction that linked education to the practical needs of local communities (this last idea was not entirely new, since reformers had promoted such an outlook during the last years of the Qing dynasty). Significantly, the new system formally valorized the use of the vernacular (*baihua*) in school instruction and textbooks, thus ending the dominance of the classical language (*wenyan*) in culture and learning. During the 1920s and 1930s, increasing emphasis was placed on the importance of mass education (*pingmin jiaoyu*), especially in rural areas. This was a time when individual reformers and innovators attempted to put their ideas into practice. Thus Tao Xingzhi opened an experimental school near Nanjing that encouraged cooperation between students and local peasants, and Liang Shuming (1893–1988) pioneered a rural reconstruction movement in Shandong Province that aimed to use schools to revitalize local communities.

Yet after the Guomindang (Nationalist Party) came to national power in 1928, schools became progressively more centrally regulated and supervised, as education was once again enlisted to serve the practical needs of the state, which included inculcation of unquestioning loyalty to the Guomindang and its ideology (associated with the thought of its founder, Sun Yat-sen). At the same time, student political activism, so much a feature of the early twentieth century, was actively discouraged. During this period, educational resources were monopolized by secondary and higher-level institutions in urban centers.

During the war of resistance against Japan (1937–1945), the Communist Party promoted mass education and literacy, pioneered by reformers in the 1920s and 1930s, and found new ways of extending education to even the remotest rural areas. In particular, the Communist Party encouraged rural communities to establish popularly managed schools (*minban xuexiao*) adapted to local conditions, united academic study with productive labor, and adopted flexible schedules and curricula. These competing approaches to education—balancing the demands of popularization (*puji*) with the raising of standards (*tigao*)—were to underpin fierce political conflict in the post-1949 communist era.

SEE ALSO *Academies (shuyuan); Kang Youwei; Socialization and Pedagogy.*

**BIBLIOGRAPHY**

Ayers, William. *Chang Chih-tung and Educational Reform in China*. Cambridge, MA: Harvard University Press, 1971.

Bailey, Paul J. *Reform the People: Changing Attitudes Towards Popular Education in Early Twentieth-Century China*. Edinburgh: Edinburgh University Press, 1990.

Bailey, Paul J. *Gender and Education in China*. London: Routledge, 2007.

Biggerstaff, Knight. *The Earliest Modern Government Schools in China*. Ithaca, NY: Cornell University Press, 1961.

Culp, Robert. *Articulating Citizenship*. Cambridge, MA: Harvard University Asia Center, 2007.

Elman, Benjamin A., and Alexander Woodside, eds. *Education and Society in Late Imperial China, 1600–1900*. Berkeley: University of California Press, 1994.

Harrell, Paula. *Sowing the Seeds of Change: Chinese Students, Japanese Teachers, 1895–1905*. Stanford, CA: Stanford University Press, 1992.

Hsiung, Ping-chen. *A Tender Voyage: Children and Childhood in Late Imperial China*. Stanford, CA: Stanford University Press, 2005.

Keenan, Barry. *The Dewey Experiment in China*. Cambridge, MA: Council on East Asian Studies, Harvard University, 1977.

Pepper, Suzanne. *Radicalism and Education Reform in 20th-Century China*. Cambridge, U.K.: Cambridge University Press, 1996.

Rawski, Evelyn. *Education and Popular Literacy in Ch'ing China*. Ann Arbor: University of Michigan Press, 1979.

Seybolt, Peter. The Yenan Revolution in Mass Education. *China Quarterly*, no. 48 (October–December 1971): 641–669.

Thøgersen, Stig. *A County of Culture*. Ann Arbor: University of Michigan Press, 2002.

Weston, Timothy. *The Power of Position: Beijing University: Intellectuals, and Chinese Political Culture, 1898–1929*. Berkeley: University of California Press, 2004.

***Paul J. Bailey***

## TEXTBOOKS AND MORAL EDUCATION, 1900–1949

Moral education and classical literacy lay at the heart of the traditional educational system, but textbooks for the modern educational system redefined moral education to incorporate values needed to shape public-spirited citizens and facilitate state-building. In the first decades of the transition, commercial presses helped shape the content of textbooks, but over time the central government played an ever-increasing role in determining content and structure.

### LATE QING TEACHING MATERIALS

With the abolition of the civil service examination and establishment of modern schools, new types of teaching materials were needed. Traditional texts for elementary education, such as the *Trimetrical Classic* and the *One Thousand Character Classic*, used rhyming phrases to introduce basic vocabulary essential for a classical Confucian education. They introduced core Chinese values such as filial piety and ritual through stories of exemplary individuals; they also included a limited amount of basic knowledge (*changshi*), history, and literature. Progressive educators and reformers in the late Qing (1644–1912) criticized the absence of specialized practical and scientific knowledge, the haphazard introduction of vocabulary, and content that had little relevance to the daily lives of young children. As the Zongli Yamen noted in 1898, "Schools in Western countries all have a fixed set of textbooks, which progress from easy to hard in an orderly manner . . . organized according to daily lessons."

From the outset, both the content and the authority to determine content were contested. In 1906 the newly established Ministry of Education (Xuebu) claimed the right to approve all textbooks and planned to publish textbooks. The ministry's conservative guidelines stressed traditional morality and ethics through reading the classics (*dujing*), veneration of Confucius, and cultivation of moral character (*shenxiu*), but it added three new items: love of country, esteem for the military, and a concern for practical knowledge.

Commercial publishers led by the Commercial Press (Shangwu Yinshuaguan) produced competing readers for language, history, and geography. In 1908 Jiang Weiqiao and Zhuang Yu brought out the first volume of the most popular text of its era, the *China National Readers* (*Zuixin guowen jiaokeshu*). These readers, the editors proclaimed, would facilitate popular education by offering systematic materials for nine grades. Young people could learn proper conduct, private and public morality, and how to speak, dress, and behave. They would discover the need for sanitation and exercise, and they would learn how to treat friends and love the country. The *China National Readers* thus incorporated strong reformist, practical, and patriotic goals, including life skills and opposition to bound feet, superstition, and opium. In addition, by starting with items that were familiar to students and presenting them in a lively fashion before introducing more difficult doctrines, the readers broke with past tradition. It is not surprising that the Commercial Press textbooks eventually accounted for almost half of all educational books in these years.

## REPUBLICAN-ERA REFORM

The Republican revolution of 1911 opened the door for further reforms. Reading the classics was eliminated from the primary-school curriculum on the grounds that morality required active practice of appropriate behavior, not "empty words." Cai Yuanpei (1867–1940), the minister of education, described a citizen's education (*guomin jiaoyu*) as taking the perspective of the student. Editors at the Commercial Press used their great freedom to introduce a new series, *Republican Readers* (*Gongheguo jiaokeshu*). Primary-school readers continued to uphold many traditional Chinese virtues, especially filiality, diligence in studies, and proper behavior. However, moral behavior now included fulfilling civic responsibilities to the nation and the public good. Not only was this the natural extension of love of family to the nation, it was evident in nature as demonstrated by the organized willingness of ants to serve the interests of the group.

With the 1922 reforms of the school system along American lines, textbooks went one step further in focusing on the child's experiences and providing life skills as opposed to conveying a set body of knowledge. Textbooks published by the commercial presses in Shanghai shifted from literary Chinese (*wenyan*) to the vernacular language. Chinese-language textbooks for the lower grades replaced essays on citizenship, history, sanitation, and geography with children's literature and other items of interest to young students. "Cultivation of moral character" (*xiushen*) as a category gave way to "citizenship," "citizen training," and "social science." Not only were the lessons intended to stir the imagination of students, they were designed to encourage individual thought. Perhaps reflecting the influence of the May Fourth movement, a 1924 fourth-grade textbook's list of five virtues consisted of helping others, equality, freedom, self-governance, and concern for the public good. At the same time, nationalistic themes made frequent appearances, although they were not yet associated with specific political parties.

In 1928 the newly victorious Guomindang Party added a more explicit political agenda by identifying Sun Yat-sen's Three People's Principles as the basis for education. The 1947 constitution defined the purpose of education as promoting a spirit of nationalism (*minzu*), self-government (democracy), and a healthy body, scientific outlook, and skills for life (people's livelihood). Guomindang-era texts echoed many of the themes of the New Life movement and ideas of self-government. Because Chinese lacked a collective strength, discriminated against women, gave priority to the family, and did not observe rules, the schools were supposed to have students participate in group activities.

According to a 1929 civics textbook, there were three building blocks for the new citizen: (1) the ancient moral codes of China, including Confucian virtues of loyalty, filial piety, and benevolence; (2) new moral and ethical codes that emphasized scientific ways of thinking, collective organization, service to the community, public sanitation, and the eradication of superstition; and (3) knowledge of China's laws, the government system, and the importance of industrialization to the nation. Lessons for first-year students began with concrete examples taken from the child's experience, focusing on cleanliness, respect for teachers and classmates, relationships with siblings, the benevolence of parents, and the importance of healthy eating. Starting around the third grade, the textbooks introduced material explaining school elections, model communities, and the activities of a local government, often in the form of plays, letters, and diaries. As the Japanese threat intensified in the 1930s, stories about encroachments increased, as did examples of young people defending Chinese sovereignty. These basic principles and approaches continued through the wartime years and the civil war with little change.

**BIBLIOGRAPHY**

Bai Limin. *Shaping the Ideal Child: Children and Their Primers in Late Imperial China.* Hong Kong: Chinese University Press, 2005.

Borthwick, Sally. *Education and Social Change in China: The Beginnings of the Modern Era.* Stanford, CA: Hoover Institution Press, 1983.

Qui Xiuxiang. *Qingmo xinshi jiaoyu de lilun yu xianshi: Yi xinshi xiaoxuetang wei zhongxin de shentao* [The Ideals and Reality of New Style Education at the End of the Qing-A Disucussion Centered on the Establishment of New Style Primary Schools]. Taibei: Zhengda Lishixi, 2000.

Si Qi. *Xiaoxue jiaokeshu fazhanshi* [History of the Development of Primary School Textbooks]. Taibei: Huatai Wenhua, 2005.

Wang Huaxin. *Qingmo Minguo shiqi zhongxue jiaoyu yanjiu* [A Study of Middle School Education in the Late Qing and Republic]. Shanghai: Huadong Shishifan Daxue Chubanshe, 2002.

Wang Jianjun. *Zhongguo jindai jiaokeshu fazhan yanjiu* [A Study of the Development of Modern Chinese Textbooks]. Guangzhou: Guangdong Jiaoyu Chubanshe, 1996.

***Arthur Lewis Rosenbaum***

## EDUCATION SINCE 1949

A massive expansion in educational access is justly celebrated as one of the major achievements of China since 1949. Nevertheless, in education policy, there was much that was not particularly new about the "New China" of the post-"liberation" era. While radical experiments with rural schooling had been conducted sporadically in Communist-controlled areas from the 1930s, once the levers of national power were within its grasp, the Chinese Communist Party (CCP) retained and reinforced the hierarchical, elitist, regular system of schooling inherited from the Nationalist regime, along with its curricular emphasis on general academic subjects, science and modernization, moral and political socialization, and a mimetic pedagogical approach. Pedagogically, indeed, despite the efforts of innovative educators inspired by the progressivism of John Dewey (1859–1952) or indigenous initiatives such as Liang Shuming's (1893–1988) rural reconstruction movement, the dominant approach under both the Guomindang (GMD) and the Communists remained very similar to that of the traditional *sishu:* rote learning of texts, combined with regular testing. This was reinforced by one of the new regime's first educational initiatives: the reinstatement of an intensely competitive system—reminiscent of the pre-1905 imperial *keju*—of national examinations (the *gaokao*) to select talented individuals to serve the state.

### MEASURED EXPANSION

The education system of the People's Republic of China (PRC) in the early 1950s differed from its Republican predecessor chiefly in its ideological content, and in the efficiency with which it was subjected to central control (remaining Western missionary schools and colleges were also closed or secularized). Both the CCP and the GMD inherited what John Fitzgerald (1996) has termed China's tradition of "pedagogical politics," with its vision of the ruler as a moralizing teacher, and the CCP shared the modernizing nationalism of the preceding regime, though with an admixture of Marxist class struggle.

Under Soviet tutelage, a major reorganization, centralization, and specialization of higher education institutions took place during the 1950s, but at the primary and secondary levels the Soviet influence was more superficial. Secondary schooling remained centered around highly selective, primarily urban "key schools," many of them established prior to 1949, and these attracted a large share of state funding. The emphasis in contemporary Soviet education policy was on the fostering of a modernizing vanguard of scientists, engineers, and technocrats crucial to building the kind of military-industrial complex that could compete with the West, but Stalinist elitism merely reinforced an already prevalent and deeply ingrained elitist ethos. Likewise, the Soviet educator Ivan Kairov's (1893–1978) vision of education as the transmission of a state-defined curriculum, leaving little scope for initiative or independence on the part of teachers or students, must have seemed old hat to most Chinese teachers. Russian was taught as the default foreign language during the 1950s, but the Sino-Soviet split of 1960 abruptly deprived it of this status, and many teachers of Russian were compelled to retrain as English teachers.

In the early years of the PRC, the teaching force of necessity consisted predominantly of individuals possessing what was now termed a "bad class background." Opportunities for postprimary education in pre-"liberation" times had been largely restricted to wealthier groups, and while the new regime needed their knowledge and skills, it was suspicious of their political leanings. The textbooks and teaching guidelines produced in Beijing by the People's Education Press (*Renmin Jiaoyu Chubanshe,* founded in 1950) thus not only provided a much-needed prop for the many poorly qualified teachers; they also catechized those unfamiliar with the tenets of the new Communist faith. Meetings and training sessions were also organized to evangelize teachers unfamiliar with the CCP message.

In party propaganda generally, as well as in school textbooks, the meaning of the new ideology was illustrated through stories of heroes exemplifying the revolutionary virtues, much as the old Confucian texts promoted exemplars of a rather different social and moral ethos. Meanwhile, in the workaday world of the local educator, model schools and model teachers were presented as exemplars of best practice—pedagogical and ideological. Considerable effort and resources were devoted to the task of promoting education in standard Chinese (*Putonghua*)—another GMD policy that the Communists pursued with greater vigor and effectiveness. This also involved much retraining of teachers, as did the simplification of the Chinese script, a Communist measure intended to facilitate the spread of literacy while marking a dramatic break with the "feudal" past.

The return in the early 1950s of peace and stability, after the turmoil of the anti-Japanese and civil wars, allowed for a rapid recovery and extension of basic schooling in war-ravaged areas of China. However, the emphasis on maintaining academic standards that characterized policy in these years meant that in many regions the party leadership felt compelled to dampen popular expectations of a rapid expansion of educational access. These expectations had been raised in areas where pre-1949 initiatives to promote modern schooling had proceeded farthest, and had also been encouraged by the CCP's own propaganda campaigns. However, qualitative concerns were reflected in a reluctance to expand state provision of schooling more rapidly than the normal schools, colleges, and universities (*shifan xuexiao, xueyuan,* and *daxue*) could supply qualified teachers to staff local schools, and policymakers were anxious to ensure that an excessively rapid spread of schooling did not encourage peasants to harbor ambitions to venture beyond their villages or counties. In the interests of social and political stability, and in line with the Soviet-style economic strategy of central planning, many within the CCP desired the schooling system to produce educated individuals no faster than they could be absorbed by modern industries, the professions, and the state bureaucracy.

Existing educational infrastructure at the postprimary level was overwhelmingly concentrated in urban areas, while state investment in rural schooling remained limited—but the *hukou* (household registration) system restricted movement from rural to urban areas in search of education or employment opportunities. In many rural areas, what basic schooling was available was often *minban* (people-managed), still relying largely on old *sishu* teachers, capable of imparting literacy according to the old methods but unfamiliar with the curriculum of the modern schools, and supported by village resources rather than state funds.

## RADICALIZATION AND EXTENSION TO THE MASSES

The relatively cautious and measured expansion of regular schooling during the early 1950s gave way from around 1957 to more radical policies prompted by frustration at what Mao and his circle felt was an unduly slow rate of progress toward industrialization and socialist modernity, and by a sense that the knowledge and skills crucial to the modernization project were still largely monopolized by the old "bad class" elites. Elitism in education and slow progress toward the socialist utopia were problems indissolubly linked in the minds of those who now sought to harness the masses to the cause of a revolutionary "Great Leap Forward." In education, the Great Leap marked a dramatic shift away from the emphasis on standards and the selection of talent, toward the rapid extension of basic education to the "broad masses," including adults (targeted by ambitious literacy campaigns). In Mao's phraseology, it was now better to be "red" than "expert."

In an analysis of the history of schooling in Shandong's Zouping County, Stig Thøgersen (2002) argues that the twenty-year period from 1957 to 1976 should be seen as characterized overall by a more radical emphasis on quantitative expansion, with a hiatus caused by the famine of the early 1960s and the subsequent period of retrenchment. Within China, this period, and particularly the years of the Cultural Revolution, is nowadays viewed as an unmitigated educational catastrophe. However, in the field of basic schooling, quite the reverse would appear to be the case, and it is important to distinguish the chaotic violence of 1966 to 1968 from the subsequent period. Literacy levels in Zouping County roughly doubled to two-thirds of the population in the period from 1964 to 1982, and work by Han Dongping (2000) and Suzanne Pepper (1996) suggests this was not unique (see national enrollment figures in Table 1). The quality of education available at postprimary level undoubtedly suffered during the Cultural Revolution, as Donald Treiman (2007) demonstrates, and higher education was particularly hard hit. However, the vehemently negative portrayal within China of the educational implications of the Cultural Revolution reflects the political struggles of the post-Mao era, as well as the elitist prejudices and often horrific personal experiences of many reform-era political and intellectual leaders.

The spectacular expansion of basic education in the pre-reform period was not due to any substantial new injection of state funding; if anything, levels of funding per student appear to have declined during the Cultural Revolution. Rather, the expansion was driven by political imperative, with production brigade commanders obliged

**Enrollment figures for different levels of education, 1949–1985**

| | School-age children entering primary school (%) | Primary school graduates entering junior high school (%) | Junior high school graduates entering senior high school (%) | Senior high school graduates entering college (%) |
|---|---|---|---|---|
| 1949 | 25.0 | — | — | — |
| 1965 | 84.7 | 44.9 | 26.4 | 45.6 |
| 1976 | 96.0 | 94.1 | 71.4 | 4.2 |
| 1980 | 93.0 | 75.9 | 43.1 | 4.6 |
| 1985 | 95.9 | 68.4 | 39.4 | 31.5 |

SOURCE: Pepper, Suzanne. *Radicalism and Education Reform in 20th-century China: The Search for an Ideal Development Model*. New York: Cambridge University Press, 1996, p. 483 (col. 1) and p. 487 (cols. 2–4); calculations are based on official Chinese sources.

*Table 1*

to find funding from collective resources, including farms or factories established by schools themselves. Pursuing education through labor was not just a slogan of the times; it was a financial necessity. Qualified teachers were assisted by large numbers of untrained *minban* instructors, many of whom were graduates of junior middle school, while intellectuals "sent down" from urban areas to learn from the peasants also taught in village schools. However, for all the radical rhetoric about learning from the masses, the traditional pedagogy persisted, reinforced by the authoritarian political context. Moreover, despite the often arduous physical labor that students and teachers were obliged to perform, the curriculum remained a general academic one, with weak vocational education.

## POST-MAO REFORM

The power struggle within the party following the death of Mao in 1976 saw "expertise" finally triumphing over "redness." The new party leadership ordered a return to the pre-Cultural Revolution system of regular schooling. Curriculum development and textbook production was recentralized, and from 1977 the annual *gaokao* was reinstated. After a decade of thwarted aspirations, the reopening or return to the *status quo ante* of senior high schools, colleges, and universities, along with the reintroduction of competitive entrance examinations, presaged a tumultuous dash for the very limited places available in higher education. Many small village schools were closed, if not for lack of funding, then for lack of teachers, many of whom were among those scrambling to enter universities or reenter the urban workforce.

Meanwhile, land-use reform and the dismantling of rural communes, along with fiscal and administrative decentralization during the early 1980s, spurred the growth of rural incomes, but also undermined the finances of many village schools, leaving educational costs to be borne increasingly by families themselves. The growing value of children's farm labor also increased the opportunity costs of schooling—even though most rural families had by now come to regard school attendance as the norm, for girls as well as boys.

Concern at an excessive neglect of basic education led the CCP leadership in 1986 to proclaim a commitment to the universalization of nine years of compulsory education, to be achieved by different deadlines in different regions of the country, depending on their level of "development." Significant progress has subsequently been made in broadening access to basic schooling. Perhaps the key factor in this has been demographic: the introduction of the one-child policy in 1979 dramatically reinforced a trend toward lower birth rates, leading to smaller primary school cohorts from the late 1980s. This has contributed to constraining growth in the demands placed on state educational funding, while also obliging families to concentrate their resources on investment in the education of fewer children.

Particularly following Deng Xiaoping's post-Tiananmen reassertion of his authority within the party, the focus of policymakers has shifted increasingly to the expansion and improvement of secondary and higher education. In the words of former president Jiang Zemin, the overriding aim now is to build up China as a "personnel great power" (*rencai qiangguo*), involving a heightened focus on fostering high skills in such areas as the sciences, technology (including information technology), foreign languages (especially English, now widely taught in urban primary schools and a compulsory subject at the university level), engineering, and national defense. Top universities and research institutes have seen particularly large state investment in these and other fields regarded as strategically important, as part of an effort to build up world-class centers of expertise. Meanwhile, as the infrastructure of state socialism (in the form of centralized manpower planning and work placements) has been progressively dismantled, so the socialist content of school and university curricula has been steadily stripped of real meaning. Over the reform period as a whole, there has been a tendency to make education less overtly or crudely political, and to attempt to relate it more closely to vocational needs and the national pursuit of economic growth and technological progress.

A discourse of "quality education" (*suzhi jiaoyu*) also emerged during the 1990s, encompassing a broad and amorphous range of concerns, including a dissatisfaction with the limitations of traditional pedagogy, and a desire to promote greater creativity and critical thinking. The latter are valued by the regime primarily for their contribution to economic competitiveness and the national capacity for scientific and technological innovation, but not for any role they might play in promoting skills or values of active, democratic citizenship. Indeed, a massive and ongoing campaign of "patriotic education" (launched in the early 1990s) has as its chief aim the promotion of uncritical, state-centered patriotism and unquestioning acceptance of party rule. Teacher training programs and curriculum guidelines increasingly attempt to encourage new pedagogical approaches that will promote student initiative and independence, but the authoritarian political context militates against effective implementation. In addition, the character of the public examination system, with the *gaokao* as its cornerstone, continues to institutionalize the traditional practice of teaching to test and rote memorization.

## RISE IN INEQUALITY

The reform era, and particularly the years since the 1990s, has witnessed an increasing divergence between provinces, regions, and urban and rural areas in terms of quality of education offered within the schooling system, as family and community wealth has become an increasingly crucial determinant of educational opportunity. This rise in inequality is in part a reflection of the growing wealth gap between coastal and metropolitan areas and the rest of the country, but it is also related to policies of fiscal decentralization pursued since the early 1980s, the dismantling of rural communes, and the decreasing economic role of old-style state enterprises with their cradle-to-grave provision of basic services (including education). This has meant that families and communities have become increasingly dependent upon their own resources to finance the costs of education, particularly as schools in poorer provinces or counties have been compelled to find methods (often extralegal) of supplementing their often inadequate state funding (an inadequacy exacerbated by endemic corruption and the misappropriation of funding intended for education).

By the early twenty-first century, public expenditure per primary student in Shanghai (the highest) was more than ten times greater than the lowest provincial figure, with the differential having doubled during the 1990s (Hannum, Park, and Cheng 2007, p. 6). Wealthy urban families can buy their way into the best state schools, or purchase a private education (either within China or overseas), but poor families in less-developed rural regions have few options.

With divergence in school facilities and resources has come divergence in teacher quality—the best urban schools recruit the best teachers, while their rural counterparts often struggle to attract good applicants. One state response to growing regional divergence has been to enable more "advanced" areas to push their students further and faster, by allowing them more scope to develop their own curricula, and by opening up the school textbook market to limited competition. Meanwhile, since 1997 the national uniformity of the *gaokao* has been compromised, with preferential quotas granted to "advanced" cities and provinces.

The problems afflicting rural educational provision apply also to the education of most minority nationalities (*shaoshu minzu*), such as the Tibetans, Yi, Zhuang, or Mongols. Despite extra state funding and preferential quotas for access to higher education, enrollment and completion rates for many minority groups remain significantly

**Selected educational transitions of rural youth by province (2000) and percentage change (1990–2000)**

| | Percentage 2000 | | | | | Difference 2000–1990 | | | | |
|---|---|---|---|---|---|---|---|---|---|---|
| | Ever attend | Grad. primary school | Attend junior high school | Grad. junior high school | Attend senior high school | Ever attend | Grad. primary school | Attend junior high school | Grad. junior high school | Attend senior high school |
| **Total** | **99.05** | **98.22** | **86.09** | **87.54** | **22.82** | **4.76** | **11.16** | **23.62** | **3.94** | **4.54** |
| Beijing | 99.69 | 100 | 95.19 | 95.1 | 68.04 | 0.59 | 2.34 | 1.78 | −0.73 | 34.71 |
| Shandong | 99.56 | 99.3 | 89.57 | 87.99 | 21.85 | 2.73 | 4.51 | 23.52 | −5.65 | 7.42 |
| Jiangxi | 99.46 | 98.56 | 88.12 | 87.3 | 20.52 | 5.1 | 23.1 | 27.86 | 14.03 | −4.4 |
| Anhui | 99.66 | 99.39 | 88.88 | 83.01 | 12.1 | 9.55 | 18.9 | 30.4 | 1.62 | −0.42 |
| Yunnan | 97.27 | 93.34 | 64 | 80.04 | 22.54 | 16.12 | 23.53 | 9.1 | 5.97 | −4.46 |
| Tibet | 56.68 | 80.82 | 32.2 | 57.14 | 25 | 37.71 | 40.82 | 12.2 | NA | NA |

SOURCE: Connelly, Rachel, and Zheng Zhenzhen. Enrolment and Graduation Patterns as China's Reforms Deepen, 1990–2000. In *Education and Reform in China*, eds. Emily Hannum and Albert Park, 64–92. New York: Routledge, 2007, pp. 88–89.

*Table 2*

below the national average. In 2000 rural rates of transition to junior high school were 97 percent in Zhejiang, but 64 percent in Yunnan, and 32 percent in Tibet (Hannum, Park, and Cheng 2007, p. 10; see also Table 2). Many exasperated Han officials and experts blame this phenomenon on the failure of many rural and minority parents to appreciate the importance of schooling, a reflection of the parents' low quality (*suzhi*). However, others point to reasons for such parents' ambivalence toward the schooling on offer, including the prohibitive costs for most of progression beyond primary school, and the heavy curricular focus on the culture and lifestyle of urban Han Chinese. Increasingly, the state is moving to concentrate educational provision for rural and minority children beyond the early primary years in larger boarding schools—partly to reduce dropout rates, and partly to enable more intensive political socialization away from the low *suzhi* environment of the village (Murphy 2004).

Official statistics show significant progress in school attendance beyond the early primary level (ages ten to eighteen): in 2000, 88.8 percent of urban boys and 89.4 percent of urban girls in this age range were in school, compared to 76.6 percent of rural boys (1990 figure: 54 percent) and 74.4 percent of urban girls (1990: 44 percent) (Hannum, Park, and Cheng 2007, p. 12). However, one rapidly expanding group tends to be ignored in such statistics: the children of migrants from rural areas to the cities. Their precise number is unknown, though a 2003 report offered a (conservative) estimate of 20 million nationally (Chen and Liang 2007, p. 117). Despite recent central government policies aimed at making urban authorities responsible for educating such children, schooling remains unaffordable for many migrant families, who often still resort to community-run *minban* schools on the precarious margins of the state system.

The changing meaning of *minban* educational provision in contemporary China graphically illustrates the ideological and infrastructural shifts of the reform era. *Minban* schools for migrants resemble in function and status the *minban* village schools of the early 1950s, when many villages funded and ran their own very basic schools in the absence of state provision (as some do today). However, in the early twenty-first century the term *minban* often functions as a euphemism for "private," and is loosely applied to a range of private or joint-venture schools and colleges. Among these are highly elitist institutions such as Dulwich College (Beijing), as well as many less-prestigious schools and colleges established to meet a burgeoning demand for secondary and higher education that the state system cannot, or will not, fulfill. Diversification in forms of provision has been particularly marked in higher education, where there has been a huge expansion in tertiary student numbers since the early 1990s, witnessing an increase in the age-participation rate from 9.8 to 21 percent in the 1998–2006 period alone (from 8.5 to over 23 million students) (Watson 2007). This has been financed largely through user fees, with state resources concentrated on the top institutes, with the consequence that while fees for the most prestigious universities are capped, private (or semiprivate) institutes of dubious quality often charge higher fees to desperate students and their parents.

Greater recognition of the scale of the challenge posed by societal inequality became a hallmark of the presidency of Hu Jintao (from 2002). Education, so crucial to personal success in the twenty-first century Chinese labor market, has reflected and reinforced the rapid growth of regional and class disparities, and measures to boost access to a decent education for the poorest thus form a key component of initiatives aimed at tackling inequality (e.g., the New Socialist Countryside [*xin shehuizhuyi nongcun*] program launched in 2006).

China's levels of education spending have been well below the rates seen in most of the East Asian tigers (South Korea, Taiwan, Singapore) during their rapid economic expansion from the 1970s to 1990s (Green et al. 2007), but in January 2008, the central government announced its intention to boost education spending from 2.79 percent to 4 percent of gross domestic product over the succeeding five years. Education played a role in bringing about growth with equality elsewhere in post-1940s East Asia; it remains to be seen whether China's government, in its pursuit of a "harmonious society," has the commitment or capacity to match this achievement.

**SEE ALSO** *Harmonious Society.*

**BIBLIOGRAPHY**

Chen Yiu Por and Liang Zai. Educational Attainment of Migrant Children: The Forgotten Story of Urbanization in China. In *Education and Reform in China,* eds. Emily Hannum and Albert Park, 117–132. New York: Routledge, 2007.

Connelly, Rachel, and Zheng Zhenzhen. Enrolment and Graduation Patterns as China's Reforms Deepen, 1990–2000. In *Education and Reform in China,* eds. Emily Hannum and Albert Park, 64–92. New York: Routledge, 2007.

Fitzgerald, John. *Awakening China: Politics, Culture, and Class in the Nationalist Revolution.* Stanford, CA: Stanford University Press, 1996.

Green, Andy, Angela Little, Sangeeta Kamat, et al. *Education and Development in a Global Era: Strategies for "Successful" Globalisation.* London: Department for International Development, 2007.

Han Dongping. *The Unknown Cultural Revolution: Educational Reforms and Their Impact on China's Rural Development.* New York and London: Garland, 2000.

Hannum, Emily, Albert Park, and Cheng Kaiming. Introduction: Market Reforms and Educational Opportunity in China. In *Education and Reform in China,* eds. Emily Hannum and Albert Park, 1–23. New York: Routledge, 2007.

Murphy, Rachel. Turning Peasants into Modern Chinese Citizens: "Population Quality" Discourse, Demographic Transition, and Primary Education. *China Quarterly* 177 (2004): 1–20.

Pepper, Suzanne. *Radicalism and Education Reform in 20th-century China: The Search for an Ideal Development Model.* New York: Cambridge University Press, 1996.

Thøgersen, Stig. *A County of Culture: Twentieth-century China Seen from the Village Schools of Zouping, Shandong.* Ann Arbor: University of Michigan Press, 2002.

Treiman, Donald. The Growth and Determinants of Literacy in China. In *Education and Reform in China,* eds. Emily Hannum and Albert Park, 135–153. New York: Routledge, 2007.

Watson, David. *Chinese Universities in the Service of Society: A Report on the China-England Study of National Policy on Higher Education Management.* London: British Council, 2007.

***Edward Vickers***

## EDUCATION IN RURAL AREAS

Throughout the twentieth century, China's educational system reflected a sharp urban-rural dichotomy, held in place by the household (*hukou*) registration system established in the 1950s. The People's Republic of China inherited a system with a scholastic, liberal, and urban ethos. Although universal basic education was a stated Republican aim, formal schooling was directed by professional elites and was largely disconnected from the lives of ordinary citizens (Price 1979; Kwong 1979). The Chinese Communist Party perpetuated rural-urban divisions by using irregular and full-time schools to simultaneously address the contradictory needs of "the masses" and the goal of national construction and production. Balancing "red and expert" missions complicated educational reform for decades.

The goal of universal basic education was tied to eradicating illiteracy. China's illiteracy rate stood between 85 percent and 90 percent at the beginning of the twentieth century and remained virtually unchanged fifty years later (Ross 2006). The uneven distribution of literacy and schooling was a function of poverty, a region's remoteness from market centers, and the reluctance of leaders to place politically empowering literacy in nonelite hands (Woodside 1992; Pepper 1996; Peterson 1997). Policies to extend education to rural residents chiefly relied on the establishment of spare-time, part-work schools that combined education with productive labor (Hu 1962; Price 1979).

### THE GREAT LEAP FORWARD AND THE CULTURAL REVOLUTION

In 1958, the official figure for elementary school enrollment was 86 million, accounting for 85 percent of the students of compulsory age (Pepper 1996, pp. 283–284). In many rural areas, however, the figure was likely below 70 percent (Price 1979, p. 213). A policy of "walking on two legs" supported the establishment of regular and irregular schools, including spare-time *minban* (self-financing, locally managed) literacy classes and schools, and tens of thousands of irregular, *minban* agricultural middle and high schools (Kwong 1979; Pepper 1996; Price 1979). Although such popularization efforts resulted in low-quality schooling, giving rise to key-point schools within the regular system, educational opportunities for rural children and adults expanded, measured by the increase in gross enrollments (Cleverley 1985; Kwong 1979).

The decade of the Cultural Revolution (1966–1976) brought widespread criticism of the country's school system as exclusionary and elitist. Key-point schools were branded as "little treasure pagodas," while regular, *minban*, and part-time rural schools expanded rapidly. Coupled with an influx into the countryside of "sent down" urban youths who frequently acted as teachers, wider educational access contributed to increased agricultural production and the democratization of village political culture at the close of the Mao era (Thøgersen 1990; Price 1979; Han 2000; Joel 2004; Pepper 1996). However, rural residents viewed irregular work-study options, which failed to provide upward social mobility, as inferior to regular schooling (Pepper 1996, p. 349). In addition, the government placed tighter restrictions on rural-urban migration to ensure that rural youths stayed in the countryside. A combination of a lack of qualified teachers and resources, closures of secondary schools and colleges, narrowly ideological pedagogy, severe disruptions in attendance and in the school calendar, and low student morale negatively affected the literacy rates of the cohort born between 1955 and 1966 (Bhola 1984; Hopkins 1986; Thøgersen 1990; Seeberg 1990; Treiman 2002). In the end, Cultural Revolution educational policies supported "the formation and reproduction of social differences" between rural and urban residents (Peterson 1997, p. 17).

### THREE DECADES OF REFORM

Beginning in the late 1970s, early reform-era policies reinscribed urban-rural divisions, putting enormous pressure on the education system's Four Modernization priorities of efficiency and excellence privileged full-time schooling and precipitated a sharp decline in rural middle-school enrollment (Pepper 1996). With the revival of key-point schools, educational resources were concentrated in cities, towns,

***Math instruction at a rural school, Yanmaidi, Sichuan province, March 18, 2005.*** *Formal education remains a struggle in many parts of rural China, due in part to a lack of classrooms, supplies, and teachers. Despite assistance from the government to ensure each student completes a minimum of nine years of schooling, many children suspend their studies to help on family farms.* AP IMAGES

and county seats, and the reinstituted national college entrance examination became one of the few means by which rural students, who perceived secondary schooling as the means to "leap over the village gate" (*tiaochu nongmen*), could enjoy urban social-welfare benefits (Hawkins 1983, p. 120; Thøgersen 1990).

The economic and social dangers of backtracking on universal basic education became apparent to state officials by the early 1980s. Rural education was plagued by poor teaching, dangerously inadequate infrastructure and facilities, and a secondary-school dropout rate ranging as high as 50 percent to 70 percent (Thøgersen 1990). Insufficient numbers and high costs of high schools, family-planning policies that exacerbated dropout rates, and a lack of effective vocational schools negatively impacted school attendance, especially of female and minority rural children (Seeberg et al. 2007).

China's nine-year Compulsory Education Law was implemented in 1986, and the net enrollment rate for primary-school-age children increased from 84.7 percent in 1985 to 99.5 percent in 2007 (Ministry of Education 2007). While less than 70 percent of primary-school graduates were admitted into junior high school during the mid-1980s, virtually all students now matriculate to junior high school (Ministry of Education 2006b). Illiteracy rates among youths and adults (ages twelve to forty), which stood at 30 percent in 1970, dropped to 20 percent in 1988, and by the early 2000s China had basically achieved nine-year compulsory education and universal functional literacy among youths and middle-aged adults (Xie 2002; Ross 2006, p. 3). The gender gap in school enrollment has also been greatly reduced (Ministry of Education 2008).

Nevertheless, rural education efforts face significant challenges. Pressure on junior middle-school students to become migrant workers explain dropout rates that reach 30 percent or higher (Lou and Ross 2008). Nearly seventy million children of migrant parents are "left behind" in homes with one or no parents, leaving rural schools overwhelmed with custodial responsibilities. At least until the economic downturn of 2008, as many as twenty million migrant children under eighteen years of age were living in cities and working as laborers, many without access to schooling (Ministry of Education 2005; *China Statistical Yearbook* 2006).

Admission to senior high school is difficult for rural students who have proportionately fewer high-school options than their urban counterparts. Many rural students who are successful in college preparatory high schools cannot take full advantage of the dramatic expansion of higher education, where gross enrollment rates were 23 percent in 2007 compared to 3 percent in the early 1990s. High college tuition on top of heavy high-school fees creates a financial burden beyond the means of poor rural families. Likewise, midwestern and western provinces have far fewer quotas for the entrance of their students into prestigious institutions of higher education.

To address educational disparity, the state has relied primarily on the decentralization of K–12 school financing. Beginning in 1986, funding was decentralized, and county- and village-level education offices gained a greater degree of decision-making power. While elite urban schools received considerable public support, financial responsibility for rural schools was left largely to local communities that relied heavily on surcharges, stipulated by the State Council to be 1.5 percent to 2 percent of the per capita net income of farmers each year. After 1995, the state recentralized some financial responsibilities through poverty-relief education-support programs (Su 2002). Rural school expansion has also been supported by initiatives such as Project Hope, launched in 1989 by the China Youth Development Foundation and aimed at pooling charitable donations to assist education, and the Spring Bud Project, launched in 1989 by the All-China Women's Federation to support impoverished female students.

Rural schools continue to struggle with funding shortfalls, debt, inferior infrastructure, and poor teaching. The 2008 Wenchuan earthquake, in which well over 10,000 students perished due to the collapse of unstable school buildings, became a symbol of lack of attention to rural schooling, in spite of improved national oversight, including county-by-county reviews of compulsory schooling, mandated since 1993. One bright spot in efforts to enhance educational equity is the Rural Compulsory Education Assured Funding Mechanism, which was established in Spring 2005 to provide free education in rural regions. The funding framework assures that spending on rural compulsory education is shared between the central government and local authorities. The central government assumes most financing responsibilities in rural education through its key policy, Two Exemptions and One Subsidy (TEOS), which provides financial support for school fees, textbooks, and boarding costs. TEOS was implemented first in the west in spring 2006 and applied to rural and urban children throughout China in the autumn of 2008. The state has finally made genuinely free universal basic education central to its efforts to "build a socialist new countryside" (Lou and Ross 2008).

## BIBLIOGRAPHY

Bailey, Paul. *Reform the People: Changing Attitudes Towards Popular Education in Early Twentieth-century China.* Edinburgh, U.K.: Edinburgh University Press, 1990.

Bhola, H. S. The Anti-illiteracy Campaigns in the People's Republic of China: From the 1950s to the 1980s. In *Campaigning for Literacy: Eight National Experiences of the Twentieth Century, with a Memorandum to Decision-makers,* ed. H. S. Bhola, 73–90. Paris: UNESCO, 1984.

Borthwick, Sally. *Education and Social Change in China: The Beginnings of the Modern Era.* Stanford, CA: Hoover Institution Press, 1983.

China Children and Teenagers' Fund. The Spring Bud Project. http://www.cctf.org.cn/.

*Zhongguo Tongji Nianjian* [China Statistical Yearbook]. Beijing: China Statistics Press, 2006.

China Youth Development Foundation. Project Hope. http://www.cydf.org.cn/.

Cleverley, John. *The Schooling of China: Tradition and Modernity in Chinese Education.* Boston: Allen & Unwin, 1985.

Fraser, Stewart E. *China: Population Education and People.* Melbourne, Australia: School of Education, La Trobe University, 1987.

Gamberg, Ruth. *Red and Expert: Education in the People's Republic of China.* New York: Schocken, 1977.

Han Dongping. *The Unknown Cultural Revolution: Educational Reforms and Their Impact on China's Rural Development.* New York: Garland, 2000.

Hawkins, John N. *Education and Social Change in the People's Republic of China.* New York: Praeger, 1983.

Hopkins, Dorothy. China's Successful Adult Literacy Campaign. *Adult Literacy and Basic Education* 10, 2 (1986): 102–116.

Hu Chang-tu. *Chinese Education under Communism.* New York: Teachers' College, Columbia University, 1962.

Joel, Andreas. Leveling the Little Pagoda: The Impact of College Examinations, and Their Elimination, on Rural Education in China. *Comparative Education Review* 48, 1 (2004): 1–48.

Kwong, Julia. *Chinese Education in Transition: Prelude to the Cultural Revolution.* Montreal: McGill-Queen's University Press, 1979.

Lou Jingjing and Heidi Ross. From Fee to Free: Achieving the Right to Education in China. *Chinese Education and Society* 41, 1 (2008): 1–7.

Ministry of Education of the People's Republic of China. "Weilai 50 nian Zhongguo jiaoyu yu renli ziyuan kaifade zhanlue gouxiang" [Strategic concepts for the development of Chinese education and human resources for the next fifty years in a country with a large population to a country with sound human resources—Report on the problems of China's education and human resources]. *Chinese Education and Society* (2005): 38/4, 61–69.

Ministry of Education of the People's Republic of China. *2005 Nian quanguo jiaoyu shiye fazhan tongji gongbao* [2005 National statistic report on the development of education]. 2006a. http://www.moe.gov.cn/edoas/website18/64/info20464.htm.

Ministry of Education of the People's Republic of China. *Geji Xuexiao Biyesheng Shengxue Lv* [Promotion Rate of Graduates of School of All Levels]. 2006b. http://www.moe.gov.cn/edoas/website18/90/info33490.htm.

Ministry of Education of the People's Republic of China. *2006 Nian jiaoyu tongji shuju: Geji gelei xuexiao xiaoshu* [2006 Statistics of education in China: Number of schools by level and type]. 2007. http://www.moe.gov.cn/edoas/website18/54/info33454.htm.

Ministry of Education of the People's Republic of China. *2007 Nian quanguo jiaoyu shiye fazhan tongji gongbao* [2007 National statistic report on the development of education].

2008. http://www.moe.gov.cn/edoas/website18/54/info1209972965475254.htm.

Niu Xiaodong. *Policy Education and Inequalities in Communist China since 1949*. Lanham, MD: University Press of America, 1992.

Pepper, Suzanne. *China's Education Reform in the 1980s: Policies, Issues, and Historical Perspectives*. Berkeley: University of California, Center for Chinese Studies, 1990.

Pepper, Suzanne. *Radicalism and Education Reform in 20th-century China: The Search for an Ideal Development Model*. Cambridge, U.K.: Cambridge University Press, 1996.

Peterson, Glen. *The Power of Words: Literacy and Revolution in South China, 1949–95*. Vancouver: University of British Columbia Press, 1997.

Price, R. F. *Education in Modern China*. 2nd ed. London: Routledge & Kegan Paul, 1979.

Rawski, Evelyn Sakakida. *Education and Popular Literacy in Ch'ing China*. Ann Arbor: University of Michigan Press, 1979.

Ross, Heidi. *UNESCO EFA Monitoring Group Report: Literacy Education in China*. Paris: UNESCO, 2006.

Seeberg, Vilma. *Literacy in China: The Effect of the National Development Context and Policy on Literacy Levels, 1949–79*. Bochum, Germany: Brockmeyer, 1990.

Seeberg, Vilma, Heidi Ross, Tan Guangyu, and Liu Jinghuan. Grounds for Prioritizing Education for Girls: The Telling Case of Left-behind Rural China. In *International Perspectives on Education and Society*; Vol. 8: *Education for All: Global Promises, National Challenges*, eds. David Baker and Alexander Wiseman, 109–154. Oxford: Elsevier Science, 2007.

Su Xiaohuan. *Education in China: Reforms and Innovations*. Beijing: China Intercontinental Press, 2002.

Thøgersen, Stig. *Secondary Education in China after Mao: Reform and Social Conflict*. Aarhus, Denmark: Aarhus University Press, 1990.

Treiman, Donald J. The Growth and Determinants of Literacy in China. California Center for Population Research, University of California, Los Angeles. On-Line Working Paper Series: Paper ccpr-005-02. 2002. http://repositories.cdlib.org/ccpr/olwp/ccpr-005-02.

Woodside, Alexander. Real and Imagined Continuities in the Chinese Struggle for Literacy. In *Education and Modernization: The Chinese Experience*, ed. Ruth Hayhoe, 23–45. New York: Pergamon Press, 1992.

Xie Goudong. Toward the Eradication of Illiteracy among Youth and Adults in China. In *Integrating Lifelong Learning Perspectives*, ed. Carolyn Medel-Añonuevo, 267–268. Hamburg, Germany: UNESCO Institute for Education, 2002.

***Heidi Ross***
***Jingjing Lou***

## KINDERGARTEN

Kindergartens in China are early childhood centers that provide education and care for children ages three to six, with programs often organized into three age groups. The first Chinese kindergarten was established in 1903 in Wuhan, the capital of Hubei Province, by the government during the Qing dynasty (1644–1912). Its curriculum and instruction were borrowed from Japan, and the principal and teachers were Japanese. The Chinese term for kindergarten, *youzhiyuan*, was taken from the Japanese *yōchien*, which was written the same way in both languages. In 1904 the provincial government in Hubei established the Guimao School System and formally included kindergarten for the first time, marking the beginning of center-based early childhood education in China.

### HISTORICAL REVIEW

Since 1949, the development of kindergartens has been closely linked to political and socioeconomic changes in China and can be roughly grouped into four periods. First, a *rapid expansion* (1949–1957) occurred when the new socialist regime encouraged women to join the labor force and rapidly developed kindergartens and nurseries in urban as well as rural areas. The major purpose of kindergartens during this period was to provide child-care services for working parents.

Second, a *chaotic* period (1958–1977) ensued when the country went through political turmoil (e.g., the Cultural Revolution) and kindergartens were closed along with other educational institutions. During this period, children were sent home and qualified teachers were sent to rural or remote areas for reeducation through labor.

Third, a period of *resurgence* (1978–1993) developed when, propelled by an open-door policy, market-economy reform, and the one-child policy that started in the late 1970s, kindergartens enjoyed unprecedented development and provided early childhood care and education to a larger number of children and parents. More importantly, a series of recommendations, regulations, and guidelines were issued to regulate kindergartens during this period. As a result, kindergartens became better regulated, and the focus of the programs changed from custodial child care to a balance between care and education (Zhu Jiaxong and X. Christine Wang, 2005).

Fourth, a *commercialization* period began in 1994 as the market economy began to take hold in China. Kindergartens were forced to commercialize. Early childhood education was eliminated from the compulsory education system and lost public funding. In addition, the early childhood education departments at different governmental levels were cut and weakened. Consequently, kindergartens were transformed into market-driven and self-funded systems.

### PROVISION AND ENROLLMENT

Corresponding to the aforementioned changes, Table 1 presents the official figures on the provision and enrollment of kindergartens from 1949 to 2005. The gross enrollment ratio for kindergarten increased rapidly in the 1990s, from

**Number of kindergartens and kindergarteners in China (1949–2005)**

| Year | Kindergartens (1,000) | Kindergarteners (100,000) |
|---|---|---|
| 1949 | 1.3 | 1.3 |
| 1950 | 1.8 | 1.4 |
| 1951 | 4.8 | 3.82 |
| 1952 | 6.531 | 4.24 |
| 1957 | 16.42 | 10.88 |
| 1962 | 17.564 | 14.46 |
| 1965 | 19.226 | 17.13 |
| 1975 | 171.749 | 62 |
| 1978 | 163.952 | 78.77 |
| 1979 | 165.629 | 87.92 |
| 1980 | 170.419 | 115.08 |
| 1981 | 130.296 | 105.62 |
| 1982 | 122.107 | 111.31 |
| 1983 | 136.306 | 114.03 |
| 1984 | 166.526 | 129.47 |
| 1985 | 172.262 | 147.97 |
| 1986 | 173.376 | 162.9 |
| 1987 | 176.775 | 180.78 |
| 1988 | 171.845 | 185.453 |
| 1989 | 172.634 | 184.7656 |
| 1990 | 172.322 | 197.22 |
| 1991 | 164.465 | 220.93 |
| 1992 | 172.506 | 242.82 |
| 1993 | 165.197 | 255.25 |
| 1994 | 174.657 | 263.03 |
| 1995 | 180.438 | 271.1233 |
| 1996 | 187.324 | 266.6327 |
| 1997 | 182.485 | 251.8964 |
| 1998 | 181.368 | 240.3034 |
| 1999 | 181.136 | 232.625 |
| 2000 | 175.836 | 224.4181 |
| 2001 | 111.706 | 202.1837 |
| 2002 | 111.752 | 203.6025 |
| 2003 | 116.39 | 200.3906 |
| 2004 | 117.899 | 208.94 |
| 2005 | 124.4 | 217.903 |

SOURCE: China National Society of Early Childhood Education (CNSECE). *BaiNian ZhongGuo YouJiao (The Centenary Chinese Preschool Education)*. Beijing: Educational Science, 2003; Ministry of Education. *ZhongGuo JiaoYu TongJi NianJian (Educational Statistics Yearbook of China 2006)*. Beijing: People's Education Press. 2006.

***Table 1***

29.9 percent of the preschoolers in 1991 to 47 percent in 1996. In 2005, when China's population exceeded an estimated 1.3 billion, there were 124,400 kindergartens and 21,790,300 kindergarteners (Ministry of Education, 2006). Noticeable disparities existed in the gross enrollment ratio between rural and urban areas, and there was an urgent need to develop early childhood education in rural areas, including full-scale kindergartens or one-year preschool programs.

## TYPES OF KINDERGARTENS

Based on different funding sources, there are four types of kindergartens in China: (1) Kindergartens serving governmental personnel at all levels are basically funded and supported by the government; (2) Kindergartens serving parents working in state-owned enterprises, companies, or factories, as well as the army, are funded by their owners and can be regarded as kindergartens indirectly owned by the state; (3) Kindergartens under the jurisdiction of street offices—the lowest level of municipal government—are self-funded with partial financial support from owners; (4) Kindergartens that are operated and supported by non-governmental organizations or private owners. Some preschool classes in the countryside are attached to primary schools and cater to the needs of children from age five to age six or seven. These four types of kindergartens vary substantially by location (i.e., rural area, county/town, or city), organizer (i.e., education department, other departments, community, or private sector), and quality (the first two types of kindergartens usually offer higher quality than the latter two).

## CURRICULA AND PEDAGOGIES

There were three paradigm shifts and major waves of curriculum reform during the twentieth century. First, the Japanese version and then the American model of kindergarten education were imported into China during the 1920s and 1940s. The Soviet model was adopted during the 1950s, and its teacher-directed and subject-based approach was widely used. Beginning in the 1980s, Chinese educators adopted the American model of child-centered curricula and pedagogies, although educational approaches based on American democracy and progressive ideals are often not congruent with Chinese culture and traditions. Thus, early teaching of reading and writing, which parents and teachers find desirable, is prohibited by China's educational authorities, leading to difficulties in implementation (Zhu Jiaxong and X. Christine Wang, 2005). Chinese researchers and practitioners of early childhood education have begun critical reflection on these borrowed ideas, and have endeavored to form culturally appropriate curricula and pedagogies, which may result in a hybrid of three cultural threads: Confucian, Communist, and Western.

## TEACHER QUALIFICATION AND PROFESSIONALISM

The minimum entrance requirement for kindergarten teachers is a diploma from a normal school (i.e., a two-year teacher-training institution that accepts middle-school graduates) or a two- or four-year college that admits high-school graduates. Directors of kindergartens usually have considerable working experience and training in administration. In 2000, among 946,448 directors and teachers, 12 percent had a two- or four-year college degree, 45 percent were normal-school graduates, 27 percent graduated from

***Kindergarten teacher with his students, Changchun, Jilin province, July 6, 2006.*** *Eliminated during the Cultural Revolution, kindergarten education reemerged in China in the late 1970s, combining early learning with child care. While traditionally a female-dominated profession, in recent years the government has encouraged the development of male teachers in kindergarten classrooms.* CHINA PHOTOS/GETTY IMAGES

vocational schools, and 17 percent and 10 percent were senior or junior secondary-school graduates, respectively (Margaret Wong and Pang Lijuan 2002).

## A TYPICAL DAY IN A CHINESE KINDERGARTEN CLASSROOM

Most urban kindergartens provide full-day service that begins at about 7:30 a.m. and ends at 5:30 p.m. Only a few kindergartens function as boarding schools, where children sleep at the center on weeknights. Classrooms are usually brightly lit, well ventilated, and equipped with a variety of learning materials, which are organized into different learning centers. Children's desks are often arranged in groups. Many activities and transition points punctuate the day, as outlined in the following summary of a typical day:

7:30-8:05, welcome and greeting

8:05-8:30, breakfast

8:30-8:45, free play, reading and chatting

8:45-9:30, theme activities

9:30-9:45, drinks

9:40-10:10, learning corner activities

10:10-11:10, outdoor activities

11:10-11:30, story time

11:30-12:00, lunch

12:00-12:10, after-lunch walk

12:10-2:30, nap

2:30-3:30, clean up, outdoor activities, and snack

3:30-4:30, subject activities (language/music/math/arts)

4:30-5:00, free play and packing up

5:00-5:30, farewell routine

Much more time is spent in teacher-directed activities than in children's free play (Roa Nirmala and Li Hui, 2008). The highly structured curriculum reflects China's cultural tradition of group-oriented collectivism.

**SEE ALSO** *Life Cycle: Infancy and Childhood.*

**BIBLIOGRAPHY**

China National Society of Early Childhood Education (CNSECE). *Bainian zhongguo youjiao* [The centenary Chinese preschool education]. Beijing: Educational Science, 2003.

Liu Yan and Feng Xiaoxia. Kindergarten Educational Reform during the Past Two Decades in Mainland China: Achievements and Problems. *International Journal of Early Years Education* 13, 2 (2005): 93–99.

Ministry of Education. *Zhongguo jiaoyu tongji nianjian* [Educational statistics yearbook of China 2006]. Beijing: People's Education Press, 2006.

Pang Lijuan and Margaret Wong. Early Childhood Education in China: Issues and Development. In *International Developments in Early Childhood Services*, eds. Lorna Chan and Elizabeth Mellor, 53–69. New York: Lang, 2002.

Rao, Nirmala, and Li Hui. "Eduplay": Beliefs and Practices Related to Play and Learning in Chinese Kindergartens. In *Play and Learning in Early Childhood Settings: International Perspectives*, eds. Ingrid Pramling Samuelsson and Marylin Fleer, 72–92. New York: Springer, 2009.

Zhu Jiaxong and X. Christine Wang. Contemporary Early Childhood Education Research in China. In *International Perspectives on Research in Early Childhood Education*, eds. Bernard Spodek and Olivia N. Saracho, 55–77. Greenwich, CT: Information Age, 2005.

***Hui Li***

## HIGHER EDUCATION BEFORE 1949

Since its beginnings in the late nineteenth century, China's modern higher-education system has passed through several structural reforms. As the country itself underwent industrialization and social transformation, higher education experienced a series of adjustments to enable it to keep pace with the need for well-trained professionals and leaders in the social and cultural domains.

### FOUNDATIONS AND EARLY GROWTH

Some scholars have argued that the early Chinese colleges originated with the language and engineering schools built as part of the Self-strengthening movement (1861–1894). A more obvious point of departure is during the period of the political movement in the 1890s that represented the voice of reformist elites in a changing China. Beiyang University (Beiyang Xi Xuetang, present-day Tianjin University) was established in 1895, followed by the Imperial University of Beijing (Jingshi Da Xuetang, present-day Beijing University or Beida) in 1898.

In the early 1900s, a comprehensive higher-education system emerged as an important part of China's first western-style educational system. Its key institutions were comprehensive universities (*da xuetang*), advanced teachers' colleges (*youji shifan xuetang*), higher specialty colleges (*gaodeng zhuanye xuetang*), and preparatory programs (*yuke*). A comprehensive university was expected to offer programs in Chinese classics, law, literature, medicine, science, agriculture, engineering, and commerce. Although graduate schools (*tongru yuan*) were planned, this part of the project was never implemented.

In the last decades of Qing rule, there were three comprehensive universities (Jingshi Da Xuetang, Beiyang Xi Xuetang, and Shanxi Da Xuetang) and a number of higher specialty colleges (including colleges of language, politics and law, commerce, agriculture, industry, and medicine) and advanced teachers' colleges distributed throughout the provinces. These institutions composed the main body of Chinese higher education. They provided various programs with flexibility for responding to China's urgent needs for economic development and social transformation. The abolition of the thousand-year-old civil service examination in 1905 made modern higher education an important avenue for old literati to develop modern identities through gaining the credentials to join a new social elite. By 1909, the three universities had 749 students, twenty-five specialty colleges had 4,525 students, and nine advanced teachers' colleges had a total of 1,580 students.

In the early Republican period (1910s), the Ministry of Education restructured higher education by abolishing the specialty colleges and preparatory programs, and building three new national universities in Wuchang, Nanjing, and Guangzhou. At the same time, the advanced teachers' colleges, now known as national higher teachers' colleges (*guoli gaodeng shifan*), were distributed throughout six educational districts (Nanjing, Wuchang, Beijing, Chengdu, Guangzhou, and Shenyang) to direct local education. In addition, in order to expand China's system of higher education, the Ministry of Education recognized private universities and colleges.

Under the warlord government from 1916 to 1927, secondary education suffered serious stagnation due to the provincial government's embezzlement of educational funds for military use. Higher education, however, with the cooperation among the Ministry of Education, national elites, and social organizations, developed rapidly during this period. The education reform of 1922 dominated by above forces stimulated both the growth of private universities and the transformation of specialty colleges into universities.

Unofficial data indicate that the government budget for higher education in 1925 was 11,473,289 yuan. In 1916 there were ten universities nationwide (including both public and private); by 1925 there were twenty-one national universities, nine provincial universities, and ten

***Chinese man studying, 1874.*** *In late nineteenth-century China, education reform became increasingly important to many leaders, particularly after humiliating conditions imposed by Western nations after the Opium Wars. Imperial officials hoped modernizing the nation's educational system would result in a stronger China, better equipped for future self-defense.* © HULTON-DEUTSCH COLLECTION/CORBIS

registered private universities, with a total of 21,483 students and 3,762 faculty and staff. During this period, many public colleges and universities, for the first time in Chinese history, opened their doors to female students. A women's teachers' college was established in 1920, becoming a women's normal university in 1924. By 1925, the total number of female students enrolled in all types of universities and colleges had reached 972.

Universities and colleges were not only training centers for professionals but also venues for social movements. Beijing University played a key role, especially in the warlord era. While he was president of Beida, Cai Yuanpei (1867–1940) carried out a policy of "tolerance and inclusion of all learnings" (*jianrong bingbao*), successfully establishing Beida's academic leadership by embracing both traditional Chinese learning and newly introduced Western learning. In the history of Chinese education, Beida provides the leading example of academic freedom and intellectual innovation. It became known as a center of enlightenment, and led both the New Culture Movement from the 1910s to the 1920s and the student movement of May 4, 1919.

## HIGHER EDUCATION UNDER THE NATIONALIST GOVERNMENT

The period of Nationalist government in Nanjing from 1927 to 1937 was another era of rapid development in higher education. According to the government's regulation of education, a comprehensive university must possess at least three of the following colleges: humanities and social sciences, science, law, education, agriculture, industry, commerce, or medicine. Professional schools, in contrast, could be established individually. Private schools had to acquire permission and registration from the government. In 1931 eighteen universities and colleges were nationally funded, twenty-one were funded by provincial governments, and thirty-seven by private sources. Together they had 38,805 students and 6,318 faculty and staff members. By 1936, the number of universities and colleges had increased to 108 with 41,922 in-school students and 11,850 faculty and staff. Funds for higher education that year reached 39,275,386 yuan.

The uneven distribution of educational resources to the provision of higher education during this period resulted in clear social discrepancies between the elite and the masses, urban and rural, and coast and hinterland. European education experts sent by the League of Nations in 1931 observed that students tended to enroll in the fields of political sciences and law rather than in the natural sciences and engineering. They concluded that students' preference for government positions continued a centuries-long tradition of Chinese literati studying for access to fame and wealth via government office.

Furthermore, the number of college students during this period accounted for a mere 0.01 percent of the population, with most students coming from wealthy urban families, leading to elitism in higher education. Because most universities and colleges were located in coastal areas and big cities, such as Beijing, Shanghai, and Nanjing, urban elites had a monopoly on educational opportunities. This concentration of higher education in cities caused serious concern among scholars nationwide that the urban schools were drawing youth away from rural areas. The fear was that rural communities would be left isolated from developed urban civilization.

In the 1930s, institutions of higher education were required by the Nationalist Party to politicize education. The Ministry of Education ordered all schools to add military training and courses on the Nationalist Party's ideology to their curricula as a means of building discipline and loyalty to the party. To reinforce control of the country's universities and colleges, the government elevated National Southeast University (Guoli Dongnan Daxue) to the rank of National Central University (Guoli Zhongyang Daxue, or Nanjing University after 1952), an institution meant to provide academic leadership. The government also established a new university, National Central Political University (Guoli Zhongyang Zhengzhi Daxue) to train party cadres and government officials.

Social movements also served to politicize education in China. In an atmosphere of surging nationalism created by successive acts of Japanese aggression in the 1930s, many college students turned to political radicalism, becoming actively involved in protests and movements of national salvation against the Nationalist government's ambiguity in the face of Japanese expansion in China.

## THE WAR YEARS AND AFTER

After the outbreak of the Anti-Japanese War in 1937, most universities and colleges moved to the "Great Rear" region in southwest China. This relocation led to another reorganization of Chinese higher education. In 1938 three of China's top universities, Beijing (Beiping) University, Qinghua (Tsinghua) University, and Nankai University, merged to become Southwest United University (Xi'nan Lianhe Daxue, or Lianda), established for the interim in Kunming, Yunnan Province. Other universities and colleges were scattered through the provinces of Yunnan, Guizhou, Sichuan, Guangxi, Shaanxi, and Gansu. During the eight years of war, Chinese higher education suffered from an absence of financial security and extreme shortages of library facilities and other equipment. Although the number of universities dropped during the war, from forty-one in 1934 to thirty-eight in 1945, the number of four-year specialty colleges increased from thirty-eight to fifty-seven, and three-year technical colleges increased from thirty-one to fifty-two over the same period. The total number of students rose from 41,922 in 1936 to 80,646 in 1945, with a budget in the latter year of 1.8 billion yuan (roughly equivalent to 1,800,000 yuan in 1936 currency).

The relocation of Chinese universities and colleges to remote regions of southwest and northwest China during the war resulted in a large-scale cultural transfer. The students and faculty of these universities and colleges, with their academic and social activities, introduced new concepts and lifestyles to local society and helped disseminate modern knowledge. These schools also left a legacy to the provinces by offering the opportunity of higher education to the youth of inland areas who previously had virtually no access. After the war, most of these universities and colleges moved back to their original bases, but they left a large number of trained teachers and facilities in the localities where they had temporarily resided. This provided the foundations for the People's Republican government's program of redistribution and dispensation inland of higher-education resources over the next decade.

The relocation of Chinese higher education during the war also marked a turning point in Chinese academia. Inspired by the diversity of local ethnic groups and the richness of their cultures, many scholars and graduate students of humanities reoriented their academic research, turning away from Western subjects to the study of Chinese local cultures and communities. Graduate studies in China before 1949 were composed of only a very small sector of higher education, mostly confined to the humanities, social sciences, and theoretical science. The number of graduate students was also small, 369 in 1947, with a later peak only of 424 in 1949.

During the Anti-Japanese War, the Chinese Communist government also established some colleges and universities in the region under its control in northern China in an effort to respond to the needs of educated youth who came to the Yan'an area to join the resistance movement, simultaneously providing manpower to the expanding Communist revolutionary base areas. The best-known institutions of this period were the Resisting Japan Political and Military Academy (Kang Ri Junzheng DaxuE), Lu Xun Academy of Arts (Lu Xun Yishu Xueyuan), Yan'an Women's College (Yan'an Nüzi Daxue), and the Marxism-Leninism Academy (Ma-Lie Zhuyi Xueyuan). Although the central task of these institutions was to train cadres for the Communist Party and governments, the educational goals, the administrative systems, the curricula, and the pedagogy of these institutions inaugurated a new tradition that became dominant in higher education after 1949.

After the Anti-Japanese War, the scale of China's higher-education system remained much the same as in the war years nationwide. With its defeat in military and political battles on the mainland, the Nationalist government moved to Taiwan, where it relocated a number of China's top universities, including Qinghua University, Jiaotong (National Chiao Tung) University, and Central Political (National Chengchi) University. The majority of universities and colleges, however, were left to the new regime on mainland. After 1949, China's higher-education system entered another chapter under the new government of the People's Republic of China.

**BIBLIOGRAPHY**

Becker, Carl. H., et al. *The Reorganization of Education in China*. Paris: League of Nations Institute of Intellectual Cooperation, 1932.

Chan, Ming K., and Arif Dirlik. *Schools into Fields and Factories: Anarchists, the Guomindang, and the National Labor University in Shanghai, 1927–1932*. Durham, NC: Duke University Press, 1991.

Cong, Xiaoping. *Teachers' Schools and the Making of the Modern Chinese Nation-State, 1897–1937*. Toronto: University of British Columbia Press, 2007.

Hayhoe, Ruth. *China's Universities, 1895–1995: A Century of Cultural Conflict*. New York: Garland, 1996.

Israel, John. *Lianda: A Chinese University in War and Revolution*. Stanford, CA: Stanford University Press, 1998.

Jiaoyu bu [Ministry of Education]. *Di yi ci Zhongguo jiaoyu nianjian* [The first yearbook on the education of China, 1932]. Reprint. Taibei: Zhuanji wenxue chubanshe, 1971.

Jiaoyu bu tongji shi [Office of Statistics, Ministry of Education]. *Quanguo gaodeng jiaoyu tongji, 1934* [Statistics of higher education, 1934]. Shanghai: Shangwu yinshuguan, 1936.

*Kangzhan yilai de gaodeng jiaoyu zhuanhao* [Special issue on higher education since the war]. *Jiaoyu zazhi* [Educational review] 31, 1 (1941).

Lin, Xiaoqing Diana. *Peking University: Chinese Scholarship and Intellectuals, 1898–1937*. Albany, NY: State University of New York Press, 2005.

Linden, Allen. Politics and Education in Nationalist China: The Case of the University Council, 1927–1928. *Journal of Asian Studies* 27, 4 (1968): 763–776.

Ou Yuanhai. Kangzhan shi nian lai Zhongguo de daxue jiaoyu [Chinese higher education in the past ten years of wartime]. *Jiaoyu jiaoyujie* [Chinese educational circle] 1, 1 (1947): 7–15.

Pepper, Suzanne. *Radicalism and Education Reform in Twentieth-century China*. New York: Cambridge University Press, 1996.

Weston, Timothy B. *The Power of Position: Beijing University, Intellectuals, and Chinese Political Cultural, 1898–1929*. Berkeley, CA: University of California Press, 2004.

Yeh, Wen-hsin. *The Alienated Academy: Culture and Politics in Republican China, 1919–1937*. Cambridge, MA: Harvard University Press, 1990.

***Xiaoping Cong***

## HIGHER EDUCATION SINCE 1949

China's higher-education system has experienced momentous change since 1949. At the start of the new regime, with Mao Zedong and Zhou Enlai leading the country, universities were nationalized and many were renamed, thus putting an end to all private higher education. The direction of higher education during the period of socialist transformation became heavily influenced by the Soviet Union, which emphasized ideological support for socialist construction, separation of universities from research institutes, highly specialized fields of study, a close link between education and labor, and university access for children of peasants and workers. Student tuition fees were abolished and graduates were allocated to work positions according to a centralized planning system. Aside from the colleges and universities under the Ministry of Education, many others were administered by respective ministries (agriculture, railroad, textiles, forestry, the post and communications, etc.) and graduates were allocated to work units under these ministries.

College and university personnel were organized into *danwei*—the basic unit of communist social life—with an "iron rice bowl" that included salary, accommodations, meals, health care, and other benefits guaranteed for life. Even after relations with the Soviet Union soured in the late 1950s, most academic exchange continued to occur with the communist block nations, and the structure of higher education remained intact.

Although the number of higher-education institutions increased moderately from 205 to 227 and enrollments grew from 166,504 to 403,176 in the seven years after 1949, the totalitarian regime of this period placed severe limits on academic freedom. In 1956 Chairman Mao launched the Hundred Flowers campaign, inviting intellectuals to air their views, but followed it with an anti-rightist crackdown the following year that punished a great many scholars and intellectuals. The pace of higher-education expansion quickened during the Great Leap Forward period (1958–1960), and by 1966 the number of colleges and universities had reached 434 with 680,000 students. Not long after that, in May 1966, Chairman Mao launched the Cultural Revolution, which threw Chinese higher education into chaos. Many professors were severely criticized, and universities were closed for several years, with devastating effects on Chinese higher education.

In June 22, 1968, the editor's note of *People's Daily* contained Mao's instruction that universities still have to be run, but with a heavy emphasis on science and engineering courses. Length of study was provisionally set at two to three years with advanced studies only lasting one year. In a report concerning enrollment submitted by Peking and Qinghua universities in 1970, it was decided that the task of workers, peasants, and soldiers was to study in university and reform them in accordance with Mao Zedong Thought. In 1972 a notification was announced to stop the practice of getting into university though the back door, but the practice continued. A week later a report in Beijing pointed out that 20 percent of university students only had an elementary school education. Thus, when colleges and universities began to reopen, examinations were eliminated, standards were ignored, enrollments shrunk, and teaching and research become judged by erratic political trends. Many academic staff and university graduates were sent off to work in rural areas to receive labor training before they were assigned to jobs. Thus, along with the graduates of urban junior and senior higher schools who were sent "up to the hills and down to the villages" to settle and start their families, most now agree that a generation of talent was lost. Higher education was left in a highly weakened and hyperpoliticized state. As China exited the Cultural Revolution, enrollments rapidly shot up from 273,000 in 1977 to 401,000 in 1978. However, a lack of facilities and qualified teachers caused plans to be scaled down to 275,000 in 1979, 281,000 in 1980, 279,000 in 1981, and 315,000 for 1982. As Deng Xiaoping came to power and launched a series of economic reforms and opened China to the outside world, higher education access and quality would gradually recover and eventually reap the positive effects of these reforms.

The shift away from a centrally planned economy brought unprecedented change to higher education. This period was also marked by a rehabilitation of intellectuals, many of whom had been sent to rural areas, and the return to urban China of many of the "sent-down youth" formerly at school before the Cultural Revolution. Examinations for entrance to higher education were reintroduced, and academic standards were greatly strengthened as the system tried to maintain an academic faculty that was both "red and expert." There was also a shift in the direction of overseas study, and Western societies with capitalist economies quickly became favored study destinations. By 1985, the number of institutions of higher education had increased to 1,016, though most only had an average enrollment of between two and three thousand students.

When the Ministry of Education was upgraded to a commission from 1985 to 1998, reforms were introduced that gave more autonomy to universities in matters of curriculum, staffing, and student selection. Higher-education gross enrollment rates of the 18–22 age group remained low from about two percent in 1980 to three percent in 1990. The student demonstrations of 1986 and 1989 ensured they would remain so as the leadership became concerned about social instability, especially exemplified by its military suppression of student demonstrations in Beijing's Tiananmen Square in 1989.

By the mid-1990s, Deng Xiaoping had made a concerted effort to rejuvenate China's economic reforms and further open the way for market forces to operate in society. For universities, this meant an upsurge in enrollments and steadily rising tuition fees, paralleled by efforts to institutionalize student loans. Colleges and universities sought to achieve economies of scale through expanded student numbers, and the gross enrollment rate rose past 4 percent.

A further expansion of enrollment rates in the late 1990s signaled a determined shift from elite to mass higher education. By this time, the job allocation system that had assigned students to jobs after graduation was being dismantled. Market forces began to take a greater role in many aspects of college and university life. Many colleges and universities shifted to formula funding, generated much of their own revenue, cooperated more with industry, ran various enterprises, borrowed capital construction

***First-year college students in Xi'an, Shaanxi province, August 23, 2005.*** *In the 1970s, Deng Xiaoping promoted modernizing China through higher education, allowing students to attend foreign institutions. Although increased government funding in the twenty-first century has led to the growth of domestic universities, many students continue to study outside of China, looking to gain experience in the Western world.* © CHINA NEWSPHOTO/REUTERS/CORBIS

funds from banks, charged higher student fees, admitted adult learners into regular higher education programs, and consolidated themselves with other institutions to attain economies of scale.

While the state Ministry of Education maintained direct control of about 3 to 4 percent of universities, over four hundred institutions of higher education formerly under the authority of various central government ministries were transferred to provincial or local education bureaus. Those directly affiliated with the State Council were cut from 367 to 111. This occurred as a result of the national policy to slim down state-owned enterprises and the central government bureaucracy. In the meantime, institutional enrollments began to balloon as scores of colleges and universities were consolidated into larger scale institutions. The average number of students in regular institutions of higher education was 3,112 in 1997, up from 1,919 in 1990, when about 80 percent of China's universities had fewer than four thousand students, and about 60 percent had fewer than three thousand students. By 2000, 612 colleges and universities were consolidated into 250 (Postiglione 2002).

The breakneck-paced expansion of Chinese higher education that began around the turn of the century is historically unprecedented. While only about 4 percent of the 18–22 age group was involved in higher education in 1995, the 2005 figure had surpassed 20 percent. For example, in 2000, there were two million new students admitted to regular higher-education institutions, those traditionally catering to secondary school graduates, though for the first time, adults over the age of twenty-five were permitted to enter these regular institutions of higher education. In 1999, 4,367,700 students were enrolled in regular higher-education programs, and 3,054,900 were enrolled in adult-education institutes. The equally large adult sector of higher education remained intact, though the boundaries between the two sectors began to blur.

The decision to expand higher education was due in part from the pressure of the growing numbers graduating from secondary school. With few exceptions, China's education system had largely settled on the 6+3+3 schooling format followed by either a four-year college and university bachelor's degree program or a two- to three-year specialized vocational-technical diploma program. The government's decision to expand higher education also aimed to stimulate the economy in the aftermath of the Asian economic crisis by getting families to spend more of their savings (and to keep more students in school during a period of rising unemployment).

***A student filming graduation ceremonies at Tsinghua University, Beijing, July 18, 2007.*** *While many young Chinese continue to attend foreign universities, the number of students at domestic institutions has risen, due in part to reforms enacted in the 1980s to rebuild an educational system dismantled during the purges of the Cultural Revolution.* CHINA PHOTOS/GETTY IMAGES

China's human resource blueprint published in 2003 set out the long-term expansion plan for higher education. Before 2010, the entrance rate for higher education would be raised from around 13 percent to over 20 percent, reaching the level of a moderately developed nation. In fact, UNESCO reported that as of July 2003, China already had highest number of college and university students in the world, followed by the United States, India, Russia, and Japan (Xing 2003), By 2007, China's largest city had a gross enrollment ratio exceeding 60 percent (Shen 2003). Between 2010 and 2020, the gross entrance rate of higher education is set to exceed 40 percent, and from 2021 to 2050 to reach at least 50 percent.

China's higher-education expansion would not have been tenable without private (or what is known as *minban,* or popularly run) higher education. While China's private higher-education institutions remained relatively weak (only some could grant degrees) and in a marginal position, they did relieve financial pressure on government and provided more opportunities to those who could pay for a higher education. In 2002, there were 320,000 undergraduates studying in private colleges and universities, accounting for only 2.2 percent of all China's undergraduates. In December 2002, the Standing Committee of the National People's Congress passed the Private Education Promotion Law of the People's Republic of China, regarded as a breakthrough in privatization of higher education in China. The new law was followed in September 2003 by the Regulations on Sino-foreign Cooperative Education of the People's Republic of China. Meanwhile, the Ministry of Education promulgated its *Opinions to Standardize and Intensify the Management of Independent Colleges Run by Regular Colleges and Universities with New Mechanisms and Models,* which aroused concern on the part of private colleges and universities because it permitted public colleges and universities to found "second-tier colleges" (e.g., independent colleges) with lower entrance-score requirements and high tuition fees. Over three hundred independent colleges were established nationwide, enrolling some 400,000 undergraduates.

Another major development concerned rising expectations for China to establish a system of world-class universities. Government support, as indicated in the so-called

211 and 985 policies, provided major financial backing to top institutions with high levels of academic promise. Enormous attention was directed at both the international rankings of top universities and the questions of how to establish and maintain a world-class university. The most visible effort to transform China's universities was the so-called Peking University reform (*Beida gaige*). The reform of the faculty-appointment system aroused strong feelings on and off campus and became a controversial social issue, as it called for external competition in hiring and a "last ranked, first fired" practice for university faculty. To maintain academic quality, the income of university teacher salaries in Chinese higher education was sharply increased. From 1982 to 2000, salaries grew by 101 percent. The average university teacher salary was said to be higher than that of other professions in China.

Although trying to be fiercely independent, colleges and universities came to reflect China's deepening international engagement, global economic rise, and growing leadership in the world. Moreover, China also recognized that it must become more involved in the growing trade in higher-education services worldwide. It approved hundreds of Sino-foreign joint ventures in higher education and set up Confucian institutes for Chinese language and culture study in many countries. At the same time, the number of international students coming to China grew, and the number of Chinese students leaving for overseas was maintained, despite the fact that only about one-quarter returned to China since the beginning of the reform period in 1979.

By the end of the first decade of the twenty-first century, China's higher-education system had become almost unrecognizable from its predecessor. However, it struggled to deal with longstanding problems like corruption in student enrollment and academic practices, as well as new challenges, such as high rates of unemployment among the enormous number of graduates thrown into the job market each year by the country's mammoth system of colleges and universities.

**BIBLIOGRAPHY**

Hayhoe, Ruth, ed. *China's Universities and the Open Door.* Armonk, NY: Sharpe, 1989.

Hayhoe, Ruth. *China's Universities, 1895–1995: A Century of Cultural Conflict.* New York: Garland, 1996.

Min Weifang (Weifang Min). China. In *Asian Higher Education: An International Handbook and Reference Guide,* eds. Gerard A. Postiglione and Grace C. L. Mak, 37–55. Westport, CT: Greenwood, 1997.

Min Weifang (Weifang Min). Chinese Higher Education: The Legacy of the Past and the Context of the Future. In *Asian Universities: Historical Perspectives and Contemporary Challenges,* eds. Philip Altbach and Toru Umakoshi, 53–84. Baltimore, MD: Johns Hopkins University Press, 2004.

Pepper, Suzanne. *Radicalism and Education Reform in 20th Century Education: The Search for an Ideal Development Model.* New York: Cambridge University Press, 1996.

Postiglione, Gerard A. Chinese Higher Education at the Turn of the Century: Expansion, Consolidation, and the Globalization. In *Higher Education in the Developing World: Changing Contexts and Institutional Responses,* eds. David Chapman and Ann Austin, 149–166. Westport, CT: Greenwood, 2002.

Postiglione, Gerard A. Higher Education in China: Perils and Promises for a New Century. *Harvard China Review* (2005): Volume 5, Number 2: 138–143.

Shen Zuyun (Zuyun Chen). Shanghai jiang shuaixian shixian gaodeng jiaoyu puji hua: 2002 nian gaodeng jiaoyu maoruxuelu yida 51%, 5 nianhou jiangda 60% yishang [Shanghai will take the lead in the massification of higher education: Gross enrollment rate reaches 51 % in 2002 and set to move beyond 60 % in five years]. *China Education Daily,* February 17, 2003. http://www.jyb.com.cn/gb/2003/02/17/zy/jryw/1.htm.

Xing Dan (Dan Xing). Zhongguo gaodeng jiaoyu guimo shouci chaoguo meiguo yueju shijie diyi [The scale of higher education in China surpasses the United States for the first time, leaping to first position in the world]. *Eastday News* June 24, 2003. http://news.eastday.com/epublish/gb/paper148/20030624/class014800014/hwz968718.htm.

Yang Rui (Rui Yang). *The Third Delight: The Internationalization of Higher Education in China.* London and New York: Routledge, 2002.

***Gerard A. Postiglione***

## CHRISTIAN UNIVERSITIES AND COLLEGES

Education was a significant aspect of the Protestant missionary endeavor in China. Robert Morrison (1782–1834), who arrived in China in September 1807, was a pioneer in this field. Morrison was the first Protestant missionary sent by London Missionary Society. After working for ten years in Macau and Guangzhou (Canton) without having won a single soul, he submitted the Ultra-Ganges Mission Plan to the London Missionary Society in 1817. Among other things, he proposed to set up a school in Malacca (Melaka) in present-day Malaysia to reach overseas Chinese there, pending the opening of China (Harrison 1979, pp. 22–23).

Though the Christian movement was vested with full consciousness of being global and universal, missionaries in China had to interact with local situations and develop in the process a new approach suited to the Chinese culture. For instance, when the Anglo-Chinese College was established in Malacca in 1818, Morrison stated that the school should have a dual purpose. On the one hand, it would carry out the London Missionary Society's aim "of spreading Christ's Gospel into China." On the other hand, it gave expression to Morrison's hope that he could advance from merely preaching the gospel to promoting the Sino-Western cultural exchange, hence the name Anglo-Chinese College (Wu Yixiong 2000, pp. 318–335). This college became the first research center in Southeast Asia to engage in such a cultural exchange.

The extension of missionary activities in China itself was made possible by the Treaty of Nanjing, signed in 1842, whereby Hong Kong was ceded to Great Britain and five other ports were opened for trade and missionary activities, including Shanghai, Ningbo, Xiamen (Amoy), Fuzhou, and Guangzhou. Missionaries began to establish mission schools at the primary and secondary levels in the five ports; these institutions gradually developed into Christian universities and colleges.

According to the records of the first missionary conference held at Shanghai in 1877, many missionaries at that time remained hesitant about the relevance of educational work in China, simply because: (1) it was not directly related to the Christian mission; (2) education was concerned with secular knowledge, which could be harmful to the teaching of the Christian gospel; and (3) many believed the money received from missionary societies should be spent for direct evangelistic work and not for secular work such as running schools. To counter these views, missionaries who were in favor of education, such as Calvin Mateer (1836–1908), argued that "mission schools were for evangelization" and "education was the means and tools for evangelism" (Mateer 1877, p. 171). It was only at the second missionary conference held in Shanghai in 1890 that a significant number of missionaries showed themselves convinced of the value and validity of Christian education in China. Indeed, missionary education did not begin to experience significant development until the end of the nineteenth century.

## CHRISTIAN EDUCATION IN TWENTIETH-CENTURY CHINA

After the turn of the twentieth century, Christian education became a booming enterprise in China. Interestingly, the Boxer Uprising led missionaries to realize that Chinese people needed to be better educated if they were to be less hostile to foreigners and missionaries. Between 1907 and 1920, the number of Christian schools in China increased threefold, and the student population reached as high as 245,000. In higher education, only 199 students were enrolled in a handful of Christian colleges in 1900, but by 1920 there were sixteen Christian colleges with 1,700 students (Stauffer 1922). The Christian educational enterprise in China was growing so rapidly that by the 1920s it was almost independent of the missionary enterprise, especially with regard to school administration and curriculum.

After 1920, Christian higher education entered a different phrase. The Burton Education Commission report of 1922 issued a new directive concerning Christian education in China—namely, to be "more Efficient, more Christian and more Chinese." This coincided with the rise of the anti-Christian movement and the "reclaim educational sovereignty" movement in China, which quickened the sinicization of Christian schools. As a result, the Chinese government issued a number of regulations to prevent missionary schools from propagating religion and to ensure Chinese leadership or strong participation in the schools (Wallace 1926, pp. 227–228). These were strict, yet sensible demands from the government, and in his report to the Board of Trustees, John Leighton Stuart (1876–1962), the president of Yenching (Yanjing) University in Beijing, explained to the trustees that "the nationalist movement is thoroughly reasonable and its demands are only those which any self-respecting people have a right to make" (UB Archives 1927, p. 299).

In response to the government regulations issued in 1925, many Christian colleges were registered with the government between 1927 and 1930, and by 1935 most of China's Christian colleges were registered. The most significant changes after registration were the appointment of Chinese presidents and an increase in the number of Chinese on the management boards. Christian colleges were consequently now under Chinese management and were targeted at serving the Chinese people. As a result, there were radical changes in the teaching programs and the curriculum, as the schools began to attempt to meet the needs and demands of Chinese society. In the early years, the missionaries followed a Western model of education, placing emphasis on Western sciences, theology, and religious education (Lutz 1972, pp. 71–72). Missionaries gradually realized, however, that the schools should also include Chinese language, culture, and national studies in their curriculum. In addition, courses on other religious traditions, such as Buddhism, Daoism, and the religious thought of Confucius (551–479 BCE), were offered, along with the teachings of Zhuangzi (fourth century BCE) and comparative studies of different systems of thought, particularly their contrast with Christianity.

As early as the 1920s, Yenching University was offering an astonishingly eclectic array of elective courses on such topics as religious ideas in ancient Chinese poetry, Indian philosophy, modern religious thought, Buddhism, Daoism, Islam, and Confucianism (see *Yenching University Bulletin* 1929–1930; Ng 2003, pp. 56–81). Moreover, new faculties were established in such fields as law, journalism, forestry, engineering, medical sciences, and commerce and business management at many of China's Christian colleges, most of which were upgraded to university status according to the government requirements (Lutz 1971). Indeed, some Christian colleges became nationally known for their first-class teaching and research in certain specialized fields, such as journalism at Yenching University, law at Suzhou University, forestry at Nanking (Nanjing) and Lingnan universities, library sciences at Central China (Huazhong) University, and English and engineering at St. John's University in Shanghai (Ng 2006, pp. 192–193).

## CHRISTIAN SCHOOLS IN THE PEOPLE'S REPUBLIC

At the time of the establishment of the People's Republic of China in 1949, the original thirteen Protestant Christian universities, as well as three Roman Catholic universities, were still in existence. The Protestant universities could be classified into three categories (*Educational Review* [1933] 1987, pp. 143–145):

Christian universities run by individual missionaries or Christians:

- Lingnan University in Guangzhou

Christian colleges or universities run by individual denominations or mission boards:

- University of Shanghai (Kujiang) (American Baptist Mission)
- St. John's University in Shanghai (American Protestant Episcopal Church)
- Hangzhou University (American Presbyterian Mission)
- Soochow (Suzhou) or Dongwu University in Suzhou (Methodist Episcopal Church, South)
- South China Women's (Huanan) University in Fuzhou (Methodist Episcopal Mission)

Interdenominational Christian colleges or universities:

- Yenching University in Beijing (Methodist Episcopal Mission, American Board of Commissioners for Foreign Missions, American Congregationalists, English Congregationalists, and American Presbyterian Mission)
- Shandong Christian (Cheeloo) University in Jinan (American Presbyterian Mission and English Baptist Mission)
- University of Nanking (Jinling) in Nanjing (Methodist Episcopal Mission, American Presbyterian Mission, and United Christian Mission)
- Ginling Women's College in Nanjing (American Baptist Mission, Disciples of Christ, Methodist Episcopal Mission, North and South, and American Presbyterian Mission)
- Central China (Huazhong) University in Wuhan (American Protestant Episcopal Church, London Missionary Society, Wesleyan Methodist Mission, American Reformed Church, and Yale Foreign Missionary Society)
- West China Union (Huaxi) University in Sichuan (American Baptist Church Mission, Friends' Foreign Mission Association of Great Britain and Ireland, Methodist Church of Canada [later United Church of Canada], Methodist Episcopal Mission, and Church Missionary Society of England)
- Fukien (Fujian) Christian University in Fuzhou (Church Missionary Society, American Board of Commissioners for Foreign Missions, Reformed Church in America, and Methodist Episcopal Mission)

After the Korean War began in 1950, all Christian schools in China were forced to close (He Di 1989). These schools did not continue to operate on the Chinese mainland after 1952, but the faculty and students of some of them moved to Taiwan, Hong Kong, and Southeast Asia, and from there continued the work of providing a Christian education to Chinese society. In university education, Taiwan's Fu Jen Catholic University and Suzhou (Dong Wu) University represent examples of institutions that were relocated from the mainland. Later, Chinese Christians in Taiwan established Tung Hai (Dong Hai) University and Chung Yuan Christian University to continue indigenous Christian education in Taiwan. In 1999, when Taiwan's Fu Jen Catholic University celebrated the seventieth anniversary of its founding, it was tracing its history back to its establishment in Beiping (Beijing) in 1929. Hong Kong also had Chung Chi College, which was established to continue the ideals of the former thirteen Protestant Christian universities in China, the badges and symbols of which hung on the two sides of the alter of the college chapel (Ng 2001; Ng 2003, pp. 108–134, 304–316). Later, Baptist College and Lingnan College were established in Hong Kong.

In the mid-1970s, Chung Chi College, Hong Kong Baptist College, and Lingnan College joined the Association of Christian Universities and Colleges in Asia, becoming the three universities to represent Hong Kong's Christian institutes of higher education. When Hong Kong was returned to China in 1997, Hong Kong's Christian schools, including Chung Chi College (a college of the Chinese University of Hong Kong from 1963), Hong Kong Baptist University (renamed in 1995), and Lingnan University (renamed in 1999) were restored to the motherland and became the three Christian universities and colleges located constitutionally within the public educational system of the Hong Kong Special Administration Region of the Peoples' Republic of China.

After the changes that came about in 1952, mainland scholars ceased to have any interest in the China's Christian educational enterprise, but serious reflection on Christian education continued in Taiwan and Hong Kong and overseas. After China began to implement an open-door policy in the 1980s, mainland professors and scholars gradually become interested in research into Christianity, including the study of Christian higher education in China. On the Chinese mainland, more than ten universities had established independent departments for the study of religion by the turn of the century, or offered special courses of religious studies in relevant departments. The topic of Christian higher education in China has thus received more attention from the academia. Chinese scholars in recent years have sought new insights into Christian educational activities in China, and reflected on Christianity in new ways, including from the perspective of "glocalization" (Ng 2006).

**SEE ALSO** *Morrison, Robert.*

**BIBLIOGRAPHY**


Burton Education Commission. *Christian Education in China: A Study Made by an Educational Commission Representing the Mission Boards and Societies Conducting Work in China.* New York: Foreign Missions Conference of North America, 1922.

*Educational Review* 9, 1 (March 1933). In *Diguo zhuyi qinhua jiaoyu shi ziliao: jiaohui jiaoyu* [Materials on the educational history of invasion of the imperialism in China: Church education], ed. Li Chu Cai, 143–145. Beijing: Science of Education Press, 1987.

Harrison, Brian. *Waiting for China: The Anglo-Chinese College in Malacca, 1818–1843.* Hong Kong: Hong Kong University Press, 1979.

He Di. Yenching University and the Modernization of Chinese Education. Paper delivered at the First International Conference on the History of the Pre-1949 Christian Universities in China, Wuhan Central China Normal University, 1989.

Li Chu Cai, ed. *Diguo zhuyi qinhua jiaoyu shi ziliao: Jiaohui jiaoyu* [Materials on the educational history of the invasion of imperialism in China: Church education]. Beijing: Science of Education Press, 1987.

Lutz, Jessie. *China and the Christian Colleges, 1850–1950.* Ithaca, NY: Cornell University Press, 1971.

Mateer, Calvin. The Relation of Protestant Missions to Education. *Records of the General Conference of the Protestant Missionaries of China held at Shanghai.* Shanghai: Organizing Committee of the General Conference of the Protestant Missionaries of China, 1877.

Ng, Peter Tze Ming. *Wushi nianlai Chongji xueyuan de jidujiao jiaoyu* [Chung Chi College and its Christian education in the past fifty years]. Hong Kong: Centre for the Study of Religion and Chinese Society, Chung Chi College, Chinese University of Hong Kong, 2001.

Ng, Peter Tze Ming. Cong zongjiao jiaoyu dao zongjiao yanjiu: Yanjing daxue zongjiao jiaoyude kaocha. In *Jidu zongjiao yu Zhongguo daxue jiaoyu* [Christianity and university education in China], 56–81. Beijing: Chinese Social Sciences Press, 2003.

Ng, Peter Tze Ming. *Quanqiu diyuhua shijiaoxia de jidujiao daxue* [Christian higher education in China as seen from the perspective of glocalization]. Taibei, Taiwan: Cosmic Light, 2006.

Stauffer, Milton T., ed. *The Christian Occupation of China.* Shanghai: China Continuation Committee, 1922.

Tao Feiya, and Peter Tze Ming Ng. *Jidujiao daxue yu guoxue yanjiu* [Chinese studies in Christian colleges in China]. Fuzhou: Fujian Educational Press, 1998.

United Board for Christian Higher Education Archives (UB Archives). Minutes of the Board of Trustees of Peking University (December 9, 1927). New Haven, CT: Yale Divinity School Special Collections.

Wallace, Edward. Christian Education in China: A Report. In *China Christian Year Book*, ed. Frank Rawlinson, 227–228. Shanghai: Christian Literature Society, 1926.

Wu Yixiong. *Zai Zongjiao yu shisu zhijian: Jidu xinjiao chuanjiaoshi zai huanan yanhaide zaoqi huodong yanjiu* [Between religion and the secular: Study of the early activities of missionaries in South China]. Guangzhou: Guangdong Jiaoyu Chubanshe, 2000.

*Yenching University Bulletin.* Colleges of Arts and Letters: Announcement of Courses, 1929–1930. Yenching University Archives, Yj29022, Peking University.

Zhang Kaiyuan, and Arthur Waldron, eds. *Zhongxi wenhua yu jiaohui daxue* [Christian universities and Chinese–Western cultures]. Wuhan: Hubei Educational Press, 1991.


*Peter Tze Ming Ng*

## ADULT EDUCATION

Despite China's advanced civilization, 80 percent of the population, especially women, remained illiterate in 1949 (Chakrabarti 1998). The task of spreading literacy to the countryside began in the 1930s in the Communist-controlled provinces (Yao 1987), a process accelerated from 1949 with the provision of "spare-time" literacy and basic education programs for working people. After the setback of the Cultural Revolution and its aftermath (1966–1976), there was a renewed focus on adult education with a number of major educational policy directives between 1987 and 1995 to assist China's program of modernization and economic development (Wu and Ye 1997; Xie 2003). There was also a shift toward adult education as lifelong learning, with opportunities for professionals to upgrade their skills and more investment for informal community education (Jones and Wallis 1992; Cheng et al. 1999; Han 2003).

### THE DIVERSITY OF PROVISION

Adult education in China is wide in scope and diverse in nature, incorporating basic education and literacy programs, vocational on-the-job training for workers, distance learning through radio and television universities, and programs to prepare self-taught people for examinations leading to diplomas (Li 2004). It parallels the regular school system, with adult primary, secondary, and higher education provision. Although both central and provincial government are significant providers and help regulate and evaluate the quality of programs, schools have been established by a wide range of organizations, including private businesses, trade unions, and academic institutions.

## BASIC EDUCATION AND ADULT LITERACY

In 1988 the State Council issued regulations aimed at eliminating illiteracy "regardless of sex, nationality, or race." At the same time, schools were opened in rural areas to offer courses for farmers in agriculture, forestry, and fisheries, while in townships courses were offered in such areas as business, building, transportation, and services. Official statistics indicated a massive drop in illiteracy by 2001 to only 4.8 percent of those aged fifteen to fifty (Xie 2003).

## ON-THE-JOB TRAINING

More than thirty million workers each year have been receiving on-the-job training (Xie 2003) driven by the need to adapt to technological change. Independent economic studies have indicated that the financial burden for such training has shifted from government to private investment, which has contributed significantly to efficiency and productivity, as well as improving the prospects of promotion and enhanced levels of pay (Xiao 2002; Xiao and Tsang 2004).

## WIDENING PARTICIPATION IN FURTHER AND HIGHER EDUCATION

The advent of distance and online education, correspondence courses, and evening classes has provided access for students in remote areas as well as those in full-time employment (Wang and Bott 2004). Distance education was piloted in 1979 with the establishment of the Central Radio and TV University, and by 2003 more than two thousand off-campus learning centers had been established, further progress being facilitated with the creation of the China Education and Research Network (CERNET) in 1994 and the rapid growth in the Internet and computer technology (Wang and Kreysa 2006). Students are able to access lectures through video and receive additional support through printed study materials and face-to-face tutorials with local instructors.

A parallel development has been the emergence of the self-taught examination system, allowing open access to examinations at various levels. The system came under the regulation of the State Council in 1988 to ensure parity of standards with regular full-time student provision (Zhou 2006). Education through distance learning and the self-taught system has proved flexible and cost-effective for both government and students.

## CONTINUING POST-UNIVERSITY EDUCATION

A national strategy for post-university continuing education was launched in 1987 to upgrade the skills of administrators and other professional groups through short-term training and "spare-time" study. The results have been significant in the education profession by reducing the percentage of unqualified or underqualified teachers in primary and junior middle schools. There are incentives for teachers to undergo further training by linking pay scales to qualifications and responsibilities (Li 1999), including special allowances for elite "model teachers" (*te ji*). A prestigious masters degree in subject teaching, combining on-the-job training and off-the-job university study, was also introduced in 1997 (Wang 2004; Gu 2006).

Significant developments are taking place in the upgrading of skills and knowledge in other professions, drawing where necessary on the expertise of overseas universities through partnership, knowledge transfer, and sponsorship by such bodies as the China Medical Board (New York), as in the case of nursing education (Sherwood and Liu 2005).

Increased investment in the training of lawyers (Hu 1999; Wang 2000; Mo and Li 2002; Ji 2006) has become important for a number of reasons. In 2004, Zhang Fusen, the Minister of Justice, highlighted the acute shortage of lawyers, especially in remote rural areas (Liu 2004), along with a sharp increase in demand for legal services in advanced urban areas related to finance, real estate, intellectual property, foreign-related services and labor disputes. Significant efforts have therefore been made to expand and diversify legal training, ranging from prestigious university law schools to radio and TV universities and various vocational institutions offering short courses. The impetus behind such provisions has been a pragmatic response to increased demand. While there have been improved opportunities to enter the legal profession, there are serious concerns about the impact of the expansion on quality and the future status of the legal profession. Even in the case of fully qualified lawyers, there is an urgent need to enhance and update their skills. They need to become familiar with more diverse legal systems since the incorporation of Macau and Hong Kong within the republic; there is a need to modernize teaching methods in law schools; and since China's open-door policy there has been a need to improve the language skills of lawyers to deepen their understanding of international and comparative law.

## CONCLUSION

The overall impact of these developments in adult education is difficult to quantify and requires further research. There have been significant achievements, but there are also challenges. More investment is needed to increase participation rates, especially for disadvantaged groups, including the poor in remote rural areas. Opportunities for continued lifelong learning beyond the mere acquisition of literacy skills will be needed to prevent people relapsing into illiteracy (Xie and Zhang 2003). The quality as well as the quantity of provision also requires serious attention, including a gradual move away from teacher-centered, content-based, test-driven approaches to more flexible, student-centered, self-directed learning (Wang and Kreysa 2006).

**SEE ALSO** *Illiteracy.*

**BIBLIOGRAPHY**


Chakrabarti, Sreemati. Women and Adult Literacy in China. Indira Gandhi National Centre for the Arts. 1998. http://www.ignca.nic.in/ks_41036.htm.

Cheng Kai-Ming, Jin Xinhuo and Gu Xiaobao. From Training to Education: Lifelong Learning in China. *Comparative Education* 35, 2 (1999): 119–130.

Colletta, Nat J. *Worker-Peasant Education in the People's Republic of China: Adult Education During the Post-revolutionary Period.* Washington, DC: World Bank, 1998.

Gu, M. The Reform and Development of Teacher Education in China. International Center for Teacher Education. 2006. http://www.icte.ecnu.edu.cn?EN/show.asp?id=547.

Han Min. Social Transformation and Lifelong Learning in China: Observation from Adult Education. National Centre for Educational Development Research, Institutional Policy Seminar, Seoul, Korea, June 24–26, 2003. http://www.unesco.org/iiep/eng/research/highered/lifelrn/china.pdf.

Hu Jiaxiang. Challenging Chinese Legal Education: Lessons to Be Learned from Britain. UK Centre for Legal Education. 1999. http://www.ukcle.ac.uk/interact/lili/1999/hu.html.

Huang Shiqi. Nonformal Education and Modernization. In *Education and Modernization: The Chinese Experience*, ed. Ruth Hayhoe, 141–180. New York: Pergamon Press, 1992.

Huang Yongchang. Continuing Medical Education for the Health Professions in China. *Journal of Continuing Education in the Health Professions* 11, 3 (1991): 251–255.

Hunter, Carmen S., and Martha McKee Keehn, eds. *Adult Education in China.* London: Croom Helm, 1995.

Ji Weidong. Legal Education in China: A Great Leap Forward for Professionalism. *Kobe University Law Review* 39 (2006): 1–22.

Jones, David, and John Wallis. Adult Education in China: An Enquiry into Reasons for Attending. *International Journal of Lifelong Education* 11, 1 (1992): 25–40.

Lee, Doris. Web-based Instruction in China: Cultural and Pedagogical Implications and Challenges. *Educational Technology Research and Development* 52, 1 (2004): 101–105.

Li Defeng. Modernization and Teacher Education in China. *Teaching and Teacher Education* 15, 2 (1999): 179–192.

Li Lanqing. *Education for 1.3 Billion: Former Chinese Vice Premier Li LanQing on 10 Years of Education Reform and Development.* Beijing: Foreign Language Teaching and Research Press/Pearson Education Asia, 2004.

Liu Xiaosen. Ren min ri bao, er ling ling si nian san yue san shi yi ri, di shi si ban, zuo zhe. *People's Daily*, 14th edition, March 31, 2004.

Mo, J.S. and Li, W. Legal Education in the People's Republic of China. *Journal of the History of International Law* 4, 1 (2002): 176–203.

Sherwood, Gwen, and Liu Huaping. International Collaboration for Developing Graduate Education in China. *Nursing Outlook* 53, 1 (2005): 15–20.

Wang, Victor, and Paul Bott. Modes of Teaching of Chinese Adult Educators. *Perspectives: The New York Journal of Adult Learning* 2, 2 (2004): 32–51.

Wang, Victor, and Peter Kreysa. Instructional Strategies of Distance Education Instructors in China. *Journal of Educators Online* 3, 1 (2006): 1–25.

Wang Weiguo. A Brief Introduction to Legal Education in China. Conference of International Legal Educators, Florence, Italy, May 24–27, 2000. http://www.aals.org/2000international/english/chinaintro.htm.

Wang, Ying Jie. Patterns of Development of Chinese Teacher Education in a Reform Context. In *Reform of Teacher Education in the Asia-Pacific in the New Millennium: Trends and Challenges*, ed. Yin Cheong Cheng, King Wai Chow and Magdalena Mo Ching Mok, 63–79. London: Kluwer Academic Publishers, 2004.

Wu, H., and Ye, Q. Lifelong Learning in the People's Republic of China. In *Lifelong Learning: Policies, Practices, and Programs*, ed. Michael J. Hatton, 346–359. Toronto: Humber College, 1997.

Xiao Jin. Determinants of Salary Growth in Shenzhen, China: An Analysis of Formal Education, On-the-job Training, and Adult Education with a Three-level Model. *Economics of Education Review* 21, 6 (2002): 557–577.

Xiao Jin and M. C. Tsang. Determinants of Participation and Non-participation in Job-related Education and Training in Shenzhen, China. *Human Resource Development Quarterly* 15, 4 (2004): 389–420.

Xie Guodong. Adult Education in China: Present Situation, Achievements, and Challenges. DVV International. 2003. http://www.iiz-dvv.de/.

Xie Guodong and Zhang Zhupeng. Meeting the Basic Learning Needs of the Newly Literate: China's Post-literacy Education for the Early 21st Century. *International Review of Education* 49, 6 (2003): 621–629.

Yao Zhongda. Adult Education Theory and Development in China. *Adult Education: International Perspectives from China*, ed. Chris Duke, 13–18. London: Croom Helm, 1987.

Yu Bo and Xu HongYan. *Adult Higher Education: A Case Study of Workers' Colleges in the People's Republic of China.* Paris: International Institute for Educational Planning, UNESCO, 1988.

Zhang Xiang Dong and Michael D. Stephens, ed. *University Adult Education in China.* Nottingham, U.K.: University of Nottingham Department of Adult Education, 1992.

Zhou Ji. *Higher Education in China.* Singapore: Thomson, 2006.


***Michael D. Wilson***

*The author would like to acknowledge the advice of Lin Zheng of the University of Portsmouth, and Sun Lijuan of Zhongnan University of Economics and Law (ZUEL) on certain aspects of Chinese legal education, and to Fang Man, of the University of Leeds, for providing assistance with translation.*

## MORAL EDUCATION

China can be described as a "pan-moralist" society. This pan-moralism, however, is not mainly about individual morality; it must be seen in a social context because it is heavily concerned with proper behavior and social order under Confucianism as well as Communism.

### ETYMOLOGY OF MORAL EDUCATION

The classical character for moral or virtue—*de* 德—originally was comprised of three elements, one connoting crossroads or change on the left, perhaps alluding to the changeability or malleability of man, a seeing eye at the top right connoting public gaze, and heart or mind at the bottom connoting self-cultivation. According to Confucianism, the mind is capable of knowing the rules of proper behavior or "rites" (*li* 礼), evaluating the situation based on such knowledge, and commanding proper action. In other words, the mind is fully capable of evaluating a situation and acting correctly. This innate capability of distinguishing between right and wrong is strengthened by education. In some interpretations, the classical character for education—*jiao* 教—depicts a man with a whip in his hand on the right held over a child with books on the left. Education thus connotes order and discipline.

### THE "MORAL SCIENCE" OF MODEL LEARNING

The model learning (*mofan jiaoyu*) theory of moral education is of a more recent date, but was already evident in the biographies of virtuous men and women. Today it is seen as a conscious strategy by the state of social and moral engineering or social control with "Chinese characteristics." During the socialist era this has been developed into an allegedly rational "moral science" meant to bring harmony and stability to a changing society, and to improve the "quality" (*suzhi*) of the people. The Chinese dominant theory of learning is based on the principle that we are all capable of learning from exemplary models, whether intentional or not. Model emulation thus became the principal means of education. An element of constant repetition is present in order to form stabilizing habits that bind individuals to society, and these habits are modelled after exemplary heroes. Much emphasis is therefore put on presenting the right model in order to inculcate the right behavior. Traditionally, exemplary models could be historical heroes, ancestors, imperial officials, virtuous widows, teachers, and so on. Even during periods of massive attacks on Confucianism, such as the Cultural Revolution, repetitive emulation of exemplary heroes was strongly propagated together with constant recitation of Mao quotations. During the Maoist years of war and revolution, the Chinese were indoctrinated with the examples of soldiers sacrificing themselves for the collective (for example, Dong Cunrui [1929–1948], Wang Jie [1942–1965]), and "do-gooders" such as Lei Feng (1940–1962), a model soldier and peacetime hero constantly doing selfless deeds for his comrades. The example of Lei Feng is still widely used in children's education, but with modernization the Communist model heroes have faded. Whatever their effect on people's minds, such heroes achieved something like a Communist "sainthood" over the years.

### MORAL ACTIVITIES, MORAL CAMPAIGNS, AND EXEMPLARY DETERRENCE

On the macro level there were mass activities or movements (*huodong*) and campaigns (*yundong*) by which the whole country could be mobilized in order to implement correct attitudes and political aims. The modernization program that began in 1978 set "spiritual civilization" (*jingshen wenming*) on an equal footing with "material civilization" (*wuzhi wenming*). Even the Chinese judiciary is meant to be educative: The practices of sentencing rallies (*gongpan dahui*), in which alleged criminals are paraded publicly, and the draconian campaigns of "hard strikes" (*yanda*) against crime, are based on the deterrence principle of learning by negative example.

**SEE ALSO** *Life Cycle: Infancy and Childhood; Socialization and Pedagogy.*

**BIBLIOGRAPHY**

Bakken, Børge. *The Exemplary Society: Human Improvement, Social Control, and the Dangers of Modernity in China.* Oxford, U.K.: Oxford University Press, 2000.

Munroe, Donald. *The Concept of Man in Early China.* Stanford, CA: Stanford University Press, 1969.

***Børge Bakken***

## WOMEN'S EDUCATION

Formal education for women in China was not available until the mid-nineteenth century, although curricula for women's education were developed earlier, and private and home-based education for women is mentioned in literature. The content of women's education mainly comprised literature and the arts, norms and rites, and skills such as needlework, spinning, and weaving. A small number of girls, mainly from better-off families, were enrolled in private and home-based schools.

Missionaries introduced formal education for Chinese women in the mid-nineteenth century, mainly in coastal and more developed cities. Forty missionary schools for girls were opened in the 1844–1898 period. The number of students involved increased dramatically over the turn of twentieth century; the number of female students in Christian schools was 576 in 1869, 2,064 in

1877, and 4,373 in 1902. The curriculum in missionary schools covered mostly primary- and secondary-education topics, with an emphasis on English and religion. Most of the girls enrolled were from poor families or were orphans. Some missionary schools later became Chinese-run schools, and missionary-school graduates were among the earliest career women and schoolteachers in China. Missionary schools had a higher proportion of girl students compared to state-run schools. For example, in 1921, 31 percent of missionary primary-school students were girls, while the proportion was less than 5 percent in public primary schools.

The first indigenous girls' school, the Classic Uprightness Girls' School (Jingzheng Nüxue), was founded in May 1898 in Shanghai by Chinese gentry reformers, including Liang Qichao (1873–1929). The school had sixteen students at the beginning and forty students by the end of the year. There was a public discussion on women's education in early twentieth-century China, with stronger voices advocating education for women, and requests for public schools for girls by reformers and activists such as Qiu Jin (1875–1907), the famous female revolutionary. An order issued by the government on girls' education in early 1906 opened a door for women's public education; more schools, including public schools for girls, opened during the following several years, and more girls enrolled. There were more than five hundred girls' schools with over twenty thousand students in 1908, compared to only seventy-one girls' schools and fewer than two thousand students in 1905. Meanwhile, vocational education for women began to rise, a major component of which was teacher training. Education reform in 1912 specified that girls and boys need not go to separate primary schools, and although students were still to attend separate schools by gender in secondary and higher education, courses and curriculum should follow the same system.

Chinese students began to study abroad in the late nineteenth century, with a few women among them. Several women studied in the United States before 1894, and more joined the increasing number of international students in Japan later. It is estimated that about one hundred of the female international students in Tokyo in 1907 were from China. More Chinese students, including some women, studied in Europe and the United States after 1907.

## MORE PUBLIC EDUCATION FOR WOMEN AFTER THE MAY FOURTH MOVEMENT (1919)

The May Fourth movement of 1919 marked an important turning point in the history of education in China, and also in the development of women's education. Elites promoted the rights of women to equality regarding educational access and opportunities, and called for a change in feudal education ideology. Remarkable progress was made in several areas, including the establishment of the first advanced educational institution for women, the Women's Normal College of Beijing; coeducation for male and female students in secondary and tertiary education; and the development of secondary vocational education. The purpose and content of women's education were reconceived, so that the aim of educating women was not only to produce worthy mothers and good wives (*xianqi liangmu*) but to engender women's liberation and independence. The government promoted women's education during the late 1920s and early 1930s, and more girls gained access to primary and secondary education. The share of female students in secondary education stood at 8 percent in the 1929–1930 school year, but had risen to 15 percent by the 1930–1931 school year. The proportion of female students was even higher in secondary teacher-training programs, about 33 percent in the 1930–1931 school year.

## THE CAMPAIGN TO ELIMINATE ILLITERACY

After the establishment of the People's Republic of China in 1949, women were encouraged to go to school and to participate in socioeconomic activities. More girls were enrolled in schools, and more women learned to read as a result of national campaigns in the 1950s to eliminate illiteracy in rural and urban China. Figure 1 displays the impact of the campaign for women—a significant decrease in the illiteracy rates for women aged thirty-five to forty-five in the year of 1982. The promotion of primary education reduced illiteracy among young women by 1990. A further drop in the illiteracy rate by 2000 among those aged fifteen to nineteen suggests the success of China's education system for girls during the last two decades of the twentieth century.

The progress of education reform in China was interrupted during the decade of the Cultural Revolution (1966–1976). Girls' access to and completion of primary and secondary education was strongly related to local economic development, family resources, and educational resources, compared to that of boys. There was a wider gender gap in primary and secondary education in rural China.

## EFFORTS TOWARD GENDER EQUITY IN EDUCATION ACCESS

The Law of Compulsory Education, enacted in 1986, defined a nine-year compulsory-education program for all students. Governmental and nongovernmental programs, national and international projects, as well as local policies encouraged girls to enroll and complete primary and secondary school in less-developed rural areas, and the efforts have been integrated into poverty-alleviation

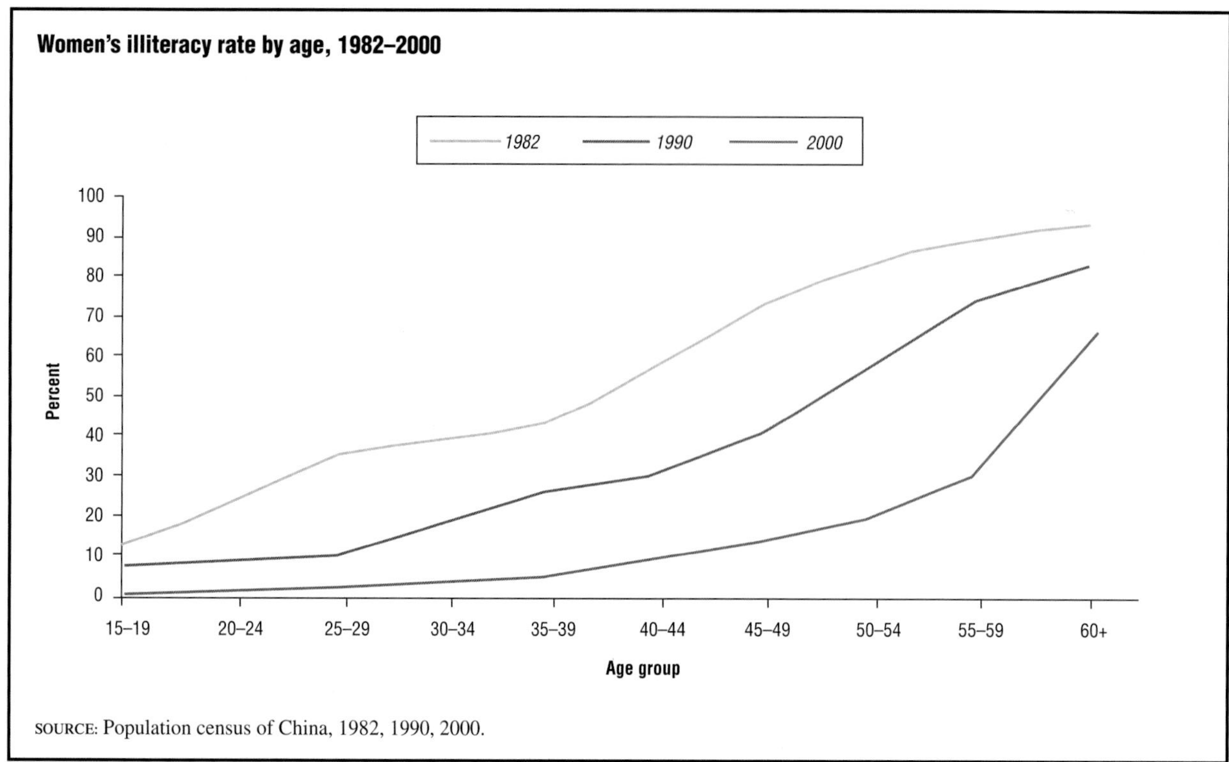


SOURCE: Population census of China, 1982, 1990, 2000.

*Figure 1*

programs. The female education issue has been linked to women's empowerment, women's benefits and rights, and social development. More girls were enrolled in primary school, and the gender gap in enrollment rates for boys and girls became negligible after years of effort. Primary school enrollment rates have remained above 95 percent since the mid-1980s, and reached 99 percent in 2000, for both boys and girls.

The gender gap between primary-school completion and secondary-school enrollment narrowed during the last two decades of the twentieth century and the beginning of the twenty-first century, especially in rural areas. Figure 2 shows the structure of educational attainment for the male and female populations in 1982, 1990, and 2000, according to the results of three national censuses. Females caught up with males in primary and secondary education, as well as in advanced education. The average years of schooling for women in 2005 was 7.3, and for men was 8.4, with a 1.1-year difference; in 1990 the number was 5.5 for women and 7.4 for men, almost a two-year difference.

More than 50 percent of students in vocational education are women, mainly due to gender segregation in certain occupations. For example, more girls received vocational training as nurses and schoolteachers. There were 1,600 women's vocational schools and three women's vocational colleges in China by 2003.

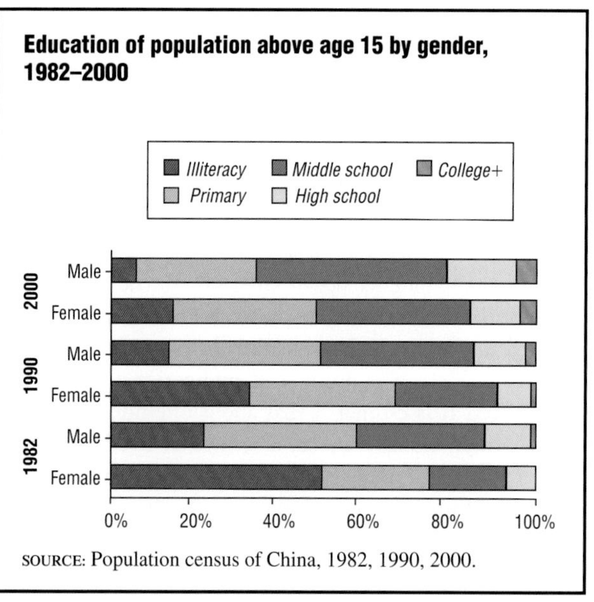


SOURCE: Population census of China, 1982, 1990, 2000.

*Figure 2*

The proportion of female students in college was 17.8 percent in 1947, 26.9 percent in 1965, 39.7 percent in 1999, and 48.1 percent in 2006. The percentage of female students in postgraduate programs reached a historical high in 2006, with 46.4 percent in masters programs and 33.9 percent in Ph.D. programs. The share of female students varies among different universities and is related to the distribution of university programs in different areas. Although the college-admission test system does not take gender into account, there has been significant gender segregation in study areas among college students: More female students study linguistics, literature, and history in college, and more female students are enrolled in postgraduate programs in medical schools and in the arts and humanities. In 2007 an increase in female university students in science and technology was observed.

**SEE ALSO** *Illiteracy; Missionaries; Women, Status of.*

**BIBLIOGRAPHY**


Bailey, Paul J. *Gender and Education in China: Gender Discourses and Women's Schooling in the Early Twentieth Century*. New York: Routledge, 2007.

Liu Jucai. *Zhongguo jindai funu yundongshi* [The women's movement in modern China]. Beijing: Zhongguo Funu Chubanshe, 1989.

Luo Suwen. *Nuxing yu jindai Zhongguo shehui* [Women and modern China]. Shanghai: Shanghai Renmin Chubanshe, 1996.

Ma Wanhua. Zhongguo nuxing gaodengjiaoyu fazhan de lishi: Xianzhuang yu wenti [History, current status, and problems of women's advanced education in China]. *Jiaoyu fazhan yanjiu* [Education development research] 3 (2005): 1–5.

Population Census Office under the State Council and National Bureau of Statistics of China. Tabulation on the 1990 Population Census of the Peoples' Republic of China. Beijing: China Statistics Press, 1993.

Population Census Office under the State Council and Department of Population, Social, Science, and Technology Statistics, National Bureau of Statistics of China. Tabulation on the 2000 Population Census of the Peoples' Republic of China. Beijing: China Statistics Press, 2002.

Shi Jinghuan. Jiaoyu, fuquan yu fazhan: 95′ shifuhui yilai Zhongguo funu jiaoyu yanjiu huigu [Education, empowerment, and development: Review of women's education research since 1995 World Women's Conference]. *Funu yanjiu luncong* [Collection of women's studies] 1 (2007): 59–66.

Xiong Xianjun. *Zhongguo nuzi jiaoyushi* [History of women's education in China]. Taiyuan, PRC: Shanxi Jiaoyu Chubanshe, 2006.


***Zheng Zhenzhen***

## POLICY AND ADMINISTRATION SINCE 1976

In line with its long tradition of a centralized polity, China has run a centralized system for educational administration since 1949. Under the direct leadership of the State Council, the Ministry of Education (MOE) was established on November 1, 1949, renamed as the State Commission of Education on June 18, 1985, and had its original name restored on March 10, 1998. With nineteen administrative offices, the MOE's major responsibilities include, but are not limited to, the major tasks delineated below.

First, the MOE initiates and makes national policies, regulations, and strategic plans for educational development, scientific research, and language work, and coordinates policy implementation and evaluation. Second, it serves as a central governmental agency in full charge of educational administration, coordination, evaluation, and supervision. For example, it establishes national standards for schools at all levels from kindergarten to graduate school, with regard to school leadership and management, campus infrastructure and teaching facilities, teacher certification, curricula, textbooks, examination standards and requirements, teaching programs, and degrees. Third, the MOE budgets and manages annual national expenditures for the country's educational system (including formal and informal education) and scientific research. It is also the legal recipient and agency on behalf of the central Chinese government for the management of educational aid, donations, or loans received from international funders. Fourth, the MOE enforces and supervises the nationwide implementation of nine-year compulsory education and adult literacy activities. Fifth, it makes annual plans for student recruitment in postsecondary education systems, and administers unified national examinations—for example, the national college entrance examinations, the certification examinations for adult self-learners, and the certification examinations for teaching Chinese as a foreign language. Sixth, the MOE takes responsibilities for planning, regulating, and evaluating teacher education, technical and vocational education and training, and minority education. Seventh, it approves and oversees the establishment and administration of private schools, especially private higher education institutions. Finally, it collects and publishes annual national data for education.

In addition, the MOE carries out the Communist Party of China's political initiatives, mainly with regard to ideological education, political supervision, and campaigns. It also coordinates with the Education, Science, Culture, and Public Health Committee of the National People's Congress; the State Steering Committee of Science, Technology, and Education; the State Council's Academic Degree Committee; the State Development and Reform Commission; and China's National Commission for UNESCO (United Nations Educational, Scientific, and Cultural Organization).

The administration of education in China is structured in a top-down, pyramidal model. Parallel with the MOE at the national level, provincial bureaus of education are set up

**Expansion of China's tertiary education, 1991–2007**

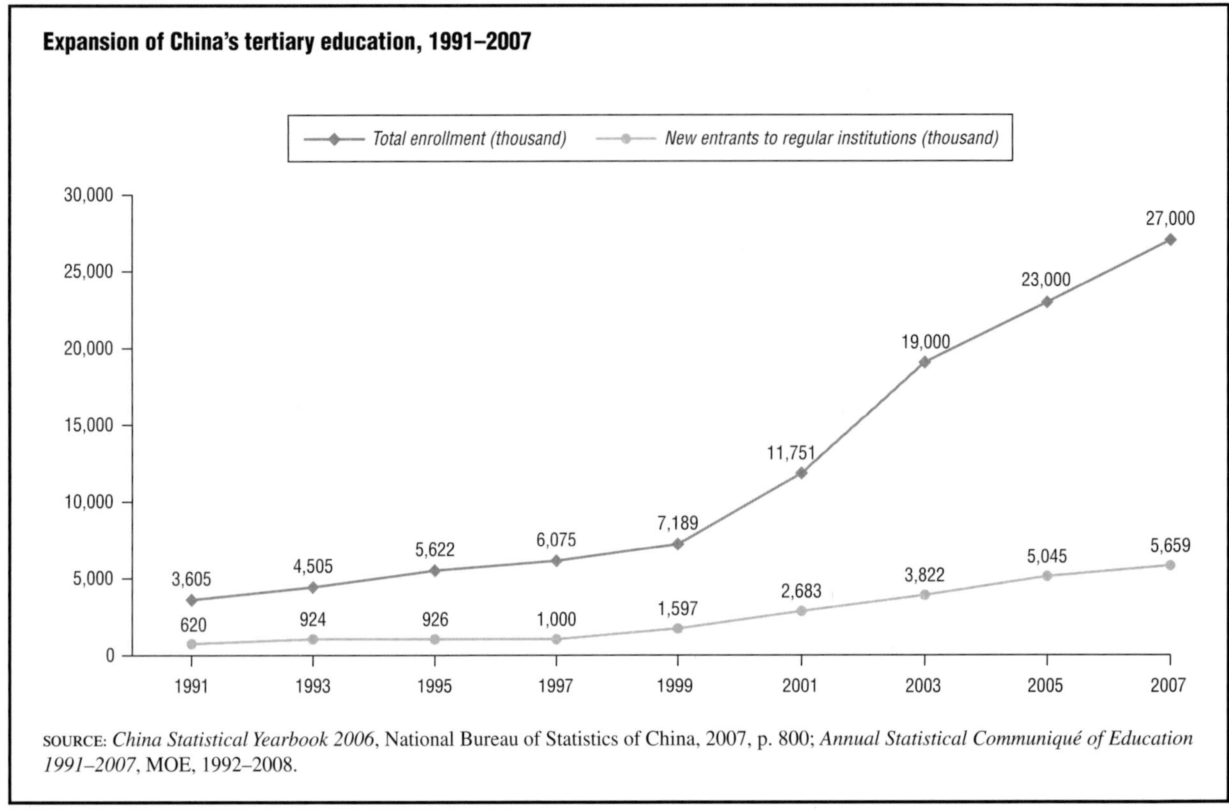


SOURCE: *China Statistical Yearbook 2006*, National Bureau of Statistics of China, 2007, p. 800; *Annual Statistical Communiqué of Education 1991–2007*, MOE, 1992–2008.

*Figure 1*

in every province, autonomous region, and municipality. Similarly, city or county offices of education within a province, autonomous region, or municipality are established for local educational administration. The provincial and local offices of educational administration mainly function as implementation or coordination agencies for national educational policies, plans, and regulations, though they also have authority to make policies, regulations, strategic plans, and annual budgets for local educational development.

## NATIONAL POLICIES FOR EDUCATION

Since 1976, the Chinese government has enacted several important laws, such as the Degree Ordinance (1981), the Compulsory Education Law (1986), the Teachers Law (1993), the Educational Law (1995), and the Higher Education Law (1998). Based on them, the MOE has further promulgated more than two hundred regulations or policies for various initiatives. Such policies as the establishment and funding of key schools, the expansion of the higher education system, and the regulation of private (*minban*) education have significantly changed China's educational system.

**The Establishment and Funding of Key Schools** From the early 1950s to the early 1980s, almost all schools in China had to rely on public funding wholly from a governmental budget, because receiving funding from the private sector was prohibited. In order to direct public funding toward a better quality of schooling, the Chinese government put in place a key-school system in 1952, which gave development priority to a limited number of schools, usually located in the downtown areas of big cities or provincial capitals. In the early 1980s, this system was further enhanced due to the political and socioeconomic demand for excellence.

The key-school system has significantly differentiated development opportunities among schools and has disadvantaged the majority of schools, which tend to have less funding available for their development and a lower social status. Naturally, the key-school system also led to unequal learning opportunities for most students. In the mid-1990s, heated debates broke out on these issues, and forced the MOE to gradually abandon the key-school system. Since then, the Chinese government has endeavored to weaken the system, but the former key schools still remain significantly privileged.

**The Expansion of the Higher Education System** China has had the largest national higher education system in the

**Private education in China, 1997–2006**

| | | | 1997 | 2000 | 2003 | 2006 |
|---|---|---|---|---|---|---|
| **Institution** | Higher education | Regular | 20 | 37 | 173 | 596 |
| | | Other | 1,095 | 1,282 | 1,104 | 994 |
| | Secondary education | Regular | 1,702 | 3,316 | 6,330 | 7,796 |
| | | Vocational | 689 | 999 | 1,435 | 2,570 |
| | Primary education | | 1,806 | 4,341 | 5,676 | 6,161 |
| | Preschool education | | 24,643 | 44,317 | 55,500 | 75,426 |
| **Enrollment (in thousands)** | Higher education | Regular | 16 | 68 | 810 | 2,805 |
| | | Other | 1,190 | 982 | 1,004 | 939 |
| | Secondary education | Regular | 546 | 1,495 | 3,979 | 6,418 |
| | | Vocational | 184 | 303 | 817 | 2,297 |
| | Primary education | | 522 | 1,308 | 2,749 | 4,121 |
| | Preschool education | | 1,349 | 2,843 | 4,802 | 7,757 |

SOURCE: Data for 1997 and 2000 are as collected in the PRC's Ministry of Education Department of Development and Planning and Shanghai Institute of Educational Sciences (Eds.), *2002 Green Paper on Non-Governmental Education in China* (Shanghai Education Publishing House, 2003), pp. 9–19. Data for 2003–2006 are collected from *Annual Statistical Communiqué of Education 1991–2007* (MOE, 2004–2007).

*Table 1*

world since 2003. In the early 1990s, China began to gradually expand its higher education system at a moderate pace. Since the late 1990s, the pace of expansion has radically accelerated due to sociopolitical demand and a push for greater domestic expenditure. In 1991 only 3.5 percent of the relevant age group, those between eighteen and twenty-two, benefited from any form of higher education. This reached 10.5 percent in 1999 and 22 percent in 2006, with over twenty-five million students enrolled. The average size of regular higher education institutions has quadrupled from 2,074 students in 1992 to 8,148 students in 2006. The number of tertiary students per 100,000 inhabitants has quintupled from 304 in 1991 to 1,816 in 2006. Private higher education has contributed significantly to this radical expansion, with a rapid increase in enrollment from 1.2 million students in 1,115 institutions in 1997 to 3.7 million students in 1,590 institutions in 2006.

**The Regulation of Private (*Minban*) Education** China adopted a state- or public-run model for education from the early 1950s to the early 1980s. The 1982 constitution mandates that the government is solely responsible for funding and administering all types of schools, though funding and administration by nongovernment sectors are encouraged. Since the late 1980s, the Chinese government has begun to deregulate private education through the Interim Regulations on Privately-Run Schools (1987), which was upgraded into the Promotion Law of Privately Run Schools in 2002. These regulations designate private education as a public good instead of a profitable business, and set the tone for the establishment and administration of private schools. Table 1 shows the rapid development and expansion of private education in China since 1997.

These national policies have brought about remarkable institutional changes in China's education in terms of quantity, diversity, and technology, but Chinese policymakers and administrators have also been greatly challenged by such serious issues as equity, quality, accountability, decentralization, marketization, and globalization.

**BIBLIOGRAPHY**


Li Jun (Jun Li) and Lin Jing (Jing Lin). China's Higher Education Expansion: A Policy Analysis from a Rational Framework. In *Worldwide Transformation of Higher Education*, eds. David. P. Baker and Alexander W. Wiseman. Oxford: Elsevier Science, 2008.

Ministry of Education of the PRC. *Quangguo Jiaoyu Shiye Fazhan Tongji Gongbao 2005* (*Annual Statistical Communiqué of Education 2005*). Beijing: Author, 2007.

Ministry of Education of the PRC. *Zhongguo Jiaoyu Tongji Nianjian 2005* (*Educational Statistics Yearbook of China 2005*). Beijing: People's Education Press, 2006.

National Bureau of Statistics of China. *Zhongguo Tongji Nianjian* 2006 (*China Statistical Yearbook 2006*). Beijing: China Statistics Press, 2007.


***Jun Li***

## COST OF EDUCATION SINCE 1978

Since the launch of economic reform in the late 1970s, China has experienced significant transformations in the context of rapid economic growth. Realizing the importance of education to further development, the Chinese government has repeatedly promised to invest in education.

**Public education expenditure as a percent of GDP**

unit: billion *yuan*

| Year | Gross domestic product | Government appropriation for education* | Percentage (%) |
|---|---|---|---|
| 1992 | 2,663.8 | 72.9 | 2.74 |
| 1995 | 5,847.8 | 141.2 | 2.41 |
| 1999 | 8,206.8 | 228.7 | 2.79 |
| 2000 | 8,946.8 | 256.3 | 2.86 |
| 2001 | 9,731.5 | 305.7 | 3.14 |
| 2002 | 10,517.2 | 349.1 | 3.32 |
| 2003 | 11,739.0 | 385.1 | 3.28 |
| 2004 | 15,987.8 | 446.6 | 2.79 |

*Government appropriation for education includes the expenditure of central and local governments on education.

SOURCE: National Bureau of Statistics of China (NBSC), 2005.

*Table 1*

Although the government has tried to allocate more financial resources to support education, the reality has clearly suggested that educational financing and provision have increasingly relied on nonstate sources; hence, citizens in mainland China have generally regarded educational financing as a financial burden (Mok Ka Ho and Lo Yat Wai 2007).

## SHIFTING FINANCIAL BURDENS TO FAMILIES AND INDIVIDUALS

In the early 1980s, Deng Xiaoping remarked that the Chinese government would raise its investment in education by allocating up to 4 percent of the gross domestic product (GDP) to educational development. Since the 1980s, the Chinese economy has demonstrated consistent growth with an average growth rate of 9 to 10 percent annually. Nonetheless, budgetary allocation on education, though fluctuating, has been low (see Table 1). Even the State Council of the People's Republic of China has openly recognized the insufficiency of government funding for education. In response to this concern, the Eleventh Five-Year Plan (2006–2010) calls on governments at all levels to make the development of education a strategic priority and "to commit to a public education system that can be accessed by all" (Li 2007).

The accompanying graph, detailing national educational expenditure by sector, shows the consistent growth in educational expenditure financed by the nonstate sector despite the increase in the state's contribution. According to statistics provided by the China Education and Research Network, the state's share in national educational expenditure has declined when compared to contributions from the nonstate sector (see accompanying graph highlighting national educational expenditure as a percentage, by sector). In this policy context, educational financing and provision have begun to rely more on the nonstate sector, which gets contributions from social groups, individuals, and local communities.

Table 2 details the increase in contributions from social groups and individuals from 2000 to 2004, with steady growth from 6,289 million yuan to 25,901 million yuan. During this period, a number of charities and nongovernmental organizations developed programs, such as the Hope Program, to create educational opportunities for Chinese children, particularly those living in rural areas.

Although there are no official statistics indicating how much household income is being spent on education, expenditures related to education are becoming increasingly important to the consumption of Chinese residents, both urban and rural. Attaching great weight to education, many urban families send their children to private tutors or classes after school or during weekends, while some families in rural China struggle to save or borrow money to send their children to urban areas for education. Regional disparities in economic development have resulted in different educational experiences and educational inequalities in China.

## NEW DIRECTIONS

The Chinese government has recognized the problem of educational inequalities, and Premier Wen Jiabao introduced measures to address the issue. During the Sixteenth National Congress, the Chinese Communist Party made education a priority compared to other policy areas in the Eleventh Five-Year Plan (2006–2010). One priority, among the various goals, was the implementation of the "Two Basics" project to universalize nine-year compulsory education and to eradicate illiteracy among the middle-school students in the rural areas of western China. Regarding educational financing, the government decided to waive in 2006 all tuition and fees for students from rural areas of western China in order to release parents' from the heavy burden of educational expenses. The same policy was introduced to central and eastern China in 2007 (China Education and Research Network 2006).

In 2007 Wen Jiabao announced an educational investment plan in his government report. A total of 85.85 billion yuan was allocated to education in 2007, a 41.7 percent increase over the previous year. In order to uphold the principle of educational equality, part of the funding was used to enhance the access of children from poor families to education. In addition, the government has continued to provide free textbooks to students from lower socioeconomic backgrounds, along with living allowances for those studying in boarding schools. About 150 million

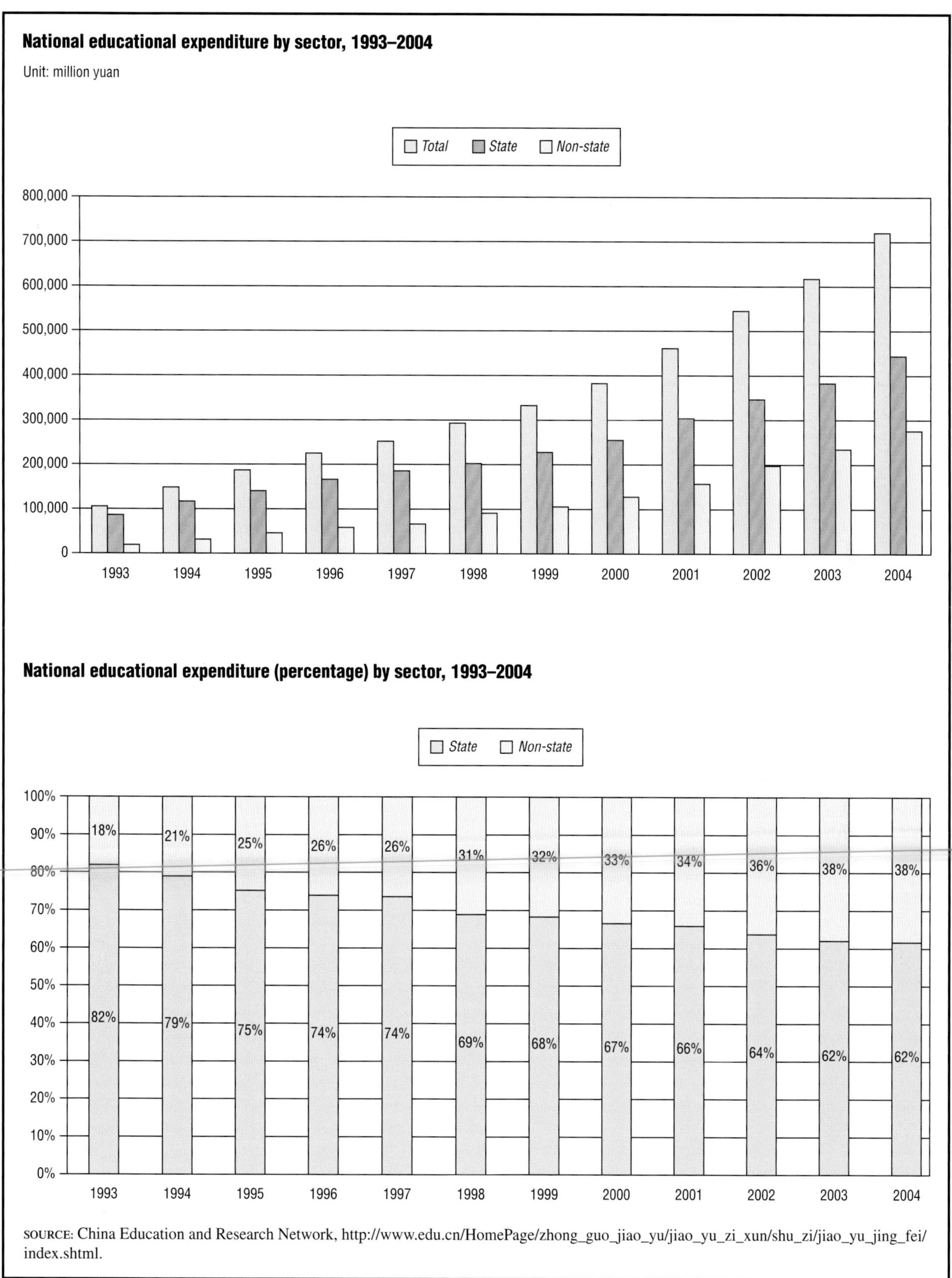
National educational expenditure by sector, 1993–2004
Unit: million yuan
Total
State
Non-state
800,000
700,000
600,000
500,000
400,000
300,000
200,000
100,000
0
1993
1994
1995
1996
1997
1998
1999
2000
2001
2002
2003
2004
National educational expenditure (percentage) by sector, 1993–2004
State
Non-state
100%
90%
80%
70%
60%
50%
40%
30%
20%
10%
0%
18%
21%
25%
26%
26%
31%
32%
33%
34%
36%
38%
38%
82%
79%
75%
74%
74%
69%
68%
67%
66%
64%
62%
62%
1993
1994
1995
1996
1997
1998
1999
2000
2001
2002
2003
2004
SOURCE: China Education and Research Network, http://www.edu.cn/HomePage/zhong_guo_jiao_yu/jiao_yu_zi_xun/shu_zi/jiao_yu_jing_fei/index.shtml.

*Figure 1*

**Educational expenditure (contributions from social groups and individuals, and social donations)**

| | Total | | Social groups and individuals | | Social donations | |
|---|---|---|---|---|---|---|
| Year | Million yuan | % of total | Million yuan | % of total | Million yuan | % of total |
| 2000 | 334,904 | 100% | 6,289 | 1.63% | 12,586 | 4.81% |
| 2001 | 384,908 | 100% | 8,585 | 2.23% | 11,395 | 2.96% |
| 2002 | 463,766 | 100% | 12,809 | 2.76% | 11,288 | 2.43% |
| 2003 | 548,002 | 100% | 17,255 | 3.15% | 12,727 | 2.32% |
| 2004 | 620,827 | 100% | 25,901 | 4.17% | 10,459 | 1.68% |

SOURCE: *China Educational Finance Statistical Yearbook* (2000–2004).

*Table 2*

rural households with school-age children benefit from these programs (*People's Daily*, March 5, 2007).

**BIBLIOGRAPHY**

China Education and Research Network. The Educational Development during the 10th 5-Year Plan. 2006. http://www.edu.cn/news_1461/.

China Education and Research Network. http://www.edu.cn/ (sources from various years of 1994–2005).

Li Rui. Casualties of the Rush to Profit from Schooling. *South China Morning Post*, January 27, 2007.

Ministry of Education of the People's Republic of China. *China Educational Finance Statistical Yearbook 2005*. Beijing: Zhongguo Tongji Chubanshe, 2005.

Ka Ho Mok and Yat Wai Lo. The Impacts of Neo-liberalism on China's Higher Education. *Journal for Critical Education Policy Studies* 5, 1 (2007). http://www.jceps.com/.

National Bureau of Statistics of China. *China Statistical Yearbook* (2000–2004). Beijing: Zhongguo Tongji Chubanshe, 2000–2004.

Wen Jiabo. Zengjia jiaoyu taozi [Increase state investment in education], *People's Daily*, 5 March 2007.

***Ka Ho Mok***

## PRIVATE SCHOOLS SINCE 1980s

There were no private schools in China prior to the reform era that began in the late 1970s. Private schools, like the emergence of private businesses, were not creations based on official blueprints of development. Private schools gradually evolved as a response to popular demand for education in the more liberal political atmosphere of the new era. In the late 1970s, the central government exhorted schools to engage in profit-making activities to make up for shortfalls in their operating funds. Among other money-making activities, state schools offered additional classes above the quota set by the government. In an environment where private initiatives were tolerated, and with no rules to the contrary, individuals offered private tuition to anyone who needed help to prepare for the newly restored admission exams for universities and other levels of education.

By the 1990s, these disparate individual and organized efforts offering education for a fee coalesced into the establishment of private schools at every level of education. There are no accurate statistics on the number of these schools. In 1994, the Xinhua News Agency reported that among the 40,000 private educational establishments, there were 16,990 kindergartens, 4,030 primary schools, 851 middle schools, and 800 colleges and universities. These schools were located in major urban centers and their suburbs. The majority were nursery and primary schools providing care to children whose parents were too busy to look after them. Some were tutorial schools preparing candidates who were not enrolled in public schools but intended to take the public school exams. Other private schools provided job training for the opportunities available in the new economy. Some drilled students in English to prepare them to go abroad, while others offered another chance for education to those ousted from the very competitive public school system. Many private schools were operated by individuals; some were retired teachers. Others were owned by corporations, while others were "schools within schools," that is, private schools run by public schools.

Since education is a public good, the presence of schools offering services only to those who could afford them was anathema to China's long-held socialist political philosophy. In addition, some private schools were considered "elitist," and labeled as such not for their academic standing but for the hefty fees they charged. Other private schools were fly-by-night operations that took their clients' money but did not deliver the services advertised. The presence of such schools triggered intense debate in China's education circles. Opponents condemned the elitist boarding schools, accessible only to the very rich, and attacked the for-profit institutions for betraying the public trust and not serving the public good. Defenders argued that the private schools mobilized resources available at the grassroots, and supplied a demand for education that the government could not meet. As China's economic reform progressed in the late 1990s, some proponents bravely argued that there was nothing wrong with making money through education.

Advocates for private education won the day. Official recognition of China's private schools came with the state council's promulgation of the Regulations for the Operation of Schools Run by Social Forces in 1997. The regulations stipulated requirements for private schools, provided guidelines for their operation, including the disposal of "profit," and offered some protection to clients. The labeling of these schools as "schools run by social forces" (*shehui liliang banxue*), rather than "private schools" (*siren banxue* or *siren xuexiao*), is significant. Because the government still considered China socialist, it could not bring itself to refer to these schools as *private*.

By 2003 the government had become even more positive in its support of private schools and passed the Law on the Promotion of Private Education. In Chinese, however, this legislation continued to refer to the schools as *shehui liliang banxue*, not *siren banxue*. In the same year, the government passed legislation on Chinese-foreign Cooperation in Running Schools, clearing the way for foreign investment in Chinese education. The official position, however, remained ambivalent if not contradictory. In 2004 the minister of education located schools in the social-service sector, rather than the economic sector. Thus, schools were regarded as administrative units in the Chinese governing system to provide public services, rather than economic units to produce goods or make money.

Nevertheless, private schools are in China to stay. In 2005 the Ministry of Education reported that there were more than 86,000 private schools in China, but made no mention of the number of schools with Chinese-foreign proprietorship. This was because joint ventures in education remained largely shared educational programs between foreign and existing Chinese schools. Among the private schools, there were 68,835 kindergartens, 6,242 primary schools, 4,608 junior high schools, 3,175 senior high schools, and 252 institutions of higher learning. Private kindergartens constituted over half of all kindergartens in China, while private schools at the other levels made up only 2.7 percent of the schools in the country. Together, these private institutions served approximately 21,680,000 students, or only 1 percent of all students in the country.

The significance of private schools is not so much in their number but in what they represent. Their presence represents a radical departure from the Chinese Communist Party's monopoly of education. Private schools provide types of learning different from the government-mandated curriculum. In addition, they signify the presence in society of a propertied social stratum, if not a propertied social class, that can afford to pay for the expensive education of its children. More important, whatever the official posturing on the issue, the presence of these schools reflects government tolerance of different forms of proprietorship, even in education, within China's system of market socialism.

**BIBLIOGRAPHY**

Kwong, Julia, et al., eds. Private Schools in China. Spec. Issue. *Chinese Education and Society* 29, 3 (1996).

Kwong, Julia, et al., eds. Private Schools in China. Spec. Issue. *Chinese Education and Society* 29, 5 (1996).

Lin Jing. *Social Transformation and Private Education in China.* Westport, CT: Praeger, 1999.

Ngok, King-lun, and Julia Kwong. "Globalization and Educational Restructuring in China." In *Globalization and Educational Restructuring in the Asia Pacific Region*, eds. Kaho Mok and Anthony Welch, 160–188. New York: Palgrave Macmillan, 2003.

***Julia Kwong***

## EDUCATION THROUGH LABOR, REFORM THROUGH LABOR

*Laojiao* (education through labor) and *laogai* (reform through labor) are two terms often associated with China's correction system. The former refers to the treatment of detainees guilty of minor transgressions who are put under administrative detention for less than four years in China's correction system; the latter refers to the treatment of perpetrators of more serious crimes who have been sentenced by the court and held in detention for longer periods. The former inmates are under the jurisdiction of the police, better known as the *gong an* (public security), and the latter are under the procuratorate. The difference between the two terms *laojiao* and *laogai* is semantic and bureaucratic; the principle and nature of the treatment are the same. In both cases, the targets have made "mistakes" and are to be changed or rehabilitated—whether one calls it *jiao* (education) or *gai* (reform)—through participation in labor (*lao*).

Some social scientists have attributed the emphasis on labor in correction to Soviet influences; others pointed to the financial returns from the work of these detainees. But a more fundamental reason for its adoption comes from the Marxist ideology. According to the socialist dogma, from a macro societal perspective the economy is the foundation on which the superstructure, including ideology, emerges. At an individual level, a person's behavior and beliefs are shaped by one's work experience. Doing manual labor or working alongside the proletariat will instill an appreciation of work and produce "class feeling" (an appreciation of the working class). In periods of heightened political fervor such as the Cultural Revolution, all citizens, especially the younger generation, were encouraged to work in the backward regions to show their commitment to the country and the Communist ideology. In the case of *laojiao* and *laogai*, the deviants would change their outlooks or undergo thought reform through participating in labor.

## CRIMES AND INCARCERATION RATES

In the highly politicized and controlled Chinese society, prisoners may not have broken any law as we understand it. Some are incarcerated for committing theft, robbery, or violent crimes, but others are there because they have inadvertently or openly disagreed with, defied, or criticized the positions or policies taken by the Communist government or Party. In addition, the definition of serious crimes has changed over time. In the late 1970s a person embezzling 2,000 yuan would be prosecuted in court; now the same offense would be handled internally in the workplace and the offender sent to *laojiao*. In this "prosecution" process the accused have few or no rights, and no channel of appeal. In 2005 and 2007 there were proposals before the National People's Congress (*quanguo renmin daibiao dahui*) to integrate this process into the judicial system.

The Chinese government considers information on prisons and prisoners to be sensitive, even more so than crime statistics. Estimates of the number of such institutions fluctuate between fewer than 1,000 to more than 5,000; a recent statistic counted 310 *laojiao* centers in the country. Information on the number incarcerated over time and the percentage of political prisoners is also hard to find. Between 1949 and 1965 the crime rate averaged about 46.4 per 100,000 in the population; data were not available during the Cultural Revolution; and between 1979 and 1993, it averaged about 90 per 100,000. Relying on crime statistics as a rough indicator of the incarceration trend suggests that the incarceration rate was high when the Communists took power in 1949, dropped in the 1960s, and rose again in the reform era. The incarceration rate, like the crime rate, was especially high in years of intense political campaigns such as the *Sanfan Wufan* (Three-anti and Five-anti campaigns of 1951–1952) and the *Fanyou Yundong* (anti-rightist campaign of 1957). It spiked again in 1984 with the renewed crackdown on crimes and in 1989 in the aftermath of the Tiananmen Incident in 1989. In the more open political climate of the reform era, the Chinese government reported 1.2 million in prison, or an incarceration rate of 107 per 100,000; by 2007 it had risen to 118 per 100,000.

## RATIONALE AND PROCEDURE

The goal of the Chinese correction system has always been to "cure the sickness and save the person." The purpose of *laogai* or *laojiao,* therefore, is to provide psychological support, moral education, discipline, and skills required by the inmates upon their release. Until legal reform in the 1980s, the terms *prisoners* and *prison* were rarely used. Instead, prisoners were referred to as targets of reform or reeducation incarcerated in *laogai chang suo* (sites for reform through education). Even with the legal reforms, the 1994 Prison Law and the 2003 Provisions of Prisoners' Education and Reform still emphasized the education of prisoners through labor. Indeed, article 69 of the Prison Law stipulated that all able-bodied prisoners have to work.

The daily routine of the detainees or prisoners is highly regimented. Their movements are closely monitored by the guards, who keep detailed reports of their behavior. Detainees spend most of the day working and the evenings in study. They work on the shop floor, on farms, in mines, or in construction, and industrial accidents among prisoners are not unusual. Study programs range from political studies to literacy or skills training, and prisoners can obtain education diplomas from these programs. Under Mao, study sessions focused more on examining and discussing political documents. These political study sessions are opportunities for prisoners to show they have acquired the "right" attitudes, and prisoners, especially those accused of committing political or serious crimes, have to reflect on their "mistakes," sometimes in isolation, and to write confessions. An often repeated Chinese dictum states that those who confess are treated leniently, and those who resist, severely. Consequently, despite regulations protecting prisoners' rights, those who do not show repentance can be ill treated and even abused by their guards.

## ASSESSMENTS

The Chinese practice of reforming prisoners through labor has received mixed if not polar reviews. Memoirs of political prisoners have inevitably pointed to their unjust incarceration and the repressive forced labor in *laogai* camps. Others have criticized the Chinese government for using much of the returns of penal labor to run prisons instead of giving inmates fair remuneration for their work. Supporters and some progressive Western criminologists, in contrast, see the emphasis on education and transformation rather than punishment in China's penal system as positive; prisoners are not idle, and they have the opportunity to learn in prison. Supporters point to the low recidivism rate among Chinese prisoners (5%) compared to the double-digit rates in other countries as an indication of the success of this rehabilitation strategy. Indeed, *laojiao* and *laogai* is an emotional topic and controversial issue, and it is difficult to give a fair assessment, especially when its practice can sometimes deviate from well-intentioned theories.

**SEE ALSO** *Chinese Marxism: Mao Zedong Thought; Communist Party; Mao Zedong.*

### BIBLIOGRAPHY

Diamant, Neil J., Stanley B. Lubman, and Kevin J. O'Brien. *Engaging the Law in China: State, Society, and Possibilities for Justice.* Stanford, CA: Stanford University Press, 2005.

Du, James J. *Punishment and Reform: An Introduction to the Reform-through-labor System in the People's Republic of China.* Hong Kong: Lo Tat, 2004.

Dutton, Michael R. *Policing and Punishment in China: From Patriarchy to "the People."* Cambridge, U.K.: Cambridge University Press, 1992.

Tanner, Harold Miles. Crime and Punishment in China, 1979–1989. Ph.D. diss., Columbia University, 1994.

Troyer, Ronald J., John P. Clark, and Dean G. Rojek. *Social Control in the People's Republic of China.* New York: Praeger, 1989.

Wu, Hongda Harry. *Laogai: The Chinese Gulag.* Boulder, CO: Westview, 1992.

***Julia Kwong***

## EILEEN CHANG

SEE *Chang, Eileen (Zhang Ailing).*

## ELECTIONS AND ASSEMBLIES, 1909–1949

On October 19, 1907, an imperial edict directed provincial officials to convene consultative bureaus (*ziyiju*) that would help unite officialdom and the people through the discussion of local affairs. Such provincial bureaus, which could bring together representatives from all subprovincial jurisdictions, began to meet. Meanwhile, in Beijing, a government task force began drafting electoral regulations for the provincial assemblies (also known as *ziyiju*) that would supplant these consultative bureaus. These discussions, dominated by men who had studied in Japan and infused the regulations with ideas and plans borrowed from Japan, led to the promulgation on July 22, 1908, of election regulations.

In August 1908, the Qing court's nine-year plan of constitutional reform listed provincial assemblies, local councils (*yishihui*), and a parliament (*yiyuan*) as key arenas for political participation by Chinese citizens. In the six months preceding the elections held in the summer of 1909, about 1.7 million male citizens (about 0.4 percent of the population) were registered as eligible voters in elections that sent county representatives to the prefectural electoral colleges that selected China's 1,643 provincial assemblymen. Voters were literate men at least twenty-five *sui* old (candidates were thirty *sui* or more) who met at least one of the following requirements: employment, such as teaching, that contributed to the public good; receipt of a new-style education degree or one of the three traditional civil-service degrees; official rank; or possession of capital or property valued at 5,000 yuan or more.

On October 14, 1909, which was declared a public holiday, the newly elected assemblymen gathered in twenty-one provincial capitals to debate the issues of the day. Nationally distributed journals carried reports of the proceedings, photographs of assembly halls, and seating charts. In time, the assemblies would publish accounts of their proceedings, which could include such topics as budgets, taxation, and reform initiatives. Although officials might still see these bodies in terms of the original consultative role outlined in 1907, China's first provincial assemblies addressed a more ambitious agenda that illuminated differences between the way citizens and officials approached provincial issues. Moreover, provincial assemblies soon contributed to an empirewide debate on various constitutional issues, especially the timetable for convening a parliament.

While preparations were being made for provincial assemblies, a second set of elected bodies—subcounty councils—was authorized by regulations promulgated on January 18, 1909. These councils were to attend to education, public welfare, public works, and agricultural, industrial, and commercial development. The council electorates were much larger than those for assembly elections since men, who still needed to be literate, could vote as long as they met a much more modest tax-paying (two yuan) requirement. Similar regulations for county councils were promulgated on February 6, 1910. Like the schedule for a parliament, which had been advanced from 1916 to 1913 after a successful petition movement that culminated in November 1910, Beijing's original plan for subcounty council elections (1912–1914) was also advanced. Local councils began to be elected as early as 1909. By the end of 1911, government agencies had reported the establishment of over one thousand preparatory self-government schools (*zizhi yanjiusuo*) with at least fifty thousand students and the election of at least five thousand councils, mostly at the subcounty level. (County councils, originally scheduled to be established in 1913 to 1914, had begun to be elected by late 1910, also on the basis of an "advanced" [*tiqian*] schedule. At least three hundred were reported established by the end of 1911.)

Regulations for a national assembly (*zizhengyuan*), drawn up in 1909, described a consultative body comprised of two hundred men, half nominated by the emperor and half elected from and by provincial assemblies. Like provincial assemblies, the national assembly could discuss budgets as well as other fiscal and legal matters. Although originally conceived in the context of administrative reform, the convening of the national assembly in October 1910 was an intermediate step intended to lead to parliamentary elections that had been rescheduled for 1913.

### PARLIAMENTS IN REPUBLICAN CHINA

These efforts did not end with the 1911 revolution. Local councils and provincial assemblies continued to meet, and the long-anticipated elections for a parliament took place beginning in December 1912. Sun Yat-sen's (Sun Yixian or Sun Zhongshan) National People's Party (Guomindang) dominated the elections, whose results were thrown into turmoil with the assassination of its leading light, Song Jiaoren, in March 1913. Nevertheless, the parliament (*guohui*) convened in Beijing in April 1913 and sought to both assert its own authority and check Yuan Shikai, the reform-minded Qing official and general who was president of the Republic of China. By the fall, after Yuan had put down the so-called Second Revolution in central and southern China, he slowly pushed Sun's National People's Party to the margins and ultimately out of power. Branded as a rebel organization by Yuan in November 1913, the removal of all National People's Party members from the parliament severely diminished the body's prestige and influence.

Yuan had turned on China's first democratic experiments. By February 1914 he had abolished all levels of elected assemblies. While provincial assemblies and local councils were reconstituted in some localities later in the 1910s and 1920s, national-level regulations were absent. At the provincial level, officials who had cheered Yuan's 1914 abrogation answered to neither local nor provincial bodies. At the national level, there were putative representative bodies, but none that were elected with as large an electorate and as open and free elections as those of 1912 to 1913. These included several sessions of the 1913 parliament, with others convening in 1916 to 1917 and 1922 to 1924, as well as rival parliaments associated with various regional military leaders, such as Duan Qirui (1865–1936), who dominated the Anfu Parliament (Anfu Guohui) of 1918 to 1920. In the end, these parliaments and associated cabinets and constitutions fell short of the ideals of constitutionalism and instead have been seen as symbols of failure caused by political corruption, regional militarism, or elite factionalism.

But the late-Qing innovations and early-Republican experiments were not forgotten. Sun Yat-sen, in his *Fundamentals of National Reconstruction* (*Guomin zhengfu jianguo dagang*, 1924), called for county elections, provincial assemblies, and finally the election of a national assembly that would adopt and promulgate a constitution. Sun's reorganized Nationalist Party (Guomindang) would champion his vision after 1928, when Sun's political heir, Chiang Kai-shek (Jiang Jieshi), completed the Northern Expedition that had reunified China. Sun's vision informed the national-level attempt in the new national capital, Nanjing, in the 1930s to write a constitution, an effort that was severely disrupted by the Japanese attacks on China that culminated in the Sino-Japanese War of 1937 to 1945. Nevertheless, direct elections for a national assembly tasked with drafting a permanent constitution were held in 1936 on the eve of war. Ten years later, this body finally met and on December 25, 1946, approved a constitution that took effect on January 1, 1947. Among the elected bodies stipulated in this constitution were a National Assembly (Guomin Dahui) (responsible for constitutional revisions and selecting a president) and a law-making Legislative Yuan (Lifa Yuan).

## LEGACIES OF CONSTITUTIONALISM IN TAIWAN

Constituted on the basis of elections held in 1948, the Legislative Yuan moved to Taiwan as the mainland fell to the Communists in 1949, and it continues in existence to the present. Only in 1969 were supplementary seats added to make room for additional representatives to join those elected in 1948. Although Chiang Kai-shek never took China past the preparatory stage of "political tutelage," his son Chiang Ching-kuo (Jiang Jingguo), who ended martial law in 1987, helped usher in a period of positive democratic developments in Taiwan. In 1991 full democratic elections were held for the National Assembly, and in 1992 the Legislative Yuan was elected on the same basis. By 2000, when the National Assembly's prerogative for constitutional reforms was shifted to the Legislative Yuan (the National Assembly's power to elect a president had already been given to a national electorate in 1996), the promise of early-twentieth-century constitutionalism, when China's first councils, assemblies, and a parliament were elected, was finally realized.

**SEE ALSO** *Constitutionalism; Constitutions before 1949; Regionalism; Villages since 1800.*

**BIBLIOGRAPHY**

Chao, Linda, and Ramon H. Myers. *The First Chinese Democracy: Political Life in the Republic of China on Taiwan.* Baltimore, MD: Johns Hopkins University Press, 1998.

Fincher, John H. *Chinese Democracy: The Self-government Movement in Local, Provincial, and National Politics, 1905–1914.* London: Croom Helm, 1981.

Nathan, Andrew J. A Constitutional Republic: The Peking Government, 1916–28. In *The Cambridge History of China,* Vol. 12, ed. John K. Fairbank, 256–283. Cambridge, U.K.: Cambridge University Press, 1983.

Qian Duansheng (Ch'ien Tuan-sheng). *The Government and Politics of China.* Cambridge, MA: Harvard University Press, 1950.

Thompson, Roger R. *China's Local Councils in the Age of Constitutional Reform, 1898–1911.* Cambridge, MA: Council on East Asian Studies, Harvard University, 1995.

Young, Ernest P. Politics in the Aftermath of Revolution: The Era of Yuan Shih-k'ai, 1912–1916. In *The Cambridge History of China,* Vol. 12, edited by John K. Fairbank, 208–255 Cambridge, U.K.: Cambridge University Press, 1983.

***Roger R. Thompson***

# EMPERORS, 1800–1912

Historians of the Qing are in agreement that the emperors of the nineteenth century make a very pale comparison to the great emperors of the seventeenth and eighteenth centuries. On the surface, the judgment may be less than meaningful, since the extraordinary abilities and personal qualities of the earlier emperors could be rivaled by few rulers anywhere in the world in the early modern or modern period, and the challenges facing nineteenth-century China were also unique. Nevertheless, the nineteenth century was a time of great trouble and transformation for the empire, and the greatest of the changes were reflected in the declining role of the emperor in governance of the empire and the growing role of imperial regencies and aristocratic coalitions.

## YONGYAN, THE JIAQING EMPEROR

The death of Hongli (1711–1799), the Qianlong emperor, was a watershed for the empire. Though he had abdicated in 1796 and was incapacitated by the effects of old age, his faction of favorites, led by Heshen (1750–1799), had kept the reins of real power out of the hands of Yongyan (1760–1820), his successor. From the time he ascended the throne as the Jiaqing emperor in 1796, already aged thirty-five, Yongyan was alternately lectured and ignored by Hongli's favorites, including Heshen. Continuous and disorganized war against the various rebellions allowed the Heshen faction to deplete the imperial treasury by more than a hundred million ounces of silver in the last few years of Hongli's life. When the retired emperor died on February 12, 1799, Yongyan quickly took advantage of his new power to have Heshen and his collaborators arrested; within days, Heshen committed suicide on command of the new emperor.

The suppression in 1804 of the White Lotus Rebellion, the dredging and damming of the Yellow River, and support for the Eight Banners—the traditional Qing military force—all demanded major expenditures from the court. In the meantime, the many expensive monuments and residences built by previous emperors required large outlays to prevent them from deteriorating. For the first few years of his reign, Yongyan increased the sale of offices and ranks and maintained a high tariff on the European trade at Guangzhou, the source of about 80 percent of his income. He also became obsessed with personal frugality, eschewing any lavish court displays and any significant expenditure on his own clothing and housing. But the scale of the response was inadequate. Yongyan was unable to maintain outlays for river management, and during his reign the Yellow River flooded at least seventeen times. Bannermen deserted the garrisons and the newly created farms in the Northeast (the proper name of the three northeastern provinces of Liaoning [previously Liaodong], Jilin and Heilongjiang). Rebellions were not eradicated. A small group actually breached the security of the Forbidden City and attempted to assassinate Yongyan in 1813. And the Europeans, especially the British, were highly irritated by Yongyan's tariff rates. In 1816 they sent a mission led by William Pitt Amherst (1773–1857) to persuade the Qing court to lower the tariffs.

At nearly every turn, Yongyan seemed to be defeated by mechanisms in place before his ascension to the throne. Only a small portion of the imperial appropriation for river management actually was applied to that task; most funds disappeared into the pockets of officials, a practice that was already common in the Qianlong period. Increasing the sale of offices, which brought immediate revenue to the court, only made the problems of corruption worse, since officials who had purchased their offices felt entitled to recoup the expense through theft and the extraction of bribes. Troops of the Eight Banners despised the emperor's attempts to alleviate their insolvency by assigning them to state farms, and they abandoned the projects whenever possible. The emperor's frequent pronouncements on thrift, perhaps maliciously quoted by his detractors, gave the popular impression of a miser who was indifferent to commoners' troubles. The refusal to agree to British tariff demands, while bolstering imperial income in the short term, sowed the seeds of virulent ill will in Britain.

Yongyan's training and personality made him a weak contrast to his father at the same age. As a child, Yongyan had shown unusual intelligence and a strong scholarly bent. His father secretly named him heir apparent in 1773, but the designation was kept so secret that Yongyan's education, travel, and personal contact with his father were kept identical to those of his nine brothers. The result was that Yongyan was unprepared for the throne even at the relatively advanced age at which he achieved it, and the unusual circumstances of his father's abdication did not permit him to gain any real experience even after he became emperor. His frustration with policy matters often led him to return to his scholarly interests. He wrote a great deal, about history, manners, travel, and literature. Like his grandfather, the Yongzheng (1678–1735) emperor, Yongyan died relatively early (aged sixty) and suddenly, during a trip to the imperial retreat at Rehe.

## MINNING, THE DAOGUANG EMPEROR

Great hope was placed in Yongyan's second son, Minning (1782–1850), when he became the Daoguang emperor on Lunar New Year's Day, 1820. Like his father, Minning was a scholar by inclination and like his father he was secretly designated heir apparent. But by the time he became emperor, he also had a dashing side to his public profile. When rebels had broken into the Forbidden City in 1813, Minning had seized a musket and run down to the courtyard, where he shot two of the rebels himself. This suggestion of ferocity was evident again in 1828, when the imperial suppression of the rebellion of Xinjiang Muslim rebel, Jehangir, was followed by the rebel's public humiliation and quartering in Beijing.

These incidents aside, Minning was not distinguished for decisiveness or ruthlessness. But he had a contrasting quality that is now of great interest to historians who compare this phase of the Qing empire to similar passages in the Ottoman and Russian empires: Minning had a very strong consultative tendency. He faced many of the same crises as his father, including flooding of the unmaintained Yellow River, regional rebellion, corruption among his officials, and British dissatisfaction with trade rules. But he also faced new crises, particularly deterioration of the Grand Canal and the spread of opium addiction. In each case, he instituted a period of investigation by his officials, followed by an invitation to officials to debate proper policy courses. The information gathered was good, and the debates were searching, often systematic, and produced results that still interest modern scholars.

In less critical circumstances, these consultative trends were not unlike those that in other empires eventually produced well-grounded constitutional and representative movements. Scholars debate whether the actual policy choices made by Minning after these consultations were the wisest course. He never succeeded in getting his officials to take seriously the need to fix the problems with the Yellow River. In the case of the Grand Canal, he decided to attempt a program of expensive repairs, rather than abandon the canal altogether in favor of sea transport. With regard to opium, he considered and at length rejected the options of legalization and taxation in favor of an absolute demand for rehabilitation of the addicted, eradication of the drug, and banning of future imports. He dispatched Lin Zexu, a far more uncompromising individual than himself, to deal with the British and American merchants who were behind the smuggling of the drug. It was a miscalculation, but a complex one, since even the British government thought until a very late date that the trade was not worth fighting a war about. The Qing forces were inadequately prepared for the British attack when it came. They attempted to both repulse the overwhelming attacks and to negotiate a loser's treaty with the British. Minning and his closest court advisors were alternately enraged by and befuddled by British demands for huge indemnities and unprecedented privileges, and as they delayed responding, or remonstrated with their own negotiators, the price of settling increased.

When the war was over, Minning began, characteristically, a careful study of how the war had been lost. Under pressure to begin paying the British indemnity, he began a detailed review of the treasury accounts and finally assessed the amount that had been pilfered from the bullion stores since 1799 at ten million ounces, which he insisted that treasury officials, present and past, restore from their family fortunes. Minning permitted the local officials at Guangzhou to delay in enacting the provisions of the 1842 Treaty of Nanking (Nanjing) (and subsequent unequal treaties signed with other European powers and the United States), as he delayed in paying the impossible indemnity. At the same time, he returned to the theme of frugality, appearing in court with mended robes and lowering the salaries of his officials and the stipends of the aristocracy. The huge imperial complex at Rehe was abandoned as an imperial retreat. But with demands domestically and internationally, Minning could not catch up, and as the court neared the midcentury mark, its financial obligations were ten times its income. In 1849 the Grand Canal project was abandoned, throwing laborers and merchants into an economic depression the emperor had tried to avoid two decades earlier. Despite his failures, Minning was a figure loved by the elites for his loyalty to courtiers and his personal modesty. His funeral was remarkable for the genuine outpouring of public grief that it occasioned.

## YIZHU, THE XIANFENG EMPEROR

Minning's successor, Yizhu (1831–1861), who ruled as the Xianfeng emperor from 1851 to his death in 1861, was perhaps the truly tragic figure among the nineteenth-century emperors. His father publicly designated Yizhu as his successor in 1846, when Yizhu was fifteen years old. By the time of his accession, problems that had emerged under his father's rule were reaching crisis proportions. In 1850 the court learned of the gathering of rebels under the leadership of the Taiping visionaries in Guangxi, and dispatched troops. In ensuing months came news of repeated defeats of the imperial expeditions. The Taiping movement gathered villages, counties, and nearly whole provinces under its control as it approached the Yangzi (Changjiang) River. Yizhu turned to a talented and determined group of military strategists and local governors, who eventually contained the Taipings at the Yangzi and then at Nanjing, but could not dislodge them. Just as the court seemed to gain a small edge in the civil war in 1854, the British and French governments began to apply first political and then military pressure to have the unequal treaties of the 1840s enacted. The young emperor was unsure how to reply, and before deciding, in 1855, he received news of a massive environmental catastrophe, as the Yellow River actually changed course, resulting in nearly a million casualties.

In 1856 Britain and France took advantage of an administrative dispute at Guangzhou to declare war again. Naval assaults were swift, and at first the Qing forces, profoundly distracted by the civil war, were unable to respond. The Mongol general Sengge Rinchin (1811–1865) afforded the emperor a brief moment of hope by repulsing British and French forces as they attempted to approach Tianjin in 1859; but within months the European forces had regrouped and stormed Beijing, knocking the architectural treasures of the Qianlong emperor's summer palace at Yuanming yuan to the ground, and driving Yizhu with his family and retainers to flee to the disused imperial retreat at Rehe. His government was forced into another round of unequal treaties, this time giving the British control of Qing income from the foreign trade. With the last real source of funds for the government lost, the civil war dragging on, with deaths rising into the tens of millions, and another humiliating defeat to the Europeans confirmed, Yizhu chose to stay at Rehe. He died at Rehe the next year, aged thirty.

Yizhu's youth and the magnitude of the problems confronting him from the first day of his reign combined to foreclose any hope of real achievement, but in retrospect it is clear that his willingness—probably on the advice of his formidable advisor Sushun (d. 1861)—to allow provincial governors such as Zeng Guofan and Li Hongzhang very wide latitude in their uses of revenues and deployment of their local forces, together with a willingness to release Eight Banner officers to fight the Taipings under civilian Chinese command, had been the fundamental element in the government's containment of the Taipings at the Yangzi. Yizhu's death was the structural end of the emperorship he had inherited, but the court continued to develop, with some effectiveness, the patterns of coalition military command and civilian administration that had begun in Yizhu's time.

## ZAICHUN, THE TONGZHI EMPEROR

Just before dying, Yizhu was reported to have designated his son Zaichun (1856–1875) as his heir, and Sushun formed a regency for the six-year-old emperor. In essence, the regency would have been dominated by aristocrats who were not close relatives of the imperial family, and Sushun himself would have been the effective administrator of the empire. But an imperial clique quickly formed to undo this structure. Yizhu's brothers Yixin (1833–1898) and Yihuan (1840–1891), together with Zaichun's mother Cixi (a concubine before being raised to empress status after giving birth to Zaichun), and Yizhu's highest wife, the Empress Dowager Ci'an (1837–1881), conspired to have Sushun arrested when he led the imperial party back to Beijing; a little over a month later, Sushun was beheaded and his sympathizers purged from government.

The reign name chosen for Zaichun, Tongzhi, literally meant *joint rule*. It likely referred most directly to the partnership between Ci'an and Cixi in attempting to oversee both the boy emperor and the empire. But it also recalled the ongoing development of shared power between the imperial government and the civilian governors, creating the amalgamated military forces where Chinese, Manchu, and Mongol volunteers joined ranks against the rebels, whether Taipings (finally defeated in 1864), Nian (defeated in 1868), or Muslim (defeated at Kashgar in 1873). And by the end of Zaichun's reign in 1875 (when he was nineteen years old), it would have another meaning as well: when the British and French had declared joint victory over the Qing in 1860, the new treaties meant that a British official (in actuality one, Robert Hart (1835–1911), who served continuously from 1861 to his retirement in 1907) would collect the tariff revenues and divide them between the Qing and British governments. Debts to other Western powers were paid from the Qing treasury after the British debt was withheld. British, French, and American advisors joined the war against the Taipings, bringing rifles and grenades, and importing whole brigades of mercenaries. Foreign diplomats oversaw the creation of a new Qing diplomatic office, and conducted some negotiations themselves on behalf of the Qing empire. "Joint rule" by 1875 signified not only the new alliances within the empire, but its new, and not altogether welcome, partnership with the governments of Britain, France, and the United States.

The imperial coalition with Cixi, Ci'an, Yihuan, and Yixin cooperated with civilian governors attempting to deal with post–civil war problems of devastated agriculture, masses of refugees, and the rebuilding of the profoundly damaged urban centers of Nanjing, Hangzhou, and many other sites in the Yangzi valley and delta. But they also readily grasped the benefits of the empire's new situation. With the war over, resources were now available for rebuilding not only in the provinces but also at the capital, including the Forbidden City and the imperial pleasure grounds at the summer palace at Yihe. Trade at the many ports now part of the treaty system was governed by the British terms, but the efficient collection of funds provided the Qing court a level of revenue it had not enjoyed since the eighteenth century. At the same time, deficit financing on a large scale was now possible due to the loans provided by the newly friendly governments in Europe.

With a new sense of power, the coalition was disinclined to brook opposition from outsiders. After Sushun, the next to become a prominent victim of the coalition was Zaichun himself. In 1872 the teenaged emperor married a court woman of his own choosing, and prepared to assume personal control over his government. His first project was a major renovation of the ruined Yuanming yuan. The proposed extravagance aroused the ire of the regents. In the midst of losing all his political battles against the coalition, the young emperor contracted smallpox in 1874 and became incapacitated. He appeared to rally, but suddenly died in the first days of 1875. The direct line of the imperial successors ended with Zaichun. His mother selected his cousin Zaitian (1871–1908), a son of Yihuan, as the new emperor. A few months later Zaichun's pregnant wife died, reportedly by suicide. Officials and some family members were distraught at the fact that by choosing a cousin rather than a nephew as successor, the coalition had left Zaichun without a formal heir to worship his spirit; the official Wu Kedu (1812–1879) committed suicide at Zaichun's mausoleum at Dongling to protest the late emperor's abandonment.

## ZAITIAN, THE GUANGXU EMPEROR

With a four-year-old child on the throne as the Guangxu emperor, the coalition was free for at least a decade to steer their course around the obstacles of domestic dislocations, foreign debt, and continuing threat of attack. After 1881 they did so without Ci'an, who after years of friction with Cixi over various matters suddenly took ill and died. Yixin assumed command of the new diplomatic office. The 1860s were a time of institution building and growing success for Yixin, but it did not last. The empire's demonstrable weakness in the face of foreign aggression incited more ventures from aspiring imperialists bent upon more exactions. Yixin had to appear and sign humiliating new treaties of defeat with France and Japan. For his part, Yihuan had plans for building a modern, industrialized navy, with himself in charge. His project proceeded with apparent success until the first test of the navy's effectiveness, in 1884 against France, brought disrepute upon both Yihuan and Yixin.

In 1889 Cixi effected a marriage between Zaitian (then sixteen years old) and her own niece. Thereafter, Cixi began to direct her attentions, at least overtly, to the renovation and expansion of the new summer palace at Yihe, well funded by Yihuan from money originally appropriated for a new navy.

***The last emperor of China, Puyi, Beijing, c. 1924.*** *Throughout the nineteenth century, China's emperors faced a slew of internal and external obstacles to their reign. Natural disasters, foreign imperialism, and civil war all contributed to the collapse of the Qing dynasty in 1912.* 

But she was also keeping an eye on the maturing Zaitian, who after Yihuan's death in 1891 was beginning to talk openly about assuming control of the government. With Yihuan dead and Yixin discredited, Cixi was now the sole survivor of the old regency. In 1896 Zaitian began working with young reform activists to attempt to dislodge the power of Cixi. They proposed a complete overhaul of the government, reducing the traditional offices and support for the Eight Banners, while creating new offices to oversee the development of agriculture, industry, communications, and education. Cixi tolerated their discussions, but in 1898, when Zaitian attempted to form a political base to make himself ruler, she called upon her supporters in the military to have all his new advisors arrested and executed. Zaitian was made a virtual prisoner of Cixi at the Yihe summer palace.

Eventually Cixi's manipulation of the provincial governors and of the poor led to her virtual invitation to the Boxers to set upon the foreign communities in Beijing. In 1900 the calamity forced Cixi to flee, with her prisoner Zaitian in tow, as far as Xi'an. From there, missives to the foreign occupiers arrived, apparently signed by Zaitian, in which he accepted full responsibility for the Boxer Rebellion and subsequent damages; these letters were forged by Cixi. In 1901 the imperial entourage was permitted to return to Beijing, where Cixi extended her charm offensive to the foreign envoys and their wives, who had declined to prosecute her for her part in the Boxer debacle. She also coopted elements of Zaitian's own plans of 1898 and began to present herself as a champion of reform. For his part, Zaitian was apparently convinced that the new reform spirit Cixi had found since her escape from foreign prosecution would lead to the creation of a constitutional monarchy on the model of Meiji Japan (a hope shared by many nationalists), and he prepared himself for the role through study, including English. However, it appears that as her own end approached, Cixi carefully prepared the emperor's as well; he died one day before her, aged thirty-seven.

### PUYI, THE XUANTONG EMPEROR

Cixi had arranged for Zaitian, who was childless, to be succeeded by Yihuan's grandson, the three-year-old Puyi (1906–1967). His regency was to be headed by Yihuan's son, Zaifeng (1883–1951). The regent's ambitions ran very much along the lines of his father, to create an industrialized army and modern bureaucracy dominated by imperial uncles. Such plans probably appeared to be thwarted by the nationalist revolution that ignited in October of 1911 and led to the abdication of the child emperor in February of 1912. However, the compromise ending of the civil war left the imperial house in the Forbidden City protected and supported by a powerful clique of northern governors, and in possession of an enormous fortune in the form of the imperial treasures of sculpture, ceramics, and other art objects. As Puyi grew, the imperial household replicated many of the intrigues of past courts, as regents plotted against emperors, and reformists plotted against reactionaries, and treasuries were plundered by all. In later years, the miniature struggles within the imperial city eventually became entangled with much larger issues of Chinese nationalism, Japanese imperialism, and foreign acquisitiveness.

**SEE ALSO** *Cixi, Empress Dowager; History: Overview, 1800–1860; History: Overview, 1860–1912; Qing Restoration.*

**BIBLIOGRAPHY**

Crossley, Pamela Kyle. *Orphan Warriors: Three Manchu Generations and the End of the Qing World.* Princeton: Princeton University Press, 1990.

Hummel, Arthur, ed. *Eminent Chinese of the Ch'ing Period.* Washington, DC: U.S. Government Printing Office, 1943.

Kwong, Luke S. *A Mosaic of the Hundred Days: Personalities, Politics, and Ideas of 1898.* Cambridge, MA: Harvard University Press, 1984.

Leonard, Jane Kate. *Controlling from Afar: The Daoguang Emperor's Management of the Grand Canal Crisis, 1824–1826.* Ann Arbor: University of Michigan Press, 1996.

Liu Kwang-ching. The Ch'ing Restoration. In *The Cambridge History of China,* eds. Denis Twitchett and John K. Fairbank, Vol. 10: *The Late Ch'ing, 1800–1911,* Pt. 1, 409–490. Cambridge, U.K.: Cambridge University Press, 1978.

Mann Jones, Susan, and Philip A. Kuhn. Dynastic Decline and the Roots of Rebellion. In *The Cambridge History of China,* eds. Denis Twitchett and John K. Fairbank, Vol. 10: *The Late Ch'ing, 1800–1911,* Pt. 1, 107–162. Cambridge, U.K.: Cambridge University Press, 1978.

Rhoads, Edward J. M. *Manchus and Han: Ethnic Relations and Political Power in Late Qing and Republican China, 1861–1928.* Seattle: University of Washington Press, 2000.

Wright, Mary Clabaught. *The Last Stand of Chinese Conservatism: The T'ung-chih Restoration, 1862–1874.* Stanford, CA: Stanford University Press, 1957.

***Pamela Crossley***

## EMPLOYEES' HEALTH INSURANCE

Two major employees' health-insurance schemes were in place from the 1950s to the late 1970s. Public health insurance, funded by government budgets, covered employees in government departments, schools and universities, and the army. Labor insurance, funded by state-enterprise welfare funds, covered employees in state and some urban collective enterprises. Both schemes provided rather comprehensive healthcare coverage for those with a work unit (*danwei*).

Individual employees made no direct contributions to these insurance schemes and received free or subsidized medical treatment. These schemes also usually covered up to half of dependents' medical fees. Many work units had their own clinics or hospitals for their employees. Other work units paid hospitals directly for their employees' treatment.

The work-unit healthcare system privileged urban over rural dwellers and excluded those without a work unit from any health insurance. At the end of the 1970s, 75 percent of the urban labor force was covered by one of the mentioned insurance schemes. But they constituted only 15 percent of the country's total population. This health-insurance system became more difficult to sustain in the post-Mao reform period. A growing number of people even in urban areas fell out of the health-insurance schemes. These included the self-employed and small-business owners, people who worked for private enterprises, and people who worked for money-losing state and collective enterprises. Furthermore, market reforms substantially drove up medical costs. As a result, the government and state enterprises faced pressing financial burdens to cover employees' healthcare benefits. Social health-insurance reforms were deemed inevitable.

## EARLY REFORMS: 1980s–1990s

From the early 1980s, a series of new measures were adopted to test out alternative models. Some work units introduced copayments that required employees to be responsible for part of their medical fees, and other work units required employees to pay the full amount for their treatment and then seek reimbursement from their employers. These initial new measures were followed by risk-pooling experiments, which attempted to use newer enterprises with younger workforces to share part of the burden of older enterprises with older workforces. These uncoordinated reform practices based on the 1950s health-insurance system continued in most cities in the 1990s.

In 1994 a compulsory social health-insurance scheme was first experimented with in two cities: Zhenjiang in Jiangsu Province and Jiujiang in Jiangxi Province. This scheme was intended eventually to replace the prereform schemes altogether. It was modified and extended to a number of cities in 1995 and 1996, including Tianjin and Shanghai. Under the new scheme, a broad portion of the population was covered, including the self-employed, those working for private enterprises, and workers laid off from state enterprises. This new scheme became the prototype for the national health-insurance reform introduced in 1998.

## THE NATIONAL HEALTH INSURANCE SYSTEM SINCE 1998

A nationwide Urban Employee Basic Health Insurance System was issued by the State Council in December 1998. Intended to provide basic health insurance to all urban employees, it shifted the financial burden from the state to employers and employees. At the discretion of local governments, rural enterprises and their employees could also join the scheme, though no provision was made for rural migrants to cities. The cost-sharing arrangement was as follows: Employers had to contribute 6 to 8 percent of total wages, of which 70 percent went to a locally administered medical trust fund. The remaining 30 percent went into employees' individual accounts, with allocations varying according to age group. Younger workers got much less from employers' contributions. Each employee was given an individual medical-insurance account and was required to pay 2 percent of his wages into this account. One's medical costs were then paid for by a combination of funds from the medical trust fund, the medical-insurance account, and the employee's own money. The medical-insurance account paid for up to 10 percent of the local average annual wage, after which the medical trust fund paid alongside copayments made by the employee. Copayments were set on a sliding scale specified by local governments. However, the maximum amount that the medical trust fund paid was capped at four times the average annual wage. Any costs above this upper limit were paid by employees or their private health insurance.

This nationwide health-insurance reform thus started to shift the financial burden to a bipartite or tripartite system. There were no state subsidies in this basic health-insurance system. The state's financial contribution to medical care remained in subsidizing hospitals' expenditures. Local governments have been given some flexibility in determining the percentages of employer and employee contributions. It has been reported that all medical trust funds at the national level have managed so far to maintain a positive balance.

## IMPACTS OF THE REFORMS

Unlike the old work-unit system, this nationwide universal system basically eliminated the privileged position of employees in central government and state enterprises. Based on risk pooling through medical trust funds, the new system entitled practically all urban employees from all different sectors to the same range of health-insurance coverage, regardless of the nature and size of their workplaces. It encompassed laid-off workers and workers in money-losing state enterprises. In this sense, the new system enhanced equal access to medical care. In addition, workers in rural enterprises were in principle allowed to participate in the new system, though participation was voluntary and subject to employers' willingness to join and to the local governments' policies. So far, the system is not accessible to the entire rural population. It is limited to nonagricultural employees, and farmers are excluded.

In 1999, 49 percent of urban Chinese had health insurance, but only 7 percent of rural residents had such coverage. Since 2001 the new national health-insurance system has been implemented in some major cities, such as Shanghai, Chengdu, and Shenyang. Thus far, however, it is difficult to obtain reliable information on actual participation in this new system. Apart from the fact that participation in this scheme varies significantly from place to place, official accounts are frequently misleading and inflated (see Duckett 2004 for details).

While this new nationwide health-insurance system covers a broader portion of the population than the old one, it provides a narrower range of medical benefits. On average, individuals now have to spend more on medical treatment than in the prereform era. Indeed, health expenditures have become one of the biggest burdens for individual employees. In 2000 individual health expenditures made up 61 percent of total national health expenditures, compared to 39 percent in 1990. The privatization of some medical institutions has been driving up medical costs. The new system discriminates especially against younger age groups, who are expected to rely more on their own savings. Dependents are no longer entitled to any medical benefits. Furthermore, although the new scheme is mandatory, some very small enterprises and money-losing state enterprises cannot contribute the stipulated percentage to the medical trust funds. As a result, they either underreport wages to reduce their contributions or shift costs to employees by cutting wages. Employees working in these enterprises or in low-paying jobs thus have less in their medical-insurance accounts. They are subject to higher out-of-pocket payments. Those with very low coverage or without insurance are left with fewer options. An increasing number of patients in poor areas choose not to receive outpatient care or refuse to be hospitalized even though they should be, mainly because of their lack of ability to pay.

**SEE ALSO** *Health Care, 1800–1949; Medical Care since 1949; Rural Cooperative Medical Systems.*

**BIBLIOGRAPHY**


Bloom, Gerald, and Tang Shenglan, eds. *Health Care Transition in Urban China.* Aldershot, Hants, U.K.: Ashgate, 2004.

Duckett, Jane. State, Collectives, and Worker Privilege: A Study of Urban Health Insurance Reform. *China Quarterly* 177 (2004): 155–173.

Guo, Baogang. Transforming China's Urban Health-Care System. *Asian Survey* 43, 2 (2003): 385–403.

Hillier, Sheila, and Shen Jie. Health Care Systems in Transition: People's Republic of China. Part 1: An Overview of China's Health Care System. *Journal of Public Health Medicine* 18, 3 (1996): 258–265.


***Cheris Shun-ching Chan***

## ENCYCLOPEDIAS

The "Chinese encyclopedia" became famous through a story by the Argentinean author Jorge Luis Borges (1899–1986), which claimed that it grouped animals in such categories as "belonging to the emperor," "embalmed," or "from afar resembling flies." Sadly, the order of things in Chinese encyclopedias is more predictable. Premodern literati encyclopedias grouped things into the broad categories "heaven," "earth," and "man," and assembled under the subheadings quotations on the subject from earlier authors. Popular reference works without literary aspirations such as the early seventeenth-century *Complete Book of Ten Thousand Treasures* (*Wanbao quanshu*) adopted this order, but included summarizing articles and illustrations.

The largest printed project of the first type was the *Collection of Texts and Illustrations of Old and New Times* (*Gujin tushu jicheng,* 1726), with 10,000 chapters in 5,020 volumes. With sixty copies printed, it was meant for the use of the top echelon only. When in 1880 the British pioneer of modern Chinese-language publishing, Ernest Major (1841–1908), added lithography to his Shenbao publishing house in Shanghai, he set out to democratize and commercialize access to this treasure of Chinese learning and illustration. Because all the earlier copies had suffered from worms, fires, water, and use, Major had to splice together a complete set from different sources. Gathering subscribers in a temporary shareholding company to finance the project, he released 1,500 copies of what became known as the "major print" in 1885. In the early 1890s, the Qing court discovered the potential of the work to project Chinese culture abroad at a time when cultural flows seemed all to be going in the opposite direction. The court had copies printed as gifts to major libraries in Europe and the United States.

In the meantime, a new range of knowledge had become relevant in China—knowledge about the world, about the different political and social institutions to be found there, and about science and technology. The new encyclopedias drew on Western encyclopedias, such as Hugh Murray's *An Encyclopedia of Geography* (1834), often through an oral translation by a Westerner. Chinese encyclopedias also drew on diaries of the first Chinese ambassadors to the West; on Japanese translations of Western works, such as the 1848 edition of *Chambers's Information for the People,* which included overview articles; on new Japanese encyclopedias, such as the *Imperial Encyclopedia* (*Teikoku hyakka zensho,* 1898–1908); or on each other through reckless copying.

The peaks of encyclopedia publishing show a direct link with high tides of crisis and reform. The first occurred between 1895 and 1898, leading up to the Hundred Days' Reform, and the second occurred after the court embarked on a "new policy" (*xinzheng*) in 1901 following the Boxer upheaval. The court's new examinations included "Western knowledge," and the new encyclopedias were the only source available for preparation because schools able and willing to teach the new knowledge were still rare. About fifty or sixty, often huge, encyclopedias were published in short order. They show a level of Chinese familiarity with the West that defies common prejudice.

The Republican period saw only a few new encyclopedic works, but they were of high quality. The often reprinted two-volume *Encyclopedia for Everyday Use* (*Riyong baike quanshu*, 1919 completely revised and expanded; 1934 in three volumes) offers a systematic body of "civilized" knowledge for the new Republican citizen to replace the "unscientific" spirit of works such as the *Wanbao quanshu*. The *Handbook of Concepts of the New Culture* (*Xin wenhua cishu*, 1921; many reprints) defines China's "new culture" as exclusively Western-derived, and offers in a single volume knowledgeable introductions to the key figures and concepts of the time. Its entries are arranged with Western headings in alphabetical order from Abelard to Zwingli. The publisher was the Commercial Press in Shanghai, which also launched the Encyclopedia Book Series (Baike xiao congshu, 1923–1948), with over one hundred topical volumes along the lines of the Temple Primers or the Göschen Series.

The People's Republic of China (PRC) first provided only regularly updated handbooks with the official definitions of concepts, most importantly the completely reworked *Ocean of Terms* (*Cihai*, first edition Shanghai 1947, draft of new edition in 1961; several revisions after 1979), while generally relying for definitions and information on the *Great Soviet Encyclopedia* (*Bolshaya Sovetskaya Entsiklopediya*, 1926–1947; second edition, 1950–1958). After the Sino-Soviet split and the end of the Cultural Revolution, China produced its own *Great Chinese Encyclopedia* (*Zhongguo da baike quanshu*, 1980–1995; sixty categories). It is organized according to fields of knowledge (e.g., sports, chemistry) connected through an overall index. While setting out to be more scholarly than political, the political changes since 1980 have made many articles into historical documents. A Chinese edition of the 15th edition of the *Concise Encyclopedia Britannica* was published at about the same time (1985–1991).

The efforts of the Communist Party to retain discursive control have been challenged by free online encyclopedias such as the Chinese edition of Wikipedia, which is based outside of China, and the *Baidu baike* encyclopedia from the Chinese search engine Baidu. The Baidu abides by the rules laid down by the Propaganda Department. Wikipedia has not done so and has seen access time and again blocked by the state-of-the-art "Golden Shield" erected around PRC cyberspace to shield citizens from unapproved information and opinion.

Research on modern Chinese encyclopedias has only recently started. The focus has been on the period between 1890 and 1911.

**BIBLIOGRAPHY**

Chen Pingyuan and Milena (Dolezelova), eds. *Jindai Zhongguo de baike cishu* [Encyclopedic works of china 1870-1911]. Beijing: Peking University Press, 2007.

Zhong Shaohua. *Renlei zhishi de xin gongju: Zhong Ri jindai baikequanshu yanjiu* [New tools of human knowledge: Studies on Chinese and Japanese encyclopedias 1870-1911]. Beijing: Beijing Tushuguan Press, 1996.

***Rudolf G. Wagner***

## ENDANGERED SPECIES, PROTECTION OF

China's biological resources are among the world's richest. This is due not only to its size, but also to the tremendous diversity of habitats it provides for wild plants and animals. China has over 34,291 species of higher plants and 6,347 species of vertebrates, including numerous endemic species. However, industrialization, economic development, and human population pressure have combined to result in a rapid loss of biological diversity and an acceleration in the number of species disappearing from the earth. It is estimated that there are 4,000 to 5,000 endangered higher plants and more than 398 endangered vertebrates in China. Endangered species in China include the giant panda, golden monkey, Asian elephant, black-necked crane, and crested ibis. The pteridophyte plants *Cyrtomium bemionitis* and vertebrates *Crocodilus porosus* have become extinct in China.

### LAWS AND REGULATIONS

China is working hard to protect its endangered wildlife and their habitats. As early as 1950, the State Council promulgated Regulations on the Protection of Rare Animals and Plants. Like a number of other legal systems, the modern approach to wildlife protection emerged in the 1970s in the years following the Stockholm Declaration. Since 1980 China has adopted a series of important statutes, laws, and regulations for the protection of endangered species. The Constitution provides that the state ensures the rational use of natural resources, that it protect rare animals and plants, and that organizations and individuals may not appropriate or damage natural resources. In 1988 the National People's Congress adopted the Wild Animals Protection Law, focusing on all aspects of protection and use. This law addresses wild-animal reserves; hunting; domestication permits; the sale, purchase, and transport of state-protected wild animals and their products; and the import and export of state-protected wild animals. The Wild Plants Protection Regulations, issued in 1996, provides detailed rules for the conservation and management of wild plants. The 1997 revision of the

Criminal Law stipulated for the first time that damage to the environment and resources is a crime, and provides that illegal hunting, killing, transporting, and selling of rare and endangered species can incur heavy fines and sentences of more than ten years. On September 1, 2006, the Regulation on the Import and Export of Endangered Species become effective to protect wild fauna and flora, and to comply with the Convention on International Trade in Endangered Species of Wild Fauna and Flora. Other laws and regulations related to the protection of endangered species are the Environmental Protection Law, the Environmental Impact Assessment Law, the Forest Law, the Marine Environment Protection Law, the Grasslands Law, the Fishery Law, the Water Pollution Prevention Law, and Nature Reserves Regulations.

## ADMINISTRATION

Many ministries and agencies are involved in the protection of endangered species. The Ministry of Environmental Protection, as a national focal point of the Convention on Biological Diversity, is responsible for the overall supervision and management of biodiversity conservation in China. The Interdepartmental Joint Committee on Species Protection, headed by the Ministry of Environmental Protection and composed of representatives from sixteen other ministries and agencies under the State Council, was established in 2003 to guide and supervise the protection of species at the national level. The protection of endangered species is administered in detail by the State Forestry Administration and the Ministry of Agriculture. Both agencies have nationwide responsibility for management of endangered species, a responsibility they share with local governments. China ratified the Convention on International Trade in Endangered Species of Wild Fauna and Flora in 1981 and the Convention on Biological Diversity in 1993. Management offices have been established and scientific committees have been set up to implement the stipulations of these conventions.

***Giant panda climbing a tree, Wolong, Sichuan province.*** *A wide variety of habitats exists in China, from arid desert steppes in the north to subtropical conditions in the south, allowing for a great diversity of wildlife. As China becomes more industrialized, the central government has begun to enact greater protection of some of these environments and the endangered species they support, such as the giant pandas of central China.* © KEREB SU/CORBIS

STRATEGIES AND ACTION PLANS

China officially announced the implementation of its Biodiversity Action Plan on June 13, 1994. The Action Plan is one of the major actions taken by the government in fulfilling its obligations under the convention. The plan provides a strong basis and comprehensive guidance for dealing with the challenges of protecting biodiversity. The plan addresses goals, objectives, and tasks for conserving biodiversity. China also promulgated its Outline on National Eco-environment Protection in 2000 and its Outline on Planning for the Protection and Utilization of National Species Resources in 2007. Competent authorities also worked out specific conservation action plans for forestry, agricultural, marine, and wetlands biodiversity, so that biodiversity conservation by sectors is incorporated into the national action plan.

MEASURES TO PROTECT ENDANGERED SPECIES

In 1997–1998 China issued the *Zhongguo Binwei Dongwu Hongpishu* (China Red Book on Endangered Faunas), covering species of birds, mammals, amphibians, reptiles, and fish. In 1999 China promulgated its first batch of key national wild flora placed under protection, which included 246 flora species in 8 categories.

Recognizing that wildlife and endangered species require suitable habitats, governments at the national, provincial, and local levels created nature reserves. They were established to achieve a variety of objectives. Some were designed to focus on specific endangered species, like the panda or the red-crowned crane. Others were created to protect sensitive ecosystems or endemic plant communities. There are also marine nature reserves for aquatic animals and plants. As of the end of 2007, China has set up 2,531 nature reserves covering a total area of 385.2 million acres, or 15.2 percent of China's total land territory.

China has implemented six major forestry programs. From 2001 to 2005, implementation of China's forestry programs resulted in 64.5 million acres of new forests and 23 million acres of enclosed hills for growing trees. China's total investment reached RMB 148.195 billion. In 2001 the state established the forestry ecological compensation fund. In the next six years, the state invested RMB 10 billion in this fund. In 2006 the fund's outlay reached RMB 3 billion annually, and areas covered by it reached 99 million acres.

China established a regulatory system for sustainable utilization of wild animal and plant resources, requiring, for instance, a permit for hunting wild animals under national protection, a permit for collecting wild plants under national protection, a permit for domesticating and breeding wild animals under national protection, and approval of competent authorities for selling, purchasing, utilizing, exporting, and introducing wild animals. As a result of intensified nationwide efforts, many wild aquatic animals under national protection were rescued. To promote sustainable use of fishery resources, China instituted prohibited fishing periods, prohibited fishing areas, fishing permits, and zero-increase and declining quotas for marine fishing.

China also strengthened basic and applied research on protection and sustainable use of endangered species. Moreover, it actively participated in the implementation and negotiation of relevant international conventions, and it developed bilateral and multilateral cooperation, and cooperation with nongovernmental organizations. Through news agencies and other forms of publicity, the government has made efforts to enhance public awareness of endangered species. In addition, it undertook inspections, investigations, and prosecutions to eliminate illegal trade in endangered species.

As a result of continued efforts by both Chinese people and international communities, some wild animals and plants have increased or stabilized their populations over wider distribution areas and improved habitats. For instance, when firstly discovered in 1981, there were only 7 crested ibis, and now there are a total of 750 wild or artificially bred crested ibis. The number of Chinese alligators increased from over 200 to over 10,000, and the number of giant panda increased over 40 percent. In addition, stable artificially bred populations have been established in China for over 200 species of rare and endangered wild animals. Of 189 species of severely endangered nationally protected wild plants, 71 percent achieved stable wild populations. It is estimated that 85 percent of wildlife species, 85 percent of terrestrial ecosystems, and 65 percent of higher plant colonies are now protected. Yet some species are still critically endangered as a result of illegal hunting, poaching, logging, and smuggling activities.

**BIBLIOGRAPHY**

Watters, Lawrence, and Wang Xi. The Protection of Wildlife and Endangered Species in China. *Georgetown International Environmental Law Review* (Spring 2002).

Xu, Haigen, Jun Wu, Yan Liu, et al. Biodiversity Congruence and Conservation Strategies: A National Test. *BioScience* 58 (2008): 632–639.

Xu, Haigen, Shunqing Wang, and Dayuan Xue. Biodiversity Conservation in China: Legislation, Plans, and Measures. *Biodiversity and Conservation* 8 (1999): 819–837.

***Haigen Xu***

# ENERGY

*This entry contains the following:*

OIL AND NATURAL GAS
*Kelly Sims Gallagher*

HYDROLOGICAL POWER and WIND POWER
*Phillip Andrews-Speed*

NUCLEAR POWER
*Gregory Kulacki*

ELECTRICITY GENERATION
*Kelly Sims Gallagher*

## OVERVIEW

In 2007 China was self-reliant for about 90 percent of its commercial energy supply. Coal continued to account for about 70 percent of the national energy supply. The balance was provided by oil (21 percent), natural gas (3 percent), and hydroelectricity (6 percent). The proportion of nuclear and of other forms of renewable energy was small but growing.

The reserves of coal and the level of investment in production capacity have allowed China to meet its own needs for coal as well as to be a significant coal exporter. In 2007 China became a net importer of coal for a short period, but this is probably a transient phenomenon. In contrast, reserves of oil and natural gas are limited, and China became a net importer of oil in 1993 and of natural gas in 2006. The potential for new hydroelectricity capacity is large, but the widespread recognition of negative social and environmental impacts of the Three Gorges Dam may slow down the construction of new large dams.

From 1980 to 2000 the annual consumption of energy increased by 250 percent, from 415 to 1,060 million tons of oil equivalent, at an average rate of about 4.5 percent per year. Between 2002 and 2006 energy demand rose by a further 60 percent in just four years, equivalent to a rate of 12.5 percent each year. This soaring demand arose from a surge in economic growth and an increase in the proportional contribution of heavy industry to the economy. As a result, twenty years of declining energy intensity were reversed and the government was faced with a major policy challenge to bring energy demand under control. Though the rate of growth of demand will slow, projections suggest that China's consumption of energy will more than double by the year 2030, with significant consequences for international energy markets and the environment.

China's energy sector remains dominated by the state, in its various forms. Most energy companies remain wholly or predominantly owned by the state, at different levels of government. The oil and gas industry is monopolized by three groups—CNPC (China National Petroleum Corporation), Sinopec, and CNOOC (China National Offshore Oil Corporation)—and by their listed subsidiaries (PetroChina Ltd., Sinopec Ltd., and CNOOC Ltd.). Private-sector participation is limited to a large number of small Chinese refining and distribution companies, and to a small number of foreign investors, including Shell, BP, ExxonMobil, Agip, Chevron, Phillips, and Total. The electrical power sector is dominated by five generating companies and two grid companies spun out of the previous State Power Company. But more than 50 percent of the generating capacity is owned by a variety of other enterprises at the local government level. The coal industry is more heterogeneous and diverse, with a wide range of enterprises owned at provincial and lower levels of government, and significant private-sector participation in small-scale mines.

Since 1993 China has lacked a Ministry of Energy, or any single agency responsible for energy policy. The National Development and Reform Commission (NDRC) continues to be the dominant government body in this sector. It retains the authority to set energy prices, to approve major investments, and to develop strategies for energy conservation and energy efficiency. The Ministry of Land and Resources is responsible for issuing licenses for resource extraction and for managing environmental damage to the land. The State Environmental Protection Agency has national responsibility for environmental protection.

In response to the developing national energy challenges, the government established three new bodies to address energy policy during the 2003–2005 period: the Energy Leading Group in the State Council coordinates energy policy across all sectors of the economy; the State Energy Office provides the leading group with energy policy analysis and proposals; and the Energy Bureau of the NDRC pulls together the energy functions within this commission. In addition, the State Electricity Regulator Commission was established in 2002 to drive forward and to regulate the emerging markets in the power sector.

**BIBLIOGRAPHY**

Andrews-Speed, Philip. *Energy Policy and Regulation in the People's Republic of China.* The Hague, Netherlands: Kluwer, 2004.

Berrah, Noureddine, Feng Fei (Fei Feng), Roland Priddle, and Wang Leiping (Leiping Wang). *Sustainable Energy in China: The Closing Window of Opportunity.* Washington DC: World Bank, 2007.

Downs, Erica. *China* (Brookings Foreign Policy Studies, Energy Security Series). Washington DC: Brookings Institution, 2006.

***Philip Andrews-Speed***

## COAL

China is the largest producer and consumer of coal in the world. It has the third largest recoverable reserves, the best of which are located in the central north of the country. In 2007 production surpassed 2.3 billion tons. Only about 6 percent of the production comes from surface mines, with the rest from underground mines. The relative proportions of production from large state-owned mines, local state-owned mines, and tens of thousands of small town and village mines have varied since the founding of the People's Republic.

## COAL-MINE ACCIDENTS

Although China's coal industry was actually more dangerous in the Mao Zedong period, its rapid growth since 1980 and a more open society have focused unprecedented public attention on coal-mine accidents and fatalities.

Chart 1 shows a steady improvement in death rates per million tons output (though not in total number of deaths) from the mid 1970s to the early 1990s. But there was little further improvement before death rates began to fall in the early 2000s, at first with a relatively static number of fatalities (around six thousand) matched by rapidly increasing output, and then from 2006 with an actual drop in fatalities. China's small township and village enterprise mines have consistently been the most dangerous, followed by the local state mines, with the large state mines being relatively safe.

Although coal mining (especially underground) is an intrinsically dangerous occupation, the continuing incidence of major gas or coal-dust explosions indicates that even in the first decade of the twenty-first century, China has still not succeeded in overcoming problems largely resolved by European mines in the late nineteenth century. A series of massive disasters struck the Chinese coal-mining industry in 2005, including an explosion at Fuxin, Liaoning, causing 216 casualties—the worst mining disaster since an even larger explosion in 1960 at Datong, Shanxi, during the Great Leap Forward.

Government attempts to improve the situation through regulation have had limited success. In rural areas, attempts to close mines for safety reasons run into a coalition of (sometimes corrupt) local officials and mine owners, but also face opposition from the local population whose livelihoods depend on the mines. The state mines, though they have a much better record, were pressured for much of the 1990s by the need to reduce costs to become economically viable at a time when coal prices were not high; when coal prices improved, the profits to be made encouraged both types of mine to cut corners in order to maximize output. However, since the early 2000s, government attempts to address the situation have gradually registered some success, for example in weeding out some of the smallest and most dangerous mines.

### BIBLIOGRAPHY

Meitan Gongye Bu, Anquan Si. *Zhongguo meikuang shangwang shigu tongji fenxi ziliao huibian, 1949–1995.* Beijing: Meitan gongye chubanshe, 1998.

Wang Shaoguang. "Regulating Death at Coalmines: Changing Mode of Governance in China." *Journal of Contemporary China* 15, 46 (2006): 1–30.

Wright, Tim. "The Political Economy of Coal Mine Disasters in China: 'Your Rice Bowl or Your Life.'" *China Quarterly* 179 (2004): 629–646.

**Tim Wright**

Since the mid-1990s, in the interests of efficiency and regulation, government officials have expressed the desire to consolidate production into six to eight large coal-mining conglomerates through the merger and closure of thousands of small mines. However, realizing this goal has been difficult because of the insatiable national demand for coal to fuel China's burgeoning economy, and concomitantly, the potentially attractive earnings from involvement in the industry. Compared to eking out an existence off the land in some of the least fertile parts of the country, many farmers continue to risk their lives in horrific working conditions in order to earn what for them are substantial sums of money. The small mines are often run illegally by people who have little knowledge of mine construction and who use almost anything available to cut and shift the coal. The loss of life in these mines is notoriously high (see sidebar).

Coal accounts for almost 70 percent of China's total energy consumption. Thermal power plants, fueled mainly by coal transported by rail, generate about 80 percent of the country's total electricity. The coal industry is closely linked with heavy industries such as iron and steel, chemicals, cement, and so forth. In order to meet the country's surging demand for power, the government is investing heavily in extending the life of existing large state mines, opening new ones, modernizing and expanding the railway system, and building ever more thermal power plants.

In 2007 China became a net importer of coal. For many southern and coastal areas, sourcing of coal from abroad has become more reliable and cheaper than depending on rail shipments from the north and interior. Also, the quality of the coal is higher. Because the government wants to remain as energy self-sufficient as possible, and world oil prices are high and continue to climb, coal will remain the main form of energy for the foreseeable future, though the government is building extensive natural gas import infrastructure and many nuclear power plants, as well as major hydropower projects.

China is under considerable international pressure to drastically reduce the air pollution resulting from burning such vast amounts of coal. The traditional means of

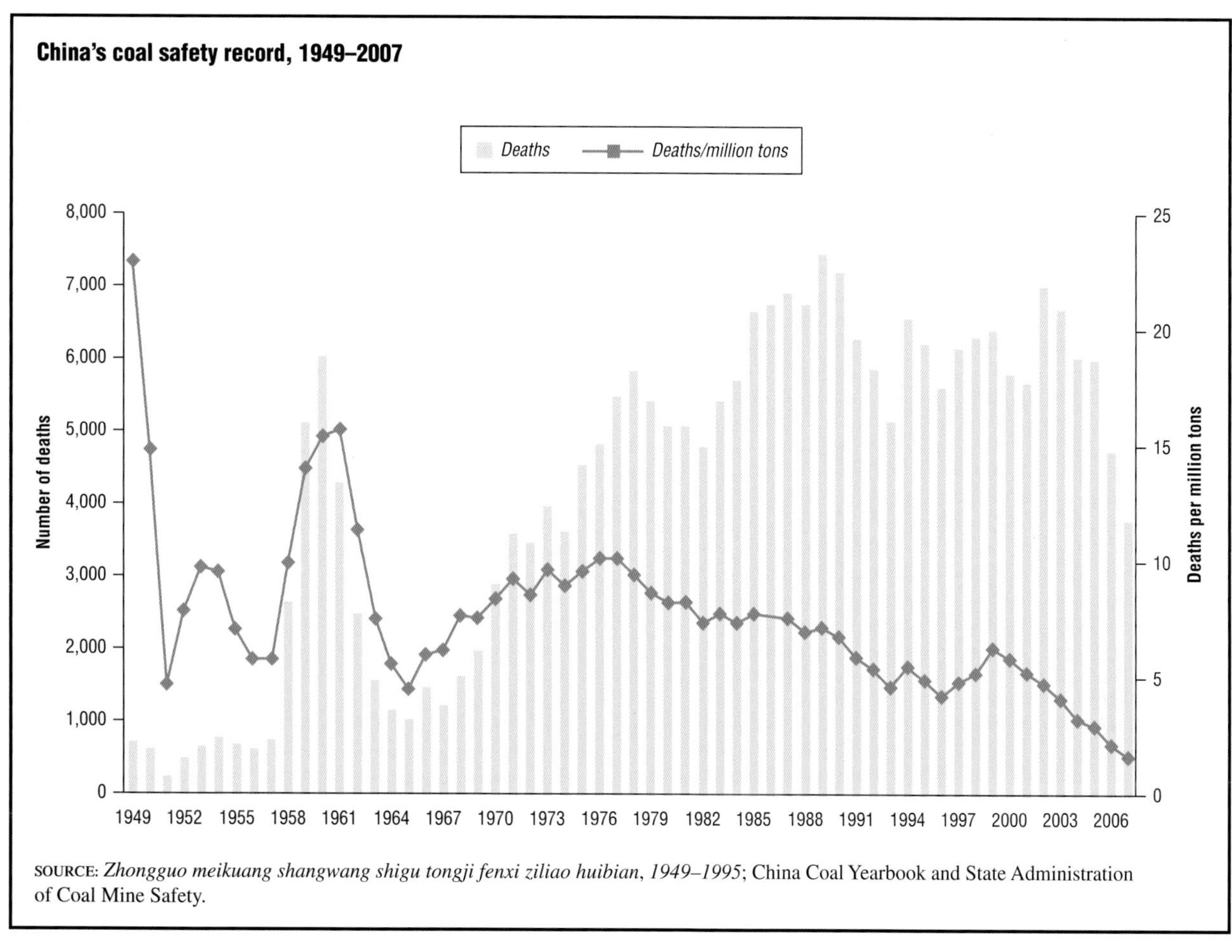


SOURCE: *Zhongguo meikuang shangwang shigu tongji fenxi ziliao huibian, 1949–1995*; China Coal Yearbook and State Administration of Coal Mine Safety.

***Figure 1***

processing requires copious amounts of water, but there are serious water shortages in the main coal-producing areas. Thus, all possible options such as clean coal, liquefaction, coal gasification, and other technologies aimed at raising the efficiency with which coal is consumed and reducing the environmental impacts of its use are all anxiously being explored.

**BIBLIOGRAPHY**

Andrews-Speed, Philip, Yang Minying, Shen Lei, and Shelley Cao. The Regulation of China's Township and Village Coal Mines: A Study of Complexity and Ineffectiveness. *Journal of Cleaner Production* 11, 2 (2003): 185–196.

Thomson, Elspeth. *The Chinese Coal Industry: An Economic History*. London and New York: RoutledgeCurzon, 2003.

Tu Jianjun (Jianjun Tu). China's Botched Coal Statistics? *China Brief* 6, 21 (2006): 8–10.

Tu Jianjun (Jianjun Tu). Coal Mining Safety: China's Achilles' Heel. *China Security* 3, 2 (2007): 36–53.

***Elspeth Thomson***

## OIL AND NATURAL GAS

China became the second-largest consumer of oil in the world in 2004, and it consumed 7.4 million barrels of oil per day in 2006. In 2008, China ranked as the third-largest oil importer after the United States and Japan. Angola became the largest source of crude oil supply to China in 2006, surpassing Saudi Arabia for the first time. Net imports of crude and refined products in 2006 were 3.4 million barrels of oil per day, about one-quarter of U.S. total net imports (BP 2007). China is not a major consumer of natural gas; natural gas accounted for less than 1 percent of total energy consumption in 2005 (National Bureau of Statistics 2007, chap. 7). China consumed only 5.4 billion cubic feet per day in 2006, equal to just 9 percent of U.S. consumption that year (BP 2007).

China is not as well endowed with oil and gas resources as it is with coal. China had 18.3 billion barrels of proven oil reserves (1.3 percent of the world total) and 53.3 trillion cubic feet of natural gas (also 1.3 percent of the world total) as of January 2006 (DOE 2006). China's largest oil-producing field, Daqing, is located in northeastern China, but it is already in decline. Oil and gas exploration is currently focused offshore and in the western provinces. Although foreign companies are permitted to undertake oil and gas exploration and production, the Chinese national oil companies are entitled to a majority share in any commercial discovery.

In 1998 the Chinese government reorganized the oil industry, forming two major vertically integrated oil and gas companies, the China National Petroleum Corporation (CNPC), with a regional dominance in the north and west, and the China Petroleum and Chemical Corporation (Sinopec), which controls most of the assets in the south and east. The China National Offshore Oil Corporation (CNOOC) is responsible for all offshore exploration and production. All three companies undertake international exploration and production, and all carried out initial public offerings of stock in the early 2000s, but the Chinese government owns a majority stake in these monolithic companies.

The Chinese government regulates retail fuel prices in the Chinese market, and it held fuel prices far below the world price even as crude oil prices soared between 2005 and 2008, putting great pressure on Chinese refineries, which still had to pay world prices to import crude. This price regulation has made it difficult for Chinese refining capacity to expand and be upgraded. Refining capacity was 6.6 million barrels per day in 2006. Only 190,000 barrels per day were added in 2007, but 400,000 additional barrels per day are projected to be added in 2008 (Dow Jones MarketWatch 2007; Chen and Bai 2008).

Most of China's oil is consumed by the transportation sector, mainly by highway vehicles, but during periods of electricity shortages, diesel use increases sharply as backup generators are put into operation. Overall, in 2005, power generation, construction, and agricultural vehicles together accounted for about 15 percent of petroleum demand, with the rest used by the transport and industry sectors. Overall, however, the transportation sector only accounts for 8 percent of total energy consumption in China (National Bureau of Statistics 2007, chap. 7). There are approximately 10 million heavy trucks, and much of China's freight is moved by truck (Bradsher 2007). China has approximately 30 million passenger cars (defined as cars, pickups, and SUVs), compared with 230 million passenger cars in the United States. Sales of cars in China have exploded during the early years of the twenty-first century. As recently as 2000, only 500,000 passenger cars were produced in China, but in 2007, Chinese sales exceeded 10 million for the first time (CATARC 2000–2007).

Due to mounting concerns about energy security, the Chinese government imposed China's first fuel-efficiency standards on passenger cars in 2005, and these were tightened to an equivalent of thirty-six miles per gallon in January 2008, although they are a weight-based standard. The Chinese government also embarked on a drive to secure oil resources around the world, purchasing oil concessions and arranging long-term contracts in countries as diverse as Angola, Sudan, and Venezuela (Lee and Shalmon 2007). CNPC has acquired exploration and production interests in twenty-one countries, and Sinopec has acquired major stakes in international fields, including the Udmurtneft field in Russia and a $2 billion investment in the Yadavaran field in Iran (DOE 2006; Kurtenbach 2007). CNOOC offered to purchase UNOCAL in 2005, but withdrew its bid due to opposition from the U.S. Congress. Instead, CNOOC has made major investments in Indonesia and Niger.

Motor vehicles have become a major source of urban air pollution as well, accounting for as much as 80 percent of air pollution in some cities (Gallagher 2006). Most of China's domestic crude is low in sulfur, but as China imports more crude oil from abroad, sulfur in fuels has become a major cause of the air-pollution problem.

China's oil consumption is expected to increase 5 percent per year through 2015, and its natural gas consumption is projected to grow 10 percent per year during the same time period (IEA 2007, reference scenario).

**BIBLIOGRAPHY**

BP. *BP Statistical Review of World Energy 2007.* London: Author, 2007.

Bradsher, Keith. Trucks Power China's Economy, at a Suffocating Cost. *New York Times*, December 8, 2007.

Chen Aizhu and Jim Bai. China Set for 400,000-bpd Oil Refinery Output Rise. Reuters. January 9, 2008.

China Automotive Technology and Research Center (CATARC). *Statistical Yearbook of Automobile Industry.* Tianjin: Author, 2000–2007.

Dow Jones MarketWatch. China's Crude Oil Imports May Rise 10.3% in 2007. March 7, 2007.

Gallagher, Kelly Sims. *China Shifts Gears: Automakers, Oil, Pollution, and Development.* Cambridge, MA: MIT Press, 2006.

International Energy Agency (IEA). *World Energy Outlook 2007: China and India Insights.* Paris: Author, 2007. Available from http://www.worldenergyoutlook.org/.

Kurtenbach, Elaine. China's Sinopec, Iran Ink Yadavaran Deal. Associated Press, *Petroleum News*, December 16, 2007.

Lee, Henry, and Dan Shalmon. Searching for Oil: China's Oil Initiatives in the Middle East. Working paper. Cambridge, MA: Belfer Center for Science and International Affairs, Kennedy School of Government, Harvard University, 2007.

National Bureau of Statistics of China. *China Statistical Yearbook 2007.* Beijing: Author, 2007.

U.S. Department of Energy (DOE), Energy Information Administration. Country Analysis Brief. December 2006.

***Kelly Sims Gallagher***

## HYDROLOGICAL POWER

China has one of the largest hydrological power resources in the world, and most of these resources are located in the southwest, with 50 percent in just three provinces—Yunnan, Guizhou, and Sichuan—and in one provincial-level municipality, Chongqing. After liberation, the country

## THREE GORGES AND GEZHOUBA DAMS

Both the Three Gorges Dam and the Gezhouba Dam are located in Yichang, Hubei Province, China. The Gezhouba Dam, completed in 1988, was the experimental dam of the Three Gorges Dam project. The Three Gorges Dam—the world largest dam project—was one of China's "state projects." The idea of the Three Gorges Dam was first proposed in 1919 by Sun Yat-sen (Sun Yixian or Sun Zhongshan). The project involved a long decision-making process, and encountered many obstacles, including war, economic issues, and prolonged government debate.

The controversy surrounding the project includes the forced displacement of people, environmental effects, and the impact on local culture and aesthetics. The losses from inundation are enormous. More than 1.2 million people had to be resettled, and twenty towns or municipal districts and 1,680 villages were wholly or partially affected by inundation (Li Heming et al. 2003; Jackson and Sleigh 2000). The environmental impacts of the dam project are related to disruption to the habitats of endangered species living in the Yangzi River—the most species-rich river in the Palearctic region (Park Young-Seuk et al. 2003; Wu Jianguo et al. 2003). Culturally, the Three Gorges area holds the complete record of successive dynasties dating back to pre-Chinese times (Qing Dai 1998). Thus the construction of the dam has had a significant impact on many cultural sites.

The main benefits of the project are flood control, power generation, and improved navigation. In the past, floods on the Yangzi killed thousands and left millions homeless. With a 22.15 billion cubic-meter capacity for flood storage, the dam can control the Yangzi's huge upstream floodwaters. Moreover, the dam has a power-generating capacity of 18,200 megawatts and will play a crucial role in the control of environmental pollution and in the development of China's economy. In terms of improved navigation, the Three Gorges Dam will increase annual one-way navigation capacity and improve navigation conditions in the dry season. Other benefits of the dam include the development of a fishery in the reservoir, as well as tourism and recreational activities.

**BIBLIOGRAPHY**

Dai Qing, ed. *Yangtze! Yangtze!* Trans. Nancy Liu et al. Ed. Patricia Adams and John Thibodeau. London: Earthscan, 1994.

Dai Qing, ed. *The River Dragon Has Come: The Three Gorges Dam and the Fate of China's Yangtze River and Its People.* Trans. Yi Ming. Ed. John Thibodeau and Philip Williams. Armonk, NY: Sharpe, 1998.

Jackson, Sukhan, and Adrian Sleigh. Resettlement for China's Three Gorges Dam: Socio-economic Impact and Institutional Tensions. *Communist and Post-Communist Studies* 33, 2 (2000): 223–241.

Li Heming, Paul Waley, and Phil Rees. Reservoir Resettlement in China: Past Experience and the Three Gorges Dam. *Geographical Journal* 167, 3 (2001): 195–212.

Park Young-Seuk, Chang Jianbo, Sovan Lek, et al. Conservation Strategies for Endemic Fish Species Threatened by the Three Gorges Dam. *Conservation Biology* 17, 6 (2003): 1748–1758.

Wu Jianguo, Huang Jianhui, Han Xingguo, et al. Ecology: Three-Gorges Dam—Experiment in Habitat Fragmentation? *Science* 300, 5623 (2003): 1239–1240.

*Mark Y. L. Wang*

embarked on a very extensive program at the commune and brigade level to construct small-scale hydropower plants. Using low technology, these plants were unreliable and incurred high line losses. Yet by 1973 the total hydro capacity had reached 10 gigawatts (GW) and provided 20 percent of electricity output. After the open-door policy was launched in 1978, the government changed the emphasis to large-scale power stations.

In 2004 China overtook Canada and Brazil to become the world's largest user of hydroelectricity. By 2007 the total installed capacity in China was 145 GW and the annual output was 490 terawatt hours (TWh). Despite this construction program, the proportion of hydroelectric capacity in China's power sector has gradually fallen from more than 30 percent in the early 1980s to about 20 percent in 2007. This decline has been largely due to the more rapid expansion of thermal power capacity. Over this period, the contribution of hydropower to China's electricity supply has declined from a peak of 24 percent in 1983, to 15 to 16 percent over the 2003–2006 period.

In 2008, in addition to the 22-GW Three Gorges Dam, more than ten dams were under construction with capacities in excess of 3 GW and which together amount to a total of more than 50 GW to be commissioned before 2017. Construction was due to start in 2008 or 2009 on a further seven dams of 3 GW or greater capacity, adding a total of 37 GW. Official plans see the national capacity rising to 200 to 240 GW by 2020.

The justification for these dams is premised on the need for flood control and, on occasions, for improved navigation for waterborne traffic, in addition to the requirement for additional energy supplies. More recently, the argument has been that this form of energy production contributes much less to the production of greenhouse gases than thermal power generation.

The construction of large dams has long been controversial in China, as it has been around the world. The arguments against the dams range from the financial and technical to the environmental and social. Three of these arguments are particularly important in China. First, the contribution of these dams to the power supply can vary from year to year depending on water flows, and fluctuates throughout the year with the seasons. As a result, China's overall load factor for its hydroelectricity industry is just 0.37, well below that of Brazil and Canada, which are 0.56 and 0.59 respectively. Secondly, the commercial viability is also diminished in China because many dams are far from the centers of demand for power.

Finally, the high population density in much of China, especially near large rivers, has exacerbated the problems of forced migration and safety. It has been estimated that by the early 1990s some ten million people had been displaced by such projects. The new Three Gorges Dam has resulted in the displacement of more than one million people. In addition, China used to have a poor record in dam safety, and many dams have collapsed. The most notorious of these was the Banqiao Dam in Henan Province, which failed during a freak flood in 1975, causing the deaths of 170,000 people and affecting eleven million. While the construction standards for the largest dams have certainly improved since then, collapses of smaller dams are reported frequently.

As a result of these and other concerns, the level of protests being voiced at newly planned dams is increasing. This may slow the rate of construction at a time when the government wishes to enhance the role of clean energy. In addition, fears exist that climate change is reducing snowfall in the Himalayas, which in turn will cause the flow of water in some of China's large rivers to decline.

**BIBLIOGRAPHY**

Jing Jun. Rural Resettlement: Past Lessons for the Three Gorges Project. *China Journal* 38 (1997): 65–92.

Martinot, Eric, and Li Junfeng. *Powering China's Development: The Role of Renewable Energy*. Washington, DC: Worldwatch Institute, 2007.

Xu Yichong (Xu Yi-chong). *Powering China: Reforming the Electric Power Industry in China*. Burlington, VT: Ashgate, 2002.

***Philip Andrews-Speed***

## WIND POWER

China has substantial wind resources, mainly located in the coastal southeastern provinces and in the northwest and northeast of the country. As part of the government's strategy to rapidly enhance the proportion of renewables in the energy supply, it has been actively promoting the development of wind power. Installed capacity has doubled each year since 2003. In 2006, 2.6 gigawatts (GW) of new capacity were installed, and a further 3.4 GW were installed in 2007, bringing the total to 6 GW. This gives China the fifth largest wind-power sector in the world, behind India. Wind power now accounts for nearly 1 percent of installed power-generating capacity. In addition to these plants that are connected to the grid, the country has more than 200,000 stand-alone turbines for local energy supply, totalling some 50 megawatts (MW).

The current national energy strategy and climate-change policy has resulted in ambitious targets being set for the expansion of wind power. Yet the industry has already exceeded the target of 5 GW set for 2010. The official target of 30 GW set for 2020 is also likely to be exceeded, and by 2030 installed capacity will probably be in the range 50 to 100 GW, accounting for 2 to 3 percent of total electricity supply.

More than forty Chinese manufacturers are active in wind power, and they provide more than 50 percent of the market. They have mainly delivered turbines with capacities of less than 1 MW, but they are rapidly scaling up. The main manufacturers are Gold Wind with 33 percent market share in 2006, Zhejiang Yuanda, Sinovel, and East Turbine. Their competitive position with respect to foreign manufacturers is helped by the legal requirement that 50 percent of the equipment in the first phase of a project must be made in China, and this rises to 70 percent in later phases. The leading foreign manufacturers are GE, Vestas, and Gamesa. The major Chinese developers are the large national power companies, which are obliged to invest in renewables: National Power Group, Huaneng, Guohua, Datang, and China Power Investment.

The Renewable Energy Law passed in 2005 requires grid companies to connect all renewable plants and to purchase all electrical power generated by these plants. Incentives for research and development were also provided to encourage the domestic manufacturing of the required technologies. Despite these positive components, the law did not provide for a feed-in tariff. Rather, the tariff for new large projects is set by competitive bidding. This has resulted in the state-owned power companies driving prices down to levels below what most would estimate to be commercially viable, and private-sector investors, both domestic and foreign, have failed to gain significant opportunities recently.

For projects not included in this bidding process, prices are set by the local pricing bureaus, also at a relatively low level but higher than that for thermal power. As a result of insufficient financial incentives and poor planning, developers have been slow to build contracted capacity, and the grid companies have been slow to connect and dispatch completed new wind-power capacity.

An added potential incentive for the construction of renewable energy capacity is the Clean Development Mechanism. By the end of 2007, seventeen wind-power projects in China had been registered under the Clean Development Mechanism, but administrative obstacles and policy ambiguity have prevented more rapid implementation.

**BIBLIOGRAPHY**

International Energy Agency. *World Energy Outlook 2007: China and India Insights*. Paris: OECD/IEA, 2007.

Martinot, Eric, and Li Junfeng. *Powering China's Development: The Role of Renewable Energy*. Washington, DC: Worldwatch Institute, 2007.

Zhang Zhongxiang. Towards an Effective Implementation of Clean Development Mechanism Projects in China. *Energy Policy* 34 (2006): 3691–3701.

***Philip Andrews-Speed***

## NUCLEAR POWER

Chinese efforts to develop commercial nuclear energy began in the 1970s, but developed slowly because of government concerns about cost and safety. A dramatic rise in the demand for electricity, the increased cost of fossil fuels, the environmental consequences of heavy reliance on coal, and increased domestic industrial capacity and technical expertise have made investments in nuclear energy more attractive to China's current planners.

In 2007 China operated eleven commercial nuclear reactors providing 62.86 billion kilowatt-hours of electricity, or about 2.3 percent of China's total electrical-energy output. Scheduled to be completed by 2020 are an additional twenty-two reactors, which will increase China's nuclear generating capacity to 40 gigawatts-electric, or 4 percent of projected national electrical-energy production. China's National Development and Reform Commission announced a target of 160 gigawatts-electric for nuclear-generation capacity by 2030. Proposals to build nineteen additional nuclear plants are currently under review, and an additional eighty-six plants have been proposed.

A leading Chinese nuclear engineer described China's initial set of eleven operating nuclear-power plants as the "United Nations of nuclear reactors." They include four French pressurized water reactors at Daya Bay and Lingao in Guangzhou, two Russian AES-91 pressurized water reactors at Tianwan in Jiangsu Provence, two Canadian CANDU 6 pressurized heavy-water reactors at Qinshan in Zhejiang Provence, and three indigenous Chinese CNP-600 pressurized water reactors at the same Qinshan site. Going forward, Chinese planning documents call for reliance on Chinese domestic design and production, with limited foreign cooperation when necessary. Only six of the next twenty-two reactors scheduled to be completed by 2020 will be of foreign design. Westinghouse signed contracts with China for four of their as yet untested third-generation AP1000, and Areva NP signed contracts for two of their advanced European pressurized water reactors. All of China's planned projects for constructing nuclear-power plants will involve a high degree of international participation with countries such as Finland, Germany, Japan, and South Korea all supplying key components.

China has six operating uranium mines producing approximately 840 metric tons per year, which is not quite sufficient to satisfy current demand. The balance is met with modest imports from Russia and Kazakhstan while China expands domestic production. China's known reserves stand at approximately 70,000 metric tons of uranium, which are sufficient to meet China's projected short-term demand. Concerns about long-term supply are expressed in Chinese efforts to acquire commercial spent-fuel reprocessing facilities. In November 2007 an agreement was concluded between the French company Areva and the China National Nuclear Corporation to conduct a feasibility study on constructing a facility for fabricating mixed-oxide fuel in China. This follows an attempt by the China National Nuclear Corporation to purchase a similar facility from Germany in 2003.

Looking toward the future, China has a comparatively vigorous research program on energy from nuclear fusion. China currently operates five experimental Tokamak fusion devices and is constructing a new experimental advanced superconducting Tokamak at the Institute of Plasma Physics in Hefei. The new Chinese Tokamak is similar to the International Thermonuclear Experimental Reactor (ITER) being built in France by an international consortium that includes China.

**BIBLIOGRAPHY**

Li Jingjing and Qu Zhen. Constructing Our National Nuclear Energy Safety Legislation System. *Proceedings of the 2006 Conference of the Environmental and Resource Law Society, China Law Society* (2006): 1518–1525.

Liu Chengan. Energy Requirements and the Future of Nuclear Energy. *Chinese Journal of Nuclear Science and Engineering* 27, 2 (2007): 106–112.

Pan Ziqiang. The Development of Nuclear Power and Emergency Response. *Radiation Protection* 27, 1 (2007): 1–5, 18.

Yu Ganglin and Wang Kan. Research on Fuel Physical Characteristics in Small Long-Life Nuclear Power Systems. *Nuclear Power Engineering* 28, 4 (2007): 5–8.

***Gregory Kulacki***

## ELECTRICITY GENERATION

China's total installed capacity for electricity was 713 gigawatts (GW) in 2007, up 91 GW from 2006. The rapidity of the recent expansion of China's electricity capacity has been unparalleled in world history. In 2000 China only had 319 GW of capacity, meaning that between 2000 and 2007, electricity capacity grew 18 percent on average annually.

According to the China Electricity Council, 74 percent of the country's electricity is derived from coal, at 526 GW in 2007. Hydropower provides 20 percent of electricity capacity, nuclear 1 percent, and wind power half of 1 percent. Although nuclear and wind power have been growing rapidly, coal is so dominant that it is unlikely that the current mix of electricity supply can be significantly altered. Natural gas is not commonly used for power generation due to the high price and lack of availability of the fuel in China.

Nationally, 96 percent of rural households have access to electricity, although in some provinces the figure is much lower, such as in Guizhou, where 80 percent of rural households lack access (*China Energy Data Book* 2004). Industry consumes the majority of electricity supplied, accounting for 74 percent of total demand (National Bureau of Statistics 2006, chap. 7). There is no national electrical grid; the regional grids are not well connected. The grid is owned and operated by the State Grid Corporation of China and the China Southern Power Grid Corporation. There are numerous major domestic electricity companies in China, the five largest of which are China Huaneng Group, China Huadian Corporation, China Guodian Corporation, China Datang Corporation, and the China Power Investment Corporation, all major state-owned enterprises.

Foreign investment into the electricity sector has been considerable, especially for equipment and service providers, although it only accounted for 2 percent of total foreign direct investment into China in 2005 (National Bureau of Statistics 2006, chap. 18). Independent power producers account for 9 percent of installed capacity in China (Woo 2005). Power generation equipment is a major source of trade between China and other countries. For the United States, for example, power generation equipment was the second-largest export to China and import from China in 2006. Siemens, Bosch, General Electric, Westinghouse, and others are all active in the Chinese electricity industry.

Overall, the efficiency of the electricity sector has improved markedly since the mid-1990s, with many new plants among the most efficient in the world. China's coal-fired power plant efficiency has improved from 27 percent in 1974 to 33 percent in 2003 (Zhao and Gallagher 2007). Still, there are many small and inefficient plants that keep the overall efficiency much lower than is desirable given the Chinese government's official target of improving the overall energy efficiency of the economy by 20 percent by 2010. The government intends to shut down many of the small plants and replace them with larger-scale, efficient plants. China's coal-burning power plants are causing severe environmental pollution, including acid rain, air pollution, water pollution, and mercury contamination. The State Environmental Protection Administration (SEPA) issued emissions standards for air pollutants from thermal power plants that took effect January 1, 2004. These standards require reductions in nitrogen oxide and sulfur dioxide emissions, but enforcement has been weak. Acid rain, caused mainly from $SO_2$ emissions from coal combustion, is estimated to cost $30 billion yuan in crop damages and $7 billion yuan in material damage annually. This damage, in turn, causes an estimated 1.8 percent of the value of the crop output, especially for vegetable crops (World Bank-SEPA 2007). The emissions standards issued by SEPA are aimed at reducing acid rain.

### BIBLIOGRAPHY

*China Energy Data Book*. Berkeley, CA: Lawrence Berkeley National Laboratory, 2004.

National Bureau of Statistics of China. *China Statistical Yearbook 2006*. Beijing: Author, 2006.

Woo Pei Yee. China's Electric Power Market: The Rise and Fall of IPPs. Working paper no. 45. Program on Energy and Sustainable Development, Stanford University, August 2005.

World Bank and SEPA, 2007. Cost of Pollution in China: Economic Estimates of Physical Damages. World Bank and China State Environmental Protection Agency, Washington D.C.: February.

Zhao Lifeng and Kelly Sims Gallagher. Research, Development, Demonstration, and Early Deployment Policies for Advanced Coal Technology in China. *Energy Policy* 35 (2007): 6467–6477.

***Kelly Sims Gallagher***

## ENTREPRENEURS SINCE 1949

In 2008 China had an estimated 150 million entrepreneurs (*qiyejia*), including freelance professionals, whose occupations ranged from street vending to real estate. According to

*Forbes* magazine, twenty eight Chinese were billionaires (Kroll 2008). The number of billionaires rocketed to sixty-six in 2007, falling back to twenty-four (excluding Hong Kong) after markets slumped worldwide in October 2008. In 2007 real estate accounted for the largest number of individual fortunes, reflecting the general rise in standards of living in urban China and aspirations for home ownership in China's growing middle class. The slump in real estate in 2008 left Liu Yongxing (b. 1948), president of the agricultural feed producer East Hope Group, China's richest man. His tale of rags to riches, from raising chickens and quails in 1982 to amassing a fortune exceeding a billion dollars by 2002, illustrates the massive expansion of entrepreneurship in China in the reform era.

Entrepreneurs fared poorly in the early decades of the Communist state. When the People's Republic of China (PRC) was established in 1949, a "national bourgeoisie" (*minzu zichan jieji*) was recognized as one of four social classes constituting the people (*renmin*) of China (the others being the petty bourgeoisie, the workers, and the peasants). This class disappeared when China was deemed to have achieved socialism in 1957. Private companies were nationalized, and private economic activities were progressively limited and then forbidden. Old prejudices—extending to more than business people—characterized the self-employed as greedy, proto-criminal, immoral, and antisocial. Stigmatized as "capitalists" or "bourgeois," they were viewed antisocialist and antirevolutionary, and effectively marginalized. In the second half of the 1950s the private sector was basically eliminated. People with connections to it were victimized during the Cultural Revolution (1966–1969).

## ENTREPRENEURS IN THE REFORM ERA

Self-employed individuals appeared on the scene again with the onset of economic reforms at the end of the 1970s, and in the second half of the 1980s larger private entrepreneurs reemerged. At that time, discussion about entrepreneurs was comparatively new because for a period no one could be recognized as an entrepreneur as such. Chinese media began to herald being an entrepreneur an honor, and managing a company was regarded as a heroic action, even if it had to be admitted that the path to successful entrepreneurship had been an extremely stony one on which many had stumbled. In 1992 Deng Xiaoping declared it to be glorious to become rich. Ten years later, in 2002, the Sixteenth Party Congress labeled entrepreneurs "socialist laborers" and permitted them to become members of the Communist Party.

Because the sociopolitical demarcation between Chinese and Western-capitalist entrepreneurs had become increasingly blurred, the Chinese entrepreneur was treated as a culturally specific type. He (and sometimes she) differentiated himself from his Western counterpart by "distinct Chinese qualities." He was, it was argued, a reformer and a hero who operated in the interests both of social needs and of increasing the social affluence of China. But it is also clear that people in China had difficulties with the term *entrepreneur*, which they coped with by declaring Chinese entrepreneurs to be socialist on the grounds that they had helped to build up the material and intellectual culture of socialism.

In terms of expertise, what was expected from entrepreneurs were leadership, organization and coordination, market flexibility, specialized training in modern company organization and management, and orientation to both the domestic and world markets. More qualified entrepreneurs were to be trained, the conditions and the environment for entrepreneurial activity were to be improved, and they were to be supported by the state. That said, entrepreneurs also had to be controlled because a relatively large amount of economic power was concentrated in their hands. Ideally, the Chinese entrepreneur should be a patriot, identifying with the political system and its core values.

## ENTREPRENEURS AND THE POLITICAL DOMAIN

In the socioeconomic constellation of China, there is a combination of the world of officialdom and the world of entrepreneurs, that is, the entry of the cadre into the domain of the company and vice versa. This results from a number of factors: the form of ownership of the company; cadres being appointed through higher levels of administration (state or collective companies); the income of the cadres (because incomes from business activities are much higher than those for work in state administration or the party); and the openings available to officials due to their connections and their positions within networks.

In addition, entrepreneurs have to become politically active in order to be able to lead their companies successfully on terrain that is legally uncertain. Politically active means that they have to strive for membership in the Communist Party or in a body with certain public protective functions (e.g., people's congresses, political consultative conferences, mass organizations). Officials or persons with close contacts to officials unquestionably possess superior starting conditions than those without such connections. The percentage of party members amongst private company owners is relatively high. Private entrepreneurs buy votes to get elected in local people's congresses or as village heads, or they buy political advocates in party committees or parliaments.

Insofar as entrepreneurs differ from other groups in their lifestyle, behavior, status consciousness, identity, and their collective image in the eyes of other groups (particularly

***Employees of a manufacturing firm discussing company ethics, Changsha, September 26, 2005.*** *In the early years of the People's Republic of China, the Communist government forbid the private ownership of businesses. However, these restrictions loosened under Deng Xiaoping and entrepreneurship became more common in China, as the government redefined such business owners as "socialist laborers," critical to the country's transformation to a market-based economy.* AP/VII/LAUREN GREENFIELD

cadres), one can speak of the formation of a new social stratum. The more successful and larger private entrepreneurs—and to some extent, less successful and smaller private entrepreneurs—possess a striking group awareness that can be clearly differentiated from other social groups. Entrepreneurs are aware of their economic importance and are not shy of articulating their interest in having a say in economic political decisions. Furthermore, although individual entrepreneurs might have particular political interests, entrepreneurs as a group have adjusted to the political system.

The status quo shows that entrepreneurs are concerned primarily with the extension and protection of their economic rights, as well as with the stabilization of their businesses. To reduce uncertainty and minimize transaction costs, they are interested in strengthening law and order. This, at present, determines their political-strategic performance. A survey of Chinese entrepreneurs in the late 1990s showed that their pivotal concern is business development, followed by the irksome problems of *guanxi* (connections; here expressed as *guanxi mafan*, "the bother of connections") and corruption. This demonstrates that these system-endemic problems are seen as a barrier to business rather than an integral part of a "Chinese enterprise culture."

To sum up, due to their increasing economic significance private entrepreneurs have developed into a social group that on the one side is embedded into the system and on the other side pressures for economic and social change. From the viewpoint of some entrepreneurs this development is inevitable, and a necessary consequence of the introduction of market economic structures.

Entrepreneurs directly articulate their own interests via entrepreneurial associations whose political influence is concentrated on formulating economic-political proposals and legislative bills. These proposals are taken seriously and are implemented in business policies at the local and central levels. Political activity by entrepreneurs as deputies to people's congresses or people's political consultative conferences is theoretically possible, but in practice much restricted. Yet, as mentioned above, since the Sixteenth Party Congress, private entrepreneurs officially have had access to Communist Party membership. This apparent contradiction is one indication of how central entrepreneurs are to the process of social transformation in contemporary China.

**SEE ALSO** *Commercial Elite, 1800–1949; Comprador; Economic Reform since 1978; Liu Hongsheng; Lu Zuofu; Rong Zongjing; Shops; Sincere Department Stores; Social Classes before 1949; Social Classes since 1978; Wing On Department Stores; Zhang Jian.*

**BIBLIOGRAPHY**

Dickson, Bruce J. *Red Capitalists in China*. Cambridge, U.K.: Cambridge University Press, 2003.

Gates, Hill. *China's Motor: A Thousand Years of Petty Capitalism*. Ithaca, NY, and London: Cornell University Press, 1997.

Heberer, Thomas. *Private Entrepreneurs in China and Vietnam: Social and Political Functioning of Strategic Groups*. Leiden, Netherlands and Boston, MA: Brill, 2003.

Heberer, Thomas. *Doing Business in Liangshan: Liangshan's New Ethnic Entrepreneurs*. Seattle, WA, and London: University of Washington Press, 2007.

Khanna, Tarun. *Billions of Entrepreneurs: How China and India Are Reshaping Their Futures and Yours*. Cambridge, MA: Harvard Business School Press, 2008.

Kroll, Luisa. World's Billionaires. *Forbes*, March 5, 2008. http://www.forbes.com/2008/03/05/richest-billionaires-people-billionaires08-cx_lk_0305intro.html.

Krug, Barbara, ed. *China's Rational Entrepreneurs: The Development of the New Private Business Sector*. London: RoutledgeCurzon, 2004.

Menkhoff, Thomas, and Solvay Gerke, eds. *Chinese Entrepreneurship and Asian Business Networks*. London: RoutledgeCurzon, 2002.

Tsai, Kellee S. *Back-Alley Banking: Private Entrepreneurs in China*. Ithaca, NY: Cornell University Press, 2002.

***Thomas Heberer***

## ENVIRONMENT

China's environment has continued to degrade under stresses imposed by a large population, rapid industrialization, and increasing rates of per capita consumption. Improving environmental awareness among the Chinese public along with increasingly competent regulation by the Chinese government has slowed but not stopped a steady decline in key environmental indicators. International agreements and activities contribute additional expertise and resources that concerned Chinese are using to confront environmental degradation, which has become one of China's most pressing domestic political and economic challenges.

### WATER SUPPLY AND QUALITY

Data collected during a comprehensive government study on the state of China's environment mandated by a decision of the State Council in 2006 and released in late 2007 describe declining groundwater resources and increasing surface-water pollution. One in four Chinese cities is experiencing measurable annual declines—greater than 0.5 meters—in groundwater resources, while most others are barely holding steady. Only 6 percent of Chinese urban centers are recording measurable annual increases in groundwater levels, while consumption in all Chinese cities continues to increase at rates commensurate with high economic growth and significant population increases from rural-to-urban migration. The quality of the groundwater available to urban residents is also starting to decline. Annual declines in groundwater quality are apparent in one out of every five Chinese cities, in contrast to improved water quality in less than one in ten. The quality of the groundwater supplies in the remaining three-quarters of Chinese urban areas is holding steady. Population centers in North and North-central China are suffering the highest declines in groundwater quality and quantity.

Chinese environmental monitoring conducted from 2006 to 2007 indicates that approximately 70 percent of China's surface water is moderately, heavily, or severely polluted and that 95 percent of the surface water flowing through China's urban areas is heavily or severely polluted. Government assessments indicate that as many as 320 million people in rural China do not have consistent access to clean drinking water. Repeated large-scale temporary water shortages caused by toxic discharges from industrial plants into three of the country's seven major river systems are key factors in those assessments. One-quarter of the surface water in China's seven major river systems is so severely polluted it is completely unusable, even for landscaping. Less than half of the surface water in these watersheds is suitable for drinking. In the Liaohe, Huaihe, Songhuajiang, and Haihe watersheds, less than one-fifth of the surface water is suitable for drinking. More than half of the surface water in the Liaohe and Haihe watersheds feeding into the Bo Hai Gulf is so severely polluted it cannot be used at all. Efforts to reclaim these two badly damaged watersheds in China's industrial Northeast have stemmed the pace of degradation but have yet to produce measurable improvements in surface-water quality.

The 2007 State Council study reported that China's lakes are more severely degraded than its river systems. Two-thirds of the water in China's twenty-seven major lakes is unsuitable for drinking, and nearly half is so severely polluted that it cannot be used for any purpose. The waters off China's considerable coastline, on the other hand, are much healthier than China's lakes and rivers. Two-thirds of China's coastal waters remain suitable for aquaculture and

***Paper factory smokestack at the edge of a contaminated lake, Xinjiang.*** *Many of the water sources inside China suffer some level of industrial pollution, leaving millions of citizens without reliable access to clean drinking water.* © BOB SACHA/CORBIS

bathing. Nearly a third of China's coastal waters are relatively unspoiled and could be designated natural maritime preserves, especially the waters off Hainan Island and the Shandong Peninsula. Only a tiny fraction of these areas, amounting to just over 1 percent of China's coastal waters, had been officially designated as natural marine preserves as of the end of 2006. One-quarter of China's coastal waters, those close to the major ports of Shanghai, Guangzhou, and Tianjin, as well as Hangzhou Bay and the Liaohe Delta, are so severely polluted they are no longer suitable for industrial use. Most of the approximately one hundred harmful algal blooms that occur in Chinese coastal waters each year occur in or near these five areas.

## AIR QUALITY

A series of studies conducted from 2000 through 2006 indicated that China's air-pollution problems are even more widespread. Sixteen of the world's top twenty cities with the highest concentrations of air pollution are in China. Nearly half of China's 559 urban centers consistently fail to meet China's national air-quality standards, which are on par with standards accepted by the World Health Organization. This is a significant improvement over the recent past, when as many as two-thirds of China's cities failed to meet these standards, indicating how dramatic China's urban air-pollution problem had become. Even with these improvements, the negative health effects on the 450 million people who live in urban China cost the national economy up to 5 percent of its annual gross domestic product (GDP), according to internal Chinese estimates.

The most serious problems are in the cities that are experiencing the highest rates of economic growth and rural-to-urban migration. Despite concerted efforts at mitigation, major cities in both North and South China from Beijing to Guangzhou showed no measurable improvements in many air pollutants, especially in the amount of total suspended particulates and sulfur dioxide. Minor improvements at the margin in some major cities are being offset by higher concentrations of air pollutants in others. From a public health perspective, most important is the lack of improvement in urban concentrations of fine particulate matter. Over half of China's major cities continue to have concentrations that present a public health risk. As a result, respiratory diseases are a leading cause of premature deaths in China.

Acid rain is becoming an increasingly serious problem, especially in the southern and eastern sections of the country responsible for most of China's agricultural output. Over a third of the entire country's surface area, and more than half of its arable land, is affected by acid rain. Nearly half of the 524 Chinese cities where acid rain is currently measured experienced some instances of acid rain, with close to one-fifth of those cities experiencing it more than three out of every four times there is measurable precipitation.

China's sulfur-dioxide emissions continue to increase, but at a slightly slower pace than in previous years, according to official Chinese estimates. These estimates indicate that annual emissions grew from 19.3 million tons in 2002 to 25.9 million tons in 2006, and emissions continue to rise but at rates lower than the rate of GDP growth. Industrial sources account for more than 95 percent of increased sulfur-dioxide emissions, with personal consumption accounting for the remaining 5 percent. The amount of particulate matter expelled into the atmosphere has remained relatively constant over the same period, registering an increase from 10.3 million tons in 2002 to 10.8 million tons in 2006.

China has made significant progress in reducing both its production and consumption of ozone-depleting substances. Chinese production of chlorofluorocarbons has dropped from 39,363 tons in 2000 to 13,079 tons in 2006, and the country's consumption of chlorofluorocarbons has dropped by an equal amount. Similar rates of decline are observable in the production and consumption of other ozone-depleting substances over the same period. China's carbon-dioxide emissions continued to increase significantly, to over 6,200 million tons in 2006.

## LAND USE AND NATURAL RESOURCES

The amount of arable land in China is declining. In the one-year period between October 2005 and October 2006, China experienced a net loss of approximately 767,000 acres of arable land. A total of 1,685,000 acres were lost to environmental degradation, construction, and natural disasters, while 918,000 were restored in rural development efforts. Environmental degradation was responsible for more than half of China's recent losses of arable land. Point-source pollution from rural enterprises, poor waste management, improper use of fertilizers and pesticides, and the dumping of urban industrial waste in rural areas has led to serious soil-contamination problems that official Chinese reports identify as a constraint on sustainable rural development. Public sanitation is also a significant problem in rural China, where 45 percent of the population still suffers from the effects of improper or inadequate treatment of human waste, although conditions are steadily improving.

While China's arable land is shrinking, despite reclamation efforts, reforestation programs are adding slightly to China's national forest cover. China ranks fifth in the world in total forested areas and sixth in the amount of forest reserves. It ranks first in the amount of reforested area. The past two quadrennial surveys of China's forest cover indicate that the percentage of total forested area expanded by a modest amount between 1994 and 2003. The rate of expansion was four-thousandths of a percentage point above the rate of population growth, indicating that despite significant absolute population increases—China added the equivalent of a third of the population of the entire United States during that eight-year period—and the attendant increased consumption of domestic wood products, the amount of forest cover per capita actually increased.

## EDUCATION AND AWARENESS

Questions have been raised, both within China and internationally, about the reliability of Chinese environmental data. There is general agreement, however, that the data continue to improve over time as the quantity and quality of the means of collecting and reporting Chinese environmental information become more transparent and standardized.

Both the Chinese public and the Chinese government are increasingly aware of the steady degradation of the Chinese environment, although their appreciation of the consequences is less pervasive. Generally low levels of education, both in the general public and in government institutions, are major impediments to the formation and implementation of effective environmental policy. Many Chinese environmental experts see improvements in both general and environmental education as the key to transforming China's environmental policies and practices.

Since the late 1980s, longstanding ideological prejudices from the Maoist era against more concerted action based in comparisons of the relative environmental damage done in the course of global industrialization by developed and nondeveloped nations have become far less salient and have all but been abandoned. Arguments over the competitive economic advantages of comparatively lax environmental standards continue, but an increasing number of Chinese experts are introducing cost-benefit analyses into high-level policy planning, where environmental costs are more accurately assessed and more deeply appreciated. Access to foreign educational opportunities, along with Chinese domestic educational investments and reforms, are making an increasing number of middle- and lower-level functionaries more knowledgeable about the environmental impacts of

***Security guard directing traffic in deteriorating conditions caused by a sand storm and air pollution, Changchun, Jilin province March 27, 2006.*** *As urban incomes rise in China, so does the number of individuals driving automobiles, adding a new layer of pollution to air already compromised by industrial toxins.* © CHINA DAILY/REUTERS/CORBIS

their decisions. Comprehensive and widespread environmental-education programs in Chinese elementary and secondary schools are increasing public awareness and laying the foundation for improved environmental competence across all sectors of the economy and society.

## MANAGEMENT AND REGULATION

Chinese and foreign observers have identified weaknesses in Chinese political organizations and government institutions that inhibit effective environmental regulation. The ability of Chinese leaders to identify problems, formulate

***Controlled burning of farm crops, Xishuangbanna region, Yunnan province March 1, 2007.*** *Once China's only tropical rainforest, the Xishuangbanna region has become home since the 1950s to fields of sugar cane, tea plants, and rubber trees. Environmental experts predict the possibility of dust bowl conditions in the area by the mid-twenty-first century, a scenario becoming increasingly common as China struggles to balance needs for arable land with responsible stewardship of natural resources.* © RYAN PYLE/CORBIS

policies, and enact regulations far outstrips the ability of government agencies to enforce them. Several political, cultural, and institutional factors inhibit the ability of increasingly competent environmental agencies to carry out their mandate.

China has a unitary national government and a single political party. Provincial and local governments are subordinate to the national government, and China's non-Communist political parties may advise but not challenge the Chinese Communist Party (CCP). Parallel lines of authority influence policy choices and enforcement behaviors in governmental, party, and state-owned commercial entities. Government positions are generally determined according to stature and influence within the CCP, creating informal lines of political and personal authority that influence the behavior and decision making of government functionaries.

This defining characteristic of contemporary Chinese political culture imposes serious constraints on the authority of China's environmental agencies, since conflicts between environmental regulations and economic, social, or even personal matters are resolved informally rather than by the formal regulations codified in the law. Greater respect for and deference to the law is a focal point of contemporary political reform in China, but China's environmental laws and regulations often lack the specificity needed to exert a decisive influence on policy decisions, especially at the local level. The Chinese legal system is becoming more effective and Chinese environmental law more well-defined. This promises to increase the impact of China's environmental laws and regulations in the future.

The structure of China's environmental institutions makes it difficult for provincial, municipal, district, and village-level environmental regulators to carry out national policy and enforce national laws and regulations. Environmental bureaus are staffed, funded, and controlled at the local level, which gives localities a high degree of autonomy over environmental policy and enforcement decisions.

China's State Environmental Protection Agency (SEPA) has limited authority over the activities of provincial, municipal, or country-level environmental agencies, and their authority is confined to providing information about the policies, laws, and regulations localities are obliged to carry out. The incentives for local government officials to aggressively oversee the environmental management of their jurisdictions are weak and often outweighed by competing priorities, especially economic ones. Environmental officials and ordinary citizens who are unhappy with the way conflicts over environmental issues are resolved have few legal means of redress, except to complain or stage public protests. In the absence of a violation of the criminal code or a breach of contract, official failures to heed environmental laws and regulations cannot be addressed in the Chinese courts.

These structural weaknesses in Chinese environmental institutions allow local officials to discount or ignore the harmful consequences of breaches of environmental laws and regulations until they reach a point where demonstrable injury to individuals or property becomes severe. Lack of public awareness and low educational attainment at the lower levels of the regulatory structure help to obscure environmental damage, which often becomes acute before it is noticed. As a result, China's environmental agencies devote most of their limited resources to crisis management rather than to the implementation of the proactive measures needed to stop and eventually reverse China's continued environmental decline. Since 2004 China has been investing about 1.5 percent of annual GDP in environmental protection, well above the 0.8 to 1.0 percent standard recommended by the United Nations Environmental Program. Getting more out of that investment is the focus of current efforts to strengthen and reform China's environmental management.

Encouraging local officials to be attentive to environmental issues is a major objective of current reforms. The Chinese leadership is building incentives into its personnel policies that encourage local officials to be proactive about the quality of their local environment. These policies also include penalties for environmental failures. An effective measure implemented and continually adjusted each year is the inclusion of environmental questions in public opinion surveys about the job performance of local officials. The surveys are conducted by the central government and are theoretically independent of any local influence. Poor scores on these surveys can result in official reprimands and may inhibit promotion to higher office. Some of the data from these surveys are released to Chinese academics for detailed study. In addition to helping police the behavior of local officials, the surveys also help the central government to identify problems and evaluate existing policy.

A bolder reform measure that has met with considerable resistance within the CCP and has yet to be implemented involves the calculation of a "green GDP" that incorporates environmental costs into the overall assessment of economic performance. The single most important criteria on which Chinese officials are evaluated is GDP growth within their jurisdiction. Including environmental criteria in the measurement of GDP would provide a powerful incentive for government officials to attend to environmental concerns, much more so than the existing opinion surveys, which are not a significant factor in decisions on promotion.

The green GDP proposal was raised by Chinese president Hu Jintao in a meeting on population and the environment in early 2004. Several months later, SEPA commissioned a study focused principally on the costs of pollution in ten jurisdictions throughout China. The report, produced in conjunction with the China National Bureau of Statistics, showed a negative cost of 3.05 percent of GDP. A second and much broader study was commissioned in 2006; this report incorporated resource depletion and involved multiple Chinese government agencies engaged in resource management, including the Water Bureau, the Forestry Bureau, and the Ministry of Land and Resources, as well as experts from the governments of Canada, Norway, and other countries working on developing methods of environmental accounting. The results were so strikingly negative they were embargoed. Several of the ten jurisdictions selected for the second study showed flat or negative growth using the expanded green GDP calculation. The report gave rise to strong opposition from the provinces for any green GDP measure to be used in evaluating the performance of government officials.

Opponents questioned President Hu's green GDP initiative on two grounds. The first was the developmental trajectories of more-advanced nations, which demonstrate that national economies need to reach a certain stage before they can afford environmental protection. This line of reasoning conflicts with nearly two decades of CCP propaganda, which consistently and emphatically rejected the notion of "polluting first and cleaning up later." Proponents of the green GDP approach recognized that China fell far short of its own propaganda, but that this was no reason to abandon an important principle. The leadership agreed, although plans to implement the green GDP measure have stalled. The debate now concerns how best to calculate a green GDP.

The first step taken to resolve this problem was a decision to conduct the first comprehensive national assessment of the sources of environmental pollution. The yearlong project began in early 2008. A special twelve-person working group was formed to carry out the assessment.

The panel is headed by Vice Premier Zeng Peiyan, State Council Assistant Secretary Zhang Ping, and the heads of SEPA and the National Bureau of Statistics.

Between 2002 and 2007 China also promulgated a series of new environmental laws, regulations, practices, and standards that more clearly define the responsibilities of individuals, enterprises, and the various layers of government in China. The law that most directly addresses the longstanding problems with enforcement of environmental regulations is a 2007 provisional decision on penalties that can be imposed not only for violations of the letter of the law but also for behavior that is deemed contrary to the intent of national policy. The decision was promulgated jointly by SEPA and the Ministry of Supervision, which has the authority to investigate and penalize government employees at every level of the system. This gives the central government, through the offices of the highest executive body, the State Council, some power to enforce environmental laws and regulations that have proven difficult to address through the courts. The law introduces greater specificity, identifying prohibited behaviors such as organizing unauthorized visits to natural reserves, interfering with the collection of environmental data, and failing to file reports on time. The law is a virtual list of all the different types of enforcement failures observed by Chinese environmental advocates in recent years. The penalties range from demotions in government rank to dismissal.

Another provisional regulation promulgated in March 2008 requires and provides guidelines for public participation in environmental impact statements for new construction. The intent of the regulation is to force enterprises and local governments involved in conducting environmental impact assessments to make the information in the assessments available to the public. This includes specifying who is conducting the new construction, who is preparing the environmental impact statement, and the names and contact information of responsible individuals. These individuals also must specify procedures and timelines for the entire process, including for the submission of public comments. The provisional regulation also forbids government officials from approving projects if compliance with these procedures is not documented in the final application for approval. The only exceptions are for projects deemed to be secret, presumably for national security reasons. A few months after these regulations were promulgated the Chinese government also updated and strengthened a 1997 law on the rights of Chinese citizens to petition officials on environmental issues.

Other environmental legislation passed between 2002 and 2008 includes a law managing the import and export of potentially invasive species, a law regulating the environmental management of scenic areas, a law on the management of electronic waste, a law governing inspection of national-level natural preserves, a law creating a permit system for the management of low-level radioactive waste, a law governing practices at biological laboratories, a law on the management of environmental monitoring, a law governing procedures for the establishment of environmental standards, and a law governing rights to petition for changes in and seek redress from decisions made by environmental administrators. All are signs that the Chinese government is making concentrated efforts to construct an increasingly specific and transparent system of environmental regulation that addresses the ambiguities that allow government officials, especially at the local level, to sidestep or ignore national directives.

China is simultaneously stepping up national efforts to compel local enforcement through periodic ad hoc interagency rectification campaigns. One effort carried out in 2007 involved 1.7 million person-hours targeted at 720,000 enterprises that uncovered 280,000 violations and resulted in the permanent closure of 3,176 firms. Despite these efforts, the number of documented serious environmental incidents continues to increase, and most major environmental indicators continue to decline. These realities, according to many Chinese environmental experts, who are supported by the current CCP leadership, are driving the elite effort to integrate environmental costs into calculations about economic growth with indicators like a green GDP.

## REFORM AND REORGANIZATION

Continued internal dissatisfaction with the government's efforts at managing environmental policy led the leadership to designate the Environmental Protection Bureau one of the five new "major bureaus" created by the Eleventh National People's Congress (2008) under a new "major bureau system." The new system consolidates the twenty-eight bureaus and agencies that previously reported directly to the State Council. According to some sources within SEPA, this reorganization will transform what had been a relatively weak environmental agency into a more influential institution with authority to shape national policy in all areas, including agricultural and energy policy, which impact the ability to carry out a much broader mandate to manage the "greater environment."

The language the State Council used to describe the new Environmental Protection Bureau's mandate describes four areas of authority: (1) to set, organize, and carry out environmental planning, policy, and standards; (2) to define and organize environmental functional areas; (3) to monitor and manage environmental pollution remediation; and (4) to coordinate and resolve major environmental problems. In the broadest sense, the language gives the bureau the ability to define the scope of its authority. The question for many observers inside and outside of China is whether or not the bureau will have the political power to impose its authority

***A motorcyclist riding through a wind farm, Dabancheng, Xinjiang August 4, 2006.*** *While robust economic growth brought prosperity for many Chinese, the resulting pollution from poorly regulated factories has become a problem for the government. Since the turn of the twenty-first century, officials have proposed legislation protective of the environment and promoted the use of renewable energy to curb pollution.* © RYAN PYLE/CORBIS

over other traditionally more influential interests, such as energy and agriculture, within the Chinese system.

## INTERNATIONAL ACTIVITIES

Chinese participation in international agreements and international environmental undertakings has had a salutary effect on the evolution of Chinese environmental protection efforts. In the years immediately after the 1972 United Nations Conference on the Human Environment, the Chinese who participated in this seminal event formed a steadily growing core of government officials who did not see environmental protection as a means by other nations to suppress or slow Chinese national development. Overcoming this longstanding ideological and negative predisposition to environmentalism took considerable effort and is recognized within China as the most significant accomplishment of the first generation of Chinese environmental leaders.

In the following decades, regular Chinese participation in the decision-making processes of international environmental organizations created a web of invested government officers, legally binding commitments, and moral obligations that exerted significant influence over Chinese domestic environmental policy and activity. This culminated in China's commitment to Agenda 21, a comprehensive plan for global sustainable development adopted by 178 governments at the 1992 Rio Conference of the United Nations Conference on Environment and Development, which cemented the principal of sustainable development in Chinese environmental planning and policy. Gradual economic and financial integration facilitated by international agreements encouraged Chinese leaders to adopt international environmental norms, standards, and practices. Educational and technical exchanges provided much-needed environmental expertise, especially during the 1980s and 1990s, when Chinese higher education was still recovering from the decade-long closure of Chinese colleges and universities during the political upheavals of the Cultural Revolution and its aftermath (1966–1976).

Many Chinese experts argue that the party leadership's capability to overcome entrenched local economic interests and strong bureaucratic resistance will depend on the involvement of an increasingly affluent and better-educated population able to support their effort to improve China's environment. The political leadership's decision to implement new laws and regulations that provide greater transparency and public access is designed to increase the possibilities for informed and timely public involvement. While China's political system imposes rigid constraints on the activities of individuals, the media, and nongovernmental organizations, China's continued integration into global economic, scientific, educational, and cultural networks is extending the reach of common environmental norms and expectations throughout Chinese society and culture. The Chinese government is cautiously facilitating contact and cooperation on environmental issues to gain much-needed leverage against recalcitrant and uneducated interests in the Chinese economy and the Chinese government. Even international environmental organizations such as Greenpeace are encouraged to operate in China, so long as they can continue to strike the government's preferred and continuously shifting balance between encouraging public participation and preventing political unrest.

China hosts an average of thirty high-level international environmental delegations each year, and more than a hundred international conferences and workshops. It sends several thousand officials overseas for short-term training and takes in an average of eighty million U.S. dollars in foreign environmental assistance.

**SEE ALSO** *China's Agenda 21; Desertification; Land Use, History of; Natural Resources; River Systems: Water Control.*

**BIBLIOGRAPHY**

Ma, Xiaoping, and Leonard Ortolano. *Environmental Regulation in China: Institutions, Enforcement and Compliance.* New York: Rowman & Littlefield, 2000.

Ministry of Environmental Protection of the People's Republic of China. http://www.mep.gov.cn.

Shapiro, Judith. *Mao's War Against Nature: Politics and the Environment in Revolutionary China.* Cambridge, U.K.: Cambridge University Press, 2001.

Sinkule, Barbara J., and Leonard Ortolano. *Implementing Environmental Policy in China.* Westport, CT: Praeger, 1995.

Smil, Vaclav. *China's Environmental Crisis: An Inquiry into the Limits of National Development.* New York: Sharpe, 1993.

***Gregory Kulacki***

# EPIDEMICS

An *epidemic* is defined as the occurrence of a disease that spreads rapidly and widely, simultaneously affecting an atypically large number of individuals within a community or region. A pandemic occurs when the disease outbreak becomes transnational or even global. A contaminated source, such as food and water, contributes to common-source epidemic diseases like cholera, dysentery, or typhoid fever. Host-to-host infections, transmitted from individual to individual directly or indirectly, include such diseases as diphtheria, tuberculosis, influenza, SARS, syphilis (and other sexually transmitted diseases), HIV/AIDS, malaria, and plague. Except for HIV/AIDS, SARS, and avian influenza, which are emergent, all the aforementioned diseases were common in pre-1949 China when the control of epidemic diseases was hampered by political instability, an underdeveloped medical and public health system, inadequate funds and health personnel, and deplorable health conditions. With the founding of the People's Republic of China, the government introduced massive public-health programs and succeeded in controlling or eradicating certain common communicable diseases. However, political, social, and economic changes since 1978 have, to some extent, adversely affected the government's anti-epidemic efforts.

## ANTI-EPIDEMIC POLICY AND CONTROL, 1949–1978

China's health policy before 1978 stressed prevention, control of epidemics and common communicable diseases, mass mobilization for health work, and an activist role for the party-state in formulating and directing health policies. The people were exhorted to participate fully in health work, and public-health activities, labeled "patriotic health campaigns," targeted such diseases as plague, smallpox, malaria, schistosomiasis, kala-azar, epidemic meningitis, and cholera. The use of mass movements to promote public-health work contributed to the successful control of many diseases. In the mid-1950s, the "anti–four pests" campaign against rodents, flies, mosquitoes, and bedbugs involved the mobilization of the population in environmental and sanitation improvements, popular health education, and the promotion of hygienic habits. The reduction of the rodent population, careful surveillance, and mass vaccination lowered the number of plague cases from 7,787 in 1949 to an average of ten to thirty in the mid-1960s. A campaign targeting infected dogs and sand flies resulted in the basic control of kala-azar in 1958. The elimination of snails—the intermediate host of schistosomiasis—and the killing of parasite ova in night soil led to the eradication of the disease in many infected areas in the late 1970s. Malaria infection rates also declined from 102 per 10,000 people in 1955 to 21.6 per 10,000 in 1958. Mass vaccination programs covering such diseases as cholera, smallpox, measles, epidemic cerebrospinal meningitis, and typhoid began in the early 1950s, and succeeded in reducing mortality and morbidity rates of many diseases. In 1961 the last case of smallpox was recorded.

The coordination and direction of the nationwide preventive and anti-epidemic structure was critical. Under the supervision of the Sanitation and Epidemic Prevention Department of the Ministry of Health was a nationwide network of anti-epidemic stations at every administrative level responsible for the prevention and surveillance of epidemics and infectious diseases, initiation of health and vaccination campaigns, training of personnel, and sanitation and environment improvements. The number of anti-epidemic stations increased from 1,626 in 1957 to 2,912 in 1975. The active involvement of the party-state in these efforts, however, meant that quite often public-health work suffered from political infighting and uncertainty that might disrupt the operation of the anti-epidemic network. For example, much of the antimalaria activity came to a halt during the Great Leap Forward in the late 1950s, and a major epidemic broke out in 1960. Similar disruptions occurred during the Cultural Revolution (1966–1969), and malaria epidemics resulted when large numbers of sent-down youths who had no immunity were relocated in the countryside and were exposed to malaria.

## POST-1978 ANTI-EPIDEMIC POLICY AND CONTROL

Economic changes in the post-1978 period have led to increased income inequality and a widening gap in power and resources between the coastal regions and the interior, as well as between urban and rural areas. They have also to some extent eroded central control over lower administrative levels. These developments were reflected in disparities in the distribution of resources: In 1986 the urban health system received 4.34 times more per capita health-service funds than the countryside, and urban areas had 2.69 times more hospital beds and 3.07 more doctors per one thousand people. State public-health funding also declined in the 1990s as the government allowed market mechanisms to determine the viability of many health programs. A bias in favor of more profitable curative medicine developed, while public-health programs suffered.

The shift to an emphasis on curative medicine resulted partly from the epidemiologic transition in the late 1970s. The disease profile changed from one dominated by communicable diseases to one characterized by increased chronic degenerative diseases such as cancer and heart disease. But the reduction in public-health funding and supervision over lower-level health work resulted in the resurgence of some of the diseases that had previously been under control. In the early 1990s, schistosomiasis remerged as a major problem. The conversion to fee-for-service, even in some public-health programs, led to a decline in nationwide immunization, and coverage in the late 1980s was only 60 percent in urban areas and 33 percent in the countryside.

The government tried to reverse these trends with the reestablishment of more central direction over public-health activities and research. The establishment of the national Center for Disease Control and Prevention (CDC) in 2002 marked the restructuring of the former anti-epidemic stations, which were now renamed CDCs and entrusted with broad public-health duties, although many of them suffered from inadequate funding and personnel. Yet they have to confront not only the resurgence of some old diseases but also emergent diseases with epidemic and even pandemic potential.

In 1985 China reported the first death of an AIDS patient. The AIDS virus was spread through transfusion of contaminated blood, prostitution, intravenous drug use, and septic blood donation and selling processes. In 2002 the government disclosed that China faced an AIDS epidemic. The following year, the Chinese government announced that an outbreak of severe acute respiratory syndrome (SARS) had occurred in Guangdong. The failure of the Chinese government to disclose fully the status of the epidemic, which had spread to Hong Kong and other parts of the country (in Beijing alone, there were an estimated one hundred to two hundred cases), revealed the breakdown of disease-monitoring and central supervision at the lower levels. Compounding these problems were the continual outbreaks of avian influenza—the virus, known as H5N1, infected a human patient for the first time in Hong Kong in 1997—in various parts of China.

It is clear that post-1978 changes seriously undermined public-health work, and the country is vulnerable not only to the resurgence of old diseases but also emergent epidemic diseases. The diminished role of the party-state in health matters, the decentralization and commercialization of health care, and the increased inequity in accessibility to care have created problems that the government in recent years is trying to address through the reassertion of control over public-health services, increased funding, and active intervention in epidemic control and prevention. For example, to deal with the HIV/AIDS problem, the government increased control over illegal drug use and prostitution, banned illegal blood collection, and provided free treatment for infected individuals. It has taken drastic action to halt the spread of the bird-flu virus by mandating the slaughter of infected birds. And it has exhibited more transparency in reporting and taking quick action in the isolation of SARS cases. It has also emphasized research and cooperated with international health agencies. Such actions would hopefully assure the continual success of China's attempt to control emergent and old epidemic diseases that have plagued the country for so long.

**SEE ALSO** *Avian Influenza; Health Care, 1800–1949; HIV/AIDS; Medicine, Western, 1800–1949; Medicine, Western, since 1949; Severe Acute Respiratory Syndrome.*

**BIBLIOGRAPHY**

Cai Jingfeng, et al., eds. *Zhongguo yixue tongshi: Xiandai zhuan* [A general history of medicine in China: Volume on the contemporary period]. Beijing: Renmin Weisheng Chubanshe, 1999.

Chen Haifeng, ed. *Chinese Health Care: A Comprehensive Review of the Health Services of the People's Republic of China.* Lancaster, U.K.: MTP Press, 1984.

World Health Organization. *Country Cooperation Strategy: WHO China Strategic Priorities for 2004–2008.* Geneva, Switzerland: World Health Organization, 2004.

Yip, Ka-che. Disease, Society, and the State: Malaria and Health Care in Mainland China. In *Disease, Colonialism, and the State: Malaria in Modern East Asian History,* ed. Ka-che Yip, 103–120. Hong Kong: Hong Kong University Press, 2009.

***Ka-che Yip***

# EPIGRAPHIC SCHOOL OF ART

In the midst of the transformations of Chinese society and culture that began in the mid-nineteenth century, a new spirit and new styles emerged from the ancient tradition of Chinese calligraphy and painting, which stepped into modern times. Calligraphers and painters who devoted themselves to innovation in culture and society steadily absorbed new ideas, selectively accepting and rejecting the heritage of traditional art. The Epigraphic school of art was identified in the Lower Yangzi River Valley beginning in the mid-nineteenth century. It involved a fundamentalist reinterpretation of the aesthetics of Chinese calligraphy and painting based upon absorption of Zhou, Qin, Han, and Wei archaeological and epigraphic studies into the practice of art.

## ISSUES INFLUENCING MODERN CHINESE CALLIGRAPHY

A review of the evolution of modern Chinese calligraphy reveals three issues that directly influenced the understanding and practice of calligraphy. The first is the competition or interaction between appreciation of *tie* and admiration for *bei*. One group of modern calligraphers primarily followed the script styles of stone steles of the Northern Wei (386–534) period (*bei*) and the stone carvings of the Qin (221–206 BCE) and Han (206 BCE–220 CE) periods in order to develop a new style of calligraphy; other artists adopted the styles of Wang Xizhi (307–365) and Wang Xianzhi (344–386) of the Jin dynasty (265–420) as found in *tie* rubbings, in an attempt to surpass their predecessors. *Tie* were calligraphy models that were based on masterpieces of standard or cursive script by famous ancient artists and had been carved in stone for the purpose of making reproduction rubbings of the calligraphy. *Bei* is the term for stone stele, and in this context usually refers to a commemorative inscription carved on a monument by artisans whose names are often not known today. Study and appreciation of the functional writing of these anonymous scribes, or *beixue*, was a trend that grew steadily in importance beginning in the eighteenth century.

The second important factor is self-consciousness about the interaction of calligraphy's practical and aesthetic functions. This means that calligraphy may either begin from the linguistic function of writing as textual record and go on to seek a harmony of utility and art, or it may separate itself from its linguistic function in order to emphasize its nature as a creative visual art.

The third factor is the balance between nature and skill. This means that the calligrapher may either break the old conventions to freely express his nature, or he may develop a new creative model within the traditional conventions, thus using his skill to attain a natural quality.

## THE WORK OF ZHAO ZHIQIAN (1829–1927) AS A CORRECTIVE TO EXAMINATION-HALL STYLE

At the beginning of the nineteenth century, *tiexue*, which followed Song (960–1279) and Ming (1368–1644) dynasty practices of emulating ink rubbings of the works of Wang Xizhi and Wang Xianzhi, was already in decline. The standard script (*kaishu* or *zhenshu*) had lost its vitality and become the *guan'geti,* examination-hall style. From the mid-eighteenth century, stone epitaphs, and particularly stone steles of the Wei period (386–556), were excavated in great numbers, providing an important corrective to the stiff and overdecorative examination-hall style. This phenomenon, along with calligraphy theory that promoted *beixue*, such as the writings of Ruan Yuan (1764–1849) and Bao Shichen (1775–1855) in the mid-nineteenth century, and a rising ideology of national self-strengthening in response to pressure on China from the Western powers, produced a trend that took virile power as its aesthetic ideal in calligraphy.

Zhao Zhiqian, who had dual status as a literatus with a complicated official career and as a professional calligrapher, painter, and seal carver, excelled at all four script styles, but specialized in standard script. His early work followed the style of Yan Zhenqing (c. 709–785), but later he accepted Bao Shichen's (1772-1855) *beixue* theories and his work shifted to a northern stele style. His standard script calligraphy was a powerful corrective to the weak, stiff, overcontrolled qualities of the examination-hall style. The combination of irregularity and order in his structures and his skillful and fluid brushwork possesses a multifaceted beauty that reflects both the partially suppressed unhappiness of the frustrated literatus and the professional artist's integration of elite and popular tastes. His pursuit of charm within power, as well as his transformation of the antique into the vernacular, is reflected also in his seal script, clerical script, and semicursive script calligraphy. Among calligraphers who followed the Northern Wei stele style, Zhao Zhiqian brought popular flavor into literati taste. With the rise of the Epigraphic school of calligraphy, Zhao Zhiqian also started to introduce some of the archaic awkwardness of ancient inscriptions into painting. Zhao Zhiqian's painting achieved an epigraphic flavor, but sometimes at the cost of liveliness. In calligraphy and also in its extension into painting, however, *jinshiqi*, or antiquarian epigrapher's taste, gradually became a very important aspect developed in the Lower Yangzi River Valley, especially in the new metropolis of Shanghai.

## WU CHANGSHI AND A NEW FORM OF REVIVALISM

Wu Changshi (1844–1927), one of the most important artists in late nineteenth- and early twentieth-century China and the leader of the later Shanghai school of painting, pioneered a new form of revivalism, in which he brought the northern stele style into seal-script calligraphy. Similar to the career of Zhao Zhiqian, whose calligraphy and seal carving preceded his painting, Wu Changshi's serious involvement in painting did not begin until long after he had taken up seal carving and calligraphy. His early calligraphy emulated Yan Zhenqing (709–785) of the Tang dynasty (618–907), but he later studied Zhong Yao (151–230) and Han and Wei stele carvings. When he was about thirty, he obtained a rubbing of Stone Drum script, *shiguwen,* from a Suzhou friend. He liked its powerful spirit, and he studied it constantly over the following half century. He used it as a stepping-stone to surpass Wei and Jin styles by reviving an even more ancient script. He studied the ancient masters but developed his own individual characteristics, with his own style as the core, synthesizing the aesthetic of calligraphy with the tastes of painting and seal carving. Wu Changshi's lifelong practice of Stone Drum script and seal carving enabled him to more naturally and spontaneously produce epigraphic effects in his painting. His works are simple and unsophisticated, monumental and well-structured, irregular and bold. His brushwork is comparatively rough, wild, and intentionally naive.

During the last stage of Wu Changshi's career, with the foundations of traditional art under attack, challenged by Western culture and education, as well as criticism from the Western-influenced New Cultural movement, the continued practice of Chinese painting had a larger communal or even national significance. At that time, an intensified consciousness of the West marked artistic pursuits, regardless of an artist's approach. Wu Changshi, instead, recalled the literati tradition, and drew his strength from his epigraphic and calligraphic heritage and from the art of seal carving. Wu Changshi's follower, Chen Shizeng (1876–1923), recognized parallels between their literati approach and the tenets of Western modernism, a convergence that was fruitful for likeminded artists later in the twentieth century.

## CONCLUSION

The Epigraphic school of art, represented by Zhao Zhiqian, Wu Changshi, and other artists, appeared in the late nineteenth and early twentieth century. During that period, Western styles of painting, from concept to technique, challenged traditional Chinese ink painting. Epigraphic study and the Epigraphic school of art, with the revival of the National Essence group, was a response to the challenge of the West. With its powerful and self-assertive style, the Epigraphic style in painting and calligraphy reflected the desire for cultural and national strength in the face of the collapse of China's imperial system.

Epigraphic artists, who imported the Qin and Han calligraphic characteristics into painting, greatly changed the concepts and brushwork of traditional literati painting, bringing with them a strong quality of two-dimensional abstraction. Epigraphic-style painting and calligraphy, particularly in the first decades of the twentieth century, may be considered the final attempt of China's Confucian-educated scholar-painters to save the tradition known as literati art.

**SEE ALSO** *Art, National Essence Movement in; Calligraphy; Literati Painting (wenrenhua); Shanghai School of Painting; Wu Changshi (Wu Junqing).*

### BIBLIOGRAPHY

Andrews, Julia, and Shen, Kuiyi. *A Century in Crisis: Modernity and Tradition in the Art of Twentieth-century China.* New York: Guggenheim Museum, 1998.

Brown, Claudia, and Chou, Ju-his. *Transcending Turmoil: Painting at the Close of China's Empire, 1796–1911.* Phoenix, AZ: Phoenix Art Museum, 1992.

Cahill, James. The Shanghai School in Later Chinese Painting. In *Twentieth-century Chinese Painting,* ed. Maybching Kao, 54–88. New York: Oxford University Press, 1988.

*Studies on Shanghai School of Painting*. Shanghai: Shanghai Calligraphy and Painting Publishing House, 2000.

***Kuiyi Shen***

## ETHNIC MINORITIES

SEE *Minority Nationalities.*

## EUROPEAN UNION, RELATIONS WITH

China and Europe have one of the longest relationships in world history. Exchange in many forms goes back centuries, but has been subject to frequent interruption due to periods of internal strife and international confrontation. The last 100 years have held to this pattern, demonstrating both diversity of interaction and also a tendency to polarize between periods of amity and mistrust.

The most significant development in the first thirty years after the founding of the People's Republic of China (1949) was the agreement to move beyond the presumed contradiction between socialist and capitalist societies in order to deal with pressing issues of world order. By the 1970s China and Europe had agreed that the Soviet Union represented a common threat, and this general accord was supplemented by the desire to normalize economic and cultural exchange. As a result, diplomatic recognition was achieved between China and the European Community in 1975, though a number of European states had pursued this earlier, notably France in 1964. Of course, there was still the potential for mistrust to prevail over amity, and this exacerbated differing responses to the collapse of Leninist systems in Europe. Europeans interpreted the collapse of Western Leninism as a triumph for civil society and for the European model of democracy and welfarist capitalism. China's response was much more equivocal, since it represented the end of Soviet hegemonism, but might also potentially lead to attempts to reverse the gains of Chinese Leninism. Consequently, in the crisis of June 1989 the Chinese leadership rigorously imposed Deng Xiaoping's cardinal principles of socialism and repressed Chinese civil society at precisely the point that European civil society was achieving its validation. The legacy of 1989 was to live on both in specific issues, such as the arms embargo imposed at that time, but also in an unspoken contradiction: Was the increasing engagement of China by Europe aimed at helping the Chinese government solve the problems of modernization, or was it aimed at bringing China to the point where Leninism gave way peacefully to enfranchisement?

### DIPLOMATIC ENGAGEMENT AFTER TIANANMEN

With the end of the Cold War, Europe made increasing efforts toward constitutional integrity. China learned to live with post-Maastricht Europe, operating on the two levels of intergovernmental bargaining and supranational institutions, not least because it hoped that this would advance a general process toward multipolarization (though Chinese analysts were rarely very specific as to what they meant by this term). Chinese assumptions in this regard were shaken by the breakup of Yugoslavia, which revealed Europe's continued dependence on U.S. military capability. China's serious concerns turned critical when the United States and Europe presumed to have the authority to create new sovereignties over Kosovo in 1999. The implications for China and its contested territories, such as Xinjiang and Tibet, were evident, but China's outrage was disregarded. Partly as a result of this, expectations of multipolarization faded, and when the next crisis of sovereign authority emerged, over Iraq in 2003, China took a more cautious stance, allowing the main contestation to be acted out among the United States, Russia, and two separate European camps.

Even as this complex strategic environment emerged, China and Europe moved to expand the means and depth of their engagement. This went through various drafts from 1995 onward, but seemed to reach a culmination with the declaration of "comprehensive strategic partner relations" in 2003. The more visible outcomes of the rapprochement were annual summits alternately in China and Europe, and a proliferating number of subordinate dialogue mechanisms that covered human rights; space, science, and technology; agriculture; industry; intellectual property rights; and much else. Two developments were particularly noteworthy. In December 2005 the two sides held their first strategic dialogue at vice ministerial level, which was clearly designed to increase transparency and understanding of strategic intentions and expectations. Secondly, negotiations opened in 2007 on a new Partnership and Cooperation Agreement that was intended to codify and coordinate the main dimensions of an increasingly interdependent relationship. Yet, with rising interdependence, there arose new policy agendas with the potential for new problems. Four areas should be emphasized: economic and environmental governance; law and civil society; technology cooperation and strategic implications; and regional integration and security.

### THE CONTEMPORARY AGENDA

By 2004 China was Europe's largest trade partner, and Europe was China's second largest after the United States. In 2007 China provided 16.2 percent of Europe's imports and took 5.8 percent of exports. Europe received 20.5

percent of China's exports and provided 12.9 percent of imports. Though Chinese exports to Europe were growing at twice the pace of its imports from Europe (26.6% and 13.4% per annum for the five years 2003–2007), Chinese analysts argued that this was due to globalization factors that were largely favorable to European consumers and corporations, notably inflation-suppressing manufactures and good investment margins. China held 4 percent of extra–European Union (EU) foreign direct investment (FDI) stock in 2007 (€124 billion), most of it intermediated through Hong Kong. Chinese inflows to the EU averaged around €2 billion per annum, again mostly from Hong Kong. Yet, Europe retained reservations about China's industrial model in two specific regards. They would not grant China "market economy" status as long as there was domestic price manipulation that permitted evident export dumping; and they raised increasing concerns about protection of European intellectual property rights. These issues of internal regulation were complemented by concerns about the external consequences of hyperindustrialization. As the most significant new contributor to the drivers of environmental change, China inevitably became the focus of European governance efforts for global sustainable development. In this way technical micro-regulation issues merged with macro-governance concerns.

A second cluster of problems lay in the area of development of civil society. Europe wanted China to pursue legal and institutional development in order to improve the quality of governance in issues that affected Europe, but they also openly advocated the legal and institutional strengthening of Chinese civil society. Europe had pressed for China to become a signatory to the International Covenant on Civil and Political Rights since the 1970s, and concern for China's human rights record remained a permanent feature of relations, either within high-level dialogues or the debates of the European Parliament. Europe made provisions in its funding programs for China, such as €20 million for the development of civil society and €10 million to deal with the problem of illegal migration under the 2002 to 2004 National Indicative Programme, only to find these were not taken up due to political sensitivity. The level of international exposure given to Chinese dissident minorities in Europe, such as the Uygur diaspora in Germany, also became a source of friction between Beijing and European countries. Beijing's decision to abandon the Eleventh European Union–China Summit scheduled for December 2008 because of the meeting between France's president Nicolas Sarkozy (b. 1955), who held the EU presidency at the time, and the Dalai Lama was continued evidence of differing interpretations of the rights of society versus the rights of states in Europe and China.

A third problem area that emerged after 2003 was the military and strategic consequences of deepening Europe-China interdependence. This focused specifically on the failed attempt in 2004 of the German and French governments to build a diplomatic consensus to end the arms sanctions imposed on China in 1989, but it also pointed to the wider problem of civilian-military overlap in technological projects such as the Galileo Satellite program. The arms sanctions remained in place due to two main pressures. Within Europe the human rights lobby argued that because the embargo was imposed because of rights violations it could be lifted only with demonstrable improvement in the rights situation, which they did not yet perceive. Outside Europe, the United States and Europe's other strategic partners in Asia, Japan and India, argued that the end of sanctions would appear to endorse China's military modernization at a time when these partners were concerned about the pace and lack of transparency of this development. The military buildup in the Taiwan Strait and the passing of the Anti-Secession Law of 2005 also informed the context in which the embargo was postponed into some indefinite future.

This then led on to the fourth area of concern—Europe's aspiration to contribute to regional governance and security in East Asia. Europe supported East Asian regional institutionalization and China's increasing interest in promoting it. Yet, there was evident contradiction between the use of nationalism as a legitimating mechanism within East Asian societies, including China, and the need to establish collective regional leadership. In circumstances where nationalism and regionalism seemed to negate one another, Europe seemed to accept that the U.S. alliance system in the western Pacific was the foundation of the regional security architecture for the foreseeable future, contradicting Beijing's aspiration that regional integration would be one means of moving East Asia into a post-U.S. era. In following this path, Europe was evidently balancing its interests in a productive relationship with China with the need to meet the concerns of other regional partners such as Japan and the Association of Southeast Asian Nations (ASEAN). On the pivotal issue of Taiwan, for example, though Europe attempted to maintain an independent posture, its position was in practice indistinguishable from that of the United States and its allies: "no independence, no forced change to the status quo."

As can be seen from each of these issue areas, the Sino-European partnership announced in 2003 was less a marriage than a hasty engagement that both sides quickly came to view as posing as many challenges as opportunities. The Chinese, in particular, were disappointed in the failure of the relationship to live up to initial expectations, and settled into a mode of cautious pragmatism. Cautious and pragmatic progress may be the most that either side can expect for the imminent future.

**SEE ALSO** *ASEAN, Relations with; East Central European States, Relations with; Germany, Relations with; United Kingdom, Relations with.*

**BIBLIOGRAPHY**

Casarini, Nicola. *Remaking Global Order: The Evolution of Europe-China Relations and Its Implications for East Asia and the United States.* Oxford, U.K.: Oxford University Press, 2009.

Kerr, David, and Liu Fei. *The International Politics of EU-China Relations.* Oxford, U.K.: Oxford University Press, 2007.

Shambaugh, David, Eberhard Sandschneider, and Zhou Hong. *China-Europe Relations: Perceptions, Policies, and Prospects.* London and New York: Routledge, 2007.

***David Kerr***

# EXAMINATION SYSTEM, 1800–1905

Late imperial Chinese civil examinations played a central role in Chinese political, social, and intellectual life from 1800 to 1905. Local elites and the imperial court continually reexamined and adjusted the classical curriculum and entertained new ways to improve the system for selecting civil officials. As a test of educational merit, civil examinations tied the dynasty and literati culture together bureaucratically. Civil examinations reflected the larger literati culture because they were already penetrated by imperial interests and local elites, who together formed the classical curriculum.

Civil examinations were an effective cultural, social, political, and educational construction that met the needs of the government while simultaneously supporting late imperial social structure. Gentry and merchant status groups were defined in part by their examination credentials. Civil examinations themselves were not an avenue for social mobility because the selection process entailed the social, political, and cultural selection of those who were elites already. Nevertheless, a social by-product was the limited circulation of lower and upper gentry, military, and merchant elites in the government. In addition, the large pool of examination failures created a rich collection of literary talent that filled ancillary roles as novelists, playwrights, pettifoggers, ritual specialists, and lineage agents. When the civil examinations were summarily eliminated by modern reformers in 1904, this event touched off the unforeseen demise of the partnership between the dynasty in power and its gentry-merchant elites. Because imperial interests and literati values were equally served, they fell together in the twentieth-century Chinese revolution.

Imperial examinations continued the long-standing commitment to the moral and cosmological teachings associated with the Learning of the Way (neo-Confucianism), which served as the state orthodoxy in official life and in literati culture. The intersections between elite social life, popular culture, religion, and the mantic arts reveal the full cultural scope and magnitude of the examination process in 1,300 counties, 140 prefectures, and 17 provinces, as well as in the capital region. These regular testing sites, which in terms of the role of police surveillance in the selection process also operated as "cultural prisons" ("prisons" that elites fought to enter), elicited the voluntary participation of millions of men—women were excluded—and attracted the attention of elites and commoners at all levels of society.

## POWER, POLITICS, AND EXAMINATIONS

Classical philosophy and imperial politics were dubious partners during the Qing dynasty (1644–1912), when Song classical interpretations remained the orthodox guidelines for the examination system. Qing appropriations of that orthodoxy as a single-minded and monocular political ideology affected politically and socially how literati learning would be interpreted and used in later dynasties. The mark of the late imperial civil system was its elaboration of the civil examination models through the impact of commercialization and demographic growth when the reach of the process expanded from metropolitan and provincial capitals to all 1,300 counties. In addition, the upsurge in numbers of candidates was marked by degree inflation at the lower levels. Palace graduate degree-holders dominated most positions of higher office. Officialdom became the prerogative of a slim minority. As the door to official appointment, civil examinations also conferred social and cultural status on families seeking to become or maintain their status as local elites.

Competitive tensions in the examination market explain the policelike rigor of the civil service examinations as a systematic and stylized educational form of cultural hegemony that elites and rulers could both support. Imperial power and bureaucratic authority were conveyed through the accredited cultural institutions of the Ministry of Rites, the Hanlin Academy, and civil examinations. Political legitimation transmitted through education succeeded because enhanced social status and legal privileges were an important by-product of the examination competition to enter the civil service.

Fixed quotas based on the ratio between successful and failed candidates demonstrated that the state saw educational access to the civil service as a means to regulate the power of elites. Government control of civil and

## CIVIL SERVICE EXAMINATIONS, 1800–1905

Operating under the aegis of the Ministry of Rites, with the emperor playing the role of chief examiner, the government of late-imperial China devoted significant time, energy, and resources to the recruitment and selection of its personnel. Central to this process was a series of examinations that began in China's myriad counties and ended within the Forbidden City in Beijing. Although the chances of ultimate success were slim—6,000 to 1, according to one estimate in the post-Taiping era—millions of Chinese men, young and old alike, vied for degrees in this highly competitive process.

The government cast a wide net. Most literate males could register and sit for the relatively noncompetitive entrance examination supervised by the education officials of their county. An estimated two million men, referred to as *tonghseng*, would make it past this first step, and most of these men would also pass the examination supervised by prefectural officials. A third examination, however, also given at the prefectural level but supervised by provincial authorities, was very competitive. The lowest examination degree, the *shengyuan,* was awarded on the basis of strict quotas established by the central government, and only one or two men out of a hundred were successful. Across the empire about 30,000 *shengyuan* degree holders, men known colloquially as *xiucai* or "flourishing talents," were advanced to the provincial-level examinations in the post-Taiping era.

In the fall these *shengyuan* traveled to their respective provincial capitals and sat for a series of three competitive examinations conducted over a period of a week under the auspices of examination officials dispatched from Beijing. At these examinations candidates toiled in cramped examination cells constructed in vast compounds, each in isolation amid thousands of others. After the third and final examination, about 1,500 men throughout China were awarded the provincial *juren* degree, also apportioned on a quota basis by province, and began their preparation for the final series of examinations held in Beijing.

Unlike the *shengyuan* degree, the *juren* degree was granted for life. Anyone who held this degree could seek the highest degree, the *jinshi.* Every three years thousands of *juren,* the number could exceed 10,000, traveled to Beijing to compete for this most-coveted metropolitan degree. Each step winnowed the group, and at the end of this process, which resembled the one for the provincial examinations, an average of only 300 men remained. A final palace examination, presided over by the emperor, ranked the men, some of whom were appointed to the prestigious Hanlin Academy. Others, through an appointment process supervised by the Ministry of Personnel, gained jobs in the bureaucracy, which had about 20,000 slots. With this final mark of distinction, *jinshi* degree holders had their names engraved on stone tablets, some of which can still be seen in the temple dedicated to Confucius in Beijing.

This "regular" route to office, and often power and prestige, was balanced by an "irregular route" that began with registering for the county-level entrance examination. After registration men could purchase a degree. These *jiansheng* were quite numerous, and after the Taiping Uprising (1851–1864) the sale of such degrees generated significant revenue for the government. The number of men with any one of these degrees, regular or irregular, has been estimated at about 1.4 million in late-nineteenth-century China.

***Roger R. Thompson***

military selection quotas was most keenly felt at the initial licensing stages for the privilege to enter the examination selection process at the county level. In 1600, there were perhaps 500,000 civil licentiates in a total population of some 150 million, or a ratio of one licentiate per three thousand persons. By 1850, with a population of 350 million, there were only some 800,000 civil and military licentiates, but still only about half a million were civil, a ratio of one per one thousand persons.

Because of economic advantages in South China (especially the Yangzi Delta but including the southeast), candidates from the south performed better on the civil examinations than candidates from less prosperous regions in the north, northwest, and southwest. To keep the south's domination of the examinations within acceptable bounds, Qing education officials maintained the official ratio of 60:40 for allocations of the highest *jinshi* (literati eligible for appointments) degree to candidates from the

**Format of provincial and metropolitan civil service examinations during the Qing dynasty, 1793–1898**

| Session no. | No. of questions |
|---|---|
| One | |
| 1. Four books | 3 quotations |
| 2. Poetry question | 1 poetic model |
| Two | |
| 1. Change | 1 quotation |
| 2. Documents | 1 quotation |
| 3. Poetry | 1 quotation |
| 4. Annals | 1 quotation |
| 5. Rites | 1 quotation |
| Three | |
| 1. Policy questions | 5 essays |

*Table 1*

south versus the north, which was slightly modified to 55:10:35 by allocating 10 percent for the central region.

The overcrowded examination hall became a contested site, where the political interests of the dynasty, the social interests of its elites, and the cultural ideals of classical learning were all compromised. Moreover, examination halls empirewide were supervised by literati officials who were in charge of the military and police apparatus when so many men were brought together to be tested at a single place. Forms of resistance to imperial prerogative emerged among examiners, and widespread dissatisfaction and corruption among the candidates at times triumphed over the high-minded goals of the classical examinations.

## LITERACY AND SOCIAL DIMENSIONS

The monopolization of "cultural resources" by local elites depended on their linguistic mastery of nonvernacular classical texts tested by the state. Imperial examinations created a written language barrier that stood between those who were allowed into the empire's examination compounds and those classical illiterates who were kept out. In a society where there were no "public" schools, education was monopolized by gentry and merchants who organized into lineages and clans to provide superior classical educations. The Mandarin vernacular and classical literacy played central roles in culturally defining high and low social status in Chinese society. The selection process permitted some circulation of elites in and out of the total pool, but the educational curriculum and its formidable linguistic requirements effectively eliminated the lower classes from the selection process. In addition, an unstated gender ideology simply assumed that women were ineligible.

Literati regularly turned to religion and the mantic arts to understand and rationalize their chances of success in the competitive local, provincial, and metropolitan examinations. Examination dreams and popular lore spawned a remarkable literature about the temples candidates visited, the dreams that they or members of their family had, and the magical events in their early lives that were premonitions of later success. Both elites and commoners used fate to describe the forces operating in the examination marketplace. The anxiety produced by examinations was a historical phenomenon, which was experienced most personally and deeply by boys and men. They encoded fate using cultural glosses that had unconscious ties to popular religion.

The civil service competition affirmed a classical curriculum that consolidated elite families into a culturally defined status group of degree-holders that shared: (1) internalization of a common classical language; (2) memorization of a shared canon of classics; and (3) a literary style of writing known as the "eight-legged essay." Elite literary culture was in part defined by the civil examination curriculum, but that curriculum also showed the impact of literati opinions about education. The moral cultivation of the literatus was a perennial concern of the imperial court as it sought to ensure that the officials it chose in the examination market would be loyal to the ruling family. For the literatus, it was important that the dynasty conformed to classical ideals that literati themselves had formulated.

The bureaucracy made an enormous financial commitment to staffing and operating the empirewide examination regime. Ironically, the chief consequence was that by 1800 examiners no longer could read each essay carefully. Final rankings, even for the eight-legged essay, appeared very haphazard as a result. While acknowledging the educational impact of the curriculum in force, one should guard against portraying weary examiners with so many papers to read as the dynasty's "thought police" inside the examination halls trying to impose orthodoxy from above. Overall, however, examiners as an interpretive community did uphold canonical standards. They marked their cognitive world according to the moral attitudes, social dispositions, and political compulsions of their day.

## FIELDS OF LEARNING

In the nineteenth century, the examination curriculum increasingly conformed to the statecraft and evidential research currents then popular. In the late eighteenth century, the Qing dynasty had initiated "ancient learning" curricular reforms to make the examinations more difficult for the increasing numbers of candidates by requiring mastery of not one but all Five Classics, which included the *Changes*, *Documents*, and *Poetry* classics, along with the *Spring and Autumn Annals* and the *Record of Rites*. In addition, the formalistic requirements of a new poetry question after 1787 gave examiners an additional tool, along with the eight-legged essay "grid," to grade papers more efficiently. The grid rigidly defined the number of words and parallel sentence patterns that students had to employ to present their arguments, and its rigidity represented, for reformers toward the end of the dynasty, the pivot of political conservatism. Later rulers failed to recognize that an important aspect of the civil examinations was the periodic questioning of the system from within that gave it credibility from without.

Literati fields of learning, such as natural studies and history, were also represented in late imperial civil examinations, particularly in the reformist era after 1860. Such inclusion showed the influence of the Qing court and its regional officials, who for political reasons widened the scope of policy questions on examinations in the 1880s and 1890s.

### DELEGITIMATION AND DECANONIZATION

Radical reforms were initiated to meet the challenges of the Taiping Uprising (1851–1864) and Western imperialism. Even the Taipings instituted their own Christian-based civil examinations in the 1850s. When the civil examinations lost their cultural luster and became an object of ridicule even among literati officials, the system was derided as an "unnatural" educational regime that should be discarded. During the 1890s and 1900s, new political, institutional, and cultural forms emerged that challenged the creedal system of the late empire and internationalized its educational institutions.

The demise of civil examinations yielded consequences the last rulers of imperial China and reformist gentry generally underestimated. The Manchu court was complicit in its own dismantling after the forces of delegitimation and decanonization were unleashed by reformist Chinese gentry, who prevailed in education circles in the 1890s and persuaded the imperial court to eliminate the institution in 1904.

Education reform and the elimination of examinations after 1905 were tied to newly defined goals of Western-style change that superseded the conservative goals of reproducing dynastic power, granting elite prestige, and affirming the classical orthodoxy. The ideal of national unity replaced dynastic solidarity, as the sprawling, multiethnic Manchu Empire became a struggling Chinese Republic. It was later refashioned as a multiethnic Communist nation in 1949. With the Republican revolution of 1911, the imperial system ended abruptly, but its demise was already ensured in 1904 when the Qing state lost control of the examination system.

The emperor, his bureaucracy, and literati cultural forms quickly became symbols of backwardness. Traditional forms of knowledge were uncritically labeled as "superstition," while "modern science" in its European and American forms was championed by new intellectuals as the path to knowledge, enlightenment, and national power. Perhaps the most representative change occurred in the dismantling of the political, social, and cultural functions of the civil examination regime in 1904 to 1905. By dismantling imperial institutions such as the civil examination system so rapidly, the Chinese reformers and early Republican revolutionaries underestimated the public reach of historical institutions that had taken two dynasties and five hundred years to build. When they delegitimated them all within the space of two decades starting in 1890, Han Chinese literati helped bring down together the Manchu dynasty and the imperial system of governance. Its fall concluded a millennium of elite belief in literati values and five hundred years of an empirewide civil service examination.

**SEE ALSO** *Education: 1800–1949; Government Administration, 1800–1912; Reform under the Qing Dynasty, 1800–1912; Taiping Uprising.*

**BIBLIOGRAPHY**

Deng Siyu. *Zhongguo kaoshi zhidu shi* [History of Chinese examination institutions]). Taipei: Student Bookstore, 1967.

Elman, Benjamin. *A Cultural History of Civil Examinations in Late Imperial China*. Berkeley: University of California Press, 2000.

He Bingdi (Ho Ping-ti). *The Ladder of Success in Imperial China: Aspects of Social Mobility, 1368–1911*. New York: Columbia University Press, 1962.

Miyazaki Ichisada. *China's Examination Hell: The Civil Service Examinations of Imperial China*. Trans. Conrad Schirokauer. New York: Weatherhill, 1976.

Shang Yanliu. *Qingdai keju kaoshi shulue* [Summary of civil examinations during the Qing period]. Beijing: Sanlian Bookstore, 1958.

Zi, Etienne. *Pratique des examens littéraires en Chine* [The Chinese literary examinations in practice]. Shanghai: Imprimerie de la Mission Catholique, 1894.

***Benjamin A. Elman***

## EXPORT PROCESSING ZONES

**SEE** *Taiwan, Republic of China.*

## EXTRATERRITORIALITY

Extraterritoriality (*zhiwai faquan*), the system by which most foreigners and their enterprises were exempt from Chinese jurisdiction and subject only to the law of their home countries, was ceded by China under the unequal treaties of the nineteenth century and became one of the defining characteristics of the treaty-port system. Nationalists later saw extraterritoriality as an infringement of China's sovereignty and made its abolition one of their earliest targets. However, the system declined slowly and came to its final end only in 1946.

## THE DEVELOPMENT OF EXTRATERRITORIALITY

To enjoy extraterritoriality means to be free from the jurisdiction of the state in which one resides. In the contemporary world, the concept survives in the form of diplomatic immunity and the immunity from local law sometimes enjoyed by foreign military stationed in allied countries. Historically, both the Chinese and the Ottoman empires had expected foreign traders to be controlled by a headman according to their own laws. The British in Guangzhou had wanted extraterritorial rights even before the Opium War because they were horrified by the use of torture to extract confessions and other aspects of Chinese criminal law. Extraterritoriality was also a feature of unequal treaties forced on Japan by the Western powers, but it was terminated there in the 1890s.

Extraterritoriality in China was established in various treaties signed in the aftermath of China's defeat in the First Opium War (1839–1842), which ceded consular jurisdiction. The Treaty of the Bogue (1843) gave British citizens in China the right to be tried under British law if they became involved in criminal cases. The French Treaty of Whampoa (Huangpu) in 1844 granted France consular jurisdiction over its citizens within the five treaty ports, and the Americans obtained consular jurisdiction over their citizens in both civil and criminal cases through the Wanghia (Wangxia) Treaty (1844). The system was subsequently extended through ad hoc arrangements, through the application of most-favored-nation treatment, and through further unequal treaties that China was forced to sign. Finally, eighteen nations—Austria-Hungary, Belgium, Brazil, Denmark, France, Germany, Great Britain, Italy, Japan, Mexico, the Netherlands, Norway, Peru, Portugal, Russia, Spain, Sweden, and the United States—benefited from extraterritorial rights. Any case in which the plaintiff was Chinese (whether an individual or a government agency) and the defendant a treaty national had to be adjudicated in the courts of the relevant treaty power. A complex system of consular courts evolved. There were seven in the foreign settlements of Shanghai alone, with Great Britain and the United States even maintaining appeal courts there.

In the foreign settlements of Shanghai, Xiamen (Amoy), and Hankou, "mixed courts" extended extraterritoriality into civil matters that should have fallen under Chinese jurisdiction: claims by foreigners against Chinese, and claims against foreigners who lacked consular jurisdiction, whether by Chinese or foreigners. These courts, formally established in the 1860s, were at first presided over by Chinese magistrates in the presence of an assessor—the foreign consul or his representative, whose influence was often paramount. The mixed courts came under absolute consular control after the 1911 revolution.

Extraterritoriality contributed to the "opening of China" by allowing foreign companies to rely on their own contract law. They could not be forced to pay Chinese taxation, and foreign banks could even issue currency free of regulation. Extraterritoriality also gave foreigners an obvious advantage in their dealings with Chinese. What caused even greater resentment was the fact that Chinese Christian converts and Chinese employed by foreigners sometimes also claimed extraterritorial rights.

The end of extraterritoriality was envisaged as early as 1902 in the Mackay Treaty, a Sino-British agreement on commercial matters. Article 12 mentioned the possibility of Great Britain giving up extraterritorial rights when "the state of Chinese laws and their administration warrant us in so doing" (Ch'en 1979, p. 332). The implied promise, though possibly not taken very seriously by the British, was an underlying influence in the legal reforms enacted in the last years of the Qing dynasty (1644–1912).

## THE DECLINE OF EXTRATERRITORIALITY

Germany and Austria-Hungary lost their extraterritorial rights when China entered World War I (1914–1918) on the side of the Allies. Soviet Russia voluntarily relinquished its rights after the Bolshevik Revolution of 1917, a move much welcomed by Chinese nationalists. However, despite Chinese diplomatic efforts, the Nine-Power Treaty (1922), signed after the Washington Conference (1921–1922), upheld the privileges of the treaty powers in China.

Between 1919 and 1925, the growth of Chinese nationalism produced ever more vocal opposition to extraterritoriality, which was viewed as an imperialist injustice. Sympathetic foreigners, such as American employees of the Young Women's Christian Association in China, individually relinquished their rights. In 1929 the Guomindang government at Nanjing declared its intention to abolish all extraterritorial jurisdictions. Several minor powers voluntarily gave up their rights. The issue was somewhat eclipsed by Japan's invasion of northeast China in 1931 and by increasing Sino-Japanese tension, culminating in the outbreak of war in 1937. In a much-changed situation, with China as their wartime ally, the United States and Great Britain agreed to terminate extraterritorial rights on January 11, 1943. Ironically, Japan had done the same just two days earlier in an agreement with its puppet government in Nanjing. France was the last country to relinquish its rights in 1946.

**SEE ALSO** *Foreign Concessions, Settlements, and Leased Territories; Imperialism; Shanghai Mixed Court.*


**BIBLIOGRAPHY**

Ch'en, Jerome. *China and the West: Society and Culture, 1815–1937*. London: Hutchinson, 1979.

Faure, David. The Mackay Treaty of 1902 and Its Impact on Chinese Business. *Asian Pacific Business Review* 7, 2 (2000): 81–92.

Feuerwerker, Albert. The Foreign Presence in China. In *The Cambridge History of China*, Vol. 11: *Republican China, 1912–1949*, eds. John K. Fairbank and Dennis Twitchett, Pt. 2, 128–192, Cambridge, U.K.: Cambridge University Press, 1983.

Garner, Karen. Redefining Institutional Identity: The YWCA Challenge to Extraterritoriality in China, 1925–30. *Women's History Review* 10, 3 (2001): 409–440.

Vincent, John. *The Extraterritorial System in China: Final Phase*. Cambridge, MA: Harvard University, East Asian Research Center, 1970.


***Delia Davin***

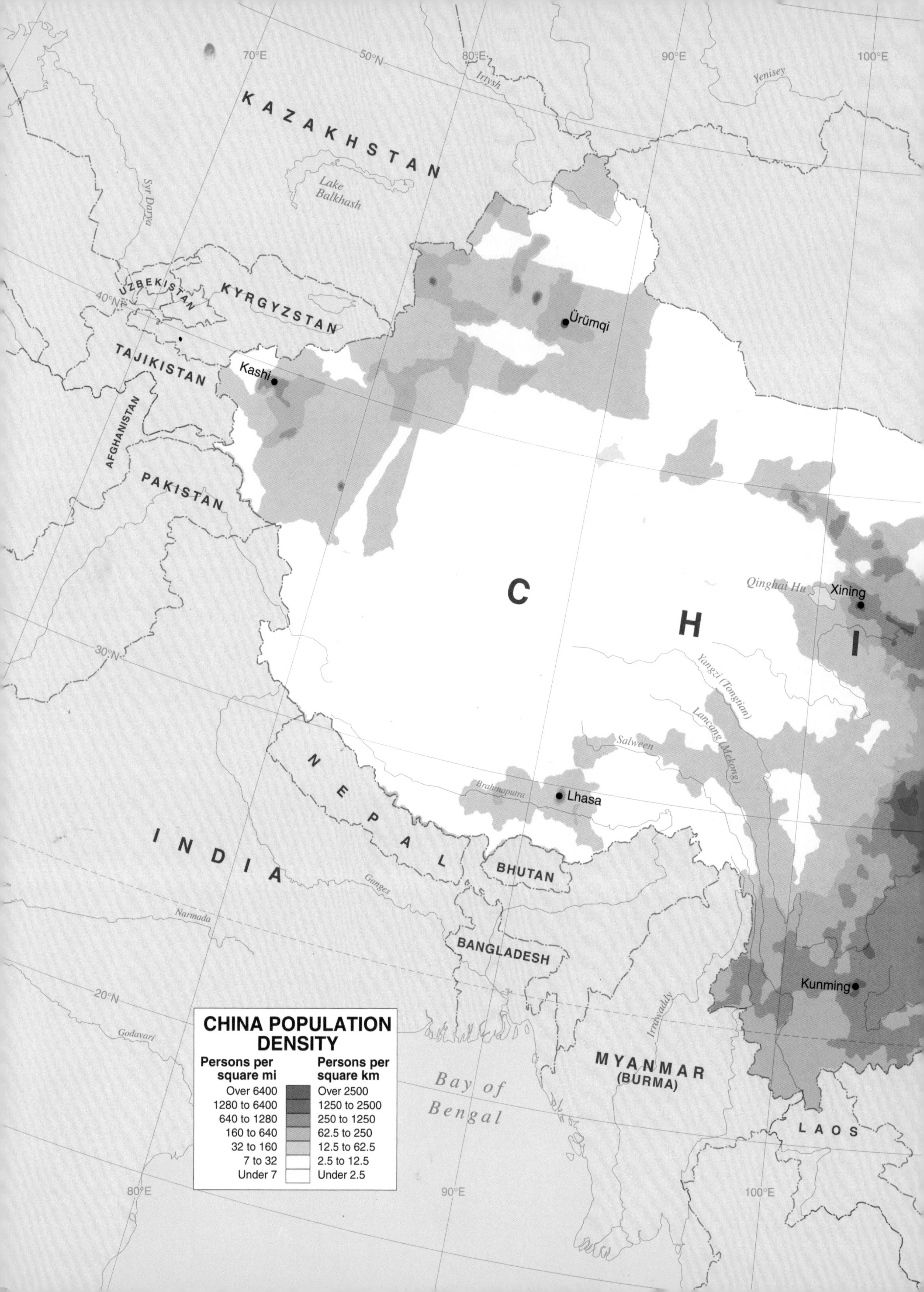
KAZAKHSTAN
Lake Balkhash
Irtysh
Yenisey
Syr Darya
UZBEKISTAN
KYRGYZSTAN
TAJIKISTAN
AFGHANISTAN
PAKISTAN
Kashi
Ürümqi
C
H
I
Qinghai Hu
Xining
Yangzi (Tongtian)
Lancang (Mekong)
Salween
Brahmaputra
Lhasa
NEPAL
INDIA
BHUTAN
Ganges
Narmada
BANGLADESH
Godavari
Irrawaddy
Bay of Bengal
MYANMAR (BURMA)
LAOS
Kunming
70°E
80°E
90°E
100°E
50°N
40°N
30°N
20°N
CHINA POPULATION DENSITY
Persons per square mi
Persons per square km
Over 6400
1280 to 6400
640 to 1280
160 to 640
32 to 160
7 to 32
Under 7
Over 2500
1250 to 2500
250 to 1250
62.5 to 250
12.5 to 62.5
2.5 to 12.5
Under 2.5